TELECOMMUNICATION
PRINCIPLES
(IN M.K.S. UNITS)

STEERABLE DIRECTIONAL RADIO AERIAL: GOONHILLY G.P.O. RADIO STATION (SEE P. 294)
(Courtesy of P.M.G.)

TELECOMMUNICATION PRINCIPLES

(IN M.K.S. UNITS)

By

R. N. RENTON, C.G.I.A., F.I.E.E.

Third edition

PITMAN PUBLISHING

Third edition 1965
Reprinted 1967
Reprinted 1969
Reprinted 1971
Reprinted 1973

SIR ISAAC PITMAN AND SONS LTD.
Pitman House, Parker Street, Kingsway, London, WC2B 5PB
P.O. Box 46038, Portal Street, Nairobi, Kenya

SIR ISAAC PITMAN (AUST.) PTY. LTD.
Pitman House, 158 Bouverie Street, Carlton, Victoria 3053, Australia

PITMAN PUBLISHING COMPANY S.A. LTD.
P.O. Box 11231, Johannesburg, South Africa

PITMAN PUBLISHING CORPORATION
6 East 43rd Street, New York, N.Y. 10017, U.S.A.

SIR ISAAC PITMAN (CANADA) LTD.
495 Wellington Street West, Toronto 135, Canada

THE COPP CLARK PUBLISHING COMPANY
517 Wellington Street West, Toronto 135, Canada

ISBN: 0 273 40951 4

621/
382 REN

16015

Text set in 10 pt Monotype Modern, printed by letterpress,
and bound in Great Britain at The Pitman Press, Bath
G3—(T.418:74)

FOREWORD

By H. Faulkner, C.M.G., B.Sc., M.I.E.E., F.I.R.E.

Telecommunication is an awkward word. I believe it was first invented at the Madrid Telegraph and Radio Conference when it was decided to combine the International Telegraph Union and the International Radio Telegraph Union into one International "Telecommunication" Union. Telecommunication has grown out of all recognition during the first half of this century and has entered very deeply into the lives of the people particularly through the telephone and broadcasting services. The basis of the study of the subject is essentially electrical and although the fundamental scientific principles of all electrical subjects are common, their application to telecommunication is, in my opinion, sufficiently different from their application to electrical power to justify a separate approach.

For example, to the Telecommunication engineer the electron is much more real than to the Power engineer. The former has direct visual evidence of its existence by the splashes it makes on the screen of a cathode-ray tube, or by the measurement of electron flow in the anode circuit of a triode. The rather exaggerated antics which have to be postulated to account for the flow of current along a conductor must make the electron seem much less real and thus demand a rather different treatment.

There is a significant psychological difference in the effect on the student if the problems illustrative of the important principles he is learning have a direct bearing on his daily working contacts, and the City and Guilds Advisory Committee had this in mind in deciding to name the subject "Telecommunication Principles." The author has followed this lead in his choice of examples most of which have been taken from telecommunication practice, and his careful working out of many such examples is a feature of the book.

The book has been written for the less mathematically minded student, but references have been made in appendixes to the short cuts provided by a use of elementary calculus for the sake of those students wishing to take the little extra trouble. The early steps in the subject have, I think wisely, been made as easy as possible to encourage the young student, and the pace is somewhat quickened in the later chapters.

It is hoped that the textbook will be welcomed by the many students of Telecommunication Engineering and especially by those taking the City and Guilds examinations in this subject, and that it will prove a real help to them in mastering the principles on which the art is based.

PREFACE TO THE THIRD EDITION

ONE might have thought that a textbook dealing with *principles* could have remained unchanged yet valid over an extended period, but such has been the pace of developments in new materials and devices for telecommunication during the last decade or two that a revised edition has become a necessity.

The most important change is the inclusion of a new Chapter, dealing with semi-conductor devices. Following the introduction of the point-contact transistor by Bardeen and Brattain in 1948, the even more remarkable work of Shockley—also of the Bell Telephone Laboratories—which resulted in the introduction of the junction transistor in all its forms, has brought into being vast new industries and has affected the lives of all of us. In such a developing field I have naturally needed to draw on many published works, to which I am pleased to make full acknowledgment. In order to limit the treatment of this subject to a single not-overlong Chapter, an endeavour has been made to concentrate upon the important principles which are of particular interest to telecommunication engineers. I am grateful to my colleagues Mr. D. Baker, Mr. H. G. Bassett and Mr. F. F. Roberts of the Post Office Research Station for proof-reading and advice on this Chapter.

Other significant changes in this new edition relate to the properties of new magnetic materials which are of recent introduction—square-loop materials and ferrites, for example—as well as to new dielectric materials.

Some additions have been made to conform to the revised examination syllabuses of the City and Guilds of London Institute and advantage has been taken to include some of the more recent Questions.

A number of new illustrations have been included: for these and related information I should like to express my appreciation to the Automatic Telephone & Electric Co. Ltd.; Mullard Ltd.; The Permanent Magnet Association; The Plessey Co. Ltd.; Standard Telephones & Cables Ltd.; The Westinghouse Brake & Signal Co. Ltd.; to the Editors of the *I.E.E. Journal* and of the *I.P.O.E.E. Journal* and to the Postmaster-General for permission to reproduce published information.

R.N.R.

LONDON, 1964

PREFACE TO THE SECOND EDITION

WHEN the first edition of this book was in preparation, the question of the general adoption of M.K.S. units was under active discussion, but no decision had at that time been taken as regards the fourth defining unit nor on the important question of rationalization.

It would then have been premature to base the original edition upon M.K.S. units, but in view of the interest and importance of the system, a brief description of the basis of the M.K.S. system was included in the Appendix on Units: this Appendix is maintained, practically unchanged, in the present edition.

In July 1950, the International Electrotechnical Commission decided in favour of adopting the rationalized system of M.K.S. Units, with the ampere as the basic electrical unit providing the relation with mechanical units. It was not until June 1953, however, that agreement was reached to base rationalization upon the values of absolute permeability and permittivity *in vacuo*. During the ensuing years, the introduction of rationalized M.K.S. units has been widely encouraged by academic and professional bodies.

In the new edition, rationalized M.K.S. units have been used throughout. Fortunate indeed is the student newly entering the field of electricity and magnetism. For his benefit the basis of units has in fact been doubly rationalized, or to use the current term, "streamlined." For him the M.K.S. units provide the most straightforward and simple single system so far devised, for the practical units—the volt, the ampere, the ohm and the rest —*are already M.K.S. units*. The earlier student already nurtured on C.G.S. electrostatic and electromagnetic units would be well advised to avoid confusion in his mind, either by discarding his earlier memories of definitions and formulae, or else by taking care to maintain a clear demarcation between the bases of the two systems. The important thing is to *use* the M.K.S. system *for itself*, not to fall into confusion from converting one system to the other: no difficulty at all need then be experienced in assimilating the M.K.S. system.

In response to requests, the course year to which each worked example seems appropriate has been indicated. It should, however, be borne in mind that this indication is in the nature of a general guide only, and it does not necessarily imply that a particular question was taken from the examination paper of the year shown. Advantage has also been taken to apply the symbols, signs and abbreviations recommended in the new British Standard 1991 Part I (1954).

R. N. R.

LONDON, 1957

PREFACE TO THE FIRST EDITION

WITH the rising momentum of development during the nineteen-thirties in the technique and practice of telecommunication, the scope of text-books dealing with this subject expanded considerably. To permit this fuller treatment in his standard text-books *Telegraphy* and *Telephony*, Mr. T. E. Herbert decided to withdraw the introductory chapters on magnetism and electricity which these books had hitherto contained, and to cover this subject-matter in a new book to be entitled *Telecommunications Electricity*. It is to these circumstances that the present book owes its conception and I should like to acknowledge my indebtedness to Mr. Herbert's guidance and mature advice in planning the book which was to have appeared under our joint authorship.

Serious work upon this book was delayed by *force majeure* until 1946—a year which coincided with the introduction of radical changes in syllabus for the City and Guilds Examinations in telecommunication subjects. The original intention to cover the earlier examination syllabus in Technical Electricity was necessarily abandoned in favour of the new syllabus and the book received its present title.

As it now stands the book sets out to describe fundamental principles underlying the practice of telegraphy, telephony, and radio, but while adhering as closely as possible to principles, nevertheless some digression has been made to point the way to practice where this has appeared desirable. The plan of the book has been drawn up to include all items in the City and Guilds Examination syllabus in *Telecommunications (Principles) Grade I*, *Grade II*, and *Grade III*.

After consideration of the mathematical standard to be assumed on the part of the potential reader, I reached the conclusion that it would be better to exclude use of the differential or integral calculus. There are, of course, two opinions on this, but from personal experience I know that there is a large body of students eager to progress beyond elementary grades in their studies who are deterred from doing so by the frequently inseparable appearance of seemingly precipitous mathematical proofs. As a compromise I have given in a separate Appendix (A.5) some of the more popular proofs which require application of the calculus. Exceptionally, use has been made in the main text of the differential coefficient dy/dx simply as an expression for rate of change: an explanation of this symbol has been given in the Appendix (A.2). A summary of the essential mathematical equipment in trigonometry and vector algebra which this book requires has also been given in the Appendix, so that the book is, in some measure, self-contained.

Chapter I is intended to give sufficient description of atomic structure and current flow for the student to attain a correct perspective for the ensuing chapters: the related Appendix D is given not so much on account of its detail, but in order to present a general picture of electron shells and the relation of physical and electrical properties to atomic structure.

From Chapter II onwards consideration of the alternating current has been associated with that of the direct current. The detailed treatment of the a.c. circuit is covered in Chapter X, where the j-notation is used alongside that of Pythagoras' Theorem. The significance of the j-operator is explained in the Appendix.

Since a chapter must have a title, Chapter XI appears under "A.C. Transmission." No one would pretend to cover so complex and exhaustive a subject within a single chapter: nevertheless I have tried here to introduce a simple approach to the concepts of characteristic impedance, attenuation, and distortion.

In Chapter XIII treatment of the electronic valve is limited to the principle of its operation and the basis of its use as oscillator, rectifier, amplifier, and modulator. A description of the metal rectifier is included, as also is the cathode-ray oscilloscope.

In common with Chapter XI, the final one on sound has an apparently ambitious title: the intention there has been to include just sufficient of the properties of sound to give an insight into acoustics in telecommunication with an appreciation of factors concerned in distortion.

I wish to acknowledge the courtesy of the Postmaster-General in permitting the use in this book of official illustrations and instructions.

I am indebted to H. R. Harbottle Esq., O.B.E., for reading proofs and offering valuable criticism and advice.

In a book of this nature I have naturally drawn upon many sources for reference and wish to record my thanks to the Council of the Institution of Post Office Electrical Engineers and to the Board of Editors of the *Institution of Post Office Electrical Engineers Journal* for permission to reproduce information from Papers read before the Institution and from articles appearing in the *Journal*. Detailed acknowledgments have been made at the conclusion of each chapter.

Opportunity has been taken to include representative worked examples throughout the book: apart from a few elementary illustrations these have been taken entirely from recent City and Guilds Examination papers in telecommunication subjects. For permission to make use of these questions and also to reproduce the examination syllabus (Appendix H) I am indebted to the City and Guilds of London Institute.

In the interests of accuracy all terms, definitions, symbols, and abbreviations have been taken from the following publications, by kind permission of the British Standards Institution—

British Standard 204 (1943): "Glossary of Terms used in Telecommunication."
British Standard 205 (1943): "Glossary of Terms used in Electrical Engineering."
British Standard 530 (1947): "Graphical Symbols for Telecommunication."
British Standard 560 (1934): "Engineering Symbols and Abbreviations."
British Standard 1409 (1947): "Letter Symbols for Electronic Valves."
British Standard 1991 : Part 1 (1954): "Letter Symbols, Signs and Abbreviations."

My thanks are due to Mr. F. W. Dopson and to Mr. R. Breach, who have prepared the line diagrams: also to Mr. C. R. Wickens and to Mr. W. A. J. Paul for many of the photographs. Finally I wish to record my gratitude for photographs and information generously supplied by The Automatic Coil Winder and Electrical Equipment Co., Ltd.; The Electric Lamp Manufacturers' Association of Great Britain, Ltd.; Ernest Turner Electrical Instruments, Ltd.; Evershed and Vignoles, Ltd.; The Plessey Co., Ltd.; Siemens Bros. & Co., Ltd.; Standard Telephones and Cables, Ltd.; Westinghouse Brake and Signal Co., Ltd.; Walter Jones & Co. (Engineers).

R. N. R.

London, 1950

CONTENTS

CONTENTS

CHAPTER I

ELECTRONS

1.1. Effects of Electricity. To the question "What is electricity?" there is no answer. Electricity is known by the results it produces: the laws which govern its behaviour have been investigated and are well established.

The effects of an electric current are threefold, namely, (i) magnetic, (ii) heating, and (iii) chemical. Conversely, electric currents are produced from the expenditure of magnetic, heat, or chemical energy.

The magnetic effect has perhaps the widest application in industry: it is the basis of electrical power generating systems and of electric traction; it has also made possible the early microphone, the telephone receiver, the electromagnet, and the relay which are the foundations of telecommunication equipment. The heating effect has a wide field in heating and lighting appliances. The also of use in electric furnaces and welding, and chemical effect is applied mainly to the use of storage battery installations for use where emergency and portable power supplies are required, and also in the electroplating industry.

The flow of an electric current in a conductor normally results in (i) the creation of a magnetic field, and (ii) the production of heat. The chemical effect results only under certain favourable conditions, requiring the presence of suitable chemical solutions.

From a knowledge of the laws governing these effects, precision instruments for measuring electrical quantities are designed (Chapter XII), though meters depending upon electro-chemical effects are not practicable for application outside the laboratory.

1.2. Construction of Matter. A knowledge of the significant points of the Electron Theory of Matter assists a fuller understanding of the various electrical phenomena. According to this theory matter cannot be disassociated from the electric charges accompanying the primary units of mass. It is therefore necessary to know something of the construction of *matter*—the name embracing all the vast number and quantities of the different substances which together comprise the universe. Matter exists in three different states, as a solid, a liquid, or a gas.

1.3. Compounds and Elements. By far the majority of the different substances available are *compounds*, that is to say, they consist of two or more different simple substances in close chemical combination. Water is a compound formed from combination of the simple substances hydrogen and oxygen: sulphuric acid is a compound formed from hydrogen, sulphur, and oxygen. Some 500 000 chemical compounds are at present known and classified.

The simple substances referred to are known as *elements*: they cannot chemically be further broken down into different substances—they contain, in fact, only themselves: a quantity of pure hydrogen contains hydrogen and only hydrogen.

The different elements at present known to occur naturally number only 92. They can exist alone, as elements, or in most cases they can combine to form compounds. All the different compound substances in existence are made up of the various possible combinations, often complex, of these 92 elements.

1.4. Molecules. If any substance is progressively subdivided to obtain the smallest possible particle of that substance without breaking it up into any constituent chemical parts and thus losing its identity, then that minute particle is known as a *molecule*; a molecule is the smallest particle of any compound or element which can exist alone. Salammoniac, for example, is a chemical combination of nitrogen, hydrogen, and chlorine (all three are normally gases) in certain fixed proportions: if the molecule of salammoniac be subdivided, then it no longer exists as such but is broken up into its constituent elements.

The molecules of any substance are in a continual state of movement, which is accelerated by any increase in temperature. In a solid, the molecules are tightly packed so that their movement is relatively confined: as the temperature is raised, the molecules move more violently until finally they achieve the mobility of the liquid state. In a liquid the molecules are less tightly packed, and much less so in a gas where the molecules achieve their maximum freedom of movement, which accounts for the more ready expansion and contraction of gases. The pressure exerted by a gas is due to the incessant bombardment by its molecules on the containing vessel.

1.5. Atoms. The *atom* is the name given to the smallest particle of an element which can take part in a chemical process. An atom cannot usually exist alone for any length of time: it will immediately combine with different atoms present to form a molecule of a chemical compound, or else unite with similar atoms, usually in pairs, to form molecules of an element. Exceptionally, however, the molecules of some substances, such as copper, or lead, contain only one atom, in which cases the molecule and the atom are identical.

A molecule therefore may consist of one atom, such as copper, written Cu (see Appendix **D**); of two or more similar atoms, for example hydrogen whose molecule contains two atoms and is written H_2; or of two or more atoms of different kinds, for example, sulphuric acid of which the molecule is written H_2SO_4 since it is made up of two atoms of hydrogen, one atom of sulphur, and four atoms of oxygen. The sulphuric acid may be broken down chemically by removing the sulphur atom and three oxygen atoms, leaving water, H_2O.

All atoms of a given element are chemically identical from whatever source they originate. The atom is indivisible in the sense that less than one of them cannot take part in a chemical reaction.

1.6. Electrons, Protons, and Neutrons. Every atom is itself constructed from minute particles, termed *electrons*, *protons*, and *neutrons*.

The electron carries a *negative* charge, equal to 1.6×10^{-19} coulombs: it is the fundamental unit of electricity. The mass of an electron, 9.1×10^{-31} kg, is due to its charge.

The proton carries a *positive* charge of 1.6×10^{-19} coulombs, i.e. of the same magnitude as the electron charge. Its mass, however, is about 1 840 times as great as that of the electron.

The neutron carries no electric charge: its mass is approximately equal to that of the proton.

All electrons are identical, no matter from what type of atom they are derived: similarly all protons are identical and so are all neutrons.

A summary of the subdivision of matter shows that the hundreds of thousands of different substances are formed from combinations, in various proportions, of 92 elements, the atoms of which, in their turn, are determined by the number and arrangement of their constituent electrons, protons, and neutrons.

In the normal state, every atom has equal numbers of electrons and protons: the charges on these being equal but opposite, the atom is then electrically neutral.

Mention of other atomic particles, for example the short-living *positron* or positive electron, is unnecessary for the present consideration.

1.7. Atomic Structure. The simplest atom, that of hydrogen, consists of one proton around which one electron moves in a fixed orbit.

The structure of most atoms is more complex, and may be likened to a minute solar system, with a central **positive nucleus surrounded by planetary** electrons revolving at high speed in definite orbits: these orbits may be elliptical or eccentric. In the atoms having more than one or two electrons these orbits exist in groups or shells, and each member of any one group moves in the type of orbit characteristic of that group.

Except for the simple hydrogen atom, the nucleus is made up of protons and neutrons in approximately equal numbers. The nucleus therefore contains practically the whole of the atomic mass, and carries a positive charge equal in magnitude to the sum of the charges carried by the extra-nuclear electrons.

The elements may be arranged in a Periodic Table proceeding step by step from a simpler element to the next higher: at each step the nuclear charge is increased by one unit and at the same time an electron is inserted in the outer part of the electronic envelope. The physical and chemical properties of an element are determined by the electronic configuration, particularly in the outermost shell. For example, the magnetic elements, iron, cobalt, and nickel occupy adjacent positions in the Periodic Table; also the alkali metals which are very active chemically—lithium, sodium, potassium, rubidium, and caesium—each have only one electron in their outermost shells.

A particular arrangement of the electrons within the shells is characteristic of a particular element. There is a maximum to the number of electrons which can be in each shell. The first or inner shell contains a maximum number of 2 electrons, the second 8, the third 18, and the fourth 32. The lightest element, hydrogen, has one electron in the first shell the first shell is completed in the element helium with two electrons. Passing from element to element through the Periodic Table, each shell gradually fills up, commencing with the inner one and proceeding outwards, but the maximum number in each shell is not always reached before the next shell begins to form. For example, when the formation of the fourth shell begins, the third shell contains only 8 electrons instead of its full complement of 18. This arrangement of the electrons within the shells is indicated for the elements in the Periodic Table in Appendix **D** along with the chemical symbols.

The space occupied by an atom is, except for the small nucleus (of radius about 10^{-12} cm) where the mass is concentrated, practically empty. The planetary electrons are separated from the nucleus by much greater distances, relatively, than are the planets of the solar system.

A simplified representation of the carbon atom is shown in Fig. 1.1. The nucleus consists of six protons intimately bound up with six neutrons, and displaying therefore a positive nuclear charge of + 6 units: around this nucleus revolve six orbital electrons in various planes, balancing the nuclear charge and making the atom as a whole electrically neutral.

The number of protons in the nucleus—equal to the number of extra-nuclear electrons—is known as the *atomic number*: one "isotope" (see below) of copper, for example, of atomic number 29 has a nucleus consisting of 29 protons and 35 neutrons, with 29 orbital electrons neutralizing the + 29 units charge on the nucleus.

Any change in the structure of the nucleus will naturally result in the formation of a different type of atom. This is well demonstrated by the element radium, an element exhibiting a phenomenon known as radio-activity, which spontaneously disintegrates by shooting out particles from the nucleus until it ultimately reaches stability in the form of lead. Any change in the nucleus involves vast transfers of energy.

It may be added that a chemically pure element often consists of a mixture of different sorts of atoms, identical in chemical properties but differing in mass owing to the differing numbers of neutrons present. These different forms of atoms are known as *isotopes*. The hydrogen isotope having twice the atomic weight of the normal hydrogen atom has one neutron in the nucleus, and is known as "heavy" hydrogen. The isotope forms of an atom, however, display the same electrical charges.

1.8. Ions. It is possible to detach an orbital electron from an atom, so leaving the atom with an excess positive charge. Alternatively the neutral atom may be given an additional orbital electron, in which case the atom assumes a negative charge.

Atoms or groups of atoms which exhibit externally an electrical charge are known as *ions*, a positive ion being deficient of one or more electrons, and a negative ion possessing one or more electrons in excess of its normal condition.

The atom has a strong tendency to remain neutral: a positive ion attracts electrons to it, and a negative ion will readily part with excess electrons.

1.9. Electric Currents. The flow of an electric current in a metal is accomplished by the drift of outer orbital electrons from atom to atom throughout the material, the atoms themselves not moving from their mean positions. It is unlikely that any electron ever moves more than the distance between two neighbouring atoms: a positive ion will attract an electron from its neighbouring atom which, itself becoming positive, then attracts an electron from the next atom, so producing the electron drift. Electric charges moving in this manner constitute an *electronic current*.

Just as the electron is considered as a particle which carries a negative charge, so in the class of solid materials known as "semiconductors" modern theory postulates the existence of a "particle" which carries a positive charge and is termed a *hole*. It is in fact a mobile vacancy which should normally be occupied by an electron. The magnitudes of the charges carried by both the electron and the hole are equal but the polarity is of opposite sign. The flow of current produced by a drift of holes is further discussed in Chapter XIV.

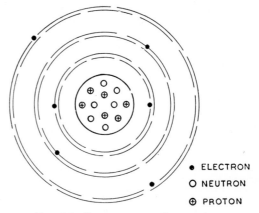

● ELECTRON
○ NEUTRON
⊕ PROTON

FIG. 1.1. STRUCTURE OF CARBON ATOM

The passage of an electric current through a fluid or gas or some solids involves the actual movement of the ions—charged atoms or charged molecules—carrying their charges. This is a case of *ionic* or *electrolytic conduction* which forms the basis of the subject-matter of Chapter IV.

By imparting sufficient velocity to the outer electrons they can be dislodged entirely from a material and made to travel through a vacuum or a gas at low pressure as a stream of free electrons: this is the basis for the operation of the electronic valve. Under certain conditions, the gas molecules may become ionized and electrolytic conduction results. This is further discussed in Chapter XIII.

1.10. Conductors, Semiconductors, and Insulators. A material which readily permits the flow of electrons is known as an electrical *conductor*: a material in which no appreciable electron drift is possible is called an *insulator*. There is, however, no perfect insulating material, just as there is no perfect conductor which permits the passage of electrons with complete freedom. All metallic conductors possess a property called "resistance," due to the free electrons, in the course of their motion through the metal, colliding from time to time with the ions, and being deflected from their path, or retarded. The fundamental difference between a conductor and a non-conductor is that the conductor contains "free" (i.e. detachable) outer electrons while the non-conductor does not. Any conduction observed in insulators (other than that occurring at breakdown) has generally been assumed to be electrolytic.

An important class of solids whose use has recently come into considerable prominence displays the property of conducting an electric current to a degree which is intermediate between the conductor and the insulator. These materials, known as *semiconductors*, may conduct by both electron currents and hole currents.

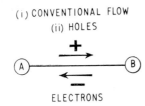

FIG. 1.2. DIRECTION OF CURRENT FLOW

1.11. Direction of Current Flow. The question of the direction of flow of an electric current may conveniently be clarified at this stage. Prior to the discovery of the electron it was necessary to postulate the direction of flow of the current: the electric current was assumed to be a flow of POSITIVE electricity *from a positive to a negative terminal.* This is still the accepted convention in practical application, and the terminals of electrical instruments are, where necessary, marked positive and negative accordingly. The flow of current by "holes," being a positive current, is naturally in the same direction as the "conventional" current.

On the other hand the Electron Theory shows that the normal electric current is actually an electron flow, i.e. a flow of NEGATIVE electricity *from a negative ion to a positive ion.*

Though these two conceptions may appear at first to be conflicting, they are not so: a positive flow from *A* to *B* (Fig. 1.2) is mathematically the same as a negative flow from *B* to *A*. No confusion should arise if it is remembered that the conventional view assumes a flow of positive electricity while the Electron Theory concerns the flow of negative electrical charges.

Except where otherwise stated, the older convention, namely the flow of positive electricity from positive to negative, is assumed throughout this book.

SUMMARY

Effects of Electricity. (i) Magnetic, (ii) Heating, (iii) Chemical. (i) and (ii) are inseparable from the flow of current.

Chemical Compound. A substance consisting of two or more elements chemically combined.

Element. A primary substance not combined with any other.

Molecule. The smallest particle which retains the identity of the substance.

Atom. The smallest particle of an element which takes part in a chemical change.

Electron. An elementary particle containing the smallest negative electric charge.

Proton. An elementary particle carrying an equivalent positive charge.

Hole. A mobile vacancy in the electronic structure of a semiconductor: can be regarded as a positive electronic charge of equal (but opposite) magnitude to that of the electron.

Atomic Structure. Electrons (−) and protons (+) carry charges of equal magnitude: protons with neutrons form a positive nucleus around which circulate electrons of sufficient number to render the atom electrically neutral.

Positive Ions. Charged atoms or groups of atoms with a deficit of orbital electrons.

Negative Ions. Charged atoms or groups of atoms with excess orbital electrons.

Electric Currents. (i) In a metal, the drift of outer orbital electrons from atom to atom; (ii) in a semiconductor the drift of conduction electrons or holes; (iii) in a fluid or gas and in some solids, the movement of ions; (iv) in a vacuum or low pressure gas, a stream of free electrons.

Conductor. A material which readily permits the flow of a current.

Insulator. A material in which no appreciable current will flow.

Semiconductor. A material whose property of permitting a flow of current lies between that of metals and insulators.

Current Direction. (i) Practical convention (also hole current)—movements of positive electricity from + to −; (ii) Electron theory—movement of negative electrons from − to +.

REFERENCES

W. G. RADLEY, C. E. RICHARDS, E. A. SPEIGHT, and E. V. WALKER: "Modern Materials in Telecommunication." *I.P.O.E.E. Journal,* **33** (1940), p. 53.

CHAPTER II

THE D.C. CIRCUIT

2.1. Current. Owing to the intangible nature of the electric current, a reference to some analogy such as that provided by a hydraulic system gives a useful idea of the character of the electric circuit: such an analogy is by no means perfect, and a warning may well be given of the danger in pushing

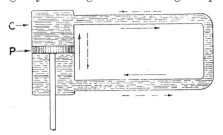

Fig. 2.1. Water Analogy—A.C.

the comparison too far and incurring the risk of deducing false conclusions.

Consider the elementary hydraulic system shown in plan in Fig. 2.1 where a simple pump, consisting of a piston P in a cylinder C, is connected to the two ends of a pipe, the whole being filled with water. While the piston is at rest the water remains stationary since there is no motive force urging it to move, although there is water present in all parts of the system: to produce motion of the water there must be applied to it a force or pressure of some sort. When the pump is actuated, the piston on its forward stroke (shown by the full arrow) produces an increase of pressure at one end of the pipe and a corresponding suction at the other end, resulting in a displacement of the water molecules along the pipe in the direction of the full arrows. The reverse piston-stroke (dotted arrow) reverses the conditions of pressure and suction, and the water molecules are now displaced in the opposite direction (dotted arrows). The reciprocating piston produces alternating surges in the water, the water being always in a state of motion (excluding of course the instantaneous positions) so long as the pump is working.

Fig. 2.2 shows a simple electrical system. An electric generator, or alternator, G, has its two terminals connected to a conducting material, say a copper wire. While the generator is at rest there is no electric flow in the wire although it abounds with electrons. When the generator is put into motion it sets up an electrical pressure difference

between its terminals, resulting in a displacement of the electrons in the conducting path. Compared with the water pump, the electric generator may be regarded as a device for pumping electrons round a conducting path, or circuit. The generator continually reverses the *direction* or *sense* of its pressure difference, the electron displacements being therefore alternately first in one direction and then in the other as shown by the full and dotted arrows. The electrons surge back and forth in the con-

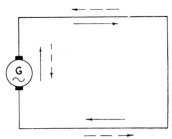

Fig. 2.2. Simple A.C. Circuit

ducting path much in the same manner as the water molecules of Fig. 2.1. The moving electrons carrying negative electric charges produce surges or currents of electricity in the conductor.

An ELECTRIC CURRENT is *the flow of electricity along any path or around any circuit.* The symbol for current is I or i.

An electric current which continually changes its direction in this manner is known as an ALTERNATING CURRENT (A.C.). Currents of this nature find considerable application in electrical practice: the natural occurrence of alternating quantities is also found, for example, in light and sound. *An alternating current is an electric current which alternately reverses its direction in a circuit in a periodic manner, the frequency being independent of the constants of the circuit.* The term frequency is applied to denote the number of times a change of direction is produced in a given interval of time—usually one second.

In Fig. 2.3 the hydraulic system includes two simple valves. On the forward piston-stroke (full arrow) the water pressure forces open the valve O and shuts the valve I; due to the pressure difference water molecules are displaced around the pipe in the direction of the full arrows. The reverse piston-stroke (dotted arrow) closes valve O and opens valve I, but does not produce any displacement of the water in the pipe. In this way the reciprocating piston produces a series of gushes or pulsations of the water in the pipe, the water being

5

constrained by the valves to move always in the same direction. With a suitable design and speed of pump, a sensibly steady unidirectional flow may be obtained.

The dynamo G of Fig. 2.4 is an electric generator fitted with a device called a commutator whose purpose may be regarded as being similar to that

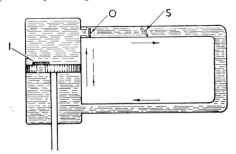

FIG. 2.3. WATER ANALOGY—D.C.

of the valves in Fig. 2.3. The dynamo maintains a steady pressure difference between its terminals—usually with a very small degree of pulsation—so producing a continuous unidirectional drift of the "free" outer electrons which constitutes the electric current flow around the circuit. The direction of current flow indicated in the diagram is the practical or positive flow. A voltaic cell

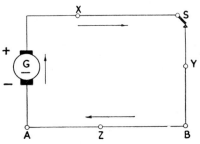

FIG. 2.4. SIMPLE D.C. CIRCUIT

(Chapter IV) is also a generator producing a unidirectional pressure difference.

An electric current of this nature, namely unidirectional, is usually known as a DIRECT CURRENT (D.C.) or sometimes as a continuous current. *A direct current is an electric current flowing in one direction only and sensibly free from pulsation.*

In passing, it should be noted that the direction of flow of positive electricity *inside* the dynamo or cell must be from the negative to the positive terminal. The path inside the generator is known as the *internal* circuit to distinguish it from the outside path or *external* circuit.

The simile has been suggested that the direct

current flows in one direction like the water of a stream, while the alternating current flows backwards and forwards like the tide in an estuary.

In the hydraulic system the flow of water can be stopped by shutting the stop-cock S (Fig. 2.3). In the electric circuit the opening of a switch S (Fig. 2.4) inserts a non-conducting material, usually air, into the path and prevents the passage of electrons: the flow of current necessitates a complete conducting path or circuit from the generator around the external circuit and back to the generator. When the external circuit is opened by a switch the generator is said to be on *open circuit*: with the circuit completed by closing the switch, a *closed circuit* is presented and current flows.

The rate of flow of water is measured by the quantity of water passing a given point in unit time, for example in gallons per hour. The intensity or strength of an electric current is similarly measured by the quantity or charge of electricity passing a given point in unit time, usually one second. The fundamental unit of electric charge is that carried by one electron, consequently the fundamental unit of current strength is a rate of flow of one electron per second. For practical purposes a unit of charge known as the COULOMB (C) is adopted, equal to the charge carried by $6\cdot28 \times 10^{18}$ electrons. The practical unit of current strength, the AMPERE, usually abbreviated to AMP (A), is a rate of flow of one coulomb per second, i.e. the current in a circuit is 1 A if $6\cdot28 \times 10^{18}$ electrons pass through any cross-section of the conductor *every second*. It is the *rate of flow* which is to be understood by the use of the term *current*. The magnitudes of currents utilized in telecommunication circuits are frequently so small as to be more conveniently expressed in terms of the subdivisions, the milliamp (mA) and the microamp (μA).

In the hydraulic system a higher rate of flow is obtainable by an increased piston speed or by using a more powerful pump. At the same time the diameter of the pipe and the amount of friction on the inner walls have a controlling effect on the rate of flow. If the pipe is of very small bore the flow of water will be correspondingly small: a large diameter pipe is capable of passing a greater quantity of water per second, but in either case the rate of flow will be still dependent upon the pressure applied by the pump.

Similarly the rate of current flow in the electric circuit is dependent, not only upon the electrical pressure applied from the generator, but also upon RESISTANCE due to the nature and dimensions of the conducting material. *Resistance is that property of a body by virtue of which it resists the flow of electricity through it, causing a dissipation of electrical energy as heat.* The symbol for resistance is R or r.

Since the rate of flow of water depends upon the size of the pipe, the question arises as to how this rate would be affected by the non-uniformity of the bore, for example if a length of pipe of smaller bore were inserted in the path. The answer is that the rate of flow will be the same at all points, the retardation through the small bore influencing the rate of flow at other parts of the path: if this were not so there would have to be continual accumulation or diminution of water at some point. *The strength of the electric current is the same at all parts of the circuit*: this is a fundamental property of the electric circuit, and an important one. If the circuit branches into two or more parts, the total strength in these branches is equal to the current leaving and returning to the generator.

2.2. Electromotive Force and Potential. To utilize a familiar example, it is known that the water of a stream rising in the hills flows downhill in its effort to reach the sea. This is due to the gravitational force acting on the mass of the water and pulling it downwards until it reaches sea-level. For the same reason, if an elevated tank of water has an open pipe near its base the water will gush out, always attempting to reach a lower level. The stored water is said to possess *potential energy*, that is to say, energy possessed by virtue of its position. The higher the tank of water is placed, the greater is its potential energy, and the water is said to be at a higher *head* or pressure compared to any water present at a lower level, possessing less potential energy (since it has not so far to fall) and therefore at a lower head. The term *head* is thus relative, and the natural flow is from the higher to the lower.

This may be illustrated by an arrangement such as that of the simple elevation shown in Fig. 2.5. If the upper tank initially contains water, there exists a difference of pressure between the two tanks, so that when the stopcock S is opened water will flow spontaneously into the lower tank via the pipe which directs it, i.e. from the higher head to the lower. It should be noted that this flow depends upon the relative heights of the tanks quite independently of which tank initially holds the greater *quantity* of water. The flow ceases when the upper tank has emptied, but this flow could be made continuous by driving the pump P to force the water which is at the lower level, against the gravitational pull, back to the upper tank from which it would continue to flow due to its potential energy. The pump imparts *kinetic energy*—or energy due to motion—to the water to force it to an elevated position where it then regains potential

energy: the water is restored to its position or higher level by virtue of the work which has been done by the pump. As the water subsequently falls, the potential energy of the water at successive points along the connecting pipe gradually falls also until it is in the lower tank and at a relative zero level: the fall of pressure is uniform.

Considering a direct current in the electric circuit, the cell or dynamo functions to produce a higher pressure or *potential* at one terminal than at the other, and a flow of current results from the higher to the lower around the external circuit. In

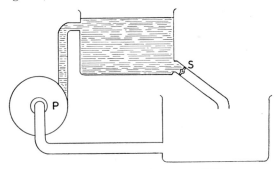

Fig. 2.5. Water Analogy—P.D.

the electric circuit, potential is analogous to level or pressure in a hydraulic system: electric potential is in fact often referred to as electric pressure. Potential is also analogous to temperature, which is the determining condition for heat to flow between one body and another at different temperatures when the two are in contact.

The current flow in a circuit is assumed to be from the positive to the negative terminal, and a point at positive potential is said to have a *higher* potential with respect to a point at negative or relatively lower potential. The flow of "free" electrons is, of course, from the point of negative potential to the point of higher potential. The production of a *potential difference* (p.d.) is thus an essential condition for the flow of current. *Potential difference denotes a difference between the electrical states existing at two points tending to cause a movement of electricity from one point to the other.* The symbol for p.d. is V or v.

In the external circuit, the magnitude of the potential falls gradually from the positive terminal to the negative, and at points along the circuit successively diminishing values of potential occur and can be measured: there is a p.d. between any two points chosen at random in the external circuit. It should also be clear that the potential of any point in the external circuit, for example the point Y in Fig. 2.4 is positive with respect to a point Z

at lower potential, but at the same time Y is negative to a point X at higher potential.

The mechanism by which a cell establishes a difference of potential at its terminals is discussed in Chapter IV, but clearly a p.d. is only obtained as the result of a consumption of energy within the generator: a force is necessary to drive the current *from low to high* potential within the generator. This force is known as the ELECTROMOTIVE FORCE (e.m.f.). *The electromotive force of a source is that force which tends to cause a movement of electricity in a circuit.* The symbol for e.m.f. is E or e.

Confusion sometimes arises between e.m.f. and p.d.: it is most important to realize that e.m.f. and p.d. are related as cause and effect. The electromotive force produces and maintains a potential difference between the terminals, and without an e.m.f. there could be no p.d. The e.m.f. and p.d. are seen to bear to one another a relationship similar to that borne between kinetic and potential energy respectively.

In the hydraulic analogy of Fig. 2.5 the potential energy acquired by the water in the upper tank would be equal to the kinetic energy imparted by the pump were it not for the losses due to friction, etc., incurred in the pump. Similarly, in the electric circuit the e.m.f. of the generator will be slightly greater than the p.d. produced owing to the inevitable losses within the generator.

Though not a strictly accurate parallel, suppose the stopcock in Fig. 2.5 is closed: the *whole* of the water is then pumped into the upper tank and a slightly greater head of water is produced compared with the head maintained while water is circulating with the stopcock open. When the electric generator is on open circuit, the p.d. becomes exactly equal to the e.m.f. since no current is flowing within the generator. This relationship between e.m.f. and p.d. is further discussed in Chapter IV.

The e.m.f. and the p.d. are measured in terms of the same unit the VOLT (V). Electrical mains supplies are being standardized at a pressure of 240 V: telephone and telegraph systems operate at 50 V and 80 V respectively: on the other hand, potential differences between points in telecommunication circuits are frequently measured in millivolts (mV) or in microvolts (μV).

The water in a river flows until it finds sea level which is regarded as the reference zero level. In a similar respect the earth—which is a good electrical conductor—is regarded as being at zero electric potential, the absolute potential of any point being referred to the zero potential of the earth. The POTENTIAL at any point is *the potential difference between that point and earth*, being positive if current tends to flow from the point *to* earth, and

negative if current would flow *from* earth to the point.

To ensure the safety of users against dangerous effects which might result from an electrical fault, such as the breakdown of insulation, it is a common practice to connect to earth all those parts of electrical appliances—i.e. the mountings and casings—with which the human body is likely to come into contact. The body will then remain at one potential—that of the earth—even when touching the electrical apparatus: consequently no current will flow through the body since there can be no difference of potential. However, the practical achievement of this safety condition requires considerable care in the design of earthing systems: it is not always possible to secure earth connexions of sufficiently low resistance to prevent, under fault conditions, the existence of considerable p.d.s between bodies nominally at earth potential. The potential of the earth in the near vicinity of an earth connexion may be altered considerably due to the passage of a fault current.[1]

In telecommunication systems, one terminal (usually the positive) of the source of e.m.f. is normally connected to earth. One advantage in doing this is that, in the electrical connexion between two distant points, the return path completing the closed circuit may be provided naturally by the earth, and the expense of providing an additional line—often of considerable length—is avoided. For instance, if in Fig. 2.4 the point A and the point B are each earth-connected, the length of wire AB becomes redundant as a return path and it can be omitted. The electrical resistance of the earth being zero, the resistance of the path AB is reduced to that of the earth connexions at A and B. There are, however, practical limitations which restrict the use of single-wire circuits with "earth-return."

2.3. Conductors. *A conductor is a body or substance which offers a low resistance to the passage of an electric current.* All materials conduct an electric current to some extent, but in many substances the resistance offered is so extremely high that such substances are regarded as insulators. In general, metals are the best conductors: the ratio of their conducting power to that of the insulating materials is of the order of 10^{17}. The electrical properties of a substance are governed by the atomic structure: though a considerable amount of investigation has been carried out, prediction of the absolute magnitude of the conductivities of different materials by deduction from theory has so far met with only partial success.

In telecommunication equipment the majority of conductors occur in the form of wires. The choice of a conducting material for any purpose usually depends upon the need for its resistance to be as low as possible, or alternatively for some applications it must be high. Equally important for such purposes as overhead lines are considerations of the mechanical properties of a wire, its tensile strength, its elasticity, its coefficient of expansion, or its weight. Sometimes it is highly important that the resistance should remain practically invariable with any change in temperature or on the other hand such a variation may be desirable. For economic reasons the final choice of a suitable conductor will be largely governed by its cost.

Pure silver possesses the best conducting properties but owing to its high cost it is ruled out for all but specialized uses. Pure copper is by far the most commonly used conductor in any electrical system since it best fulfils all general requirements; it is used in all forms of coils, in cables, and for some overhead lines.

The effect of impurities or of the deliberately added constituents in the alloys is usually to increase the resistance. Cadmium-copper, an alloy consisting of 99 per cent copper and 1 per cent cadmium, is much used for certain classes of overhead lines, its mechanical strength being superior to that of copper for only a slight increase of resistance.

Platinum, gold, and silver find considerable application in the contacts required at switching points. The main requirement here, apart from low electrical resistance, is resistance to wear, and pure platinum best fulfils this need, but owing to high cost it is used only where fairly heavy currents have to be broken, as for example, in the magnet circuits of automatic telephone switches. The standard telephone relay (Fig. 7.8) uses contacts of pure silver: for other contacts alloys comprising 7 per cent platinum, 67 per cent gold, and 26 per cent silver (P.G.S.), or 10 per cent gold and 90 per cent silver (G.S.) are used. For telegraph relays, contacts of copper-palladium and platinum-iridium alloys are used. Tungsten is used for breaking the heavy currents in motor circuits. The use of contacts provided by mercury contained in small glass tubes has been largely adopted for switching circuits working at heavy currents, at high voltages or for long contact life.

There are also instances of non-metallic conductors, the foremost in use being carbon. Apart from its negative temperature coefficient it has the important property that its resistance depends upon the applied pressure, the resistance decreasing as the applied pressure increases. The application of this property in the carbon microphone is well known, and in recent years the use of carbon in automatic voltage regulators has become common.

2.4. Insulating Materials. An essential need in any electrical equipment is for the separation or insulation of one conducting path from another. An INSULATING MATERIAL is one *which offers relatively high resistance to the passage of an electric current*: such a material is also referred to as a DIELECTRIC. It follows from this definition that all known dielectrics have a small electrical conductivity. Superpurification considerably increases the resistivity of some materials, indicating that impurities may be a major cause of dielectric conduction.

The final choice of an insulating material[2] must depend upon mechanical as well as electrical properties appropriate to its intended use. Important mechanical and physical properties to be considered may include one or more of the following: tensile, compressive, shear, and impact strength: modulus of elasticity: resistance to heat and shock: low water absorption: resistance to mineral oils, to acids, and to other chemical action; specific gravity: coefficient of linear expansion: non-inflammability: thermal conductivity and rigidity: dimensional stability: flexibility (for cables): adaptability to a wide range of moulding or machining processes: freedom from tracking (i.e. from the creation of a conducting carbon path following a high voltage discharge over the surface). Important electrical properties include adequate electric strength against breakdown under high applied voltage: low power-factor: permittivity over a range of frequencies and temperature: insulation resistance: surface and volume resistivity. Cost is naturally an important factor.

The commoner gases are the most nearly perfect insulators, but with complete absence of mechanical strength. For example, air is the insulating material for a route of overhead wires: most switching devices depend upon the insertion or bridging of an air-gap in a circuit, though in practice the conductors must be mounted upon some insulating material for rigid support, and this material enters largely into the degree of insulation obtained.

The commoner non-metallic liquids have a small *electronic* conductivity. The *ionic* conductivity of liquids varies greatly: for oils it is very small, and these are the only practicable liquid insulating materials, an important example being transformer oil, which of course also acts as a cooling medium.

Pure water is practically a non-conductor but is very slightly ionized (Chapter IV). It is, however, practically impossible to keep it free from impurities, of which even the smallest percentage highly ionizes it and renders it a comparatively good conductor. For this reason the presence of moisture is detrimental to good insulation, the water providing a path for leakage of the current. As an example, the failure of a cable is more often due to the ingress of moisture than to any other cause. Water as a surface film on insulators is harmful not because of its own (low) conductivity, but because of its power to dissolve and dissociate certain constituents of the insulator, resulting in the presence of ions with consequent electrolytic current. To overcome this, impregnation is adopted to fill all interstices which might trap moisture, and surface varnishing to keep moisture away from the surface of the insulator itself.

With solid insulating materials,[3] since there are no free electrons in pure substances (excepting metals), no electronic conduction takes place. Ionic conduction can occur, and, if appreciable, there results some change in the composition of the material.

The textiles cotton, silk, and wool are used extensively for insulating flexible conductors and in internal cables and coil windings. The insulation resistance of textiles is altered in the presence of moisture due to the development of a back-e.m.f. The presence of impurities in textiles increases the conductivity and also the tendency for corrosion by the small currents flowing. Paper is used almost exclusively to separate the conductors in multi-conductor underground cables, but by crimping the paper or by using a wrapping of string between conductor and paper the enclosed air plays an important part as the insulating material: such cables are known as air-spaced paper-core cables (A.S.P.C.).

To name but a selection from the extensive range of available insulating materials there are the natural minerals mica, asbestos, slate, and marble: or vitrified materials, glass, ceramics, and porcelain: natural and synthetic rubber: ebonite: waxes, enamels, varnishes, oils: natural resins (shellac) and synthetic resins, from the early "bakelite" to the more recent introductions either of the thermosetting or thermoplastic types. Thermosetting plastics undergo chemical change when subjected to heat and pressure: they are thus converted to an insoluble infusible state which cannot be further reformed even by the application of more intense heat and pressure. Thermoplastic[4] compounds on the other hand can be softened and re-softened indefinitely by the application of heat provided that the heat applied is insufficient to cause chemical decomposition. Many new substances are produced by a molecular process known as "polymerization." Polymerization is the building up of long-chain molecules from relatively simple molecular structures. In the case of thermosetting compounds, cross-linking of the molecules occurs. Among these materials are many variants under trade names such as "perspex" (acrylic resins), "polythene" (polymerized ethylene), "neoprene" (based upon synthetic rubber), and "polystyrene" (cellulose base). Also extensively used are papers of various grades and laminated paper or fabric boards such as S.R.B.P. (synthetic resin bonded paper).

A list of commonly employed insulating materials with their properties appears in Table 2.I. The electric properties of dielectrics are further discussed in Chapter V.

2.5. Semiconductors. On the basis of electrical conduction all solid materials can be broadly divided into three classes. If the *conductivity* σ is greater than 10^3 mho/cm the solid is called a *conductor*. Examples are copper, $\sigma = 5 \times 10^5$, and constantan, $\sigma = 2 \times 10^4$ mho/cm. The conductivity of a conductor normally falls with increasing temperature, apart from a few special alloys designed to have a conductivity practically independent of temperature.

At the other extreme is the group of solids having conductivity σ lower than 10^{-9} mho/cm and known as *insulators*. Examples are glass, $\sigma = 10^{-10}$; ebonite, $\sigma = 10^{-15}$; mica, $\sigma = 10^{-14}$; and paraffin wax, $\sigma = 10^{-17}$ mho/cm.

Some non-metallic substances have conductivities too low to justify their being called conductors and yet too large to admit them to the class of insulators. They are crystalline materials known as SEMICONDUCTORS[5] and are capable of electronic conduction by electrons and "holes." The conductivity of semiconductors lies between $\sigma = 10^{-6}$ and 10^{+3} mho/cm at normal temperatures. Their conductivity is very temperature-dependent. *rising* with an increase of temperature over a certain range: the conductivity is also directly affected by the influence of certain forms of radiation of sufficiently short wavelength such as visible light.

Semiconductors are always very slightly impure and their conductivity is influenced by the degree of impurities present. Germanium, silicon, selenium, and gallium arsenide are among the materials of most practical utility in this class.

That part of solid-state theory related to semiconductors is described in Chapter XIV in connexion with transistors. The two-electron "valence" bonds between neighbouring atoms of the pure semiconductor are intact at very low temperatures approaching absolute zero ($-273°C$): no electrons are free to move under the influence of any externally applied potential and no current flows in the material which is then an insulator. At higher temperatures the random thermal vibrations of the atoms result in the fracture of some of the valence bonds, setting free an electron from each fractured bond and leaving an incomplete one-electron bond. The freed electrons produce the condition of electrical conductivity. At $-40°C$ germanium has a *resistivity* of about 2 000 ohm-cm: at $+25°C$, with the increased thermal atomic vibrations and fracture of valence bonds resulting in more free electrons, the resistivity is about 50 ohm-cm, while at $+40°C$ the resistivity is about 30 ohm-cm. Very few of the elements are semiconductors at room temperature but there is a large number of compounds which are semiconductors.

2.6. Resistance. Resistance is measured in terms of a unit known as the OHM (Ω). *The ohm is the resistance in which a steady current of one ampere generates heat at the rate of one watt.*

The resistance of a conductor is an intrinsic property of the material and so varies for different substances according to the composition. Some standard of comparison of the resistances of different materials is necessary for design work, as well as the means of computing the numerical value of the resistance of a conductor of any size and shape. The resistance of any conductor depends upon its composition and its dimensions: it also varies with its temperature.

It has been established that the resistance of a conductor of uniform gauge and homogeneous material is directly proportional to its length and inversely proportional to its cross-sectional area. Expressed in symbols—

$$R \propto l/a$$

or

$$R = k \cdot l/a$$

where R = resistance,
l = length,
a = cross-sectional area,
k = a constant.

For example, with a given material, since R is proportional to l, it follows that if the length of wire is doubled then the resistance is doubled; on the other hand, since R is *inversely* proportional to a, if the cross-sectional area is *increased* fourfold then the resistance is *decreased* to one-quarter of its original value, assuming that all other factors remain unchanged.

TABLE 2.I

INSULATING MATERIALS

Material	Type	Surface Resistivity (MΩ/cm-square)	Volume Resistivity (MΩ/cm-cube)	Relative Permittivity at 1 kc/s (ε_r)	Power Factor $\times 10^4$ at 1 kc/s	at 60 kc/s
Insulating oil.	Oils and waxes	—	10^9	2·3	< 1	—
Petroleum jelly		—	—	2·2	< 10	< 10
Paraffin wax .		> 10^{11}	10^{11}	2·2	< 1	< 1
Beeswax		> 10^{11}	10^8	3·0	300	—
Shellac .	Natural resins	10^4	10^{10}	3 to 4	—	—
Rubber		—	—	—	—	—
Gutta percha .		—	—	3·4	80	200
Balata		—	—	3·0	40	180
Paragutta		—	—	2·6	12	20
K-gutta		—	—	2·6	4	16
Telconax		—	—	2·8	100	100
Ebonite		10^8	10^{10}	3·0	50	70
Bakelite	Synthetic resins	10^5	10^5	5	1 000	—
Bakelite laminated sheet.		10^5	10^6	5	800	—
Diakon		10^6	10^{11}	3·6	320	220
Polystyrene .		> 10^7	10^{12}	2·7	< 1	1
Cellulose acetate		10^7	—	6	300	—
Polythene		10^8	10^{11}	2·26	7	7
Mica	Ceramics and minerals	10^3	10^{10}	4·7	3	3
Quartz .		—	10^8	4·6	< 1	—
Glass .		1	10^8	5 to 7	—	100
Porcelain, glazed		100	10^8	4 to 7	—	—

In the expression $R = k \cdot l/a$, if a unit cube of a material be considered so that $l = 1$ and $a = 1$, then $R = k \cdot 1/1$ so that k is equal to the resistance of a unit cube of the material. The resistance of such a cube of any material is known as its VOLUME RESISTIVITY (or RESISTIVITY or SPECIFIC RESISTANCE). *The volume resistivity is the resistance between opposite faces of a unit cube of a given material at a given temperature.* The symbol of resistivity is ρ (see Appendix **E**).

The general expression for evaluation of resistance thus becomes

$$R = \rho \cdot l/a \quad . \quad . \quad . \quad (2.1)$$

This expression enables the resistance of a conductor to be determined by simple calculation, or alternatively any factor in the expression can be determined if the other three are known.

Table 2.II gives a list of the resistivities of the more common conducting materials. In this Table the resistance is expressed in microhms/cm-cube. From equation (2.1), $\rho = Ra/l$. Considering the dimensions (Appendix **B**) of this expression the

TABLE 2.II

RESISTIVITIES AND TEMPERATURE COEFFICIENTS
OF METALS AND ALLOYS AT 0°C

Metal or Alloy	Resistivity ($\mu\Omega$/cm-cube)	Temperature Coefficient (per °C)
Aluminium . . .	2·665	0·004 35
Aluminium, hard drawn .	2·828	0·004 0
Brass (70% Cu, 30% Zn) .	6 to 9	0·001 0
Bronze (88% Cu, 12% Sn) .	18	0·001 8
Cadmium . . .	6·85	0·003 9
Constantan (Eureka) (60% Cu, 40% Ni) . . .	51	± 0·000 01
Copper . . .	1·588	0·004 26
Copper, hard-drawn .	1·76	0·004 26
Gold	2·20	0·003 77
Invar (35% Ni-steel) . .	81	0·001 2
Iron	9·07	0·006 25
Lead	20·4	0·004 11
Manganin (84% Cu, 4% Ni, 12% Mn) . . .	46·7	0·000 015
Mercury	94·07	0·000 72
Nichrome (80% Ni, 20% Cr)	95	0·000 43
Nickel	12·3	0·006 2
Nickel silver (55–65% Cu, 7–30% Ni, 15–35% Zn) .	30	0·000 273
Phosphor bronze . .	5 to 10	—
Platinoid . . .	38	0.000 22
Platinum . . .	10·92	0·003 67
Silver	1·47	0·004 0
Tin	13·05	0·004 4
Tungsten . . .	5·48	0·004 5
Zinc	5·75	0·004 06

area a can be replaced by $l \times l$, hence $\rho = R \times l \times l/l = R \times l$, i.e. the resistivity may be expressed as the product of a resistance with a length: nowadays it is usually expressed in ohm-centimetres (Ω-cm). It is scarcely necessary to state that the above expression is only true when ρ, l, and a are expressed in terms of the same unit.

Frequently the conductor concerned is in the form of a wire of circular cross-section. Since $a = \pi d^2/4$ where $d = $ diameter,

$$R = 4\rho l/(\pi d^2)$$

or, for comparison between two wires,

$$R_1/R_2 = \rho_1 l_1 d_2{}^2/(\rho_2 l_2 d_1{}^2)$$

The resistance is thus *inversely* proportional to the *square* of the diameter.

It is sometimes desirable to use a conductor having a cross-section other than that of the simple circle and the area of the section must be correctly applied to resistance calculations. In the cases of square and rectangular sections no difficulty arises: hollow conductors are sometimes used and the area of such **a** section is $\pi(d_o{}^2 - d_i{}^2)/4$ where d_o and d_i are the outside and inside diameters respectively.

For open line wires and for cables the gauge of a wire is usually specified by its weight per unit length, and it is necessary to develop a relation between the length, weight, and resistance of a wire. In practice the various sizes of wires are denoted by their weights per mile. For instance, a single copper wire weighing 40 lb/mile (uninsulated) is termed a "40 lb copper wire."

The *total* weight (W) of a wire is directly proportional to its cubical contents, i.e. to the product of its length and cross-sectional area.

Thus, $W \propto l \times a$

Now $R \propto l/a$. Multiplying by l/l ($= 1$)

            $R \propto l \times l/(a \times l)$ or $l^2/(al)$

But $W \propto al$. $\therefore$ $R \propto l^2/W$

Thus the resistance of a wire is directly proportional to the *square* of its length and *inversely* proportional to the total weight. If two wires of the same total weight are respectively 1 and 2 yd long, then their resistances will be in the ratio 1 : 4. Not only is the length of wire greater in the second case, but its gauge is less since it is obvious that the same quantity of metal is spread over 2 yd instead of 1.

If W is the total weight of a wire of length l, then the weight w per unit length is $w = W/l$, whence $W = wl$. Since

$$R \propto l^2/W \text{ and } W = wl$$
$$R \propto l^2/(wl) \text{ or } l/w$$

The resistance of a wire is directly proportional to its length and *inversely* proportional to its weight per unit length.

As the resistance per mile of any particular kind of wire is inversely proportional to its weight per mile it will be seen that the two quantities when multiplied together will always give the same numerical result. This value is known as the *ohm-mile constant*; it is equal to 878·2 for copper and 1 045 for cadmium-copper. The resistance per mile of a 20 lb copper wire is 878·2/20 = 43·9 or 44 Ω/mile, and the resistance of a 40 lb cadmium-copper wire is 1 045/40 = 26·1 Ω/mile. A knowledge of the ohm-mile constant for any material enables the resistance per mile of any size of that wire to be readily determined.

If a telephone is situated one mile distant from the exchange, the total length of the circuit (i.e. there and back) will be two miles. For this reason line resistances are often quoted in terms of the loop-mile: thus the resistance of the 20 lb copper wire may be given as 88 Ω/loop-mile.

EXAMPLE 2.1 (A).* What length of manganin wire having a cross-sectional diameter of 0·5 mm will have the same resistance as 10 m of soft copper wire 0·1 mm in diameter? (The specific resistance of copper can be taken as 1·57 $\mu\Omega$-cm and that of manganin as 50 $\mu\Omega$-cm.) (C. & G.)

For the copper wire—

$\rho = 1\cdot57 \times 10^{-6}$ Ω-cm

$l = 1\,000$ cm

$a = \pi \,.\, 0\cdot01^2/4$ cm²

$R_c = \rho l/a$

$\quad = (1\cdot57 \times 10^3 \times 4)/(10^6 \times \pi \times 0\cdot01^2)$

$\quad = (1\cdot57 \times 4)/(10^3 \times \pi \times 0\cdot01^2)$

For the manganin wire—

$\rho = 50 \times 10^{-6}$ Ω-cm

$l = \,?$ cm

$a = \pi \,.\, 0\cdot05^2/4$ cm²

$R_m = (50 \times l \times 4)/(10^6 \times \pi \times 0\cdot05^2)$

$\quad = 2l/(10^4 \times \pi \times 0\cdot05^2)$

Since $R_c = R_m$

$(1\cdot57 \times 4)/(10^3 \times \pi \times 0\cdot01^2)$

$\quad = 2l/(10^4 \times \pi \times 0\cdot05^2)$

* (A), (B) and (C) after Example numbers indicate the course year (Appendix H) to which the Example is appropriate.

whence

$l = (1\cdot57 \times 4 \times 10^4 \times \pi \times 0\cdot05^2)/(10^3 \times \pi \times 0\cdot01^2 \times 2)$

$\quad = (1\cdot57 \times 20 \times 0\cdot05^2)/0\cdot01^2$

$\quad = 785$ cm

EXAMPLE 2.2 (A). The resistance of the wire used for a telephone line is 55 Ω/mile when the weight of the wire is 20 lb/mile. If the specific resistance of the material is 0·77 $\mu\Omega$-in., what is the cross-sectional area of the wire? What would be the resistance of a loop to a subscriber 5 miles from the exchange if wire of the same material but weighing 70 lb/mile were used? (C. & G.)

(i) $R = 55$ Ω

$\quad \rho = 0\cdot77 \times 10^{-6}$ Ω-in.

$\quad l = 1\,760 \times 36$ in.

$\quad a = \,?$ in.²

$\quad R = \rho l/a$

$\quad a = \rho l/R$

$\quad\quad = 0\cdot77 \times 1\,760 \times 36/(10^6 \times 55)$

$\quad\quad = 0\cdot000\,887$ in.²

(ii) $w_1 = 20$ lb/mile

$\quad w_2 = 70$ lb/mile

$\quad R_1 = 55$ Ω/mile

$\quad R_2 = \,?$ Ω/mile

$R_1/R_2 = w_2/w_1$

$R_2 = R_1 w_1/w_2$

$\quad = 55 \times 20/70$

$\quad = 15\cdot714$ Ω/mile

Resistance of 5-mile loop

(10 miles) $= 157\cdot14$ Ω

EXAMPLE 2.3 (A). Calculate the resistance of a 100-metre length of wire having a uniform area of 0·1 mm² if the wire is made of manganin having a resistivity of 50 $\mu\Omega$-cm.

If the wire is drawn out to three times its original length, by how many times would you expect its resistance to be increased? What other considerations may affect this factor? (C. & G.)

(i) $R = \,?$ Ω

$\quad \rho = 50 \times 10^{-6}$ Ω-cm

$\quad l = 10\,000$ cm

$\quad a = 0\cdot001$ cm²

$\quad R = \rho l/a = 50 \times 10^4 \times 10^3/10^6 = 500$ Ω

(ii)   New length $= 3l$

         New area $= a/3$

New resistance $= R'$

$$R' = \rho \times 3l \times 3/a = 9\rho l/a$$

Hence, resistance would be increased 9 times.

(iii) The solution for (ii) depends upon the stretched wire having uniform cross-sectional area throughout its length, and the resistivity remaining constant despite stretching.

EXAMPLE 2.4 (A). A copper tube, 100 m in length, has an internal diameter of 2·5 cm and wall thickness of 2 mm. If the specific resistance of copper is 1·7 $\mu\Omega$-cm, what is the resistance of the tube?

$R = ?\ \Omega$

$\rho = 1\cdot7 \times 10^{-6}\ \Omega$-cm

$l = 10^4$ cm

$a = \pi(2\cdot9^2 - 2\cdot5^2)/4$ cm².

$$R = \rho l/a = 1\cdot7 \times 10^4 \times 4/\{(10^6\pi(2\cdot9^2 - 2\cdot5^2)\}$$
$$= 0\cdot01\ \Omega$$

EXAMPLE 2.5 (A). One mile of copper wire of No. 14 gauge (diameter 0·08 in.) has a resistance of 8·5 Ω. What is its resistivity? The resistance per mile of a bronze wire of the same gauge is 18·2 Ω. What is the resistivity of the bronze?   (C. & G.)

(i) For the copper wire—

$R = 8\cdot5\ \Omega$

$\rho = ?\ \Omega$-in.

$l = 1\ 760 \times 36$ in.

$a = \pi \times 0\cdot08^2/4$ in.²

$\quad R = \rho l/a$ and $\rho = Ra/l$

$\therefore \rho = (8\cdot5\pi \times 0\cdot08^2)/(1\ 760 \times 36 \times 4)$

$\quad = 0\cdot674\ 4 \times 10^{-6}$

$\quad = 0\cdot674\ 4\ \mu\Omega$-in.

(ii) R_c for copper $= 8\cdot5\ \Omega$/mile

$\quad R_b$ for bronze $= 18\cdot2\ \Omega$/mile

$\quad R \propto \rho$

$\quad R_b/R_c = \rho_b/\rho_c$ and $\rho_b = R_b\rho_c/R_c$

$\qquad = 18\cdot2 \times 0\cdot674\ 4/8\cdot5$

$\qquad = 1\cdot444\ \mu\Omega$-in.

Notes: (i) It will be observed that where a simple comparison is being made and not a direct calculation it is unnecessary to reduce l and a to inch (or centimetre) units, provided that they are expressed in the same units (e.g. both in yards)

since the *ratio* only of these values is concerned in this instance.

(ii) Further worked examples on resistivity will be found in later sections and also at the end of Chapter II.

2.7. Conductance. It is sometimes desirable to describe a material from the point of view of its ability to conduct a current rather than from its resistance aspect. The term CONDUCTIVITY is used to denote *the reciprocal of volume resistivity,* i.e. conductivity $\sigma = 1/\rho$. In a similar manner the CONDUCTANCE is, *in the d.c. circuit, the reciprocal of resistance.* Thus conductance $G = 1/R$.

Conductance and conductivity are expressed in terms of a unit called the MHO, which is defined as *the conductance of a body having a resistance of one ohm.* As resistivity is expressed in ohm-cm, then conductivity may be expressed in (ohm-cm)$^{-1}$ or in mho/cm. If the resistivity of copper is taken as $\rho = 1\cdot588 \times 10^{-6}$ ohm-cm, the conductivity is $10^6/1\cdot588$ or $0\cdot629\ 7 \times 10^6$ mho/cm. A resistance of 10 ohms has a conductance of 1/10 mho or 0·1 mho. The International Electrotechnical Commission has proposed that the name *siemens* be given to the unit of electrical conductance. This name does not seem to have come into use, nor is the mho widely used, conductances being frequently expressed in the form (ohm-cm)$^{-1}$.

Use of the conductance rather than the resistance of a conductor frequently simplifies the solution of problems involving circuits containing resistances in parallel.

Copper wire used commercially is not chemically pure, and its resistance is increased by the presence of impurities: a conductivity of 99 per cent of that of pure (electrolytic) copper is frequently specified.

2.8. Rheostats. A set of graded resistance coils mounted in a box is one of the most useful and necessary adjuncts in electrical testing. The coils of wire of definite and accurate resistance values can be brought into circuit or cut out at will. A variable resistance is known as a rheostat.

One form of resistance box, the Rheostat F, is in common use for the purpose of adjusting the current value in a circuit: the diagram of connexions is shown in Fig. 2.6. The two radial arms of laminated phosphor-bronze make contact with selected studs of hard brass, a resistance coil being connected between each pair of studs. In the left-hand set each coil has a resistance of 400 Ω and each coil of the right-hand set has a resistance of 40 Ω. In addition, coils of 1, 2, 3, 4, 10, 20, and 4 000 Ω resistance are connected between the pairs of brass blocks which are cut to receive a tapered circular brass peg between each pair of blocks.

With all the brass pegs in position the brass blocks form a continuous conductor of negligible resistance. Removal of any peg brings into circuit the resistance coil connected between that pair of blocks, the value of each coil being engraved near the two blocks. The blocks are suitably shaped to provide facilities for removing all dust, dirt, and metallic

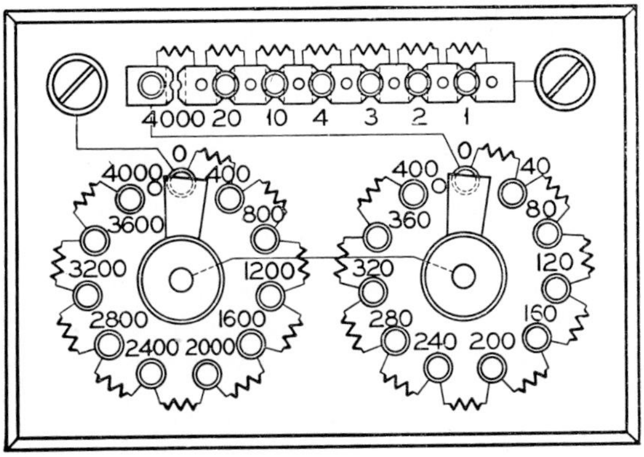

FIG. 2.7. RHEOSTAT F, 9 999 Ω
(*Courtesy of P.M.G.*)

Another form of resistance box frequently used in the Wheatstone Bridge and of a type finding other applications is the Decade resistance box shown in Fig. 2.8. This rheostat comprises four sets of ten coils each ranging from one to ten in thousands, hundreds, tens, and units respectively; the total resistance range is therefore from 1 Ω to

FIG. 2.6. CONNEXIONS OF RHEOSTAT F

filings produced by the repeated twisting of the solid pegs in their sockets. It is a matter of considerable importance that the pegs should fit tightly and that the contact surfaces and insulating gaps should be kept clean, otherwise inaccurate resistance readings will arise. All the brass contacts are mounted upon a base of ebonite, a material possessing very high insulating properties. The radial contact arms select one or more of the associated resistance coils in steps of 40 Ω or 400 Ω. By the joint use of the pegs and the radial arms any value of resistance from 1 to 8 440 Ω can be obtained in steps of 1 Ω. The box is provided with perforated metal sides to dissipate any heat which may be generated. The resistance coils are wound with platinoid wire and are correct to ± 1 per cent. The arms are arranged to avoid disconnexion of the circuit as they pass from one contact to the next.

A later form of the rheostat F —(see Fig. 2.7)—dispenses with the row of brass blocks and the associated resistance coils and has instead a total of four radial arms with sets of resistance coils for thousands, hundreds, tens, and units of ohms as in the Decade box described below. With this arrangement, resistance adjustments can be made far more quickly.

11 110 Ω in steps of 1 Ω. The construction of a set of ten coils and the method of selection by means of the dial is shown in Fig. 2.9. Each of the four units of ten coils is mounted upon an independent fitting, which consists of a central contact flange and a ring of eleven segments mounted upon an insulating support. The switch brush contains sixteen copper laminations continuous from end to end, one end of the brush making contact with the central flange and the other with the ring of segments. The switch positions are defined to the

FIG. 2.8. DECADE RESISTANCE BOX
(*Courtesy of Cambridge Instrument Co., Ltd.*)

touch by ball clicks. An ebonite knob fitted with a white pointer moving over a dial on the face of the instrument controls the movement of the switch brush. Rheostats of this type have an accuracy of one part in 1 000, and when all the pointers are set to zero, the total resistance between the terminals is only 0·007 Ω.

FIG. 2.9. CONSTRUCTION OF 10-COIL RESISTANCE
(*Courtesy of Cambridge Instrument Co., Ltd.*)

The direct-reading resistance box (Figs. 2.10 and 2.11) consists of nine uniform coils for each of the units, tens, hundreds, and thousands of ohms ranges, with a total of 9 999 Ω. Each set of coils is controlled by a separate rotary switch and each of

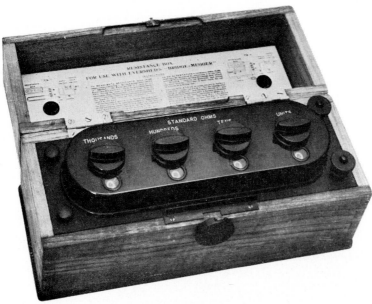

FIG. 2.10. DIRECT-READING RESISTANCE BOX
(*Courtesy of Evershed & Vignoles*)

the four switches carries a figured dial, arranged to show a single digit through a small aperture, to represent the position of the switch. The total resistance inserted by means of the switches is thus given directly by a row of figures. This resistance

box is used as a component of the "Bridge Megger" testing set.

In order to meet the requirement for a semi-variable resistance which will not be in need of

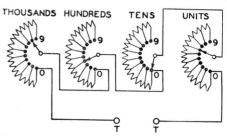

FIG. 2.11. CONNEXIONS OF DIRECT-READING
RESISTANCE BOX

frequent re-adjustment, a coil is used which has a number of sections each brought out to soldering tags, the appropriate tappings being wired to the external circuit.

2.9. Resistors. Resistors, or resistances of fixed values, a universal requirement in telecommunication equipment, are made up in various forms.

The material of which the wire for a rheostat or resistor is composed is a matter of considerable importance. Copper is quite inadmissible on account of its large variation in resistance with changes in temperature. Also, where a high resistance is required the quantity of wire necessary would render the coils very bulky or else necessitate the use of extremely fine wire, on account of the low resistivity of copper. Materials such as the alloys constantan (eureka) and manganin (a copper-nickel-manganese alloy) are frequently employed on account of their high resistivities and low temperature coefficients. The gauge should be as large as possible since this will give great accuracy of adjustment, and furthermore any heat developed will be better radiated by the larger surface area available: the size of the complete resistor also enters into the question of efficient heat radiation. In practice the questions of bulk and cost assume importance and usually the lower resistance coils are made of heavy, and the higher resistance coils of light, gauge wire. Precautions are also observed to ensure permanent accuracy: to this end stresses in the material are avoided and any residual strains removed by careful "ageing" after the coils are wound.

Resistor coils used for testing and other important purposes must be wound so as to have the lowest possible values of inherent inductance and capacitance.

Some typical forms of resistor are shown in Fig. 2.12. Those shown at (a) and (b) are used in automatic telephone and telegraph equipment: as they are small their natural inductance is low, and they are not usually wound non-inductively unless this property is required to a high degree. The ends

FIG. 2.12. RESISTORS
(Courtesy of P.M.G.)

of the wire are brought out to suitable soldering tags. The type shown at (a) is wound upon a moulded bobbin with a brass tubular centre and protected with tape, while that at (b) is wound upon a ceramic former and given a coating of varnish: it is used to carry heavier currents. These resistors are designed to dissipate the resultant heat developed from 2 W and 10 W respectively. They are general purpose resistors with an accuracy of the order of ± 2½ per cent.

The type shown at (c) is a vitreous resistor used in small power panels. This resistor is wound with fine nickel-chrome wire upon a ceramic tube. The wire is embedded in vitreous enamel and the resistor will safely dissipate 30 W if surrounded by a free air space: dust covers housing such equipment are of the ventilated type. The terminals are formed by the mechanically interlocking clips (included in the illustration) which are brazed, and shaped into suitable lugs for fixing and wiring.

Small carbon resistors, particularly suitable for use with electronic valve and transistor equipment,

are available in values ranging from 10 Ω to 10 MΩ. Two different forms of construction are used.[6]

The solid carbon rod type, Fig. 2.13, is manufactured by fusing together powdered carbon, of various grades in suitable proportions, with a small quantity of resin to act as a binder. The resulting rod or "pin" is then sprayed with a thin coating of copper on each end: the purpose of this is to provide good electrical connexion and also to limit the resistance value by controlling the axial length of the copper coating. The carbon pin is cemented into a short ceramic insulating tube. Spun brass caps fixed to short lengths of tinned copper connecting wire are then pressed on to the ends of the pin.

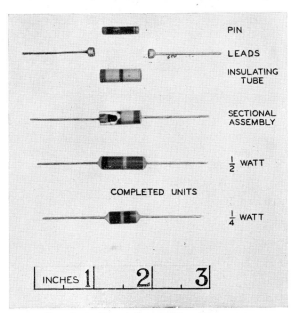

FIG. 2.13. SOLID CARBON ROD RESISTORS
(INSULATED TYPE)
(Courtesy of "I.P.O.E.E. Journal")

After drying off, the completed resistor is impregnated with wax. Alternatively, the insulating tube is omitted, and the electrical connexions are made by spinning one and a half turns of tinned copper wire round each end and dipping in solder, subsequently impregnating the resistor with wax (Fig. 2.14).

In the carbon deposit type, a ceramic rod is fed through a furnace in a controlled hydro-carbon atmosphere, resulting in a carbonaceous coating to the rod. Alternatively, prepared carbon in solution is applied to the insulating rod by spraying or dipping, some degree of resistance control being obtained by variations in the basic coating material. In both types a spiral track, of varying pitch to suit the final ohmic value, is cut into the coating to increase the length of the resistance path: connexion caps are applied as described above.

This type of resistor has a negative temperature coefficient and due to its small size is practically non-inductive: the reactance due to capacitance is also small unless used at ultra-high frequencies. It is liable to produce microphonic noise due to thermal agitation of the resistor material unless this is of good quality. Owing to the difficulty

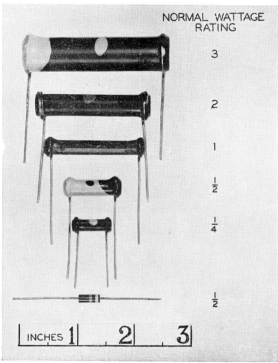

NORMAL WATTAGE
RATING

3

2

1

$\frac{1}{2}$

$\frac{1}{4}$

$\frac{1}{2}$

INCHES 1 2 3

FIG. 2.14. SOLID CARBON ROD RESISTORS
(NON-INSULATED)
(*Courtesy of "I.P.O.E.E. Journal"*)

in marking the resistance values on such small components, these resistors are painted in three colours based on a colour code to indicate the resistance value. These resistors are not suitable for use where the highest grade of accuracy is essential, being subject to tolerances of ± 5 per cent, ± 10 per cent, and ± 20 per cent. They are also available in various ratings with a maximum dissipation up to 5 W.

SILICON-CARBIDE RESISTORS.[7] Based upon the use of silicon carbide (carborundum), which is a semiconductor, a class of resistors is available whose behaviour does not follow Ohm's Law. The current is in fact proportional not directly

to the voltage but to the third, fourth, or fifth power of the applied voltage. The resistivity of the silicon-carbide *crystal itself* is of the order of 1 to 10 Ω-cm and it follows Ohm's Law approximately. When measured with normal electrodes to include the effect of contact resistance, the resistivity may range from 10 Ω-cm to 10^6 Ω-cm according to the current density. As with other semiconductors, silicon carbide displays the properties of rectification, negative temperature coefficient, photo-conductivity, and luminescence (surface glow) under appropriate conditions. Resistors of this type are in common use, under various trade names, in the form of lightning arrestors or spark quenches for the purpose of dissipating undesired energy from high voltage surges.

The silicon carbide is prepared from sand and coke subjected to very high temperature (1 780 to 2 200°C). The resistors may be made in the form of a block, disk, or rod composed of a fired mixture consisting principally of a ceramic bond and silicon-carbide crystals. The method of forming the resistors may be one of those usually employed in the ceramic industry: dry pressing using a "dry" mix, i.e. a mix with a small percentage only of moisture; extrusion using a plastic mass; or moulding or slip casting using a slurry.

After forming, the resistors are fired at a temperature depending on the bond used. The furnace treatment has a direct bearing on the final electrical characteristics.

The usual method of making an electrical connexion to the fired disk is to spray brass, zinc, or copper over the faces which are to act as contacts. Loads may be soldered to this surface, but it may be more convenient to use terminals on metal fins clamped to the resistor faces. If the resistors are liable to operation under humid conditions, which could cause the leakage current to become comparable with the normal current, they are impregnated by immersion in a suitable compound. The finished resistor is ceramic in character.

These resistors are sometimes referred to as "non-ohmic" resistors—a somewhat unfortunate choice of terminology, meant to imply that these resistors are non-linear, i.e. they do not follow Ohm's Law.

The current/voltage relation over the working range may be expressed as $V = K \times I^\beta$, K being a constant for the particular current range, and β having a value between $\frac{1}{3}$ and $\frac{1}{5}$.

2.10. Temperature Coefficient. The resistance of a conductor depends upon its temperature. The normal flow of current in any conductor usually produces a rise of temperature but resistance rise due to this cause is frequently small and can be safely ignored. Many cases occur, however, where its effects must be allowed for and indeed this variation is sometimes put to good use. Accurately designed resistors are usually marked with the temperature at which they are correct, normally $15 \cdot 5°C$ or $60°F$.

With metals the resistance increases with rise of temperature by a definite fraction of its resistance value at $0°C$. If R_t and R_0 denote the resistance values of any conductor at temperatures $t°C$ and $0°C$ respectively, the increase in resistance over the temperature range $t°$ is equal to the difference $(R_t - R_0)$ ohms: this increase expressed as a ratio to the value at $0°C$ is $(R_t - R_0)/R_0$. Dividing by t gives the fractional increase for each degree rise of temperature, i.e. $(R_t - R_0)/(R_0 t)$ and this expression is known as the TEMPERATURE COEFFICIENT (α) of the material. *The temperature coefficient of resistance is the change in the magnitude of the resistance of a substance caused by a rise of one degree centigrade in temperature and expressed as a fraction of the magnitude at $0°C$.* It may be added that bodies expand on heating and a similar (thermal) coefficient relates to the increase in length.

As it is usually desired to know what value of resistance to expect at a given temperature ($t°C$) the above expression for the temperature coefficient α may be transposed into another form—

From
$$\alpha = (R_t - R_0)/(R_0 t),$$
$$R_0 \alpha t = R_t - R_0,$$
$$R_t = R_0 + R_0 \alpha t$$
or
$$R_t = R_0(1 + \alpha t) \quad . \quad . \quad . \quad (2.2)$$

The foregoing expression is true only for small temperature increases, and if greater accuracy is required it becomes necessary to utilize the expression—
$$R_t = R_0(1 + \alpha t + \beta t^2)$$
where β is a constant determined experimentally. It will be seen that if t is small, since β itself is also small, the product βt^2 may be regarded as negligible for general purposes.

Table 2.II enumerates the temperature coefficients of the more commonly used conductors. Three interesting observations may be made. The effect of alloying metals produces a reduced temperature coefficient, so low as to be almost negligible in the case of constantan and manganin. This is a desirable feature where constancy of resistance is desired, as for example in resistors used for testing purposes. Secondly, carbon has a *negative* temperature coefficient, its resistance *falling* with

a *rising* temperature—a property which may be specially utilized. Thirdly, the coefficient for most pure metals is the same, approximately $0 \cdot 4$ per cent (centigrade).

If it is desired to compare the resistances R_1 and R_2 of two conductors at temperatures t_1 and t_2, neither being zero, then,

since
$$R_1 = R_0(1 + \alpha t_1)$$
and
$$R_2 = R_0(1 + \alpha t_2),$$
$$R_1/R_2 = \frac{R_0(1 + \alpha t_1)}{R_0(1 + \alpha t_2)}$$
$$\therefore \qquad R_1 = \frac{R_2(1 + \alpha t_1)}{1 + \alpha t_2}$$

an expression which excludes the factor R_0.

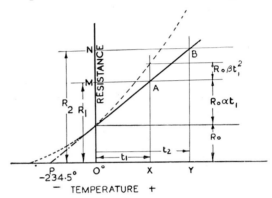

FIG. 2.15. RESISTANCE/TEMPERATURE CURVE

The variation in resistance with temperature is shown in Fig. 2.15 for copper, the full line graph being the graph of $R_t = R_0(1 + 0 \cdot 004\,26t)$. The dotted curve shows the form taken when using the expression $R_t = R_0(1 + \alpha t + \beta t^2)$: for low temperatures the difference between the dotted and full line graphs is very small.

If the full line graph is produced to meet the temperature axis at P it cuts this at $-234 \cdot 5°C$, a value known as the *absolute resistance zero for copper*. Taking any two points A and B on the graph and dropping perpendiculars to the resistance and temperature axes, OM is the resistance R_1 at $t_1°C$ (OX), and ON is the resistance R_2 at $t_2°C$ (OY). The two triangles PAX and PBY are similar so that—

$$AX/BY = PX/PY$$
or
$$R_1/R_2 = (234 \cdot 5 + t_1)/(234 \cdot 5 + t_2)$$

This expression can also be obtained as follows—
$$R_1/R_2 = (1 + 0 \cdot 004\,26t_1)/(1 + 0 \cdot 004\,26t_2).$$

2

Dividing by α/α (= 1),

$$R_1/R_2 = \left(\frac{1}{0\cdot004\ 26} + t_1\right)\bigg/\left(\frac{1}{0\cdot004\ 26} + t_2\right)$$
$$= (234\cdot5 + t_1)/(234\cdot5 + t_2)$$

The value 234·5 is the reciprocal of the temperature coefficient for copper. This expression is a very convenient one for comparing the resistances of a conductor at two different temperatures, neither being zero, if a Table showing the reciprocals of temperature coefficients is available.

EXAMPLE 2.6 (A). The filament of a 240-V metal filament lamp is to be constructed from wire having a diameter of 0·32 mm and a resistivity at 20°C of 4·3 $\mu\Omega$/cm-cube. If the temperature coefficient of resistance of the wire is 0·005 per degree centigrade, what length of filament is necessary if the lamp is to dissipate 60 W at a filament temperature of 2 420°C?   (C. & G.)

Note: The (hot) resistance R_h of a lamp is given by $R_h = $ volts²/watts, i.e. $\dfrac{V^2}{W}$, so that R_h at 2 420°C $= 240^2/60 = 960\ \Omega$.

At $t_h = 2\ 420°C$, $R_h = 960\ \Omega$;

,, $t_c = 20°C$, $R_c = ?\ \Omega$;

$\alpha = 0\cdot005$ per °C;

$\rho = 4\cdot3 \times 10^{-6}\ \Omega$/cm-cube;

$l = ?$ cm;

$a = \pi(0\cdot002)^2/4$ cm².

$R_h/R_c = (1 + \alpha t_h)/(1 + \alpha t_c)$, or

$R_c = R_h(1 + \alpha t_c)/(1 + \alpha t_h)$
$= 960(1 + 0\cdot005 \times 20)/(1 + 0\cdot005 \times 2\ 420)$
$= 960 \times 1\cdot1/13\cdot1 = 80\cdot61\ \Omega$

$l = Ra/\rho = 80\cdot61\pi(0\cdot002)^2 \times 10^6/(4 \times 4\cdot3)$
$= \underline{\underline{58\cdot86\ \text{cm}}}$

EXAMPLE 2.7 (A). The current through an electrical conductor is 1 A when the temperature of the conductor is 0°C, and 0·7 A when the temperature is 100°C. What would be the current when the temperature of the conductor is 1 200°C and what is the temperature coefficient of resistance of the conductor?   (C. & G.)

Note: The resistance is the ratio V/I

At $t = 0°C$, $R_0 = V/1\ \Omega$;

,, $t = 100°C$, $R_{100} = V/0\cdot7\ \Omega$;

,, $t = 1\ 200°C$, $R_{1\ 200} = ?$;

$\alpha = ?$

(i) $R_{100} = R_0(1 + \alpha t)$, $V/0\cdot7 = V(1 + 100\alpha)$,
$$1/0\cdot7 = (1 + 100\alpha)$$
$$100\alpha = 1/0\cdot7 - 1 = 1\cdot43 - 1 = 0\cdot43$$
$$\alpha = \underline{\underline{0\cdot004\ 3}}$$

(ii) $R_{1\ 200} = V(1 + 0\cdot004\ 3 \times 1\ 200) = V \times 6\cdot16$

The current at 1 200°C $= V/R = 1/6\cdot16$
$= \underline{\underline{0\cdot162\ \text{A}}}$.

A rise in temperature detracts from the normal efficiency of both conductors and insulators, for it decreases the conductance of the former and decreases the insulation resistance of the latter, nearly all insulating materials having a negative temperature coefficient. The effect of changes of temperature is far more marked with insulators than with conductors, for whilst an increase of 15°F would raise the resistance of a copper conductor from 1 000 Ω to 1 036 Ω, the resistance of a gutta-percha core would fall from 9 000 MΩ to 1 000 MΩ for the same rise in temperature. The equation connecting the resistance of insulating materials with temperature is exponential and varies largely with the quality as well as with the composition of the material.

Since the electrical resistance of a metal rises with the temperature it is natural to investigate the ultimate minimum resistance of a metal subjected to extremely low temperatures. It is found that the resistivity of metals tends towards a small constant value, the "residual resistance," as the temperature approaches absolute zero (− 273°C), this residual value being probably due to the presence of impurities. Some metals, notably tin, mercury and zinc lose all resistance at very low temperatures, their conductivity becoming infinite and producing the phenomenon of "superconductivity[8]": the resistance of other metals such as copper, silver, gold, nickel and iron does not vanish even at $\frac{1}{20}$ degree above absolute zero. Currents induced in a super-conducting ring persist long after the inducing source has been withdrawn and their magnitudes often reach hundreds of amps even in quite fine wires: this maximum current is limited only by the inductance of the ring. The resistance being zero, no heating effects results from the flow of current in a superconductor. In recent times *cryogenics*, the technology of conductivity at very low temperatures, has been actively developed.

THERMISTORS.[9],[10] A thermistor, or thermally sensitive resistor, is the name given to a semiconductor device which makes use of the special property of semiconductors that the resistance is highly temperature-dependent, its temperature coefficient of resistance being negative.

The resistance of a semiconductor decreases with rising temperature from R_0, its value at the absolute zero temperature, to R_T, its resistance at any temperature $T°$, according to the relation

$$R_T = R_0\, e^{-\beta t}$$

where β is a constant and e is the base of Naperian logarithms. At any constant temperature the thermistor resistance remains constant, i.e. it follows Ohm's Law. In operation resistivity changes of 500:1 or more are possible. Naturally

The two important characteristics for a particular thermistor are shown graphically in Fig. 2.16. In (a) the resistance is plotted against ambient temperature; in (b) a family of curves is drawn for voltage against current. For small currents the thermistor follows Ohm's Law as a normal (linear) resistance. A maximum voltage (V_{max}) is soon reached beyond which a *reducing* value of p.d. will bring about an *increasing* value of current, a phenomenon occurring in other aspects of electrical technology and known as *negative (incremental) resistance*. This negative resistance is not achieved unless the turnover at the maximum

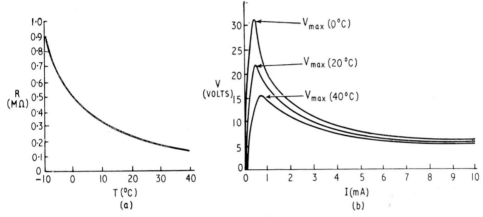

FIG. 2.16. THERMISTOR CHARACTERISTICS
(a) Resistance variation with ambient temperature
(b) Voltage/current relationship

the resistance changes with ambient (surrounding) temperature, a factor to be taken into account in use.

The thermistor finds practical application where it is desired to vary the resistance of a circuit according to the value of the applied voltage.

A suitable thermistor material is a mixture of metallic oxides such as those of nickel, manganese, and copper, fired at a high temperature (about 1 200°C). The temperature coefficient of resistance is about −4 per cent per degree centigrade. In one form commonly used a small bead of thermistor material is formed upon two platinum wires: direct or indirect heating may be used, i.e. the control current may be passed through the resistor material itself or through a separate heating element wound around but insulated from the resistor material. Thermistors are also made in the form of pellets up to $\frac{1}{2}$ in. in diameter by $\frac{1}{8}$ in. thick and silvered on the flat faces for connexions, or soldered on to a brass base. Circular rods up to $\frac{1}{4}$ in. diameter and $1\frac{1}{2}$ in. in length are also available.

p.d. (V_{max}) has first been exceeded. The graphs (b) illustrate how the value of V_{max} rises for falling ambient temperature.

2.11. Ballast Resistors. The ballast resistor, or *barretter*, is an instrument which utilizes the property of resistance variation with temperature. An iron wire in an atmosphere of hydrogen has the property of increasing its resistance considerably on reaching a critical temperature. In telephone exchanges the circuit which feeds current over the line to energize the subscriber's telephone includes a ballast resistor: its object is to keep the magnitude of this current constant, within close limits, irrespective of the resistances of the various lines which are from time to time connected to the current feeding circuit.

This ballast resistor comprises a glass envelope containing one or, for convenience frequently two, filaments of tungsten in an atmosphere of hydrogen.

The ballast action is to some extent dependent upon the gas pressure in the envelope: in the type described a particular form of construction is employed with a view to controlling the changes in density of the gas adjacent to the heated filament in order to extend the constant-current characteristic. In Fig. 2.17 is reproduced a set of curves showing how the resistance of this barretter varies

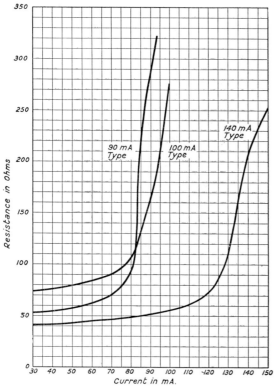

FIG. 2.17. BALLAST RESISTOR CHARACTERISTICS

with the current flowing in it, for the 90 mA, 100 mA, and 140 mA types.[11]

Similar resistors having suitable characteristics are also used in telegraph circuits, being connected in the positive and negative supply feeds to the transmitter. Their normal resistance is instrumental in preventing sparking, and should an earth contact fault on the line arise, the resistance of the barretter rises to reduce the current to a safe value: in this condition the lamp glows and indicates the fault. A ballast resistor of this type is illustrated in Fig. 2.18; it has twin filaments of tungsten contained in nitrogen.

2.12. Ohm's Law. An important relationship exists between the potential difference, the current, and the resistance of the electric circuit. Professor G. S. Ohm investigated this problem and as a result enunciated the law associated with his name.

OHM'S LAW states that *the current in any conductor at uniform temperature is directly proportional to the potential difference between its ends*. The ratio of the p.d. to the current is the resistance, and the value of the ohm is such that the resistance in ohms is equal to the ratio of the p.d. in volts to

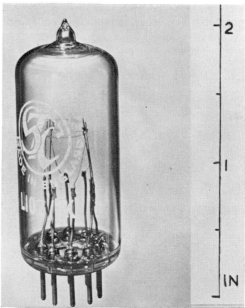

FIG. 2.18. TWIN-FILAMENT BALLAST RESISTOR
(Courtesy of S.T. & C. Ltd.)

the current in amps. Expressed in symbols the law may be given in its three dependent forms as follows—

if V = p.d. in volts,

I = current in amps,

R = resistance in ohms,

$R = V/I$, or $V = IR$, or $I = V/R$ . . (2.3)

This law may accordingly be expressed in various forms, but it is well to remember that the current is *directly* proportional to the p.d. and *inversely* proportional to the resistance. The relation applies equally to a *complete* circuit or to *any portion* of a circuit: care is necessary to apply it correctly. If any one law of the electric circuit can be said to be of greater importance than any other then undoubtedly that one is Ohm's law. So closely is this law followed that it forms the basis of the most precise methods of electrical measurement.

EXAMPLE 2.8 (A). If a p.d. of 50 V is applied to a telephone relay of 1 000 Ω resistance, what current will flow in the relay?

$$I = V/R$$
$$= 50/1\ 000 = 0\cdot050\text{ A or } 50\text{ mA}$$

EXAMPLE 2.9 (A). A p.d. of 80 V when applied to a telegraph circuit produces a current of 20 mA. What is the total circuit resistance?

$$R = V/I$$
$$= 80/0\cdot020 = 4\ 000\ \Omega$$

EXAMPLE 2.10 (A). An e.m.f. drives a current around a circuit which includes a relay of 11 Ω resistance. If the current through the relay is found to be 250 mA, what p.d. exists across the relay?

$$V = IR$$
$$= 0\cdot250 \times 11 = 2\cdot75\text{ V}$$

Note: Further calculations on Ohm's law will be found in most of the worked examples following in Chapters II, III, and IV.

The relationship established by Ohm's law enables a definition of the VOLT to be given as *that electromotive force or potential difference which, applied steadily to a conductor the resistance of which is one ohm, produces a current of one ampere.*

The foregoing explanation is based upon the behaviour of a direct current circuit, but it may be stated at this stage that Ohm's law is true also for the alternating current flowing in a *pure* resistance, i.e. one which has neither inductance nor capacitance, and is also true in its modified form for any a.c. circuit.

2.13. Resistors in Series. Circuits containing two or more resistance elements are of common occurrence: the component resistors may be interconnected in one or both of two arrangements which are known as *series* and *parallel.*

Two or more conductors are said to be connected in series when they are so connected that they are traversed by the same current, i.e. when one terminal of each conductor is joined to one terminal of an adjacent conductor in the form of a chain so that the current flows through them in succession. To calculate the value of the circuit current in accordance with Ohm's law it is necessary to know the equivalent or joint resistance of such a combination.

Fig. 2.19 shows three resistors *AB*, *BC*, and *CD* whose magnitudes are equal to R_1, R_2, and R_3 ohms respectively, connected in series: a p.d. of V volts

applied to them jointly produces a current of I amps, whose magnitude is the same in all parts of the circuit. A p.d. accordingly exists across each resistor and the sum of these separate p.d.s must be equal to the p.d. across the whole circuit.

$$\text{P.d. across } AB = V_1 = I \times R_1$$
$$\text{,,   ,,   } BC = V_2 = I \times R_2$$
$$\text{,,   ,,   } CD = V_3 = I \times R_3$$

$$\text{Total p.d. across } AD = V_1 + V_2 + V_3$$
$$= IR_1 + IR_2 + IR_3$$
$$= I(R_1 + R_2 + R_3)$$

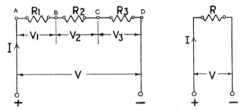

FIG. 2.19. RESISTORS IN SERIES

If R = joint resistance of R_1, R_2, and R_3, i.e. that resistance which would give the same current I from the same p.d. V,

$$V = IR$$
$$\therefore \qquad IR = I(R_1 + R_2 + R_3)$$
$$\text{and} \qquad R = R_1 + R_2 + R_3$$

The same reasoning applies to any number of resistors joined in series, so that in the general case—

$$R = R_1 + R_2 + R_3 + \ldots + R_N \quad (2.4)$$

where R is the joint resistance and R_1, R_2, etc., represent the individual resistors.

In words, *if two or more resistors are connected in series, the joint resistance of the combination is equal to the sum of the individual resistances.*

The statement that the resistance of a wire depends upon its length follows from the above law, since any wire may be regarded as a number of shorter wires joined in series.

EXAMPLE 2.11 (A). What is the joint resistance of seven resistors value 1, 2, 3, 4, 10, 20, and 4 000 Ω respectively, when they are connected in series?

$$R = R_1 + R_2 + R_3 + R_4 + R_5 + R_6 + R_7$$
$$= 1 + 2 + 3 + 4 + 10 + 20 + 4\ 000 = 4\ 040\ \Omega$$

EXAMPLE 2.12 (A). A reading of 10 V is obtained on a voltmeter of 5 000 Ω resistance when it is connected in series with a battery of negligible resistance and a telephone line which is looped at the distant end. When the 5 000 Ω voltmeter is replaced by one of 500 Ω resistance the reading is 4 V. Calculate the resistance of the line.　　(C. & G.)

Fig. 2.20 (i) and (ii) show the circuit conditions and the symbols adopted for unknown values.

(i) Taking the 5 000 Ω resistance,

$$I_1 = 10/5\,000 = 0.002 \text{ A}$$

Taking the whole circuit,

$$I_1 = E/(5\,000 + R) = 0.002$$
$$E = 0.002(5\,000 + R)$$

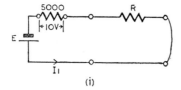

(i)

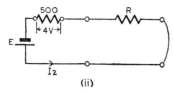

(ii)

FIG. 2.20 (Example 2.12)

(ii) Taking the 500 Ω resistance,

$$I_2 = 4/500 = 0.008 \text{ A}$$

Taking the whole circuit,

$$I_2 = E/(500 + R) = 0.008$$
$$E = 0.008(500 + R)$$

Combining the equations (i) and (ii),

$$0.002(5\,000 + R) = 0.008(500 + R)$$
$$10 + 0.002R = 4 + 0.008R$$
$$0.006R = 6 \text{ and } R = \underline{\underline{1\,000\,\Omega}}$$

EXAMPLE 2.13 (A). An electrical measuring instrument having an internal resistance of 500 Ω gives a full-scale deflexion when a current of 0.01 A is passed through it. What voltage applied to a circuit consisting of this instrument in series with an external resistor of 9 500 Ω would be required to give a full-scale deflexion?　(C. & G.)

To obtain a current of 0.01 A through resistors of 500 Ω and 9 500 Ω in series,

$$V = I(R_1 + R_2) = 0.01(500 + 9\,500)$$
$$= 0.01 \times 10\,000 = \underline{\underline{100 \text{ V}}}$$

2.14. Fall of Potential.

At this point it is possible to investigate more fully the fall of potential round the d.c. circuit. In Fig. 2.21 suppose that a large number of resistors each of equal value R ohms are connected in series, and a potential difference of V volts applied across the combination results in a flow of current of I amps in the circuit. The p.d. across any one resistor is, from Ohm's law, $V = IR$ volts: this is the p.d. across each resistor R, so that the potential falls in steps of IR volts. If this process be applied to a circuit containing an infinitely large number of resistors each of very small value (δR) ohms (see Appendix

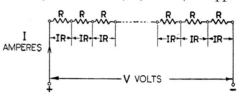

FIG. 2.21. FALL OF POTENTIAL

A.2) connected in series, then a current of I amps produces a p.d. of $I \cdot \delta R$ volts across each resistor. The condition of an infinite number of equal resistors joined in series represents a single uniform conductor, and so it is seen that the potential falls uniformly around the circuit. This is an important statement and its principle finds many practical and useful applications: some typical instances are given in the following paragraphs.

EXAMPLE 2.14 (A). Resistors of 10, 20, 30, and 40 Ω are connected in series across a p.d. of 50 V. Plot a graph showing the fall of potential around the circuit.

The joint resistance

$$R = R_1 + R_2 + R_3 + R_4$$
$$= 10 + 20 + 30 + 40 = 100 \,\Omega$$

The current $I = 50/100 = 0.50$ A

P.d. across 10 Ω = 0.5 × 10 = 5 V

,,　　,,　　20 Ω = 0.5 × 20 = 10 V

,,　　,,　　30 Ω = 0.5 × 30 = 15 V

,,　　,,　　40 Ω = 0.5 × 40 = 20 V

Fig. 2.22 (ii) shows the corresponding points plotted as a graph. The "curve" obtained is a straight line, showing that the rate of fall of potential is uniform. Across each ohm of resistance the drop in volts is 0.5 V: this follows of course from simple proportion if 50 V are to be dropped uniformly over 100 Ω. The p.d. across each resistor is also indicated in the circuit diagram (i). This type of graph is applicable to any d.c. circuit with the axes suitably calibrated. The p.d.

across each resistance element of a simple series circuit can be determined by simple proportion, without the need for evaluating the current in the above manner unless this information is specifically called for. For example, the p.d. across the resistors is proportional to their respective values of 10, 20, 30, and 40 Ω, or to their ratio 1 : 2 : 3 : 4.

Since $1 + 2 + 3 + 4 = 10$—

P.d. across $10 \, \Omega = 50 \times \frac{1}{10} = 5$ V
,, ,, $20 \, \Omega = 50 \times \frac{2}{10} = 10$ V
,, ,, $30 \, \Omega = 50 \times \frac{3}{10} = 15$ V
,, ,, $40 \, \Omega = 50 \times \frac{4}{10} = 20$ V

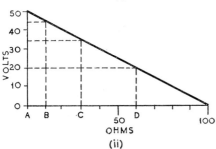

FIG. 2.22 (Example 2.14)

As the potential falls around the circuit, any point in the circuit is at a *negative* potential with respect to any other point at a higher potential, but is at the same time at a *positive* potential with respect to any other point at a lower potential: current flows from a positive to a negative potential. For example, point B is 5 V negative with respect to A, but 10 V positive with respect to C: similarly C is 10 V negative to B, but 15 V positive to D, and D is 15 V negative to C but 20 V positive to E.

The p.d. across any portion of a circuit is frequently referred to as the potential drop or VOLTAGE DROP: in the case above there is a voltage drop of 15 V across the 30 Ω resistor. *Voltage drop is the voltage between any two given points on a conductor.*

The fall of potential around a circuit may also be utilized to provide the desired operating potentials to the electrodes of an electronic valve (see Chapter XIII). In Fig. 2.23 is shown one example

where R_1, R_2, R_3, and R_4 represent the resistances of the filaments of four valves connected in series: R_5 and R_6 are additional resistors inserted to ensure the requisite potential across each filament. The current flowing in the circuit, I, is 0·5 A. The potential applied to the grid of any valve is considered with respect to the negative end of its filament. In this case the potentials applied to the

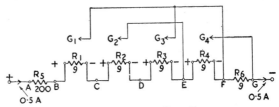

FIG. 2.23. PROVISION OF GRID POTENTIALS

grids are as follows, the filaments being of equal resistance, namely 9 Ω—

Potential G_1 = p.d. between C and F
$\quad = I(R_2 + R_3 + R_4)$
$\quad = 0·5 \times 27 = 13·5$ V
,, $\quad G_2$ = p.d. between D and $E = I(R_3)$
$\quad = 0·5 \times 9 = 4·5$ V
,, $\quad G_3$ = p.d. between E and $F = I(R_4)$
$\quad = 0·5 \times 9 = 4·5$ V
,, $\quad G_4$ = p.d. between F and $G = I(R_6)$
$\quad = 0·5 \times 9 = 4·5$ V

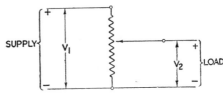

FIG. 2.24. PRINCIPLE OF POTENTIOMETER

It will be seen that the potentials at these points are all negative with respect to the filament.

2.15. The Potentiometer. This is an instrument designed to enable a definite p.d. or voltage to be "tapped off" a circuit. It comprises a three-terminal rheostat—see Fig. 2.24—forming a portion of a main circuit; by suitable adjustment of the rheostat any desired amount V_2 of the available p.d. V_1 may be applied to another circuit as required.

The principle is often applied as shown in Fig. 2.25 to obtain suitable p.d.s for application at desired points.

In telegraph circuits where "double-current" transmission is employed, the method shown in

Fig. 2.26 is sometimes used to provide the necessary positive and negative potentials. A p.d. of 160 V is maintained across a high resistance AB and a connexion is made to the "centre-point" of this resistor. The potential at the centre-tap will be 80 V due to the uniform potential drop. This centre-point is therefore 80 V *below* the 160 V

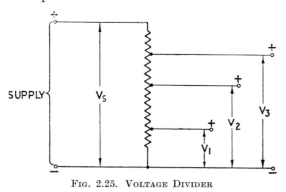

FIG. 2.25. VOLTAGE DIVIDER

potential at A, but is 80 V *above* the point of zero potential at B. It can, therefore, be regarded as a point of *relative zero potential* with respect to point A which is relatively at $+ 80$ V, and to point B which is relatively at $- 80$ V. It will be seen later that applying a potentiometer in this manner has some effect on the uniform potential drop in the

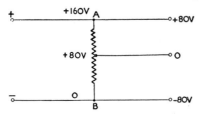

FIG. 2.26. DOUBLE CURRENT POTENTIOMETER

main resistance on account of the load being in parallel with a portion of this resistance, and the potentiometer requires careful design accordingly. The potentiometer is also used extensively in electrical measuring equipment (Chapter XII).

Slide wires are continuously variable resistors, distinct from rheostats such as the Decade which are variable in steps: the continuous variation of the slide wire is obtained by sliding-contacts working directly on the resistance wire.

The 1 000-Ω slide wire used for fault localization consists of one portion which is variable in steps together with another which is continuously variable. It is not a simple rheostat, but is designed as a potential divider, and is arranged so that the resistance value between the two main terminals

remains constant irrespective of variation of setting of the controls. The connexions are illustrated in Fig. 2.27, from which it will be seen that each of the sliding contacts connected to the hundreds, tens, units, and tenths dials always bridges two complete coils, and that the value of the bridging resistance (the lower order) is equal to the series

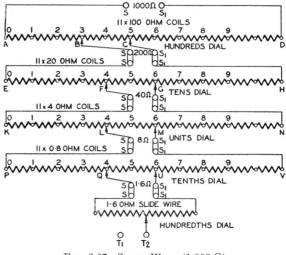

FIG. 2.27. SLIDE WIRE (1 000 Ω)

resistance of the two bridged coils. This results in the effective resistance of the two bridged coils being reduced to that of one, so that whatever the dial settings may be, the resistance across S and S_1 remains constant.

By removing the straps S–S and S_1–S_1 at the 200-Ω position a 200-Ω slide wire is obtained on the same principle: in a similar manner, a 40-Ω or 8-Ω slide wire may be obtained. This is a great convenience since for most tests it is necessary that the slide wire should be of a resistance comparable to that of the circuit connected to it.

If a p.d. V volts is applied across the 1 000-Ω terminals S–S_1, than the p.d.s across the 200-Ω, 40-Ω, 8-Ω and 1·6-Ω sections are 0·1 V, 0·01 V, 0·001 V and 0·000 1 V respectively. In the diagram the following p.d.s are tapped off—

Between	$AB = 0·3 \times 1·0$ V	$= 0·3$ V
,,	$EF = 0·4 \times 0·1$ V	$= 0·04$ V
,,	$KL = 0·4 \times 0·01$ V	$= 0·004$ V
,,	$PQ = 0·4 \times 0·001$ V	$= 0·000\ 4$ V
,,	$QT_2 = 0·5 \times 0·000\ 1$ V	$= 0·000\ 05$ V

$$0·344\ 45 \text{ V}$$

$$\frac{\text{p.d. between } A\text{–}T_2}{\text{p.d. between } S\text{–}S_1} = \frac{344·45}{1\ 000}$$

This is the ratio read off the dials. It should be appreciated that the dial readings are potentials and not resistances.

2.16. Resistors in Parallel. If both terminals of a resistor are joined respectively to both terminals of one or more other resistors so that the current divides and flows through them all simultaneously, the resistors are said to be connected in parallel. In Fig. 2.28, the several resistors R_1, R_2, R_3, R_4, . . ., R_N are connected in parallel across two points at a potential difference V volts. This is the p.d. across *each* resistor so that the resultant currents flowing, I_1, I_2, I_3, I_4, . . ., I_N respectively, may be deduced for each path from Ohm's law and have the following values—

$$I_1 = V/R_1, \ I_2 = V/R_2, \ I_3 = V/R_3,$$
$$I_4 = V/R_4, \ I_N = V/R_N$$

These currents must combine to flow together in the main circuit which includes the source of electrical energy, and since the *total* current I is the same in all parts of the circuit,

$$I = I_1 + I_2 + I_3 + I_4 + \ldots + I_N$$

Let the equivalent resistance of this parallel combination be R ohms.

Then $\quad I = V/R$

but $\quad I = I_1 + I_2 + I_3$
$$+ I_4 + \ldots + I_N$$
$$= V/R_1 + V/R_2 + V/R_3$$
$$+ V/R_4 + \ldots + V/R_N$$

i.e. $\quad V/R = V/R_1 + V/R_2 + V/R_3$
$$+ V/R_4 + \ldots + V/R_N$$

whence $1/R = 1/R_1 + 1/R_2 + 1/R_3$
$$+ 1/R_4 + \ldots + 1/R_N \quad . \quad (2.5)$$

In words, *if two or more resistors are joined in parallel, the reciprocal of the equivalent resistance is equal to the sum of the reciprocals of the separate resistances.* It should be noted that $1/R$ is the *reciprocal*, not the actual value, of the equivalent resistance.

The conductance is defined as the reciprocal of the resistance and it is probably simpler to remember that *the total conductance of a number of paths in parallel is equal to the sum of their separate conductances.* If G (= $1/R$) denotes the total conductance, and G_1, G_2, G_3, G_4, . . ., G_N the separate conductances ($G_1 = 1/R_1$, etc.) then,

$$G = G_1 + G_2 + G_3 + G_4 + \ldots + G_N$$

The magnitude of the current in each one of the parallel paths may be determined by either of two methods—

Method (i). From Ohm's law, as stated above,

$I = V/R$ for the main circuit and
$I_1 = V/R_1$, $I_2 = V/R_2$, $I_3 = V/R_3$, $I_4 = V/R_4$, etc., for the branching paths.

Method (ii). Since

$$V/R = I = VG_1 + VG_2 + VG_3$$
$$+ VG_4 + \ldots + VG_N$$

the total current divides so that the current in each path is directly proportional to the conductance of the path.

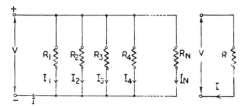

FIG. 2.28. RESISTORS IN PARALLEL

The use of method (i) is preferable if the *applied p.d.* is known: method (ii) is quicker if the *main current* is known. Both methods are shown in the following example.

EXAMPLE 2.15 (A). If five resistors of 2, 4, 8, 16, and 32 Ω respectively are connected in parallel, what is the equivalent resistance of the combination? What current flows in each path due to a p.d. of 16 V?

By Method (i)

If the joint resistance is R,

$$1/R = \tfrac{1}{2} + \tfrac{1}{4} + \tfrac{1}{8} + \tfrac{1}{16} + \tfrac{1}{32}$$
$$= (16 + 8 + 4 + 2 + 1)/32 = \tfrac{31}{32}$$

whence $R = \tfrac{32}{31}$ or $1 \cdot 03 \ \Omega$

Current in $\ 2 \ \Omega$ path $= \tfrac{16}{2} = 8$ A

$\quad$,, $\qquad 4 \ \Omega \quad$,, $\ = \tfrac{16}{4} = 4$ A

$\quad$,, $\qquad 8 \ \Omega \quad$,, $\ = \tfrac{16}{8} = 2$ A

$\quad$,, $\qquad 16 \ \Omega \quad$,, $\ = \tfrac{16}{16} = 1$ A

$\quad$,, $\qquad 32 \ \Omega \quad$,, $\ = \tfrac{16}{32} = 0 \cdot 5$ A

By Method (ii)

Total conductance $G = \frac{1}{2} + \frac{1}{4} + \frac{1}{8} + \frac{1}{16} + \frac{1}{32}$

$\qquad\qquad = (16 + 8 + 4 + 2 + 1)/32$

$\qquad\qquad = \frac{31}{32}$

$\therefore \qquad\qquad R = \frac{32}{31} = 1.03\ \Omega$

Total current $= VG = 16 \times \frac{31}{32}$ A

and $I_1 : I_2 : I_3 : I_4 : I_5$

$\quad = G_1 : G_2 : G_3 : G_4 : G_5$

$\quad = \frac{1}{2} : \frac{1}{4} : \frac{1}{8} : \frac{1}{16} : \frac{1}{32}$

$\quad = 16 : 8 : 4 : 2 : 1$

Now, $16 + 8 + 4 + 2 + 1 = 31$

Current in $\ 2\ \Omega$ path $= (16 \times \frac{31}{32}) \times \frac{16}{31} = \underline{\underline{8\ \text{A}}}$

$\quad,, \qquad 4\ \Omega \quad ,, \ = (16 \times \frac{31}{32}) \times \frac{8}{31} = \underline{\underline{4\ \text{A}}}$

$\quad,, \qquad 8\ \Omega \quad ,, \ = (16 \times \frac{31}{32}) \times \frac{4}{31} = \underline{\underline{2\ \text{A}}}$

$\quad,, \qquad 16\ \Omega \quad ,, \ = (16 \times \frac{31}{32}) \times \frac{2}{31} = \underline{\underline{1\ \text{A}}}$

$\quad,, \qquad 32\ \Omega \quad ,, \ = (16 \times \frac{31}{32}) \times \frac{1}{31} = \underline{\underline{0.5\ \text{A}}}$

Note. Method (ii) would not normally be used to solve this problem, but is given for purposes of illustration.

Three usefully remembered points arise from the relationship given above for resistances in parallel—

(i) The equivalent resistance of any number of *paralleled* resistors is always *less than* the value of the smallest resistance. For example, if two resistors of $5\ \Omega$ and $95\ \Omega$ respectively are connected in parallel then the joint resistance must be less than the smaller resistance, $5\ \Omega$.

(ii) If *two* (only) resistors are connected in parallel, the joint resistance is equal to the *product divided by the sum* of the resistances. For, let R = the joint resistance of two resistors R_1 and R_2 joined in parallel. Then—

$$1/R = 1/R_1 + 1/R_2 = (R_2 + R_1)/(R_1 R_2)$$
$$R = R_1 R_2/(R_1 + R_2) = \text{product/sum} \quad . \quad (2.6)$$

Hence the equivalent resistance of the two conductors of $5\ \Omega$ and $95\ \Omega$ resistance, referred to above, when connected in parallel is

$$(5 \times 95)/(5 + 95) = 475/100 = 4.75\ \Omega$$

(i.e. less than $5\ \Omega$).

(iii) If a number N of *equal* resistors R' ohms are connected in parallel, the equivalent resistance R is equal to R'/N.

For, $1/R = 1/R' + 1/R' + 1/R' + \ldots N$

$\qquad = (1 + 1 + 1 + \ldots N)/R' = N/R'$

or $R = R'/N$

For example, if 5 resistors each of $450\ \Omega$ resistance are connected in parallel, the joint resistance is equal to $450/5 = 90\ \Omega$.

The statement that the resistance of a conductor is inversely proportional to the cross-sectional area follows from the relation given above for resistors in parallel, for any conductor may be regarded as being made up from a number of thinner wires joined together in parallel.

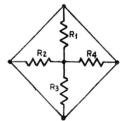

FIG. 2.29 (Example 2.16)

A resistor is sometimes connected in parallel with an instrument possessing resistance, say a meter or a coil, in order to divert a portion of the main current from flowing through the instrument: a resistor used in this manner is known as a *shunting resistance* or simply as a *shunt*.

EXAMPLE 2.16 (A). In the resistance network shown in Fig. 2.29, $R_1 = R_2 = 2R_3 = 2R_4$ and the resistance of all connecting leads is negligible. If a battery of 2·4 V is connected across R_4 and the total current drawn from the battery is 0·6 A, what is the value of each resistance?
(*C. & G.*)

The resistances are all in parallel, therefore joint resistance R is given by

$$1/R = 1/R_1 + 1/R_2 + 1/R_3 + 1/R_4$$
$$= 1/(2R_4) + 1/(2R_4) + 1/R_4 + 1/R_4$$
$$= (1 + 1 + 2 + 2)/(2R_4) = 6/(2R_4) = 3/R_4$$

i.e. $3R = R_4$

Since $\qquad V = 2.4\ \text{V, and } I = 0.6\ \text{A,}$

$\qquad\qquad R = V/I = 2.4/0.6 = 4$

$\qquad\qquad R_4 = R_3(= 3R) = \underline{\underline{12\ \Omega}}$

$\qquad\qquad R_1 = R_2(= 2R_3) = \underline{\underline{24\ \Omega}}$

EXAMPLE 2.17 (A). A given length of wire has a resistance of $30\ \Omega$. The wire is cut into three equal lengths and these are connected in parallel. What is the combined resistance of the three pieces? (*C. & G.*)

Resistance of each equal piece $= 30/3 = 10\ \Omega$.

Joint resistance of these three lengths in parallel $= 10/3 = \underline{\underline{3.3\ \Omega}}$.

2.17. Resistors in Series and Parallel. Many circuits which have to be considered do not consist of a simple arrangement of resistors in series or in parallel, but are a combination of the two arrangements. To evaluate the equivalent resistance in such a case it is necessary first to determine the joint resistance of each set of paralleled resistors present, and then to treat the circuit as a simple series circuit. A few worked examples will make the procedure clear.

EXAMPLE 2.18 (A). The circuit diagram in Fig. 2.30 (i) represents the conditions on the third conductor of a subscriber's line termination at the metering stage of a call on a manual telephone exchange. What is (a) the equivalent resistance of the circuit, (b) the current in the main circuit, (c) the potential at the point M, and (d) the current in the 50 Ω resistor?

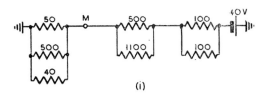

(i)

(ii)

FIG. 2.30 (Example 2.18)

The three resistances of 40, 50, and 500 Ω may be replaced by a single resistance R_1 whose value is given by

$$1/R_1 = 1/40 + 1/50 + 1/500$$
$$= (25 + 20 + 2)/1\,000 = 47/1\,000$$

whence $R_1 = 1\,000/47 = 21\cdot3\ \Omega$

The joint value R_2 of the two resistors of 500 and 1 100 Ω in parallel is equal to their product divided by their sum, i.e.

$$R_2 = (1\,100 \times 500)/(1\,100 + 500)$$
$$= 550\,000/1\,600 = 343\cdot8\ \Omega$$

The joint resistance R_3 of the two equal resistors in parallel is equal to $100/2 = 50\ \Omega$.

The circuit may now be redrawn in its equivalent form (ii) which is a simple series circuit.

(a) The total resistance

$$= 21\cdot3 + 343\cdot8 + 50 = 415\cdot1\ \Omega$$

(b) The current $I = 40/415\cdot1 = 96\cdot4\ \text{mA}$

(c) The potential at

$$M = IR_1 = 0\cdot096 \times 21\cdot3 = 2\cdot04\ \text{V}$$

(d) The current in the 50 Ω resistor

$$= 2\cdot04/50 = 0\cdot040\,8 = 41\ \text{mA}$$

EXAMPLE 2.19 (A). Fig. 2.31 shows the sleeve circuit conditions established when a plug is connected with a subscriber's line jack at an "A" position in a central battery exchange. Calculate the p.d. across the CO relay. (C. & G.)

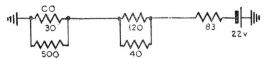

FIG. 2.31 (Example 2.19)

Joint resistance of

$$30 \text{ and } 500\ \Omega = 30 \times 500/(30 + 500)$$
$$= 15\,000/530 = 28\cdot3\ \Omega$$

Joint resistance of

$$40 \text{ and } 120\ \Omega = 40 \times 120/(40 + 120)$$
$$= 4\,800/160 = 30\ \Omega$$

Total circuit resistance

$$= 28\cdot3 + 30 + 83 = 141\cdot3\ \Omega$$

P.d. across CO relay (30 Ω)

$$= 22 \times 28\cdot3/141\cdot3 = 4\cdot4\ \text{V}$$

EXAMPLE 2.20 (A). A battery of 40 V is joined in series with a resistor of 3 960 Ω and a relay of 200 Ω across which is shunted a resistor R. What is the value of R if the current through the relay is 2 mA? (C. & G.)

The circuit is shown in Fig. 2.32.

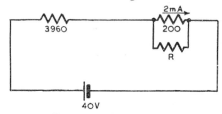

FIG. 2.32 (Example 2.20)

P.d. across 200 Ω relay

$$= 0\cdot002 \times 200 = 0\cdot4\ \text{V}$$

P.d. across 3 960 Ω

$$= 40 - 0\cdot4 = 39\cdot6\ \text{V}$$

Current in 3 960 Ω

$$= 39\cdot6/3\,960 = 0\cdot01\ \text{A}$$

Current through resistance R
$$= 0\cdot01 - 0\cdot002 = 0\cdot008 \text{ A}$$

Resistance of R
$$= 0\cdot4/0\cdot008 = 50 \ \Omega$$

EXAMPLE 2.21 (A). In the circuit below (Fig. 2.33) calculate—

(i) The currents flowing at points X and Y.
(ii) The p.d. between the points X and Z. (C. & G.)

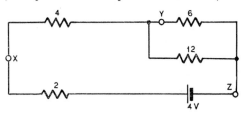

FIG. 2.33 (Example 2.21)

(i) Joint resistance of $6 \ \Omega$ and $12 \ \Omega$ in parallel
$$= 6 \times 12/(6 + 12) = 72/18 = 4 \ \Omega$$

Total circuit resistance
$$= 2 + 4 + 4 = 10 \ \Omega$$

Current flowing at X
$$= 4/10 = 0\cdot4 \text{ A}$$

P.d. across 6 and $12 \ \Omega$ resistors
$$= 4 \times 0\cdot4 = 1\cdot6 \text{ V}$$

Current flowing at Y
$$= 1\cdot6/6 = 0\cdot267 \text{ A}$$

(ii) P.d. across $4 \ \Omega$ resistor
$$= 4 \times 0\cdot4 = 1\cdot6 \text{ V}$$

P.d. across 6 and $12 \ \Omega$ resistor
$$(= 4 \ \Omega) = 1\cdot6 \text{ V}$$

P.d. across XZ
$$= 1\cdot6 + 1\cdot6 = 3\cdot2 \text{ V}$$

EXAMPLE 2.22 (A). In the circuit in Fig. 2.34, what is—

(i) The total current taken from the battery?
(ii) The current flowing through R_2?
(iii) The voltage drop across R_3?
(iv) The current in R_1? (C. & G.)

Joint resistance of R_3, R_4, and R_5
$$= 1/(\tfrac{1}{4} + \tfrac{1}{4} + \tfrac{1}{2}) = 1 \ \Omega$$

Joint resistance of R_2, R_3, R_4, and R_5
$$= 2 + 1 = 3 \ \Omega$$

Joint resistance of R_1, R_2, R_3, R_4, and R_5
$$= 2 \times 3/(2 + 3) = 6/5 \ \Omega$$

(i) The total current taken from the battery
$$= 6 \times \tfrac{5}{6} = 5\cdot0 \text{ A}$$

(ii) The current flowing through R_2
$$= \tfrac{6}{3} = 2 \text{ A}$$

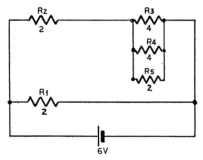

FIG. 2.34 (Example 2.22)

(iii) The p.d. across R_3

$\quad$ = (current flowing through R_2) $\times$ (joint resistance of R_3, R_4, and R_5) $= 2 \times 1 = 2 \text{ V}$

(iv) The current flowing in R_1
$$= \tfrac{6}{2} = 3 \text{ A}$$

EXAMPLE 2.23 (A). Calculate the current supplied by the battery to the network given below, Fig. 2.35 (i) and (ii), and the current flowing in BD. What resistance connected between AD will reduce this latter current to zero? If AD were short-circuited, what current would flow in BD? (C. & G.)

(i) $\quad$ Joint resistance of $BC = \tfrac{10}{2} = 5 \ \Omega$

$\quad$ Total circuit resistance $= 5 + 5 = 10 \ \Omega$

Current supplied by battery $= \tfrac{2}{10} = 0\cdot2 \text{ A}$

(ii) Current in $BD = \tfrac{1}{2} \times 0\cdot2 = 0\cdot1 \text{ A}$

(iii) Let the resistance to be connected between AD be X ohms. For current in BD to become zero, B and D must be at the same potential.

P.d. from A to $B = (\tfrac{5}{15}) \times 2 = \tfrac{2}{3} \text{ V}$

,, $\quad$,, $\quad A$ to $D = \{X/(5 + X)\} \times 2 = \tfrac{2}{3} \text{ V}$

$$2X/(5 + X) = \tfrac{2}{3}, \ 6X = 10 + 2X, \text{ whence}$$
$$X = \tfrac{10}{4} = 2\cdot5 \ \Omega$$

(iv) Resistance between DB

$$= \tfrac{5}{2} = 2 \cdot 5 \ \Omega$$

Resistance of DBC

$$= 2 \cdot 5 + 10 = 12 \cdot 5 \ \Omega$$

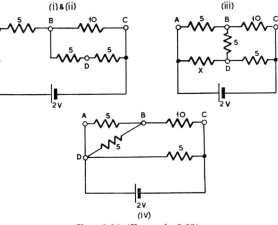

FIG. 2.35 (Example 2.23)

Current in DBC

$$= 2/12 \cdot 5 = 0 \cdot 16 \ \text{A}$$

$\therefore$ Current in BD

$$= \tfrac{1}{2} \times 0 \cdot 16 = 0 \cdot 08 \ \text{A}$$

Note: (iii) would normally be solved as a balanced Wheatstone bridge (Example 2.31).

2.18. Cabling and Wiring. The conductors used for connecting items of electrical equipment to one another and to the source of electrical energy are designed to offer the lowest resistance compatible with economy in cost. This is necessary to avoid wasteful heating and power losses (see Chapter III), and also to limit the potential drop in the connecting wires to ensure that sufficient p.d. is available to operate the equipment. The safe current capacity of a conductor is that maximum current which will not develop heat at a greater rate than it can be dissipated without producing an undue rise in temperature. The size of a conductor used for cabling and wiring is determined by the condition that it must not produce an appreciable potential drop and is based upon considerations of the current density—the ratio of the current to cross-sectional area—in the conductor. In an automatic telephone exchange the bus bars feeding power from the battery room to the apparatus racks are of rectangular-section copper of sufficient

area to limit the total drop in positive and negative leads to a maximum of one volt.

For normal calculations the resistance of correctly designed connecting wires can often be neglected when it is small in comparison with other resistance values in the circuit. In some cases, for

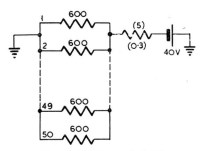

FIG. 2.36 (Example 2.24)

example testing circuits, the resistance of the connecting wires is comparable with other parts of the circuit and special care must then be taken to allow for this condition.

The effect of excessive resistance in the connecting leads is shown by the following example.

EXAMPLE 2.24 (A). In a manual telephone exchange the calling lamps have a resistance of 600 Ω each. If 50 of these lamps were fed in parallel from a 40 V supply over a common distribution lead having a resistance of 5 Ω, what is the potential difference across the lamps, and the current in each lamp (*a*) when 5 lamps are glowing, (*b*) when 50 lamps are glowing? If the resistance of the lead is reduced to 0·3 Ω, what is the p.d. across the lamps and the current per lamp for (*a*) and (*b*)?

The arrangement of the circuit is shown in Fig. 2.36.

(*i*) *Resistance of leads* $= 5 \ \Omega$.

	5 Lamps		50 Lamps
Joint resistance of lamps	$= 600/5$	$= 120 \ \Omega$	$600/50 = 12 \ \Omega$
Joint resistance of lamps and leads	$= 120 + 5$	$= 125 \ \Omega$	$12 + 5 = 17 \ \Omega$
P.d. across lamps	$= 40 \times 120/125$	$= \underline{38 \cdot 4 \ \text{V}}$	$40 \times 12/17 = \underline{28 \cdot 2 \ \text{V}}$
Current per lamp	$= 38 \cdot 4/600$	$= \underline{64 \ \text{mA}}$	$28 \cdot 2/600 = \underline{47 \ \text{mA}}$

(*ii*) *Resistance of leads* $= 0 \cdot 3 \ \Omega$

Joint resistance of lamps and leads	$= 120 + 0 \cdot 3$	$= 120 \cdot 3 \ \Omega$	$12 + 0 \cdot 3 = 12 \cdot 3 \ \Omega$
P.d. across lamps	$= 40 \times 120/120 \cdot 3$	$= \underline{39 \cdot 9 \ \text{V}}$	$40 \times 12/12 \cdot 3 = \underline{39 \ \text{V}}$
Current per lamp	$= 39 \cdot 9/600$	$= \underline{66 \cdot 5 \ \text{mA}}$	$39/600 = \underline{65 \ \text{mA}}$

It is seen that with a high resistance distribution lead the p.d. across the lamps fluctuates considerably with the number of lamps in circuit and the current available to operate each lamp falls heavily as the number of lamps in circuit is increased. This illustrates the need for using a distribution lead having a low resistance (i.e. a suitable cross-sectional area in relation to its length) commensurate with the current load which it may be called upon to carry.

In telephone systems the electrical energy required to operate a private branch exchange

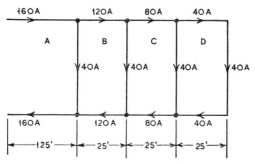

FIG. 2.37 (Example 2.25)

(P.B.X.) is, under suitable conditions, supplied over a line from the main exchange. For this purpose a p.d. of 30 V is usually available at the main exchange. The P.B.X. equipment is designed to operate down to a minimum p.d. of 12 V. The maximum line resistance which can be permitted for this purpose is then easily calculated. From a knowledge of the size of the P.B.X. the anticipated maximum number of simultaneous connexions can be determined. The resistances of the various components are known so that a figure for the maximum current to be carried is readily obtained. Calling this I amps, the permissible resistance R for the line or "power lead" is fixed by the maximum allowable potential drop in the line, i.e. 30–12 V.

$$\dot{R} = V/I = (30\text{--}12)/I = 18/I \ \Omega$$

In practice, the line resistance may be reduced to this figure by "bunching" if necessary, i.e. by connecting in parallel two or more wires to obtain the desired resistance.

EXAMPLE 2.25 (A). The power distribution system at an automatic exchange consists of a pair of uniform copper conductors, negative and positive, carried close together for 200 ft. There are four tees, 25 ft apart, from the conductors, to feed current to the automatic equipment, the first tee being 125 ft from the battery supply end of the conductors. If the current required at each tee is 40 A, find the cross-sectional area that the conductors

must have in order to ensure that the maximum drop in them shall not exceed 1 V. The specific resistance of copper may be taken as 0·64 μΩ/in.-cube.   (C. & G.)

Fig. 2.37 shows the conditions to be met.
The resistance of a conductor is $\rho l/a$ and the voltage drop $V = IR = I\rho l/a = \rho/a \times Il$.

Tabulating—

Section	I (A)	l (in.)	Il
A	160	$250 \times 12 = 3\,000$	48×10^4
B	120	$50 \times 12 = 600$	$7{\cdot}2 \times 10^4$
C	80	$50 \times 12 = 600$	$4{\cdot}8 \times 10^4$
D	40	$50 \times 12 = 600$	$2{\cdot}4 \times 10^4$

Total p.d.
$$= \Sigma(I\rho l/a) = (\rho/a) \cdot \Sigma(Il) \ . \ . \ . \text{(see Appendix A.2)}$$
$$= (0{\cdot}64/10^6 a)(48 + 7{\cdot}2 + 4{\cdot}8 + 2{\cdot}4)10^4$$
$$= (0{\cdot}64/10^2 a) \times 62{\cdot}4 = 1 \text{ V by specification}$$
$$\therefore a = 0{\cdot}64 \times 62{\cdot}4/100 = \underline{0{\cdot}399 \text{ in.}^2}$$

2.19. Insulation Resistance of Lines.

An overhead wire is supported at intervals of 60 yd or so by means of poles and an insulator is fitted at each pole to limit the current which would flow from the wire to the earth or into another wire. The insulation resistance of the insulator itself is of the order of 1 000 MΩ or more. If the effect of successive insulators is considered, however, it is seen that all the insulators are in parallel with one another, and a section of the line may be represented by the equivalent circuit of Fig. 2.38: it is

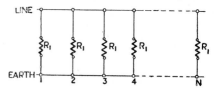

FIG. 2.38. INSULATION RESISTANCE OF A LINE

assumed that the insulation resistance of the air is infinite so that leakage of the current occurs only at the insulators. Suppose that the insulation resistance R_1 of each of the N insulators is approximately the same; then the equivalent insulation resistance R of the whole line is given by $R = R_1/N$. For instance, if the insulation resistance of a single insulator were 1 000 MΩ, the insulation resistance of a length of line comprisng 500 insulators would be 1 000/500 = 2·0 M. Ωi

In other words the overall insulation resistance of the line is reduced as the number of insulators is increased: the insulation resistance decreases with increase in the length of the line. For a cable a similar reasoning applies but here the conductor and the insulating material are in contact at an infinitely large number of points.

It is usual to assume that the insulation resistance is uniform along a section of the line and to express this as insulation resistance per unit length—normally in megohms per mile. The overall insulation resistance of any line then may be considered as due to the equivalent resistance of a number of separate paths, each one mile apart, in parallel.

EXAMPLE 2.26 (A). What is the insulation resistance of a line in a 40-mile length of main cable having an insulation resistance of 10 000 MΩ/mile?

This may be considered as 40 resistances each of 10 000 MΩ in parallel and so would have an overall insulation resistance of 10 000/40 = 250 MΩ.

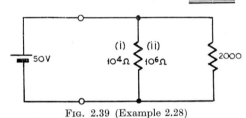

FIG. 2.39 (Example 2.28)

EXAMPLE 2.27 (A). The measured insulation resistance of a 50-mile line is found to be 100 MΩ; what is the insulation resistance per mile?

The overall insulation resistance R may be considered to be due to N paths each of R_1 ohms in parallel. $R = R_1/N$ or $R_1 = NR$, i.e. insulation resistance = 50 × 100 = 5 000 MΩ/mile.

Notes: (i) The overall insulation resistance of a line is calculated by dividing the insulation resistance per mile by the number of miles.

(ii) The insulation resistance of a section of line is usually assumed to act at the centre of that section.

EXAMPLE 2.28 (A). An overhead line of negligible resistance has permanently connected to it a load of 2 000 Ω. The insulation resistance between the wires of the line is 10 000 Ω. The circuit is supplied by a secondary battery of 50 V, 10 Ah. For how long will the battery supply the load without recharging, and by how much will this time be increased if the insulation resistance is raised to 1 MΩ? It may be assumed that the voltage of the battery remains constant through the discharge. (C. & G.)

The circuit conditions are shown in Fig. 2.39.

(i) With insulation resistance = 10 000 Ω

Joint resistance

$$= 10\ 000 \times 2\ 000/12\ 000 = 20\ 000/12\ \Omega$$

Current from battery

$$= 50 \times 12/20\ 000 = 0.03\ \text{A}$$

A battery of 10 Ah (§4.4) will last for 10/0.03 = 333.3 hr.

(ii) With insulation resistance 1 MΩ.

Joint resistance

$$= 10^6 \times 2\ 000/1\ 002\ 000 = 1\ 996\ \Omega$$

Current from battery

$$= 50/1\ 996 = 0.025\ \text{A}$$

A battery of 10 Ah will last for 10/0.025 = 400 hr.

Increase of discharge time = 400 − 333 = 67 hr (approx.).

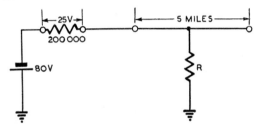

FIG. 2.40 (Example 2.29)

EXAMPLE 2.29 (A). A battery giving a constant terminal p.d. of 80 V and a voltmeter of 200 000 Ω resistance are used in making a "wire to earth" insulation test on one wire of a telephone line five miles in length. If a reading of 25 V is obtained, what is the insulation resistance of the wire in megohms per mile? (C. & G.)

Note: Neglect the conductor resistance of the wire and assume that the insulation resistance is "lumped" at the centre (see Fig. 2.40). If the p.d. across the voltmeter is 25 V, the p.d. across the insulation resistance R is 80 − 25 = 55 V. Then since p.d. is proportional to resistance—

$$R/200\ 000 = \tfrac{55}{25}$$
$$R = 200\ 000 \times \tfrac{55}{25} = 440\ 000\ \Omega$$

Insulation resistance per mile = 440 000 × 5 = 2.2 MΩ.

2.20. True and Apparent Line Resistance. It is important that the precise meanings of the terms insulation resistance and conductor resistance should be appreciated. The true conductor resistance of a wire is the resistance of the wire itself as determined from its dimensions and its resistivity ($R = \rho l/a$). The true insulation resistance of a wire is the equivalent resistance of all the shunt paths along which a current can escape or leak from it: for an open line wire it is the equivalent resistance offered by all the insulators to the passage of current over their surfaces. The true conductor resistance and the true insulation resistance are entirely separate entities, but with the measurements normally made it is actually the *apparent* conductor resistance and the *apparent* insulation resistance which are observed and the two measurements are interdependent. The apparent conductor

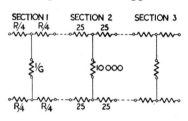

(a)

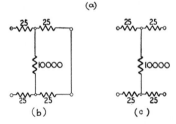

(b)   (c)

FIG. 2.41. CONDUCTOR AND INSULATION RESISTANCES
OF A LINE

resistance is the true conductor resistance modified by the value of the true insulation resistance, and the apparent insulation resistance is the true insulation resistance modified by the value of the true conductor resistance. The apparent insulation resistance is always higher than the true value: this is brought about by the effect of inclusion of conductor resistance in series. The apparent conductor resistance is always lower than the true value, due to the shunting effect of the insulation resistance.

Consider a pair of wires forming an external line circuit. As shown in Fig. 2.41 (a) the uniformly distributed conductor resistance may be considered as being "lumped" in series sections, and the distributed insulation resistance may similarly be assumed to act as though it were concentrated in shunt at the mid-point of each section. If the sections are infinitely small in length then this assumption becomes true. Suppose that for each section the true conductor loop resistance is 100 Ω, and the true insulation resistance is 10 000 Ω: these values are shown in the diagram.

To measure the loop resistance of a line the far

end is *short-circuited*, i.e. the two wires are joined together at the distant end by a conductor of zero resistance. The insulation resistance is measured with the far end *open-circuited*, i.e. the two wires are insulated from one another throughout.

The measured loop resistance of one section is that shown in Fig. 2.41 (b) and is equal to

$$25 + 25 + (50 \times 10\ 000)/(50 + 10\ 000)$$
$$= 50 + 49 \cdot 75 = 99 \cdot 75 \ \Omega$$

The measured insulation resistance of one section —Fig. 2.41 (c)—is $25 + 10\ 000 + 25 = 10\ 050\ \Omega$.

Similar evaluations for two, three, four, and five sections have been made and are shown tabulated below together with the calculated true values.

No. of Sections	Conductor Resistance		Insulation Resistance	
	True	Apparent	True	Apparent
1	100	99·75	10 000	10 050
2	200	198	5 000	5 095
3	300	292	3 333	3 450
4	400	380	2 500	2 640
5	500	462	2 000	2 170

An appreciable discrepancy between the true and apparent values occurs only when the true values of conductor resistance and insulation resistance are comparable. Normally the insulation resistance of a line is very much higher than the values assumed for the numerical example and in most cases the difference between true and apparent (or measured) values may be ignored.

The true and apparent values of conductor resistance and insulation resistance are given by the following expressions where C is the conductor resistance and I is the insulation resistance in ohms, and the suffixes t and a denote the true and apparent values respectively.

$$C_t = \sqrt{I_a C_a}/2 \times \log_e \frac{\sqrt{I_a} + \sqrt{C_a}}{\sqrt{I_a} - \sqrt{C_a}} \text{ ohms}$$

$$I_t = 2\sqrt{I_a C_a} \div \log_e \frac{\sqrt{I_a} + \sqrt{C_a}}{\sqrt{I_a} - \sqrt{C_a}} \text{ ohms}$$

2.21. Attenuation. It will be observed that in a telecommunication circuit which includes a line the current flowing at the sending end of a circuit does not all pass through the receiving termination, but some of it returns to the source by the leakage paths provided by the insulation resistance progressively along the line. Such an effect is known as *attenuation*, and from its nature it follows a logarithmic law. In the d.c. circuit the relation between the values of the current sent, I_s, and the current received, I_r, is given by

$$I_r = I_s \cdot e^{-\beta l}$$

where $e =$ the base of natural logarithms $(= 2{\cdot}718)$,

$l =$ the length of line, and

$\beta =$ the "attenuation coefficient" per unit length.

The attenuation coefficient is dependent upon the values of conductor resistance and insulation resistance and is in fact equal to $\sqrt{RG}$, where R is the *true* conductor resistance in ohms per unit length; and G is the conductance, in mhos per unit length, due to the insulation resistance, and is usually known as the *leakance*. The unit length is usually the mile. For alternating currents the effects of inductance and capacitance have to be considered and the calculations are more complex. This subject is more fully dealt with in Chapter XI.

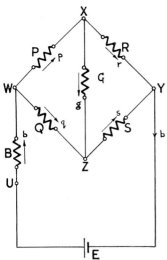

FIG. 2.42. BRIDGE NETWORK

2.22. Kirchhoff's Laws. It has been shown in Example 2.18 and others how the equivalent resistance of a somewhat complex circuit comprising resistances connected both in series and parallel arrangements can be calculated from the application of Ohm's law. By this process all parallel elements are reduced to their equivalent value and the circuit is then treated as a simple series circuit: as a result the current flowing in any part of the circuit is found by a direct application of Ohm's law.

This direct method fails when the more complex circuits, or *networks* as they are termed, are encountered. For instance the network of Fig. 2.42 does not permit of solution in this manner due to the presence of the bridging element XZ and recourse must be had to the methods available by the application of Kirchhoff's two laws.

KIRCHHOFF'S FIRST LAW states that *the algebraic sum of the currents meeting at any point of a network is zero*. This law is axiomatic for there would be

an accumulation at a junction point unless the currents flowing towards that point were balanced by, or equal to, the currents flowing away from it. The First Law may be summarized as*—

$$\Sigma(i) = 0 \text{ at any junction point} \quad . \quad (2.7)$$

The meaning of this rule is illustrated by a reference to Fig. 2.43 where P is the meeting point of the six paths carrying the currents i_1, i_2, i_3, i_4, i_5, and i_6. Since the *algebraic* sum is to be considered, suppose that it is decided to give a positive sign to currents flowing *towards* the point and a negative sign to currents flowing *away from* the point. Then i_2, i_5, and i_6 are negative and i_1, i_3, and i_4, are positive. The algebraic sum of these is zero so that

$$i_1 + i_3 + i_4 - i_2 - i_5 - i_6 = 0$$

or

$$i_1 + i_3 + i_4 = i_2 + i_5 + i_6$$

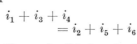

FIG. 2.43. KIRCHHOFF'S FIRST LAW

To apply this law to the network of Fig. 2.42 where the magnitudes of the currents flowing in the resistances P, Q, R, S, B, and G are denoted by the letters p, q, r, s, b, and g respectively, it is first necessary to decide upon the direction of the current flow at each of the junction points W, X, Y, and Z. Knowing that the point U is at a positive potential with respect to point Y, the arrows can readily be inserted with the exception of those for the direction of the current g. The direction of g is not known unless it is ascertained whether X or Z is at the higher potential, and for any similar case where a current direction cannot be assessed at sight it is necessary to assume the direction: if the assumption is subsequently proved to be erroneous this will become apparent by a solution giving a *negative* value to the magnitude of the current, indicating that the current flows in a direction opposite to that assumed.

The following equations can now be written down, assuming that the current g flows from X to Z—

At point W,

$$b - p - q = 0, \text{ or } q = b - p$$

At point X,

$$p - r - g = 0, \text{ or } r = p - g$$

* For use of Σ, see Appendix **A.2** (ii).

At point Z,

$$g + q - s = 0, \text{ or } s = g + q = (g + b - p)$$

At point Y,

$$r + s - b = 0, \text{ or } r + s = b,$$
$$\text{or } (p - g) + (g + b - p) = b$$
$$\text{or } b = b$$

The object in applying this First Law is to reduce the number of unknown currents to its true minimum: for example, s is not independently unknown for it is known in terms of g, b, and p as shown above (at point Z). Furthermore the final point (Y in this problem) acts as a check ($b = b$) against possible errors due to confusion of $+$ and $-$ signs. Worked examples are given below.

KIRCHHOFF'S SECOND LAW states that *in any mesh of a network the algebraic sum of the e.m.f.s is equal to the algebraic sum of the products of the resistances and the respective currents of the separate parts.* In short, for any mesh or closed part of the circuit,*

$$\Sigma E = \Sigma(IR) . \quad . \quad . \quad (2.8)$$

In effect this second law is simply a particular yet invaluable application of Ohm's law to a portion of the circuit.

The product of the current and resistance of any path gives the p.d. acting in that path so that it may be said that in any mesh of a network the algebraic sum of the e.m.f.s is equal to the algebraic sum of the p.d.s across the separate parts.

By a mesh is meant a complete closed circuit, and in Fig. 2.44 all the seven possible meshes into which the network of Fig. 2.42 can be divided have been shown separately in (a) to (g).

Attention has been drawn to the distinction between e.m.f. and p.d.: this difference must be clearly appreciated to apply the second law correctly. In Fig. 2.44 (a) there is one source only of e.m.f. (E) but a p.d. may exist across each resistance element: the same remark applies to the meshes shown in (b), (c), and (d); while the remaining meshes shown at (e), (f), and (g) do not contain any source of e.m.f. Applying this second law to each mesh in turn produces the equations given below, care being taken to allot the correct sign to each p.d. in accordance with the direction of the current—

(a) In mesh $UWXY$, $E = Bb + Pp + Rr$
(b)   ,, $UWZY$, $E = Bb + Qq + Ss$
(c)   ,, $UWXZY$, $E = Bb + Pp + Gg + Ss$
(d)   ,, $UWZXY$, $E = Bb + Qq - Gg + Rr$

* For use of Σ, see Appendix **A.2** (ii).

(e) In mesh $WXYZ$, $0 = Pp + Rr - Ss - Qq$
(f)   ,, WXZ $0 = Pp + Gg - Qq$
(g)   ,, XYZ, $0 = Rr - Ss - Gg$

The derivation of these expressions—at least for (a), (b), (c), and (d)—is fairly obvious from the diagrams since it is merely an illustration of the uniform fall of potential around the circuit. By

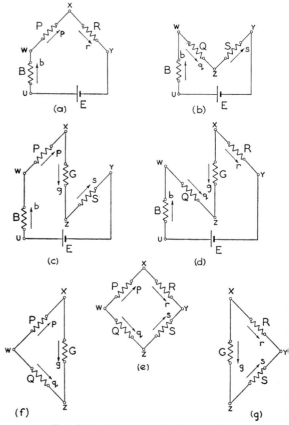

FIG. 2.44. KIRCHHOFF'S SECOND LAW

this method the foregoing seven equations, which, however, are not all independent, are obtained: some of the terms will be known from given data, and, provided that a number of equations equal to the number of unknown terms is available, the unknown terms can be evaluated by solution of these simultaneous equations. It is not necessary to utilize all the seven equations given above, these having been shown for illustration of all the meshes existing. In solving such a problem discrete selection of the meshes containing the unknowns is required. A typical solution of the currents in a network is given in the worked example, following.

In the above analysis, the letters p, q, r, s, b, and g, have been used to denote current values for convenience in illustration of the application of the second law. It is apparent that not all of these are unknown, and in fact the first law enables all the currents to be expressed in terms of three values I, i_1, and i_2 as shown in Fig. 2.45. The current I in the main circuit will divide at point W. Suppose i_1 flows in the path WX: since the total current is the same in all parts of the circuit, or alternatively by the first law since the algebraic sum of the currents is zero, the current flowing in WZ must be $I - i_1$. Similarly, i_1 divides at X and if i_2 denotes the current which flows in the path XZ, then the current flowing in XY is $i_1 - i_2$. The current in ZY is equal to $I - i_1 + i_2$, i.e. the sum of $(I - i_1)$ and i_2. At point Y the currents $(i_1 - i_2)$ and $(I - i_1 + i_2)$ unite and together equal I, the main current, as would be expected.

EXAMPLE 2.30 (A). In Fig. 2.45, what is the strength of the current in each part of the circuit?

From the first law—

Let current in the path $UW = I$
"   "   "   " $WX = i_1$
∴   "   "   " $WZ = I - i_1$,
for $I - i_1 - (I - i_1) = 0$

Let current in the path $XZ = i_2$ (assumed to flow from X to Z)

∴ current in the path $XY = i_1 - i_2$,
for $i_1 - i_2 - (i_1 - i_2) = 0$

and therefore,

Current in the path $ZY = (I - i_1 + i_2)$,
for $(I - i_1) + i_2 - (I - i_1 + i_2) = 0$

These currents together with the resistance values are indicated in the diagram.

From the second law—

In mesh $UWXY$,

$$2I + 12i_1 + 8(i_1 - i_2) = 2$$
$$2I + 20i_1 - 8i_2 = 2$$
$$I + 10i_1 - 4i_2 = 1 \quad . \quad . \quad . \quad \text{(i)}$$

In mesh WXZ,

$$12i_1 + 10i_2 - 6(I - i_1) = 0$$
$$- 6I + 18i_1 + 10i_2 = 0$$
$$- 3I + 9i_1 + 5i_2 = 0 \quad . \quad . \quad \text{(ii)}$$

In mesh XYZ,

$$8(i_1 - i_2) - 16(I - i_1 + i_2) - 10i_2 = 0$$
$$- 16I + 24i_1 - 34i_2 = 0$$
$$- 8I + 12i_1 - 17i_2 = 0 \quad . \quad \text{(iii)}$$

Multiplying (i) by 3, $3I + 30i_1 - 12i_2 = 3$
Adding (ii), $- 3I + 9i_1 + 5i_2 = 0$
$$39i_1 - 7i_2 = 3 \quad \text{(iv)}$$

Multiplying (ii) by 8,
$$- 24I + 72i_1 + 40i_2 = 0$$

Multiplying (iii) by 3,
$$- 24I + 36i_1 - 51i_2 = 0$$

Subtracting, $36i_1 + 91i_2 = 0$
$$i_1 = - 91i_2/36$$

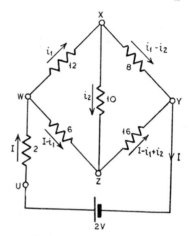

FIG. 2.45 (Example 2.30)

Substituting in (iv),

$$- (39 \times 91i_2)/36 - 7i_2 = 3$$
$$- 1\,183i_2 - 84i_2 = 36$$
$$i_2 = - 36/1\,267$$
$$= - 0 \cdot 028\,4 \text{ A}$$
$$\text{or} - 28 \cdot 4 \text{ mA}$$

The negative sign indicates that a current of 28·4 mA flows in the direction from Z to X, i.e. in opposite sense to the assumed direction: but note that $(- 28 \cdot 4)$ must be used as the value for i_2 in evaluating the remaining currents.

$$i_1 = - 91i_2/36 = - 91 \times (- 28 \cdot 4)/36 = 71 \cdot 8 \text{ mA}$$

From (i), $I = 1 - 10i_1 + 4i_2$
$$= 1 - (10 \times 0 \cdot 071\,8)$$
$$+ (4 \times - 0 \cdot 028\,4)$$
$$= 1 - 0 \cdot 718 - 0 \cdot 113\,6$$
$$= 1 - 0 \cdot 831\,6$$
$$= 0 \cdot 168\,4 \text{ A or } 168 \cdot 4 \text{ mA}$$

Current in

$$UW = I = 168{\cdot}4 \text{ mA}$$
$$WX = i_1 = 71{\cdot}8 \text{ mA}$$
$$XY = i_1 - i_2 = 71{\cdot}8 - (-28{\cdot}4) = 100{\cdot}2 \text{ mA}$$
$$ZY = I - i_1 + i_2 = 168{\cdot}4 - 71{\cdot}8 + (-28{\cdot}4)$$
$$= 68{\cdot}2 \text{ mA}$$
$$WZ = I - i_1 = 168{\cdot}4 - 71{\cdot}8 = 96{\cdot}6 \text{ mA}$$
$$XZ = i_2 = 28{\cdot}4 \text{ mA (from } Z \text{ to } X)$$

Since an applied e.m.f. of 2 V produces a total current of 168·4 mA, the equivalent resistance R of

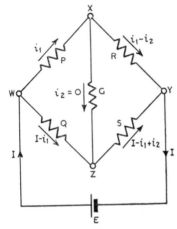

FIG. 2.46 (Example 2.31)

the combined network is given by $R = V/I$ $= 2/0{\cdot}168 = 11{\cdot}9 \ \Omega$. Deducting the 2-$\Omega$ resistance of the path UW gives a value of $9{\cdot}9 \ \Omega$ for the equivalent resistance of the network across the points WY, a value which cannot be computed by the simple series-parallel approach.

It is interesting to investigate what governs the direction of the current in the path XZ, i.e. the current in the resistance G. In the two paths WXY and WZY the fall of potential will be equal because the two paths are connected in parallel across the same p.d. at the points W and Y. Obviously for every point in the path WXY there will be a corresponding point at the same potential in the path WZY. If X and Z were such a pair of points at the same potential, i.e. no p.d. existed between X and Z, *no current would flow in the path XZ*. With Z fixed and X moved slightly nearer the high potential end (i.e. towards W) a current would flow from X to Z; and with Z still fixed and X moved towards the low potential end Y a current would now flow from Z to X. This important principle forms the basis of certain measuring

circuits known as *null* or *balanced* methods, of which the Wheatstone bridge is the most commonly used. It is important to note that in the balanced state X and Z represent any pair of points at the same potential.

EXAMPLE 2.31 (A). Draw the circuit of a simple Wheatstone bridge, and applying Kirchhoff's Laws to the various branches, determine the conditions for no deflexion in the galvanometer.   (*C. & G.*)

Note: The galvanometer is the bridging path XZ (G ohms). Using the symbols denoted in Fig. 2.46, then if $i_2 = 0$, applying Kirchhoff's laws—

In mesh WXZ, $0 = Pi_1 + 0 - Q(I - i_1)$

  or $Pi_1 = Q(I - i_1)$ or $P/Q = (I - i_1)/i_1$

In mesh XYZ, $0 = R(i_1 - 0) - S(I - i_1 + 0) + 0$

  or $Ri_1 = S(I - i_1)$ or $R/S = (I - i_1)/i_1$,

whence $P/Q = R/S \, [= (I - i_1)/i_1]$

This then is the condition that no current shall flow in the path XZ, i.e. that the points X and Z shall be at the same potential.

Note: The same conclusion can be reached from the direct application of Ohm's law by considering the fall of potential along WXY and WZY: since the path XZ, *in the balanced case*, carries no current it can be ignored. If X and Z are to be at the same potential then the

  p.d. across WX = p.d. across WZ and
  „   „ XY = p.d. „   „ ZY,

or $\dfrac{\text{p.d. across } WX}{\text{p.d. across } XY} = \dfrac{\text{p.d. across } WZ}{\text{p.d. across } ZY}$

Since $i_2 = 0$ and the p.d.s are equal to the products of the resistances and currents flowing in them—

$$Pi_1/(Ri_1) = Q(I - i_1)/\{S(I - i_1)\} \text{ or } P/R = Q/S$$

i.e. $PS = QR$ or $P/Q = R/S$

EXAMPLE 2.32 (A). In the circuit in Fig. 2.47 (i), if $I_1 = 0{\cdot}5$ A and $I_2 = 0{\cdot}1$ A, determine the values of R_1 and R_2 and the current flowing through each of the resistances.   (*C. & G.*)

Let the current in R_1 be I amps.

By Kirchhoff's first law (see diagram (ii))—

Current in $AD = (0{\cdot}5 - I)$
  „ $BC = (I - 0{\cdot}1)$
  „ $DC = (0{\cdot}5 - I + 0{\cdot}1) = 0{\cdot}6 - I$

By Kirchhoff's second law (see diagram (ii))—
In mesh ABD,

$$IR_1 + (10 \times 0.1) - 10(0.5 - I) = 0$$
$$IR_1 + 1 - 5 + 10I = 0$$
$$IR_1 + 10I = 4 \qquad . \qquad . \qquad . \qquad \text{(i)}$$

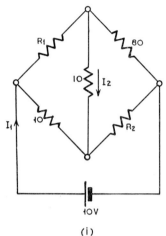

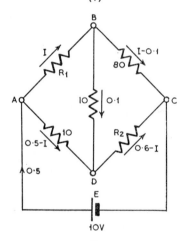

(i)

(ii)

Fig. 2.47 (Example 2.32)

In mesh $ABCE$,

$$IR_1 + 80(I - 0.1) = 10$$
$$IR_1 + 80I - 8 = 10$$
$$IR_1 + 80I = 18 \qquad . \qquad . \qquad \text{(ii)}$$

Combining (i) and (ii),

$$IR_1 + 10I = 4$$
$$IR_1 + 80I = 18$$
$$70I = 14 \text{ and } I = 0.2 \text{ A}$$

Substituting for $I = 0.2$ in (i),

$$0.2R_1 + (10 \times 0.2) = 4$$
$$0.2R_1 = 4 - 2$$
$$R_1 = 10 \ \Omega$$

In mesh $ADCE$, $(0.5 - I)10 + (0.6 - I)R_2 = 10$

Substituting $I = 0.2$,

$$(0.5 - 0.2)10 + (0.6 - 0.2)R_2 = 10$$
$$3 + 0.4R_2 = 10$$
$$R_2 = (10 - 3)/0.4$$
$$= 17.5 \ \Omega$$

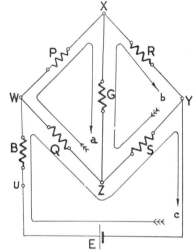

Fig. 2.48. Maxwell's Method

Current in $AB = I = 0.2$ A

„ $BC = (I - 0.1) = 0.1$ A

„ $AD = (0.5 - I) = 0.3$ A

„ $DC = (0.6 - I) = 0.4$ A

2.23. Maxwell's Method. The solution of complicated networks by the method of Example 2.30 is apt to be tedious, and Maxwell suggested the assumption of *cyclic currents* flowing in each mesh, in order to facilitate calculation. The cyclic currents all flow in the same direction, i.e. either all clockwise or all anti-clockwise.

In Fig. 2.48 the same network as for Fig. 2.44 is used and cyclic currents of magnitudes a, b, and c are assumed to flow in each mesh in the direction shown by the arrow. The current flowing in any *conductor* which is included in two separate meshes is therefore equal to the algebraic sum of the cyclic currents flowing through it due to the separate meshes. For instance the current flowing in the resistance G is due to a current a (in the mesh WXZ) together with a current of $-b$ (in the mesh XYZ). Applying Kirchhoff's second law in this manner gives the following expressions for the meshes indicated in Fig. 2.48, each mesh being traversed in the same (clockwise) direction.

Mesh $UWXY$. $Bc + Pa + Rb = E$

,, $UWZY$. $Bc + Q(c-a) + S(c-b) = E$

,, $UWXZY$. $Bc + Pa + G(a-b)$
$+ S(c-b) = E$

,, $UWZXY$. $Bc + Q(c-a) + G(b-a) + Rb$
$= E$

,, $WXYZ$. $Pa + Rb + S(b-c)$
$+ Q(a-c) = 0$

,, WXZ. $Pa + G(a-b) + Q(a-c) = 0$

,, XYZ. $Rb + S(b-c) + G(b-a) = 0$

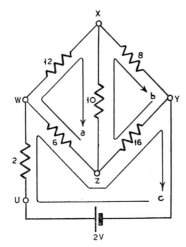

FIG. 2.49 (Example 2.33)

EXAMPLE 2.33 (A). Solve Example 2.30 by the use of Maxwell's cyclic currents.

The cyclic currents a, b, and c are assumed to flow in a clockwise direction as shown in Fig. 2.49.

From Kirchhoff's second law—
In mesh $UWXY$,
$$2c + 12a + 8b = 2,$$
$$\text{or } 6a + 4b + c = 1 \quad . \quad . \quad \text{(i)}$$

In mesh WXZ,
$$12a + 10(a-b) + 6(a-c) = 0,$$
$$\text{or } 14a - 5b - 3c = 0 \quad . \quad \text{(ii)}$$

In mesh XYZ,
$$8b + 16(b-c) + 10(b-a) = 0,$$
$$\text{or } -5a + 17b - 8c = 0 \quad . \quad \text{(iii)}$$

Multiplying (i) by 3,
$$18a + 12b + 3c = 3$$
Adding (ii), $\quad 14a - 5b - 3c = 0$
$$32a + 7b = 3 \quad . \quad . \quad \text{(iv)}$$

Multiplying (ii) by 8, $112a - 40b - 24c = 0$
Multiplying (iii) by 3, $-15a + 51b - 24c = 0$
Adding, $\quad\quad 127a - 91b = 0 \quad \text{(v)}$
$$a = 91b/127$$

Substituting in (iv),
$$32 \times 91b/127 + 7b = 3$$
$$2\,912b + 889b = 381$$
$$b = 381/3\,801 = 0{\cdot}100\,2 \text{ A}$$
$$\text{or } 100{\cdot}2 \text{ mA}$$
$$a = (91 \times 381)/(127 \times 3\,801)$$
$$= 0{\cdot}071\,8 \text{ A or } 71{\cdot}8 \text{ mA}$$

From (i), $c = 1{\cdot}0 - (4b + 6a)$
$$= 1{\cdot}0 - (0{\cdot}400\,8 + 0{\cdot}430\,8)$$
$$= 1{\cdot}0 - 0{\cdot}831\,6$$
$$= 0{\cdot}168\,4 \text{ A or } 168{\cdot}4 \text{ mA}$$

Current in $UW = c = 168{\cdot}4$ mA

,, $WX = a = 71{\cdot}8$ mA

,, $XY = b = 100{\cdot}2$ mA

,, $ZY = c - b = 168{\cdot}4 - 100{\cdot}2$
$$= 68{\cdot}2 \text{ mA}$$

,, $WZ = c - a = 168{\cdot}4 - 71{\cdot}8$
$$= 96{\cdot}6 \text{ mA}$$

,, $XZ = a - b = 71{\cdot}8 - 100{\cdot}2$
$$= (-28{\cdot}4) = 28{\cdot}4 \text{ mA flowing}$$
$$\text{from } Z \text{ to } X$$

It is necessary to observe special care in applying the signs indicating the current direction, and also to avoid confusion between the direct application of Kirchhoff's laws and the method of Maxwell's cyclic currents.

Note: Examples of networks including more than one e.m.f. are given in Chapters IV and VIII.

EXAMPLE 2.34 (A). In the circuit (Fig. 2.50), if the current at the point A is 100 mA and there is no deflexion in the galvanometer, what are the values of the resistors R_1 and R_2? (*C. & G.*)

(i) Since there is no current in the galvanometer, the 0·1 current flows also through the 90 Ω resistor.

$$V = IR,\ 10 = 0{\cdot}1(R_1 + 90) = 0{\cdot}1R_1 + 9$$
$$R_1 = (10 - 9)/0{\cdot}1 = 10 \text{ Ω}$$

(ii) Again, since there is no current in the path YZ, Y and Z must be at the same potential, or, in other words, the p.d. between X and Y is equal to the p.d. between X and Z.

P.d. between X and $Y = 10 \times 0.1$
$$= 1 \text{ V} = \text{p.d. between } X \text{ and } Z$$

Current in $XZ = 1/5 = 0.2$ A

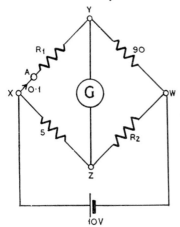

Fig. 2.50 (Example 2.34)

Now, p.d. between Z and $W = 10 - 1$
$$= 0.2 R_2 \text{ and } R_2 = 9/0.2 = \underline{45 \, \Omega}$$

Note: The second part of this problem would normally be solved by the Wheatstone bridge relation as follows—

$R_1/5 = 90/R_2$, $R_2 = 5 \times 90/R_1$
$$= 5 \times 90/10 = \underline{45 \, \Omega}$$

Additional Examples

EXAMPLE 2.35 (A). Two relays A and B are connected in series with each other between battery terminals giving a constant p.d. of 49 V. When a voltmeter of 500 Ω resistance is connected across A and B in turn, the readings obtained are 14 and 28 V respectively. Calculate the individual resistances of A and B. *(C. & G.)*

Let A and B be the resistances in ohms of the two relays (Fig. 2.51).

Voltmeter across A

Current in $A = 14/A$
,, 500 $\Omega = 14/500$
,, $B = 35/B$

$I_1 = (14/A + 14/500) = 35/B$
$(7\,000 + 14A)/500A = 35/B$
$(1\,000 + 2A)/500A = 5/B$
$(500 + A)/250A = 5/B$
$500B + AB = 1\,250A$
$AB = 1\,250A - 500B$. (i)

Voltmeter across B

Current in $B = 28/B$
,, 500 $\Omega = 28/500$
,, $A = 21/A$

$I_2 = 21/A = (28/B + 28/500)$
$21/A = (14\,000 + 28B)/500B$
$3/A = (2\,000 + 4B)/500B$
$3/A = (500 + B)/125B$
$375B = 500A + AB$
$\therefore \quad AB = 375B - 500A$ . . . (ii)

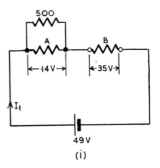

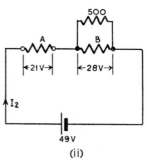

Fig. 2.51 (Example 2.35)

Combining (i) and (ii),
$1\,250A - 500B = 375B - 500A$
$1\,750A = 875B$ and $2A = B$

Substituting $B = 2A$ in (i),
$2A^2 = 1\,250A - 1\,000A$
$$= 250A$$
$\therefore \quad 2A(A - 125) = 0$
$$A = \underline{125 \, \Omega}$$
$$B = 2A = \underline{250 \, \Omega}$$

EXAMPLE 2.36 (A). One pole of a 24-V battery of negligible resistance is connected to earth and the other pole is connected to one end, A, of a line wire of high insulation resistance and having a conductor resistance of 1 000 Ω. A relay of 500 Ω resistance is connected between the wire and earth at the distant end and the minimum current required to hold this relay operated is 10 mA. Determine the line resistance from A of two points on the line such that if an earth fault of 600 Ω resistance occurred anywhere in between these points the relay would release. (*C. & G.*)

See Fig. 2.52.

The current in the relay must be 10 mA.

Let x ohms be the distance (in ohms) of the fault point(s) from A.

The p.d. across XE,

$$V_{XE} = 0 \cdot 010(1\ 000 - x + 500)$$
$$= 0 \cdot 010(1\ 500 - x)$$

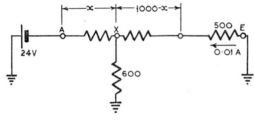

FIG. 2.52 (Example 2.36)

The current in the 600 Ω fault, I_{600}

$$= 0 \cdot 010(1\ 500 - x)/600$$

Total current $I = 0 \cdot 010 + 0 \cdot 010(1\ 500 - x)/600$

P.d. across AX,

$$V_{AX} = x\{0 \cdot 010 + 0 \cdot 010(1\ 500 - x)/600\}$$

$$V_{XE} + V_{AX} = 24 = 0 \cdot 010(1\ 500 - x)$$
$$+ 0 \cdot 010x\{1 + (1\ 500 - x)/600\}$$

$$2\ 400 = 1\ 500 - x + x$$
$$+ x(1\ 500 - x)/600$$
$$x(1\ 500 - x) = 900 \times 600 = 540\ 000$$
$$x^2 - 1\ 500x + (750)^2 = (750)^2 - 540\ 000$$
$$(x - 750)^2 = 22\ 500$$
$$x = 750 \pm \sqrt{22\ 500}$$
$$= 750 \pm 150 = \underline{\underline{600}} \text{ or } \underline{\underline{900}}\ \Omega$$

EXAMPLE 2.37 (A). An overhead power line, 10 000 m long, carries a current of 950 A. It is made up of a central steel wire circular in cross-section and 1 cm in diameter, round which is drawn an aluminium tube 1 cm internal diameter and 2 cm external diameter. If the specific resistances of steel and aluminium are 19·2 and 3·2 $\mu\Omega$/cm-cube respectively, determine—

  (i) the current flowing in the steel wire;
 (ii) the relative resistances of the steel and aluminium;
(iii) the difference in potential between the two ends of the line.   (*C. & G.*)

Steel	Aluminium
$\rho = 19 \cdot 2 \times 10^{-6}$	$3 \cdot 2 \times 10^{-6}\ \Omega$/cm-cube
$l = 10^6$	10^6 cm
$a = \pi/4$	$\pi(2^2 - 1^2)/4 = 3\pi/4$ cm^2

For steel,
$$R = \rho l/a = (19 \cdot 2 \times 10^6 \times 4)/(10^6 \pi)$$
$$= 24 \cdot 443\ \Omega$$

For aluminium,
$$R = (3 \cdot 2 \times 10^6 \times 4)/(10^6 \times 3\pi) = 1 \cdot 358\ \Omega$$

Resistance of steel/resistance of aluminium
$$= 24 \cdot 44/1 \cdot 358 = \underline{\underline{18/1}}$$

Current in steel wire $= 950 \times 1/19 = \underline{\underline{50\ \text{A}}}$

Considering the steel wire, $V = IR = 50 \times 24 \cdot 44$
$$= \underline{\underline{1\ 222\ \text{V}}}$$

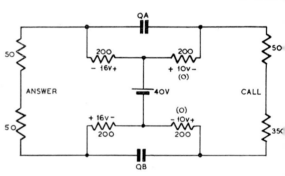

FIG. 2.53 (Example 2.38)

EXAMPLE 2.38 (A). A 40-V central battery transmission bridge consists of four impedance coils each of 200 Ω resistance and two line-capacitors. The external line resistance is 50 Ω on the answering side and 350 Ω on the calling side, the resistance of the terminating telephones being 50 Ω in each case. (*a*) What is the steady voltage across each capacitor when the telephones are in circuit, and (*b*) what would be the effect on the capacitors if the 350 Ω line were suddenly disconnected?   (*C. & G.*)

The circuit conditions are shown in Fig. 2.53. QA and QB are the capacitors.

Answering Side

Total resistance
$$= 200 + 50 + 50 + 200 = 500\ \Omega$$

Proportion of total voltage dropped across each 200 Ω resistance $= 200/500 = 2/5$.

P.d. across each 200 Ω resistance $= 2/5 \times 40$
$= 16$ V.

Calling Side

Total resistance

$$= 200 + 50 + 350 + 200 = 800 \ \Omega$$

Proportion of total voltage dropped across each $200 \ \Omega$ resistance $= 200/800 = \frac{1}{4}$.

P.d. across each $200 \ \Omega$ resistance $= \frac{1}{4} \times 40 = 10$ V.

(*a*) Hence p.d. across QA = p.d. across QB $= 16 - 10 = \underline{6 \text{ V}}$.

When the $350 \ \Omega$ line is disconnected, no current flows in the calling side and the p.d. across each $200 \ \Omega$ resistance on the calling side falls to zero.

(*b*) Hence p.d. across QA = p.d. across QB $= 16 - 0 = \underline{16 \text{ V}}$.

EXAMPLE 2.39 (A). The resistance in ohms of a metal filament lamp used on a 250 V d.c. supply is given by the expression $R = 43(1 + 0.005t)$ where t is the temperature of the filament in degrees centigrade. What is (*a*) the current through the lamp at the instant of switching on if the room temperature is 20°C, and (*b*) the current through the lamp when the filament attains its normal working temperature of 2 700°C ?   (*C. & G.*)

(*a*) $R_{20} = 43(1 + 0.005 \times 20) = 43(1.1)$
     $= 47.3 \ \Omega$
   $I_{20} = 250/47.3 = \underline{5.29 \text{ A}}$

(*b*) $R_{2 \ 700} = 43(1 + 0.005 \times 2 \ 700)$
       $= 623.5 \ \Omega$
   $I_{2 \ 700} = 250/623.5 = \underline{0.4 \text{ A}}$

EXAMPLE 2.40 (A). A circuit containing a heater having a constant resistance of 36 Ω is to be supplied from a d.c. source which varies between 20 and 30 V. It is necessary to maintain the current in the heater within the limits 0.25 and 0.3 A despite this variation in supply voltage. This is done by adding a series resistance to the circuit with a high temperature coefficient of resistance of 0.002 per °C relative to its resistance at room temperature.

Calculate the maximum and minimum values of the series resistor that are necessary to meet the specified conditions.

What rise in temperature in the resistor will give the required range of control ?   (*C. & G.*)

The circuit consists of two resistors in series. The variable resistor r has a resistance which depends upon its temperature.

When the voltage is at its minimum of 20 V, the current will have the minimum tolerable value of 0.25 A. Then by Ohm's Law if r_1 is this minimum value of the variable resistor,

$$20 = 0.25(36 + r_1), \ r_1 + 36 = 20/0.25$$
$$r_1 = 80 - 36 = \underline{44 \ \Omega}$$

When the voltage is at maximum, 30 V, the current will be maximum, 0.3 A. If r_2 is the maximum value of the variable resistor,

$$30 = 0.3(36 + r_2), \ r_2 + 36 = 30/0.3$$
$$r_2 = 100 - 36 = \underline{64 \ \Omega}$$

The resistance r is related to its temperature t by the expression

$$r_t = r_0(1 + \alpha t)$$

where $\alpha =$ the temperature coefficient of resistance,

   $t =$ the temperature rise in °C,

   $r_0 =$ the initial resistance,

and $r_t =$ the resistance at t°C.

Now $r_0 = 44 \ \Omega$, $r_t = 64 \ \Omega$ and $\alpha = 2 \times 10^{-3}$.

The rise in temperature t°C is given by—

$$64 = 44(1 + 0.002t), \ 64 - 44 = 88 \times 10^{-3}t$$
$$20 = 88 \times 10^{-3} \times t$$
$$t = 20 \times 10^3/88 = \underline{227.2°C}$$

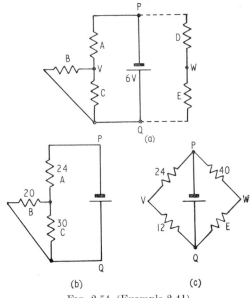

FIG. 2.54. (Example 2.41)

EXAMPLE 2.41 (A). Three resistors A, B, and C are connected as shown in Fig. 2.54 (*a*) across a 6-V battery. Calculate the battery current.

A second circuit consisting of two resistors D and E is now added across the battery, as shown by the dotted connexions in Fig. 2.54 (*a*). It is then found that the potential difference between V and Q is equal to that between W and Q. Calculate the value of resistor E. $A = 24 \ \Omega$, $B = 20 \ \Omega$, $C = 30 \ \Omega$, $D = 40 \ \Omega$.   (*C. & G.*)

In Fig. 2.54(*b*) the total resistance across the battery is the single resistance which is equivalent to *A*, *B*, and *C*.

Resistors *B* and *C* in parallel can be replaced by a single resistance *r* ohms, where

$$r = 20 \times 30/50 = 12 \ \Omega$$

The equivalent resistance across the battery $= 12 + 24 = 36 \ \Omega$. Then from Ohm's Law,

$$\text{the battery current} = 6/36 = 0\cdot167 \text{ A}$$

When resistors *D* and *E* are added across the battery the circuit can be redrawn as in Fig. 2.54(*c*). Resistor *E* has a value such that the potential difference across *VQ* equals that across *WQ*. The circuit is equivalent to a balanced Wheatstone bridge and there will be no potential difference between *V* and *W*.

The ratios of the two resistors on each of the two sides will therefore be equal, the current in *PW* being equal to that in *WQ*, and the current in *PV* being equal to that in *VQ*.

$$24/12 = 40/E, \ E = 40 \times 12/24 = 20 \ \Omega$$

EXAMPLE 2.42 (A). A resistance thermometer takes the form of a Wheatstone bridge in which one arm is a coil of wire that changes in resistance in proportion to its temperature. The bridge circuit contains two 100-Ω resistors as ratio arms. A resistor, adjustable from 50 to 100 Ω, makes the third arm, and the coil provides the fourth arm of the bridge. The coil has a resistance of 60 Ω at 20°C. When the coil is heated, the adjustable resistor must be increased by 5 Ω to restore the balance of the bridge circuit.

If the temperature coefficient of resistance of the coil is 0·05 per cent per °C, what is the temperature of the coil? (*C. & G.*)

The circuit of the measuring device is that of a Wheatstone bridge with an adjustable resistor *r* and a thermometer coil of resistance *R*. As the ratio arms are fixed at 100 Ω, then for balance

$$r/100 = R/100, \text{ i.e. } r = R$$

$$\text{At 20°C, } R = r = 60 \ \Omega$$

At t°C, the unknown temperature of the coil, *r* is adjusted to 65 Ω. Therefore *R* has also become 65 Ω, due to an increase of resistance with rise of temperature.

If α is the temperature coefficient of resistance of the coil of wire in the thermometer, then the resistance R_t of the coil at t°C $= R_0 \ (1 + \alpha t)$, where R_0 is the resistance at 0°C.

If *T* is the *rise* in coil temperature and R_{20}

is the coil resistance at 20°C, then the resistance at $(T + 20)$°C is given by—

$$R_{T+20} = R_{20}(1 + \alpha T)$$

Now, $R_{T+20} = 65 \ \Omega$, and $R_{20} = 60 \ \Omega$

Since $\alpha = 0\cdot05$ per cent,

$$65 = 60(1 + 0\cdot000\ 5T)$$
$$T = (65 - 60)/(0\cdot000\ 5 \times 60)$$
$$= 10\ 000/60 = 167°C$$

This is the rise in temperature. The temperature of the coil is $T + 20 = 187$°C.

EXAMPLE 2.43 (A). Resistors of 15, 5, and 3 Ω are connected as shown in Fig. 2.55 (*a*). Calculate the current flowing in the 5-Ω resistor when a 2-V battery is connected between the points *A* and *E*.

The battery is now removed and the points *A* and *E* are joined together. Find the voltage that must now be applied between the points *C* and *D* to give a current of 100 mA in the 15-Ω resistor, and calculate the resulting battery current. (*C. & G.*)

When a 2-V battery is connected across *AE* the total resistance in circuit is $15 + 5 \ \Omega$. The current in the 5-Ω resistor, $I = 2/20 = 0\cdot1$ A.

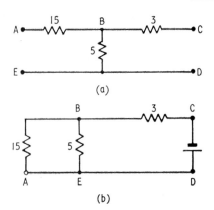

FIG. 2.55. (Example 2.43)

When the points *A* and *E* are joined together and a voltage is applied between *C* and *D*, the circuit can be redrawn as shown in Fig. 2.55(*b*).

As the current in the 15-Ω resistor is 0·1 A, the voltage across *AB* is $V_{AB} = 0\cdot1 \times 15 = 1\cdot5$ V

$$\text{Current in 5-}\Omega \text{ resistor} = 1\cdot5/5 = 0\cdot3 \text{ A}$$

$$\text{Battery current} = \text{current in the 3-}\Omega \text{ resistor}$$
$$= 0\cdot1 + 0\cdot3 = 0\cdot4 \text{ A}$$

Voltage across CD = voltage across AB + voltage across BC
$$= 1\cdot5 + (0\cdot4 \times 3) = 2\cdot7 \text{ V}$$

EXAMPLE 2.44 (A). Eight resistors, one of which is adjustable, are employed in the network shown in Fig. 2.56 (a), the 4-V and 2-V batteries being connected as shown. A milliammeter connects the points A and C.

Calculate, using Kirchhoff's Laws, or otherwise,

(a) the value of R to give zero current in the galvanometer,

(b) the two battery currents.   (C. & G.)

(a) When there is no deflexion in the meter, there can be no p.d. across it. Therefore the voltages across AB and CB must be equal. The equivalent circuit of the portion of the network on the side AB is as in Fig. 2.56(b). The two

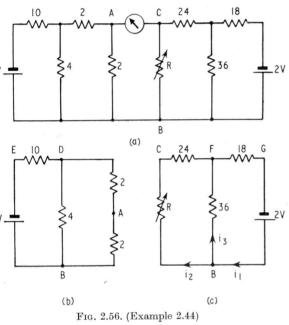

(a)

(b)   (c)

FIG. 2.56. (Example 2.44)

equal arms between D and B have a resultant resistance 2 Ω. The total resistance between E and B is 12 Ω.

Voltage across $DB = (2/12) \times 4 = \frac{2}{3}$ V

When no current is taken at A,

the voltage across $AB = (2/4) \times (\frac{2}{3}) = \frac{1}{3}$ V

On the right-hand part of the circuit the value of R to give $\frac{1}{3}$ V across CB is required.

Referring to Fig. 2.56(c), in mesh $GBCFG$
$$2 = 18i_1 + i_2(24 + R) \qquad . \qquad (i)$$

In mesh $GBFG$,
$$2 = 18i_1 + 36i_3 \qquad . \qquad . \qquad (ii)$$
$$\text{Also } i_1 = i_2 + i_3 \qquad . \qquad . \qquad (iii)$$

Substituting for i_3 in (ii),
$$2 = 18i_1 + 36(i_1 - i_2) \qquad . \qquad (iv)$$
$$2 = 54i_1 - 36i_2 \qquad . \qquad . \qquad (v)$$

Also $i_2 R = \frac{1}{3}$ or $i_2 = 1/3R$

Multiply (i) by 3 and subtract (v)—
$$6 = 54i_1 + i_2(72 + 3R)$$
$$2 = 54i_1 - 36i_2$$
$$\overline{\qquad 4 = i_2(108 + 3R) \qquad}$$

Substitute $i_2 = 1/3R$
$$4 = \frac{108 + 3R}{3R}$$
$$12R - 3R = 108$$
$$R = \underline{\underline{12 \ \Omega}}$$

(b) Total resistance across 4-V battery = 12 Ω

Current in 4-V battery = $4/12 = \underline{\underline{\tfrac{1}{3}A}}$

Total resistance across 2-V battery = 36 Ω

Current in 2-V battery = $2/36 = \underline{\underline{1/18 \ A}}$

SUMMARY

Potential Difference. A difference between the electrical states at two points tending to cause a movement of electricity from one point to the other.

Electromotive Force. The force which tends to cause a movement of electricity in a circuit.

Ohm. The resistance in which a steady current of one ampere generates heat at the rate of one watt.

Volume Resistivity (ρ). The resistance between opposite faces of a unit cube of a given material at a given temperature.

Conductor Resistance. $R = \rho l/a$ ohms   . (2.1)

Conductance. $G = 1/R$ mhos.

Temperature Coefficient of Resistance (α). The change in resistance, caused by a rise of $1°C$ in temperature, expressed as a fraction of the magnitude at $0°C$.

Resistance and Temperature.
$$R_t = R_0(1 + \alpha t): R_1/R_2 = (1 + \alpha t_1)/(1 + \alpha t_2) \quad (2.2)$$

Ohm's Law. $I = V/R: V = IR: R = V/I:$ Applies to a whole circuit or to a part of a circuit   .   .   .   .   .   . (2.3)

Volt. That e.m.f. or p.d. which, applied steadily to a conductor the resistance of which is 1 ohm produces a current of 1 A.

Resistors in Series.

$$R = R_1 + R_2 + R_3 + \ldots + R_N. \quad . \quad (2.4)$$

Resistors in Parallel.

(i) $1/R = 1/R_1 + 1/R_2 + 1/R_3 + \ldots + 1/R_N.$ (2.5)

or $\quad G = G_1 + G_2 + G_3 + \ldots + G_N.$

(ii) Two resistors only, $R = \text{product/sum}$. (2.6)

(iii) N equal resistances (R' each), $R = R'/N.$

Kirchhoff's Laws.

(i) At any point, $\Sigma(i) = 0$ . . . (2.7)

(ii) In any closed circuit, $\Sigma(E) = \Sigma(IR)$. (2.8)

REFERENCES

1. E. F. H. GOULD: "A Note on the Behaviour of the Earth as an Electrical Conductor," *I.P.O.E.E. Journal*, **3**(1944), p. 118.
2. G. E. HAEFELY: "Electrical Insulating Materials," *I.E.E. Journal*, **88 Part I** (1941), p. 179.
3. W. G. RADLEY, E. A. SPEIGHT, C. E. RICHARDS, and E. V. WALKER: "Modern Materials in Telecommunication," *I.P.O.E.E. Journal*, **35** (1942), p. 84.
4. E. E. L. WINTERBORN: "Plastics in Cables," ibid., **51** (1958), p. 33.
5. W. G. RADLEY et alii: "Modern Materials in Telecommunications," ibid., **34** (1942), p. 179.
6. F. C. CARTER: "The Production of Fixed Carbon Resistors," ibid., **36** (1943), p. 6.
7. F. ASHWORTH, W. NEEDHAM, and R. W. SILLARS: "Silicon-carbide Non-ohmic Resistors," *I.E.E. Journal*, **93 Part I** (1946), p. 385.
8. W. G. RADLEY et alii: "Modern Materials in Telecommunication," *I.P.O.E.E. Journal*, **34** (1941), p. 72.
9. W. T. GIBSON: "Thermistor Production," ibid., **46** (1953), p. 34.
10. F. A. WILSON: "The Use of Thermistors," ibid., **50** (1957), p. 98.
11. F. B. CHAPMAN: "The Use of Ballast Resistance in Transmission Bridges," ibid., **26** (1933), p. 140.

CHAPTER III

POWER AND ENERGY

3.1. Energy. The energy aspect of the electric circuit is extremely important. Power and telecommunication systems are fundamentally concerned with the transfer of electrical energy from one point —the generator or transmitter—to another—the load or receiver; this must be done with as little energy loss as possible in order to promote a high efficiency and so reduce production costs and tariffs.

Energy is the capability for performing work. If a machine or device possesses energy it can, by releasing the whole or a part of that energy, perform work. Conversely, work must be performed on the device to impart energy to it. Accordingly, work and energy are interchangeable and are measured in the same units.

Energy exists in various forms, the most common being mechanical, electrical, chemical, or in the form of heat, light, or sound. Energy may be either *kinetic* or *potential*, the former being the energy due to motion and the latter due to position or state. An electric motor when revolving possesses kinetic energy which is converted to work when the motor is coupled up to drive a machine. The earlier forms of telegraph transmitter were driven either by a falling weight or by a clock spring: both the elevated weight and the wound spring possess potential energy by virtue of their position or condition respectively, and they perform work on the transmitter when their energy is released. Conversely, work must be performed to raise the weight or rewind the spring when all the energy has been consumed.

The following definitions are added for reference. The unit in which energy is measured is the JOULE: *it is the energy expended when a force of 1 newton is exerted through a distance of 1 metre.*

The NEWTON (N), *a unit of force, is that force which, acting on a mass of 1 kilogramme, gives to it an acceleration of 1 metre per second per second.*

3.2. Energy Conversion. According to the Conservation of Energy theorem the amount of energy in the universe is constant: energy can be neither created nor destroyed. Different forms of energy are interchangeable, and when energy disappears in one form it reappears in another.

Present theory postulates that the mass of a body is due to its energy and that energy and mass are interchangeable.

Electrical energy in small quantities is obtained by the release of chemical energy from a voltaic cell. In larger amounts it is produced from the mechanical energy applied to a generator, the mechanical energy in turn deriving ultimately from the chemical energy of combustion of coal, oil, or petrol, or from the heat energy released by fission of the atomic nucleus. In favourable circumstances the natural energy of wind, of falling water

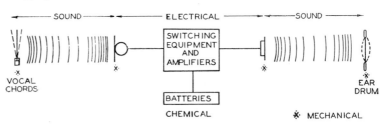

FIG. 3.1. ENERGY FORMS IN A TELEPHONE SYSTEM

or of the sun is used.

In converting from one form of energy to another, it is not possible to ensure that all the energy appears in the desired form. For instance, in utilizing an electric motor, most of the applied electrical energy appears in the desired form of mechanical energy; some electrical energy, however, is unavoidably used up in producing heat in the machine, light in the sparking which occurs at the brushes, and sound in the characteristic hum of the rotating machine. Electrical energy is consumed in reversing the magnetic field, and of the total mechanical energy produced some is lost in overcoming friction in the bearings and brushes and air resistance before the useful energy output can be made available. In the design of such converting machinery, the restriction of energy losses to a minimum is a major consideration.

3.3. Energy in Telecommunication. In a telephone system energy is initially used up in vibrating the vocal chords to produce sound energy in the air (Fig. 3.1): the vibrating air particles impinging upon the diaphragm of the microphone set it in motion to control or modulate the release of electrical energy from a battery. The electrical energy is fed to the transmission line which transfers it from section to section and through switching equipment ultimately to the receiver. At this stage the electrical energy produces magnetic and subsequently mechanical energy to vibrate the receiver diaphragm which produces sound energy to vibrate the ear-drum and so communicate information to the brain. The line system and electrical equipment are all designed to pass on the energy as efficiently as possible by themselves consuming the minimum of energy in the process, this loss being made good by amplifiers drawing their energy from batteries.

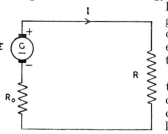

FIG. 3.2. TRANSFER OF POWER

A telegraph system utilizes mechanical energy controlled from a keyboard to release electrical energy into the line for subsequent conversion to mechanical energy by means of an electro-magnet to control a printing mechanism: or, in photo-telegraphy, light reflected from each minute portion of a picture controls electrical energy which, after propagation over the transmission medium, controls light energy at a remote point.

3.4. Electrical Energy. In the electric circuit work is performed whenever a quantity of electricity flows between two points. If the quantity is Q coulombs and the p.d. between two points is V volts, the work done is equal to the product $Q \times V$ and it results in the expenditure of electrical energy W equal to QV joules.

Since $Q = It$ the energy

$$W = VQ = VIt \text{ joules} . \qquad . \quad (3.1)$$

Using the three forms of Ohm's law, since $V = IR$,

$$W = IR \times It = I^2Rt \text{ joules}$$

or, since $I = V/R$,

$$W = V \times (V/R) \times t = V^2t/R \text{ joules}$$

These expressions are true provided that V is in volts, I is in amps, R is in ohms, and t is in seconds. The two first forms are found most useful in solving energy problems: the energy may be calculated for the whole or for a portion of the circuit by proper selection of the values V, I, and R.

The *electron-volt* is the energy required to move one electron between two points having a p.d. of one volt: the electron-volt = $1 \cdot 6 \times 10^{-19}$ joules.

The joule is sometimes known as the *watt-second*, so that it is convenient to remember that the energy

$$W = VIt \text{ watt-seconds}$$

3.5. Power. Power is the rate at which work is done. A certain amount of energy may be consumed in one hour or in two hours: in the first instance the rate of energy consumption (i.e. the power) is twice as great as when spread over two hours. Power is therefore equal to energy divided by time.

The electrical unit of power is the WATT (W). *The watt is the power when energy is expended at the rate of one joule per second.* Since the joule is one newton-metre (N-m), the watt is equal to one newton-metre per second.

In power systems kilowatts (kW) or megawatts (MW), and in telecommunication systems milliwatts (mW), microwatts (μW), or picowatts (pW), are units often more conveniently employed (Appendix **F**).

The power

$$P = energy/time = VIt/t = VI \text{ watts} \quad (3.2)$$

Substituting $V = IR$,

$$P = IR \times I = I^2R \text{ watts}$$

or substituting $I = V/R$,

$$P = V \times V/R = V^2/R \text{ watts}$$

The transfer of power from a generator to a load is depicted in Fig. 3.2. The generator e.m.f. is E volts, and R_0 ohms is its internal resistance: the load resistance is R ohms. The circuit current I amps is

$$I = E/(R + R_0)$$

the power in the load is

$$P = I^2R = E^2R/(R + R_0)^2$$

It can be proved that the condition for maximum transfer of power from generator to load is that

$$R = R_0$$

EXAMPLE 3.1 (A). An electric lamp is rated at 60 W for a 240-V supply. What is its resistance? If used with a voltage of 210 V, what power would it take, assuming that its resistance remains constant? (*C. & G.*)

(i) $W = V^2/R$

$\qquad R = V^2/W = 240^2/60 = 57\ 600/60$

$\qquad\ \ = 960\ \Omega$

(ii) $W = V^2/R$

$\qquad\ \ = 210^2/960 = 44\ 100/960 = 46 \text{ W}$

EXAMPLE 3.2 (A). A dynamo giving an output of 10 kW is sending a current of 50 A through a resistance. What is (*a*) the value of this resistance in ohms, and (*b*) the voltage of the dynamo? (*C. & G.*)

(*a*) $W = I^2R$

$R = W/I^2 = 10\,000/50^2 = 4\ \Omega$

(*b*) $W = VI$

$V = W/I = 10\,000/50 = 200\ \text{V}$

EXAMPLE 3.3 (A). A resistor A is connected in series with paralleled resistors B and C, and the combination is joined to the terminals of a 40-V battery. If the watts dissipated in A, B, and C are 8, 6, and 2 respectively, what are the individual values of the resistances? (*C. & G.*)

The circuit diagram is shown in Fig. 3.3.

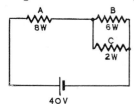

FIG. 3.3 (Example 3.3)

Since the power in $A = 8\ \text{W} = $ the power taken jointly by B and C, the joint resistance of B and C must equal that of A, and p.d. across $A = $ p.d. across (B and C) $= 20\ \text{V}$.

Hence, for A,

$W = V^2/R = 20^2/R = 8$

$R = 20^2/8 = 400/8 = 50\ \Omega$

for B,

$W = V^2/R$

$R = V^2/W = 20^2/6 = 400/6 = 66 \cdot 67\ \Omega$

for C,

$W = V^2/R$

$R = V^2/W = 20^2/2 = 400/2 = 200\ \Omega$

EXAMPLE 3.4 (A). A circuit consisting of three resistors of 50 Ω, 100 Ω, and 300 Ω respectively, joined in parallel, is connected in series with a fourth resistor across a 20-V d.c. supply. What is the value of the fourth resistor if the power dissipated in heating the 50 Ω resistor is 2 W? In which of the three paralleled resistors is the most heat generated? (*C. & G.*)

The circuit diagram is shown in Fig. 3.4.

Joint resistance of the three resistors in parallel—

$1/R = 1/50 + 1/100 + 1/300$

$= (6 + 3 + 1)/300 = 10/300$

$R = 300/10 = 30\ \Omega$

For 50 Ω resistance, $W = V^2/R$,

$V = \sqrt{(WR)} = \sqrt{(2 \times 50)} = \sqrt{100} = 10\ \text{V}$

Hence p.d. across unknown resistor must be $(20 - 10) = 10\ \text{V}$, and since this is equal to the p.d. across the paralleled resistors the unknown resistor must be equal to the joint value of these resistors, i.e. to 30 Ω.

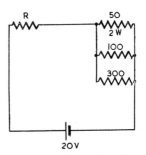

FIG. 3.4 (Example 3.4)

Since $W = V^2/R$, for a given p.d. the power is inversely proportional to the resistance: most power is dissipated in the 50 Ω resistor.

EXAMPLE 3.5 (A). A house is equipped with ten 250-V, 50-W lamps and twenty 250-V, 25-W lamps which are wired in parallel. What is the resistance presented to the supply mains when all lamps are switched on? (*C. & G.*)

Resistance of one 50-W lamp at 250 V,

$R = V^2/W = 250^2/50 = 62\,500/50 = 1\,250\ \Omega$

Resistance of ten 50-W lamps in parallel

$= 1\,250/10 = 125\ \Omega$

Resistance of one 25-W lamp

$= V^2/W = 250^2/25 = 62\,500/25 = 2\,500\ \Omega$

Resistance of twenty 25-W lamps in parallel

$= 2\,500/20 = 125\ \Omega$

Joint resistance of 125 Ω and 125 Ω in parallel

$= 125/2 = 62 \cdot 5\ \Omega$

Alternative method—

Total power of all lamps

$= (10 \times 50) + (20 \times 25) = 500 + 500$

$= 1\,000\ \text{W}$

$R = V^2/W = 250^2/1\,000 = 62\,500/1\,000$

$= 62 \cdot 5\ \Omega$

EXAMPLE 3.6 (A). If, in the circuit shown in Fig. 3.5, the total current drawn from the cell (which has negligible internal resistance) is 1·5 A, what is the resistance of x, and what power is dissipated in each resistor? (*C. & G.*)

Joint resistance of 3 and 1·5 Ω in parallel—

R = product/sum = $(3 \times 1·5)/(3 + 1·5)$
  = $4·5/4·5 = 1$ Ω

Total value of known resistors = $1 + 1 = 2$ Ω
Current taken by this path = $V/R = 2/2 = 1$ A
Current taken by $x = 1·5 - 1 = 0·5$ A
Resistance of $x = V/I = 2/0·5 = 4$ Ω

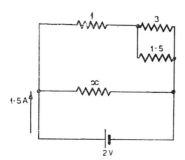

Fig. 3.5 (Example 3.6)

Power in 4 Ω resistor = $V^2/R = 2^2/4 = 4/4 = 1$ W

  „   1 Ω   „   = $I^2R = 1^2 \times 1 = 1$ W

P.d. across 3 and 1·5 Ω resistors = p.d. across 1 Ω resistor = 1 V

Power in 3 Ω resistor = $V^2/R = 1^2/3 = \frac{1}{3}$ W

  „   1·5 Ω „   = $V^2/R = 1^2/1·5 = \frac{2}{3}$ W

EXAMPLE 3.7 (A). A resistor is designed to dissipate 1 kW when connected across a 200-V d.c. supply. Calculate its resistance.
  Two such resistors can be connected either (a) in series or (b) in parallel across the 200-V supply. What will be the power dissipated in each case?
  Draw a circuit, with switches that will give either series or parallel connexion of these two resistors, as might be used in an electric heater having provision for low- or high-power rating.   (C. & G.)

$$W = I^2R = E^2/R$$

If $W = 1\ 000$ W and $E = 200$ V,

$$R = 200^2/1\ 000 = 40\ \Omega$$

The two 40-Ω resistors in series give an equivalent resistance of 80 Ω.

  Power dissipated = $200^2/80 = 500$ W

When the two resistors are in parallel, each is connected directly across the 200-V supply.
Power dissipated in each resistor
$$= 200^2/40 = 1\ 000\ \text{W}$$
Total power dissipated in the two resistors
$$= 2 \times 1\ 000 = 2\ 000\ \text{W} = 2\ \text{kW}$$

The series-parallel switch for a heater having low and high power could be connected as shown

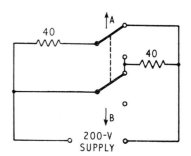

Fig. 3.6. (Example 3.7)

in Fig. 3.6. Two switches are required, mechanically interconnected so as to operate together. In position A the resistors are in parallel and in position B they are in series.

EXAMPLE 3.8 (A). Five valves have their filaments connected as shown in Fig. 3.7 (a). Four valves of type A each require 6 V, 0·3 A. Valve B requires 6 V, 0·15 A.
  Calculate the values of R_1 and R_2 to give the correct valve operating conditions when a 17-V d.c. supply is connected across the terminals XY of the network.
  What is the power dissipated in R_1 and R_2 respectively?
(C. & G.)

As the valves A all require 6 V, a total of 12 V must be maintained across the conductors PQ (Fig. 3.7(b)). The voltage drop across R_2 is 6 V with 0·15 A flowing.

$$R_2 = 6/0·15 = 40\ \Omega$$

The total current from the three parallel circuits
$$= 0·3 + 0·3 + 0·15 = 0·75\ \text{A}$$

The voltage drop in $R_1 = 17 - 12 = 5$ V when the current is 0·75 A.

$$R_1 = 5/0·75 = 20/3 = 6·67\ \Omega$$

The power dissipated in R_1
$$= 5^2 \times 3/20 = 75/20 = 3·75\ \text{W}$$

The power dissipated in $R_2 = 6^2/40 = 0·9$ W

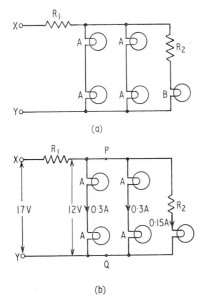

(a)

(b)

FIG. 3.7. (Example 3.8)

EXAMPLE 3.9 (A). A bay of telecommunication equipment operating from a two-wire d.c. supply requires 2 000 W at 200 V at its input terminals. The bay is 600 ft distant, measured along the cable, from the supply main outlet. A second bay, fed from the same cable but situated 300 ft nearer to the supply main, requires 2 500 W at 250 V. The resistance of the cable employed is 0·2 Ω per 100 ft of each conductor.

What resistance must be connected in series with one of the feeders to give correct voltage conditions at both bays?

What supply voltage is necessary? (C. & G.)

The circuit is shown in Fig. 3.8.

The current supplied to bay $A = 2\ 000/200 = 10$ A
The current supplied to bay $B = 2\ 500/250 = 10$ A
The resistance in the feeders connecting B to A

$$= 2 \times 300 \times 0\cdot2/100 = 1\cdot2\ \Omega$$

As the voltage at bay A must be 200 V and at bay B must be 250 V, a drop of 50 V must be achieved in the two conductors of feeder AB under working conditions. A current of 10 A flows in AB. The loop resistance between A and B must be $50/10 = 5\ \Omega$. Of this $1\cdot2\ \Omega$ will be already in the conductor resistance. The additional resistance to be inserted in AB is

$$5 - 1\cdot2 = \underline{3\cdot8\ \Omega}$$

The total current drawn from the supply mains will be the sum of the currents for both bays of equipment

$$= 10 + 10 = 20\ \text{A}$$

The loop conductor resistance between B and the supply is also $1\cdot2\ \Omega$. A current of 20 A in $1\cdot2\ \Omega$ gives a voltage drop of

$$20 \times 1\cdot2 = 24\ \text{V}$$

The supply mains voltage required is 24 V greater than that across the feeder at B.

$$\text{Supply voltage} = 250 + 24 = \underline{274\ \text{V}}$$

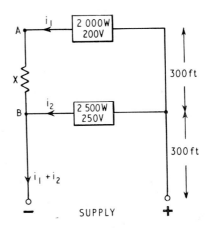

FIG. 3.8. (Example 3.9)

EXAMPLE 3.10 (A). A de-icing equipment fitted to a radio aerial consists of a length of resistance wire arranged so that when a current is passed through it parts of the aerial become warm. The resistance wire dissipates 1 250 W when 50 V are maintained across the ends. It is connected to a d.c. supply by 300 ft of twin copper wire, each conductor of which has a resistance of 0·002 Ω per foot.

Calculate—
(a) the current in the resistance wire,
(b) the power lost in the copper connecting wire,
(c) the supply voltage required to maintain 50 V across the heater resistance itself. (C. & G.)

Since the de-icing resistor dissipates 1 250 W with 50 V across it,

$$W = VI,\ 1\ 250 = 50I,\ I = \underline{25\ \text{A}}$$

As the supply leads consist of 300 ft of twin wire, the total length of single conductor is 600 ft.

The total resistance of the supply leads
$$= 600 \times 0\cdot002 = 1\cdot2\ \Omega$$

The leads carry a current of 25 A.

Power lost in these leads
$$= I^2R = 25^2 \times 1\cdot2 = \underline{750\ \text{W}}$$

3

The voltage drop in these leads
$$= IR = 25 \times 1 \cdot 2 = 30 \text{ V}$$

Total supply voltage required = voltage across de-icing resistor + drop in leads
$$= 50 + 30 = \underline{80 \text{ V}}$$

EXAMPLE 3.11 (A). An electric heater made from 10 ft of resistance wire which has a resistance of 0·6 Ω per foot at room temperature shows a temperature rise of 500°C when connected to a 27-V supply. The temperature rise can be assumed to be proportional to the power dissipated, and the temperature coefficient of the resistance wire can be taken as constant at 0·001 per °C. Calculate the supply voltage needed to run the heater with a temperature rise of 400°C. (C. & G.)

The resistance of the heater at room temperature $= 10 \times 0 \cdot 6 = 6 \text{ Ω}$. At $t°$ above room temperature the resistance
$$= R_0(1 + \alpha t) = 6(1 + 0 \cdot 001 t)$$

The power dissipated in R ohms when a voltage E is across it $= E^2/R$ watts and as the temperature rise is proportional to power,
$$t = k \times E^2/R \qquad . \qquad . \qquad \text{(i)}$$

When $E = 27$ V, $t = 500°C$, and when $t = 500°C$ the heater resistance will rise to
$$6(1 + 0 \cdot 001 \times 500) = 9 \text{ Ω}$$

From (i),
$$500 = k \times 27^2/9 \text{ and } k = 500/81$$

When $t = 400°C$ the resistance
$$= 6(1 + 0 \cdot 001 \times 400) = 8 \cdot 4 \text{ Ω}$$

From (i), putting $k = 500/81$, $t = 400°C$, and $R = 8 \cdot 4 \text{ Ω}$,
$$400 = (500/81) \times (E^2/8 \cdot 4)$$
$$E^2 = 18^2 \times 1 \cdot 68, \ E = \underline{23 \cdot 3 \text{ V}}$$

3.6. B.O.T. Unit.
From the above relationship for power, energy = (power × time): for the electrical energy-unit the *watt-second* is the same as the joule. Similarly the watt-hour, the energy expended in one hour when the power is one watt, is a unit frequently employed.

The unit on which the tariff for electric power supply is based is the kilowatt-hour (kWh) and it is known as the *Board of Trade Unit*, or simply as the UNIT. This B.O.T. unit, 1 kWh, is equal to 1 000 Wh or 36×10^5 Wsec. It should be observed that this is an energy unit, not a power unit.

EXAMPLE 3.12 (A). The insulation resistance of the electric power wiring system in a house is 10^6 Ω; the supply is at 200 V. Calculate the cost per year of the leakage if one B.O.T. unit costs one shilling.

Energy $W = V^2 t/R$
$$= (200^2 \times 365 \times 24)/(1\ 000 \times 10^6)$$
$$= 0 \cdot 35 \text{ kWh}$$
Cost at 1/– per kWh $= \underline{\underline{0 \cdot 350/-}}$ or $\underline{\underline{4 \cdot 20\text{d.}}}$

3.7. Efficiency.
In a machine used for energy conversion, the ratio of useful power produced (the output) to the total power required to produce it (the input) is known as the efficiency (η) of the system: it is usually expressed as a percentage. Hence—

Efficiency
$$\eta = (\text{useful power}/\text{total power}) \times 100\%$$
$$= (\text{output}/\text{input}) \times 100\%$$

Owing to inevitable losses, the efficiency is always less than 100 per cent: this figure is approached as closely as possible by careful design of equipment.

The total power is equal to the sum of the useful power produced plus the power used in overcoming losses. Therefore—

$$\% \text{ efficiency } (\eta) = \frac{(\text{useful power} \times 100)}{(\text{useful power} + \text{losses})}$$
$$= \frac{(\text{output} \times 100)}{(\text{output} + \text{losses})}$$

This is often a more useful form for calculation, as for example in motors and generators, because the two powers must be expressed in terms of the same unit.

EXAMPLE 3.13 (A). A certain exchange requires for its operation 49 kWh per day. Two similar batteries are provided and are used on alternate days, each battery supplying the exchange on one day and being recharged on the following day. The average watt-hour efficiency of each battery is 70 per cent, and charging is completed in 8 hr by means of a motor generator which is run for 6 hr at full output with an overall efficiency of 80 per cent, and for 2 hr at one-half of full output with an overall efficiency of 75 per cent. Calculate the total energy in kilowatt-hours drawn from the supply mains during a charging period of 8 hr. (C. & G.)

Energy used per day for the exchange = 49 kWh

Energy output per battery discharge = 49 kWh

Since efficiency = output/input, input = output/efficiency, and total energy input to battery at $\eta = 70\%$ is $49 \times 100/70 = 70$ kWh. This is the total energy output of the generator per charge.

If power output of generator at full load $= P$ kW, then

total kilowatt-hours $= (P \times 6) + (0 \cdot 5P \times 2) = 70$

whence $7P = 70$ and $P = 10$ kW.

(*a*) Energy output from generator at full-load for 6 hr $= 10 \times 6 = 60$ kWh.

Energy input to generator at full-load for 6 hr (at $\eta = 80\%$) $= 60 \times 100/80 = 75$ kWh.

(*b*) Energy output from generator at half full-load for 2 hr $= 5 \times 2 = 10$ kWh.

Energy input to generator at half full-load for 2 hr (at $\eta = 75\%$) $= 10 \times 100/75 = 13\cdot33$ kWh.

Energy from supply mains during 8 hr
$$= 75 + 13\cdot3 = 88\cdot3 \text{ kWh.}$$

3.8. Energy Conversion Equivalents.

An amount of energy in one form if fully converted into another will still retain the same magnitude. Each form of energy is measured in units most convenient to that system and the units of each system are directly related to one another. For the present consideration, the most important relationships are those between (i) electrical and heat energies, (ii) electrical and mechanical energies.

Heat, being a form of energy, is preferably measured in joules: another unit commonly used is the CALORIE (small calorie or gramme calorie) which is *the quantity of heat required to raise the temperature of* 1 *g of water, at* 15°C, *by* 1°C. *A calorie is approximately equivalent to* 4·18 *J.* Other heat units are the KILOCALORIE (great calorie), *a unit of heat equal to* 1 000 *cal,* and the BRITISH THERMAL UNIT (B.Th.U.), *the quantity of heat required to raise the temperature of* 1 *lb of water from* 60°F *to* 61°F. *A British Thermal Unit is equivalent to* 1 054 *J.*

It is useful to note that 1 cal is approximately equivalent to 4·2 J, or conversely that 1 J is equivalent to $1/4\cdot2 = 0\cdot24$ cal.

Mechanical power can be measured by the product of a mass in pounds times the height in feet through which it is raised in unit time, i.e. in foot-pounds per second. The BRITISH HORSE POWER (h.p.) is equal to 550 ft-lb/sec, or 33 000 ft-lb/min.

550 ft-lb/sec
$$= 550/2\cdot2 \times 12/39\cdot37 \text{ kg-m/sec}$$
$$= 550/2\cdot2 \times 12/39\cdot37 \times 9\cdot81 \text{ N-m/sec}$$
$$= 746 \text{ N-m/sec} = 746 \text{ watts}$$

The electrical equivalent is thus 1 h.p. $= 746$ W, or 1 kW $= 1\cdot34$ h.p. It should be noted that these are power units.

EXAMPLE 3.14 (A). A 250-V d.c. motor develops 2 h.p. with an efficiency of 80 per cent. What is the current taken from the supply? (*C. & G.*)

2 h.p. is equivalent to $2 \times 746 = 1\ 492$ W.

Efficiency $\eta = $ output/input
$$\text{input} = \text{output}/\eta$$
$$= 1\ 492 \times 100/80 = 1\ 865 \text{ W}$$
$$I = W/V = 1\ 865/250 = \underline{\underline{7\cdot46 \text{ A}}}$$

EXAMPLE 3.15 (A). What is the maximum current obtainable from an engine-driven 50-V d.c. generator when the engine develops 5 h.p., if the efficiency of the generator is then 85 per cent? (*C. & G.*)

5 h.p. is equivalent to $5 \times 746 = 3\ 730$ W

$$\eta = \text{output}/\text{input}$$
$$\text{output} = \eta \times \text{input}$$
$$= 85 \times 3\ 730/100 = 3\ 170\cdot5 \text{ W}$$
$$W = VI$$
$$I = W/V = 3\ 170\cdot5/50 = \underline{\underline{63\cdot4 \text{ A}}}$$

3.9. Heat Generation.

In a simple conductor the whole of the electrical energy is converted into heat. Heat is invariably generated when a current flows in any conductor, but unless this heat is specifically desired, as for instance in heating appliances, the conductor is so designed, i.e. by limiting its resistance, that the heat generated shall be negligible. Production of unwanted heat is disadvantageous for two reasons: firstly it represents a waste of energy, and secondly any considerable increase of temperature in electrical equipment is deleterious to the insulating material as well as producing an attendant fire risk.

The amount of heat produced is defined by JOULE'S LAW, a principle enunciated by Joule in regard to the heating of a conductor carrying a current, namely that *the heat produced by a current I flowing through a resistance R for a time t is proportional to* I^2Rt. If I is in amps, R in ohms and t in seconds, the electrical energy is I^2Rt joules (watt-seconds) and the heat produced is I^2Rt joules or, applying Joule's equivalent, this energy is equal to

$$I^2Rt/4\cdot2 \text{ calories of heat} \qquad . \quad (3.3)$$

From this expression the heat generated by a current of I amps flowing for t seconds in a conductor of R ohms resistance can be calculated, or alternatively, any of the factors can be calculated if the other three are known. This does not give any indication of the temperature rise, however, unless it is known how much of the heat so generated is lost. A body assumes a steady temperature when the heat imparted to it is exactly balanced by the heat lost due to conduction, convection, and radiation. Resistors in which excessive undesired heat is liable to be generated are usually wound with larger gauge wire, as the increased surface area has a greater emissivity or heat radiating power: further an uninsulated conductor will radiate its heat more readily than one enclosed in insulating covering. With certain instruments which unavoidably generate heat, rectifiers for example, it is necessary to provide adequate ventilation to dissipate the heat by convection currents and prevent damage from heat to the instrument itself and also to neighbouring components. Large power installations are frequently cooled by oil or water.

The heat gained or lost by a body is equal to the product $ms\theta$ kilocalories, where m kilogrammes is the mass of the body, $\theta°$ is the change in temperature, and s is a constant for the substance, known as the *specific heat*: for water, $s = 1$.

When a wire is heated it expands: by utilizing a wire of suitable resistance and coefficient of thermal expansion, the current heating it may be measured by the resultant expansion of the wire, which produces movement of a pointer over a calibrated scale. This is the principle of the hot-wire class of measuring instruments designed for measuring current and p.d.

EXAMPLE 3.16 (A). A lighted lamp is completely immersed in a jar containing 6 000 g of water and after 5 min. the temperature of the water has increased by 3°C. What is the wattage of the lamp? (*C. & G.*)

Total heat gained by water

= mass × specific heat × temperature rise

= 6 000 × 1 × 3 = 18 000 cal

Heat gained per second

= 18 000/(5 × 60) = 60 cal

Electrical energy per second

= power = 60 × 4·2 = 252 W

EXAMPLE 3.17 (A). If a heat coil of 5 Ω resistance is required to operate when it is absorbing 75 J/min, what is its equivalent operating current? (*C. & G.*)

75 J/min = 75/60 J/sec = 5/4 W

$$W = I^2 R$$

$$I = \sqrt{W/R} = \sqrt{5/(4 \times 5)}$$

$$= \sqrt{\tfrac{1}{4}} = \tfrac{1}{2} A$$

3.10. Lamps. Until recent times the electric lamp has depended upon the heating effect of the current but other principles, described below, are now being utilized for illumination purposes.

METAL FILAMENT LAMPS. One of the commonest applications of the heating effect of the current is in the electric lamp in which the current flowing in a fine wire, or *filament*, raises it to incandescence. An illustration showing the constructional details of a filament lamp is given in Fig. 3.9A. The thin tungsten filament within a glass bulb is supported upon wires radiating from a central glass pillar fused into a glass tube. The two ends of the filament are led to insulated terminals in a metal cap which is cemented to the bulb. The connecting wires passing through the glass tube must have the same coefficient of expansion as glass so that the junction between them remains gas-tight: this is ensured by using, within the seal, a copper tube with an iron core. The connexion wires from the seal to the filament are usually of nickel, and from the seal to the terminals are of copper. In manufacture, air is pumped out of the glass bulb which is then filled with an

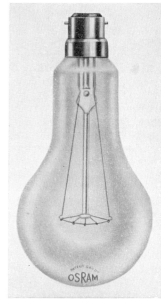

FIG. 3.9A. METAL FILAMENT LAMP
(*Courtesy of Electric Lamp Manufacturers Association*)

inert gas such as argon or nitrogen to prevent oxidization and volatilization of the heated filament which would considerably reduce the life of the filament: sufficient gas is admitted to produce atmospheric pressure when the lamp is burning.

The amount of light produced depends upon the temperature to which the current raises the filament, which in turn depends upon the power consumption (VI): for a constant voltage, the power depends upon the current, or is *inversely* proportional to the resistance ($= \rho l/a$), consequently the illumination is inversely proportional to the filament length and directly proportional to the square of the diameter. Convection currents set up in the gas tend to cool the filament, and to reduce this effect the filament consists of a closely spiralled wire in which form the proximity of adjacent turns prevents excessive loss of heat. In the "coiled-coil" design of lamp this coiled filament is itself wound into an open coil (see Fig. 3.9B) to assist in maintaining the filament temperature.

The working temperature of the filament at

white heat is about 2 700°C at which temperature the amount of light energy emitted represents only about 2 per cent efficiency, a good deal of the energy consumed being dissipated as heat. The illumination from this type of lamp is of the order of two candle-power per watt.

The filaments of lamps are designed to carry a specified current safely, and the lamps are rated at the voltage which will ensure this current and at the corresponding wattage which is a measure of the light intensity. If the rated current is exceeded by using the lamp on an excessively high voltage supply, the temperature rise will usually cause the filament to melt (the melting point of tungsten is 3 655°C). The cold resistance of a lamp is very different from the value of its resistance when hot (see Example 2.6).

FLUORESCENCE.[1] The electric discharge lamp or fluorescent tube, recently introduced widely for illumination purposes, is essentially a mercury vapour lamp in which the energy radiated by the mercury vapour in the ultra-violet (invisible) region of the spectrum is absorbed by fluorescent powder coatings on the inside of the tube, and converted to energy in the visual range. Minute particles of some substances have the property of acting as frequency changers and by a careful selection of substances radiations within the ultra-violet region may be converted into light at various frequencies (colours) within the visible frequency range. A large number of powders will respond very effectively to radiations at the frequency of ultra-violet light, and according to the characteristics of each will convert to a certain wavelength and hence a particular colour in the visual spectrum. By using a combination of powders in suitable proportions a near-daylight, or light of other desired colour can be produced. About 60 per cent of the input power can be converted into ultra-violet light of which some 5 per cent is changed into visible light. The fluorescent lamp has about three times the efficiency of the coiled-coil filament lamp.

A fluorescent tube comprises a coiled-coil tungsten filament fitted at either end of the tube: the

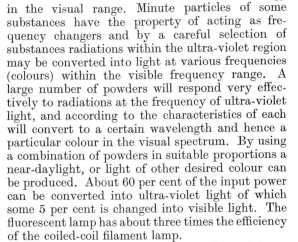

FIG. 3.9B. "COILED COIL" FILAMENT

tungsten is coated with oxides of the alkaline earth metals on account of their electron-emitting properties. A metal plate is welded to each filament to carry a share of the current when either end-electrode is acting as an anode. The inner surface of the tube is coated with a layer of the selected fluorescent powders. The tube contains argon gas at low pressure and also mercury vapour produced from a small globule of mercury inserted into the tube.

The elementary circuit of such a lamp is shown in Fig. 3.10. In common with all mercury discharge lamps it is necessary to have a current

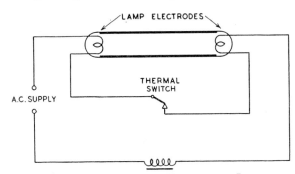

FIG. 3.10. PRINCIPLE OF FLUORESCENT LAMP

limiting device in series. An automatic starting device is incorporated, the essential function of which is to produce a high voltage impulse to start the discharge. This starting switch may take the form of a bi-metallic strip which opens a pair of contacts when a certain temperature is attained. It will be seen from the diagram that the choke, electrodes, and starting switch are all joined in series initially. When the main circuit is closed the electrodes are heated and ionization commences. After about two seconds, by which time the electrodes are sufficiently heated, the starting switch opens sharply and, due to the inductance of the choke, a voltage surge is produced across the lamp which, assisted by ionized gas in the vicinity of the hot electrode at each end, operates the lamp by causing an ionization discharge between the electrodes. The argon in the tube facilitates starting because of the relatively low voltage at which this gas ionizes and becomes conducting. The initial discharge is through the argon gas: the arc produced quickly vaporizes the mercury and the current is then carried entirely by the mercury vapour. If operated on d.c. supplies a protective resistance must be used in series with the choke which now functions only to provide the starting impulse: the power loss in the controlling equipment is about equal to that taken by the lamp,

consequently the arrangement becomes unecono-
mical.

ELECTROLUMINESCENCE.[2] When an alternating
electric field is applied across a thin dielectric
layer containing special phosphor materials, the
whole layer will glow from the direct conversion
of electrical energy into light energy: this effect
is termed *electroluminescence* and it is the basis
of a number of lighting applications such as indicator lamps or illuminated signs. Several materials,
e.g. silicon carbide, exhibit electroluminescence
but the zinc-sulphide phosphors are the most
important for this purpose. These are prepared by
heating a mixture of pure precipitated zinc sul-
phide with copper compounds and fluxes to a

In the organic type, the phosphor and a light-
reflecting powder are held in organic resins on a
glass base which has a transparent conducting
film on the surface adjacent to the phosphor
layer. An electrode, either of evaporated metal or
of conducting paint, is applied to the reflecting
surface of the phosphor layer, followed by layers
of paraffin wax and aluminium foil to act as moisture barriers.

Typically these lamps when energized from a
240-V, 50-c/s supply have an efficiency of the
order of 1 lumen per watt. These lamps may be
smoothly dimmed to extinction simply by varying
the applied voltage. Other phosphor materials may
be used for lamps excited from d.c. supplies.

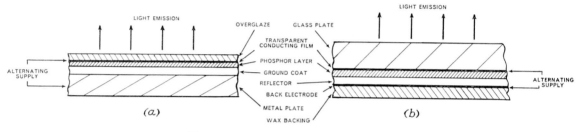

FIG. 3.11. ELECTROLUMINESCENT LAMPS
(*a*) Ceramic type. (*b*) Organic type

temperature of about 1 000°C. The electroluminescent properties depend upon the proportions of copper and halide* ions: predominantly
blue, green, or yellow light may be produced.

The electroluminescent lamp is essentially a
luminous capacitor. There are two basic forms,
known as the ceramic and the organic types:
the essential details of construction are illustrated
in Fig. 3.11.

In the ceramic type, a thin layer (about 0·002
in.) of ceramic enamel or *frit* is fused on to a thin
sheet of iron. This ground coat of ceramic must be
white to act as a reflector of light and must have a
high permittivity in order to absorb sufficient
power. To this ground coat is applied a thin layer
(0·001 in.) of the phosphor material in a second
ceramic frit which must however be transparent
and also non-conducting. The upper surface of
this layer is made electrically conductive by spraying with a solution of a tin salt: it must also be
transparent. A final protective ceramic coating
is then applied; this "overglaze" is transparent
and possesses a high degree of insulation resistance.
Electrical connexions are applied to the two conducting layers.

* Halides are the binary compounds of the halogen
elements (i.e. fluorine, bromine, iodine, and chlorine).

3.11. Fuses. A fuse is invariably fitted in an
electrical circuit to disconnect it in the event of a
fault condition which would be liable to damage
the apparatus due to excessive current. A fuse
consists essentially of a short length of conductor
such as platinoid, phosphor-bronze, etc., having a
reasonable resistance value and a low melting point.
The heat developed in the fuse by the normal
circuit current produces very little increase in
temperature, but the excessive current flowing
under fault conditions raises the temperature above
the melting point of the fuse wire which thereby
disconnects the circuit. The fuse wire is usually
enclosed in some such material as porcelain
(Fig. 3.12 (*a*)), asbestos (Fig. 3.12 (*b*)), or glass to
avoid the risk of fire from the molten metal which
may disintegrate violently. For telegraph or telephone equipment, power distribution fuses usually
have the fuse wire soldered between two springs so
that when the fuse blows electrical and visual indication will be immediately given to assist in
rapid localization of the faulty fuse: this type of
fuse is illustrated in Fig. 3.13 which shows the
fuse (i) when normal, and (ii) when blown.

The maximum current which a circuit is designed
to carry safely is usually about half the fusing
current. Fuses should always be fitted as closely

s possible to the source of supply in order to protect all parts of the circuit.

3.12. Conversions from Electrical Energy.

When current flows through any form of circuit the

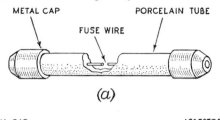

(a)

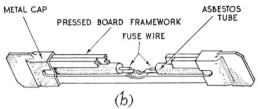

(b)

FIG. 3.12. LINE FUSES
(*a*) Porcelain type. (*b*) High insulation asbestos type.

whole of the electrical energy is converted into some other form of energy. If a current of I amps flows for t seconds in a circuit consisting of a *pure resistance* R ohms, the electrical energy I^2Rt is

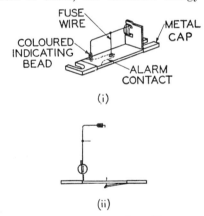

(i)

(ii)

FIG. 3.13. ALARM TYPE FUSES

entirely converted into heat energy. Every form of conversion from electrical energy other than to the production of heat energy results in the generation of a *counter-e.m.f.*, i.e. an e.m.f. which opposes the applied e.m.f. originally producing the current.

In a circuit possessing inductance L henrys (Chapter VII) and carrying a current I amperes, energy is expended in building up the magnetic field initially but not in maintaining it: this energy, equal to $\frac{1}{2}LI^2$ joules, is wholly restored when the current ceases and the field collapses.

Similarly in a circuit possessing capacitance C farads (Chapter V) at a p.d. of V volts, the energy, equal to $\frac{1}{2}CV^2$ joules, used in charging the capacitance is restored to the circuit when the capacitance is subsequently discharged.

In both of these cases, a counter e.m.f. is generated in building up the magnetic field or the electrostatic charge.

When electrical energy is converted into either chemical (Chapter IV) or mechanical energy (Chapter IX), the conversion takes place by driving a current I amperes against a *counter-e.m.f.* E volts: this back-e.m.f. is invariably present in these cases. The energy EIt joules consumed in overcoming this back-e.m.f. is entirely absorbed in producing chemical energy (as in the case of charging a secondary cell) or in producing mechanical energy (as with the electric motor).

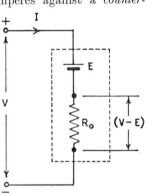

FIG. 3.14. LOAD CIRCUIT WITH BACK E.M.F.

Fig. 3.14 shows a source of electrical energy at a p.d. of V volts applied across a load which includes a back-e.m.f. E volts and inherent internal resistance R_0 ohms: this load may represent either a secondary cell or an electric motor. If I is the circuit current, the total *power* supplied to the load is VI watts. The net or effective voltage in the circuit is $(V - E)$ volts. The power dissipated as heat is the product of this voltage and the current, and is equal to $(V - E)I$ watts. The difference between the total power supplied, VI watts, and the power used in developing heat, $(V - E)I$ watts, is transformed into chemical or mechanical power. This latter power is

$$(VI) - (V - E)I = EI \text{ watts}$$

so that it may be stated that when a current I amperes is driven against a back-e.m.f. E volts, the electrical power transformed into chemical or mechanical power is EI watts. The following power equation applies—

$$VI = I^2R_0 + EI \text{ watts}$$

3.13. Thermo-E.M.F.

The THERMO-ELECTRIC EFFECT (SEEBECK EFFECT) *is an effect sometimes associated with the name of Seebeck, namely that an e.m.f. arises due to a difference of temperature between two junctions of dissimilar materials in the same circuit.* The e.m.f. developed in this manner is known as a thermo-e.m.f. The magnitude of this e.m.f. differs for various pairs of metals and increases as the temperature of the junction is raised. Such an arrangement of conductors constitutes a *thermo-couple.*

Fig. 3.15 shows two junctions formed by copper and iron conductors: an e.m.f. exists at each end

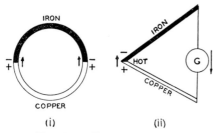

FIG. 3.15. THERMO-JUNCTION

in the direction from copper to iron (i) and if both junctions are at the same temperature these e.m.f.s are equal and no current flows. If one of the junctions is heated (ii) the e.m.f. at this end increases and a current flows around the circuit in the direction copper to iron at the hotter end. The e.m.f. reaches a maximum at some critical temperature depending upon the combination used. A circuit comprised of some different conducting material may be inserted between the two metals at the cold junction without affecting the e.m.f. generated.

A thermo-couple is employed mainly as the basis for current measuring instruments being particularly valuable at the higher frequency alternating currents. In thermo-couple measuring instruments, the current to be measured is led through a wire in contact with one junction of the couple. The heat generated by the current in the wire raises the temperature of this junction and generates an e.m.f. which is measured by a sensitive instrument connected between the unheated ends of the couple.

This thermo-couple e.m.f. is due to two factors, (i) the Peltier e.m.f. which is the e.m.f. existing across the heated junction, and (ii) the Thomson e.m.f. which is due to the temperature gradient along each of the wires taken separately. The Seebeck effect is the algebraic sum of the Peltier and Thomson e.m.f.s. The Peltier effect is reversible, i.e. a current passed through a junction of dissimilar metals will warm *or cool* the junction according to the direction of the current: these effects are independent of the normal I^2R or Joule heating.

SUMMARY

Newton (N). The unit of force—that force which acting upon a mass of 1 kilogramme gives to it an acceleration of 1 metre per second^2.

Energy. The capability for performing work.

Joule. The energy expended when a force of 1 newton is exerted through a distance of 1 metre.

1 joule = 1 watt-second = 1 newton-metre.

Electrical Energy.

$$W = VIt = I^2Rt = V^2t/R \text{ joules} \quad . \quad (3.1$$

Power. The rate of doing work or of expending energy. 1 watt = 1 joule/sec = 1 newton-metre/second.

Electric Power.

$$\text{Energy/time} = VI = I^2R = V^2/R \text{ watts} \quad . \quad (3.2$$

B.O.T. Unit. (Energy) = 1 kWh.

Efficiency.

$$\eta = (\text{output/input}) \times 100\%$$
$$= [\text{output/(output + losses)}] \times 100\%.$$

Calorie. The heat required to raise the temperature of 1 g of water from 15°C to 16°C.

Kilo-calorie (Great Calorie). 1 kcal = 1 000 cal.

British Thermal Unit. The quantity of heat required to raise the temperature of 1 lb of water from 60°F to 61°F.

Joule's Equivalent.

1 cal = 4·2 J: 1 J = 0·24 cal

Horse-power. 1 h.p. = 746 W.

Heat Generated

$$= VIt = I^2Rt \text{ joules}$$
$$= VIt/4·2 = I^2Rt/4·2 \text{ cal} \quad . \quad (3.3$$

REFERENCES

1. S. E. PUGH: "Fluorescent Lighting," *I.P.O.E.E. Journal,* **37** (1944), p. 65.
2. P. W. RANBY and P. J. CLEWER: "Current Applications of Electroluminescence," *Transactions of the Illuminating Engineering Society,* **25** (1960), p. 167.

CHAPTER IV

CELLS

In this chapter the chemical effect of the current is considered. An important practical application is the storage of chemical energy in such a manner that on release it is readily and efficiently converted to electrical energy.

For convenience the chapter is divided into sections dealing with electro-chemistry, voltaic cells, primary cells, secondary cells and grouping cells.

ELECTRO-CHEMISTRY

4.1. Electrolysis. The flow of current in a metallic conductor takes place without producing any change in the material of the conductor in which it flows: it is an *electronic* current, sometimes known as a conduction current.

Most fluids, and also certain metallic solids which permit the passage of an electric current are decomposed in the process: chemical action results from the flow of current and the conducting material is split up to form different substances. In this form of current flow, the current is conveyed by particles of the substance, each particle carrying a small charge of positive or negative electricity and moving through the path from one terminal to the other. Such a flow is known as an *electrolytic* current, or a convection current, and the charged particles—charged atoms or groups of atoms—are called ions.

Many chemical compounds when in solution or in a molten state behave in this way and as such they are known as ELECTROLYTES. An electrolyte *is a conducting medium or solution in which the electric current flows by virtue of chemical changes or decomposition and the consequent movement and discharge of ions.* The process, namely *the production of chemical changes by ionic migration and discharge,* is termed ELECTROLYSIS.

4.2. Ionization. When certain chemical compounds are dissolved in water, some of the molecules are broken up into two component ions carrying equal positive and negative charges. For example, if copper sulphate crystals are dissolved in water, copper atoms each carrying a positive charge (i.e. copper ions) are formed, together with sulphate ions each with an equal negative charge. The process of formation of ions is known as IONIZATION.

4.3. Electrolysis of Water. Water (a chemical compound of hydrogen and oxygen) is a suitable fluid for demonstrating the occurrence of electrolysis,

but, as pure water is not a good conductor, it is preferable to improve its conductivity by adding, for example, a few drops of sulphuric acid.

Consider a vessel containing a dilute solution of sulphuric acid in which are placed two platinum plates (Fig. 4.1). Normally no chemical action occurs between the acid and the platinum, but if the platinum plates are connected to a source of e.m.f., bubbles of gas—hydrogen and oxygen—

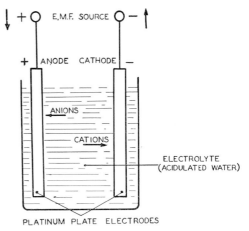

FIG. 4.1. ELECTROLYSIS

will rise from the proximity of the platinum plates on the passage of an electric current.

The metallic* conductor, in this case the platinum plate, by means of which electrons pass to or from the electrolyte is called the ELECTRODE. It is necessary to distinguish between the two electrodes, and the names ANODE and CATHODE are given to the positive and negative electrodes respectively: the (positive) current enters the electrolyte at the anode (A) and leaves at the cathode (C), so that the direction of current flow is $A \rightarrow C$. These details are indicated in the illustration of Fig. 4.1 which represents a particular form of ELECTROLYTIC CELL.

The electrolysis of the acidulated water is pictorially represented in fuller detail in Fig. 4.2. Before a current is passed (i) the sulphuric acid (H_2SO_4) contains a large number of positive and negative ions, the opposite charges being equal and exactly neutralizing one another. Each positive

* This definition also includes the conductor carbon.

ion is a positively charged atom of hydrogen: each negative ion is a group of one sulphur atom and four oxygen atoms together carrying a double negative charge. One molecule of the electrolyte may be represented as shown below, the + and − indices indicating the charge—

$$H_2SO_4 = H_2{}^{++} + SO_4{}^{--}$$

When the electrodes are connected to a source of e.m.f., the anode and cathode are subjected to

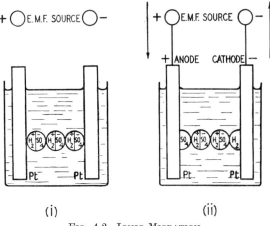

FIG. 4.2. IONIC MIGRATION

a difference of potential. The positive hydrogen ions are attracted to the negative cathode, and the negative sulphate ions, or *sulphions*, (SO_4), migrate to the anode—Fig. 4.2 (ii). When the ions come into contact with the oppositely charged electrode, they immediately lose their charges. Each pair of hydrogen atoms forms a molecule of hydrogen which is liberated at the cathode. The sulphions at the anode are incapable of independent existence and cannot react with the platinum. Instead, they react with the water present forming more sulphuric acid and liberating at the anode oxygen atoms which also pair to form molecules—

$$SO_4 + H_2O \rightarrow H_2SO_4 + O$$

The hydrogen ions do not travel to the cathode in the form of bubbles of gas but by a process of linkages, each hydrogen ion displacing a similar ion from the adjacent sulphuric acid molecule until the cathode is reached.

The ions are named according to the electrode to which they migrate (see Fig. 4.1). *The ion which carries the negative charge (against the direction of the current) and delivers it at the anode is called the* ANION: *the ion which carries the positive charge (in the direction of the current) and delivers it at the cathode is the* CATION.

The formation of hydrogen on the cathode results in a *counter*-e.m.f.

A solution of copper sulphate in which are immersed two copper plates to serve as electrodes may also be subjected to electrolysis by the passage of a current. In this case the cations are copper, and on losing their charge copper atoms are liberated. These copper atoms are deposited upon the copper cathode which gradually becomes coated with a film of electrolytic copper and consequently increases in mass.

The anions are sulphions which are able to combine with the copper atoms of the anode to form molecules of copper sulphate and pass into the solution. This loss of copper atoms from the anode results in a reduction in its mass, and the net effect of the electrolysis in this case is to transfer pure copper from the anode to the cathode, the strength of the electrolyte remaining constant.

A similar process occurs during the electrolysis of a silver nitrate solution with silver anodes, and most metals can be subjected to electrolysis in suitable electrolytes. It will be observed that the metallic ion travels with the current from the positive to the negative electrode and is deposited on the cathode.

If the two electrodes were connected to a source of alternating current, each would become an anode and a cathode in turn, so that any electrolytic action during one half-cycle would be reversed during the ensuing half-cycle: consequently the aggregate effect of an alternating current applied to an electrolytic cell would be zero.

Consideration of the direction of flow of electrons in the external circuit enables the ANODE to be defined as *an electrode by which electrons leave an electrolyte*; and the CATHODE as *an electrode by which electrons enter an electrolyte*.

4.4. Quantity. The extent of the electrolytic action depends upon the quantity of electricity which flows. To understand what is meant by quantity it may be useful to refer again to the hydraulic analogy: the quantity of water passing any point in the pipe is determined by the product of the rate of flow and the duration of time considered, i.e. the volume of the water passing. Unit quantity would be equal to the volume of a stationary column of water (in a pipe of unit diameter) of length equal to the distance covered by the water in unit time.

Similarly by a quantity of electricity is meant the product of the rate of flow and the time. The COULOMB (C) is *the unit of quantity of electricity in the practical system* and it is defined as *the quantity of electricity passing in a second when the mean current is one ampere*. The coulomb is one ampere-second and Quantity (coulombs) = Current amperes) × Time (seconds) or $Q = I \times t$. Conversely, the ampere is a rate of flow of one coulomb per second.

Another commonly employed unit of quantity of electricity is the AMPERE-HOUR (Ah), equal to 3 600 C.

4.5. Faraday's Laws. Faraday enunciated the two fundamental principles of electrolysis, namely–

(1) *The chemical effect resulting from electrolysis is directly proportional to the quantity of electricity which has passed through the electrolyte.*

(2) *The quantity of each substance chemically changed, or liberated, at an electrode by the passage of a definite quantity of electricity is directly proportional to the equivalent weight* of the substance.*

From the first law—

$$m \propto It = k \cdot It$$
$$\text{or } m \propto Q = k \cdot Q$$

if m = mass of element liberated (grammes),

I = current (amps),

t = time (seconds),

Q = quantity (coulombs),

k = a constant.

If $I = 1$ and $t = 1$, so that the quantity flowing is equal to unity, then $m = k \times 1 \times 1$, or $m = k$: in other words this constant k is *the mass of the substance undergoing electro-chemical change due to the passage of one coulomb* and it is known as the ELECTRO-CHEMICAL EQUIVALENT of the substance. The electro-chemical equivalent is usually denoted by z and is measured in grammes per coulomb. The electro-chemical equation is therefore $m = zIt$. The electro-chemical equivalents of a number of elements are given in Table 4.I.

TABLE 4.I

ELECTRO-CHEMICAL EQUIVALENTS

Element	Electro-chemical Equivalent (g/C)
Copper . . .	0·000 329 3
Gold . . .	0·000 680 8
Hydrogen . . .	0·000 010 4
Nickel . . .	0·000 304 0
Silver . . .	0·001 118 0
Zinc . . .	0·000 338 7

From Faraday's second law, if the electro-chemical equivalent for one element is accurately determined, then the electro-chemical equivalent

* The *equivalent weight* is the mass of a substance which, in a specified chemical reaction, combines with or replaces 8 g of oxygen.

of any other element can be determined from its chemical equivalent. The chemical equivalent is the ratio of the *atomic weight* to the *valency*: these values are known for all the elements.

EXAMPLE 4.1 (A). A metal object with a total surface area of 64 cm² is to be copper-plated to a depth equivalent to a uniform deposit of 0·15 g/cm². If a current of 0·8 A is to be used, how long would the plating process take? The electro-chemical equivalent of copper is 0·000 329 g/C.   (*C. & G.*)

Mass of copper to be deposited
$$= 0 \cdot 15 \times 64 = 9 \cdot 6 \text{ g}$$
$$9 \cdot 6 = zIt = 0 \cdot 000\ 329 \times 0 \cdot 8t$$
$$t = 9 \cdot 6 \times 10^5/26 \cdot 32 = 36\ 480 \text{ sec} = \underline{10 \text{ hr } 8 \text{ min}}$$

EXAMPLE 4.2 (A). An electrolytic tank filled with a solution of silver nitrate is to be used to silver-plate a copper article. If a steady current of 1 A deposits 6·71 g of silver in 1 hr 40 min, calculate the electro-chemical equivalent of silver.   (*C. & G.*)

$$m = zIt, \quad 6 \cdot 71 = z \times 1 \times 6\ 000$$
$$z = 6 \cdot 71 \times 10^{-3}/6 = 1 \cdot 118 \times 10^{-3}$$
$$\text{or } \underline{0 \cdot 001\ 118 \text{ g/C}}$$

EXAMPLE 4.3 (A). A direct current is passed between two electrodes which are immersed in a solution of copper sulphate. After 30 min it is found that one electrode has increased in weight by 0·594 g. Calculate the amount of current flowing. (The electro-chemical equivalent of copper is 0·000 33 g/C.)   (*C. & G.*)

$$m = 0 \cdot 594 \text{ g},$$
$$z = 0 \cdot 000\ 33 \text{ g/C},$$
$$t = 30 \times 60 = 1\ 800 \text{ sec}.$$
$$I = ? \text{ A},$$
$$m = zIt,$$
$$I = m/(zt)$$
$$= 0 \cdot 594/(0 \cdot 000\ 33 \times 1\ 800)$$
$$= 0 \cdot 594/0 \cdot 594$$
$$= \underline{1 \cdot 0 \text{ A}}.$$

EXAMPLE 4.4 (A). In a refinery for the production of electrolytic copper, the p.d. between the plates in each vat is 3 V. What is the cost of the power used per kilogramme of copper refined if the power costs 0·5d. per kWh? 1 A deposits 1·2 g of copper per hour.

Current required to deposit 1 000 g of copper per hour = 1 000/1·2 A.

Power per hour = $3 \times 1\ 000/1 \cdot 2$ W
$$= 3/1 \cdot 2 \text{ kW}$$

Cost at 0·5d./kWh = $3 \times 0 \cdot 5/1 \cdot 2 = 1 \cdot 5/1 \cdot 2$
$$= \underline{1 \cdot 25 \text{d.}}$$

4.6. Current. If the mass of a cathode be carefully weighed before and after being subjected to electrolysis under controlled conditions of known time and current strength, the value of the current can be readily determined from Faraday's first law: alternatively, the mass of a gas liberated can be measured for this purpose. *An electrolytic cell when arranged for the measurement of the quantity of electricity passing by the accurate measurement of one or more of the products of electrolysis* is called a COULOMETER. The earlier name, *voltameter*, is falling into disuse owing to its similarity to, and possible confusion with, *voltmeter*.

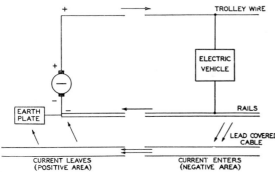

FIG. 4.3. ELECTROLYTIC CORROSION

Electro-plating is an example of the use of electrolysis to deposit a layer of the pure metal from an anode of the desired metal upon another material arranged as a cathode. This method is frequently adopted, for example, to deposit a protective film upon parts of electrical apparatus to prevent corrosion.

In the process known as *anodizing*, films of insulating oxides are produced on aluminium and light alloys, for protective purposes, by deposition on these metals used as the *anodes* in suitable solutions. Electrolysis has also been applied to detect telegraph signals by the discoloration of chemically treated paper upon the passage of the received current.

4.7. Electrolytic Corrosion. An instance of a deleterious effect of electrolysis sometimes occurs in the electrolytic corrosion of lead covered underground cables. Where these cables are laid in the vicinity of electric railways or tramways in which the uninsulated rails are utilized to form part of the circuit, if the return path through the rails is inefficient, a portion of the current leaves the rails,[1] usually at points remote from the power station, and it will flow in the conducting path offered by the lead sheath of the cables—see Fig. 4.3. Eventually—generally near the power station—this current will leave the cable sheath to

return to the source: due to the presence of moisture, that part of the lead sheath at which the current leaves becomes an anode, and lead is carried away from the sheath with the current. There is a tendency for this current to be confined to small areas, and as a result of this electrolytic corrosion the lead is gradually eaten away until the moisture is enabled to penetrate the cable and destroy the insulation. The positions where conditions are favourable for the current to enter and leave the cable sheath are known as negative and positive areas respectively. It will be apparent that trouble of this nature can only occur with d.c. operated traction systems. Currents may also be set up in the lead sheath with similar results due to natural differences of earth potential in the various soils through which the cables pass.

Typically these straying currents may reach a magnitude of 10 to 20 mA: according to Faraday's Law a current of 10 mA could erode 0·75 lb of lead in one year. These harmful effects can be combatted in various ways according to the particular circumstances—(i) the cable may be bonded to an earth plate in order that the current will leave the sheath only at that point: (ii) insulating gaps may be left in the lead sheath at appropriate points to prevent the flow of sheath current: (iii) reactive magnesium electrodes (anodes) may be buried in the ground and connected to the cable by an insulated wire; the magnesium being more positive than lead in the electro-chemical series, the cable sheath becomes a cathode in relation to the surrounding earth, i.e. current flows from the magnesium electrode through the earth *to* the cable sheath and electrolytic corrosion cannot occur. The wire connecting the cable sheath to the magnesium electrode completes the circuit. This method is termed *cathodic protection*.[2] The same result may be achieved by applying a negative potential to the lead sheath from a mains-driven rectifier either to neutralize or to reverse the sheath current.

VOLTAIC CELLS

4.8. Simple Voltaic Cell. In the electrolytic cells of the type described in the preceding pages, the electrical energy applied from an external source is converted to chemical energy. By a suitable choice of materials an electrolytic cell can be arranged to produce a process which is the reverse of this—namely to convert chemical energy to electrical energy and generate an e.m.f. *A source of electrical energy depending on chemical action and complete in itself* is termed a VOLTAIC CELL. *It has two electrodes each of which is immersed in an electrolyte and reacts therewith to produce an e.m.f.*

A simple voltaic cell comprises an electrode of zinc and one of copper immersed in an electrolyte of dilute sulphuric acid: the copper electrode acquires a positive potential and the zinc electrode a negative potential, generating an e.m.f. of approximately 1 V. If the electrodes are joined by a wire as shown in Fig. 4.4, a continuous current will flow in this conductor from the copper to the zinc, the path being completed from the zinc to the copper within the electrolyte.

The zinc is at a lower potential than the copper, but the current is driven through the electrolyte from the low potential to the high potential electrode due to the electromotive force of the electro-chemical action, in a manner comparable to that of the hydraulic pump described earlier.

The zinc electrode is an anode and is sometimes referred to as the electro-positive element, but it is the negative terminal of the cell: the copper electrode is a cathode, and negative element, but is the positive terminal of the cell. This apparent conflict of ideas becomes clear if the external and internal circuits of the cell are considered separately.

When the current flows, electro-chemical action results, bubbles of hydrogen appear at the copper electrode, and the zinc electrode is gradually dissolved into the electrolyte. The amount of zinc consumed or converted into a chemical compound of zinc when known currents are supplied by the cell for definite periods can be calculated from Faraday's first law.

The positively charged hydrogen atoms, or ions, migrate to the copper electrode giving up their positive charges and combining in pairs to form molecules of free hydrogen, which is liberated at the copper electrode.

The negatively charged sulphions move to the zinc electrode where they give up their negative charges and unite with one atom of zinc—

$$Zn + SO_4 \rightarrow ZnSO_4$$

In this way positive and negative potentials are imparted to the copper and zinc electrodes respectively due to the dissociation of the electrolyte. This chemical action maintains the e.m.f. until the zinc has all been dissolved away or until the acid has been completely dissociated. With this simple form of cell the strength of the current rapidly decreases, owing to the two effects known as *local action* and *polarization* which occur.

The name PRIMARY CELL is given to *a voltaic cell for the direct conversion of chemical energy into electrical energy, characterized by the consumption of the more electropositive of the two elements forming the cell. For all practical purposes a primary cell is irreversible.*

4.9. E.M.F. of a Cell. If a plate of pure zinc is immersed in dilute sulphuric acid, no discernible chemical action occurs, but the zinc electrode at once acquires a potential difference with respect to the electrolyte with which it is in contact, this p.d. being known as an *electrode potential*. The negative ions of the electrolyte are attracted to the zinc plate and a negative charge is quickly built up on the zinc electrode, until its potential becomes so negative that further attraction of the ions ceases. This particular value is the electrode potential for zinc in a sulphuric acid electrolyte and is equal to

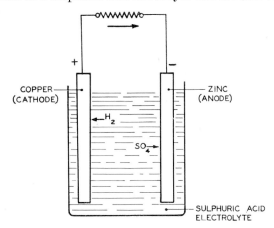

FIG. 4.4. SIMPLE VOLTAIC CELL

— 0·62 V. In a similar manner, the copper immersed in the sulphuric acid acquires an electrode potential of + 0·46 V, due to the hydrogen ions. The e.m.f. between the terminals of the cell is due to the sum of these electrode potentials, i.e. 0·62 + 0·46 or 1·08 V.

Elements can be arranged in an electro-chemical series which for the commoner elements is in the order magnesium, zinc, lead, tin, bismuth, antimony, iron, copper, mercury, silver, platinum, carbon: of any pair taken to form the electrodes of a voltaic cell the metal appearing earlier in the list will form the negative terminal: furthermore, the more widely apart in this series are the metals chosen, the greater is the resulting e.m.f. With a view to obtaining the maximum e.m.f., the metals zinc and carbon are chosen for the Leclanché cell which gives an e.m.f. of about 1·5 V, the zinc being the negative terminal.

The e.m.f. of a voltaic cell, depending as it does upon the sum of the two electrode potentials, is determined only by the nature of the electrodes and the electrolyte: it is independent of the physical dimensions of the cell.

4.10. Local Action. Commercial zinc usually

contains a small amount of impurities mainly in the form of iron, carbon, tin, and arsenic. If an electrode of such composition is inserted in a sulphuric acid solution, chemical action commences and the zinc is gradually dissolved away, irrespective of whether the cell is furnishing a current to an external circuit or not. This action is due to the dissimilar metals present, for example the zinc and the particles of iron, forming minute voltaic cells. The zinc and iron are in contact with one another and also with the electrolyte, and the small local circulating currents result in the liberation of hydrogen and the eating away of the zinc. When the cell is delivering current, this local action represents a waste of energy because these local currents are not available to the external circuit: when the cell is not delivering current, the local action continues and the life of the cell is thereby shortened.

This effect is a serious drawback from a practical point of view, but it can be overcome by amalgamating the zinc with mercury. If the zinc plate is dipped into mercury, the zinc particles on the surface dissolve in the mercury but the impurities do not. A film consisting of particles of pure zinc dissolved in mercury is formed on the surface of the electrode. The impurities are prevented by the mercury from access to the electrolyte, and local action is eliminated. As the surface zinc is dissolved into the electrolyte during use of the cell, further particles of zinc from within the plate dissolve into the mercury to maintain the process. With a zinc rod treated in this manner, no chemical action occurs whether the cell is delivering current or not. For manufacturing purposes, to achieve the same result it is usually preferable to add a small percentage of mercury to the zinc which is to be used for the electrodes.

4.11. Polarization. When a simple voltaic cell is supplying current, some of the hydrogen liberated rises to the surface and escapes into the atmosphere but some remains adhering to the copper plate. After a time the copper plate is so completely covered with bubbles of hydrogen that it is no longer in good contact with the electrolyte. The hydrogen, the electrolyte, and the zinc form a secondary voltaic combination in which the zinc is at a *higher* potential than the hydrogen, and an e.m.f. is set up which tends to drive a current in the reverse direction. Such an e.m.f. which opposes the normal flow of current in a circuit is termed a *back-e.m.f.* or a *counter-e.m.f.* The reduction in contact area between the copper and electrolyte also increases the internal resistance of the cell.

This action of the hydrogen covering the copper electrode and producing a counter-e.m.f. is known as POLARIZATION, and its effect is to reduce the e.m.f. available at the cell terminals to a very low value.

The occurrence of polarization is inherent in simple voltaic cells, and before such a cell can be put to any practical use it is imperative to overcome the ill effects of the presence of hydrogen.

Many forms of primary cell have been designed with a view to the prevention of polarization either by removing the hydrogen as it forms on the electrode, or alternatively by preventing it from forming or from reaching the electrode. Any added substance whose function is to minimize electrolytic polarization is known as a *depolarizer* or as a *depolarizing agent*. The differences between the various types of cell lie mainly in the methods by which this depolarization is effected.

Polarization also occurs during electrolysis and if, for example, in the electrolysis of water, the applied current is cut off, a back-e.m.f. of polarization could be measured, whose magnitude, however, rapidly decreases. For this reason continuous electrolysis cannot be effected unless the p.d. applied to the electrodes exceeds the *decomposition voltage*, i.e. unless it is great enough to overcome the value of the e.m.f. due to polarization. For the decomposition of water this value is about 1·5 V. With copper electrodes in a copper sulphate electrolyte, however, no back-e.m.f. is actually apparent because polarization e.m.f.s are produced at each electrode and, being of equal magnitude and opposite sense, they neutralize one another.

4.12. Internal Resistance. The laws which govern the resistance of a solid conductor may be applied to the electrolyte. In a cell the length of the electrolyte path is the distance between the plates, and the cross-sectional area is the average area of the immersed surfaces. The resistance of the electrolyte largely governs the *internal resistance* of the cell, and this increases directly with the distance between the electrodes and inversely with the superficial immersed area of the electrodes. The internal resistance also depends upon the nature of the electrolyte, and as a cell ages, deterioration of the electrolyte tends to increase the internal resistance. The internal resistance and therefore the current which can be supplied by a cell accordingly depend upon its dimensions.

It is essential to keep the internal resistance of a cell as low as possible, for when the cell is delivering current the potential difference between the terminals falls due to the potential drop across the internal resistance of the cell.

When a cell is on open circuit, i.e. there is no external circuit and no current flowing, the full e.m.f. of the cell appears as the p.d. across the terminals: there is no voltage drop inside the cell while there is no current flowing.

When a cell is on closed circuit, i.e. a current is flowing in an external circuit, the same current flowing in the internal circuit produces a potential drop inside the cell, and, as part of the generated e.m.f. is used up in driving the current through this resistance, the *terminal p.d.* is less than the *generated e.m.f.* by an amount equal to the internal voltage drop.

The relation between these values can be calculated from Ohm's law. If E volts is the generated

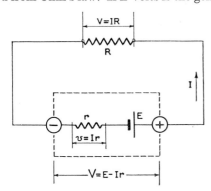

FIG. 4.5. EFFECT OF INTERNAL RESISTANCE

e.m.f. (i.e. the sum of the electrode potentials) r ohms is the internal resistance of the cell, and I amps the current flowing in an external resistance R ohms, the terminal p.d. V volts is obtained as follows (see Fig. 4.5)—

Internal potential drop $v = Ir$ volts

Terminal p.d., $V = (E - v) = (E - Ir)$. (4.1)

The generated e.m.f. is absorbed in two stages, (i) in driving a current I through the internal resistance r, and (ii) in driving the same current through the external resistance R. These two potential drops $v = Ir$ and $V = IR$ are together equal to the generated e.m.f. E, or

$$E = v + V = Ir + IR = I(r + R)$$

for the circuit current $I = E/(R + r)$. As the value of the current I increases, the internal potential drop Ir increases and the terminal p.d. falls. When current is being drawn from the cell, the terminal p.d. is always less than the e.m.f.

The internal resistance is considered as acting in series with the cell e.m.f. as shown in Fig. 4.5.

From the equation $V = E - Ir$, $Ir = E - V$ and $r = (E - V)/I$. This expression is used to define the INTERNAL RESISTANCE of a cell as the

instantaneous value of the ratio, to the current passing, of the difference between the e.m.f. generated and the potential difference between the terminals of the cell.

EXAMPLE 4.5 (A). Three secondary cells, A, B, C, each of 2 V e.m.f., have internal resistances of 0·1, 0·2, and 0·3 Ω respectively. When the cells are connected in series to supply a certain load, a current of 2·5 A flows. For these conditions calculate—

(a) the voltage across the terminals of each battery,
(b) the voltage across the terminals of the load.

(C. & G.)

With a current of 2·5 A the voltages necessary to overcome the internal resistances will be respec-

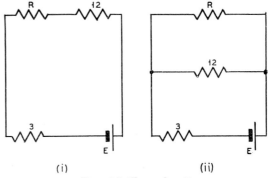

FIG. 4.6 (Example 4.7)

tively $(2·5 \times 0·1)$, $(2·5 \times 0·2)$, and $(2·5 \times 0·3)$ = 0·25, 0·50, and 0·75 V. The effective voltage across the terminals of each battery will be $(2·0 - 0·25)$, $(2·0 - 0·50)$, and $(2·0 - 0·75)$ V respectively, i.e.—

$$1·75, 1·5 \text{ and } 1·25 \text{ V}$$

The total load voltage
$$= 1·75 + 1·5 + 1·25 = 4·5 \text{ V}$$

EXAMPLE 4.6 (A). A cell of internal resistance 0·5 Ω and e.m.f. 1·4 V is connected to a resistor of 40 Ω. What current flows in the circuit?

Total resistance $= R + r = 40 + 0·5 = 40·5$ Ω.

Current $= E/(R + r) = 1·4/40·5 = 0·034\ 6$ A.

EXAMPLE 4.7 (A). A resistor R is connected first in series and then in parallel with a meter of 12 Ω resistance. When a battery having an internal resistance of 3 Ω is applied to the combination the reading on the detector is found to be the same in each case. Calculate the value of R.

(C. & G.)

See the circuit diagram in Fig. 4.6. Let E be the e.m.f. of the battery.

(i) Circuit current = current in meter
$$I_1 = E/(R + 12 + 3)$$
$$= E/(R + 15)$$

(ii) Joint resistance of the two resistors in parallel = product/sum = $12R/(12 + R)$.

Current from battery,

$$I = E \div \{3 + 12R/(12 + R)\}$$
$$= E \div (36 + 3R + 12R)/(12 + R)$$
$$= E(12 + R)/(36 + 15R)$$

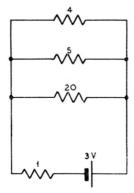

FIG. 4.7 (Example 4.8)

This current divides in proportion to the conductances, hence current in 12 Ω path,

$$I_2 = I \times R/(12 + R)$$
$$= \{E(12 + R)/(36 + 15R)\} \times \{R/(12 + R)\}$$
$$= ER/(36 + 15R)$$

But $I_1 = I_2$,

$$E/(R + 15) = ER/(36 + 15R)$$
$$R(R + 15) = 36 + 15R$$
$$R^2 + 15R = 36 + 15R$$

whence $R^2 = 36$ and $R = 6\ \Omega$

EXAMPLE 4.8 (A). A battery having an e.m.f. of 3 V and an internal resistance of 1 Ω is connected across three resistors of 4, 5, and 20 Ω which are joined in parallel. What is the total current taken from the battery and the current through each resistor? In which of the three parallel resistors is most heat generated? Give the reason for your statement. (C. & G.)

Equivalent value of paralleled resistors (see Fig. 4.7)—

$$1/R = \tfrac{1}{4} + \tfrac{1}{5} + \tfrac{1}{20} = (5 + 4 + 1)/20 = 10/20$$
$$R = 20/10 = 2\ \Omega$$

Total current from battery, $I = 3/(2 + 1) = 1\cdot0$ A

Conductance ratio $= \tfrac{1}{4} : \tfrac{1}{5} : \tfrac{1}{20} = 5 : 4 : 1$ and $5 + 4 + 1 = 10$

Current in $4\ \Omega = 1 \times 5/10 = 0\cdot5$ A

,, $5\ \Omega = 1 \times 4/10 = 0\cdot4$ A

,, $20\ \Omega = 1 \times 1/10 = 0\cdot1$ A

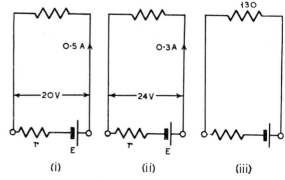

FIG. 4.8 (Example 4.9)

Heat generated $= V^2t/(4\cdot2R)$ g cal: for a constant p.d. the heat is proportional to $1/R$, consequently most heat is generated in the lowest resistor, i.e. in the 4 Ω resistor.

EXAMPLE 4.9 (A). The p.d. at the terminals of a Leclanché battery is 20 V when the battery is supplying a current of 500 mA, and 24 V when the current is 300 mA. Calculate the current the battery would supply when connected to a resistor of 130 Ω. (C. & G.)

The circuit diagrams are given in Fig. 4.8.

Let E volts and r ohms be the e.m.f. and the internal resistance of the battery.

(i) $V = E - Ir$, $20 = E - 0\cdot5r$

(ii) $24 = E - 0\cdot3r$

Subtracting, $4 = 0\cdot2r$, $r = 20\ \Omega$

From (i) $E = 20 + 0\cdot5r = 20 + (0\cdot5 \times 20)$
$$= 20 + 10 = 30\ V$$

(iii) $I = E/(R + r) = 30/(130 + 20)$
$$= 30/150 = 0\cdot2$ A

EXAMPLE 4.10 (A). When a voltmeter of 600 Ω resistance is connected to a battery of primary cells the reading obtained is 48 V. When a resistor of 120 Ω is connected in parallel with the voltmeter the reading falls to 40 V. Calculate (a) the e.m.f. and (b) the internal resistance of the battery. (C. & G.)

The circuit diagrams are given below in Fig. 4.9.

Let the e.m.f. and the internal resistance of the battery be E volts and r ohms respectively.

(i) Current $= V/R = 48/600 = 0{\cdot}080$ A

$V = E - Ir,\ 48 = E - 0{\cdot}08r$

(ii) Joint resistance of 600 Ω and 120 Ω,

$R = \text{product}/\text{sum} = (600 \times 120)/(600 + 120)$
$= 72\,000/720 = 100\ \Omega$

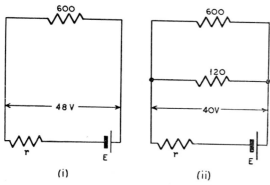

FIG. 4.9 (Example 4.10)

Current from battery $= V/R = 40/100 = 0{\cdot}4$ A
$$V = E - Ir$$
$$40 = E - 0{\cdot}4r$$
and from (i),
$$48 = E - 0{\cdot}08r$$

Subtracting, $8 = 0{\cdot}32r,\ r = 8/0{\cdot}32 = 25\ \Omega$
$$E = 40 + 0{\cdot}4r = 40 + (0{\cdot}4 \times 25)$$
$$= 40 + 10 = 50\ \text{V}$$

EXAMPLE 4.11 (A). A dry cell supplies a current of 100 mA when connected across a resistor of 9 Ω and a current of 50 mA when connected across a resistor of 23 Ω. Assuming that the internal resistance of the cell remains constant, what is the e.m.f. of the cell? (C. & G.)

See the circuit diagrams of Fig. 4.10.

Let E volts and r ohms be the e.m.f. and the internal resistance of the dry cell.

(i) $V = IR = 0{\cdot}1 \times 9 = 0{\cdot}9$ V
$V = E - Ir,\ 0{\cdot}9 = E - 0{\cdot}1r$

(ii) $V = IR = 0{\cdot}05 \times 23 = 1{\cdot}15$ V
$V = E - Ir,\ 1{\cdot}15 = E - 0{\cdot}05r$

Multiplying (i) by 0·5,
$$0{\cdot}45 = 0{\cdot}5E - 0{\cdot}05r$$
$$0{\cdot}70 = 0{\cdot}5E$$
$$E = 1{\cdot}4\ \text{V}$$

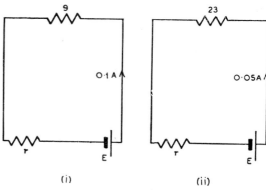

FIG. 4.10 (Example 4.11)

EXAMPLE 4.12 (A). If 50 telegraph circuits each of 500 Ω resistance are connected to a battery with e.m.f. of 24 V and internal resistance of 20 Ω, calculate the current flowing in one circuit when (a) the key on this circuit only is depressed, (b) the keys on all 50 circuits are depressed simultaneously. (C. & G.)

See the circuit diagrams of Fig. 4.11.

(i) $I = 24/(20 + 500) = 24/520 = 0{\cdot}046$ A

(ii) Resistance of 50 circuits each 500 Ω in parallel $= 500/50 = 10\ \Omega$

Total current $= 24/(20 + 10) = 24/30$
$$= 4/5\ \text{A}$$
Current per circuit $= 4/(5 \times 50) = 4/250$
$$= 0{\cdot}016\ \text{A}$$

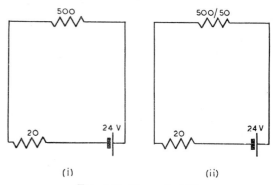

FIG. 4.11 (Example 4.12)

EXAMPLE 4.13 (A). A battery of 100 V and internal resistance 1 Ω is connected across an external resistance of 10 Ω. What would be the change of p.d. across this resistance if a second resistance of equal value is connected in parallel? What power would be drawn from the supply in the second case? (C. & G.)

The circuit diagrams are given in Fig. 4.12.

(i) Current $I = E/(R + r) = 100/(10 + 1)$

$$= 100/11$$

P.d. across $1\ \Omega = Ir = 100/11$ V

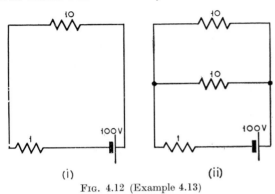

FIG. 4.12 (Example 4.13)

(ii) Joint resistance of two parallel resistors each $10\ \Omega = 10/2 = 5\ \Omega$

Current $I = E/(R + r) = 100/(5 + 1) = 100/6$

P.d. across $1\ \Omega = Ir = 100/6$

Change of p.d. across $1\ \Omega$

$= $ change of p.d. across $10\ \Omega$

$= (100/6 - 100/11) = (1\ 100 - 600)/66$

$= 500/66 = \underline{7\cdot58}$ V

Power $= V^2/R = (100 - 100/6)^2/5$

$= \{(600 - 100)/6\}^2 \div 5$

$= (250/3)^2 \div 5 = 62\ 500/(9 \times 5)$

$= 1\ 390$ W $= \underline{1\cdot39\ \text{kW}}$

4.13. Calculation of E.M.F. from Thermo-chemical Relations. The electrical energy produced in a cell results from the transformation of chemical energy. When the corresponding chemical energy change takes place *without* the generation of electrical energy, the energy is released in the form of heat. The electrical energy resulting from the electro-chemical action is therefore equivalent to the heat energy resulting from the purely chemical action. From a knowledge of the heat of chemical transformation, the e.m.f. of a cell can be calculated.

For example, in the simple voltaic cell, the chemical action consists of the combination of the zinc with the sulphuric acid and the decomposition of the water.

The heat evolved when 65 g of zinc (i.e. the *gramme-equivalent*, or the number of grammes equal to the number expressing the atomic weight) combine with sulphuric acid $= 108\ 000$ g cal.

The heat absorbed by the decomposition of 18 g of water (the gramme-equivalent of water)

$$= 69\ 000 \text{ g cal}$$

Total heat evolved per gramme of zinc

$$= (108\ 000 - 69\ 000)/65$$
$$= 39\ 000/65 \text{ g cal}$$

The electro-chemical equivalent of zinc is $0\cdot000\ 338\ 7$ g/C, and the heat equivalent of this mass is

$$(39\ 000 \times 0\cdot000\ 338\ 7)/65 \text{ g cal}$$

From the mechanical equivalent of heat at $4\cdot2$ J/g cal the energy is

$$(39\ 000 \times 0\cdot000\ 338\ 7 \times 4\cdot2)/65 \text{ J}$$

This energy is equivalent to the product of the e.m.f. and the quantity, and since the quantity considered for $0\cdot000\ 338\ 7$ g of zinc is unity,

$$E = (39\ 000 \times 0\cdot000\ 338\ 7 \times 4\cdot2)/65 = 0\cdot9 \text{ V}$$

In the general case, if h is the heat evolved (as specified above) in calories per gramme, z is the electro-chemical equivalent in grammes per coulomb, and J is the mechanical equivalent of heat in joules, then the e.m.f.

$$E = Jhz \text{ volts}$$

The back-e.m.f. developed from the electrolysis of water can be calculated from this expression: given $J = 4\cdot2$, $h = 34\ 000$, and z for hydrogen $= 0\cdot000\ 010\ 4$,

$$E = (4\cdot2 = 34\ 000 \times 0\cdot000\ 010\ 4) = 1\cdot49 \text{ V}$$

PRIMARY CELLS

4.14. The Leclanché Cell. The chief characteristics of a good cell are—

1. High e.m.f.
2. Low internal resistance.
3. Absence of polarization.
4. Absence of local action.
5. Low initial cost.
6. Low cost of renewals.
7. Large amount of energy between renewals.
8. Little attention required.
9. No injurious fumes liberated.
10. Materials easily and safely handled.
11. Small dimensions.

There is no form of cell which completely fulfils all these conditions, each of which is of high importance. Conditions (6) and (7) mean that the cost of a given quantity of electrical energy should be as low as possible, and conditions (7) and (8) specify that the labour cost of maintenance shall be small. The relative importance of the above properties naturally depends upon the purpose to which the cell is to be put, and for telecommunication requirements the Leclanché cell more nearly approaches these conditions than any other form of primary cell.

If a Leclanché cell is heavily or continuously worked, then polarization occurs and the e.m.f. varies, but after a short period of rest the hydrogen is absorbed and the cell is again ready for use. The Leclanché cell is eminently satisfactory for intermittent work at a suitable current strength.

Though comparatively cheap in initial cost and requiring little attention, the Leclanché cell is nevertheless an expensive source of electrical energy, and its use is practically confined to local circuits and to isolated installations.

The containing vessel of the Leclanché cell consists of a square glass jar, ending in an almost circular collar shaped to admit the zinc rod. The collar and a portion of the jar itself are usually heavily coated with ozokerite to arrest creeping of the electrolyte.

The positive electrode is a plate of carbon capped with a brass terminal. The shank of this terminal is tinned, fitted into holes in the carbon and a lead alloy is run into the holes and around the head of the carbon: this alloy expands on cooling, ensuring a good contact between terminal and carbon. The head is then soaked in hot paraffin wax which seals the pores in the carbon and prevents the electrolyte from corroding the lead.

The negative electrode is in the form of a zinc rod cast upon a copper wire, which is insulated where it emerges from the zinc and forms one terminal of the cell. The zinc rod tapers towards either end from the centre as illustrated in Fig. 4.13: this gives the most economical shape of the cathode. A small percentage of mercury is added to the zinc during manufacture to prevent local action. Two zinc rods are used in the larger cells.

The depolarizer is powdered manganese dioxide (graded to a size which will pass through a sieve of 50 but not of 60 meshes to the square inch) and is mixed with powdered gas carbon in the proportion of 70 per cent manganese dioxide and 30 per cent carbon to improve the conductivity of the depolarizer.

To maintain the depolarizer in intimate contact with the carbon plate, a porous container is used: until recently this generally took the form of an unglazed earthenware pot but nowadays it is more usually a sack made in textile fabric. A little of the depolarizer is placed in the bottom of the

porous container and moistened with the electrolyte. The carbon rod stands centrally in the container and is surrounded by the depolarizer mixture which is firmly tamped down as it is added. A covering of marine glue, in which a small ventilating hole is made, keeps the carbon and depolarizer in place. The sack is reinforced by a lapping of string. Fig. 4.13 illustrates the complete sack element comprising carbon electrode and depolarizer.

The electrolyte is ammonium chloride (sal-ammoniac) made up by dissolving from two to four ounces of ammonium chloride to each pint of

FIG. 4.13. ZINC ROD AND SACK TYPE ELEMENT FOR LECLANCHÉ CELL
(*Courtesy of P.M.G.*)

water, the stronger solution being used for heavily worked cells. The completed cell appears as shown in Fig. 4.14. The porous pot must be saturated before the cell is ready for use since it must allow free access between the carbon and the electrolyte, its purpose being to hold the carbon and the depolarizer firmly together.

Consideration of the chemical actions which take place when the cell is delivering current will show that free ammonia gas is generated, and this has a deleterious effect upon surrounding metal work. The evolution of the gas necessitates free ventilation in any battery compartment which may be used and evaporation of the solution is therefore facilitated.

To permit a cell to be sealed with the object of retarding evaporation of the electrolyte, manganese chloride is substituted for ammonium chloride in cells where the energy is discharged over a period of several months. With manganese chloride electrolyte no free gas is evolved so that the cells can be safely sealed, thereby practically stopping evaporation and at the same time preventing the oxidation which takes place when manganese chloride is exposed to the atmosphere. If a cell containing manganese chloride is not sealed, the zinc rod becomes coated with an oxide which increases the internal resistance of the cell.

FIG. 4.14. LECLANCHÉ CELL
(*Courtesy of P.M.G.*)

The e.m.f. of a Leclanché cell is about 1·5 V when new, decreasing during the life of the cell to a useful limit of 1·0 V: the internal resistance of a good cell may be as low as 0·5 Ω but this value increases as the cell ages. The use of manganese chloride as the electrolyte gives a slightly higher e.m.f.

With the cell idle no chemical action takes place, but when the cell is on closed circuit the chemical components are redistributed in the following manner—

(1) WITH AMMONIUM CHLORIDE (NH$_4$Cl) ELECTROLYTE. The electrolyte consists of positively charged ammonium ions (NH$^+$) and negatively charged chlorine (Cl$^-$) ions.

At the negative plate the chlorine ions give up their charges to the zinc and enter into chemical combination, forming zinc chloride (ZnCl$_2$) which passes into solution with the electrolyte—

$$Zn + 2Cl \rightarrow ZnCl_2$$

At the positive plate the ammonium ions give up their charges to the carbon with which, however, they do not react chemically: instead they break up into ammonia gas and hydrogen—

$$2NH_4 \rightarrow 2NH_3 + H_2$$

The hydrogen atoms freed unite in pairs to form molecules and would normally cause polarization.

At the depolarizer the manganese dioxide (MnO$_2$) gives up oxygen to react with the hydrogen and form water, producing a lower oxide of manganese (Mn$_2$O$_3$—manganese sesquioxide) in the process—

$$2MnO_2 + H_2 \rightarrow Mn_2O_3 + H_2O$$

(2) WITH MANGANESE CHLORIDE ELECTROLYTE (MnCl$_2$). The electrolyte consists of positively charged manganese ions (Mn$^+$) and negatively charged chlorine ions (Cl$^-$).

At the negative plate the chlorine ions give up their charges to the zinc and enter into chemical combination forming zinc chloride which passes into solution with the electrolyte—

$$Zn + 2Cl \rightarrow ZnCl_2$$

At the positive plate the manganese ions give up their charges to the carbon and react with the manganese dioxide depolarizer to form a lower oxide of manganese in the process—

$$Mn + 3MnO_2 \rightarrow 2Mn_2O_3$$

4.15. The Leclanché Air Depolarized Cell.

In this type of cell the positive electrode is a cylindrical block of very porous carbon fitted with a terminal. The zinc rod electrode is insulated from the carbon block by holding the two together with rubber bands twisted into the form of a figure 8, the presence of the twisted rubber ensuring a gap between the elements. The electrolyte is either manganese chloride or ammonium chloride.

The chemical action of this cell differs from that described above only in the depolarizing action. The upper portion of the carbon block is not immersed in the electrolyte and the air is free to diffuse into the interior of the porous carbon block. The ammonia and hydrogen gases produced at the positive electrode collect in the pores of the carbon block where, due to the catalytic properties of carbon, the hydrogen unites with the oxygen of the atmosphere to form water, the extreme porosity of the carbon allowing the ammonia gas to escape. The carbon element remains dry owing to the presence of a colloidal film between the carbon and the electrolyte, and this film also ensures a good electrical contact between the two, with the result that the cell has a low internal resistance. Since air is employed as the depolarizer, it is necessary to provide adequate ventilation for the cell.

Compared with the sack type cell, the air depolarized cell has a lower internal resistance and a longer life, i.e. a greater ampere-hour capacity: the e.m.f., however, is less and polarization occurs more readily.

4.16. Dry Cells. The question of portability and other considerations of convenience render the fluid electrolyte type of cell unsuitable for some requirements. For these purposes it is necessary to make use of the so-called dry cell which is a modification of the Leclanché cell and has precisely the same electro-chemical reactions.

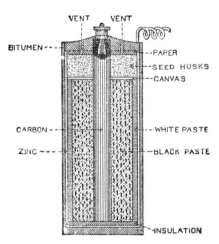

FIG. 4.15. DRY CELL
(*Courtesy of A.E.I. Ltd.*)

A dry cell may be defined as a primary cell in which the electrolyte is applied in the form of a paste so that it does not flow out if the cell be inverted. The cell is sealed except for a small vent. In comparison with the fluid electrolyte of an ordinary cell, this perhaps justifies, or at all events extenuates, the generic title given to this class of cell. If, however, the materials were actually dry the cell would, by reason of its enormously high resistance, be incapable of supplying a current. The storage of dry cells prior to use is a matter of some concern for if they were allowed to become dry they would fail after very little service.

A typical dry cell is illustrated in Fig. 4.15, and Fig. 4.16 gives a cross-sectional view showing the construction. The cell has a zinc container in the form of a cylindrical vessel to which is soldered an insulated copper wire to serve as the negative terminal. The positive electrode is a carbon rod fitted with a terminal in the manner described for the wet Leclanché cell: this rod is placed centrally in the zinc container, standing upon a disk of insulating material to prevent direct contact between the two electrodes. The depolarizer, closely surrounding the carbon, consists of the carbon and manganese dioxide mixture moistened with ammonium chloride solution producing a black paste. The electrolyte, a solution of ammonium chloride

FIG. 4.16. SECTION OF DRY CELL
(*Courtesy of A.E.I. Ltd.*)

mixed with such materials as flour or plaster of paris to form a white paste, is filled between the depolarizer and the zinc case. A space left above the pastes is filled with ground cork or wheat husks to receive the gases and moisture liberated. The whole is contained in a case of cardboard impregnated with paraffin wax. The top of the cell is sealed with bitumen through which are pierced two small holes for the gases to escape.

4.17. Maintenance of Leclanché Cells. During the life of the cell, the zinc, the electrolyte, and the depolarizer gradually become exhausted: a good cell is designed so that under average working conditions these three will fail simultaneously. A cell is considered faulty if its e.m.f. falls below 1 V or if its internal resistance exceeds 2 Ω.

The effect of too weak an electrolyte is to hasten the formation of crystals on the zinc, whilst too strong an electrolyte leads to creepage of the solution. The early formation of large crystals on the zinc indicates that excessively large currents are being taken from the cell, while smaller currents continued over too long a period result in smaller crystals. These crystals raise the internal resistance and form more readily as the electrolyte becomes weaker. Any incrustation forming on the zinc or the porous element should be removed.

The ozokerite normally prevents any creepage of the electrolyte. If creepage does occur, it produces corrosion which is difficult to eliminate, hence care is necessary to keep the exposed elements dry. The electrolyte should be maintained at the correct level by topping-up with more electrolyte of a suitable strength depending upon the estimated current taken from the cell.

The electrical connexions should be kept clean and tight and covered with a film of petroleum jelly to prevent corrosion. The cells should stand upon dry wood to prevent leakage of the current to earth: if damp situations cannot be avoided, the cells should be placed in wooden boxes which stand upon earthenware insulators. In a wet cell the zinc rod, sack element, and electrolyte will each need replacing at intervals: with a dry cell it is not practicable to replace individual components and the complete cell must be renewed when failure occurs.

The application of suitable electrical tests indicates the condition of a cell at any time during its life. A measurement of the e.m.f. of the cell when on open circuit shows whether the carbon, zinc, and electrolyte are in order but does not take into account either internal resistance or polarization. The internal resistance can be calculated from the value of the p.d. when the cell is supplying a known current. The state of the depolarizer can be determined by taking a heavy current from the cell and ascertaining whether the cell immediately regains its open-circuit e.m.f. when the external circuit is disconnected.

The usual test applied to primary cells is as follows.

(i) Measure the open circuit e.m.f. of the cell*: let this be E_1 volts.

(ii) Connect a 2 Ω resistor across the cell and measure the terminal p.d.—V volts.

(iii) Remove the resistor from across the cell

* The e.m.f. may be measured sufficiently accurately for this test using a high resistance voltmeter.

after one minute and measure the e.m.f. immediately the resistor is disconnected: call this E_2 volts.

The value of E_1 indicates the state of the electrodes and electrolyte.

The values of V and E_1 enable the internal resistance r to be calculated, for the current is

$$I = E_1/(2 + r)$$

and the voltage drop across the internal resistance is

$$Ir = E_1 r/(2 + r) = (E_1 - V)$$

from which r may be found.

The difference between E_1 and E_2 indicates the back-e.m.f. of polarization. E_2 should not be less than 1·2 V.

4.18. Sizes of Cells. The e.m.f. of a cell is entirely independent of its dimensions, but the internal resistance of a cell and the amount of electrical energy it will deliver depend upon the size of the cell. It will be obvious that, given two cells, of similar type but of different size, the larger cell will furnish a given current for a longer period than a smaller one. Not only so but at any period during the discharge the larger cell is subjected to a less severe test since its resources (i.e. the quantities of active chemical materials) are much greater.

With any type of cell the quantity of electricity it will deliver—that is, the *capacity* of the cell—varies considerably according to the strength of the discharge current: the higher the current the lower the capacity. The extent of the variation is indicated for typical cells in Table 4.II below.

TABLE 4.II

LECLANCHÉ TYPE CELLS: CAPACITY AND ENERGY AT GIVEN DISCHARGE RATES

Discharge Rate (mA)	WK1	WK2	WK4	DR2	DS1	
50	215	50	20	40	150	Capacity (Ah)
100	180	42	15	36	135	
200	135	30	10	27	100	
—	200	75	40	45	135	Energy (Wh)
—	100	50	20	50	150	Discharge rate (mA)

In accordance with the British Standards Specification for Leclanché type primary cells, cells are designated by two letters and a number. The significance of the letters is as follows—

W = Wet cell:	R = Round cell:
D = Dry cell:	S = Square cell:
K = Sack type element:	I = Inert cell.
P = Porous pot cell:	

The method of determining the capacity of a given type of cell consists in discharging the cell, at a mean current strength corresponding to the size of the cell, through a copper coulometer. The capacity in ampere-hours is computed from the increase in weight of the copper cathode of the electrolytic cell.

Contrary to the behaviour of Leclanché and other wet cells, dry cells, when worked at small discharge rates of a long period, give a lower ampere-hour capacity than the rated values. This is due to the tendency of the cells to dry out, which entails their rejection owing to high internal resistance before the elements can be fully used up.

The internal resistance of a cell is only roughly proportional to its size when the cell is of homogeneous construction. In the case of the simple voltaic cell for example, the rule holds good, but in the case of the Leclanché and dry cells an increase in the size of the cell means that, although the areas of the electrodes are increased, the distance between the zinc and carbon plates is also increased and the resistance therefore tends to remain uniform.

4.19. The Inert Cell.
The construction and action of an inert cell are similar to those of the dry Leclanché cell except that all the ingredients are initially in the solid state and are completely enclosed. The cell is inactive and incapable of producing a current until water is added (through a vent provided with a stopper) to form an electrolyte with the chemicals contained in the cell.

The inert cell is not so efficient as the dry cell but it has the advantage that it deteriorates less rapidly while being kept in stock. The e.m.f. and the internal resistance have approximately the same values as those given for the dry cell.

4.20. The Standard Cell.
Since the e.m.f. of a voltaic cell depends upon the nature of the materials forming the electrodes and electrolyte, it is possible to construct a cell whose e.m.f. can be utilized as a standard reference for voltage measurement if the condition of the cell is carefully controlled.

The Muirhead standard cells utilize an acid cadmium-sulphate electrolyte with cadmium-mercury amalgam in the negative limb and mercury (together with a layer of mercurous sulphate) in the positive limb. Complete security of contents is ensured by the use of porous disks of high molecular-weight polythene which hold the chemical constituents firmly in position. The e.m.f. is within the range 1·018 58 to 1·018 64 volts (at 20°C) with an accuracy of 0·001 per cent. The e.m.f. value is reproducible at any given temperature, and with accurate temperature control the e.m.f. will vary less than $\pm$ 1 μV per year. The e.m.f.

at temperatures other than 20°C is capable of accurate calculation.

SECONDARY CELLS[3]

4.21. Elements of Secondary Cells.
A secondary cell, or ACCUMULATOR, is a *voltaic cell which is reversible and which, after discharge, can be brought back approximately to its initial (charged) chemical condition by passing a current through it in the direction opposite to that of discharge.* A primary cell, on the other hand, is for all practical purposes irreversible.

Secondary cells in general use are of the lead-acid type, that is to say they have electrodes of lead immersed in an electrolyte of dilute sulphuric acid in a suitable container, but many differences in detail occur in the various types. The chemical action in every lead-sulphuric acid cell is the same. When fully charged, the active material on the positive plate is peroxide of lead, whilst that on the negative plate is spongy lead. On discharge an increasing proportion of the active material of both positive and negative plates is converted to lead sulphate. On charge the positive plate assumes a rich chocolate colour, and the colour of the negative plate is light grey. When the cells are discharged, the true shade of colour of the positives grows somewhat lighter: the fact of the sulphation occurring gradually throughout the material accounts for its not showing itself in the form of a grey colour upon the plates.

These principles of the secondary cell are illustrated in Fig. 4.17 which shows the general conditions of a cell both when charged and discharged.

4.22. Chemistry of Secondary Cells.
The full chemistry of secondary cells is not known with any degree of certainty at the present time, notwithstanding the fact that many eminent chemists have devoted much study to it. The *double sulphation theory* is still generally accepted as a close approximation to the probable facts, since the calculated voltage of a secondary cell from thermo-chemical reactions postulated accords roughly with the observed voltage.

DISCHARGE. When the cell is in the charged state, the active material of the positive plate is lead peroxide (PbO_2) and that of the negative plate is metallic lead (Pb) in a spongy state. As the cell discharges (Fig. 4.17 (i)) the positive hydrogen ions of the sulphuric acid (H_2SO_4) move through the electrolyte to the positive plate (cathode) where they give up their charges: the free hydrogen reacts to reduce the lead peroxide to lead monoxide (PbO) which then combines with the sulphuric acid to form lead sulphate ($PbSO_4$)—

Positive Plate (i.e. the plate which is normally at

the higher potential, and which forms the anode during charge).

$$PbO_2 + H_2 \rightarrow PbO + H_2O$$
$$PbO + H_2SO_4 \rightarrow PbSO_4 + H_2O$$

The negative sulphions travel to the negative plate and combine with the lead to form lead sulphate—

Negative Plate.

$$Pb + SO_4 \rightarrow PbSO_4$$

The two conditions of the cell when fully charged and discharged are—

CHARGED			DISCHARGED		
+ plate	electrolyte	− plate	+ plate	electrolyte	− plate

$$PbO_2 + 2H_2SO_4 + Pb \rightleftharpoons PbSO_4 + 2H_2O + PbSO_4$$

In practice the chemical changes indicated above do not extend to the limit of the available material, the charge and discharge each being stopped before the whole of the active material has undergone chemical change. Lead sulphate to a slight extent

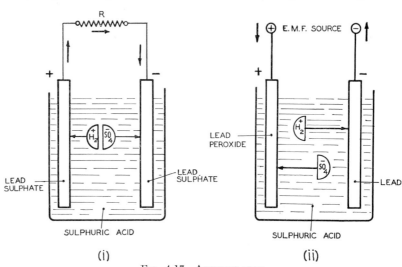

FIG. 4.17. ACCUMULATOR
(i) On discharge. (ii) On charge.

Thus lead sulphate is formed on both plates: this is not the ordinary lead sulphate which is insoluble, but probably a more complex compound.

CHARGE. When the cell is being recharged (Fig. 4.17 (ii)), the hydrogen ions move to the negative plate (now the cathode) and the sulphions to the positive plate. The chemical actions are then the reverse of those given above, and may be written—

Positive Plate.

$$PbSO_4 + SO_4 + 2H_2O \rightarrow PbO_2 + 2H_2SO_4$$

Negative Plate.

$$PbSO_4 + H_2 \rightarrow Pb + H_2SO_4$$

In considering the migration of the ions in the two cases, it should be remembered that on *discharge* the cell is a voltaic cell (H⁺ to positive electrode—see Fig. 4.4.); but on *charge* the cell is undergoing electrolysis (H⁺ to negative plate—see Fig. 4.2).

is therefore always present in both plates when charged.

As the cell approaches full charge, the amount of lead sulphate present on the plates is insufficient to combine with all the ions reaching the plates. As a result some of the water of the electrolyte is decomposed: hydrogen gas is liberated at the negative plate whilst oxygen is given off at the positive plate from the combination of the sulphion with water, forming also sulphuric acid—

$$SO_4 + H_2O \rightarrow H_2SO_4 + O$$

The stage at which the evolution of oxygen and hydrogen takes place is known as *gassing* and indicates that the cell is practically fully charged.

4.23. Construction of Plates. The lead used for the plates is termed corroded lead, as the surface rapidly oxidizes and turns to a grey colour when exposed to the atmosphere. It is soft and has little tensile strength. The lead should be in the pure state and should not contain more than 0·005 per cent of foreign material. The active material—i.e. that portion of a plate in which chemical changes are wrought by the passage of an electric current —may be supplied either by forming it by electrolytic action on the plate itself, or by applying it mechanically in the form of a paste. Modern practice favours Planté formed positives with Fauré pasted negatives, the formed negative having disappeared almost entirely. Improvements in Planté plates have for their objects the simplification of the forming process, design of the plates to reduce and resist stresses, and an increase in the active

FIG. 4.18. PLANTÉ POSITIVE PLATE (CHLORIDE)

surface. With pasted plates the problem is chiefly in the direction of securing better adherence between the plate and the paste.

4.24. Planté Positive Plates. The Planté plate (Fig. 4.18) consists of a pure lead casting with deep, finely divided, vertical grooves in its surface to render its developed area large in comparison with its superficial area. The active area may be increased up to ten times in this manner. Some plates have a core or diaphragm formed midway through the plates from which the leaves or laminae formed by the grooves stand out. Others are without a core and the grooves pass through the plate so that it is possible to see through the unformed grid if it is held up to the light. Cross-sections of these two types are shown in Figs. 4.19A and 4.19B.

Planté plates usually maintain their capacity until the end of their useful life. Although some material is lost from the surface due to gassing, it

is replaced by the formation of further lead peroxide from the underlying lead. Lead peroxide is of lower density than lead, and the formation of lead peroxide is accompanied by an increase in the volume of the active material: this results in the active material exerting a stress upon the lead,

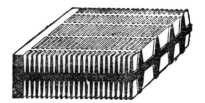

FIG. 4.19A. SECTION OF PLANTÉ PLATE WITH CORE

causing it to expand. Due to the vertical laminations most of the expansion occurs in this direction and the length of the plates increases slightly with use. The horizontal ribs spaced at intervals give stability to the plates.

Negative plates are seldom made by the Planté process.

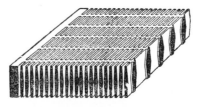

FIG. 4.19B. SECTION OF PLANTÉ PLATE WITHOUT CORE

4.25. Rosette or Manchester Positive Plates. This type of plate forms an intermediate class between the Planté and Fauré plates, since the active material is not formed actually on the plate itself nor is it applied in the form of a paste: it is formed on spirals of lead tape fixed in the grid.

It is constructed of an antimonial lead plate containing a large number of round holes which are countersunk on both sides of the plate so as to provide for expansion of the active material during forming. Into these holes are forced rolls or rosettes of soft corrugated lead upon which is formed the active material by a process similar to that used for Planté plates. This type of plate is illustrated in Fig. 4.20.

4.26. Fauré Plates. There are two types of pasted plate—the ordinary type and the box type. The former class is used for both positive and negative plates, the box type being used largely for negative plates.

In the *ordinary type* the plate consists of an antimonial lead grid, the addition of antimony producing an alloy of greater tensile strength and less subject to electro-chemical corrosion than lead. The use of this alloy also facilitates the manufacturing process of the grids. The active material in the form of a paste is applied mechanically to the grids: the ingredients of this paste differ somewhat for the positive and negative plates which are otherwise generally similar in construction. A negative plate of this type is illustrated in Fig. 4.21.

For the *box type* two antimonial lead grids are used, each with horizontal and vertical ribs forming

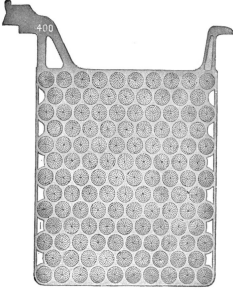

FIG. 4.20. ROSETTE POSITIVE PLATE (CHLORIDE)

FIG. 4.21. PASTED NEGATIVE PLATE
(*Courtesy of P.M.G.*)

(PbO) and red lead or minium (Pb_3O_4) are used for negative and positive plates respectively. Small quantities of substances known as reducing,

squares of about $1\frac{1}{2}$ in. sides. On one side of each grid is burned a sheet of perforated lead with about 150 holes to the square inch: each grid therefore forms a shallow tray divided into square compartments. One grid is cast with a number of rivets at suitable points and the other has holes in corresponding positions. The active material is heaped up in each compartment of one of the grids, the other grid is placed in position on top and the two halves are riveted together. This form of construction is clearly illustrated in Fig. 4.22 where one corner of the plate is shown opened up.

With this box construction the electrolyte has easy access to the active material through the perforated lead, and this allows the paste to be more spongy and porous than with the ordinary type.

4.27. Active Material. The active material is manufactured chiefly from lead oxides: litharge

FIG. 4.22. BOX NEGATIVE PLATE (CHLORIDE)

porosity, hardening, expanding, and cementing agents are added.

The reducing agent, usually ammonium sulphate, is added to accelerate formation of the active material. After the paste has set, the porosity agent—frequently sugar or magnesium sulphate—is dissolved and leaves the paste in a porous state to facilitate subsequent electro-chemical action. The hardening agent, which may be glycerine, tapioca, or carbolic acid, binds the ingredients of the mixture together, consolidating the paste, making it durable, and increasing its conductivity. The texture of the plate influences the capacity per unit area, the allowable rates of charge and discharge, and the life. Soft plates generally give greater capacity per unit area, but have a shorter life than hard plates. Expanding agents of such composition as graphite, or ground pumice, are usually confined to use in box negatives and minimize the tendency of the lead particles to consolidate, which would cause a reduction in plate capacity. After the ingredients have been thoroughly mixed in a dry state, the cementing agent—dilute sulphuric acid—is applied and the paste is transferred immediately to the grids. The plate with the active material is then subjected to a gradual and uniform drying process.

The grid of the positive plate plays an important part in conducting the current since the resistivity of the paste is considerably higher than that of lead.

4.28. Demi-Planté Positive Plates.

A positive plate known as the demi-Planté, or semi-Planté, is sometimes used in small or medium sized stationary cells. It is a combination of the Fauré and Planté types, starting its life by using active material which has been pasted on to it, but later, having lost the pasted material, it utilizes active material which has gradually been produced electrolytically from the lead of the plate. The plate is usually made of pure lead similar to that used for Planté plates. Grooves are produced on both sides but unlike those of the Planté type plates they are horizontal and of greater width. A few vertical ribs are provided to strengthen the plate. The grooves are filled with paste similar to that used for Fauré plates, and the forming process is also similar.

The developed area of the lead frame of a plate of this type is less than that of a similarly dimensioned Planté plate on account of the smaller number of grooves. Consequently it is not so suitable for use in cells which are required for heavy discharges. A further disadvantage is that the horizontal grooves cause lateral expansion of the plates, a direction in which space in the containers is limited.

4.29. Forming Process for Planté Positive Plates.

The formation process consists in electrolytically converting the substance or surface of an unformed plate into the maximum quantity of active material.

In the *three-stage process* the plates to be formed are first immersed in dilute sulphuric acid to which is added small percentages of *forming agents*: these forming agents may be acetic, nitric, or hydrochloric acid, or salts of these acids, and accelerate formation by corroding the lead and allowing a higher current density than if the electrolyte contained dilute sulphuric acid only. The forming agents produce a thin film of a lead compound which is converted to lead sulphate by the sulphuric acid. A current is passed through the electrolyte from the plates being formed to dummy plates used as cathodes. The resultant electrolysis converts the lead sulphate to lead peroxide and the process is continued until a coating of lead peroxide between $\frac{1}{64}$ in. and $\frac{1}{32}$ in. thick is produced. The amounts of forming agents added are gauged so that none remains in the electrolyte on the completion of this first stage.

The second stage consists in reversing the direction of the current, so that the lead peroxide coating is reduced to spongy lead: all traces of forming agent are then removed, and the plates are washed.

For the third stage the electrolyte is renewed and the direction of the current is again reversed. The spongy lead is reconverted to lead peroxide, and forming is complete.

4.30. Forming Process for Pasted Plates.

The plates are immersed in tanks of dilute sulphuric acid and a current is passed from the positives (anodes) to the negatives (cathodes). The action of the sulphuric acid converts the lead oxide to lead sulphate and as a result of electrolysis this is converted to lead peroxide on the anodes and spongy lead on the cathodes. The process is continued until practically the whole of the lead sulphate has been converted: about 3 per cent of lead sulphate remains which cannot readily be removed and this acts as a binder for the active material.

On completion of the forming process the positive plates can be put into storage, but the negative plates would rapidly oxidize from exposure to the air and so are partially discharged so as to give them a protective film of lead sulphate. Before the plates can be put into service, it is necessary to subject them to a prolonged charge—the *initial charge*—to remove the oxides and sulphates from the negative plates.

4.31. The Electrolyte.

The specific gravity of a substance is its relative density compared with the density of water at 4°C: since 1 m³ of water at 4°C

weighs 1 000 kg, the specific gravity of water is
1 000.

Concentrated sulphuric acid has a specific
gravity of 1 840, and for use in secondary cells it is

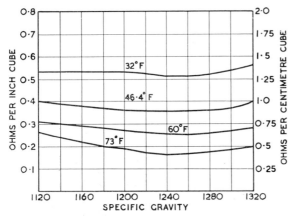

FIG. 4.23. RESISTIVITY OF ELECTROLYTE

diluted with distilled water. For the satisfactory
operation of secondary cells it is not essential for
the electrolyte to be of any definite specific gravity,
provided it is within the limits of 1 100 to 1 300. If

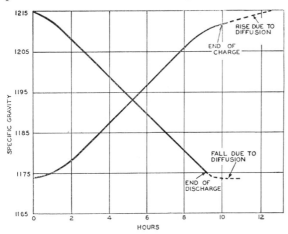

FIG. 4.24. SPECIFIC GRAVITY VARIATIONS
(CONSTANT CURRENT)

below this limit, damage may be caused by the
plates becoming hydrated, whilst, if above, the
plates are liable to be corroded.

The resistance of a sulphuric acid solution varies
with the specific gravity and with the temperature:
Fig. 4.23 shows the extent of this variation over
the gravity range commonly encountered. Electrolyte having a specific gravity of about 1 215
(when the cells are fully charged) is generally found

to be most suitable for stationary types of cells
for portable cells a higher specific gravity ofter
reaching 1 280 is employed.

The electrolyte must be chemically pure and it
is especially important that it should be free from
iron.

The chemical equations show the formation of
sulphuric acid on charge and of water on discharge
The effect of this is to produce a rise and fall of the
specific gravity of the electrolyte during charge
and discharge of the cell. According to Faraday's
laws the quantity of charge and discharge (in
ampere-hours) is related directly
to the mass of water and sulphuric acid liberated by the
electro-chemical action. Hence
the specific gravity of the electrolyte is proportional to the state
of charge of the cell. The voltage of a cell remains fairly
constant during discharge, consequently the specific reading is a
valuable indication to the state
of a cell during charge or discharge.

Fig. 4.24 shows the variation
which occurs in the specific
gravity while a cell is being
charged and discharged at a
constant current strength. There
is a slight lag in the specific
gravity changes owing to the
time required for the diffusion of
the electrolyte. This is shown
by the dotted lines which illustrate the continuance of change
in the specific gravity after the charge and dis
charge have been terminated. Some flattening of
the curve towards the end of the charge will be
discerned: this is due to the reduced amount of
active material remaining to be converted.

An instrument used to measure the specific
gravity of the electrolyte is known as the *hydro*
meter. One type of hydrometer frequently used for
this purpose is shown in Fig. 4.25: its range is
from 1 170 to 1 220. The instrument consists of a
weighted glass bulb with a calibrated stem which
sinks into the electrolyte to a depth depending
upon the specific gravity. With the hydrometer
alone it is difficult to take accurate reading;
because the electrolyte forms a meniscus around
the stem due to surface tension. The celluloid float
is used to obviate this difficulty by raising the
cursor line or reading point above the level of the
electrolyte. The hydrometer is specially calibrated
in conjunction with the float.

FIG. 4.25
HYDROMETER WITH
FLOAT
(Courtesy of Lucsmart)

The specific gravity varies inversely with the temperature. Hydrometer readings are corrected to their equivalent value at 60°F by allowing ± 0·4 for each degree above or below 60°F respectively. A thermometer is floated in the electrolyte to enable the temperature to be readily and accurately determined.

Some portable cells are provided with a type of specific gravity indicator in the form of coloured beads or a pivoted arm similar in appearance to a clock hand. These indicators provide only an approximate indication of the specific gravity of the electrolyte, and the degree of accuracy is reduced if the current varies from the appropriate rate for the cell.

Due to the decomposition of water during the gassing stage of the charging process, the level of the electrolyte in the cell gradually falls and it is necessary to maintain the specific gravity at the correct value by occasionally topping up with distilled water: the level of the electrolyte must always be sufficient to cover the tops of the plates fully.

The decrease in specific gravity during discharge of the cell is known as the specific gravity *range*. The quotient of the ampere-hour capacity divided by the specific gravity range is the *specific gravity constant*. These values are obtained from a test discharge taken when the cell is first installed.

4.32. Construction of Cells. To obtain a useful capacity it is usually necessary to employ several plates in a cell. The plates of like polarity are burned to a lead bar, the group of plates being referred to as a *section*: when placed in the cell the positive and negative plates interleave, the number of plates in the negative section being always one more than the number of positive plates in order to make use of all the positive surface and to avoid buckling.

Separators are placed between adjacent plates in order to minimize the risk of adjacent plates coming into contact with each other if buckling or displacement occurs. In the larger cells the separators are glass tubes held in position by guides on the negative plates: these guides may be seen on the plate shown in Fig. 4.21. The glass tubes rest upon the bottom of the container and protrude above the surface of the electrolyte sufficiently to support glass plates used for the purpose of arresting the loss of acid through spraying when the cell is gassing. The diameter of the glass tubes is equal to the spacing between the plates—approximately half an inch. For smaller cells separators of ebonite, p.v.c., rubber, or glass wool are used.

For small cells the containing vessel consists of a glass box either sealed or open. A complete cell

in open glass box is illustrated in Fig. 4.26, which clearly shows the glass rods. Constructional details are shown in Fig. 4.27. Cells of a capacity exceeding 300 Ah are contained in wooden tanks lined with chemically pure lead. Cells of this type are shown in Fig. 4.28 which demonstrates the size of these larger cells. Recent experience has shown that wrapped ebonite containers may have certain

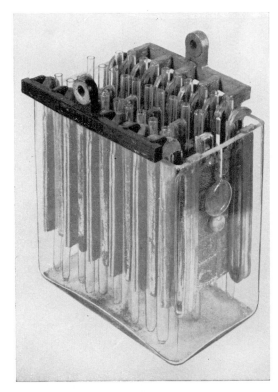

FIG. 4.26. SECONDARY CELL, 300 AH (D.P.)

advantages for large stationary cells. The plates of the smaller cells are supported by their projections on the edges of the glass container: in the lead-lined tanks the plates rest on glass slabs to insulate them from the lead lining. The depth of the container is proportioned to allow below the plates a clear space in which sediment may accumulate for a considerable time without touching the plates.

The end negative plates have a tendency to fan out causing the positive plates to be overworked on the upper surface: as a result there is a tendency for the positives to break away or to come into contact with the tank lining. To prevent this it is usual to insert end springs of hard lead between the end of the containing box and the outer negative plates, supplemented in the case of lead-lined tanks by glass separators between the springs and the plates. These springs are clearly shown in the illustration of Fig. 4.26.

An enclosed type of cell has recently been introduced for service in small telephone exchanges:

is followed by a uniform and more gradual rise a. the specific gravity of the electrolyte rises and the potential of the positive plate increases: a furthe abrupt rise occurs towards the end of the charge when the process is becoming largely one of the electrolysis of water. As the curves show, this fina

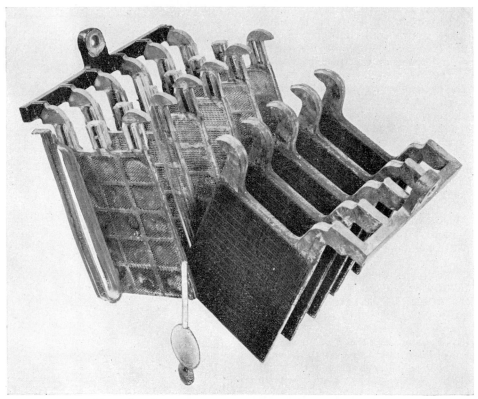

FIG. 4.27. CONSTRUCTIONAL DETAILS OF SECONDARY CELL
(*Courtesy of P.M.G.*)

with the closed container there is no risk of the acid spray due to gassing causing corrosion of adjacent equipment. A specially designed vent permits the escape of the gases liberated but successfully prevents the escape of acid spray. With open type cells a separate room is required to house the cells on account of the corrosion which would be produced on nearby apparatus.

4.33. Voltage Changes. Fig. 4.29A shows how the cell voltage undergoes change when a charging current is applied: a series of curves is shown for different charging rates. In each case the quantity of charge given is approximately the same, so that the longer the charging period the lower is the current strength. At first the e.m.f. rises abruptly due chiefly to a polarization counter-e.m.f.: this

e.m.f. of the cell, depending upon the rate of de. composition of the water, increases with the strength of the charging current and a value of 2·65 V or more may be reached: this value, however, drops to about 2·15 V immediately the termination of the charge prevents further electrolysis.

The corresponding e.m.f. changes for the discharge of the cell at various rates are shown in Fig. 4.29B. If the cell is left on open circuit after being charged, the voltage falls from 2·15 V to a value of the order of 2·05 V. This value drops gradually throughout the discharge due to the fall in the plate potentials and in the specific gravity of the electrolyte. The discharge should not be continued after the cell voltage has reached a figure of 1·83 V. The sharper voltage fall in the case of

FIG. 4.28. DUPLICATE 50-VOLT TELEPHONE EXCHANGE BATTERIES (CHARGE-DISCHARGE WORKING)

(Courtesy of P.M.G.)

heavy discharges is influenced by the lag in diffusion of the denser electrolyte from the pores of the plates.

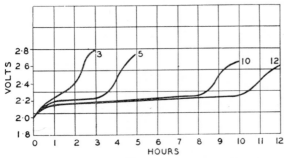

FIG. 4.29A. VOLTAGE VARIATIONS DURING CHARGE

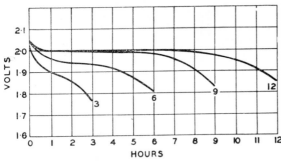

FIG. 4.29B. VOLTAGE VARIATIONS DURING DISCHARGE

4.34. Capacity of Cells. The capacity of any cell is not a fixed quantity but varies with the length of the period over which the discharge is spread, and to a lesser extent depends upon the temperature. The capacity of a cell is always stated in conjunction with the discharge period for which that capacity holds good: the period is referred to as the *rate*. The 9-hour rate is usually standardized for cells used in telegraph offices and telephone exchanges, but a 10-hr rate has recently been recommended by the British Standards Institution.

The ampere-hour capacity of a cell depends mainly upon the quantity and character of the active material and the specific gravity of the electrolyte. The quantity of active material is proportional to the size, thickness, and number of plates. It is found that for a given plate and any specified discharge rate there is a particular specific gravity of the electrolyte which gives the maximum capacity. The design of the plates, the porosity of the active material, and the temperature affect the rate of diffusion of the electrolyte. During discharge the density of the electrolyte in the pores of the active material is reduced and, unless the rate of diffusion is sufficient to make good this loss of density, the cell ceases to function. The capacity

is affected by the rate of chemical action, i.e. by the discharge rate, and is reduced for an increase in the discharge rate. Fig. 4.30 shows the percentage ampere-hour capacity of a given cell at different discharge rates, based upon the rated capacity when discharged over a 9-hr period.

The effect of an increase in temperature is to increase the e.m.f., and to reduce the resistance of the electrolyte and increase its rate of diffusion; this results in a greater capacity being obtained from the cell before its terminal p.d. falls to the minimum specified value. Corrections are made for temperature, usually to a figure of 60°F: in this case the corrected capacity for the 9-hr rate is ∓ 0.5 per cent for each degree above or below 60°F.

4.35. Internal Resistance of Secondary Cells
The internal resistance depends primarily upon the total plate area and the distance between the

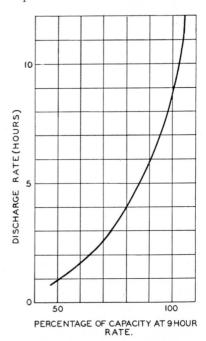

FIG. 4.30. CAPACITY VARIATIONS WITH DISCHARGE RATE

plates, and also upon the type of separator and the specific gravity and temperature of the electrolyte. The resistance of a secondary cell with $\frac{1}{2}$ in. glass tube separators is given approximately by the formula—

Internal resistance (ohms)

$= 0.25/$rated ampere-hour capacity

his gives a resistance of approximately 0·001 for cell of 300 Ah capacity with correspondingly maller values for larger cells. This low value gives he secondary cell one of its important advantages ver the primary cell. The voltage drop due to the tternal resistance is very small at the normal discharge rates and consequently the terminal p.d. is ractically constant with fairly wide changes of urrent.

4.36. Charging. The first charge which a cell eceives after being filled with electrolyte is termed he *initial* charge. Subsequent charges are either *rdinary* charges or *equalizing* charges. Equalizing harges are given periodically for the purpose of aaking good any deficiencies in the previous rdinary charges, to bring all cells to a uniformly illy charged condition and to reduce the possility of the formation of obdurate sulphate and s injurious effects.

In the INITIAL CHARGE the cells are filled with ifficient electrolyte of sp. gr. 1 215 to cover the lates by ⅛ in., and immediately given a prolonged harge commencing at about one half the normal tte (i.e. at the 18-hr rate). Frequent readings are taken of the specific gravity which gradually falls: hen the specific gravity has passed the minimum alue, the charging current is increased to the 9-hr tte and maintained at this figure until each cell eaches a uniform voltage of 2·65 V with all plates assing freely and the specific gravity remains con- cant for two hours. The charge is then terminated, nd after giving at least one hour for diffusion to ecome complete, the specific gravity is adjusted to value between 1 210 and 1 215.

For an ORDINARY CHARGE it is preferable to harge at about double the normal rate until assing commences: this enables a large part of ae charge to be given in a comparatively short me, and almost the whole energy is used in fectively charging the cells. When the voltage f the cell rises to 2·35 V, gassing commences and ae charging rate must be reduced since excessive assing tends to loosen and dislodge the active aaterial and the charging energy is largely wasted a decomposing the water of the electrolyte. To- ards the end of the charge the specific gravity acreases at a lower rate (see Fig. 4.24) due to the ifficulty in converting the remaining lead sul- hate: the greater part of the energy is causing assing and is consequently being used inefficiently. rdinary charges are therefore terminated before the ll is fully charged, generally after about 93 per cent f the full specific gravity range has been reached.

Pasted plate cells which are being "floated" aould receive four hours' gassing charge (over- aarge) each month to drive off antimony from the negative plates. This is necessary to avoid "poisoning"—the tendency for the antimony to separate from the lead and migrate from the positive grid to the negative active material (poisoned negatives) at very low charging rates.

EQUALIZING CHARGES are carried out in the same manner as ordinary charges but are continued until the specific gravity reaches a value which remains constant for one or two hours.

All specific gravity readings are corrected for a temperature of 60°F.

Undercharging results in lead sulphate being left on the plates, and if repeatedly undercharged, a cell loses capacity.

Overcharging produces excessive gassing, dis- lodging the active material and reducing the life of the plates. Particles of active material lodging on the negative plates are converted to lead and may accumulate sufficiently to bridge the gap between the positive and negative plates, producing internal short circuits. Excessive charging may also cause the plates to buckle.

4.37. Discharging. The discharge rate of a secondary cell is that constant current output which will discharge the cell in a certain number of hours. Thus with the 9-hr rate the capacity of the cell would be fully discharged in 9 hr.

The *assigned* capacity of a cell, upon which the maintenance of the cell is based, is derived from the result of a test discharge. From this test dis- charge the specific gravity range is determined. At the low rates of discharge used in telecommuni- cation installations the decrease of specific gravity with discharge may be taken as being proportional to, and a measure of, the number of ampere-hours discharged. The decrease in specific gravity by one hydrometer division represents approximately the discharge of a certain number of ampere-hours, known as the *ampere-hours per hydrometer division* at any part of the discharge. The residual capacity of a cell can thus be determined from the hydro- meter readings and a knowledge of the specific gravity range and the ampere-hours per hydro- meter division. Thus if a cell has an assigned capacity of 1 000 Ah and the specific gravity range is 50 divisions on the hydrometer, the ampere- hours per hydrometer division = 1 000/50 = 20. If the specific gravity after the last equalizing charge was 1 213 and the observed specific gravity at a given instant during a normal discharge is 1 180, the fall in specific gravity is (1 213 — 1 180) = 33 divisions. The remaining range available until full discharge is (50 — 33) = 17 divisions and this at 20 Ah per division represents 20 × 17 = 340 Ah.

The discharge should be stopped when the

4

specific gravity falls to a value which is equal to the specific gravity reached on the last equalizing charge less the specific gravity range.

Voltage and current readings are also taken during the discharge, for this information affords a means of keeping check on the capacity of the cell: the ultimate voltage reached depends upon the discharge rate. At the 9-hr rate a minimum voltage of 1·83 V should be reached—any value below this would indicate that the cell was losing capacity.

Under-discharging tends to produce sluggishness and a reduction in the capacity of the cell. Moreover, since repeated under-discharging necessitates more frequent charging, the ill-effects of gassing will be more pronounced.

Over-discharging has a serious effect on cells by producing an excessive amount of lead sulphate which cannot readily be removed and causes buckling of the plates.

4.38. Faults. If the cells receive careful treatment, faults are not likely to develop until after considerable service, but if maintenance attention is unsatisfactory, faults may be numerous and the life of the plates is reduced. The more common types of fault are sulphation, buckling, short circuits, corrosion, and decrease of specific gravity.

Sulphation is usually the result of overdischarging or insufficient charging: in this event the lead sulphate undergoes a physical change, gradually developing into larger and hardened crystals —a form which cannot be converted by charging. Plates affected in this way become lighter in colour, gas prematurely on charge, and lose capacity: they may be located by the cadmium test described below. Such plates cannot be satisfactorily reconditioned but some improvement may be effected by prolonged charging at a low rate.

Buckling is chiefly limited to positive plates and is caused by unequal stresses set up in various parts of a plate owing to uneven work, due, for instance, to partial sulphation or excessive charging or discharging. Excessive charging produces a larger amount of active material than the plate is designed to carry and this may not be distributed evenly. The lead base of the plate is also weakened and buckling consequently occurs. Buckling once commenced becomes progressively worse since both sides of the plate are not equidistant from the neighbouring plates and the uneven work is aggravated. For this reason buckling should be remedied in the early stages by removing and carefully straightening the affected plates with the application of pressure between two pieces of wood.

A short-circuit, or internal contact between the plates of opposite polarity, causes the plates to discharge internally, so lowering the voltage and specific gravity. Such a fault may be due to buckled plates or to *treeing*, i.e. an accumulation of spongy lead on the negative plates caused by disintegration of active material from excessive gassing, the suspended particles being carried to the negative plate as lead. The affected plates will be apparent by the presence of an excessively large potential drop across two widely separated points of the plate surface. If the trouble is caused by buckling, the plates must be straightened, or if due to treeing the growth must be carefully removed by means of a scaling stick. After removal of the fault the cell requires careful charging to restore it to normal.

Corrosion is liable to occur at the bolted connexions between adjacent cells and produce high resistance: it is frequently caused by a film of acid spray which promotes electro-chemical action. For this reason the connexions should be kept clean and tight and smeared with petroleum jelly. High resistance may also be caused by loose connexions owing to the plastic flow of the lead. Such faults may be located by the voltage drop across the connexions or by the presence of heat at these points.

Decrease in specific gravity may arise from the chemical reactions with the sediment deposited in the bottom of the tank as a result of excessive gassing: acid spraying while gassing and the occurrence of sulphation are also possible causes.

Contact between the plates and the lead lining of the container causes the lead lining to take the same colour as the plate with which it is in contact: the potential difference between the lining and either plate, which should normally be 1·6 V and 0·4 V for the positive and negative plate respectively, will be reduced.

4.39. Cadmium Testing. Cadmium testing is a useful method of determining the relative conditions of the positive and negative plates in a cell. Its commonest application is when a cell is low in capacity and it is desired to find whether this is due to a weak positive or a weak negative section.

Cadmium is a metal inert chemically to sulphuric acid and when inserted into the electrolyte of a cell it takes up a definite voltage with respect to the sulphuric acid. Hence the voltage between the positive plate and the cadmium electrode can be measured, and likewise the voltage between the negative group and the cadmium. The algebraic sum of these readings is, of course, the terminal voltage of the cell.

The cadmium electrode (Fig. 4.31) is in the form of a rod 2–3 in. long and contained in a perforated bonite sheathing in order to insulate it from contact with the plates. It should be immersed in the electrolyte between the centre plates of the cell and allowed to soak for an hour before the tests are made. All the cells should be brought into a thoroughly charged condition by giving them an equalizing charge, and the cadmium test applied towards the end of a discharge at the 9-hr rate. When the cell voltage has fallen to 1·9 V, the cadmium potentials should be read at intervals, while the discharge is continued down to 1·5 V. Owing to the possibility of polarization of the cadmium electrode, some inaccuracy in measuring

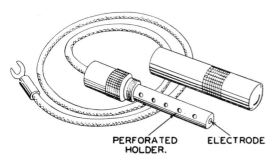

PERFORATED   ELECTRODE
HOLDER.

FIG. 4.31. CADMIUM TESTING ELECTRODE

the cadmium-to-positive potential may arise: consequently it is usual to obtain these values from the algebraic difference between the cell voltage and the negative-to-cadmium voltage.

On open circuit when the cell is giving, say, 2·05 V, the voltage between positive and cadmium will usually read about 2·20 V, and between negative and cadmium about 0·15 V, the cadmium then being negative to both the positive and negative groups. Towards the end of the discharge when the terminal voltage is, say, 1·85 V, the positive-to-cadmium reading will usually be between 2·03 V and 2·05 V, and the negative-to-cadmium between 0·18 V and 0·20 V. The positive-to-cadmium voltage thus falls gradually during discharge while the negative-to-cadmium voltage rises. If the positive voltage falls below or the negative voltage rises above these figures, the element in question is thus revealed to be weak, so that this test can readily be applied to any cell which has fallen below the minimum permissible voltage on a discharge test. In general, the plates which are failing are indicated by an appreciable and progressive change in the voltage readings.

4.40. Efficiency of Cells. The amount of energy obtainable from a secondary cell is always less than the amount of energy required to charge it.

The efficiency of a cell is considered in two respects, namely the ampere-hour (quantity) and the watt-hour (energy) efficiencies.

The ampere-hour efficiency of a cell is *the ratio of the quantity of electricity available during discharge to the quantity of electricity required during charge, under the conditions of a specified test*, or—

$$\eta = \left[\frac{(\text{ampere-hours discharge})}{(\text{ampere-hours charge})}\right] \times 100\%$$

Similarly, the watt-hour efficiency of a cell is *the ratio of the amount of energy available during discharge to the amount of energy required during charge under the conditions of a specified test*, or—

$$\eta = \left[\frac{(\text{watt-hours discharge})}{(\text{watt-hours charge})}\right] \times 100\%$$

Typical figures for the ampere-hour and watt-hour efficiencies are 90 per cent and 70 per cent respectively. The difference in these values may be attributed to the presence of internal resistance, and to the mean voltage on charge being greater than the mean voltage during discharge.

4.41. Alkaline Cells. If a battery of secondary cells is allowed to supply a load while at the same time it is actually being charged, the terminal voltage across the load will rise due to the battery voltage increasing from the nominal 2·0 V per cell up to 2·6 V per cell: such a wide variation in supply voltage is usually undesirable. In certain automatically controlled power plants where the charge and discharge overlap, the voltage at the bus-bars is maintained at a sensibly constant value by switching into circuit as required one or more cells whose e.m.f. opposes that of the main battery. In a telephone exchange the power supply must not be subjected to even a momentary interruption, and this necessitates switching these opposing, or counter-e.m.f., cells in and out of circuit by short-circuiting them during the switching operation. This procedure would be harmful to lead acid cells, and alkaline type cells are used for this purpose.

With this type of cell no formation of the plates takes place, all the energy applied to the cell being dissipated in heat and in decomposing the water of the electrolyte. No energy is stored in the plates and the cells can be short-circuited without harm.

With inert electrodes, a molecular layer of liberated gases from water electrolysis covers them and transforms them into gas electrodes, generating a definite e.m.f. in opposition to that which called the gases into being. Potassium hydroxide is used as the electrolyte to give a lower internal resistance.

Two views of this cell are shown in Fig. 4.32. The cell consists of an electrode assembly suspended from a lid within a glass jar containing the electrolyte, which consists of pure potassium hydroxide (KOH) solution diluted to a specific gravity of 1 190 approximately. The electrode assembly consists of a large number of thin nickel-plated mild-steel plates, interleaved in the manner of ordinary secondary cell plates and connected alternately to two posts, which are extended to form the two terminals of the cell. It is immaterial which post is used as the positive and which as the negative

under the lid, which consists of a lower portion of ebonite, a rubber gasket, and a top portion, also of ebonite, and these three sections are clamped between nuts on the upper portions of the terminal posts and washers resting on the shoulders of the posts. The rubber gasket serves to provide a gas-tight joint with the top of the glass box, so that all the gases evolved during the working of the cell are forced to escape via a special vent-plug fitted in the centre of the lid. This vent plug has wide

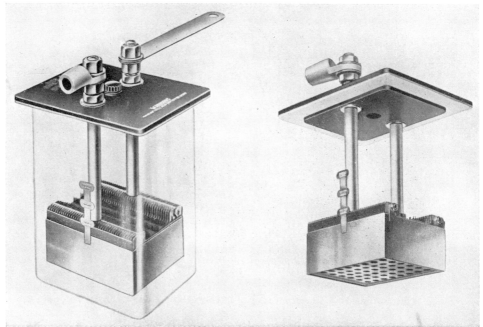

FIG. 4.32. ALKALINE TYPE CELLS
(*Courtesy of P.M.G.*)

terminal. The plates connected to the opposite posts are spaced by ebonite separators made in the form of a very narrow **U**. The separators are prevented from moving sideways by suitable projections formed in the plates, and are prevented from falling by resting on the base of a rectangular metal sleeve which encloses the complete plate assembly and is, incidentally, in contact with one of the terminals. To prevent contact between the edges of the plates and the inside of the sleeve, which would short-circuit the cell, a thin strip of ebonite is inserted between each end wall of the sleeve and the edges of the plates. The sleeve is open at the top and is provided with a sufficient number of holes in the bottom to allow free circulation of the electrolyte.

The terminal posts are provided with shoulders

passages, so that the velocity of flow of the gases is low; consequently very little spray is carried out of the cell, although it is quite normal for gassing or frothing to take place inside owing to the fact that most of the energy spent in the cell is dissipated in decomposing the water of the electrolyte.

Whilst all the parts of the cell below the lid are given a nickel plated finish to resist chemical action of the electrolyte, the terminal nuts and washers fitted on the posts projecting through the lid are lead plated to reduce the risk of corrosion when the cells are used in the same room as secondary cells of the lead-acid type. For convenience in checking the level of the electrolyte, a suitable indicator is fitted within the cell in the form of a strip of metal which is attached to the sleeve enclosing the plate assembly and carries markings to show the minimum permissible level, the maximum level, and the level at which the nominal specific gravity of 1 190 applies.

The decomposition of water predominates, and the electrodes occupy only a relatively small part of the cell container as it is essential to provide ample covering by the electrolyte, leaving space for the frothing which occurs: periodical topping up with distilled water is necessary to maintain the level between the limits indicated as these determine the specific gravity range and so govern the voltage. Owing to the hydrogen generated, naked lights should never be used near to these cells.

The voltage across the cell terminals is 2·0 V at a nominal loading of 0·11 A/in.² of plate, decreasing slightly if the current falls below the rated value. The cells are made up in various sizes.

Mention may be made of the NICKEL-IRON type of cell. This cell is constructed of steel plates with nickel oxide as the active material on the positives in an electrolyte of potassium hydroxide. The e.m.f. of a newly charged cell is about 1·4 V, falling to 1·0 V during discharge. The efficiency is lower than that for a lead acid cell, the nickel-iron cell having an energy efficiency of about 55 per cent and a quantity efficiency of about 70 per cent: its capacity is also more variable with temperature changes. The main advantages of the nickel-iron cells are their greater mechanical robustness and their ability to withstand greater discharging and charging currents. Their main field of application is in traction work.

The nickel-cadmium type, employing a mixture of iron and cadmium for the negative electrode, has the same general characteristics as the nickel-iron cell.

There is also the silver-zinc cell in which the positive electrode is of silver oxide, the negative electrode is zinc, and the electrolyte is a 45 per cent solution of potassium hydroxide. This cell has a very good power/weight ratio but it is naturally expensive in first cost.

GROUPING CELLS

4.42. Cells in Series. The maximum e.m.f. obtainable from a voltaic cell is about 2·0 V, and as this is insufficient for most requirements two or more cells must usually be grouped together. A combination of two or more cells electrically connected and employed as a single unit is called a battery. As with resistors there are similarly three ways in which cells may be arranged, (i) in series, (ii) in parallel, and (iii) in a series-parallel combination sometimes referred to as *multiple-arc*.

In the series arrangement the unlike terminals of adjacent cells are connected together in the manner of Fig. 4.33 (i) which illustrates three cells having e.m.f.s of E_1, E_2, and E_3 respectively. The free terminal of each end cell forms a terminal of the battery.

In the left-hand cell the positive terminal is E_1 volts positive with respect to the negative terminal (the battery terminal). In the centre cell the positive terminal is E_2 volts positive to the negative terminal, which is, however, at the same potential as the positive terminal of the first cell. Consequently there is a joint e.m.f. of $(E_1 + E_2)$ volts across the

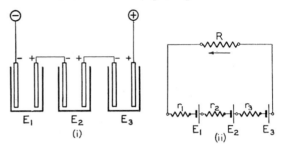

FIG. 4.33. CELLS IN SERIES

outer terminals of the first two cells. Similarly the negative terminal of the right-hand cell is at a potential of $(E_1 + E_2)$ volts above the negative battery terminal, so that the e.m.f. of the whole battery is $(E_1 + E_2 + E_3)$ volts.

For any battery of n cells of e.m.f. E_1, E_2, . . ., E_N respectively in series, the joint e.m.f.

$$E_T = E_1 + E_2 + \ldots + E_N$$

i.e. the total e.m.f. is equal to the sum of the separate e.m.f.s: if all the cells are of a similar type having an e.m.f. of E volts per cell, $E_T = nE$, i.e. the total e.m.f. is equal to the e.m.f. of one cell multiplied by the number of cells.

The internal resistances r_1, r_2, etc., of the individual cells also act in series, so that the joint internal resistance of the battery

$$r_T = r_1 + r_2 + \ldots + r_N$$

or if all cells have equal values r of internal resistance, $r_T = nr$.

If such a battery is applied to an external resistance R (Fig. 4.33 (ii)), the total e.m.f. $= nE$ and the total internal resistance $= nr$, so that the current is given by

$$I = nE/(R + nr)$$

EXAMPLE 4.14 (A). If 6 cells each having an e.m.f. of 1·5 V and an internal resistance of 1 Ω are joined in series, what current flows in an external resistance of 10 Ω?

Total e.m.f $= 6 \times 1.5 = 9.0$ V

Total internal resistance $= 6 \times 1.0 = 6.0$ Ω

$$I = 9.0/(10 + 6) = \underline{\underline{0.56 \text{ A}}}$$

EXAMPLE 4.15 (A). How many cells, each having an e.m.f. of 1·5 V and an internal resistance of 0·2 Ω, would be required to pass a current of 1·5 A through a resistance of 40 Ω? (C. & G.)

Let N be the number of cells joined in series.

Then total e.m.f. $= 1.5N$ and $r = 0.2N$

$$I = E/(R + r)$$
$$1.5 = 1.5N/(40 + 0.2N)$$
$$60 + 0.3N = 1.5N, \; 1.2N = 60, \; N = 60/1.2$$
$$= \underline{\underline{50 \text{ cells}}}$$

EXAMPLE 4.16 (A). If N cells, each having an e.m.f. E volts and an internal resistance r ohms, are joined in series through an external resistance R ohms, then the current I is equal to the e.m.f. of each cell multiplied by the number of cells and divided by the aggregate resistance, both external and internal. Find a formula expressing N in terms of r, R, E and I. Through what external resistance would 20 cells, for each of which E is 1·016 V and r is 0·45 Ω, drive a current of 0·8 A when arranged in series?

$$\text{Total e.m.f.} = NE$$
$$\text{Total internal resistance} = Nr$$
$$\text{Current } I = NE/(R + Nr)$$
$$IR + INr = NE$$
$$NE - INr = IR$$
$$N(E - Ir) = IR$$
$$N = \underline{\underline{IR/(E - Ir)}}$$

From $IR = N(E - Ir)$, $R = N(E - Ir)/I$

$\therefore \quad R = 20\{1.016 - (0.8 \times 0.45)\}/0.8$
$$= 20(1.016 - 0.36)/0.8$$
$$= 20(0.656)/0.8 = 13.12/0.8 = \underline{\underline{16.4 \ \Omega}}$$

4.43. Cells in Parallel.
In this arrangement all the positive electrodes are connected together and all the negative electrodes are also joined together as shown in Fig. 4.34 (i). All the electrodes of like polarity are at the same potential and so the e.m.f. of the battery is the same as that of a single cell. The internal resistances are in parallel so that if there are m similar cells the joint internal resistance of the battery equals r/m ohms. When connected to an external resistance R (Fig. 4.34 (ii)) the current is $I = E/(R + r/m)$.

The total current flowing in the external circuit is provided in equal proportions by the individual cells, and the output of current from each cell is

reduced accordingly. This may be of importance where a heavy current is required.

If the cells connected in parallel are not identical, it is usually necessary to apply Kirchhoff's laws.

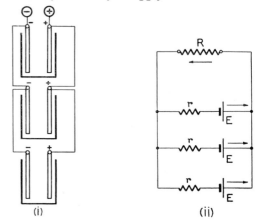

FIG. 4.34. CELLS IN PARALLEL

EXAMPLE 4.17 (A). If six cells each of 1·5 V e.m.f. and 1 Ω internal resistance are joined in parallel, what current flows in an external resistance of 10 Ω?

Total e.m.f. $= 1.5$ V

Total internal resistance $= 1.0/6 = 0.17 \ \Omega$

$$I = 1.5/(10 + 0.17) = 1.5/10.17 = \underline{\underline{0.15 \text{ A}}}$$

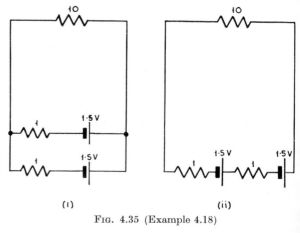

FIG. 4.35 (Example 4.18)

EXAMPLE 4.18 (A). Two cells each having an e.m.f. of 1·5 V and an internal resistance of 1 Ω are joined in parallel and are connected across a resistance of 10 Ω. What current flows through the resistance? What current would flow if the two cells were joined in series and were connected across the same resistance? (C. & G.)

The circuit diagrams are shown in Fig. 4.35 (i) and (ii).

(i) The joint internal resistance $= \frac{1}{2} = 0.5\ \Omega$.

The total e.m.f. is that of one cell, i.e. 1.5 V

Total current $= E/(R + r) = 1.5/(10 + 0.5)$
$$= 1.5/10.5 = \frac{1}{7} = 0.143\ \text{A}$$

(ii) $I = E/(R + r) = 3.0/(10 + 1 + 1) = \frac{3}{12}$
$$= 0.25\ \text{A}$$

EXAMPLE 4.19 (A). Two primary batteries having e.m.f.s of 20 V and 21 V, and internal resistances of 20 and 28 Ω respectively are connected in parallel. When the resistance of the external circuit has a certain value X ohms, the current supplied by each of the batteries is the same. Find this value of X. (C. & G.)

The circuit diagram is given in Fig. 4.36.

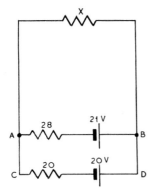

FIG. 4.36 (Example 4.19)

Let the current from each battery be I amps.

Then current in X is $2I$ amps.

P.d. across $X = 2IX =$ p.d. across $AB =$ p.d. across CD

„ „ $AB = E - Ir = 21 - 28I = 2IX$

„ „ $CD = 20 - 20I = 2IX$

$21 - 28I = 20 - 20I$, $8I = 1$ and $I = \frac{1}{8}$ A

Taking p.d. across AB, $21 - 28/8 = 2X/8$
$$35/2 = 2X/8$$

$$X = (35 \times 8)/(2 \times 2) = 70\ \Omega$$

EXAMPLE 4.20 (A). Two primary cells each having an e.m.f. of 1.4 V and a resistance of 0.4 Ω are (i) joined in parallel, (ii) joined in series, and connected across a resistance of 0.6 Ω. Find the current which flows in each case. (C. & G.)

The circuit diagrams are shown in Fig. 4.37.

(i) Total e.m.f. $= 1.4$ V
Total internal resistance $= 0.4/2 = 0.2\ \Omega$
Current $= 1.4/(0.6 + 0.2) = 1.4/0.8$
$$= 1.75\ \text{A}$$

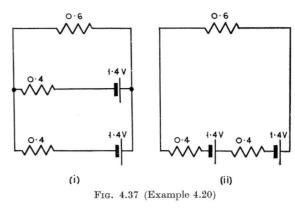

FIG. 4.37 (Example 4.20)

(ii) Total e.m.f. $= 2.8$ V
Total internal resistance $= 0.8\ \Omega$
Current $= 2.8/(0.6 + 0.8) = 2.8/1.4 = 2.0\ \text{A}$

EXAMPLE 4.21 (A). Two cells each having an e.m.f. of 2 V but having internal resistances of 0.3 and 0.2 Ω respectively are joined in parallel and are connected across a resistance of 0.68 Ω. What current flows through this resistance, and what current is drawn from each cell? (C. & G.)

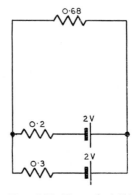

FIG. 4.38 (Example 4.21)

The circuit diagram is shown in Fig. 4.38.

The joint internal resistance
$$= (0.2 \times 0.3)/(0.2 + 0.3)$$
$$= 0.06/0.5 = 0.12\ \Omega$$

The total e.m.f. $= 2.0$ V

Current
$$= 2/(0.68 + 0.12) = 2/0.8 = \underline{\underline{2.5 \text{ A}}}$$

P.d. across $0.68 \ \Omega$
$$= IR = 2.5 \times 0.68 = 1.7 \text{ V}$$

Drop across internal resistance of battery
$$= 2 - 1.7 = 0.3 \text{ V}$$

Current in $0.2 \ \Omega$
$$= 0.3/0.2 = \underline{\underline{1.5 \text{ A}}}$$

Current in $0.3 \ \Omega$
$$= 0.3/0.3 = \underline{\underline{1.0 \text{ A}}}$$

4.44. Cells in Series-Parallel. This arrangement consists in connecting in parallel two or more batteries each made up of an equal number of cells joined in series. In Fig. 4.39 six cells have been

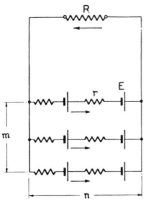

FIG. 4.39. CELLS IN SERIES-PARALLEL

arranged as three two-cell batteries in parallel and connected to an external resistance R.   he total e.m.f. E is equal to that of one series-battery or $E_T = nE$, n being the number of cells in series. The total internal resistance r_T of m such batteries in parallel is equivalent to m resistances, each equal to nr, in parallel, or $r_T = nr/m$. The current is

$$I = \frac{nE}{R + nr/m}$$

EXAMPLE 4.22 (A). If six cells each of e.m.f. 1.5 V and $1.0 \ \Omega$ internal resistance are arranged in three rows each of two cells per row, what current flows in an external resistance of $10 \ \Omega$?

$$\text{Total e.m.f.} = 2 \times 1.5 = 3.0 \text{ V}$$
$$\text{Total internal resistance} = (2 \times 1.0)/3 = 0.67 \ \Omega$$
$$I = 3.0/(10 + 0.67)$$
$$= \underline{\underline{0.28 \text{ A}}}$$

If the six cells were arranged in *two* rows each o three cells then—

$$\text{Total e.m.f.} = 3 \times 1.5 = 4.5 \text{ V}$$
$$\text{Total internal resistance} = (3 \times 1.0)/2 = 1.5 \ \Omega$$
$$I = 4.5/(10 + 1.5)$$
$$= 4.5/11.5 = \underline{\underline{0.39 \text{ A}}}$$

EXAMPLE 4.23 (A). A battery which is required to pass a current of 0.25 A through a resistance of $88 \ \Omega$ has to b assembled from cells each having an e.m.f. of 1.5 V an an internal resistance of $0.5 \ \Omega$. How many cells woul be required ?   (C. & G.

To pass a current of 0.25 A through a resistanc of $88 \ \Omega$ requires a p.d. of $V = IR = 0.25 \times 88$ $= 22$ V. Cells will therefore have to be arrange in series.

For N cells, total e.m.f. $= 1.5N$ V and tota internal resistance $= 0.5N \ \Omega$.

$$I = E/(R + r),$$
$$0.25 = 1.5N/(88 + 0.5N)$$
$$22 + 0.125N = 1.5N, \quad 1.5N - 0.125N = 22$$
$$1.375N = 22, \quad N = 22/1.375 = \underline{\underline{16 \text{ cells}}}$$

EXAMPLE 4.24 (A). A small manual exchange is to be served by means of primary cells, each cell having an e.m.f. of 1.5 V and an internal resistance of $0.5 \ \Omega$. The maximum current required is 2 A and the p.d. at the battery terminals must be kept within the limits 25–30 V. Calculate the number of cells required.   (C. & G.)

At "No-load," the maximum p.d. ($=$ e.m.f. must be 30 V.

Number of cells required in series
$$= 30/1.5 = 20 \text{ cells}$$

The internal resistance of this battery will be $20 \times 0.5 = 10 \ \Omega$.

At "Full-load," potential drop in battery $= 30 - 25 = 5$ V.

Total battery current $= 2$ A.

Permissible battery resistance
$$= V/I = 5/2 = 2.5 \ \Omega$$

To achieve this value, four similar batteries each of $10 \ \Omega$ resistance must be connected in parallel $(10/4 = 2.5)$.

Hence battery consists of 4 paralleled rows each of 20 cells in series and total number of cells $= 4 \times 20 = \underline{\underline{80 \text{ cells}}}$.

4.45. Reversed Cells. If in joining a number of cells in series any of the cells is reversed, the total

.m.f. will be reduced, but the total internal resistance will be unaffected. The e.m.f. will be equal to the e.m.f. of the larger number acting in one direction less the e.m.f. of the smaller number acting in the opposite direction.

If n cells each of e m.f. E are to be joined in series to form a battery of e.m.f. nE and one cell is accidentally reversed, then the battery e.m.f. is $(n-1)E$ volts less E volts due to the reversed cell, i.e. $(n-2)E$ volts, or two cells are deficient, the reversed cell neutralizing the e.m.f. of one other cell.

EXAMPLE 4.25 (A). A battery of 20 cells in series is connected to an external resistance of 580 Ω. Each cell has an e.m.f. of 1·5 V and an internal resistance of 1 Ω. Calculate the voltage across the terminals of the battery. By how much would this voltage be reduced if, owing to an error, one of the cells were connected in opposition to the remaining cells? What would be the p.d. across the reversed cell? (C. & G.)

Total e.m.f.
$$= 20 \times 1\cdot5 = 30 \text{ V}$$

Total internal resistance
$$= 20 \times 1 = 20 \ \Omega$$

External resistance
$$= 580 \ \Omega$$

Potential drop across 580 Ω
$$= (30 \times 580/600) = (30 \times 29)/30 = \underline{29 \text{ V}}$$

With one cell reversed—

Total e.m.f.
$$= 18 \times 1\cdot5 = 27 \text{ V}$$

Total internal resistance
$$= 20 \ \Omega$$

Potential drop across 580 Ω
$$= (27 \times 580/600) = 27 \times 29/30 = 26\cdot1 \text{ V}$$

Reduction in p.d.
$$= (29 - 26\cdot1) = \underline{2\cdot9 \text{ V}}$$

Circuit current $= V/R = (26\cdot1/580)$ A

P.d. across 1 Ω $= 1 \times 26\cdot1/580 = 0\cdot045$ V (due to current)

Actual p.d. $=$ e.m.f. $+$ p.d.
$$= (1\cdot5 + 0\cdot045) = \underline{1\cdot545 \text{ V}}$$

EXAMPLE 4.26 (A). Twelve cells, each 1·5 V and $\frac{1}{2}$ Ω internal resistance, are connected in series with an external resistance of 18 Ω. What is the current in the circuit? If four of the cells are connected in opposition to the others, what current will flow in the circuit? (C. & G.)

Total e.m.f. $= 12 \times 1\cdot5 = 18$ V
Total internal resistance $= 12 \times 0\cdot5 = 6$ Ω
External resistance $= 18$ Ω
$$I = E/(R + r)$$
$$= 18/(18 + 6) = 18/24$$
$$= 0\cdot75 \text{ A}$$

With four cells connected in opposition—

Total e.m.f. $= (12 - 8)1\cdot5 = 6$ V
Total internal resistance $= 6$ Ω
$$I = 6/(18 + 6) = 6/24$$
$$= 0\cdot25 \text{ A}$$

EXAMPLE 4.27 (A). Four primary cells arranged in series, each having an e.m.f. of 1·5 V and an internal resistance of 0·5 Ω. are connected to an external resistance of 28 Ω. If one of the cells were reversed, what would be the reading on a voltmeter connected across this cell? (C. & G.)

Total e.m.f.
$$= (4 - 2)1\cdot5 = 3 \text{ V}$$

Total internal resistance
$$= 4 \times 0\cdot5 = 2 \ \Omega$$

External resistance
$$= 28 \ \Omega$$
$$I = E/(R + r) = 3/(28 + 2) = 0\cdot1 \text{ A}$$

P.d. across reversed cell due to current
$$= 0\cdot1 \times 0\cdot5 = 0\cdot05 \text{ V}$$

Total p.d. across cell
$$= 1\cdot5 + 0\cdot05 = \underline{1\cdot55 \text{ V}}$$

4.46. Counter-E.M.F. Cells. It is sometimes desirable to connect one or more cells in opposition to a main battery in order to provide an alternative current supply at an e.m.f. lower than that provided by the main battery. The cells connected in a circuit in this manner, namely in such a way that their e.m.f. opposes the flow of current through them, are termed *counter-e.m.f. cells*. The current always flows through these cells in the charging direction, consequently secondary cells are employed and they are always fully charged: the counter-e.m.f. of each cell is approximately 2·6 V.

An example of such an arrangement is shown in Fig. 4.40 where cells are inserted in opposition to a 50-V main exchange battery to provide a 30-V supply for feeding power to private branch exchanges: no charging facilities are necessary for these counter-e.m.f. cells. For a main 50-V battery 25 cells are used: the counter-e.m.f. battery consists of 7 cells.

It will be observed that the alternative p.d. could not be provided satisfactorily by a potential-dropping resistance on account of the fluctuating voltage which would result from variations in the load.

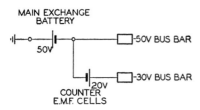

MAIN EXCHANGE
BATTERY

50V

-50V BUS BAR

20V
COUNTER
E.M.F. CELLS

-30V BUS BAR

FIG. 4.40. COUNTER-E.M.F. CELLS

4.47. Grouping Cells for Maximum Current.

The series method of connecting cells is normally used to form a battery, the parallel arrangement being actually equivalent to a single cell of larger dimensions. The three Examples (4.14, 4.17, and 4.22) given earlier demonstrate that a given number of cells can be made to furnish different values of current in the same external resistance depending on how the cells are connected.

The maximum current which can be obtained from any particular cell is reached when the cell is *short-circuited* (i.e. joined to an external circuit of zero resistance) and is equal to its e.m.f. divided by its internal resistance. Similarly, if a thousand such cells be placed in series and short-circuited, the maximum current will be still the same, for whilst the e.m.f. has been increased a thousandfold the internal resistance has been similarly increased. If it is desired to obtain a larger current from the cells, they must be placed in parallel. Every cell which is added increases the current for although the e.m.f. remains the same the internal resistance is reduced by every additional cell.

If the current produced by a number of cells joined up in series and flowing through a circuit of relatively *high resistance* is considered, it will at once be seen that the internal resistance of the cells is insignificant in comparison with the high external resistance. Each cell added in series will increase the current flowing in the circuit. Upon the other hand, the effect of joining cells in parallel is to reduce the total internal resistance, and this is of no consequence in comparison with the external resistance. The e.m.f. remains the same and consequently the addition of cells in parallel means no practical increase in the current available. It does, however, mean that each cell supplies only its proportion of the total current.

In order to obtain the maximum current from the minimum number of cells, the cells should be joined in series when the external resistance is large in comparison with that of the cell; whilst for a low external resistance the cells should be joined in parallel. Between the extremes already discussed come the cases when series-parallel arrangements are necessary. The rule relating to the grouping of cells is that the arrangement of cells which gives *an internal resistance most nearly approximating to the external resistance* will furnish the maximum current (see also §**3.5**). This statement is demonstrated mathematically below using the symbols of §**4.44**.

For the series-parallel arrangement,

$$I = \frac{nE}{R + nr/m} = \frac{mnE}{mR + nr}$$

Since mn (the total number of cells) and therefore mnE is constant, I will be *greatest* when $(mR + nr)$ has its *lowest* value. Now $(mR + nr)$ can be rewritten as

$$(\sqrt{mR} - \sqrt{nr})^2 + 2\sqrt{nmRr}$$

and since the squared term cannot have a negative value, the magnitude of the expression is least when $(\sqrt{mR} - \sqrt{nr})^2$ is zero, i.e. when

$$\sqrt{mR} = \sqrt{nr} \text{ or } R = nr/m$$

(nr/m is the internal resistance.)

The arrangement which produces the maximum current is that in which the internal resistance is geometrically (not arithmetically) nearest to the external resistance. For example, two battery arrangements having internal resistances of 10 Ω and 40 Ω respectively would produce equal currents in an external resistance of 20 Ω for 10 : 20 = 20 : 40. It follows, however, that the voltage drop in the battery is then equal to the voltage drop in the external resistance. The efficiency of the arrangement—the ratio of useful power to total power—is only 50 per cent.

The total number of cells, N, equals nm and the above condition is sometimes put in the form $n = \sqrt{(NR/r)}$.

For, as $nr/m = R$, $nr = mR$, $n = mR/r$,

$$n^2 = nmR/r = NR/r \text{ or } n = \sqrt{(NR/r)}$$

EXAMPLE 4.28 (A). How should 120 cells, each of e.m.f. 1·5 V and internal resistance 3 Ω, be arranged in order to pass a maximum current in an external resistance of 10 Ω? What is the value of this current?

If there are n cells in each row, and m rows $nm = 120$, or $m = 120/n$. For maximum current $nr/m = R$, or $nr \times n/120 = R$, $(n^2 \times 3)/120 = 10$,

$^2 = 400$ or $n = 20$, i.e. there should be 6 rows of 0 cells per row.

$$I = \frac{nE}{R + nr/m} = \frac{20 \times 1 \cdot 5}{10 + \dfrac{20 \times 3}{6}} = \frac{30}{10 + 10}$$

$$= 1 \cdot 5 \text{ A}$$

EXAMPLE 4.29 (A). Twelve voltaic cells each having a oltage of 1·5 and an internal resistance of 3 Ω are con-ected in a series-parallel arrangement to an external esistance of 9 Ω. The current is given by the expression $= 1 \cdot 5x/(\frac{1}{4}x^2 + 9)$ amps, where x is the number of cells series. Calculate the values of I as given by the formula or values of x from 4 to 8 and plot a curve of I against x. /hat arrangement of the cells makes the current a maximum and what is the relation between the internal nd external resistance? (C. & G.)

The values of I for values of x from 4 to 8 are alculated in the following table—

x	$1 \cdot 5x$ (a)	$\frac{1}{4}x^2 + 9$ (b)	$I \; (= a/b)$
4	6·0	13·0	0·462
5	7·5	15·25	0·492
6	9·0	18·0	0·500
7	10·5	21·25	0·494
8	12·0	25·0	0·480

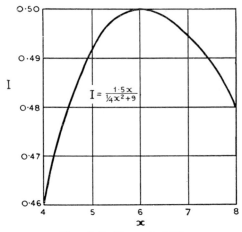

FIG. 4.41 (Example 4.29)

The required curve is plotted in Fig. 4.41, nd shows that the maximum current is reached /hen x (the number of cells in series) = 6. In this ase there are two such rows in parallel.

Total resistance of one row = $6 \times 3 = 18$ Ω

Joint resistance of two rows in parallel = $18/2$ = 9 Ω

In this condition the internal and external resistances are equal.

EXAMPLE 4.30 (A). How many Leclanché cells each hav-ing an e.m.f. of 1·4 V and an internal resistance of 1·25 Ω would be required to send a current of 100 mA through a resistance of 459 Ω ? Find the maximum current which could be sent, using the same number of cells, through a resistance of 5 Ω. (C. & G.)

The maximum current is obtained when the internal resistance of the battery is equal to the external resistance. As the external resistance is large (459 Ω) it will be necessary to connect all the cells in series.

Let N = required number of cells.

Total e.m.f. = $1 \cdot 4N$ V

Total internal resistance = $1 \cdot 25N$ Ω

External resistance = 459 Ω

Current = 0·1 A

$$I = E/(R + r)$$
$$0 \cdot 1 = 1 \cdot 4N/(459 + 1 \cdot 25N)$$
$$45 \cdot 9 + 0 \cdot 125N = 1 \cdot 4N$$
$$1 \cdot 4N - 0 \cdot 125N = 45 \cdot 9$$
$$1 \cdot 275N = 45 \cdot 9, \; N = 45 \cdot 9/1 \cdot 275$$
$$N = 36 \text{ cells}$$

Using the same number of cells with an external resistance of 5 Ω, the cells must be arranged so that their internal resistance is as nearly as possible equal to 5 Ω.

Let the number of cells per row be n

Let the number of rows be m

$mn = 36$ and $n = 36/m$

Total internal resistance = $nr/m = 5$.

Substituting $n = 36/m$ and $r = 1 \cdot 25$,
$$36 \times 1 \cdot 25/m^2 = 5,$$
$$\therefore m^2 = (36 \times 1 \cdot 25)/5 = 36 \times 0 \cdot 25 = 9 : m = 3.$$

$n = 36/m = 36/3 = 12$

Battery would consist of 3 rows each of 12 cells. Under these conditions total internal resistance = $(12 \times 1 \cdot 25)/3 = 5$ Ω.

Total e.m.f. = $12 \times 1 \cdot 4 = 16 \cdot 8$ V
$$I = 16 \cdot 8/(5 + 5) = 1 \cdot 68 \text{ A}$$

4.48. Unlike Cells in Parallel—Application of Kirchhoff's Laws. If cells connected in parallel have dissimilar e.m.f. and internal resistance, the simple rule given in §**4.43** for parallel cells is only approximately correct, and it becomes necessary to apply Kirchhoff's laws.

In Fig. 4.42 two cells of e.m.f. e_1 and e_2 and internal resistance r_1 and r_2 respectively are connected to an external resistance of R ohms: the currents furnished by each cell are i_1 and i_2 respectively.

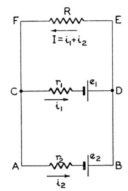

FIG. 4.42. UNLIKE CELLS IN PARALLEL

By Kirchhoff's first law,
$$I = i_1 + i_2$$

By Kirchhoff's second law for mesh $CDEF$,
$$e_1 = i_1r_1 + IR = i_1r_1 + (i_1 + i_2)R \qquad (i)$$

For mesh $ABEF$,
$$e_2 = i_2r_2 + IR = i_2r_2 + (i_1 + i_2)R \qquad (ii)$$

From (i)
$$i_1 = (e_1 - IR)/r_1$$

and from (ii)
$$i_2 = (e_2 - IR)/r_2$$

From these two expressions the values of the e.m.f.s, currents, or resistances can be calculated, given sufficient data. In the event of one of the paralleled cells being reversed, the sign of the currents concerned will naturally be changed.

EXAMPLE 4.31 (A). Find the current supplied by each battery in the circuit given in Fig. 4.43.

Let the currents be i_1 and i_2 as shown.

In mesh $ABEF$,
$$20 = 4(i_1 - i_2) + 10i_1 = 14i_1 - 4i_2 \qquad (i)$$

In mesh $DFEC$,
$$12 = -4(i_1 - i_2) + 8i_2 = -4i_1 + 12i_2 \qquad (ii)$$

Multiplying (i) by 3,
$$60 = 42i_1 - 12i_2$$

Adding (ii),
$$72 = 38i_1$$
$$i_1 = 72/38 = \underline{\underline{1.895 \text{ A}}}$$

From (i),
$$4i_2 = 14 \times 1.895 - 20 = 26.53 - 20$$
$$i_2 = 6.53/4 = \underline{\underline{1.632 \text{ A}}}$$

The current in the external resistance is $(i_1 - i_2)$ $= (1.895 - 1.632) = 0.263$ A.

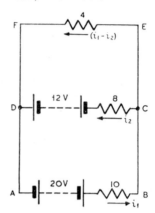

FIG. 4.43 (Example 4.31)

EXAMPLE 4.32 (A). A battery having an e.m.f. of 24 V and an internal resistance of 0.005 Ω is connected in parallel with another battery having an e.m.f. of 24.5 V and an internal resistance of $0.005\,5$ Ω. The two batteries supply current to an external resistance of 0.045 Ω. Calculate the current passing in each battery and the voltage applied to the external circuit.   (C. & G.

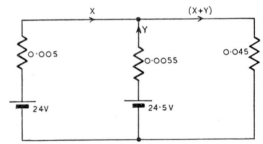

FIG. 4.44 (Example 4.32)

Let current from each battery be X and Y amps as shown in Fig. 4.44. Then by Kirchhoff's first law, current in load resistance is $X + Y$ amps.

Applying Kirchhoff's second law—
$$24 = 0.005X + 0.045(X + Y)$$
$$= 0.05X + 0.045Y \qquad (i)$$
$$24.5 = 0.005\,5Y + 0.045(X + Y)$$
$$= 0.045X + 0.050\,5Y \qquad (ii)$$

Multiplying (i) by 0.9,
$$21.6 = 0.045X + 0.040\,5Y \qquad (iii)$$

Subtract from (iii):

$$24·5 = 0·045X + 0·050\ 5Y$$
$$2·9 = 0·01Y,\quad Y = 290\ \text{A}$$

Substituting $Y = 290$ in (iii),

$$21·6 = 0·045X + 11·745,$$
$$21·6 − 11·745 = 0·045X,\quad X = 9·855/0·045$$
$$= 219\ \text{A}$$

P.d. across load, $V = IR = 0·045(X + Y)$
$$= 0·045(290 + 219)$$
$$= 0·045 × 509 = 22·905\ \text{V}$$

The floating battery principle involves two e.m.f.s connected in parallel.

Cases also occur in telegraph and telephone circuits where double battery networks arise from the signalling conditions at two ends of a line. A typical case is the Bridge Duplex telegraph circuit for which a full solution of a practical case is given below.

EXAMPLE 4.33 (A). Calculate the current flowing in each path of the Bridge Duplex telegraph circuit in Fig. 4.45.

The following data are used—

Line resistance = 1 000 Ω
Receiver circuit resistance = 8 200 Ω
Bridge arms resistance = 3 000 Ω
Balance resistance = 3 500 Ω
Internal resistance of battery = 100 Ω
E.m.f. of battery = 100 V

Using Maxwell's cyclic currents, and dividing each equation by 100 the solution tabulated below is obtained.

Equation		=	Batteries in Opposition	Batteries in Combination	
p-mesh	$66p - 30x - 35y$	=	1	1	(i)
x- ,,	$-30p + 142x - 82y$	=	0	0	(ii)
y- ,,	$-35p - 82x + 244y - 82z - 35q$	=	0	0	(iii)
z- ,,	$-82y + 142z - 30q$	=	0	0	(iv)
q- ,,	$-35y - 30z + 66q$	=	−1	1	(v)
Adding	$p + 30x + 10y + 30z + q$	=	0	2	(vi)
(i) × 10	$660p - 300x - 350y$	=	10	10	
(ii) × 22	$-660p + 3\ 124x - 1\ 804y$	=	0	0	
Adding	$2\ 824x - 2\ 154y$	=	10	10	(vii)
(vi) × 66	$66p + 1\ 980x + 660y + 1\ 980z + 66q$	=	0	132	
(i) × 1	$66p - 30x - 35y$	=	1	1	
Subtract	$2\ 010x + 695y + 1\ 980z + 66q$	=	−1	131	(viii)
(v)	$-35y - 30z + 66q$	=	−1	1	
(viii) − (v)	$2\ 010x + 730y + 2\ 010z$	=	0	130	(ix)
(vii) × 1 005	$2\ 838\ 120x - 2\ 164\ 770y$	=	10 050	10 050	
(ix) × 1 412	$2\ 838\ 120x + 1\ 030\ 760y + 2\ 838\ 120z$	=	0	183 560	
Subtract	$3\ 195\ 530y + 2\ 838\ 120z$	=	− 10 050	173 510	(x)
(iv) × 22	$- 1\ 804y + 3\ 124z - 660q$	=	0	0	
(v) × 10	$- 350y - 300z + 660q$	=	− 10	10	
Add	$- 2\ 154y + 2\ 824z$	=	− 10	10	(xi)
(xi) × 1 005	$- 2\ 164\ 770y + 2\ 838\ 120z$	=	− 10 050	10 050	
(x)	$3\ 195\ 530y + 2\ 838\ 120z$	=	− 10 050	173 510	
Subtract	$5\ 360\ 300y$	=	0	163 460	
From (vii)	y (line)	=	0	0·030 5 A or 30·5 mA	
	x (bridge arm)	=	3·54 mA	26·8 mA	
	z (,, ,,)	= −	3·54 mA	26·8 mA	
	p (battery)	=	16·76 mA	43·5 mA	
	q (,,)	= −	16·76 mA	43·5 mA	
	$q - z$ (bridge arm)	=	− 13·22 mA	16·7 mA	
	$p - x$ (,, ,,)	=	13·22 mA	16·7 mA	
	$y - x$ (receiver)	=		3·7 mA	
	$y - z$ (,,)	=		3·7 mA	
	$p - y$ (balance)	=		13·0 mA	
	$q - y$ (,,)	=		13·0 mA	

(The negative signs indicate currents in the reverse direction from those assumed by the cyclic arrows.)

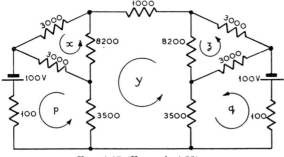

Fig. 4.45 (Example 4.33)

4.49. Charging Circuit. Cells may be given a *constant voltage charge*, i.e. a charge characterized by the application of a constant difference of potential to the terminals of the battery; or given a *constant current charge*—a charge characterized by controlled constant current through the battery. A modification of the latter method in general use is to commence charging the battery at the $4\frac{1}{2}$-hr rate (constant current) until gassing commences and thereafter to charge at constant current at the 9-hr rate: by this method the charging process is completed in a shorter time, and no harm is done to the cells.

Cells which are idle gradually lose their capacity by local action. To overcome this it is necessary to apply a steady charge with a very small current, so calculated as to compensate for the losses due to local action, allowing the battery to be constantly maintained in a fully charged condition: this steady charge at a low rate is known as a *trickle charge*.

With a constant voltage charge, the (back) e.m.f. of the battery rises during charge, consequently the magnitude of the charging current is automatically reduced as the charge proceeds.

In constant-current charging a rheostat must be connected in series with the battery or else a voltage regulator used with the charging generator so that the charging current may be maintained at the correct value. Since the opposing e.m.f. of the secondary battery varies from 1·83 V to 2·6 V per cell while being charged, a fairly wide variation of voltage is necessary quite apart from any changes from the normal charging rate.

When a battery is undergoing charge, the applied p.d. must exceed that of the opposing e.m.f. of the battery by an amount sufficient to drive the required current through the total resistance of the circuit. If the opposing e.m.f. of the cells is E volts, the p.d. of the charging supply is V, and the *total* resistance of the circuit is R, the resulting current

$$I = (V - E)/R$$

EXAMPLE 4.34 (A). What p.d. will be required at the commencement and end of charging an 11-cell battery at a constant current of 200 A, if the resistances of the charging source is 0·02 Ω, the leads 0·03 Ω, and the battery 0·04 Ω?

Resistance of circuit $= 0{\cdot}02 + 0{\cdot}03 + 0{\cdot}04$

$$= 0{\cdot}09\ \Omega$$

At beginning, $E_B = 1{\cdot}83 \times 11 = 20{\cdot}13$ V

P.d. in excess of 20·13 V to drive 200 A through 0·09 Ω

$$= 200 \times 0{\cdot}09 = 18\ \text{V}$$

P.d. of supply

$= (20{\cdot}13 + 18) = \underline{\underline{38{\cdot}13\ \text{V}}}$, at commencement of charge

At end $E_B = 2{\cdot}6 \times 11 = 28{\cdot}6$ V

P.d. to drive 200 A through 0·09 Ω $= 18$ V

P.d. of supply

$= (28{\cdot}6 + 18) = \underline{\underline{46{\cdot}6\ \text{V}}}$, at end of charge

EXAMPLE 4.35 (A). A 50-V exchange battery has a capacity of 400 Ah and an ampere-hour efficiency of 88 per cent. The voltages at the battery terminals required to maintain a constant charging current are 52 at the commencement of the charge and 70 at the end of the charge. It is desired to recharge the battery completely at a constant current from 120-V d.c. supply mains in $6\frac{1}{2}$ hr, using a series resistor of which part is variable. Calculate the current-carrying capacity required for the resistor units, and the values in ohms of the fixed and variable portions respectively. (*C. & G.*)

Total charge required

$$= (400 \times 100)/88 = 5\ 000/11\ \text{Ah}$$

During $6\frac{1}{2}$ hr at constant current, charging current

$$= 5\ 000/(11 \times 6{\cdot}5) = 70\ \text{A}$$

Current-carrying capacity of resistor units

$$= \underline{\underline{70\ \text{A}}}$$

Battery e.m.f. at beginning of charge $= 52$ V

Supply voltage $= 120$

Voltage to be dropped in series resistor

$$= (120 - 52) = 68\ \text{V}$$

Charging resistor to drop 68 V at 70 A

$$= V/I = 68/70 = 0{\cdot}971\ \Omega$$

Battery e.m.f. at end of charge $= 70$ V

Voltage to be dropped in series resistor
$$= (120 - 70) = 50 \text{ V}$$

Charging resistor to drop 50 V at 70 A
$$= V/I = 50/70 = 0.714 \ \Omega$$

This is the minimum series resistance required and it can therefore be the *fixed portion* $= \underline{0.714 \ \Omega}$

Variable portion $=$ maximum resistance
$$- \text{ fixed portion}$$
$$= 0.971 - 0.714 = \underline{0.257 \ \Omega}$$

EXAMPLE 4.36 (A). A telephone repeater station requires a continuous current of 5 A at a minimum voltage of 25 V which is supplied from a secondary battery. If this battery has to be fully charged in a period of 10 hr every seventh day, what is the required power output and voltage range of the charging generator? (*C. & G.*)

Minimum permissible voltage per cell $= 1.83$ V

Minimum battery voltage $= 25$ V

Number of cells required
$$= 25/1.83 = 13.6 \text{ or } 14 \text{ cells}$$

If battery is to be fully charged in a period of 10 hr every seventh day, discharge must last for 6 days and 14 hr $= (6 \times 24) + 14 = 158$ hr.

Capacity to discharge 5 A at this rate
$$= 5 \times 158 = 790 \text{ Ah}$$

Charge required at 90% efficiency
$$= (790 \times 100)/90 = 878 \text{ Ah}$$

To complete this charge in 10 hr at constant current requires a charging current of $878/10 = 88$ A.

Battery voltage at commencement of charge
$$= 14 \times 1.83 = 25.62 \text{ V}$$

Battery voltage at end of charge
$$= 14 \times 2.65 = 37.1 \text{ V}$$

Voltage range of charging generator
$$= \underline{25 \text{ V to } 38 \text{ V}}$$

Power output $= 38 \times 88$
$$= \underline{3.344 \text{ kW}}$$

EXAMPLE 4.37 (A). A 60-V, 100 Ah output secondary battery is charged from a 100-V d.c. supply through a series resistance. What is the approximate cost of one full charge if the battery is in good condition and the cost of the electricity is 1d./kWh? (*C. & G.*)

At an ampere-hour efficiency of 90 per cent, charge required $= (100 \times 100)/90 = 111$ Ah.

Energy required during charge
$$= VIt = 100 \times 111 = 11.1 \text{ kWh}$$

Cost at 1d./kWh
$$\underline{\underline{11.1\text{d.}}}$$

EXAMPLE 4.38 (A). What would be the maximum voltage required at the generator terminals to charge a typical battery of 11 cells at a normal rate of 200 A if the resistance of the charging panel equipment and busbars is $0.01 \ \Omega$? (*C. & G.*)

Maximum e.m.f. per cell at end of charge $= 2.6$ V

Total battery e.m.f. at 2.6 V per cell
$$= 11 \times 2.6 = 28.6 \text{ V}$$

Voltage drop in series equipment of $0.01 \ \Omega$ at 200 A
$$= IR = 0.01 \times 200 = 2 \text{ V}$$

Maximum voltage at terminals of charging generator
$$= \text{battery e.m.f.} + \text{p.d. in series equipment}$$
$$= 28.6 + 2 = \underline{\underline{30.6 \text{ V}}}$$

EXAMPLE 4.39 (A). A secondary battery consists of 20 cells in series, each having an e.m.f. of 1.8 V when discharged, and 2.6 V when charged. The internal resistance of each cell can be assumed to be constant and equal to $0.1 \ \Omega$. If a charging supply of 80 V is available, calculate the value of the variable series resistor required to maintain the charging current at a constant value of 10 A throughout the charging period. (*C. & G.*)

Battery e.m.f. at commencement of charge
$$= 20 \times 1.8 = 36 \text{ V}$$

Battery e.m.f. at end of charge
$$= 20 \times 2.6 = 52 \text{ V}$$

Internal voltage drop in cells ($0.1 \ \Omega$ each) at 10 A $= IR$
$$= 20 \times 0.1 \times 10 = 20 \text{ V}$$

Voltage to be dropped in series resistor at commencement of charge
$$= 80 - (36 + 20) = 24 \text{ V}$$

Voltage to be dropped in series resistor at end of charge
$$= 80 - (52 + 20) = 8 \text{ V}$$

Resistance required to drop 24 V at 10 A
$$= V/I = 24/10 = 2.4 \ \Omega$$

Resistance required to drop 8 V at 10 A
$$= V/I = 8/10 = 0{\cdot}8\ \Omega$$

The charging resistor must be variable between $0{\cdot}8\ \Omega$ and $2{\cdot}4\ \Omega$.

EXAMPLE 4.40 (A). The p.d. between the poles of a partly charged battery when it is being charged at 80 A is 51·5 V. The charging current is then stopped and the p.d. falls to 51 V. Calculate the p.d. between the poles of the battery when it is discharged at 160 A. (C. & G.)

Drop in voltage during charge
$$= (51{\cdot}5 - 51) = 0{\cdot}5\ \text{V}$$

Resistance for this drop at 80 A
$$= V/I = 0{\cdot}5/80\ \Omega$$

P.d. in this resistance at 160 A
$$= IR = (160 \times 0{\cdot}5)/80 = 1{\cdot}0\ \text{V}$$

P.d. at terminals when delivering 160 A
$$= 51 - 1 = 50\ \text{V}$$

EXAMPLE 4.41 (A). A battery charging unit has the circuit shown in Fig. 4.46 (a). It consists of a dynamo giving a steady output of 24 V d.c. independent of load, an ammeter, and a series resistor R adjustable from 0 to 10 Ω. The battery to be charged is connected to the terminals BC as shown, and while charging it has a back-e.m.f. of 14 V and an internal resistance of 2 Ω. Determine—

(a) the maximum charging current which can be given to the battery,

(b) the value of R necessary to give a charging current of 2 A.

For case (b) how much electrical power is lost in R and how much in the internal resistance of the battery? What happens to the remainder of the electrical power supplied by the dynamo? (C. & G.)

The current flowing in the circuit is that produced by the difference between the dynamo and battery voltages acting in a purely resistive circuit containing only the battery resistance of 2 Ω and the resistance R. This equivalent circuit is shown in Fig. 4.46(b).

(a) For maximum current R must be a minimum, i.e. $R = 0$.

Maximum charging current $= 10/2 = 5\ \text{A}$

(b) For a charging current of 2 A,
$$R + 2 = 10/2,\ R = 5 - 2 = 3\ \Omega$$

The energy dissipated in R
$$= I^2R = 2^2 \times 3 = 12\ \text{W}$$

The energy dissipated in the battery resistance of 2 Ω
$$= 2^2 \times 2 = 8\ \text{W}$$

Total resistance losses $= 12 + 8 = 20\ \text{W}$

Dynamo output $= E \times I = 24 \times 2 = 48\ \text{W}$

Of this 48 W, 20 W are lost as heat in the resistive part of the circuit: the remaining power of 28 W is converted into chemical energy in charging the battery.

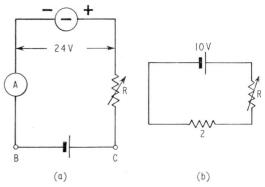

FIG. 4.46. (Example 4.41)

Details of charging circuits and equipment will be found in Chapter VIII.

4.50. Battery Floating. The present tendency for utilizing secondary cell batteries in telegraph offices and telephone exchanges is to avoid charging and discharging the cells: instead, an amount of electrical energy approximately equal to that required by the load is supplied by a d.c. generator (or rectifier) connected in parallel with the cells which are normally idle, neither gaining nor losing in electrical energy.

The process is known as *floating*: the cells are floated at 2·15 V at which value the condition of the cells remains stable. The presence of the battery across the generator assists in voltage control: also the capacity of the cells is available to meet any emergency due to stoppage of the external electricity supply, and is usually designed to provide 24 hr reserve. The main advantages of this method are (i) increased life of the plates due to the absence of gassing and of wear and tear of the plates by constant charging and discharging, (ii) less maintenance necessary, and (iii) a 50 per cent reduction in the capacity of the plates necessary for a given reserve, since the battery is always fully charged and no duplicate battery is required.

The basic connexions for a floating battery system utilizing a d.c. generator are depicted in

Fig. 4.47. In operation the output of the generator(s) is varied to keep pace with the load, but the

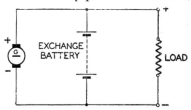

FIG. 4.47. FLOATING BATTERY

rapid fluctuations in load usually result in the flow of slight charging and discharging currents. To overcome this and also the slight loss of capacity (about 1 per cent) of an idle battery due to local action, a trickle charge is applied to the battery. In the practical application of a floating system, several alternative methods are available.

The floating system comprises two dissimilar e.m.f.s in parallel, and a solution of the current values involves the use of Kirchhoff's laws. Equipment details and also worked examples on battery floating circuits are given in Chapter VIII.

SUMMARY

Electrolysis of Water. $H_2O \rightarrow H_2$ (− electrode) + O (+ electrode).

Anode. Electrode by which *electrons* leave an electrolyte.

Cathode. Electrode by which *electrons* enter an electrolyte.

Coulomb. The quantity of electricity passing in 1 sec when the mean current is 1 A.

Faraday's Laws. (1) The chemical effect resulting from electrolysis is directly proportional to the quantity of electricity which has passed through the electrolyte.

(2) The quantity of each substance chemically changed or liberated at an electrode by the passage of a definite quantity of electricity is directly proportional to the equivalent weight of the substance.

Electro-chemical Equivalent (z). The mass of the substance undergoing electro-chemical change due to the passage of 1 C.

Mass Liberated by Electrolysis. $m = zQ = zIt$ g.

Simple Voltaic Cell. $Zn + H_2SO_4 \rightarrow H_2$ (+ electrode) + $ZnSO_4$ (− electrode).

Local Action. Due to minute voltaic cells within cell due to impurities.

Polarization. Due to formation of hydrogen film on positive electrode.

Internal Resistance (r). $E = IR + Ir$, or $1 = E/(R + r)$.

Leclanché Cell.

$$Zn + 2NH_4Cl \rightarrow 2NH_3 + H_2 \text{ (+ electrode)}$$
$$+ ZnCl_2 \text{ (− electrode)}$$

(Depolarizer) $2MnO_2 + H_2 \rightarrow Mn_2O_3 + H_2O$

Secondary Cells. Charged:

PbO_2 (+ plate) + $2H_2SO_4$ + Pb (− plate). Discharged:

$PbSO_4$ (+ plate) + $2H_2O$ + $PbSO_4$ (− plate).

Efficiency.

Quantity: $\dfrac{\text{Ampere-hour discharge}}{\text{Ampere-hour charge}} \times 100\%$

Energy: $\dfrac{\text{Watt-hour discharge}}{\text{Watt-hour charge}} \times 100\%$

Cells in Series. (i) E.m.f. = sum of separate e.m.f.s (ii) Internal resistance = sum of separate internal resistances.

Cells in Parallel. (i) E.m.f. = e.m.f. of one cell (if identical). (ii) Internal resistance = r/m (m similar cells in parallel).

Cells in Series-parallel. (i) E.m.f. = $n \times E$ (n similar cells in series). (ii) Internal resistance = nr/m (m similar parallel rows).

Maximum Current. When external resistance = internal resistance, $(R = r)$.

Charging Cells. V (source) = E (cells) + IR.

REFERENCES

1. P. B. FROST: "The Leakage of Direct Current and Potential Gradients in the Ground," *I.P.O.E.E. Journal*, **43** (1950). p. 125.
2. J. GERRARD: "Cathodic Protection of Underground Cables," ibid., **44** (1951), p. 71.
3. L. H. CATT: "Secondary Cells for British Post Office Telecommunications," *I.P.O.E.E. Printed Paper No.* **218** (1960),

CHAPTER V

ELECTROSTATICS

5.1. Electrification by Friction. Electrostatics is the science of electric charges at rest, including momentary charging and discharging currents. Prior to the discovery of the voltaic cell in the year 1800, there was no practical method of maintaining a continuous supply of electrical energy: consequently electrodynamics, the study of forces resulting from electricity in motion, i.e. the electric current, was unknown. Earlier methods of producing electric charges, known as far back as the year 600 B.C., depended upon some form of friction. The material commonly used to produce electricity by friction was amber, whose Greek name is *electron*.

If an ebonite rod is rubbed with fur it will be found that both ebonite and fur are capable of attracting small fragments of paper: this is due to electrification—the production of electric charges upon the ebonite and the fur as a result of the friction. Electric charges are produced in this manner in most materials. As one practical instance, in large telegraph offices where message forms are circulated amongst the operating positions by conveyor belts, the message forms show a tendency to adhere to the canvas belts on account of the electric charges produced in the moving belting.

5.2. Law of Attraction and Repulsion. If an electrified ebonite rod is carefully suspended by a silk thread and a second electrified ebonite rod is brought near to it, the suspended rod will be deflected away as the result of a force of repulsion which exists between the two ebonite rods. On the other hand, if a glass rod, which has been electrified by rubbing it with silk, is brought near to the suspended ebonite rod, a force of attraction is demonstrated between the two rods. Evidently there are two kinds of electric charge, and they are referred to as positive and negative electric charges.

A force of repulsion exists between two positively charged bodies (e.g. two charged glass rods) or between two negative charges (e.g. two charged ebonite rods): a force of attraction exists between positively and negatively charged bodies. In brief, like charges produce repulsion, and unlike charges produce attraction.

5.3. Application of Electron Theory. In terms of the Electron Theory, the effect of friction between the ebonite and the fur is to detach "free" orbital electrons from the fur, these electrons then being

acquired by the molecules of the ebonite. This leaves the fur with a deficit of electrons (positive charge $+ Q$) and the ebonite acquires an excess of electrons (negative charge $- Q$). The charges on both fur and ebonite are of equal magnitude, since their respective charges are due to the transfer of a number of electrons from one material to the other: this can be confirmed in a simple manner by experiment. Similarly for any other pair of materials, for example the glass and the silk, equal and opposite charges are produced on the two materials.

5.4. Conductors and Insulators. The ebonite, fur, glass, and silk considered above come under the heading of insulators and consequently the charge produced upon each shows no tendency to spread or to be conducted throughout the material, the charge remaining locally within the area where friction occurred. On the other hand, if a rod of brass or other conducting material is charged by friction, the charge will spread uniformly throughout the conducting material. In charging a conductor by friction it is essential to mount it in some insulating material, or *dielectric*, otherwise if the conductor is held in the hand the charge will be conducted away to earth through the body.

5.5. Coulomb's Law. If two small insulated conductors (Fig. 5.1) are charged and placed near to one another, a force of attraction (unlike charges) or repulsion (like charges) will exist

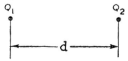

Fig. 5.1. Inverse Square Law

between them. As the result of measurement, it has been found that this force is directly proportional to the product of the charges, and *inversely* proportional to the *square* of the distance between them. This is COULOMB'S LAW. In symbols, if the charges are Q_1 and Q_2 coulombs respectively and the distance separating the charged conductors is d metres, the force F is given by

$$F = Q_1 Q_2 / (4\pi\varepsilon d^2) \text{ newtons} \qquad . \quad (5.1)$$

In any medium, for given charges the force is inversely proportional to the square of the distance between them: doubling or trebling the distance between the charged conductors results in a *reduction* of the force to one-quarter or one-ninth respectively.

The COULOMB is the unit of quantity of electric charge. The coulomb, as a quantity of electrostatic charge, is a considerable amount and the force which would result if $Q_1 = Q_2 = 1$ coulomb and $d = 1$ metre would be enormous (almost one million tons if air were the dielectric). In practical cases the charges would be measured in microcoulombs. The symbol ε denotes the *permittivity* of the medium separating the charges.

5.6. Permittivity. The force exerted between two charged conductors depends not only upon the magnitude of the charges and their distance apart, but also upon the nature of the dielectric which separates them. In the general expression for the force, $F = Q_1 Q_2/(4\pi\varepsilon d^2)$ newtons, ε is a factor known as the ABSOLUTE PERMITTIVITY of the dielectric medium.

TABLE 5.I

RELATIVE PERMITTIVITY (ε_r)

Material	ε_r
Air	1·0
Paraffin wax	2·0 to 2·2
Ebonite	2·0 to 4·0
Transformer oil . . .	2·2 to 2·3
Polythene	2·3
Pure rubber	2·34
Resin	2·5
Paragutta	2·7
Shellac	2·7 to 3·7
Wax impregnated paper . .	2·8 to 3·8
Beeswax	3·0
Gutta-percha . . .	3·4
Glass	3 to 9
Diakon	3·6
Bakelite	4 to 6·5
Porcelain	4 to 7
Mica	5 to 7
Aluminium oxide film . .	7·7 to 12·6
High capacitance ceramics . .	80 to 95

In a perfect vacuum, or in "free space," this absolute permittivity is usually termed the *permittivity of free space*: sometimes it is called the *electric space constant* or the *primary electric constant*. For this fundamental consideration, the permittivity of free space is designated by ε_0 and it has the value

$$\varepsilon_0 = 8{\cdot}854 \times 10^{-12}$$

The dimension of ε_0 is farads/metre. This quantity ε_0 frequently appears in calculations on electrostatic problems and it is useful to have some idea of how the value $\varepsilon_0 = 8{\cdot}854 \times 10^{-12}$ arises.

The velocity c of electromagnetic waves in free space is 3×10^8 metres/second. The permittivity of free space ε_0, together with a further constant μ_0 usually known as the *permeability of free space*, or sometimes as the *magnetic space constant* or the *primary magnetic constant*, is related to the velocity c in accordance with the expression

$$\mu_0\varepsilon_0 = 1/c^2$$

From this relationship,

$$\varepsilon_0 = 1/(\mu_0 c^2) \text{ farads/metre}$$

As a basic postulation in the establishment of the rationalized M.K.S. system of units (see Appendix **B** (vii)), the permeability of free space μ_0 is given the value

$$\mu_0 = 4\pi \times 10^{-7} \text{ henry/metre}$$

Substituting this value for μ_0 in the above relationship gives

$$\begin{aligned}
\varepsilon_0 &= 1/(\mu_0 c^2) \\
&= 1/(4\pi \times 10^{-7} \times 3 \times 10^8 \times 3 \times 10^8) \\
&= 10^{-9}/36\pi \\
&= 0{\cdot}008\,854 \times 10^{-9} \\
&= 8{\cdot}854 \times 10^{-12} \text{ farads/metre}
\end{aligned}$$

For any medium other than free space, the (absolute) value of its permittivity is different from ε_0. For example a particular wax may have a permittivity which is twice as great as that of free space and so equal to $2\varepsilon_0$ or $2 \times 8{\cdot}854 \times 10^{-12}$. For all dielectrics in common use it is convenient to determine their permittivity relative to that of free space. The wax quoted above would be said to have a *relative permittivity* of 2·0.

Relative permittivity for any material is designated by ε_r: this is simply a number or ratio. For any medium the *absolute* value of permittivity ε is then given by

$$\varepsilon = \varepsilon_r\varepsilon_0 \text{ farads/metre}$$

The relative permittivity of air is approximately equal to 1·0, so that its absolute value $\varepsilon = \varepsilon_r\varepsilon_0$ is approximately equal to ε_0 since $\varepsilon_r \simeq 1$, i.e. the absolute permittivity of air may be regarded as equal to $8{\cdot}854 \times 10^{-12}$ farads/metre.

Table 5.I gives the *relative* permittivities ε_r for a number of the more common dielectric media. In making calculations it will usually be necessary to use the absolute value of permittivity ε obtained from $\varepsilon = \varepsilon_r\varepsilon_0$. It will be found however that formulae are frequently written in the form $\varepsilon_r \varepsilon_0$ rather than in the form ε in order to draw attention to this point and prevent confusion. The use of ε_r and ε_0 in calculation is demonstrated in the worked examples later in the present chapter.

Relative permittivity ε_r was formerly known by the name *dielectric constant* or *specific inductive capacity*.

5.7. Induction. If a positively charged conductor A (Fig. 5.2) is brought near to a second conductor BC which is insulated but initially uncharged, equal negative and positive charges will be produced at B and C respectively: electrons of the second conductor are attracted towards the positively charged conductor, producing an excess of electrons (negative charge) at B and a deficit of electrons (positive charge) at C. When the charged conductor A is removed, electrons in the second conductor revert to their original distribution and this conductor now shows no evidence of any electric charge.

This phenomenon whereby a charge appears on

FIG. 5.2. ELECTROSTATIC INDUCTION FROM POSITIVE CHARGE

a hitherto uncharged conductor due to the proximity of a charged conductor is known as ELECTROSTATIC INDUCTION, and the charge gained by the second conductor is an induced charge. The positive and negative charges induced at B and C must be equal in magnitude, but, since B is nearer to A,

FIG. 5.3. ELECTROSTATIC INDUCTION FROM NEGATIVE CHARGE

a net force of attraction results between the charged conductor A and the inductively charged conductor BC. From this it follows that a force of attraction exists between any charged conductor and an uncharged conductor as a result of the induced charges.

If, on the other hand, the conductor A is given a negative charge (Fig. 5.3) it will repel the electrons from the uncharged conductor, resulting in an accumulation of electrons at C and a deficit at B so that the induced charges will appear as shown in the diagram, a force of attraction again being present.

Consideration will show that should two charged conductors be brought close together each will induce a charge on the other, and further, that any variations in the charge on either conductor will induce corresponding changes in the charge on the other. The practical effect of this induction on telegraph and telephone lines is discussed later.

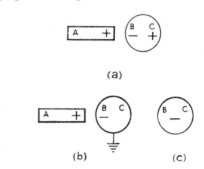

FIG. 5.4. CHARGING NEGATIVELY BY INDUCTION

5.8. Charging by Induction. Fig. 5.4 (a) shows a positively charged conductor A brought near to an initially uncharged conductor BC: induction results exactly as explained in connexion with Fig. 5.2. If the conductor BC is now connected to earth (Fig. 5.4 (b))—touching it with the finger is sufficient for this purpose—electrons will flow into BC from the earth to neutralize the positive charge at C. When the earth connexion and then the charging conductor A are both removed, BC will retain a negative charge (Fig. 5.4 (c)) distributed uniformly, due to the electrons which flowed in from the earth. In this way a negative charge is produced on BC.

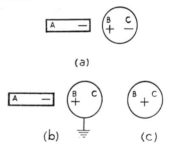

FIG. 5.5. CHARGING POSITIVELY BY INDUCTION

In a similar manner, a positive charge can be produced in BC by first charging A negatively: connecting BC to earth in this case causes electrons to flow from C to earth to neutralize the charge at C, leaving BC positively charged when the earth connexion and the inducing charge are removed. This case is illustrated in Fig. 5.5.

5.9. Charge Density. The density of a charge, indicated by the symbol D, is equal to the magnitude of the charge per unit area. If a charge of Q coulombs is distributed over an area A square metres, the charge density D is

$$D = Q/A \text{ coulombs/metre}$$

It is found from experiment that a charge does not spread uniformly over a conductor, unless it is

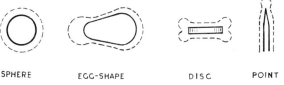

SPHERE   EGG-SHAPE   DISC   POINT

FIG. 5.6. CHARGE DENSITY

of spherical form, but tends to accumulate at the areas of greatest curvature. This is illustrated, in one plane, for various shapes of conductors in Fig. 5.6, where the charge density is proportional to the height of the dotted line above the conductor. This factor accounts for the use of pointed lightning conductors where it is required to collect the maximum charge.

When a conductor is charged, tests prove that the charge resides on the outside surface of the conductor, whether it is hollow or solid. This is demonstrated by Faraday's classic Butterfly Net experiment. A cotton or silk net is charged and the charge is found to reside on the outside only. The net is then turned inside out and the charge is again found to reside only on what has now become the outside of the net.

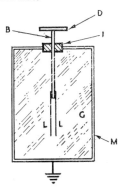

FIG. 5.7. GOLD-LEAF ELECTROSCOPE

5.10. The Electroscope. An electroscope is an instrument used for detecting the presence of an electric charge: it can also be used for distinguishing between positive and negative charges.

One type of such an instrument, the gold-leaf electroscope, is illustrated in Fig. 5.7. It has two strips of gold leaf (LL) attached to a vertical brass rod (B), the other end of which terminates in a horizontal thin brass disk (D). The leaves and part of the rod are enclosed within, and carefully insulated at (I) from a metal case (M) with glass (G) back and front. The metal case, which screens the gold leaves against draughts, is connected to earth: in the event of excessive charge, the leaves touch the case and are discharged to prevent damage. The action of the instrument depends upon induced charges.

In order to detect the presence of a charge on a given conductor it is brought near to the brass disk. If the conductor is charged, an induced charge appears on the gold leaves, and they diverge (Fig. 5.8 (a)): if the conductor carries no charge,

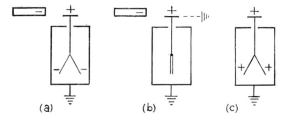

(a)   (b)   (c)

FIG. 5.8. CHARGING ELECTROSCOPE POSITIVELY

then there is naturally no induction and no movement of the leaves. To determine the sign of the charge being tested it is first necessary to charge the electroscope.

To charge the instrument positively, a charged ebonite rod (negative) is brought near to the electroscope disk (see Fig. 5.8 (a)). This induces a positive charge on the disk and a negative charge on the leaves, in the manner described earlier. The leaves diverge due to their mutual repulsion. The disk is then earth-connected by touching it with the finger, so leaving it positively charged; the leaves lose their charge so that they collapse (Fig. 5.8 (b)). When the finger is removed from the disk and the ebonite rod is then removed, the positive charge spreads to the leaves and they diverge again. The instrument is now charged positively (Fig. 5.8 (c)).

To determine the sign of a charge on a body, it is brought near to the disk. If it is a positive charge, the positive induced charge on the leaves increases and so does their divergence. On the other hand the presence of a negatively charged body near the disk decreases the charge on the leaves and decreases the divergence of the leaves. It is important that the presence of a charge be first detected by the uncharged electroscope before attempting to determine its sign because if an uncharged body were brought near to the charged electroscope the divergence of the leaves would decrease owing to induction from the electroscope to the uncharged body: hence an uncharged body would give the same result as a body carrying a charge opposite in sign to that of the electroscope.

Alternatively, the instrument can be charged negatively by using a charged glass rod (positive) instead of ebonite. The indications would then be the opposite of those described for the positively charged electroscope.

A piece of apparatus known as a *proof plane* is sometimes used to transfer some of the charge from the body under investigation. The proof plane is simply a small brass disk fixed to an insulating handle. To test the presence and sign of the charge on a body it is touched with the disk of the proof plane which acquires part of its charge (if any): the proof plane is then allowed to touch the electroscope disk. This procedure is useful, for example, in testing for the presence of a charge inside a hollow conductor.

5.11. The Electric Field. If a charged conductor is placed at any point, a second charged conductor brought anywhere near to it will experience a mechanical force, either of attraction or repulsion. Consequently it is reasonable to consider that an electric force, capable of producing mechanical force, exists in the region surrounding the charged conductor. *The space in the neighbourhood of a charged body, throughout which an electric charge would experience a mechanical force* is referred to as the ELECTRIC FIELD. The presence of an electric field also causes a movement or displacement of charge on conductors present in that field.

The strength of the electric field, or the ELECTRIC FORCE, denoted by the symbol E, is measured by the *potential gradient* present in the field. For example, if the potentials at two points in an electric field are V_1 and V_2 volts, then the potential difference between these points is $V = (V_1 - V_2)$ volts: suppose that these points are separated by a very small distance d, measured in metres, so that the field may be considered uniform between the points. Then this potential difference V falls uniformly between these points and the potential gradient is equal to $-V/d$ volts/metre. The electric field strength E is then said to be

$$E = -V/d \text{ volts/metre} . \qquad . \quad (5.2)$$

The reason for the negative sign is that the potential V *decreases* as the distance d *increases*, both being measured in the same direction from the same point.

It is stated in Table 5.II that the dielectric strength of air is 30 kV/cm. As an example, if this voltage $V = 30$ kV were applied across two electrodes placed at a distance $d = 1$ cm apart, the resulting electric field strength, or electric force, would be

$$E = V/d$$
$$= 30 \times 10^3/10^{-2}$$
$$= 3 \times 10^6 \text{ volts/metre}$$

At the other extreme, when planning sites for radio transmitters, measurements of electric field strength are made at suitable remote receiving stations: the field strength values in such cases are measured in millivolts/metre or in microvolts/metre.

Since a force has direction as well as magnitude, the direction of the electric force at any point in the

FIG. 5.9. ELECTRIC FIELD: ISOLATED CHARGES

field must be stated. It is defined as the direction in which a *positive* charge placed at that point would tend to move.

The state of the field surrounding a conductor is illustrated by plotting *lines of electric force*. The direction of a line at any given point indicates the

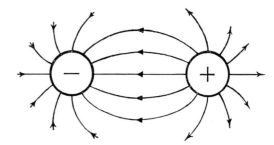

FIG. 5.10. ELECTRIC FIELD: UNLIKE CHARGES

direction of the field at that point, i.e. the direction in which a positive charge would tend to move if placed at that point.

The lines of force for typical fields are illustrated in Fig. 5.9 for isolated positive and negative charges; in Fig. 5.10 for adjacent unlike charges; and in Fig. 5.11 for adjacent similar charges. It should not be forgotten that these diagrams can show the field in one plane only, whereas in effect the field exists in three dimensions. It is convenient to picture each line as always endeavouring to contract so as to take the shortest path, while at the same time exerting a lateral force of repulsion on adjacent lines. All lines of force leave a positive charge and terminate upon a negative charge.

The electric force E is also measured by the mechanical force which it exerts upon a charge

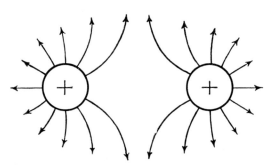

FIG. 5.11. ELECTRIC FIELD: SIMILAR CHARGES

placed at any point. The electric force at a point is one unit if a charge of one coulomb placed at this point experiences a force of one newton. Consequently a charge of Q coulombs would experience a force of Q newtons at a point where the field intensity is one unit, and a force $Q \times E$ newtons at a point where the field intensity is E units. With this conception, the field strength is expressed in *newtons/coulomb*: newtons per coulomb are of the same dimension as volts per metre. In these circumstances then the force is

$$F = QE \text{ newtons/coulomb} \qquad . \quad (5.3)$$

5.12. Electric Flux. The dielectric surrounding a charged conductor is in a state of electric strain owing to the opposition which it offers to the electric force exerted by the charged conductor. When a conductor is introduced into the field, the strain at that point disappears due to the charge which is induced on the conductor. This strain is known as the induction, the displacement or the FLUX, which may be defined as *the quantity of electricity displaced across a given area in a dielectric. The total flux displaced across a surface enclosing a charge is equal to the charge.*

Lines of induction or flux can be drawn to indicate the direction of the electric flux or displacement in the field surrounding a charged conductor: the direction of these lines for any normal dielectric is the same as the direction of the lines of force, so that Figs. 5.9, 5.10, and 5.11 represent also the fields of induction for these particular cases.

The unit of electric flux is the amount of electric flux associated with unit charge, namely with a

charge of one coulomb. It is, however, measured as an intensity, in terms of the charge of electricity moved per unit area, and so known as the *displacement density*, or as the *electric flux density*: it is designated by the symbol D. The unit of area is the square metre. Accordingly, for any area A square metres the flux density is

$$D = Q/A \text{ coulombs/square metre} \quad . \quad (5.4)$$

For a given charge Q and a given area A, the value of the flux density D is *independent of the nature of the medium* separating two charged conductors. Under the same conditions however, the magnitude of *the electric force E varies with the nature of the dielectric*. For any dielectric medium there is an important relation between the displacement D and the electric force E which can be verified experimentally. The ratio of D to E is the permittivity ε, a relationship which can be written for the general case

$$\varepsilon = \varepsilon_r \varepsilon_0 = D/E \text{ farads/metre} \qquad . \quad (5.5)$$

It follows that if the electric force *were maintained at a constant value* while the dielectric medium were changed from one material to another, the electric flux density would change with the material, i.e. if $E = k$, $D \propto E$. This relationship is used to define the RELATIVE PERMITTIVITY of a dielectric medium as *the ratio of the electric flux density produced in the medium to that produced in free space by the same electric force.*

The total flux from an electric charge is denoted by the symbol Ψ, so that $\Psi = DA$ and $\Psi = Q$ numerically.

It may be added that the flux density D is a mathematical concept which is postulated for practical purposes. The electric force E is primarily due to the charge Q or to the potential V which has caused it to exist. E and D may be regarded as being related as cause and effect. The factor ε_0 is a unit-defining constant.

5.13. Potential. The unit of potential is measured in terms of the energy expended in moving a charge against a force of repulsion.

In considering the field around a charged conductor (Fig. 5.12), if the conductor is positively charged, a positive charge at the point A will experience a force of repulsion, and energy will have to be expended to move it to point B which is at a higher potential than A. Similarly C is at a higher potential than B, and further energy is expended in moving the charge from B to C against the force of repulsion.

If one joule of energy is expended in moving a positive charge of one coulomb between two points against a force of repulsion, the potential difference between the two points is one volt.

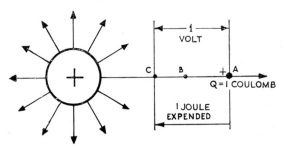

FIG. 5.12. UNIT OF POTENTIAL

5.14. Lines of Potential. Lines can be drawn joining together all points in a field which are at the same potential: they are known as *equipotential* lines. For an isolated charged spherical conductor the potential at all points distant r_1 metres from the centre of the sphere will be equal, and similarly all points distant r_2, r_3, etc., will be at

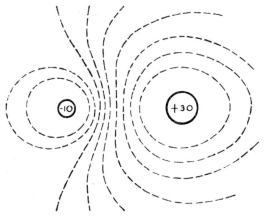

FIG. 5.13. EQUIPOTENTIAL LINES

the same potentials respectively. The surfaces of equipotential—surfaces throughout which no p.d. exists—will consequently be a series of concentric spheres, and a diagram illustrating this would be a series of concentric circles. The lines of equipotential for a field containing two or more charged conductors could be plotted as the result of calculations: a typical case is illustrated in Fig. 5.13.

The action of the gold-leaf electroscope may be explained in terms of potential. The disk and leaves acquire a positive (or negative) potential under the influence of a nearby positive (or negative) charge, the containing case remaining at earth potential:

due to the difference of potential between the leaves and the case, there is a force of attraction which causes the leaves to diverge. When the instrument is first given a positive or negative charge, the effect of bringing a like or unlike charge near to the disk is to increase or decrease, respectively, the potential of the disk and leaves: a greater or smaller divergence is then produced.

The induction due to a nearby charge (see Fig. 5.2) may also be explained by considering potential. In Fig. 5.14 is shown the positively

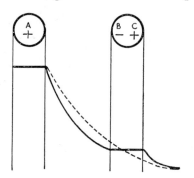

FIG. 5.14. POTENTIAL OF INDUCED CHARGE

charged conductor A: the dotted line shows the decrease of potential as the distance from A increases. When the conductor BC is placed in this field, the left-hand side B is at a higher potential than the right-hand side C: current flows in the conductor BC due to this potential difference until the potentials at B and C are equalized. The end B is now at a negative potential compared with the space surrounding it, and the end C is at a positive potential relative to the surrounding space. The modified potential fall is shown by the full line curves.

Charges induced in this manner are a common cause of interference with speech in telephone lines. If the charged source A represents one wire of an a.c. power transmission system, induced charges would cause hum in a receiver connected to the telephone line represented by BC.

5.15. Capacitance. The electrical CAPACITANCE of a conducting body is *the property by virtue of which a quantity of electricity has to be imparted to it to produce a difference of potential between it and the surrounding bodies.* Capacitance is denoted by the symbol C.

The hydraulic analogy may again be employed to draw a parallel between the capacity of a vessel and electrical capacitance. If two cylindrical vessels of different diameters are supplied with equal quantities of water, the level will be higher in the vessel of smaller diameter: similarly if two conductors of different sizes are charged with equal quantities of electricity, the electrical level, or potential, of the smaller conductor will be raised to a higher degree than the potential of the larger conductor.

As the charge on a conductor is increased, its potential rises, the potential V being proportional to the charge Q. At the same time, the smaller the conductor the more rapidly its potential rises for given increments in Q. The potential V is directly proportional to the quantity of charge Q, and inversely proportional to the capacitance C, or $V = Q/C$. This important expression may also be shown as

$$Q = VC \text{ or } C = Q/V \quad . \quad . \text{ (5.6)}$$

The capacitance of a conductor is therefore a measure of the ratio of its charge to its potential, when all neighbouring conductors are at zero potential.

The practical unit of capacitance is the FARAD: it is *that capacitance which requires a charge of one coulomb to raise its potential by one volt.* The farad is a unit considerably larger than the capacitance met with in practical conductors and capacitors, whose values are normally expressed in microfarads (μF) or picofarads ($\mu\mu$F or pF).

In the expression $C = Q/V$, the terms must be expressed in farads, coulombs, and volts respectively.

The capacitance of a conductor depends primarily upon its size and shape and upon the nature of the dielectric which surrounds it: it is also influenced by the presence of neighbouring charges.

It may be observed that a spherical conductor having a capacitance of one farad would have a radius of 9×10^9 cm, equal to $5 \cdot 5 \times 10^7$ miles. The capacitance of the earth, if regarded as a spherical conductor of 4 000 miles radius, is equal to about 715 μF.

When a charged conductor is connected to two or more other conductors, whether charged or uncharged, the combined charge will be re-distributed between the conductors so that they each acquire the same potential. Since $Q = CV$, V being constant $Q \propto C$ and the re-distribution of charge will be in direct proportion to the several capacitances.

5.16. The Capacitor. The potential of a charged conductor is increased due to the proximity of a second similarly charged conductor, and decreased by the proximity of a conductor carrying a charge of opposite sign. In the latter case, for a given charge this *reduction* in potential will *increase* the capacitance of the conductor because the product $VC \ (= Q)$ is constant.

This principle is usefully employed in the condenser, or CAPACITOR, which is a device for increasing the electrical capacitance of a conductor to store electrical energy as electric stress in a dielectric. In its simplest form, the capacitor consists of two flat metal plates separated by a thin layer of dielectric. If these conductors are connected to the terminals of a battery (Fig. 5.15), the two plates will acquire equal positive and negative charges: the charge on each plate will tend to lower the potential of the other, thus increasing the capacitance of the plates, and allowing a greater charge to flow into the capacitor.

The quantity of electricity on the positive plate is known as the charge on the capacitor. When the

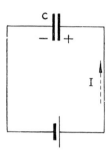

FIG. 5.15. SIMPLE CAPACITOR CIRCUIT

plates are brought to the same potential, by removing the e.m.f. and joining the plates by a conductor, the capacitor is said to be discharged.

For precise calculations, the insulation resistance of a capacitor must often be taken into account: a capacitor can be completely represented as a capacitance and a resistance joined either in series or in parallel.

In telecommunication equipment capacitors are used for a variety of purposes: for example, telegraph circuits employ capacitors to store electrical energy during certain short time intervals and restore it to the circuit when required to improve waveform. In telephone circuits, capacitors are frequently used to prevent the continuous flow of direct currents while permitting the "flow" of alternating currents. In a.c. circuits, capacitors are utilized to provide impedances of the required magnitudes and phase angles. A frequent use of the capacitor, in conjunction with the resistor, is to provide given time intervals.

5.17. The Parallel Plate Capacitor. In the parallel plate capacitor the plates are so close together that the field between them can be regarded as uniform. If the charge density is D, the surface area of *one side of one plate* is A square metres, the distance between the plates is d metres, and the permittivity is ε, the total charge Q may be calculated from

$$D = Q/A \quad . \quad \text{(equation 5.3)}$$

and is $Q = DA$ coulombs.

The p.d. V between the plates may be calculated from

$$E = V/d \quad . \quad \text{(equation 5.4)}$$

whence $\qquad V = Ed$

but from $\qquad D/E = \varepsilon \quad . \quad \text{(equation 5.6)}$

$$E = D/\varepsilon$$

whence $\qquad V = Ed = Dd/\varepsilon$

The capacitance

$$C = Q/V = DA \div Dd/\varepsilon$$
$$= \varepsilon A/d = \varepsilon_r \varepsilon_0 A/d \text{ farads} \qquad . \quad (5.7)$$

This shows that the capacitance of a capacitor is directly proportional to the plate area and to the permittivity, and inversely proportional to the thickness of the dielectric.

In the foregoing expressions it should be noted that A and d are in metre units, ε_r is the relative permittivity (see Table 5.I), and ε_0, the permittivity of free space, is equal to $8 \cdot 854 \times 10^{-12}$.

EXAMPLE 5.1 (A). What quantity of electricity will produce a difference of potential of 200 V between the plates of a capacitor of 5 μF? Compare the magnitudes of two capacitors, one having two circular plates 4 cm diameter and $\frac{1}{2}$ mm apart, and the other having two square plates 5 cm each side and $\frac{3}{4}$ mm apart. (C. & G.)

(i) $\quad V = 200$ V

$\qquad C = 5 \times 10^{-6}$ F

$\qquad Q = ?$

$\qquad C = Q/V$

$\qquad Q = CV = 5 \times 10^{-6} \times 2 \times 10^2$

$\qquad\qquad = 10^{-3}$ coulombs or $\underline{1\,000 \ \mu\text{C}}$

(ii) $\quad A_1 = \pi 4^2/4 = 4\pi$ cm^2

$\qquad A_2 = 5 \times 5 = 25$ cm^2

$\qquad d_1 = 0 \cdot 05$ cm

$\qquad d_2 = 0 \cdot 075$ cm

$\qquad C_1 = ?$

$\qquad C_2 = ?$

$\qquad C \propto A/d$

$C_1/C_2 = A_1 d_2/(A_2 d_1)$

$\qquad = (4\pi \times 0 \cdot 075)/(25 \times 0 \cdot 05) = 3 \cdot 77/5$

$\qquad = 0 \cdot 75$, i.e. the capacitances are in the ratio $\underline{3 : 4}$

EXAMPLE 5.2 (A). A simple capacitor, consisting of two insulated parallel plates, has a capacitance of $0 \cdot 001$ μF and receives a charge of 1 μC. What is the p.d. between the plates? What would be the capacitance if the area of each plate were trebled and the spacing between the plates halved? (C. & G.)

(i) $\quad C = Q/V$

$\qquad V = Q/C = 10^{-6}/10^{-9}$

$\qquad\qquad = \underline{1\,000 \text{ V}}$

(ii) $\quad A_1 = A$

$\qquad A_2 = 3A$

$\qquad d_1 = 2d$

$\qquad d_2 = d$

$\qquad C_1 = 10^{-9}$ F

$\qquad C_2 = ?$

$C_1/C_2 = A_1 d_2/(A_2 d_1) = (A \times d)/(3A \times 2d)$

$\qquad = \frac{1}{6}$, i.e. the capacitance would be increased six-fold to $\underline{0 \cdot 006 \ \mu\text{F}}$

EXAMPLE 5.3 (A). A variable capacitor of $1\,000$ $\mu\mu$F is charged to a p.d. of 100 V. The plates of the capacitor are then separated by means of an insulated rod so that the capacitance is reduced to 300 $\mu\mu$F. Would you expect the p.d. across the capacitor to have changed, and if so by how much? (C. & G.)

$C = Q/V$. For a constant value of Q, $V \propto 1/C$. If the capacitance is *reduced* by 10/3, the charge remains constant and the potential difference therefore *increases* by 10/3 to $100 \times 10/3 = 333$ V, i.e. increases by $(333 - 100) = \underline{233 \text{ V}}$.

EXAMPLE 5.4 (A). If a capacitor is to have a value of $0 \cdot 1$ μF and the paper utilized for the dielectric is 4 cm wide by $0 \cdot 02$ mm thick with a relative permittivity of $2 \cdot 25$, what length of paper would be required? (C. & G.)

$$C = 0 \cdot 1 \ \mu\text{F}$$
$$A = (l \times 0 \cdot 04) \text{ m}^2$$
$$\varepsilon_r = 2 \cdot 25$$
$$\varepsilon_0 = 8 \cdot 854 \times 10^{-12}$$
$$d = 0 \cdot 02 \times 10^{-3} \text{ m}$$
$$C = \varepsilon_r \varepsilon_0 A/d \text{ F}$$
$$= \varepsilon_r \varepsilon_0 wl \times 10^6/d \ \mu\text{F}$$

where l and w are the length and width of the dielectric.

$$l = C \times d/(\varepsilon_r \varepsilon_0 w \times 10^6)$$
$$= 0.1 \times 0.02 \times 10^{-3}/$$
$$(2.25 \times 8.854 \times 10^{-12} \times 0.04 \times 10^6)$$
$$= 200/79.7 = \underline{\underline{2.51 \text{ m}}}$$

EXAMPLE 5.5 (A). A capacitor consisting of two air-spaced parallel plates, each of effective area 1 000 cm² spaced 0·1 cm apart, is connected across a constant-voltage source of 500 V. Calculate the charge on the capacitor.

The permittivity of free space in M.K.S. units is 8·854 $\times 10^{-12}$ F/m. (C. & G.)

In air,

$C = \varepsilon_0 A/d$ farads

$A = 1\,000 \times 10^{-4}$ m²

$d = 0.1 \times 10^{-2}$ m

$\varepsilon_0 = 8.854 \times 10^{-12}$ F/m

$V = 500$ V

$$C = \frac{8.854 \times 10^{-12} \times 1\,000 \times 10^{-4}}{0.1 \times 10^{-2}}$$
$$= 885.4 \times 10^{-12} \text{ F}$$
$Q = CV = 885.4 \times 10^{-12} \times 500 = \underline{\underline{0.442\,7 \ \mu\text{C}}}$

EXAMPLE 5.6 (A). A parallel-plate capacitor has two metal plates, each of effective area 500 cm². Calculate its capacitance when the distance between the plates is adjusted to 0·5 cm.

A constant charging current of 2 μA is supplied to this capacitor. Calculate (a) for how many microseconds this charge must continue in order to raise the potential difference between the plates to 1 000 V. (b) Using the same two capacitor plates and the same charging current flowing for the same time as in (a) what alteration is necessary in the capacitor to ensure that the potential difference between the plates rises to twice the value obtained in (a)?

The permittivity of free space should be taken as 8·854 $\times 10^{-12}$ in M.K.S. units. (C. & G.)

In air,

$$C = \varepsilon_0 A/d = \frac{8.854 \times 10^{-12} \times 500 \times 10^{-4}}{5 \times 10^{-3}}$$
$$= 88.54 \times 10^{-12} = \underline{\underline{88.54 \ \mu\mu\text{F}}}$$

(a)
$$V = 1\,000 = Q/C = It/C$$
$$= \frac{2 \times 10^{-6} \times t \times 10^{-6}}{88.54 \times 10^{-12}}$$
$$t = 1\,000 \times 88.54/2 = \underline{\underline{44.27 \text{ msec}}}$$

(b) $2V = 2Q/C$, and since the charge Q will be unchanged when the alteration to the capacitor is made,

$$2V = Q/(C/2), \text{ i.e. } C \text{ must be halved}$$

The capacitance is inversely proportional to the distance between the plates so that the plates must be separated by twice the spacing, i.e. by 1·0 cm.

EXAMPLE 5.7 (A). Calculate the capacitance between two air-spaced parallel plates each of effective area 150 cm² spaced 1 mm apart. A potential difference of 100 V is maintained between the plates. What is

(a) the electric field strength between the plates,
(b) the charge held by the capacitance?

This capacitor is connected in a circuit which gives it a steady charging current of 1·0 μA. Draw a graph showing the relation between the voltage across the capacitor and the time during which the charging current has been flowing. Show values on your axes.

The permittivity of free space in M.K.S. units is 8·854 $\times 10^{-12}$ F/m. (C. & G.)

The capacitance $C = \varepsilon_r \varepsilon_0 A/d$ farads where $\varepsilon_r = 1$ for air

$\varepsilon_0 = 8.854 \times 10^{-12}$ F/m

$A = 150 \times 10^{-4}$ m²

$d = 10^{-3}$ m

$C = (1 \times 8.854 \times 10^{-12} \times 150 \times 10^{-4})/10^{-3}$
$= 133 \times 10^{-12}$ F $= \underline{\underline{133 \ \mu\mu\text{F}}}$

(a) The electric field strength (or electric force) in the dielectric is the electric potential gradient (or potential drop per unit length) across it. If a potential difference of V volts is maintained between the parallel plates of the capacitor d metres apart, the potential gradient

$$= V/d \text{ volts/metre}$$

When $V = 100$ V and $d = 10^{-3}$ m,

the electric field strength $= 100/10^{-3} = 10^5$ V/m

(b)
$$Q = CV = 133 \times 10^{-12} \times 100 = \underline{\underline{0.013\,3 \ \mu\text{C}}}$$

The charge Q coulombs from a current i flowing for t seconds is

$$Q = i \times t \text{ coulombs}$$

The p.d. is

$$V = Q/C = i \times t/C = (i/C) \times t$$
$$= \frac{10^{-6} t}{133 \times 10^{-12}} = 10^6 t/133 = \underline{\underline{7\,500t}}$$

This relationship can be represented by a straight line with a gradient such that the voltage increases steadily at a rate of 7 500 volts/second, as shown in Fig. 5.16.

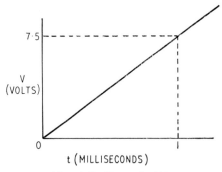

FIG. 5.16. (Example 5.7)

5.18. Dielectric Strength. If the potential difference across the dielectric separating a pair of charged conductors is excessive, the dielectric will break down and become a conductor.

The application of a normal voltage across a dielectric produces a small current: if the applied voltage is increased, the current increases also, proportionally at first, then less rapidly. With further increase of applied voltage the current rises with increasing rapidity and a stage is reached where the resistance of the dielectric suddenly falls to a low value with an enormous increase of current. The current flows as a spark or arc and the dielectric is punctured or broken down.

The property of an insulating material which enables it to withstand an electrical stress is termed the DIELECTRIC STRENGTH: it is measured by the maximum stress which an insulating material can successfully withstand, expressed usually in kilovolts per millimetre or centimetre thickness of the dielectric under specified conditions. The approximate dielectric strengths of various dielectrics are given in Table 5.II.

The mechanism of this breakdown is somewhat obscure: at some critical value of p.d. the force of attraction between the electrons in the dielectric and the positive plate exceeds the force with which the atoms of the dielectric retain their electrons. This p.d. imparts sufficient velocity for the orbital electrons to move through the dielectric. The breakdown will occur at a point in the dielectric either where the electric field is strongest or where the dielectric is weakest, neither being entirely homogeneous: in a solid the dielectric is punctured but in a liquid or gas dielectric the puncture is self-healing when the excessive voltage is removed.

TABLE 5.II

DIELECTRIC STRENGTHS

Material	kV/cm
Air	30
Mineral oils . . .	50– 80
Glass	75–300
Ebonite	270–400
Pure rubber . . .	330
Paraffin wax . . .	600
Mica	600–750
Gutta-percha . . .	830
Lead glass	1 000
Beeswax	1 100

The occurrence of spark and brush discharge depends upon the radius of curvature of the electrodes and is brought about more readily with a small radius.

The breakdown produces ionization which forms a conducting path between the conductors: in this event a continuous arc may be formed which, moreover, can then be maintained by a lower p.d. or over a greater distance. To avoid this occurrence on switchgear used for breaking heavy currents, various devices may be employed. In one form a "magnetic blow-out" is used: this utilizes a magnetic field which has the property of deflecting the arc to such an extent that it is curved sufficiently for its actual path to exceed the distance over which the arc can be maintained.

To obtain the maximum value of a capacitance, the thickness d of the dielectric must be as small as possible, but the value chosen must be a compromise with the thickness required to ensure adequate electric strength of the insulating material employed.

The phenomenon of electric breakdown is used to safeguard telephone and telegraph equipment against possible damage from lightning discharges. Lightning protectors, or spark gap arrestors are connected between line and earth at the point where external lines enter a building. The usual type consists of two small carbon blocks, one connected to the line wire and the other to earth. The two blocks are held in mechanical contact but they are separated electrically by a thin film of anti-dust varnish covered by a cellulose acetate insulating varnish applied to the contact face of each block to give a separation of about 0·004 in.

The surge voltage from a lightning discharge breaks down the varnish dielectric and forms a low resistance discharge path between line and earth, which has a greater conductance than the electrical equipment which it protects. The varnish coating self-healing when the lightning surge ceases. These protectors normally operate at voltages between 500 V and 750 V.

Gas-filled discharge tubes have the advantage that, for a given voltage, the electrodes may be more widely spaced than in air.

5.19. Dielectric Absorption. When a charged capacitor is discharged and then rested for a few minutes it will exhibit a further but smaller residual charge. This is believed to be due to a slight absorption of the charge by the dielectric itself. Although there is no general drift of electrons through the dielectric from one electrode to the other, a movement of electricity does occur. The electrons while remaining bound to the positive nucleus of the atom are moved from their mean equilibrium positions under the influence of the electric field. When in this state the dielectric is said to be polarized.

The electrons in the dielectric are strained towards the positively charged plate and a limited number of electrons from the negatively charged plate will enter the dielectric. The initial discharge of the capacitor neutralizes the charge on the plates, after which the small charge held in the dielectric moves on to the plates.

5.20. Dielectric Loss. Since there is no perfect insulating material the dielectric has a finite resistance and will carry a small leakage current. The total dissipation of energy which occurs in an insulating material when it is subjected to an alternating electric stress is known as the DIELECTRIC LOSS. With high grade capacitors this factor is negligible in many cases, but in a.c. work it must often be taken into account, particularly at high frequencies since it influences the phase angle. The insulation resistance of a capacitor is usually expressed in terms of its product with the capacitance. A usual specification for paper dielectric capacitors requires an insulation resistance of 300 MΩ-μF, after one minute's electrification at 100 V and at a temperature of 15°C. For a 2 μF capacitor, this is equivalent to an insulation resistance of not less than 150 MΩ. The reference to one minute's electrification is essential since, on account of dielectric absorption, the capacitor requires a measurable interval of time to become fully charged.

5.21. Capacitors. A 2 μF Mansbridge type of capacitor in general use is illustrated in Fig. 5.17. The conductor is formed from spraying finely divided tin upon one side of a sheet of paper: two such sheets of metallized paper are interleaved with and enclosed within two sheets of paper, impregnated with paraffin wax to reduce water absorption and improve the space factor. The whole is then rolled up into a compact form, compressed, and, after extracting all traces of moisture, sealed with insulating material such as bitumen into a damp-proof metal case. Copper strips making contact with the conducting surfaces of the two rolled "plates" are connected to two soldering tags.

Two sheets of metallized paper about 20 ft long and 3 in. wide by 0·000 5 in. thick are required to give a capacitance of 2 μF: the interleaving paper, of thickness about 0·000 5 in., is 3½ in. wide to permit of overlapping the conductors and minimizing the possibility of dielectric breakdown at

FIG. 5.17. MANSBRIDGE CAPACITOR
(*Courtesy of P.M.G.*)

the edges of the conductors. After manufacture the capacitors are subjected to tests for insulation resistance, capacitance, and dielectric strength. The insulation resistance is usually measured at 300 V after one minute's electrification to allow for dielectric absorption. The values of capacitance and safe working voltage are marked upon the metal case. This type of capacitor is relatively cheap to construct in a variety of values, but the losses become high above about 10 kc/s.

It is now generally recognized that capacitance, loss angle (the angle by which the angle of lead of the current falls short of 90°), insulance and voltage breakdown are all dependent upon temperature, time, frequency and the magnitude of the applied voltage. It is important to appreciate that when subjected to electric stress, capacitors are not the completely static devices which they appear to be: when connected to a d.c. source a small conduction current will be present in the capacitor. This current comprises electronic and ionic components in which the latter predominate due to the inevitable presence of impurities: products of electrolysis may react with the dielectric to produce further ionizable matter which in the early life of the capacitor is harmlessly disposed of by inhibitors which occur naturally in the dielectric but which become exhausted in course of time.

Ionic conduction, however, increases cumulatively until dielectric failure finally results from the conduction current becoming great enough to cause excessive local heating. The ionic conduction varies approximately as the logarithm of the temperature, and the life of a capacitor allowed to work at a high temperature may be considerably reduced unless the capacitor is specifically designed for that purpose.

In the design of a capacitor, the protection of the dielectric against moisture is an essential requirement. For small units used under normal conditions waxes and bitumens suffice as a sealing element, and the terminal wires serve also to hold the capacitors in position. On heavier units clamp plates of synthetic resin bonded paper (S.R.B.P.) may be used for mounting to prevent strain on the connecting wires. With increase of size the use of a metal container surrounding a bitumen-protected unit is common practice. The efficacy of enclosed capacitors is impaired, however, unless special attention is paid to the design of the projecting terminal tags.

Fully sealed capacitors with paper dielectric may include an oil filling to prevent the formation of voids—small gas or vacuum pockets in the dielectric caused by the contraction of waxes if subjected to temperature changes—which would result in points of increased electric stress where in effect the breakdown voltage would be decreased.

CERAMIC CAPACITORS. Ceramic as a dielectric is suited to use at high frequencies, is hard and durable, and it can be formed into robust capacitor units: the electrical properties are appreciably dependent upon frequency, temperature and applied voltage, and the application of ceramic capacitors is restricted to uses where accuracy of capacitance is unimportant. Ceramic materials fall into two main groups: (i) those based upon the use of pulverized rutile (titanium oxide) and characterized by high values of permittivity (up to $\varepsilon_r = 90$) but with comparatively high power loss: (ii) steatite, a form of the mineral talc (magnesium silicate), having good mechanical properties, which permit accurate shaping by grinding and polishing, with a permittivity of about $\varepsilon_r = 6\cdot5$ and a low dielectric loss.

SILVERED MICA CAPACITORS. Mica as a dielectric combines high permittivity with a low loss, both of these qualities being substantially independent of frequency and applied voltage.

Ruby mica is a mineral occurring naturally in a form which can be split into thin sheets or laminations to a thickness of about 0·001 in.: careful selection is necessary to eliminate imperfections and select the high quality which is essential for this purpose.

In the silvered mica class of capacitors, finely divided silver in a carrier material is sprayed or painted upon small sheets of pure mica. The silver glaze is applied to both sides of the mica with a short gap left on either side to separate the two electrodes. Fig. 5.18 illustrates the process by which, for example, two, four or eight electrodes may be cut from a given size of mica. These capacitor "plates" are then stacked in the desired numbers and the connecting wires soldered or otherwise secured to the opposite ends. Each capacitor is individually measured for capacitance, which can be adjusted to a fine tolerance (± 1 per cent) by scraping away some of the silvered surface. Finally the silvered mica stack is sealed in a container which may be of wax for ordinary use, or a synthetic resin moulding for tropical rating: for more arduous duty the stack may be enclosed in a sealed metal container with internal seals for the connecting wires to give the maximum protection against the ingress of moisture. Due to the high degree of bonding which can be achieved between the mica and the silver coating the stability with time and temperature of this class of mica capacitor is of a high order. The silver coating is very thin and on account of its resistance it is not suited for use on heavy current capacitors for which purpose metal-foil electrodes are preferable.

POLYSTYRENE CAPACITORS.[1] Capacitors with polystyrene as the dielectric are used extensively in high-grade electrical filters. Polystyrene is a synthetic plastic derived from polyethylene. It is strong and flexible from being stretched in two directions while still hot and soft from the forming process and cooled while under tension. The resulting film has a thickness of about 0·000 5 in. or less. Its permittivity $\varepsilon_r = 2\cdot5$: it has very high dielectric strength, very low power factor, very high insulation resistance, and is almost non-hygroscopic.

The conventional wound-construction is used in the preparation of polystyrene capacitors, with two foils usually of aluminium interleaved with two polystyrene film spacers (Fig. 5.19). Flat tinned-copper connecting leads are spot-welded to the metal foils. The polystyrene capacitor has a negative temperature coefficient of capacitance, a property which can be used in frequency-filters

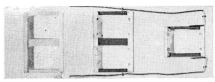

Approximately ⅛ actual size

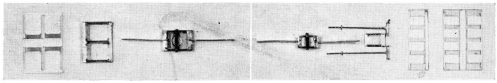

Approximately ¼ actual size   Approximately 1½ actual size

⅛ actual size   ¼ actual size   1½ actual size   ⅛ actual size   ⅛ actual size
SUPER TROPICAL   TROPICAL

FIG. 5.18. SILVERED MICA CAPACITORS
(Courtesy of Standard Telephones & Cables Ltd.)

to neutralize the positive coefficient of the ferrite core inductors used to complete the filter.

FERRO-ELECTRICITY. A class of materials, of which barium tartanate is an example, has been termed *ferro-electric* on account of the property of

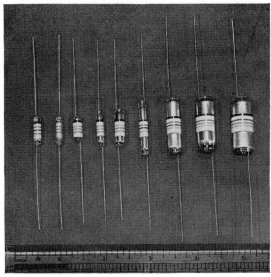

FIG. 5.19. POLYSTYRENE CAPACITORS
(Courtesy of Automatic Telephone & Electric Co., Ltd.)

hysteresis between applied voltage and the resulting electric charge.

These materials contain no iron, as the name ferro-electric might otherwise imply, but the name has been chosen to indicate the close resemblance between electric polarization and the magnetization of ferromagnetic materials. Ferro-electricity is rather a rare phenomenon. *Anti-ferro-electricity,* the analogue of anti-ferromagnetism, also exists in a number of chemical compounds. Barium tartanate is characterized by a high value of initial permittivity and it is used as the dielectric in ceramic capacitors. When made from single crystals a rectangular hysteresis loop results which can be used for signal information storage, as described in connexion with magnetic materials having rectangular hysteresis loops.

5.22. Variable Capacitors. These capacitors are usually constructed from two sets of multiple plates carefully insulated from one another, the dielectric being generally air, though mica, oil, or other materials are occasionally used for special purposes. The variation of capacitance is obtained by rotating one set of plates—the moving vanes—within the fixed vanes, so producing a change in overlapping or effective area. Slow motion reduction gearing is frequently incorporated to obtain precise settings of the vanes. The moving vanes carry a pointer moving over a 180° calibrated scale.

With the usual semicircular plates the capacitance at any given setting is proportional to the angle swept out by the pointer ($C \propto A$). For radio work it is often more convenient for the rotation of the plates to be proportional to the frequency or wavelength to which the capacitance is being adjusted. This is achieved by special shaping of the plates so that the swept area of the plates bears the required ratio to the angle of rotation.

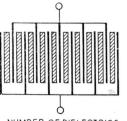

NUMBER OF DIELECTRICS = N
NUMBER OF PLATES = (N+1)

FIG. 5.20. MULTI-PLATE CAPACITOR

In calculating the capacitance value of a multi-plate capacitor, the effective area of one set of plates has to be considered. In a two-plate capacitor, the charge and hence the area of *one* side of *one* plate only enters into the expression for calculating capacitance. For the multi-plate pattern, the area of one side of each pair of plates has to be considered: the number of plates connected to one terminal is normally one greater than the number of plates connected to the other (Fig. 5.20).

For purposes of calculation the total plate area A is equal to the number of dielectric layers (n) multiplied by the surface area (a) of one side of one plate, or $A = na$: the *total* number of plates will be ($n + 1$). This is made clear in the following worked example and also in Example 5.26.

EXAMPLE 5.8 (A). A parallel plate capacitor consists of 11 plates each having an effective area of 100 cm² and spaced 0·02 mm apart. If the capacitance is 0·25 μF, what is the relative permittivity of the dielectric? If the capacitor receives a charge of 50 μC what is the p.d. developed across the plates?
(C. & G.)

$$A = (11 - 1)100 = 10^{-1}\,\text{m}^2$$
$$d = 0\cdot02\,\text{mm} = 2 \times 10^{-5}\,\text{m}$$
$$C = 0\cdot25 \times 10^{-6}\,\text{F}$$
$$\varepsilon_r = ?$$
$$\varepsilon_0 = 8\cdot854 \times 10^{-12}$$

(i) $C = \varepsilon_0\varepsilon_r A/d$
$$\varepsilon_r = Cd/A\varepsilon_0 = 0\cdot25 \times 10^{-6} \times 2 \times 10^{-5}/$$
$$(10^{-1} \times 8\cdot854 \times 10^{-12})$$
$$= 50/8\cdot854 = 5\cdot65$$

(ii) $$V = Q/C = 50/0\cdot25 = 200\,\text{V}$$

5.23. Non-inductive Capacitors. With the Mansbridge type of capacitor, the charge on the adjacent turns results in inductance. For capacitors of negligible inductance a modified method of construction is adopted in which the metallized paper "plates" overlap the dielectric at the ends—that is to say, one plate at either end of the dielectric—and copper strips make contact with every turn of the rolled conductor. Conductor resistance and power loss are also reduced by this form of construction.

5.24. Capacitors with Inherent Resistance. In spark quench circuits, where the energy of the spark must be consumed, it is necessary to use a resistor with a capacitor. It is sometimes convenient to incorporate this resistance with the capacitor by using plates of a suitable alloy possessing a higher resistivity than the usual conductor.

5.25. Electrolytic Capacitors.[2],[3] During recent years an electrolytic type of capacitor has come into extensive use for certain purposes in telecommunication equipment. Its principle depends upon the formation of a dielectric film upon a metal anode by electro-chemical action.

The elements of an electrolytic capacitor are shown in Fig. 5.21. The capacitor consists of two electrodes and an electrolyte: upon the anode a thin dielectric film is formed

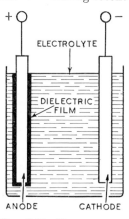

FIG. 5.21. ELEMENTS OF ELECTROLYTIC CAPACITOR

during the manufacturing process. This thin film has a high dielectric strength. In use, the negative electrode serves only to make contact with the outer surface of the dielectric film via the electrolyte: this contact is by electrolytic conduction, which gives the name to this class of capacitor. The electrolyte ensures also a continuous reforming of the dielectric film should this become deteriorated either by chemical action when the capacitor is lying idle for long periods, or by the application of excessive voltages.

The initial forming process is carried out in a separate forming bath. A high initial current flows but drops rapidly as the film forms. The water present in the electrolyte—usually ammonium borate—is dissociated into hydrogen which is liberated at the cathode, and oxygen ions which at the anode form an oxide layer on the metal electrode: the full composition of this layer is not accurately known. In use this coated anode must always remain positive, since the film will tend to be destroyed if the polarity is reversed: for this

...son the terminals of electrolytic capacitors ... always marked + and − and their correct ...nnexion in a circuit must be carefully observed. Aluminium is found to be a suitable metal for ...e electrodes: the basic material used for the ...ctrolyte is usually boric acid. Three main ...pes of construction have been adopted resulting ... the forms known as wet, semi-dry, and dry. A ...ajor problem in design is to produce the maxi-...um effective surface of film on the anode—a ...oblem somewhat similar to that of producing ...aximum surface of active material in secondary ...ll plates. To this end, various methods of ribb-...g, corrugating, perforating, roughening, or etch-...g the anode have been employed in the wet type: ...uminium foils for the dry types are usually pre-...red by an embossing or etching process which ...ay produce a fourfold increase in surface area.

It is essential for the metal of the electrodes ...d internal leads to be at least 99·99 per cent pure ... prevent possibility of chemical action with the ...ctrolyte during idle periods.

For the film-forming process, the selection of the ...rticular electrolyte and its dilution are deter-...ined by the requirements for producing a strong ...d stable film, on which the current density and ...e forming voltage also have an influence by ...ntrolling the rate of film formation. The forming ...ltage is usually about 10 per cent higher than ...e rated working voltage. The thickness of the ...m is roughly proportional to the forming ...ltage: the thinner the film, the greater the capa-...tance—$C \propto 1/d$—but a certain minimum thick-...ess is necessary to give adequate dielectric ...rength.

The composition of the working electrolyte may ...e different from that used in the forming process, ...r it has only to repair any possible defects occur-...ng in the film: it is important, however, that it ...ould have a low resistance in order to avoid ...ndue losses.

In the so-called dry type two foils and two ...pacers are rolled together (see Fig. 5.22) in the ...annner adopted for paper dielectric capacitors, ...nd held with tape or a rubber band. The foils ...ave a smaller width than the spacers to prevent ...ossible contact or dielectric breakdown at the ...dges. The best thickness for the foils is found to be ...f the order of 0·004 in. for the positive (bearing ...he dielectric film) and 0·002 in. for the negative, ...he positive foil being suitably treated to increase ...ts active surface area. The spacer is made of ...issue paper: it provides mechanical separation ...etween the foils and also holds the electrolyte.

Connexion between the foils and terminals is ...made by folding over the foil ends for direct connexion to the terminals: the connexions are thus integral with the foils and the use of joints within the electrolyte is avoided. One foil end is connected to a central insulated terminal, the other may be connected to the metal can which is used as the container. It should be noted that, although a metal container is frequently used and connected electrically to the negative electrode, this container does not form the cathode of the capacitor. The rolled sections are wrapped in waxed or oiled paper and carefully sealed in the container with wax or bitumen to prevent ingress of moisture.

The chief advantage of the electrolytic capacitor is the considerable capacitance which is made available in a small space and at a relatively low cost. This is mainly due to the thinness of the dielectric film and to the fairly high value of relative permittivity, which for aluminium oxide lies between 9 and 10. With this class of capacitor the leakage current is greater, compared with "solid" dielectric capacitors, due jointly to the lower specific insulation resistance of the dielectric film and also to the much larger capacitance present in a given space.

After a long period of idleness, a small reforming current flows until any deterioration of the dielectric film is made good. Both the capacitance and the leakage current tend to increase as the temperature increases.

The losses as measured by the power-factor are much higher for electrolytic capacitors, and may be between 2 and 40 per cent compared with less than 1 per cent for the solid dielectric type of capacitor.

A capacitance of 8 μF needs to have a total anode surface area of at least 70 in.^{2} With the present design of electrolytic capacitors, a safe working voltage up to about 550 V is possible: for use with greater voltages it is necessary to connect two or more capacitors in series. When ripple is present it is important that the combined peak value of d.c. voltage plus ripple should not exceed the working voltage: furthermore the ripple magnitude must not be so great as to reverse the polarity on alternate half-cycles.

By building up a capacitor with two electrodes, *each* coated with a dielectric layer, the capacitor becomes non-polarized—it has similar properties to the application of positive and negative poten-tials in either direction A thicker spacing is re-quired on account of the greater peak voltage, and the capacitance for given physical dimensions is reduced since both films are then in series. With an increase of frequency the capacitance falls and the power-factor rises. The electrolytic capacitor therefore, apart from specialized a.c.

5

applications, finds its greatest use in d.c. and low-frequency equipment, particularly in ripple-smoothing circuits.

After considerable use, the capacitance falls and the losses rise, so limiting the life of the capacitor: some deterioration also takes place during "shelf" life as with dry cells.

The construction of the tantalum-foil capacito follows that of the aluminium type: the tantalum and tantalum-oxide film are chemically inert an extremely resistant to corrosion. The woun tantalum unit is inserted into a silver capsule an impregnated under vacuum with the electrolyte.

Solid or sintered-anode tantalum capacito

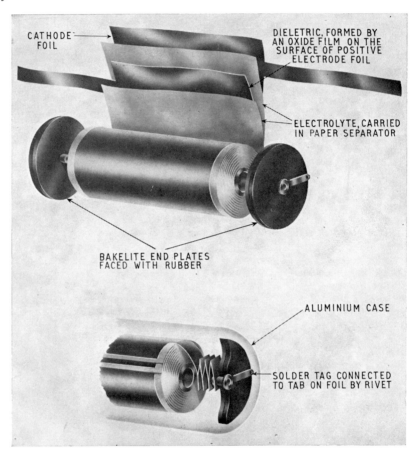

FIG. 5.22. CONSTRUCTIONAL DETAILS OF ELECTROLYTIC CAPACITOR
(Courtesy of Automatic Telephone & Electric Co. Ltd.)

TANTALUM CAPACITORS. Electrolytic capacitors with tantalum-foil electrodes have been recently introduced. Compared with the aluminium type, while more costly the tantalum capacitor has a much higher relative permittivity ($\varepsilon_r = 27$), improved characteristics, greater stability in performance, and an improved storage life. Tantalum electrolytic capacitors are largely used with transistor equipment where working voltages are very low and capacitance values require to be relatively large on account of the low impedances involved.

are made from tantalum powder which is compacte to form a pellet around a tantalum terminal wir (Fig. 5.23): this is then sintered at very high tem perature and low pressure so that particles joi together without melting and the pellet presents large surface area. The porous tantalum is the formed with a tantalum-pentoxide film by elec trolysis after which all traces of electrolyte ar removed. Contact is made with this by a semi conductor, manganese dioxide. The all-dry con struction is completed by a cathode connexio of a layer of carbon and a metallized coating. Th uter case, which forms the cathode connexion, is usually of silver. The sintered tantalum capacitor has a very high capacitance/volume ratio and a low inductance.

A wet sintered-anode tantalum capacitor is also available. The construction follows that of the dry

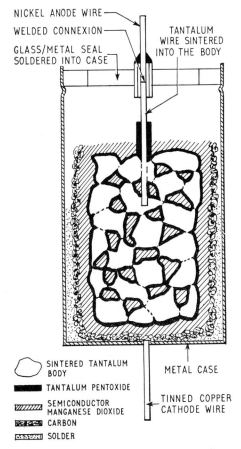

NICKEL ANODE WIRE
WELDED CONNEXION
GLASS/METAL SEAL
SOLDERED INTO CASE
TANTALUM WIRE SINTERED INTO THE BODY

SINTERED TANTALUM BODY
TANTALUM PENTOXIDE
SEMICONDUCTOR MANGANESE DIOXIDE
CARBON
SOLDER
METAL CASE
TINNED COPPER CATHODE WIRE

FIG. 5.23. DRY SINTERED-ANODE TANTALUM CAPACITOR
(*Courtesy of Standard Telephones & Cables Ltd.*)

design but uses a wet electrolyte which may be either sulphuric acid or a neutral solution such as lithium chloride. The sintered types are hermetically sealed.

5.26. Capacitors in Series. If two or more capacitors are connected in series, the joint or effective capacitance of the combination is equal to the reciprocal of the sum of the reciprocals of the separate capacitances.

In Fig. 5.24 three capacitors of C_1, C_2, and C_3 units of capacitance respectively are connected in series across a supply at a p.d. of V volts. When the circuit is closed, electrons from the negative

terminal will flow to charge one plate of capacitor C_3 negatively: an equal number of electrons will be repelled from the second plate of this capacitor (leaving it positively charged) to the electrically connected plate of capacitor C_2 giving it an equal negative charge. A similar electron flow will charge

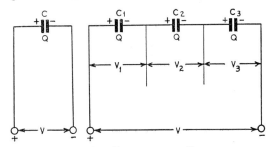

FIG. 5.24. CAPACITORS IN SERIES

the second plate of capacitor C_2 positively and produce equal and opposite charges on the plates of capacitor C_1. Each capacitor in the series combination will carry an equal charge Q units. If the p.d.s across the three capacitors are V_1, V_2, and V_3 respectively, then

$$V_1 = Q/C_1, \quad V_2 = Q/C_2, \quad \text{and} \quad V_3 = Q/C_3$$

The total applied p.d.

$$V = V_1 + V_2 + V_3 = Q/C_1 + Q/C_2 + Q/C_3$$
$$= Q(1/C_1 + 1/C_2 + 1/C_3)$$

The p.d. across the equivalent capacitor carrying this same charge Q is

$$V = Q/C$$

so that

$$Q/C = Q(1/C_1 + 1/C_2 + 1/C_3)$$

or $$1/C = 1/C_1 + 1/C_2 + 1/C_3 \qquad . \quad (5.8)$$

This expression for the joint value of capacitors in *series* is of similar form to that for resistors in *parallel*. The equivalent value of a number of capacitors in series is less than the value of the smallest of the individual capacitors.

For two capacitors C_1 and C_2 only, in series, the joint capacitance is calculated from

$$1/C = 1/C_1 + 1/C_2 = (C_2 + C_1)/(C_1 C_2)$$

or $$C = C_1 C_2/(C_1 + C_2) = \text{product/sum}$$

For N equal capacitors C' in series, the equivalent capacitance C is given by

$$1/C = 1/C' + 1/C' + 1/C' + \ldots = N/C'$$

or $$C = C'/N$$

EXAMPLE 5.9 (A). A $2\,\mu$F capacitor is connected in series with a second capacitor and the capacitance of the combination is $1\cdot2\,\mu$F. What is the value of the second capacitor?   (C. & G.)

$$C = \text{product/sum}$$
$$= C_1C_2/(C_1 + C_2)$$
$$CC_1 + CC_2 = C_1C_2$$
$$C_1C_2 - CC_2 = CC_1$$
$$C_2(C_1 - C) = CC_1$$
$$C_2 = CC_1/(C_1 - C)$$
$$= (1\cdot2 \times 2)/(2 - 1\cdot2) = 2\cdot4/0\cdot8$$
$$= 3\,\mu\text{F}$$

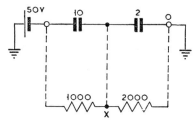

FIG. 5.25 (Example 5.10)

EXAMPLE 5.10 (A). Two capacitors of $10\,\mu$F and $2\,\mu$F respectively are joined in series. One end of the series is earthed and the other end joined to a 50 V exchange battery. What will be the charge held by each capacitor? The larger capacitor is then shunted by $1\,000\,\Omega$ and the smaller by $2\,000\,\Omega$; will the charges be altered, and if so, what will now be the charge on each?   (C. & G.)

Joint capacitance = product/sum

$$= (10 \times 2)/(10 + 2) = 20/12\,\mu\text{F}$$
$$Q = CV = (20/12) \times 50$$
$$= (1\,000/12)\mu\text{C} = 83\cdot3\,\mu\text{C}$$

This will be the charge on *each* capacitor.

The voltage drop in the shunting resistances will be uniform, so that the potential at point X (see Fig. 5.25) will be $33\frac{1}{3}$ V.

When shunted the p.d. across the $10\,\mu$F capacitor becomes

$$(50 \times \tfrac{1}{3}) = 50/3\text{ V}$$

and the p.d. across the $2\,\mu$F capacitor becomes

$$(50 \times \tfrac{2}{3}) = 100/3\text{ V}$$
$$Q_1 = C_1V_1 = 10 \times 50/3 = 166\cdot67\,\mu\text{C}$$
$$Q_2 = C_2V_2 = 2 \times 100/3 = 66\cdot67\,\mu\text{C}$$

EXAMPLE 5.11 (A). Two capacitors of $2\cdot5\,\mu$F and $3\cdot5\,\mu$F respectively are connected in series. What is their joint capacitance? If the two capacitors in series are connected to the terminals of a 60 V battery with the positive

terminal joined to earth, what will be the charge on each capacitor and the potential of each of the terminals? Show in a diagram the potentials across the capacitors.

(C. & G.)

(i) $C = \text{product/sum}$
$$= (\tfrac{5}{2} \times \tfrac{7}{2}) \div (\tfrac{5}{2} + \tfrac{7}{2})$$
$$= 35/(4 \times 6)$$
$$= 35/24 = 1\cdot46\,\mu\text{F}$$

(ii) With the capacitors in series they will have the same charge

$$Q = VC = 60 \times 35/24 = 87\cdot5\,\mu\text{C}$$

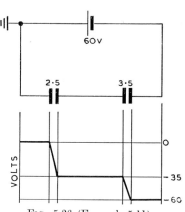

FIG. 5.26 (Example 5.11)

From $V = Q/C$, $V \propto 1/C$. The p.d. across each capacitor is therefore in inverse proportion to its capacitance. Their capacitances are in the proportion $C_1/C_2 = \frac{5}{7}$ (and $7 + 5 = 12$)

$$V_1 = 60 \times 7/12 = 35\text{ V}$$
$$V_2 = 60 \times 5/12 = 25\text{ V}$$

Fig. 5.26 shows the capacitors and the p.d.s across them.

EXAMPLE 5.12 (A). Two capacitors of $0\cdot02\,\mu$F and $0\cdot04\,\mu$F are connected in series across a 100 V d.c. supply. What would be the voltage developed across each capacitor if the insulation resistance of each capacitor is (a) infinitely great, (b) $1\,\text{M}\Omega$?   (C. & G.)

(a) Since the capacitors are in series they will have equal charges and the p.d. across each obeys $V \propto 1/C$. Their capacitances are in the ratio $C_1/C_2 = \frac{1}{2}$.

P.d. across $0\cdot02\,\mu$F capacitor
$$= 100 \times \tfrac{2}{3} = 66\cdot7\text{ V}$$

P.d. across $0\cdot04\,\mu$F capacitor
$$= 100 \times \tfrac{1}{3} = 33\cdot3\text{ V}$$

(b) Since the insulation resistance of each capacitor is the same, the potential at point X in Fig. 5.27 will be 50 V and the p.d. across each capacitor will be the same, i.e. 100/2 or 50 V.

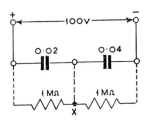

Fig. 5.27 (Example 5.12)

5.27. Capacitors in Parallel. Fig. 5.28 shows three capacitors of C_1, C_2, and C_3 units respectively connected in parallel across a source of p.d. of

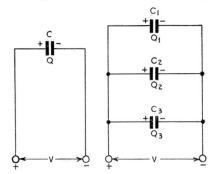

Fig. 5.28. Capacitors in Parallel

V volts. In this arrangement the p.d. across each capacitor is the same, V volts, and the charge taken by each capacitor, Q_1, Q_2, and Q_3, depends upon its capacitance ($Q \propto C$ if V is constant). The equivalent capacitance of C units would carry a charge

$$Q = Q_1 + Q_2 + Q_3 = C_1 V + C_2 V + C_3 V$$

But, for the equivalent capacitance $Q = CV$, hence

$$CV = C_1 V + C_2 V + C_3 V$$

and

$$C = C_1 + C_2 + C_3 + \ldots \quad . \quad (5.9)$$

Thus for any number of capacitors connected in parallel the joint capacitance is equal to the simple sum of the individual capacitances. This expression for capacitors in *parallel* is of similar form to that for resistors in *series*.

A multi-plate capacitor, such as the variable capacitor, is in effect an assembly of equal capacitors in parallel.

EXAMPLE 5.13 (A). Two capacitors of 2 μF and 4 μF are connected (a) in series, (b) in parallel. What is the joint capacitance in each case?   (C. & G.)

(a) $C = \text{product/sum} = (2 \times 4)/(2 + 4)$
     $= \frac{8}{6} = 1.33\ \mu\text{F}$

(b) $C = 2 + 4 = 6\ \mu\text{F}$

EXAMPLE 5.14 (A). Two capacitors when connected in series are found to have a capacitance of 2.4 μF. The value of one of the capacitors is known to be 4 μF; what is the capacitance of the other? If the capacitors are connected in parallel, what will be the capacitance?

(C. & G.)

In series, $C = \text{product/sum} = C_1 C_2/(C_1 + C_2)$
$$CC_1 + CC_2 = C_1 C_2$$
$$C_1 C_2 - CC_2 = CC_1$$
$$C_2(C_1 - C) = CC_1$$
$$C_2 = CC_1/(C_1 - C)$$
$$= (2.4 \times 4)/(4 - 2.4)$$
$$= 9.6/1.6 = 6\ \mu\text{F}$$

If joined in parallel the joint capacitance $= 4 + 6 = 10\ \mu\text{F}$

EXAMPLE 5.15 (A). A capacitor of 5 μF, charged to a p.d. of 100 V, is connected in parallel with a similar uncharged capacitor. What quantity of electricity would flow into the second capacitor and to what voltage would it be charged?   (C. & G.)

(i) $Q = CV = 5 \times 100 = 500\ \mu\text{C}$

The charge will be shared equally by the two equal capacitors, the charge in each being

$$Q = 500/2 = 250\ \mu\text{C}$$

(ii) $V = Q/C = 250/5 = 50\ \text{V}$

EXAMPLE 5.16 (A). Two capacitors each consist of two plates separated the same distance apart in air. The first capacitor has square plates having 6-in. sides and is charged with 10 units of electricity to a p.d. of 200 V. The second capacitor has square plates having 12-in. sides and is uncharged. What would be the charge and potential of each capacitor if the two capacitors were connected in parallel?   (C. & G.)

For these capacitors,

$$C \propto A, \ C_1/C_2 = 6^2/12^2 = 36/144 = \tfrac{1}{4}$$

If the two capacitors are joined in parallel, their p.d.s become equal and the charge is shared in direct proportion to their capacitances.

Charge on first capacitor $= 10 \times \tfrac{1}{5} = 2$ units

Charge on second capacitor $= 10 \times \tfrac{4}{5} = 8$ units

When in parallel the joint capacitance of the 1-unit and 4-unit capacitors becomes

$$1 + 4 = 5 \text{ units}$$

Since $C = Q/V$ as Q remains the same and C is increased from 1 to 5 the p.d. (across each capacitor) becomes reduced to $\frac{1}{5}$ of its value originally, i.e. to $200/5 = \underline{\underline{40 \text{ V}}}$

EXAMPLE 5.17 (A). A capacitor is made from three parallel plates separated 0·5 cm from each other, the outer two plates being connected together. What would be the effect on the capacitance if the middle plate were moved to a distance of 0·25 cm from the top plate? (C. & G.)

The three-plate capacitor is equivalent to two capacitors in parallel. When the separation is 0·5 cm, assume that the capacitance of "each" capacitor is C so that the combined capacitance of the original capacitor is $2C$.

Now

$$C \propto 1/d, \; C_1/C_2 = d_2/d \text{ and } C_2 = C_1 d_1/d_2$$

When the middle plate is moved to 0·25 cm from the top plate (i.e. to 0·75 cm from the bottom plate)—

For 0·25 cm spacing, capacitance
$$= C \times 0·5/0·25 = 2C$$

For 0·75 cm spacing, capacitance
$$= C \times 0·5/0·75 = 2C/3$$

Joint capacitance of $2C$ and $2C/3$ in parallel
$$= 2·67C$$

Ratio of initial and modified capacitances
$$= 2·67C/2C = 1·33$$

i.e. capacitance is increased 1·33 times.

5.28. Screening. If a charged conductor is completely surrounded by an earth-connected conductor, lines of induction from the charged conductor end upon the surrounding conductor which provides their path to earth. Consequently, the charged conductor has no electric field outside the surrounding conductor which forms an *electrostatic* screen for the region outside it.

A conductor can be screened against inducing charges from an *outside* source by completely surrounding it with a conductor: it is not essential for this screen to be earth-connected. Lines of induction reaching the screen will not pass to the interior provided the screen is at the same potential throughout, because lines of induction must connect two points at different potentials. The lines cannot leave the screen to pass inside for they could only terminate again upon the screen, i.e. at the same potential.

Such screening has extremely important applications in the design of telecommunication equipment, to prevent changes of the charge on one conductor from inducing interfering charges on adjacent conductors. Particularly is this so in carrier telephone and radio equipment which use high-frequency alternating currents, and satisfactory operation of the equipment depends upon the electrostatic screening of components by enclosing them in earth-connected metal containers.

In underground cables designed for carrier telephony, the "go" and "return" pairs working in opposite directions are screened from one another, frequently by running them in separate cables, while in high-grade speech and music circuits special pairs are screened from other pairs by enclosing them in a helical wrapping of metallized paper or thin metal foil.

Where electrostatic screening is required between the windings of mains transformers, a sheet of copper foil is wrapped over the primary winding and connected to earth: it is important that this screen should not form a short-circuited turn.

5.29. Self-capacitance of Coils. In a coil carrying a current, the adjacent turns are at slightly different potentials so producing a self-capacitance between the turns and also between each turn and earth, with air, the insulating covering and coil former as the dielectric. The capacitance results in dielectric absorption of energy and production of heat which may be appreciable at the higher frequencies. To reduce this capacitance to a minimum, low-loss insulating materials are used and various forms of winding are adopted with a view to introducing equal but oppositely charged capacitances which will cancel out. The self-capacitance of small carbon resistors is usually negligible.

5.30. Valve Inter-electrode Capacitance. Due to their proximity the electrodes in an electronic valve possess mutual capacitances which are undesirable on account of the energy fed from one electrode to another. This effect can be overcome by introducing a neutralizing capacitance in the external circuit, or more satisfactorily by use of the screen grid valve.

With high-frequency currents it is also necessary to screen the valve as a whole from electrostatic coupling with adjacent conductors: this is done either by enclosing the valve in an earth-connected metal container, or by spraying the bulb with metal and connecting this coating to earth.

5.31. Capacitance of Cables. The capacitance

value of a single-conductor underground or submarine cable can be calculated from

$$C = \frac{2\pi\varepsilon_r\varepsilon_0}{\log_e (R/r)} \text{ farads/metre length}$$

where r metres and R metres are respectively the inner and outer radii of the dielectric.

For two parallel overhead wires the capacitance

$$C = \frac{2\pi\varepsilon_r\varepsilon_0}{\log_e (d/r)} \text{ farads/metre length}$$

where r metres is the radius of each conductor and d metres the distance between them.

The capacitance to earth of a single overhead wire is given by

$$\frac{2\pi\varepsilon_r\varepsilon_0}{\log_e (2h/r)} \text{ farads/metre length}$$

where r metres is the radius of the conductor and h metres the height of the conductor above the earth.

h/r	$2h/r$	$\log_e (2h/r)$ $= 2\cdot302\,6 \times \log_{10} (2h/r)$	$1\cdot8 \log_e (2h/r)$	$C = \dfrac{10\,000}{1\cdot8 \log_e (2h/r)}$
1 000	2 000	$2\cdot302\,6 \times 3\cdot301\,0 = 7\cdot600\,9$	13·68	730·98
2 000	4 000	,, $\times 3\cdot602\,1 = 8\cdot294\,1$	14·93	669·79
3 000	6 000	,, $\times 3\cdot778\,2 = 8\cdot699\,6$	15·66	638·55
4 000	8 000	,, $\times 3\cdot903\,1 = 8\cdot987\,2$	16·18	618·02
5 000	10 000	,, $\times 4\cdot000\,0 = 9\cdot210\,4$	16·58	603·12
6 000	12 000	,, $\times 4\cdot079\,2 = 9\cdot392\,7$	16·91	591·43
7 000	14 000	,, $\times 4\cdot146\,1 = 9\cdot546\,9$	17·18	582·10
8 000	16 000	,, $\times 4\cdot204\,1 = 9\cdot680\,4$	17·42	574·12
9 000	18 000	,, $\times 4\cdot255\,3 = 9\cdot798\,2$	17·64	566·90
10 000	20 000	,, $\times 4\cdot301\,0 = 9\cdot903\,6$	17·83	560·91

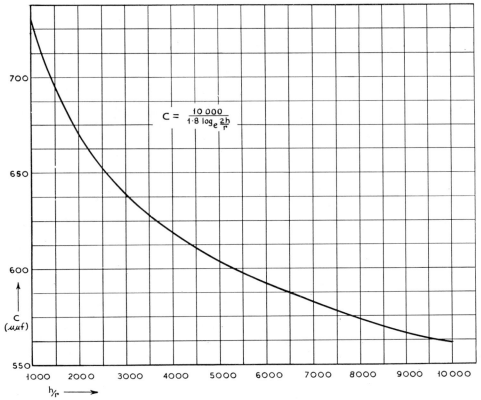

FIG. 5.29. (Example 5.18)

EXAMPLE 5.18 (B). If the capacitance of a horizontal wire of length l cm is $\dfrac{l}{1\cdot8\log_e(2h/r)}\mu\mathrm{F}$, where h/r is the ratio of the height above earth to the radius of the wire, plot a curve showing the relationship between the capacitance and h/r as the latter varies between the limits 1 000 to 10 000. Take l as 10 000 cm. When the wire is in its highest position, what increase in its length would be needed to make the capacitance equal to its value at the lowest height? (C. & G.)

The curve is plotted in Fig. 5.29 from the tabulated results.

For the capacitance to be equal to 730·98 when $h/r = 10\ 000$,

$$730\cdot98 = l/17\cdot83, \quad l = 730\cdot98 \times 17\cdot83$$
$$= 13\ 033\cdot3 \text{ cm}$$

$$\text{Increase in length} = (13\ 033 - 10\ 000)$$
$$= 3\ 033 \text{ cm}$$

5.32. Effects of Line Capacitance. It cannot be too strongly emphasized that every conductor possesses capacitance, both between itself and the earth as a conductor, and also between itself and

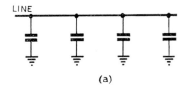

(a)

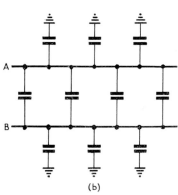

(b)

FIG. 5.30. CAPACITANCE OF LINES

neighbouring conductors: this applies particularly to line and cable circuits. The presence of inherent capacitance between conductors is usually undesirable and it is necessary to neutralize its presence in some way.

The capacitance of a telephone or telegraph line can be represented as shown in Fig. 5.30 which indicates (a) the wire-to-earth capacitance present in a single wire circuit with earth return, and (b) the capacitance from wire to wire, and from each wire to earth in a metallic pair. The capacitance is normally distributed uniformly along the line. In a multiple-line overhead route or in a multiple pair underground cable, capacitance exists between each wire and every other wire as well as between each wire and earth. Main underground cables are generally designed on a quad basis, and the possible wire-to-wire and wire-to-earth capacitances within each quad are depicted in Fig. 5.31.

The capacitance of overhead lines is usually negligibly small, but in underground cables the capacitance is by no means negligible owing to the

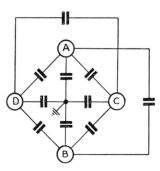

FIG. 5.31. CAPACITANCES OF CABLE QUAD

much closer spacing of the conductors, i.e. to the low value of dielectric thickness, and partly due to the presence of paper as well as air for the dielectric. In submarine cables the presence of this capacitance introduces serious disadvantages which have to be overcome for the satisfactory propagation of telephone and telegraph signals.

The distributed capacitance introduces shunt paths, particularly at the higher frequencies, for the a.c. signals in the line to return to the transmitting source without passing through the receiving termination, resulting in *attenuation* and also in *phase displacement*.

Apart from this attenuation and distortion produced, special precautions have to be taken to prevent or reduce to negligible magnitude the incidence of electrical interference of one circuit with another by electrostatic induction. Electromagnetic induction also produces interference between adjacent circuits, but the effects of electrostatic induction are by far the more serious.

Fig. 5.32 shows one wire of a disturbing line represented by the conductor A: due to the telephone or telegraph signals passing, A is being subjected to continuous changes in charge. Each change induces a corresponding change on the eighbouring line represented by the conductors 'D, and, if C is nearer to A than D is, induced urrents will flow in the receiver terminating CD vith the result that signals transmitted over A are iable to be overheard on the CD circuit. This lefect, known as *cross-talk*, is overcome by methods lepending upon equalizing the capacitances beween AC and AD so that the currents in C and D re balanced out.

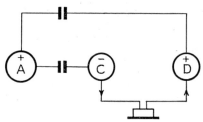

FIG. 5.32. CROSS-TALK FROM ELECTROSTATIC
INDUCTION

In overhead lines the required result is obtained oy transposing the wires at intervals so that, for example, as shown in Fig. 5.33 the wires C and D re on the average equidistant from A: in practice he details of transposition of the line wires are omewhat more complex.

In underground cables, the use of twisted pairs

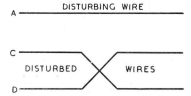

FIG. 5.33. TRANSPOSITION OF LINE WIRES

vith suitable variation in adjacent "quads" provides the required transposition, but, despite the greatest care in design and manufacture, variations nevitably occur in the separation of adjacent conluctors so that the several capacitances are unequal over a length of line. The electrostatic coupling is most severe between circuits which are most closely situated in the cable cross-section since small rregularities in spacing produce relatively larger capacitance unbalance: also there are no intervening conductors to produce a screening effect. Considerable reduction in cross-talk is achieved by carefully selecting pairs to be jointed in successive cable lengths from the results of precise capacitance measurements on all pairs of the cable. In other cases, notably for working at carrier frequencies the same result is achieved by adding capacitance to those wires of lower value to build up all conluctors to approximately equal capacitance values:

this is carried out by terminating all cable pairs upon a frame and connecting capacitors of the required values across the desired conductors.

5.33. Energy. If a charge of Q coulombs raises the potential of a capacitance C farads to V volts, the energy W stored in the field is given by the expression

$$W = VQ/2 = Q^2/2C = CV^2/2 \text{ joules} \quad (5.10)$$

The derivation of this expression may be demonstrated in the following manner. The p.d. across a capacitor, initially zero, gradually rises to V volts due to a charge of Q coulombs: the average p.d. is $V/2$ and the energy required to charge it is

$$V/2 \times I \times t = QV/2 \text{ joules}$$

Between a pair of oppositely charged plates in a capacitor there is a force of attraction. If this force is F newtons and d metres is the distance separating the plates, the work done if the plates are allowed to come together is equal to the product $F \times d$: this is equal to the energy stored in the plates, $CV^2/2$, hence

$$Fd = CV^2/2 \text{ joules}$$

This force of attraction between two charged plates provides the basis for operation of the electrostatic voltmeter.

EXAMPLE 5.19 (A). A 2 μF capacitor is charged to a p.d. of 1 000 V. What is the amount of energy stored in the capacitor? If this charged capacitor is connected in parallel with an uncharged 3 μF capacitor, what will be the p.d. and the total energy stored after connexion? Explain the reason for any difference in the energy stored in the two cases.   (*C. & G.*)

$$W = CV^2/2 = \tfrac{1}{2} \times 2 \times 10^{-6} \times 10^3 \times 10^3$$
$$= \underline{\underline{1 \text{ J}}}$$

$$Q = CV = 2 \times 10^{-6} \times 10^3 = 2 \times 10^{-3} \text{ C}$$

When the capacitors are joined in parallel the p.d. across each becomes equal and the joint capacitance $= 2 + 3 = 5 \ \mu$F.
The total Q remains the same.

$$V = Q/C = (2 \times 10^{-3})/(5 \times 10^{-6})$$
$$= \underline{\underline{400 \text{ V}}}$$

The total energy now becomes

$$CV^2/2 = \tfrac{1}{2} \times 5 \times 10^{-6} \times 400^2$$
$$= \underline{\underline{0 \cdot 4 \text{ J}}}$$

The remainder of the energy $(1 \cdot 0 - 0 \cdot 4 = 0 \cdot 6 \text{ J})$ is dissipated as heat in the conductors due to an oscillatory discharge when the charged and uncharged capacitors are connected together.

EXAMPLE 5.20 (A). A variable capacitor has a maximum capacitance of 1 000 pF and a minimum capacitance of 100 pF. When in the maximum position it is charged to 1 000 V. The charging supply is then disconnected and the capacitor turned to the minimum position. What was the original energy and the final energy stored in the capacitor? Explain the reason for any difference. (*C. & G.*)

At maximum capacitance

$$W = CV^2/2 = \tfrac{1}{2} \times (10^3 \times 10^{-12}) \times (10^3 \times 10^3)$$
$$= 1/2\,000 = \underline{0{\cdot}000\,5 \text{ J}}$$

$$Q = CV = 10^3 \times 10^{-12} \times 10^3 = 1 \ \mu\text{C}$$

At minimum capacitance Q is the same and

$$V = Q/C$$
$$= 10^{-6}/(10^2 \times 10^{-12}) = \underline{10\,000 \text{ V}}$$

$$W = CV^2/2 = \tfrac{1}{2} \times (10^2 \times 10^{-12}) \times (10^4 \times 10^4)$$
$$= 1/200$$
$$= \underline{0{\cdot}005 \text{ J}}$$

The increase of electrical energy at the lower capacitance is due to the work done in separating the plates.

EXAMPLE 5.21 (A). In Example 5.8, what is (a) the energy stored, and (b) the force of attraction between adjacent plates? (*C. & G.*)

$$\left.\begin{array}{l} V = 200 \text{ V} \\ C = 0{\cdot}25 \times 10^{-6} \text{ F} \\ \varepsilon_r = 5{\cdot}65 \\ d = 2 \times 10^{-5} \text{ m} \\ A = 10^{-1} \text{ m}^2 \end{array}\right\} \text{from Example 5.8}$$

(a) Energy

$$W = CV^2/2 = \tfrac{1}{2} \times 0{\cdot}25 \times 10^{-6} \times 200^2$$
$$= \underline{0{\cdot}005 \text{ J}}$$

(b) Energy stored in capacitor = force × distance.

$$CV^2/2 = F \times d$$
$$F = CV^2/2d$$
$$= \varepsilon_r \varepsilon_0 A V^2/2d^2$$
$$= (5{\cdot}65 \times 8{\cdot}854 \times 10^{-12} \times 10^{-1} \times 200^2)/$$
$$\qquad\qquad\qquad (2 \times 4 \times 10^{-10})$$
$$= 8{\cdot}854 \times 5{\cdot}65 \times 5$$
$$= \underline{250 \text{ newtons}}$$

EXAMPLE 5.22 (A). Four perfect capacitors are connected as shown in Fig. 5.34 to the three terminals ABC.
(a) Calculate the value of capacitance that would be measured across terminals BC.
(b) Terminals B and C are now connected together. What capacitance would be measured across AB?

(c) Find the energy stored in the whole circuit in the second condition when a 100-V battery is connected across AB. (*C. & G.*)

(a) The capacitance C_1 measured across BC will be that of the four capacitors connected in series—

$$1/C_1 = 1/2 + 1/3 + 1/1 + 1/5 = 61/30$$
$$C_1 = 30/61 = \underline{0{\cdot}492 \ \mu\text{F}}$$

(b) When B and C are joined, the capacitance across AB will consist of the capacitance (C_2) across AC in parallel with that (C_3) across AB in Fig. 5.34.

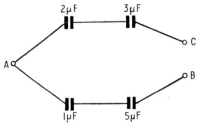

FIG. 5.34. (Example 5.22)

Across AC, $1/C_2 = 1/2 + 1/3 = 5/6$
$$C_2 = 6/5 = 1{\cdot}2 \ \mu\text{F}$$

Across AB, $1/C_3 = 1/1 + 1/5 = 6/5$
$$C_3 = 5/6 = 0{\cdot}83 \ \mu\text{F}$$

If C_4 is the value of C_2 and C_3 in parallel,

$$C_4 = C_2 + C_3 = 6/5 + 5/6 = 61/30 = \underline{2{\cdot}03 \ \mu\text{F}}$$

(c) The energy stored in the circuit in (b) will be the same as that which would be stored in the equivalent capacitance, 2·03 μF—

$$W = \tfrac{1}{2}CV^2 = \tfrac{1}{2} \times 2{\cdot}03 \times 10^{-6} \times 100^2$$
$$= 10{\cdot}15 \times 10^{-3} \text{ joules}$$
$$= \underline{10{\cdot}15 \text{ mJ}}$$

EXAMPLE 5.23 (A). Two capacitors, having capacitances of 1 and 2 μF respectively and negligible leakage, are each charged to 100 V. What is (a) the charge, (b) the energy stored in each capacitor?
Will these values be altered if, after the source has been disconnected, the two charged capacitors are connected in parallel?
The two capacitors initially uncharged are connected in series across the 100-V source. Calculate—
(c) the capacitance of the two in series,
(d) the voltage across each capacitance,
(e) the energy stored in each. (*C. & G.*)

(a) From $Q = CV$, the charge on the 1-μF capacitor

$$= 1 \times 10^{-6} \times 100 = \underline{10^{-4} \text{ C}}$$

he charge on the 2-μF capacitor

$$= 2 \times 10^{-6} \times 100 = \underline{\underline{2 \times 10^{-4} \text{ C}}}$$

(b) From $W = \frac{1}{2}CV^2$,

1e energy stored in the 1-μF capacitor at 100 V

$$= 10^{-6} \times 100^2/2 = \underline{\underline{0 \cdot 005 \text{ J}}}$$

he energy stored in the 2-μF capacitor

$$= 2 \times 10^{-6} \times 100^2/2$$

$$= \underline{\underline{0 \cdot 01 \text{ J}}}$$

Vhen the capacitors are connected in parallel iere will be no change in these energy values ecause, as both capacitors are charged to 100 V lready, there will be no interchange of potential or of charge.

(c) If C farads is the effective capacitance of the vo capacitors in series,

$$1/C = 1/1 + 1/2 = 3/2 \text{ and } C = \underline{\underline{2/3 \ \mu\text{F}}}$$

(d) As the two capacitors C_1 and C_2 have equal harge Q when connected in series,

$$Q = C_1 V_1 = C_2 V_2$$

here V_1 and V_2 are the p.d.s across C_1 and C_2 espectively.

$$V_1/V_2 = C_2/C_1 \text{ and}$$

$$\frac{V_1}{(V_1 + V_2)} = \frac{C_2}{(C_1 + C_2)}, \ V_1 = \frac{C_2(V_1 + V_2)}{(C_1 + C_2)}$$

$$V_1 = 100 \times 2/3 = \underline{\underline{66 \cdot 7 \text{ V}}}$$

$$V_2 = \frac{C_1(V_1 + V_2)}{(C_1 + C_2)} = \underline{\underline{33 \cdot 3 \text{ V}}}$$

(e) The energy stored in the 1-μF capacitor at 6·7 V

$$= \frac{1}{2} \times 10^{-6} \times 66 \cdot 7^2 = \underline{\underline{2 \cdot 22 \text{ mJ}}}$$

'he energy stored in the 2-μF capacitor at 33·3 V

$$= \frac{1}{2} \times 2 \times 10^{-6} \times 33 \cdot 3^2 = \underline{\underline{1 \cdot 11 \text{ mJ}}}$$

EXAMPLE 5.24 (A). A 10-μF capacitor is charged from , 100-V battery. The battery is then removed. Calculate he energy stored in the capacitor.

Two other capacitors, of 5 and 3 μF joined in series, re now connected across the terminals AB of the charged apacitor. Determine—

(a) the total capacitance across AB,
(b) the p.d. across each of the three capacitors. Assumng that no leakage of charge occurs, find—
(c) the energy stored in each capacitor.   (C. & G.)

If $C = 10 \times 10^{-6}$ farads, and $V = 100$ V, the energy stored

$$= \frac{1}{2}CV^2 = \frac{1}{2} \times 10^{-5} \times 10^4 = \underline{\underline{0 \cdot 05 \text{ J}}}$$

(a) The capacitors are connected as shown in Fig. 5.35(a). If C_1 is the equivalent of the 5-μF and 3-μF capacitors in series, then

$$1/C_1 = 1/5 + 1/3 = 8/15$$
$$\text{and} \qquad C_1 = 15/8 = 1 \cdot 875 \ \mu\text{F}$$

If C_2 is the equivalent of 1·875 μF in parallel with 10 μF (see Fig. 5.35(b)), then

$$C_2 = 1 \cdot 875 + 10 = \underline{\underline{11 \cdot 875 \ \mu\text{F}}}$$

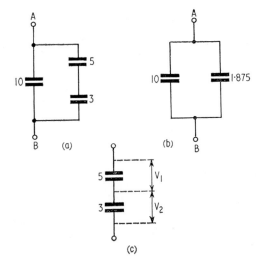

FIG. 5.35. (Example 5.24)

(b) The total charge given to the 10-μF capacitor from the 100-V battery is, from $Q = CV$,

$$Q = 10 \times 10^{-6} \times 100 = 10^{-3} \text{ C}$$

This charge remains constant but is redistributed when the three capacitors are connected.

When the shunt capacitance equivalent to 1·875 μF is connected, the charge of 10^{-3} C is contained in 11·875 μF. If V_{AB} is the new p.d. across AB, and the 10-μF capacitor,

$$V_{AB} = Q/C = 10^{-3}/(11 \cdot 875 \times 10^{-6})$$
$$= 1\ 000/11 \cdot 875 = \underline{\underline{84 \cdot 21 \text{ V}}}$$

The charge taken by the two capacitors in series must be equal, because electrons flow out of the one into the other.

$$C_1 V_1 = C_2 V_2$$

$$5V_1 = 3V_2 \text{ (see Fig. 5.35(c))}$$

$$V_1/V_2 = 3/5$$

$$\frac{V_1}{V_1 + V_2} = \frac{3}{5+3} = 3/8$$

$$V_1 + V_2 = V_{AB} = 84.21 \text{ V}$$

$$V_1 = 84.21 \times 3/8 = \underline{31.58 \text{ V}}$$

$$V_2 = 84.21 - 31.58 = \underline{52.63 \text{ V}}$$

flowing between the capacitors during the re adjustment of charges.)

5.34. Time-constant. The time required t charge a capacitor depends not only upon it capacitance C farads and upon the applied p.d V volts but also upon the value of any series resis tance R ohms present in the circuit. In the un charged state, the p.d. across the capacitor is zero but immediately it commences to acquire a charge its p.d. reaches some value v, which Fig. 5.36 show to be in the nature of a back-e.m.f. The availabl charging potential is reduced to $(V - v)$ and, if is constant and v gradually increases as the chargin

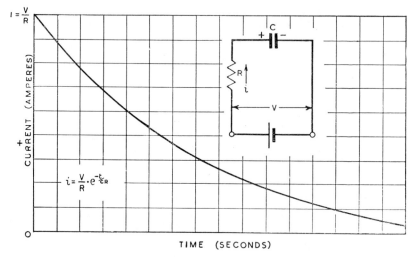

FIG. 5.36. CAPACITOR CHARGE CURRENT

(c) Energy $W = \frac{1}{2}CV^2$.

In 10-μF capacitor, energy stored

$$= \frac{1}{2} \times 10 \times 84.21^2 \times 10^{-6}$$

$$= \underline{0.035\ 46 \text{ J}}$$

In 5-μF capacitor, energy stored

$$= \frac{1}{2} \times 5 \times 31.58^2 \times 10^{-6}$$

$$= \underline{0.002\ 49 \text{ J}}$$

In 3-μF capacitor, energy stored

$$= \frac{1}{2} \times 3 \times 52.63^2 \times 10^{-6}$$

$$= \underline{0.00\ \ 4\ 16 \text{ J}}$$

(It will be noted that the total energy now in the three capacitors is 0.042 11 J: the energy ori ginally in the 10-μF capacitor before sharing the charge was 0.05 J. The difference between these energies has been dissipated in heat by the current

proceeds, the charging p.d. $(V - v)$ gradually falls reaching zero when the capacitor is fully charge and $v = V$. The charging current commences at maximum value and falls to zero, varying as show by the curve in Fig. 5.36. The value of the curren at any instant will, by Ohm's law, depend upon th magnitude of the resistance R present, and afte any particular elapsed time t' seconds will be equa to

$$i' = (V - v')/R$$

where v' denotes the "back-e.m.f." after t' second charging.

The solution to this equation is

$$\boldsymbol{i = (V/R)e^{-t/(CR)}} \qquad . \qquad . \ (5.11$$

where $e = 2.718$ (the base of natural logarithms When $t = 0$, $-t/CR = 0$, and $e^{-0} = 1$, so that has its maximum value, $i = V/R$: theoretically reaches zero when $t = \infty$, which may be confirme by substituting $t = \infty$ in the expression for i.

If the capacitor is discharged by shunting it and removing the charging p.d., the p.d. across the capacitor gradually falls and so does the current strength. The instantaneous value of the current strength on discharge is given by the expression—

$$i = -(V/R) \cdot e^{-t/(CR)} \quad . \quad . \quad (5.12)$$

The negative sign for the current indicates the reversal of current direction consequent on discharge. This current curve is given in Fig. 5.37.

The expression for the discharge may be readily produced from the charging equation if the capacitor is considered to be discharged by the application

The curves of variations of q with time during charge and discharge are similar to those for the growth and decay of current in an inductance (see Chapter VII) and are given in Figs. 5.38 and 5.39 respectively.

Expressions for the instantaneous value of the voltage may be derived by dividing the equations for quantity by the capacitance C, for $v = q/C$.

During charge,

$$v = V(1 - e^{-t/(CR)}) \quad . \quad . \quad (5.15)$$

and during discharge,

$$v = V \cdot e^{-t/(CR)} \quad . \quad . \quad (5.16)$$

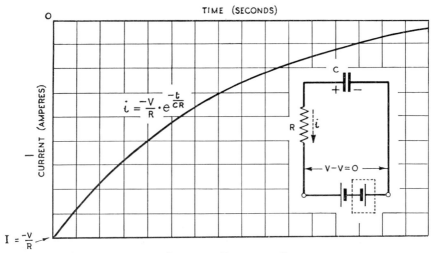

FIG. 5.37. CAPACITOR DISCHARGE CURRENT

of an equal and opposite p.d., $-V$. Because the capacitor is fully charged, the current $i_1 = 0$ due to the original source $(+V)$; and is

$$i_2 = (-V/R) \cdot e^{-t/(CR)}$$

for the added p.d. $(-V)$. Hence the net current is

$$i \ (= i_1 + i_2) = 0 - (V/R) \cdot e^{-t/(CR)}$$
$$= (-V/R) \cdot e^{-t/(CR)}$$

Although the *current* value *diminishes* with time for both charge and discharge, the magnitude of the charge is of course increasing on charge and decreasing on discharge. If q is the instantaneous magnitude of the charge whose final or maximum value is $Q \ (= CV)$, then during charge,

$$q = CV(1 - e^{-t/(CR)}) \quad . \quad . \quad (5.13)$$

and during discharge

$$q = CV \cdot (e^{-t/(CR)}) \quad . \quad . \quad (5.14)$$

For a particular charging period $t = CR$,

$$q = CV \cdot (1 - e^{-\frac{CR}{CR}}) = CV \cdot (1 - e^{-1})$$
$$= CV \cdot (e - 1)/e = CV \cdot (2 \cdot 718 - 1 \cdot 0)/2 \cdot 718$$
$$= 0 \cdot 632 CV = 0 \cdot 632 Q$$

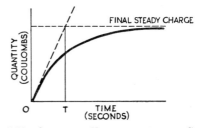

FIG. 5.38. QUANTITY VARIATION DURING CHARGE

The time for the quantity of charge to reach $0 \cdot 632$ of its maximum value (Q) is known as the TIME-CONSTANT, and in seconds it is numerically equal to the product CR, provided C and R are expressed in farads and ohms respectively.

The time-constant is equal to the time which would be required to charge (or discharge) the capacitance if the initial charging (or discharging) rate were maintained. For, considering the charge, the initial current $I = V/R$ coulombs/second. The total charge $Q = CV$ coulombs and since $t = Q/I$, the time required to charge the capacitance at a constant current of V/R would be

$$t = CV \div V/R = CR \text{ seconds}$$

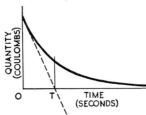

FIG. 5.39. QUANTITY VARIATION DURING DISCHARGE

For practical purposes it may be taken that the final value of the current or charge is reached after a period equal to five times the value of the time-constant.

One useful application of this constant lies in the facility for comparing one cable circuit with another.

The shunted capacitor, with suitable values of C and R, is used in telegraph signalling and in electronic valve circuits for the practical utilization of particular time intervals.

EXAMPLE 5.25 (A). A capacitor of 1 000 μF capacitance is charged to a p.d. of 200 V. If the capacitor is discharged in 1/1000 sec, what is the average value of the current during discharge?   (C. & G.)

$$Q = CV = 10^3 \times 10^{-6} \times 200 = 0\cdot2 \text{ C}$$
$$Q = It, \; I = Q/t = 0\cdot2 \times 1\,000 = \underline{200 \text{ A}}$$

EXAMPLE 5.26 (B). A 0·02 μF capacitor receives a charge of 20 μC. What energy is stored in the capacitor? If the capacitor is made up of parallel plates each having an area of 1 130 cm² and placed 1 mm apart in air, how many plates are used?
Indicate by a curve drawn approximately to scale how the p.d. across the capacitor will diminish with time if the capacitor has an insulation resistance of 1 000 MΩ
(C. & G.)

$$\varepsilon_r = 1,$$
$$\varepsilon_0 = 8\cdot854 \times 10^{-12}$$
$$a = 1\,130 \text{ cm}^2 = 0\cdot113 \text{ m}^2$$
$$d = 1 \text{ mm} = 10^{-3} \text{ m}$$
$$C = 0\cdot02 \times 10^{-6} \text{ F}$$
$$(n + 1) = \text{ number of plates.}$$

(i) $W = CV^2/2 = Q^2/(2C)$
    $= (20^2 \times 10^{-12})/(2 \times 0\cdot02 \times 10^{-6})$
    $= \underline{0\cdot01 \text{ J}}$

(ii) $C = \varepsilon_r\varepsilon_0 A/d \text{ F}$
    $= \varepsilon_r\varepsilon_0 na/d \text{ F}$
    $n = Cd/(\varepsilon_r\varepsilon_0 a)$
    $= 0\cdot02 \times 10^{-6} \times 10^{-3}/$
        $(8\cdot854 \times 10^{-12} \times 1 \times 0\cdot113)$
    $= 20$

Number of plates
    $= 20 + 1 = \underline{21 \text{ plates}}$

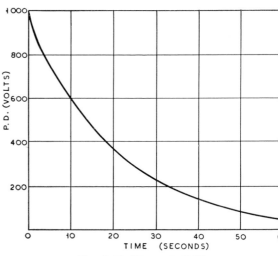

FIG. 5.40. (Example 5.26)

(iii) P.d. across capacitor $v = V \cdot e^{-t/(CR)}$

Initial p.d. $= V = Q/C = 20/0\cdot02 = 1\,000 \text{ V}.$
    $v = 1\,000e^{-t/(CR)}$

Taking the two values $t = 10$ and $t = 50$ sec for an approximate curve, and substituting the value $R = 1\,000 \text{ M}\Omega = 10^9 \text{ }\Omega$:

when $t =$	10 sec	50 sec
$v =$	606·5 V	82 V

The curve is drawn in Fig. 5.40.

EXAMPLE 5.27 (B). A 2 μF capacitor charged to a p.d. of 150 V is connected with an uncharged 4 μF capacitor. To what voltage would the combination be charged? Draw a curve approximately to scale showing how the voltage would decrease with time if the insulation resistance of each capacitor is 2 MΩ.   (C. & G.)

On the charged capacitor

$$Q = CV = 2 \times 10^{-6} \times 150 = 300 \text{ }\mu\text{C}$$

When the capacitors are connected together the total charge remains the same: the joint capacitance becomes $2 + 4 = 6\ \mu\text{F}$.

$$V = Q/C = 300/6 = \underline{50\ \text{V}}$$

The joint insulation resistance is $1\ \text{M}\Omega = 10^6\ \Omega$. On discharge the p.d. $v = V \cdot e^{-t/(CR)}$ where $V = 50 = $ initial p.d.

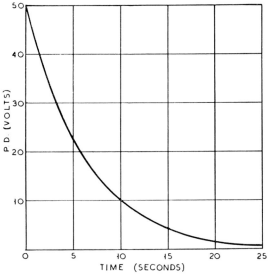

FIG. 5.41. (Example 5.27)

Substituting $C = 6 \times 10^{-6}\ \text{F}$, and $R = 10^6\ \Omega$,

$$v = V \cdot e^{-t/(CR)} = 50 \cdot e^{-t/6}$$

from which the following values may be obtained—

t (seconds)	.	0	1	4	6	12	24
v (volts)	.	50	42·3	25·7	18·4	6·8	0·9

Fig. 5.41 is plotted from these figures.

EXAMPLE 5.28 (B). A battery having an e.m.f. of 200 V and negligible internal resistance is connected across a capacitor of 0·1 μF and a resistor of 1 MΩ joined in series. Calculate the value of the current flowing in the circuit (a) at the instant when the connexion is made, (b) 0·1 sec later. What will be the voltage across the capacitor in the latter case?   (C. & G.)

(a) At the instant when the connexion is made, there is no p.d. across the capacitor and the full applied e.m.f. is available across the resistance

$$I = 200/10^6 = \underline{0·2\ \text{mA}}$$

(b) The p.d. across the capacitor at any instant t seconds after the connexion is made is

$$v = V(1 - e^{-t/(CR)})$$

Substituting $V = 200$, $t = 0·1$ sec, $C = 0·1\ \mu$F, and $R = 10^6\ \Omega$—

$$v = 200(1 - e^{-\frac{0·1}{0·1}}) = 200(1 - 1/2·718) = 126\ \text{V}$$

At this instant, the p.d. across the resistance is $200 - 126 = 74$ V.

$$i = v/R = 74/10^6 = \underline{0·074\ \text{mA}}$$

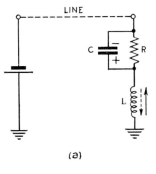

(a)

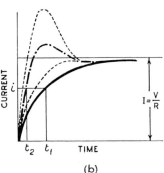

(b)

FIG. 5.42. ACTION OF SHUNTED CAPACITOR

5.35. The Shunted Capacitor. It is shown in Chapter VII that the rate of rise of current in a circuit possessing electromagnetic inductance L is reduced due to the production of a back-e.m.f.: this back-e.m.f. is initially almost of equal magnitude to the applied e.m.f., and it falls gradually with time to permit the current to reach its Ohm's law value. This *rate* of rise is enhanced by the presence of a series resistor R, and the full line curve in Fig. 5.42 (b) shows the growth of current with time under these conditions.

In telegraph signalling this effect delays the response of the inductive receiving instrument until the operating current reaches a sufficient value— the value assumed to be i in the figure. The rise (and decay) of the current can be hastened by shunting a capacitor C across the series resistor R (Fig. 5.42 (a)). At the instant of application of the signalling battery, the capacitor plates are both at the same potential and the resistor R is virtually short-circuited. The capacitor commences to charge rapidly, and as the charge is built up the p.d. across the capacitor (and also across the resistor) rises. The current in the inductive receiving instrument L is the sum of the currents in the resistor and in the capacitor, and it takes the form shown in the chain-dotted curve (Fig. 5.42 (b)). In this way the operating value of the current, i, is reached in the much shorter time t_2, compared with time t_1 without the capacitor. The rate of the initial current growth depends upon the value of the capacitance used, and the dotted curves show

the later sections of the line, the practical result of which is that there is a transient time during which the current is delayed in attaining its full value at the receiving end of the cable while it is progressively charging up the cable capacitance. The fact that this received current I_R is also less in magnitude than the sent current I_S due to leakage currents is not considered here.

When the sending battery is disconnected a similar time interval is required for the energy stored by the cable capacitance to discharge through the receiving instrument Z, and the cessation of the current at the receiving end is thus also delayed. This factor limits the frequency with

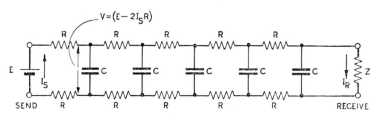

Fig. 5.43. Signalling on Cable Circuit

the effects of using larger or smaller values of capacitance. The maximum current may exceed the Ohm's law value.

When the sending battery is disconnected on the termination of a signal the capacitor discharge current (Fig. 5.42 (a)—dotted arrow) opposes the prolonging current (full arrow) produced by the inductance and results in a quicker cessation of the signal.

5.36. Propagation Velocity of Cables. A cable circuit possesses *distributed* capacitance and resistance: such a circuit may be represented as shown in Fig. 5.43 where each section containing $2R$ and C represents a short length of the line.

When a signalling battery is applied to the sending end of the cable, the p.d. across the capacitance of the first section is initially zero: this p.d. rises slowly as the capacitance becomes charged, ultimately attaining its final value $V = E - 2I_S R$.

The p.d. applied to the second section of cable is always the p.d. across this first capacitance, hence the p.d. applied to charge the second section of the cable commences at zero and rises gradually to reach its final value. In other words, the capacitance of the first section must be fully charged before the maximum p.d. V is available to charge the second section. The second section takes longer to charge than it would have done had the full p.d. for this section been immediately applied. Similar delay occurs in the successive charging of

which telegraph signals can follow one another, for the growth and decay of one signal must be completed before a subsequent signal is transmitted: otherwise the decay curve of one signal would be overlapped by the growth of the next signal, and the signals lose their identity, e.g. several short signals would be received as one long signal.

This factor limits the working speed of a cable, the speed being dependent upon the product CRl^2, C and R being the capacitance and resistance per unit length, and l being the length of line. On the longer submarine cables the received current may take several seconds to attain its maximum value, and signalling over such cables accordingly calls for special receiving instruments and methods of transmission.

In the "double-current" system of transmission, each signal is terminated by a reversal of the sending battery instead of by its disconnexion, the reversal of potential hastening the discharge of the cable.

Summary

Like Charges. Cause repulsion.

Unlike Charges. Cause attraction.

Coulomb's Law.
$$F = Q_1 Q_2 / (4\pi \varepsilon d^2) \text{ newtons} \qquad . \quad (5.1)$$

Electric Force.
$$E = - V/d \text{ volts/metre} . \qquad . \quad (5.2)$$

Mechanical Force.
$$F = QE \text{ newtons/coulomb} \qquad . \quad (5.3)$$

Electric Flux Density.
$$D = Q/A \text{ coulombs/metre}^2 \qquad . \quad (5.4)$$

Permittivity.
$$\varepsilon = \varepsilon_r \varepsilon_0 = D/E \text{ farads/metre}$$
$$\varepsilon_0 = 8 \cdot 854 \times 10^{-12} \text{ farads/metre} \quad (5.5)$$

Capacitance (C). Of a conductor—the property of a conductor which requires a quantity of electricity to be imparted to it to raise its potential.
$$C = Q/V \qquad . \qquad . \qquad . \quad (5.6)$$

Farad. Unit of capacitance requiring 1 C to raise its potential by 1 V.

Parallel Plate Capacitor.
$$C = \varepsilon_r \varepsilon_0 A/d \text{ farads} \qquad . \qquad . \quad (5.7)$$

$A = na$, where n = number of dielectric layers: number of plates = $(n + 1)$: a = area of one side of one plate in square metres.

Capacitors in Series.
$$1/C = 1/C_1 + 1/C_2 + 1/C_3 + \ldots \quad (5.8)$$

Two capacitances only, C = product/sum. N similar capacitances C', $C = C'/N$.

Capacitors in Parallel.
$$C = C_1 + C_2 + C_3 + \ldots \qquad . \quad (5.9)$$

Energy. $\qquad W = CV^2/2 \text{ joules} \qquad . (5.10)$

Time-constant. $t = CR$ seconds.

During charge,
$$i = (V/R) \cdot e^{-t/(CR)} \qquad . \qquad . \qquad . (5.11)$$
$$q = CV \cdot (1 - e^{-t/(CR)}) \qquad . \qquad . \qquad . (5.13)$$
$$v = V \cdot (1 - e^{-t/(CR)}) \qquad . \qquad . \qquad . (5.15)$$

During discharge,
$$i = -(V/R) \cdot e^{-t/(CR)} \qquad . \qquad . \qquad . (5.12)$$
$$q = CV \cdot e^{-t/(CR)} \qquad . \qquad . \qquad . (5.14)$$
$$v = V \cdot e^{-t/(CR)} \qquad . \qquad . \qquad . (5.16)$$

REFERENCES

1. F. McCABE: "Polystyrene Dielectric Capacitors," *A.T.E. Journal*, **15** (1959), p. 237.
2. D. S. MARGOLIS and J. H. COZENS: "Electrolytic Capacitors," ibid., **15** (1959), p. 245.
3. A. A. NEW: "Electrolytic Capacitors and their Reliability," *I.P.O.E.E. Journal*, **55** (1962), p. 115.

CHAPTER VI

MAGNETISM

6.1. Magnetic Properties. Iron and steel, and to a much smaller extent nickel and cobalt, are the chief materials capable of acquiring the properties of magnetism.

A material is said to be magnetized if it displays the following properties: (i) when freely suspended it comes to rest in a line running approximately north and south, (ii) it is able to impart magnetism to other magnetic materials, and (iii) it exerts a force upon other magnetized materials.

Natural magnetic ores occur in small amounts in certain parts of the earth in the form of magnetite, but for commercial use all magnets have their magnetic property conferred upon them by electrical means.

For practical purposes, magnets are usually required in the shape either of a short bar; or more commonly, when it is necessary to have the two ends, or poles, close together, magnets are made in the form of a **U**—the so-called horse-shoe magnet. The poles are those parts of a magnet from which the external magnetic effects appear to emanate. A magnet always has its N pole clearly marked by stamping the letter N upon it, or by painting the north end red, or by some other suitable distinguishing mark for the N pole.

The earth itself behaves as a huge magnet with its poles approximately at the north and south geographical poles of the earth. When a bar magnet is freely suspended, that end which points to the earth's north pole is known as the north pole (N) of the magnet: the other end is its south pole (S). More correctly these magnet poles are called the north-seeking and south-seeking poles respectively, but the word "seeking" is usually omitted.

6.2. Law of Attraction and Repulsion. If a magnet is suspended or pivoted and a second magnet is brought near to it, the suspended magnet will be deflected.

If a N-pole approaches the N-pole of the suspended magnet, the latter is deflected away from the approaching magnet: repulsion also occurs if the S-pole of a second magnet is brought near to the S-pole of the suspended magnet. On the other hand, the N-pole of the suspended magnet is deflected towards the S-pole of a magnet brought near to it; and similarly the S-pole of the suspended magnet will be attracted by a N-pole. The general rule for the influence of one magnet upon

another is that like poles repel one another whilst attraction results between unlike poles.

This law illustrates the need for bearing in mind that the correct name for the N-pole of a magnet is a "north-seeking pole," because the earth's north pole would repel, not attract, a true north pole: nevertheless north poles and south poles are the terms accepted generally for "north-seeking" and "south-seeking" poles.

6.3. The Inverse Square Law. This law involves the consideration of an isolated magnetic pole: it is not possible to obtain a N-pole without its accompanying S-pole, but the required condition can be approximated by considering a long magnet and neglecting the effect of the distant pole.

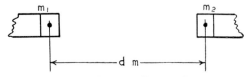

FIG. 6.1. INVERSE SQUARE LAW

If two isolated poles of strength m_1 and m_2 units respectively are placed at a distance of d metres apart (Fig. 6.1), the force F of attraction (unlike poles) or of repulsion (like poles) between them varies directly as the product of the pole strengths and inversely as the square of the distance d metres between the poles.

In symbols, the expression for the force is

$$F = m_1 m_2 / 4\pi\mu d^2 \text{ newtons}. \qquad . (6.1)$$

where μ is the *permeability*.

This law is determined from the results of experimental measurements. The pole strengths m_1 and m_2 are measured in *webers*, a unit which is defined in § **7.10.**

6.4. Magnetization by Contact. If a piece of unmagnetized steel is brought into contact with a magnet, the steel itself becomes a magnet capable of magnetizing other pieces of iron or steel: furthermore it will be found on removing the steel that it has retained its magnetic properties. The degree of magnetism imparted by simple contact is somewhat feeble, but it can be strengthened by using the following method. The bar of steel to be magnetized is laid upon a table and one pole of a strong bar magnet is drawn along its length, repeatedly and always in the same direction, being lifted well clear of the magnet between successive strokes. The end of the steel bar at which the pole of the magnet leaves it will acquire a polarity opposite to that of the magnet pole. The polarity produced is

FIG. 6.2. MAGNETIZATION BY CONTACT

indicated in Fig. 6.2 where the dotted line shows the path taken by the magnet.

6.5. Magnetic Induction. It is not essential for contact with a magnet to take place in order to produce magnetic properties in a piece of iron or steel. This can be readily demonstrated using a small compass needle as an indicator. The compass needle consists of a short thin piece of magnetized steel with a hard bearing at its centre resting on a pointed vertical pivot. A bar magnet is placed upon a bench at such distance from a compass needle as to have little effect upon it. If a piece of unmagnetized steel, or preferably iron, is now interposed between the magnet and the compass needle, the needle will be immediately deflected showing that the iron bar has become magnetized by induction. Furthermore, if the permanent magnet is removed, the compass needle will not return to its original position, indicating that the iron bar has retained some induced magnetism. The direction

FIG. 6.3. MAGNETIZATION BY INDUCTION

of the induced magnetism is shown in Fig. 6.3, and it is always such that the adjacent poles of the inducing magnet and the induced magnet are dissimilar.

The attraction of unmagnetized pieces of iron and steel by a magnet is brought about by magnetic induction occurring in pieces of iron or steel lying adjacent to a magnet: the induction of dissimilar poles, as described above, results in a force of attraction in conformity with the law of attraction and repulsion.

6.6. Residual Magnetism and Coercive Force. Iron and steels of different grades, and also the

various magnetic alloys, differ in the extent to which they respond to magnetic treatment. Steel is more difficult to magnetize than soft iron, but once magnetized it retains its magnetism more readily than does soft iron, which quickly loses its magnetism unless completely undisturbed. Magnetism can be removed from a magnet by impact, or vibration, by raising the temperature, or by a suitable degree of magnetic induction in the reverse direction.

The magnetism which remains in a substance after the magnetizing force has been removed is known as RESIDUAL MAGNETISM: the degree to which it retains this magnetism (after saturation) is termed the retentivity or REMANENCE. Soft iron has a higher remanence than steel provided that it is completely undisturbed.

The power to retain magnetism in spite of such subsequent treatment as impact, etc., after the magnetizing force has been withdrawn is measured by the COERCIVITY. Steel has a greater coercivity than iron.

A PERMANENT MAGNET may be defined as *a body which, having been magnetized, retains a substantial portion of its magnetization.* In telecommunication equipment such as magneto-generators, telephone receivers, and polarized relays which require permanent magnets, steels or steel alloys with high degrees of remanence and coercivity are employed. Soft iron with low coercivity is used for the cores of relays and transformers where it is necessary that the magnetism shall disappear quickly when the magnetizing force is removed.

6.7. Position of Poles. The presence of a magnet pole is observed to be spread over an end region of the magnet, but a magnet pole may be considered

FIG. 6.4. POSITION OF POLES

as though concentrated at a resultant point, in much the same way as the weight of a body may be assumed to be concentrated at its centre of gravity. The positions of these two points for any magnet can readily be determined by placing the magnet upon a sheet of paper and putting a compass needle successively in three positions near to one end: the continuation of the axis of the compass needle in each position will give three lines meeting in a point which is the resultant point or pole of the magnet (Fig. 6.4). The procedure is then repeated for the other pole of the magnet. The pole is the point or region towards which lines of force converge, or at which resultant magnetic forces may be considered to act.

Under certain conditions of magnetization, poles are exhibited within the magnet, and may take the form shown in Fig. 6.5. A pole occurring on a part of a permanent magnet remote from either free end is known as a *consequent pole*: the presence of consequent poles may be revealed by exploring the length of the magnet with a small compass needle.

N	SS	NN	S

FIG. 6.5. CONSEQUENT POLES

For some purposes, ring-shaped magnets (Fig. 6.6 (*a*)) are required: normally they exhibit no free poles. Ring-shaped magnets are also used with two short pole-pieces connected across a diameter (Fig. 6.6 (*b*)): in this case the magnet is equivalent to two horse-shoe magnets in parallel.

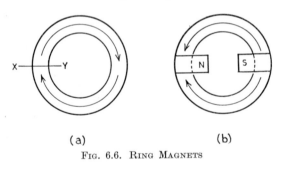

(a)   (b)

FIG. 6.6. RING MAGNETS

The distance between the poles of a magnet is known as the *magnetic length l* of the magnet and it is usually about 0·9 times the overall length of the magnet.

The product of this length l metres with the strength m webers of either pole is known as the magnetic moment M, so that $M = ml$.

6.8. Intensity of Magnetization. The intensity of magnetization within the magnet, denoted by the symbol J, is the ratio of the pole strength m webers to the cross-sectional area A m^2 of the magnet. In symbols,

$$J = m/A \text{ webers/m}^2$$

Multiplying this by $l/l \; (= 1)$ gives

$$J = (m \times l)/(A \times l) = M/V$$

the volume V of the magnet being equal to the product Al. The INTENSITY OF MAGNETIZATION may be defined as *the magnetic moment per metre*^{3}.

6.9. The Magnetic Field. A magnet influences the state of the medium for some distance around it: the affected region, namely *the space in the neighbourhood of a magnet throughout which the forces due to the magnet can be detected* is known as the MAGNETIC FIELD. The condition of the medium before the magnet is applied becomes changed when a magnet is introduced, for in the latter case a force will at once act upon any magnet pole placed in the field. The field may be termed a field of magnetic force, since a mechanical force will act upon any magnet pole (or induced pole) in that field.

The strength or intensity of the field is known as the MAGNETIZING FORCE and denoted by the symbol H. Magnetizing force is measured in *ampere-turns/metre*.

6.10. Lines of Force. To describe any force fully the direction in which it acts must be stated as well as its magnitude. The direction of the influences acting in a magnetic field may be demonstrated by drawing *lines of magnetic force*: a LINE OF MAGNETIC FORCE is *a line drawn in a magnetic field such that its direction at every point is the direction of the magnetic force at that point*.

Two convenient methods are available for plotting the lines of force in a magnetic field. In the first method, with the magnet laid upon a large sheet of paper, a small compass needle is moved about the field, commencing at the N-pole and finishing at the S-pole. A dot is marked upon the paper coincident with the tip of the N-pole of the compass, the compass then being moved so that its S-pole coincides with this dot. A repetition of this process will produce a series of dots which, when joined together, will form the line of force shown in Fig. 6.7.

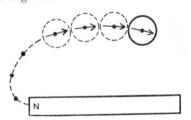

FIG. 6.7. PLOTTING LINES OF FORCE

An alternative method is to place a sheet of glass or cardboard over the magnet and to sprinkle iron filings on the sheet: when the sheet is gently vibrated the individual filings having become small magnets will set themselves in the direction of the field at all points, and as a whole will give a picture of the lines of force. Fig. 6.8 shows the disposition of the lines of force for the simple bar and horse-shoe magnets. Figs. 6.9 and 6.10 show the lines of force for two simple arrangements of magnets, the attractions and repulsions between unlike and like poles being clearly indicated. Points occur, symmetrically disposed between similar poles, where the magnetizing forces due to the two like

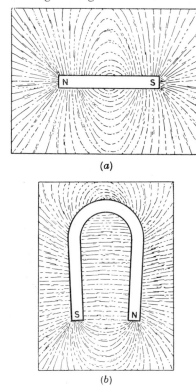

(a)

(b)

FIG. 6.8. MAGNETIC FIELD OF MAGNET
(*a*) Bar magnet. (*b*) Horse-shoe magnet.

poles are equal in magnitude but opposite in direction: the resultant force at these points is zero and a compass needle placed here would come to rest in any position with equal facility. Such points are termed *neutral points*: they are indicated at *X* in Figs. 6.9 (*a*) and 6.10 (*a*) and (*b*). It should not be forgotten that these diagrams show the conditions in one plane only, whereas the field exists in three dimensions throughout the medium surrounding the magnet. It is helpful to imagine that the lines of force tend to contract and take the shortest possible path between poles, at the same time exerting a mutual lateral force of repulsion. Within a magnet the magnetizing force is in the opposite direction to the magnetic flux: this is apparent if consideration is given to the direction

which a unit north pole *inside* the iron would take, i.e. from the N-pole to the S-pole. A permanent magnet is continuously subjected to a *demagnetizing force* which tends to restore the magnet to its original state prior to being magnetized. For this reason it is customary to keep bar magnets, while not in use, in pairs with soft iron end pieces, or *keepers* (*K*), as shown in Fig. 6.11,

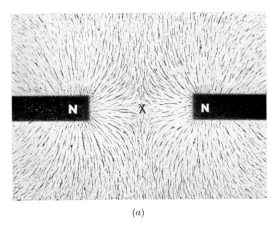

(a)

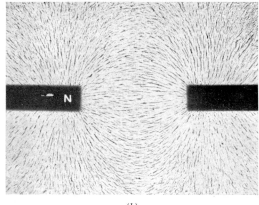

(b)

FIG. 6.9. MAGNETIC FIELD OF TWO BAR MAGNETS,
AXES IN LINE
(*a*) Like poles adjacent. (*b*) Unlike poles adjacent.

an arrangement which produces a continuous magnetic path with no free poles, and no demagnetizing force.

6.11. Terrestrial Magnetism. Unlike the geographical poles, the positions of the earth's magnetic poles are not constant but are subject to a continuous variation. The earth's magnetic meridian, that is, a line passing along the axis of a compass needle, makes an angle with the true geographic meridian at any point, this angle being known as the *declination*. The declination varies at different parts of the surface of the earth, being zero in some places, and at any point it is subject to slight annual variation. The angle of declination together with the annual variation is marked on all ordnance survey maps: at Greenwich the declination is of the order of 15°. In addition to the regular variation, more violent changes in

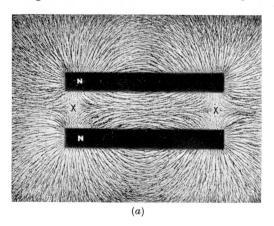

(a)

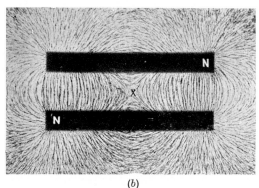

(b)

FIG. 6.10. MAGNETIC FIELD OF TWO BAR MAGNETS, AXES PARALLEL

(a) Like poles adjacent. (b) Unlike poles adjacent.

declination due to magnetic storms and probably originating in sun spots are occasionally experienced: while these storms persist they frequently interfere with the signalling on telegraph and telephone lines as a result of induced e.m.f.s, and also interfere with radio reception.

The earth's magnetic field is not everywhere parallel to the earth's surface. For example, immediately above the N and S magnetic poles of the earth the field is almost entirely vertical and at points near to the earth's geographical equator the field is practically horizontal. The angle which the field makes with the horizontal plane is known

as the *angle of dip*: it can be readily measured by means of an instrument known as the *dip needle*. This instrument is essentially a compass needle accurately balanced and pivoted on a *horizontal* pivot, with a calibrated scale behind it from which the angle of dip can be read directly.

For measurement of dip, the dip needle must first be placed in the magnetic meridian and with

FIG. 6.11. BAR MAGNETS WITH KEEPERS

its N-pole pointing towards the north. As with declination, magnetic dip is also subject to continuous small changes. At Greenwich the angle of dip is approximately 66°.

The dip needle indicates the direction of the earth's total magnetic field at the point under consideration. With magnetic measuring instruments

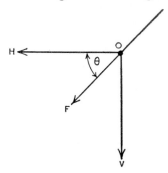

FIG. 6.12. ANGLE OF DIP

such as the magnetometer it is only the horizontal component of this total field which is being considered. In Fig. 6.12, if OF is the position taken up by the dip needle, $\theta°$ being the angle of dip, the horizontal component H and the total field F are related by the expression $H = F \cos \theta$: similarly the vertical component V is given by $V = F \sin \theta$.

6.12. Magnetic Flux. The magnetic field may be regarded as a field of induction or *flux* on account of the induced magnetism experienced by any magnetic material placed in that field, due to the magnetizing force present. The notion of magnetic flux has to be distinguished from the notion of magnetic force. The conception of lines of magnetic induction, or lines of magnetic flux, is used to show the direction of the magnetic flux at any point in the field.

The symbol for magnetic flux is Φ, and it is measured in terms of a unit called the WEBER.

The amount of magnetic flux per metre² over a small area (the area being in the position which gives a maximum value for the flux) is known as the magnetic FLUX DENSITY. The symbol for flux density is B and it is measured in webers/metre². For an area A metres² over which a total flux Φ webers is uniformly distributed, the flux density is

$$B = \Phi/A \text{ webers/metre}^2*$$

6.13. Permeability. A piece of iron or steel placed in a magnetic field becomes magnetized by

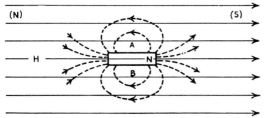

FIG. 6.13. FIELDS DUE TO INDUCING AND INDUCED MAGNETS

induction. The inducing and induced fields are indicated in Fig. 6.13. The parallel lines represent a small uniform portion of the inducing field whose magnetizing force is H ampere-turns/metre:* this field runs in the direction from left to right across the diagram. The piece of iron becomes a magnet and its field of force is shown by the dotted lines. The summation of the two fields, namely the original field H and the field due to the induced magnet, results in the distorted field of Fig. 6.14. It can be seen that the two fields are, in general, in opposition in the regions A and B, and assist one another in the regions near to the poles. The general effect is as though the lines of force tend to crowd into the iron which provides a better path than the surrounding air for the magnetic lines.

The ratio of the magnetic flux density produced in a medium to that produced in a vacuum by the same magnetizing force is known as the RELATIVE PERMEABILITY of the medium: it is denoted by the symbol μ_r. Being a ratio, μ_r is dimensionless, i.e. it is just a number. The (absolute) permeability of a vacuum, usually referred to as the (absolute) *permeability of free space*, and sometimes as the

* The weber, ampere-turn, and henry are defined in Chapter VII.

magnetic space constant or *primary magnetic constant* has, in order to establish the rationalized system of M.K.S. units, been given the value $4\pi \times 10^{-7}$ and the dimension henry/metre: it is designated by the symbol μ_0, thus

$$\mu_0 = 4\pi \times 10^{-7} \text{ henry/metre}*$$

The relationship of μ_0 to a comparable unit-defining constant ε_0, the *permittivity of free space*, or the *primary electric constant*, used in calculations of electrostatics problems has been described in Chapter V.

From the definition given above for relative permeability, it is clear that the *absolute permeability* for any magnetic material is obtained by multiplying the relative permeability μ_r by the

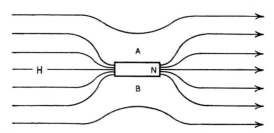

FIG. 6.14. COMBINED FIELD OF INDUCING AND INDUCED MAGNETS

factor μ_0. Absolute permeability for any material is denoted by μ, thus

$$\mu = \mu_r \mu_0 \text{ henry/metre}$$

Following these definitions can be stated the most important relationship established between permeability, flux density, and magnetizing force. The ABSOLUTE PERMEABILITY of a material or medium is *the ratio of the magnetic flux density to the magnetizing force producing it.*

Expressed in symbols, if a magnetizing force H ampere-turns/metre produces a flux density of B webers/square metre in a material, then for that material the absolute permeability

$$\mu = B/H, \text{ or } B = \mu H, \text{ or } H = B/\mu.$$

More usefully, for the purpose of making calculations the expression may be written as

$$\mu = \mu_r \mu_0 = B/H \text{ henry/metre} \quad . \quad (6.2)$$

This property of permeability and its expression as the ratio of induced flux to magnetizing force are of the utmost importance in the study and application of magnetic materials. The permeability of air is taken as $\mu_r = 1$. Steel and iron have relative permeability values of the order of several thousands, enabling them to produce large flux densities from small magnetizing forces.

It is important to appreciate that the relative permeability of a ferromagnetic material is not a constant value, but that μ_r *varies with the value*

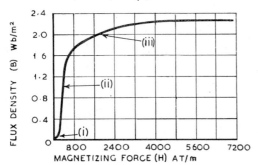

FIG. 6.15. PERMEABILITY (*B-H*) CURVE

of H: this is well demonstrated by the permeability curves which follow.

It is possible by electrical means to produce magnetic fields of any desired strength *H* ampere-turns/metre and also to measure the resultant

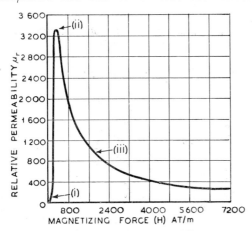

FIG. 6.16. PERMEABILITY (μ_r-*H*) CURVE

flux density *B* webers/square metre induced in any magnetic material placed in that field: from the ratio *B/H* the permeability can then be calculated. In selecting magnetic materials for industrial purposes it is essential to know their magnetic properties, and permeability curves are produced for this purpose.

A typical permeability curve for a magnetic material, initially unmagnetized, is illustrated in Fig. 6.15. The permeability, being the ratio *B/H*, is determined by the *slope* of the curve (Appendix **A 2**) and it is seen that this curvature is not in

general of constant value: as *H* is increased steadily there are three distinct stages in the corresponding change in *B*.

The permeability, measured by the slope, (i) rises slowly at first, (ii) increases rapidly to reach a maximum value at the steepest part of the curve, and then (iii) falls away towards zero as the curve flattens out almost horizontally. This variation in relative permeability with values of *H* is apparent in the corresponding graph of Fig. 6.16 where values of μ_r, obtained from Fig. 6.15, are plotted against values of *H*. It will be seen from the magnetic theory that once all the elementary magnets constituting the material are brought into line then no increase in flux can be expected from further increases in the value of magnetizing force, for the material has become magnetically saturated. This saturation, which is exhibited in the later portion of the curve of Fig. 6.15, and shows practically no increase in values of *B* in this specimen for values of *H* greater than 4 000, is a characteristic feature of permeability curves.

In electromagnetic equipment such as transformers, chokes, etc., it is necessary for changes of magnetizing force to control consequent changes in flux density: for these purposes the saturation portion of the curve must be definitely excluded from use, for if the value of *H* exceeds the point at which saturation commences, no further increase in the value of *B* will follow from further increases in the value of *H*.

6.14. Hysteresis. The properties of residual magnetism and coercive force are important factors in the selection of any magnetic material and

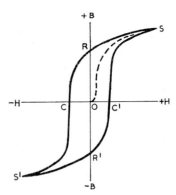

FIG. 6.17. HYSTERESIS LOOP

produce practical effects requiring special consideration when the material is taken through a "cycle" of magnetization.

In Fig. 6.17 the dotted line *OS* is the permeability curve plotted for a certain sample of soft

ron (initially unmagnetized) by gradually increasing the value of H in successive steps and
measuring the corresponding values of B. If the
value of H is now reduced to zero by successive
stages, then it is found that the curve does not
retrace its original path but instead follows some
such path as SR. This is due to the property of
residual magnetism and for this case it is seen that,
when H has been reduced to zero, the value of the
residual magnetism is represented on the scale by
the ordinate OR.

If the polarity of the magnetizing force is now
reversed to give negative values of H—i.e. a reversed field—it is found that H must be increased
negatively to the value represented by OC before
the value of the flux falls to zero: OC is a measurement of the coercive force.

Further negative increments in H cause the flux
to approach saturation at the point S'. If the value
of H is now reduced to zero the curve cuts the axis
at point R' where the degree of residual magnetism
is again apparent. Increases of H over a range of
positive values cause the curve to cut the H axis
at C', at which the flux has again fallen to zero,
and subsequently to complete the loop at the
point S. During further cycles of magnetization
the curve retraces the path $SRCS'R'C'$.

The net result of this magnetizing cycle is that
once the specimen has been initially magnetized
(the dotted curve), the flux value B lags everywhere
behind the corresponding values of the magnetizing
force H. The name given to this lagging of B
behind H is MAGNETIC HYSTERESIS, which may be
defined as *the phenomenon by which the magnetization
of some materials depends not only on the present
magnetizing force but also on the previous magnetic
state. It causes a dissipation of energy, the "hysteresis
loss" when the material is subjected to cyclic magnetization.* The hysteresis loss is discussed below.

Fig. 6.18 shows a group of magnetization curves
for a certain sample of steel. The initial permeability curve on the sample when unmagnetized is
shown by the dotted line OA. The inner loops of
this diagram are obtained by taking the same
specimen through more restricted ranges of values
of H, namely, by reversing the magnetizing force
before saturation is reached. If a vertical line YY'
is drawn intersecting these loops, it is seen that
seven different values of B are obtained for the one
value of H. This serves to emphasize that the
value of the permeability $\mu\ (= B/H)$ is defined
with respect to the initial magnetization of a
specimen—the curve OA. The other values of B
corresponding to this value of H include the
previous treatment suffered by the specimen, and
the effects of residual magnetism.

In Fig. 6.17 the ordinate OR is the magnitude of
the residual magnetism present when the magnetizing force is reduced to zero *after having been at
saturation point.* This value is described as the
REMANENCE—*the remanent flux density obtained
when the initial magnetization reaches the saturation
value of the material.*

If the full magnetizing force for saturation has
not been applied to the specimen, the magnitude
of the residual magnetism when H reaches a zero
value is termed the REMANENT FLUX DENSITY—i.e.
*the magnetic flux density remaining in a sub-
stance when, after an initial magnetization, the magnetizing force is reduced to zero. The remanent flux
density depends on the initial magnetization.* Thus

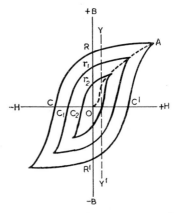

FIG. 6.18. GROUP OF MAGNETIZATION CURVES

in the curves of Fig. 6.18, the values Or_1 and Or_2
represent values of remanent flux density, not of
remanence.

The ordinates OC_1 and OC_2 in Fig. 6.18 are the
magnitudes of the reversed magnetizing forces
required to reduce the remanent values of flux
density to zero. Any one of these values is known
as the COERCIVE FORCE, namely *the demagnetizing
force required to reduce the magnetic flux density in a
substance from the remanent value to zero. It depends
on the initial magnetization.*

The particular value of coercive force measured
by the ordinate OC in Fig. 6.17—i.e. after the
specimen has been magnetically saturated—is
termed the COERCIVITY, which is defined as *the
value of the coercive force when the initial magnetization has the saturation value for the substance.*

Typical hysteresis loops for the general case of a
soft magnetic material, and a permanent magnet
material are illustrated in Figs. 6.19 and 6.20
respectively: the general shapes of these curves
immediately reveal the magnetic natures of the

materials by the wide divergence in their values of coercivity. In comparing these curves attention should be paid to the scales used, particularly on the H axis.

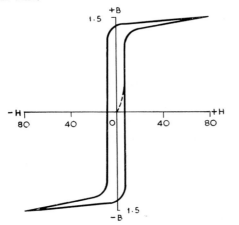

FIG. 6.19. HYSTERESIS LOOP FOR SOFT MAGNETIC MATERIAL

When a magnetic material is taken through cycles of magnetization by reversal of the direction of magnetizing force, considerable energy is expended in effecting the mechanical distortion

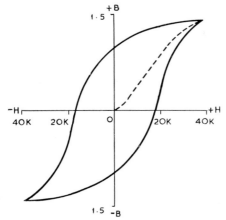

FIG. 6.20. HYSTERESIS LOOP FOR PERMANENT MAGNET MATERIAL

suffered during magnetization and demagnetization. The energy absorbed reappears as heat in the material. In designing electrical equipment which is subject to changing magnetizing forces, particular attention has to be paid to the hysteresis effect, both from the point of view of reducing the energy losses to a minimum and of avoiding excessive increases in temperature.

The MAGNETIC HYSTERESIS LOOP (or B–H loop) is *the name given to the closed figure formed by plotting the values of the magnetic flux density B in a magnetic material against the magnetizing force H when the latter is taken through a complete cycle. The hysteresis loss is proportional to the area of this loop.* The magnetic fields of alternating currents and rotating machines are continuously reversing: to limit the magnitude of the energy wasted by hysteresis, the magnetic material used is specially selected with a minimum area of hysteresis loop (see Fig. 6.19).

The hysteresis loss of a specimen can be determined from a knowledge of the area of the loop but for machines it is preferable to apply the formula due to Steinmetz. For every magnetic cycle reaching a maximum flux density B_{max} webers/metre^2 the hysteresis loss per metre^3 of the material is equal to $nB^{1.6}_{max}$ joules, where n is a factor known as the *hysteresis constant*. If the magnetizing force makes f cycles per second, and the volume of the magnetic material is v metre^3, the hysteresis loss is equal to

$$nfvB^{1.6}_{max} \text{ joules per second} = nfvB^{1.6}_{max} \text{ watts}$$

The hysteresis coefficient depends upon the material. It will be noted that the hysteresis loss increases with frequency and also depends upon the maximum flux density.

Using the area of the loop as the basis of calculation, if B and H are expressed in webers/metre^2 and ampere-turns per metre respectively the work done per cycle per metre^3 is equal to (area of loop) joules: if v metre^3 is the volume of the magnetic material and f cycles per second the frequency, then the hysteresis loss

$$= fv(\text{area of loop}) \text{ watts}$$

6.15. Magnetic Materials.[1] The majority of substances belong to one of two classes, termed *paramagnetic* and *diamagnetic*.

A paramagnetic material has a constant permeability slightly greater than that of a vacuum. A rod of paramagnetic material when placed in a strong magnetic field would tend to set itself with its length parallel to the direction of the field. Examples of paramagnetic materials are glass, platinum, palladium, oxygen.

A diamagnetic material has a permeability less than that of a vacuum: a rod of diamagnetic material would tend to set itself at right angles to the direction of a magnetic field, the direction of induced polarity being such as to cause repulsion. This class includes the metals antimony, mercury, zinc, tin, lead, and copper. Diamagnetism is not a very conspicuous magnetic phenomenon and so far it has no significant practical application.

Iron, cobalt, nickel and their alloys are separately classified as *ferromagnetic* materials, characterized by hysteresis and a high permeability which varies with the magnetizing force.

Ferromagnetic materials may be conveniently divided into two classes: (*a*) the "magnetically soft" materials used for the various forms of electromagnets such as relays, transformers, loading coils, and for the magnetic circuits of generators and motors; (*b*) the "magnetically hard" materials used for permanent magnets. For all applications of magnetic materials, stability of properties is very important, and the material should be capable of formation to the required shape easily, i.e. the mechanical properties must be borne in mind.

6.16. Non-magnetic Alloys. Non-magnetic alloys can be produced although one or more of the contituents may in themselves be magnetic. Such materials are frequently required for use as "magnetic insulators" in or near a magnetic circuit.

One such alloy under the name of "Nomag" is a cast-iron alloy containing 10 per cent nickel and 6 per cent manganese: its relative permeability is 1·03. Brass is a well-known non-magnetic alloy having a relative permeability of 1·0. Gun metal is another non-magnetic alloy. A steel containing about 25 per cent nickel is also non-magnetic.

6.17. Magnetically Soft Materials.[2],[3] These materials can be easily magnetized but they quickly lose their magnetism when the magnetizing force is removed. They are characterized by high maximum permeability, low coercivity and low hysteresis loss.

In the selection of a magnetic material for a specific purpose, six qualities have to be considered. They are (1) permeability, (2) remanence, (3) coercivity, (4) saturation point, (5) electrical resistivity, and (6) constancy of characteristics with age and use. The important factor hysteresis is accounted for in this list, being dependent upon the relative values of remanence and coercivity. Electrical resistivity should be as high as possible as it is of importance in reducing the magnitude of eddy currents. The limitations of hysteresis and resistivity naturally assume the greatest significance in magnetic fields due to alternating currents.

The last few decades have seen the development of magnetic materials possessing magnetic properties far in excess of any which were previously known. At the close of the nineteenth century the various grades of soft iron available had a maximum relative permeability of about 3 000: the losses due to hysteresis and eddy currents were high and tended to increase with ageing.

Among the earlier alloys, a 4 per cent silicon alloy, known as "Stalloy," was produced with a maximum relative permeability of about 3 600 and with a resistivity about five times that of iron: the possible reduction in eddy current losses was thus considerable. The presence of silicon renders the impurities less soluble in iron and improves stability. One of the uses for stalloy was for the diaphragms of telephone receivers. Stalloy at present produced has a maximum relative permeability of about 9 500, reduced losses, and a performance which improves with age. With specially controlled methods of preparation, silicon

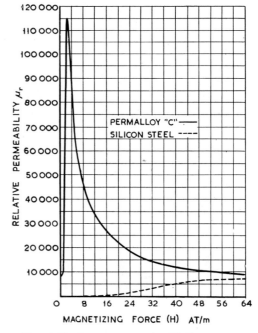

FIG. 6.21. PERMEABILITY (μ_r-H) CURVES FOR PERMALLOY C AND ANNEALED SILICON STEEL
(*Courtesy of I.P.O.E.E.*)

alloys with maximum relative permeability values up to 60 000 and with high resistivity and low hysteresis have been produced.

A series of alloys with a high nickel content[4] was subsequently produced under the name of "Permalloys." One such alloy contains 78·5 per cent nickel and 21·5 per cent iron. A study of Fig. 6.21 reveals the high value of initial relative permeability, over 100 000, of permalloy "C." The related *B-H* curves are given in Fig. 6.22 for permalloy C and silicon steel. The relative permeability (μ_r-B) for some newer and older materials is strikingly contrasted in Fig. 6.23: the hysteresis curves for the same materials are shown in Fig. 6.24. These graphs include mumetal

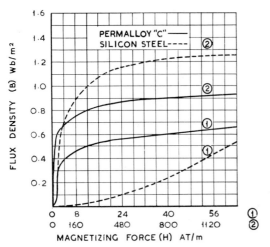

FIG. 6.22. PERMEABILITY (*B-H*) CURVES FOR
PERMALLOY C AND ANNEALED SILICON STEEL
(*Courtesy of I.P.O.E.E.*)

The high initial permeability of the nickel iron alloys is an important characteristic producing high flux densities with very low values of magnetizing force. Comparative values of relative permeability for equal values of magnetizing force for the following materials show this valuable property of the nickel-iron alloy—hard steel 40, low carbon dynamo steel 200, best soft iron 250, silicon steel 400, and special nickel-iron alloys up to about 120 000.

The nickel-iron alloys show certain disadvantage in their low saturation values, in their comparatively low electrical resistivities, and the high

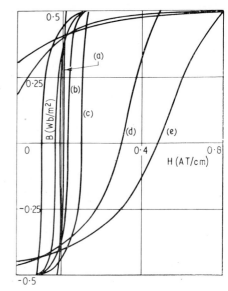

FIG. 6.24. HYSTERESIS CURVES FOR MATERIALS IN FIG. 6.2
(*Courtesy of I.E.E.*)

with initial relative permeability of 20 000 to 30 000, reaching a maximum of 90 000; and supermalloy with an initial relative permeability of about 120 000 and a maximum of about 900 000.

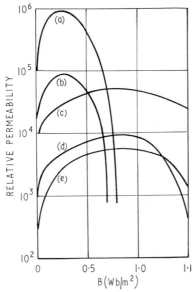

FIG. 6.23. PERMEABILITY (*μ_r-B*) CURVES FOR VARIOUS
MATERIALS

(*a*) Supermalloy.
(*b*) Mumetal.
(*c*) Grain-oriented silicon-iron in rolling direction ($3\frac{1}{4}$ per cent Si).
(*d*) Hot-rolled 4 per cent silicon-iron.
(*e*) Hot-rolled dynamo iron.
(*Courtesy of I.E.E.*)

degree of sensitivity of the magnetic properties to heat treatment and mechanical work. This has led to the development of various alloys containing a third element for the introduction of certain beneficial properties. Among these may be mentioned manganese and aluminium for the purpose of deoxidizing the alloys; silicon, chromium and copper to raise the electrical resistivity; cobalt and vanadium to improve the constancy of permeability in varying magnetic fields; cobalt to reduce hysteresis loss; manganese to reduce coercivity and assist forgeability, and molybdenum to increase the initial permeability and improve the uniformity of the alloy. The foregoing list is by no means comprehensive. Correct heat treatment is an essential factor in the production of all soft magnetic alloys, to prevent residual stresses and strains in the material. Purity of the materials other essential condition for impurities promote deleterious effects in all soft magnetic materials, and manufacturing technique has to be carefully controlled so that both in the alloying process and the subsequent heat treatment metallic and gas impurities are kept to a minimum.

The alloy "Mumetal" is a nickel-iron alloy containing in addition about 6 per cent copper: it has a slightly lower initial permeability than the simple (binary) nickel alloys but shows a higher electrical resistivity.

One extensive application of the nickel-iron alloy has been in the "loading" of submarine cables. A

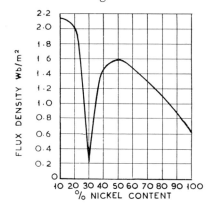

FIG. 6.25. VARIATION OF FLUX DENSITY WITH NICKEL CONTENT
(Courtesy of I.P.O.E.E.)

continuous nickel-iron wire wrapped around the copper conductor increased its inductance to offset the harmful effect of cable capacitance: this type of loaded cable permitted a much greater speed of signalling compared with the unloaded cable. The alloy is also employed for the cores of inductance coils used for loading underground cable circuits, permitting a useful reduction in the size of the coil compared with the use of an iron core. For high-frequency use in carrier working, about 4 per cent of chromium is included in the alloy to increase the resistivity.

Nickel-iron alloys are also used largely in the construction of moving-iron measuring instruments for which purpose the alloys combine the desirable properties of low hysteresis loss and high permeability. Another application is in magnetic screens.

A wide variation of magnetic and electrical properties is available within the nickel-iron range: Figs. 6.25, 6.26, and 6.27 show the variations in flux density, resistivity, and hysteresis loss with nickel content. Alloys of very different properties may thus be selected from the nickel-iron series of alloys.

A series of nickel-iron alloys which include a percentage of cobalt to reduce the hysteresis loss is available under the name of "perminvar": this material exhibits a constancy of permeability at low values of magnetizing force in addition to its

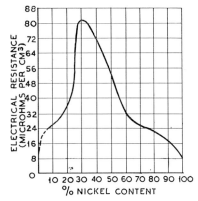

FIG. 6.26. VARIATION OF ELECTRICAL RESISTIVITY WITH NICKEL CONTENT
(Courtesy of I.P.O.E.E.)

low hysteresis loss and high resistivity. This feature is strikingly shown in the hysteresis loops of Fig. 6.28. The use of perminvar is particularly suited to high-frequency work, but it is restricted to cases where low magnetizing forces are applied

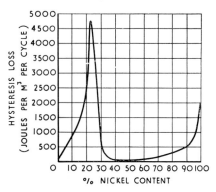

FIG. 6.27. VARIATION OF HYSTERESIS LOSS WITH NICKEL CONTENT
(Courtesy of I.P.O.E.E.)

and a relatively low permeability is acceptable. A typical composition is 45 per cent nickel, 23 per cent iron, 25 per cent cobalt, and 7 per cent molybdenum.

Another class of magnetic alloys is the cobalt-iron series. Its main property is the high saturation value of flux density which may be attained at reasonably low values of magnetizing force. This is demonstrated in Fig. 6.29 where the cobalt-iron sample has almost reached saturation (at over 2·3 webers/metre², while for the same magnetizing force the iron is far from its possible saturation value of 2·2 webers/metre². The curve shows the permeability of the alloy to be higher than for the

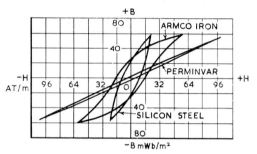

FIG. 6.28. HYSTERESIS LOOPS OF PERMINVAR, SILICON IRON, AND ARMCO IRON
(*Courtesy of I.P.O.E.E.*)

iron at values of flux density greater than 1·3 webers/metre².

The addition of about 2 per cent vanadium to facilitate fabrication and reduce brittleness produces the alloy "permendur," used for the receiver diaphragms in hand micro-telephones. Its

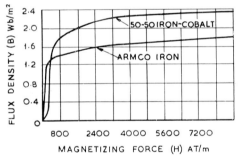

FIG. 6.29. PERMEABILITY CURVES (*B-H*) OF COBALT IRON AND PURE IRON
(*Courtesy of I.P.O.E.E.*)

particularly valuable feature is the high permeability values at high flux densities.

Magnetic cores subjected to alternating fluxes produce considerable losses and lowering of efficiency due to eddy currents. At low frequencies the use of insulated stampings of high resistivity reduces the magnitude of these losses.

For higher frequencies magnetic *dust cores* have been developed. For the cores of loading coils and transformers, electrolytically deposited iron powdered into fine grains was originally used. The dust is covered with an insulating film by chemical

or electro-chemical treatment and then compressed under high pressure. A maximum relative permeability of about 500 was obtained, but the resistivity being about 60 times that of ordinary iron, considerably reduced eddy current losses.

With the nickel-iron alloys, the admixture of certain elements renders the alloys brittle so that they can be crushed into a dust of fineness of less than a 200 mesh. The dust particles are coated with a thin tenacious layer of insulating material and the whole is then fabricated at high pressure into the required shape of core, followed by the requisite heat treatment. The completed core must have adequate mechanical strength to withstand the subsequent coil winding operation.

Wide control of the magnetic quality of the finished core is possible by suitable adjustment of the grade and proportion of alloy and binding material with, if required, a certain proportion of inert spacing material. The introduction of innumerable small non-magnetic gaps reduces the permeability of the magnetic core and results in very high magnetic stability.

The permeability curves of dust cores closely approximate to straight lines and in this respect they behave as air cores.

The relatively high permeability at low values of magnetizing force combined with low hysteresis and eddy current loss available in modern dust cores from high-grade magnetic materials, has led to the use of these alloys in dust cores of chokes and transformers at telecommunication frequencies giving improved characteristics and a greater fidelity of reproduction of the original waveform. The "*Q*" value can be made to the same order from 50 c/s to 50 Mc/s using different core types and grades of material.

The properties of a number of the soft magnetic alloys are summarized, with details of their composition, in Table 6.I.

6.18. Ferrites.[5],[6] In recent years a new class of magnetic materials, which are non-metallic has been developed for practical use: these materials are called *ferrites*. The outstanding feature of ferrites is their high value of resistivity—they are in fact insulators—as a result of which their losses due to the flow of eddy currents are negligibly low. Cores of complex shapes can be moulded from these new materials (Fig. 6.30): for many purposes the use of laminated cores or dust cores can be superseded and an improved performance obtained with a much reduced space requirement.

Ferrite materials are based upon the natural ferrite "lodestone" or magnetite. This complex oxide of iron ($FeO.Fe_2O_3$—known as ferrous ferrite) contains ions of iron in both divalent

TABLE 6.I

SOFT MAGNETIC MATERIALS

	Composition (per cent)				Relative Permeability μ_r		Saturation Flux Density (Wb/m²)	Remanence (Wb/m²)	Coercivity (AT/m)	Resistivity ($\mu\Omega$·cm)
	Fe	Ni	Co	Other Elements	Initial	Maximum				
Cast iron . .	95	—	—	C 3, Si 2	—	600	—	0·53	368	30
Magnetic iron .	99·94	—	—	—	250	5 500	2·15	1·3	80	10
Magnetic iron purified in hydrogen	99·98	—	—	—	25 000	27 500	2·15	1·36	4	10
Stalloy . .	96	—	—	Si 4	400	6 700	2·0	1·2	4	60
Nickel . .	0·4	99·0	—	Cu 0·2	110	600	0·61	0·36	272	8
Permalloy 78·5 .	20·9	78·5	—	Mn 0·6	900	105 000	1·07	0·6	4	16
Mumetal . .	20	74	—	Cu 5, Mn 1	7 000	80 000	0·85	0·6	4	42
Permalloy B .	50	50	—	—	2 000	12 000	1·6	—	—	55
Permalloy C .	16	79	—	Mo 4	22 000	70 000	0·85	0·5	4	55
Permendur .	50	—	50	—	800	5 000	2·45	1·4	160	7
2 V-Permendur .	49	—	49	V 2	800	4 500	2·4	1·4	160	26
45/25 Perminvar	29·4	45	25	Mn 0·6	365	1 800	1·55	0·33	112	19
7/70 Perminvar .	22·4	70	7	Mn 0·6	850	4 000	1·25	0·24	48	16
Supermalloy .	16	78	—	Mn 0·5 Mo 5	50 000	300 000	0·75			

and trivalent forms. The divalent ions are entirely replaced, for example partly by zinc and partly by nickel resulting in a solid solution of mixed ferrites having very good electrical and magnetic properties. Other ferrites containing manganese-zinc are extensively used for loading coils, filter inductances, and transformers. Magnesium-manganese ferrites having rectangular permeability (B/H) curves are used for storage cores.

The preparation of ferrites follows a process

FIG. 6.30. SELECTION OF FERRITE CORES

(*Left back,* various sizes of pot core; *right back and side,* cores for television and radio sets; *centre front,* storage cores; *left front,* transformer E and U cores.)

(*Courtesy of Mullard Ltd.*)

similar to that for ceramic materials, involving the firing at about 1 200°C of a pulverized mixture of the oxides with a suitable binder. This results in a very hard black and ceramic-like material which can be ground, machined, or drilled: it is chemically inert and unaffected by changes in humidity. An interesting comparison of certain properties between typical ferrites and conventional soft magnetic materials is given in Table 6.II. From this Table it is seen that ferrites have

TABLE 6.II

FERRITES

Characteristic	Magnetically Soft Ferrites	Ferromagnetic Materials
Initial Permeability	10 to 6 000	10 to 10^5
Maximum Permeability	100 to 11 000	10^3 to 10^6
Saturation Flux Density (Wb/m²)	0·15 to 0·5	1·4
Residual Flux Density (Wb/m²)	0·08 to 0·45	—
Resistivity (Ω-cm)	10 to 10^8	(10 to 100) $\times\ 10^{-6}$
Permittivity	15 to 150 000	—
Curie Temperature	From 80°C upwards	750°C (iron)

values of permeability which though quite high are yet not so high as in the better of the ferromagnetic materials of the conventional type: also the Curie temperature is much lower, indicating a sensitivity in performance to temperature rise.

Inductors using ferrite cores have a positive temperature coefficient of inductance: in frequency filters this can however be offset by associating the ferrite-cored inductors with capacitors having the dielectric polystyrene, a material which has a negative temperature coefficient of capacitance. The permittivity of the ferrites can also be very high, but their outstanding characteristic is their extremely high resistivity.

6.19. Magnetic Materials with Rectangular Hysteresis Loops.[7]

Some new materials, both metals and ferrites, have recently been developed with magnetic characteristics giving them a hysteresis loop which is of approximately rectangular shape. This form of hysteresis loop has opened up important new possibilities in application: for example it gives a means of storing information represented by binary signals, from the two stable remanent states of the material.

A typical rectangular hysteresis loop has the form shown in Fig. 6.31 in which H_M and B_M are the maximum values of the applied magnetic field and corresponding flux density: B_R and H_C are the retentivity and the coercivity respectively.

Characteristic features of this rectangular hysteresis loop are (i) a high retentivity ratio B_R/B_M, which may reach 95 per cent: (ii) a *high*, constant value of dB/dH, the rate of change of flux, along the sides, or irreversible parts, of the loop; this ratio dB/dH is termed the *differential permeability*, μ_d: (iii) a *low*, constant value of dB/dH along the top and bottom, or reversible parts, of the loop: and (iv) fairly square corners to the "loop."

Materials which exhibit a rectangular hysteresis loop, when the field is in the correct direction, include single crystals and certain polycrystalline materials such as grain-oriented nickel-iron and

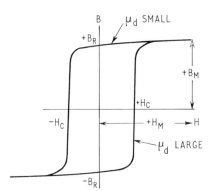

FIG. 6.31. A RECTANGULAR HYSTERESIS LOOP

silicon-iron, certain nickel-iron alloys heat-treated in a magnetic field, the mumetal class of alloys of very fine gauge, and certain of the ferrites.

The particular shape of the rectangular loop can be explained by the domain theory of ferromagnetism (see Fig. 6.42). If the field is low, the boundaries between the domains move so that those domains whose vectors are most nearly parallel to the field vector grow at the expense of the others. This is a reversible process, so that if the field is removed the boundaries return to their original positions. Increasing the field causes further movement of the boundaries, but now the movements are much larger, and irreversible. Finally, when all the vectors are more or less parallel to the field vector, a further increase in the field causes the domain vectors to rotate into line with the field vector; this rotational process is reversible. The characteristics of some commercial materials having rectangular hysteresis loops are displayed in Table 6.III.

In a storage device now extensively used for switching purposes a small core is made up in the form of a ring (0·50 in. outside diameter × 0·30 in. inside diameter × 0·15 in. long) of manganese-magnesium ferrite: this core can be

TABLE 6.III

MAGNETIC MATERIALS WITH RECTANGULAR HYSTERESIS LOOPS

Material	Resistivity $(\Omega\text{-cm})$	Initial Permeability μ_r	Maximum Permeability μ_r	Saturation Flux Density B_M (Wb/m²)	Remanence B_R (Wb/m²)	B_R/B_M	Coercivity H_C (AT/m)
H.C.R. alloy	40×10^{-6}	1 000	60 000	1·56	1·48	0·95	16
Permalloy F	26×10^{-6}	400 — 2 000	250 000	1·35	1·31	0·97	4
Permenorm	45×10^{-6}	850	95 000	1·48	1·44	0·97	7
Deltamax	51×10^{-6}	400 — 1 700	130 000	1·50	1·45	0·97	8
Ferramic S1	2×10^{7}	40	515	0·18	0·16	0·90	119
Ferramic S2	—	49	1 300	0·20	0·18	0·90	56
Ferroxcube D1	—			0·23	0·22	0·96	100

threaded or wound with wires for electrical control. The required energizing field, $+H_M$ or $-H_M$, is applied by a brief electrical pulse: the ferrite core will then remain in one or other of its stable remanent states, represented by $+B_R$ or $-B_R$. Due to the high degree of remanence the electrical energy is required only to change the magnetic state of the core but not to maintain it. The resultant state of the flux, $+B_R$ or $-B_R$, can later be ascertained by electrical examination at any desired time. For example, suppose an examining pulse applies a field of $-H_M$: if the core had been left with "positive" remanence $(+B_R)$ the examining pulse would drive the loop from $+B_R$ to $-B_M$ and result in a flux change of $(B_M + B_R)$: if on the other hand the core had been left with "negative" remanence $(-B_R)$ the same examining pulse $(-H_M)$ would result in a very small flux change of $(B_M - B_R)$ only. If the hysteresis loop is substantially rectangular the factor $(B_M - B_R)$ approaches zero. A change in flux generates an e.m.f. in any conductor influenced by the flux (see Chapter VII), the e.m.f. being proportional to the rate of flux change. Discrimination between the two states is then afforded by the generation of a significant e.m.f. in the one case compared with virtually zero voltage in the other. This device represents an "on-off" or binary switch without any moving parts. It may be operated at extremely high speed from the expenditure of very little electrical energy. Typical characteristics are for the device to operate from an electrical pulse equivalent to 1 ampere-turn and to respond with a switching time of 1 to 5 μsec. In practical applications large stores are made up from a matrix of such cores: a typical instance is a square matrix having 32 rows each containing 32 cores and measuring about 2·5 in. × 2·5 in., giving a store of 1 024 binary elements or "bits." Such a store is illustrated in Fig. 6.32: the complete store unit is shown at (a), while (b) shows the core detail.

(a) 1 024-bit store

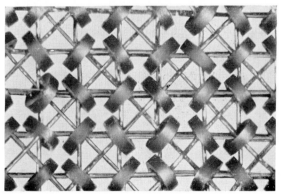

(b) Core detail

FIG. 6.32. FERRITE-CORE MATRIX
(Courtesy of the Plessey Co. Ltd.)

6.20. Grain-oriented Magnetic Materials. For some time it has been known that single crystals of iron, nickel, and cobalt can be more easily magnetized in some directions than others, an effect termed *magnetocrystalline anisotropy* (*iso* means equal, *aniso* is unequal). The permeability graphs of Fig. 6.33 show this for iron magnetized at (*a*) high and (*b*) low field strengths in the three directions indicated by the inset cube: the cube edge direction *A* shows the easiest magnetization, the face diagonal *B* is more difficult, with the cube diagonal *C* the most difficult. For nickel this order

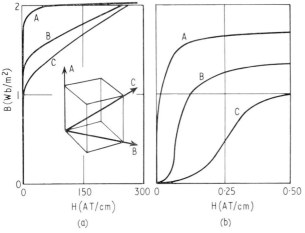

FIG. 6.33. MAGNETIZATION CURVES FOR 3·85 PER CENT SILICON-IRON SINGLE CRYSTALS SHOWING DIRECTIONAL PROPERTIES

(*a*) At high field strengths
(*b*) At low field strengths
(Courtesy of I.E.E.)

is reversed. Other magnetic alloys show comparable characteristics.

This behaviour fits in well with the domain theory. In a single crystal the domain vectors are all parallel to one of the directions of magnetization—parallel to one of the cube edges in the iron crystal—this arrangement involving the least energy.

In polycrystalline materials the crystals are oriented at random so that the direction of the applied field corresponds to the easiest direction of magnetization for only a small proportion of them.

Single crystals cannot readily be produced on a large scale, and for commercial production of magnetic material with the directional properties of the single crystal it has been found more practicable to prepare polycrystalline sheet material in which all the individual crystals are aligned.

The term *grain-oriented* is usually employed to describe certain kinds of magnetically soft (i.e. permeable) iron-alloy strip in which the crystals

or grains are deliberately oriented in a preferred direction in order to enhance one or more magnetic properties in the direction traversed by the flux. Such properties may include the permeability particularly at high flux densities, the hysteresis losses, and especially the combination of high retentivity and low coercivity. Grain-oriented materials should not be confused with "domain oriented" or "magnetically-annealed" materials.

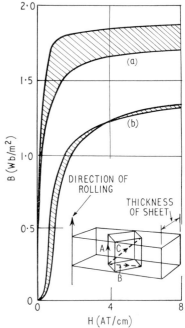

FIG. 6.34. PERMEABILITY (*B/H*) CURVES
(*a*) Cold-rolled grain-oriented 3¼ per cent silicon-iron
(*b*) Hot-rolled 4 per cent silicon-iron
(Courtesy of I.E.E.)

the latter are usually magnetically hard and used for permanent magnets: domain orientation is achieved by the application of a magnetic field during cooling through the Curie temperature.

To prepare the sheet, a billet of 50/50 nickel iron alloy is severely cold-rolled: this causes the grains or crystals of the metal to become long and thin and to take up a particular alignment in the sheet. Cores are then prepared by spirally winding tape from this sheet upon a ceramic former which is then annealed at a temperature of 1 000–1 200°C. This annealing may take place in a magnetic field. The resulting material has a rectangular hysteresis loop and can be most easily magnetized in three directions—(i) the rolling direction, (ii) at right-angles to this but in the rolling plane,

ii) perpendicular to the rolling plane. Commercially this is termed H.C.R. (Heavily Cold-Rolled)
alloy—see Table 6.III. From its directional properties it can be used either in the form of spiral
cores or made in the form of stampings.

Silicon-iron alloys with 3–4 per cent silicon are
produced by a somewhat different cold-rolling
process and only two favourable directions occur:
these are longitudinal and transverse in the plane
of rolling. The objective of the silicon-iron alloy
is a material having a high permeability and low
hysteresis losses. These properties are contrasted
in Fig. 6.34 against a near-similar alloy produced
by the hot-rolled process.

6.21. Permanent Magnets.[8] Materials suitable
for permanent magnets are characterized by high
values of remanence and coercivity. It follows
that the hysteresis loss will be high and such
materials usually have relatively low values of permeability, properties which are associated with a
hard magnetic material (see Fig. 6.20). The
mechanical hardening by cold work, by quenching
or by the addition of alloying constituents produces
considerable internal strains. Use of the term
"magnetic hardness" applied to materials suitable
for permanent magnets arises from the frequent
association of their characteristics with mechanical
hardness.

Considerable improvement has taken place in
the properties of permanent magnets produced
during the last few decades. The earlier permanent
magnets of glass hard steel containing about 1 per
cent carbon were very susceptible to temperature
variations and to mechanical shock and vibration:
their successful operation necessitated excessive
dimension ratios. The tungsten steel magnets also
in use contained about 6 per cent tungsten, with
fractional percentages of carbon and chromium.

In the chrome steel series the addition of 1 per
cent chromium to the steel increased its coercivity
and permitted hardening by quenching in oil
instead of water, thus reducing the risk of quenching cracks: the coercivity was of the order of 3 000
or 4 000 ampere-turns/metre. This chrome steel
was largely used in magneto generators and polarized bells and needed somewhat large dimensions
in order to retain its magnetic strength. The
coercivity was increased slightly by the use of 4 per
cent chromium which produced a steel to replace
the earlier 6 per cent tungsten steel which was
water quenched.

Cobalt steel marked a decided advance in permanent magnet steels. The alloy containing 35 per
cent cobalt, 7–8 per cent tungsten and 3 per cent
chromium has a coercivity equal to three times
that of the 4 per cent chrome steel, but, owing to

its greater cost, alloys containing a lower percentage
of chromium were more commonly used. The
cobalt alloy permitted the use of magnets of reduced length and mass and also facilitated the
manufacturing process. Magnets of cobalt steel
have been used for the later magneto generators
and polarized bells and for the short bar magnet
used in the receiver of the hand micro-telephone.
Other applications are in moving-coil loud speakers
and in lightweight electromagnetic pick-ups. The

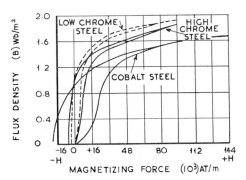

FIG. 6.35. PERMEABILITY (B-H) AND DEMAGNETIZATION
CURVES FOR CHROME STEELS AND COBALT STEELS

(Courtesy of I.P.O.E.E.)

demagnetization curves in Fig. 6.35 illustrate the
relative coercivities of the chromium steels and
cobalt steels.

The latest permanent magnet steels are the alloys
containing aluminium and nickel. The alloy known
as "Alni" consists of 13 per cent aluminium, 24 per
cent nickel, 4 per cent copper, and 59 per cent iron:
it has a coercivity equal to more than double that
of cobalt steel. This higher coercivity is accompanied by a lower remanence so that a greater
cross-sectional area of magnet must be used for
the same flux density: the magnets may, however,
be made shorter, the higher coercivity giving a
greater resistance to self-demagnetization. In use
the alloy is usually made in the form of small
blocks and the magnetic circuit is completed by
means of suitably shaped pole pieces of magnetically soft material.

Another aluminium-nickel alloy, "Alnico" steel,
of which the nominal composition is aluminium
10 per cent, nickel 18 per cent, cobalt 12 per cent,
copper 6 per cent, and iron 54 per cent, has a still
higher value of coercivity: the remanence is greater
than that of alni steel, but lower than that of the
cobalt or tungsten steels. These properties are well
illustrated in the demagnetization curves of
Fig. 6.36.

These aluminium-nickel steels are utilized in many types of electrical instruments, where the consequent saving in space and weight are advantageous. The receivers for hand micro-telephones embody short magnets of alni steel with (soft) pole pieces of "invar"—a 36 per cent nickel-iron alloy with low hysteresis losses.

The advances made in the development of permanent magnet steels[9] are illustrated by the photograph of Fig. 6.37 which shows the relative sizes of bar magnet necessary in various alloys to

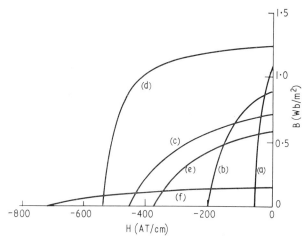

FIG. 6.36. DEMAGNETIZATION CURVES OF SOME PERMANENT MAGNET MATERIALS

(a) Tungsten steel (6% W, 0·9% C).
(b) Cobalt steel (35% Co, 3·5% Cr, 3% W, 1% C).
(c) Alnico (10% Al, 18% Ni, 12% Co, 6% Cu).
(d) Alcomax III (8% Al, 13·5% Ni, 24·5% Co, 3% Cu, 1% Nb).
(e) Iron powder.
(f) Vectolite (30% Fe_2O_3, 44% Fe_3O_4, 26% Co_2O_3).

Courtesy of I.E.E.)

produce a flux density of 0·5 webers/metre² in an air-gap 2 mm long by 4 cm² cross-sectional area. The superiority of the newer alloys is also demonstrated in Figs. 6.38 and 6.39, which show the relation between percentage retained magnetization against demagnetization by a.c. fields and by impact.

The values of remanence and coercivity for the various permanent magnet steels are shown in Table 6.IV. The mechanical properties of the newer alloys differ considerably from those of the earlier magnet steels, necessitating a very different procedure in hardening and fabricating.

The new alloy Ticonal (titanium, cobalt, nicke, aluminium and iron) has a coercivity nearly 50 pe

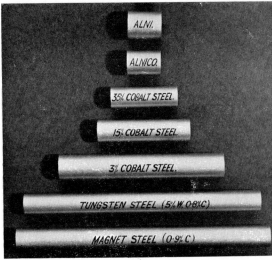

FIG. 6.37. RELATIVE SIZES OF BAR MAGNETS IN VARIOUS ALLOYS TO PRODUCE A SPECIFIED FLUX DENSITY
(Courtesy of "I.P.O.E.E. Journal")

cent higher than alnico and also an appreciabl higher remanence.

The mechanical hardness of permanent magne

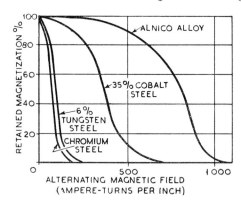

FIG. 6.38. DECREASE IN MAGNETIZATION WITH ALTERNATING DEMAGNETIZING FIELD FOR VARIOUS PERMANENT MAGNET STEELS
(Courtesy of "Nickel Bulletin")

materials is such that they can only be worked b grinding. To overcome this difficulty, sma magnets of intricate shape are now made by powde metallurgy:[10] the alloy is prepared by mixin the finely-powdered constituents and pressing th mixture to the shape of the finished part. Th

TABLE 6.IV

MAGNETIC PROPERTIES OF SOME PERMANENT MAGNET MATERIALS

Material	Remanence B_R (Wb/m²)	Energy Product BH_{max} (AT-Wb/m³) (thousands)	Coercivity H_C (AT/m) (thousands)	Remarks
Alcomax II	1·3	43	46·2	
*Alcomax II SC	1·37	47	47·7	
Alcomax III	1·26	43	51·8	
*Alcomax III SC	1·32	48·5	55·7	
*Columax	1·35	59·6	59·0	Anisotropic
Alcomax IV	1·15	36	59·7	* = crystal oriented
*Alcomax IV SC	1·22	41·5	62·0	
Hycomax I	0·9	25·5	65·6	
Hycomax II	0·85	32	95·6	
Hynico II	0·60	14·3	71·6	
Alnico (High Rem.)	0·80	13·5	39·8	
Alnico (Normal)	0·72	13·5	44·6	
Alnico (High Coercivity)	0·65	13·5	49·3	Isotropic
Alni (High Rem.)	0·62	10·0	38·2	
Alni (Normal)	0·56	10·0	46·1	
Alni (High Coercivity)	0·50	10·0	54·0	
35% Cobalt steel	0·90	7·55	19·9	
15% Cobalt steel	0·82	4·90	14·3	
9% Cobalt steel	0·78	4·00	12·7	
6% Cobalt steel	0·75	3·50	11·55	
3% Cobalt steel	0·72	2·8	10·35	
2% Co, 4% Cr steel	0·98	2·55	6·35	
6% Tungsten steel	1·05	2·4	5·18	
Chromium steel	0·98	2·26	5·58	
Feroba I	0·22	7·9	135	Isotropic barium ferrite
Feroba II	0·39	25·4	135	Anisotropic barium ferrite

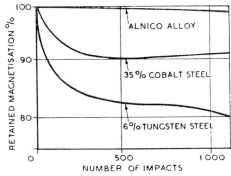

FIG. 6.39. DECREASE IN MAGNETIZATION WITH
MECHANICAL IMPACT FOR VARIOUS PERMANENT
MAGNET STEELS
(*Courtesy of "Nickel Bulletin"*)

pressings are then sintered in hydrogen at temperatures up to 1 400°C.

In another approach some very useful permanent magnet materials have been obtained by alloying.

The most important of these contain about 60 per cent copper with 20 per cent nickel and 20 per cent iron, from which the name *cunife* is derived. The properties of these materials, and of others containing vanadium, are listed in Table 6.V.

A portion of the hysteresis loop for a hard magnetic material showing the values of remanence B_R and coercivity H_C is given in Fig. 6.40: this portion of the hysteresis loop bounded by the remanence and coercivity values is known as the *demagnetization curve*. A magnetic circuit always includes a small working air-gap in which it is desired to set up a strong magnetic flux. The introduction of this air-gap reduces the working flux density from the remanence value B_R to some such value as B_D shown by the working point W. This reduction in flux density to the value B_D could equally well have been attained by applying a demagnetizing force H_D.

The energy which a given volume of magnet

TABLE 6.V

PROPERTIES OF SOME DUCTILE AND OTHER PERMANENT MAGNET MATERIALS

Alloy	Fe	Ni	Cu	Other	H_c (AT/m) (thousands)	B_R (Wb/m²)	BH_{max} (AT-Wb/m³) (thousands)
Cunife 1	20	20	60		44	0·54	13·5
Cunife 2	27·5	20	50	Co 2·5	21	0·73	6·4
Magnetoflex 20	20	20	60		33	0·52	7·2
Cunico 1	—	21	50	Co 29	53	0·34	6·4
Vicalloy	38	—	—	Co 52⎫ V 10⎭	24	0·9	8·0
Magnetoflex 35	35	—	—	Co 52⎫ V 13⎭	32	0·85	14·5
Alcomax II	55·5	11	4·5	Co 21⎫ Al 8⎭	46	1·24	35·0
Alnico IV	56	27	—	Co 5⎫ Al 12⎭	53	0·6	10·0

steel can set up in the working air-gap of a given external magnetic circuit depends upon the particular shape of the demagnetizing curve for the material and upon the actual working point on that curve: the working point can be controlled by the dimension ratio chosen for the magnet.

Two important relations can be proved connecting the values of B_D and H_D with the physical

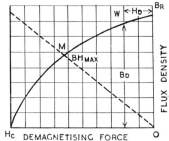

FIG. 6.40. DEMAGNETIZATION CURVE
(Courtesy of I.P.O.E.E.)

dimensions, A the cross-sectional area and l the length of the magnet. These relations are that (1) the product Al, which is the volume of the magnet, is inversely proportional to the product $B_D H_D$, or $V = Al \propto 1/(B_D H_D)$; (2) the ratio of l to A is proportional to the ratio of B_D to H_D, or $l/A \propto B_D/H_D$. The ratio l/A is known as the *dimension ratio* of the magnet. These two variable factors, the product $B_D H_D$ and the ratio B_D/H_D which are related to the volume and to the dimension ratio of the magnet are fundamental factors in permanent magnet design. From the first relationship it is clear that when $B_D H_D$ is a maximum, the volume of the magnet required is a minimum, so that a maximum value of $B_D H_D$ will give the

optimum design for least weight and cost o material.

Table 6.VI shows for a typical modern magne alloy the product and ratio of B and H over th range of the demagnetization curve. It will b seen that the product BH increases to a maximun value at, in this particular case, $H = 26\,400$.

This maximum value for any curve is designate BH_{max} and it is a critical factor in the design o permanent magnets. It follows that the greate the value of BH_{max} for a material, the greater i

TABLE 6.VI

H	B	BH	B/H
0	0·72	0	
8 000	0·67	5 360	$8·4 \times 10^{-5}$
16 000	0·6	9 600	$3·8 \times 10^{-5}$
24 000	0·5	12 000	$2·1 \times 10^{-5}$
32 000	0·3	9 600	$0·9 \times 10^{-5}$
40 000	0	0	0

its magnetic efficiency per unit volume. In magne design the values of B_D and H_D are chosen cor responding to the value BH_{max}; the dimension of the magnet may then be determined from th foregoing relationships. In certain cases, however it may be preferable to depart from this optimun condition in order to obtain a larger dimensio ratio, because the lower the value of H_D, the mor stable and permanent the magnet is likely to be It will be seen from Table 6.VI that a lower value of H_D will correspond to a higher value of the rati B_D/H_D and consequently to a higher value of th dimension ratio l/A. This explains why a long thin magnet is more resistant to externa lemagnetizing influences than is a short thick magnet of the same material.

The values of BH_{max} for the various magnet steels are given in Table 6.IV.

The determination of BH_{max} may be made by graphical construction from the demagnetizing curve. If a rectangle is drawn upon the ordinates OB_R and OH_C (Fig. 6.40) the intersection of the diagonal (from the origin) of this rectangle with the curve gives the value at which BH_{max} arises. In Fig. 6.40 this is the point M which occurs approximately midway along the demagnetizing curve. It will be seen that the co-ordinates of this point M depend upon the shape of the demagnetizing curve (i.e. upon the material) as well as upon the value of B_R and H_C.

In order that the flux density shall be reasonably high the demagnetizing force H_D must be appreciably less than the coercivity H_C. For the older alloys such as tungsten steel with a coercivity of 5 200 ampere-turns/metre, the safe maximum allowable value of H_D on this account is limited to a fraction of this value: for the newer alloys with coercivities of the order of 40 000 ampere-turns/metre, much greater values of H_D are permissible without excessive reduction of flux density B_D, and in consequence, much shorter magnets of the newer materials can be used without serious demagnetization.

6.22. Magnetic Theory. The earlier molecular theory of magnetization held to account for the magnetic phenomenon suggested that each molecule of a magnetic material is itself a minute permanent magnet. In the unmagnetized state these molecules, oriented entirely at random, in effect form themselves into closed chains, as indicated in Fig. 6.41 (*a*), the N-pole of each molecule neutralizing the equal but opposite effect of the S-pole of a neighbouring molecule: consequently no polarity is exhibited externally, and the material appears to be unmagnetized.

The effect of magnetizing the material is gradually to align all the molecules in the same direction so that free poles are exhibited at the two ends as shown in Fig. 6.41 (*b*). In case (*b*) a state of magnetic saturation has been reached when no further magnetization could be produced in the material by any further increase in the magnetizing force because all the molecules have been completely aligned. Between the two states shown at (*a*) and (*b*) the substance shows successive degrees of magnetization due to the gradual alignment of the molecular magnets as the magnetizing force is steadily increased from zero to the saturation value.

Inside the magnet every molecular N-pole is near to and assisted by a similar molecular S-pole, but at the ends of the magnet free molecular poles occur, imparting polarity to the magnet. There is a certain amount of fanning out at the ends due to the lateral repulsion of the similar free molecular poles: this is confirmed in the shape of the external magnetic field (Fig. 6.8). If subjected to heat treatment or vibration, the molecules tend to return to their original closed chains—very readily in the case of soft iron—and the presence of magnetism externally disappears.

The more obvious evidence supporting this theory is that if a bar magnet is broken into pieces

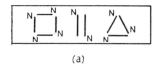

(a)

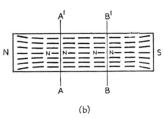

(b)

FIG. 6.41. MOLECULAR THEORY OF MAGNETIZATION

—as at AA' and BB' in Fig. 6.41 (*b*)—each piece becomes in itself a complete magnet with free north and south poles.

Other important supports to this theory are as follows—

(1) The various degrees of susceptibility and of remanence possessed by the various qualities of iron and steel. The greater molecular rigidity of hard steel requires a greater coercive force to effect a change of magnetic condition—in other words it is more difficult to magnetize and demagnetize.

(2) The effect of vibration or any molecular disturbance on magnetization or demagnetization. Magnetization is assisted by light blows on the material while under the influence of the magnetizing force. Magnets are weakened by rough usage or by the molecular disturbance of great heat.

(3) The production of heat and molecular noises in a piece of magnetic material subjected to rapid changes of magnetization. The molecules can be heard to move and the energy used in overcoming the friction opposing the movement, and which causes the hysteresis loss is transformed into heat.

(4) The alteration in the size and shape of a magnetic material due to magnetization. This

phenomenon of a relation between magnetization and mechanical strain is known as MAGNETO-STRICTION.

(5) The tendency to reach magnetic saturation when all the molecules have been brought into alignment.

(6) Iron loses its elasticity and its magnetization at the same critical temperature, the CURIE POINT.

Magnetostriction and the Curie point are discussed below.

If the molecular magnets referred to consist of single atoms or relatively small molecular groups, the material exhibits paramagnetic properties, including zero remanence.

The molecular theory of magnetism does not explain why the molecules of certain materials only should be magnets. According to modern theory the *spinning electron* is regarded as the ultimate magnetic particle. An electron in motion is equivalent to an electric current and it sets up a magnetic field. In addition to its orbital motion, a spin about its own axis is attributed to the electron. Within each electron shell an electron may spin in one of two directions, opposite in sense. Within any completed shell, i.e. a shell containing an even number of electrons occupying all available positions, half of the electrons have positive spin and half have negative spin: the resultant magnetic moment is therefore zero. The magnetic materials are those with an incomplete third shell, showing a resultant electron spin and a magnetic moment.

As an example, iron has only 14 out of a possible 18 electrons in the third shell. Of these 14 electrons, 9 have positive and 5 have negative spins, showing a resultant positive spin of $+4$. The magnetic elements which occur in adjacent positions in the Periodic Table (Appendix **D**) are chromium, manganese, iron, cobalt, and nickel: each has a resultant electron spin and so exhibits the magnetic phenomenon. All shells except the third contain as many electrons spinning in the one direction as in the other.

For ferromagnetism to arise, it is necessary that, in addition to the existence of resultant electron spin, the resultant spins of neighbouring atoms should be oriented in the same direction. This requirement is not fulfilled by the atoms of such elements as platinum and palladium, consequently they are not ferromagnetic although they have incomplete inner shells.

If atoms are brought together in a metallic form the spinning electrons of adjacent atoms interact. By a process known as "exchange interaction" the magnetic moments associated with the atoms may be aligned so that they act together to give a total resultant magnetic moment *or* they act

in opposition to give a zero resultant magnetic moment. When the magnetic moments assist one another to give a resultant magnetic moment the material is *ferromagnetic*. If they act in opposition to give zero resultant magnetic moment the metal is *anti-ferromagnetic*.

Ferrites consist of two or more chemical compounds which become ionized (Chapter IV)—i.e. the number of orbital electrons has been changed. The ions of these compounds may or may not have a resultant magnetic moment depending upon the elements concerned. If they do have resultant magnetic moments they are mutually in opposition but owing to the fact that a ferrite crystal structure exists in two distinct forms—known as the *octahedral* and *tetrahedral* forms, of which the former predominates—the compensation is partial only and a resultant magnetic moment is present. Though actually anti-ferromagnetic by nature this form of incompletely-compensated ferro-magnetism is termed *ferrimagnetism*. Summarizing, if the magnetic moments in each ion or atom of a material are distributed in a haphazard manner the material is paramagnetic: if the spins are parallel and aid one another the material is ferro-magnetic: when the spins are anti-parallel, if the balance is not complete the material is ferri-magnetic, but if the balance is perfect the material is anti-ferromagnetic.

The modern view of ferromagnetic phenomena is that they are due to atomic, rather than molecular, effects. In the ferromagnetic materials—iron and steel, for example—it is generally agreed that the elementary magnetic units consist of much larger groups of atoms, each group containing something like 10^{14} atoms. These cohering groups of atoms are known as *domains*. Within the domain the magnetic moments of all atoms are completely aligned so that the domain itself is magnetically saturated.

The fact that an increase in flux density is only accomplished by an increase in magnetizing force—i.e. that saturation cannot be immediately attained by the application of a small magnetizing force—is explained by the ferromagnetic material having different properties in different directions; this property also explains the phenomena of remanence, coercivity, and hysteresis.

If the applied magnetizing force is in a particular direction—*a direction of easiest magnetization*—with reference to the crystal structure, the permeability is a maximum, and a maximum flux density results. There are six directions of easiest magnetization, namely those along three mutually perpendicular axes, each in two senses. In the un-magnetized state, each domain is assumed to be magnetized to saturation in one of these directions of easiest magnetization. The net magnetization is, however, zero, because of the random distribution of the various domains.

A theoretical explanation to the form of the permeability curve would therefore be given by Fig. 6.42, which should not, however, be regarded as other than a highly diagrammatic representation. In this diagram, (a) represents a piece of unmagnetized iron, each square indicating a domain: the arrows, circles, and crosses represent the six directions of easiest magnetization, the circles and crosses indicating the two senses of direction

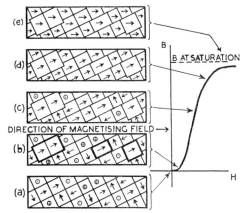

FIG. 6.42. STATE OF DOMAINS DURING MAGNETIZATION
(*Courtesy of "I.P.O.E.E. Journal"*)

mutually perpendicular to the arrows. The direction of applied magnetizing force will not in general be parallel to one of these directions.

A small applied magnetizing force will be unable to change the orientations of any domain, and it is believed that the domain most nearly in the direction of magnetizing force will grow in size at the expense of neighbouring domains farther from alignment with the magnetizing force (b). Only a small increase in flux density will result, corresponding to the initial permeability.

As the magnetizing force increases, the orientations of other domains will change *abruptly*, one by one, to a more favourable direction of easy magnetization (c): this results in a greater rate of increase of flux density, and corresponds to the steeper middle portion of the permeability curve.

The abrupt orientation of the domains is accomplished by sudden re-orientations of all the electron spins in the domain from one direction of easy magnetization to another, and it is a discontinuous process. This *Barkhausen effect* may be observed by winding a coil around a ferromagnetic specimen and connecting the coil through an amplifier to a

telephone receiver: as the magnetizing field applied to the specimen is gradually increased, however slowly and smoothly it is varied, a series of clicks is heard in the receiver indicating that the changes in magnetic induction are discontinuous. This stage is completed at (d) where the sample is essentially one large domain.

When the discontinuous process is completed, the direction of magnetization changes smoothly from the direction of easiest magnetization into parallelism with the applied magnetizing force. The material at this stage is magnetized to saturation (e). This final smooth orientation corresponds to the final (saturation) portion of the curve.

The domain theory assumes that the magnetic moments of the elementary magnets remain constant, and that an increase in flux density is brought about by changes in the inclination of their magnetic axes to the direction of the magnetizing force.

Thermal agitation tends always to produce a random distribution in the alignment of the resultant electron spins between neighbouring atoms. At a certain critical temperature, known as the CURIE POINT, this disturbance is sufficient for a ferromagnetic material to lose its magnetism completely. For iron the Curie point is 770°C. At the other extreme, saturation is obtained with very small magnetizing forces at low temperatures in the neighbourhood of absolute zero (− 273°C). At normal temperatures, an increase in intensity of magnetization is only obtained by applying sufficient magnetizing force to overcome the forces of the normal thermal agitation.

The Curie temperatures for 6 per cent tungsten, 35 per cent cobalt, and nickel-iron alloys are all in the region 710°–760°C, which approximate to the corresponding change point (770°C) for iron. Nevertheless the forms of the curves relating decrease in magnetization with increase in temperature are vastly different (Fig. 6.43) and show the superiority of the newer alloys in their performance at temperatures up to the Curie point.

The phenomenon of MAGNETOSTRICTION—the small change produced in the length of a piece of material as a result of magnetization—helps to explain the relation between mechanical hardness and magnetic hardness. Such changes in dimensions are opposed by the normal internal forces and energy must therefore be expended in producing them. There is little doubt that this is the main cause of hysteresis loss.

Mechanical hardness depends upon the development of internal strains. The larger the strains the more stable is the magnetization and the larger the value of coercive force required to disturb it.

Fig. 6.44 illustrates the Joule effect of magneto-striction for specimens of various materials under the influence of an increasing magnetizing force. The effect is most marked with nickel, and the

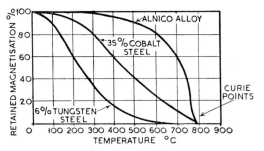

FIG. 6.43. RELATIVE DECREASE IN MAGNETIZATION WITH TEMPERATURE FOR VARIOUS PERMANENT MAGNET STEELS, SHOWING CURIE POINTS
(*Courtesy of "Nickel Bulletin"*)

sudden application of a large magnetizing force induces a loud click from the material. Nickel-iron alloys show intermediate values of contraction and at about 80 per cent nickel the effect practically

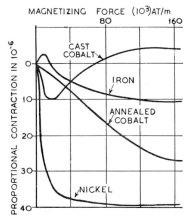

FIG. 6.44. RELATIVE MAGNETOSTRICTION FOR VARIOUS METALS

vanishes: this is approximately the composition of one of the permalloys, the hysteresis loss of which is very much less than for either nickel or iron separately.

A piece of material subjected to a magnetizing field will acquire a different flux according to whether or not an external strain is applied.

6.23. Magnetic Screening. The introduction of a piece of soft iron into a magnetic field causes flux lines to concentrate in the iron, leaving the field weaker elsewhere (Fig. 6.14). The effect of an iron

ring or of a cylinder placed in a magnetic field is indicated in Fig. 6.45: a region enclosed by a soft iron ring is screened to a considerable extent from the effects of the field and would be almost completely screened inside a closed iron container. There is little tendency for flux lines to leave the iron and pass through an air medium, only to return again to the same iron path.

Magnetic screening is of frequent application in telecommunication equipment to prevent undesirable magnetic interference between adjacent components. Such items as relays and calling indicators are frequently fitted into soft iron covers which preclude the possibility of false operation

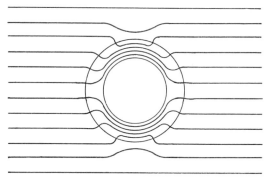

FIG. 6.45. MAGNETIC SCREEN

from a neighbouring field and at the same time exclude dust from the moving parts and from the insulating material. They are normally earth connected and may also act as electrostatic screens.

6.24. Force Between Magnet Poles. If a closed iron ring (Fig. 6.6 (*a*)) is subjected to a magnetizing force in the direction of its circumference it will become magnetized in the manner indicated in the diagram, forming a closed path showing no external poles. External poles can be produced by cutting a small gap in the ring, as at XY.

If the gap is small enough, a uniform field will exist across it, the flux density in this gap being equal to B webers/metre^2. Suppose that the gap length is increased by a small amount x metres, the current being increased at the same time so that the flux density remains constant in value. No energy change then takes place in the system and if P newtons is the force of attraction between the pole surfaces, then the energy stored in the added volume of air-gap must have been derived from the work done by the force of P newtons acting through the distance x metres, namely Px joules. This energy is equal to the energy per unit volume

$B^2/2\mu_0$ multiplied by the volume of this added air-gap Ax: hence

$$P \times x = B^2/2\mu_0 \times A \times x$$

and

$$P = B^2 A/2\mu_0 \text{ newtons} \qquad . \quad (6.3)$$

This expression may be utilized, for example, to calculate the pull on the armature of a relay (see Examples 7.3 and 7.7). It will be noted that the pull is proportional to the *square* of the flux density. If an instrument exerts a pull due to two air-gaps, as for example in the telephone receiver (see Fig. 15.23), the pull is $B^2A/2\mu_0$ newtons for *each* air-gap. If the medium were other than air, and of relative permeability μ_r, the pull would be $B^2A/2\mu_r\mu_0$ newtons.

6.25. Energy Stored in the Magnetic Field.

In the air-gap considered above, since $\mu_r \simeq 1$, the B-H graph is a straight line and the area under the graph is a triangle whose area is $\frac{1}{2}BH$: this area represents the energy stored per unit volume in the magnetic field so that

$$W = \tfrac{1}{2}BH = B^2/2\mu_0 \text{ joules/m}^3$$

Summary

Law of Attraction and Repulsion. Like poles produce repulsion. Unlike poles produce attraction.

Inverse Square Law.

$$F = m_1 m_2/4\pi\mu_r\mu_0 d^2 \text{ newtons} \qquad . \quad (6.1)$$

Magnetic Flux (Φ). The magnetic induction in a material due to a magnetizing force. $\Phi = BA$ webers.

Flux Density (B). Magnetic flux per metre². $B = \Phi/A$ webers/metre².

Permeability (μ). The ability of a material to produce magnetic flux.

$$\mu = \mu_r\mu_0 = B/H \text{ henry/metre} \qquad . \quad (6.2)$$
$$\mu_0 = 4\pi/10^7 \text{ henry/metre}$$

Residual Magnetism. (*Remanent flux density.*) The magnetism remaining in a substance after the magnetizing force has been withdrawn.

Remanence (B_R). The residual flux density after the initial magnetization reaches saturation.

Coercive Force. The demagnetizing force necessary to reduce the residual magnetism to zero.

Coercivity (H_C). The demagnetizing force necessary to reduce the remanence to zero after the initial magnetization reaches saturation.

Hysteresis. In a magnetization cycle, the lagging of B behind H.

Hysteresis Loop. The closed figure formed by plotting B against H through a magnetizing cycle.

Hysteresis Loss. The energy absorbed in taking a magnetic material through cycles of magnetization: the loss is proportional to the area of the hysteresis loop.

Soft Magnetic Material. Characterized by high permeability, low coercivity and low hysteresis loss.

Permanent Magnet Material. Characterized by high remanence and high coercivity.

Pull Between Magnet Surfaces.

$$P = B^2A/2\mu_r\mu_0 \text{ newtons} . \qquad . \quad (6.3)$$

Magnetic Energy. $W = B^2/2\mu_r\mu_0$ joules/metre³

REFERENCES

1. F. Brailsford, D. A. Oliver, D. Hadfield, and G. R. Polgreen: "Magnetic Materials," *I.E.E. Journal, Part I,* **95** (1948), p. 522.
2. C. E. Morgan: "The Development of Magnetic Materials," *I.P.O.E.E. Paper No.* **168.**
3. F. Brailsford: "Modern Ferromagnetic Materials," *I.E.E. Journal,* **5** (1959), p. 417.
4. *The Nickel Bulletin,* April, 1938.
5. W. A. Turner: "An Introduction to Soft Magnetic Ferrites," *A.T.E. Journal,* **14** (1958), p. 72.
6. M. O. Williams: "Magnetically Soft Ferrites," ibid., **14** (1958), p. 129.
7. B. G. Parkin: "Magnetic Materials with Rectangular Hysteresis Loops," *I.P.O.E.E. Journal,* **48** (1955), p. 1.
8. D. A. Oliver: "Permanent Magnets," *Magnetism* (Institute of Physics), 1938, p. 71.
9. W. G. Radley, C. E. Richards, E. A. Speight, and E. V. Walker: "Modern Materials in Telecommunication: Part 4, Magnetic Materials," *I.P.O.E.E. Journal,* **34** (1941), p. 19.
10. G. W. Eastwood: "Ductile Permanent Magnet Materials," ibid., **53** (1961), p. 262.

CHAPTER VII

ELECTROMAGNETISM

7.1. Directions of Current and Magnetic Field.
Whenever an electric current flows in a conductor, a magnetic field is produced in the medium surrounding the conductor. This phenomenon may be readily demonstrated by placing a compass needle near to a current-carrying conductor: it will also be found that a reversal in the direction of current reverses the deflexion of the needle.

For a straight conductor the lines of force take the form of concentric circles around the conductor, i.e. the current and the magnetic field are in planes

(a)   (b)

FIG. 7.1. DIRECTIONS OF CURRENT AND MAGNETIC FIELD

at right angles to one another. If a vertical conductor is passed through a horizontal sheet of card on which iron filings are sprinkled, the passage of a fairly heavy current in the conductor will, assisted by lightly vibrating the card, cause the iron filings to set themselves in well-defined circles concentric with the conductor.

Simple rules have been formulated which relate the direction of current and field. Maxwell's "Corkscrew Rule" is perhaps the most readily remembered. When a corkscrew is in use it has two distinct motions—the rotating movement applied to the handle together with the resulting movement in the direction of its length. According to MAXWELL'S RULE—*if a right-handed corkscrew could be screwed into the conductor, the direction of the current is represented by the longitudinal movement of the corkscrew, and the direction of the magnetic field is represented by the direction of rotation.*

Alternatively, there is AMPÈRE'S RULE: "imagine a man to be swimming in the conductor in the direction of the current with his face towards a compass needle: then the N-pole of the compass needle is deflected towards his left hand."

It will be noted that both rules are applicable to either direction of the current. An alternating current produces a continuously reversing field.

For the representation of electromagnetic fields the conventions of Fig. 7.1 are adopted. The small

circle is the cross-section of a conductor. The cross (Fig. 7.1 (*a*)) represents the rear-end view of a feathered arrow to indicate a current flowing away from the eye of the reader, i.e. into the paper. The dot (Fig. 7.1 (*b*)) represents the end view of the point of the arrow, indicating a current flowing towards the observer, i.e. from out of the paper. Application of the Corkscrew Rule enables the direction of the concentric fields to be indicated. The field is clockwise when the current flows away from the observer: anti-clockwise when the current flows towards the observer.

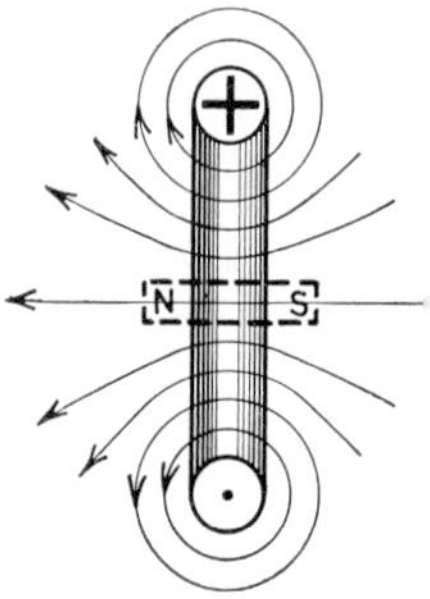

7.2. The Solenoid. The field may be made more intense if the conductor is bent into the form of a loop. Either half of the loop is represented in Fig. 7.2, which shows how the field becomes concentrated within the loop: it will be observed that the field so produced is

FIG. 7.2. MAGNETIC FIELD OF CIRCULAR CONDUCTOR

equivalent to that of a short bar magnet (shown dotted at *NS* in the diagram) placed at right angles to the loop.

The step which naturally follows is to wind the conductor into a number of loops forming a *solenoid*. The field of the solenoid is shown in Fig. 7.3, which is simply an extension of Fig. 7.2. It will be seen that the field due to a solenoid is identical with that of a bar magnet placed inside the solenoid, and indicated at *NS* by the dotted line. The field immediately between two adjacent turns tends to become cancelled out, so giving to the solenoid field its characteristic shape.

The polarity of a solenoid is best deduced from the Corkscrew Rule, but from Fig. 7.3 it is seen that if the solenoid, viewed from one end, carries a current in a clockwise direction, then that end is a S-pole: and alternatively, if viewed from the end where the current is in a counter-clockwise direction, that end is a N-pole.

7.3. Magnetizing Force of Electromagnetic Field.
The magnetizing force H at any point near a conductor carrying a current I amperes is directly dependent upon the strength of the current which causes the magnetic field to be established: the

magnetizing force is also inversely proportional to the length l metres of the magnetic path being considered. In symbols

$$H = I/l$$

In the more general case, the conductor is wound into the form of a solenoid having N turns each carrying the current I amperes: then if the length of the magnetic path is l metres the magnetizing force is

$$H = NI/l \text{ ampere-turns/metre} \qquad . \quad (7.1)$$

In the case of a single conductor ($N = 1$) such as that shown in Fig. 7.1, the magnetizing force at any point depends upon the length of the magnetic

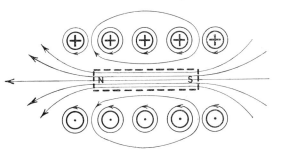

FIG. 7.3. MAGNETIC FIELD OF SOLENOID

path containing the point. For example at any point on one of the circles shown, the length of the path is $2\pi r$ metres if r metres is the radius of the circle. The magnetizing force at any point on the circle is then

$$H = NI/l = I/2\pi r \text{ ampere-turns/metre}$$

The value of H is seen to be greatest for points nearest to the conductor when r has its minimum value and the magnetic path-length, $2\pi r$, is least.

The number of turns N being simply a number, the magnetizing force is sometimes stated simply in terms of *amperes per metre*.

The expression $H = NI/l$ ampere-turns/metre is of considerable practical importance and is used as the basis for design of electromagnets and relays. The length l metres is the total length of the magnetic path.

It should be noted that an increase in the number of turns, by increasing the resistance, reduces the current from a given voltage unless compensated by using a wire of greater cross-sectional area.

EXAMPLE 7.1 (A). Calculate the approximate intensity of the magnetic field at the centre of an air-cored solenoid 10 cm long wound with 20 turns per cm and carrying a direct current of 5 A. (*C. & G.*)

$$l = 10 \text{ cm} = 0 \cdot 1 \text{ m}$$
$$N = 20 \times 10 = 200 \text{ turns}$$
$$I = 5 \text{ A}$$
$$H = NI/l = 200 \times 5/0 \cdot 1$$
$$= \underline{\underline{10\ 000 \text{ AT/m}}}$$

7.4. Flux Density of a Solenoid. If the solenoid is wound upon a ferromagnetic core having a relative permeability μ_r (at a magnetizing force H), the flux density

$$B = \mu H$$
$$= \mu_r \mu_0 H \qquad . \qquad . \qquad \text{(equation 6.2)}$$
$$= \mu_r \mu_0 NI/l \text{ webers/metre}^2$$

A definition of the weber is given in § **7.10**.

The use of a magnetically soft core material having a high initial relative permeability together with a winding of many turns permits a comparatively high flux density to be obtained from a relatively low current. Furthermore the practical convenience is afforded by "switching" the flux on or off with the current, of varying the flux by controlling the current, and also of reversing the flux by reversing the current. Relays and electromagnets, used so extensively in telecommunication equipment, depend upon these principles for their operation.

EXAMPLE 7.2 (A). An iron rod, circular in cross section, 1 m long, is bent into a closed ring and is wound with 1 000 turns of insulated wire. What is the flux density in the iron, if a current of 2 A is passed through the wire and the relative permeability of the iron is 500? (*C. & G.*)

$$N = 1\ 000 \text{ turns}$$
$$I = 2 \text{ A}$$
$$l = 1 \text{ m}$$
$$\mu_r = 500$$
$$\mu_0 = 4\pi \times 10^{-7}$$
$$H = NI/l$$
$$= 1\ 000 \times 2/1 = 2\ 000 \text{ AT/m}$$
$$B = \mu H = \mu_r \mu_0 H$$
$$= 500 \times 4\pi \times 2\ 000/10^7$$
$$= 0 \cdot 4\pi = \underline{\underline{1 \cdot 257 \text{ Wb/m}^2}}$$

7.5. The Magnetic Circuit. The complete closed path followed by any group of lines of magnetic flux, i.e. from the N-pole to the S-pole externally, and from the S-pole to the N-pole inside the magnet or coil, is known as the *magnetic circuit*; it lends itself to consideration in a similar manner to the electric circuit.

Fig. 7.4 shows a soft iron ring of mean length l metre and cross-sectional area A metre² uniformly wound with N turns and carrying a current of I amperes. A coil of this type is known as a *toroid*: it has no external magnetic circuit and no free poles. This form of coil is used in certain transformers and in loading coils. The directions of the current and the flux are indicated in the diagram.

The magnetizing force

$$H = NI/l \text{ ampere-turns/metre}$$

The flux density

$$B = \mu H = \mu_r \mu_0 H$$
$$= \mu_r \mu_0 NI/l \text{ webers/metre}^2$$

The total flux

$$\Phi = BA = \mu_r \mu_0 ANI/l \text{ webers}$$

This expression may be rewritten as

$$\Phi = NI \div l/(\mu_r \mu_0 A) \text{ webers}$$

The term NI, which is the source of the magnetic flux, is known as the MAGNETO-MOTIVE FORCE by analogy to *e.m.f.* which is the source of an electric current. The magneto-motive force is denoted by M (sometimes by F) and expressed simply in ampere-turns, thus

$$M = NI \text{ ampere-turns} \quad . \quad . \quad (7.2)$$

The term $(l/\mu_r \mu_0 A)$ is termed the RELUCTANCE. It is denoted by the symbol S (sometimes by R) and, on account of its derivation from the above expression, it is measured in ampere-turns/weber, so that

$$S = l/(\mu_r \mu_0 A) \text{ ampere-turns/weber} \quad . \quad (7.3)$$

In the above expressions, l metres is the total length of the magnetic path.

The equation of the magnetic circuit may therefore be written—

Flux = magneto-motive force/reluctance

or in symbols,

$$\Phi = M/S \quad . \quad . \quad . \quad (7.4)$$

In its other two forms—

$$M = \Phi S \text{ or } S = M/\Phi$$

This equation is of similar form to Ohm's law for the electric circuit. The m.m.f., comparable to e.m.f., is the factor responsible for producing a difference of *magnetic potential*—the difference in the magnetic states existing at two points which produces a magnetic field between the two points and sets up a flux in the magnetic circuit.

The magnitude of the flux depends upon the value of the reluctance of the circuit: the reluctance

$S = l/(\mu_r \mu_0 A)$ is analogous to electrical resistance $R = \rho l/a$ or to $R = l/(\sigma a)$, where σ is the conductivity, showing the correspondence of magnetic permeability to electrical conductivity. The flux, however, is not an actual flow comparable to the electron drift in the electric circuit: furthermore the reluctance is not constant for a given magnetic path, since the value of μ_r varies with the magnetizing force.

Reluctance is defined as the ratio of the m.m.f. acting in the magnetic circuit to the resultant magnetic flux.

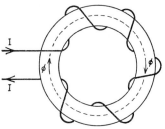

FIG. 7.4. MAGNETIC CIRCUIT

7.6. Reluctance. If a small air-gap is cut into the ring (Fig. 7.4) the reluctance of the air-gap must be separately considered. Its reluctance is $l/(\mu_r \mu_0 A)$ where $\mu_r = 1$; compared with a ferromagnetic path whose relative permeability may have a value of several thousands, it will be seen that the reluctance of even a very short air-gap reaches a high value (see Example 7.4). In magnetic instruments air-gaps are restricted to the minimum length necessary to permit the moving parts to function, and careful attention is paid to ensuring good magnetic joints between component parts of the magnetic circuit to exclude even minute undesired air-gaps.

In a simple magnetic circuit made up of several different materials acting in series, for example the core, yoke, armature, and working air-gap of a relay (Fig. 7.9), the total reluctance is equal to the simple sum of the separate reluctances, or

$$S = S_1 + S_2 + S_3 + \ldots$$
$$= l_1/(\mu_1 A_1) + l_2/(\mu_2 A_2) + l_3/(\mu_3 A_3) + \ldots \quad (7.5)$$

where μ_1, μ_2, and μ_3 are each of the form $\mu = \mu_r \mu_0$.

Where magnetic paths occur in parallel, it is necessary to determine the reluctance of each path: the flux in each path will then be equal to the m.m.f. across that path divided by its reluctance, care being taken to ensure that the m.m.f. considered is actually that applied across the path.

The name RELUCTIVITY is given to the reciprocal of relative permeability, i.e. it is equal to $1/\mu_r$.

The name PERMEANCE *is given to the reciprocal of* RELUCTANCE, *i.e. permeance* $= \mu_r \mu_0 A / l$ webers/ampere-turn.

EXAMPLE 7.3 (B). The following particulars are taken from the magnetic circuit of a relay—

Mean length of iron circuit	$= 20$ cm
Length of air-gap	$= 2$ mm
Number of turns on core	$= 8\,000$
Current through coil	$= 50$ mA
μ_r for the iron	$= 500$

Neglecting leakage, what is the flux density in the air-gap? If the area of the core is 0·5 cm², what is the pull exerted on the armature?　　　　(*C. & G.*)

For air,
$$S_A = 2 \times 10^{-3}/(1 \times 4\pi \times 10^{-7}A) = 10^4/(2\pi A)$$
For iron,
$$S_I = 0 \cdot 2/(500 \times 4\pi \times 10^{-7}A) = 0 \cdot 2 \times 10^4/(2\pi A)$$
Total
$$S = S_A + S_I = 10^4/(2\pi A) + (0 \cdot 2 \times 10^4)/(2\pi A)$$
$$= (1 \cdot 2 \times 10^4)/(2\pi A)$$
$$\text{M.m.f.} = NI$$
$$= 8\,000 \times 0 \cdot 05 = 400 \text{ AT}$$
$$\Phi = \text{M.m.f.}/S$$
$$= 400 \div (1 \cdot 2 \times 10^4)/(2\pi A)$$
$$= 800\pi A/(1 \cdot 2 \times 10^4)$$
$$B = \Phi/A$$
$$= 800\pi/(1 \cdot 2 \times 10^4) = 2\pi/30$$
$$= 0 \cdot 209 \text{ Wb/m}^2$$

$$\text{Pull} = B^2 A/2\mu_0$$
$$= (2\pi/30)^2 \times 0 \cdot 5 \times 10^{-4} \div 2 \times 4\pi \times 10^{-7}$$
$$= 10\pi/36$$
$$= 0 \cdot 872 \text{ newtons.}$$

EXAMPLE 7.4 (B). In a certain relay the total length of iron in the magnetic circuit is 100 times the total length of the air-gaps and the relative permeability for the iron is 1 000. Taking the cross-sectional area of the air-gaps to be the same as that of the iron, what proportion of the overall reluctance of the magnetic circuit do these gaps represent?　　　　(*C. & G.*)

Using the suffixes A for air and I for iron—
$$l_I = 100 l_A, \ A_I = A_A$$
$$S = S_A + S_I = l_A/A_A + 100 l_A/(1\,000 A_A)$$
$$= l_A/A_A + l_A/(10 A_A) = 11 l_A/(10 A_A)$$
$$S_A/S = l_A/A_A \div 11 l_A/(10 A_A) = \underline{10/11}$$

i.e. the air-gaps represent 10/11 or 91 per cent of the total circuit reluctance.

EXAMPLE 7.5 (B). The magnetic circuit of a certain relay is equivalent to that provided by a round iron rod of 0·8 cm² cross-section and 15 cm in length, bent into a circle, with its ends 0·05 cm apart. Calculate the ampere-turns required to produce a total flux of 50 μWb in the iron, its relative permeability under these conditions being 3 000.　　　　(*C. & G.*)

$$\Phi = 50 \times 10^{-6} \text{ Wb}$$

Iron	Air
$l_I = 0 \cdot 15$ m	$l_A = 5 \times 10^{-4}$ m
$\mu_I = 3\,000 \times 4\pi \times 10^{-7}$	$\mu_A = 4\pi \times 10^{-7}$
$A_I = 0 \cdot 8 \times 10^{-4}$ m²	$A_A = 0 \cdot 8 \times 10^{-4}$ m²

$$S_I = l_I/\mu_I A_I$$
$$= 0 \cdot 15/(3\,000 \times 4\pi \times 10^{-7} \times 0 \cdot 8 \times 10^{-4})$$
$$= 0 \cdot 5 \times 10^7/3 \cdot 2\pi$$
$$S_A = l_A/\mu_A A_A$$
$$= 5 \times 10^{-4}/(4\pi \times 10^{-7} \times 0 \cdot 8 \times 10^{-4})$$
$$= 5 \times 10^7/3 \cdot 2\pi$$
$$S = S_I + S_A = 5 \cdot 5 \times 10^7/3 \cdot 2\pi$$
$$\Phi = NI/S$$
$$NI = \Phi S = 50 \times 10^{-6} \times 5 \cdot 5 \times 10^7/3 \cdot 2\pi$$
$$= \underline{275 \text{ AT}}$$

EXAMPLE 7.6 (B). A soft iron bar, 30 cm long, is bent into the form of a ring but with the ends separated 0·1 cm apart in air. The bar is wound with 500 turns of wire through which is passed a direct current of 0·5 A. What is the flux density in the air-gap between the ends of the bar if the relative permeability of the iron under these conditions is 250?　　　　(*C. & G.*)

$$N = 500$$
$$I = 0 \cdot 5 \text{ A}$$

Iron	Air
$l_I = 0 \cdot 3$ m	$l_A = 10^{-3}$ m
$A_I = A$	$A_A = A$
$\mu_I = 250 \times 4\pi \times 10^{-7}$	$\mu_A = 1 \times 4\pi \times 10^{-7}$

$$S_I = 0 \cdot 3/(250 \times 4\pi \times 10^{-7}A)$$
$$= 1 \cdot 2 \times 10^4/(4\pi A)$$
$$S_A = 10^{-3}/(4\pi \times 10^{-7}A)$$
$$= 10^4/(4\pi A)$$
$$S = S_I + S_A$$
$$= 2 \cdot 2 \times 10^4/(4\pi A)$$
$$M = NI$$
$$= 500 \times 0 \cdot 5 = 250 \text{ AT}$$
$$\Phi = M/S = 250 \times 4\pi A/(2 \cdot 2 \times 10^4)$$
$$= \pi A/22$$

$$B = \Phi/A = \pi/22$$
$$= 0.14 \ \text{Wb/m}^2$$

EXAMPLE 7.7 (B). Calculate the approximate pull on the armature of a relay having the following characteristics—

Mean length of iron circuit	= 30 cm
Total length of air-gaps	= 3 mm
Number of turns on core	= 10 000
Mean cross-sectional area of iron circuit	= 0.6 cm²
Current through coil	= 50 mA
μ_r for the iron	= 600

It may be assumed for this purpose that the area of the air-gap is equal to the mean cross-sectional area of the iron circuit. (C. & G.)

Iron	Air
$l_I = 0.3$ m	$l_A = 0.3 \times 10^{-2}$
$A_I = 0.6 \times 10^{-4}$	$A_A = 0.6 \times 10^{-4}$
$\mu_I = 600 \times 4\pi \times 10^{-7}$	$\mu_A = 4\pi \times 10^{-7}$

$$S_I = l_I/\mu_I A_I$$
$$= 0.3/(600 \times 4\pi \times 10^{-7} \times 0.6 \times 10^{-4})$$
$$= 10^9/48\pi$$
$$S_A = 0.3 \times 10^{-2}/(4\pi \times 10^{-7} \times 0.6 \times 10^{-4})$$
$$= 6 \times 10^9/48\pi$$
$$S = S_I + S_A$$
$$= 7 \times 10^9/48\pi$$
$$M = NI$$
$$= 10^4 \times 0.05 = 500 \ \text{AT}$$
$$\Phi = M/S$$
$$= 500 \times 48\pi/(7 \times 10^9)$$
$$= 24\pi/(7 \times 10^6) \ \text{Wb}$$
$$B = \Phi/A$$
$$= 24\pi/(7 \times 10^6 \times 0.6 \times 10^{-4})$$
$$= 4\,000\pi/(7 \times 10^4) \ \text{Wb/m}^2$$
$$\text{Pull} = B^2 A/2\mu_0$$
$$= 16 \times 10^6\pi^2 \times 0.6 \times 10^{-4}/$$
$$(49 \times 10^8 \times 2 \times 4\pi \times 10^{-7})$$
$$= 12\pi/49$$
$$= 0.76 \ \text{N}$$

7.7. Magnetic Leakage. If a magnetizing coil is wound over a portion only of the magnetic circuit, a certain amount of magnetic leakage occurs due to flux lines passing from one part of the iron to another by paths which do not include the working air-gap where the maximum flux is required: in consequence, the flux in the air-gap will be appreciably less than the flux at any point of the magnet. The part of the magnetic flux which follows a path in which it is ineffective for the purpose desired is termed the leakage flux.

If this leakage flux is denoted by Φ_L and the useful flux in the air-gap by Φ_U, the total flux Φ_T generated by the m.m.f. must be

$$\Phi_T = \Phi_L + \Phi_U$$

The ratio of useful flux to total flux

$$= \Phi_U/\Phi_T = (\Phi_T - \Phi_L)/\Phi_T$$

is known as the LEAKAGE FACTOR: its value will be always less than one.

Due to the fringing of the flux at the air-gaps the cross-sectional area at each gap is effectively increased, with consequent reduction in the reluctance of the air-gap. The effective reluctance in such a case is equal to the actual reluctance multiplied by the leakage factor.

Magnetic leakage is analogous to the electrical leakage due to imperfect insulation: it is impossible to procure in the magnetic circuit the high standard for magnetic "insulation" usually obtained for electrical insulation, and the occurrence of magnetic leakage must always be taken into account in designing magnetic instruments.

EXAMPLE 7.8 (B). The core of a certain telephone relay is 6 cm in length and has a cross-sectional area of 0.7 cm²; the yoke has an effective length of 7 cm and a cross-sectional area of 0.8 cm²; the armature has an effective length of 1.5 cm and a cross-sectional area of 0.4 cm². The effective lengths of the air-gaps are 0.001 cm at the heel end, 0.03 cm at the knife edge or hinge, and 0.2 cm at the armature. Calculate the total reluctance of the magnetic circuit, assuming that the relative permeability for the iron parts is constant at 3 000 and that the factor to be applied to the air-gaps to correct for fringing is 0.7. (C. & G.)

	l (m)	A (m²)	μ_r
Core (C)	0.06	7×10^{-5}	3 000
Yoke (Y)	0.07	8×10^{-5}	3 000
Arm. (A)	0.015	4×10^{-5}	3 000
	10^{-5}	7×10^{-5}	1
Air-gaps (G)	3×10^{-4}	8×10^{-5}	1
	2×10^{-3}	7×10^{-5}	1

$$\mu_0 = 4\pi \times 10^{-7}$$
$$S_C = 0.06/(3\,000 \times 4\pi \times 10^{-7} \times 7 \times 10^{-5})$$
$$= 10^7/14\pi = 2.28 \times 10^5$$

$$S_Y = 0.07/(3\,000 \times 4\pi \times 10^{-7} \times 8 \times 10^{-5})$$
$$= 7 \times 10^7/96\pi = 2.32 \times 10^5$$
$$S_A = 0.015/(3\,000 \times 4\pi \times 10^{-7} \times 4 \times 10^{-5})$$
$$= 10^7/32\pi = 0.995 \times 10^5$$
$$S_1 = 10^5(2.28 + 2.322 + 0.995)$$
$$= 5.6 \times 10^5$$
$$S_G = (10^7/4\pi)[10^{-5}/(7 \times 10^{-5}) + (3 \times 10^{-4})/$$
$$(8 \times 10^{-5}) + (2 \times 10^{-3})/(7 \times 10^{-5})]$$
$$= (10^7/4\pi)[1/7 + 15/4 + 200/7]$$
$$= (10^7/4\pi)[0.14 + 3.75 + 28.57]$$
$$= 258.4 \times 10^5$$

Effective reluctance of air-gaps
$$= (258 \times 10^5 \times 0.7)$$
$$= 180.6 \times 10^5$$

Total reluctance
$$= 10^5(5.6 + 180.6)$$
$$= 186.2 \times 10^5 \text{ AT/Wb}$$

7.8. Electromagnets and Relays. An electromagnet is a piece of apparatus embodying a ferromagnetic core which is only strongly magnetized

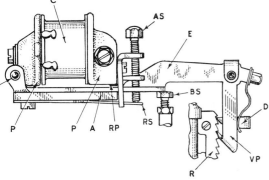

FIG. 7.5. ELECTROMAGNET FOR SELECTOR SWITCH

when an electric current passes through a winding surrounding the core. Dependent upon requirements the electromagnet is frequently fitted with an armature, a suitably shaped piece of ferromagnetic material arranged in such a way as to be displaced by the magnetic action of the electromagnet.

An electromagnet from a selector switch used in automatic telephone exchanges is illustrated in Fig. 7.5. The coil C is fitted with a soft iron core extended to form the pole pieces PP. The armature A is pivoted at H leaving a small working air-gap. The armature extension E carries a pivoted and sprung pawl VP which engages with the teeth of a ratchet R on successive operations of the

electromagnet and so positions the selector switch. The detent D holds the ratchet in position. A quick release is brought about by the restoring spring RS fitted to the armature and tensioned by the adjusting screw AS. A backstop BS limits the maximum armature movement. An important detail is the brass residual plate RP which ensures a minute air-gap when the armature is fully attracted: this limits the minimum value of reluctance and prevents the armature from "sticking," due to residual magnetism, when the current supply is disconnected.

The telephone bell in common use is a polarized

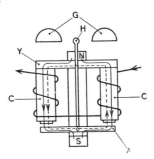

FIG. 7.6. POLARIZED MAGNETO BELL

electromagnet whose armature is fitted with a hammer playing between two bell gongs (Fig. 7.6): it is operated by an alternating current. This *magneto bell* consists essentially of two iron-cored solenoids CC having a common yoke Y and a centrally pivoted armature A which are magnetically polarized by a strong permanent magnet NS. Under the influence of the permanent magnet flux alone (shown by the full lines) the armature in its central position is attracted towards both pole faces with equal force, but if displaced slightly it will move to the nearer pole, since the unequal air-gaps will have upset the equal distribution of flux. The electromagnet windings are connected in series, assisting one another magnetically so that with the current flowing in a given direction the magnetic flux (shown by the dotted lines) is increased at one pole while the flux at the other pole face is decreased. Hence the armature is attracted to one side and the hammer H strikes one of the gongs G. When the current through the coils is reversed the relative strengths of the attractive forces at the two pole faces are reversed causing the armature to be tilted in the opposite direction so that the hammer strikes the other gong. In this manner the passage of an alternating current through the coils causes the hammer to strike each gong alternately.

A polarized electromagnet from a teleprinter is

illustrated in Fig. 7.7. A U-shaped permanent magnet NS is fitted with shaped pole pieces PP enclosing the electromagnet coils CC. The armature A is symmetrically disposed with respect to the four pole faces and is pivoted centrally at H. Movements of the armature extension E, limited by the stops M and S, are communicated to the teleprinter mechanism.

The full lines indicate the two parallel paths of the flux due to the permanent magnet. Since the

midpoint of the air-gap, the attractive force increases owing to the progressive shortening of the gap and reduction in the reluctance. The redistribution of the flux when the armature reaches the S stop is indicated in Fig. 7.7 (b).

It will be observed that the armature movement of a polarized electromagnet is dependent upon the current direction; this is true for all polarized instruments, for example, the telephone receiver.

Another characteristic of polarized instruments

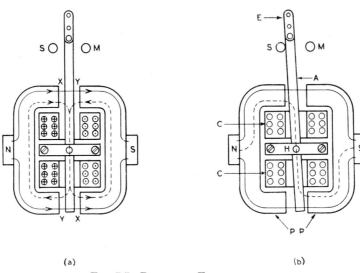

(a)   (b)

FIG. 7.7. POLARIZED ELECTROMAGNET

magnetic circuit is symmetrical the armature is pulled with equal force ($B^2A/2\mu_0$ newtons) towards each pole face, and so would tend to remain midway in the air-gap, i.e. it is neutral; in practice the armature extension remains with equal facility against either stop.

The dotted line indicates the path taken by the flux due to a unidirectional current in the coils. Examination of the flux lines in the four gaps shows that in two gaps (XX in Fig. 7.7 (a)), the permanent and electromagnet fluxes are additive while in the other two gaps (YY) the fluxes are in opposition. As a result the forces of attraction between the armature and the pole faces at XX exceed those between the armature and the pole faces at YY and as a consequence the armature extension moves to the stop S.

When the current in the coils is reversed, the flux direction shown by the dotted line also reverses and the flux density in the gaps at YY is now greater, resulting in movement of the armature extension to the stop M. In either direction of movement, as soon as the armature passes the

is their great sensitivity, demonstrated in the following manner. Let P be the flux density in the gap due to the permanent magnet, and E be the flux produced by the line current in the electromagnet. The tractive force on an armature is equal to $B^2A/2\mu_0$ newtons. In the polarized instrument the working flux B is $(P \pm E)$, hence the tractive force is proportional to $(P \pm E)^2 = P^2 \pm 2PE + E^2$. With an unpolarized instrument, the tractive force is proportional only to E^2. The polarized instrument therefore provides the additional tractive force proportional to $(P^2 \pm 2PE)$. The tractive force due to the current in the polarized electromagnet is greater than that due to the current in the non-polarized magnet by the term $\pm 2PE$. The value of P can be made large in comparison with E, consequently the value $\pm 2PE$ is much greater than E^2: moreover, the term $2PE$ is directional. The reason for the greater sensitivity of the polarized instrument is apparent. Roughly speaking, the permanent magnet may be regarded as providing the tractive force, the electromagnet determining the direction of movement.

A relay is an electrically operated device for opening and closing circuits.

A photograph of a standard telephone type relay appears in Fig. 7.8. The magnetic circuit (together with the "buffer block") is shown in Fig. 7.9. This

FIG. 7.8. TELEPHONE TYPE RELAY
(*Courtesy of P.M.G.*)

circuit comprises the soft iron core and the yoke with a knife edge termination upon which the armature is hinged. The core is that part of the magnetic circuit which is within the winding. The

FIG. 7.9. MAGNETIC CIRCUIT OF TELEPHONE TYPE
RELAY
(*Courtesy of P.M.G.*)

yoke is a piece of ferromagnetic material not surrounded by windings, forming a fixed part of the magnetic circuit and serving to complete that circuit.

The constructional details are indicated in Fig. 7.10 where C is the coil winding terminating in soldering tags T. The pole face P—the terminal surface of the core from which surface the useful flux emerges—is enlarged to ensure a big cross-sectional area to the working gap and so reduce its

reluctance. The retaining spring S holds the armature A in position upon the knife-edge of the yoke Y when the relay is mounted upon its side. Various combinations of insulated contact springs CS may be fitted and these are tensioned against the shaped

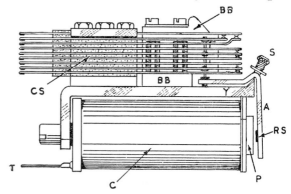

FIG. 7.10. DETAILS OF TELEPHONE TYPE RELAY
(*Courtesy of P.M.G.*)

buffer block BB to give adequate contact pressure. The armature is fitted with a small non-magnetic residual stud RS to ensure a small air-gap and prevent retention of the armature by remanent

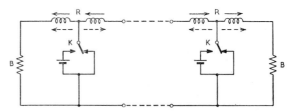

FIG. 7.11. DUPLEX TELEGRAPH CIRCUIT

flux: in certain relays an adjustable residual screw with a locknut is fitted. This pattern of relay incorporates many features designed to reduce fault liability, such as twin contacts of pure silver, and efficient magnetic joints from yoke to core and yoke to armature to exclude unwanted air-gaps at these points.

A differentially-wound relay is one having two windings excited by direct current and so arranged that the electromagnetic effects are opposed. Such a relay is employed to respond to special signalling requirements. A common application is in the duplex telegraph circuit (Fig. 7.11) where it is required to transmit signals over a line in both directions simultaneously and independently. The relay R has two equal windings, which produce equal fluxes for equal currents. The circuit at each station includes a balance network B which in each case is electrically equivalent to the line circuit plus the distant terminal circuit: when either key K is closed to the left-hand contact, equal currents flow in the line winding and balance winding of the home relay in opposing directions (dotted arrows) and each relay is unresponsive to operations by the key connected to its centre-point. The relays are not differentially connected with respect to the distant key, the current from which (full arrows) flows in both the line winding and balance winding of the relay in the same assisting directions.

7.9. Flux Linkage. From the instant when the closing of a switch allows the current to flow in a conductor, each magnetic line of flux starts from a point source at the centre, growing to a circle, the circular lines increasing in number until the field reaches its full intensity. While the field is being established the expanding circular flux lines cut the conductor. If the conductor is in the form of a solenoid, then every flux line may cut every turn of the coil.

It is often more convenient to consider the number of *linkages* occurring, a linkage being one flux line linked with one turn of the conductor. The total number of linkages is equal to the product of the number of turns and the number of magnetic flux lines. For example, 100 linkages result from 100 flux lines cutting one turn; from one flux line cutting 100 turns; from ten flux lines cutting ten turns or from any other combination of lines and turns whose product is 100.

When a flow of current ceases, the magnetic flux collapses and the occurrence of linkages is repeated, but this time in the opposite sense, since the flux is now decaying instead of growing.

It is important to appreciate that in the d.c. circuit flux linkage occurs only during the short transient period while the flux is changing: once the flux has either reached the steady state or decayed to zero no further linkages take place. In the a.c. circuit flux linkage is a continuous process.

7.10. Electromagnetic Induction. When the magnetic flux linking a conductor is changing, an e.m.f. is induced whose magnitude is proportional to the rate of change of flux. This extremely important statement is known as FARADAY's LAW. The magnitude of the induced e.m.f. is one unit when the rate of change of flux is also unity. The unit of flux has been selected such that unit rate of change of flux with time produces unit e.m.f. The unit of e.m.f. is the volt and the unit of time is the second. The name given to the unit of flux is the WEBER (Wb) which may therefore be defined as *that magnetic flux which, when cut by a conductor in one second, would induce an e.m.f. of one volt.* The weber is a large unit and it is sometimes more

convenient to employ the milliweber (mWb) or the microweber (μWb).

The induction of an e.m.f. in this manner may be readily observed by using two separate conductors or coils, one to produce the inducing flux and the other to exhibit the induced e.m.f. Fig. 7.12 shows a circuit arrangement in which a coil P is connected in series with a switch and rheostat to a battery: an adjacent coil S is simply connected across a galvanometer having a central zero, to indicate the presence and direction of a current.

When the switch is closed, current flows in the coil P in the direction indicated by the full line

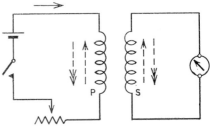

FIG. 7.12. ELECTROMAGNETIC INDUCTION

arrow. The flux due to this current cuts the turns of coil S, causing a momentary deflexion on the galvanometer.

On opening the switch, the collapse of flux produces further linkages with coil S; the galvanometer is again momentarily deflected, this time in the reverse direction.

These deflexions occur when current in coil P is switched on or off, the galvanometer indicating an absence of induced e.m.f. while a steady current flows in coil P.

The above description refers to the e.m.f. induced in a neighbouring coil, but since whatever flux cuts coil S must also cut the coil P itself, e.m.f.s are in fact induced similarly in coil P. The coil connected to the battery and producing the flux is known as the primary coil (P): that connected to the galvanometer and said to be electromagnetically coupled to P is the secondary coil (S). *If the change of magnetic flux is due to a variation in the current flowing in the same circuit, the phenomenon is known as* SELF-INDUCTION: *if due to a change of current flowing in another circuit it is known as* MUTUAL INDUCTION.

Since any change in flux linkage induces an e.m.f., electromagnetic induction occurs not only when the current is started and stopped, but also when it is increased or decreased. Manipulating the rheostat of Fig. 7.12 while the switch is closed will produce deflexions in the galvanometer, in a forward direction when the current increases and reversed when the current is reduced. The flow of an alternating current, being of continuously changing magnitude, is always accompanied by induced e.m.f.s and the importance of this effect in the a.c. circuit is considerable.

A change in flux linkage brought about by the *motion of a conductor* in a uniform magnetic field is the principle of e.m.f. induction used in most forms of rotary generator (Chapter VIII).

Changes in flux linkage may also be brought about by changes in reluctance: an e.m.f. is induced by any disturbance of the magnetic circuit even though the current remains constant. This principle is used in some forms of a.c. generator, such as the tone generator.

Though the expression "induced current" is in common use, it should be noted that the e.m.f. induced in a conductor will only give rise to a current provided that the conductor forms part of a closed electrical circuit.

7.11. Direction of Induced E.M.F.
The galvanometer deflexions referred to above establish experimentally the direction of the induced e.m.f.s in the secondary circuit and by inference in the primary circuit also.

When the current is switched on, the galvanometer deflexion indicates that the induced e.m.f. in the secondary circuit is in the direction shown by the dotted arrow (Fig. 7.12). The primary coil P is also cut by this same flux and an e.m.f. is simultaneously induced in a like direction in the primary circuit. It will be seen at once that this induced e.m.f. in the primary circuit opposes the battery current: it is in fact a back-e.m.f.

On switching off the current, the induced e.m.f.s in both primary and secondary circuits are as indicated by the double-headed arrows. The e.m.f. induced in the primary circuit tends to prolong the battery current, or to oppose its cessation.

This is summed up in an important rule for establishing the direction of an induced e.m.f., namely LENZ'S LAW, which states that *the direction of an induced e.m.f. is always such as to oppose the cause which produces it*. That this must be so is clear from a consideration of the primary circuit, for an induced e.m.f. acting in the same direction as the applied current would continuously build up the current and so create a supply of energy.

7.12. Inductance.
The property of a conductor by virtue of which induction occurs—i.e. an e.m.f. is induced in it due to flux linkage when the current changes—is known as INDUCTANCE. The greater the e.m.f. for a given current change, the higher is the value of inductance. A magnetic field always accompanies the flow of current in a conductor, consequently any conductor inherently possesses the property of inductance to some extent.

When the e.m.f. induced in the current-carrying conductor itself is being considered (the coil P of Fig. 7.12) the conductor or coil is said to possess SELF-INDUCTANCE (symbol L): where electromagnetic induction occurs between adjacent conductors the property is referred to as MUTUAL INDUCTANCE (symbol M).

The self-inductance of a conductor is small unless it is wound in the form of a coil: the presence of a ferromagnetic core by increasing the flux also tends to increase the inductance.

The mutual inductance of two conductors is also small unless either they are in the form of coupled coils, or else the conductors run parallel for a considerable distance as, for example, in transmission lines.

Inductance is measured by the rate at which the linkages change resulting from a unit change of current, for upon this depends the magnitude of the e.m.f. induced. The practical unit of inductance, the HENRY (H), is that *inductance which produces an e.m.f. of one volt when the current is changing at the rate of one ampere per second*. Since an e.m.f. of one volt is induced for a flux-linkage of one weber-turn per second, the henry is *that inductance producing one weber-turn per ampere*. In symbols

$$L = N\Phi/I \text{ henrys}$$

The henry is the practical unit for both self and mutual inductance. As with other units, submultiples are used—the millihenry (mH) and the microhenry (μH)—when more convenient.

The property of self-inductance is to induce an opposing e.m.f. whenever the current changes and thereby to oppose any change in the current flowing in the coil. An inductance coil, or *inductor*, is for this reason frequently known as a choke coil, or simply as a *choke*. This choking effect is of importance when a pulsating d.c. voltage or an a.c. voltage is applied, the choke offering a strong opposition to the current changes.

The behaviour of an inductor may be compared to the mechanical inertia of a flywheel. As in starting up the rotation of a flywheel mechanical energy must be applied, so also in an inductor the expenditure of electrical energy is necessary to overcome the back-e.m.f. and start the current. When the full current is established, or the flywheel is rotating, the only energy required is that necessary to overcome the electrical resistance and the mechanical friction respectively, both of these amounts being small in well-designed equipment. When the flywheel stops, it delivers up the whole of its kinetic energy: the collapse of the magnetic flux when the current is stopped results in the original energy being restored to the circuit. The function of both inductor and flywheel is to oppose energy fluctuation.

EXAMPLE 7.9 (B). A coil having 1 000 turns produces a flux of 10 mWb when carrying a direct current of 10 A. What is the inductance of the coil assuming that all the flux threads all the turns? (C. & G.)

$$\text{Linkages} = N\Phi$$
$$= 1\,000 \times 10^{-2}$$

$$\text{Linkages per ampere} = N\Phi/I$$
$$= 1\,000 \times 10^{-2}/10$$
$$= 1\,\text{H}$$

7.13. Magnitude of Induced E.M.F.

The induced e.m.f. is, by Faraday's law, proportional to the rate of change of flux. Measured in volts, the e.m.f.

$$E = -\ (\textit{rate of change of linkages}) \text{ volts}$$
$$= -\ \textit{rate of change of } N\Phi \text{ volts}$$

Assuming the number of turns to remain constant, if Φ_1 webers is the flux at an instant of time t_1, and Φ_2 webers is the flux at an instant t_2, shortly after, the flux changes by $(\Phi_2 - \Phi_1)$ webers in a time interval $(t_2 - t_1)$ seconds: the rate of flux change is

$$(\Phi_2 - \Phi_1)/(t_2 - t_1) \text{ webers/sec}$$
and
$$E = -\ \{N(\Phi_2 - \Phi_1)/(t_2 - t_1)\} \text{ volts}$$

Using the calculus notation (Appendix **A-2**),

$$E = -\ N(d\Phi/dt) \text{ volts} \qquad . \qquad . \ (7.6)$$

In words, to find the induced voltage, multiply the number of turns by the rate of change of flux, in webers/second.

The negative sign for the above expression signifies the force of Lenz's law, i.e. the production of a back-e.m.f.

The flux is proportional to the current, consequently the induced e.m.f. is proportional to the rate of change of current. In terms of inductance, the e.m.f. induced is one volt when the current changes at the rate of one ampere per second in a coil of one henry inductance. The induced e.m.f. is thus proportional to both the value of the inductance and to the rate of change of the current. If the current at an instant t_1 is i_1 amperes and it has changed to a value of i_2 amperes at an instant t_2 shortly afterwards, the current change $(i_2 - i_1)$ amperes occurs in $(t_2 - t_1)$ seconds and the rate of change of current is, therefore, $(i_2 - i_1)/(t_2 - t_1)$ amperes per second. For an inductance of L henrys, the induced e.m.f.

$$E = -\ \{L(i_2 - i_1)/(t_2 - t_1)\} \text{ volts}$$
or $$E = -\ L(di/dt) \text{ volts} \qquad . \ (7.7)$$

In words, the induced voltage is calculated by multiplying the inductance in henrys by the rate of change of current in amperes per second.

It will be observed that if the value of $(i_2 - i_1)$ is negative the induced e.m.f. is positive, indicating a forward or prolonging induced e.m.f. when the current is falling.

For two coupled coils whose mutual inductance is M henrys,

$$E = M(i_2 - i_1)/(t_2 - t_1) \text{ volts}$$
$$= M(di/dt) \text{ volts} \qquad . \qquad . \ (7.8)$$

The negative sign is usually omitted for a mutually induced e.m.f. as the secondary circuit does not carry the primary current: it will be borne in mind, however, that the directions of self and mutually induced e.m.f.s are the same.

EXAMPLE 7.10 (A). A direct current of 1 A is passed through a coil of 5 000 turns and produces a flux of 100 μWb. Assuming that all the flux threads all the turns what is the inductance of the coil? What would be the voltage developed across the coil if the current were interrupted in 1/1 000 sec? (C. & G.)

$$\text{Inductance } L = \text{flux linkages/ampere}$$
$$= N\Phi/I$$
$$= 5 \times 10^3 \times 10^{-4}/1$$
$$= 0.5\,\text{H}$$

Rate of change of current
$$= di/dt = 1 \div 1/1000 = 1\,000 \text{ A/sec}$$

Induced e.m.f.
$$= L \cdot di/dt = 0.5 \times 1\,000 = 500\,\text{V}$$

EXAMPLE 7.11 (A). An iron rod 2 cm in diameter and 20 cm long is bent into a closed ring and is wound with 3 000 turns of wire. It is found that when a current of 0.5 A is passed through this coil the flux density in the iron is 0.5 Wb/m². Assuming that all the flux links with every turn of the coil, what is the relative permeability of the iron?

What voltage would be developed across the coil if the current through the coil is interrupted and the flux in the iron falls to 10 per cent of its former value in 0.001 sec? (C. & G.)

$$l = 0.2\,\text{m}$$
$$A = \pi \times 10^{-4}\,\text{m}^2$$
$$N = 3\,000$$
$$I = 0.5\,\text{A}$$
$$B = 0.5\,\text{Wb/m}^2$$

$$H = NI/l$$
$$= (3\,000 \times 0.5)/0.2$$
$$= 7\,500\,\text{AT/m}$$

$$\mu = \mu_r\mu_0 = B/H$$
$$= 0.5/7\,500$$

$$\mu_r = \mu/\mu_0$$
$$= 0.5/7\,500 \div (4\pi \times 10^{-7})$$
$$= 500/3\pi = \underline{\underline{53}}$$

$$\Phi = BA$$
$$= 0.5 \times \pi \times 10^{-4}\,\text{Wb}$$

Change of flux, $(\Phi_2 - \Phi_1)$
$$= 0.5\pi \times 10^{-4} \times 0.9$$

Linkages $= (\Phi_2 - \Phi_1)N$
$$= 0.5\pi \times 10^{-4} \times 0.9 \times 3 \times 10^3$$
$$= 0.135\pi$$

Rate of change of linkages
$$= N(\Phi_2 - \Phi_1)/(t_2 - t_1)$$
$$= 0.135\pi/0.001$$

Induced e.m.f.
$$= 0.135\pi \times 10^3$$
$$= \underline{\underline{424\,\text{V}}}$$

7.14. Inductors in Series. If several inductors L_1, L_2, L_3, etc., are joined in series, being so spaced or magnetically screened that their mutual inductance is zero, the joint inductance

$$L = L_1 + L_2 + L_3 + \dots \qquad . \ (7.9)$$

It will be noted that this expression is of similar form to that for resistors in series.

The derivation of this expression is as follows. If the current in the inductors is changing at the rate di/dt* amperes per second the e.m.f. induced in each coil is proportional to $L(di/dt)$, etc.: since the inductors are connected in series, the total e.m.f. is the sum of the separate e.m.f.s, or

$$E = \{L_1(di/dt) + L_2(di/dt) + L_3(di/dt) + \dots\} \text{ volts}$$
$$= di/dt(L_1 + L_2 + L_3 + \dots) \text{ volts}$$

The e.m.f. induced in the single equivalent inductor L is $L \cdot (di/dt)$ volts, hence

$$L \cdot (di/dt) = (L_1 + L_2 + L_3 + \dots)di/dt$$

or
$$L = L_1 + L_2 + L_3 + \dots$$

If the series connected inductors are so placed that mutual induction occurs, this must be taken into consideration. For two inductors L_1 and L_2 henrys joined in series and so arranged that their mutual inductance is M henrys, the joint inductance L is given by

$$L = L_1 + L_2 \pm 2M \qquad . \qquad (7.10)$$

* For use of di/dt see Appendix **A.2.**

Use of the $+$ and $-$ signs in expression (7.10) depends upon whether the two inductors are connected so that the mutually induced e.m.f. assists or opposes the e.m.f. of self-induction. Fig. 7.13 illustrates the alternative connexions. Full arrows show the current; dotted arrows show the back e.m.f. of self-induction; double-headed arrows show the mutually induced e.m.f. which is in the opposite direction to the applied p.d. in the primary circuit.

This expression may be derived by considering two inductors L_1 and L_2 so arranged that their mutual inductance is M. In Fig. 7.13 (a) their

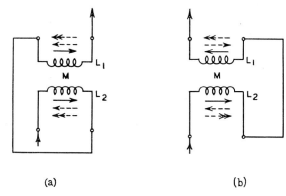

(a)   (b)

FIG. 7.13. INDUCTORS IN SERIES WITH MUTUAL INDUCTION

e.m.f.s of self-induction and mutual induction are additive: the total e.m.f. induced in L_1 is therefore

$$E = (L_1 \cdot di/dt + M \cdot di/dt) \text{ volts}$$
$$= (L_1 + M)di/dt \text{ volts}$$

Similarly the total e.m.f. induced in L_2 is

$$(L_2 \cdot di/dt + M \cdot di/dt) \text{ volts}$$

The total e.m.f. induced in L_1 and L_2 is

$$(L_1 + L_2 + 2M) \cdot di/dt$$
$$= L(di/dt)$$

whence $\qquad L = (L_1 + L_2 + 2M)$

If the *connexions* to either coil are reversed the e.m.f.s of self and mutual induction are in opposition (see Fig. 7.13 (b)), consequently

$$L = (L_1 + L_2 - 2M)$$

EXAMPLE 7.12 (A). Two coils of 100 mH and 200 mH have a total inductance of 360 mH when connected in series. If the coils are disconnected and a current which varies at the rate of 100 A/sec is passed through one coil, what voltage is induced in the other coil?   (*C. & G.*)

Since the combined inductance is greater than the sum of the individual inductances, the coils are in series assisting.

$$L = L_1 + L_2 + 2M$$
$$360 = 100 + 200 + 2M$$
$$M = (360 - 300)/2 = 30 \text{ mH}$$

Induced e.m.f. $= M \times$ rate of change of current
$$= 30 \times 10^{-3} \times 100 = 3 \text{ V}$$

7.15. Inductors in Parallel. The equivalent inductance L of several inductors L_1, L_2, L_3, . . . in parallel and possessing no mutual inductance is given by

$$1/L = 1/L_1 + 1/L_2 + 1/L_3 \quad . \ (7.11)$$

For two inductors (only) in parallel, if $M = 0$,

$$1/L = 1/L_1 + 1/L_2 = (L_2 + L_1)/L_1 L_2$$
or $$L = L_1 L_2/(L_1 + L_2) \quad . \quad . \ (7.12)$$

i.e. the combined inductance is equal to the product divided by the sum of the separate inductances.

For N equal inductors L' in parallel ($M = 0$), the combined inductance L is determined from

$$1/L = 1/L' + 1/L' + 1/L' + . . . = N/L'$$
or $$L = L'/N \quad (7.13)$$

It will be observed that these expressions are of similar form to those for resistors in parallel. The method of derivation is given below.

For inductors in parallel and with negligible mutual inductance, if the current in each branch at a given instant is i_1, i_2, i_3, respectively, the total current

$$i = i_1 + i_2 + i_3 + . . .$$
and
$$di/dt = di_1/dt + di_2/dt + di_3/dt + . . .$$

The e.m.f.s induced in the separate coils are $L_1(di_1/dt)$, $L_2(di_2/dt)$, $L_3(di_3/dt)$, and these e.m.f.s must be equal since the coils are connected in parallel. Hence

$$E/L_1 = di_1/dt, \ E/L_2 = di_2/dt, \ E/L_3 = di_3/dt$$

The e.m.f. induced in the single equivalent inductor L will be

$$E = L \cdot di/dt, \text{ whence } E/L = di/dt$$

Since $di/dt = di_1/dt + di_2/dt + di_3/dt + . . .$
$$E/L = E/L_1 + E/L_2 + E/L_3 + . . .$$

whence

$$1/L = 1/L_1 + 1/L_2 + 1/L_3 + . . .$$

If two inductors L_1 and L_2, connected in parallel, are so coupled that their mutual inductance is M, the joint inductance

$$L = (L_1 L_2 - M^2)/(L_1 + L_2 \mp 2M) \quad (7.14)$$

In the denominator, the upper sign $(-)$ is used if the inductors *aid* one another: the lower sign $(+)$ is used if the inductors are in *opposition*.

In the particular case where the two inductors are equal, $L_1 = L_2$, and

$$L = (L_1{}^2 - M^2)/(2L_1 \mp 2M)$$
$$= (L_1 + M)(L_1 - M)/2(L_1 \mp M)$$
or $$L = (L_1 \pm M)/2 \quad . \quad . \quad . \quad . \ (7.15)$$

In the numerator, the upper sign $(+)$ refers to inductors aiding; the lower sign $(-)$ to inductors opposing. It will be seen that care is essential in the use of the signs.

With two equal inductors L' in parallel and possessing mutual inductance M, if the current in each coil is changing at the rate of di/dt amperes per second, the e.m.f. induced equally in each coil will be $L' \cdot di/dt \pm M \cdot di/dt$, depending upon whether the self and mutually induced e.m.f.s are additive or in opposition. The equivalent single inductance L carrying a current $2i$ will have an induced e.m.f.

$$E = 2L \cdot di/dt = L' \cdot di/dt \pm M \cdot di/dt$$

whence

$$2L = L' \pm M \text{ and } L = (L' \pm M)/2$$

Example 7.13 (A). Two coils have inductances of 250 μH and 100 μH respectively. They are placed so that their mutual inductance is 50 μH. What will be their joint inductance (a) in series aiding, (b) in series opposing, (c) in parallel aiding, (d) in parallel opposing? (*C. & G.*)

$$L_1 = 250 \ \mu\text{H}, \ L_2 = 100 \ \mu\text{H}, \ M = 50 \ \mu\text{H}$$

(a) $L = L_1 + L_2 + 2M = 250 + 100 + 100$
$$= 450 \ \mu\text{H}$$

(b) $L = L_1 + L_2 - 2M = 250 + 100 - 100$
$$= 250 \ \mu\text{H}$$

(c) $L = (L_1 L_2 - M^2)/(L_1 + L_2 - 2M)$
$$= (25\,000 - 2\,500)/(250 + 100 - 100)$$
$$= 22\,500/250 = 90 \ \mu\text{H}$$

(d) $L = (L_1 L_2 - M^2)/(L_1 + L_2 + 2M)$
$$= 22\,500/450 = 50 \ \mu\text{H}$$

7.16. Inductance of a Solenoid. The total flux in a solenoid is

$$\Phi = BA = \mu_r \mu_0 ANI/l \text{ webers}$$

If this flux links with every turn of the solenoid, the number of *linkages*

$$N\Phi = \mu_r \mu_0 AN^2 I/l \text{ weber-turns}$$

The inductance L in henrys, which is in weber-turns per ampere is

$$L = \mu_r \mu_0 A N^2 I / I l$$
$$= \mu_r \mu_0 A N^2 / l \text{ henrys} \qquad . \qquad . \ (7.16)$$

Substituting $S = l / \mu_0 \mu_r A$,

$$L = N^2 / S \text{ henrys}$$

It will be noted that the inductance is proportional to the *square* of the number of turns.

If the solenoid is air-cored, $\mu_r = 1$, and

$$L = \mu_0 A N^2 / l \text{ henrys}$$

The above expression for inductance is rarely suitable for direct application because most inductors are relatively short and the field is not uniform: also for a ferromagnetic core the demagnetizing effect is appreciable. From this general expression empirical formulae are derived for the various forms of inductor.

7.17. Mutual Inductance of Two Solenoids.

When two coils are electromagnetically coupled, if the primary coil has N_1 turns, the flux in the primary coil is

$$\Phi = \mu_r \mu_0 A N_1 I / l$$

If *all* this flux links with the N_2 turns of the secondary coil the number of linkages is

$$N_2 \Phi = \mu_r \mu_0 A N_1 N_2 I / l$$

and the mutual inductance

$$M = \mu_r \mu_0 A N_1 N_2 / l \text{ henrys} \qquad . \ (7.17)$$

Should two coupled coils have unequal numbers of turns, the flux per ampere set up in the coil having the greater number of turns would be greater than that due to one ampere flowing in the coil of fewer turns, the flux being proportional to the ampere turns: on the other hand, the flux produced by the larger coil would link with the fewer turns of the smaller coil. Consequently for the consideration of mutual inductance of the coupled coils it is immaterial which coil is regarded as the primary and which the secondary.

7.18. Influence of Current on Inductance.

The value of the inductance of a coil depends upon the linkages per ampere: the inductance of an air-cored coil is independent of the current flowing, the flux being proportional to the magnetizing force ($H = NI/l$) and to the current since $\mu_r = 1$.

In an inductor with a ferromagnetic core the inductance will remain constant only so long as operation takes place on the straight portion of the permeability curve. If the current is allowed to reach a value such that the core becomes magnetically saturated, the flux is no longer proportional to the magnetizing force and to the current: consequently the number of linkages per ampere and hence the inductance falls as saturation is approached.

In telecommunication equipment, inductors frequently carry alternating current superimposed upon a direct current. Suppose a small D.C. is passed through an inductor producing a magnetizing force equal to H_1 (Fig. 7.14): if a small A.C. is superimposed on this D.C. the resultant

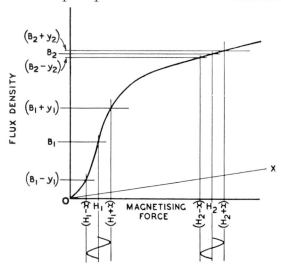

Fig. 7.14. Effect of Current on Inductance

magnetizing force varies between the values ($H_1 \pm x$), producing changes in flux density from ($B_1 + y_1$) to ($B_1 - y_1$). This is a comparatively large change in flux density and accordingly the inductance of the coil is high. If now the D.C. is increased until the magnetizing force reaches the value H_2, almost saturating the core, superimposing the same A.C. will produce the same change in magnetizing force ($H_2 \pm x$) but the changes in flux density between ($B_2 + y_2$) and ($B_2 - y_2$) are now very small: the inductance of the coil is consequently very much reduced.

It is important therefore to restrict the current flowing in an inductor to the prescribed value; inductors with ferromagnetic cores are usually rated for a given d.c. value and if this is exceeded the inductance is liable to fall; this observation applies particularly to those frequent cases when an inductor carries both D.C. and A.C.

Inductors, and more particularly transformers, which carry an A.C. superimposed upon a D.C. usually have an air-gap left in the magnetic circuit, and the μ_r curve approaches a straight line (OX in Fig. 7.14). This is due to the fact that the reluctance of the air-gap will be considerably higher than that of the iron, and also the air-gap does not become saturated. Whatever the value of the direct current, the change in flux density due to a superimposed A.C. remains approximately constant, and so also does the inductance. One example of this construction is in the induction coil used in the subscriber's telephone set. Such a coil usually requires less iron and less copper and a reduction in losses results.

7.19. Eddy Currents. In addition to the e.m.f. induced in the windings of an inductor, e.m.f.s will always be induced in any adjacent conducting material while it is subjected to flux changes, for example, in the core and armature of an electro-magnet. As a result eddy currents will circulate in the mass of the core and armature in an infinite number of parallel paths.

An EDDY CURRENT is defined as *a local current induced in a conducting body by a varying or a relatively-moving magnetic field.*

The production of eddy currents is a serious dis-advantage, firstly because energy is expended in producing them, and secondly because the eddy currents develop heat and may cause an undesirable temperature rise. In a.c. circuits eddy currents are continuously induced, consequently their presence is a much more serious matter here than in the simple d.c. circuit.

It is not possible to prevent the induction of eddy currents but their magnitude can be restricted by providing a high resistance path : for this reason

FIG. 7.15. SLOW ACTING RELAYS
(*Courtesy of P.M.G.*)

high resistivity is a desirable characteristic in the soft magnetic materials when carrying alternating fluxes.

The cores of instruments such as transformers which are subjected to alternating fluxes are always subdivided by constructing them from thin lami-nated sheets or stampings, each one insulated from its neighbour by a film of insulating varnish. On account of the relative directions of magnetic flux and eddy currents, this lamination has very little effect on the magnetic path but offers the maximum resistance to eddy currents. The path of the eddy

currents includes these insulating gaps in series, and the gaps afford a considerable reduction in the magnitude of the eddy currents. In some forms of inductor the core consists of a bundle of insulated iron wires. For the higher frequency currents, dust cores or ferrites are employed. The use of a special high permeability iron, such as *mumetal*, for the stampings reduces the losses by reducing the

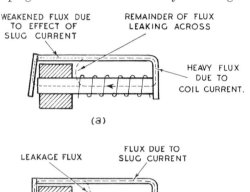

FIG. 7.16. RELAY FITTED WITH ARMATURE END SLUG
(*a*) Operating. (*b*) Releasing.

dimensions required for the iron circuit. The plates of capacitors are sometimes made of a high resistivity alloy to reduce the magnitude of eddy currents.

On the other hand, conditions are sometimes made deliberately favourable to the generation of eddy currents for some particular purpose. One such application is in promoting the slow action of relays. For this purpose a thick copper ring or *slug* is fitted over one end of the core in a portion of the winding space (Fig. 7.15). This slug provides a closed path of low resistance.

With a slug fitted at the armature end of the core, when the winding is energized the flux com-mences to build up in the core (Fig. 7.16 (*a*)) but owing to this rising flux in the portion of the core enclosed by the slug, eddy currents will circulate in the slug : by Lenz's law the flux due to these eddy currents opposes the main flux.

The effect of this is to cause a larger proportion of the winding flux to leak from the core to the yoke without traversing the armature gap. As the rate of change of the flux in the slugged portion of the core dies down, the eddy currents in the slug subside and a greater portion of the winding flux can then pass through the complete circuit of core and armature. When this flux reaches a sufficiently high value the armature will operate. Fig. 7.17 illustrates the variation of current and flux in a relay during the operating period. Operating lags up to about 100 msec can be obtained in this manner.

When the circuit of the winding is disconnected

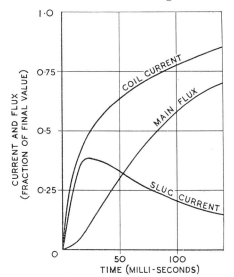

FIG. 7.17. RISE OF CURRENT AND FLUX IN SLOW OPERATING RELAY

Fig. 7.16 (b)) the previously steady current drops to zero but the flux is now prolonged due to the eddy currents induced in the slug which, according to Lenz's law, tend to oppose the decay of flux. Owing to the flux leakage between the core and the yoke, the flux caused by the eddy currents in the slug will tend to be confined to the portion of core near the slug. This portion contains the armature, and flux in the armature air-gap will be maintained for the maximum time. Release lags up to 350 msec can be obtained in this manner.

If the slug is fitted at the heel end—the core end remote from the armature (Fig. 7.18)—the operating time of the relay is but little affected by the presence of the slug because of the tendency for the winding flux to avoid entering the slug appreciably, but to leak across to the yoke instead. When the current ceases, the flux will tend to circulate round the heel end of the relay, the leakage path in effect acting as a shunt on the armature circuit ; in consequence, the flux value at which the relay releases will be reached slightly more rapidly compared with the relay fitted with an armature-end slug. This type of relay is thus fast in operating but slow in releasing.

7.20. Skin Effect. In conductors carrying high-frequency alternating currents practically the whole of the current is confined to the surface or *skin* of the conductor, very little current flowing in the centre portion of the conductor.

The SKIN EFFECT is *an electromagnetic effect occurring in a conductor when carrying an alternating current, namely, that the current density is greater at the surface of the conductor than in the centre. In the case of very high frequencies the current may be practically confined to the surface.*

When a conductor carries a current some of the magnetic flux exists within the conductor and this portion links with the centre of the conductor while not linking with the material nearer the surface. As a result, the inductance of the conductor is greater at the centre than at parts nearer the surface because of the greater number of flux linkages occurring in the centre portion as the flux grows and decays. With alternating currents at the higher frequencies, particularly at radio frequencies, the property of the inductance in opposing current changes is sufficiently great to affect the flow of current, most of which flows in the

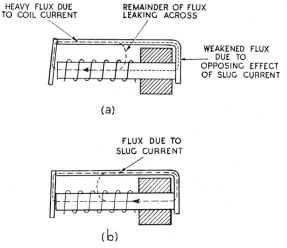

FIG. 7.18. RELAY FITTED WITH HEEL END SLUG
(a) Operating. (b) Releasing.

surface of the conductor where it meets with less opposition, i.e. impedance.

The consequence of this skin effect is that the effective cross-sectional area of a given conductor is reduced at high frequencies : the high-frequency resistance of a conductor may be several hundred times greater than the resistance offered to a direct current or low-frequency alternating current, and it increases with the *square* of the frequency. For a thin wire, the current distribution is more nearly uniform owing to the relatively greater portion of the flux linking with the cross-section of the conductor for a given current; consequently the skin effect and increased resistance to high frequencies is not so marked.

For radio-frequency work hollow or flat strip conductors are often employed; another method adopted to reduce losses is to use *litzendraht*—stranded wires in which each strand is separately insulated and appears in turn at the centre and surface of the bunch of paralleled conductors.

In telephone transmission systems, signalling relays are bridged across the speech circuit: it is essential that these relays present a high impedance at speech frequencies to minimize their shunting effect, yet their d.c. resistance must be kept at a low value.

The inductance of a relay can be increased by the use of a highly permeable material in the core. Care has to be exercised, however, as in most materials of this type permeability is very high at low values of magnetizing force but falls off rapidly as the magnetizing force is increased. In the relays under consideration, the flux consists of a small rapidly varying component superimposed on a larger steady flux. The extent to which the rapidly varying flux penetrates the core is very small owing to the skin effect, and the voice-frequency flux is restricted to the surface. The necessary increase in inductance, and consequently in impedance, can be attained by providing a highly permeable material near the surface of the core. Nickel iron is used for this purpose and is applied to the core in the form of three sleeves (Fig. 7.19): in addition to its high permeability, at low values of magnetizing force nickel iron possesses high resistivity, thus reducing eddy currents with a further increase in inductance. A further reduction in eddy currents is obtained by leaving a longitudinal gap in each sleeve (Fig. 7.19 (a)) and fitting the sleeves so that these gaps do not coincide (Fig. 7.19 (b)).

7.21. Inductors. The practical application of inductors lies naturally in a.c. equipment, or in d.c. circuits where unsteady or pulsating currents are present. Inductors are used in a variety of forms suitable for different purposes: they may be broadly divided into two categories depending upon whether the core is air or a ferromagnetic material. The range extends from small radio frequency coils carrying a few microamperes to the large silicon iron cored coils designed to carry over 2 000 A and weighing almost a ton: the latter are used in floating battery installations for smoothing the generator ripple.

An important feature in the design of inductors is the reduction of losses: these may be classed as I^2R losses (copper losses), hysteresis losses, eddy current losses, and dielectric losses.

I^2R losses, due to the power expended in driving the current through the resistance of the inductor winding, are reduced by keeping the resistance as low as possible: inductors carrying high frequency currents are wound with stranded wire, tube or strip.

Hysteresis losses, present only in inductors with ferromagnetic cores, show the need for using a core material having a small area of hysteresis loop.

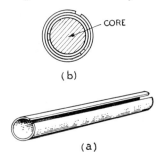

FIG. 7.19. NICKEL IRON SLEEVES FOR RELAY

Losses due to eddy currents are considerably reduced by subdivision of the core and by using a core material of high resistivity. At the higher frequencies it is often necessary to use an air core to reduce losses. There is also a power loss due to eddy currents in the conductor itself: by opposing the main magnetic field, eddy currents also reduce the inductance.

Energy losses in inductors are caused by the induction of eddy currents in adjacent conducting material; methods to minimize these losses include the careful spacing of components and the restriction of external magnetic fields by compact design or by the use of toroids where these are suitable. The use of magnetic screening cans for coils is effective provided that they are thin, of high resistivity material and not too near the inductor, for the screening can will itself absorb energy by eddy currents: a radius of about twice that of the enclosed inductor is desirable for a screening can.

Dielectric losses also occur at high frequencies due to the self-capacitance between every turn and every other turn, and between each turn and earth. The dielectric is the insulating covering, if employed, for the conductor and the former upon which the coil is wound: the power absorbed by the dielectric is converted to heat. The use of low loss dielectrics, minimum insulating material on the conductor and special design of winding to reduce self-capacitance, limits the losses due to dielectrics.

In Fig. 7.20 are illustrated different stages in the production of toroidal coils using dust cores. The illustration includes the cores themselves, screened loading coils used to offset the effects of cable capacitance, and toroidal inductors used as components in electric wave filters for carrier telephone equipment.

Variable inductors depend upon control of the

7.22. Time-constant. In a circuit possessing inductance, a direct current does not attain its Ohm's law value instantaneously; the current in building up to its full value is subjected to a delay which depends upon the ratio of resistance to inductance present in the circuit.

Fig. 7.21 shows a circuit containing inductance L henrys in series with resistance R ohms which

FIG. 7.20. TOROIDAL CORES AND COILS
(*Courtesy of "I.P.O.E.E. Journal"*)

factors N and μ_r. A common method is to use a winding which is tapped at suitable intervals and to select the appropriate number of turns by the

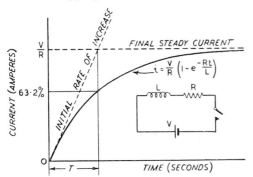

FIG. 7.21. GROWTH OF CURRENT IN INDUCTOR

use of a radial switch. Another form of variable inductor utilizes an adjustable core.

The *variometer* consists of two series-connected coupled coils whose total inductance can be varied by adjusting the coupling and hence the mutual inductance.

includes the resistance of the inductor. When the switch is closed to apply a p.d. of V volts across the circuit, the initial flow of current in the inductor results in a back-e.m.f. E volts of self-induction, so that the net available voltage to drive the current i amperes through the circuit is not V but is reduced to $(V - E)$ volts: the magnitude of the current is then $i = (V - E)/R$. This back-e.m.f. E equals $-L \cdot di/dt$* and it has its maximum value when the ratio di/dt is a maximum, i.e. at the instant of closing the circuit when the current changes from zero to some finite value: the magnitude of the back-e.m.f. E falls gradually until the current reaches its maximum steady value, when $E = 0$ and $i = (V - 0)/R = V/R$, the Ohm's law value.

The magnitude of the current at any instant is equal to

$$i = (V - E)/R = \{V - L(di/dt)\}/R$$

This is a differential equation whose solution is

$$i = \frac{V}{R}(1 - e^{-Rt/L}) \quad . \quad . \ (7.18)$$

* For use of di/dt, see Appendix **A.2.**

From this expression, known as the HELMHOLTZ EQUATION, the value of the current i amperes at any instant t seconds after closing the circuit can be calculated: R ohms is the total circuit resistance, L henrys the total inductance, and $e = 2.718$ is the base of the Naperian system of logarithms. The curve in Fig. 7.21 shows the current i amperes plotted against the time t seconds according to this expression.

It will be seen that this expression is Ohm's law, $I = V/R$, modified by the factor $(1 - e^{-Rt/L})$. To attain the full current value V/R it is necessary that $(1 - e^{-Rt/L})$ should be equal to 1, i.e. that $e^{-Rt/L}$ should equal 0: this requirement is satisfied only when $t = \infty$, but in all practical cases the steady value of the current is very nearly attained after five times the "time-constant" (see below).

When the impressed voltage V is removed the magnetic field collapses, restoring energy to the circuit and so inducing an e.m.f. which prolongs the current: this is apparent in the sparking which occurs at the contacts breaking an inductive circuit. If a closed circuit is provided for the induced e.m.f., for example, by short-circuiting the supply voltage instead of disconnecting it, the current will decay exponentially as shown on the curve of Fig. 7.22, which is symmetrical with the curve of Fig. 7.21.

It may be convenient to consider that the cessation of current in a closed circuit is brought about by inserting an equal but opposite supply voltage $-V$. The steady current reached due to the

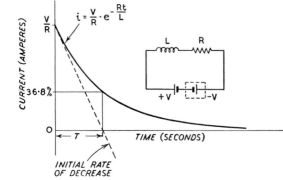

FIG. 7.22. DECAY OF CURRENT IN INDUCTOR

original voltage $+V$ is $i = +V/R$. From equation (7.18) the current due to the newly applied voltage $-V$ is $-\dfrac{V}{R}.(1 - e^{-Rt/L})$. The total current due to the voltage $(+V - V)$ is therefore

$$i = +\frac{V}{R} - \frac{V}{R}(1 - e^{-Rt/L})$$

$$= \frac{V}{R} - \frac{V}{R} + \frac{V}{R} . e^{-Rt/L}$$

or $\qquad i = \dfrac{V}{R} . e^{-Rt/L} \qquad . \qquad . \qquad . \quad (7.19)$

This is the expression determining the magnitude of the decaying current at any instant, and used for producing the graph of Fig. 7.22.

The inductive properties of circuits are conveniently compared by determination of the relative times taken for the current to increase to a given proportion (63·2 per cent) of the final value.

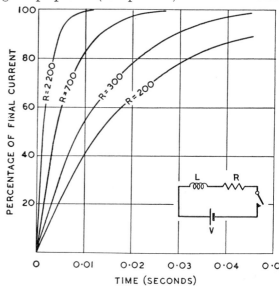

FIG. 7.23. EFFECT OF R/L RATIO ON GROWTH OF CURRENT

The time in seconds for the current to reach 63·2 per cent of its full (Ohm's law) value is known as the TIME-CONSTANT: *this time in seconds is equal to the ratio* L/R *where* L *henrys is the circuit inductance and* R *ohms is the total resistance in circuit.*

Substituting $t = L/R$ in the Helmholtz equation gives—

$$i = \frac{V}{R} . (1 - e^{-1}) = \frac{V}{R} . (1 - 1/e)$$

$$= \frac{V}{R} . \frac{(e - 1)}{e} = \frac{V}{R} . \frac{(2.718 - 1)}{2.718}$$

$$= \frac{V}{R} . (0.632) = 63.2\% I$$

The time-constant of a circuit is also the time which would be required for the current to attain its final value if the initial rate of change were steadily maintained. This time T is indicated in the two curves, Figs. 7.21 and 7.22. Considering the growth of current, the applied voltage V at every instant must overcome (i) the voltage drop iR in the circuit; (ii) the back-e.m.f. $- L \cdot (di/dt)$.

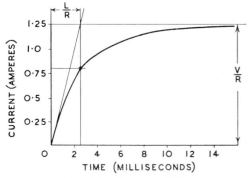

FIG. 7.24 (Example 7.14)

The initial current i is negligibly small so that $iR = 0$ and $V = L \cdot di/dt$, or $di/dt = V/L$. If this rate of rise V/L were maintained steadily for T seconds, then to attain the final current V/R, $I = T \cdot V/L$ and this must equal V/R. Consequently $TV/L = V/R$, or $T = L/R$.

In telephone and telegraph signalling circuits, relays and electromagnets are required to respond to currents of short duration; in the design of such circuits attention has to be paid to the gradual rise of the current and consequent delay in response of the relay. The series of curves in Fig. 7.23 demonstrates the increase in *rate of growth* of the current by increasing the total circuit resistance to reduce the ratio L/R. The final value of current will naturally become less as the resistance is added, and it should be noted that the ordinate denotes percentage of final value. Series resistance is usually added in machine telegraph circuits to ensure the quick response of relays and electromagnets. The use of the shunted capacitor in sharpening telegraph signals has already been discussed.

EXAMPLE 7.14 (B). What is the time-constant of a circuit consisting of an inductance of 100 mH in series with a resistance of 40 ohms? Draw a curve approximately to scale showing how the current would build up in this circuit when 50 V D.C. is applied. (C. & G.)

Time-constant $= L/R = 10^{-1}/40$
$$= 0.002\ 5 \text{ or } 2.5 \text{ msec}$$

An approximate curve is given in Fig. 7.24 from the following data—

(i) Final current $= V/R = 50/40 = 1.25$ A.

(ii) The initial slope is that which would reach the final value in 2.5 msec.

(iii) The current after 2.5 msec is $0.632I = 0.632 \times 1.25 = 0.79$ A.

EXAMPLE 7.15 (B). A relay having an inductance of 2 H and a resistance of 200 Ω has an operating current of 6.5 mA. Compare the times which elapse after the application of the battery before the relay operates when—

(a) A battery of 2 V is applied directly to the coil.
(b) A battery of 10 V is applied through a resistance of 800 Ω.
(c) A battery of 50 V is applied through a resistance of 4 800 Ω.

Give curves illustrating the rate of rise in each case. (For the purpose of this question take $1/e = 0.35$.)

(C. & G.)

From $i = \dfrac{V}{R} \cdot (1 - e^{- Rt/L})$ where $i = 6.5/1\ 000$—

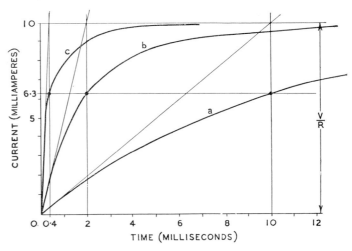

FIG. 7.25 (Example 7.15)

(a) $V = 2, R = 200, L = 2, V/R = 2/200$
$$= 10 \text{ mA}.$$

$$\frac{6.5}{1\ 000} = \frac{10}{1\ 000} \cdot (1 - e^{- 200t/2})$$

$$\frac{6.5}{1\ 000} = \frac{10}{1\ 000} \cdot (1 - e^{- 100t})$$

$$10e^{- 100t} = 3.5$$

$$e^{- 100t} = 0.35$$

Since $1/e = e^{-1} \simeq 0.35$, $e^{-100t} = e^{-1}$

whence

$$100t = 1 \text{ and } t = 1/100 = \underline{\underline{10 \text{ msec}}}$$

(b) $V = 10$, $R = 1\,000$, $L = 2$, $V/R = 10$ mA.

$e^{-1\,000t/2} = 0.35$, $e^{-500t} = e^{-1}$

$$500t = 1,\ t = 1/500 = \underline{\underline{2 \text{ msec}}}$$

(c) $V = 50$, $R = 5\,000$, $L = 2$, $V/R = 10$ mA.

$e^{-5\,000t/2} = 0.35$, $e^{-2\,500t} = e^{-1}$

$$2\,500t = 1,\ t = 1/2\,500 = \underline{\underline{0.4 \text{ msec}}}$$

t	Rt/L	$-\dfrac{Rt}{L}\cdot\log_{10} e$	$e^{-Rt/L}$	$1 - e^{-Rt/L}$	i
0·0	0·0	0·0 0·0	1·0	0·0	0·0
0·000 5	0·25	− 0·108 $\bar{1}$·892	0·779 8	0·220 2	0·440 4
0·001	0·50	− 0·216 $\bar{1}$·784	0·608 1	0·391 9	0·783 8
0·001 5	0·75	− 0·324 $\bar{1}$·676	0·474 2	0·525 8	1·051 6
0·002	1·00	− 0·434 $\bar{1}$·567	0·369 0	0·631 0	1·262 0
0·002 5	1·25	− 0·541 $\bar{1}$·459	0·287 7	0·712 3	1·424 6
0·003	1·50	− 0·648 $\bar{1}$·352	0·224 9	0·775 1	1·550 2
0·003 5	1·75	− 0·757 $\bar{1}$·242	0·174 6	0·825 4	1·650 8
0·004	2·00	− 0·866 $\bar{1}$·134	0·136 1	0·863 9	1·727 8

From the curve plotted in Fig. 7.26 the time taken for the current to reach 1·26 A is $\underline{\underline{0.001\ 98 \text{ sec}}}$

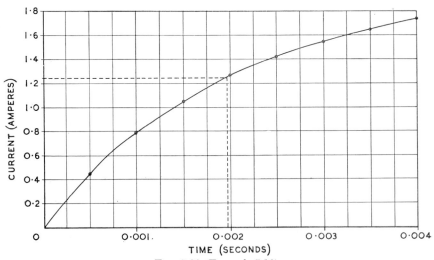

Fig. 7.26 (Example 7.16)

The approximate curves for these three cases are drawn in Fig. 7.25 from the following data—

(a) $L/R = 2/200 = 10$ msec   Time to reach
(b) $L/R = 2/1\,000 = 2$ msec   6·32 mA, and to reach 10 mA at
(c) $L/R = 2/5\,000 = 0.4$ msec   initial rate of rise.

Use of the approximation $1/e = 0.35$ results in the time taken to reach 6·5 mA having the same solution as the time to reach 6·32 mA (the time-constant).

EXAMPLE 7.16 (B). The current in a circuit comprising resistance and inductance can be represented by the expression $i = \dfrac{V}{R}\cdot(1 - e^{-Rt/L})$.

If $V = 120$ V, $R = 60\ \Omega$, $L = 0.12$ H, $e = 2.71$, plot a curve showing the value of i as t varies from 0·0 to 0·004 sec. From your curve find the time taken for the current to reach 1·26 A.   (C. & G.)

EXAMPLE 7.17 (B). The current at any moment discharging in a circuit can be represented by the expression $i = \dfrac{V}{R}\cdot e^{-Rt/L}$. From this expression, deduce the ratio of the values of the current when $t = 0$ and $t = L/R$.

If $V/R = 2$ and $R/L = 500$, plot a curve for the following ratios of t: 0, 0·001, 0·002, 0·003, 0·004, and use this curve to prove the accuracy of the ratio.   (C. & G.)

$$i = \frac{V}{R}\cdot e^{-Rt/L}$$

When $t = 0$, $i_0 = (V/R) \times e^0 = V/R$

When $t = L/R$, $i_T = (V/R) \times e^{-1} = (V/R) \times (1/e)$

$$i_0/i_T = e = \underline{\underline{2.718}}$$

For the graph $i = 2e^{-500t}$—

t (sec) .	.	0	0·001	0·002	0·003	0·004
i (amp) .	.	2·0	1·213	0·736	0·446	0·271

The curve is given in Fig. 7.27.

When $t = 0$, $i_0 = 2$

when $t = L/R = 1/500 = 0.002$

$i_T = 0.736$ and $i_0/i_T = 2/0.736 = 2.718$

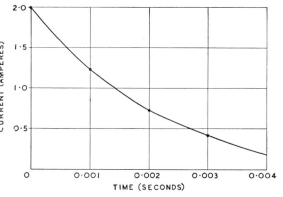

FIG. 7.27 (Example 7.17)

EXAMPLE 7.18 (B). A coil having a resistance of 200 Ω and a constant inductance of 2 H is connected across a 50 V battery supply. Reckoning time from the instant at which the circuit is closed, find (a) the value which the current will have reached after a period equivalent to the time constant of the coil, and (b) the rate at which the current will then be increasing.   (C. & G.)

If $t = L/R$, $i = 0.632 . V/R = 0.632 \times 50/200$
$= 0.158$ A

At this instant, the voltage used in overcoming the resistance

$= iR = 0.158 \times 200 = 31.6$ V

Back-e.m.f.

$= 50 - 31.6 = 18.4$

From $E = L . di/dt$,

$di/dt = E/L = 18.4/2 = 9.2$ A/sec

EXAMPLE 7.19 (B). A certain relay of 2 000 Ω resistance will just operate when connected in series with a resistance of 500 Ω to battery terminals giving a constant voltage. When the series resistance is removed and the relay is connected directly to the battery terminals it operates in 15 msec. Calculate the inductance of the relay.
(C. & G.)

Current at which relay operates $= V/2\,500$ A.
Final current value $= V/2\,000$ A.
Current after 15 msec,

$$\frac{V}{2\,500} = \frac{V}{2\,000} . (1 - e^{-2\,000 \times 0.015/L})$$

$2\,000/2\,500 = 1 - e^{-30/L}$

$e^{-30/L} = 0.2$, $e^{+30/L} = 5$

$30/L = \log_e 5 = 2.301 . \log_{10} 5 = 1.609\,4$

$L = 30/1.609\,4 = 18.6$ H

EXAMPLE 7.20 (B). Give the modified form of Ohm's law that is applicable to calculations of the instantaneous values of an impulsing current. If 50 V be applied to a relay having an inductance of 750 mH and a resistance of 500 Ω, calculate the time in milliseconds needed for the current to rise to 50 mA.   (C. & G.)

$$i = \frac{V}{R} . (1 - e^{-Rt/L})$$

$0.05 = (50/500) \times (1 - e^{-500t/0.75})$

$0.5 = 1 - e^{-666t}$, $0.5 = e^{-666t}$

$666t = \log_e 2$, $666t = 0.694$, $t = 0.001$ sec

EXAMPLE 7.21 (B). An impulsing relay having a resistance of 400 Ω and an inductance of 16 H is adjusted to operate with a current of 15 mA. What will be the operating lag of the relay when it is connected in series with a non-inductive resistance of 1 200 Ω and a battery of 48 V ? ($\log_{10} e = 0.434\,3 : \log_{10} 2 = 0.301\,0$.)   (C. & G.)

$$i = \frac{V}{R} . (1 - e^{-Rt/L})$$

$0.015 = \dfrac{48}{400 + 1\,200} . (1 - e^{-1\,600t/16})$

$0.015 = 0.030(1 - 1/e^{100t})$

$\frac{1}{2} = 1 - 1/e^{100t}$, $\frac{1}{2} = (e^{100t} - 1)/e^{100t}$

$e^{100t} = 2e^{100t} - 2$, $e^{100t} = 2$

$100t \log_{10} e = \log_{10} 2$, $100t \times 0.434\,3 = 0.301\,0$

$t = 0.301\,0/43.43 = 0.006\,9 = 6.9$ msec.

EXAMPLE 7.22 (B). A certain relay has a winding of 15 000 turns with a resistance of 1 000 Ω and its operating current is 8 mA. The reluctance of the magnetic circuit may be taken as constant at a value of 8.75×10^6 AT/Wb, and it may be assumed that there is no leakage of flux. Calculate the inductance of the relay and the time required for the current to reach its operating value when a potential of 50 V is applied to the circuit.   (C. & G.)

$L = \mu_r \mu_0 A N^2/l = N^2/S$
$\quad = 15^2 \times 10^6/(8.75 \times 10^6) = 25.7$ H

$$i = \frac{V}{R} . (1 - e^{-Rt/L})$$

$iR = V(1 - e^{-Rt/L})$

$iR = V - V . e^{-Rt/L}$

$V/e^{Rt/L} = V - iR$

$e^{Rt/L} = V/(V - iR)$

$(Rt/L) . \log_{10} e = \log_{10}\{V/(V - iR)\}$

$Rt/L = \log_{10}\{V/(V - iR)\} \div \log_{10} e$

$t = \dfrac{L}{R} . \left\{ \log_{10} . \left(\dfrac{V}{V - iR} \right) \right\} \div \log_{10} e$

7

$$V - iR = 50 - (0\cdot008 \times 1\,000) = 50 - 8$$
$$= 42$$
$$t = (25\cdot7/1\,000) \times \log_{10} 50/42$$
$$\div 0\cdot434\,3$$
$$= 0\cdot025\,7 \times \log_{10}(50/42) \div 0\cdot434\,3$$
$$= 0\cdot025\,7 \times 0\cdot075\,6/0\cdot434\,3$$
$$= 0\cdot025\,7 \times 0\cdot174\,4 = 0\cdot004\,48$$
$$= 4\cdot5 \text{ msec}$$

EXAMPLE 7.23 (B). A relay has a resistance of 400 Ω and its operating current is 15 mA. There are 14 000 turns in the relay coil and the magnetic circuit may be assumed to have a constant reluctance of $1\cdot175 \times 10^7$ AT/Wb.

Calculate the inductance of the relay and the time taken for the current to reach its operating value, when the relay is connected in series with a resistor of 400 Ω and a p.d. of 50 V is applied to the combination. The effect of magnetic leakage may be neglected.   (C. & G.)

$$L = \mu_r\mu_0 A N^2/l = N^2/S$$
$$= 196 \times 10^6/(1\cdot175 \times 10^7)$$
$$= 16\cdot68 \text{ H}$$

$$i = \frac{V}{R} \cdot (1 - e^{-Rt/L})$$

$$iR = V - Ve^{-Rt/L} = V - V/e^{Rt/L}$$
$$V/e^{Rt/L} = V - iR, \quad e^{Rt/L} = V/(V - iR)$$
$$Rt/L = \log_e\{V/(V - iR)\}$$
$$t = (L/R) \times \log_e \{V/(V - iR)\} \text{ sec}$$
$$= \frac{16\cdot68}{(400 + 400)} \times \log_e\left(\frac{50}{50 - 0\cdot015 \times 800}\right)$$
$$= 0\cdot0208 \times \log_e 1\cdot315 = 0\cdot0208 \times 0\cdot273\,7$$
$$= 5\cdot7 \text{ msec}$$

EXAMPLE 7.24 (B). A telephone relay has a resistance of 1 000 Ω and an inductance of 25 H. The relay will just operate with a current of 16 mA and it releases when the current falls to 5 mA. Calculate the time lags in operating and in releasing when the relay is working directly across 50 V d.c. supply terminals. Assume that the inductance remains constant and also that under release conditions the relay is short-circuited.   (C. & G.)

Operating
$$i = \frac{V}{R} \cdot (1 - e^{-Rt/L})$$
$$\frac{16}{1\,000} = \frac{50}{1\,000} \cdot (1 - e^{-1\,000t/25})$$
$$16 = 50 - 50 \cdot e^{-40t}$$
$$50/e^{40t} = 50 - 16 = 34$$
$$e^{40t} = 50/34 = 1\cdot47$$
$$40t = \log_e 1\cdot47 = 0\cdot385\,26$$
$$t = 0\cdot385/40 = 0\cdot009\,6$$
$$= 9\cdot6 \text{ msec}$$

Releasing
$$i = \frac{V}{R} \cdot e^{-Rt/L}$$
$$\frac{5}{1\,000} = \frac{50}{1\,000} \cdot e^{-1\,000t/25}$$
$$5 = 50 \cdot e^{-40t} = 50/e^{40t}$$
$$e^{40t} = 50/5 = 10$$
$$40t = \log_e 10 = 2\cdot302\,6$$
$$t = 2\cdot302\,6/40 = 0\cdot057\,56$$
$$= 57\cdot6 \text{ msec}$$

EXAMPLE 7.25 (B). A certain relay which has a resistance of 1 000 Ω and an inductance of 10 H will just operate when the current reaches a value of 25 mA. What time interval will elapse before the relay operates when a potential of 50 V is applied to its terminals?   (C. & G.)

$$i = \frac{V}{R} \cdot (1 - e^{-Rt/L}),$$
$$\frac{25}{1\,000} = \frac{50}{1\,000} \cdot (1 - e^{-1\,000t/10})$$
$$25 = 50 - 50 \cdot e^{-100t}$$
$$50 \cdot e^{-100t} = 50 - 25 = 25$$
$$e^{-100t} = 25/50, \quad e^{100t} = 2$$
$$100t = \log_e 2 = 0\cdot693\,15$$
$$t = 0\cdot006\,9 = 6\cdot9 \text{ msec}$$

7.23. Energy of Magnetic Field. Energy is expended while a magnetic field is built up in an inductance L; none is required to maintain the field itself but electrical energy (I^2Rt), entirely converted to heat, is of course required to maintain the current I in the resistance R of the conductor. When the field collapses the whole of the initial energy is restored to the circuit. It is frequently convenient for calculation purposes, to consider any inductor as being made up of pure inductance L acting in series with its pure resistance R.

The energy expended in building up a magnetic field in an inductance L is equal to

$$LI^2/2 \text{ joules} \qquad . \qquad . \quad (7.20)$$

where I is the final steady current.

EXAMPLE 7.26 (A). In Example 7.10, what would be the maximum voltage developed across the coil if a capacitor of 10 μF were connected across the switch breaking the d.c. supply?   (C. & G.)

In Example 7.10, $I = 1$ A, $L = 0\cdot5$ H.

The energy stored in a capacitor is
$$\tfrac{1}{2}CV^2 = \tfrac{1}{2}LI^2$$
$$V^2 = LI^2/C$$
$$V = I\sqrt{(L/C)}$$
$$= 1(0\cdot5 \times 10^6/10)^{\frac{1}{2}} = 10^2\sqrt{5} = 223\cdot6 \text{ V}$$

EXAMPLE 7.27 (A). A capacitor of 1 μF charged to a p.d. 100 V is connected across a coil having an inductance 1 mH and negligible resistance. What is the maximum rrent which can flow in the coil?　(C. & G.)

Energy in charged capacitor $= \frac{1}{2}CV^2$

Energy stored in coil $= \frac{1}{2}LI^2$

$$\frac{1}{2}CV^2 = \frac{1}{2}LI^2, \quad I^2 = CV^2/L$$

$$I = V\sqrt{(C/L)}$$

$$= 100\sqrt{(10^{-6}/10^{-3})} = \underline{\underline{3\cdot16 \text{ A}}}$$

7.24. Non-inductive Resistors.

Any conductor ossesses the property of self-inductance to some xtent due to the linkages set up by the flux. A

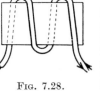

FIG. 7.28.
NON-INDUCTIVE
RESISTOR

conductor may, however, be wound in such a manner as to neutralize the flux and consequently to reduce the inductance to zero. If the conductor is looped back upon itself from a point midway along its length, the flux due to one half of the conductor will be completely neutralized by the equal and opposite flux due

o the other half. Accordingly a non-inductive re-stor, a frequent requirement for testing and other urposes, may be produced by winding it upon a ormer with the conductor doubled, as indicated n Fig. 7.28.

7.25. Spark Quench Circuits.

If an inductive ircuit is disconnected, the collapsing flux restores nergy to the circuit, and when the switch contacts pen the current is rapidly brought to zero: the nduced e.m.f. frequently reaches a high value due o the rapid change in linkages. While the distance etween the receding contacts is small this voltage sually exceeds the dielectric strength of the air nd a spark travels across the gap to complete the ircuit.

In highly inductive circuits this sparking may be erious from three points of view. Fisrtly the high oltage, though of short duration, may be in excess f the dielectric strength of the conductor covering nd damage the insulating material: or the exces-ive current may damage the insulating material n account of the heat produced.

Secondly, the spark carries with it small par-icles of material from the switch contacts, causing hem to be pitted or gradually eaten away, at the ame time covering them with an oxide film which vill produce a high resistance contact when they re subsequently closed. In extreme cases arcing nay occur and prevent the circuit from being dis-onnected by the switch contacts. In telegraph nd telephone relays whose contacts may operate

millions of times in the course of a year, this spark-ing and arcing would have serious results if per-mitted to occur.

Thirdly, interference is caused with adjacent radio equipment each time sparking occurs, due to the radiation of electromagnetic energy.

Spark quench circuits are fitted to switching con-tacts where necessary to prevent this sparking. In the simplest case the inductor may be shunted by a non-inductive resistor, so that when the power supply is disconnected the inductor has a per-manently closed circuit (Fig. 7.29 (a)) and the induced current (shown by the dotted arrows) cir-culates in the circuit formed by L and R in series. If L represents a relay or electromagnet then the shunt path, in prolonging the flux, will delay the release of the armature. The simple shunt is not always desirable from circuit design considerations.

Another common form of spark quench circuit consists of a non-inductive resistor R in series with a capacitor C connected across the switching con-tacts (Fig. 7.29 (b)). The resistor limits the mag-nitude of the current flowing due to the induced e.m.f., and absorbs the energy: the capacitor is necessary to avoid placing a d.c. shunt path across the inductor. The contacts are frequently of specially hard material such as platinum or

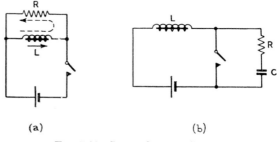

(a)　　　　　　　　　(b)

FIG. 7.29. SPARK QUENCH CIRCUITS

tungsten. The values chosen for C and R depend upon the circuit constants and the contact material: in the general case of telephone and telegraph switch-ing contacts, a capacitor of 1 μF in series with a non-inductive resistor of 10 Ω for silver contacts and 200 Ω for platinum contacts is usually found to be satisfactory. In some cases the capacitor may be used alone, but a current limiting resistor is usually necessary. The current in the spark quench circuit of this type is oscillatory.

Other devices depend upon the use of metal rectifiers and varistors. To avoid radio interference it is sometimes necessary to fit special tuned suppressor circuits.

With heavy currents a magnetic quench is some-times used.

7.26. Electromagnetic Interference. Telephone and telegraph circuits running on parallel routes possess mutual inductance. As a result the fluctuating direct currents or alternating currents constituting the telegraph or telephone signals flowing in any one circuit (the *disturbing* circuit) introduce corresponding e.m.f.s in any adjacent circuits (the *disturbed* circuits). The practical effect of this is to produce interference or *cross-talk* between the circuits so that signals from one circuit would be overheard in another. This is overcome in cables by using twisted pairs of conductors. The principle of this is similar to that of the non-inductive resistor: the two conductors of each pair being on the average the same distance from any disturbing circuit have equal and opposite disturbing fluxes linking them, the induced e.m.f.s being neutralized in the twisted pair. The lay—the length occupied by a twist—is varied for each layer of conductors. With overhead lines, the same result is effected by transposing the position of the wires on the same poles at intervals. In practice the cross-talk due to electromagnetic induction is not serious at voice frequencies but causes appreciable cross-talk in carrier cables, requiring special balancing facilities at the cable terminations to reduce this cross-talk.

7.27. Vibratory Power Converters. The principle of electromagnetic induction is conveniently applied for the purpose of obtaining power supplies at relatively high voltages from a low voltage source.

The magnitude of an induced e.m.f. depends upon the rate of change of the flux. If an iron core is enclosed by primary and secondary windings, the rapid opening and closing of the primary circuit will induce in the secondary winding a high voltage which will be further increased if the

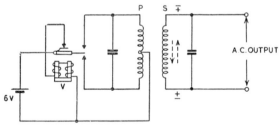

FIG. 7.30. RINGING VIBRATOR

secondary winding has a large number of turns. From Fig. 7.12 it is clear that the induced e.m.f. is an alternating one, being reversed when the primary circuit is closed, and forward when the primary circuit is opened.

One application of this principle is in the ringing vibrator (Fig. 7.30) used in small telephone exchanges. The operation of the vibrator portion *V*

is similar to that of the well-known trembler bell. The vibrator consists simply of an electromagnet whose armature when operated disconnects its own circuit: in restoring, the armature again closes its own circuit, resulting in a continuous state of vibration. The mass of the armature, or *tuned reed*, is designed to give a specific frequency of vibration.

An extension of the reed plays between two contacts and connects the 6-V battery alternately to the two balanced parts of the primary coil. The current flows alternately in each half of the

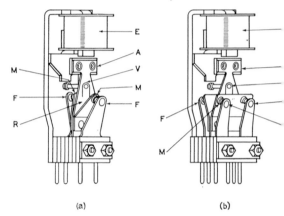

(a)   (b)

FIG. 7.31. VIBRATORY POWER CONVERTERS
(a) Non-synchronous. (b) Synchronous.

winding in opposite directions, consequently the effect of breaking the circuit of the one half winding is assisted by making the circuit of the other half winding. As indicated by the arrows a continuously reversing e.m.f. is generated in the secondary winding.

Vibratory power converters are also used extensively for providing, from a low voltage battery, the high tension d.c. voltages required for operating radio equipment. The output from a vibrator is fundamentally alternating: rectification to produce a d.c. output is effected either by (i) the use of a metal rectifier, or (ii) in the synchronous type by the use of vibrating change-over contacts in the secondary circuit which operate in synchronism with the primary circuit contacts.

The construction of both types is illustrated in Fig. 7.31. Each comprises a free steel reed *R*: to this is attached a soft-iron armature *A* which is attracted by the electromagnet *E*. The pair of platinum contacts *V* is connected in series with the magnet winding to drive the vibrator, the contacts being closed when the reed is stationary. The frequency of vibration is of the order of 100 c/s depending upon the characteristics of the reed. A pair of tungsten contacts *M* is attached to the reed and when the mechanism is functioning the moving contacts engage intermittently with the insulated fixed contacts F. The synchronous type has an additional set of contacts S which operate in synchronism with the first set, but are arranged to close later and open earlier, the object of this sequence being to prolong the life of the contacts.

The principle of operation of the non-synchronous type is similar to that of the ringing vibrator (Fig. 7.30).

The circuit arrangement of the synchronous vibrator, shown in Fig. 7.32, is of the voltage-

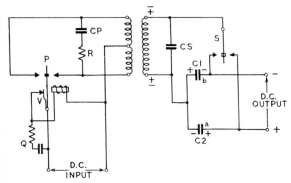

FIG. 7.32. SYNCHRONOUS VIBRATOR WITH VOLTAGE DOUBLING CIRCUIT

doubling type, and differs from Fig. 7.30 by the inclusion of rectifying contacts S and storage capacitors C_1 and C_2. Owing to synchronism between the contacts in the primary and secondary circuits, the spring S changes over at the instant when the e.m.f. in the secondary winding is reversing. At the instant when S opens its left-hand contact, assuming that the upper terminal of the secondary winding is at negative potential, the capacitor C_1 is charged with the polarity indicated: when S closes its right-hand contact the reversed e.m.f. in the secondary winding is applied in series with the charge on C_1 across the d.c. output terminals. In this way one of the capacitors receives each half-cycle a charge which in the following half-cycle is added in series with the (reversed) secondary e.m.f. and applied across the output terminals. For each complete vibration of the reed, two unidirectional pulses are delivered to the output circuit: smoothing equipment is usually required at the output terminals.

The capacitor CP and resistor R act as a spark quench to moderate the rate of decay of primary current at the instant of contact break, and together with the capacitor CS limits the magnitude of undesirable voltage peaks in both the primary and secondary circuits. The slight sequencing of the

contacts P and S ensures that the secondary circuit is always open at the intervals of make and break of the contacts P, so that the full primary current is not broken by the P contacts. A spark quench

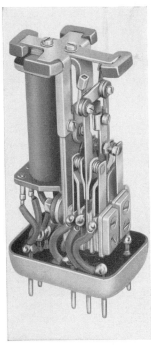

FIG. 7.33. VIBRATORY POWER CONVERTER
(*Courtesy of "I.P.O.E.E. Journal"*)

circuit Q is also fitted across the vibrator drive contacts.

A photograph of a vibrator appears in Fig. 7.33.

SUMMARY

Corkscrew Rule. If a right-handed corkscrew could be screwed into the conductor, the direction of the current is represented by the longitudinal movement of the corkscrew, and the direction of the magnetic field is represented by the direction of rotation.

Magnetizing Force.

$$H = NI/l \text{ ampere-turns/metre} \qquad . \quad (7.1)$$

Flux Density.

$$B = \mu H = \mu_r \mu_0 H$$
$$= \mu_r \mu_0 NI/l \text{ webers/metre}^2$$

Total Flux. $\quad \Phi = BA$ webers

Magneto-motive Force.

$$M = NI \text{ ampere-turns} . \qquad . \quad (7.2)$$

Reluctance.
$$S = l/(\mu_r\mu_0 A) \text{ ampere-turns/weber} . \quad (7.3)$$
Magnetic Circuit.

Flux = m.m.f./reluctance
$$\Phi = M/S \quad . \qquad . \qquad . \qquad . \quad (7.4)$$
Reluctances in Series.
$$S = S_1 + S_2 + S_3 + \dots \quad . \quad (7.5)$$

Faraday's Law. When the magnetic flux linking a conductor is changing, an e.m.f. is induced whose magnitude is proportional to the rate of change of flux.

Lenz's Law. The direction of an induced e.m.f. is always such as to oppose the cause which produces it.

Electromagnetic Induction. The production of an e.m.f. in a circuit by a change of magnetic flux through the circuit. If the change of magnetic flux is due to a variation in the current flowing in the same circuit the phenomenon is known as *self-induction*; if due to a change of current flowing in another circuit, as *mutual induction*.

Self-inductance. The property of a circuit by virtue of which self-induction occurs.

Mutual Inductance. The property of circuits by virtue of which mutual induction occurs.

Henry. That inductance which produces an e.m.f. of one volt when the current is changing at the rate of one ampere per second.

Induced E.M.F.

$$E = -N . d\Phi/dt \text{ volts} \quad . \qquad . \quad (7.6)$$
$$E = -L . di/dt \text{ volts} \quad . \qquad . \quad (7.7)$$
$$E = M . di/dt \text{ volts} \quad . \qquad . \quad (7.8)$$

Inductors in Series $(M = 0)$.

$$L = L_1 + L_2 + L_3 + \dots \quad . \qquad . \quad (7.9)$$

(Two inductors only),
$$L = L_1 + L_2 + 2M \text{ (aiding)}$$
(Two inductors only),
$$L = L_1 + L_2 - 2M \text{ (opposing)}$$
$$\left. \right\} \quad . (7.10)$$

Inductors in Parallel $(M = 0)$.
$$1/L = 1/L_1 + 1/L_2 + 1/L_3 + \dots \quad . \quad (7.11)$$

$(M = 0,$ two inductors only),
$$L = L_1 L_2/(L_1 + L_2) \quad . \qquad . \qquad . \quad (7.12)$$
$(M = 0,$ N similar inductors),
$$L = L'/N \qquad . \qquad . \qquad . \quad (7.13)$$

(Two inductors only),
$$L = (L_1 L_2 - M^2)/(L_1 + L_2 - 2M) \text{ (aiding)}$$
(Two inductors only),
$$L = (L_1 L_2 - M^2)/(L_1 + L_2 + 2M) \text{ (opposing)}$$
$$\left. \right\} \quad (7.14)$$

(Two equal inductors),
$$L = (L_1 + M)/2 \text{ (aiding)}$$
(Two equal inductors),
$$L = (L_1 - M)/2 \text{ (opposing)}$$
$$\left. \right\} \quad . (7.15)$$

Inductance of Solenoid.
$$L = \mu_r\mu_0 A N^2/l \text{ henrys}$$
$$= N^2/S \text{ henrys} \qquad . \qquad . \quad (7.16)$$

Mutual Inductance of Two Solenoids.
$$M = \mu_r\mu_0 A N_1 N_2/l \text{ henrys} \qquad . \quad (7.17)$$

Eddy Currents. Local currents induced in a conducting body by a varying or relatively-moving magnetic field.

Skin Effect. In a conductor carrying an a.c.: an effect whereby the current density is greater at the surface of the conductor than in the centre.

Growth of Current.
$$i = \frac{V}{R} . (1 - e^{-Rt/L}) \qquad . \qquad . \quad (7.18)$$

Decay of Current.
$$i = \frac{V}{R} . e^{-Rt/L} \qquad . \qquad . \quad (7.19)$$

Time-constant (T). The time taken for the current to attain 63·2 per cent of its final value. $T = L/R$ seconds.

Energy of Magnetic Field.
$$W = \tfrac{1}{2}LI^2 \text{ joules} \qquad . \qquad . \quad (7.20)$$

REFERENCES

1. G. R. POLGREEN: "Magnetic Dust Cores," *I.P.O.E.E. Journal*, **37** (1944), p. 1.
2. L. S. DISTIN: "Modern Vibratory Power Converters," ibid., **39** (1946), p. 53.

CHAPTER VIII

GENERATORS

8.1. E.M.F. Induced by a Moving Conductor. The induction of an e.m.f. from the changes in flux linkage of a conductor, due in turn to current changes, was discussed in Chapter VII. An e.m.f. will always be generated from changes in flux linkage by whatever means these changes are brought about. An e.m.f. can be equally well induced in a conductor by moving it in a constant field, or by varying a magnetic field with respect to a stationary conductor: both of these methods are used in the design of machines for generating electrical energy.

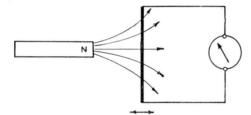

Fig. 8.1. Induction of E.M.F.

Fig. 8.1 shows a conductor placed in a magnetic field and connected to a sensitive galvanometer. If the magnet is moved, a deflexion will be shown on the galvanometer *while this movement takes place.* Furthermore, if the magnet is moved towards the conductor, the deflexion is in the opposite sense from that obtained when the magnet recedes from the coil. Similar deflexions will be obtained if the conductor is moved and the magnet remains stationary. In general, any relative movement between a magnetic field and a conductor produces an e.m.f.

8.2. Magnitude of Induced E.M.F. The magnitude of the e.m.f. is by Faraday's law proportional to the rate at which the flux linkage changes. If the flux Φ changes by the small amount $d\Phi$ in an interval of time dt, the rate of change of flux is the ratio $d\Phi/dt$ and the induced e.m.f. is

$$E = d\Phi/dt \text{ volts}$$

When a conductor of length l m is moving with a velocity v m/sec and cutting a flux of uniform density B Wb/m² at right angles (Fig. 8.2), the area swept out by the conductor each second will be $l \times v$ m²: the linkages per second will be

$$B \times l \times v \text{ Wb/sec}$$

Hence the induced e.m.f.

$$E = Blv \text{ volts}$$

If the conductor is not cutting the flux at right angles, the direction of conductor motion with respect to the flux must be taken into consideration. In Fig. 8.3 a conductor is shown moving with a velocity v m/sec acting at an angle $\theta°$ to the direction of the flux. This velocity can be considered as being made up of two components (Appendix **A.4**), $v \cos \theta$ m/sec parallel to the flux and $v \sin \theta$ m/sec perpendicular to the field. The

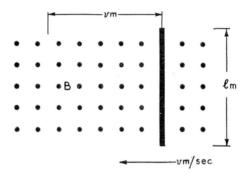

Fig. 8.2. E.M.F. of Moving Conductor

former component, $v \cos \theta$, being parallel to the field does not result in any linkages, but the latter component, $v \sin \theta$, is at right angles to the flux. The general expression for the induced e.m.f. becomes

$$E = Blv \sin \theta \text{ volts} \qquad . \qquad (8.1)$$

When the conductor moves at right angles to the field, $\theta° = 90$ and $\sin \theta = 1$, so that

$$E = Blv \text{ volts}$$

When $\theta° = 0$, $\sin \theta = 0$ and $E = 0$. The length l is the effective length of the conductor in the field.

8.3. Direction of Induced E.M.F. The direction of the induced e.m.f. in relation to the motion and to the field may be deduced from an application of Lenz's law. The current which flows in a conductor as a result of the induced e.m.f. will establish its own magnetic field and this must be in such a direction that it sets up a force opposing the motion which produces it.

In Fig. 8.4 the direction of the original flux is shown by the vertical lines F and the direction of conductor motion by the horizontal arrow M. The concentric field due to the current induced in the conductor must be clockwise, so that a combination of the inducing and induced fields produces the field shown in Fig. 8.5. Regarding the lines of force

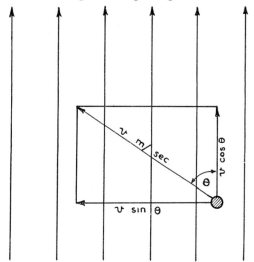

FIG. 8.3. VELOCITY COMPONENTS

in this diagram from the conception of their tendency to contract and to repel one another laterally, a resultant force indicated by the dotted arrow arises to oppose the motion which induced the e.m.f. This establishes the direction of the induced current, indicated by the cross in the diagram (see Fig. 7.1).

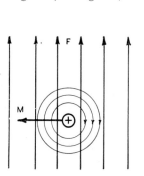

FIG. 8.4. DIRECTION OF INDUCED E.M.F.

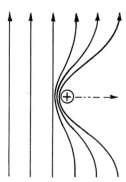

FIG. 8.5. FORCE OPPOSING MOTION OF CONDUCTOR

The relative directions of the motion, the inducing flux, and the current are conveniently remembered by application of FLEMING'S RIGHT-HAND RULE. *Extend the thumb and first two fingers of the right hand mutually at right angles: then if the thumb represents the direction of motion and the first finger that of the flux, the second finger will point in the direction of the induced current.* These three directions mutually at right angles are represented in Fig. 8.6 by the three edges at one corner of a cube, and may be compared with the directions c

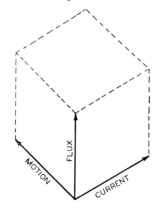

FIG. 8.6. FLEMING'S RIGHT-HAND RULE

Fig. 8.4. The following mnemonic assists in applying Fleming's rule—

thu$M$b—Motion
First—Flux
se$C$ond—Current

(Since a *left*-hand rule is introduced in Chapter IX it is convenient to remember that the rIght-hand rule determines current (I).)

8.4. E.M.F. Induced in Rotating Coil. A conductor formed into a rectangular coil is shown in Fig. 8.7 rotating in a uniform parallel field in

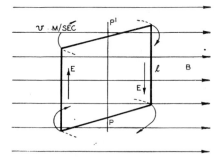

FIG. 8.7. COIL ROTATING IN UNIFORM PARALLEL FIELD

clockwise direction with an angular velocity of v m/sec around the axis PP': the same frame is shown in plan in Fig. 8.8. While it rotates the direction of its velocity is always tangential to the circular path swept out by the vertical limbs. If at any instant this velocity makes an angle $\theta°$ with

e direction of the flux, the active component
erpendicular to the field is $v \sin \theta$ m/sec. If the
agnetic flux density is B webers/m² the induced
m.f. in each vertical limb of the coil is

$$E = Blv \sin \theta \text{ volts}$$

nce the vertical limbs are cutting the flux in
pposite directions, Fleming's right-hand rule
ows that the induced e.m.f.s are also in opposite
rections as indicated in both diagrams. These
ertical limbs form in effect two conductors con-
ected in series and Fig. 8.7 shows that these
m.f.s are additive, the total e.m.f. being

$$2E = 2Blv \sin \theta \text{ volts}$$

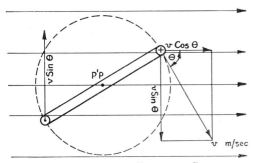

FIG. 8.8. PLAN OF ROTATING COIL

If the frame is replaced by a coil having Z vertical
onductors the induced e.m.f. will be

$$E = BlvZ \sin \theta \text{ volts}$$

The e.m.f. induced when a coil rotates at constant
elocity in a uniform parallel field is always pro-
ortional to $\sin \theta$, $\theta°$ being the angle swept out as
ie coil rotates. The magnitude of the e.m.f. is
ontinuously varying and also changing its direc-
on—it is in fact an alternating e.m.f.: this is
irther discussed in Chapter X.

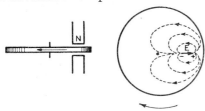

FIG. 8.9. EDDY CURRENTS

Any conductor, that is to say any mass of metal,
hich rotates in a magnetic field will be subject to
iduced e.m.f.s. Fig. 8.9 shows in elevation and
lan a metal disk rotating between the poles of a
nagnet placed eccentrically. With the disk rota-
ng in a clockwise direction (viewed from above)
nd the magnet polarity shown in the diagram, the

direction of the induced e.m.f. E will, by Fleming's
right-hand rule, be that marked by the arrow in
the plan view. Eddy currents circulate in the mass
of the metal as indicated by the dotted lines.

EXAMPLE 8.1 (A). The armature of a generator consists
of a coil of 20 turns of wire which is wound longitudinally
on a drum 10 cm long and 6 cm in diameter. If this
armature is rotated at a speed of 2 000 r.p.m. in a magnetic
field of 10 webers/m², what is the maximum voltage
developed across the ends of the coil?   (C. & G.)

$Z = 20$
$l = 0·1$ m
$d = 0·06$ m
$n = 2\ 000/60$ r.p.s.
$B = 10$ Wb/m²

Peripheral velocity $V = \pi \times 0·06 \times 2\ 000/60$ m/sec
$\qquad\qquad\qquad = 2\pi$ m/sec

$$\begin{aligned}
\text{Max e.m.f. } E &= BlvZ \\
&= 10 \times 0·1 \times 2\pi \times 20 \\
&\qquad \times 2 = 80\pi \\
&= 251·4 \text{ V}
\end{aligned}$$

EXAMPLE 8.2 (A). A coil of wire wound with 20 turns in
the form of a square having 10 cm sides is rotated at a
speed of 1 200 r.p.m. in a uniform magnetic field of
0·2 webers/m². What is the voltage developed across
the ends of the coil when the angle between the plane of
the coil and the direction of the magnetic field is (a) 0°,
(b) 30°, (c) 90°?   (C. & G.)

$Z = 40$
$N = 1\ 200$ r.p.m.
$l = 0·1$ m
$B = 0·2$ Wb/m²
$v = 2\pi \times 0·05 \times 1\ 200 \div 60$ m/sec
$\quad = 6·28$ m/sec

$$\begin{aligned}
E &= BlvZ \sin \theta = 0·2 \times 0·1 \times 6·28 \\
&\qquad \times 40 \sin \theta \\
&= 5 \sin \theta
\end{aligned}$$

(a) $\theta = (90 - 0) = 90$, $\sin 90 = 1$, $E = \underline{5 \text{ V}}$

(b) $\theta = (90 - 30) = 60$,
$\qquad\qquad\qquad \sin 60 = 0·86$, $E = \underline{4·3 \text{ V}}$

(c) $\theta = (90 - 90) = 0$, $\sin 0 = 0$, $E = \underline{\underline{0}}$

8.5. The Direct Current Generator. The d.c.
generator (or dynamo) is a machine which when
driven by mechanical power causes the rotation of
a system of conductors in a magnetic field to
generate an e.m.f. and maintain a d.c. output voltage. The dynamo comprises two main parts, the
field magnets to produce the flux and the armature
which carries the moving conductors.

The field magnets are designed to produce an
intense magnetic flux to be cut by the rotating

conductors. In very small machines the field is satisfactorily produced by a strong permanent magnet, but in all other machines the field is produced by electromagnets. The field magnet windings may be energized or *excited* by an external source of d.c. energy, but it is more usual to use a portion of the energy generated by the machine itself for this purpose.

The armature consists of a soft-iron drum on the

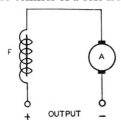

FIG. 8.10. SERIES-WOUND D.C. GENERATOR

surface of which are fixed the conductors to be rotated between the pole-pieces of the field magnets. The clearance or air-gap between armature and pole-pieces is made as small as possible in order to reduce the reluctance of the magnetic circuit to a minimum. For this reason the pole-pieces are shaped so as to be concentric with the armature. Due to the shape of the pole-pieces and the use of a soft-iron armature the flux in the gap

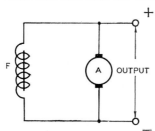

FIG. 8.11. SHUNT-WOUND D.C. GENERATOR

is mainly radial so that the rotating conductors will cut the flux at right angles.

An integral part of the armature is the *commutator* which consists of a number of copper segments insulated from one another with mica and connected electrically to the armature conductors with which they rotate: electrical contact is made with the rotating conductors by means of conducting brushes which press on to the commutator segments. At the same time the commutator ensures that the generated e.m.f. is always applied unidirectionally across the generator terminals, although this e.m.f. in each rotating conductor is itself alternating.

To energize the field windings from the armature the field winding F and armature winding A may be connected in series or in parallel according to requirements. In the former case the machine is known as a series-wound generator, and in the latter as a shunt-wound generator: these connexions are depicted in Figs. 8.10 and 8.11.

For some purposes a compound-wound machine is used which has its field winding in two sections, one connected in series and the other in parallel with the armature winding. The electrical connexions of the two possible arrangements of this

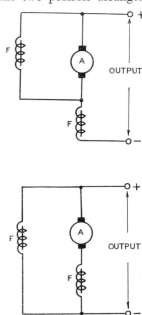

FIG. 8.12. COMPOUND-WOUND D.C. GENERATOR
(a) Short shunt. (b) Long shunt.

type are shown in Fig. 8.12: in the *short-shunt* method (Fig. 8.12 (a)) the series winding carries the output current only; in the *long-shunt* type (Fig. 8.12 (b)) the series winding carries the full armature current.

In telecommunication equipment where the desired characteristic of the d.c. generator is constant p.d. for battery charging or floating the shunt-wound machine is employed.

8.6. The Armature Circuit. Fig. 8.13 shows two conductors TT revolving in a clockwise direction in a magnetic field. The conductors are joined in series by means of the rear connexion R and extended at the front to two collecting rings CC: two brushes BB connected to terminals maintain contact with the rotating conductors via the rings.

Application of Fleming's right-hand rule to the

rotating conductors shows that the descending and ascending conductors generate e.m.f.s which are in opposite directions but which combine in driving a current around any circuit connected to the terminals. However, when each ascending conductor in turn becomes a descending conductor, and vice versa, the e.m.f. in that conductor reverses: the terminal voltage is consequently an alternating one, changing direction at every half revolution of the conductors.

The slip rings are replaced in Fig. 8.14 by a

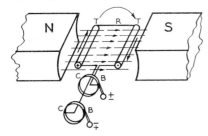

FIG. 8.13. A.C. GENERATOR

commutator consisting of two insulated semi-circular contact strips (CC). With correct location of the brushes, each conductor through its commutator segment becomes changed over to the opposite brush at the instant when the direction of its induced e.m.f. falls to zero and reverses. Consequently, although the e.m.f. in the conductor is still alternating, one terminal of the machine is always at a positive potential with respect to the

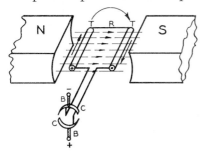

FIG. 8.14. D.C. GENERATOR

other, and a unidirectional current will flow in any external circuit applied to the terminals.

The variation of e.m.f. at the brush terminals during one revolution takes the form shown by the full line in Fig. 8.15, the dotted line indicating the reversed e.m.f. in the winding during alternate half revolutions. The actual shape of the e.m.f. curves depends upon the flux distribution, since at constant armature speed this distribution entirely governs the rate of flux change. In any case the

e.m.f. will fall to zero twice per revolution at the instant when the conductor velocity is parallel to the flux, and the current delivered to the external circuit will be a pulsating one.

By using a winding consisting of many conductors and a number of commutator segments spaced evenly around the armature, the pulsations

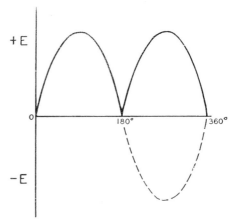

FIG. 8.15. COMMUTATION

may be reduced to a negligible amount. Fig. 8.16 shows the effect of doubling the number of conductors and spacing them 90° apart. When one pair of conductors has zero e.m.f. the other pair is generating its maximum e.m.f., and if the separate e.m.f.s shown at E_1 and E_2 are added at every

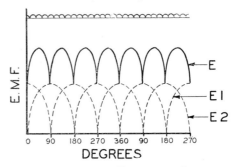

FIG. 8.16. EFFECT OF INCREASING ARMATURE CONDUCTORS

instant, the curve E is produced which has no zero value. The result of employing an even greater number of conductors is indicated by the upper line showing the production of an almost constant e.m.f. with but slight ripple.

Fig. 8.17 shows an arrangement of twelve conductors joined to an equal number of commutator segments with brushes at BB. All conductors under the influence of the N-pole have an induced e.m.f. opposite to that in the conductors under the S-pole. If the front of each conductor were joined to the *rear* of its counter-clockwise neighbour, then, assuming that these connecting wires did not

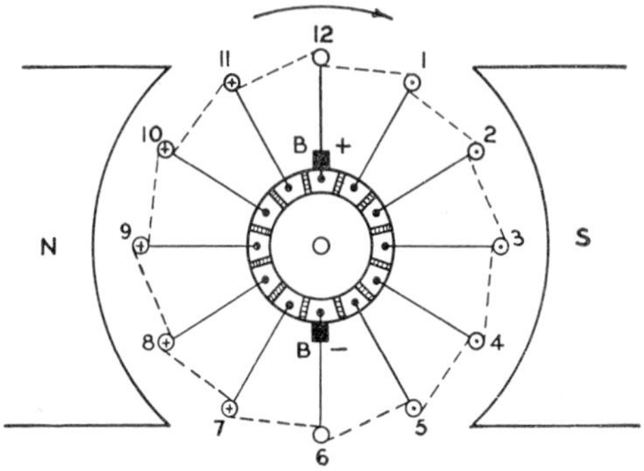

FIG. 8.17. PATHS IN ARMATURE CIRCUIT

themselves generate any e.m.f., the e.m.f.s of conductors under either pole would assist one another. This is perhaps more readily visualized in the diagram of Fig. 8.18 where the e.m.f. in each conductor is represented by the symbol for a voltaic cell. The resultant effect is equivalent to

The resistance of one path is $Zr/2$ ohms and since two equal paths are in parallel the joint armature resistance is $Zr/4$ ohms. The term armature resistance is usually taken to include armature winding

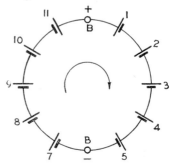

FIG. 8.18. E.M.F.s IN ARMATURE CONDUCTORS

commutator segments, brushes and contact resistance. Armature resistance is analogous in its effects to the internal resistance of a voltaic cell and it is kept as low as possible.

8.7. Armature Construction. The arrangement of conductors given in Fig. 8.17 is not a practicable one. The design of an armature winding is a

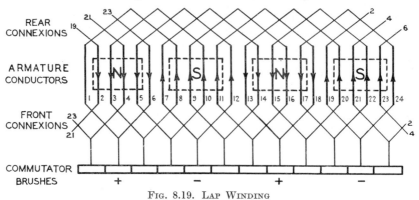

FIG. 8.19. LAP WINDING

two series-batteries joined in parallel: there are two parallel paths in this particular armature winding.

The brushes make contact with each conductor in turn while its e.m.f. is zero and reversing: at this instant, too, a pair of conductors becomes short-circuited while the brush is momentarily bridging two adjacent commutator segments (Fig. 8.17).

If Z is the total number of active conductors each generating an e.m.f. E volts and of resistance r ohms, the generated e.m.f. is $ZE/2$ volts. For a given external circuit taking I amperes each conductor carries $I/2$ amperes.

complex problem, but the general arrangement may be briefly given.

A conductor under one pole is normally connected to a conductor influenced by opposite polarity so that their e.m.f.s mutually assist. Connexions between conductors are effected at the rear of the armature, and also at the front where conductors are connected to each other and to the commutator segments.

There are two alternative methods of connecting armature conductors together, resulting in what are known as *lap* and *wave* windings. A winding is best illustrated by a development diagram. The distance between two conductors which are connected together, expressed in terms of armature conductors, is known as the *pitch*; the back and front pitches are not necessarily equal, and may be positive or negative, that is to say a conductor

rise in temperature of the machine due to eddy currents is limited. The insulating non-magnetic layers have little influence on the magnetic circuit since the direction of the flux, being at right angles

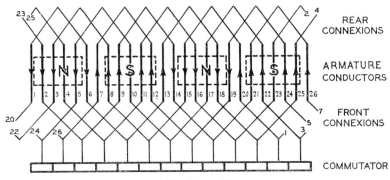

Fig. 8.20. Wave Winding

may be joined to another conductor ahead or behind it in the direction of rotation.

In a lap winding (Fig. 8.19) the back pitch is positive and the front pitch is negative as the winding progresses. A wave winding (Fig. 8.20) has both pitches positive. A wave winding has two parallel paths through the armature. In a lap winding the number of parallel paths produced is equal to the number of poles. The armature winding of a bi-polar machine consequently results

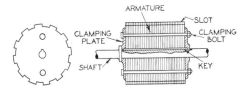

Fig. 8.21. Armature Construction

in two parallel paths irrespective of the winding method employed.

Armature conductors are fitted in the circumference of a soft-iron drum which is of laminated construction from a number of firmly clamped thin flat disks of the shape shown in Fig. 8.21. These disks are insulated from one another by coatings of insulating varnish or by thin sheets of prepared paper. The object of this design is to minimize the magnitude of eddy currents by providing a high-resistance path. Eddy currents are induced in the soft-iron core in a direction parallel to the length of the conductors: in this direction they encounter the high resistance of the insulating layers between laminations in series and their magnitude is considerably reduced. In this way considerable energy wastage is avoided and the

to the direction of induced e.m.f., encounters all these disks magnetically in parallel to one another.

The conductors are fitted into slots, two or more conductors to a slot and carefully insulated from the core and from one another; they are held in position by wedges, for not only does the centrifugal force tend to throw them out, but also there

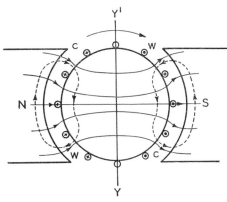

Fig. 8.22. Armature Reaction

is a considerable mechanical force acting upon them when they carry a current. With the conductors carried in slots the length of the air-gap, and hence the magnetic circuit reluctance, can be considerably reduced.

8.8. Armature Reaction. The flux due to the field magnets is symmetrical about a line midway between the poles. This is the line YY', in Fig. 8.22, which is the *magnetic neutral axis*. When the armature is delivering current the armature conductors set up their own field, the general shape of which is that shown by the dotted loops. This flux superimposed upon the main flux due to the field magnets produces a distorted field which is weakened in the regions marked W and concentrated in the regions C. The combined field (Fig. 8.23) results in a shifting of the magnetic neutral axis in the direction of rotation from YY' to NA. This alteration in the effective excitation in a machine, due to the magnetomotive forces set up by the current in the armature winding, is known as ARMATURE REACTION. The extent of armature reaction depends upon the magnitude of the armature current; the position of the magnetic neutral axis is not stable unless this current is constant. This disadvantage affects the brush position, but it may be overcome by fitting compoles.

8.9. Commutation. A portion of the armature winding is connected electrically between each pair of adjacent commutator segments (see Fig. 8.17). As these segments approach a brush this portion of the winding is carrying one half of the total armature current; an instant later these two segments together with this portion of the armature winding are momentarily short-circuited by the brush. After passing the brush, this portion of the winding again carries half of the total current but now in the reverse direction.

The armature, running in an intense magnetic field, possesses considerable self-inductance, the effect of which is to oppose this variation and reversal of current in the armature conductors concerned. As a result of self-inductance the current changes are retarded and the commutator segment passes the brush before the current has fallen to zero. There is uneven current distribution in the brush owing to the changing area of commutation contact and considerable sparking takes place at the commutator segment after passing the brush.

Both of these effects produce overheating of the commutator and brushes, and at the same time the burning and pitting caused by the sparking damage the good contact surfaces required. These defects are partly overcome by the use of hard carbon brushes having a somewhat high contact resistance which in effect deflects the delayed current through the lower resistance path of the armature winding concerned.

8.10. Brush Position. The desirable position for fitting the brushes is such that they should be in contact with conductors lying outside the magnetic field and inducing no e.m.f. This position would normally be along the line YY' (Fig. 8.23), but the occurrence of armature reaction shifts the magnetic neutral axis to NA (unless "compoles" are fitted) and it is necessary to advance the brushes, i.e. in the direction of armature rotation, to this position. The ideal brush position necessarily varies with

current output since this controls the extent of armature reaction: the brush carriers are capable of a certain amount of adjustment.

In addition to the brush shift demanded by armature reaction a further shift is needed to reduce sparking at the commutator. The brushes are given a further slight advance to CC' so that an opposing e.m.f. shall be induced in that portion of the winding which is undergoing short-circuit in order to neutralize the delaying effect of self-inductance.

Owing to the advance in the brush position the conductors in the region YY' (Fig. 8.23) will now

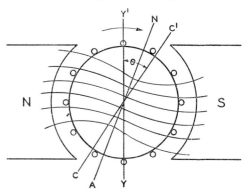

FIG. 8.23. BRUSH POSITION

carry current, which is moreover in such a direction that the field they produce will be almost in direct opposition to the main field. The field is thereby weakened and the conductors lying within this region are termed *armature demagnetizing turns*.

This demagnetization increases with the armature current and with the angle of advance $\theta°$. If the total number of conductors in the armature is Z, there are $Z/360$ conductors per degree and hence $4Z\theta/360$ demagnetizing conductors or $2Z\theta/360$ demagnetizing turns.

8.11. Compoles. Compoles (also known as commutating poles, or interpoles) are small auxiliary poles set centrally between the main poles of a commutating machine. Their polarity is the same as the adjacent main pole ahead, in the direction of rotation. They are shown in the illustration of Fig. 8.24 which indicates the main constructional features of a four-pole machine. The compole windings carry the whole current of the armature, with which they are connected in series. The field due to the compole windings is directly proportional to the armature current and it is in the opposite direction to the field produced by the armature. With a suitable number of turns on the compoles the armature reaction is reduced to zero;

in this event the magnetic field provided by the field magnets is restored to its initial undistorted state and the brushes can be fitted on the axis YY'.

If a few additional turns are wound on the compoles their field exceeds that produced by the armature windings, and the conductors being short-circuited by the brushes cut the compole flux and have induced in them an e.m.f. opposite to the e.m.f. of self-induction. This abolishes the need for

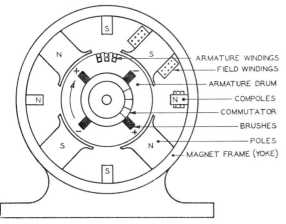

FIG. 8.24. FOUR-POLE MACHINE WITH COMPOLES

any advancement of the brushes on account of commutation difficulties and also allows low resistance brushes to be used. Since the conductors in the region YY' will not now lie in a magnetic field, there are no demagnetizing turns and the main field is entirely unaffected by the armature field. In practice it is economical to adopt the use of compoles only in the larger machines which are usually of the multi-polar type. The illustration of Fig. 8.25 shows the compoles, together with brush and commutator details, of a large machine.

8.12. E.M.F. of a Bi-polar D.C. Generator. The e.m.f. induced in a conductor is

$$E = Blv \text{ volts}$$

where B webers/m² is the flux density, l m is the effective length of the conductor, and v m/sec is the conductor speed at right angles to the flux. If the armature rotates at n r.p.s. and the conductors sweep out a circle of radius r m, the velocity

$$v = 2\pi rn \text{ m/sec}$$

and the e.m.f. generated by each conductor is

$$E = 2\pi Blrn \text{ volts}$$

If $\theta°$ is the angle subtended by the pole face at the centre of the armature and Z is the total number of conductors, the number of active conductors

cutting the flux is $Z\theta/360$. (Only one-half of the conductors needs to be considered since there are two armature paths in parallel, hence $\theta°$ and not $2\theta°$ is the angle concerned.)

FIG. 8.25. MULTI-POLAR D.C. GENERATOR SHOWING COMPOLES, COMMUTATOR, AND BRUSHES
(Courtesy of P.M.G.)

E.m.f. induced by all the active conductors in one half winding

$$= 2\pi BlrnZ\theta/360$$
$$= (2\pi r\theta l/360) \times BnZ$$

But $2\pi r \times (\theta/360) \times l$ m² is the area a of the field of one pole face, hence

$$2\pi r\theta lB/360 = Ba = \Phi \text{ webers}$$

the flux per pole. The equation for the e.m.f. of a bi-polar generator is therefore

$$E = \Phi nZ \text{ volts}$$

or if the speed is N r.p.m.,

$$E = (\Phi NZ/60) \text{ volts}$$

8.13. Multi-polar Machines. In a rotating conductor the e.m.f. reverses each time the conductor comes under the influence of a different pole. For a machine with more than one pair of poles this necessitates one set of brushes for each pair of poles. All positive brushes will be at the same potential and they are connected together and to the machine positive terminal: similarly all negative brushes are connected together and to the negative terminal.

The increase in the number of poles together with a possible change in the number of parallel paths in the winding must be taken into consideration in the e.m.f. equation. With a lap winding the number of parallel paths in the winding is always equal to the number of poles: this type of winding is used when heavy currents are to be taken from the dynamo, so reducing the current carried by each conductor.

A wave winding invariably has two parallel paths: this method of winding, in which half of the conductors act in series, is used where a high voltage machine is required.

The armature resistance will be determined according to the numbers of conductors and parallel paths.

If p is the total number of poles (excluding compoles) and A is the number of parallel paths, the general e.m.f. equation for any d.c. generator becomes

$$E = \Phi n Z \times p/A \text{ volts} . \quad . \quad (8.2)$$

For a lap winding, $p = A$, and

$$E = \Phi n Z \text{ volts}$$

For a wave winding, $A = 2$, and

$$E = \Phi n Z P \text{ volts}$$

where P is the number of *pairs of poles*.

For a bipolar machine, whether wave or lap wound, $p = A = 2$, and

$$E = \Phi n Z \text{ volts}$$

8.14. The Shunt-wound D.C. Generator Circuit.

The connexions of the shunt-wound d.c. generator with a load resistance R_L ohms are shown in Fig. 8.26. E is the e.m.f. generated in the armature

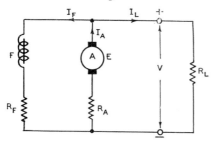

FIG. 8.26. CIRCUIT OF SHUNT-WOUND D.C. GENERATOR

conductors. I_F and I_A amperes are respectively the field and armature currents: the resistances of the field and armature are R_F and R_A ohms respectively; the terminal p.d. is V volts and the load current I_L amperes.

The generated e.m.f. is

$$E = \Phi n Z \times p/A \text{ volts}$$

The voltage drop in the armature, analogous to the voltage drop due to the internal resistance of a voltaic cell, is $I_A R_A$. The voltage equation for terminal p.d. is thus

$$V = E - I_A R_A \text{ volts}$$

The armature provides current not only for the load, but for the field also, hence the current equation is

$$I_A = I_L + I_F$$

The field current is $I_F = V/R_F$ amperes. The armature current is

$$I_A = (E - V)/R_A$$

The load current is

$$I_L = V/R_L$$

The above simple equations enable all the various voltages and currents to be calculated for a shunt dynamo from sufficient data. The conditions are identical with those of a battery (Fig. 4.5) with a shunting resistance R_F in addition to the load.

The shunt-wound d.c. generator is employed where the requirement is for a constant p.d. at a uniform speed. In practice the terminal voltage falls off slightly if the load current is increased by decreasing the load resistance. Fig. 8.27 is a characteristic curve, known as the *external characteristic*, showing how the terminal voltage changes as the load current is varied.

When the dynamo is started up the remanent flux of the poles is sufficient for the generation of a small e.m.f.: this small e.m.f. provides a current for the field, and in this way the field and the e.m.f. are quickly built up.

The field is wound of many turns and its resistance is relatively high in order to draw little

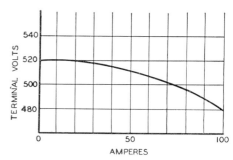

FIG. 8.27. CHARACTERISTIC CURVE OF SHUNT-WOUND D.C. GENERATOR

current from the armature. The resistances of the armature conductors and of the compoles are made as low as possible, both from the point of view of reducing the internal voltage drop and also limiting the I^2R (or copper) losses and generation of heat in the windings. When the generator is on open circuit, the armature current is the field current only ($I_A = I_F + 0$) and since I_F is small the ternal voltage drop $I_A R_A$ is small: the terminal oltage on no-load is practically equal to the e.m.f. enerated.

When current is being delivered to the load, the acreased armature current causes a greater internal oltage drop and the terminal p.d. accordingly falls s the load current increases. Additional factors, owever, accentuate the falling characteristic of he shunt-wound generator. Firstly as the terminal .d. falls with increasing load current, the field urrent ($= V/R_F$) also falls due to the internal oltage drop, and the resulting drop in the flux Φ rings about a decrease in the generated e.m.f. econdly, if the generator is not fitted with com- oles the demagnetizing effect of the armature urrent results in a further reduction in flux and in enerated e.m.f.

Despite the slightly falling characteristic, the hunt-wound d.c. generator is regarded as a onstant voltage machine.

The rated full-load current is that at which the aaximum permissible temperature is reached: his is usually 40°C, at which temperature the heat s dissipated as fast as it is generated.

The difference in terminal p.d. between no-load nd full-load, expressed as a percentage of the *no-* oad voltage, is known as the REGULATION, i.e. oltage regulation

$$= \frac{\text{(no-load p.d.} - \text{full-load p.d.)}}{\text{no-load p.d.}} \times 100 \text{ per cent}$$

or example in the curve of Fig. 8.27 the voltage egulation is

$(520 - 480)/520 \times 100$ per cent $= 7\cdot69$ per cent

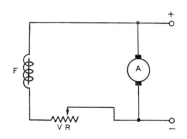

FIG. 8.28. VOLTAGE CONTROL

8.15. Voltage Control. In order to adjust the erminal p.d. within desired limits either Φ or N in ae e.m.f. equation must be varied. It is usually ndesirable to change the speed of the machine and ae field flux is therefore made capable of adjust- ent by fitting a *shunt-field rheostat* or regulator in ·ries with the field circuit to control the field

current. The arrangement of a voltage regulator (VR) is shown in Fig. 8.28. An increase in this resistance will bring about a reduction of field current and of flux and thus of generated e.m.f. and terminal p.d.

Various methods of automatically controlling the voltage within close limits have also been de- veloped. One type of automatic voltage regulator depends upon the decrease produced in the resis- tance of carbon when it is subjected to increased mechanical pressure. The carbon pile C (Fig. 8.29) consists of a stack of annular carbon rings whose resistance is variable over a wide range by varying the applied pressure. The electromagnet winding E is energized from the governed voltage: its armature move- ment controls the pressure applied to the carbon pile whose initial compression is supplied by a spring. An increase of current in E pro- duces a reduction in pressure and an increase in resistance of the pile. The carbon pile is inserted in series with the generator field. Applied to a shunt-wound d.c. generator, when the current load in- creases, the terminal p.d. of the generator falls slightly; the automatic voltage regu- lator then increases the

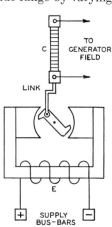

FIG. 8.29. CARBON PILE REGULATOR

current in the dynamo field, allowing the generated e.m.f. to rise and to restore the bus-bar voltage to its normal value. Conversely a decrease in load current causes a slight rise in voltage at the bus-bars and the automatic voltage regulator reduces the field current and generated e.m.f.

Another automatic voltage regulator in common use is of the dynamometer form of moving coil instrument: the "pointer" of the regulator varies a rheostat in series with the field winding.

8.16. Dynamo Losses and Efficiency. When the armature is delivering current the rotating con- ductors are cutting the field flux, and according to Lenz's law a force is set up which tends to oppose the rotation. This force must be overcome by the driving engine or motor, and in fact the energy which the engine uses up in this manner is exactly equal to the electrical energy generated.

In addition there are various energy losses in- troduced in the process of energy conversion, and the engine must perform additional work equivalent to the energy losses involved. These losses are known as *rotational losses*.

The following are included in rotational losses: (i) Friction losses in the bearings and in the commutator and brushes; also the air resistance (windage) in the narrow air-gap. These losses are approximately proportional to the speed of rotation. (ii) Eddy current losses in the laminations of the armature: this energy loss is proportional to n^2B^2 where n is the number of revolutions per second and B is the flux density. (iii) Hysteresis losses. The armature laminations are subjected to a complete cycle of magnetization in passing each pair of poles and this hysteresis effect results in an energy loss which depends upon the speed of rotation. The hysteresis loss is proportional to $nB^{1.6}$. Hysteresis and eddy current losses are grouped together under the description *core loss* (*iron loss*).

With the generator running at constant speed the rotational losses will be constant if the flux density is constant. It has already been seen that the flux varies with armature current, but it is usually assumed that the rotational losses are constant irrespective of armature and load current changes; since these losses are very small compared with the generator energy output at full-load, this assumption does not produce appreciable error.

Of the electrical energy generated, not all of this is available for delivery to the external load. A certain amount of energy known as the I^2R *loss* (copper loss) is wasted inside the machine itself. The I^2R loss is made up of the power losses: (i) In the armature winding, brushes and commutator, equal to $I_A{}^2R_A$ watts. This power is all converted into heat and this loss increases considerably (i.e. with the square of the current) as the generator output increases: at full-load it is by far the greatest of the losses. (ii) In the field windings $I_F{}^2R_F$ watts. This power is also converted entirely into heat but it decreases slightly as the generator output increases owing to the falling off in terminal voltage and in field current I_F. The field losses being relatively small, they are usually considered constant at all loads.

The energy conversion losses may be conveniently tabulated as follows—

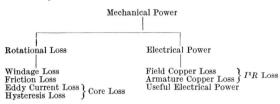

If the terminal p.d. is V volts and the load current is I amperes, the power delivered to the load is VI watts. The mechanical power driving the generator is equal to the useful electrical power $+ I^2R$ loss $+$ rotational loss. The dynamo efficiency is thus—

$$\eta = (\text{output/input}) \times 100\%$$
$$= \frac{VI \times 100}{VI + I^2R \text{ loss} + \text{rotational loss}}\%$$

In the larger machines the losses represent only a small proportion of the full-load power output and the efficiency may be of the order of 95 per cent. This high efficiency falls off considerably with smaller machines down to as low as 60 per cent. With the exception of the armature copper loss all the other losses are approximately the same at no-load and full-load—hence the economic desirability of running the machine at full-load as far as possible.

EXAMPLE 8.3 (A). What is the maximum current obtainable from an engine-driven 50 V d.c. generator when the engine developed 5 h.p. if the efficiency of the generator is then 85 per cent? (C. & G.)

$$\text{Power input} = (5 \times 746) \text{ watts}$$
$$\text{Power output} = (5 \times 746 \times 0.85) \text{ watts}$$
$$\text{Maximum current} = W/V = 5 \times 746 \times 0.85/50$$
$$= \underline{63.4 \text{ A}}$$

8.17. Battery Charging and Floating. The shunt-wound type of d.c. generator is commonly employed for charging secondary cells on account of its approximately constant terminal voltage.

In the series-wound d.c. generator the armature current flows in the field also, resulting in an increase in flux and in terminal voltage as the armature current (i.e. the load current) rises until saturation is reached, after which the terminal voltage tends to fall for any further increase in armature current.

In applying the shunt-wound generator to a battery certain safeguards must be introduced into the charging circuit. It is necessary to include an automatically operated *circuit-breaker* to disconnect the charging circuit in the event of some dangerous condition arising. The circuit-breaker is a device operated electromagnetically if (i) the charging current becomes excessive (overload), or (ii) the generator voltage falls below that of the battery. The latter condition could arise, for example, from any stoppage of the electric power or fuel supply to the machine or engine which drives the generator. In this event current from the battery would flow back to the generator and drive it as a motor with consequent damage to the battery.

A typical charging circuit is shown in Fig. 8.30. After the generator has been started and run up to full working speed, the circuit breaker CB is closed y hand. The circuit breaker consists essentially of switch with a powerful releasing spring and it is etained in the closed position by a trigger: this rigger is capable of being withdrawn by the perated armature of either the overload *OL* or the everse current *RC* electromagnets. The overload oil is adjusted to operate at slightly higher than he maximum charging current. The reverse urrent coil is polarized by connecting one winding cross the charging circuit: any reversal of current a the series connected winding occasioned by the attery discharging into the generator causes

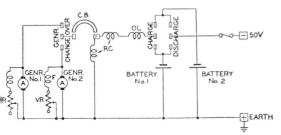

FIG. 8.30. BATTERY CHARGING CIRCUIT

nmediate operation of the reverse coil magnet nd release of the circuit breaker. The field egulator *VR* is for adjusting the terminal voltage f the generator. A rheostat may be connected in eries with the battery to control the charging urrent, or this control may be entirely effected rom adjustment of the generator voltage.

Modern methods in utilization of secondary atteries in telephone exchanges and repeater tations and in telegraph offices tend to abandon he charge-discharge system and utilize a floating ystem instead. In the floating system, the enerator is permanently connected across the attery and supplies the load at the bus-bars. The attery is necessary only to supply the load in the vent of a power failure putting the generator out f service, for which purpose it has a relatively mall capacity sufficient to carry the load for 4 hours: it also assists in stabilizing the output oltage.

The battery receives no appreciable charge or lischarge but loses its charge slightly while idling: arious methods are available to overcome this oss, such as dividing the battery capacity and iving a trickle charge to each half during alternate veeks.

Two or more generators of different outputs can e joined in parallel to cope with the larger variaions in load. The smaller variations are met by he automatic voltage regulator.

The circuit arrangement for a typical floating

system employing two generators and a divided battery are indicated in Fig. 8.31. An essential item of equipment is the inductor (*I*) (§ 7.21) to smooth out the generator ripple which would otherwise produce a steady hum in telephone circuits: the inductor functions by inducing a back-e.m.f. to oppose the ripple e.m.f. of the generator and it must be of adequate dimensions to carry the full-

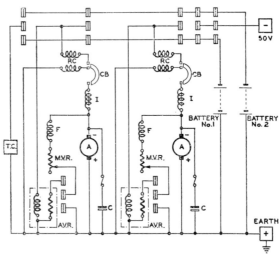

FIG. 8.31. FLOATING BATTERY CIRCUIT

load current. The smoothing is assisted by the use of large electrolytic capacitors (*C*) across the generators which charge up to the voltage crests of the ripple and discharge into the load as the peak voltage falls. Details of the smoothing equipment vary with each power installation. The diagram includes the connexions of the manual voltage regulator (*MVR*), the automatic voltage regulator (*AVR*) and the output terminals of the trickle charger (*TC*).

EXAMPLE 8.4 (A). A shunt-wound generator and a battery are connected in parallel to supply an exchange. The resistance of the generator armature is $0.006\ \Omega$, and the internal resistance of the battery is $0.005\ \Omega$.

Calculate the current supplied by the generator when its e.m.f. is 0.75 V greater than that of the battery, and the exchange is taking 510 A. The field current may be neglected.

What is the maximum value of the exchange load current that could be supplied wholly by the generator, assuming that its e.m.f. remained 0.75 V greater than that of the battery? (*C. & G.*)

The circuit diagram is given in Fig. 8.32.

Applying Kirchhoff's first law, if the load current is 510 A and the battery current (charging) is *I* amperes, the generator current is $(I + 510)$ amperes.

Applying Kirchhoff's second law to the left-hand mesh—

$$0.75 = 0.005\,I + 0.006(I + 510)$$
$$0.75 = 0.011\,I + 3.06$$
$$I = (0.75 - 3.06)/0.011$$
$$= -210 \text{ A (i.e. the battery}$$
$$\text{is discharging)}$$

Generator current $= 510 + I = 510 - 210$
$$= 300 \text{ A}$$

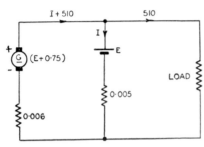

FIG. 8.32 (Example 8.4)

Maximum voltage which can be dropped in the generator before its p.d. is equal to the e.m.f. of the battery $= 0.75$.

Current in generator to produce this p.d. $= 0.75/0.006 = 125$ A

If the current exceeds this figure the generator p.d. becomes equal to the battery e.m.f. and the latter then assists in supplying the load.

EXAMPLE 8.5 (A). A shunt-wound generator and a battery are connected in parallel to supply an exchange. The resistance of the generator armature is $0.01\ \Omega$ and the battery has an internal resistance of $0.015\ \Omega$. Neglecting

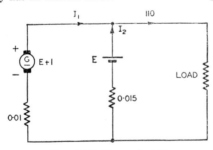

FIG. 8.33 (Example 8.5)

the field current, find the current supplied by the generator when its e.m.f. is 1 V in excess of that of the battery, and the total output to the exchange is 110 A.   (C. & G.)

By Kirchhoff's first law (see Fig. 8.33),

$$I_1 + I_2 = 110. \quad I_2 = (110 - I_1)$$

Applying Kirchhoff's second law to the left-hand mesh—

$$E + 1 - E = 0.01\,I_1 - 0.015\,I_2 = 1$$
$$1 = 0.01\,I_1 - 0.015(110 - I_1)$$
$$1 = 0.01\,I_1 + 0.015\,I_1 - 1.65$$
$$0.025\,I_1 = 2.65$$
$$I_1 = 2.65/0.025 = \underline{\underline{106 \text{ A}}}$$

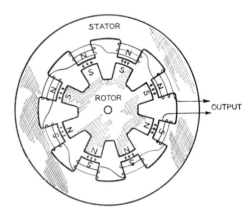

FIG 8.34. PRINCIPLE OF INDUCTOR GENERATOR

8.18. A.C. Generators. Machines giving an a.c. output are extensively employed over a wide range of outputs, and according to different design principles. The smaller a.c. generators, or alternators, are of generally similar design to the d.c. machine.

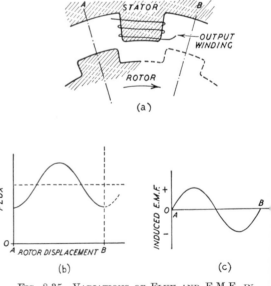

FIG. 8.35. VARIATIONS OF FLUX AND E.M.F. IN INDUCTOR GENERATOR

with the substitution of continuous slip-rings for a commutator.

For high-voltage machines it is more usual to use a rotating field and a stationary armature, referred to as the *rotor* and *stator* respectively. The field is energized by direct current fed through slip-rings and the alternating e.m.f. is generated in the stationary armature windings.

Alternators with low-voltage output are in common use in telecommunication systems. One

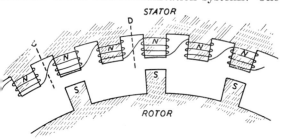

FIG. 8.36. OUTPUT WINDINGS OF MULTI-FREQUENCY GENERATOR

such machine is employed in automatic telephone systems to generate the signalling tones. In the "inductor" type of machine (Fig. 8.34) the rotor consists simply of a laminated soft-iron toothed disk and it carries no windings, being magnetized

by induction from the stator. Both the field and output windings are on poles on the inner periphery of the soft-iron stator. The field windings (not shown in the illustration) are energized from the

exchange d.c. supply and the flux produced links with the output windings. The flux linkage is varied by the constantly changing reluctance of

FIG. 8.37. FOUR-FREQUENCY GENERATOR: STATOR
(Courtesy of P.M.G.)

the magnetic circuit as the rotor teeth pass the poles, the reluctance rising and falling as the length of the air-gap changes.

FIG. 8.38. FOUR-FREQUENCY GENERATOR: ROTOR
(Courtesy of P.M.G.)

The displacement of a rotor tooth in passing a stator pole from position A to position B is indicated in Fig. 8.35 (*a*). The corresponding flux variation is shown in Fig. 8.35 (*b*), the flux rising from a minimum to a maximum value and falling again to a minimum as the rotor tooth passes the rotor teeth and the rotor speed. The machine shown in Fig. 8.34 runs at a speed of 1 000 r.p.m.

FIG. 8.39. 18-FREQUENCY GENERATOR: ROTOR WITH DRIVING
MOTOR ARMATURE
(Courtesy of Walter Jones)

FIG. 8.40. 18-FREQUENCY GENERATOR: STATOR SHOWING OUTPUT
AND FIELD WINDINGS
(Courtesy of Walter Jones)

pole. The actual rate of change of flux, and consequently the waveform is governed by the shapes of the rotor teeth and pole faces. The generated e.m.f. (Fig. 8.35 (c)) alternates at a frequency which is equal to the product of the number of so that with eight teeth the frequency is $8 \times 1\,000/60 = 133.3$ c/s, the value chosen for the "ringing" tone. The polarity of the four lower poles is opposite to that of the upper poles: the winding directions are accordingly reversed and the coils connected in series so that the e.m.f.s in the separate windings are additive.

It is not essential to have equal numbers of stator poles and rotor teeth provided that the pitches are such that the flux variations at all output windings are in synchronism. In general, provided the method of winding illustrated in Fig. 8.34 is adopted, the frequency is equal to $(N \times n)$ c/s, where N is the number either of rotor teeth or stator poles (whichever is the greater) and n is the rotational speed in revolutions per second.

In some inductor machines, alternate stator poles are wound in reverse directions and the rotor teeth have twice the angular pitch of the stator poles (Fig. 8.36). In this case, a complete cycle is generated when a rotor tooth travels past two adjacent stator poles (from C to D). The frequency of the generated e.m.f. is then equal to the product of the speed and the number of rotor teeth. This method is adopted in the four-frequency generator used for telephone junction signalling at 400, 600, 750, and 900 c/s. The stator of this machine is illustrated in Fig. 8.37: the four sets of rotor teeth are shown in Fig. 8.38. The 400 c/s tone is generated by a rotor having 24 teeth, the common shaft rotating at a speed of 1 000 r.p.m.

Similar machines fitted with 18 rotors and 18 sets of stator poles are used for generating the a.c. output at the 18 different frequencies employed in modern voice-frequency multi-channel telegraph systems; the rotor assembly, which includes the armature of the d.c. driving motor and a centrifugal speed-governor, is illustrated in Fig. 8.39. The 18 separate stator windings (Fig. 8.40) have a common exciting field; by designing the generator so that the reluctance of the magnetic circuit through each stator and rotor pair remains constant as the rotors revolve, inductive interference between the separate output circuits is prevented.

8.19. The Hall Effect. When a current flows in a homogeneous conductor, there is the well-known potential fall (IR) along its length. In Fig. 8.41 the current I amperes flows in the direction of the x-ordinate and there is a potential drop in the direction of current flow. In a transverse direction, the y-ordinate, there is no potential difference between the two points PP', provided that these points are accurately positioned at equal (electrical) distances from the same end of the conductor.

If now a magnetic field is applied to produce a flux density B Wb/m² in a direction which is mutually at right-angles to both the direction of current flow and to the transverse axis PP'—i.e. the magnetic field is applied in the direction of

the z-ordinate, it is found that an e.m.f. is generated in the transverse direction PP'. The generation of this e.m.f. in these circumstances is known as the *Hall effect*. It is due to the magnetic deflexion of the charged particles flowing in the conductor.

If the conductor is in fact a semiconductor the charged particles are electrons (n-type semiconductor) or holes (p-type semiconductor). The deflexion occurs in opposite directions according to whether the semiconductor is p-type or n-type. For a given conventional direction of current, the electrons and holes would be flowing in opposite

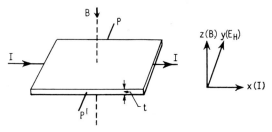

FIG. 8.41. HALL EFFECT

directions, and the Hall voltage is of opposite polarity for n-type and p-type semiconductors.

The magnitude of the Hall voltage E_h is determined by $E_h = BJR_h$, where B is the flux density, J is the current density in the conductor, and R_h is the "Hall constant." The intensity $J = I/t$, t being the thickness of the conductor in the z-direction: the Hall voltage is inversely proportional to the thickness of the conductor.

SUMMARY

Induced E.M.F.

$$E = Blv \sin \theta \text{ volts} \qquad . \qquad . \ (8.1)$$

Fleming's Right-hand Rule.

thuMb—Motion
First—Flux
seCond—Current.

Armature Reaction. The alteration in the effective excitation in a machine due to the magneto-motive forces set up by the current in the armature winding.

Compoles. Auxiliary poles so situated between the main poles of a commutating machine as to produce an auxiliary flux at the place through which the conductors under commutation are moving, for the purpose of facilitating commutation.

Generated E.M.F.

$$\left.\begin{array}{l} E = \Phi n Z \text{ volts} \\ \quad\quad \text{(lap winding)} \\ E = \Phi n Z P \text{ volts} \\ \quad\quad \text{(wave winding)} \\ P = \text{pairs of poles} \end{array}\right\} \quad . \quad\quad . \quad\quad . \quad\quad . \quad (8.2)$$

Shunt-wound D.C. Generator. Terminal voltage $V = E - I_A R_A$.

Load current $I_L = I_A - I_F$.
Field current $I_F = V / R_F$.

Voltage Regulation.

$$\frac{(\text{no-load p.d.} - \text{full-load p.d.})}{\text{no-load p.d.}} \times 100\%.$$

Mechanical Power.

rotational loss + electrical power

Rotational Loss. Friction loss + eddy current loss ($\propto n^2 B^2$) + hysteresis loss ($\propto n B^{1.6}$).

Electric Power. Field copper loss ($I_F{}^2 R_F$) + armature copper loss ($I_A{}^2 R_A$) + useful power (VI).

CHAPTER IX

THE D.C. MOTOR

9.1. Action of a Magnetic Field upon an Energized Conductor. Whenever a conductor carrying a current is influenced by a magnetic field (other than its own) a mechanical force is exerted upon the conductor. Upon this effect depends the operation of electric motors and also of certain types of measuring instruments, telephone receivers, and microphones.

If two straight conductors, each carrying a current, are placed parallel to one another and adjacent, a force of attraction or repulsion will

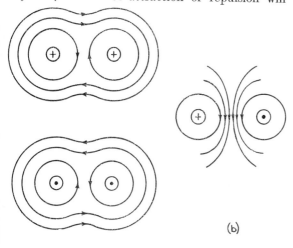

(a)

(b)

Fig. 9.1. Force between Two Parallel Conductors

exist between them. If the two currents flow in the *same* direction, the force will be one of *attraction*: conversely, currents flowing in *opposite* directions will produce a force of *repulsion* between the conductors. Fig. 9.1 shows the magnetic fields in the two cases with respect to the current directions, using the conventions given in Fig. 7.1. In Fig. 9.1. (*a*) the two fields neutralize one another in the region between the two conductors, and the conception whereby the lines of force contract shows the production of a force tending to bring the conductors nearer to one another. In Fig. 9.1 (*b*) it will be seen that the concentration of the field between the conductors and the lateral repulsion of the lines of force gives rise to a mechanical force which tends to separate the conductors.

Fig. 9.2. shows a conductor carrying a current

and a single line of force of its magnetic field. This field is clockwise and a unit north pole N placed near to the conductor would, if free to move, rotate in a clockwise direction around the conductor. Conversely, if the magnet pole is fixed and the conductor free to move, the conductor would

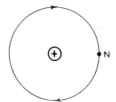

Fig. 9.2. Force on Unit N-Pole

rotate round the magnet pole, also in a clockwise direction. Reversing the direction of the current would reverse the direction of the field due to it and also the motion of the pole or of the conductor.

The existence of a mechanical force can be

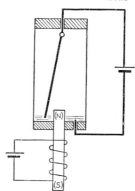

Fig. 9.3. Motion of Energized Conductor in Magnetic Field

demonstrated using the apparatus illustrated in Fig. 9.3. A wide vertical glass tube, corked at either end, has one pole of the core of a strong solenoid inserted through the lower cork which supports a layer of mercury. Through the upper cork is inserted a metal hook from which is suspended a thick copper wire: the lower end of the wire dips into the mercury by means of which it is maintained in electrical contact with the battery via a copper wire inserted through the lower cork. If the movable conductor carries a fairly heavy current, it will rotate in a clockwise direction, viewed from above, when the solenoid circuit is closed. Reversing the direction of the current in either the solenoid or the conductor will reverse

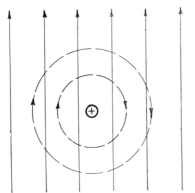

FIG. 9.4. ENERGIZED CONDUCTOR IN MAGNETIC FIELD

the direction of rotation of the conductor: reversal of the direction of the currents in both solenoid and conductor will maintain the original clockwise direction of rotation.

The force which produces this motion is the result of the interaction between two magnetic fields—that due to the solenoid and that due to

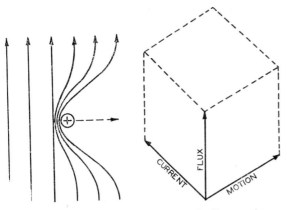

FIG. 9.5. FORCE ON ENERGIZED CONDUCTOR

FIG. 9.6. FLEMING'S LEFT-HAND RULE

the energized conductor. A conductor carrying a current and situated in a magnetic field always experiences a mechanical force, unless the conductor is actually parallel to the direction of the magnetic field. In the design of instruments depending upon this principle the conductors are usually placed so that they cut the field at right angles in order to exert the maximum force.

9.2. Magnitude of Force. If a conductor carrying a current of I amperes is placed in a magnetic field

of flux density B webers/metre^2, and l metre is the length of the conductor perpendicular to the field, the force acting upon the conductor is given by

$$F = BIl \text{ newton} \qquad . \qquad . \quad (9.1)$$

This expression is the basis for calculations on electric motors, and on electrical instruments using the same principle.

For two parallel conductors placed d metres apart and carrying currents I_1 and I_2 amperes, the force (per metre length) is

$$F = 2 \times 10^{-7} I_1 I_2 / d \text{ newton/metre}. \quad (9.2)$$

This is AMPERE'S LAW. From this law, by writing $I_1 = I_2 = 1$ ampere and $d = 1$ metre, the ampere is fundamentally defined as *that constant current which, when maintained in each of two rectilinear, infinitely-long, parallel conductors of negligible cross-section, situated in a vacuum and separated by one metre, would produce between these conductors a force equal to 2×10^{-7} newtons per metre length.*

9.3. Direction of Force. In Fig. 9.4 the conductor carrying a current is placed at right angles to a uniform parallel field. The clockwise field due to the current is shown by dotted circles. These two fields cannot exist separately and if their values are added together at every point the resultant field will be of the form illustrated in Fig. 9.5. If the usual conception is applied of lines of force endeavouring to shorten themselves and

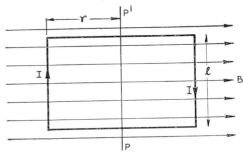

FIG. 9.7. TORQUE ON COIL IN UNIFORM PARALLEL FIELD

at the same time to repel one another laterally, the force tending to move the conductor to the right, and shown by the dotted line, is clearly indicated.

The relative directions of current, magnetic field and motion are summarized in FLEMING'S LEFT-HAND RULE. *Extend the thumb and the first and second fingers of the left hand mutually at right angles: then if the first finger represents the direction of the magnetic flux, and the second finger represents the direction of the current, the thumb will point in the direction of the motion of the conductor*. These directions are represented in Fig. 9.6 by the three edges at the corner of a cube. The rule is conveniently memorized by the mnemonic—

thuMb—Motion
First—Flux
seCond—Current

Since a right-hand rule is enunciated in §**8.3**, it is useful to remember that the le*F*t-hand rule indicates the *F*orce acting on a conductor.

9.4. Torque Acting upon Energized Coil. A conductor formed into a rectangular frame of height l metre and width $2r$ metre, carrying a current of I amperes is shown in Fig. 9.7, pivoted on the axis PP' in a magnetic field of flux density B webers/metre². A plan of this conductor, which is initially in a plane parallel to the field, is shown in Fig. 9.8.

A force $F = BIl$ newton will act upon each of the vertical limbs of the conductor, and (from Fleming's left-hand rule) this force will tend to rotate the coil in a clockwise direction. In the initial position there is no force whatever acting upon either of the horizontal limbs because they are parallel to the field.

The term *torque* indicates the turning moment, or turning effect, of a force. If a force F newtons acts at a perpendicular distance d metres from a pivot, the torque T is equal to the product Fd newton-metre. Consequently the greater the distance d, the greater is the torque. If two parallel forces F act to produce a combined torque on the same pivot at a radius d. the system of forces constitutes a *couple*: the torque due to the couple is equal to $2F \times d$ or to $F \times 2d = 2Fd$ newton-metre.

The value of the torque T acting upon both vertical limbs in the initial position—the thick line in Fig. 9.8—is equal to

$$T = 2Fr = 2BIlr \text{ newton-metre}$$

As soon as the coil commences to rotate, however, the perpendicular distance r becomes $r \cos \theta$ where $\theta°$ is the angle between field and coil. In this position, shown by the thin line in Fig. 9.8, the torque is

$$T = 2BIlr \cos \theta \text{ newton-metre}$$

Under the influence of this torque the conductor will rotate through an angle of 90° and then come to rest: in this position, although the forces on the vertical limbs remain the same, the torque is zero because $r \cos 90° = 0$. These forces simply tend to pull the vertical limbs apart: in Fig. 9.8 the dotted line shows the conductor in its final position after rotating through an angle of 90°. In the final position, forces also act upon both horizontal limbs tending to pull them apart, in fact

this force commences to act as soon as rotation begins to develop an angle between the horizontal limbs and the magnetic field.

Fig. 9.8 also shows that as the coil rotates, the magnetic flux passing through it steadily increases, reaching a maximum when the coil attains its final steady position after rotating through 90°. Any conductor carrying a current and situated in a

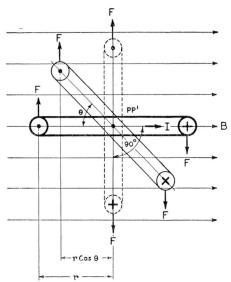

FIG. 9.8. PLAN OF ENERGIZED COIL

magnetic field tends to alter its position so that the flux passing through it will be a maximum.

If the frame is replaced by a coil having Z turns, each turn will be cut by the flux and the force acting on the coil will be

$$F = 2BIlZ \text{ newton}$$

the torque will be

$$T = 2BIlZr \cos \theta \text{ newton-metre}$$

As $l \times 2r$ is the area of the coil a, the torque

$$T = BIZa \cos \theta \text{ newton-metre}$$

This expression applies to a coil of any shape.

EXAMPLE 9.1 (A). What is the force exerted on a wire 20 cm long carrying a direct current of 2 A when placed in a uniform field of 1 weber/m² whose direction is perpendicular to the wire? If the wire were bent back on itself to form a narrow loop having parallel sides 9 cm long and 2 cm apart, what would be the magnitude and direction of the resulting force on the loop?   (*C. & G.*)

$$F = BIl = 1 \times 2 \times 0.2$$
$$= 0.4 \text{ newton}$$

With the wire bent into a narrow loop (see Fig. 9.9), l becomes 9 cm, and

$$F = 1 \times 2 \times 0.09 = \underline{0.18 \text{ newton}}$$

This is the force on each 9 cm limb of the loop, i.e. there is a torque of $2Fr = 2 \times 0.18 \times 0.01 = 0.003\,6$ newton-metre. The direction of the force on each limb according to Fleming's left-hand rule is indicated in Fig. 9.9, showing a clockwise torque (viewed from above) about the line YY'.

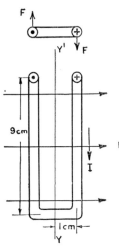

FIG. 9.9 (Example 9.1)

EXAMPLE 9.2 (A). (a) A straight conductor, which is at right-angles to a uniform magnetic field of 500 mWb/m² carries a direct current of 10 A. What is the force on a 10-cm length of the conductor?

(b) In a milliammeter the moving coil is square with 2-cm sides and 100 turns. It rotates so as to cut a uniform radial magnetic field with a strength of 2 Wb/m². Calculate the deflecting force on the coil when it is carrying 10 mA. (C. & G.)

(a) $F = B \times I \times l = 500 \times 10^{-3} \times 10 \times 10 \times 10^{-2} = \underline{0.5 \text{ newton}}$

(b) The force on each conductor cutting the field

$$= B \times I \times l = 2 \times 10 \times 10^{-3} \times 2 \times 10^{-2}$$
$$= 4 \times 10^{-4} \text{ newton}$$

The radial distance to each conductor is 10^{-2} metres.

Torque due to one conductor = force × radius

$$= 4 \times 10^{-4} \times 10^{-2} = 4 \times 10^{-6} \text{ newton-metres}$$

For 100 turns there will be 200 effective conductors.

Total deflecting torque $= 200 \times 4 \times 10^{-6}$
$$= 8 \times 10^{-4} \text{ newton-metres}$$

9.5. The D.C. Motor. The electric motor is a machine for converting electrical energy into mechanical energy. The design and construction of a d.c. motor have much in common with the d.c. generator, and, in fact, a very small machine may be used indiscriminately for either purpose. The d.c. motor has field magnets, armature conductors fitted on a laminated soft-iron core, brushes and commutator. The commutator is necessary to ensure reversal of the current in the conductors each time they come under the influence of an opposite polarity. The armature may be lap-wound or wave-wound. The connexions between armature and field magnets may be such as to produce a series-wound, shunt-wound or compound-wound motor, depending upon the desired characteristics. In the present chapter only those features which are peculiar to the d.c. motor will be treated.

Direct current from some external source is fed to the field magnet and armature windings. The armature conductors, carrying a current in an intense radial magnetic field, are subjected to a force whose direction is determined by Fleming's left-hand rule. For example, if current were fed to the d.c. generator illustrated in Fig. 8.22 in the direction there indicated with the same direction of magnetic field, the armature would be subjected to a torque and rotate in a counter-clockwise direction. With armature current and field in the same direction respectively in a d.c. generator and a motor, their rotations will be in opposite directions.

Directly the armature commences to rotate its conductors cut the magnetic flux and an e.m.f. is induced in the armature. From Lenz's law or from Fleming's right-hand rule, this is shown to be a counter-e.m.f., opposing the p.d. applied to drive the motor. The magnitude of this counter e.m.f. E is that of the equivalent generator, namely

$$E = \Phi n Z \times p/A \text{ volts}$$

The applied p.d. must be sufficient to overcome the back-e.m.f. E volts and also to supply an additional voltage $I_A R_A$ to drive the armature current I_A through the resistance R_A of the armature. The effective p.d. across the armature becomes $(V - E)$ volts, and the armature current is $I_A = (V - E)/R_A$. This gives the voltage equation for the d.c. motor,

$$V - E = I_A R_A, \text{ or } V = E + I_A R_A$$

9.6. Motor Torque and Speed. The torque T is proportional to the armature current I_A: if the mechanical load on the motor is increased the armature torque must increase: the armature current increases to develop this additional torque. By an automatic variation of armature current, therefore, the armature torque adjusts itself to meet any change in the mechanical load.

The armature current, $I_A = (V - E)/R_A$, can increase only at the expense of a decrease in E, the other factors being constant.

The e.m.f., $E = \Phi n Z$, can only decrease as a result of a reduction in the speed n. The field flux, depending upon the field current $I_F = V/R_F$ remains sensibly constant with the applied p.d.

Summarizing, an increase in load and in torque

T demands a rise in armature current I_A. This is obtained by a reduction in back-e.m.f. E causing a decrease in the speed n. The two important factors for any motor are, therefore, (i) torque depends upon armature current, and (ii) back-e.m.f. depends upon speed. These four factors, torque, armature current, back-e.m.f., and speed are interdependent.

The total torque of the motor can be calculated from

$$T = BIlr \text{ newton-metre}$$

taking into account the number of conductors, but the same information is more readily obtained from energy considerations.

If the voltage equation $V = E + I_A R_A$ is multiplied through by the armature current I_A, the power equation for the armature circuit,

$$VI_A = EI_A + I_A^2 R$$

is obtained. The first term VI_A is the total power applied to the armature. $I_A^2 R_A$ is the power dissipated as heat in the armature, and EI_A is the power converted into mechanical power. In words, power input to armature = mechanical power + heat developed.

If n r.p.s. is the rotational speed of the armature, the distance moved by the conductors every second is $2\pi rn$ ft/sec, r feet being the radius of the circle swept out by the rotating conductors. For a force F pounds on the conductors, the work done per second (the product of force × distance per second) is $2\pi rnF$ ft-lb/sec. The torque $T = Fr$ in foot-pounds, hence the work done is $2\pi nT$ ft-lb/sec. The unit of mechanical power is the horse-power (h.p.): one h.p. = 550 ft-lb/sec. Hence the horse-power of a motor = $2\pi nT/550$. The electrical equivalent of one h.p. is 746 W, hence motor h.p. = $EI_A/746$ and $2\pi nT/550 = EI_A/746$, whence the torque

$$T = 550EI_A/(2\pi n \times 746) = 0.117\frac{E}{n} \times I_A \text{ ft-lb}$$

The ratio E/n is known as the induction factor Ψ giving a relationship between torque and armature current,

$$T \propto \Psi I_A$$

Since $E = \Phi nZP$ volts (wave-wound), or $E = \Phi nZ$ volts (lap-wound) the induction factor is $P\Phi Z$ for a wave-wound machine and ΦZ for a lap-wound or bi-polar machine.

9.7. Position of Brushes. The field due to the current in the conductors produces armature reaction. For the same direction of rotation of a generator and a motor with similar magnetic fields, the armature currents flow in opposite directions: this follows from consideration of the left- and right-hand rules. In the d.c. motor the brushes must therefore be *retarded* on account of armature reaction. Also due to the current direction the effect of armature inductance necessitates a further retardation of the brushes to give sparkless commutation. The same consideration shows that if *compoles* are fitted, the polarity of a motor compole must be the same as that of the main pole immediately *behind* it.

9.8. The Shunt-wound D.C. Motor Circuit. Fig. 9.10 shows the electrical connexions of the d.c.

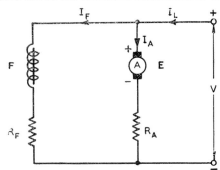

FIG. 9.10. SHUNT-WOUND MOTOR CIRCUIT

shunt-wound motor. The field current is I_F amperes, the armature current is I_A amperes: the resistance of the field and armature are R_F and R_A ohms respectively. The p.d. of the source of electrical energy is V volts and the total current taken by the motor, the load current, is I_L amperes. The counter-e.m.f. is E volts.

The load current energizes both field and armature, giving the current equation $I_L = I_F + I_A$.

The p.d. of the source of supply must overcome both the back-e.m.f. E volts and the voltage drop of the armature circuit, $I_A R_A$, so that the voltage equation is $V = E + I_A R_A$. The magnitude of the back-e.m.f. E volts is that of the equivalent generator, so that $E = \Phi nZ$ volts for lap-wound and bi-polar motors and $E = \Phi nZP$ for a wave-wound motor.

The field current $I_F = V/R_F$, and the armature current is $I_A = (V - E)/R_A$ amperes.

The characteristics of the shunt-wound d.c. motor are that its speed is fairly constant at all loads and that its torque is approximately proportional to the armature current. The applied p.d. across the motor terminals being constant, the field current and flux will be constant in a motor fitted with compoles. From the torque equation $T = 0.117\frac{E}{n}.I_A$, since the ratio E/n is constant if the flux is constant, the torque is proportional to the armature current.

An increase in load requiring an increase in torque causes the armature current I_A to increase and therefore produces an increase in voltage drop $I_A R_A$. The applied voltage V being constant, the increased voltage drop can only be obtained by a reduction in E which necessitates in turn a decrease in speed. The speed therefore falls as the load increases, but in practice, so long as the armature is rotating, $I_A R_A$ is very small compared with V and the speed at full-load is little less than the speed at no-load.

If the motor is not fitted with compoles, the brushes will be retarded and some of the conductors will produce a demagnetizing field which increases with current. The field is thus weakened as the load and torque increase. Now the torque is proportional to ΦI_A and from this it follows that if an increase of torque reduces the value of Φ, I_A has to increase more rapidly: in other words, the torque increases rather more slowly than the armature current.

The weakening of the field due to the demagnetizing turns also affects the motor speed, for to generate the same back-e.m.f. in a weakened field the motor will have to rotate faster. As a result the speed-torque characteristic is rather improved due to the presence of demagnetizing turns.

The difference in speed at no-load and full-load, expressed as a percentage of the no-load speed is known as the SPEED REGULATION. Thus, speed regulation

$$= \left\{ \frac{(\text{speed at no-load} - \text{speed at full-load})}{\text{no-load speed}} \right\}$$
$$\times\ 100 \text{ per cent}$$

9.9. Speed Control. From the voltage equation, $V = E + I_A R_A$, E being proportional to the speed, it is apparent that speed can be controlled by variation of the armature current I_A; the applied p.d. V being constant, a fall in armature current I_A would give an increase in back-e.m.f. E and therefore in speed n. This method is wasteful in power owing to the high value of I_A and it also reduces the torque.

The motor is normally regulated by the inclusion of a rheostat in the field circuit to control the field current and flux. At a given load, decreasing the field results in an *increase* in speed because the armature must rotate at a greater speed to produce the same back-e.m.f. The resistance in the field circuit is therefore *increased* to *raise* the speed of the motor.

To reverse the direction of rotation of the motor it is necessary to reverse the direction either of the field or of the armature current (Fleming's left-hand rule). If both field and armature current are reversed, the direction of motion remains unchanged. From this consideration, it is clear that the d.c. shunt-wound motor could, in principle, be energized satisfactorily from an a.c. supply. A.c. commutator motors are used for many purposes: the details of their design are necessarily influenced by additional factors peculiar to the a.c. circuit.

While the motor is running, the armature current is limited by the back-e.m.f. generated. If a motor at rest were connected direct to the full supply voltage, then owing to the absence of any back-e.m.f. the armature current I_A would be equal to

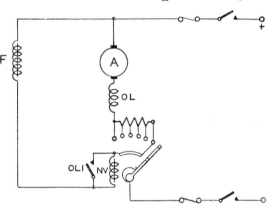

FIG. 9.11. MOTOR STARTER

V/R_A; R_A being very small, the armature current would be dangerously excessive. For this reason, all but the very small motors have a starting rheostat included in the armature circuit. The motor is started up with the whole of this rheostat in circuit and the resistance is gradually cut out as the motor gains speed and generates a back-e.m.f.

Two additional safeguards to the motor must also be provided. Firstly, if the electrical supply should temporarily fail after the motor has been started up, it must be ensured that when the supply is restored the armature will not be left across the supply mains with all the starting resistance cut out of circuit. Secondly, should such an excessive mechanical load be encountered that the armature current would increase to an unsafe value, the motor must be automatically disconnected from the supply source.

The connexions of a typical motor starter circuit incorporating these safeguards are given in Fig 9.11. When the main switch is closed the electrical supply is connected through fuses to the starting circuit. The rheostat handle is advanced step by step, fully energizing the field at once and gradually utting out the starting resistance from the arma-ture circuit as the motor speed increases. When he starting resistance is completely cut out, the ontrolling handle is held in this position against a owerful restoring spring by the no-volt electro-magnet NV included in series with the field. This lectromagnet will only be energized as long as urrent flows in the field circuit: if any failure ccurs in the power supply the no-volt electro-magnet becomes de-energized and the rheostat andle is returned by its restoring spring to the arting position.

In series with the armature is inserted a low-esistance overload relay OL: this is adjusted so

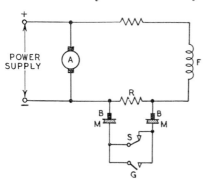

FIG. 9.12. SHUNT-WOUND MOTOR CIRCUIT WITH
SPEED GOVERNOR

hat it will not operate on the normal full-load rmature current, but any current in excess of this auses the closing of its contacts $OL1$: these con-acts are arranged to short-circuit the no-volt lectromagnet and so release the starter handle to isconnect the power supply. It will be observed rom the diagram that the motor field is never dis-onnected, but when de-energized it forms part of closed circuit which includes both electro-agnets, the starting resistance, and the armature. 'he field, possessing considerable inductance, would enerate a dangerously high e.m.f. of self-induction ere its circuit disconnected.

Where the maintenance of a constant speed with uctuating load is essential—in the printing tele-raph machine, for example—an automatically perating speed governor is incorporated in the 1otor. In the teleprinter the governor employed of the centrifugal type and is a totally enclosed nit mounted upon the spindle of the motor with vhich it revolves. Electrical connexions between he governor and the field circuit are provided by 1eans of two brushes BB which make contact with wo metallic rings MM mounted on the governor ase (see Fig. 9.12).

When the motor is at rest, the starting contact spring S short-circuits the governor resistor. The object of this device is to provide maximum field current and torque at starting. As soon as the governor reaches a certain speed which is well below normal, the spring moves outwards by centrifugal action and these contacts do not then affect normal operation of the governor.

The governor contacts G are connected across the governing resistor R in the motor field circuit. When the motor speed is below normal, the governor contacts are held apart by the pull of a powerful spring on the contact arm. The increase in resistance of the field circuit reduces the field current and flux to a comparatively low value and causes the motor to accelerate. As soon as the speed rises above normal, the pull of the governor spring is overcome by centrifugal force, the contact arm moves outwards and the governor contacts G close, short-circuiting the governing resistor. The consequent rise of current in the field winding of the motor causes the speed to decrease below normal until the reduced centrifugal force enables the governor spring to regain control of the contact arm and separate the contacts: the speed now again increases. These variations of speed above and below normal occur rapidly and continuously during the operation of the motor, but their mag-nitude is small and for practical purposes the speed may be regarded as constant. By this means the motor speed has a maximum variation of ± 0.5 per cent.

9.10. Motor Losses and Efficiency. If the total current taken by the motor is I_L amperes at a p.d. of V volts, the power input to the motor is VI_L watts. Part of this power is dissipated as heat in the field and armature due to the I^2R losses, $I_A{}^2R_A$ and $I_F{}^2R_F$. The remaining power EI_A is converted into mechanical power. The useful power is equal to this gross power less the power consumed in overcoming the rotational losses. The mechanical output is therefore

$$VI_L - I^2R \text{ loss} - \text{rotational loss}$$

and the efficiency $\eta = (\text{output}/\text{input}) \times 100\%$

$$= \{(VI_L - I^2R \text{ loss} - \text{rotational loss})/VI_L\} \times 100\%$$

In this expression, the mechanical output is stated in terms of electrical power.

The armature loss $I_A{}^2R_A$ increases with load. The field loss $I_F{}^2R_F$ is constant. The rotational loss is approximately constant at all loads.

EXAMPLE 9.3 (A). A shunt-wound d.c. motor takes 10 A from a 250-V supply on full-load. The resistance of the shunt field is 125 Ω and the armature resistance is 0·025 Ω.

Neglecting other than copper losses, calculate the efficiency of the machine and its full-load output in horse-power.

(C. & G.)

$$I_F = V/R_F = 250/125 = 2 \text{ A}$$
$$I_A = I_L - I_F = 10 - 2 = 8 \text{ A}$$

Field copper loss
$$= I_F^2 R_F = 2^2 \times 125 = 500 \text{ W}$$

Armature copper loss
$$= I_A^2 R_A = 8^2 \times 0 \cdot 025 = 1 \cdot 6 \text{ W}$$

Total I^2R loss
$$= 501 \cdot 6 \text{ W}$$

Input power
$$= VI = 250 \times 10 = 2 \; 500 \text{ W}$$
$$\eta = \text{output} \times 100\%/\text{input}$$
$$= (VI - I^2R \text{ loss}) \times 100\%/VI$$
$$= 100(2 \; 500 - 501 \cdot 6)/2 \; 500 \simeq \underline{\underline{80\%}}$$

Useful power
$$= 2 \; 000 \text{ W}$$
$$\text{H.p.} = 2 \; 000/746 = \underline{\underline{2 \cdot 68 \text{ h.p.}}}$$

EXAMPLE 9.4 (A). A d.c. motor operating from a 400-V supply is driving a d.c. generator having a shunt-connected field winding of 125 Ω resistance. This generator is supplying a current of 12 A at 250 V to a number of lamps. Calculate the percentage of the total power available at the brushes that is dissipated in the field winding.

If the overall efficiency of the generator is known to be 75 per cent, and the efficiency of the d.c. motor alone is 70 per cent, calculate the current and power drawn by the d.c. motor from the 400-V supply. (C. & G.)

The useful output of the generator into the lamp load is 12 A at 250 V

$$= 12 \times 250 = 3 \; 000 \text{ W}$$

The power dissipated into the field is

$$250^2/125 = 500 \text{ W}$$

The total power passing through the brushes is

$$3 \; 000 + 500 = 3 \; 500 \text{ W}$$

The percentage power dissipated in the field winding

$$= (500/3 \; 500) \times 100 = \underline{\underline{14 \cdot 28 \text{ per cent}}}$$

For the generator with an efficiency of 75 per cent—

$$\frac{\text{Useful output power to load}}{\text{Total input power to generator}} = \frac{75}{100}$$

Total input power to generator
$$= (100/75) \times 3 \; 000 = 4 \; 000 \text{ W}$$

This is the electrical equivalent to the mechanical power driving the generator, i.e. it is the useful power output of the motor.

For the motor of efficiency 70 per cent—

$$\frac{\text{Useful output power}}{\text{Input power from mains}} = \frac{70}{100}$$

Input power to motor
$$= (100/70) \times 4 \; 000 = 5 \; 714 \text{ W}$$

This power is drawn from 400-V mains supply.

$$\text{Supply current} = 5 \; 714/400 = 14 \cdot 285 \text{ A}$$

9.11. The Rotary Converter and Dynamotor

The power plant installed for energizing telecommunication equipment normally consists of shunt-wound generators driven from electric motors connected to the a.c. or d.c. supply mains; in buildings where mains supplies are not available, as for example in certain remote repeater stations, the generators are driven from prime movers, usually diesel engines.

Many types of machine are available wherein the motor and generator windings are fitted on a single armature fluxed from a common field: such machines are fitted either with two separate commutators or with one commutator and one set of slip rings. Their purpose is essentially to convert D.C. to A.C. or vice versa, or to convert from one d.c. voltage to another, by applying the input voltage to drive the motor. Such machines are not used for stepping up or down a.c. voltages owing to the much greater efficiency and simplicity of the *transformer* or stationary converter.

A rotary converter is defined as *a synchronous machine with a single armature winding having commutator and slip rings for converting A.C. into D.C. or vice versa.*

A dynamotor, or rotary transformer, is *a machine combining both motor and generator action in one magnetic field, but having two separate armature windings with independent commutators.*

With high output machines of high efficiency, the mechanical coupling of motor and generator is a satisfactory arrangement economically. With the smaller machines having an efficiency of say 80 per cent, the overall efficiency of such a motor generator set would be 80 per cent × 80 per cent = 64 per cent only. The use of a combined machine such as the rotary converter promotes a higher overall efficiency and reduced cost by reducing the separate losses of motor and generator.

SUMMARY

Ampere's Law.

$$F = BIl \text{ newton} \quad . \qquad . \qquad . \qquad . \quad (9.1)$$

$$F = 2 \times 10^{-7} I_1 I_2 / d \text{ newton/metre} . \quad (9.2)$$

Fleming's Left-hand Rule.

        thuMb—Motion
        First—Flux
        seCond—Current

Torque on Energized Coil.

$$T = 2BIlZr \cos \theta \text{ newton-metre}$$

Shunt-wound D.C. Motor.

$$I_L = I_A + I_F$$
$$I_F = V/R_F$$
$$I_A = (V - E)/R_A$$
$$V = E + I_A R_A$$

Horse-power. Motor h.p. $= 2\pi n T / 550 = VI/746$

Efficiency.

$$\eta = \{(VI - I^2R \text{ loss} - \text{rotational loss})/VI\} \times 100\%$$

CHAPTER X

ALTERNATING CURRENTS

COMPARED with the d.c. circuit, the a.c. circuit is complicated by the fact that the continuously changing current magnitude induces back e.m.f.s in any inductance and capacitance present: as a result, opposition additional to conductor resistance is presented to the flow of current whose rise and fall does not necessarily occur in step with the voltage, i.e. the question of phase has to be considered.

MAGNITUDE AND PHASE

10.1. Sine Waveform. By waveform is meant the shape of the graph representing the instantaneous values of a periodically varying quantity plotted against time.

In Fig. 10.1, a conductor P shown in end view is rotating in a clockwise direction at a steady angular

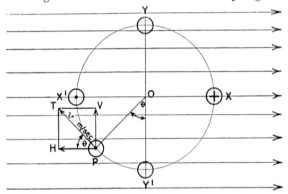

FIG. 10.1. GENERATION OF ALTERNATING E.M.F.

velocity in a uniform parallel magnetic field. The circular velocity v m/sec is at every instant tangential to the circular path described by the rotating conductor, and it can be resolved into two right-angled components in the directions PV and PH (see Appendix **A.4**).

If $\theta°$ is the angle made at any instant between the conductor P and its starting point on the axis YY', then $\angle TPH$ is also $\theta°$ (from geometrical relationships,

$$\angle TPH + \angle TPV = \angle VPT + \angle VPO = 90°$$

and

$$\angle TPH = \angle VPO = \theta°).$$

The horizontal component of velocity PH is v $\cos \theta$ and the vertical component PV is $v \sin \theta$.

The horizontal component is always parallel to the magnetic field and consequently at no time is instrumental in producing an induced e.m.f. On the other hand, the vertical component $v \sin \theta$ being always at right angles to the field gives an induced e.m.f.

$$E = Blv \sin \theta \text{ volts}$$

In other words, since B, l (the length of the conductor), and v are constant, the induced e.m.f. proportional to $\sin \theta$.

In Fig. 10.2 is plotted the graph of $\sin \theta$ for values of θ from $0°$ to $360°$, and this to a suitable vertical scale also represents the magnitude of the e.m.f. induced as the conductor rotates. The sine curve passes through all values between $+1$ and -1. Similarly the graph showing the induced e.m.f. passes through all values between positive and negative maxima, including zero values. The reversal in the direction of induced e.m.f. is apparent from application of Fleming's right-hand rule to Fig. 10.1. When the rotating conductor ascending the induced e.m.f. may be regarded as positive: when the conductor is descending the direction of the induced e.m.f. is reversed since the motion ($v \sin \theta$) is reversed, the field remaining unchanged. At points Y and Y' the magnitude of the vertical velocity component is instantaneously zero, the induced e.m.f.s at these instants being also zero. At points X and X', the vertical velocity

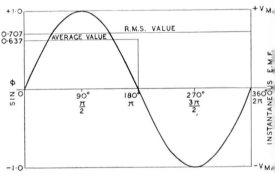

FIG. 10.2. SINUSOIDAL SINE-WAVE GRAPH

component has its maximum value and the horizontal velocity component is now zero: accordingly the induced e.m.f. at these instants has maximum value.

An electric current which alternately reverses its direction in a circuit in a periodic manner (the frequency being independent of the constants of the circuit) is termed an ALTERNATING CURRENT.

It should be observed that (i) any conductor which rotates in a magnetic field will generate an e.m.f. of alternating form since the relative direction of the motion with respect to the field alternates: also (ii) the resulting e.m.f. will be of sine waveform or *sinusoidal*, only provided that *l* and *v* remain constant and *B* is uniform and parallel as assumed above.

In rotary generators *l* and *v* are constant, but the distribution of magnetic flux encountered by the conductors and hence the value of *B* is usually not uniform, in which case the waveform of the induced e.m.f. does not follow the pure sine curve.

Fig. 10.3 shows the waveform of the output from a telephone hand generator driven at constant speed, the waveform being somewhat distorted from the pure sine curve owing to a non-uniform field. It is, however, convenient to adopt the sine wave for ease in calculation, and this is justified by the statement of Fourier's Theorem (§**11.11**). Throughout Chapters X and XI, a sine waveform is assumed except where a contrary statement is made.

10.2. Frequency. The waveform of Fig. 10.2 is produced by the conductor in moving through one

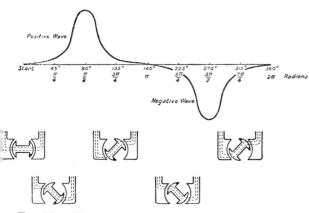

FIG. 10.3. WAVEFORM OF OUTPUT FROM TELEPHONE HAND GENERATOR

complete revolution, and this will be repeated for each successive revolution. The complete series of changes taking place in the value of a recurring variable quantity during a period is known as the CYCLE. In the sine waves of Fig. 10.4 one cycle is completed between the points *A* and *B*, these two

points having the same value and they are also changing in the same direction: the cycle may commence at any value, and a complete cycle is also performed between any pair of points such as *C* and *D*. In the course of one cycle, the magnitude passes through all its values, both positive and negative. Between *A* and *X* the magnitude has passed through all its positive values only, and *AX* therefore represents one half-cycle.

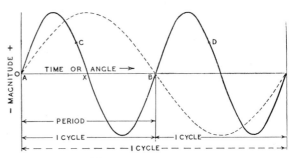

FIG. 10.4. FREQUENCY

The number of e.m.f. cycles experienced by a rotating conductor is equal to the number of revolutions only in the case of a bipolar machine. In the four-pole machine of Fig. 10.5 it will be seen that the relative motion between conductor and flux alternates twice per revolution, so producing two cycles per revolution. The number of cycles per revolution is equal to the number of pairs of poles.

The number of cycles performed per second is termed the FREQUENCY. Frequency, for which the symbol is *f*, is expressed in cycles per second, abbreviated to c/s or sometimes represented by the symbol $\sim$. In high-frequency work the kilocycle per second (kc/s), the megacycle per second (Mc/s), or the gigacycle per second (Gc/s) are more conveniently employed. In telecommunication systems, alternating currents at frequencies between the limits 17 c/s for a ringing generator and 50 Gc/s or more for high-frequency radio and television work are employed. The output frequency of a multipolar alternator is equal to the product of the number of revolutions per second and the number of pairs of poles.

In Fig. 10.4 the full line curve has a frequency equal to twice that shown by the dotted curve because its magnitude passes through two cycles in the time required for one cycle by the dotted curve.

The ANGULAR FREQUENCY denotes *the product of*

the frequency of a sinusoidal phenomenon and the factor 2π. The symbol for angular frequency is ω and it is measured in radians per second, so that

$$\omega = 2\pi f \qquad . \qquad . \qquad . \quad (10.1)$$

A variable quantity, the characteristics of which are reproduced at equal intervals is said to be PERIODIC, *and the minimum interval after which the same characteristics recur is known as the* PERIOD. The period is measured in seconds and expressed by the symbol T. The period is the time in seconds required to perform one cycle. In Fig. 10.4 the length AB represents one period for the full line curve, where the abscissa scale is in time units. Frequency is sometimes expressed as periods per second or p.p.s.

The frequency is the reciprocal of the period, i.e.

$$f = 1/T, \text{ or } T = 1/f \quad . \qquad . \quad (10.2)$$

For example, an alternating quantity whose frequency is 50 c/s has a period of 1/50 sec or 0·020 sec.

10.3. Phase. Phase refers to the fraction of the whole period which has elapsed, measured from some fixed origin, usually a zero value. The term PHASE DIFFERENCE (phase displacement) is used to distinguish between two periodic alternating quantities whose frequencies are equal. They are said to be *in phase* if they reach corresponding values simultaneously, for example if their zero values correspond when their magnitudes are changing in the same directions; or *out of phase* to denote that they do not reach corresponding values simultaneously. Phase difference may be measured in time, or, more usually as an angle, denoted by the symbol ϕ.

In Fig. 10.6, the two graphs $OABCD$ and $OMBND$ are in phase because they pass through their zero or maximum values together, although their magnitudes differ. The two graphs $OABCD$ and $JEFGH$ are out of phase to the extent of 60°, this being the angular distance between their zero values. The graph $OABCD$ is said to lead the curve $JEFGH$ by 60°, or alternatively $JEFGH$ lags 60° behind $OABCD$, depending upon which graph is taken as the standard of reference. When the phase angle is exactly 90° the two waves are said to be in *quadrature*. The curves $OMBND$ and $OPBQD$ are 180° out of phase, or in *antiphase*: although their zero values coincide the magnitudes are not changing in the same direction at these zero values.

If two alternating quantities have the same waveform—for example, both are sine waves— they may differ in three respects: (i) frequency, (ii) phase, and (iii) magnitude.

10.4. Maximum or Peak Value. As the magnitude of an alternating e.m.f. or current is continuously varying, an expression for the magnitude cannot be given simply as for a direct current or voltage. The a.c. magnitude may be expressed in one of four different ways according to requirements: these are known as *maximum, instantaneous, average,* and *r.m.s.* values.

The term maximum value is self-explanatory in a conductor rotating in a parallel uniform field

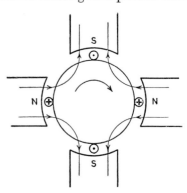

FIG. 10.5. MULTI-POLAR GENERATOR

this value would be the magnitude of the induced e.m.f. when the conductor is cutting the flux at right angles. In Fig. 10.6, maximum values are shown by the ordinates AX and MX for those particular alternating quantities. Maximum or peak voltages have to be considered where the question of insulation of conductor arises. The positive and negative maximum values are normally, but not necessarily, numerically equal.

Maximum values are designated by the capital letters with the subscript $_{max}$: E_{max} and V_{max} denote peak e.m.f.s and p.d.s and I_{max} is a peak current.

10.5. Instantaneous Value. The instantaneous value is the value of a varying quantity at a particular instant of time. It is measured by the ordinate to the curve at the instant chosen: this implies the need for stating at what point on the curve the instantaneous value is taken. For example, it might be the value at 45° after zero when the current is rising (OY in Fig. 10.6); or at 0·001 sec after a zero value.

The general symbols used to express instantaneous values are the small letters e and v for voltages and i for currents.

For a voltage or current varying sinusoidally $v = k \sin \theta$ or $i = k' \sin \theta$. At $\theta = 90°$ when maximum values have been attained $\sin \theta° = \sin 90° = 1$

$v = k$ and $i = k'$. Since this is to be the maximum value in each case, $k = V_{max}$ and $k' = I_{max}$. Instantaneous values may therefore be written—

$$e = E_{max} \sin \theta, \, v = V_{max} \sin \theta$$
$$i = I_{max} \sin \theta \quad . \quad . \quad . \quad . \quad (10.3)$$

when $\sin \theta = 0$, ($\theta = 0°$, $180°$, or $360°$), e, v, and i are each equal to zero.

It is often convenient to calculate the instantaneous values in terms of the time interval which

similar form for E or V, the second expression i_2 lagging ϕ radians behind the first, i_1. Referring to Fig. 10.6, if the expression for the curve $OMBND$ is $i_1 = I_1 \sin \omega t$, where $I_1 = MX$, the expression for the curve $JEFGH$ is $i_2 = I_2 \sin (\omega t - \phi)$ this curve passing through all its instantaneous values ϕ radians (60° in this case) later than the corresponding values for the curve of i_1. A leading quantity would be represented by

$$i_3 = I_3 \sin (\omega t + \phi)$$

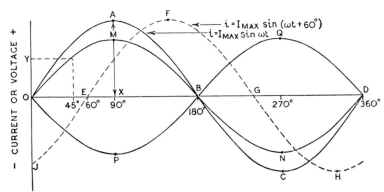

FIG. 10.6. PHASE DIFFERENCE

has elapsed from a zero value rather than in terms of the angle developed. The angle $\theta°$ is $360°$ or 2π radians per cycle, and if the frequency is f c/s, the angle develops at the rate of $2\pi f$ radians every second. After a lapse of time equal to t seconds, the angle θ will be $2\pi ft$ radians. The following equations may be written, substituting $\theta = 2\pi ft$ in expression (10.3)—

$$e = E_{max} \sin 2\pi ft, \, v = V_{max} \sin 2\pi ft$$
$$i = I_{max} \sin 2\pi ft \quad . \quad . \quad . \quad . \quad (10.4)$$

the angle $2\pi ft$ in each case being measured in radians. The term $2\pi f$ is the *angular frequency* ω, so that substituting $\omega = 2\pi f$, equations (10.4) are frequently written—

$$e = E_{max} \sin \omega t, \, v = V_{max} \sin \omega t$$
$$i = I_{max} \sin \omega t \quad . \quad . \quad . \quad . \quad (10.5)$$

the angle (ωt) being again in radians.

If two alternating quantities of equal frequency and maximum values I_1 and I_2 (or E_1 and E_2, or V_1 and V_2) have a phase displacement of ϕ radians, their instantaneous values i_1 and i_2 may be written as $i = I_1 \sin \omega t$ and $i_2 = I_2 \sin (\omega t - \phi)$, and in a

EXAMPLE 10.1 (A). If a sine wave current of maximum value 10 A alternates at 50 c/s what is its value at (i) 0·005 sec, (ii) 0·002 sec, (iii) 0·01 sec after its zero value?

$$I_{max} = 10 \text{ A}, f = 50 \text{ c/s}$$
$$\omega = 2\pi f = 100\pi \text{ radn/sec}$$

(i) $i = I_{max} \sin \omega t$
$= 10 \sin (100\pi \times 0·005) \text{ radn}$
$= 10 \sin \pi/2 \text{ radn} = 10 \sin 90° = \underline{10 \text{ A}}$

(i.e. the curve passes through its maximum value at 0·005 sec).

(ii) $i = 10 \sin (100\pi \times 0·002) \text{ radn}$
$= 10 \sin (100\pi \times 0·002 \times 360/2\pi)°$
$= 10 \sin 36° = 10 \times 0·587 \, 8 = \underline{5·88 \text{ A}}$

(iii) $i = 10 \sin (100\pi \times 0·01) = 10 \sin \pi$
$= 10 \times 0 = \underline{0}$

(i.e. the curve passes through a zero value at $t = 0·01$ sec, which would be expected from (i)).

EXAMPLE 10.2 (A). An a.c. voltage is defined by the following expression: $e = 100 \sin 5\,000t$. What is the instantaneous value of the voltage 1/250 sec after the beginning of a cycle? What is the time occupied by one complete cycle? (*C. & G.*)

When $t = 1/250$

$$e = 100 \sin 5\ 000/250$$
$$= 100 \sin 20 \ (\text{radn})$$
$$= 100 \sin (20 \times 180/\pi)^\circ$$
$$= 100 \sin 1\ 146^\circ$$
$$= 100 \sin (1\ 146 - 3 \times 360)^\circ$$
$$= 100 \sin 66^\circ = \underline{\underline{91\cdot36 \text{ V}}}$$

$$\omega = 2\pi f = 5\ 000, f = 5\ 000/2\pi$$
$$t = 1/f = 2\pi/5\ 000 = \underline{0\cdot001\ 26 \text{ sec}}$$

10.6. Average Value. This is the mean value taken over one half-cycle. Consideration of average values is mainly confined to calculations in connexion with rectifiers. The symbols used to denote average values are E_{av} and V_{av} for voltages and I_{av} for currents.

For a sine waveform the average value is equal to $0\cdot637 \left(= \dfrac{2}{\pi} \right)$ of the maximum (peak) value, or—

$$E_{av} = 0\cdot637\ E_{max}, \ V_{av} = 0\cdot637\ V_{max}$$
$$I_{av} = 0\cdot637\ I_{max} \qquad . \qquad . \qquad . \qquad (10.6)$$

For example, if the maximum value of a sine wave current is 10 A, the average value over one half-cycle is 6·37 A. In other words, the same effect would be produced by a current rising sinusoidally from zero to 10 A and falling to zero or by a steady current of 6·37 A maintained for an equal period of time. The average value is indicated in Fig. 10.2.

If the waveform is other than sinusoidal, the average value must be separately calculated for each case, either from a knowledge of the mathematical expression for the waveform and applying the integral calculus; or graphically by the method of Simpson's rule, which consists in erecting a number of ordinates to meet the curve, measuring these and determining their arithmetic mean.

EXAMPLE 10.3 (A). If the average value of a sine wave voltage is 159 V, what is the peak value?

$$V_{av} = 0\cdot637\ V_{max}$$
$$V_{max} = V_{av}/0\cdot637 = 159/0\cdot637 = \underline{\underline{250 \text{ V}}}$$

10.7. R.M.S. or Effective Value. This is defined as the square root of the mean value of the squares of the instantaneous values taken over one complete cycle.

R.M.S. or EFFECTIVE values of voltage and current are denoted simply by the capital letters E or V and I respectively. The r.m.s. value is indicated by most forms of a.c. measuring instrument and it is most generally used for calculations the appearance in a.c. work of the symbols E, V and I may always be taken to indicate the effective values.

The r.m.s. value for a sine curve is equal to $0\cdot707 \ (= 1/\sqrt{2})$ of the peak value, or—

$$E = 0\cdot707\ E_{max}, \ V = 0\cdot707\ V_{max}$$
$$I = 0\cdot707\ I_{max} \qquad . \qquad . \qquad . \qquad (10.7$$

This means, for example, that a steady current of 7·07 A will produce or consume the same amount of *power* (e.g. the same heating effect) as a sine wave alternating current of maximum value 10 A when maintained for an equal time period. The r.m.s. value is indicated in Fig. 10.2.

The mean value of a sine curve taken over a complete cycle is zero, for the sum of all the instantaneous values during one half-cycle is nullified by an equal but opposite sum in the subsequent half-cycle. A simple mean value cannot be used for the complete cycle.

All squared quantities are positive, so that if all instantaneous values over one complete cycle are squared, then a mean value of these squares can be found. The square root of this mean will then give an effective value—the *root-mean-square* (r.m.s.) value—for the current or voltage.

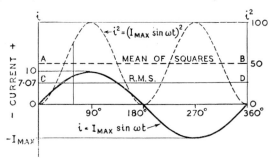

FIG. 10.7. R.M.S. VALUE

In Fig. 10.7 the full line graph represents one cycle of a sine wave current $i = I_{max} \sin \omega t$. By taking a number of instantaneous values, squaring these and plotting the squared values, the dotted graph is obtained: this is the graph

$$i^2 = (I_{max} \sin \omega t)^2$$

and it is always positive. The mean value of the dotted curve occurs at the dotted line AB about which the curve will be seen to be symmetrical

is value is still the *square* of a current. Taking
the square root of the magnitude OA gives the full
line CD (magnitude OC) which is the *root of the
mean of the squares*—the r.m.s. value.

In the diagram a simple value $I_{max} = 10$ A has
been taken. The curve for $i^2 = (10 \sin \omega t)^2$ reaches
a peak value of 100: the mean value for this is,
by symmetry, equal to one half of the peak value,
or 50. Taking the square root of this gives an
r.m.s. value of 7·07 A, i.e. 0·707 times the peak
value.

It should be noted that the values obtained
above for $I_{av}(= 0.637 \, I_{max})$ and $I(= 0.707 \, I_{max})$
are correct only for the pure sine waveform.

The ratio of r.m.s. to average value is termed the
FORM FACTOR. For a sine waveform this is

r.m.s./average
$$= I_{max}/\sqrt{2} \div 2I_{max}/\pi = \pi/(2\sqrt{2})$$
$$= 1.11(= 0.707/0.637)$$

EXAMPLE 10.4 (A). An alternating voltage has an r.m.s.
value of 230 V. What is the peak value?

$$V = 0.707 \, V_{max}$$
$$V_{max} = V/0.707 = 230/0.707 = 325 \text{ V}$$

EXAMPLE 10.5 (A). What is the effective value of an alternating current having a perfectly rectangular waveform
and a maximum value of 1 A? How would the heating
effect of this current compare with that of a direct current
having a steady value of 0·5 A?   (C. & G.)

For a rectangular waveform the instantaneous
value of the current is at all times equal to the
maximum value, so that the effective value is also
1 A.

$$\frac{\text{Heating effect of A.C.}}{\text{Heating effect of D.C.}} = 1^2/0.5^2 = 4/1$$

EXAMPLE 10.6 (A). Compare the heating effect when
flowing in equal resistances, of a direct current of 2 A
with that of an A.C. having a maximum value of 2 A.
What would be the effect on the amount of heat produced
in each case if a capacitor were inserted in series with each
resistance?   (C. & G.)

Heat $= I^2 Rt$ joule.
The direct current, $I_D = 2$ A.
The r.m.s. value of the A.C., $I_A = 2/\sqrt{2}$.
Heat due to D.C./Heat due to A.C.
$$= 2^2 \div (2/\sqrt{2})^2 = 4 \times 2/4 = 2/1.$$

i.e. the D.C. has twice the heating effect of the A.C.

The effect of the capacitor in the d.c. circuit is
to limit the production of heat to the short charging
period and thereafter prevent the flow of current.
In the a.c. circuit, no power is absorbed by the
capacitor, consequently the heat produced in the

circuit by a given current is the same irrespective
of whether the capacitor is in circuit or not (assuming a negligible power loss in the capacitor).

EXAMPLE 10.7 (A). A coil of wire, having a resistance of
10 Ω and consisting of 100 turns in the form of a square
of 20 cm sides is rotated at a speed of 2 000 r.p.m. in
a uniform magnetic field of 0·05 Wb/m² and at right
angles to the field. The extremities of the coil are connected across a resistance of 20 Ω.

What is (a) the effective value of the current which
flows through the 20 Ω resistance, (b) the instantaneous
value of the current through the resistance when the
plane of the coil is at an angle of 30° to the direction of
the magnetic field?   (C. & G.)

Peripheral velocity of frame
$$v = 2\pi \times 0.1 \times 2\,000/60$$
$$= 20\pi/3 \text{ m/sec}$$

Velocity of coil perpendicular to field (see
Fig. 10.8)
$$= \text{v} \cos \theta = (20\pi/3) \times \cos \theta \text{ m/sec}$$

For each active conductor
$$E = Blv \cos \theta \text{ volts}$$
$$= (0.05 \times 0.2 \times 20\pi/3) \times \cos \theta$$
$$= (0.2\pi/3) \times \cos \theta \text{ volts}$$

For 100 turns (i.e. 200 active conductors)
$$E = (200 \times 0.2\pi/3) \times \cos \theta$$
$$= 40\pi \cos \theta/3 = 41.9 \cos \theta \text{ volts}$$

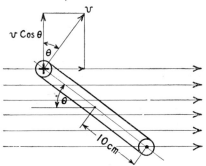

FIG. 10.8. (Example 10.7)

(a) Total resistance
$$= 20 + 10 = 30 \text{ Ω}$$

Instantaneous current
$$= 41.9 \cos \theta/30 = 1.39 \cos \theta \text{ A}$$

Maximum value
$$= 1.39 \text{ A}$$

R.m.s. value
$$= 1.39 \times 0.707 = 0.98 \text{ A}$$

(b) Instantaneous value when $\theta = 30°$,
$$= 1·39 \cos 30° = 1·39 \times 0·866 = \underline{\underline{1·21 \text{ A}}}$$

Simple A.C. Circuits

10.8. Circuit with Pure Resistance. Fig. 10.9 (a) shows an a.c. generator connected to a load consisting of a pure resistance, i.e. one with negligible self-inductance and self-capacitance. As the p.d. across the resistor terminals alternates, the resistance remaining constant, the resultant current

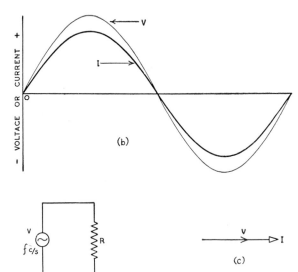

(b)

(a)

(c)

FIG. 10.9. CIRCUIT WITH PURE RESISTANCE

rises and falls in accordance with Ohm's law, which may be written as follows for peak, instantaneous, average, and r.m.s. values—

$$I_{max} = V_{max}/R, \quad i = v/R$$
$$I_{av} = V_{av}/R, \quad \text{or } I = V/R \qquad . \qquad . (10.8)$$

The current rises and falls in phase with the voltage: the phase angle $\phi = 0°$ for a pure resistance. The voltage and current graphs are given in Fig. 10.9 (b). The corresponding vector diagram is drawn in Fig. 10.9 (c): the phase angle being zero, V and I are drawn along the same straight line to suitable scales.

EXAMPLE 10.8 (A). A p.d. of 30 V r.m.s. is maintained across a pure resistance of 600 Ω. What is the r.m.s. current?

$$I = V/R = 30/600 = \underline{\underline{0·05 \text{ A}}}$$

EXAMPLE 10.9 (A). What current is taken from the 250 V 50 c/s a.c. mains by a 500 W heater element?

Two such heater elements are connected in parallel and the combination is joined in series with a similar element across the a.c. mains. What is the voltage across the single element and the total power consumed if the resistance of the heater element remains constant?

(C. & C.)

$$I = W/V = 500/250 = \underline{\underline{2 \text{ A}}}$$

$$R = V/I = 250/2 = 125 \ \Omega$$

Resistance of two similar elements in parallel
$$= 125/2 = 62·5 \ \Omega$$

Combined resistance of the three elements
$$= 125 + 62·5 = 187·5 \ \Omega$$

Current in circuit
$$= 250/187·5 = 4/3 \text{ A}$$

Voltage across single element
$$= IR = (4/3) \times 125 = \underline{\underline{166·6 \text{ V}}}$$

Total power
$$= I^2R = (4/3)^2 \times 187·5 = \underline{\underline{333·3 \text{ W}}}$$

10.9. Circuit with Pure Inductance. An inductance must inherently possess resistance too, but the resistance value may be made relatively so small as to be negligible for all but the lowest frequencies; in any case it is convenient firstly to consider the effect of an alternating current on a pure inductance and to consider later the effect of added resistance.

The action of an inductor in producing a counter e.m.f. depends upon a change of current, and the presence of inductance in a.c. circuits where the current varies continuously assumes a far greater importance than in the d.c. circuit where its effect is remarked only during transient periods.

Fig. 10.10 (a) shows an inductance of L henry maintained at a p.d. of V volts at f c/s. The resultant current, I amperes, is shown by the thick line in the accompanying graphs (Fig. 10.10 (b)).

In the same diagram is plotted the rate of change of the current, shown by the dotted line. This rate of change di/dt is equal to the slope of the current curve: it is zero when the current is at its maximum values, and the current is changing at the maximum rate when its magnitude is passing through a zero value. This produces a cosine curve (the dotted curve), or in other words the rate of change of current follows a sine curve which is 90° ahead of the current curve.

The induced e.m.f. $E \ (= -L \cdot (di/dt)$ volts) proportional to the rate of change of current, but t is of opposite sign since it is a counter-e.m.f.: its magnitude is shown, to an appropriate scale, by he chain dotted line.

In order to drive the current I around the circuit, the applied p.d. V must be always equal and opposite to the back e.m.f. E, and it is shown by the fourth curve (the thin line) in the diagram.

This demonstrates that, in an a.c. circuit containing inductance only, the voltage and current do not pass through their corresponding values simultaneously. For a pure inductance the current always lags 90° behind the voltage. The vector diagram is given in Fig. 10.10 (c) where the phase

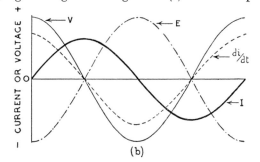

(b)

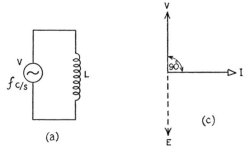

(a)   (c)

FIG. 10.10. CIRCUIT WITH PURE INDUCTANCE

angle ϕ (between the current and the voltage) equals 90°.

If the voltage is expressed by
$$v = V_{max} \sin \theta$$
the current
$$i = I_{max} \sin (\theta - \pi/2)$$

The magnitude of the current depends upon (i) the inductance and (ii) the frequency, these two factors governing the magnitude of the back-e.m.f. $e \propto - L \cdot di/dt$). The current $I = V/\omega L$ or $\omega L = V/I$. This is a form of Ohm's law and the term ωL, being the ratio V/I, is measured in ohms, if L is in henrys, V is in volts, and I in amps: it is not the usual "ohmic" or conductor resistance but it is the opposition due to the back-e.m.f. produced, and it is known as the REACTANCE. Re-

actance is defined as *the component of the applied voltage in quadrature with the current, divided by the current.* Inductive reactance is denoted by the symbol X_L so that
$$X_L = \omega L = 2\pi fL = V/I \qquad . (10.9)$$

This expression may be derived in the following manner. Since $t = 1/f$ and there are *four changes* per cycle, the time for each change is $1/4f$ seconds.

Average rate of change of current
$$di/dt = I_{max} \div 1/4f = 4fI_{max} \text{ amp/sec}$$
$$V_{av} = L \cdot di/dt = 4fI_{max}L = V_{max} \times 2/\pi$$
$$I_{max} = 2V_{max}/(4\pi fL) = V_{max}/(2\pi fL)$$
or
$$V/I = 2\pi fL$$

The component of an alternating current (or voltage) which is IN PHASE with the voltage (or current) is referred to as the ACTIVE voltage or current. The component which is in QUADRATURE is termed the REACTIVE component.

EXAMPLE 10.10 (A). Calculate the reactance, and the current flowing, when an inductor of 10 H is connected across a 110 V supply alternating at 50 c/s.
$$\omega = 2\pi 50 = 100\pi = 314 \text{ radn/sec.}$$
$$X_L = \omega L = 314 \times 10 = \underline{\underline{3\,140\ \Omega}}$$

$$I = V/X_L = 110/3\,140 = \underline{\underline{0\cdot035\ \text{A}}}$$

(The current lags 90° behind the applied voltage.)

EXAMPLE 10.11 (A). Two coils have self-inductance of 5 H and 10 H respectively. What will be their reactance at a frequency of 50 c/s when connected (a) in series, (b) in parallel? (C. & G.)
$$\omega = 2\pi f = 2\pi \times 50 = 100\pi \text{ radn/sec}$$

(a) The joint inductance of the two coils in series is
$$L = L_1 + L_2 = 5 + 10 = 15 \text{ H}$$
$$X_L = \omega L = 100\pi \times 15 = \underline{\underline{4\,710\ \Omega}}$$

(b) The joint inductance of the two coils in parallel is
$$L = L_1 L_2/(L_1 + L_2)$$
$$= (10 \times 5)/(10 + 5) = 50/15 = 3\cdot3 \text{ H}$$
$$X_L = \omega L = 100\pi \times 3\cdot3 = \underline{\underline{1\,045\ \Omega}}$$

EXAMPLE 10.12 (A). What would be the effective (r.m.s.) value of the current through a coil of 20 mH and of negligible resistance if connected across the voltage supply $e = 100 \sin 5\,000t$? (C. & G.)

From $e = 100 \sin 5\,000t$, $E_{max} = 100$ V and
$$\omega = 5\,000 \text{ radn/sec}$$
$$E = 0\cdot707 \times 100 = 70\cdot7 \text{ V}$$
$$X_L = \omega L = 5\,000 \times 20 \times 10^{-3} = 100\ \Omega$$
$$I = E/X_L = 70\cdot7/100 = \underline{\underline{0\cdot707\ \text{A}}}$$

10.10. Circuit with Pure Capacitance. Before proceeding to a fuller investigation of the current of Fig. 10.11(a), where a p.d. of V volts at a frequency f c/s is maintained across a capacitance C farads, it is desirable to consider the nature of the circuit current. The current flowing "through" a capacitor is a fairly common expression, but, apart from the small leakage current, an alternating current is unable to flow through a dielectric. In the a.c. circuit, as the voltage rises the capacitor charges up until its p.d. reaches the peak value of the generator voltage. Subsequently the capacitor discharges, recharges with opposite polarity, and after again discharging the cycle is repeated. The circuit current consists of alternate charging, discharging, and recharging currents.

In Fig. 10.11 (b), the applied voltage V, the rate of change of charge, dq/dt, and the current I are shown in their phase relationships. At the instant when the applied voltage commences to rise positively from zero, the rate at which the voltage changes (i.e. the slope of the voltage curve) is a maximum. Since the charge Q is proportional to the voltage V for a constant value of capacitance C ($C = Q/V$), the rate of increase of the charge is also a maximum at this instant; in other words, the current has its maximum value when the voltage is passing through a zero value. As the voltage rises, the rates at which both voltage and charge increase diminishes and the current falls. When the voltage is no longer increasing, having reached its maximum value, the current is zero. As the voltage falls, the charge decreases resulting in a discharging or reversed current; the voltage falling at an ever-increasing rate results in an increase of current which reaches its maximum value as the voltage falls to zero. This procedure is repeated with change of sign in the next half-cycle and it will be seen that with a pure capacitance the current (the thick line) passes through all its values 90° ahead of the corresponding voltage changes (the thin line).

Summarizing the above, for a sinusoidal voltage curve ($v = V_{max} \sin \omega t$), the rate of change of voltage gives a cosine curve. The rate of change of charge (dq/dt) is a cosine curve because V is proportional to Q, and since $I = Q/t$, the curve for the current i is also a cosine curve, leading the voltage sine curve by 90°.

As the charge builds up on the capacitor its p.d. at every instant is equal but of opposite polarity to that of the applied p.d. For a pure capacitance the current always leads the applied voltage by 90°. The vector diagram is given in Fig. 10.11 (c) showing the phase angle ($\phi = 90°$) between voltage and current.

If the voltage is expressed by

$$v = V_{max} \sin \theta$$

the current equation is

$$i = I_{max} \sin (\theta + \pi/2)$$

The ratio of voltage to current, $V/I = X_C$, is the CAPACITIVE REACTANCE. This reactance $X_C = -1/(\omega C)$ ohms, where C is in *farads*. The form of Ohm's law for this circuit is—

$$I = V/X_C = -V\omega C = -2\pi f C V$$
$$\text{or} \qquad V = I X_C = -I/(\omega C) \qquad . \qquad . \quad (10.10)$$

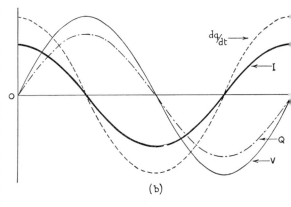

(b)

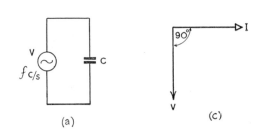

(a)   (c)

FIG. 10.11. CIRCUIT WITH PURE CAPACITANCE

Capacitive reactance is regarded as negative (the voltage lags by 90°) to distinguish it from inductive reactance, which is positive (voltage leads by 90°).

This expression for reactance may be derived in the following manner.

The charge $Q_{max} = C V_{max}$.

The *total* change of charge $= 4C V_{max}$ per cycle (four changes).

At f c/s ($= 1/t$), the charge per second $= 4fC V_{max}$ (coulombs per second), $I_{av} = 4fC V_{max}$.

$$\text{But} \qquad I_{av} = \left(\frac{2}{\pi}\right) \times I_{max}$$

$$\text{or} \qquad I_{max} = I_{av} \times \left(\frac{\pi}{2}\right)$$

e. $$I_{max} = 4fCV_{max} \times \pi/2 = 2\pi fC V_{max}$$

nd (r.m.s.) $I = 2\pi fCV$

r $$X_C = V/I = \frac{1}{2\pi fC}$$

It should be noted that in a.c. circuits, the reactance, and accordingly the current, will depend upon the frequency as well as upon the other factors L and C (and V).

EXAMPLE 10.13 (A). What is the reactance of a 2 μF capacitor at (i) 50 c/s, (ii) 800 c/s, and (iii) what current flows when this capacitor is connected across a 230 V, 50 c/s supply?

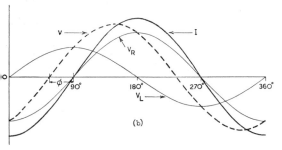

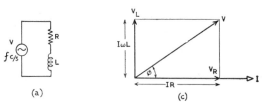

FIG. 10.12. CIRCUIT WITH RESISTANCE AND INDUCTANCE IN SERIES

(i) $\omega = 2\pi f = 2\pi 50 = 314$ radn/sec

$X_C = 10^6/(314 \times 2) = 1\ 592\ \Omega$

(ii) $\omega = 2\pi 800 \simeq 5\ 000$ radn/sec

$X_C = 10^6/(2 \times 5 \times 10^3) = \underline{100\ \Omega}$

(iii) $I = V/X_C = 230/1\ 592 = \underline{0\cdot 144\ A}$

(The voltage lags 90° behind the current.)

EXAMPLE 10.14 (A). What would be the result of connecting a capacitor of 5 μF across a 250 V, 50 c/s a.c. supply? (C. & G.)

$\omega = 2\pi f = 100\pi$ radn/sec

$X_C = 1/(\omega C) = 10^6/(100\pi \times 5) = 2\ 000/\pi$

$I = V/X_C = 250\pi/2\ 000 = \underline{0\cdot 393\ A}$

EXAMPLE 10.15 (A). An alternating voltage defined by the expression $e = 200 \sin 100\ \pi t$ is applied across a capacitor of 0·5 μF. What is (a) the voltage to which the capacitor is charged 1/30 sec after switching on, (b) the energy stored in the capacitor when the voltage across it attains its maximum value? (C. & G.)

(a) At $t = 1/30$ sec

$v = 200 \sin (100\pi/30$ radn)

$100\pi/30$ radn $= (100\pi/30) \times (180/\pi)$ degrees

$= 600° = 360° + 240°$

$v = 200 \sin 240° = 200 \sin 60°$

$= 200 \times 0\cdot 866 = \underline{173\cdot 2\ V}$

(b) $V_{max} = 200$

$W = CV^2/2$

$= \frac{1}{2} \times 0\cdot 5 \times 10^{-6} \times 2^2 \times 10^4 = 10^{-2}$

$= \underline{0\cdot 01\ J}$

SERIES CIRCUITS

10.11. Resistance and Inductance in Series. In Fig. 10.12 (a) the resistance R ohms is the total circuit resistance including the conductor resistance of the inductor L henrys, with which it acts in series. The circuit current is I amperes resulting from an applied p.d. V volts at a frequency f c/s.

The applied voltage V may be considered as being made up of two components, (i) it must maintain a p.d. across the resistance and this p.d. $V_R = IR$ is in phase with the current, (ii) it must maintain across the inductance a p.d. $V_L = IX_L = I\omega L$: this p.d. leads the current by 90°.

These two voltage components V_R and V_L, having a phase difference of 90°, are shown in the vector diagram (Fig. 10.12 (c)): the applied voltage V is the vector sum of these two components and has the phase angle ϕ with respect to the circuit current.

For a circuit comprising resistance and inductance only, the phase angle must always lie between the values 0° (if $L = 0$) and 90° (if $R = 0$), the current always lagging behind the applied voltage.

The current and p.d.s may be calculated as follows*—

$$V = (V_R^2 + V_L^2)^{\frac{1}{2}} = V_R + jV_L$$
$$= \{(IR)^2 + (\omega LI)^2\}^{\frac{1}{2}} = IR + j\omega LI$$
$$= I(R^2 + \omega^2 L^2)^{\frac{1}{2}} = I(R + j\omega L)$$

and $I = V/(R^2 + (\omega L)^2)^{\frac{1}{2}} = V/(R + j\omega L)$ (10.11)

The vector sum of the resistance and reactance,

$$(R^2 + \omega^2 L^2)^{\frac{1}{2}} = R + j\omega L$$

is termed the *impedance*.

* For the use of "j" see Appendix **A.4.**

The phase angle ϕ by which the current lags behind the voltage is calculated from the construction of Fig. 10.12 (c):

$$\tan \phi = I X_L /(IR) = \omega L / R$$

or in the more usual notation,

$$\phi = \tan^{-1} \omega L / R$$

The phase differences are shown from the graphs in Fig. 10.12 (b) for the p.d.s V_R and V_L which are $90°$ out of phase; the current I which is in phase

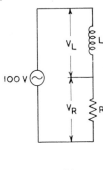

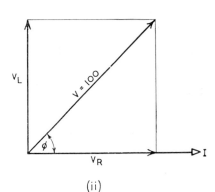

(i)

(ii)

FIG. 10.13 (Example 10.17)

with V_R; and the applied voltage V which leads the current by the angle ϕ.

EXAMPLE 10.16 (B). The operating coil of a relay, having an inductance of 8 mH and a resistance of 30 Ω is connected across a 5 V, 800 c/s a.c. supply. What would be the current through the coil and the phase angle of the current relative to the applied voltage? (C. & G.)

The relay may be regarded as being made up of a resistance and inductance connected in series.

$$\omega = 2\pi f = 2\pi \cdot 800 \simeq 5\,000 \text{ radn/sec}$$
$$X = \omega L = 5\,000 \times 8 \times 10^{-3} = 40 \ \Omega$$
$$I = V/(R^2 + X^2)^{\frac{1}{2}} = 5/(30^2 + 40^2)^{\frac{1}{2}} = 5/50$$
$$= 0 \cdot 1 \text{ A}$$

$$\phi = \tan^{-1} X_L/R = \tan^{-1} 40/30 = \tan^{-1} 1 \cdot 3$$
$$= 53° \ 8' \text{ (lagging)}$$

EXAMPLE 10.17 (B). The voltage across a circuit consisting of an inductance and a resistance in series is 100 V. If the resulting voltage across each of the components is the same, what is the value of this voltage? Explain your answer by means of a diagram. (C. & G.)

Using the symbols in the circuit diagram Fig. 10.13 (i), since $V_L = V_R$

$$V = (V_R^2 + V_L^2)^{\frac{1}{2}} = \sqrt{2} \cdot V_R = 100$$
$$V_R = 100/\sqrt{2} = 100\sqrt{2}/2 = 70 \cdot 7 \text{ V}$$

FIG. 10.13 (ii) shows the required diagram.

EXAMPLE 10.18 (B). A ringing machine has a virtual voltage of 75 at a frequency of 16 c/s. The machine is applied to an electromagnet having an effective resistance of 40 Ω and an inductance of 2 H. What is the virtual current? Calculate the time lag between the current and the e.m.f. (C. & G.)

$$\omega = 2\pi f = 32\pi = 100$$
$$X_L = \omega L = 100 \times 2 = 200 \ \Omega$$
$$I = V/(R^2 + X_L^2)^{\frac{1}{2}} = 75/(40^2 + 200^2)^{\frac{1}{2}}$$
$$= 75/41\,600^{\frac{1}{2}} = 75/204 = 0 \cdot 367 \text{ A}$$

$$\phi = \tan^{-1} X_L/R = \tan^{-1} 200/40$$
$$= \tan^{-1} 5 = 79°$$
$$T = 1/f = 1/16 \text{ sec for } 360°$$
time for $79° = 1/16 \times 79/360$
$$= 0 \cdot 014 \text{ sec}$$

10.12. Resistance and Capacitance in Series.

circuit comprising a resistor R ohms in series with a capacitor C farads connected across a source of supply V volts at a frequency of f c/s is shown in Fig. 10.14 (a): the resistor R may include the equivalent insulation resistance of the capacitor.

To maintain a current of I amperes the applied voltage must provide two components, (i) a voltage $V_R = IR$ across the resistance, and in phase with the current, and (ii) a voltage $V_C = IX_C = -I/(\omega C)$ lagging $90°$ behind the current. These two components V_R and V_C having a phase difference of $90°$ are shown in the vector diagram Fig. 10.14 (c). The applied voltage V is the vector sum of these two components and has the phase angle ϕ with respect to the circuit current.

For a circuit comprising resistance and capacitance only, the phase angle must always lie between the values $0°$ (if $C = 0$) and $-90°$ (if $R = 0$), the current changes leading the applied voltage.

The current and p.d.s may be calculated as follows—

$$V = (V_R^2 + V_C^2)^{\frac{1}{2}} \qquad = V_R - jV_C$$

$$= \left\{ (IR)^2 + \left(-\frac{I}{\omega C}\right)^2 \right\}^{\frac{1}{2}} = IR - jI/(\omega C)$$

$$= I\left\{ R^2 + \left(-\frac{1}{\omega C}\right)^2 \right\}^{\frac{1}{2}} = I\{R - j/(\omega C)\}$$

$$I = V / \left\{ R^2 + \left(-\frac{1}{\omega C}\right)^2 \right\}^{\frac{1}{2}} = V/\{R - j/(\omega C)\} \tag{10.12}$$

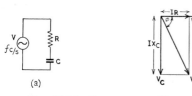

(b)

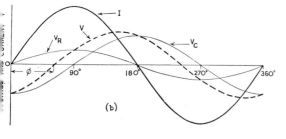

(a)

(c)

FIG. 10.14. CIRCUIT WITH RESISTANCE AND CAPACITANCE IN SERIES

The vector sum of the resistance and reactance

$$\left\{ R^2 + \left(-\frac{1}{\omega C}\right)^2 \right\}^{\frac{1}{2}} = \{R - j/(\omega C)\}$$

is termed the *impedance*. The term $(-j/(\omega C))$ may be multiplied by $j/j(= 1)$, producing $(-j^2/(j\omega C))$: since $-j^2$ is equal to $+1$, this impedance may be written as $\{R + 1/(j\omega C)\}$.

The phase angle ϕ by which the current leads the applied voltage is calculated from Fig. 10.14 (c):

$$\tan \phi = IX_C/(IR) = -1/(\omega CR)$$
$$\text{or} \qquad \phi = \tan^{-1}\{-1/(\omega CR)\}$$

the angle being always negative.

The phase differences are shown in Fig. 10.14 (b) for the p.d.s V_R and V_C which are 90° out of phase; the current I which is in phase with V_R; and the applied voltage V which lags behind the current by the angle ϕ.

EXAMPLE 10.19 (B). A circuit consists of a capacitor of μF and a resistance of 200 Ω connected across a supply

of 1·0 V at 800 c/s. Calculate (i) the reactance, (ii) the phase angle, (iii) the current flowing, (iv) the p.d. across the resistance, (v) the p.d. across the capacitor.

$$\omega = 2\pi f = 2\pi \cdot 800 \simeq 5\,000 \text{ radn/sec}$$

(i) $X_C = 1/(\omega C) = 10^6/(2 \times 5\,000) = \underline{100\ \Omega}$

(ii) $\phi = \tan^{-1} X_C/R = \tan^{-1} - 1/(\omega CR)$
$$= \tan^{-1} - 100/200 = \underline{-27°}$$

(iii) $I = V/(R^2 + X_C^2)^{\frac{1}{2}} = 1/(200^2 + 100^2)^{\frac{1}{2}}$
$$= 1/223 = \underline{0·004\,4 \text{ A}}$$

(iv) $V_R = IR = 0·004\,4 \times 200 = \underline{0·88 \text{ V}}$

(in phase with the current)

(v) $V_C = IX_C = 0·004\,4 \times 100 = \underline{0·44 \text{ V}}$

(lagging 90° on the current)

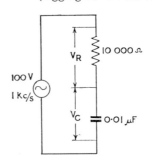

(i)

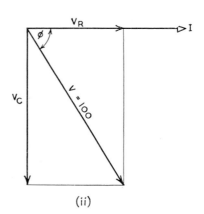

(ii)

FIG. 10.15 (Example 10.20)

EXAMPLE 10.20 (B). A resistor of 10 000 Ω and a capacitor of 0·01 μF are connected in series. If 100 V at a frequency of 1 kc/s are applied across the circuit, what is the drop of potential across (a) the resistor, and (b) the capacitor? Find the value of the tangent of the angle between the applied voltage and the voltage across the resistance. (C. & G.)

$$\omega = 2\pi f = 2\pi \,.\, 10^3$$

$$X_C = 1/(\omega C) = 10^6/(2\pi \times 10^3 \times 0.01)$$
$$= 10^5/2\pi = 1.59 \times 10^4$$

$$I = V/(R^2 + X_C{}^2)^{\frac{1}{2}}$$
$$= 100/\{10^8 + (1.59 \times 10^4)^2\}^{\frac{1}{2}}$$
$$= 100/\{10^8 + (2.53 \times 10^8)\}^{\frac{1}{2}}$$
$$= 100/\{10^8(1 + 2.53)\}^{\frac{1}{2}}$$
$$= 100/\{10^4 \times (3.53)^{\frac{1}{2}}\} = 1/188$$
$$= 0.005\ 3 \text{ A}$$

(a) P.d. across resistor

$$= V_R = IR = 0.005\ 3 \times 10^4 = \underline{\underline{53 \text{ V}}}$$

(b) P.d. across capacitor

$$= V_C = IX_C = 0.005\ 3 \times 1.59 \times 10^4$$
$$= \underline{\underline{84.5 \text{ V}}}$$

(c) Tan ϕ (see vector diagram Fig. 10.15)

$$= V_C/V_R = 84.5/53 = \underline{\underline{1.59}}$$

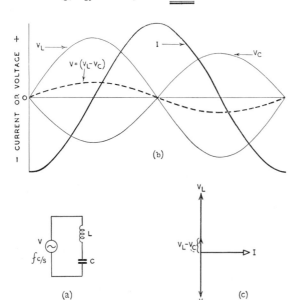

(b)

(a)

(c)

FIG. 10.16. CIRCUIT WITH INDUCTANCE AND CAPACITANCE IN SERIES

10.13. Inductance and Capacitance in Series. The circuit diagram for this case is shown at Fig. 10.16 (a) and the vector diagram at 10.16 (c).

The p.d.s across the inductance ($V_L = IX_L$) and capacitance ($V_C = -IX_C$), being respectively $+ 90°$ and $- 90°$ out of phase with the current can be added algebraically and the applied voltage

$$V = V_L - V_C = IX_L - IX_C$$
$$= I(X_L - X_C) = I\{\omega L - 1/(\omega C)\}$$

The current

$$I = V/(X_L - X_C)$$
$$= V/\{\omega L - 1/(\omega C)\} \qquad . \qquad . \ (10.13)$$

The phase angle is either $+ 90°$ (if $\omega L - 1/(\omega C)$ is positive) or $- 90°$ (if $\omega L - 1/(\omega C)$ is negative).

The graphs are shown at Fig. 10.16 (b).

10.14. Impedance. The vector sum of the resistance and reactance in a circuit is termed the IMPEDANCE, which is defined as *the ratio of the r.m.s. e.m.f. in a circuit to the r.m.s. current which is produced thereby*. The symbol for impedance is Z and it is measured in ohms. Thus

$$Z = (R^2 + X^2)^{\frac{1}{2}} = R + jX$$

where X is the algebraic sum of X_L and X_C so that the full expression for impedance is

$$Z = \left\{ R^2 + \left(\omega L - \frac{1}{\omega C} \right)^2 \right\}^{\frac{1}{2}}$$
$$= R + j\{\omega L - 1/(\omega C)\}$$

The impedance of any portion of a circuit may also be determined by adding vectorially the appropriate values of R and X.

The full statement of an impedance must include its phase angle, which may have a value of $\pm 90°$ or any intermediate value, as well as its magnitude. An impedance is usually written in the form $Z\underline{/\phi}$ if ϕ is positive (inductive circuit), or as $Z\overline{\backslash \phi}$ if ϕ is a negative angle (capacitive circuit).

For the a.c. circuit the complete expression of Ohm's law is

$$I = V/Z, \text{ or } V = IZ, \text{ or } Z = V/I \quad (10.14)$$

This expression is the same as for the d.c. circuit writing Z instead of R: it should be noted that Z is dependent upon frequency as well as upon the values of R, L, and C.

An impedance Z together with its two components R and X can be represented by the sides of a right-angled triangle, termed the *impedance triangle*. The impedance triangle is formed by drawing to scale two sides at right angles to represent the values of R (horizontally) and X (vertically) and completing the third side which represents the impedance Z to the same scale (Fig

10.17): the angle ϕ is the phase angle. Alternatively the triangle may be constructed from a knowledge of the appropriate three dimensions—sides or angles—which determine a triangle. The two cases are illustrated in Fig. 10.17 for (a) positive angle (X_L drawn vertically upward), and (b) negative angle (X_C drawn vertically downward). Using the trigonometrical solutions for triangles, any of the unknown circuit elements—impedance,

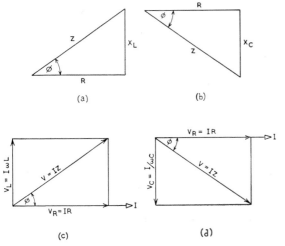

reactance, etc.—can be calculated from sufficient data.

The sides of the impedance triangle are parallel to the corresponding voltage vectors: the sides of the triangle are in fact obtained by dividing each of the voltages V, V_R, and V_X by the common series current I. The voltage vector diagrams are shown for reference at (c) and (d) in Fig. 10.17.

The impedance of an inductor increases with the frequency: at high frequencies the resistance may become negligible in comparison with the reactance.

The dielectric resistance of a capacitor acts in shunt with the capacitance, though its effect may be replaced by an equivalent series resistance (see Example 10.51) giving the same impedance and phase angle. The impedance of a capacitor falls as the frequency increases: at very high frequencies quite low values of self-capacitance provide low-impedance (shunt) paths which are usually undesirable and whose elimination necessitates special consideration in the practical design of equipment.

EXAMPLE 10.21 (B). A certain telephone receiver has an impedance of 400 Ω with an angle of lag of 70° when an alternating current with a frequency of 800 c/s is passing. Calculate the effective resistance and inductance at this frequency. (C. & G.)

See the impedance triangle in Fig. 10.18.
$$\omega = 2\pi f = 2\pi . 800 \simeq 5\,000 \text{ radn/sec}$$
$$\omega L = Z \sin \phi$$
$$5\,000\,L = 400 \sin 70 = 400 \times 0.939\,7$$
$$L = 400 \times 0.939\,7/5\,000 = 0.075 \text{ H}$$

$$R = 400 \cos 70 = 400 \times 0.342$$
$$= 136.8 \,\Omega$$

EXAMPLE 10.22 (B). When an alternating voltage of 10 V at a frequency of 500 c/s is applied across an iron-cored coil having an inductance of 0·1 H the current is found to lag behind the applied voltage by 81°. With the aid of a vector diagram determine the effective resistance of the coil and the value of the current. (C. & G.)

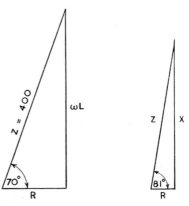

FIG. 10.18 (Example 10.21) FIG. 10.19 (Example 10.22)

$$\omega = 2\pi f = 2\pi . 500 = 3\,146 \text{ radn/sec}$$
$$X = \omega L = 3\,146 \times 0.1 = 314.6 \,\Omega$$

From the impedance triangle given in Fig. 10.19,
$$R = 314.6/\tan 81° = 314.6/6.313\,8 = 49.75 \,\Omega$$

$$Z = 314.6/\sin 81° = 314.6/0.987\,7 = 318 \,\Omega$$
$$I = V/Z = 10/318 = 0.031\,4 \text{ A}$$

EXAMPLE 10.23 (B). The impedance of a series circuit consisting of a resistor and an inductor is 200 Ω when the frequency is 500 kc/s. If the value of the resistance is 100 Ω, what is the value of the inductance? (C. & G.)

$$Z^2 = R^2 + X^2, \quad 200^2 = 100^2 + X^2$$
$$X^2 = (4 \times 10^4) - (1 \times 10^4) = 3 \times 10^4$$
$$X = 10^2 . \sqrt{3} = 173.2 \,\Omega$$
$$X = 2\pi f L$$
$$L = X/(2\pi f)$$
$$= 173.2 \times 10^6/(6.28 \times 5 \times 10^5) \ (L \text{ in } \mu H)$$
$$= 1\,732/31.4 = 55.1 \,\mu H$$

EXAMPLE 10.24 (B). The impedance of a certain relay at 796 frequency is increased from $7\,780/54°$ to $19\,290/72°$ by fitting nickel sleeves over the core. Calculate the inductance and the effective resistance of the relay with and without the sleeves. (*C. & G.*)

See the impedance triangles in Fig. 10.20.

$$\omega = 2\pi f = 2\pi \,.\, 796 \simeq 5\,000 \text{ radn/sec}$$

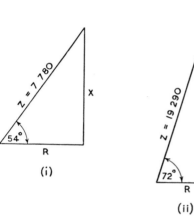

FIG. 10.20 (Example 10.24)

(i) *Without sleeves.*

$$\omega L = 7\,780 \sin 54°$$
$$L = 7\,780 \times 0·809\,0/5\,000 = \underline{1·259 \text{ H}}$$

$$R = 7\,780 \cos 54° = 7\,780 \times 0·587\,8$$
$$= \underline{4\,573 \ \Omega}$$

(ii) *With sleeves.*

$$\omega L = 19\,290 \times \sin 72°$$
$$L = 19\,290 \times 0·951\,1/5\,000 = \underline{3·667 \text{ H}}$$

$$R = 19\,290 \cos 72° = 19\,290 \times 0·309\,0$$
$$= \underline{5\,960 \ \Omega}$$

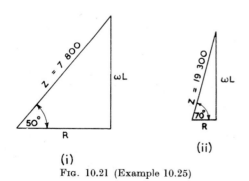

FIG. 10.21 (Example 10.25)

EXAMPLE 10.25 (B). The impedance of a relay, as measured at 796 c/s (i.e. 5 000 radn/sec) was increased from $7\,800/50°$ to $19\,300/70°$ by the use of three nickel iron sleeves. Calculate the corresponding values of the inductance. (*C. & G.*)

See the impedance triangles in Fig. 10.21.

$$\omega = 5\,000$$

(*a*) $\omega L_1 = 7\,800 \sin 50°$
$$L_1 = 7\,800 \times 0·766/5\,000 = \underline{1·2 \text{ H}}$$

(*b*) $L_2 = 19\,300 \times \sin 70°/5\,000$
$$= 19\,300 \times 0·939\,7/5\,000 = \underline{3·63 \text{ H}}$$

EXAMPLE 10.26 (B). A circuit consists of a resistance of 100 Ω in series with an inductance. When the frequency of an applied voltage changes from 200 kc/s to 500 kc/s, the impedance doubles in value. Calculate the value of the inductance. (*C. & G.*)

At $f = 200$ kc/s, $\omega_1 = 4\pi \times 10^5$ radn/sec
At $f = 500$ kc/s, $\omega_2 = 10\pi \times 10^5$ radn/sec
$$Z_1 = (R^2 + \omega_1^2 L^2)^{\frac{1}{2}}$$
$$Z_2 = (R^2 + \omega_2^2 L^2)^{\frac{1}{2}}$$
But $$Z_2 = 2Z_1$$
$$R^2 + \omega_2^2 L^2 = 4R^2 + 4\omega_1^2 L^2$$
$$L^2(\omega_2^2 - 4\omega_1^2) = 3R^2$$
$$L^2 = 3R^2/(\omega_2^2 - 4\omega_1^2) = 3 \times 10^4/\{(100\pi^2 \times 10^{10})$$
$$- (4 \times 16\pi^2 \times 10^{10})\}$$
$$= 3 \times 10^4/(36\pi^2 \times 10^{10})$$
$$L = (\sqrt{3} \times 10^2 \times 10^6)/(6\pi \times 10^5) \ \mu\text{H}$$
$$= 1\,732/6\pi = \underline{93 \ \mu\text{H}}$$

EXAMPLE 10.27 (B). Draw an impedance triangle approximately to scale for a circuit having resistance and inductance which, when connected to 200 V a.c. mains,

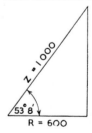

FIG. 10.22 (Example 10.27)

takes a current of 200 mA and absorbs 24 W. If the frequency of the supply is 50 c/s, what is the inductance of the circuit? (*C. & G.*)

$$Z = V/I = 200/0·2 = 1\,000 \ \Omega$$
$$P = I^2 R$$
$$R = P/I^2 = 24/0·2^2 = 24/0·04$$
$$= 600 \ \Omega$$
$$\phi = \cos^{-1} R/Z = \cos^{-1} 600/1\,000 = \cos^{-1} 0·6$$
$$= 53° \ 8'$$

The impedance triangle is drawn approximately to scale for the sides 600 and 1 000 and the included angle 53° 8′. (See Fig. 10.22.)

$$X_L = (Z^2 - R^2)^{\frac{1}{2}} = (1\ 000^2 - 600^2)^{\frac{1}{2}} = 800\ \Omega$$

(This value may be read off the scaled triangle.)

$$X_L = \omega L$$
$$L = X_L/\omega = 800/(2\pi \cdot 50)$$
$$= 800/314 = \underline{2 \cdot 54}\ \mathrm{H}$$

EXAMPLE 10.28 (B). A coil of constant inductance is connected to an alternating supply at a frequency of 50 c/s and the current flowing is noted. When a 2 μF capacitor, of negligible resistance, is joined in series with the coil the value of the current is the same as before. Calculate the inductance of the coil.

If the coil has a resistance of 80 Ω, find the total impedance of the circuit. (C. & G.)

With the coil only, impedance $= (R^2 + \omega^2 L^2)^{\frac{1}{2}}$
With the coil and capacitor, impedance

$$= \left\{ R^2 + \left(\omega L - \frac{1}{\omega C} \right)^2 \right\}^{\frac{1}{2}}$$

Since the current is the same in the two cases,

$$\left\{ R^2 + \left(\omega L - \frac{1}{\omega C} \right)^2 \right\}^{\frac{1}{2}} = (R^2 + \omega^2 L^2)^{\frac{1}{2}}$$

whence

$$\omega^2 L^2 = \{ \omega L - 1/(\omega C) \}^2$$
$$\text{and}\quad \omega L = \pm \{ \omega L - 1/(\omega C) \}$$

The positive root is inadmissible, because $1/(\omega C)$ is not equal to zero.

$$\omega L = - \{ \omega L - 1/(\omega C) \}, \quad 2\omega L = 1/(\omega C)$$
$$L = 1/(2\omega^2 C) = 10^6/(2 \times 100^2 \pi^2 \times 2)$$
$$= 10^6/(10^4 \times 4\pi^2) = 25/\pi^2 = \underline{2 \cdot 532}\ \mathrm{H}$$

$$Z = \left\{ R^2 + \left(\omega L - \frac{1}{\omega C} \right)^2 \right\}^{\frac{1}{2}} = \{ R^2 + (-\omega L)^2 \}^{\frac{1}{2}}$$
$$= (R^2 + \omega^2 L^2)^{\frac{1}{2}}$$
$$= \{ 80^2 + (314 \times 2 \cdot 532)^2 \}^{\frac{1}{2}} = (80^2 + 795^2)^{\frac{1}{2}}$$
$$= 800\ \Omega$$

$$\phi = \tan^{-1} \omega L/R = \tan^{-1} 795/80 = \tan^{-1} 9 \cdot 937$$
$$= 84° \text{ (negative since } X \text{ is negative)}$$

Impedance $= \underline{800\backslash 84°}$

EXAMPLE 10.29 (B). A circuit consisting of a resistance of 50 Ω, an inductance of 10 H, and a capacitance of 1 μF in series is found to pass 1 A with a certain applied e.m.f.

alternating at 50 c/s. What will it pass with the same e.m.f. alternating at 100 c/s? (C. & G.)

$$\omega_1 = 100\pi\ \mathrm{radn/sec}$$
$$Z = \left\{ R^2 + \left(\omega L - \frac{1}{\omega C} \right)^2 \right\}^{\frac{1}{2}}$$
$$Z_{50} = \{ 50^2 + (3\ 142 - 10^6/314 \cdot 2)^2 \}^{\frac{1}{2}}$$
$$= (50^2 + 41^2)^{\frac{1}{2}} = 63\ \Omega$$
$$\omega_2 = 200\pi\ \mathrm{radn/sec}$$
$$Z_{100} = \{ 50^2 + (6\ 283 - 10^6/628 \cdot 3)^2 \}^{\frac{1}{2}}$$
$$= (50^2 + 4\ 692^2)^{\frac{1}{2}} = 4\ 693\ \Omega$$

Since V is constant, $I \propto 1/Z$,

$$I_{50}/I_{100} = Z_{100}/Z_{50}$$
$$I_{100} = I_{50} \times Z_{50}/Z_{100} = 1 \times 63/4\ 693$$
$$= 0 \cdot 013\ 4\ \mathrm{A}$$

10.15. Resistance, Inductance, and Capacitance in Series.

The general case of the a.c. series circuit is shown in Fig. 10.23 (a). The applied voltage has the three components (i) $V_R = IR$, across the resistance R and in phase with the current I; (ii) $V_L = I\omega L$ across the inductance L, leading the current by 90°; (iii) $V_C = -I/(\omega C)$ across the capacitance C, lagging 90° behind the current (Fig. 10.23 (b)).

The two latter components V_L and V_C being relatively 180° out of phase, with their vectors lying in the same straight line, may be treated algebraically: the total reactance voltage V_X is equal to their algebraic sum, or $V_X = V_L - V_C$. There are three possible results from this. (i) If $V_L > V_C$, V_X is positive and ϕ is positive, lying between 0° and 90°: this vector diagram is shown in Fig. 10.23 (c). (ii) If $V_L < V_C$, V_X is negative and ϕ is negative, lying between 0° and $-90°$: this vector diagram is shown in Fig. 10.23 (d). (iii) If $V_L = V_C$, $V_X = 0$ and $\phi = 0$: this special case of *resonance* is discussed in §10.17.

The applied voltage V

$$= (V_R^2 + V_X^2)^{\frac{1}{2}}$$
$$= \{ V_R^2 + (V_L - V_C)^2 \}^{\frac{1}{2}} = V_R + j(V_L - V_C)$$
$$= \left\{ (IR)^2 + \left(I\omega L - \frac{I}{\omega C} \right)^2 \right\}^{\frac{1}{2}}$$
$$= \left\{ IR + jI \left(\omega L - \frac{1}{\omega C} \right) \right\}$$
$$= I \left\{ R^2 + \left(\omega L - \frac{1}{\omega C} \right)^2 \right\}^{\frac{1}{2}}$$
$$= I \left\{ R + j \left(\omega L - \frac{1}{\omega C} \right) \right\}$$

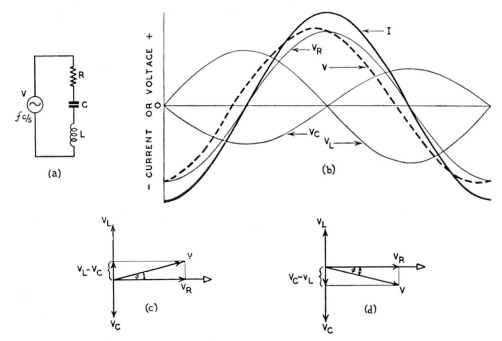

(a)

(b)

(c)   (d)

FIG. 10.23. CIRCUIT WITH RESISTANCE, INDUCTANCE, AND CAPACITANCE IN SERIES

The final expression within the brackets is the IMPEDANCE,

$$Z = \left\{R^2 + \left(\omega L - \frac{1}{\omega C}\right)^2\right\}^{\frac{1}{2}}$$

$$= R + j\{\omega L - 1/(\omega C)\} \qquad . \quad (10.15)$$

and the current

$$I = V/Z = V/\left\{R^2 + \left(\omega L - \frac{1}{\omega C}\right)^2\right\}^{\frac{1}{2}}$$

$$= V/\left\{R + j\left(\omega L - \frac{1}{\omega C}\right)\right\}$$

The phase angle ϕ by which the current leads or lags behind the voltage is

$$\phi = \tan^{-1} X/R = \tan^{-1}(X_L - X_C)/R$$

$$= \tan^{-1}\{\omega L - 1/(\omega C)\}/R \qquad . \qquad (10.16)$$

The phase angle is $+ 90°$ if $R = C = 0$; is 0 if $\omega L = 1/(\omega C)$; is $- 90°$ if $R = L = 0$; is positive if $\omega L > 1/(\omega C)$; and negative if $\omega L < 1/(\omega C)$.

EXAMPLE 10.30 (B). A capacitor of 2 μF, a resistor of 50 Ω, and an inductor of 6 H are connected in series. What current will flow when an e.m.f. of 200 V r.m.s. at 50 c/s is applied to the circuit?   (C. & G.)

$$I = V/\left\{R^2 + \left(\omega L - \frac{1}{\omega C}\right)^2\right\}^{\frac{1}{2}}$$

$$\omega L = 100\pi \times 6 = 600\pi \ \Omega$$

$1/(\omega C) = 10^6/(2 \times 100\pi) = 10^4/2\pi \ \Omega$

$$I = 200/\{50^2 + (600\pi - 10^4/2\pi)^2\}^{\frac{1}{2}}$$

$$= 200/\{50^2 + (1\ 885 - 1\ 592)^2\}^{\frac{1}{2}}$$

$$= 200/297 = \underline{\underline{0{\cdot}674 \text{ A}}}$$

$$\phi = \tan^{-1} X/R = \tan^{-1} 293/50$$

$$= \tan^{-1} 5{\cdot}86 = \underline{\underline{80° \ 18'}} \ \text{(current lagging}$$
since $X_L > X_C$)

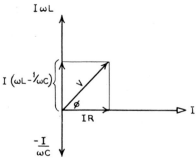

FIG. 10.24 (Example 10.30)

EXAMPLE 10.31 (B). A circuit containing capacitance C, inductance L, and resistance R all in series, is connected to an alternating supply of e.m.f. E. Derive an expression for the current in the circuit, and give its value when $C = 100 \ \mu$F, $L = 2$ H, $R = 100 \ \Omega$, and $E = 1\ 400$ V and the supply frequency is $100/2\pi$ c/s.   (C. & G.)

The current

$$I = E \Big/ \left\{ R^2 + \left(\omega L - \frac{1}{\omega C} \right)^2 \right\}^{\frac{1}{2}}$$

(see §**10.15** for derivation)

$$\omega = 2\pi f = 2\pi \times 100/2\pi = 100 \text{ radn/sec}$$
$$\omega L = 100 \times 2 = 200 \ \Omega$$
$$1/(\omega C) = 10^6/(100 \times 100) = 100 \ \Omega$$
$$I = 1\ 400/\{10^4 + (200 - 100)^2\}^{\frac{1}{2}}$$
$$= 1\ 400/(10^4 + 10^4)^{\frac{1}{2}} = 1\ 400/(100\sqrt{2})$$
$$= 14\sqrt{2}/2 = \underline{\underline{9 \cdot 89 \text{ A}}}$$

$$\phi = \tan^{-1} 100/100 = \tan^{-1} 1 = \underline{\underline{45°}}$$

(current lagging, since $\omega L > 1/(\omega C)$)

EXAMPLE 10.32 (B). A coil having an inductance of 1 mH and a resistance of 5 Ω is connected in series with a capacitor of 10 μF. What would be the current flowing through this circuit if an a.c. voltage of 100 V is applied having a frequency of (i) 5 000/2π c/s, (ii) 10 000/2π c/s? (C. & G.)

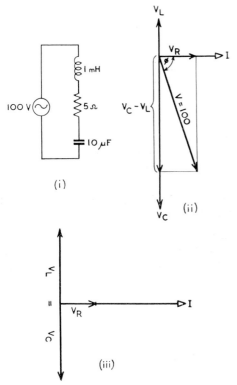

FIG. 10.25 (Example 10.32)

(i) (See diagram (ii) of Fig. 10.25)
$$\omega = 2\pi f = 2\pi \times 5\ 000/2\pi$$
$$= 5 \times 10^3 \text{ radn/sec}$$
$$X_L = \omega L = 5 \times 10^3 \times 10^{-3} = 5 \ \Omega$$

$$X_C = 1/(\omega C) = 10^6/(5 \times 10^3 \times 10) = 20 \ \Omega$$
$$R = 5 \ \Omega$$
$$I = V/\{R^2 + (X_L - X_C)^2\}^{\frac{1}{2}}$$
$$= 100/\{5^2 + (5 - 20)^2\}^{\frac{1}{2}}$$
$$= 100/(25 + 225)^{\frac{1}{2}} = 100/(250)^{\frac{1}{2}}$$
$$= 100/(5\sqrt{10}) = 20\sqrt{10}/10 = \underline{\underline{6 \cdot 324 \text{ A}}}$$

$$\phi = \tan^{-1} X/R = \tan^{-1} 15/5 = \tan^{-1} 3 \cdot 0$$
$$= \underline{\underline{71° \ 30'}} \text{ (current leading since } X_L < X_C)$$

(ii) (See diagram (iii) of Fig. 10.25)
$$\omega = 2\pi f = 10^4 \text{ radn/sec}$$
$$X_L = \omega L = 10^4 \times 10^{-3} = 10 \ \Omega$$
$$X_C = 1/(\omega C) = 10^6/(10^4 \times 10) = 10 \ \Omega$$
$$R = 5 \ \Omega$$
$$I = 100/\{5^2 + (10 - 10)^2\}^{\frac{1}{2}} = 100/5 = \underline{\underline{20 \text{ A}}}$$

$$\phi = \tan^{-1} X/R = \tan^{-1} 0/5 = \underline{\underline{0°}}$$

Note. Since $X_L = X_C$, the circuit current is determined by the value of the resistance only and the circuit is at *resonance*.

EXAMPLE 10.33 (B). An alternating current of 0·5 A is passed through a circuit consisting of a coil having an inductance of 10 mH and a resistance of 10 Ω which is connected in series with a capacitor of 2 μF. If the voltage developed across the capacitor is 50 V, what is the voltage developed across the coil? Illustrate your answer by a vector diagram drawn approximately to scale. (C. & G.)

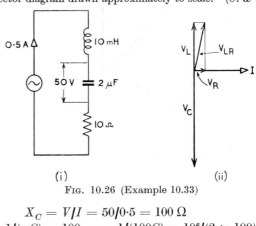

FIG. 10.26 (Example 10.33)

$$X_C = V/I = 50/0 \cdot 5 = 100 \ \Omega$$
$$1/(\omega C) = 100, \ \omega = 1/(100C) = 10^6/(2 \times 100)$$
$$= 5\ 000 \text{ radn/sec}$$
$$X_L = \omega L = 5\ 000 \times 10^{-2} = 50 \ \Omega$$

Voltage across L
$$= IX_L = 0 \cdot 5 \times 50 = 25 \text{ V}$$

Voltage across R
$$= IR = 0 \cdot 5 \times 10 = 5 \text{ V}$$

Voltage across coil (see Fig. 10.26)

$$= (5^2 + 25^2)^{\frac{1}{2}} = (25 + 625)^{\frac{1}{2}} = (650)^{\frac{1}{2}}$$
$$= 25 \cdot 5 \text{ V}$$

EXAMPLE 10.34 (B). An inductor L, a capacitor C, both of negligible resistance, and a non-inductive resistor R

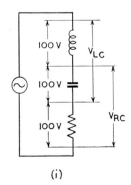

(i)

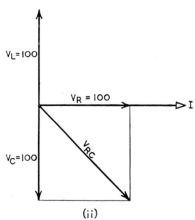

(ii)

FIG. 10.27 (Example 10.34)

are joined in series in the order named across alternating supply mains. When a voltmeter is connected across L, C, and R in turn the reading is 100 V in each case. What readings would be obtained (a) across L and C, and (b) across C and R? If the frequency be 50 c/s and C is of 2 μF capacitance, find the values of L and R.

(C. & G.)

The vector diagram (Fig. 10.27) shows the phase difference between the voltages across R, L, and C.

(a) Since the voltages across L and C are 180° out of phase, the voltage across L and C jointly = $V_{LC} = 100 - 100 = 0$ V

(b) The voltages across R and C are 90° out of phase; voltage across R and C jointly = V_{RC}
$$= (100^2 + 100^2)^{\frac{1}{2}} = 10^2 \times \sqrt{2} = 141 \cdot 4 \text{ V}$$

$$\phi = \tan^{-1} V_C / V_R$$
$$= \tan^{-1} 100/100 = \tan^{-1} 1 = 45°$$

Since

$$V_L = V_C, \ \omega L I = I/(\omega C) \text{ and}$$
$$L = 1/(\omega^2 C)$$
$$= 1/\{(100\pi)^2 \times 2 \times 10^{-6}\} = 10^2/2\pi^2$$
$$= 5 \cdot 07 \text{ H}$$

Since $\qquad V_R = V_L, \ IR = \omega L I$
and $\qquad R = \omega L = 100\pi \times 5 \cdot 07 = 1\ 595\ \Omega$

EXAMPLE 10.35 (B). A capacitor of 4 μF is connected in series with a resistance of 400 Ω. This combination is connected in series with two inductors in parallel of values 10 H and 5 H respectively. What current will flow through the resistance when an e.m.f. of 100 V r.m.s. at 50 c/s is applied to the circuit? (C. & G.)

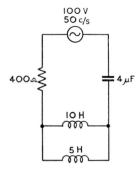

FIG. 10.28 (Example 10.35)

See the circuit diagram of Fig. 10.28. For two inductors in parallel,

$$L = L_1 L_2 / (L_1 + L_2)$$
$$= 10 \times 5/(10 + 5) = 50/15 = 10/3 \text{ H}$$
$$\omega = 2\pi f = 2\pi \times 50 = 314 \text{ radn/sec}$$
$$\omega L = 314 \times 10/3 = 1\ 047\ \Omega$$
$$1/(\omega C) = 10^6/(314 \times 4) = 796\ \Omega$$
$$I = E / \left\{ R^2 + \left(\omega L - \frac{1}{\omega C} \right)^2 \right\}^{\frac{1}{2}}$$
$$= 100/\{400^2 + (1\ 047 - 796)^2\}^{\frac{1}{2}}$$
$$= 100/(400^2 + 251^2)^{\frac{1}{2}}$$
$$= 100/(4 \cdot 72 \times 10^2) = 0 \cdot 212 \text{ A}$$

$$\phi = \tan^{-1} X/R = \tan^{-1} 251/400$$
$$= \tan^{-1} 0 \cdot 628 = 32° 7'$$

(current lagging, since $X_L > X_C$)

EXAMPLE 10.36 (B). A radio-frequency voltage is applied across a circuit comprising resistance, capacitance, and inductance in series. If the voltage across each of the three components is 100, what is the voltage across the whole circuit? Illustrate your answer with a diagram.

(C. & G.)

See the circuit and vector diagrams, Fig. 10.29.

Since the voltages across L and C are 180° out of phase and therefore cancel out, the applied voltage across the whole circuit is 100 V in phase with the current.

Note. This is a *resonant* circuit.

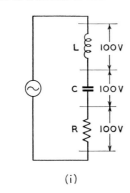

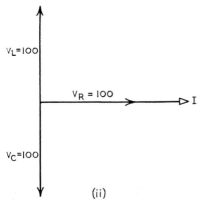

(i)

(ii)

FIG. 10.29 (Example 10.36)

EXAMPLE 10.37 (B). What is the impedance at a frequency of 900 kc/s of a circuit consisting of a capacitor of $0{\cdot}000\,2\ \mu$F in series with a coil of $200\ \mu$H inductance and 25 Ω resistance?

(C. & G.)

$$Z = R + j\{\omega L - 1/(\omega C)\}$$
$$\omega = 2\pi \times 9 \times 10^5 = 5{\cdot}655 \times 10^6$$
$$X_L = \omega L = 5{\cdot}655 \times 10^6 \times 2 \times 10^{-4}$$
$$= 1\,131\ \Omega$$
$$X_C = 1/(\omega C) = 1/(5{\cdot}655 \times 10^6 \times 2 \times 10^{-10})$$
$$= 884\ \Omega$$
$$X = \omega L - 1/(\omega C) = 1\,131 - 884 = 247\ \Omega$$

$$Z = (25^2 + 247^2)^{\frac{1}{2}} = 248{\cdot}2\ \Omega$$
$$\phi = \tan^{-1} 247/25 = \tan^{-1} 9{\cdot}88 = 84{\cdot}2°$$
$$\text{Impedance} = 248{\cdot}2\underline{/84{\cdot}2°}$$

10.16. Impedances in Series.

The rule for determining the joint impedance of a number of separate impedances in series is similar to that for resistors in series—

$$Z = \text{vector sum } (Z_1 + Z_2 + Z_3 + \ldots + Z_N)$$
$$= (R_1 + R_2 + R_3 + \ldots + R_N)$$
$$\quad + j(X_1 + X_2 + X_3 + \ldots + X_N)$$
$$= \{(\Sigma R)^2 + (\Sigma X)^2\}^{\frac{1}{2}}$$

The phase angle of the equivalent impedance, $\phi = \tan^{-1} \Sigma X/\Sigma R$. To find the sum of a number of impedances in series it is necessary to resolve each impedance into its two components. For an impedance Z/ϕ', from the impedance triangle (Fig. 10.17)—

$$R' = Z' \cos \phi', \text{ and } X' = Z' \sin \phi', \text{ so that}$$
$$Z = \{(\Sigma Z \cos \phi)^2 + (\Sigma Z \sin \phi)^2\}^{\frac{1}{2}} \text{ and}$$
$$\phi = \tan^{-1} (\Sigma Z \sin \phi)/(\Sigma Z \cos \phi)$$

EXAMPLE 10.38 (B). Two relays D and I are connected in series with each other across a telephone line. At a particular frequency, the individual impedances of the relays are as follows—

Relay $D = 16\,000\underline{/75°}\ \Omega$;

Relay $I = 5\,000\underline{/50°}\ \Omega$.

Calculate the combined impedance of the two relays. Give the result in the form Z/ϕ.

(C. & G.)

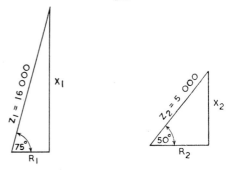

FIG. 10.30 (Example 10.38)

$$Z = Z_1 + Z_2 = (R_1 + jX_1) + (R_2 + jX_2)$$
$$= R_1 + R_2 + j(X_1 + X_2)$$

From the impedance triangles, Fig. 10.30,

$$X_1 = 16\,000 \sin 75° = 16\,000 \times 0{\cdot}965\,9$$
$$= 15\,454\ \Omega$$
$$R_1 = 16\,000 \cos 75° = 16\,000 \times 0{\cdot}258\,8$$
$$= 4\,140{\cdot}8\ \Omega$$

$X_2 = 5\ 000 \sin 50° = 5\ 000 \times 0{\cdot}766 = 3\ 830\ \Omega$

$R_2 = 5\ 000 \cos 50° = 5\ 000 \times 0{\cdot}642\ 8$

$\qquad = 3\ 214\ \Omega$

$X = X_1 + X_2 = 15\ 454 + 3\ 830 = 19\ 284\ \Omega$

$R = R_1 + R_2 = 4\ 141 + 3\ 214 = 7\ 355\ \Omega$

$\phi = \tan^{-1} X/R = \tan^{-1} 19\ 284/7\ 355 = 69° 7'$

$Z = (X^2 + R^2)^{\frac{1}{2}} = (19\ 284^2 + 7\ 355^2)^{\frac{1}{2}}$

$\qquad = 20\ 640\ \Omega$

Combined impedance $= \underline{\underline{20\ 640/69° 7'}}$

10.17. Series Resonant Circuit. In the series circuit (Fig. 10.23) the impedance

$$Z = R + j\{\omega L - 1/(\omega C)\}$$

This may be written as

$$Z = R + \frac{(1 - \omega^2 LC)}{j\omega C}$$

At the critical frequency which makes $\omega L = 1/(\omega C)$, (case (iii) referred to in §**10.15**), $\omega^2 LC = 1$, so that $Z = R$, and

$$X = \{\omega L - 1/(\omega C)\} = 0$$

The phase angle

$$\phi = \tan^{-1} X/R = 0/R = 0$$

In other words, (i) the impedance has its minimum value, equal to R, (ii) the current has its maximum value, $I = V/R$, and (iii) the voltage and current are in phase. Under these conditions, namely when the inductive reactance X_L is equal to the capacitive reactance X_C, the circuit is said to be RESONANT. The particular frequency for which $X_L = X_C$ is termed the RESONANT FREQUENCY, and is usually designated f_r.

A vector diagram for the series resonant circuit is given in Fig. 10.31 (*a*). The essential condition for resonance being that $\omega L = 1/(\omega C)$,

$$\omega^2 = (2\pi f_r)^2 = 1/(LC)$$

so that the resonant frequency

$$f_r = \frac{1}{2\pi(LC)^{\frac{1}{2}}} \qquad . \qquad . \ (10.17)$$

Curves showing the variation of reactance with frequency are given in Fig. 10.31 (*b*). Inductive reactance is directly proportional to the frequency $(X_L = \omega L)$; capacitive reactance is *inversely* proportional to frequency $(X_C = 1/(\omega C))$. The combined reactance X is the algebraic sum of these curves and this variation with frequency is shown by the dotted line. At the resonant frequency $X_L = X_C$ and $X = 0$. The dotted curve illustrates that at frequencies below resonance X and ϕ are negative. $(X_C > X_L)$: at frequencies above resonance, X and ϕ are positive $(X_L > X_C)$.

The graph Z_s of Fig. 10.32 is a *resonance curve* for the series circuit, showing the variation of impedance with frequency. The minimum value

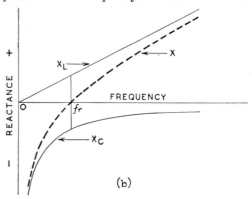

(b)

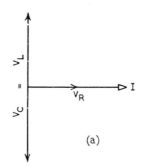

(a)

FIG. 10.31. VARIATION OF REACTANCE WITH FREQUENCY

of the impedance $(Z = R)$, and the resonant frequency (f_r) at which this occurs, are indicated. The impedance increases at frequency values above or below resonance. At very low frequencies it is nearly equal to the capacitive reactance; at high frequencies it approaches the inductive reactance.

The series resonant circuit giving maximum current and minimum impedance at the resonant frequency is known as an *acceptor circuit*. Acceptor circuits are frequently employed in a.c. work particularly at carrier and radio frequencies where they are used to "tune-in" a given frequency, by suitable adjustment of the inductance or capacitance, discriminating by an increased impedance against other signals of undesired frequency. More commonly the resonant circuit is desired to offer a minimum impedance to a band of frequencies, for which purpose the tuned circuit forms the basis of the frequency filter.

It will be seen from the vector diagram (Fig. 10.31 (a)) that, although at resonance the circuit reactance is zero, nevertheless p.d.s. are built up across both the inductance and capacitance present. These voltages V_L and V_C are equal, and the acceptor circuit is in a state of *voltage resonance*.

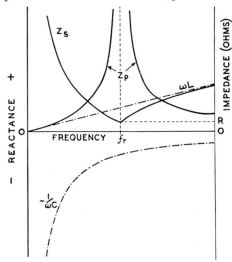

FIG. 10.32. RESONANCE CURVES

The current having its maximum value, these p.d.s.

$$V_L = I\omega L, \text{ and } V_C = - I/(\omega C)$$

may have values greatly in excess of the supply voltage, so that in practice resonant circuits must often be carefully avoided, or alternatively insulation of adequate dielectric strength must be provided. The reason for these high voltages is that V_L and V_C are 180° out of phase; consequently the energy from the collapsing magnetic field is available to assist in charging the capacitance. When the capacitance discharges, this energy is available to assist in re-establishing the magnetic field, the only energy lost being that absorbed in generating heat in the circuit resistance. At the resonant frequency the alternations occur just at the instants required for the collapsing magnetic field to reinforce the capacitor charge, and vice versa.

A simple mechanical analogy of resonance is provided by the pendulum which can be set swinging to a large amplitude from a series of minute forces, provided that these impulses are properly timed in their application at the resonant frequency of the particular pendulum: if the impulses are not so timed, the pendulum fails to build up a large swing.

EXAMPLE 10.39 (B). Assuming that a magneto bell has a constant inductance of 12·5 H and a resistance of 1 000 Ω, calculate (a) the joint impedance of the bell and 2 μF capacitor in series at "ringing" frequency (100 radn/sec), and (b) the frequency at which this circuit element would be in a state of resonance. (C. & G.)

(a) $R = 1\,000\ \Omega$

$\omega L = 100 \times 12\cdot5 = 1\,250\ \Omega$

$1/(\omega C) = 10^6/(100 \times 2) = 5\,000\ \Omega$

$$Z = \left\{ R^2 + \left(\omega L - \frac{1}{\omega C} \right)^2 \right\}^{\frac{1}{2}}$$

$$= \{1\,000^2 + (1\,250 - 5000)^2\}^{\frac{1}{2}}$$

$$= (1\,000^2 + 3\,750^2)^{\frac{1}{2}} = \underline{3\,880\ \Omega}$$

$$\phi = \tan^{-1} X/R = \tan^{-1} 3\,750/1\,000$$

$$= \tan^{-1} 3\cdot75$$

$$= \underline{-75°\,6'} \text{ (negative because } 1/(\omega C) > \omega L)$$

(b) $\omega L = 1/(\omega C),\ \omega^2 = 1/(LC),\ \omega = 1/(LC)^{\frac{1}{2}}$

$f_r = 1/\{2\pi(LC)^{\frac{1}{2}}\}$

$$= \frac{1}{6\cdot28 \times (12\cdot5 \times 2 \times 10^{-6})^{\frac{1}{2}}}$$

$$= \frac{10^3}{6\cdot28 \times 25^{\frac{1}{2}}}$$

$$= 200/6\cdot28 = \underline{31\cdot6 \text{ c/s}}$$

EXAMPLE 10.40 (B). A series tuned circuit has a capacitance of 0·2 μF. What must be its inductance in order that resonance shall occur at a frequency of 500 kc/s? (C. & G.)

For resonance,

$\omega L = 1/(\omega C)$

$L = 1/(\omega^2 C) = 1/(4\pi^2 f^2 C)$

$\quad = 1/(4\pi^2 \times 5^2 \times 10^{10} \times 0\cdot2 \times 10^{-6})$

$\quad = 1/(0\cdot2\pi^2 \times 10^6) = \underline{0\cdot51\ \mu\text{H}}$

EXAMPLE 10.41 (B). A resonant circuit consists of a coil having an inductance of 1 000 μH and a high-frequency resistance of 20 Ω in series with a variable capacitor which may be assumed free from loss. An e.m.f. of 1 V at a frequency of 100 kc/s is induced into the coil from a nearby circuit. What will be the value of the capacitance to produce resonance with this e.m.f. and what will then be the p.d. across this capacitor? (C. & G.)

At resonance,

$\omega L = 1/(\omega C)$

$C = 1/(\omega^2 L) = 1/(4\pi^2 \times 10^{10} \times 10^{-3})$

$\quad = 10^{-6}/40\pi^2 = \underline{0\cdot002\,54\ \mu\text{F}}$

At resonance,

$$I = V/R = 1/20 \text{ A}$$
$$V_C = I/(\omega C)$$
$$= 1/(2\pi \times 10^5 \times 0.002\ 54 \times 10^{-6} \times 20)$$
$$= 1/(4\pi \times 0.002\ 54)$$
$$= 31.4 \text{ V}$$

EXAMPLE 10.42 (B). A circuit is tuned to a frequency of 1 000 kc/s when its capacitance is 0·05 μF. What is its inductance?   (C. & G.)

At resonance,

$$\omega L = 1/(\omega C)$$
$$L = 1/(\omega^2 C) = 1/(4\pi^2 f^2 C)$$
$$L = 10^6/(4\pi^2 \times 10^{12} \times 0.05) = \underline{\underline{0.507\ \mu\text{H}}}$$

EXAMPLE 10.43 (B). A resistor, a capacitor, and a variable inductor are connected in series across 200 V a.c. mains, the frequency being 50 c/s. The maximum current which can be obtained by varying the inductance is 314 mA, and the pressure across the capacitor, which has a negligible resistance, is then 250 V. Calculate the values of the capacitance, the resistance, and the inductance of the circuit.   (C. & G.)

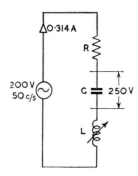

FIG. 10.33 (Example 10.43)

The circuit conditions are shown in Fig. 10.33. $\omega = 314$ radn/sec. Since the current has its maximum value, the circuit is at resonance and $Z = R$.

$$R = V/I = 200/0.314 = \underline{\underline{637\ \Omega}}$$

The p.d. across the capacitance

$$V_C = I/(\omega C) = 250$$
$$C = I/(\omega V_C) = 0.314/(314 \times 250)$$
$$= \underline{\underline{4 \times 10^{-6} \text{ F}}}$$

$$\omega L = 1/(\omega C)$$
$$L = 1/(\omega^2 C) = 10^6/\{(100\pi)^2 \times 4\} = \underline{\underline{2.5 \text{ H}}}$$

EXAMPLE 10.44 (B). The current flowing through a circuit consisting of R ohms, L microhenrys, and C microfarads in series is 0·5 A when a voltage of 30 V is applied at the resonant frequency of the circuit and is 0·3 A when the frequency of the applied voltage is doubled. What is the reactance of the circuit in the second case, and the phase angle between the applied voltage and the resulting current? Illustrate your answer by vector diagrams.
                     (C. & G.)

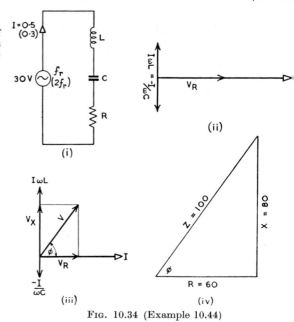

FIG. 10.34 (Example 10.44)

The circuit is shown in Fig. 10.34 (i).
At resonance (Fig. 10.34 (ii))

$$\omega L = 1/(\omega C) \text{ and}$$
$$R = V/I$$
$$= 30/0.5 = 60\ \Omega$$

When the frequency is doubled (iii)

$$Z = V/I = 30/0.3 = 100\ \Omega$$
$$\text{Reactance } X = (Z^2 - R^2)^{\frac{1}{2}} = (100^2 - 60^2)^{\frac{1}{2}}$$
$$= 80\ \Omega \text{ (iv)}$$

$$\phi = \tan^{-1} X/R = \tan^{-1} 80/60$$
$$= \tan^{-1} 1.33 = \underline{\underline{53^\circ\ 8'}}$$

The angle is positive because at frequencies greater than the resonant frequency, $\omega L > 1/(\omega C)$. When the frequency is doubled, ωL is doubled and $1/(\omega C)$ is halved. The vector diagram and impedance triangle are given in Fig. 10.34 (iii) and (iv).

EXAMPLE 10.45 (B). A circuit consisting of a non-reactive resistance R ohms, an inductance L henrys, and a capacitance C farads joined in series, is connected across a source of alternating current which has a constant sinusoidal voltage output of 1 V over the range of frequencies concerned. If $R = 1\,000\,\Omega$, $L = 0.2$ H, and $C = 0.2 \times 10^{-6}$ F, determine the frequency at which the r.m.s. voltage across L equals that across C. What is the value of this voltage? What is the voltage across R and the power absorbed by the circuit at this frequency?

(C. & G.)

Voltage across $L = \omega L I$.

,,   ,, $C = I/\omega C$.

When these are equal, $\omega L = 1/(\omega C)$ and $\omega^2 = 1/(LC)$, or $\omega = 1/(LC)^{\frac{1}{2}}$.

$$\omega = 1/(0.2 \times 0.2 \times 10^{-6})^{\frac{1}{2}} = 10^3/0.2$$
$$= 5\,000 \text{ radn/sec}$$
$$f = 5\,000/2\pi = \underline{\underline{796 \text{ c/s}}}$$

At resonance,

$$I = V/R = 1/1\,000 = 0.001 \text{ A}$$
$$V_C = V_L = \omega L I = 5\,000 \times 0.2 \times 0.001$$
$$= \underline{\underline{1 \text{ V}}}$$

$$V_R = IR = 0.001 \times 1\,000 = \underline{\underline{1 \text{ V}}}$$

At resonance, power, $P = I^2R = 10^{-6} \times 10^3$
$= \underline{\underline{0.001 \text{ W}}}$

Parallel Circuits

In the *series* circuit, where the current is the same at all parts of the circuit, it is convenient to use the current as the reference vector and to draw the various voltage vectors at suitable phase angles to the current line.

In the parallel circuit, the p.d. across the several branches is the same, the current usually differing in magnitude and phase in each branch.

Accordingly, for *parallel* circuits it is convenient to draw the *voltage* vector horizontally as the reference vector and to set off the currents in the various branches at the appropriate phase angles. A leading current (capacitance) will then appear in the first quadrant, whilst a lagging current (inductance) will appear in the fourth.

10.18. Resistance and Inductance in Parallel. Fig. 10.35 (a) shows a circuit where a p.d. of V volts at a frequency of f c/s is maintained across a resistor R ohms in parallel with an inductor L henrys which has negligible resistance.

The current in the resistor is $I_R = V/R$ amperes, in phase with the applied voltage. The current flowing in the inductive path is $I_L = V/(\omega L)$, lagging $90°$ on I_R and on V. The vector diagram is given in Fig. 10.35 (b).

The total current I

$$= (I_R^2 + I_L^2)^{\frac{1}{2}} \qquad = I_R - jI_L$$
$$= \left\{(V/R)^2 + \left(\frac{V}{\omega L}\right)^2\right\}^{\frac{1}{2}} = V/R - jV/(\omega L)$$
$$= V\left\{(1/R)^2 + \left(\frac{1}{\omega L}\right)^2\right\}^{\frac{1}{2}} = V\{1/R - j/(\omega L)\}$$
$$= V(1/R + 1/j\omega L) \qquad . \qquad . \qquad . \qquad . \quad (10.18)$$

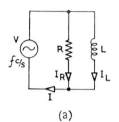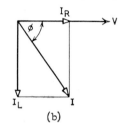

Fig. 10.35. Parallel Circuit—Resistance and Inductance

From the vector diagram,

$$\phi = \tan^{-1} I_L/I_R = \tan^{-1}\{V/(\omega L) \div V/R\}$$
$$= \tan^{-1}\frac{R}{\omega L}$$

The total impedance of the circuit is $Z = V/I = 1/(1/R + 1/j\omega L)$.

EXAMPLE 10.46 (B). A resistor of 1 500 Ω and an inductor of 5 H are connected in parallel across a 50 c/s a.c. supply of 1 000 V r.m.s. What will be the total current taken from the mains?

(C. & G.)

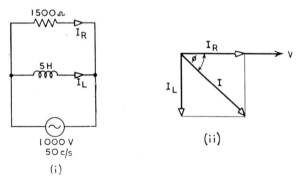

Fig. 10.36 (Example 10.46)

The circuit and vector diagrams are given in Fig. 10.36.

$$\omega = 100\pi$$

Current in resistor,

$$I_R = V/R = 1\,000/1\,500 = 0.66 \text{ A}$$

Current in inductance,

$$I_L = V/(\omega L) = 1\,000/(100\pi \times 5)$$
$$= 2/\pi = 0.64 \text{ A}$$

Total current I

$$= (I_R{}^2 + I_L{}^2)^{\frac{1}{2}} = (0.66^2 + 0.64^2)^{\frac{1}{2}}$$
$$= (0.435\,6 + 0.409\,6)^{\frac{1}{2}} = 0.845\,2^{\frac{1}{2}}$$
$$= \underline{\underline{0.92 \text{ A}}}$$

$$\phi = \tan^{-1} I_L/I_R = \tan^{-1} 0.64/0.66$$
$$= \tan^{-1} 0.969\,6 = \underline{\underline{44° \, 7'}}$$

10.19. Resistance and Capacitance in Parallel.
The circuit and vector diagrams for this arrangement are given in Fig. 10.37: the power loss in the
capacitor is assumed to be negligible.

The active current, in the resistor R, is $I_R = V/R$,
in phase with the applied voltage. The reactive

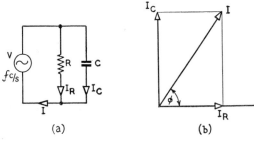

(a)   (b)

Fig. 10.37. Parallel Circuit—Resistance and
Capacitance

current, in the capacitor C, is $I_C = \omega CV$, leading
by 90° on the applied voltage and on the current I_R.

The total current from the supply I

$$= (I_R{}^2 + I_C{}^2)^{\frac{1}{2}} \qquad = I_R + jI_C$$
$$= \{(V/R)^2 + (\omega CV)^2\}^{\frac{1}{2}} = (V/R + j\omega CV)$$
$$= V\{(1/R)^2 + (\omega C)^2\}^{\frac{1}{2}} = V(1/R + j\omega C)$$
$$\qquad\qquad\qquad\qquad\qquad\qquad (10.19)$$

The phase angle

$$\phi = \tan^{-1} I_C/I_R$$
$$= \tan^{-1} (\omega CV \div V/R) = \tan^{-1} \omega CR$$

The total circuit impedance is

$$Z = V/I = 1/(1/R + j\omega C)$$

EXAMPLE 10.47 (B). Two separate circuits, the first consisting of a capacitor of $1 \mu F$ in parallel with a resistor of
200Ω, the second consisting of a capacitor and a resistor
in series, are connected in turn across an a.c. supply of
which $\omega = 2\pi f = 5\,000$ radn/sec. The value of the
current and the phase angle of the current relative to
the applied voltage are found to be exactly equal in each

case. What are the values of capacitance and resistance
in the second circuit?
Illustrate each case by a vector diagram.   (C. & G.)

Impedance of capacitance arm (Fig. 10.38 (i))

$$= 1/(\omega C)$$
$$= 1/(5\,000 \times 1 \times 10^{-6})$$
$$= 200 \, \Omega$$

From vector diagram (ii),

$$\tan \phi = I_C/I_R = V\omega C \div V/R$$
$$= \omega CR = 200/200 = 1$$

i.e. angle of lead = 45°.
Since $\phi = 45°$, $I_C = I_R$ and total current
$= \sqrt{2} \, . \, I_R$.

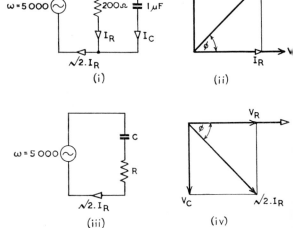

Fig. 10.38 (Example 10.47)

The currents and the power-factors being the
same in the series and parallel circuits, the power
losses are equal, and (diagram (iii))

$$I_R{}^2 \times 200 = (\sqrt{2} \, . \, I_R)^2 \times R, \text{ or } R = \underline{\underline{100 \, \Omega}}$$

For the series circuit (diagram (iv)),

$$\tan \phi = V_C/V_R = I/(\omega C) \div IR = 1/(\omega CR)$$
$$= 1 \text{ (from above), or } C = 1/(\omega R)$$

Substituting $\omega = 5\,000$, and $R = 100$,

$$C = 1/(5\,000 \times 100) \text{ farads,}$$
$$= 10^6/(5\,000 \times 100) \, \mu F = \underline{\underline{2 \, \mu F}}$$

EXAMPLE 10.48 (B). What is the impedance at 50 c/s,
100 c/s, and 200 c/s of a capacitor of $2/\pi \mu F$ shunted by
a resistor of $1\,000 \Omega$?   (C. & G.)

Assume a voltage of V volts applied across the combination (see diagram (i) of Fig. 10.39).

$$I_R = V/R$$
$$I_C = V \div 1/(2\pi fC) = 2\pi fCV$$
$$I = (I_R{}^2 + I_C{}^2)^{\frac{1}{2}} = \{(V/R)^2 + (2\pi fCV)^2\}^{\frac{1}{2}}$$
$$= V\{(1/R)^2 + (2\pi fC)^2\}^{\frac{1}{2}} = V/Z$$
$$Z = 1/\{(1/R)^2 + (2\pi fC)^2\}^{\frac{1}{2}}$$
$$\phi = \tan^{-1} 2\pi fCV \div V/R$$

(see vector diagram (ii))
$$= \tan^{-1} 2\pi fCR$$

If $C = 2 \times 10^{-6}/\pi$ F and $R = 1\,000\ \Omega$
$$Z = 1/\{(1/10^6) + (2\pi f \times 2/10^6\pi)^2\}^{\frac{1}{2}}$$
$$= 1/\{(1/10^6) + (4f/10^6)^2\}^{\frac{1}{2}}$$
$$= 1/(10^6/10^{12} + 16f^2/10^{12})^{\frac{1}{2}}$$
$$= 10^6/(10^6 + 16f^2)^{\frac{1}{2}}\ \Omega$$
$$\phi = \tan^{-1}\{2\pi f \times 2/(10^6 \cdot \pi) \times 10^3\}$$
$$= \tan^{-1} 4f/10^3$$

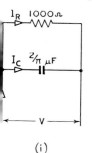

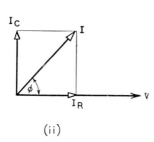

FIG. 10.39 (Example 10.48)

(i) When

$$f = 50$$
$$Z = 10^6/(10^6 + 16 \cdot 50^2)^{\frac{1}{2}}$$
$$= 10^6/(10^6 + 4 \cdot 10^4)^{\frac{1}{2}} = 10^4/104^{\frac{1}{2}}$$
$$= 980 \cdot 6\ \Omega$$

$$\phi = \tan^{-1} (4 \times 50/10^3) = \tan^{-1} 0 \cdot 2$$
$$= 11° 19'$$

(ii) When

$$f = 100$$
$$Z = 10^6/(10^6 + 16 \cdot 10^4)^{\frac{1}{2}} = 10^4/116^{\frac{1}{2}}$$
$$= 928 \cdot 3\ \Omega$$

$$\phi = \tan^{-1} (4 \times 100/10^3) = \tan^{-1} 0 \cdot 4$$
$$= 21° 48'$$

(iii) When

$$f = 200$$
$$Z = 10^6/(10^6 + 16 \cdot 200^2)^{\frac{1}{2}} = 10^4/164^{\frac{1}{2}}$$
$$= 780 \cdot 9\ \Omega$$

$$\phi = \tan^{-1} (4 \times 200/10^3) = \tan^{-1} 0 \cdot 8$$
$$= 38° 37'$$

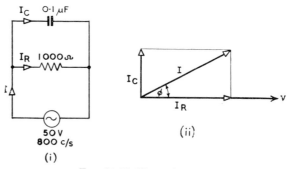

FIG. 10.40 (Example 10.49)

EXAMPLE 10.49 (B). A circuit consisting of a capacitor of $0 \cdot 1\ \mu$F shunted by a $1\,000\ \Omega$ resistor is connected across a 50 V, 800 c/s supply. What is—

    (a) the impedance presented to the supply,
    (b) the instantaneous current drawn from the supply when the applied voltage reaches its maximum value,
    (c) the phase angle of the supply current relative to the applied voltage?

Illustrate your answer by vector diagrams.   (C. & G.)

See the circuit and vector diagrams in Fig. 10.40.

$$X_C = 1/(\omega C) = 10^6/(5\,000 \times 0 \cdot 1) = 2\,000\ \Omega$$
$$I_C = 50/2\,000 = 0 \cdot 025\ \text{A}$$
$$R = 1\,000\ \Omega,\ I_R = 50/1\,000 = 0 \cdot 050\ \text{A}$$

Total current,
$$I = (I_R{}^2 + I_C{}^2)^{\frac{1}{2}}$$
$$= (0 \cdot 050^2 + 0 \cdot 025^2)^{\frac{1}{2}} = 0 \cdot 056\ \text{A}$$

(a) Total impedance,
$$Z = V/I = 50/0 \cdot 056 = 894\ \Omega$$

(b) The capacitor current leads the applied voltage by 90°, and is therefore zero when the applied voltage has its maximum value, i.e. $50\sqrt{2}$: at this instant, the total current is that through the resistance $= 50\sqrt{2}/1\,000 = 0 \cdot 070\ 7$ A.

(c) The phase angle
$$\phi = \tan^{-1} I_C/I_R = \tan^{-1} 0 \cdot 025/0 \cdot 050$$
$$= \tan^{-1} 0 \cdot 5 = 26° 34'\ \text{(leading)}$$

EXAMPLE 10.50 (B). A sinusoidal alternating voltage, having an effective value of 100 V and a frequency of 50 c/s is applied across a resistor of 200 Ω and a capacitor of 4 μF which are connected in parallel. Draw approximately to scale a graph showing the variation of the applied voltage and resulting currents throughout one complete cycle and the relative phase relationships, and show how the instantaneous values can more simply be obtained from a vector diagram. (C. & G.)

Total current

$$I = (I_R^2 + I_C^2)^{\frac{1}{2}} = (0{\cdot}5^2 + 0{\cdot}126^2)^{\frac{1}{2}}$$
$$= 0{\cdot}515 \text{ A}$$
$$i = 0{\cdot}515\sqrt{2} \sin(314t + \phi)$$
$$= 0{\cdot}729 \sin(314t + \phi)$$

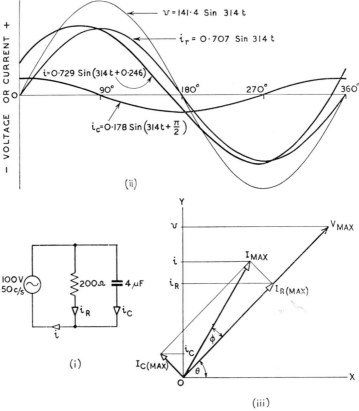

FIG. 10.41 (Example 10.50)

See the circuit diagram (i) in Fig. 10.41.

$f = 50$ c/s, $\omega = 2\pi . 50 = 314$ radn/sec
$V = 100$, $V_{max} = 100\sqrt{2} = 141{\cdot}4$ V
$v = 141{\cdot}4 \sin 314t$

Current through resistance
$I_R = V/R = 100/200 = 0{\cdot}5$ A
$i_R = 0{\cdot}5\sqrt{2} \sin 314t = 0{\cdot}707 \sin 314t$

Current in capacitor
$I_C = V\omega C = 100 \times 314 \times 4 \times 10^{-6}$
$= 0{\cdot}126$ A
$i_C = 0{\cdot}126\sqrt{2} \sin(314t + \pi/2)$
$= 0{\cdot}178 \sin(314t + \pi/2)$—the current leading the voltage by $\pi/2$ radn

where

$\phi = \tan^{-1} I_C/I_R = \tan^{-1} 0{\cdot}126/0{\cdot}5$
$= \tan^{-1} 0{\cdot}252 = 14° 6' = 0{\cdot}246$ radn
or, $i = 0{\cdot}729 \sin(314t + 0{\cdot}246)$

Diagram (ii) shows the graphs over one complete cycle for the variations of v, i_R (in phase), i (leading by 90°) and i (leading by 14° 6').

The instantaneous values may be readily obtained from the vector diagram (iii) where the applied voltage V_{max}, used as the reference vector is drawn at an angle θ, ($\theta = 2\pi ft = 314t$), for any desired instantaneous time t to be considered. The maximum values of the currents $I_{R\,max}$, I_{Cmax} and I_{max}, are drawn at the appropriate phase angle

n the usual manner. The projections shown will
hen cut the vertical axis at the required instan-
aneous values, because the axis lengths cut off by
hese projections are proportional to $\sin \theta$, i.e.
$\cdot = V_{max} \sin \theta$, $i_R = I_{R\ max} \sin \theta$, $i_C = I_{C\ max} \sin$
$\cdot$, and $i = I_{max} \sin \theta$.

EXAMPLE 10.51 (B). The losses in a capacitor can be
epresented by either a series or shunt resistance. Deduce
n expression for the relationship between the two equiva-
ent resistances.   (C. & G.)

Using the symbols shown in the diagram,
'ig. 10.42, impedance of series circuit,

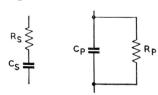

FIG. 10.42 (Example 10.51)

$$Z_S = R_S - j/(\omega C_S) = R_S + 1/(j\omega C_S)$$

mpedance of parallel circuit,

$$Z_P = 1/(1/R_P + j\omega C_P)$$

Since

$$Z_S = Z_P,\ R_S + 1/(j\omega C_S) = 1/(1/R_P + j\omega C_P)$$
$$(j\omega C_S R_S + 1)/(j\omega C_S) = R_P/(1 + j\omega C_P R_P)$$
$$j\omega C_S R_P = j\omega C_S R_S + j\omega C_P R_P + 1$$
$$- \omega^2 C_S C_P R_S R_P$$

Equating active and reactive components,

$$\omega^2 C_S C_P R_S R_P = 1 = \omega^2 C_S R_S (C_P R_P) \quad . \quad \text{(i)}$$
$$C_P R_P = C_S R_P - C_S R_S$$
$$= C_S (R_P - R_S) \quad . \quad . \quad \text{(ii)}$$

Substituting (ii) in (i),

$$\omega^2 C_S R_S (R_P - R_S) C_S = 1$$
$$\omega^2 C_S{}^2 R_S R_P - \omega^2 C_S{}^2 R_S{}^2 = 1$$
$$R_P = (1 + \omega^2 C_S{}^2 R_S{}^2)/(\omega^2 C_S{}^2 R_S)$$
$$= \underline{1/(\omega^2 C_S{}^2 R_S) + R_S}$$

10.20. Inductance and Capacitance in Parallel.
'he circuit and vector diagrams are shown in
'ig. 10.43 : it is assumed that there is no resistance
n either branch.
Using the values indicated in the diagram,
$_L = V/(\omega L)$, lagging 90° behind V. $I_C = \omega C V$,
eading V by 90°. These currents are 180° out of
bhase with one another and can be added algebraically.

The total current

$$I = I_L + I_C$$
$$= |V/\omega L - \omega C V|$$
$$= V(1/j\omega L + j\omega C) \quad . \quad \text{(10.20)}$$

and it will lag or lead exactly 90° with respect to
the applied voltage depending upon whether (i)

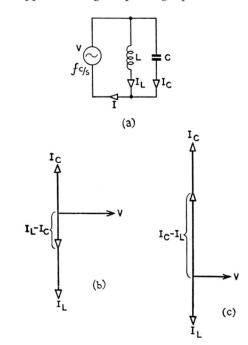

FIG. 10.43. PARALLEL CIRCUIT—INDUCTANCE
AND CAPACITANCE

$I_L > I_C$ (lag), Fig. 10.43 (b), or (ii) $I_L < I_C$ (lead),
Fig. 10.43 (c).
The particular case where $I_L = I_C$ is dealt with
in § **10.22.**

EXAMPLE 10.52 (B). An inductance of $1/\pi$ mH and a
capacitance of $0\cdot 1/\pi\ \mu$F, are connected in parallel across
an a.c. supply. If the frequency is 100 kc/s and the
value of the current in the inductance arm is 1 A, find—

   (a) the voltage across the parallel circuit,
   (b) the current in the capacitance arm,
   (c) the total current in the common external circuit.
                      (C. & G.)

See Fig. 10.44.

(a) $X_L = \omega L = 2\pi \times 10^5 \times (1/\pi) \times 10^{-3}$
$$= 200\ \Omega$$

Supply voltage $= V = V_L = I\omega L = 1 \times 200$
$$= \underline{200\ V}$$

(b) $X_C = 1/(\omega C) = 10^6/(2\pi \times 10^5 \times 0\cdot1/\pi)$

　　　$= 50\ \Omega$

　　$I_C = V/X_C = 200/50 = \underline{\underline{4\ A}}$

(c) $I = I_L - I_C = 1 - 4 = \underline{\underline{3\ A}}$

（leading by 90° since $I_C > I_L$).

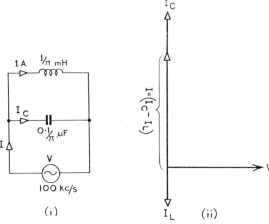

Fig. 10.44 (Example 10.52)

10.21. Resistance, Inductance, and Capacitance in Parallel.

The circuit and vector diagrams are shown in Fig. 10.45: it is assumed that the resistance is of negligible value in the inductor and capacitor branches.

The active current is

　$I_R = V/R$, in phase with the applied voltage

The capacitance current

　$I_C = \omega C V$, leads the voltage by 90°

The current in the inductance

　$I_L = V/(\omega L)$, lags 90° behind the voltage

The total reactive current

$$I_X = I_C - I_L = \omega C V - V/\omega L$$
$$= V(\omega C - 1/\omega L)$$

The total circuit current I

$$= (I_R{}^2 + I_X{}^2)^{\frac{1}{2}} = I_R + jI_X$$
$$= \{I_R{}^2 + (I_C - I_L)^2\}^{\frac{1}{2}} = I_R + j(I_C - I_L)$$
$$= \{(V/R)^2 + (\omega C V - V/\omega L)^2\}^{\frac{1}{2}}$$
$$= \frac{V}{R} + j\omega C V + V/j\omega L$$
$$= V\left\{\left(\frac{1}{R}\right)^2 + (\omega C - 1/\omega L)^2\right\}^{\frac{1}{2}}$$
$$= V(1/R + j\omega C + 1/j\omega L) \qquad . \quad (10.21)$$

The phase angle

$$\phi = \tan^{-1}(I_C - I_L)/I_R$$
$$= \tan^{-1}(V\omega C - V/\omega L) \div V/R$$
$$= \tan^{-1} R(\omega C - 1/\omega L)$$

The total impedance

$$Z = V/I = 1/(1/R + 1/j\omega L + j\omega C)$$

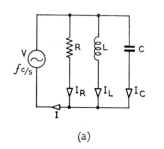

(a)

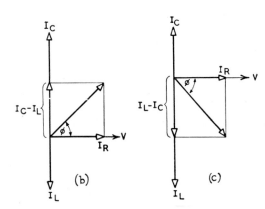

(b)　　　　　　　　(c)

Fig. 10.45. Parallel Circuit—Resistance, Inductance, and Capacitance

Example 10.53 (B). A 50 c/s a.c. supply at a pressure of 100 V is applied across a resistance of 1 000 Ω, an inductance of 0·5 H and of negligible resistance, and a capacitance of 10 μF, all of which are connected in parallel. What is the total current drawn from the supply and what is the phase angle of this current relative to the applied voltage? Illustrate your answer by a vector diagram.
(C. & G.)

Using the symbols in Fig. 10.46 (i)—

$I_R = V/R = 100/1\ 000 = 0\cdot10\ A$

$I_L = V/(\omega L) = 100/(100\pi \times 0\cdot5) = 0\cdot637\ A$

$I_C = V\omega C = 100 \times 100\pi \times 10^{-5} = 0\cdot314\ A$

$I_X = I_L - I_C = 0\cdot637 - 0\cdot314 = 0\cdot323\ A$

Total current

$$= (0.1^2 + 0.323^2)^{\frac{1}{2}} = \underline{\underline{0.337\ 6\ A}}$$

$$\phi = \tan^{-1} 0.323/0.1 = \tan^{-1} 3.23 = \underline{\underline{72°\ 46'}}$$

(current lagging since $I_L > I_C$)

The vector diagram is shown in Fig. 10.46 (ii).

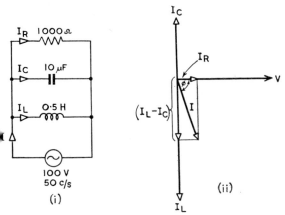

FIG. 10.46 (Example 10.53)

10.22. Parallel Resonant Circuit. In the circuit diagram of Fig. 10.47 (a), containing pure inductance and pure capacitance in parallel, the par-

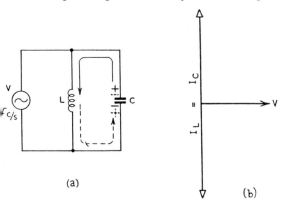

(a)

(b)

FIG. 10.47. PARALLEL RESONANT CIRCUIT

ticular case has to be considered when $I_L = I_C$ Fig. 10.47 (b)). For this condition, $V/(\omega L) = \omega C V$ numerically and

$$\omega_r = 1/(LC)^{\frac{1}{2}} \text{ or } f_r = \frac{1}{2\pi(LC)^{\frac{1}{2}}}$$

At this frequency, the supply current, $I = I_L - I_C$, becomes equal to zero and the impedance, $Z = V/I = V/0$, is infinitely great.

A parallel circuit tuned to resonance is known as a REJECTOR CIRCUIT, and it is used to offer maximum impedance and so exclude signal currents at the resonant frequency, or more commonly, over a band of frequencies.

Since in this ideal case there is no resistance present to incur I^2R losses, once the magnetic field in the inductance, or the charge on the capacitor has been established, there is a complete repeated interchange of energy between the capacitance and the inductance, and no energy whatever is drawn from the source of supply. Although the supply current is zero, a maximum current circulates within the local circuit between the inductance and capacitance: the value of this current is

$$I_C = \omega C V = V/(\omega L) = I_L$$

and the rejector circuit is in a condition of *current resonance*.

The circuit tuned to resonance has the property of storing energy in an oscillating state, changing regularly from the kinetic energy of the magnetic field to the potential energy of the capacitor charge and back again at the natural frequency. The capacitor in its fully charged state (Fig. 10.47 (a)) will proceed to discharge its energy through the inductance, resulting in the current shown by the full line arrow until the capacitor is completely discharged. At this instant the energy is entirely magnetic and the current continues in the same direction (shown by the dotted arrow) supplied by the energy from the now decaying field, to build up a p.d. of reversed polarity across the capacitor. When all the energy has been transferred from the inductor to the capacitor, the p.d. across the capacitor has its original magnitude but is now reversed in sign and the current has decayed to zero. The process then reverses and repeats itself indefinitely, cycle after cycle if there is no resistance present to absorb energy.

In the practical case the circuit resistance will not be negligible and a small amount of power is drawn from the supply to make good the I^2R losses.

10.23. Rejector Circuit with Resistance. In the practical rejector circuit it is necessary to consider the conductor resistance of the inductor, though in a high-grade coil the resistance element may be negligible at the higher frequencies.

Fig. 10.48 shows the rejector circuit with resistance in the inductance branch. Considering this branch as a simple series circuit, its current

$$I_{RL} = V/(R^2 + \omega^2 L^2)^{\frac{1}{2}}$$

and the phase angle

$$\phi = \tan^{-1} \omega L/R$$

in this type of circuit the value of R is small compared with ωL and ϕ will be practically $90°$.

This current can be split up into two right-angled components $I_{RL}\cos\phi$, the active component, and $I_{RL}\sin\phi$, the reactive component lagging $90°$ on the voltage (Fig. 10.48 (b)). It is this latter component $I_{RL}\sin\phi$ (not the total current I_{RL}) which must be equal to I_C to produce resonance.

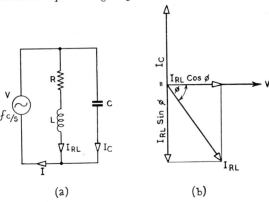

(a) (b)

FIG. 10.48. REJECTOR CIRCUIT WITH RESISTANCE

For resonance $I_C = I_{RL}\sin\phi$, where $I_C = \omega CV$.

From the impedance triangle (Fig. 10.17 (a)) for the inductor branch

$$\sin\phi = X/Z = \omega L/(R^2 + \omega^2 L^2)^{\frac{1}{2}}$$

Substituting this expression for $\sin\phi$, and

$$V/(R^2 + \omega^2 L^2)^{\frac{1}{2}} \text{ for } I_{RL}$$

$$I_{RL}\sin\phi = V/(R^2 + \omega^2 L^2)^{\frac{1}{2}}$$
$$\times \omega L/(R^2 + \omega^2 L^2)^{\frac{1}{2}}$$
$$= \omega LV/(R^2 + \omega^2 L^2)$$

Since $I_C = I_{RL}\sin\phi$
$$\omega CV = \omega LV/(R^2 + \omega^2 L^2)$$

Dividing by ωV—

$$C = L/(R^2 + \omega^2 L^2)$$
$$L = CR^2 + \omega^2 L^2 C$$
$$\omega^2 L^2 C = L - CR^2$$
$$\omega^2 = (L - CR^2)/(L^2 C) = 1/(LC) - R^2/L^2$$
$$\omega_r = \{1/(LC) - R^2/L^2\}^{\frac{1}{2}}$$

and $f_r = \dfrac{1}{2\pi} \cdot \{1/(LC) - R^2/L^2\}^{\frac{1}{2}}$. (10.22)

(*Note.* Putting $R = 0$ in this expression gives

$f_r = \dfrac{1}{2\pi(LC)^{\frac{1}{2}}}$ —the result obtained for the circuit considered in §**10.22**.)

The resonance curve obtained from plotting Z against f has the form shown by the graph Z_P in

Fig. 10.32, the impedance having a maximum value at f_r.

EXAMPLE 10.54 (B). A parallel circuit consists of two arms, one containing resistance and inductance in series and the other containing capacitance. The impedance across the circuit at resonant frequency is measured. The three elements are then placed in series and the impedance at resonant frequency again measured. The impedance in the first case was found to be much higher than in the second case. Explain these facts by the aid of vector diagrams.

If the value of the two impedances were 10 000 Ω and 100 Ω respectively, calculate the ratio of the inductance to capacitance. (C. & G.)

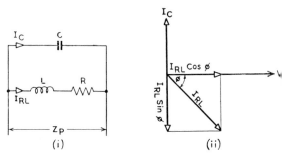

(i) (ii)

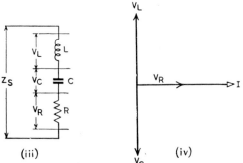

(iii) (iv)

FIG. 10.49 (Example 10.54)

For the parallel circuit—

Using the symbols shown in the circuit diagram in Fig. 10.49:

Capacitance current,

$$I_C = V\omega C, \text{ leading by } 90°$$

Inductor current,

$$I_{RL} = V/(R^2 + \omega^2 L^2)^{\frac{1}{2}}, \text{ lagging by}$$
$$\phi = \tan^{-1}\omega L/R$$

In the vector diagram (ii), I_{RL} is resolved into its two components,

$$I_R = I_{RL}\cos\phi, \text{ in phase with } V$$
$$I_L = I_{RL}\sin\phi, \text{ lagging } 90° \text{ on } V$$

At resonance, $I_C = I_{RL} \sin \phi$, and the total current $I = I_{RL} \cos \phi$.

Total impedance of parallel circuit

$= Z_P = V/I = V/(I_{RL} \cos \phi)$
(where $\cos \phi = R/\{(R^2 + \omega^2 L^2)^{\frac{1}{2}}\}$)
$Z_P = V \div \{V/(R^2 + \omega^2 L^2)^{\frac{1}{2}} \times R/(R^2 + \omega^2 L^2)^{\frac{1}{2}}\}$
$= (R^2 + \omega^2 L^2)/R$

Also, $I_C = I_{RL} \sin \phi$, where
$\sin \phi = \omega L/(R^2 + \omega^2 L^2)^{\frac{1}{2}}$

In Example 10.16, $L = 8$ mH, $R = 30 \, \Omega$, $V = 5$ V, $\omega = 5\,000$ radn/sec, $I = 0.1$ A, and $\phi = 53° 8'$ (lagging).

The current I may be resolved into the two components $I \cos \phi$ in phase with the applied voltage, and $I \sin \phi$ lagging 90° behind the applied voltage—see Fig. 10.50 (i).

By connecting a capacitance C_P in parallel with the coil to take a leading current equal to $I \sin \phi$, the total supply current would then be in phase

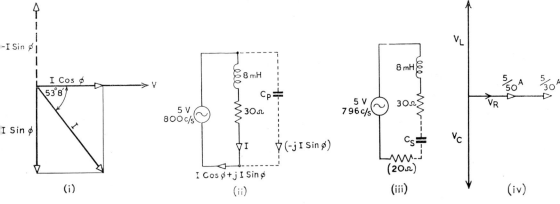

Fig. 10.50 (Example 10.55)

$V\omega C = \{V/(R^2 + \omega^2 L^2)^{\frac{1}{2}} \times \omega L/(R^2 + \omega^2 L^2)^{\frac{1}{2}}\}$
$= V\omega L/(R^2 + \omega^2 L^2)$
or, $\omega C = \omega L/(R^2 + \omega^2 L^2)$
$R^2 + \omega^2 L^2 = \omega L/\omega C = L/C$
But $Z_P = (R^2 + \omega^2 L^2)/R$ (above) $= \underline{L/(CR)}$

For the series circuit—
Using the symbols in diagram (iii), Fig. 10.49.
At resonance, $V_L = \omega L I$ (leading I by 90°) is equal to $V_C = I/(\omega C)$ (lagging 90° on I).
The total voltage $V = V_R = IR$ (in phase—see vector diagram (iv)).
Total impedance of series circuit $Z_S = V/I$ $= IR/I = \underline{R}$.

If the ratio L/C is high compared with R, the impedance of the rejector circuit must be high compared with the impedance of the acceptor circuit (both at f_r).

$Z_P = 10\,000 = L/(CR)$
$Z_S = 100 = R$
$L/C = L/(CR) \times R = 10\,000 \times 100 = \underline{10^6}$

EXAMPLE 10.55 (B). In Example 10.16, how could the phase angle be reduced to zero without altering the value of the current passing through the coil when the relay is operated from the same a.c. supply? (C. & G.)

with the applied voltage, the current through the coil remaining unchanged (diagram (ii)).

$I_C = I \sin \phi = 0.1 \times \sin 53° 8'$
$= 0.1 \times 0.8 = 0.08$ A
$I_C = V\omega C_P$
$C_P = I_C/(\omega V) = 0.08/(5 \times 5\,000)$
$= \underline{3.2 \, \mu F}$

Alternatively, a *series* capacitor C_S could be used to produce resonance (see diagrams (iii) and (iv)).

$\omega L = 1/(\omega C_S)$
$C_S = 1/(\omega^2 L) = 1/(25 \times 10^6 \times 8 \times 10^{-3})$
$= 1/(2 \times 10^5) = \underline{5 \, \mu F}$

To give the same current at resonance, the total resistance $R = V/I = 5/0.1 = 50 \, \Omega$, i.e. an additional 20 Ω resistor should be connected in series with the 5 μF capacitor and with the relay.

10.24. Admittance. In d.c. parallel circuits it is found convenient in certain cases to perform calculations in terms of conductance rather than resistance.

The reciprocal of an impedance is known as the ADMITTANCE, designated by the symbol Y, where $Y = 1/Z$ mhos. As with impedance, admittance is

9

a complex quantity and it has the two parts CONDUCTANCE (G) and SUSCEPTANCE (B). These components, also measured in mhos, have a phase difference of $90°$ so that

$$Y = (G^2 + B^2)^{\frac{1}{2}} = G + jB \quad . \ (10.23)$$

The values of the conductance and susceptance are calculated from

$$G = R/Z^2 \text{ and } B = -X/Z^2 \quad . \ (10.24)$$

These values of G and B are obtained as follows—

$$
\begin{aligned}
Y = 1/Z &= 1/(R + jX) \\
&= (R - jX)/\{(R + jX)(R - jX)\} \\
&= (R - jX)/(R^2 + X^2) = (R - jX)/Z^2 \\
&= R/Z^2 + j(-X)/Z^2 = G + jB
\end{aligned}
$$

whence $G = R/Z^2$ and $B = -X/Z^2$
If $X = 0$, $G = R/(R^2 + 0) = 1/R$; and if $R = 0$, $B = X/(0 + X^2) = 1/X$.

Admittance calculations facilitate the solution of networks with parallel branches where any branch includes resistance as well as inductance or capacitance.

To evaluate the total current in a parallel circuit, each branch is first treated as a series circuit, with a phase angle which may lie anywhere between $+ 90°$ and $- 90°$: the branch currents are split up into their components $I \cos \phi$ and $I \sin \phi$. The active and reactive components respectively of the several branches may then be added algebraically and their resultant determined (see Appendix **A.4**), i.e. the load current

$$I = \{(\Sigma I \cos \phi)^2 + (\Sigma I \sin \phi)^2\}^{\frac{1}{2}}$$

The phase angle for the network is then

$$\phi = \tan^{-1} (\Sigma I \sin \phi)/(\Sigma I \cos \phi)$$

and its impedance $Z = V/I$.

An admittance triangle with the two components conductance and susceptance may be drawn in a similar manner to the impedance triangle, but its position will be inverted with respect to the corresponding impedance triangle.

From $Y = R/Z^2 + j(-X)/Z^2$ (above)
and $\quad X = (X_L - X_C)$
$$
\begin{aligned}
j(-X/Z^2) &= j\{-(X_L - X_C)/Z^2\} \\
&= j(X_C/Z^2 - X_L/Z^2) = j(B_C - B_L)
\end{aligned}
$$

where the suffix C or L denotes capacitive or inductive, hence

$$Y = G + jB = G + j(B_C - B_L)$$

and the *susceptance* has a *positive* sign if the capacitance predominates: in the impedance equation,

the *reactance* has a *negative* sign if the capacitan⟨ce⟩ predominates; or $X = X_L - X_C$ but $B = B_C - B$⟨_L⟩

It should be observed that capacitance gives ⟨a⟩ negative sign to reactance but a positive sign ⟨to⟩ susceptance.

EXAMPLE 10.56 (B). A coil having an inductance 0.4 H and an effective resistance of $100 \ \Omega$ is connected parallel with a non-inductive resistance of $141 \ \Omega$ acro⟨ss⟩ a sinusoidal a.c. supply having a frequency of 40 c⟨/s⟩

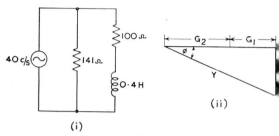

(i)
FIG. 10.51 (Example 10.56)

With the aid of a vector diagram, determine the approx⟨i-⟩ mate impedance (modulus and angle) of the comple⟨te⟩ circuit. (C. & G⟨.⟩)

See the circuit diagram (i) in Fig. 10.51.

$$X_L = 2\pi f L = 2\pi \times 40 \times 0.4 = 32\pi = 100 \ \Omega$$

Inductive path—

Impedance Z_1
$$= (100^2 + 100^2)^{\frac{1}{2}} = 100\sqrt{2}$$

Conductance G_1
$$= R_1/Z_1^2 = 100/(10^4 \times 2) = 1/200$$

Susceptance B_1
$$= X_1/Z_1^2 = 100/(10^4 \times 2) = 1/200$$

Non-inductive path—

Impedance Z_2
$$= 141$$

Conductance G_2
$$= R_2/Z_2^2 = 141/141^2 = 1/100\sqrt{2} = \sqrt{2}/200$$

Susceptance B_2
$$= X_2/Z_2^2 = 0$$

Joint conductance, G
$$
\begin{aligned}
&= G_1 + G_2 = 1/200 + \sqrt{2}/200 \\
&= 2.41/200 \text{ (see diagram (ii))}
\end{aligned}
$$

Joint susceptance, B
$$= B_1 + B_2 = 1/200$$

Joint admittance, Y

$$= (G^2 + B^2)^{\frac{1}{2}} = (2 \cdot 41^2 / 200^2 + 1/200^2)^{\frac{1}{2}}$$
$$= (5 \cdot 81 / 200^2 + 1/200^2)^{\frac{1}{2}} = (6 \cdot 81 / 200^2)^{\frac{1}{2}}$$
$$= 2 \cdot 61 / 200$$

Joint impedance, Z

$$= 200 / 2 \cdot 61 = \underline{\underline{76 \cdot 5 \ \Omega}}$$

$$\phi = \tan^{-1} B/G = \tan^{-1} (1/200 \times 200/2 \cdot 41)$$
$$= \tan^{-1} 0 \cdot 414 \ 9 = \underline{\underline{22° \ 32'}}$$

10.25. Impedances in Parallel. For impedances in parallel the combined impedance is calculated from

$$1/Z = \text{vector sum}$$
$$(1/Z_1 + 1/Z_2 + 1/Z_3 + \ldots + 1/Z_N)$$

which is equivalent to

$$A = \text{vector sum } (A_1 + A_2 + A_3 + \ldots + A_N)$$
$$= (G_1 + G_2 + G_3 + \ldots + G_N)$$
$$\quad + j(B_1 + B_2 + B_3 + \ldots + B_N)$$
$$= \Sigma(G) + j\Sigma(B) = \{(\Sigma G)^2 + (\Sigma B)^2\}^{\frac{1}{2}}$$
$$= A = 1/Z$$

The resonant frequency of the rejector circuit with resistance may be determined from calculation of the combined impedance—

Impedance of inductor branch, Z_{RL}

$$= R + j\omega L$$

Impedance of capacitor branch, Z_C

$$= -j/(\omega C)$$

Combined impedance, Z

$$= Z_{RL} Z_C / (Z_{RL} + Z_C)$$
$$= \frac{-j}{\omega C} (R + j\omega L) / \left\{ R + j\left(\omega L - \frac{1}{\omega C} \right) \right\}$$

Multiply by

$$\left\{ R - j\left(\omega L - \frac{1}{\omega C} \right) \right\} / \left\{ R - j\left(\omega L - \frac{1}{\omega C} \right) \right\}$$

$$Z = \frac{\begin{aligned} &\{-jR^2/(\omega C) + RL/C - RL/C - j\omega L^2/C \\ &\quad + R/(\omega^2 C^2) + jL/(\omega C^2)\} \end{aligned}}{\left\{ R^2 + \left(\omega L - \frac{1}{\omega C} \right)^2 \right\}}$$

$$= \frac{R/(\omega^2 C^2) + j\{L/(\omega C^2) - \omega L^2/C - R^2/(\omega C)\}}{R^2 + \{\omega L - 1/(\omega C)\}^2}$$

For resonance Z must be non-reactive, i.e. the term in j must be equal to zero, and

$$L/(\omega C^2) - \omega L^2/C - R^2/(\omega C) = 0$$

Multiply by ωC^2—

$$L - \omega^2 L^2 C - CR^2 = 0$$
$$\omega^2 L^2 C = L - CR^2$$
$$\omega^2 = \{1/(LC) - R^2/L^2\}$$
$$f_r = \frac{1}{2\pi} \cdot \{1/(LC) - R^2/L^2\}^{\frac{1}{2}}$$

Substitution of $\omega^2 = \{1/(LC) - R^2/L^2\}$ in the expression for impedance gives $Z = L/(CR)$.

EXAMPLE 10.57 (B). A circuit consists of two branches in parallel. One branch consists of an inductance L in series with a resistance R, the other branch consists of a capacitor

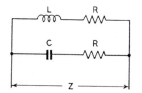

FIG. 10.52 (Example 10.57)

C in series with a resistor R. If $L/C = R^2$, prove that the impedance of the circuit is independent of frequency and equal to R.　　　　　　(C. & G.)

See Fig. 10.52.

In branch containing L, impedance,

$$Z_L = R + j\omega L$$

In branch containing C, impedance,

$$Z_C = R + 1/(j\omega C)$$

If joint impedance $= Z$, then

$$\frac{1}{Z} = \frac{1}{(R + j\omega L)} + \frac{1}{R + 1/(j\omega C)}$$
$$= 1/(R + j\omega L) + j\omega C/(j\omega C R + 1)$$

But $L/C = R^2$, $L = CR^2$

$$\frac{1}{Z} = 1/(R + j\omega C R^2) + j\omega C/(j\omega C R + 1)$$
$$= 1/\{R(1 + j\omega C R)\}$$
$$\quad + j\omega C/(j\omega C R + 1)$$
$$= (1 + j\omega C R)/\{R(1 + j\omega C R)\} = 1/R$$
$$\underline{\underline{Z = R}} \ \text{(i.e. independent of frequency)}$$

EXAMPLE 10.58 (B). Calculate the impedance of the circuit given in Fig. 10.53.

Path BCE—

$$Z_1 = (R^2 + X^2)^{\frac{1}{2}} = (20^2 + 30^2)^{\frac{1}{2}}$$
$$= (400 + 900)^{\frac{1}{2}} = 36 \ \Omega$$
$$Y_1 = 1/Z_1 = 1/36 = 0 \cdot 027 \ 8 \ \text{mho}$$
$$\phi_1 = \tan^{-1} X/R = \tan^{-1} 30/20 = 56 \cdot 3°$$

Path BDE—

$$Z_2 = (5^2 + 60^2)^{\frac{1}{2}} = (25 + 3\,600)^{\frac{1}{2}} = 3\,625^{\frac{1}{2}}$$
$$= 60.2\ \Omega$$
$$Y_2 = 1/Z_2 = 1/60.2 = 0.016\,6\ \text{mho}$$
$$\phi_2 = \tan^{-1} 60/5 = 85.2°$$

Joint path BE—

Horizontal component

$$= 0.027\,8 \cos 56.3° + 0.016\,6 \cos 85.2°$$
$$= 0.016\,7$$

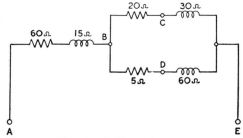

Fɪɢ. 10.53 (Example 10.58)

Vertical component

$$= 0.027\,8 \sin 56.3° + 0.016\,6 \sin 85.2°$$
$$= 0.039\,7$$
$$Y_3 = \{(0.016\,7)^2 + (0.039\,7)^2\}^{\frac{1}{2}} = 0.043\ \text{mho}$$
$$Z_3 = 1/Y_3 = 1/0.043 = 23.3\ \Omega$$
$$\phi_3 = \tan^{-1} 0.039\,7/0.016\,7 = 67.2°$$
$$R_3 = 23.3 \cos 67.2 = 9.0\ \Omega$$
$$X_3 = 23.3 \sin 67.2 = 21.5\ \Omega$$

Total circuit AE—

$$R_4 = 60 + 9 = 69\ \Omega$$
$$X_4 = 15 + 21.5 = 36.5\ \Omega$$

Impedance

$$Z_4 = (69^2 + 36.5^2)^{\frac{1}{2}} = \underline{\underline{78.1\ \Omega}}$$

$$\phi_4 = \tan^{-1} 36.5/69 = \underline{\underline{27.9°}}$$

POWER

10.26. Power. In a.c. systems, unless the load consists of a pure resistance or a resonant circuit, the load current I and supply voltage V are out of phase and the true power cannot be determined from the simple product VI.

This product VI is known as the APPARENT POWER and it is expressed not in watts but in *volt-amps* (VA), or in *kilovolt-amps* (kVA): it is not a true measure of the power consumed in the circuit, for the voltage and current are not in phase.

In Fig. 10.54 are shown the voltage and current graphs for a circuit containing pure inductance. If the instantaneous values of V and I are multiplied together—with due respect to the sign—the power curve (shown shaded) is obtained. This curve has alternative positive and negative values and it is symmetrical about the zero line. The (positive) power consumed in building up the magnetic field during one quarter-cycle of the current is restored to the circuit during the following quarter-cycle ("negative" power) when the current is falling and

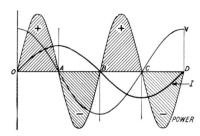

Fɪɢ. 10.54. Power in Pure Inductance

the magnetic field is decaying. The power consumed by an inductor of negligible resistance is zero. The field is fully established at the instants denoted by A and C and completely decayed at B and D.

Similar graphs for the circuit with pure capacitance are shown in Fig. 10.55. The power con-

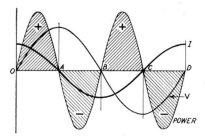

Fɪɢ. 10.55. Power in Pure Capacitance

sumed in charging a capacitor during one quarter-cycle is restored to the circuit during the next quarter-cycle and the total power absorbed during a cycle is zero. In the graphs given, the capacitor is fully charged at the instants denoted by A and C, and fully discharged at the instants B and D.

In an a.c. circuit all the power consumed is due to the current flowing through the resistance and it is equal to the product of the current I and the p.d. V_R across the resistance Fig. 10.56 (*a*) shows the general case of an a.c. circuit where power is fed into a load impedance $Z/\underline{\phi}$. In the vector diagram

Joint admittance, Y

$= (G^2 + B^2)^{\frac{1}{2}} = (2\cdot41^2/200^2 + 1/200^2)^{\frac{1}{2}}$
$= (5\cdot81/200^2 + 1/200^2)^{\frac{1}{2}} = (6\cdot81/200^2)^{\frac{1}{2}}$
$= 2\cdot61/200$

Joint impedance, Z

$= 200/2\cdot61 = \underline{\underline{76\cdot5 \ \Omega}}$

$\phi = \tan^{-1} B/G = \tan^{-1} (1/200 \times 200/2\cdot41)$
$= \tan^{-1} 0\cdot414 \ 9 = \underline{\underline{22° \ 32'}}$

10.25. Impedances in Parallel. For impedances in parallel the combined impedance is calculated from

$1/Z =$ vector sum
$\qquad (1/Z_1 + 1/Z_2 + 1/Z_3 + \ldots + 1/Z_N)$

which is equivalent to

$A =$ vector sum $(A_1 + A_2 + A_3 + \ldots + A_N)$
$\quad = (G_1 + G_2 + G_3 + \ldots + G_N)$
$\qquad + j(B_1 + B_2 + B_3 + \ldots + B_N)$
$\quad = \Sigma(G) + j\Sigma(B) = \{(\Sigma G)^2 + (\Sigma B)^2\}^{\frac{1}{2}}$
$\quad = A = 1/Z$

The resonant frequency of the rejector circuit with resistance may be determined from calculation of the combined impedance—

Impedance of inductor branch, Z_{RL}

$= R + j\omega L$

Impedance of capacitor branch, Z_C

$= -j/(\omega C)$

Combined impedance, Z

$= Z_{RL}Z_C/(Z_{RL} + Z_C)$
$= \dfrac{-j}{\omega C}(R + j\omega L)/\left\{ R + j\left(\omega L - \dfrac{1}{\omega C}\right)\right\}$

Multiply by

$\left\{R - j\left(\omega L - \dfrac{1}{\omega C}\right)\right\}\bigg/\left\{R - j\left(\omega L - \dfrac{1}{\omega C}\right)\right\}$

$Z = \dfrac{\begin{aligned}&\{-jR^2/(\omega C) + RL/C - RL/C - j\omega L^2/C\\&\quad + R/(\omega^2 C^2) + jL/(\omega C^2)\}\end{aligned}}{\left\{R^2 + \left(\omega L - \dfrac{1}{\omega C}\right)^2\right\}}$

$= \dfrac{R/(\omega^2 C^2) + j\{L/(\omega C^2) - \omega L^2/C - R^2/(\omega C)\}}{R^2 + \{\omega L - 1/(\omega C)\}^2}$

For resonance Z must be non-reactive, i.e. the term in j must be equal to zero, and

$L/(\omega C^2) - \omega L^2/C - R^2/(\omega C) = 0$

Multiply by ωC^2—

$L - \omega^2 L^2 C - CR^2 = 0$
$\omega^2 L^2 C = L - CR^2$
$\omega^2 = \{1/(LC) - R^2/L^2\}$
$f_r = \dfrac{1}{2\pi} \cdot \{1/(LC) - R^2/L^2\}^{\frac{1}{2}}$

Substitution of $\omega^2 = \{1/(LC) - R^2/L^2\}$ in the expression for impedance gives $Z = L/(CR)$.

EXAMPLE 10.57 (B). A circuit consists of two branches in parallel. One branch consists of an inductance L in series with a resistance R, the other branch consists of a capacitor

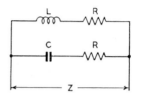

FIG. 10.52 (Example 10.57)

C in series with a resistor R. If $L/C = R^2$, prove that the impedance of the circuit is independent of frequency and equal to R. (C. & G.)

See Fig. 10.52.

In branch containing L, impedance,

$\qquad Z_L = R + j\omega L$

In branch containing C, impedance,

$\qquad Z_C = R + 1/(j\omega C)$

If joint impedance $= Z$, then

$\dfrac{1/Z = \dfrac{1}{(R + j\omega L)} + \dfrac{1}{R + 1/(j\omega C)}}{}$
$\qquad = 1/(R + j\omega L) + j\omega C/(j\omega CR + 1)$

But $L/C = R^2$, $L = CR^2$

$1/Z = 1/(R + j\omega CR^2) + j\omega C/(j\omega CR + 1)$
$\quad = 1/\{R(1 + j\omega CR)\}$
$\qquad + j\omega C/(j\omega CR + 1)$
$\quad = (1 + j\omega CR)/\{R(1 + j\omega CR)\} = 1/R$
$\underline{\underline{Z = R}}$ (i.e. independent of frequency)

EXAMPLE 10.58 (B). Calculate the impedance of the circuit given in Fig. 10.53.

Path BCE—

$Z_1 = (R^2 + X^2)^{\frac{1}{2}} = (20^2 + 30^2)^{\frac{1}{2}}$
$\quad = (400 + 900)^{\frac{1}{2}} = 36 \ \Omega$
$Y_1 = 1/Z_1 = 1/36 = 0\cdot027 \ 8$ mho
$\phi_1 = \tan^{-1} X/R = \tan^{-1} 30/20 = 56\cdot3°$

Path BDE—

$$Z_2 = (5^2 + 60^2)^{\frac{1}{2}} = (25 + 3\ 600)^{\frac{1}{2}} = 3\ 625^{\frac{1}{2}}$$
$$= 60\cdot2\ \Omega$$
$$Y_2 = 1/Z_2 = 1/60\cdot2 = 0\cdot016\ 6\ \text{mho}$$
$$\phi_2 = \tan^{-1} 60/5 = 85\cdot2°$$

Joint path BE—

Horizontal component

$$= 0\cdot027\ 8 \cos 56\cdot3° + 0\cdot016\ 6 \cos 85\cdot2°$$
$$= 0\cdot016\ 7$$

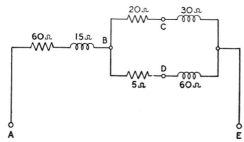

FIG. 10.53 (Example 10.58)

Vertical component

$$= 0\cdot027\ 8 \sin 56\cdot3° + 0\cdot016\ 6 \sin 85\cdot2°$$
$$= 0\cdot039\ 7$$
$$Y_3 = \{(0\cdot016\ 7)^2 + (0\cdot039\ 7)^2\}^{\frac{1}{2}} = 0\cdot043\ \text{mho}$$
$$Z_3 = 1/Y_3 = 1/0\cdot043 = 23\cdot3\ \Omega$$
$$\phi_3 = \tan^{-1} 0\cdot039\ 7/0\cdot016\ 7 = 67\cdot2°$$
$$R_3 = 23\cdot3 \cos 67\cdot2 = 9\cdot0\ \Omega$$
$$X_3 = 23\cdot3 \sin 67\cdot2 = 21\cdot5\ \Omega$$

Total circuit AE—

$$R_4 = 60 + 9 = 69\ \Omega$$
$$X_4 = 15 + 21\cdot5 = 36\cdot5\ \Omega$$

Impedance

$$Z_4 = (69^2 + 36\cdot5^2)^{\frac{1}{2}} = \underline{78\cdot1\ \Omega}$$

$$\phi_4 = \tan^{-1} 36\cdot5/69 = \underline{\underline{27\cdot9°}}$$

POWER

10.26. Power. In a.c. systems, unless the load consists of a pure resistance or a resonant circuit, the load current I and supply voltage V are out of phase and the true power cannot be determined from the simple product VI.

This product VI is known as the APPARENT POWER and it is expressed not in watts but in *volt-amps* (VA), or in *kilovolt-amps* (kVA): it is not a true measure of the power consumed in the circuit, for the voltage and current are not in phase.

In Fig. 10.54 are shown the voltage and current graphs for a circuit containing pure inductance. If the instantaneous values of V and I are multiplied together—with due respect to the sign—the power curve (shown shaded) is obtained. This curve has alternative positive and negative values and it is symmetrical about the zero line. The (positive) power consumed in building up the magnetic field during one quarter-cycle of the current is restored to the circuit during the following quarter-cycle ("negative" power) when the current is falling and

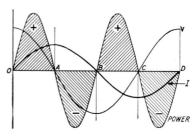

FIG. 10.54. POWER IN PURE INDUCTANCE

the magnetic field is decaying. The power consumed by an inductor of negligible resistance is zero. The field is fully established at the instants denoted by A and C and completely decayed at B and D.

Similar graphs for the circuit with pure capacitance are shown in Fig. 10.55. The power con-

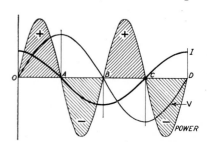

FIG. 10.55. POWER IN PURE CAPACITANCE

sumed in charging a capacitor during one quarter-cycle is restored to the circuit during the next quarter-cycle and the total power absorbed during a cycle is zero. In the graphs given, the capacitor is fully charged at the instants denoted by A and C, and fully discharged at the instants B and D.

In an a.c. circuit all the power consumed is due to the current flowing through the resistance and it is equal to the product of the current I and the p.d. V_R across the resistance. Fig. 10.56 (a) shows the general case of an a.c. circuit where power is fed into a load impedance Z/ϕ. In the vector diagram

Fig. 10.56 (*b*)) the applied voltage V has the two components $V_R = V \cos \phi$ (in phase with the current) and $V_X = V \sin \phi$ (in quadrature). The p.d. across the resistor is $V_R = V \cos \phi$, and the power absorbed in the resistance, i.e. the *true power*, is

$$V_R I = VI \cos \phi \quad . \qquad . \ (10.25)$$

The graph for the case of a lagging current ($\phi \neq 90°$) is shown at Fig. 10.56 (*c*). The power

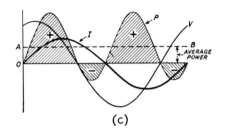

(c)

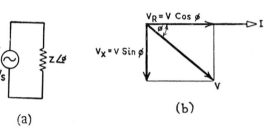

(a)

(b)

Fig. 10.56. Power in A.C. Circuit

graph (shown shaded) is obtained from the product of the instantaneous values of v and i: this has negative values which are not equal to the positive values. The average power is equal to the magnitude OA, the power graph being symmetrical about the line AB.

The ratio *true power/apparent power = watts/volt-amps* $= VI \cos \phi / VI = \cos \phi$ (for a sine wave) is known as the power-factor (p.f.): its value must always lie between ± 1 and it is of the utmost significance in the economics of a.c. power supply systems. In the impedance triangles (Fig. 10.17), the power factor is determined from $\cos \phi = R/Z$.

If the load power factor is low on account of a preponderance of capacitive or inductive reactance, the supply generator and the transmission system carry heavy currents without a corresponding useful power in the load. Power-factor correction, to bring the phase angle as nearly as possible to zero, is applied to a.c. loads to reduce the supply current: for example, in an installation employing induction motors drawing a lagging current, capacitors are

connected across the load terminals to reduce the power factor.

In capacitors whose resistance is not negligible, the power loss can be expressed in terms of the power-factor, which is a direct indication of the ratio of resistance to impedance at a given frequency.

Example 10.59 (B). A coil has an inductance of 0·025 H. When a 100 V, 50 c/s potential is impressed across the coil the current flowing is 10 A. What are the resistance and the power-factor of the coil? (*C. & G.*)

$$Z = V/I = 100/10 = 10 \ \Omega$$
$$Z^2 = R^2 + \omega^2 L^2$$
$$R^2 = Z^2 - \omega^2 L^2$$
$$\quad = 10^2 - (100\pi)^2 \times 0·025^2 = 100 - 61·5$$
$$\quad = 38·5 \ \Omega$$
$$R = \sqrt{38·5} = \underline{6·2 \ \Omega}$$

Power-factor
$$= \cos \phi = R/Z = 6·2/10 = \underline{0·62}$$

Example 10.60 (B). An alternating current of 1 A at a frequency of 800 c/s flows through a coil the inductance of which is 2·5 mH and the resistance of which is 5 Ω. What is the p.d. across the coil, the power absorbed in the coil, and the power factor? (*C. & G.*)

$$Z = (R^2 + \omega^2 L^2)^{\frac{1}{2}}$$
$$\omega = 2\pi f = 2\pi \times 800$$
$$\quad = 5\ 000 \text{ radn/sec}$$
$$Z = (5^2 + 5\ 000^2 \times 2·5^2 \times 10^{-6})^{\frac{1}{2}}$$
$$\quad = (25 + 156·3)^{\frac{1}{2}} = 13·52 \ \Omega$$
$$V = IZ = 1 \times 13·52 = \underline{13·52 \text{ V}}$$

Power, $P = I^2 R = 1^2 \times 5 = \underline{5 \text{ W}}$

P.f. $= \cos \phi = R/Z = 5/13·52 = \underline{0·37}$

Example 10.61 (B). A magneto bell and capacitor are connected in series across 75 V a.c. terminals, the frequency being 17 c/s. At this frequency the impedance of the bell is $2\ 000\underline{/45°}$ and the capacitor may be regarded as a pure capacitance of 2 μF. Calculate the current passing through the bell and capacitor and the power-factor of the combination. (*C. & G.*)

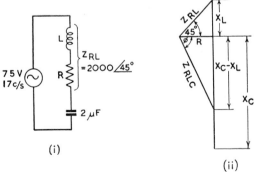

Fig. 10.57 (Example 10.61)

See the circuit diagram and impedance triangles in Fig. 10.57.

$$Z_{RL} = 2\,000\underline{/45°}$$
$$R = 2\,000\cos 45 = 2\,000/\sqrt{2} = 2\,000\sqrt{2}/2$$
$$= 1\,414\ \Omega$$
$$X_L = 2\,000\sin 45 = 2\,000/\sqrt{2} = 1\,414\ \Omega$$
$$X_C = 1/(\omega C) = 10^6/(2\pi \times 17 \times 2) = 4\,680\ \Omega$$

Total circuit impedance,

$$Z_{RLC} = \{1\,414^2 + (1\,414 - 4\,680)^2\}^{\frac{1}{2}}$$
$$= 3\,556\ \Omega$$

Current,

$$I = V/Z = 75/3\,556 = \underline{0\cdot021\ \text{A}}$$

$$\text{P.f.} = \cos\phi = R/Z = 1\,414/3\,556$$
$$= \underline{0\cdot399}$$

EXAMPLE 10.62 (B). A magneto bell and a 2 μF capacitor when connected in series across a 75 V, $16\frac{2}{3}$ c/s supply

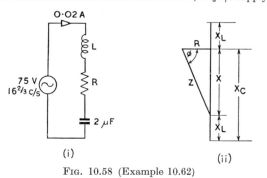

FIG. 10.58 (Example 10.62)

take a leading current of 20 mA and the power absorbed is 0·6 W. Calculate the inductance of the bell. (C. & G.)

Power $P = VI\cos\phi = 0\cdot6$ W
$$VI = 75 \times 0\cdot020 = 1\cdot5\ \text{VA}$$
$$\cos\phi = VI\cos\phi/(VI) = 0\cdot6/1\cdot5 = 0\cdot4$$
$$\phi = 66° 25'$$

Total impedance,

$$Z = V/I = 75/0\cdot020 = 3\,750\ \Omega$$

Total reactance (Fig. 10.58),

$$X = Z\sin\phi = 3\,750 \times \sin 66° 25'$$
$$= 3\,750 \times 0\cdot916\,5 = 3\,437\ \Omega$$
$$X_C = 1/(\omega C) = 10^6/(2\pi \times 16\cdot6 \times 2) = 4\,775\ \Omega$$
$$X_L = X_C - X = 4\,775 - 3\,437 = 1\,338\ \Omega$$
$$= \omega L$$
$$L = 1\,338/(2\pi \times 16\cdot6) = \underline{12\cdot79\ \text{H}}$$

EXAMPLE 10.63 (B). Two inductive coils A and B are connected in parallel across a 200 V a.c. supply. At the supply frequency coil A has a resistance of 400 Ω and a reactance of 300 Ω, and coil B has a resistance of 600 and a reactance of 800 Ω. Find the total current taken from the supply and the power-factor of the combination.
(C. & G.)

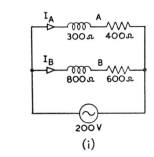

(i)

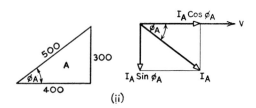

(ii)

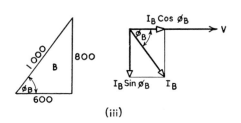

(iii)

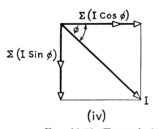

(iv)

FIG. 10.59 (Example 10.63)

See Fig. 10.59 (i).

$$I_A = V/(R + jX) = 200/(400^2 + 300^2)^{\frac{1}{2}}$$
$$= 200/500 = 0\cdot4\ \text{A}$$
$$I_B = V/(R + jX) = 200/(600^2 + 800^2)^{\frac{1}{2}}$$
$$= 200/1\,000 = 0\cdot2\ \text{A}$$

Coil A. (Diagram (ii).)

$I_A \sin \phi_A = 0.4 \times \frac{3}{5} = 0.24$ A

$I_A \cos \phi_A = 0.4 \times \frac{4}{5} = 0.32$ A

Coil B. (Diagram (iii).)

$I_B \sin \phi_B = 0.2 \times 0.8 = 0.16$ A

$I_B \cos \phi_B = 0.2 \times 0.6 = 0.12$ A

Diagram (iv).

$I_A \cos \phi_A + I_B \cos \phi_B$

$\qquad = 0.32 + 0.12 = 0.44$ A

$I_A \sin \phi_A + I_B \sin \phi_B$

$\qquad = 0.24 + 0.16 = 0.40$ A

$I = (0.44^2 + 0.40^2)^{\frac{1}{2}} = (0.193\ 6 + 0.160)^{\frac{1}{2}}$

$\qquad = (0.353\ 6)^{\frac{1}{2}} = \underline{\underline{0.594\ 6\ \text{A}}}$

P.f. $= \cos \phi = 0.44/0.59 = \underline{\underline{0.74}}$

EXAMPLE 10.64 (B). When an inductive coil is connected across 250 V 50 c/s mains the current taken is 0.5 A
a power-factor of 0.6. Calculate the total current taken

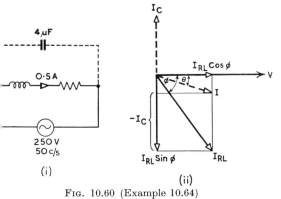

(i)

FIG. 10.60 (Example 10.64)

om the mains and the power-factor when a 4 μF capacitor
connected in parallel with the coil.   (*C. & G.*)

See the circuit and vector diagrams in Fig. 10.60.

$I_{RL} \cos \phi = 0.5 \times 0.6 = 0.3$ A

$I_{RL} \sin \phi = (0.5^2 - 0.3^2)^{\frac{1}{2}} = 0.4$ A

Capacitor current,

$\quad I_C = V\omega C = 250 \times 2\pi \times 50 \times 4 \times 10^{-6}$

$\qquad = \pi/10 = 0.314$ A

Total reactive current

$\quad = (I_{RL} \sin \phi - I_C)$

$\quad = (0.4 - 0.314) = 0.086$ A (lagging)

Active current

$\quad = I_{RL} \cos \phi = 0.3$ A

Total current, I

$\quad = (0.086^2 + 0.3^2)^{\frac{1}{2}} = (0.097\ 4)^{\frac{1}{2}} = \underline{\underline{0.31\ \text{A}}}$

New p.f. $= \cos \theta$

$\quad = I_{RL} \cos \phi / I = 0.3/0.31 = \underline{\underline{0.96}}$

EXAMPLE 10.65 (B). A battery charging generator is
driven by a single phase induction motor running from a
400 V a.c. supply. At full load the motor takes 25 A at a
power-factor of 0.6.

Calculate the total current taken from the supply, and
the power-factor at full load when a capacitor having a
reactance at the supply frequency of 32 Ω is connected
in parallel with the motor.   (*C. & G.*)

The circuit is shown in diagram (i) and the vector
diagram at (ii), in Fig. 10.61, where $\cos \phi = 0.6$
(i.e. $\phi = 53° 8'$).

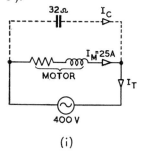

(i)

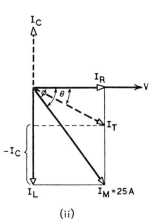

(ii)

FIG. 10.61 (Example 10.65)

The motor current I_M may be resolved into two
components, I_R in phase with the supply voltage
and I_L lagging 90° behind the supply voltage.

$I_R = I_M \cos \phi = 25 \cos 53° 8' = 25 \times 0.6$

$\qquad = 15$ A

$I_L = I_M \sin \phi = 25 \sin 53° 8' = 25 \times 0.8$

$\qquad = 20$ A

The current taken by the capacitor, $I_C = V/X_C$ $= 400/32 = 12.5$ A, leading by $90°$ on the applied voltage.

Reactive current

$$= I_L - I_C = 20 - 12.5 = 7.5 \text{ A}$$

Total current I

$$= \{I_R^2 + (I_L - I_C)^2\}^{\frac{1}{2}} = (15^2 + 7.5^2)^{\frac{1}{2}}$$
$$= \underline{16.77 \text{ A}}$$

New p.f. $= \cos \theta$

$$= I_R/I = 15/16.77 = \underline{0.89}$$

EXAMPLE 10.66 (B). An exchange charging set is run by a single-phase induction motor from a 400 V, 50 c/s supply. Under full-load conditions the motor takes a current of 50 A at a power-factor of 0.72. Find the total current and the power-factor at full-load when a 100 μF capacitor is connected in parallel with the motor. (C. & G.)

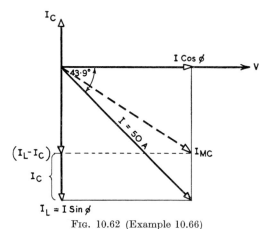

FIG. 10.62 (Example 10.66)

The current lags behind the voltage by $\phi°$, where $\cos \phi = 0.72$, i.e. $\phi = \cos^{-1} 0.72 = 43.9°$.

From the vector diagram, Fig. 10.62,
Active component of motor current

$$I_R = I \cos \phi = 50 \times 0.72 = 36 \text{ A}$$

Reactive component

$$I_L = I \sin \phi = 50 \sin 43.9° = 50 \times 0.693 4$$
$$= 34.67 \text{ A}$$

Total current taken by motor

$$= 50 = (36 + j34.67) \text{ A}$$

Current taken by 100 μF capacitor at 400 V

$$I_C = V\omega C = 400 \times 100\pi \times 100 \times 10^{-6}$$
$$= 4\pi = 12.57 \text{ A}$$

Total load current of motor + capacitor

$$I_{MC} = 36 + j(34.67 - 12.57) = 36 + j22.1$$
$$= (36^2 + 22.1^2)^{\frac{1}{2}} = \underline{42.3 \text{ A}}$$

P.f. $= \cos \phi = 36/42.3 = \underline{0.85}$

EXAMPLE 10.67 (B). The voltage applied to a coil havi̇ a resistance of 100 Ω and an inductance of 0.319 H represented by the expression $v = 100 \sin (2\pi 50t)$. Fi̇ a corresponding expression for the current and calculȧ the average value of the power taken by the coil. (C. &

The general expression for the instantaneȯ voltage is $v = V_{max} \sin 2\pi ft$.

General expression for the instantaneous curre̊

$$i = I_{max} \sin (2\pi ft - \phi)$$
$$= \frac{V_{max}}{Z} \sin (2\pi ft - \phi), \text{ where } \phi \text{ is the phȧ}$$

angle between V and I (current lagging).

If $R = 100 \Omega$ and $L = 0.319$ H

$$Z = (R^2 + \omega^2 L^2)^{\frac{1}{2}}$$
$$= \{100^2 + (100 \times \pi \times 0.319)^2\}^{\frac{1}{2}}$$
$$= (100^2 + 100^2)^{\frac{1}{2}} = 141.4 \Omega$$
$$\phi = \tan^{-1} \omega L/R = \tan^{-1} 100/100 = \tan^{-1}$$
$$= 45° = \pi/4 \text{ radn}$$
$$I_{max} = V_{max}/Z = 100/141.4 = 1/\sqrt{2} = 0.707$$

The expression for the instantaneous value of t̊ current is $i = \underline{0.707 \sin (2\pi 50t - \pi/4)}$.

The power,

$$P = VI \cos \phi, \text{ where } V = V_{max}/\sqrt{2};$$
$$I = I_{max}/\sqrt{2}$$
$$= 1/(\sqrt{2} \times \sqrt{2}) = \tfrac{1}{2}, \text{ and } \cos 45° = 1/\sqrt{2}$$
$$P = 100/\sqrt{2} \times \tfrac{1}{2} \times 1/\sqrt{2} = 100/4 = \underline{25 \text{ W}}$$

EXAMPLE 10.68 (B). Two coils A and B are connected turn across 200 V alternating supply mains. The curre̊ in each case is 400 mA, but A absorbs 48 W while absorbs 64 W. What would be the current taken å the total power absorbed if A and B were connected series across the mains? (C. &

The power in each coil is absorbed by the re̊ tance element of the coil.

Power $= P = I^2 R$, $R = P/I^2$. Impedance $Z = V$

Resistance of coil A,

$$R_A = 48/0.4^2 = 300 \Omega$$

Resistance of coil B,

$$R_B = 64/0.4^2 = 400 \Omega$$

Impedance of coil A,

$$Z_A = 200/0.4 = 500 \Omega$$

mpedance of coil B,

$$Z_B = 200/0\cdot4 = 500\ \Omega$$

Reactance of coil A,

$$X_A = (500^2 - 300^2)^{\frac{1}{2}} = 400\ \Omega$$

Reactance of coil B,

$$X_B = (500^2 - 400^2)^{\frac{1}{2}} = 300\ \Omega$$

(The reactance values are apparent from the mpedance triangles (Fig. 10.63) of sides proportional to 3, 4, and 5.)

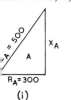 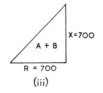

FIG. 10.63 (Example 10.68)

When the two coils are joined in series—

Total resistance

$$= R_A + R_B = 300 + 400 = 700\ \Omega$$

Total reactance

$$= X_A + X_B = 400 + 300 = 700\ \Omega$$

Total impedance

$$Z = (700^2 + 700^2)^{\frac{1}{2}} = 990\ \Omega$$

Current

$$I = V/Z = 200/990 = \underline{\underline{0\cdot202\ \text{A}}}$$

Power

$$= P = I^2R = 0\cdot202^2 \times 700 = \underline{\underline{28\cdot57\ \text{W}}}$$

EXAMPLE 10.69 (B). The current in a coil A connected to a 200 V a.c. supply is 400 mA and the power dissipated is 64 W. When a second coil B is joined in series with A the current is 200 mA and the total power dissipated is 24 W. Find the impedances of A, B, and $A + B$ respectively in the form Z/θ. (C. & G.)

In the circuit diagram (i) of Fig. 10.64—
Impedance of coil A, $Z_A = V/I = 200/0\cdot4 = 500\ \Omega$.
Power absorbed (in resistance element R_A) of coil A, $P_A = I^2R_A$, $R_A = P_A/I^2 = 64/0\cdot4^2 = 64/0\cdot16 = 400\ \Omega$.
From the impedance triangle, diagram (ii), $\phi_A = \cos^{-1} 400/500 = \cos^{-1} 0\cdot8 = 37°$.
Impedance of coil $A = 500/37°$.

In circuit diagram (iii)—
Joint impedance of coils $A + B$, $Z_{AB} = V/I = 200/0\cdot2 = 1\ 000\ \Omega$.
Power absorbed in resistance elements (R_{AB}) of coils A and B, $P_{AB} = I^2R_{AB}$, $R_{AB} = P_{AB}/I^2 = 24/0\cdot2^2 = 24/0\cdot04 = 600\ \Omega$.

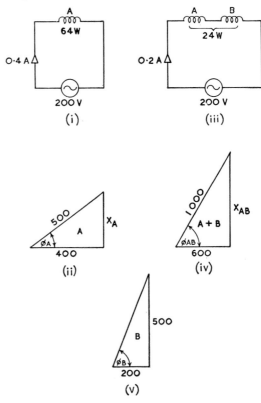

FIG. 10.64 (Example 10.69)

From the impedance triangle, diagram (iv) $\phi_{AB} = \cos^{-1} 600/1\ 000 = \cos^{-1} 0\cdot6 = 53°$.
Impedance of coils A and B in series
$$= \underline{\underline{1\ 000/53°}}$$

From the impedance triangle, diagram (ii),

$$X_A = (500^2 - 400^2)^{\frac{1}{2}} = 300\ \Omega$$

From the impedance triangle, diagram (iv),

$$X_{AB} = (1\ 000^2 - 600^2)^{\frac{1}{2}} = 800\ \Omega$$

Reactance of coil B,

$$X_B = 800 - 300 = 500\ \Omega$$

Resistance of coil B,

$$R_B = R_{AB} - R_A = 600 - 400 = 200\ \Omega$$

Impedance of coil B,

$$Z_B = (200^2 + 500^2)^{\frac{1}{2}} = 539 \ \Omega$$

From the impedance triangle, diagram (v),

$$\phi_B = \tan^{-1} 500/200 = \tan^{-1} 2\cdot5$$
$$= 68°$$

Impedance of coil B

$$= 539/68°$$

EXAMPLE 10.70 (B). What values of resistance and capacitance in series would produce the same impedance and phase angle at a frequency of 796 c/s ($\omega = 5\ 000$ radn/

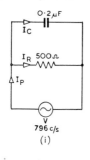
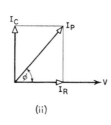

$$\text{0·2}\,\mu\text{F}$$

(i)

(ii)

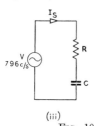
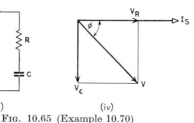

(iii)   (iv)

FIG. 10.65 (Example 10.70)

sec) as a resistor of $500 \ \Omega$ and a capacitor of $0\cdot2 \ \mu\text{F}$ connected in parallel?

In each case if an alternating voltage of 200 V at a frequency of 796 c/s is applied, what would be the real power consumed? Illustrate your answer by vector diagrams.   (C. & G.)

Parallel circuit (diagrams (i) and (ii) of Fig. 10.65)

$$X_C = 1/(\omega C) = 10^6/5\ 000 \times 0\cdot2 = 1\ 000 \ \Omega$$
$$I_C = V/1\ 000$$
$$R = 500 \ \Omega, \ I_R = V/500$$
$$\text{Tan}\ \phi = I_C/I_R = 500/1\ 000 = 0\cdot5$$

Since $I_R = 2I_C$ or $I_C = I_R/2$, the total current

$$I_P = (I_R^2 + I_R^2/4)^{\frac{1}{2}}$$
$$= I_R(5/4)^{\frac{1}{2}}$$

At $V = 200$, $I_R = 200/500$

$$\text{Power} = VI_R = 200 \times 200/500 = 80 \ \text{W}$$

Series circuit (diagrams (iii) and (iv)).

Since the impedances of the series and parallel circuits are to be equal, the total current in each circuit would be the same for a given applied voltage; also since the phase angles (and therefore the power-factors) are the same, the power losses in the two circuits will be equal.

For the parallel circuit,

$$P = 500 \ I_R^2$$

For the series circuit,

$$P = I_S^2 R = I_R^2 \times 5/4 \times R = 5I_R^2 R/4$$
$$500I_R^2 = 5I_R^2 R/4, \ R = 400 \ \Omega$$

$$\text{Tan}\ \phi = V_C/V_R$$
$$= 1/(\omega CR), \ C = 1/(\omega R \tan \phi)$$

Substituting

$$\omega = 5\ 000, \ R = 400, \text{ and } \tan \phi = 0\cdot5$$
$$C = 1/(\omega R \tan \phi)$$
$$= 1/(5\ 000 \times 400 \times 0\cdot5) = 1/10^6 = 1 \ \mu\text{F}$$

The power absorbed is the same as for the parallel circuit, i.e. 80 W.

EXAMPLE 10.71 (B). When an inductor and a resistor are connected in series, it is found that the current passing at a fixed frequency of 100 kc/s is half that passing when the resistance alone is in circuit, the applied voltage remaining constant. What is the power-factor of the inductor-resistor circuit?

If the value of the resistance is $100 \ \Omega$, what must be the value of the capacitor needed in series with the inductance and resistance to restore the current to the same value as when the resistance alone was in circuit?
                                      (C. & G.)

See the circuit and vector diagrams in Fig. 10.66.

(Diagram i). Voltage $= V$, current $= I$. Impedance, $Z_{RL} = (R + j\omega L) = V/I$

(Diagram ii). Voltage $= V$, current $= 2I$

Impedance,

$$Z_R = R = V/2I$$
$$Z_{RL} = 2Z_R = 2R$$

(Diagram iii).   P.f. $= \cos \phi = R/Z_{RL} = R/2R$
$= \frac{1}{2} = 0\cdot5$

(Diagram iv). To restore current to original value, i.e. to restore impedance to R, ωL must equal $1/(\omega C)$, or $C = 1/(\omega^2 L)$.

From the vector diagram (iii)

$$\omega^2 L^2 = Z_{RL}{}^2 - R^2 = 4R^2 - R^2 = 3R^2$$
$$\omega L = R\sqrt{3} = 100\sqrt{3}$$
$$C = 1/(\omega \times \omega L) = 1/(2\pi \times 10^5 \times 100\sqrt{3})$$
$$= 1/(20\pi\sqrt{3} \times 10^6) = \underline{0\cdot009\ 2\ \mu F}$$

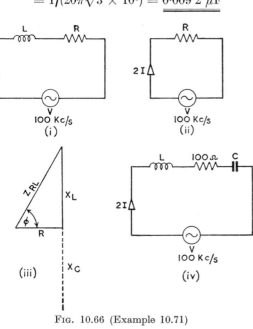

FIG. 10.66 (Example 10.71)

EXAMPLE 10.72 (B). If the product of the equivalent series resistance and the capacitance of a capacitor at a certain frequency is 20×10^{-10} and the power-factor is ·001, at what frequency was the measurement made?
(C. & G.)

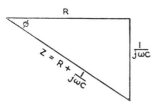

FIG. 10.67 (Example 10.72)

See the impedance triangle, Fig. 10.67.

Simple A.C. Circuits—

The power-factor

$$= \cos \phi = R/\{R + 1/(j\omega C)\}$$
$$= j\omega CR/(j\omega CR + 1)$$
$$= \omega CR/(\omega CR + 1)$$
$$\omega CR = \omega CR \cos \phi + \cos \phi,$$
$$\omega CR - \omega CR \cos \phi = \cos \phi$$
$$\omega = \cos \phi/\{CR(1 - \cos \phi)\}$$
$$= 0\cdot001 \times 10^{10}/(20 \times 0\cdot999)$$
$$= 10^7/19\cdot98$$
$$f = \omega/(2\pi) = 10^7/(19\cdot98 \times 6\cdot28)$$
$$= \underline{79\cdot6\ kc/s}$$

SUMMARY

Angular Frequency. $\omega = 2\pi f$.
Frequency and Period. $f = 1/T$.
Instantaneous Value.

$$i = I_{max} \sin \theta = I_{max} \sin 2\pi ft = I_{max} \sin \omega t$$
$$v = V_{max} \sin \theta = V_{max} \sin 2\pi ft = V_{max} \sin \omega t$$

(Angle in *radians* if ω or $2\pi f$ is employed.)

Phase Displacement.

$$i = I_{max} \sin \omega t : \quad v = V_{max} \sin (\omega t \pm \phi)$$

(ϕ radians is phase angle by which current leads or lags on voltage.)

Average Value. (Sine waveform for half cycle),

$$I_{av} = 0\cdot637\ I_{max} = (2/\pi)I_{max}$$
$$V_{av} = 0\cdot637\ V_{max} = (2/\pi)\ V_{max}$$

R.M.S. or Effective Value. (Sine waveform, for complete cycle—the equivalent d.c. power effect)—

$$I = 0\cdot707 I_{max} = (1/\sqrt{2})I_{max}$$
$$V = 0\cdot707 V_{max} = (1/\sqrt{2})V_{max}$$

Form Factor. R.M.S./Average $= (1/\sqrt{2}) \div (2/\pi)$ $= 1\cdot11$ (sine wave).

Active Component. Component of current (voltage, power) in phase with voltage (current).

Reactive Component. Component of current (voltage, power) in quadrature with voltage (current).

Circuit	Reactance X	Current I	Voltage V	Phase Angle ϕ
Pure R	0	V/R	IR	0
Pure L	$X_L = j\omega L$	$V/X_L = V/(\omega L)$	$IX_L = I\omega L$	$90°$ (I lags)
Pure C	$X_c = -j/(\omega C)$ or $1/(j\omega C)$	$V/X_c = -V\omega C$	$IX_c = -I/(\omega C)$	$90°$ (I leads)

(Capacitance gives − sign to reactance.)

Series Circuits—

Circuit	X	Z	ϕ	I	V_R	V_L	V_C
$R + L$	$j\omega L$	$R + j\omega L$	$\tan^{-1} \omega L/R$	$V/(R + j\omega L)$	IR	$I\omega L$	—
$R + C$	$-j/(\omega C)$	$R - j/(\omega C)$	$\tan^{-1}\{-1/(\omega CR)\}$	$V/\{R - j/(\omega C)\}$	IR	—	$-I/(\omega C$
$L + C$	$j\{\omega L - 1/(\omega C)\}$	$j\{\omega L - 1/(\omega C)\}$	$\tan^{-1} \pm 90°$	$V/\{\omega L - 1/(\omega C)\}$	—	$I\omega L$	$-I/(\omega C$
$R + L + C$	$j\{\omega L - 1/(\omega C)\}$	$R + j\{\omega L - 1/(\omega C)\}$	$\tan^{-1}\left(\dfrac{\omega L - 1/(\omega C)}{R}\right)$	$V/[R + j\{\omega L - 1/(\omega C)\}]$	IR	$I\omega L$	$-I/(\omega C$

Simple Parallel Circuits—

Circuit	I_R	I_L	I_C	I	ϕ	Y
$R + L$	V/R	$V/(\omega L)$	—	$V(1/R + 1/j\omega L)$	$\tan^{-1} R/\omega L$	$1/R + 1/j\omega L$
$R + C$	V/R	—	ωCV	$V(1/R + j\omega C)$	$\tan^{-1} \omega CR$	$1/R + j\omega C$
$L + C$	—	$V/(\omega L)$	ωCV	$V(1/j\omega L + j\omega C)$	$\tan^{-1} \pm 90°$	$1/j\omega L + j\omega C$
$R + L + C$	V/R	$V/(\omega L)$	ωCV	$V(1/R + 1/j\omega L + j\omega C)$	$\tan^{-1} R(\omega C - 1/\omega L)$	$1/R + 1/j\omega L + j\omega C$

Impedance Triangle.

$$Z^2 = R^2 + X^2,\ X = Z \sin \phi,\ R = Z \cos \phi$$

Acceptor Circuit.

$$\omega L = 1/(\omega C),\ \omega_r = 1/(LC)^{\frac{1}{2}},$$
$$f_r = 1/\{2\pi(LC)^{\frac{1}{2}}\},\ Z = R,\ \phi = 0,\ I = V/R$$

Rejector Circuit.

$$\omega L = 1/(\omega C),\ \omega_r = 1/(LC)^{\frac{1}{2}},\ f_r = 1/\{2\pi(LC)^{\frac{1}{2}}\}$$
$$Z = \infty,\ \phi = 0,\ I = 0$$

Rejector Circuit with Resistance.

$$I_C = I_L \sin \phi,\ f_r = \frac{1}{2\pi}\left(\frac{1}{LC} - \frac{R^2}{L^2}\right)^{\frac{1}{2}}$$

Admittance.

$$1/Z = Y = (G^2 + B^2)^{\frac{1}{2}},\ G = R/Z^2,\ B = -X/Z^2$$

Susceptance. $B = -X/Z^2,\ B = B_C - B_L$
(Capacitance gives $+$ sign to B_C.)

Power. Apparent power $= VI$ volt-amps.

True power $= VI \cos \phi$ watts.

Power-factor. P.f. $= \cos \phi =$ true power/apparent power $= R/Z$ (sine wave).

CHAPTER XI

A.C. TRANSMISSION

11.1. Principle of the Transformer. The transformer is a static instrument which utilizes the phenomenon of electromagnetic induction. It consists essentially of two closely coupled insulated coils, usually wound upon a laminated ferromagnetic core. Its function is to transform an alternating potential in the primary winding to any desired voltage in the secondary winding. Since the power values ($V \times I$) in the two windings must be approximately equal (differing only on

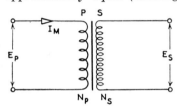

Fig. 11.1. SIMPLE TRANSFORMER

account of losses), an increase in voltage (V) from one winding to the other must be accompanied by a corresponding decrease in current (I) between the windings: consequently a transformation in impedance ($Z = V/I$) also occurs.

In telecommunication systems transformers are used in power equipment for voltage transformation and for isolating communications plant from the electric supply mains: for this purpose, transformers are characterized by the fact that they are designed for operation at a high voltage and a low fixed frequency—usually 240 V, 50 c/s. More extensively, transformers are used for impedance matching, that is to say, for connecting together two networks or circuits of different impedance so that a maximum transfer of power from one to the other can be achieved: these transformers usually operate at low voltages but over a wide frequency range.

A transformer is defined as *a piece of apparatus without continuously moving parts, which by electromagnetic induction transforms alternating or intermittent voltage or current in one winding into alternating or intermittent voltage and current in one or more other windings, usually at different values of voltage or current.*

11.2. Transformation Ratios. A simple transformer is shown in Fig. 11.1 with primary and secondary windings P and S respectively. If an alternating voltage E_P is applied to the primary

winding, an alternating magnetic flux is produced which links with the turns of the secondary winding. This flux variation induces an e.m.f. E_S of similar waveform in the secondary winding. If no magnetic leakage occurs, the rate of change of flux is the same for each turn of both the primary and secondary windings and the e.m.f. per turn is the same for each. If the primary and secondary windings have N_P and N_S turns respectively,

$$E_P/N_P = E_S/N_S \text{ or } \frac{E_P}{E_S} = \frac{N_P}{N_S}$$

If the secondary is wound with a greater number of turns than the primary, the induced secondary e.m.f. is greater than the applied primary voltage and the instrument is referred to as a *step-up* transformer. The above ratio is exactly true only for an ideal transformer with no magnetic leakage, but it is usually accurate within 1 per cent for all practical transformers.

If the secondary winding is on open circuit, the primary winding is simply an inductor and a relatively small current, the magnetizing current, I_M, flows. For a winding of high inductance L the reactance ωL has a high value, particularly in comparison with R, the conductor resistance of the primary winding. This results in a high impedance, i.e. a small magnetizing current, and also a phase angle approaching 90°.

When a load is applied to the secondary terminals a current I_S will flow in the secondary circuit. According to Lenz's law this induced current produces in the core an opposing magnetic flux which would reduce the original flux. If the primary voltage is applied at a constant value, this flux reduction cannot occur and an increased primary current (I_B) must flow to neutralize the counter flux of the secondary. If the relatively small magnetizing current be ignored, the ampere-turns NI in the primary and secondary windings are always equal in magnitude, and opposite in direction. Since $N_P I_P = N_S I_S$, the ratio of primary and secondary currents is equal to the reciprocal of the turns ratio, or

$$\frac{N_P}{N_S} = \frac{I_S}{I_P} = \frac{E_P}{E_S} \quad . \quad . \quad (11.1)$$

The phase angle between E_P and I_P on the primary side is approximately equal to the phase angle of the load impedance.

The vector diagram for a step-up transformer on load (ignoring losses) is given in Fig. 11.2. The voltage E_P applied to the primary winding produces a small magnetizing current

$$I_M = E_P/(R + j\omega L)$$

which is practically in quadrature with the applied

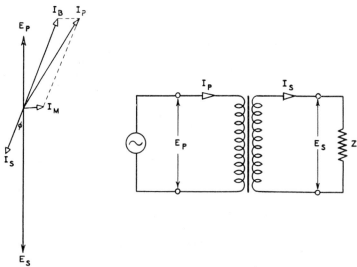

FIG. 11.2. VECTOR DIAGRAM FOR SIMPLE TRANSFORMER

voltage. This magnetizing current induces a secondary e.m.f.,

$$E_S = E_P \times N_S/N_P$$

which is in phase with the primary back-e.m.f., i.e. 180° out of phase with the applied voltage E_P. The secondary load current I_S ($= E_S/Z$ approximately) has the phase angle ϕ of the load impedance—a lagging current being shown in the diagram. This secondary current causes an increased (balancing) current

$$I_B = I_S \times N_S/N_P$$

to flow in the primary winding in opposite phase to I_S. The vector sum of I_B and I_M gives the primary current I_P.

11.3. Impedance Matching. In Fig. 11.3 (a) is shown a generator with a constant output voltage E applied across the primary winding of a transformer: the secondary is closed by an impedance Z. The turns ratio $N_P/N_S = n$. The induced e.m.f. in the secondary is E/n and the secondary current $I_S = E/(nZ)$. Neglecting the magnetizing current, the current in the primary circuit is

$$I_P = \frac{1}{n}\left(\frac{E}{nZ}\right) = \frac{E}{n^2 Z}$$

This is the current which would flow if the generator were connected directly across an impedance of modulus $n^2 Z$. In other words $n^2 Z$ is the equivalent impedance of the transformer plus secondary load Z when "viewed" from the input terminals (XY) this equivalent circuit is shown in Fig. 11.3 (b).

The use of a transformer enables the modulus of the impedance presented by a given circuit to be altered to any desired value by a judicious selection of the value n: by connecting a transformer of suitable turns ratio n between two different impedances Z_1 and Z_2 it is possible to make Z_1 and Z_2 appear to be equal to one another. From the relationship above, the impedance ratio may be expressed as

$$n = \sqrt{\frac{Z_1}{Z_2}} \qquad . \quad (11.2)$$

where $n > 1$ and $Z_1 > Z_2$, or in other words, the higher impedance is connected to the winding with the greater number of turns.

The maximum transfer of power from one circuit to another requires that the two circuits shall have equal impedance. This problem is fundamental to telecommunication systems: for example, in a telephone system, power from the microphone is transferred to the distant receiver through switching equipment, amplifiers and various sections of lines. Each link in the connexion has a particular impedance governed by certain individual design requirements: to feed maximum power from one link to the next it is often necessary to insert transformers for the purpose of impedance-matching between each pair of adjacent links.

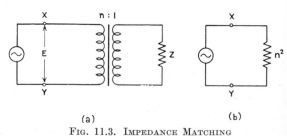

(a)   (b)

FIG. 11.3. IMPEDANCE MATCHING

EXAMPLE 11.1 (C). A transformer having 1 000 turns on the primary winding and 200 turns on the secondary winding has a resistance of 250 Ω connected across the secondary terminals. What is the apparent a.c. resistance of the transformer and resistance measured across the primary terminals?   (C. & G.)

$$n = \sqrt{\frac{Z_1}{Z_2}} \text{ and } Z_1 = n^2 Z_2$$

$$= \frac{1\,000^2 \times 250}{200^2} = \underline{6\,250\ \Omega}$$

11.4. Transformer Losses. Energy losses occur in transformers due to eddy currents, hysteresis, magnetic leakage, and conductor resistance. A study of the losses is simplified by considering the equivalent circuit of a practical transformer based

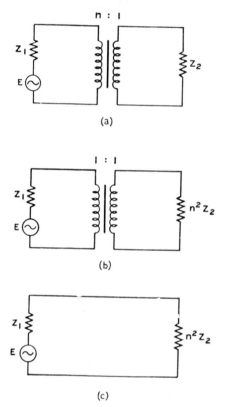

(a)

(b)

(c)

FIG. 11.4. CONVERSION OF TRANSFORMER RATIO

upon the conception of a perfect transformer[1] of unit ratio.

The transformer in Fig. 11.4 (a) having a turns ratio $n : 1$ is interposed between a generator having an internal impedance Z_1 and a load impedance Z_2. By replacing the load impedance Z_2 by an impedance equal to $n^2 Z_2$ the transformer may be regarded as having unity ratio (Fig. 11.4 (b)): in fact, since the primary and secondary voltages are now equal, the generator and load impedance may be shown directly connected as in Fig. 11.4 (c).

The magnetizing current (I_M) produces a shunt loss between generator (Z_1) and load ($n^2 Z_2$). If L_M is the inductance of the primary winding when the secondary winding is open-circuited, this shunt loss is equal to ωL_M. This loss is indicated in the equivalent transformer circuit of Fig. 11.5. The shunt loss ($2\pi f L_M$) is greatest at low frequencies, diminishing with increasing frequency until ultimately it becomes negligible. The inductance must accordingly be high enough to avoid excessive shunting loss at the lowest frequencies to be transmitted.

In addition to the quadrature magnetizing current, the primary winding also takes a small in-phase current to supply the core losses—hysteresis and eddy current losses. Since this iron loss is a power loss which develops heat in the core, it may be represented by the high resistance R_L

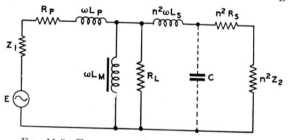

FIG. 11.5. EQUIVALENT CIRCUIT OF TRANSFORMER

in shunt with ωL_M. Both of these losses increase with frequency, the eddy current loss being proportional to the square of the frequency. Nevertheless, for an audio-frequency transformer the resistance R_L may be assumed to be practically constant for frequencies up to about 2 000 c/s and also for variations in applied voltage. This is because the total iron losses increase almost as the square of the flux density but the flux density falls with the frequency: for voltage changes the power loss in R_L varies as the square of the applied voltage. At frequencies greater than 2 000 c/s the presence of eddy currents tends to prevent the flux from penetrating beneath the surface layer of the core laminations.

It is impossible to ensure complete linkage between all flux lines and both primary and secondary conductors. The flux leakage produces leakage inductance L_P and L_S acting in series with the primary and secondary circuits respectively. These leakage reactances ωL_P and $n^2 \omega L_S$ (for the unity ratio transformer) are included in the diagram of Fig. 11.5. Finally the conductor resistance series losses R_P and $n^2 R_S$ are included in the primary and secondary circuits. The leakage reactance losses increase with frequency: the conductor loss is independent of frequency.

This combination of losses results in a frequency response graph of the form shown in Fig. 11.6 under conditions of correct matching. (The loss is expressed as the logarithmic ratio of the input and output powers, the *decibel*.) The extent of the losses depends upon the terminating impedances Z_1 and Z_2, for with a low value of terminating impedance a given shunting loss will be less serious

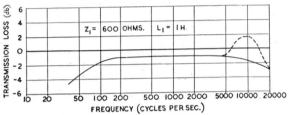

FIG. 11.6. TRANSMISSION LOSS OF AUDIO-FREQUENCY
TRANSFORMER

than for a high impedance termination: similarly the series loss will be more pronounced for a low impedance termination.

At the lower frequencies the loss is mainly that of the shunt reactance (ωL_M): over the middle of the frequency range the loss is attributable to the

For a power transformer carrying a full-load current, the vector diagram in Fig. 11.7 (*a*) includes the losses: the symbols are those shown in Fig. 11.7 (*b*) for an ideal transformer with the losses added externally. The applied primary voltage V_P is reduced by the voltage drops $I_P R_P$ (in phase with the primary current I_P) and $I_P \omega L_P$ (in quadrature) to the value E_P applied to the perfect transformer. This primary voltage E_P is stepped down in the secondary winding to E_S ($= E_P/n$) but this value is reduced by the voltage drops $I_S R_S$ (in phase with the secondary current I_S) and $I_S \omega L_S$ (in quadrature) to V_S, the secondary terminal voltage applied across the load impedance Z. The secondary current I_S ($= V_S/Z$) acting at the load phase angle ϕ produces the primary balancing current I_B which together with the magnetizing current I_M (whose phase angle approaches $90°$) makes up the primary current I_P.

The secondary terminal voltage will fall off as the load current increases. The difference between the values of the secondary terminal voltage at no-load and at full-load, expressed as a ratio to the no-load p.d. is termed the *regulation*, or—

percentage regulation

$$= \frac{100 \,(\text{p.d. at no-load} - \text{p.d. at full-load})}{(\text{p.d. at no-load})}$$

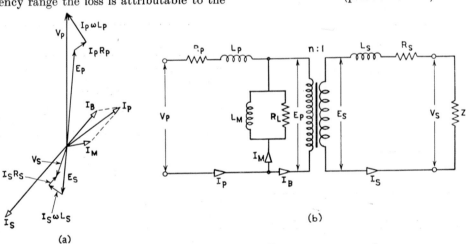

(a)

(b)

FIG. 11.7. VECTOR DIAGRAM FOR POWER TRANSFORMER, WITH LOSSES

series and shunt resistances ($R_P + n^2 R_S$) and R_L and so is largely independent of frequency. At the upper frequencies the loss is governed by the series reactances ($\omega L_P + n^2 \omega L_S$). The design of an audio-frequency transformer necessitates a compromise between shunt and series losses to produce a comparatively flat response graph over the desired frequency range.

The regulation of a power transformer is generally less than 4 per cent.

Transformer efficiency (η) is measured by the ratio of output power to input power and expressed as a percentage, or

$$\eta = \frac{\text{output power}}{\text{input power}} \times 100\%$$

$$= \frac{\text{power supplied by secondary}}{\text{total power supplied to primary}} \times 100\%$$

$$= \frac{V_S I_S \cos \phi_S \text{ watts}}{V_P I_P \cos \phi_P \text{ watts}} \times 100\%$$

The difference between input and output powers is accounted for by the core loss and I^2R (copper) loss: these losses can be made very small compared with the full-load power and high efficiencies of 98–99 per cent are obtainable in all but the smaller transformers. The efficiency may also be expressed as

$$\eta = \frac{\text{input power} - \text{losses}}{\text{input power}} \times 100\%$$

11.5. Transformer Construction.

Transformers are employed to serve a wide field of requirements ranging from miniature audio-frequency and high-

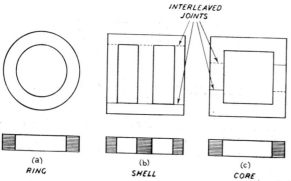

INTERLEAVED JOINTS

FIG. 11.8. TYPES OF TRANSFORMER CORES

(a) RING   (b) SHELL   (c) CORE

frequency instruments to vast power transformers handling millions of volt-amperes. The essential components of any transformer are the core and the windings.

The more usual shapes of ferromagnetic cores are shown in Fig. 11.8. The main requirements of the core are minimum magnetic length and losses, with maximum cross-section and winding space.

The ring or toroid core (Fig. 11.8 (a)), made from winding iron wire into a ring, from thin laminations stamped from sheet core material, from iron dust in a suitable binding compound, or from ferrite, has the main advantage that the core can be jointless and the leakage inductance is small if the windings are evenly distributed. The winding of such a transformer is attended with complication and it is not possible to fill the winding space completely.

The shell type of core (Fig. 11.8 (b)) is commonly employed since its form closely approaches that of the ring core. It consists of E- and I-shaped

laminations, of 0·015 in. or less in thickness, which are assembled in pairs in alternate order (Fig. 11.9) so as to produce interleaved joints which add very little to the mean length of the magnetic path. This form of construction enables the coils to be first wound upon a bobbin and the core stampings to be afterwards assembled in and about the bobbin. The assembled core and bobbin takes the

FIG. 11.9. CONSTRUCTION OF SHELL TYPE CORE

form shown in Fig. 11.10 in which the flux distribution is also indicated by the dotted lines: the flux density in the centre limb being twice that in the outer limbs, the cross-sectional areas are proportioned accordingly.

In the "core" type sometimes used (Fig. 11.8 (c)) the windings can be placed upon separate limbs and complete electrical isolation is obtainable between the primary and secondary. This is advantageous if high voltages are being used but a comparatively high magnetic leakage results from this

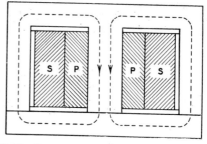

FIG. 11.10. TRANSFORMER WINDING ON SHELL TYPE CORE

arrangement. By placing one half of each winding upon either limb in the manner shown in Fig. 11.11 the leakage inductance is reduced although the protection feature is lost. In addition, however, this *astatic* winding neutralizes the effect of a uniform interfering field, an advantage which is not shared by the shell type.

The core material should have a high permeability to enable a large value of inductance to be easily obtained: the hysteresis and eddy current losses should be as low as possible. Nickel-iron and silicon-iron alloys are commonly used. Alloys of the former type reach saturation at comparatively low flux densities but this is not serious at the low powers applied to audio-frequency transformers: high inductance is obtainable with low winding resistances and the series and shunt losses are reduced. Transformers, particularly those with a high turns ratio, are frequently enclosed in a

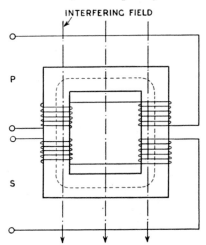

FIG. 11.11. ASTATIC TRANSFORMER WINDING

screening case of nickel-iron alloy to minimize the effect of stray magnetic fields from adjacent components.

Dust cores or ferrites are used for the high frequencies of carrier and radio systems. The usual

are most suitable for use at the high flux densities of power transformers, whereas the nickel-irons having very high permeabilities at low flux densities are suitable for low power audio-frequency

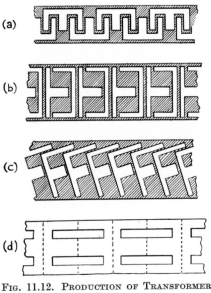

FIG. 11.12. PRODUCTION OF TRANSFORMER CORE STAMPINGS

transformers and also for the inductor elements of frequency filters.

A common thickness for the stampings is

TABLE 11.I

Material	Relative Permeability		Satura-tion Flux Density (Wb/m²)	Total Loss (Watts per lb at 50 c/s)			Resistivity (×10⁸Ω-m)	Nominal Thick-ness (inches)	Com-parative Price
	Initial	Max.		0·01 Wb/m²	0·1 Wb/m²	1·0 Wb/m²			
Mild steel	250	5 000	2·1	—	—	1·5	10	0·014	1
Silicon steel—									
2 Si + 98 Fe	300	6 000	1·8	—	0·1	0·63	55	0·014	2
Nickel iron—									
50 Ni + 50 Fe	1 800–2 400	10 000–20 000	1·6	0·000 07	0·005	0·32	55	0·015	10
80 Ni + 20 Fe	10 000–30 000	50 000–100 000	0·8	0·000 016	0·002 2	—	60	0·015	16
36 Ni + 64 Fe	1 500–2 000	6 000–8 000	1·3	0·000 05	0·009	—	90	0·015	—

shapes are toroids and cups with a central cylindrical core: in the latter, the winding is slipped into the annular space and an end plate of core material is fitted to provide a closed magnetic circuit.

The more important properties of a number of transformer core materials are given in Table 11.I, from which it will be evident that the silicon steels

0·015 in., but thicknesses of 2 mils, 5 mils, and 8 mils are also available, the thinner laminations being used for high-frequency transformers. It is of interest to note the methods adopted[2] to reduce stastage of the processed material at the stamping wage (see Fig. 11.12). From strips of the material E-shaped laminations are usually stamped in pairs the corresponding Is being cut all in a row: T- and U-shapes are interlinked, and Fs are stamped in echelon. Wastage is completely avoided in the arrangement shown in Fig. 11.12 (*d*), but the restricted winding space which results increases the I^2R loss. In this latter method, the Is are stamped out and the strip then sheared across the dotted lines to form the Es. After stamping, a thin coat of a cellulose paint is sprayed upon one or both sides of each lamination to provide the necessary

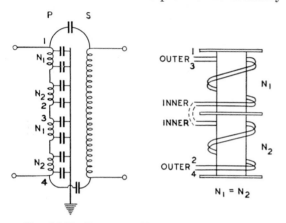

FIG. 11.13. BALANCED TRANSFORMER WINDING

insulation: in some processes this insulation is provided by a controlled heat treatment which produces an oxide layer upon the metal.

For certain purposes windings with accurate centre-points are required; the two parts of the winding about this centre-tap must be accurately balanced, not only for inductance, but also for resistance and for self-capacitance to earth. The equality of the number of turns on either side of the centre-point is assured by means of a bifilar winding: a few non-inductive turns may be added to one half-winding to balance the resistances if necessary.

The distributed capacitances are balanced by winding the bifilar conductor in two equal parts in opposite directions and connecting together the inner ends of the sections (Fig. 11.13). Capacitance between the primary and secondary windings may be reduced by fitting an earthed screen between these windings. This may take the form of an earthed copper foil which encircles the primary winding but has an insulated lap joint so as to avoid making a closed winding. Alternatively a layer of wire may be used with one end connected to earth. On small power transformers such screening may be used to minimize the danger of contact between primary and secondary.

The self-capacitances which exist between turns and between layers will produce resonances with the main and leakage inductances. Such resonances cause the loss/frequency response to depart from linearity (see the dotted resonance curve in Fig. 11.6) and special sectionalized methods of winding may be necessary to reduce the self-capacitances.

11.6. Transformers Carrying Direct Currents. In some applications transformers are required to carry a small direct current in addition to the normal alternating current. This polarizing current reduces the inductance and increases the loss at low frequencies. A small air-gap in the magnetic circuit reduces the polarizing flux in the core and increases its a.c. permeability.

With an air-gapped core it is important that the winding should be disposed about the air-gap, i.e. at the point of maximum reluctance, otherwise the leakage inductance will be high. The flux distribution for alternative positions of the winding is shown in Fig. 11.14 at (*a*) and (*b*): the air-gap

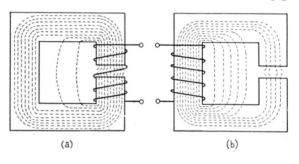

(a)   (b)

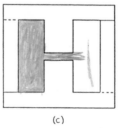

(c)

FIG. 11.14. TRANSFORMER CORES WITH AIR-GAP

position for a shell core constructed from F-shaped stampings is shown at (*c*).

Due to the irregular shape of the magnetic hysteresis loop the flux changes do not faithfully follow the changes of magnetizing force, i.e. waveform distortion occurs from the production of harmonic frequencies (odd harmonics only if the core is unpolarized) For the same reason intermodulation may also occur between simultaneously applied frequencies of different values.

These effects are minimized by the employment of air-gaps and by restriction of the magnetizing force to the linear portion of the *B-H* graph.

11.7. The Auto-transformer. In the auto-transformer only one winding is used, with a tapping to which the primary or secondary circuit is connected according to whether a step-up or step-down ratio is required. In the step-down transformer shown in Fig. 11.15 the whole winding *AB* forms the transformer primary and the tapped portion *CB* constitutes the secondary winding. The turns

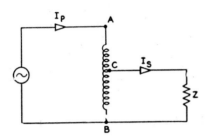

FIG. 11.15 AUTO-TRANSFORMER

ratio is the ratio of the primary turns to the secondary turns—the ratio *AB/CB* in the diagram.

The common section *CB* of the winding carries both the primary and secondary currents: these currents being in opposition, the net current in the common section is equal to their difference. As a result the I^2R loss is reduced compared with a normal transformer under similar loading. This reduction in loss is greatest for small transformers with a low turns-ratio. The fact that the primary and secondary windings are not insulated from one another may be disadvantageous for certain applications.

11.8. Resonance in Coupled Circuits. Two a.c. circuits are said to be coupled when they are so linked that energy is transferred from one circuit to the other.

The two circuits coupled are usually tuned to resonance at the same frequency, i.e. the product *LC* is the same for each. With the coupled circuits it is found that resonance occurs at *two* frequencies. The existence of two resonant frequencies arises from the fact that in a coupled circuit there are two paths in which the currents can oscillate.

One of these frequencies may be that at which each of the component circuits would resonate on its own $\left(f_r = \omega_r/(2\pi) = \dfrac{1}{2\pi\sqrt{LC}} \right)$: the other frequency is dependent upon the degree of coupling employed. This degree is expressed by the COUPLING COEFFICIENT, denoted by the symbol *K*: it is

equal to the ratio of the amount of coupling actually present to the maximum possible coupling. As a consequence the value of *K* cannot exceed 1. The coupling coefficient is defined as *the ratio of the mutual or common impedance component of two circuits, to the square root of the product of the totals, in the two circuits, of the impedance components of the same kind. (Impedance components may be inductive, capacitive, or resistive.)*

Coupled circuits may be conveniently classified, according to the nature of the path connecting one to the other, into three categories—

(i) Direct coupling through an impedance not included in either circuit.

(ii) Direct coupling through an impedance common to both circuits.

In the first two categories the coupling impedance may be a resistance, an inductance, or a capacitance.

(iii) Indirect coupling through a field of force common to both circuits. The field may be either

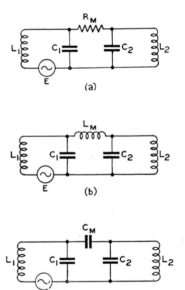

FIG. 11.16. CIRCUITS COUPLED THROUGH AN IMPEDANCE NOT INCLUDED IN EITHER CIRCUIT

magnetic or electric but the latter is infrequently used.

CATEGORY (i). The three types of circuit in the first category are illustrated in Fig. 11.16: the coupling impedance is the resistance R_M, the inductance L_M, or the capacitance C_M. The resistance of the inductors is assumed to be negligible in comparison with their reactance.

where two resonant circuits are coupled electromagnetically by a mutual inductance M henrys Fig. 11.20). With this arrangement two resonant frequencies again result whose values may be derived from the following expression—

$$v = \frac{1}{\sqrt{[LC(1 \pm K)]}}, \text{ where } K = \frac{M}{\sqrt{L_1 L_2}}. \quad (11.3)$$

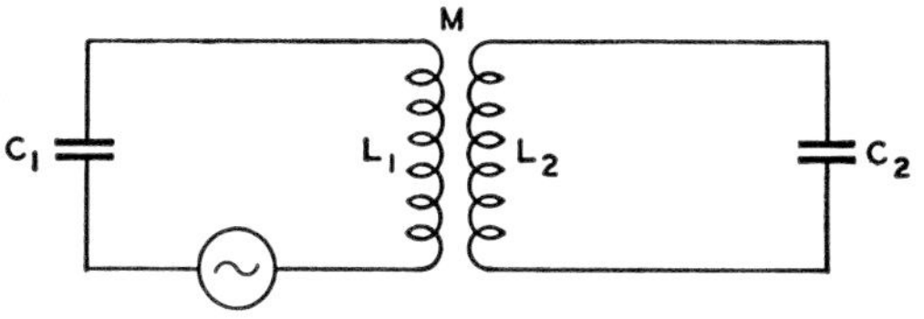

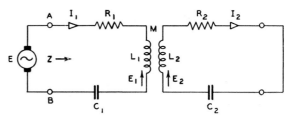

FIG. 11.20. CIRCUITS COUPLED BY MUTUAL INDUCTANCE

With electromagnetic coupling, the only applicable relationship is

$$L_1 C_1 = L_2 C_2 = LC = 1/\omega_r^2$$

The double-peaked resonance curves for three different values of the coupling inductance M are given in Fig. 11.21. Values of M, and therefore of

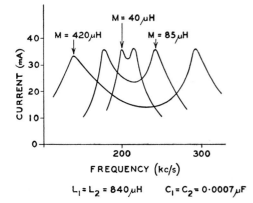

FIG. 11.21. RESONANCE CURVES FOR CIRCUITS COUPLED ELECTROMAGNETICALLY

K also, will vary according to the degree of coupling.

Circuits are said to be *tightly* or *loosely* coupled together according to whether the proportion of energy transferred from one to the other is large or small, i.e. depending upon whether K is large or small. For electromagnetic coupling M and K may be increased by moving the coupled coils more closely together so that an increased proportion of the primary flux links with the secondary coil.

The expression

$$M = N_1 N_2 A \mu_0 \mu_r / l$$

for mutual inductance assumes that all the primary flux links with the secondary coil. On this assumption—

$$M^2 = \frac{N_1^2 N_2^2 A^2 \mu_0^2 \mu_r^2}{l^2}$$

$$= \frac{N_1^2 A \mu_0 \mu_r}{l} \times \frac{N_2^2 A \mu_0 \mu_r}{l}$$

$$= L_1 L_2$$

and $\qquad M = \sqrt{L_1 L_2}$

This is the maximum possible mutual inductance between the circuits and M cannot be greater than $\sqrt{L_1 L_2}$. In any practical case it is impossible to avoid flux leakage and $M < \sqrt{L_1 L_2}$ so that $\frac{M}{\sqrt{L_1 L_2}} = K$ is less than 1.

One advantage arising from the use of coupled circuits is the increased frequency range or

FIG. 11.22. IMPEDANCE OF INDUCTIVELY-COUPLED CIRCUITS

"bandwidth" over which the impedance is low when compared with the resonance curve of the single tuned circuit (Fig. 10.32). By suitable design the trough between the peaks may be smoothed out to give an almost linear response over the frequency range utilized by a telegraph or telephone channel.

11.9. Impedance of Coupled Circuits. When two a.c. circuits are inductively coupled the effective impedance of the primary circuit is modified by the influence of the secondary circuit components.

Two circuits electromagnetically coupled by their mutual inductance M are shown in Fig. 11.22. The primary circuit comprises the elements R_1 ohms, L_1 henrys, and C_1 farads: it is energized from a generator of e.m.f. E volts at a frequency of f c/s $[= \omega/(2\pi)]$. The secondary circuit components have values of R_2 ohms, L_2 henrys, and C_2 farads. The primary impedance without regard to the secondary circuit is Z_1 ohms: the secondary impedance is Z_2 ohms. The circuit currents are I_1 amperes in the primary and I_2 amperes in the secondary. The e.m.f. induced in the secondary coil is E_2 volts: the back-e.m.f. in the primary circuit has a magnitude of E_1 volts.

The e.m.f. induced in the secondary circuit by the current I_1 flowing in the primary circuit is $\omega M I_1$: since it is $180°$ out of phase with the current I_1 it may be written as: $E_2 = -j\omega M I_1$.

The current flowing in the secondary circuit is

$$I_2 = E_2/Z_2 = -j\omega M I_1/Z_2$$

The back-e.m.f. induced in L_1 by the current I_2 is

$$E_1 = j\omega M I_2 = j\omega M(-j\omega M I_1/Z_2) = \omega^2 M^2 I_1/Z_2$$

The applied e.m.f. E must be equal to the sum of the two voltage components (i) the p.d. due to the current I_1 flowing in the impedance Z_1, and (ii) the back-e.m.f. E_1 induced by the secondary. Accordingly,

$$E = I_1 Z_1 + E_1 = I_1 Z_1 + \omega^2 M^2 I_1/Z_2$$
$$= I_1(Z_1 + \omega^2 M^2/Z_2)$$

The effective impedance Z_{eff} of the whole circuit "viewed" from the input terminals (AB) is equal to the ratio of the applied e.m.f. E to the resulting current I_1 so that—

$$Z_{eff} = E/I_1 = Z_1 + \omega^2 M^2/Z_2 \quad . \quad (11.4)$$

In other words, the impedance looking into the primary terminals (AB) is equal to the impedance of the primary circuit itself

$$[Z_1 = R_1 + j\omega L_1 + 1/(j\omega C_1) = R_1 + jX_1]$$

together with an impedance equal to $\omega^2 M^2/Z_2$ reflected from the secondary circuit.

Writing $Z_1 = R_1 + jX_1$ and $Z_2 = R_2 + jX_2$ in the above expression (11.4)—

$$Z_{eff} = Z_1 + \omega^2 M^2/Z_2 = R_1 + jX_1 + \frac{\omega^2 M^2}{R_2 + jX_2}$$

Multiplying the second term by $(R_2 - jX_2)$ to clear the j-operator from the denominator (see Appendix **A.4**)—

$$Z_{eff} = R_1 + jX_1 + \frac{\omega^2 M^2 R_2}{R_2{}^2 + X_2{}^2} - \frac{j\omega^2 M^2 X_2}{R_2{}^2 + X_2{}^2}$$

Finally, on re-arranging the vectors, the effective primary impedance is—

$$Z_{eff} = R_1 + R_2\left(\frac{\omega^2 M^2}{R_2{}^2 + X_2{}^2}\right)$$
$$+ j\left(X_1 - X_2\frac{\omega^2 M^2}{R_2{}^2 + X_2{}^2}\right) \quad . \quad (11.5)$$
$$= R_1 + R_2\left(\frac{\omega^2 M^2}{Z_2{}^2}\right) + j\left(X_1 - X_2\frac{\omega^2 M^2}{Z_2{}^2}\right)$$

From the above may be written—

Effective resistance

$$R_{eff} = R_1 + R_2\left(\frac{\omega M}{Z_2}\right)^2 \quad . \quad (11.6$$

Effective reactance

$$X_{eff} = X_1 - X_2\left(\frac{\omega M}{Z_2}\right)^2 \quad . \quad (11.7$$

It is apparent that the effect of the secondar load is always to increase the resistive componen of Z_{eff}: the reactive component may be increase or decreased, depending upon the frequency.

At the resonant frequency for the secondar circuit, $X_2 = 0$ and

$$Z_{eff} = R_1 + \omega^2 M^2/R_2 + jX_1$$

For direct coupled circuits of the type shown i Fig. 11.19 the values of R_{eff}, X_{eff}, and Z_{eff} ma be obtained by substituting ωL_m (inductiv coupling) or $1/(\omega C_m)$ (capacitive coupling) for ωM in the above expressions.

EXAMPLE 11.2 (C). The inductances of two inductivel coupled coils A and B are 0.002 and 0.032 H respectively and the coupling coefficient is 0.75. Regarding the resis tance of the coil A as negligible, what will be the ope circuit voltage across the terminals of coil B when 0.5 V is applied across the terminals of A? (C. & G.

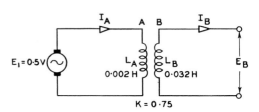

FIG. 11.23 (Example 11.2)

See the diagram in Fig. 11.23.

$$I_A = E/(R + j\omega L_A) = 0.5/(\omega \times 0.002)$$
$$= 250/\omega \text{ A}$$
$$M = K\sqrt{L_A L_B} = 0.75\sqrt{(0.002 \times 0.032)}$$
$$= 0.006 \text{ H}$$
$$E_B = \omega M I_A = \omega \times 0.006 \times 250/\omega = \underline{1.5 \text{ V}}$$

EXAMPLE 11.3 (C). A high-frequency ammeter coupled to an oscillatory circuit by means of an air-core transformer. The primary winding carries 100 A a 100 000 c/s. The secondary circuit has a total inductanc of 20 μH and a mutual inductance with the primary 1 μH. If the resistance of the secondary circuit includin the meter is 4 Ω, what current will flow through the mete (C. & G

$f = 10^5$ c/s

$\omega = 2\pi \times 10^5$ radn/sec

$L_2 = 2 \times 10^{-5}$ H

$R_2 = 4\ \Omega$

$M = 10^{-6}$ H

$I_1 = 100$ A

$\omega M = 2\pi \times 10^5 \times 10^{-6} = 0.2\pi\ \Omega$

$Z_2 = R_2 + j\omega L_2 = 4 + j(2\pi \times 10^5 \times 2 \times 10^{-5})$

$\quad = (4^2 + 16\pi^2)^{\frac{1}{2}} = 13.2\ \Omega$

$I_2 = E_2/Z_2 = \omega M I_1/Z_2 = 0.2\pi \times 100/13.2$

$\quad = 4.76$ A

EXAMPLE 11.4 (C). A circuit consisting of a capacitor of $0.001\ \mu$F and an inductor of $500\ \mu$H is coupled magnetically with a second circuit consisting of a capacitor of $0.000\ 5\ \mu$F and an inductor of $1\ 000\ \mu$H. The mutual inductance between the coils is $100\ \mu$H and the resistances of the primary and secondary coils are $15\ \Omega$ and $35\ \Omega$ respectively. What is the effective series impedance of the primary circuit at a frequency of 200 kc/s? (*C. & G.*)

$f = 2 \times 10^5$ c/s

$\omega = 4\pi \times 10^5$ radn/sec

$R_1 = 15\ \Omega$

$L_1 = 5 \times 10^{-4}$ H

$C_1 = 10^{-9}$ F

$M = 10^{-4}$ H

$R_2 = 35\ \Omega$

$L_2 = 10^{-3}$ H

$C_2 = 5 \times 10^{-10}$ F

Primary Circuit

$R_1 = 15\ \Omega$

$X_1 = \omega L_1 - 1/(\omega C_1)$

$\quad = 4\pi \times 10^5 \times 5 \times 10^{-4} - \dfrac{1}{4\pi \times 10^5 \times 10^{-9}}$

$\quad = 200\pi - 796 = 628 - 796 = -168\ \Omega$

Secondary Circuit

$R_2 = 35\ \Omega$

$X_2 = \omega L_2 - 1/(\omega C_2)$

$\quad = 4\pi \times 10^5 \times 10^{-3} - \dfrac{1}{4\pi \times 10^5 \times 5 \times 10^{-10}}$

$\quad = 1\ 257 - 1\ 591 = -334\ \Omega$

$Z_2 = (35^2 + 334^2)^{\frac{1}{2}}$

$\quad = (0.122 \times 10^4 + 11.15 \times 10^4)^{\frac{1}{2}}$

$\quad = (11.27 \times 10^4)^{\frac{1}{2}} = 336\ \Omega$

Effective resistance

$\quad = R_1 + R_2(\omega M/Z_2)^2$

$\quad = 15 + 35\left(\dfrac{16\pi^2 \times 10^{10} \times 10^{-8}}{336^2}\right)$

$\quad = 15 + 4.88 = 19.88\ \Omega$

Effective reactance

$\quad = X_1 - X_2(\omega M/Z_2)^2$

$\quad = -168 - (-334)\left(\dfrac{16\pi^2 \times 10^{10} \times 10^{-8}}{336^2}\right)$

$\quad = -168 + 46.6 = -121.4\ \Omega$

Effective impedance

$\quad = (R^2 + X^2)^{\frac{1}{2}} = (19.88^2 + 121.4^2)^{\frac{1}{2}}$

$\quad = (3.94 \times 10^2 \times 147 \times 10^2)^{\frac{1}{2}}$

$\quad = 10(150.9)^{\frac{1}{2}} = 123\ \Omega$

EXAMPLE 11.5 (C). Two circuits each consisting of an inductance of $160\ \mu$H, a resistance of $10\ \Omega$ and a capacitor of $0.001\ \mu$F are coupled by a mutual inductance between the inductors of $2\ \mu$H.

If an e.m.f. of 100 V r.m.s. at 400 000 c/s is applied in series with one circuit, what will be the currents in the circuits? (*C. & G.*)

$f = 4 \times 10^5$ c/s

$\omega = 2\pi f = 2.51 \times 10^6$ radn/sec

$E = 100$ V

$R_1 = R_2 = 10\ \Omega$

$L_1 = L_2 = 1.6 \times 10^{-4}$ H

$C_1 = C_2 = 10^{-9}$ F

$M = 2 \times 10^{-6}$ H

$X_1 = X_2 = \omega L_1 - 1/(\omega C_1)$

$\quad = 2.51 \times 10^6 \times 1.6 \times 10^{-4}$

$\qquad - \dfrac{1}{2.51 \times 10^6 \times 10^{-9}}$

$\quad = 401 - 398 = 3\ \Omega$

$Z_2{}^2 = 10^2 + 3^2 = 109\ \Omega$

$\omega^2 M^2 = (2.51^2 \times 10^{12}) \times (4 \times 10^{-12}) = 25.4\ \Omega$

Effective resistance

$\quad = R_1 + R_2(\omega^2 M^2/Z_2{}^2)$

$\quad = 10 + 10(25.4/109) = 12.33\ \Omega$

Effective reactance

$\quad = X_1 - X_2(\omega^2 M^2/Z_2{}^2)$

$\quad = 3 - 3(25.4/109) = 2.3\ \Omega$

Effective impedance

$\quad = (12.33^2 + 2.3^2)^{\frac{1}{2}}$

$I_1 = E/Z = \dfrac{100}{(12.33^2 + 2.3^2)^{\frac{1}{2}}} = 8$ A

$I_2 = E_2/Z_2 = \omega M I_1/Z_2 = (25.4/109)^{\frac{1}{2}} \times 8$

$\quad = 3.88$ A

11.10. Free and Forced Oscillations. Alternating or oscillatory currents may be produced in a tuned circuit from a source either within or without the circuit.

Taking the latter case first, the alternating current in a circuit is supplied and maintained from some external generator, the frequency of the current being governed by that of the generator supply. Such circuits are said to be in a state of FORCED OSCILLATION: this type of circuit was assumed throughout Chapter X. Forced oscillations are defined as *oscillations in a system which are maintained by an external supply of energy and which have the frequency of the external supply.*

by the symbol f_0 to distinguish it from the resonant frequency f_r of a circuit subject to forced oscillations.

The natural frequency of a circuit is

$$f_0 = \frac{1}{2\pi}\sqrt{\left(\frac{1}{LC} - \frac{R^2}{4L^2}\right)} \qquad . \quad (11.8)$$

When a charged capacitor is connected across an inductor of low resistance the p.d. across the capacitor causes a current to flow in the circuit, shown by the full arrow in Fig. 11.24 (a). The magnitude of the current depends upon the values of resistance and inductance in the circuit, the current commencing from zero and attaining a maximum value. At this stage the capacitor is

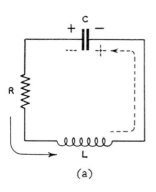
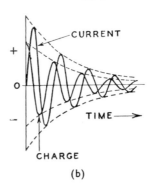
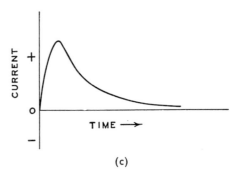

(a)   (b)   (c)

FIG. 11.24. FREE OSCILLATION

The resonant frequency f_r of such a system is

$$f_r = 1/(2\pi\sqrt{LC}) \cdot \qquad . \quad (10.17)$$

for the series circuit, and

$$f_r = \frac{1}{2\pi}\sqrt{\left(\frac{1}{LC} - \frac{R^2}{L^2}\right)} \qquad . \quad (10.22)$$

for the parallel circuit with resistance R in the inductive branch.

If a charged capacitor is allowed to discharge in a circuit which includes an inductor, an oscillatory current will flow due to the interchange of energy between the electric field and the electromagnetic field. If the circuit receives no continuous supply of energy from any external source, the frequency of the oscillatory current will depend only upon the coefficients (L, C, and R) of the circuit. Alternating currents produced in this manner are known as FREE OSCILLATIONS and defined as *oscillations in a system having capacitance, inductance, and resistance, of which the frequency is solely dependent on the constants of the system.* The frequency at which free oscillations occur is termed the *natural frequency* of the circuit and is denoted

completely discharged and its energy is transferred to the magnetic field of the inductor. With no external influence to maintain the p.d. across the inductor, the magnetic field commences to collapse, inducing an e.m.f. which tends to maintain the current in the *same* direction as before (the dotted arrow in Fig. 11.24 (a)). This current recharges the capacitor but with a polarity reversed from that existing originally. The current falls from its maximum value to zero when the capacitor is again fully charged. This process is now repeated with the current in the opposite direction and a continuous interchange of energy occurs between the capacitor and the inductor.

The energy stored in a capacitance C farads charged to a p.d. V volts is $CV^2/2$ joules: the energy stored in an inductance L henrys in which a current I amperes flows is $LI^2/2$ joules. If no resistance is present in the circuit then

$$CV^2/2 = LI^2/2$$

In the practical case energy is dissipated in the circuit resistance R with each flow of current and successive peak values of the current are reduced due to this loss of energy: the current takes the form of a damped sinusoidal oscillation. (Some energy may also be lost by electromagnetic radiation. A graph of the current plotted against time will appear as shown in Fig. 11.24 (*b*). This current will oscillate at the natural frequency of the circuit,

$$f_0 = \frac{1}{2\pi}\sqrt{\left(\frac{1}{LC} - \frac{R^2}{4L^2}\right)}$$

If I_1, I_2, I_3 . . . are the successive peak current values, the ratio $I_1/I_2 = I_2/I_3 = \ldots$ is constant.

From the above expression it is apparent that if R is small compared with L, then

$$f_0 \simeq 1/(2\pi\sqrt{LC}) = f_r$$

Furthermore, if $R^2/(4L^2) = 1/(LC)$, (i.e. if $R = 2\sqrt{L/C}$), the value of f_0 becomes zero; and if $R^2/(4L^2) > 1/(LC)$ (i.e. if $R > 2\sqrt{L/C}$), the root

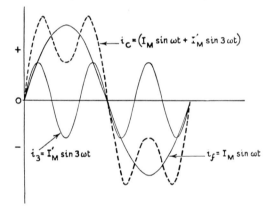

FIG. 11.25. COMPLEX WAVE: FUNDAMENTAL PLUS THIRD HARMONIC

f_0 of the equation is imaginary. In both of these cases, namely $R = 2\sqrt{L/C}$ and $R > 2\sqrt{L/C}$, the current will not be oscillatory and the discharging current from the capacitor decays gradually from its maximum value to zero (Fig. 11.24 (*c*)).

11.11. Complex Waveform. The waveforms which represent speech and telegraph signals are of complex shape. Nevertheless if they repeat the same pattern, complex waveforms can be analysed into two or more components each of which is itself of pure sine-wave form. It is for this reason that a.c. theory and line transmission theory can be developed upon the assumption of a pure sine-wave form.

The construction of complex waveforms is demonstrated more easily by graphical synthesis rather than by analysis. In Fig. 11.25 is shown a sine-wave current $i_f = I_{max} \sin \omega t$, of peak value

I_{max} and frequency $\omega/(2\pi)$ c/s: the second current shown, having a smaller amplitude and three times the frequency of i_f may be represented by $i_3 = I'_{max} \sin 3\omega t$. If the two voltages which produce these currents are applied simultaneously to a simple circuit, the instantaneous total current may be determined by adding the ordinates of the component current waves at successive instants: this

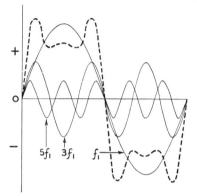

FIG. 11.26. COMPLEX WAVE: FUNDAMENTAL PLUS THIRD AND FIFTH HARMONICS

produces the complex waveform of the dotted line which may be written

$$i_c = (I_{max} \sin \omega t + I'_{max} \sin 3\omega t)$$

In any complex waveform the lowest frequency component is known as the *fundamental frequency*: other sinusoidal components whose frequencies are

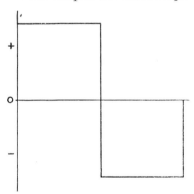

FIG. 11.27. SQUARE-TOPPED WAVEFORM

exact multiples of the fundamental frequency are called *harmonics*. In Fig. 11.25 i_f has the fundamental frequency $f_1 = \omega/(2\pi)$, while i_3 is a third harmonic of frequency $f_3 = 3\omega/(2\pi)$. A component of frequency $f_4 = 4\omega/(2\pi)$ would be a fourth harmonic: the first harmonic coincides with the fundamental frequency.

A complex waveform containing fundamental frequency f_1, third harmonic frequency $3f_1$ and fifth harmonic frequency $5f_1$ is built up in Fig. 11.26: this shows the general symmetrical wave-

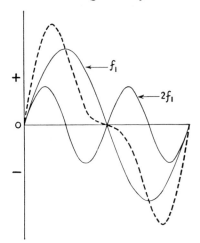

FIG. 11.28. COMPLEX WAVEFORM: FUNDAMENTAL PLUS SECOND HARMONIC

form produced by the presence of *odd* harmonic frequencies, and, in the limit, if all odd harmonic frequencies up to infinity are taken the "square-

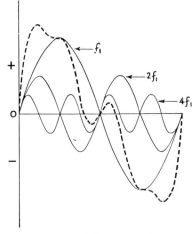

FIG. 11.29. COMPLEX WAVEFORM: FUNDAMENTAL PLUS SECOND AND FOURTH HARMONICS

topped" waveform (Fig. 11.27) originated by most forms of telegraph transmitter is produced.

Complex waves which include even harmonic frequencies only are shown in Fig. 11.28 for second harmonic and fundamental; and in Fig. 11.29 for the addition of the fourth harmonic frequency.

Finally, in Fig. 11.30 is shown the complex wave form resulting from the addition of componen sine-waves at 500 c/s, 1 000 c/s and 1 500 c/s.

Harmonic components of a complex wave ma differ from the fundamental in three ways: (i) i relative peak values, (ii) in frequency, and (iii) i phase displacement. It will be noted that th complex wave or "group" repeats its instantaneou values at the fundamental frequency.

The complete analysis of a complex wave i stated by FOURIER'S THEOREM: *any complex wav which is a repeating function can be split up int*

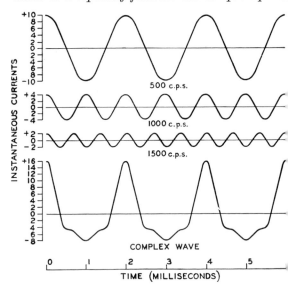

FIG. 11.30. COMPLEX WAVEFORM: FUNDAMENTAL PLUS SECOND AND THIRD HARMONICS

components each of which is a pure sine wave whos frequency is some whole-number multiple of the fund mental frequency. The mathematical expression fo a complex wave is—

$$y = A_0$$
$$+ A_1 \sin \omega t + A_2 \sin 2\omega t + A_3 \sin 3\omega t + \ldots$$
$$+ B_1 \cos \omega t + B_2 \cos 2\omega t + B_3 \cos 3\omega t + \ldots$$

The term A_0 is a non-alternating componen which, as for any other component, may or ma not be present in a given complex wave. Th presence of the cosine terms allows for the phas difference between harmonic components (Appen dix **A**.4).

11.12. Distortion. If the relative peak value frequencies, or phase displacements of one or mor components present in a complex wave are sub jected to change in any way, the original waveforr will not be preserved.

The response of any reactive network to an alternating current varies with the frequency: consequently when a complex wave is transmitted by such a network the characteristics of the components may undergo change. *The change in waveform which occurs between two points in a transmission system* is known as DISTORTION. Such distortion may arise from a variety of causes.

In the propagation of complex waves along a transmission line the series and shunt reactive elements produce an attenuation loss which varies with frequency: in a transmission line with the correct terminating impedance this attenuation increases with the frequency. *Distortion which is due to a variation of loss (or gain) with frequency* is known as ATTENUATION DISTORTION. In Fig. 11.25 the peak values of the fundamental and third

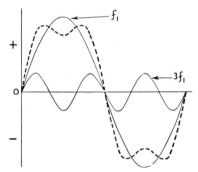

FIG. 11.31. ATTENUATION DISTORTION

harmonic frequencies are in the ratio $2:1$. The same pair of frequencies but with their amplitudes now in the ratio $4:1$ are present in Fig. 11.31. Comparison between the complex waveforms produced in these two cases illustrates the lack of definition produced in a simple case of attenuation distortion.

The time required to propagate energy over a given length of transmission line varies with the frequency: the lower frequencies being propagated at a greater velocity, the higher frequencies will lag with respect to the lower frequencies at the receiving end. *Distortion due to variation of the propagation time of the system with frequency* is referred to as DELAY DISTORTION. The distortion due to development of a phase angle ϕ between the fundamental and third harmonic frequencies due to differences in transmission time will be seen from comparison between the complex waveforms of Figs. 11.32 and 11.25, the components being in phase in the latter case. The human ear is, however, incapable of detecting the *relative phases* of the components of a complex tone and consideration of phase distortion is necessary only in certain systems, such as television.

Another form of distortion occurs where the output of a system is not proportional to variations in the magnitude of the applied signal. For example, variations in flux density (B) may not proportionately follow the changes in magnetizing force (H) due to the variation of permeability (B/H) with different values of magnetizing force. NON-LINEAR DISTORTION is the name given to *distortion which occurs due to the transmission properties of a system being dependent upon the instantaneous magnitude of the transmitted signal*. Distortion due to this cause gives rise to *amplitude distortion* by changing the proportionality between instantaneous values of input and output signals; and to *harmonic distortion* by the introduction of

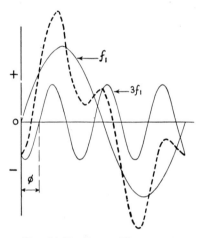

FIG. 11.32. DELAY DISTORTION

spurious harmonics causing a change in waveform between input and output signals. It is also a common cause of *intermodulation*.

Asymmetric distortion which leads to the generation of even harmonic frequencies (Figs. 11.28 and 29) is characteristic of certain types of thermionic valve and dryplate rectifiers. If two separate input frequencies p and q are applied to such a device it also leads to the production of "second order" frequencies equal to the sum $(p + q)$ and difference $(p - q)$ of the applied frequencies. Higher order terms $(2p \pm 2q$, etc.) are also introduced but for various reasons the $(p - q)$ difference frequency is the most serious.

Symmetrical distortion, which is a characteristic of certain types of thermionic valve, ferromagnetic cores, etc., and which leads to the generation of odd harmonics (Figs. 11.25 and 26), also leads to the generation of summation and difference terms of the "third order" $(2p \pm q)$. Higher order terms are also produced but here again the terms other than the difference frequency $(2p - q)$ can usually be ignored.

11.13. Primary Coefficients. A transmission line possesses the attributes RESISTANCE (R ohms), INDUCTANCE (L henrys), CAPACITANCE (C farads) and leakage admittance or LEAKANCE (G mhos), which together determine the transmission properties of the line. These four characteristics are commonly known as the PRIMARY COEFFICIENTS, or as *primary constants*—the latter a somewhat misleading term since for a given line all four factors are liable to variation with frequency, temperature, and humidity. The increase in conductor resistance at high frequencies due to skin effect has already been noted: leakance increases with frequency, whilst inductance falls slightly as the frequency

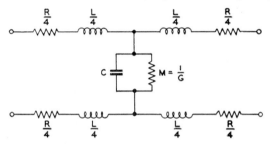

FIG. 11.33. PRIMARY COEFFICIENTS: BALANCED LINE

is raised. Capacitance is practically independent of frequency. For audio frequencies the values do not depart greatly from the d.c. (i.e. zero frequency) value but variations may be appreciable at carrier and radio frequencies.

With an increased humidity, leakance increases, and capacitance tends to do likewise owing to the high permittivity of water: resistance and inductance are independent of humidity.

Resistance increases with a rise in temperature, the values of the other three coefficients being practically independent of temperature.

The values of the primary coefficients for a loop-mile of 20 lb underground cable are as follows: resistance 88 Ω, inductance 10^{-3} H, capacitance $0 \cdot 054 \times 10^{-6}$ F, and leakance 10^{-6} mhos. Formerly the loss in any transmission line was expressed by its equivalence in Miles of "Standard" 20 lb Cable (M.S.C.) having the foregoing characteristics.

These primary coefficients are normally *distributed* uniformly in a transmission line: a section of a two-wire balanced line may be represented by the network shown in Fig. 11.33 which becomes an exact statement of conditions when the section is made sufficiently small. The resistance R ohms and inductance L henrys (per section) are shown

distributed in elements each equal to $R/4$ and L respectively: the capacitance C farads and lea ance G mhos are assumed to act at the midpoi of the section. Where the balanced condition do not apply, the section of line may be represente by Fig. 11.34: due to the lack of symmetry t

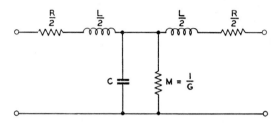

FIG. 11.34. PRIMARY COEFFICIENTS: UNBALANCED LI

unbalanced line is more susceptible to electr magnetic and electrostatic interference.

If direct current transmission only is being co sidered, and that in the "steady state"—i.e. aft all transients due to the build-up or decay perio of starting or stopping the current have elapsed the balanced and unbalanced line sections may represented by Figs. 11.35 (*a*) and 11.35 (*b*) respe tively. In this case the effects of resistance a

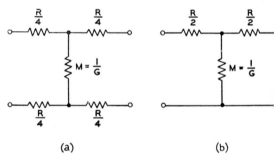

(a)   (b)

FIG. 11.35. STEADY STATE LINE CONDITION

leakance only need to be taken into account sin charging and discharging currents and inducti effects are absent, or $L = C = 0$.

If attention is first given to the non-reactive li a simplified approach to the study of line tran mission is possible. It is the *distribution* of seri and shunt elements in "ladder" formation whi leads to the relative complexities of transmissi studies when contrasted with simple series a parallel circuits.

11.14. Characteristic Resistance. The two e treme terminations for a line are (i) when it short-circuited, and (ii) when it is open-circuited.

In Fig. 11.36 two sections of a non-reactive li

re illustrated having a conductor resistance of $R = 100\ \Omega$ per loop section and an insulation resistance $M = 10\ 000\ \Omega$ per section (i.e. a leakance of $1/10^4$ or 10^{-4} mhos). Though this combination of values is unlikely to be encountered in a prac-

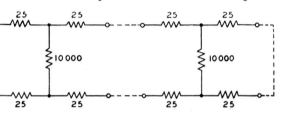

FIG. 11.36. EVALUATION OF CHARACTERISTIC RESISTANCE

cal line it permits of simple calculations for purposes of demonstration.

If the receiving end of the first section is short-circuited (Fig. 11.37 (a)) the resistance R_{c1} measured at the sending end is made up of $(2 \times 25)\ \Omega$

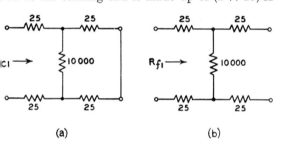

(a)   (b)

FIG. 11.37. EXTREME LINE TERMINATIONS
(a) Short circuited.   (b) Open circuited.

in series with $10\ 000\ \Omega$ which is shunted by $(2 \times 25)\ \Omega$, or—

$$R_{c1} = 25 + 25 + \frac{10^4 \times 50}{10^4 + 50}$$

$$= 50 + \frac{5 \times 10^5}{10\ 050} = 99\text{·}7\ \Omega$$

With the receiving end open-circuited (Fig. 11.37 (b)), the resistance R_{f1} measured at the sending end is $25 + 10^4 + 25 = 10\ 050\ \Omega$.

For an increasing number of sections joined in series the equivalent resistance at the sending end terminals may be readily calculated, when the receiving end is short-circuited or *closed* (R_c), or when it is open-circuited or *free* (R_f). Consider two such sections and let the numerical suffix denote the number of sections involved, i.e. $R_{c1} = 99\text{·}7\ \Omega$ and $R_{f1} = 10\ 050\ \Omega$. For two sections (Fig. 11.36) with the distant end closed, R_{c2} is made up from

$(R/4 + R/4)$ in series with a shunted circuit, the two paths in which are (i) M and (ii) $R/4 + R/4$ in series with R_{c1}.

Accordingly,

$$R_{c2} = R/2 + \frac{M \times (R/2 + R_{c1})}{M + R/2 + R_{c1}}$$

Similarly for the open-circuited line—

$$R_{f2} = R/2 + \frac{M \times (R/2 + R_{f1})}{M + R/2 + R_{f1}}$$

The results of successively evaluating from these two expressions the open and closed resistances up to the first 16 sections are given in Table 11.II: the increase in conductor resistance with the number of sections is tempered by the shunting effect of the leakage resistance and vice versa.

TABLE 11.II

Section	Resistance with Far End Closed (ohms)	Resistance with Far End Open (ohms)
1	100	10 050
2	198	5 100
3	292	3 450
4	380	2 640
5	462	2 170
6	537	1 870
7	605	1 660
8	665	1 500
9	717	1 400
10	762	1 310
11	800	1 250
12	833	1 200
13	862	1 160
14	885	1 130
15	905	1 105
16	920	1 085

These values of R_c and R_f are plotted against the number of sections in the graph of Fig. 11.38. It is at once apparent that these two values are approaching the same figure—in this case $1\ 000\ \Omega$ —which would be exactly reached only if an infinite number of sections were taken—i.e. if the line were infinitely long. In other words if this particular line were infinitely long its resistance measured at the sending end would be $1\ 000\ \Omega$, quite independently of whatever termination existed at the receiving end.

Similarly any uniform line, were it infinitely long, would have a resistance measured at the sending end which is independent of the far-end termination. This value is known as the CHARAC-TERISTIC RESISTANCE, denoted by the symbol R_0.

The series elements R tend to increase this resistance, whilst the shunt elements $(M = 1/G)$ tend to reduce its value. The characteristic resistance R_0 is equal to the geometric mean of the series and shunt resistances (R and M) or—

$$R_0 = \sqrt{R/G} \qquad . \qquad . \quad (11.9)$$

In the example taken,

$$R_0 = \sqrt{R/G} = \sqrt{10^2 \times 10^4} = 1\,000 \; \Omega$$

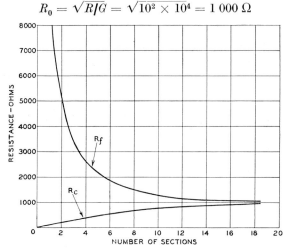

FIG. 11.38. CHARACTERISTIC RESISTANCE

The characteristic resistance is also equal to the geometric mean of the open and closed resistances (Table 11.II) or

$$R_0 = \sqrt{R_c R_f} \qquad . \qquad . \quad (11.10)$$

Here R_c and R_f refer to a *finite* line: this relationship is employed in the practical determination of R_0 from the measured values of R_c and R_f.

The characteristic resistance R_0, being determined by two of the primary coefficients (R and G), is referred to as a *secondary coefficient*.

11.15. Characteristic Impedance.

For transmission of a.c. power, the reactive line with all four primary coefficients (Fig. 11.33) must be considered. The application of pure sine-wave form is assumed in the remaining sections of this chapter.

The series impedance per section is

$$Z = (R + j\omega L) \text{ ohms}$$

The shunt *leakance* or admittance for each section is

$$Y = \left(1/M + \frac{1}{1/(j\omega C)}\right) = (G + j\omega C) \text{ mhos}$$

In the same way that the d.c. line has a characteristic resistance related to the series resistance

and shunt conductance, the reactive transmission line has a characteristic impedance Z_0 which related to the series and shunt reactive elements—

$$Z_0 = \sqrt{Z/Y} = \sqrt{\frac{R + j\omega L}{G + j\omega C}} \quad . \quad (11.1$$

It is apparent that the characteristic impedance varies with the frequency and, being a complex quantity, it has modulus and angle. This angle usually negative for telephone and telegraph cable circuits owing to the preponderance of capacitance but it may have a positive value for a "loaded" line.

If Z_c and Z_f are the measured impedances of *finite* line when the distant end is short-circuited closed (Z_c) and open-circuited or *free* (Z_f)—

$$Z_0 = \sqrt{Z_c Z_f} \quad . \quad . \quad (11.1$$

This relationship is used for the practical determination of the characteristic impedance of a line from measurements of Z_c and Z_f.

If a uniform line were of infinite length its impedance measured at the sending end would the characteristic impedance (Z_0) and this has particular magnitude, depending upon values the primary coefficients but independent of the terminating condition. Such a line may be represented by Fig. 11.39 (a). If this line were cut at

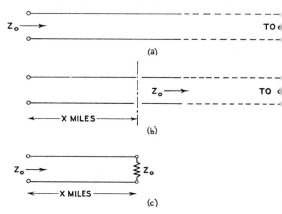

FIG. 11.39. LINE TERMINATED BY CHARACTERISTIC IMPEDANCE

finite distance, x miles, from the sending end, the remaining length would still be infinite and impedance remain equal to Z_0 when measured the direction away from the sending end (Fig. 11.39 (b)). If the *finite* section of this line is no terminated with an impedance equal to Z_0—the (characteristic) impedance of the infinitely long line (Fig. 11.39 (c))—the finite line then appears om the sending end *as though it were of infinite ngth*, and simulates the behaviour of an infinitely ng line of similar distributed constants.

It follows that the characteristic impedance, hich is the impedance of a uniform line of infinite ngth, may be defined as *the impedance of a uniform finite line measured at the sending end when e receiving end is closed with the same impedance.*

The fact that any actual uniform line can be ade to appear, at the sending end, as though it ere infinitely long, is of considerable practical aportance. The characteristic impedance

$$(Z_0 = \sqrt{Z_c Z_f})$$

any uniform finite line can be computed from easurements made of Z_c and Z_f: provided that ie line is terminated by its particular value of aaracteristic impedance Z_0 it will then behave as aough it were infinitely long. The importance of iis lies in the uniform transfer of power which can ake place in such a line.

If power were applied at the sending end of a iiform line of infinite length, this power would be ogressively transmitted from section to section the line, each section dissipating its toll of power ss, the amount of transmitted power gradually id smoothly falling until it ultimately became ro at an infinite distance from the sending end. the practical case, a uniform finite line correctly rminated by its characteristic impedance permits ower applied at the sending end to be transmitted id, after uniform dissipation producing a pro- essive and steady diminution of power in the ie, the available power at the receiving end is moothly and completely absorbed by the terminal ad impedance (Z_0).

It is well known that in the transmission of light, me reflexion of light energy always occurs when iy change of medium (a "reflecting surface") is icountered. Similarly in the propagation of und energy, echoes are produced by reflexion on eeting a change in the medium.

A transmission line is the medium for the propa- ation of electrical energy representing telephone id telegraph signals. For a uniform line termi- ited by its characteristic impedance this energy constantly transmitted (though not without some ssipation loss) and absorbed in the distant end ithout any reflexion. *The load Z_0 behaves as ough it were a smooth continuation of the uniform ie.* For a terminal impedance different from the aaracteristic value Z_0 the arriving energy meets a abrupt change in the impedance of the medium id partial reflexion of the incident energy takes ace. The reflected energy is thus lost to the ceiving load: in travelling back to the sending

end it also interferes with the forward transmission of energy.

Reflexion will also occur from any point in the line where non-uniformity occurs. All the energy available at a point normally passes that point for onward transmission towards the load: if any im- pedance irregularity occurs some of the energy is reflected back to the source and so is not available to be transmitted into the receiver load.

The insertion of an impedance-matching trans- former between line terminals and receiving load may be necessary so that the combination presents an impedance equal to Z_0: any intermediate equip- ment inserted in the line—amplifiers, for example —must also be arranged to present an impedance equal to the characteristic impedance of the line.

For the steady state d.c. circuit (Fig. 11.35), termination of the line by its characteristic resis- tance (R_0) is also necessary to avoid reflexion losses.

For an unloaded line at voice frequencies $R \gg \omega L$ and $\omega C \gg G$: the approximation $Z_0 = \sqrt{R/(\omega C)}$ may be used in such a case.

For a loaded line and also at high frequencies $\omega L \gg R$ and $\omega C \gg G$ so that R and G may be neglected and Z_0 becomes equal to $\sqrt{\omega L/(\omega C)}$ or $Z_0 = \sqrt{L/C}$, the phase angle being zero. This approximation for characteristic impedance is used in calculations at carrier and radio frequencies.

Unless a contrary statement is made the ter- mination of a line by its characteristic impedance is assumed in the remaining sections of this chapter. The characteristic impedance of a tele- phone line is approximately 600 Ω.

A transmission line may be represented by a reactive network possessing similar characteristics.

EXAMPLE 11.6 (C). A high-frequency transmission line consists of a pair of open wires having a distributed capacitance of 0·01 μF per mile and a distributed induc- tance of 3 mH per mile. What is the characteristic impedance of the line?   (C. & G.)

At high frequencies,

$$Z_0 \simeq \sqrt{L/C} = \sqrt{\frac{3 \times 10^{-3}}{0 \cdot 01 \times 10^{-6}}} = 548 \ \Omega$$

EXAMPLE 11.7 (C). A high-frequency open wire trans- mission line has a distributed capacitance of 0·02 μF per mile and a distributed inductance of 7·2 mH per mile. What is the characteristic impedance of the line?   (C. & G.

$$Z_0 \simeq \sqrt{L/C} = \sqrt{\frac{7 \cdot 2 \times 10^{-3}}{0 \cdot 02 \times 10^{-6}}} = \sqrt{3 \cdot 6 \times 10^5}$$
$$= 600 \ \Omega$$

11.16. Attenuation. In the course of the propagation of electrical energy along a line, I^2R losses occur in the series elements, whilst in the shunt elements, in addition to the power dissipation losses, some of the current returns to the source without passing into the receiving end load. Consequently a reduction or *attenuation* in power, voltage, and current occurs progressively along the line. In long lines the amount of power lost in the line may greatly exceed that delivered at the receiving end.

The occurrence of attenuation in the d.c. transmission line may be examined by assuming the application of a steady p.d. of 10 V to the non-reactive line of Fig. 11.40 terminated by its char-

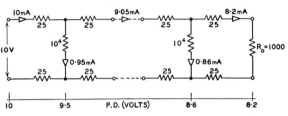

FIG. 11.40. D.C. LINE CORRECTLY TERMINATED

acteristic resistance R_0. The resistance presented at the sending end is 1 000 Ω—the characteristic resistance—and with a sending end voltage of $V_S = 10$ V, the current entering the line is

$$I_S = V_S/R_0 = 10/1\,000 = 10 \text{ mA}$$

The potential drop in the first two 25-Ω resistances is $0.01 \times 50 = 0.5$ V. This gives a p.d. across the mid-point of the first section equal to $(10 - 0.5) = 9.5$ V.

At this point the current divides between the series and shunt paths. The shunt current is $I = 9.5/10\,000 = 0.95$ mA. Of the 10 mA (I_S) which enters the first section, the amount leaving this section and passed on to the second section is $I_R = (10 - 0.95) = 9.05$ mA. The p.d. applied across the second section is $9.5 - (50 \times 0.009\,05) = 9.05$ V.

By similar calculation, the p.d. available at the mid-point of the second section is found to be reduced to 8·6 V ($= 9.05 - 50 \times 0.009\,05$). The leakage current is $8.6/10\,000 = 0.86$ mA, and the current passed on to the third section is $(9.05 - 0.86) = 8.2$ mA.

The approximate evaluation of voltages and currents for sixteen sections produces the figures given in Table 11.III. (The ratio V/I for any section is the characteristic resistance.) These values are plotted in the graph of Fig. 11.41. This graph is not a straight line—it is in fact a logarith-

mic curve and an infinite number of sections wou be required before the voltage and current fell zero. The *amount* of current lost at each shu

TABLE 11.III

Section	P.D. Across Section (V)	Current Entering Section (mA)
1	10·0	10·0
2	9·05	9·05
3	8·2	8·2
4	7·4	7·4
5	6·7	6·7
6	6·1	6·1
7	5·5	5·5
8	5·0	5·0
9	4·5	4·5
10	4·0	4·0
11	3·7	3·7
12	3·3	3·3
13	3·0	3·0
14	2·7	2·7
15	2·4	2·4
16	2·2	2·2

element is not the same for each section. The sar *proportion* of current is, however, lost in ea section, that is to say, the ratio (current ent ing/current leaving) is the same for each secti

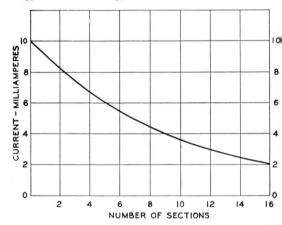

FIG. 11.41. VOLTAGE AND CURRENT ATTENUATION

In the example taken, the proportion I_S/I_R each section is roughly 10/9 or 1·1, i.e. one-ten of the current is lost at each section and nine-ten is transmitted (see Table 11.III). The attenuati follows the same mathematical law as that gove ing the rate of decay of current in an inductor the discharge of a capacitor. In the present case

$$I_S/I_R = e^{\alpha l} \text{ or } I_S = I_R e^{\alpha l}$$

or
$$I_R = I_S e^{-\alpha l} \qquad . \qquad . \qquad . \quad (11.$$

here e ($= 2 \cdot 718$) is the base of natural logarithms, is the length of line in miles, and α is termed the ATTENUATION COEFFICIENT per mile. (The negative index indicates that the function is a diminishing one.) The attenuation coefficient is a factor which expresses the proportion of current (or voltage or power) which is lost in unit length of line: although its dimension is a number, the attenuation coefficient is expressed in terms of a logarithmic unit called the *neper* or more usually by the *decibel*.

The product αl of the attenuation coefficient (α per mile) and the length of line (l miles) is a measure of the transmission efficiency of the line.

The voltage (V) and power (P) attenuations may be similarly expressed using the suffix S or R to denote sending or receiving end—

$$V_S/V_R = e^{\alpha l}, \text{ or } V_S = V_R e^{\alpha}$$

$$V_R = V_S e^{-\alpha l} \quad . \quad . \quad . \quad (11.14)$$

$$P_S/P_R = e^{2\alpha l}, \text{ or } P_S = P_R e^{2\alpha l}$$

$$P_R = P_S e^{-2\alpha l} \quad . \quad . \quad . \quad (11.15)$$

In the foregoing expressions I_S and I_R, V_S and V_R, or P_S and P_R may represent the currents, e.m.f.s, or powers at any two points in a uniform line separated by a distance l miles.

For a uniform line correctly terminated by its characteristic impedance, then at any point in the line the impedance looking towards the receiving end is always the same, namely Z_0: it follows that the ratio V/I at any point along such a line is always the same and equal to Z_0.

The attenuation coefficient is clearly determined by the primary constants: the relationship is—

$$\alpha = \sqrt{RG} \quad . \quad . \quad (11.16)$$

In the example taken in Fig. 11.36, $R = 100$ and $G = 10^{-4}$,

whence $\quad \alpha = \sqrt{10^2 \times 10^{-4}} = 10^{-1} = 0 \cdot 1$

EXAMPLE 11.8 (C). The voltages at the sending and receiving ends of a line terminated by its characteristic impedance are $1 \cdot 0$ and $0 \cdot 25$ V respectively. What would be the received voltage if the length of the line is increased by 50 per cent? (*C. & G.*)

If a voltage V_S is applied to the sending end of a line of length l closed by Z_0, the received voltage $V_1 = k \times V_S$. The voltage at the end of a second similar section joined in series would be $V_2 = k \times V_1 = k^2 V_S$; and at the end of a third such section in series would be $V_3 = k V_2 = k^3 V_S$.

The line quoted may be regarded as having a length $2l$ before extension and $3l$ ($= + 50\%$) after extension so that $k^2 = V_2/V_S = 0 \cdot 25/1$, whence $k = 0 \cdot 5$.

After extending the line,

$$V_3 = 0 \cdot 5 \times 0 \cdot 25 = \underline{0 \cdot 125 \text{ V}}$$

11.17. Propagation Coefficient. In the d.c. transmission line the ratio (sent current/received current) $= I_S/I_R = e^{\alpha l}$, where α, the attenuation coefficient, is equal to $\sqrt{RG}$.

For the a.c. transmission line similar relationships apply but with the series and shunt *reactances* taken into account. Due to the presence of inductance and capacitance in the line, the current leaving any section will not normally be in phase with the current which entered the section. The exponential coefficient which relates the sent and received currents (the attenuation coefficient in the non-reactive line) must for the reactive line take the form of a complex number which relates not only to the *magnitude* of the sent and received currents but also to their *phase difference*.

For the current ratio—

$$I_S/I_R = e^{\gamma} \text{ or } I_R = I_S e^{-\gamma l} \quad . \quad (11.17)$$

In place of the simple attenuation coefficient applied to the d.c. case, the alternating currents are related exponentially by a complex quantity termed the PROPAGATION COEFFICIENT (γ), where for the steady state

$$\gamma = \sqrt{(R + j\omega L)(G + j\omega C)} \quad . \quad (11.18)$$

i.e. the value of the propagation coefficient depends upon the primary coefficients R, L, C, and G, *and varies with the frequency* [$f = \omega/(2\pi)$].

Similarly, for the voltage and power ratios—

$$V_S/V_R = e^{\gamma l} \text{ or } V_R = V_S e^{-\gamma l} \quad . \quad (11.19)$$

$$P_S/P_R = e^{2\gamma l} \text{ or } P_R = P_S e^{-2\gamma l} \quad . \quad (11.20)$$

The propagation coefficient being a complex factor can be split up into its "in-phase" and "quadrature" components and written as—

$$\gamma = \alpha + j\beta$$

In this expression, α is the ATTENUATION COEFFICIENT and β is termed the PHASE-CHANGE COEFFICIENT.

Taking the natural logarithms of the terms in the expression $I_S/I_R = e^{\gamma l}$,

$$\log_e(I_S/I_R) = \gamma l$$

if l is taken as equal to one mile, the complex propagation coefficient

$$\gamma = \log_e(I_S/I_R) \text{ per mile}$$

The propagation coefficient is accordingly defined as *the natural logarithm of the vector ratio of the steady state amplitudes of a wave at a specified frequency, at points in the direction of propagation separated by unit length.*

Notes. (i) The transmission line is assumed to be uniform and correctly terminated by its characteristic impedance.

(ii) The in-phase component of the propagation coefficient determines the change of magnitude of the voltages or currents and is known as the *attenuation coefficient.*

(iii) The quadrature component of the propagation coefficient determines the change of phase of the voltages or currents and is known as the *phase-change coefficient.*

The propagation coefficient γ, the attenuation coefficient α, and the phase-change coefficient β, together with the characteristic impedance Z_0, are known as the four SECONDARY COEFFICIENTS: in each case their values depend upon the magnitudes of the primary constants and *vary with the frequency.*

Expressions for evaluating the attenuation coefficient and phase-change coefficient in terms of the primary coefficients and the frequency may be obtained from the expression given above for the propagation coefficient, namely—

$$\gamma = \alpha + j\beta = \sqrt{(R + j\omega L)(G + j\omega C)}$$

Squaring these expressions—

$$\gamma^2 = (\alpha + j\beta)^2 = (R + j\omega L)(G + j\omega C)$$
$$\alpha^2 + 2j\alpha\beta - \beta^2 = RG - \omega^2 LC + j\omega(RC + LG)$$

Equating the in-phase and quadrature components—

$$\alpha^2 - \beta^2 = RG - \omega^2 LC \quad . \quad . \quad \text{(i)}$$
and $$2\alpha\beta = \omega(RC + LG) \quad . \quad . \quad \text{(ii)}$$

Using the device—

$$(\alpha^2 - \beta^2)^2 = \alpha^4 - 2\alpha^2\beta^2 + \beta^4$$
$$(\alpha^2 + \beta^2)^2 = \alpha^4 + 2\alpha^2\beta^2 + \beta^4$$
$$= \alpha^4 - 2\alpha^2\beta^2 + \beta^4 + 4\alpha^2\beta^2$$
$$= (\alpha^2 - \beta^2)^2 + (2\alpha\beta)^2$$

and substituting in (i) and (ii) above—

$$(\alpha^2 - \beta^2)^2 + (2\alpha\beta)^2$$
$$= (RG - \omega^2 LC)^2 + \omega^2(RC + LG)^2$$
$$= R^2G^2 + \omega^4 L^2C^2 - 2\omega^2 LCRG + \omega^2 R^2 C^2$$
$$\quad + \omega^2 L^2 G^2 + 2\omega^2 LGRC$$
$$= R^2(G^2 + \omega^2 C^2) + \omega^2 L^2(G^2 + \omega^2 C^2)$$
$$= (R^2 + \omega^2 L^2)(G^2 + \omega^2 C^2)$$
$$(\alpha^2 + \beta^2)$$
$$= \sqrt{(R^2 + \omega^2 L^2)(G^2 + \omega^2 C^2)} \quad . \quad . \quad \text{(iii)}$$

$$\alpha^2 - \beta^2$$
$$= (RG - \omega^2 LC) \quad . \quad . \quad . \quad . \quad ($$

Adding (i) and (iii)—

$$\alpha^2 + \beta^2 + \alpha^2 - \beta^2 = 2\alpha^2$$
$$= \sqrt{(R^2 + \omega^2 L^2)(G^2 + \omega^2 C^2)} + (RG - \omega^2 LC)$$

whence $\alpha =$

$$\sqrt{\tfrac{1}{2}\left[\sqrt{(R^2 + \omega^2 L^2)(G^2 + \omega^2 C^2)} + (RG - \omega^2 LC\right.}$$
$$(11.2$$

Subtracting (i) from (iii)—

$$\alpha^2 + \beta^2 - \alpha^2 + \beta^2 = 2\beta^2$$
$$= \sqrt{(R^2 + \omega^2 L^2)(G^2 + \omega^2 C^2)} - (RG - \omega^2 LC)$$

whence $\beta =$

$$\sqrt{\tfrac{1}{2}\left[\sqrt{(R^2 + \omega^2 L^2)(G^2 + \omega^2 C^2)} - (RG - \omega^2 LC\right.}$$
$$(11.2$$

The above relationships for α and β (per mil enable these secondary coefficients to be evaluate in terms of the primary coefficients (per mile) an the frequency (c/s).

For an unloaded cable at voice frequencie $R \gg \omega L$ and $\omega C \gg G$ which leads to th following approximation for the propagation c efficient—

$$\gamma = \sqrt{R\omega C}.$$

11.18. Attenuation Coefficient. The expressio for the attenuation coefficient α in terms of the pr mary coefficients, derived from the inphase con ponent of the complex propagation coefficien is given by $\alpha =$

$$\sqrt{\tfrac{1}{2}\left[\sqrt{(R^2 + \omega^2 L^2)(G^2 + \omega^2 C^2)} + (RG - \omega^2 LC\right.}$$
$$(11.2$$

The value of α is given in *nepers*: R is in ohm L in henrys, C in *farads*, G in *mhos*, and ω radn/sec.

Attenuation in itself is not detrimental for, pr vided that the energy level of signals is not allowe to fall to the point where it becomes comparab with cross-talk interference and noise, any pow loss can be made good by amplification. Lon distance circuits are in fact designed to opera with "zero-loss" from end to end by making th amplifier gains equal to the line losses.

As a result of the rise in value of the attenuatic coefficient with increasing frequency, harmor components of a complex wave will suffer i creasing attenuation according to their frequenc attenuation distortion is introduced by the li unless special measures are taken to counteract th

The attenuation of a line may be rendered pra tically independent of frequency over a given fr quency range by the addition of inductance to th line, a process termed "loading."

Long transmission lines equipped with amplifiers are terminated by *attenuation equalizers*: this equalizer is a tuned network whose attenuation/frequency characteristic is the inverse of that of the line requiring equalizing. The equalizer ensures that all frequencies are transmitted by the combined line and equalizer with equal attenuation, and so corrects attenuation-distortion. The employment of equalizers is also essential to successful carrier working.

The graph of Fig. 11.42 shows the general shape

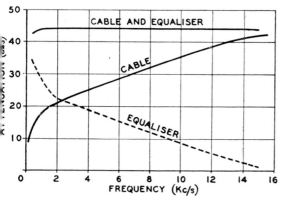

FIG. 11.42. ATTENUATION/FREQUENCY CHARACTERISTICS OF SUBMARINE CABLE WITH AND WITHOUT EQUALIZER

of the attenuation/frequency characteristic for an equalizer designed for use on a particular unloaded submarine cable: the attenuation/frequency characteristic of the combined cable and equalizer is also plotted.

For certain types of transmission line it is possible to derive simplified approximations for the attenuation coefficient by making appropriate assumptions. For example, in the d.c. steady state condition, $L = C = 0$ and

$$\alpha = [\tfrac{1}{2}(RG + RG)]^{\frac{1}{2}} = \sqrt{RG}$$

(i) *For a normal ("unloaded") cable at voice frequencies* (up to about 3 kc/s), $\omega C \gg G$ and $R \gg \omega L$.

From $2\alpha^2 =$

$$\sqrt{(R^2 + \omega^2 L^2)(G^2 + \omega^2 C^2)} + (RG - \omega^2 LC)$$

$$\alpha^2 \simeq \sqrt{R^2 \omega^2 C^2} + (RG - \omega^2 LC)$$
$$= R\omega C\{1 + G/(\omega C) - \omega L/R\},$$
where $\qquad G/(\omega C) \ll 1$ and $\omega L/R \ll 1$
$$= R\omega C$$

whence $\qquad \alpha = \sqrt{\dfrac{R\omega C}{2}}$

(ii) *For a "loaded" cable* (§**11.21**) *at voice frequencies*, where $\omega L \gg R$ and $\omega C \gg G$—

$$\alpha = \frac{R}{2}\sqrt{\frac{C}{L}} + \frac{G}{2}\sqrt{\frac{L}{C}}$$

(*Note.* Since the loaded cable acts as a low-pass filter, its characteristics in the neighbourhood of the cut-off frequency differ considerably from those of a uniform line and this approximation is permissible only for frequencies up to 0·7 of the cut-off frequency.)

(iii) *For an unloaded cable at carrier frequencies* ($f > 30$ kc/s), $\omega L \gg R$ and $\omega C \gg G$: provided that the primary coefficients are uniformly distributed—

$$\alpha = \frac{R}{2}\sqrt{\frac{C}{L}} + \frac{G}{2}\sqrt{\frac{L}{C}}$$

(*Note.* At frequencies between 2 kc/s and 20 kc/s, ωL is comparable to R and no convenient approximation is possible.)

EXAMPLE 11.9 (C). Calculate the attenuation coefficient of an open-wire line having the following primary constants per mile: $R = 8\cdot8\ \Omega$, $L = 3\cdot6$ mH, $C = 0\cdot009\ \mu$F, and $G = 2\ \mu$mhos, when the angular velocity is 5 000 radn/sec. (*C. & G.*)

$$R = 8\cdot8\ \Omega$$
$$C = 0\cdot009 \times 10^{-6}\ \text{F}$$
$$G = 2 \times 10^{-6}\ \text{mhos}$$
$$L = 3\cdot6 \times 10^{-3}\ \text{H}$$
$$\omega = 5\ 000\ \text{radn/sec}$$
$$\omega C = 5 \times 10^3 \times 0\cdot009 \times 10^{-6}$$
$$\qquad = 45 \times 10^{-6}\ \text{mhos}$$
$$\omega L = 5 \times 10^3 \times 3\cdot6 \times 10^{-3} = 18\ \Omega$$
$$(R + j\omega L) = (8\cdot8^2 + 18^2)^{\frac{1}{2}} = (77\cdot44 + 324)^{\frac{1}{2}}$$
$$\qquad = 401\cdot44^{\frac{1}{2}} = 20\cdot03\ \Omega$$
$$(G + j\omega C) = (2^2 \times 10^{-12} + 45^2 \times 10^{-12})^{\frac{1}{2}}$$
$$\qquad = 10^{-6}(4 + 2\ 025)^{\frac{1}{2}}$$
$$\qquad = 45\cdot04 \times 10^{-6}\ \text{mhos}$$
$$\alpha = \sqrt{\tfrac{1}{2}[\sqrt{(R^2 + \omega^2 L^2)(G^2 + \omega^2 C^2)} + (RG - \omega^2 LC)]}$$
$$= [\tfrac{1}{2}\{(20\cdot03 \times 45\cdot04 \times 10^{-6}) + (8\cdot8 \times 2 \times 10^{-6}$$
$$\qquad - 25 \times 10^6 \times 3\cdot6 \times 10^{-3} \times 0\cdot009 \times 10^{-6})\}]^{\frac{1}{2}}$$
$$= [\tfrac{1}{2}\{(902 \times 10^{-6})$$
$$\qquad + (17\cdot6 \times 10^{-6} - 10^{-6} \times 810)\}]^{\frac{1}{2}}$$
$$= [\tfrac{1}{2}\{(902 \times 10^{-6}) - (792\cdot4 \times 10^{-6})\}]^{\frac{1}{2}}$$
$$= [\tfrac{1}{2}(109\cdot6 \times 10^{-6})]^{\frac{1}{2}} = 10^{-3}\sqrt{54\cdot8}$$
$$= 7\cdot403 \times 10^{-3}$$
$$= 0\cdot007\ 4\ \text{neper/mile}$$

An alternative method of solution is given below—

$$\omega L/R = 18/8\cdot8 = 2\cdot045$$

$$\omega C/G = 45 \times 10^{-6}/(2 \times 10^{-6}) = 22\cdot5$$

$$\gamma^2 = (R + j\omega L)(G + j\omega C)$$

$$\underline{/\tan^{-1} \omega L/R + \tan^{-1} \omega C/G}$$

$$= [(8\cdot8^2 + 18^2)(2^2 \times 10^{-12} + 45^2 \times 10^{-12})]^{\frac{1}{2}}$$

$$\underline{/\tan^{-1} 2\cdot045 + \tan^{-1} 22\cdot5}$$

$$= 10^{-6}(401\cdot44 \times 2\ 029)^{\frac{1}{2}}\underline{/63\cdot9° + 87\cdot45°}$$

$$\gamma = 10^{-3}(401\cdot44 \times 2\ 029)^{\frac{1}{4}}\ \underline{/(63\cdot9° + 87\cdot45°)/2}$$

$$= 10^{-3} \times 30\cdot04\ \underline{/75\cdot67°}$$

$$\alpha = \gamma \cos \theta$$

$$= 0\cdot030\ 04 \cos 75\cdot67°$$

$$= 0\cdot030\ 04 \times 0\cdot247\ 48$$

$$= \underline{\underline{0\cdot007\ 4 \text{ neper/mile}}}$$

11.19. Phase-change Coefficient. In the course of propagation along a transmission line an alternating current is subjected to changes in its phase angle.

A definite time elapses between the application of a p.d. at the sending end and the arrival of the resulting current at any given point along the line. The delay experienced by the current at any point in reaching the corresponding instantaneous value to that at the sending end is due to the time required to establish the magnetic and electric fields of the distributed inductance and capacitance by the currents flowing through the line resistance.

While the initial current is travelling towards this point the current at the sending end will be passing through some portion of its alternating cycle. It follows that, in general, there will be a phase difference between the currents at any two points along the line.

For example, at the instant when the current at the sending end has a maximum positive value, then owing to the time taken to propagate energy along the line, the current at a point n miles from the sending end may be at a zero value and about to increase positively, i.e. it is lagging 90° behind the sending end current, having just reached the value which was impressed a quarter of a cycle previously. At a distance of $2n$ miles from the sending end the current will have its maximum negative value: at $3n$ miles the current has a zero value, being about to increase negatively. At $4n$ miles the two currents, impressed and received, will both be exactly at their maximum positive values with, however, a complete cycle in phase difference. Over the distance $4n$ miles an entire

wave or cycle of instantaneous values has been completed: this physical length—$4n$ miles in the present case—is described as one WAVELENGTH (λ) of propagation.

The vector diagram shown in Fig. 11.43 may be employed to convey a picture of the propagation of a pure sine wave through a distance of one wavelength. The modulus of the vector is subjected to a gradual reduction in amplitude at the rate determined by the attenuation coefficient. At the same time, the phase angle—indicated by the rotating vector—undergoes continual change at the rate determined by the phase-change coefficient.

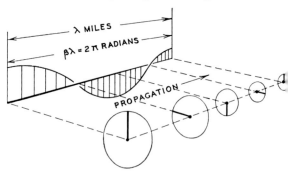

FIG. 11.43. ATTENUATION AND PHASE CHANGE ALONG TRANSMISSION LINE

The phase-change coefficient β is the phase displacement which occurs in unit length of the line it is measured in radians per mile. The expression for the phase-change coefficient β derived from the quadrature component of the complex propagation coefficient is given by $\beta =$

$$\sqrt{\tfrac{1}{2}[\sqrt{(R^2 + \omega^2 L^2)(G^2 + \omega^2 C^2)} - (RG - \omega^2 LC)]}$$

$$(11.22)$$

It is apparent that the value of β for any line depends upon the primary coefficients R ohms, L henrys, C farads, and G mhos (all per mile) and also varies with the frequency.

Due to the dependence of the phase-change coefficient upon frequency, harmonic components of a complex wave travel at different velocities, arrive at different times, and in the steady state assume different phase relationships from those at the sending end, i.e. phase distortion will arise. In systems where it is essential to preserve correct phase relationships, phase compensating networks may be used to ensure either that the component frequencies are transmitted at equal velocities, or to ensure that they assume correct steady state phase relationships.

For certain types of transmission line it is possible

to derive simplified approximations for the phase change coefficient by making appropriate assumptions. For example in the d.c. steady state condition, $\omega = L = C = 0$ and—

$$\beta = [\tfrac{1}{2}(RG - RG)]^{\frac{1}{2}} = 0$$

(i) *For an unloaded cable at voice frequencies* (up to about 3 kc/s), $\omega C \gg G$ and $R \gg \omega L$—

$$2\beta^2 = \sqrt{(R^2 + \omega^2 L^2)(G^2 + \omega^2 C^2)} - (GR - \omega^2 LC)$$

$$\simeq \sqrt{R^2 \omega^2 C^2} - (GR - \omega^2 LC)$$

$$= R\omega C\{1 - G/(\omega C) + \omega L/R\}$$

where $G/(\omega C) \ll 1$ and $\omega L/R \ll 1$

$$= R\omega C$$

$$\beta = \sqrt{\frac{R\omega C}{2}}$$

(ii) *For a loaded cable at voice frequencies,* $\omega L \gg R$ and $\omega C \gg G$ so that—

$$\beta = \omega\sqrt{LC}$$

(*Note.* This approximation is permissible only for frequencies up to 0·7 of the cut-off frequency.)

(iii) *For an unloaded cable at carrier frequencies* ($f > 30$ kc/s), $\omega L \gg R$ and $\omega C \gg G$, and

$$\beta = \omega\sqrt{LC}$$

After the impressed current wave has travelled l miles along the line the phase displacement, referred to the angle at the sending end, will be βl radians: after a distance equal to one wavelength (λ miles) has been traversed the phase displacement is $\beta\lambda$ and is equal to 360° or 2π radians. Consequently

$$\beta\lambda = 2\pi \text{ or } \lambda = 2\pi/\beta \text{ miles} \qquad . \text{ (11.23)}$$

EXAMPLE 11.10 (C). At a frequency of 500 kc/s a cable has the following primary constants: $R = 37\ \Omega$, $L = 0\cdot52$ mH, $G = 2\ 800\ \mu$mhos, and $C = 0\cdot202\ \mu$F, all per nautical mile. Calculate the attenuation and phase-change coefficients. (C. & G.)

In this example $\omega L \gg R$ and $\omega C \gg G$.

$$\alpha = \frac{R}{2}\sqrt{\frac{C}{L}} + \frac{G}{2}\sqrt{\frac{L}{C}}$$

$$= \frac{37}{2}\sqrt{\frac{0\cdot202}{520}} + \left(\frac{2\ 800}{2}\sqrt{\frac{520}{0\cdot202}}\right) \times 10^{-6}$$

$$= 0\cdot364 + 0\cdot071 = \underline{\underline{0\cdot435 \text{ neper/naut. mile}}}$$

$$\beta = \omega\sqrt{LC} = 0\cdot5 \times 6\cdot28\sqrt{520 \times 0\cdot202}$$

$$= \underline{\underline{32\cdot2 \text{ radn/naut. mile}}}$$

11.20. Velocity of Wave Transmission. Wave transmission is the propagation of a *change of condition* from one point to another progressively through a medium. In a telephone transmission line the changing condition which is propagated is electrical power varying sinusoidally at one or more constant frequencies. At any point in the line the power has a definite value at a definite instant of time, but in general it varies continuously with distance and with time.

Telecommunication systems also make use of wave transmission by electromagnetic radiation in space (radio waves) and by mechanical transmission of sound in air.

When a steady voltage is suddenly applied at the sending end of a line, the true *wave velocity* v_W is that of the *initial disturbance* or *wave front*, and

$$v_W = 1/\sqrt{LC} \text{ miles/sec} \qquad . \text{ (11.24)}$$

L henrys and C farads (both per mile) being the primary coefficients of the line. This velocity is independent of both resistance and leakance: if the line is loaded the value of L is artificially increased and the wave velocity is correspondingly reduced. It will be observed that no question of frequency arises in the conception of the velocity of wave propagation, this velocity being a property of the transmission system itself and independent of the nature of the wave disturbance.

The arrival of the wave front at any point indicates the termination of the *transient period* at that point (for which period $v_W = 1/\sqrt{LC}$) and the commencement of the *steady state*. When steady state conditions obtain, as the phase is propagated down the line at β radn/mile, the change of phase in one second is $\omega = 2\pi f$ radians. Accordingly, the phase velocity

$$v_P = \omega/\beta \text{ miles/sec} . \qquad . \text{ (11.25)}$$

Since
$$\lambda = 2\pi/\beta \qquad . \qquad . \text{ (11.23)}$$
$$\beta = 2\pi/\lambda$$

and
$$v_P = \omega/\beta = \omega\lambda/(2\pi) = \lambda f \quad \text{(11.26)}$$

giving a steady state relationship between wavelength (λ) and frequency (f) in terms of the phase velocity v_P, which is useful in its application to radio waves as well as to line transmission.

The phase velocity v_P is a function of the frequency. When the frequency is infinitely high, the phase velocity v_P becomes equal to $1/\sqrt{LC}$, i.e. it is equal to the wave velocity v_W. Also, in the distortionless condition $RC = LG$,

$$v_P = 1/\sqrt{LC} = v_W$$

and the phase velocity is independent of frequency. In general, however, the phase velocity varies with the frequency, $v_P = \omega/\beta$.

The velocity with which *energy* is propagated entails a third velocity known as the envelope or GROUP VELOCITY. The group velocity is different in value from both the wave and phase velocities, so long as the phase velocity varies with frequency. The group velocity (equal to $d\omega/d\beta$) does not differ greatly from the phase velocity.

If the velocity is unduly low, the time which elapses between the transmission of a speech signal and its reception at the distant end of a long line may be appreciable. An excessive propagation time on long cable circuits would have a disturbing effect upon telephonic conversation: on this account cable circuits used for internationally switched connexions are designed to have an overall propagation time not exceeding 250 milliseconds.

If a transmission line behaved as a pure resistance (Fig. 11.35) electrical energy would be transmitted along it with the speed of light (186 000 miles/sec). With the presence of inductance and capacitance, the higher their values the greater is the phase-change coefficient and the lower the phase velocity for a given frequency.

At high frequencies $\omega L \gg R$ and $\omega C \gg G$ so that

$$\beta \simeq \omega\sqrt{LC}$$

and

$$v = \omega/\beta \simeq 1/\sqrt{LC}$$

For a cable pair in vacuo, $1/\sqrt{LC}$ is equal to the velocity of light. The capacitance C depends upon the permittivity ε_0 and the inductance upon the permeability μ_0: the limiting velocity for $1/\sqrt{LC}$ becomes equal to $\left(\text{velocity of light} \times \dfrac{1}{\sqrt{\mu_0\varepsilon_0}}\right)$.

For a normal type of multi-conductor air-spaced paper-core underground cable ($\mu = 1$), this maximum velocity is about 125 000 miles/sec.

EXAMPLE 11.11 (C). Compute for a frequency of 796 c/s the propagation coefficient, attenuation and phase-change coefficients, the velocity of propagation, the wavelength and the characteristic impedance of a small gauge non-loaded cable circuit having the following constants per mile: $R = 176\ \Omega$, $C = 0.065\ \mu\text{F}$, inductance and leakage conductance both negligible. (*C. & G.*)

$$\left.\begin{array}{l} R = 176\ \Omega \\ L = 0 \\ C = 0.065 \times 10^{-6}\ \text{F} \\ G = 0 \end{array}\right\} \text{per mile}$$

$$\omega = 2\pi \times 796 = 5\ 000\ \text{radn/sec}$$

$R\omega C = 176 \times 5\ 000 \times 0.065 \times 10^{-6} = 0.057\ 2$

$\gamma = (R\omega C)^{\frac{1}{2}}\ \underline{/45^\circ} = (0.057\ 2)^{\frac{1}{2}}\ \underline{/45^\circ}$

$\quad = 0.24\ \underline{/45^\circ}$

$\alpha = (R\omega C/2)^{\frac{1}{2}} = (0.057\ 2/2)^{\frac{1}{2}} = 0.028\ 6^{\frac{1}{2}}$

$\quad = 0.169\ \text{neper/mile}$

$\beta = (R\omega C/2)^{\frac{1}{2}} = 0.169\ \text{radn/mile}$

$v = \omega/\beta = 5\ 000/0.169 = 29\ 560\ \text{miles/sec}$

$\lambda = 2\pi/\beta = 6.28/0.169 = 37.15\ \text{miles}$

$Z_0 = \sqrt{R/(\omega C)} = \left(\dfrac{176 \times 10^6}{5\ 000 \times 0.065}\right)^{\frac{1}{2}}$

$\quad = 10^3(176/325)^{\frac{1}{2}} = 735.8\ \overline{\backslash 45^\circ}\ \Omega$

EXAMPLE 11.12 (C). The primary coefficients of a coaxial (high-frequency) cable at a frequency of 1 Mc/s are as follows: $R = 55\ \Omega$, $L = 440\ \mu\text{H}$, $G = 2\ 200\ \mu\text{mhos}$, and $C = 0.085\ \mu\text{F}$, all per mile.

Calculate the attenuation coefficient, characteristic impedance and propagation velocity of the cable. (*C. & G.*)

At 1 Mc/s,

$$\begin{cases} \omega L = 2\pi \times 10^6 \times 440 \times 10^{-6} = 2\ 765\ \Omega \\ \omega C = 2\pi \times 10^6 \times 0.085 \times 10^{-6} = 0.533\ \text{mhos.} \end{cases}$$

Since $\omega L \gg R$ and $\omega C \gg G$ the following approximate formulae can be used with considerable accuracy—

$Z_0 = \sqrt{L/C} = \sqrt{440/0.085} = \sqrt{5\ 176}$

$\quad = 71.94\ \Omega$

$\alpha = \dfrac{R}{2}\sqrt{\dfrac{C}{L}} + \dfrac{G}{2}\sqrt{\dfrac{L}{C}} = \dfrac{R}{2Z_0} + \dfrac{GZ_0}{2}$

$\quad = \dfrac{27.5}{71.94} + \dfrac{1\ 100 \times 71.94}{10^6}$

$\quad = 0.382\ 5 + 0.079 = 0.461\ 5\ \text{neper/mile}$

$$(= 4.01\ \text{db/mile})$$

Propagation velocity $v = 1/\sqrt{LC}$

$\quad = \dfrac{10^6}{\sqrt{440 \times 0.085}}$

$\quad = 163\ 500\ \text{miles/sec}$

EXAMPLE 11.13 (C). A sinusoidal voltage of frequency 800 c/s is applied to the end of a long uniform transmission line. At a point one mile from the sending end the voltage is reduced by 20 per cent and the phase is retarded by 20°

termine—

(a) the ratio between the voltages measured at points four miles and six miles respectively from the sending end,

(b) the phase difference between the voltages at these two points,

(c) the phase velocity of the wave,

(d) the wavelength. *(C. & G.)*

(a) $V_R/V_S = e^{-\alpha l} = 80/100$

nce $l = 1$ mile, $e^{-\alpha} = 0.8$

Between points 4 miles and 6 miles distant from e sending end, i.e. $l = 2$ miles, $e^{-2\alpha} = 0.8^2 = 0.64$. Ratio between voltages at these two points is : **0.64**.

(b) The phase difference is retarded by $20°$ per le: the phase difference between the two points $2 \times 20° = \underline{40°}$.

(c) $v = \omega/\beta$ where $\omega = 5\,000$ and $\beta = 20/57.3$ radn
$v = 5\,000 \times 57.3/20 = \underline{14\,400\text{ miles/sec}}$

(d) $\lambda = 2\pi/\beta = 6.28 \times 57.3/20 = \underline{18\text{ miles}}$

(i) Distance from Sending End (miles)	(ii) Phase Angle (degrees)	(iii) Attenuation (db)	(iv) $\log_{10} I_1/I_2$ (1/20 of col. (iii))	(v) I_2/I_1 (1/antilog of col. (iv))
0	0	0	0	1.0
1	30	1	0.05	0.894
2	60	2	0.1	0.79
3	90	3	0.15	0.71
4	120	4	0.2	0.635
5	150	5	0.25	0.567
6	180	6	0.3	0.5
7	210	7	0.35	0.446
8	240	8	0.4	0.398
9	270	9	0.45	0.355
10	300	10	0.5	0.317
11	330	11	0.55	0.282
12	360	12	0.6	0.25
13	390	13	0.65	0.224
14	420	14	0.7	0.199
15	450	15	0.75	0.177
16	480	16	0.8	0.158
17	510	17	0.85	0.141
18	540	18	0.9	0.125
19	570	19	0.95	0.112
20	600	20	1.0	0.1
21	630	21	1.05	0.089
22	660	22	1.1	0.08
23	690	23	1.15	0.0708
24	720	24	1.2	0.0625

EXAMPLE 11.14 (C). A very long, uniform, transmission e has an attenuation of 1 db/mile and a phase-change efficient of $\pi/6$ radians/mile.

By means of graphs show how the magnitude and phase the current at any point varies along the first 24 miles of line. At what distance from the sending end would the rrent be in phase with the sending end?

What would be the effect of disconnecting the line a point 6 miles from the sending end? *(C. & G.)*

The variations of the magnitude and phase of the rrent along the uniform transmission line have en calculated and are shown in the following table. From the table it is apparent that the line rrent is in phase with that at the sending end at , 24, . . . miles from the sending end.

If the line were disconnected at a point 6 miles m the sending end there would be no current this point. The current which was there before e disconnexion is sent back (reflected) towards e sending end. In its return journey it will be enuated in precisely the same manner as the ginal current in its progress down the line prior the disconnexion. The current at any point will en be the vector sum of the initial incident and ulting reflected current at that point.

In Fig. 11.44 a polar diagram has been plotted licating by the full line how the magnitude and e phase of the current changes in its progress ng the line. The dotted curve shows how the rrent varies after the line is disconnected 6 les from the sending end.

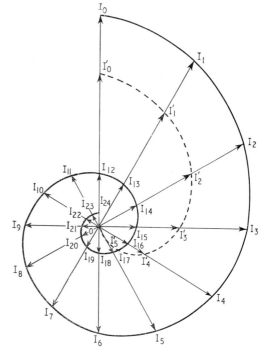

FIG. 11.44. (Example 11.14)

11.21. Distortionless Line. The self-inductance of the conductors in a cable is normally low—approximately one millihenry per mile: the inductive reactance at speech frequencies may be regarded as negligible in comparison with the resistance. The self-capacitance on the other hand is considerable—of the order of 0·054 μF/mile: its effect is serious in increasing the attenuation and phase-change coefficients and the propagation time, all of which are variable with frequency and contribute to signal distortion.

The inductive reactance at speech frequencies is very small compared with that of the capacitance. This results in a large phase angle between the voltage and current and hence for a given power and applied voltage the line current is high. Due to the high current the power lost in the line resistance is correspondingly high.

If the inductance is increased the inductive and capacitive reactances are made more comparable and the improved power factor allows the same power to be transmitted with a smaller current, i.e. the attenuation is reduced. Furthermore the phase change introduced by inductance is opposite to that produced by capacitance: the capacitive charging currents are satisfied without the withdrawal of energy from the source and the phase-change coefficient is reduced. Attenuation-distortion and phase-distortion are both reduced by the addition of inductance to a line. The propagation velocity $v \simeq 1/\sqrt{LC}$ is, however, reduced if the inductance is increased.

In order to reduce distortion it has been customary to add inductance to a line. The process is referred to as "loading" and it may be effected by one of two methods. Underground cables are loaded by the insertion of inductance coils ("loading" coils) at intervals along the route. Submarine cables when loaded have inductance added by wrapping a close spiral of a ferromagnetic wire around the conductor: the method is expensive but the employment of coil loading is not practicable in sea cables.

Loading coils take the form of toroids (Fig. 7.20): identical coils are inserted in each wire of a pair in order not to disturb the balanced condition of the primary coefficients. The main electrical requirements of the coils are low conductor resistance, high insulation resistance, low self-capacitance, magnetic stability, i.e. the value of the inductance must not change with time or current, and non-interference between coils of neighbouring circuits.

In a coil-loaded or "lump-loaded" line the uniform distribution of the primary coefficients is no longer maintained: to avoid reflexions it is essential that the coils are closely and accurately spaced

along the line. Even so each section of a loaded li is equivalent to a low-pass filter and the attenuatio of such a line rises sharply at the *cut-off frequen* determined by the values of inductance and capa tance present. The formulae given for the propag tion, attenuation and phase-change coefficients not apply to a coil-loaded cable pair owing to t non-uniform distribution of the inductance: t expressions may, however, be used for frequenci remote from the cut-off frequency, i.e. up to abo 0·7 of the cut-off frequency.

The attenuation frequency graph for a 20 cable loaded with 120 mH coils (the inductance

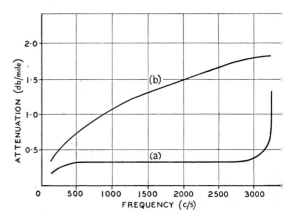

FIG. 11.45. ATTENUATION/FREQUENCY CHARACTERIST FOR 20 LB CABLES

(a) Loaded (120 mH at 1·136 miles). (b) Unloaded.

both A-wire and B-wire windings in series aidin at intervals of 2 000 yd is shown in Fig. 11.45: this example the attenuation commences to increa sharply at about 3 000 c/s. The correspondin characteristic for the same cable unloaded is al shown.

It has been determined that the number of loa ing coils must not be less than π coils per wav length for the highest frequency which is to transmitted. Considering only the cut-off frequen f_0, if the required coil spacing is d miles then

$$d = \lambda/\pi \text{ or } \lambda = \pi d$$

But $\quad \lambda = 2\pi/\beta$ and since $\beta = \omega\sqrt{LC}$,

$$\lambda = \frac{2\pi}{\omega\sqrt{LC}} = \frac{1}{f_0\sqrt{LC}} = \pi d$$

and $\quad f_0 = \dfrac{1}{\pi d\sqrt{LC}}$

where L and C are in henrys and farads per mi

espectively. For a continuously loaded line $d = 0$
nd

$$f_0 = \frac{1}{\pi \times 0\sqrt{LC}} = \infty$$

.e. the cut-off frequency is infinitely high.

If the primary constants were related so that
$RC = LG$ (i.e. if $R/L = G/C$), then substitution of
his equality in the expressions for the attenuation
nd phase-change coefficients leads to the follow-
ng results—

$$\alpha = \sqrt{RG}$$

nd

$$\beta = \omega\sqrt{LC}$$

In the first expression, $\alpha = \sqrt{RG}$, the attenua-
ion coefficient is independent of frequency—it is
quivalent to the d.c. case: all frequencies would
e equally attenuated and there would be no
ttenuation-distortion.

From the second expression, $\beta = \omega\sqrt{LC}$, since
he propagation velocity $v = \omega/\beta$,

$$v = \frac{\omega}{\omega\sqrt{LC}} = 1/\sqrt{LC}$$

e. the velocity is the same for all frequencies and
o phase distortion would occur.

Substitution of the relationship $LG = RC$ in the
xpression for characteristic impedance

$$\left(Z_0 = \sqrt{\frac{R + j\omega L}{G + j\omega C}}\right)$$

eads to the result—

$$Z_0 = \sqrt{R/G} = \sqrt{L/C}$$

e. the characteristic impedance is also independent
f frequency and behaves as a pure resistance with
ero phase angle. The characteristic impedance is,
owever, increased by loading: this has the effect
f raising the voltage on the line and leads to
ncreased cross-talk interference between adjacent
nes.

In the practical design of a cable, $R/L \gg G/C$.
he desired equality $R/L = G/C$ may be approached
ither by increasing G or by increasing L, the values
f R and C being already as low as is economically
ossible. To increase the leakance G would raise
ower losses and attenuation in addition to intro-
ucing maintenance difficulties: for the purpose of
orrecting distortion the addition of inductance is
referable.

It is, however, impracticable to add sufficient
nductance to produce the equality $LG = RC$ for,
part from the economic aspect, any increase in
nductance will be accompanied by a rise in resis-
ance also, due to the coils themselves. The design
of a loaded line becomes a matter for compromise
governed by the desired cut-off frequency and the
maximum permissible attenuation over the transmitted frequency range.

Prior to the advent of the electronic amplifier,
long underground circuits (of comparatively low
resistance) were loaded with 250 mH coils at
2 000 yd intervals in order to obtain sufficiently low
attenuation: this produced a cut-off frequency of
some 2 350 c/s with an effective upper frequency
limit of rather less than 2 000 c/s. Modern standards
demand a transmission range up to 3 400 c/s together with a high velocity of propagation: these
characteristics are obtained by the use of lighter
gauge conductors loaded with 44 mH coils at
2 000 yd spacing and equipped with amplifiers and
equalizers. For high grade music circuits requiring
a frequency transmission band up to 10 000 c/s,
10 mH coils spaced at 1 000 yd were formerly
employed, but such circuits are nowadays unloaded
and are equipped with attenuation equalizers.

Present-day utilization of main cable circuits is
by multi-channel systems employing carrier currents at high frequencies: the use of loading in such
cases is not permissible on account of the wide
frequency range to be transmitted.

EXAMPLE 11.15 (C). Compute for 796 frequency, the
attenuation coefficient of a cable circuit before and after
loading with 0·12 H coils at 1·136 miles spacing. The coefficients per mile are: loop resistance 88 Ω, capacitance =
0·065 μF, natural inductance and leakage conductance both
negligible. Use approximate formulae and allow 5 Ω for
the resistance of a loading coil. (*C. & G.*)

(i) *Before loading*

$$\left.\begin{array}{l} R = 88 \ \Omega \\ C = 0\cdot065 \times 10^{-6} \ \text{F} \\ L = 0 \\ G = 0 \end{array}\right\} \text{per mile}$$

$$\omega = 5 \ 000 \ \text{radn/sec}$$

$$\begin{aligned} \alpha &= \sqrt{R\omega C/2} \\ &= (0\cdot5 \times 5 \times 10^3 \times 88 \times 0\cdot065 \times 10^{-6})^{\frac{1}{2}} \\ &= \underline{0\cdot119 \ 6 \ \text{neper/mile}} \end{aligned}$$

(ii) *After loading*

$$\left.\begin{array}{l} R = 88 + 5/1\cdot136 = 92\cdot4 \ \Omega \\ C = 0\cdot065 \times 10^{-6} \ \text{F} \\ L = 0\cdot12/1\cdot136 \ \text{H} \\ G = 0 \end{array}\right\} \text{per mile}$$

$$\omega = 5 \ 000 \ \text{radn/sec}$$

$$\begin{aligned} \alpha &= \frac{R}{2}\sqrt{\frac{C}{L}} = 46\cdot2(0\cdot65 \times 10^{-6} \times 1\cdot136/0\cdot12)^{\frac{1}{2}} \\ &= \underline{0\cdot036 \ 2 \ \text{neper/mile}} \end{aligned}$$

EXAMPLE 11.16 (C). A cable pair is loaded with 6 mH coils at intervals of 1 000 yd for operation at frequencies up to 16 kc/s. At this frequency the primary coefficients of the cable are $R = 72\ \Omega$, $L = 1\cdot0$ mH, $C = 0\cdot065\ \mu$F, $G = 50\ \mu$mhos, all per mile loop, and the effective resistance of each coil is $4\cdot5\ \Omega$. Estimate approximately the attenuation per mile of the loaded cable. (C. & G.)

$$R = 72 + (4\cdot5 \times 1\ 760)/1\ 000$$
$$= 79\cdot92\ \Omega$$
$$L = 1\cdot0 + (6\cdot0 \times 1\ 760)/1\ 000\ \text{mH}$$
$$= 11\cdot56 \times 10^{-3}\ \text{H}$$
$$G = 50 \times 10^{-6}\ \text{mhos}$$
$$C = 0\cdot065 \times 10^{-6}\ \text{F}$$
per mile

At 16 kc/s
$$\omega L = 2\pi \times 16 \times 10^3 \times 11\cdot56 \times 10^{-3}$$
$$= 1\ 161\cdot4\ \Omega$$
$$\omega C = 2\pi \times 16 \times 10^3 \times 0\cdot065 \times 10^{-6}$$
$$= 6\ 531 \times 10^{-6}\ \text{mhos}$$

Since $\omega L \gg R$ and $\omega C \gg G$, the following expression may be used in this case as an approximation—

$$\alpha \simeq \frac{R}{2}\sqrt{\frac{C}{L}} + \frac{G}{2}\sqrt{\frac{L}{C}}$$

$$= \frac{79\cdot92}{2}\sqrt{\frac{0\cdot065 \times 10^{-6}}{11\cdot56 \times 10^{-3}}}$$

$$+ \frac{50 \times 10^{-6}}{2}\sqrt{\frac{11\cdot56 \times 10^{-3}}{0\cdot065 \times 10^{-6}}}$$

$$= (9\cdot46 \times 10^{-2}) + (1\cdot05 \times 10^{-2})$$

$$= 0\cdot105\ 1\ \text{neper}$$

11.22. The Neper.

From the expression $I_S/I_R = e^{\alpha l}$ (equation (11.13)), $\alpha l = \log_e (I_S/I_R)$. The product αl is the attenuation (or gain) of a transmission system and when evaluated from the natural or *naperian logarithm of the current ratio* of input and output currents the loss or gain is expressed in terms of a unit called the NEPER.

If $l = 1$ mile, then $\alpha = \log_e (I_S/I_R)$ is the attenuation coefficient expressed in nepers/mile. In general the attenuation of any line is equal to $\log_e (I_S/I_R)$ nepers.

For any two points in a uniform line terminated by its characteristic impedance the voltage ratio is equal to the current ratio for the same two points, so that the attenuation in this case may also be expressed as $\log_e(V_S/V_R)$ nepers.

Under the same conditions the power ratio between two points is

$$P_S/P_R = I_S^2 Z_0/(I_R^2 Z_0) = (I_S/I_R)^2$$

since $(I_S/I_R) = \sqrt{P_S/P_R} = \frac{1}{2}\log_e(P_S/P_R)$

the attenuation may also be expressed as

$$\tfrac{1}{2}\log_e(P_S/P_R)\ \text{neper}$$

The neper is a large unit and its sub-multiple the DECINEPER—one-tenth of a neper—is more commonly used: the above expressions can then be rewritten as—

Loss in decinepers

$$= 10 \log_e(I_S/I_R)$$
$$= 10 \log_e(V_S/V_R)$$
$$= 5 \log_e(P_S/P_R) \qquad . \qquad . \ (11.2?)$$

For a circuit in which a gain of power occurs, i.e. one which includes an amplifier, it is preferable to use the ratio output current I_o (voltage V_o or power P_o) to input current I_i (voltage V_i or power P_i) so that the ratio is greater than unity and the logarithm of the ratio remains positive—

Gain in decinepers

$$= 10 \log_e(I_o/I_i)$$
$$= 10 \log_e(V_o/V_i)$$
$$= 5 \log_e(P_o/P_i) \qquad . \qquad . \ (11.2?)$$

The neper, a unit based upon the natural logarithm of the ratio of two currents is used mainly by the Administrations of continental countries.

11.23. The Decibel.

The transmission unit used in this country and in the U.S.A. is the DECIBEL (dB) equal to one-tenth of the BEL. This unit is derived from the *common* logarithm of the ratio of the *powers* at any two points in a line, and the transmission loss is expressed as—

$$\log_{10}(P_S/P_R)\ \text{bels or}\ 10 \log_{10}(P_S/P_R)\ \text{decibels}$$

For the uniform line terminated by its characteristic impedance the ratio of the powers at any two points is—

$$P_S/P_R = I_S^2 Z_o/(I_R^2 Z_o) = (I_S/I_R)^2$$

it is also equal to

$$V_S^2/Z_o \div V_R^2/Z_o = (V_S/V_R)^2$$

Since the ratio

$$P_S/P_R = (I_S/I_R)^2 = (V_S/V_R)^2$$

the attenuation loss in bels is equal to—

$$\log_{10}(P_S/P_R) = 2 \log_{10}(I_S/I_R) = 2 \log_{10}(V_S/V_R)\ \text{bels}$$

In most practical cases the gain or loss is usually less than 10 bels so that it becomes more convenient to use the *decibel*. The loss between two points in a line may therefore be evaluated from—

Loss in decibels

$$= 10 \log_{10}(P_S/P_R) = 20 \log_{10}(I_S/I_R)$$
$$= 20 \log_{10}(V_S/V_R) \qquad . \qquad . \ (11.2?)$$

he current and voltage ratios being used only where infinite line conditions apply or suitable allowance is made for change in impedance.

For a circuit in which there is a net gain it is convenient to consider a ratio greater than unity with the gain expressed as a positive logarithm. If he suffix i or o refers to the input or output then—

Gain in decibels

$$= 10 \log_{10}(P_o/P_i) = 20 \log_{10}(I_o/I_i)$$
$$= 20 \log_{10}(V_o/V_i) \quad . \quad . \quad . \quad (11.30)$$

he current and voltage ratios again only being applicable to infinite line conditions or suitable allowance made for change in impedance.

A gain or loss in decibels can be converted into decineper units and vice versa according to the relationship between common and natural logarithms.

A given loss or gain expressed in decinepers is

$$\tfrac{1}{2} \times 10 \log_e \frac{P_1}{P_2} \text{ decinepers}$$

The *same* loss expressed in decibel units is

$$10 \log_{10} \frac{P_1}{P_2} = 10 \times 0.434\,3 \log_e(P_1/P_2) \text{ decibels}$$

$$(\log_{10}e = 0.434\,3)$$

Hence, $5 \log_e(P_1/P_2)$ decinepers

$$= 4.343 \log_e(P_1/P_2) \text{ decibels}$$

whence $\dfrac{\text{decibels}}{\text{decinepers}} = \dfrac{5}{4.343} = 1.151$

i.e. $\qquad 1 \text{ db} = 1.151 \text{ dn}$

and conversely,

$$1 \text{ dn} = 1/1.151 = 0.868\,6 \text{ db}$$

Both the neper and the bel are logarithmic units: the use of such units is desirable since the natural unit of transmission loss is itself a logarithmic ratio. Telephone communication is normally effected over a number of component links switched together, attenuation losses occurring in the lines and switching plant, with gains introduced by any amplifiers in the circuit. Evaluation of the overall transmission efficiency on linked circuits tends to be a cumbersome process if normal power units are employed. Using logarithmic units the overall attenuation or gain can be determined simply by taking the *algebraic sum* of the transmission equivalents of the circuit components: this is subject to the provision that there are no reflexion losses, i.e. the same characteristic impedance is maintained throughout.

Should reflexion of energy occur in transmission from one part of the circuit to another due allowance must be made in computation. For example, suppose a certain telephone circuit consists of lines with a total attenuation of 45 db and includes two amplifiers giving transmission gains of 12 db and 14 db respectively: in addition an average loss of 1 db occurs at each of six switching points and 2 db are allowed for reflexion loss. The total attenuation amounts to 45 (lines) + 6 (switching points) + 2 (reflexion) = 53 db. The total gain is 12 + 14 (amplifiers) = 26 db. The net loss is 53 − 26 = 27 db—an adequate overall volume efficiency for good commercial speech transmission.

The decibel and the neper are not power units but simply the logarithm of a power (voltage or current) ratio: they have therefore no dimension— they are just numbers. In testing transmission lines a power of one milliwatt into 600 Ω resistive impedance at the sending end is commonly employed as a reference value: the power at any point along a line is then "n db below (or above) 1 mW," and it is referred to as the *transmission level* at that point. The abbreviation *dbm* is used to indicate this power level with reference to 1 mW.

EXAMPLE 11.17 (C). If 1 W is applied at the sending end of a line and 0·25 W is delivered at the receiving end, what is the power loss expressed in (a) nepers, (b) decibels?

It is assumed that the current at the sending and receiving ends are flowing into equal impedances.

Loss in nepers

$$= \tfrac{1}{2} \log_e(P_S/P_R) = \tfrac{1}{2} \log_e(1/0.25) = \tfrac{1}{2} \log_e 4$$
$$= 2.303 \times \tfrac{1}{2} \log_{10} 4 = \underline{0.693 \text{ neper}}$$

Loss in decibels

$$= 10 \log_{10}(P_S/P_R) = 10 \log_{10} 4 = \underline{\underline{6.02 \text{ db}}}$$

EXAMPLE 11.18 (C). The input impedance of a certain piece of telephone equipment is a non-inductive resistance of 500 Ω. Its output terminals are connected across a non-inductive resistance of 50 Ω. It is found that when an alternating voltage of 10 V is applied across the input, a current of 10 mA flows in the output resistance. Find the power loss in the apparatus in decibels.   (C. & G.)

Input power $= V_S^2/R = 100/500 = 0.2$

Output ,, $= I_R^2 R = 0.000\,1 \times 500 = 0.05$

Loss $= 10 \log_{10}(P_S/P_R)$

$\qquad = 10 \log_{10}(0.2/0.05)$

$\qquad = 10 \log_{10} 4 = \underline{\underline{6.02 \text{ db}}}$

EXAMPLE 11.19 (C). A low-frequency amplifier has a gain of 56 db. The input circuit is 600 Ω resistive impedance and the output is arranged for a load of 10 Ω. What will be the current in the load when an alternating potential of 1 V is applied at the input? (C. & G.)

Input power to amplifier

$$= V^2/R = 1/600 \text{ W}$$

$$\text{Gain} = 10 \log_{10}(P_o/P_i)$$

$$56 = 10 \log_{10}\left(\frac{P_o}{1/600}\right)$$

$$5 \cdot 6 = \log_{10} 600 P_o$$

$$600 P_o = \text{antilog } 5 \cdot 6 = 3 \cdot 981 \times 10^5$$

$$P_o = \frac{3 \cdot 981 \times 10^5}{600} = 663 \cdot 5 \text{ W}$$

$$P_o = I^2 R = I^2 \times 10 = 663 \cdot 5$$

$$I = \sqrt{66 \cdot 35} = 8 \cdot 15 \text{ A}$$

EXAMPLE 11.20 (C). An attenuator inserted in a transmission line introduces a loss of 60 db: what is this loss in nepers? (C. & G.)

$$5 \log_e(P_S/P_R) = 10 \log_{10}(P_S/P_R)$$
$$= 10 \times 0 \cdot 434 \, 3 \log_e(P_S/P_R)$$

$$1 \text{ db} = \frac{5}{10 \times 0 \cdot 4343} = 1 \cdot 151 \text{ dN}$$

$$60 \text{ db} = 1 \cdot 151 \times 60/10 = 6 \cdot 906 \text{ nepers}$$

EXAMPLE 11.21 (C). Calculate the current and the voltage drop in a 600 Ω resistance in which the power dissipated is (a) 10 db above, and (b) 20 db below one milliwatt. Compute the ratios of voltages and currents when equal powers are dissipated in 600 Ω and 1 200 Ω resistors. (C. & G.)

(a) $$10 \text{ db} = 10 \log_{10}(P_S/P_R)$$
whence $$\log_{10}(P_S/P_R) = 1$$
and power ratio $$P_S/P_R = 10$$
i.e. 10 db above one milliwatt = 10 mW

$$I^2 R = W$$

$$I^2 = W/R = 10 \times 10^{-3}/600 = 1/(6 \times 10^4)$$

$$I = 10^{-2}(1/6)^{\frac{1}{2}} = \sqrt{6}/600 = 2 \cdot 449 \, 5/600$$
$$= 4 \cdot 08 \text{ mA}$$

$$VI = W$$

$$V = W/I = \frac{10 \times 10^{-3}}{4 \cdot 08 \times 10^{-3}}$$
$$= 10/4 \cdot 08 = 2 \cdot 45 \text{ V}$$

(b) $$20 \text{ db} = 10 \log_{10}(P_S/P_R)$$
whence $$\log_{10}(P_S/P_R) = 2, \text{ and } P_S/P_R = 100$$
i.e. 20 db below 1 mW = 1/100 mW

$$I^2 R = W$$

$$I^2 = W/R = \frac{1}{100 \times 10^3 \times 600} = \frac{1}{60 \times 10^6}$$

$$I = 10^{-3}(1/60)^{\frac{1}{2}} = 0 \cdot 129 \text{ mA}$$

$$V = W/I = \frac{1}{100 \times 10^3 \times 0 \cdot 129 \times 10^{-3}}$$
$$= \frac{1}{12 \cdot 9} = 0 \cdot 077 \, 5 \text{ V}$$

With equal powers into 600 Ω and 1 200 Ω

$$I_1^2 \times 600 = I_2^2 \times 1 \, 200$$

$$I_1/I_2 = \sqrt{1 \, 200/600} = 1 \cdot 414/1$$

(where I_1 is the current in the 600 Ω resistor).

$$V_1^2/600 = V_2^2/1 \, 200$$

$$V_1/V_2 = \sqrt{600/1 \, 200} = 1/1 \cdot 414$$

(where V_2 is the p.d. across the 1 200 Ω resistor)

EXAMPLE 11.22 (C). At a frequency of 60 kc/s the primary coefficients of a 40 lb carrier cable are as follows all per mile loop: $R = 75 \, \Omega$, $L = 1 \cdot 0 \text{ mH}$, $C = 0 \cdot 060 \, \mu\text{F}$, $G = 250 \, \mu\text{mhos}$. Calculate the attenuation in decibels for a 20-mile cable length. (C. & G.)

At 60 kc/s

$$\begin{cases} \omega L = 2\pi \times 60 \times 10^3 \times 10^{-3} = 376 \, \Omega \\ \omega C = 2\pi \times 60 \times 10^3 \times 0 \cdot 06 \times 10^{-6} \\ \qquad = 0 \cdot 022 \, 6 \text{ mho} \end{cases}$$

For these values, $\omega L > R$ and $\omega C > G$ and the attenuation is given with sufficient accuracy by—

$$\alpha = \frac{R}{2}\sqrt{\frac{C}{L}} + \frac{G}{2}\sqrt{\frac{L}{C}}$$

$$= \frac{75}{2}\sqrt{\frac{0 \cdot 06}{10^3}} + \frac{250}{2 \times 10^6}\sqrt{\frac{10^3}{0 \cdot 06}}$$

$$= (37 \cdot 5 \times 0 \cdot 007 \, 75) + (125 \times 129)10^{-6}$$

$$= 0 \cdot 290 \, 5 + 0 \cdot 016 \, 1 = 0 \cdot 306 \, 6 \text{ neper/mile}$$

Attenuation of 20-mile length

$$= 0 \cdot 306 \, 6 \times 20 \times 8 \cdot 686 = 53 \cdot 3 \text{ db}$$

EXAMPLE 11.23 (C). A cable circuit is loaded with 22 mH coils at 1·136 miles spacing. Calculate the attenuation in decibels of a 50-mile section at 3 000 c/s if the cable coefficients per mile are $R = 45\ \Omega$, $L = 1\cdot2$ mH, $C = 0\cdot065\ \mu$F, and $G = 5\ \mu$mhos. The power-factor of the coils is $0\cdot006$.   (C. & G.)

Power-factor $= \cos\phi = 0\cdot006$

Since this is very small, $\cos\phi \simeq R/(\omega L)$ and
$R \simeq \omega L \cos\phi = 2\pi \times 3\,000 \times 22 \times 10^{-3} \times 0\cdot006$
$= 2\cdot49\ \Omega$

$R = 45 + 2\cdot49/1\cdot136 = 47\cdot19\ \Omega$

$C = 0\cdot065 \times 10^{-6}$ F

$L = (1\cdot2 + 22/1\cdot136) \times 10^{-3} = 20\cdot56 \times 10^{-3}$ H

$G = 5 \times 10^{-6}$ mhos

For a loaded cable, $\omega L \gg R$ and $\omega C \gg G$, and

$$\alpha \simeq \frac{R}{2}\sqrt{\frac{C}{L}} + \frac{G}{2}\sqrt{\frac{L}{C}}\ \text{nepers/mile}$$

$$\simeq \frac{47\cdot19}{2}\sqrt{\frac{0\cdot065 \times 10^{-6}}{20\cdot56 \times 10^{-3}}}$$

$$+ \frac{5}{2 \times 10^6}\sqrt{\frac{20\cdot56 \times 10^{-3}}{0\cdot065 \times 10^{-6}}}$$

$$= (23\cdot6 \times 1\cdot78 \times 10^{-3}) + (2\cdot5 \times 0\cdot562 \times 10^{-3})$$

$$= 0\cdot042 + 0\cdot001\,41 = 0\cdot043\,4\ \text{neper/mile}$$

For a 50-mile section of line, loss in decibels
$= 50 \times 8\cdot686 \times 0\cdot043\,34 = \underline{18\cdot9\ \text{db}}$

11.24. Radio Communication.
In this section some of the fundamental features of radio propagation are briefly described.

ELECTROMAGNETIC RADIATION

When a.c. power at voice frequencies is applied at the sending end of a uniform transmission line a certain amount is lost by line attenuation and practically all of the remainder is delivered at the receiving end: some power, however, leaves the transmission line and is *radiated* into space in the form of electromagnetic waves. At such low frequencies the effect of radiation is negligible, but as the frequency is raised the proportion of radiated power increases and it can be detected over great distances for frequencies of 10 kc/s and upwards.

Electromagnetic waves are normally propagated from a source in every direction and they provide the vehicle for radio communication: the radiation of heat and light are also dependent upon electromagnetic waves at extremely high frequencies. Radio communication is effected by the generation, in radiating circuits, of alternating currents at suitable frequencies, a radiating circuit being essentially one from which the maximum energy is dissipated in the form of electromagnetic waves. The familiar aerial or antenna which forms the radiating circuit has capacitance and inductance as its chief electrical properties.

On leaving the aerial, electromagnetic waves are entirely independent of the equipment in which they are generated. In this respect, radiated energy differs from that of the ordinary magnetic field which has no existence apart from the magnet to which it owes its origin, and also from the electric field which cannot exist independently of the electric charge with which it is associated.

The electromagnetic field is continually in motion and acts as though it had electric and magnetic components: its motion is twofold—a translational velocity outward from the source and an oscillatory motion in a plane perpendicular to the direction of propagation. The oscillatory magnetic and electric components are mutually perpendicular and both lie in the plane which is normal to the direction of propagation. The frequency of the oscillatory motion is that of the source. The velocity of propagation is equal to $1/\sqrt{\mu_0\varepsilon_0}$ where μ_0 is the permeability and ε_0 is the permittivity of free space. In free space the wave velocity is approximately equal to 3×10^8 m/sec or $186\,000$ miles/sec, commonly known as the speed of light: this velocity is quite independent of frequency.

For electromagnetic radiation in free space the relationship between frequency f c/s and wavelength λ meters is—

$$f \times \lambda = v = 3 \times 10^8\ \text{m/sec,}$$

from which

$$f = (3 \times 10^8)/\lambda\ \text{c/s and}\ \lambda = (3 \times 10^8)/f\ \text{m}$$

Tuned circuits are employed for the generation, emission, and reception of radio waves: the resonant frequency of such a circuit is

$$f = \frac{1}{2\pi\sqrt{LC}}\ \text{c/s}$$

if L is in henrys and C is in farads.

For radio frequencies the circuit inductance is usually measured in microhenrys and the capacitance in microfarads so that

$$f = \frac{10^6}{2\pi\sqrt{L'C'}}\ \text{c/s}$$

L' being now in μH and C' in μF. The wavelength

$$\lambda = v/f\ \text{metres} = (3 \times 10^8 \times 2\pi\sqrt{L'C'})/10^6$$

or $\lambda = 1\,885\sqrt{L'C'}$ metres   .   .   . (11.31)

For purposes of nomenclature it is convenient to group frequencies into bands, each band referring to waves having similar propagation characteristics for which similar techniques can be used. The internationally agreed classification is given in Table 11.IV.

TABLE 11.IV
FREQUENCY BANDS FOR RADIO TRANSMISSION

Band No.	Frequency Range (lower limit exclusive — upper limit inclusive)	Designation
4	3 to 30 kc/s	V.L.F. Very low frequency
5	30 to 300 kc/s	L.F. Low frequency
6	300 to 3 000 kc/s	M.F. Medium frequency
7	3 to 30 Mc/s	H.F. High frequency
8	30 to 300 Mc/s	V.H.F. Very-high frequency
9	300 to 3 000 Mc/s	U.H.F. Ultra-high frequency
10	3 to 30 Gc/s	S.H.F. Super-high frequency
11	30 to 300 Gc/s	E.H.F. Extra-high frequency
12	300 to 3 000 Gc/s	—

EXAMPLE 11.24 (C). (i) State the relation between the frequency and wavelength of a radio wave. (ii) What are the frequencies corresponding to radio signals of wavelengths 20 km, 150 m, and 10 cm? (C. & G.)

(i) $f = v/\lambda$ c/s, where v is in metres/sec and λ in metres

(ii) $\lambda = 20 \times 10^3$ m: $f = \dfrac{3 \times 10^8}{2 \times 10^4} = 1.5 \times 10^4$

$$= 15 \text{ kc/s}$$

$\lambda = 150$ m: $f = \dfrac{3 \times 10^8}{1.5 \times 10^2} = 2 \times 10^6$

$$= 2 \text{ Mc/s}$$

$\lambda = 10$ cm: $f = \dfrac{3 \times 10^8}{0.1} = 3 \times 10^9$

$$= 3 000 \text{ Mc/s}$$

EXAMPLE 11.25 (C). An air-dielectric fixed capacitor and an inductor are found to resonate at a wavelength of 500 m. The capacitor and inductor are immersed in oil and it is then found that they resonate at 750 m. What is the permittivity of the oil? (C. & G.)

$f \propto 1/\sqrt{LC}$ and $\lambda \propto \sqrt{LC}$ or $\lambda \propto \sqrt{C}$

Let C_1 and C_2 be the capacitances with air and oil dielectrics respectively.

$\lambda_1{}^2/\lambda_2{}^2 = C_1/C_2$ and $C_2 = C_1\lambda_2{}^2/\lambda_1{}^2$
$$= (C_1 \times 750^2)/500^2 = 2.25C_1$$

Since $C \propto k$, the permittivity of the oil is 2.25.

EXAMPLE 11.26 (C). A tuned circuit consists of a capacitor of 0·000 5 μF and an inductor of 1 mH. What is the wavelength to which it will resonate?

What will be the effect on the wavelength of adding a capacitor of 0·000 3 μF in series with the original capacitor and an inductor of 0·4 mH in parallel with the original inductor? (C. & G.)

$L = 10^3 \ \mu$H and $C = 0.000\ 5 \ \mu$F

$\lambda = 1\ 885\sqrt{LC} = 1\ 885\sqrt{10^3 \times 5 \times 10^{-4}}$

$$= 1\ 885\sqrt{0.5} = 1\ 885 \times 0.707$$

$$= 1\ 334 \text{ m}$$

Joint value of the two capacitors in series

$$= \frac{0.000\ 5 \times 0.000\ 3}{0.000\ 5 + 0.000\ 3} = (15 \times 10^{-8})/(8 \times 10^{-4})$$

$$= 1.875 \times 10^{-4} \ \mu\text{F}$$

Joint value of the two inductors in parallel

$$= (0.4 \times 1)/(0.4 + 1) = 0.4/1.4 = 0.285\ 7 \text{ mH}$$

$$= 285.7 \ \mu\text{H}$$

$\lambda = 1\ 885\sqrt{285.7 \times 1.875 \times 10^{-4}}$

$$= 1\ 885\sqrt{535 \times 10^{-4}}$$

$$= 1\ 885 \times 23.15 \times 10^{-2} = 436 \text{ m}$$

EXAMPLE 11.27 (C). An aerial tunes to 450 m with an inductance of 100 μH in series and tunes to 600 m with an inductance of 200 μH in series. What is the capacitance and the inductance of the aerial? (C. & G.)

$\lambda = 1\ 885\sqrt{LC}$ m

(L and C in μH and μF)

$450 = 1\ 885\ (L_1 C)^{\frac{1}{2}}$; $450^2 = 1\ 885^2 L_1 C$

$600 = 1\ 885\ (L_2 C)^{\frac{1}{2}}$; $600^2 = 1\ 885^2 L_2 C$

$L_1/L_2 = 450^2/600^2$; $L_1 = 450^2 L_2/600^2$

But $L_2 - L_1 = 200 - 100 = 100$ and

$$L_2 = L_1 + 100$$

$$L_1 = 450^2(L_1 + 100)/600^2$$

$$600^2 L_1 = 450^2 L_1 + (450^2 \times 100)$$

$$L_1(600^2 - 450^2) = (450^2 \times 100)$$

$$L_1 = \frac{450^2 \times 100}{600^2 - 450^2} = 128.57 \ \mu\text{H}$$

Aerial inductance $= 128.57 - 100 = 28.57 \ \mu$H

$$C = 450^2/(1\ 885^2 L_1)$$

$$= 450^2/(1\ 885^2 \times 128.57)$$

$$= 0.000\ 443 \ \mu\text{F} = 443 \text{ pF}$$

LONG WAVES (LOW FREQUENCY)

In general, radio waves are emitted in every direction from a transmitting aerial. Those waves which are propagated in a direction parallel to the earth's surface and known as ground waves or *direct* waves, are subjected to attenuation by imperfect conduction at the surface of the earth. This attenuation of the electromagnetic wave is due to the induction of high-frequency currents in the earth's surface and it varies according to the nature of the surface over which the wave is passing: attenuation is greatest over very dry soil, whilst the direct wave has its maximum range when propagated over sea water. In either case the attenuation increases with frequency and for long range transmission by the direct wave the employment of low frequencies (i.e. long waves) is necessary. Even so the effective range of transmission by direct waves is restricted due to attenuation, but the fading effect referred to later is not present with the direct wave.

SHORT WAVES (HIGH FREQUENCY)

Long distance radio communication at high frequencies is profoundly effected by the existence of electrified layers situated some 100 km and more above the surface of the earth and forming concentric shells with it. This region, known as the *ionosphere*, consists of low pressure gases which are ionized, mainly by ultra-violet light from the sun.

Ionized layers are found to occur mainly in one group at about 90–150 km above the earth's surface, and known as the *E* layers; and also in a second group at an altitude of about 150–250 km, these being termed the *F* layers. The *E* layer functions as a good conductor at the lower frequencies and with the earth it forms a spherical wave guide within which the long waves are largely confined. The shorter waves penetrate the *E* layer and are returned by reflexion at or bending within the *F* layers. The extent of the ionization, or free electron density, varies with the height above the earth owing to the reduction in density of the atmosphere with altitude: it also varies as between day and night due to its dependence upon sunlight. The variations with time are greater in the lower (*E*) layer where the ionized gas is more dense than in the upper layers: in the upper (*F*) layers the ionized condition persists longer after sunset.

In the same way that a ray of light is deflected or *refracted* due to a change of velocity in passing from one medium to another (e.g. from air to glass) the phase velocity of radio waves is increased on passing into a region of increasing electron density. When the front of a radio wave encounters an ionized region, its velocity being increased its path is refracted away from the region. The amount of refraction depends upon the rate of change of electron density encountered by the wavefront, that is to say it depends upon the incidence angle of the wavefront. At small angles of incidence the wave is bent out of the ionized region with but little penetration: for increased angles of incidence the wave may travel some distance within the ionosphere before being progressively refracted sufficiently to return to earth: while for greater angles still the incident wave may be refracted from an outer *F* layer or again it may pass upwards through the ionosphere and be lost.

Electromagnetic waves which are propagated upwards from the surface of the earth enter the ionosphere where, according to (i) their frequency, (ii) their angle of incidence, and (iii) the state of ionization, they experience varying degrees both of attenuation and also of bending by refraction: as a result these waves may be returned to the earth's surface at great distances from the source and with a considerable proportion of their original energy.

According to their angle of incidence, waves of the same frequency will be refracted differently, follow separate paths and so return to earth at various distances from the transmitter.

The attenuation suffered by electromagnetic waves within the ionosphere is greatest for the lower frequencies being inversely proportional to the square of the frequency: it is also greater in the lower layers than in the upper, and increases during daylight owing to the greater electron density.

Over great distances reception may be due to multiple reflexions between earth and ionosphere: in such cases attenuation occurs not only within the ionosphere but also on reflexion at the earth's surface, where scattering too may occur.

Considering again the direct wave, as the total attenuation increases with the distance from the transmitter a limit is reached when little or no radiated energy can be detected: beyond this limit exists a zone usually termed the *skip distance* which extends to the point where radiated energy begins to arrive at the earth's surface after reflexion from the ionosphere. This state of affairs is indicated in Fig. 11.46 which shows the skip distance where either no signals are received at all, or else very weak signals only, these being due to scattered re-radiation from the upper ionized layers. (The shape of the service area of the direct wave of course approaches that of a circle and the skip distance in effect covers a belt around this area.)

The refraction increases considerably during daylight and the skip distance for a given frequency is least during the middle period of the day. Seasonal variations occur also, skip distance being greatest during winter and increasing with high latitudes.

Over long terrestrial distances daylight, and

therefore ionization conditions also, will vary: the degree of ionization near to the points of transmission and reception is of greater importance than that at intermediate points, the controlling factor being the condition near to the darkest end of the transmission path where bending for a given frequency is least.

For reliable short wave (H.F.) communication over distances beyond the range of the direct wave it is necessary to select the transmission frequency which gives sufficient refraction in the ionosphere, without excessive attenuation, to reflect the wave to earth at the desired location of the receiver. To

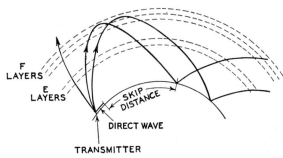

Fig. 11.46. Refraction of Short Radio Waves

maintain communication between two widely separated points it is often necessary to change the transmission frequency during a 24-hr period and also with the seasons.

Rapid fluctuations in the condition of the ionized layers cause variations in attenuation: as a consequence received signals may be subject to rapid fluctuations in strength, an effect known as *fading*. At locations where the limit of satisfactory reception from the direct wave is approached fading may also be produced by the superposition of reflected waves of fluctuating intensity. Fading may also occur on account of the variations in the length of the path taken by the reflected wave. Two or more separate modes of propagation may occur from a single emission, for example signals may arrive at a receiving aerial after n reflexions at the F layer and also after $(n + 1)$, $(n + 2)$, ... reflexions. These different multipath signals, travelling different distances between the transmitting and receiving points, have different transmission times and arrive with different delays causing mutual interference. Special techniques for reception are required to combat the effects of multipath transmission.

Fading may be counteracted by the use of a special design of transmitting aerial from which the radiated energy is emitted mainly in a horizontal direction. In addition, most radio receivers are

equipped with an automatic gain control feature whereby the output signal remains sensibly constant despite fluctuations in input signal strength. In "diversity reception" two or more aerials are used, spaced from one another by 500 ft or more: the outputs from the separate receiving equipment may then be combined or the strongest signal at any instant may be automatically selected.

V.H.F., U.H.F., AND S.H.F. TRANSMISSIONS[3],[4]

At very high frequencies radio waves follow quasi-optical paths and signal fading does not normally occur.

With relation to the curved surface of the earth the effective horizon for radio waves is slightly beyond the normal optical horizon, by a factor of about 1·33. This results from refraction in the lower regions of the earth's atmosphere due to the relative permittivity of the atmosphere, which is charged with water vapour, being somewhat greater than unity: with increased height and decreasing atmospheric pressure the relative permittivity and refractive index of the air decrease. As a result the radio waves are subjected to a refraction which bends the waves slightly away from the earth's surface and extends the radio horizon. This method of propagation is now employed extensively for the normal provision of telegraph, telephone, and television circuits over "radio-relay" or "line-of-sight" systems. At a suitable site towards the limit of the radio horizon a back-to-back directional receiving-transmitting aerial system acts as a radio-relay station, collecting the arriving signals and retransmitting them after amplification towards the next radio horizon. The carrier frequency is also changed at each retransmission station to prevent interference between the incoming and outgoing signals. The altitude of the transmitting and receiving aerials which are highly directional, must be sufficient to ensure adequate clearance above any intervening obstacles which would otherwise intersect the line of sight. These radio-relay systems operate within the frequency range 30 to 1 200 Mc/s—the V.H.F., U.H.F., and S.H.F. bands. Such systems working at frequencies beyond 1 000 Mc/s are referred to as *microwave* systems. In microwave systems wide frequency bands are available which can be used for multiplex transmission by up to 1 000 telephone channels or one or two television channels. A transmitted power of 10 watts is adequate for such systems and relay stations are spaced at 25 to 30 miles apart. With V.H.F. and U.H.F. radio-relay systems the available bandwidth is less; consequently fewer telephone channels are possible, say 60

20: relay stations in these systems are spaced at about 60 miles.

Scattering of radio waves can occur whenever there is a marked change in the refractive index of the transmission medium. The mechanism of scatter is not yet fully understood but radio waves scattered from the *troposphere*—the name given to the lower part of the earth's atmosphere, in which temperature decreases with height— result in the propagation of very small amounts of energy well beyond the normal radio horizon for the frequency concerned. Tropospheric scatter (or "forward scatter" or "beyond-the-horizon" scatter) transmission is used commercially in certain circumstances at frequencies in the range 300 to 5 000 Mc/s, mainly in cases where a site for a radio-relay station is impracticable—e.g. over a large expanse of sea. Considerable transmitted power is required, involving large aerial systems: the bandwidth available is not very great and relatively few telephone channels are possible from this method.

AERIAL RADIATION PATTERNS

For general radio broadcasting purposes it is desired that electromagnetic energy from an aerial be radiated equally in all directions. For point-to-point radio communications the transmitting aerial is designed so that maximum energy is radiated in a particular direction, i.e. towards the receiving aerial which is also designed to have complementary directional properties. The directional properties of an aerial may be determined by design and confirmed from field-strength measurements. These properties are demonstrated by the *radiation pattern* or polar diagram for an aerial. Such a diagram is the curve plotted from the locus of polar co-ordinates $A \angle \theta$ in which the magnitude A is proportional to the field strength at a constant (large) distance from the aerial in any direction θ.

For the ideal case of an *isotropic* aerial—i.e. a hypothetical aerial radiating energy equally in all directions—the radiation pattern would be a circle in any plane (Fig. 11.47 (a)). The radiation pattern may be plotted from the *aerial gain* in all directions. The term "gain" is used to express the value of the directional property of an aerial. A radio aerial, being a "passive" component (one without any internal source of energy), cannot produce gain in the sense of increasing the power fed to it. A directional effect can be obtained by designing the aerial system to confine the radiated energy to a narrow beam (e.g. as in Fig. 11.48 (a)) in the desired direction, with very little energy radiated in other directions. The term "gain" is then applied to the ratio of the energy in the

direction of maximum radiation to the energy that would be radiated by the isotropic aerial giving the same total radiated power. If this ratio is G, the gain is expressed as $10 \log_{10} G$ decibels.

The radiation pattern for an aerial has the same shape whether used for radiating or for receiving. Some typical radiation patterns for various simple arrangements of aerial are given in Fig. 11.47. In (a) for a vertical half-wave dipole aerial the radiation pattern in the horizontal plane is a circle, indicating equal radiation in all directions in this plane. For the horizontal half-wave dipole

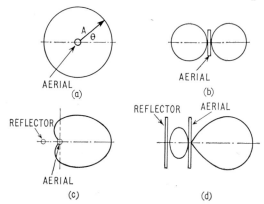

FIG. 11.47. RADIATION PATTERNS FOR SIMPLE AERIALS
(a) Vertical ½-wave dipole.
(b) Horizontal ½-wave dipole.
(c) As (a) with reflector added.
(d) As (b) with reflector added.

aerial (b) the radiation pattern, again in the horizontal plane, consists of two equal touching circles, indicating maximum radiation in, say, east and west directions, zero radiation to north and to south, with intermediate values in all other directions according to the magnitude A in any direction θ. The other two patterns (c) and (d) are again for the cases (a) and (b) but now modified due to the addition of reflecting radiators: the radiation patterns in (c) and (d) will vary according to the relative lengths of aerial and reflector and also according to the distance between them.

Although it is not possible to discuss aerial design here, some further examples of radiation patterns are shown in Fig. 11.48. At (a) is the pattern for a broadside array of vertical elements used in H.F. transmissions: (b) is a typical pattern in the horizontal plane of the ubiquitous multi-element Yagi array with a number of vertical directive elements, used for V.H.F. and U.H.F. work: (c) is for a rhombic aerial (i.e. an array in the shape of a rhomboid) used for H.F. and V.H.F. work: (d) is for a "vertical slot aerial" (with characteristics similar to Fig. 11.47 (b)). At (e) four vertical slots spaced around the periphery of a vertical cylinder give a pattern which is suitable for broadcasting, being almost omnidirectional.

For microwave systems parabolic dish aerials are generally used, with a parallel beam for energy concentrated at the focus. The aerial feed for a parabolic dish is at the focus. The feed with its

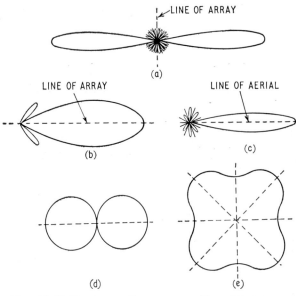

FIG. 11.48. RADIATION PATTERN FOR DIRECTIONAL AERIALS

(a) Broadside array of vertical elements.
(b) Multi-element Yagi.
(c) Rhombic.
(d) Vertical slot.
(e) Four vertical-slot broadcast.

supporting structure obscures a part of the aperture of the dish and causes a certain amount of scattering giving minor lobes in unwanted directions to the radiation pattern. The radiation pattern and arrangement of such an aerial are shown in Fig. 11.49.

For radio-communication via earth satellites, large steerable directional aerials are necessary. At the Post Office station at Goonhilly in Cornwall (see *Frontispiece*) an 85-ft diameter steerable parabolic dish aerial, weighing 870 tons, is used.[5] The dish can be steered over the entire hemisphere above the horizontal plane. This aerial is used for simultaneous transmission and reception, the frequencies being of the order of 6 000 Mc/s and 4 000 Mc/s respectively with a bandwidth of some 50 Mc/s. A large dish is necessary to collect the maximum energy (even so the received power

from a distant satellite is extremely low, of the order of micro-microwatts); and also to send maximum power in the desired direction (the beam is

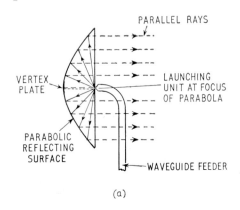

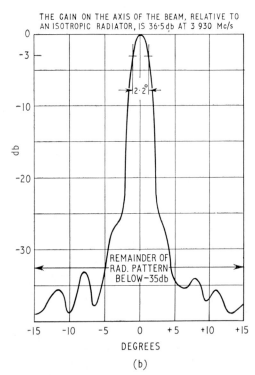

FIG. 11.49. PARABOLIC DISH AERIAL (7 FT)

(a) Action.   (b) Radiation pattern.

very narrow, only some 9 minutes of arc at 6 000 Mc/s).

11.25. Selectivity. An essential feature in the design of receiving equipment for radio and multichannel line systems is the ability to discriminate between the wanted signal and signals at other frequencies: this property in a tuned circuit is termed the SELECTIVITY.

The impedance of a reactive circuit varies with the frequency: at resonance it has a minimum value ($Z = R$) for the series circuit and is a maximum for the parallel circuit (Fig. 10.32). The resonant frequency depends upon the product LC and the minimum or maximum impedance at that frequency depends upon the value of the circuit resistance R.

The *rate* at which the impedance of a tuned circuit varies with the frequency above and below

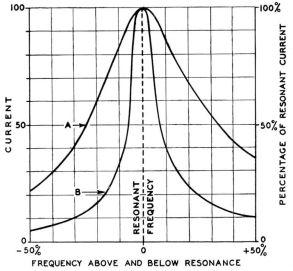

FIG. 11.50. CHARACTERISTICS OF TUNED CIRCUITS

the resonant frequency depends upon the value of R and upon the ratio of L to C. Provided that the product LC is kept constant, the ratio L/C may be varied without changing the resonant frequency. With the series circuit, the higher the ratio L/C is made the greater is the selectivity or sharpness of tuning, i.e. the smaller is the current (from a constant supply voltage) at a given deviation above or below the resonant frequency.

At non-resonant frequencies

$$Z = R + j\{\omega L - 1/(\omega C)\}$$

If R and the product LC are both kept constant but L/C is varied, then both ωL and $1/(\omega C)$ increase as the ratio L/C is increased: consequently at any frequency the difference $|\omega L - 1/\omega C|$ and the impedance rise as L/C increases. The currents in two tuned circuits are plotted against frequency in Fig. 11.50: the tuned circuit having graph A as its characteristic has a low L/C ratio compared with

the circuit relating to graph B. The current (left-hand ordinate) at, for example, 50 per cent above and below the resonant frequency, is appreciably higher in circuit A.

In the parallel tuned circuit the selectivity improves as the ratio C/L is increased.

With a tuned circuit in which the resonant frequency is adjustable—for example by the use of a variable capacitor—the selectivity is necessarily variable over the tuning range.

A flatter selectivity curve also results if the circuit resistance is increased while maintaining the ratio L/C as well as the product LC constant. Using the right-hand ordinate of the same figure, graph A relates to a circuit having a higher resistance than the circuit whose characteristic is shown by graph B. At unwanted frequencies the percentage of the resonant current value is greater with a high resistance tuned circuit.

At resonance the impedance Z is equal to R and the current is equal to V/R. At non-resonant frequencies, $Z = R + j |\omega L - 1/(\omega C)|$ and the current is V/Z. The ratio (current at resonance)/(current at non-resonance)

$$= V/R \div V/Z = Z/R = \frac{R + j|\omega L - 1/(\omega C)|}{R}$$

$$= 1 + \frac{j|\omega L - 1/(\omega C)|}{R}$$

This ratio is seen to increase as R decreases.

The selectivity of a tuned circuit must be related to the purpose for which the system is to be used. Distortion will occur if the selectivity is excessive. High fidelity and sharp selectivity being incompatible, the design of a tuned circuit may be necessarily a compromise between the two requirements unless the frequency separation between adjacent communication channels is adequate. Whatever the frequency bandwidth to be accepted by the tuned circuit, it is desirable that the graph should rise and fall steeply at the limits of frequency to be accepted, otherwise interference from unwanted signals at adjacent frequencies may be serious.

The quality of an inductor or capacitor which enables a high selectivity to be obtained is measured by the Q-*factor* which is the ratio of the reactance to the circuit resistance at the resonant frequency, i.e.

$$Q = \omega L/R \text{ or } 1/(\omega CR)$$

In the series circuit at the resonant frequency, if E is the applied voltage, the current $I = E/R$. The p.d. across the inductive element is

$$V = \omega LI = \omega LE/R$$

whence $\qquad V/E = \omega L/R = Q$

The Q-factor is thus equal to the ratio of the "resonant" voltage (V) to the applied voltage (E). The selectivity as defined by the ratio (current at resonant frequency/current at non-resonant frequency) is directly proportional to the Q-factor.

In the parallel circuit at resonance

$$Z \simeq L/(CR) = \omega L/(\omega CR) = Q/(\omega C) = Q(\omega L)$$

in other words the impedance of the parallel circuit is Q times the reactance of each branch of the circuit. The selectivity defined as the ratio (impedance at resonant frequency/impedance at non-resonant frequency) is directly proportional to the Q-factor.

The Q-factor is also defined as the ratio of the frequency of resonance to the bandwidth between those frequencies, greater and lower than the resonant frequency, which are known as the "half-power points," i.e. between those frequencies at which the response of the resonant structure differs by 3 db from that at resonance.

Losses in capacitors may be due to either the plates or the dielectric: d.c. losses in the plates are important at low frequencies but eddy losses in the plates and other metal surfaces are more serious. The dielectric losses in paper capacitors are greater than those using mica as the dielectric, though the losses in mica are important at high frequencies. Q-factors from 100 to 300 are common with paper dielectric and from 1 000 to 3 000 for mica capacitors, the Q-value decreasing as the frequency rises. With the dielectric "polystyrene" recently produced a Q-factor as high as 10 000 at a frequency of 500 kc/s is obtained.

In inductors using laminated iron cores the Q-value may not exceed 50 even at voice frequencies: with dust-cores, Q-values of the order of 200 to 300 may be obtained at voice and carrier frequencies.

EXAMPLE 11.28 (C). The Q-factor of a coil at a frequency of 1 000 kc/s is 100 and the inductance is 100 μH. What is the series resistance at this frequency? (*C. & G.*)

$$Q = X/R = \omega L/R = 2\pi f L/R$$

where f is in c/s, L in henrys, and R in ohms.

$$R = 2\pi f L/Q = 6 \cdot 28 \times 10^6 \times 10^2 \times 10^{-6}/10^2$$
$$= \underline{\underline{6 \cdot 28 \ \Omega}}$$

11.26. Impedance Networks. Reactive and non-reactive networks are used for a variety of purposes in transmission equipment. Fixed and variable attenuators—usually non-reactive—are employed to insert a known loss in a path without introducing distortion or change of impedance: an attenuator of fixed loss is usually known as a *pad*. Balance networks or artificial lines—normally reactive—are

required to simulate the characteristics of transmission lines. Reference has already been made to networks for attenuation equalization and phase equalization: suitable networks or pads are also used for impedance matching. An important class of network, which is essentially reactive, is the filter.

A network commonly takes the form of a *quadripole*, having only two pairs of terminals. A quadripole is said to be symmetrical when it is electrically equivalent to that obtained by interchanging the input terminals with the output terminals, and is

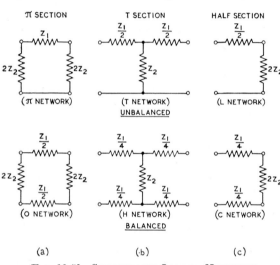

FIG. 11.51. SYMMETRICAL LADDER NETWORKS
(*a*) π-section. (*b*) T-section. (*c*) Half-section.

dissymmetrical (asymmetrical) when this is not the case.

The uniform line has been compared in Fig. 11.33 to a recurrent network made up from a plurality of simple networks joined together on an "image" impedance basis and producing no reflexions at the junctions.

Networks may be broadly divided into three classes, and according to the form of their construction they are known as (i) ladder networks (Fig. 11.51), (ii) lattice (Fig. 11.52 (*a*)) or bridge networks (Fig. 11.52 (*b*)), and (iii) bridged-T networks (Fig. 11.53).

Ladder networks (Fig. 11.51) are further named according to the letter simulated by their diagrammatic layout. The π-, T-, and L-networks shown in the upper half of the diagram are of the unbalanced type, that is to say their series impedance is entirely contained in one wire only of the pair. The corresponding balanced types—the O-, H-, and C-networks—are shown in the lower half of the diagram : these have one-half of the series impedance in either wire of the pair to preserve symmetry and reduce interference. The L-networks and C-networks are in effect equivalent to one half of the T- and H-networks respectively and they are usually referred to as half-sections.

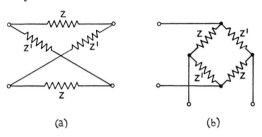

FIG. 11.52. SYMMETRICAL NETWORKS
(a) Lattice. (b) Bridge.

For calculation purposes it is usual to designate the *total series* impedance per section by the symbol Z_1, and the *total shunt* impedance per section by Z_2. For design purposes evaluations are more conveniently made upon the unbalanced networks as the

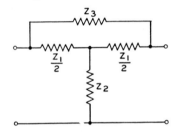

FIG. 11.53. BRIDGED-T NETWORK

calculated values of the elements can then be readily distributed equally between the two wires of a balanced structure is required. In each case the total series (Z_1) and total shunt (Z_2) impedances per section are indicated in Fig. 11.51.

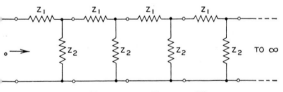

FIG. 11.54. RECURRENT LADDER NETWORK

The general case of a uniform line may be represented by a recurrent series of L-sections (Fig. 11.54). A single section may then be obtained by cutting the recurrent network either (i) midway along a series element, which then produces the T-section (Fig. 11.55 (a)) and whose impedance is

referred to as the mid-series impedance, or (ii) *midway* in the shunt element, producing the π-section (Fig. 11.55 (b)) whose impedance is then termed the mid-shunt impedance.

At the end of a line, when a termination is to be made it becomes necessary to employ a half-section of one form or the other to preserve symmetry and avoid reflexions. A typical case is presented by the

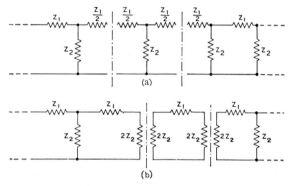

FIG. 11.55. FORMATION OF (a) T-NETWORK,
(b) π-NETWORK

coil-loaded line, the end sections of which are either of normal length terminated upon a half-value loading coil, or else are loaded normally but of one-half the usual length.

Reference has been made to the use of networks for the purpose of impedance matching. The impedance of a quadripole may differ according to whether it is measured across the input or the out-

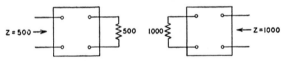

FIG. 11.56. ITERATIVE IMPEDANCE

put terminals. In Fig. 11.56, the quadripole shown measures 500 Ω impedance when measured from the left-hand (input) terminals, and the impedance is 1 000 Ω when measured from the right-hand (output) terminals : in each case the network is fitted with the appropriate matching termination. *In a quadripole, the value of the impedance measured at one pair of terminals when the other pair of terminals is terminated with an impedance of the same value is* termed the ITERATIVE IMPEDANCE. In general, iterative impedances are different for the two pairs of terminals of a network, as indicated in the diagram. When the two iterative impedances are equal, their common value is called the *characteristic impedance* of the network.

On the other hand, the IMAGE IMPEDANCES of a quadripole are defined as *the two impedances which are such that when ONE of them is connected across the appropriate pair of terminals of the network the OTHER is presented by the other pair of terminals.* Thus in Fig. 11.57, the impedance measured across the input terminals is $1\ 000\ \Omega$ when the output terminals are terminated by $100\ \Omega$: but the impedance across the output ter-

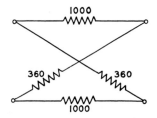

----- TERMINATION FOR Z = 100

—·—·— TERMINATION FOR Z = 1000

FIG. 11.57. IMAGE IMPEDANCES

minals of the same network measures $100\ \Omega$ when the input terminals are terminated with $1\ 000\ \Omega$. There are then no terminal reflexions. When the two image impedances are equal their common value is equal to the characteristic impedance of the network.

EXAMPLE 11.29 (C). Determine the characteristic resistance of the lattice network shown in Fig. 11.58.
(C. & G.)

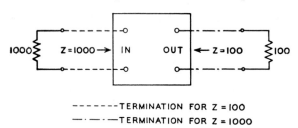

FIG. 11.58 (Example 11.29)

Using the expression $R_0 = \sqrt{R_f R_c}$—

$$R_f = \frac{1\ 360}{2}$$

$$= 680\ \Omega$$

$$R_c = \frac{1\ 000 \times 360}{1\ 000 + 360} + \frac{1\ 000 \times 360}{1\ 000 + 360}$$

$$= \frac{2 \times 360\ 000}{1\ 360} = 529\ \Omega$$

$$R_0 = \sqrt{R_f R_c} = \sqrt{680 \times 529} = \sqrt{360\ 000}$$

$$= 600\ \Omega$$

EXAMPLE 11.30 (C). An asymmetrical T-pad has series arms $300\ \Omega$ and $500\ \Omega$ respectively and a shunt arm $100\ \Omega$ resistance. Determine the image and iterative impedances of the pad. (C. & G.)

See the diagrams, Fig. 11.59.

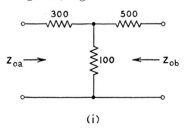

(i)

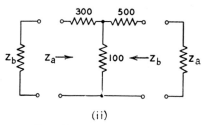

(ii)

FIG. 11.59 (Example 11.30)

(i) *Image Impedances*

(a) Seen from the left the image impedance is the characteristic impedance—

$$Z_{oa} = \sqrt{Z_c Z_f} \text{ where } Z_c = 300 + \frac{500 \times 100}{500 + 100}$$

$$= 300 + \frac{50\ 000}{600} = 383\cdot3$$

and $Z_f = 300 + 100 = 400$

$$Z_{oa} = \sqrt{383\cdot3 \times 400} = \sqrt{153\ 320} = 391\cdot4\ \Omega$$

(b) Seen from the right—

$$Z_c = 500 + \frac{300 \times 100}{300 + 100} = 500 + \frac{30\ 000}{400} = 575$$

$$Z_f = 600$$

$$Z_{ob} = \sqrt{575 \times 600} = \sqrt{345\ 000} = 587\cdot3\ \Omega$$

(ii) *Iterative Impedances*

(a) Seen from the left, let this be Z_a, then

$$Z_a = 300 + \frac{(500 + Z_a)100}{500 + Z_a + 100}$$

$$600Z_a + Z_a{}^2 = 150\ 000 + 300Z_a + 30\ 000$$
$$+ 50\ 000 + 100Z_a$$

$$Z_a{}^2 + 200Z_a - 230\ 000 = 0$$

$$Z_a = \frac{-200 \pm \sqrt{200^2 + 920\,000}}{2}$$

$$= -100 \pm \sqrt{240\,000} = \underline{\underline{389\ \Omega}}$$

(b) Seen from the right, let this be Z_b, then

$$Z_b = 500 + \frac{(300 + Z_b)100}{300 + Z_b + 100}$$

$$300Z_b + Z_b^2 + 100Z_b = 150\,000 + 500Z_b$$
$$+ 50\,000 + 30\,000 + 100Z_b$$

$$Z_b^2 - 200Z_b - 230\,000 = 0$$

$$Z_b = \underline{\underline{589\ \Omega}}$$

EVALUATION OF T-NETWORK

The T-network being of common application, the evaluation of its characteristic impedance (Z_0) in terms of the series (Z_1) and shunt (Z_2) impedances may be taken as a typical example of this class of problem. Referring to Fig. 11.60, if the T-section is terminated by Z_0 its characteristic impedance across the input terminals will also be equal to Z_0.

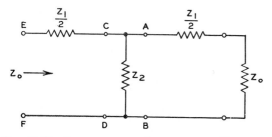

Fig. 11.60. Characteristic Impedance of T-section

Looking towards the termination, the impedance across AB—

$$Z_{AB} = Z_1/2 + Z_0$$

and the impedance across CD—

$$Z_{CD} = \frac{Z_2 \times Z_{AB}}{Z_2 + Z_{AB}} = \frac{Z_2(Z_1/2 + Z_0)}{Z_2 + Z_1/2 + Z_0}$$

and the impedance across EF—

$$Z_{EF} = Z_0 = Z_1/2 + Z_{CD}$$

$$Z_0 = Z_1/2 + \frac{Z_2(Z_1/2 + Z_0)}{Z_2 + Z_1/2 + Z_0}$$

$$= \left[\frac{\dfrac{Z_1 Z_2}{2} + \dfrac{Z_1^2}{4} + \dfrac{Z_1 Z_0}{2} + \dfrac{Z_1 Z_2}{2} + Z_2 Z_0}{Z_2 + Z_1/2 + Z_0}\right]$$

$$Z_0 Z_2 + Z_0 Z_1/2 + Z_0^2$$
$$= Z_1 Z_2/2 + Z_1^2/4 + Z_1 Z_0/2 + Z_1 Z_2/2$$
$$+ Z_2 Z_0$$

$$Z_0^2 = Z_1 Z_2 + Z_1^2/4$$

$$Z_0 = \sqrt{Z_1 Z_2 + Z_1^2/4} \qquad \cdot \quad \cdot \quad \cdot \quad (11.32)$$

POWER TRANSFER

In order to achieve the maximum transfer of power from a source of e.m.f. E (which has an internal impedance Z ohms) into a load impedance (Z_0 ohms) the internal and load impedances should be of equal modulus ($Z = Z_0$) and their reactive components should be of opposite sign. The same

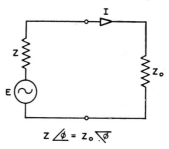

$$Z\ \underline{/\phi} = Z_0\ \underline{\diagdown\phi}$$

Fig. 11.61. Condition for Maximum Transfer of Power

condition applies to the transfer of power from one network to another.

The current from the generator (e.m.f. $= E$ volts) into the load in Fig. 11.61 is

$$I = \frac{E}{Z + Z_0}$$

The power in the load impedance is

$$I^2 Z_0 = \frac{E^2 Z_0}{(Z + Z_0)^2}\ \text{watts}$$

A proof is readily available (using the differential calculus) that for $I^2 Z_0$ to have its greatest value, then Z must be equal to Z_0. A similar relationship holds for the d.c. circuit.

In Fig. 11.62 graphs are plotted showing the effect of departure from matched impedance conditions when Z_0 and its phase angle ϕ are in turn varied. In the graphs Z is taken as 600 Ω and its angle as $-45°$. The graphs reach their maximum values when $Z_0 = 600\ \Omega$ and the phase angle is $+45°$. It will be seen that the peak values are not particularly sharp, nor are the graphs symmetrical about the peak values. In Fig. 11.63 the loss in decibels (the central column) is given for various values of load resistance R connected to a 600 Ω

generator: this loss represents the ratio of the power in R to the power wasted in the source.

The effect of interpolating a network between a generator and a load—or between two other networks—may be measured by the INSERTION LOSS

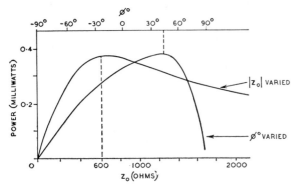

FIG. 11.62. EFFECT OF MISMATCHED IMPEDANCE

(or gain) expressed in decibels. For example, if the power delivered to a load is P_1 when connected direct to a generator and is reduced to P_2 when a

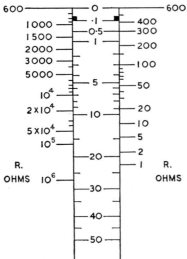

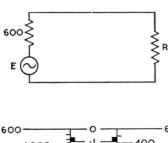

FIG. 11.63. LOSS IN DECIBELS DUE TO MISMATCHED
IMPEDANCES

network is inserted between generator and load, the insertion loss is equal to $10 \log_{10}(P_1/P_2)$ decibels.

The effect of mismatched impedances may also be measured in decibels by the REFLEXION LOSS (or gain). For instance if P_1 is the power transmitted into the load when correctly matched and P_2 is the power delivered to the load when mismatched, the reflexion loss is equal to $10 \log_{10}(P_1/P_2)$ decibels.

EXAMPLE 11.31 (C). Show that the maximum power that can be obtained from a source having an internal impedance $R + jX$ and open-circuit voltage E is equal to $E^2/4R$.

An a.c. source having a non-reactive internal impedance of 300 Ω is connected across the input terminals of the network given in Fig. 11.64 (a). What would be the value of the load resistance across the output terminals for maximum output power, and the insertion loss of the network with this load? (C & G.)

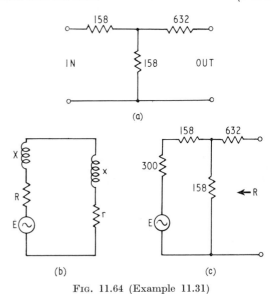

FIG. 11.64 (Example 11.31)

Suppose a load of $z = r + jx$ is connected across the source. Then with reference to Fig. 11.64 (b) the load current is

$$I = \frac{E}{R + jX + r + jx}$$

$$= \frac{E}{\sqrt{(R+r)^2 + (X+x)^2}} \bigg/ \tan^{-1}\frac{X+x}{R+r}$$

The power dissipated in the load is

$$W = I^2 r = \frac{E^2 r}{(R+r)^2 + (X+x)^2}$$

W will be maximum when $X + x = 0$, i.e. when $X = -x$; in other words the load should have a reactance equal and opposite to that of the source. Under this condition,

$$W = \frac{E^2 r}{(R + r)^2} = \frac{E^2 r}{R^2 + 2Rr + r^2}$$

$$= \left(\frac{E^2}{R}\right) \cdot \frac{1}{R/r + 2 + r/R}$$

$$= \left(\frac{E^2}{R}\right) \cdot \frac{1}{4 + (R/r - 2 + r/R)}$$

$$= \left(\frac{E^2}{R}\right) \frac{1}{4 + (\sqrt{R/r} - \sqrt{r/R})^2}$$

W will be maximum when

$$\sqrt{R/r} - \sqrt{r/R} = 0, \text{ i.e. when } r = R$$

In this case

$$W_{max} = \underline{\underline{E^2/4R}}$$

When the a.c. source is applied across the input terminals of the network, as in Fig. 11.64 (c), the resistance R measured across the output terminals will be

$$R = 632 + \frac{158 \times 458}{158 + 458} = 632 + \frac{158 \times 458}{616}$$

$$= 632 + 117 \cdot 4 = \underline{\underline{750 \ \Omega}}$$

The maximum power will be transferred from the network to the load when the load resistance is 750 Ω.

When the a.c. source is directly applied to this resistance, the current in the resistance is

$$I_1 = \frac{E}{300 + 750} = \frac{E}{1\ 050} \text{ amperes}$$

where E is the e.m.f. of the source.

When the network is inserted between the source and the load the load current will be

$$I_2 = \frac{158}{1\ 540} \cdot \frac{E}{300 + 158 + \{(158 \times 1\ 382)/1\ 540\}}$$

$$= \frac{E}{\{(458 \times 1\ 540)/158\} + 1\ 382} = \frac{E}{5\ 846}$$

Insertion loss of the network

$$= 20 \log_{10} \times \frac{(E/1\ 050)}{(E/5\ 846)} = 20 \log_{10} 5 \cdot 567$$

$$= 20 \times 0 \cdot 745\ 6 = \underline{\underline{14 \cdot 912 \text{ db}}}$$

EXAMPLE 11.32 (C). Deduce the formulae for the transmission losses due to the insertion of (a) series impedance, and (b) shunt impedance at a point where the impedance of the line in one direction is Z_1 and in the other Z_2.

Assume that the inserted apparatus does not alter the e.m.f. acting in the transmitter.

Determine the loss at 300 c/s due to a series 1 μF capacitor when $Z_1 = 400 \ \Omega$ and $Z_2 = 1\ 200 \ \Omega$. (C. & G.)

See the diagrams in Fig. 11.65.

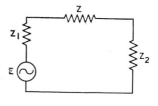

(a)

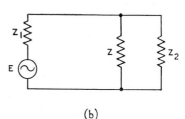

(b)

FIG. 11.65 (Example 11.32)

(a) *Insertion loss due to series impedance Z*

P.d. across Z_2 without series impedance Z is

$$V_1 = \frac{EZ_2}{Z_1 + Z_2}$$

P.d. across Z_2 with series impedance Z is

$$V_2 = \frac{EZ_2}{Z_1 + Z_2 + Z}$$

$$\text{Loss ratio} = \frac{V_1}{V_2} = \frac{Z_1 + Z_2 + Z}{Z_1 + Z_2} = 1 + \frac{Z}{Z_1 + Z_2}$$

$$\text{Insertion loss} = 20 \log_{10} \left(1 + \frac{Z}{Z_1 + Z_2}\right) \text{ db}$$

(b) *Insertion loss due to shunt impedance Z*

P.d. across Z_2 without shunt impedance Z is

$$V_1 = \frac{EZ_2}{Z_1 + Z_2}$$

P.d. across Z_2 with shunt impedance Z is

$$V_2 = \frac{E\left(\dfrac{ZZ_2}{Z + Z_2}\right)}{Z_1 + \left(\dfrac{ZZ_2}{Z + Z_2}\right)}$$

$$= \frac{E \cdot ZZ_2}{Z_1 Z + Z_1 Z_2 + ZZ_2}$$

Voltage ratio $\dfrac{V_1}{V_2} = \dfrac{Z_2(Z_1Z + Z_1Z_2 + ZZ_2)}{(Z_1 + Z_2)ZZ_2}$

$$= 1 + \dfrac{Z_1Z_2}{Z(Z_1 + Z_2)}$$

Insertion loss $= 20 \log_{10}\left(1 + \dfrac{Z_1Z_2}{Z(Z_1 + Z_2)}\right)$

(c) *Insertion loss due to series* 1 μF *capacitor*

$Z_1 = 400,\ Z_2 = 1\ 200,\ Z = -j/(\omega C)$

$$= \dfrac{(-j \times 10^6)}{300 \times 6\cdot 28}$$

$$= -j \cdot 531$$

Insertion loss $= 20 \log_{10}\left(1 - \dfrac{j \cdot 531}{1\ 600}\right)$

$$= 20 \log_{10}(1 - j \cdot 0\cdot 332)$$

$$= 20 \log_{10}(1\cdot 053) = \underline{0\cdot 448\ \text{db}}$$

EXAMPLE 11.33 (C). A 600-Ω generator is connected to a 150-Ω load via an impedance matching resistance pad as shown in Fig. 11.66. Calculate the values of the resistors, the attenuation (i.e. the image attenuation coefficient) of the matching pad and its insertion loss. (C. & G.)

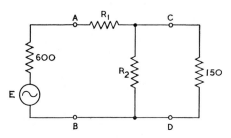

FIG. 11.66 (Example 11.33)

The impedance seen either way at AB is to be 600 Ω and that at CD is to be 150 Ω.

At AB—

$$R_1 + \dfrac{150R_2}{150 + R_2} = 600$$

$150R_1 + R_1R_2 + 150R_2 = 90\ 000 + 600R_2$

$150R_1 - 450R_2 + R_1R_2 = 90\ 000$ . . (i)

At CD—

$$\dfrac{R_2(R_1 + 600)}{R_2 + R_1 + 600} = 150$$

$R_1R_2 + 600R_2 = 150R_2 + 150R_1 + 90\ 000$

$150R_1 - 450R_2 - R_1R_2 = -90\ 000$. (ii)

Subtracting (ii) from (i), $R_1R_2 = 90\ 000$ and $R_1 = 90\ 000/R_2$.

Substituting in (i),

$$\dfrac{150 \times 90\ 000}{R_2} - 450R_2 + \dfrac{90\ 000R_2}{R_2} = 90\ 000$$

and $R_2{}^2 = \dfrac{150 \times 90\ 000}{450} = 30\ 000$

$$R_2 = \sqrt{30\ 000} = \underline{173\cdot 2\ \Omega}$$

$$R_1 = 90\ 000/173\cdot 2 = \underline{519\cdot 6\ \Omega}$$

Attenuation in decibels

$$= 10 \log_{10}\left(\dfrac{\text{power at } AB}{\text{power at } CD}\right)$$

For a unit current at AB, the current at CD is

$$\dfrac{1 \times R_2}{150 + R_2} = \dfrac{173\cdot 2}{323\cdot 2}$$

$$= 0\cdot 536$$

Power at AB, $(= I^2R) = 1 \times 600$

Power at CD $= (0\cdot 536)^2 \times 150$

Attenuation $= 10 \log_{10}\left(\dfrac{600}{0\cdot 536^2 \times 150}\right)$

$$= \underline{11\cdot 43\ \text{db}}$$

Insertion loss

$$= 20 \log_{10}\left(\dfrac{\text{current at } CD \text{ before insertion}}{\text{current at } CD \text{ after insertion}}\right)$$

Assuming unit e.m.f. at the generator—

Current at CD before insertion

$$= 1/750$$

Current at CD after insertion

$$= 0\cdot 536 \times \dfrac{1}{600 + 600}$$

Insertion loss $= 20 \log_{10}\left(\dfrac{1\ 200}{750 \times 0\cdot 536}\right)$

$$= \underline{9\cdot 48\ \text{db}}$$

ATTENUATOR NETWORKS

For the various forms of attenuator networks formulae have been developed relating the shunt and series elements to the characteristic impedance to give any desired loss in decibels. In calculation on attenuators the symbols Z_1 and Z_2 are frequently used to denote the value of *each* element—not necessarily the value per section. To avoid ambiguity, in the following examples the symbols Z

and Y are used throughout to denote *each* series and shunt element separately.

Design formulae for the two common unbalanced networks are given below, N being the voltage or current ratio (input/output)—

For the T-section: *For the π-network:*

$$X = R_0 \cdot \left(\frac{N-1}{N+1}\right) \qquad X = R_0 \cdot \frac{(N^2-1)}{2N}$$

$$Y = R_0 \cdot \left(\frac{2N}{N^2-1}\right) \qquad Y = R_0 \cdot \left(\frac{N+1}{N-1}\right)$$

The above expressions for the T-section elements may be conveniently obtained with the aid of Kirchhoff's Laws, as follows. (For derivation of the π-section equations see Example 11.37.)

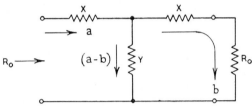

FIG. 11.67. DESIGN OF T-ATTENUATOR

Using Fig. 11.67 in which the current ratio $a/b = N$—

In the left-hand mesh—

$$aX + (a-b)Y - aR_0 = 0$$
$$NbX + (Nb-b)Y - NbR_0 = 0 \text{ (putting } a=Nb)$$
$$NX + (N-1)Y - NR_0 = 0 \qquad . \qquad . \quad \text{(i)}$$

In the right-hand mesh—

$$bX + bR_0 + Y(b-a) = 0$$
$$bX + bR_0 + Y(b-Nb) = 0 \text{ (putting } a=Nb)$$
$$X + R_0 + Y(1-N) = 0$$

and multiplying by N,

$$NX + NR_0 + NY(1-N) = 0 \qquad . \qquad . \quad \text{(ii)}$$

Subtracting (i) from (ii)—

$$2NR_0 - (N-1)Y + NY(1-N) = 0$$
$$2NR_0 - NY + Y + NY - N^2Y = 0$$
$$2NR_0 - Y(N^2-1) = 0$$
$$Y(N^2-1) = 2NR_0$$
$$Y = R_0 \cdot \frac{2N}{N^2-1}$$

Substituting for Y in (i)—

$$NX + \frac{2R_0N(N-1)}{(N^2-1)} - NR_0 = 0$$

$$X + \frac{2R_0(N-1)}{(N+1)(N-1)} - R_0 = 0$$

$$X = R_0 - \frac{2R_0}{N+1} = R_0\left(1 - \frac{2}{(N+1)}\right)$$

$$X = R_0 \cdot \left(\frac{N-1}{N+1}\right)$$

EXAMPLE 11.34 (C). A d.c. generator having a resistance of 600 Ω supplies current to a 600 Ω load. Design a resistance network of T-formation having a characteristic resistance of 600 Ω which, when connected between the generator and the load, will reduce the load current to

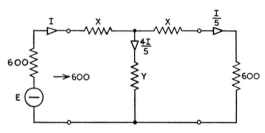

FIG. 11.68 (Example 11.34)

one-fifth of its initial value. In what proportion would the load current be reduced if two such networks were connected in series between the generator and the load?

(*C. & G.*)

See the diagram, Fig. 11.68, where the series and shunt resistor elements are denoted by X and Y respectively.

(i) The generator current will be the same with or without the T-network since $R_0 = 600$ Ω in each case. This current divides between shunt (Y) and load (600) in proportion to their conductances.

$$\frac{I/5}{4I/5} = \frac{Y}{X+600}$$

$$4Y = X + 600, \text{ or } X = 4Y - 600 \quad . \qquad . \quad \text{(i)}$$

(ii) The joint resistance across the generator terminals is 600 Ω—

$$X + \frac{(X+600)Y}{(X+600+Y)} = 600$$

$$X^2 + 600X + XY + XY + 600Y$$
$$= 600X + 360\,000 + 600Y$$

$$X^2 + 2XY - 360\,000 = 0 \quad . \qquad . \qquad . \quad \text{(ii)}$$

Substituting (i) in (ii)

$$(4Y - 600)^2 + 2Y(4Y - 600) - 360\,000 = 0$$
$$16Y^2 - 4\,800Y + 360\,000$$
$$\qquad\qquad + 8Y^2 - 1\,200Y - 360\,000 = 0$$
$$24Y^2 - 6\,000Y = 0$$
$$24Y(Y - 250) = 0, \ Y = \underline{\underline{250\ \Omega}}$$

$$X = 4Y - 600 = 1\,000 - 600 = \underline{\underline{400\ \Omega}}$$

Each such network (when closed by R_0) will absorb $\frac{4}{5}$ and transmit $\frac{1}{5}$ of the current: if two of these networks were inserted between generator and load, the load current would be $\frac{1}{5} \times \frac{1}{5} = \frac{1}{25}$ of the generator current (i.e. $\frac{1}{25}$ of the load current when no networks are present).

Alternative solution using the formula—

$$I_S/I_R = N = 5$$
$$X = R_0 \cdot \left(\frac{N-1}{N+1}\right) = 600(4/6) = \underline{\underline{400\ \Omega}}$$
$$Y = R_0 \cdot \left(\frac{2N}{N^2-1}\right) = 600(10/24) = \underline{\underline{250\ \Omega}}$$

EXAMPLE 11.35 (C). A variable attenuator includes five T-section pads, each of 600 Ω characteristic impedance and 2 db attenuation, which may be inserted in tandem as required. Calculate the input impedance—
    (*a*) with one pad only inserted and the output terminals short-circuited, and
    (*b*) with all five pads inserted and the output terminals open-circuited.
(The series and shunt arms of a T-section pad are $R_0 \cdot \left(\frac{N-1}{N+1}\right)$ and $R_0 \cdot \left(\frac{2N}{N^2-1}\right)$ respectively where N is the ratio (input voltage)/(output voltage), when terminated by the characteristic resistance (R_0).)   (*C. & G.*)

For each pad—

$$20 \log_{10} N = 2, \text{ or } \log_{10} N = 0 \cdot 1, \text{ whence}$$
$$N = 1 \cdot 259$$
$$X = R_0 \cdot \left(\frac{N-1}{N+1}\right) = 600 \left(\frac{0 \cdot 259}{2 \cdot 259}\right)$$
$$= \underline{\underline{68 \cdot 8\ \Omega}}$$
$$Y = R_0 \cdot \left(\frac{2N}{N^2-1}\right) = 600 \left(\frac{2 \times 1 \cdot 259}{1 \cdot 259^2 - 1}\right)$$
$$= \frac{1\,200 \times 1 \cdot 259}{0 \cdot 585} = \underline{\underline{2\,582\ \Omega}}$$

(*a*) The input impedance of one pad short-circuited (see Fig. 11.69 diagram (*a*)) is—
$$Z = 68 \cdot 8 + \frac{68 \cdot 8 \times 2\,582}{68 \cdot 8 + 2\,582} = 68 \cdot 8 + 67$$
$$= \underline{\underline{135 \cdot 8\ \Omega}}$$

(*b*) Total attenuation of five pads in tandem = 10 db.

$$20 \log_{10} N = 10 \text{ and } \log_{10} N = 0 \cdot 5, \text{ whence}$$
$$N = 3 \cdot 162\,3$$
$$X = R_0 \cdot \left(\frac{N-1}{N+1}\right) = 600 \left(\frac{2 \cdot 162\,3}{4 \cdot 162\,3}\right)$$
$$= 312\ \Omega$$
$$Y = R_0 \cdot \left(\frac{2N}{N^2-1}\right) = \frac{600 \times 6 \cdot 324\,6}{9}$$
$$= 422\ \Omega$$

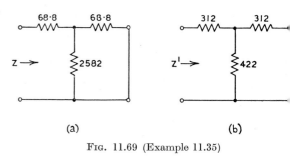

FIG. 11.69 (Example 11.35)

The input impedance of five pads open-circuited (see Fig. 11.69 (*b*)) is—

$$Z = 312 + 422 = \underline{\underline{734\ \Omega}}$$

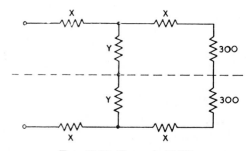

FIG. 11.70 (Example 11.36)

EXAMPLE 11.36 (C). Compute the values of the series and shunt elements of an H-type attenuator having characteristic impedance of 600 Ω and a loss of 40 db.   (*C. & G.*)

See the diagram, Fig. 11.70.
This calculation can be conveniently made by supposing the H-network to be made up from the two T-networks about the dotted line and using the formulae for the T-network, the attenuations for the H- and T-networks being the same.
Then, $20 \log_{10} N = 40$, or $\log_{10} N = 2$, whence $N = 100$.

For the T-attenuator—

$$X = Z_0 \cdot \left(\frac{N-1}{N+1}\right) = \frac{300 \times 99}{101} = 294 \ \Omega$$

$$Y = Z_0 \cdot \left(\frac{2N}{N^2-1}\right) = \frac{300 \times 200}{10^4-1} = 6 \ \Omega$$

For the H-attenuator—

Series element $= X = \underline{294 \ \Omega}$

Shunt element $= 2Y = \underline{\underline{12 \ \Omega}}$

EXAMPLE 11.37 (C). A resistance network of π configuration is to have a characteristic resistance of R_0 ohms and an attenuation of D decibels. Derive expressions for the resistances of the arms and evaluate these when $R_0 = 600 \ \Omega$ and $D = 20$ db. (C. & G.)

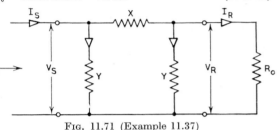

FIG. 11.71 (Example 11.37)

See the diagram, Fig. 11.71.

Let $N = V_S/V_R = I_S/I_R$

$$I_S = \frac{V_S}{R_0} = \frac{V_S}{Y} + \frac{V_R}{Y} + \frac{V_R}{R_0}$$

$$= \frac{V_S}{Y} + \frac{V_S}{NY} + \frac{V_S}{NR_0}$$

$$\qquad \dots \text{(putting } V_R = V_S/N)$$

$$\frac{1}{R_0} = \frac{1}{Y} + \frac{1}{NY} + \frac{1}{NR_0}$$

$$\frac{1}{R_0} - \frac{1}{NR_0} = \frac{1}{Y} + \frac{1}{NY}$$

$$\frac{N-1}{NR_0} = \frac{N+1}{NY}$$

$$Y = R_0 \cdot \left(\frac{N+1}{N-1}\right)$$

Also, the p.d. across X is $V_S - V_R$—

$$I_S = \frac{V_S}{R_0} = \frac{V_S}{Y} + \frac{V_S - V_R}{X}$$

$$= \frac{V_S}{Y} + \frac{V_S}{X} - \frac{V_S}{NX}$$

$$\frac{1}{R_0} = \frac{1}{X} - \frac{1}{NX} + \frac{N-1}{R_0 \cdot (N+1)}$$

$$\qquad \dots \text{(putting } V_R = V_S/N)$$

$$\frac{1}{R_0} - \frac{N-1}{R_0 \cdot (N+1)} = \frac{N-1}{NX}$$

$$\frac{N+1-N+1}{R_0(N+1)} = \frac{N-1}{NX}$$

$$\frac{2}{R_0(N+1)} = \frac{N-1}{NX}$$

$$X = \frac{R_0(N+1)(N-1)}{2N}$$

$$= R_0 \cdot \frac{(N^2-1)}{2N}$$

Substituting $R_0 = 600$ and $N = 10$ (from $20 \log_{10} N = 20$)—

$$X = 600 \times 99/20 = \underline{\underline{2\ 970 \ \Omega}}$$

$$Y = 600 \times 11/9 = \underline{\underline{733 \ \Omega}}$$

11.27. Thévenin's Theorem. The use of Thévenin's theorem enables certain classes of complex network to be quickly solved.

This theorem states—

In any system of arbitrary linear conductors (in which the current in every branch is proportional to the impressed voltage) the current in any branch is that which would result should an e.m.f., equal to the p.d. which would appear across the break if the branch were opened, be introduced into the branch and all other e.m.f.s be removed.

Stated in other words, the theorem says that—

The current in any branch z of a network may be determined by replacing the remainder of the network by a generator whose e.m.f. is V and internal impedance Z, where V and Z are the values measured at the terminals of z when that branch is opened, i.e. the generator is on open-circuit. The current in the branch z is then given by

$$I = V/(Z + z)$$

As an example of the use of Thévenin's theorem, the condition for balance of the Wheatstone Bridge may be determined. Using the diagram and symbols of Fig. 2.42 for the bridge network and examining the conditions in the bridging arm XZ—

Let the p.d. between the points W and Y be V volts when the branch XZ is opened.

The p.d. between points W and X is $V.P/(P + R)$

The p.d. between points W and Z is $V.Q/(Q + S)$

Hence p.d. across branch XZ (when open) is

$$V.\{P/(P + R) - Q/(Q + S)\}$$

If R' is the external resistance to an e.m.f. in the branch XZ, then by Thévenin's theorem the current g in the branch XZ is given by

$$g = \frac{V}{G + R} \left(\frac{P}{P + R} - \frac{Q}{Q + S} \right)$$

$$= \frac{V}{G + R'} \left\{ \frac{PQ + PS - PQ - QR}{(P + R)(Q + S)} \right\}$$

$$= \frac{V}{G + R'} \left\{ \frac{PS - QR}{(P + R)(Q + S)} \right\}$$

For $g = 0$, then $PS = QR$, the condition for balance of the bridge circuit.

EXAMPLE 11.38 (C). State Thévenin's theorem. The network shown in Fig. 11.72 (a) is connected to a source of 1 V e.m.f. and 40 Ω resistance. Find the value of the load resistance Z which will absorb maximum power and the value of that power. Calculate the insertion loss of the network under these conditions.   (C. & G.)

Thévenin's theorem may be stated as follows—

If an impedance Z is connected between any two points of a circuit, the resulting steady-state current I through the impedance can be obtained by dividing the potential difference V between the two points, before Z is connected, by the sum of Z and Z', where Z' is the impedance of the circuit measured between the two points. In other words, the two points of the circuit can be regarded as a source of a.c. which has an e.m.f. V and an internal impedance Z'.

Then, $\qquad I = \dfrac{V}{Z + Z'}$

Applying this theorem to the question, in Fig. 11.72 (b) the p.d. V and impedance Z' measured across the open-circuited terminals of the network, when the source is connected across the other two terminals, are obtained as follows—

$$V = \frac{100}{100 + 60 + 40} \times 1 = \tfrac{1}{2} \text{ V}$$

$$Z' = 60 + \frac{100\,(60 + 40)}{100 + 60 + 40} = 110 \; \Omega$$

The open-circuited network of (b) can be replaced by the circuit of (c) where $V = \tfrac{1}{2}$ and $Z' = 110$. Maximum power would be obtained from the network if the resistance Z of the load were also 110 Ω.

The p.d. across Z is now 0·25 V, i.e.

$$0·5 \times \frac{110}{110 + 110}$$

The value of this maximum power is

$$W_2 = \frac{(1/4)^2}{110} = 0·57 \text{ mW}$$

The power W_1 delivered to the load of 110 Ω were it connected directly across the source as in (d), would be

$$W_1 = \frac{\left(\dfrac{110}{150} \times 1 \right)^2}{110} = \frac{110}{150^2} = 4·9 \text{ mW}$$

Insertion loss of the network $= 10 \log_{10} W_1/W_2$

$$= 10 \log_{10} 4·9/0·57 = 10 \log_{10} 8·6 = 9·35 \text{ db}$$

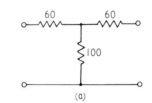

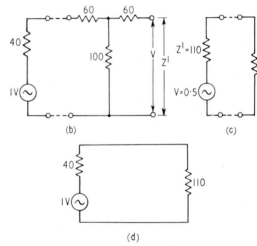

Fig. 11.72 (Example 11.38)

11.28. Bandwidth Requirements.

The theoretical width of the frequency bandwidth requirement for any specific purpose depends upon the rate at which information is to be transmitted. According to Shannon[6],[7] the amount of information M which can be sent in a given system is

$$M = (1 + P/N)^{TW}$$

where M = the number of independent message items, which may be identified in time T, bandwidth W, and signal/noise ratio P/N. This assumes ideal conditions, for example that a filter has a

near phase-characteristic in the pass band and
n infinite cut-off at the critical frequency. In
ractice some allowance must be made for the
cceptable imperfections of practical, commercial
lter design.

In telegraphy the bandwidth requirement is
roportional to the telegraph modulation rate.
or the standard 50 baud* systems, equivalent to
)/2 or 25 c/s, and corresponding to 66·6 words
er minute with 7·5 unit teleprinters, if double-
ideband amplitude-modulated transmission is
sed, which is normally the case for these narrow-
and systems, then the theoretical need is for
- 25 c/s either side of the carrier frequency, i.e.
) c/s. Practical filter design necessitates perhaps
) c/s bandwidth. For other reasons, related to
ie prevention of interference between neigh-
ouring channels, a value of 120 c/s is standardized
or the frequency spacing: this enables higher
iodulation-rates to be used—up to 100 bauds
: even more if a slightly impaired performance
in be accepted or if special methods of signal
etection are used.

The frequencies associated with either natural or
ommercial speech and with musical sounds are
iscussed in Chapter XV. For telephone speech
bandwidth of approximately 3 kc/s, placed be-
veen 300 and 3 400 c/s, has been standardized.
i multiplex telephone systems single-sideband
orking is adopted for reasons of economy and tele-
hone channels are assembled within the frequency
iectrum spaced at 4 kc/s apart to allow for filter
laracteristics. Exceptionally, for highly expen-
ve plant such as long submarine cables equipped
ith submerged amplifiers, higher-grade filters
re used with a spacing of 3 kc/s between channels.

For music transmission a bandwidth from about
) c/s to 15 kc/s is desirable, but limits of 50 c/s
) 9 kc/s or 10 kc/s (or even less) are sometimes
sed as a compromise.

For television transmissions other factors are
ivolved. With the persistence of vision of the
uman eye, if a picture is repeated 25 times a
icond it will not appear as a series of disconnected
ienes. In the 405-line system the scene being
ilevised is explored or scanned in 405 separate
ontiguous horizontal lines: assuming that the
spect ratio of the picture (the width to height
itio) is 4/3, then for equal resolution in both
imensions the total number of picture "elements"
er horizontal line would be $(405 \times 4/3)$. This
isults in a total number of picture elements equal

to $25 \times 405 \times (405 \times 4/3)$. The occurrence of a
pair of black and white picture elements constitutes an alternating cycle, so that the maximum
fundamental frequency likely to be encountered
is $\frac{1}{2} \times 25 \times 405^2 \times 4/3 = 2\,733\,750$ c/s, say 2·75
Mc/s.

For the 625-line television system the maximum
fundamental frequency is $\frac{1}{2} \times 25 \times 625^2 \times 4/3$
$= 6·5$ Mc/s. For television in colour, additional
chromatic information must be transmitted and a
significantly increased bandwidth is required.

For automatic data-processing using electronic
computers, data may be transmitted over telecommunication circuits at low speeds (50 to 200
bauds) over telegraph circuits, at medium speeds
(up to 2 000 bauds or so) over telephone circuits,
or at high speeds (for example 40 kilobauds) over
a wideband "group" (e.g. 48 kc/s) of telephone
circuits.

Present-day utilization of long-distance transmission lines, whether for telephonic or telegraphic
use, is based upon the provision of a large number
of separate *channels of communication* over a
single physical circuit—normally one for each
direction of transmission: this is achieved by
allotting a separate frequency range to each
channel and requires that the transmission system
has available a sufficiently wide frequency spectrum
for multi-channel operation.

Currents at voice frequencies are transposed to
their allotted frequency band by a process of *modulation* (see Chapter XIII) at the sending end of the
line: the inverse process of *demodulation* is carried
out by the receiving equipment. In modulation
the signal information contained in the basic
band or baseband is applied to a carrier current
whose frequency is such that, as a result of the
modulation process, the signal information from
the basic band now lies within the range allotted
to that particular channel, different carrier frequencies being essential for each channel of communication upon the same physical circuit.

The resultant waveform in the line when many
channels are engaged in transmission at the same
time becomes complex. In the main line, the signals
of individual channels have lost their identity
which must be restored in the receiving equipment
by separating out the frequencies proper to each
channel. By virtue of the difference in response of a
reactive network to currents of different frequencies, the arriving signals can be applied to a number of tuned networks connected in parallel,
each of which accepts currents at its channel
frequencies and rejects currents at all other frequencies. A tuned network designed for this
purpose is known as a FREQUENCY FILTER which

---

* The speed in bauds is the reciprocal of the duration of
ie shortest or unit telegraph element, when timed in
iconds. For example, at 50 bauds the length of a unit
ement is $1/50 = 0·020$ seconds.

is defined as *a network designed to transmit currents of frequencies within one or more frequency bands and to attenuate currents of other frequencies.*

Using normal unloaded underground cable balanced pairs, carrier systems can provide 24 telephone circuits, whilst with coaxial-tube type cables several hundred telephone circuits and one television circuit can be operated over a pair of such tubes.

11.29. Frequency Filters.[8],[9] Apart from the availability of a wideband frequency transmission system with modulating and demodulating equipment, the operation of carrier current systems is dependent upon frequency filters possessing suitable characteristics. In fact modern technique in reproduction of sound and a.c. signals generally relies to an increasing extent upon the employment of frequency filters for a variety of purposes.

Three main classes of filter are in common use. The LOW-PASS FILTER is one having a single transmission band extending from zero frequency up to the cut-off frequency, i.e. to the frequency at which the attenuation rises from approximately zero to a very high value and the filter in effect ceases to transmit.

The HIGH-PASS FILTER has a single transmission band extending from the cut-off frequency up to infinite frequency. (In this connexion the terms low and high are of course used in a purely relative sense.)

The BAND-PASS FILTER is one having a single transmission band, neither of the cut-off frequencies being zero or infinite.

In addition there is the BAND-STOP FILTER: this filter, which is of limited application, has a single *attenuation* band, neither of the cut-off frequencies being zero or infinite.

Apart from possessing the requisite attenuation/frequency characteristic, since the filter has to transmit energy at certain frequencies from a source of power into a load, it is desirable that the characteristic impedance should be reasonably constant within the transmission band and equal to the load impedance.

Dependent upon the desired characteristics, two common forms of each class of filter are available. The simple basic filter section, known as the "constant-k" type, has an impedance which varies over the transmission range: when working between fixed values of impedance reflexion losses occur at all but one frequency, and these losses may be considerable as mismatching increases: for the same reason the sharpness of cut-off is limited, and the attenuation does not reach an infinitely high value except at $f_0 = 0$ or $f_0 = \infty$. As far as possible,

filters are operated under image impedance conditions to reduce reflexion losses.

In the basic filter, the series and shunt arms consist of either a simple inductance or a simple capacitance, consequently they are inverse reactances and the product of the series (Z_1) and shunt (Z_2) impedances is constant with change of frequency i.e. $Z_1 Z_2 = k^2$, where k is known as the *nominal surge impedance*, defined below.

The second form, the *m-derived* filter has the advantage that the impedance is sensibly constant over the transmission range: also the attenuation rises sharply to an infinitely high value at a frequency just beyond the cut-off frequency. This filter has the disadvantage, however, that after rising to an extremely high value the attenuation falls again to a relatively low value in the attenuation range.

Two or more filter sections may be inserted in series between a generator and its load impedance to increase the attenuation against unwanted frequencies and improve the signal discrimination: the basic and derived filters may be used in combination to obtain correct impedance matching together with the required attenuation characteristic.

The form taken by a basic single section low-pass filter is shown in Fig. 11.73 (*a*). The series inductor elements have an impedance which increases with frequency while the reactance of the shunt capacitors decreases as the frequency rises (see Fig. 10.32). As the frequency of the applied signal increases less energy will be transferred through the series impedance to the load and more will be shunted by the capacitance. At a particular frequency—which is related to the proportions of series inductance and shunting capacitance—the attenuation increases sharply: a typical attenuation/frequency graph for the low-pass filter is given in Fig. 11.73 (*b*).

In the high-pass filter (Fig. 11.74 (*a*)) the arrangement of capacitance and inductance is reversed from that employed for the low-pass filter. The inductance provides a low impedance shunt path at the lower frequencies whilst the reactance of the series capacitance falls as the frequency rises. Attenuation is high at the lower frequencies until the cut-off value of frequency (f_0) is reached. The attenuation/frequency characteristic for the high-pass filter is shown plotted in Fig. 11.74 (*b*).

A band-pass filter results from the combination of a low-pass with a high-pass filter if the critical frequencies are arranged to overlap (i.e. if the cut-off frequency for the high-pass filter is lower than the cut-off frequency for the low-pass filter). The arrangement of the elements for a band-pass filter is shown in Fig. 11.75 (*a*) which is equivalent to a combination of Fig. 11.73 (*a*) with Fig. 11.74 (*a*) he attenuation characteristic of the band-pass lter is given in Fig. 11.75 (b) which suggests omparison with Figs. 11.73 (b) and 11.74 (b).

A band-stop filter has the reactance elements components, cannot dissipate energy. Neglecting losses, its impedance at any frequency is either *purely resistive* (its L/C ratio) or *purely reactive*: it may be resistive over certain bands of frequency

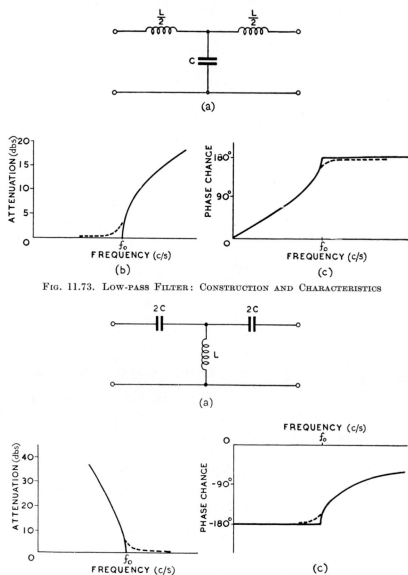

Fig. 11.73. Low-pass Filter: Construction and Characteristics

Fig. 11.74. High-pass Filter: Construction and Characteristics

rranged in the form shown in Fig. 11.76 (a). High ttenuation over a given frequency band (Fig. 1.76 (b)) is mainly due to the zero impedance eries-resonant) shunt circuit $L_2 C_2$.

A filter, consisting primarily of pure reactive and reactive over other bands. When the impedance is resistive, power is absorbed from the source of supply and necessarily passed on to the load since power cannot be absorbed in the reactances of the filter. The frequencies for which this occurs give

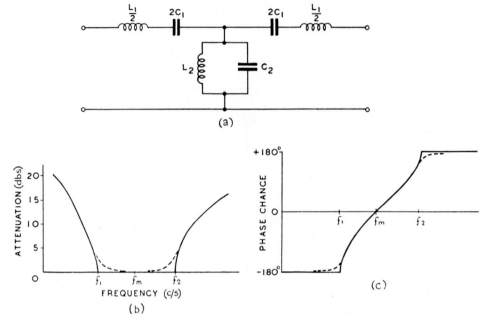

(a)

(b)

(c)

FIG. 11.75. BAND-PASS FILTER: CONSTRUCTION AND CHARACTERISTICS

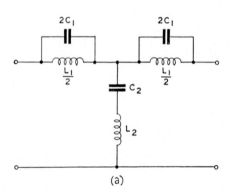

(a)

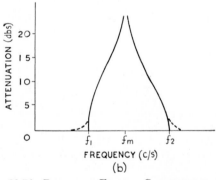

(b)

FIG. 11.76. BAND-STOP FILTER: CONSTRUCTION AND
CHARACTERISTICS

the *transmission band* of the filter: if the filter is
terminated by its image impedance so that no
reflexion occurs there can be no loss in the filter
apart from that due to the power loss occasioned by
impure reactance (e.g. resistance of the inductors).
On the other hand when the filter impedance is
purely reactive, no power can be taken from the
source by the filter and hence none can be passed
on to the load: this occurs at frequencies within
the *attenuation band*.

The foregoing can be summarized in this statement: *When the characteristic impedance is unreal
the filter attenuates; but when (i.e. at another frequency) the impedance is real the filter has a transmission band.* The evaluation of the cut-off frequency of a filter involves an examination of the
characteristic impedance and determination of the
boundary frequency at which the impedance
changes from real to unreal.

The basic filters described here are T-sections to
which Equation 11.32 is applicable, namely the
mid-series impedance—

$$Z_0 = \sqrt{Z_1 Z_2 + Z_1^2/4}$$

THE LOW-PASS FILTER. Taking firstly the low-
pass filter and substituting $Z_1 = j\omega L$ (series) and
$Z_2 = 1/(j\omega C)$ (shunt)—

$$Z_0 = \sqrt{\frac{j\omega L}{j\omega C} - \frac{\omega^2 L^2}{4}} = \sqrt{\frac{L}{C}} \sqrt{1 - \frac{\omega^2 LC}{4}}$$

r.m.s.): this calibration holds good so long as the waveform is reasonably pure, and moreover the scale shape of the d.c. instrument will not be distorted.

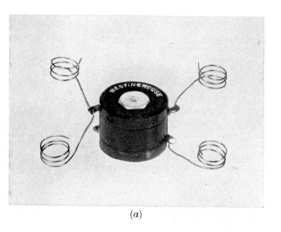

(a)

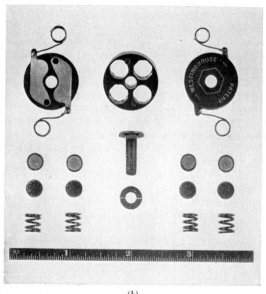

(b)

FIG. 12.23. INSTRUMENT-PATTERN FULL-WAVE
METAL RECTIFIER
(a) Complete four-element unit. (b) Constructional details.
(*Courtesy of Westinghouse Brake & Signal Co.*)

For the measurement of higher ranges of alternating current it is necessary to use a current transformer (Fig. 12.25), a shunt being unsuitable for the purpose. This is on account of the introduction of temperature errors and also due to the fact that a shunted meter forms, in effect, a rectifier-voltmeter of very low range connected across a

shunt, with the attendant disadvantages mentioned below for the low-range voltmeter. The current range can be extended as required by suitable choice

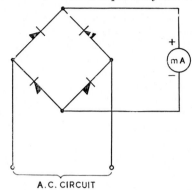

FIG. 12.24. A.C. MILLIAMMETER—RECTIFIER TYPE

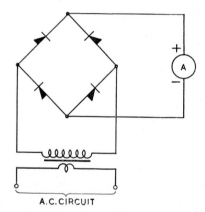

FIG. 12.25. A.C. AMMETER—RECTIFIER TYPE

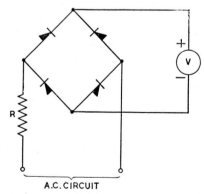

FIG. 12.26. A.C. VOLTMETER—RECTIFIER TYPE

and adjustments of the turns ratio of the transformer.

For use as an a.c. voltmeter (Fig. 12.26) it is

necessary to insert a series non-inductive resistor comparable to the method employed in adapting a moving-coil ammeter to serve as a d.c. voltmeter.

For low-voltage a.c. readings it is preferable to use a potential transformer (Fig. 12.27) to step up the voltage to a high value: the forward resistance of the rectifier will otherwise become an appreciable fraction of the whole resistance of the meter and, since the resistance of the rectifier varies with the current passing through it, the scale shape would be distorted.

In use, the moving-coil instrument must always be connected to the rectifier before the a.c. source

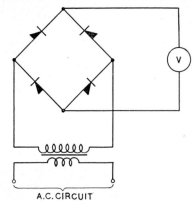

FIG. 12.27. LOW RANGE A.C. VOLTMETER—
RECTIFIER TYPE

is applied: if this is not done, the full voltage is developed across the rectifiers on account of there being no path across the d.c. terminals of the bridge, and the rectifiers will suffer damage from the overload.

The rectifier instrument has the same robustness as the moving-coil instrument and is free from the disadvantage of small overload capacity shown by the thermo-electric class of a.c. instrument. On account of its low power consumption the current or potential transformer—when employed—can be quite small. For the same reason, the rectifier instrument is admirably suited to measurements at audio frequencies, the frequency error being negligible up to 100 kc/s: above this frequency the self-capacitance of the rectifier elements acts as a shunt and reduces the deflexion at the higher frequencies.

If the waveform of the supply being measured is not sinusoidal, errors will occur according to the extent by which the form factor deviates from the value (1·11) for which the meter is normally calibrated: this error is further increased by waveform distortion caused by the rectifier itself at low voltages. The characteristics of metal rectifiers

vary somewhat with temperature and errors result if the instrument is used at temperatures greatly different from that used for calibration. To a certain extent the rectifier elements are liable to deteriorate with age.

EXAMPLE 12.7 (B). A single-plate metal rectifier, a moving-coil ammeter, and a thermo-junction ammeter are connected in series across a 2-V supply. The rectifier has a forward resistance of 20 Ω, an infinite reverse resistance and the resistance of the ammeters can be neglected. When the supply is D.C. the ammeters give identical readings. When the supply is A.C. at 50 c/s and 2 V r.m.s. the readings on the two meters are different.
Explain the reason for the difference and calculate the actual meter readings.
What will be the readings when the alternating supply has a square waveform of peak value 2 V? (*C. & G.*)

The moving-coil instrument can operate only when a unidirectional current flows in its coil. If it is to read alternating current, the current must be made unidirectional by a rectifier in the meter circuit. The deflecting torque on the coil at any instant is proportional to the instantaneous current, but the meter movement has too much inertia to vibrate at the frequency of the alternating current, and it will assume a steady deflexion proportional to the *average* value of the current in the coil.

The thermo-couple meter reading depends upon the temperature difference between two junctions and so gives a deflexion proportional to the heating effect of a current, i.e. to its r.m.s. value. It indicates the average power.

When the supply is D.C., both meters read the same: the current is $2/20 = 100$ mA.

When the supply is 50 c/s, the rectifier will suppress alternate half-cycles: the current through both meters is a series of positive half-cycles. The thermo-couple meter will read the average power represented by these half-cycles. The power in a half-cycle is equal to half the power in a full cycle. The thermo-couple meter indicates the current representing half the power of a whole sine wave, i.e. half the r.m.s. value for the whole sine-wave and so will show a reading of 50 mA.

Since the moving-coil meter reads the average value of the current it is necessary to know the average value of a sine wave which has alternate half-cycles of zero amplitude. The average value of a sine wave is $\{(2/\pi) \times \text{peak value}\}$ over a half-cycle. Over the adjacent half-wave intervals there will be zero current as the voltage is reversed: the average over a whole cycle

$$= \tfrac{1}{2} \times (2/\pi) \times \text{peak value} = \text{peak value}/\pi$$

In this expression Z_0 is real so long as $\omega^2 LC/4 < 1$: is unreal if $\omega^2 LC/4 > 1$. The cut-off frequency is therefore given by $\omega^2 = 4/(LC)$, or—

(for the low-pass filter), $f_0 = \dfrac{1}{\pi\sqrt{LC}}$. (11.33)

Alternatively,

since $\quad Z_1/Z_2 = \dfrac{j\omega L}{1/(j\omega C)} = -\omega^2 LC$

It may be stated that if the ratio Z_1/Z_2 is positive the filter will attenuate: if the ratio Z_1/Z_2 is nega-

Taking the nominal impedance $Z_0 = \sqrt{\dfrac{L}{C}}$ together with the expression $f_0 = \dfrac{1}{\pi\sqrt{LC}}$ enables the values of L and C to be calculated.

By multiplication—

$$Z_0 \times f_0 = \sqrt{\dfrac{L}{C}} \times \dfrac{1}{\pi\sqrt{LC}} = \dfrac{1}{\pi C} \text{ whence}$$

(for the low-pass filter), $C = \dfrac{1}{\pi f_0 Z_0}$ farads . (11.35)

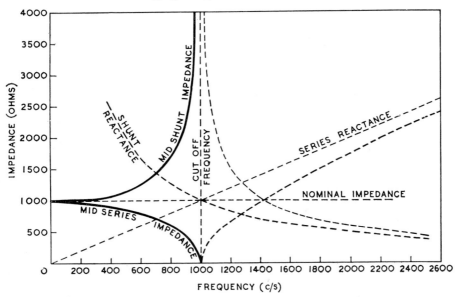

FIG. 11.77. BASIC LOW-PASS FILTER: VARIATION OF IMPEDANCE WITH FREQUENCY

tive and has a magnitude less than 4 (i.e. lies between 0 and -4) the filter will *not* attenuate.

At very low frequencies, i.e. if $\omega \simeq 0$,

$$Z \simeq \sqrt{\dfrac{L}{C}} \cdot (1 - 0) = \sqrt{\dfrac{L}{C}}$$

The value $\quad Z_0 = \sqrt{\dfrac{L}{C}}.$ . . (11.34)

is known as the *nominal impedance*, and this value is designed to equal the load impedance. It is clear that the value of Z_0 varies as the frequency $[\omega/(2\pi)]$ increases and the impedance matching deteriorates as the frequency rises from zero to the cut-off frequency. The variation in impedance with frequency is plotted in the graph of Fig. 11.77 from the relation $Z_0 = \sqrt{\dfrac{L}{C}}\sqrt{1 - \dfrac{\omega^2 LC}{4}}$.

By division—

$$Z_0/f_0 = \sqrt{\dfrac{L}{C}} \times \pi\sqrt{LC} = \pi L, \text{ whence}$$

(for the low-pass filter), $L = \dfrac{Z_0}{\pi f_0}$ henrys . (11.36)

It will be recollected that these values are based upon the total reactance per section, so that in a T-filter each inductor is $L/2$ (unbalanced) or $L/4$ (balanced).

EXAMPLE 11.39 (C). It is desired to insert a T-type low-pass filter having a cut-off frequency of 3 000 c/s in a line of 600 Ω characteristic impedance. Compute the values of the series and shunt elements of a suitable filter section assuming non-dissipative elements. (C. & G.)

$$L = Z_0/(\pi f_0) = \dfrac{600}{3\cdot14 \times 3\,000} = \dfrac{1}{15\cdot7}$$

$$= 0\cdot063\,694 = \underline{63\cdot7 \text{ mH}} \text{ (per section)}$$

$$C = \frac{1}{\pi f_0 Z_0} = \frac{1}{3\cdot 14 \times 3\,000 \times 600} = \frac{1}{5\cdot 652 \times 10^6}$$

$$= \underline{0\cdot 177 \ \mu\text{F}} \ (\text{per section})$$

Any frequency filter has a propagation coefficient and so introduces a phase change, which in the low-pass filter increases from zero at $f = 0$, to $180°$

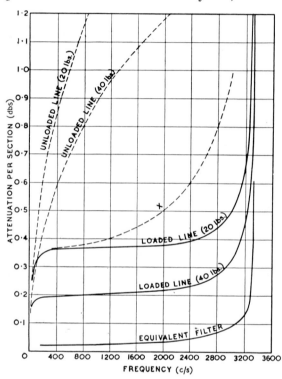

FIG. 11.78. EQUIVALENCE OF LOADED LINE AND
LOW-PASS FILTER

(π radians) at the cut-off frequency and remains at $180°$ within the attenuation range: this variation is plotted in Fig. 11.73 (c).

A coil-loaded transmission line behaves as a low-pass filter due to its construction. Its primary coefficients are, however, partly distributed and partly "lumped" whereas those of the filter section are not distributed at all.

The attenuation/frequency characteristics (per loading section) for 20 lb and 40 lb cable conductors, both loaded and unloaded, are plotted in Fig. 11.78. The lowest graph relates to the equivalent filter section having the same values of inductance and capacitance as the loading coil section: it includes the loading coil resistance, but excludes the conductor resistance of the line. The graph marked X

is the characteristic which would be obtained from the 20 lb loaded cable if all its elements were lumped. The phase change of the loaded line is practically identical with that of the corresponding filter.

Over the middle of the pass range there is little difference between the behaviour of the loaded line and the low-pass filter except that the line attenuation is much greater than the corresponding filter attenuation due to the presence of line resistance. For the same reason the cut-off point is more obscure with the loaded line. At the lower frequencies ($\omega \to 0$) the loaded line has similar characteristics to the unloaded line.

THE HIGH-PASS FILTER. In the high-pass filter the series reactance is $Z_1 = 1/(j\omega C)$ and the shunt reactance is $Z_2 = j\omega L$. Substituting these values in the expression for the mid-series impedance $Z_0 = \sqrt{Z_1 Z_2 + Z_1^2/4}$, gives—

$$Z_0 = \sqrt{\frac{j\omega L}{j\omega C} - \frac{1}{4\omega^2 C^2}} = \sqrt{\frac{L}{C}}\sqrt{1 - \frac{1}{4\omega^2 LC}}$$

This expression has a value which changes from real to unreal when $4\omega^2 LC = 1$, i.e. when $\omega^2 = \frac{1}{4LC}$ and—

(for the high-pass filter), $f_0 = \dfrac{1}{4\pi\sqrt{LC}}$. (11.3)

The characteristic impedance varies with the frequency according to the expression above: at very high frequencies when $\omega = \infty$,

$$Z_0 = \sqrt{\frac{L}{C}}\sqrt{1 - 0} = \sqrt{\frac{L}{C}}, \text{ the nominal impedance}$$

From combination of the nominal impedance $Z_0 = \sqrt{\dfrac{L}{C}}$ with the cut-off frequency, $f_0 = \dfrac{1}{4\pi\sqrt{LC}}$ by multiplication—

$$Z_0 \times f_0 = \sqrt{\frac{L}{C}} \times \frac{1}{4\pi\sqrt{LC}} = \frac{1}{4\pi C}$$

whence

(for the high-pass filter), $C = \dfrac{1}{4\pi Z_0 f_0}$ farads (11.3)

By division—

$$Z_0/f_0 = \sqrt{\frac{L}{C}} \times 4\pi\sqrt{LC} = 4\pi L$$

whence

(for a high-pass filter), $L = \dfrac{Z_0}{4\pi f_0}$ henrys   . (11.3)

These values are the totals per section, so that for a T-section filter each capacitor has a value of $2C$ (unbalanced) or $4C$ (balanced).

The high-pass filter introduces a phase change of $-180°$ over the range $f = 0$ to $f = f_0$: this angle falls to zero as the frequency rises from f_0 to ∞ Fig. 11.74 (c)).

EXAMPLE 11.40 (C). A high-pass filter for $600\,\Omega$ terminations is required to cut off below 20 000 c/s. Compute the values of the shunt and series elements. (C. & G.)

$$L = Z_0/(4\pi f_0) = \frac{600}{4\pi \times 2 \times 10^4} = \frac{3}{1\cdot257 \times 10^3}$$

$$= \underline{2\cdot39 \text{ mH}} \text{ (per section)}$$

$$C = \frac{1}{4\pi f_0 Z_0} = \frac{1}{4\pi \times 2 \times 10^4 \times 600}$$

$$= \frac{1}{150\cdot72 \times 10^6} = \underline{0\cdot006\ 65\ \mu\text{F}} \text{ (per section)}$$

THE BAND-PASS FILTER. In the band-pass filter (Fig. 11.75) there are two cut-off frequencies, f_1 and f_2. The elements are designed to produce resonance at the geometric mean frequency f_M ($f_M = \sqrt{f_1 f_2}$). The series circuit has zero impedance at the resonant frequency, whilst the shunt circuit has infinitely high impedance at this frequency.

Above the resonant frequency (f_M) the series reactance is positive (inductive) and the shunt reactance is negative (capacitive) so that the network acts as a low-pass filter: below the resonant frequency the series reactance is negative (capacitive), the shunt reactance is positive (inductive) and the filter acts as a high-pass filter.

By a similar method to that employed for the low-pass and high-pass filters, the following expressions may be obtained for the band-pass filter, using the symbols given in Fig. 11.75—

$$Z_0 = \sqrt{\frac{L}{C}}$$

$$f_1 \text{ and } f_2 = \frac{1}{2\pi}\left(\sqrt{\frac{1}{L_1 C_2} + \frac{1}{L_2 C_1}} \mp \frac{1}{\sqrt{L_1 C_2}}\right) \quad (11.40)$$

$$L_1 = \frac{Z_0}{\pi(f_2 - f_1)} \text{ henrys} \quad . \quad . \quad (11.41)$$

$$L_2 = \frac{Z_0}{4\pi}\left(\frac{1}{f_1} - \frac{1}{f_2}\right) \text{ henrys} \quad . \quad (11.42)$$

$$C_1 = \frac{1}{4\pi Z_0}\left(\frac{1}{f_1} - \frac{1}{f_2}\right) \text{ farads} \quad . \quad (11.43)$$

$$C_2 = \frac{1}{\pi Z_0 (f_2 - f_1)} \text{ farads} \quad . \quad (11.44)$$

The attenuation/frequency characteristics of the band-pass filter are shown in Fig. 11.75 (b). The phase change introduced by the band-pass filter (Fig. 11.75 (c)) is $-180°$ from $f_0 = 0$ to the lower critical frequency. In the pass range the phase shift varies from $-180°$ at f_1 to $+180°$ at f_2 passing through zero at f_M: the phase angle remains at $+180°$ from f_2 up to $f = \infty$.

In the practical filter, power losses occur in the components. The effect of resistance in the inductors is to absorb power and increase the attenuation of the pass band especially as the cut-off frequency is approached: this effect of resistance is indicated by the dotted lines in the attenuation/frequency graphs given above. The full line curves are for the ideal case assuming that the filter elements are resistance-free and also that the filter operates between impedances equal to the iterative impedance. The effect of a pure resistance termination is to produce a further rounding-off in the characteristic. In the attenuation band the presence of power losses in components limits the impedance at resonance and this restricts the attenuation at the critical frequency.

11.30. Derived Filters. A serious disadvantage arising with the simple basic filter section is the variable impedance shown over the pass band. By the addition of other elements to the basic filter a derived filter is produced which has a much more constant impedance value over the pass band. Furthermore the derived filter has a much sharper cut-off than the simple filter section, though this is accompanied by a fall in attenuation as the frequency is further varied beyond the cut-off point.

In the derived form of mid-series low-pass filter (Fig. 11.79 (a)) a portion of the series impedance is inserted in the shunt arm and the values of the normal inductance and capacitance are reduced. Such a filter is known as the *series-derived* type, in contrast to the *shunt-derived* type (Fig. 11.79 (b)) in which a portion of the shunt capacitance is inserted in the series arm.

If the series impedance is reduced by changing the inductance from L henrys to mL henrys ($m < 1$), and the shunt impedance is raised by *reducing* the capacitance from C farads to mC farads, then it is found that inductance in the shunt arm must be $\left(\dfrac{1-m^2}{4m}\right)$. L in order to produce the desired constancy of impedance. A similar modification for the shunt-derived filter is indicated by the values marked in Fig. 11.79 (b). At the resonant frequency the inductance and capacitance in the shunt arm provide a path of nearly zero impedance and so produce an extremely high attenuation at this critical frequency (f_c). A more detailed consideration of this filter is too involved to appear here, but the graphs of Fig. 11.80 are of interest:

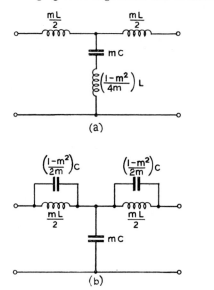

(a)

(b)

FIG. 11.79. DERIVED LOW-PASS FILTER
(a) Series-derived. (b) Shunt-derived.

here the impedance of the series-derived low-pass filter is plotted against frequency for various values of m. In particular the value of $m = 0.6$ is seen to

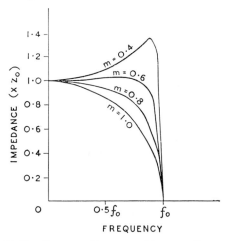

FIG. 11.80. DERIVED LOW-PASS FILTER: IMPEDANCE-FREQUENCY GRAPHS FOR VARIOUS VALUES OF m

give the smoothest impedance value over the transmission band: the value $m = 1$ relates of course to the basic (constant-k) filter impedance already shown graphically in Fig. 11.77.

Corresponding modifications can be made to produce derived high-pass and band-pass filters. Attenuation/frequency characteristics for the derived filters are given in Fig. 11.81. The special attenuation characteristics of derived sections can be employed to obtain almost any type of desired attenuation/frequency graph in the attenuating

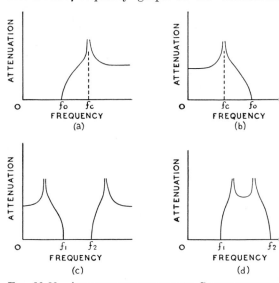

FIG. 11.81. ATTENUATION-FREQUENCY CHARACTERISTICS
OF DERIVED FILTERS
(a) Low-pass. (b) High-pass. (c) Band-pass. (d) Band-stop.

range by suitable combination of basic and derived filter sections.

The physical appearance of a band-pass filter used for discriminating between the channel frequencies at the receiving end of the line in the multi-circuit telegraph system is illustrated in Fig. 11.82; the arrangement of the circuit components is shown in Fig. 11.83. This filter comprises two basic band-pass sections connected in series, the two additional capacitors in each section are for impedance transformation to enable more convenient values of the normal shunt components to be produced.

Using improved magnetic and dielectric materials now available a similar filter with equal or improved performance would now occupy rather less than one-quarter of the volume: nevertheless Fig. 11.82 shows clearly its relationship to the filter circuit of Fig. 11.83.

The attenuation/frequency characteristic for a set of eighteen band-pass receiving filters is plotted in Fig. 11.84.

11.31. Crystal Filters.[10],[11] The quartz vibrator may be used as a resonator in the frequency filter

FIG. 11.82. RECEIVING CHANNEL FILTER

(Courtesy of P.M.G.)

account of its electrical network equivalence e Fig. 15.40) a quartz crystal can be used to place some inductor-capacitor circuits in certain sses of frequency filters. The great advantage crystal filters over networks of electrical elents lies in the high equivalent L/C ratio of the

design when using only quartz resonators. The ratio f_r/f_a which determines the frequency bandwidth in the transmission range has a maximum value determined by the physical dimension ratios available: there is also the practical impossibility of producing crystals which represent extreme

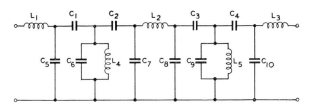

FIG. 11.83. RECEIVING CHANNEL FILTER (SCHEMATIC)

sonant circuits, their low loss (i.e. high Q value) d the stable impedance/frequency characteristic ich is obtainable from mass-produced crystals. a result of this it is possible to produce crystal ters with exceedingly sharp cut-off regions and th very high attenuation outside the transmis- n band. These filters are highly selective and proach the ideal characteristic.

There are, however, certain limitations in filter

values of the equivalent electrical elements. The presence of secondary resonances may also restrict the filter performance. The frequency range over which crystal filters are suitable is of the order of 50 kc/s to 600 kc/s. The first limitation sets the maximum bandwidth of the transmission range at about 0.8 per cent of the mean frequency if crystals and capacitors only are employed in the filter structure, e.g. a 4 kc/s channel bandwidth could

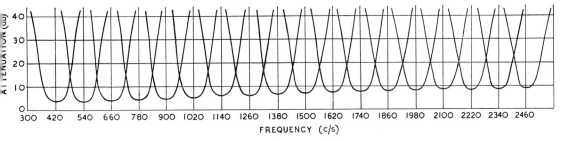

FIG. 11.84. ATTENUATION CHARACTERISTICS OF RECEIVING FILTERS FOR 18-CIRCUIT TELEGRAPH SYSTEM

not be obtained at a carrier frequency less than 500 kc/s: it is, however, possible to increase the ratio f_r/f_a by added inductance.

A typical attenuation/frequency characteristic for a band-pass filter is plotted in the graph of Fig. 11.85 which shows also the lattice-type circuit employed.

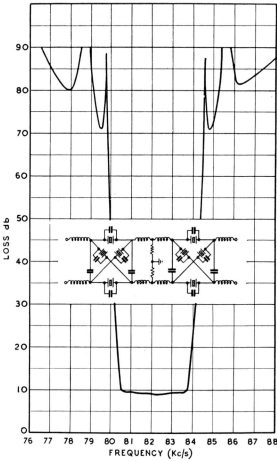

FIG. 11.85. ATTENUATION/FREQUENCY CHARACTERISTIC OF CRYSTAL FILTER

(*Courtesy of "I.P.O.E.E. Journal"*)

SUMMARY

Transformer Ratio

$$n = \frac{N_P}{N_S} = \frac{E_P}{E_S} = \frac{I_S}{I_P} = \sqrt{\frac{Z_P}{Z_S}} \quad \text{(11.1 and 11.2)}$$

Transformer Efficiency

$$\eta = \frac{\text{output power}}{\text{input power}} \times 100\%$$

$$= \frac{V_S I_S \cos \phi_S}{V_P I_P \cos \phi_P} \times 100\%$$

$$= \frac{\text{input power} - \text{losses}}{\text{input power}} \times 100\%$$

Circuits Coupled by Mutual Inductance

Resonant frequency, $f_r = \dfrac{1}{2\pi\sqrt{LC(1 \pm K)}}$

Coupling factor, $\quad K = \dfrac{M}{\sqrt{L_1 L_2}}$. (11.

Impedance of Coupled Circuits

$Z_{eff} = Z_1 + \omega^2 M^2/Z_2$ . . . . (11.

$R_{eff} = R_1 + R_2(\omega M/Z_2)^2$ . . . (11.

$X_{eff} = X_1 - X_2(\omega M/Z_2)^2$ . . . (11.

Forced Oscillations

$$f_r = \frac{1}{2\pi\sqrt{LC}} \quad \dots \text{ (series circuit)}$$

$$f_r = \frac{1}{2\pi}\sqrt{\frac{1}{LC} - \frac{R^2}{L^2}} \quad \dots \text{ (parallel circuit)}$$

Free Oscillations

$$f_0 = \frac{1}{2\pi}\sqrt{\frac{1}{LC} - \frac{R^2}{4L^2}} \quad . \quad . \quad \text{(11.}$$

Fourier's Theorem

$$y = A_0 + A_1 \sin \omega t + A_2 \sin 2\omega t + A_3 \sin 3\omega t$$
$$+ \ .$$
$$+ B_1 \cos \omega t + B_2 \cos 2\omega t + B_3 \cos 3\omega t$$
$$+ \ .$$

Attenuation Distortion

Distortion which is due to a variation of loss (gain) with frequency.

Delay Distortion

Distortion due to variation of the propagati time of the system with frequency.

Non-linear Distortion

Distortion due to the transmission properties a system being dependent upon the instantaneo magnitude of the transmitted signal.

Primary Coefficients

Resistance (R), Capacitance (C), Inductance (L and Leakance (G).

Characteristic Resistance (R_0)

The resistance of a uniform infinite line.

$$R_0 = \sqrt{R/G} = \sqrt{R_c R_f} \quad \text{(11.9 and 11.10)}$$

Characteristic Impedance (Z_0)

The impedance of a uniform infinite line—or, the impedance of a uniform finite line measured at the sending end when the receiving end is closed with the same impedance.

$$Z_0 = \sqrt{\frac{R + j\omega L}{G + j\omega C}} = \sqrt{Z_c Z_f} \quad \text{(11.11 and 11.12)}$$

Attenuation

$$I_R = I_S \cdot e^{-\gamma} \qquad . \qquad . \quad (11.17)$$
$$V_R = V_S \cdot e^{-\gamma l} \qquad . \qquad . \quad (11.19)$$
$$P_R = P_S e^{-2\gamma l} \qquad . \qquad . \quad (11.20)$$

Propagation Coefficient

$$\gamma = \alpha + j\beta = \sqrt{(R + j\omega L)(G + j\omega C)} \quad . \quad (11.18)$$

Attenuation Coefficient $\alpha =$

$$\sqrt{\tfrac{1}{2}[\sqrt{(R^2 + \omega^2 L^2)(G^2 + \omega^2 C^2)} + (RG - \omega^2 LC)]}$$
$$(11.21)$$

Phase-change Coefficient $\beta =$

$$\sqrt{\tfrac{1}{2}[\sqrt{(R^2 + \omega^2 L^2)(G^2 + \omega^2 C^2)} - (RG - \omega^2 LC)]}$$
$$(11.22)$$

Secondary Coefficients

Characteristic resistance (R_0), Characteristic impedance (Z_0), Propagation coefficient (γ), Attenuation coefficient (α) and Phase-change coefficient (β).

Approximations for Attenuation Coefficient

(i) Unloaded cable at V.F.

$$(\omega C \gg G, \text{ and } R \gg \omega L), \ \alpha = \sqrt{\frac{R\omega C}{2}}$$

(ii) Loaded cable at V.F. $\left.\right)$ $(\omega C \gg G, \text{and } \omega L \gg R)$

(iii) Unloaded cable at carrier frequencies $\left.\right\}$ $\alpha = \dfrac{R}{2}\sqrt{\dfrac{C}{L}} + \dfrac{G}{2}\sqrt{\dfrac{L}{C}}$

Approximations for Phase-change Coefficient

(i) Unloaded cable at V.F.

$$(\omega C \gg G \text{ and } R \gg \omega L), \ \beta = \sqrt{\frac{R\omega C}{2}}$$

(ii) Loaded cable at V.F. $\left.\right)$ $(\omega C \gg G, \text{ and } \omega L \gg R)$

(iii) Unloaded cable at carrier frequencies $\left.\right)$ $\beta = \omega\sqrt{LC}$

Wavelength

$$\lambda = 2\pi/\beta \text{ miles} \qquad . \qquad . \quad (11.23)$$

Phase Velocity

$$v = \omega/\beta = \lambda f \qquad . \qquad . \quad (11.26)$$

Transmission Units (Z_0 Conditions)

(i) In nepers: Gain or loss
$$= \log_e(I_S/I_R) \left[= \log_e(V_S/V_R) = \tfrac{1}{2}\log_e(P_S/P_R)\right]$$

(ii) In decinepers: Gain or loss
$$= 10 \log_e(I_S/I_R), \ [= 10 \log_e(V_S/V_R)$$
$$= 5 \log_e(P_S/P_R)] \quad . \quad (11.27)$$

(iii) In bels: Gain or loss
$$= \log_{10}(P_S/P_R), \ [= 2 \log_{10}(V_S/V_R)$$
$$= 2 \log_{10}(I_S/I_R)]$$

(iv) In decibels: Gain or loss
$$= 10 \log_{10}(P_S/P_R) \ [= 20 \log_{10}(V_S/V_R)$$
$$= 20 \log_{10}(I_S/I_R)] \quad . \quad (11.29)$$

$$1 \text{ db} = 1 \cdot 151 \text{ dn} : 1 \text{ dn} = 0 \cdot 868\,6 \text{ db}$$

Electromagnetic Radiation

$$\lambda = 1\,885 \sqrt{L'C'} \text{ metre } (L' \text{ in } \mu\text{H}, \ C' \text{ in } \mu\text{F})$$
$$(11.31)$$

Selectivity

$$Q = \omega L/R \ [\text{or } Q = 1/(\omega C R)]$$

T-network

$$Z_0 = \sqrt{Z_1 Z_2 + \frac{Z_1^2}{4}} \quad . \qquad . \qquad . \quad (11.32)$$

$$Z_1 = \text{series impedance} \left.\right\} \text{ per section}$$
$$Z_2 = \text{shunt impedance}$$

Attenuators

$$\text{T-section, } X = R_0 \left(\frac{N-1}{N+1}\right), \ Y = R_0 \left(\frac{2N}{N^2-1}\right)$$

$$\pi\text{-section, } X = R_0 \frac{(N^2-1)}{2N}, \ Y = R_0 \left(\frac{N+1}{N-1}\right)$$

$$N = \text{voltage or current ratio}$$
$$X = \text{series impedance} \left.\right\} \text{ each element}$$
$$Y = \text{shunt impedance}$$

Low-pass Filter

$$f_0 = \frac{1}{\pi\sqrt{LC}} \cdot \qquad . \qquad . \quad (11.33)$$

$$Z_0 = \sqrt{L/C} \quad . \qquad . \qquad . \quad (11.34)$$

$$C = 1/(\pi f_0 Z_0) \qquad . \qquad . \quad (11.35)$$

$$L = Z_0/(\pi f_0) \qquad . \qquad . \quad (11.36)$$

High-pass Filter

$$f_0 = 1/(4\pi\sqrt{LC}) \qquad . \qquad (11.37)$$

$$Z_0 = \sqrt{L/C}$$

$$C = 1/(4\pi Z_0 f_0) \qquad . \qquad (11.38)$$

$$L = Z_0/(4\pi f_0) \qquad . \qquad (11.39)$$

$$\left.\begin{array}{l} C = \text{capacitance} \\ L = \text{inductance} \end{array}\right\} \text{per section}$$

$$L_1 = \frac{Z_0}{\pi(f_2 - f_1)} \qquad . \qquad (11.4$$

$$L_2 = \frac{Z_0}{4\pi}\left(\frac{1}{f_1} - \frac{1}{f_2}\right) \qquad . \qquad (11.4$$

$$C_1 = \frac{1}{4\pi Z_0}\left(\frac{1}{f_1} - \frac{1}{f_2}\right) \qquad . \qquad (11.4$$

Band-pass Filter

$$f_1, f_2 = \frac{1}{2\pi}\left(\sqrt{\frac{1}{L_1 C_2} + \frac{1}{L_2 C_1}} \mp \frac{1}{\sqrt{L_1 C_2}}\right) \qquad . \qquad (11.40)$$

$$C_2 = \frac{1}{\pi Z_0 (f_2 - f_1)} \qquad . \qquad (11.4$$

REFERENCES

1. E. V. D. GLAZIER: "Transformers for Telecommunications," *I.P.O.E.E. Printed Paper No.* **176.**
2. F. C. CARTER: "The Production of Magnetic Laminations," *I.P.O.E.E. Journal,* **36** (1943), p. 65.
3. C. F. FLOYD: "An Introduction to Waveguides and Microwave Radio Systems," *I.P.O.E.E. Paper No.* **214** (1956
4. J. H. H. MERRIMAN: "The Place of V.H.F., U.H.F., and S.H.F. Radio Links in a Developing Area," *I.P.O.E. Journal,* **56** (1963), p. 149.
5. F. J. D. TAYLOR: "Large Steerable Microwave Aerials for Communication with Artificial Earth Satellites," *ibid* **55** (1962), p. 152.
6. C. E. SHANNON: "A Mathematical Theory of Communication," *Bell System Technical Journal,* July–Oct. 1948.
7. D. GABOR: "Theory of Communication," *I.E.E. Journal,* **93 Part III** (1946), p. 429.
8. G. J. S. LITTLE: "Electric Wave Filters," *I.P.O.E.E. Printed Paper No.* **143.**
9. R. J. HALSEY: "The Design and Construction of Electric Wave Filters," *I.P.O.E.E. Printed Paper No.* **147.**
10. C. F. BOOTH and C. F. SAYERS: "The Production of Quartz Resonators for the London-Birmingham Coaxial Cab System," *I.P.O.E.E. Journal,* **31** (1939), p. 245.
11. R. L. CORKE: "Crystal Filters," *ibid.,* **37** (1945), p. 113.

CHAPTER XII

METERS AND MEASUREMENTS

THE laws relating to electric phenomena having been scientifically determined, precision measuring instruments may be designed and calibrated by utilizing the effects of the electric currents.

12.1. Design Principles. The majority of electrical measuring instruments depend upon the magnetic effect of the current for their operation, though the heating effect is of common application and particularly useful in a.c. instruments at high frequencies. Electro-chemical instruments have little practical application. An important class of voltmeter which consumes no power is that dependent upon the force between two conductors carrying a static electric charge.

Apart from the electrostatic voltmeter, most electrical measuring instruments are in effect current measuring devices, that is to say that the force responsible for their deflexion depends upon the magnitude of the current they carry though their scales may be calibrated in units of p.d., of resistance, or of power.

The reading of most electrical instruments is dependent upon observing the exact position attained by an indicating pointer against a calibrated scale: this scale may be considerably extended when a reflected beam of light is used as the pointer. An important class of precision instrument, however, of which the Wheatstone bridge is a classic example, depends upon a non-deflexional or *null* method.

In a measuring instrument, the deflecting torque produced by the current being measured is opposed by a controlling torque which tends to maintain the pointer opposite the zero mark on the scale: the scale reading indicated by the pointer is the current value for which these two torques are equal and opposite. A suitable restoring torque may be provided preferably by the energy of a coiled spring, or sometimes by gravity.

If readings are to be taken quickly, some form of damping is essential to overcome the tendency of the moving system to oscillate about the point where the torques are balanced: such damping is conveniently afforded by facilitating the production of eddy currents, or by pneumatic methods if the presence of a magnetic field for the purpose is undesirable.

For the greatest accuracy to be attained and maintained a maximum torque should be produced by the moving system whose mass, however, should be kept at a minimum to reduce pivot friction: a high torque/mass ratio is a good criterion of design. Accurate balance of the movement is of first importance, particularly in portable instruments which are used in the horizontal and vertical position indiscriminately. Rigidity and robustness are also important features.

External means are usually provided for the mechanical adjustment of the moving system so that the pointer can be reset exactly to zero should this become necessary. It is perhaps unnecessary to add that measuring instruments should at all times be treated with the greatest care if the accuracy of the delicate moving system is to be maintained and the magnetic properties are to retain their essential stability.

Most current measuring instruments—an exception is the moving-coil class—will operate with either direct or alternating currents. If the deflecting torque is proportional to the first power of the current $(T \propto \pm I)$, the direction of the deflexion is obviously dependent upon current direction and the pointer of such an instrument will tend to follow the reversals of alternating currents: such instruments naturally have a linear scale—one which is evenly divided throughout its range. Most instruments have a deflexion which is proportional to the square of the current $\{T \propto (\pm I)^2 = + I^2\}$, the deflexion then being always positive: such instruments, which will read alternating currents, have a square-law scale whose divisions tend to become crowded at the lower end, though by a controlled distortion of the magnetic field or other influence the scale on these instruments can be made approximately linear.

A linear scale is most easily read by the average observer on account of its greater everyday familiarity: moving coil instruments and wattmeters follow this law, $y = x$, whose graph is plotted for comparison in Fig. 12.1 (*a*).

A square-law graph, $y = x^2$, is plotted in Fig. 12.1 (*b*) to show the derived scale: as mentioned above this is the law fundamentally followed by the majority of instruments though means may be adopted to open out their scales. Apart from the crowding at the lower values some difficulty arises in interpolating intermediate unmarked values with any degree of accuracy.

Another scale sometimes encountered is the logarithmic law scale, $y = \log x$, plotted in Fig. 12.1 (c) to show its derivation: it is less easy to read than a linear scale. It is found in some ohmmeters and in decibelmeters and is, of course, the slide rule scale.

According to the particular requirements, various grades of accuracy apply to measuring instruments: these grades may be classed as (i) standard, (ii) substandard, (iii) first grade, (iv) second grade, and (v) commercial low grade. There is no advantage in

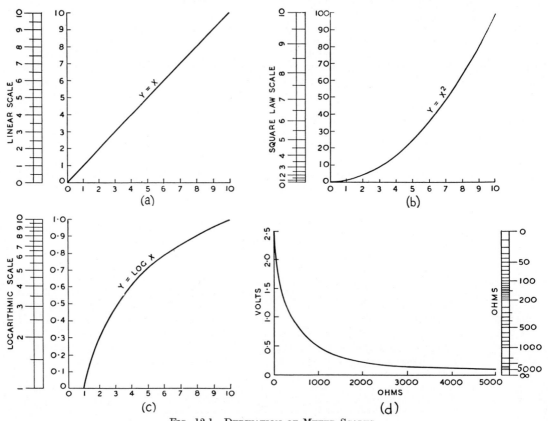

FIG. 12.1. DERIVATION OF METER SCALES
(a) Linear. (b) Square-law. (c) Logarithmic. (d) Ohmmeter.

The scale in Fig. 12.1 (d) is for an ohmmeter.

Instruments available for a.c. measurement are further classified according to whether they are suitable for (i) power supply frequencies (16–100 c/s), or (ii) audio frequencies (100 c/s to 10 000 c/s), or (iii) radio frequencies (10 kc/s and upwards). The effects of self-inductance and self-capacitance tend to impair accuracy at the upper frequencies.

Voltmeters incorporating electronic valves are particularly useful at audio and radio frequencies for both r.m.s. and peak value measurements: they have the added advantage of their ability to amplify the power available before measurement.

Cathode-ray oscilloscopes employing an electron beam of negligible inertia as the indicator, are available for a variety of measurements and tests.

using a higher grade instrument than necessitated by the requirements of the results.

In practice all commercial instruments have their scale calibrated from a sub-standard instrument which in turn is periodically checked against an approved standard.

The design of an instrument should be such that it consumes a minimum of power from the circuit for its operation: again, since meters are frequently arranged to be switched in and out of the circuits requiring measurement, it is important that the circuit constants be disturbed as little as possible by the introduction of the meter.

In the following paragraphs are quoted the approximate ranges for which each class of instrument is suitable: this does not mean, of ourse, that the entire range is covered by a single instrument.

12.2. Moving-coil Instruments. This instrument, which is essentially for d.c. use, may be designed as an amperemeter (ammeter) or as a voltmeter. It is a fairly robust instrument and for general work cannot be surpassed for accuracy and reliability.

Its operation depends upon the force acting on a conductor when it carries a current and is placed in a magnetic field: the assembly of essential components is illustrated in Fig. 12.2. A permanent magnet NS, suitably shaped to give a compact instrument, provides a powerful magnetic field between the pole-pieces PP shaped to produce a cylindrical air-gap. A high grade permanent magnet is used which has previously been "aged" to preclude risk of subsequent variation in flux density. A soft iron cylindrical core C is screwed into the base of the instrument concentrically with the pole faces. This core serves to concentrate the magnetic field within the narrow gap and ensures that this field is everywhere radial and uniform within the gap: in this way the conductors moving in a (restricted) circular path will always cut a uniform field *at right angles*, producing a maximum torque which will be constant for any position of the conductor. The conductor, of copper wire, is wound into a coil upon a rectangular frame F of aluminium, set normally at the angle illustrated. The movement is restricted to the use of the uniform portion of the field: the air-gap is made as small as possible to limit the reluctance of the magnetic field. The coil frame is pivoted in jewelled bearings and controlled by spiral phosphor bronze springs CS fitted at front and back: these springs provide the restoring torque and also serve to make electrical connexion with the moving coil. To minimize the effect of temperature changes these springs are arranged to work in opposition to one another: in the zero position the springs are in equilibrium and as the pointer is deflected one spring is wound up and the other unwound. The moving system carries a light pointer which travels across the calibrated scale, the extremities of travel being limited by two stops: a small weight is fitted to counter the effect of the pointer and preserve the balance of the moving system. The pointer is set to zero by turning an external screw which controls the fixed point of one of the restoring springs.

Further details of the construction will be seen from the photographs in Fig. 12.3. The complete instrument is shown at (a), and at (b) the complete moving system from which the method of supporting the iron core will be seen: (c) shows the component parts.

The current to be measured (I amperes) sets up a force (F newton) on each conductor of the coil such that $F = BIl$ newton where B is the flux density (Wb/m²) and l m is the effective length of a con-

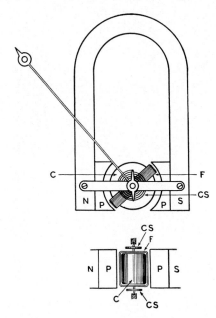

Fig. 12.2. Moving-coil Meter—Construction

ductor. If the coil has N turns ($= 2N$ conductors) of radius r m, the deflecting torque

$$T = Fr \propto 2BIlNr \text{ N-m}$$

the product $2rl$ is the area A m² of the coil, so that in general

$$T \propto BINA \text{ N-m}$$

Turns may be varied so that a full scale deflexion is reached with as little as 0·1 mA in a commercial instrument and with a fraction of a microampere in a suspension type laboratory instrument. In the absence of restoring springs, the coil would set itself at right angles to the magnetic field with any value of current sufficient to overcome the inertia of the moving system. When the coil is deflected through an angle $\theta°$, if T' N-m is the torque required to twist the restoring springs through 1°, the total restoring torque is $T'\theta$. The pointer comes to rest at the position where the deflecting and restoring torques balance, i.e. when $T'\theta = BINA$.

The inertia of the system tends to cause the moving pointer to overshoot and, on account of the restoring torque, to oscillate about the correct reading. The eddy currents induced in the aluminium frame set up an opposing force tending

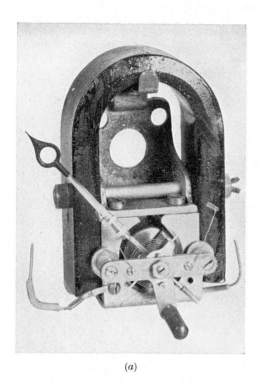

(a)

(b)

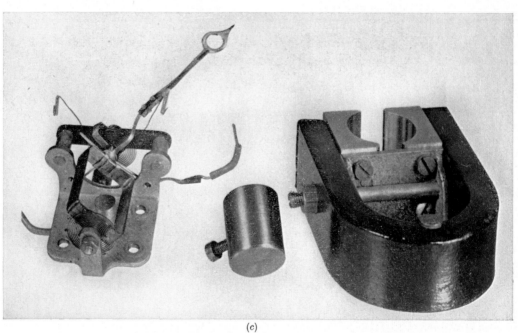

(c)

FIG. 12.3. MOVING-COIL METER SHOWING COMPONENTS
(Courtesy of P.M.G.)

to resist all movement: this damping renders the instrument "dead-beat" and enables readings to be taken without delay.

When enclosed in an iron case or suitably-screened the moving-coil instrument is unaffected by stray magnetic fields.

In the expression $T \propto BINA$, all the factors B, N, and A are constant for any given instrument and the deflexion is directly proportional to the current (I): the scale is accordingly linear. The terminals of a moving-coil instrument are clearly marked $+$ and $-$ and care must be taken to connect the meter in circuit correctly. If an alternating current is applied to such an instrument its pointer tends to follow each half-cycle, but on account of the inertia of the moving system a slight vibration about the zero point occurs and that only at low frequencies. With the addition of a metal rectifier the moving-coil instrument is used to measure alternating currents or voltages: it may also be used for the same purpose in association with a thermocouple.

The moving-coil instrument is adapted by suitable choice of resistance value to serve either as a voltmeter or as an ammeter. In a common form of high grade instrument a full-scale deflexion is produced by a current of 10 milliamperes. Provided this current *in the moving coil* is not exceeded the meter may be shunted and used to measure higher currents, or fitted with a series resistance to enable high voltages to be measured.

The moving coil is of copper which has a temperature coefficient of resistance of about 0·4 per cent per degree centigrade. If the instrument is unshunted an increase in resistance consequent upon temperature rise is accompanied by an increased p.d. and there is no error in current indication. If a shunt is used having a negligible temperature coefficient the combination will be correct at only one temperature: this source of error is avoided by joining a "swamping" resistance of eureka or constantan in series with the copper winding so that the resistance of the copper is about one quarter of the whole. In this way a possible error of about 0·4 per cent per degree centigrade can be reduced to less than 0·1 per cent per degree centigrade, as the springs and magnet both weaken slightly with increase of temperature. In voltmeters the series resistance is itself a swamp and the temperature error is quite negligible.

For some purposes the normal position of the coil is arranged to lie midway along the air-gap to produce a scale with a central zero. A milliammeter of this type used for double current telegraph circuits, is illustrated in Fig. 12.30.

Owing to the intense magnetic field of the permanent magnet the number of ampere-turns required for the coil is small and a sensitive instrument results. The "resistance per volt" can be made high to produce a low power consumption. The field of use of the moving-coil meter is wide: instruments of this class may be used to measure currents from a few microamperes to some thousands of amperes, and from microvolts to kilovolts. For the lower readings the moving system is suspended to avoid pivot friction and obtain the requisite sensitivity.

12.3. Ammeters. An ammeter is inserted in series with a circuit under test so that the current being measured passes through the instrument. The ammeter resistance must be low compared with the circuit resistance so that the current will not be appreciably reduced and the voltage drop and power loss introduced by the meter will not be excessive: care should be taken not to overload the meter nor to exceed the full-scale deflexion.

If a heavy current is to be measured the ammeter may be shunted so that a known proportion of the circuit current flows through the meter: in reading the meter due allowance is then made for the current diverted through the shunt.

By the use of two or more alternative shunts the range of certain ammeters may be extended. As the resistance of an ammeter shunt is normally of a very low order, especial care has to be taken in its electrical connexion to the meter, or the shunt resistance may be materially altered and accuracy of measurement impaired: in power switchboards shunts are frequently wired permanently in series with selected portions of the equipment and by means of a switch the ammeter (functioning actually as a millivoltmeter) is connected across any desired shunt. When shunts are selected by a switch it is very necessary that the switch should have a reliable action with a constant low resistance value: a variation of a few microhms may affect the accuracy of shunts for heavy currents. If external shunts are used care must be taken to ensure that the leads supplied with the shunt are used as their resistance is included in the calibration.

An ammeter shunt frequently carries a heavy current which produces a temperature rise: to preserve accuracy shunts are made from a material such as manganin which has a low temperature coefficient of resistance. The heat dissipating property of a shunt is a feature of its design.

If a moving-coil meter were shunted by a resistance of equal value to the moving coil, the coil and the shunt would each carry one half of the circuit current and the scale reading would require multiplication by two.

The problem of evaluating the shunt required for any particular case becomes one of diverting from the moving system the current in excess of that required to give a full-scale deflexion: alternatively the combined resistance of the shunted meter must show a value to maintain at full current the correct p.d. across the meter.

Referring to Fig. 12.4 if the meter current is

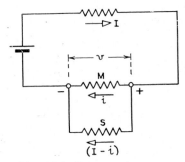

FIG. 12.4. SHUNTED AMMETER

i amps and the total current is I amps, the balance $(I - i)$ flows in the shunt: the joint resistance R ohms of the meter (M ohms) shunted by S ohms s $R = \dfrac{MS}{M + S}$. The p.d. across the meter is $v = IR = iM$, from which the current ratio

$$\frac{I}{i} = \frac{M}{R} = \frac{M(M + S)}{MS} = \frac{(M + S)}{S}$$

In other words, to reduce the meter current to $1/n$ of the main current, a shunt having a resistance equal to $1/(n - 1)$ times the meter resistance must be applied.

The addition of a shunt reduces the meter circuit resistance from M to $MS/(M + S)$. This reduction in circuit resistance is equal to

$$M - \frac{MS}{M + S} = \frac{M^2}{M + S}$$

a compensating resistance of this value must be added in series with the main circuit if it is undesirable to disturb the total circuit resistance.

Evaluations of shunt resistance, which require only the application of Ohm's law, are given in the worked examples which follow.

A *universal shunt* is used in conjunction with highly sensitive galvanometers in order to prevent damage by the passage of heavy currents through the movement. This shunt has a number of resistors of different value joined in series: any resistance value can be selected by a movable contact arm thus making it possible to vary the multiplying power according to requirements.

The advantage of this arrangement lies in the fact that the values of the various resistors do not need to bear any fixed relation to the resistance of the galvanometer being used: this is achieved from the arrangement by which the sum of the shunt

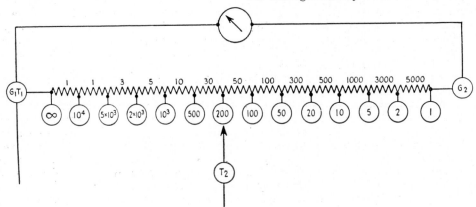

FIG. 12.5. UNIVERSAL SHUNT

This ratio, $I/i = (M + S)/S = n$, is the "multiplying power" of the shunt, i.e. it is the number by which the current reading on the meter (i) is multiplied to give the current value of the main circuit ($I = ni$).

From the ratio $(M + S)/S = n$,

$$(M + S) = nS, \text{ and } M = S(n - 1)$$

$$\text{or } S = M/(n - 1)$$

resistance plus the resistance placed in series with the galvanometer coil is maintained at a constant value.

The arrangement of a universal shunt is shown in Fig. 12.5 which indicates the values of the various resistors and the multiplying power at each adjustment. The shunt has three terminals: the galvanometer is joined across the pair ($G_1 G_2$) embracing the whole of the resistors, and the external circuit under est is connected between the common terminal G_1T_1 and the movable contact switch (T_2). With the switch in the infinity position no current flows in the galvanometer.

The expression deduced above shows that the multiplying power

$$n = \frac{\text{(meter resistance + shunt resistance)}}{\text{shunt resistance}}$$

In the universal shunt the sum $(M + S)$ is constant and the multiplying power of the shunt is inversely proportional to the resistance of the shunt.

12.4. Voltmeters. The terminals of a voltmeter are connected across the two points whose potential difference is to be measured. To avoid drawing excessive current from the supply terminals and lowering the p.d. at the points to be measured, it is necessary for a voltmeter to possess a high value of

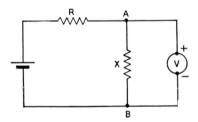

FIG. 12.6. METHOD OF CONNECTING VOLTMETER TO LOAD

resistance in comparison with that of the circuit being measured: this will also ensure that the power (V^2/R) absorbed by the meter is kept to a minimum.

In measuring the p.d. across a resistor X (Fig. 12.6) the shunting effect of the voltmeter reduces the resistance across the points AB: the circuit current increases, the potential drop across R increases and the p.d. to be measured across the points AB falls due to the presence of the voltmeter. The degree of inaccuracy of the measurement depends upon the relationship between the voltmeter resistance and the value of X: provided that the meter resistance is high compared with that of the load resistance X, the shunting effect and the error will be small.

Voltmeter resistances are expressed in "ohms per volt" for full-scale deflexion: for example, a voltmeter whose terminals present a resistance of 50 000 Ω and whose full-scale deflexion corresponds to a reading of 50 V has a resistance of 1 000 Ω per volt.

Most voltmeters show a deflexion which is proportional to the current (or to the square of the current) flowing in the moving system (the electro-

static type is a notable exception). If a full-scale deflexion requires a current of I amperes, since the resistance R ohms of the moving system is constant, it follows that a p.d. of $V = IR$ *across the moving system* will always produce a full-scale deflexion: the ratio of p.d. to current being constant the deflexion will be proportional to the p.d. (or to the square of the p.d.) and the scale can be calibrated in volts.

The range of a voltmeter may be extended by connecting a fixed resistor in series with it: for example, if a voltmeter of 5 000 Ω resistance is joined in series with a 5 000 Ω resistor and the combination joined across a source of p.d., only one-half of this p.d. will appear across the meter terminals, and the scale reading would require multiplication by two to give the correct value.

The problem of calculating the series resistance

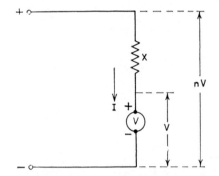

FIG. 12.7. EXTENDING THE RANGE OF A VOLTMETER

necessary to extend the range of a voltmeter may be regarded from the viewpoint of dropping the excess volts in the series resistance, or alternatively, as a question of adding sufficient series resistance to limit the full-scale current to its correct value when the increased p.d. is applied.

Referring to Fig. 12.7 suppose that I amperes is the current required to produce a full-scale deflexion of V volts on a given instrument: the resistance of the meter is R ohms and $R = V/I$. Now suppose that it is desired to extend the voltmeter range to read nV volts $(n > 1)$. To limit the p.d. across the meter to V volts it is necessary to drop the excess voltage, $nV - V = V(n - 1)$ volts, across the resistor X ohms: at a current of I amperes the value of the series resistance is given by

$$X = \frac{V(n - 1)}{I} \text{ ohms}$$

Alternatively to maintain the current at I amperes when the total p.d. applied is nV volts the total resistance will need to be nV/I ohms. The voltmeter resistance is equal to V/I so that the value of the added resistance is

$$\frac{nV}{I} - \frac{V}{I} = \frac{V(n-1)}{I} \text{ ohms}$$

Evaluations of this nature, which require only the application of Ohm's law are demonstrated in the worked examples which follow.

EXAMPLE 12.1 (A). A moving-coil milliammeter has a resistance of 12·5 Ω and gives its full deflexion for 15 mA. How can it be arranged to measure (a) up to 1·5 A, (b) up to 30 V ?   (C. & G.)

The full-scale p.d. across the moving coil is $0·015 \times 12·5 = 0·187\ 5$ V.

(a) *To measure* 1·5 A :

The excess current $= (1·5 - 0·015) = 1·485$ A should be diverted through a shunt, the p.d. across the shunt being 0·187 5 V and its resistance being $R = 0·187\ 5/1·485 = 0·126\ 3\ \Omega.$

(Alternative solution—

If $\quad I =$ total current (1·5 A) \
$\quad i =$ meter current (0·015 A) \
$I - i =$ shunt current (1·485 A) \
$\quad M =$ meter resistance (12·5 Ω) \
$\quad S =$ shunt resistance ;

$$\frac{I-i}{i} = \frac{M}{S}, \quad \frac{1·485}{0·015} = \frac{12·5}{S}$$

$$S = \frac{0·015 \times 12·5}{1·485} = 0·126\ 3\ \Omega)$$

(b) *To measure* 30 V :

The excess p.d. $(= 30 - 0·187\ 5 = 29·812\ 5)$ must be dropped in an added series resistance R carrying a current of 0·015 A.

$$R = 29·812\ 5/0·015 = 1\ 987·5\ \Omega$$

(Alternative solution—

Total resistance to produce current of 0·015 A with a p.d. of 30 V $= 30/0·015 = 2\ 000\ \Omega.$

Moving coil resistance $\ = 12·5\ \Omega$

Added series resistance $= 2\ 000 - 12·5$

$$= 1\ 987·5\ \Omega)$$

EXAMPLE 12.2 (A). A moving-coil milliammeter has a resistance of 5 Ω and gives a full-scale deflexion with a current of 50 mA. Explain how this instrument could be adapted to measure—

    (i) a direct current of 5 A, \
    (ii) a direct voltage of 20 V.   (C. & G.)

(i) *To measure* 5 A :

A current of 0·05 A flows in the moving coil and 4·95 A must be diverted through a shunt. \
    P.d. across 5 Ω moving coil with 0·05 A

$$= 0·05 \times 5 = 0·25 \text{ V}$$

P.d. across S Ω shunt with 4·95 A

$$= 4·95 \times S = 0·25$$

$$S = 0·25/4·95$$

$$= 0·050\ 5\ \Omega$$

(ii) *To measure* 20 V :

The excess voltage $(20 - 0·25)$ must be dropped by a series resistance R ohms carrying the coil current of 0·05 A.

$$R = \frac{20 - 0·25}{0·05} = \frac{19·75}{0·05} = 395\ \Omega$$

EXAMPLE 12.3 (A). The resistance of the moving-coil system of a combined ammeter and voltmeter is 10 Ω, and a full-scale deflexion is obtained when a current of 10 mA passes through the coil. \
Calculate the value of the resistance which would be required in each case to make the full-scale readings represent (a) 2·5 V, and (b) 50 mA, and show how each resistance should be connected.   (C. & G.)

P.d. across moving system $= 0·01 \times 10 = 0·1$ V.

(a) *To read* 2·5 V :

The excess p.d. $= (2·5 - 0·1) = 2·4$ V must be dropped at a current of 0·01 A across an added series resistance equal to $2·4/0·01 = 240\ \Omega.$

(b) *To read* 50 mA :

A shunt resistance must be added to divert the excess current $(0·05 - 0·01) = 0·04$ A. With a p.d. of 0·1 V, shunt resistance $= 0·1/0·04 = 2·5\ \Omega.$

12.5. Moving-iron Instruments.

There are two distinct types of moving-iron instrument: they differ according to whether deflexion is produced by attraction or by repulsion. The former makes use of the attraction of iron in the electromagnetic field of a current-carrying solenoid: the latter depends upon the mutual repulsion of two similarly magnetized pieces of iron within an energized solenoid, one being fixed and the other movable.

In each type the iron forms but a small part of the magnetic circuit: consequently the air-path reluctance is high with the result that power consumption is high, and the instrument, unless well screened, is susceptible to the influence of stray magnetic fields.

The principle of the attraction type is shown in

Fig. 12.8. A light soft iron vane V is pivoted eccentrically near to one face of a solenoid CC: the vane carries a light pointer capable of movement over a calibrated scale. When a current flows in the solenoid the vane becomes magnetized by induction and as a consequence it is attracted towards the centre of the solenoid. The opposing torque is provided by a spiral spring CS. A small air piston A is carried upon the moving system and is capable of movement against an air cushion within a curved cylinder: this provides the damping device. Alter-

current in the coil: since the force of repulsion is proportional to the product of these pole strengths, the deflexion is fundamentally dependent upon the square of the current. The flux density does not follow the current changes exactly over the working range: also, the inductance and the repulsive force fall off as the distance between the fixed and moving irons increases ($f \propto 1/d^2$): the result of this is to give a slightly more uniform scale.

Some improvement in the form of scale is obtained by the use of specially shaped pieces of

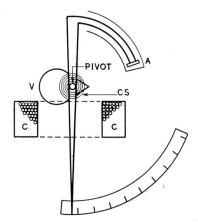

FIG. 12.8. PRINCIPLE OF MOVING-IRON METER: ATTRACTION TYPE

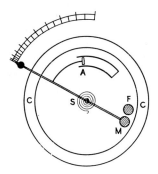

FIG. 12.9. PRINCIPLE OF MOVING-IRON METER: REPULSION TYPE

natively damping may be effected by eddy currents induced in a conducting disk which is fixed to the same spindle as the magnetic vane and, on deflexion, rotates between the poles of a permanent magnet.

The magnetizing force of the solenoid is proportional approximately to the current and so is the pole strength induced in the vane. The deflecting force, which is proportional to the product of the magnetic intensities of solenoid and vane becomes proportional to the square of the current. The meter scale is fundamentally a square law one, but by suitable shaping of the vane the scale may be made to approach a linear law.

In the repulsion type of instrument (Fig. 12.9) two thick soft iron wires are placed close together within an air-cored solenoid (CC), with their lengths parallel to the axis of this coil. One iron wire (F) is fixed to the instrument case, the other (M) being pivoted and carrying the pointer. When a current flows in the solenoid the iron pieces are magnetized similarly by induction and their mutual repulsion provides the deflecting force. The controlling force is provided by the spiral spring S. Damping is normally by air piston (A). The pole strength of each iron is approximately proportional to the

iron instead of simple bars. The design of such an instrument is shown in Fig. 12.10 (a), the moving and fixed iron pieces M and F being shown in plan in Fig. 12.10 (b) and in developed form in Fig. 12.10 (c). The fixed iron covers a larger arc than the moving iron and it is shaped narrower at one end than at the other: when the solenoid is energized the moving iron is repelled towards the narrower end of the fixed iron. The controlling spring is shown at CS: B is an adjustable balance weight and Z is the zero adjustment lever. Damping is effected by the air piston and chamber at A.

Moving-iron instruments may be designed either as voltmeters or as ammeters. They may be employed for measuring either direct or alternating currents since their deflexion is independent of current direction: in the former case (D.C.) the direction of current flow through the instrument is of course immaterial. When used for A.C. the instrument measures r.m.s. values.

Used as a voltmeter, as with the moving-coil instrument a swamping non-inductive resistance of low temperature coefficient is used in series with the solenoid to reduce temperature error. With this instrument a further gain is presented by this since the inductance is also swamped, which reduces the frequency error and the difference between d.c. and a.c. readings. Shunts may be used to increase the current range in both d.c. and a.c. instruments of this class.

The main advantages of the moving-iron instrument are its relative simplicity and cheapness for

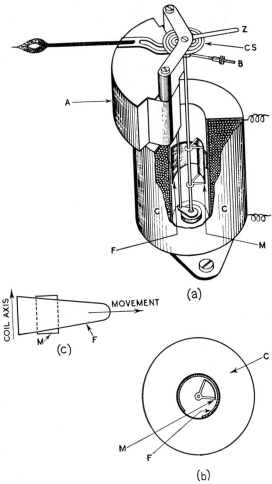

(a)

(c)

(b)

FIG. 12.10. MOVING-IRON METER: CONSTRUCTION
OF REPULSION TYPE

production, and its robust character: the coil being fixed it can be readily wound to suit its purpose. On the other hand the power consumption of moving-iron instruments is somewhat high and their accuracy does not equal that of the moving-coil instrument. Moving-iron instruments are subject to slight error if used in the vicinity of stray magnetic fields. They are also liable to hysteresis errors, a given current value giving a smaller reading when the current is rising than when it is falling, though these errors are largely overcome by the employment of nickel iron alloys of low hysteresis.

Their inductance is relatively high and they are not independent of frequency on account of their hysteresis and eddy current effects. They are also affected by changes in coil resistance with variation of temperature. For these reasons, as an a.c. instrument the moving-iron meter is most suited to power supply frequencies of approximately sine-wave form.

The moving-iron instrument operates equally well on D.C. or A.C. and first grade accuracy is possible. On a.c. measurements the scale reads r.m.s. values but errors may occur with a waveform containing harmonics which reach saturation in the permeability curve. Moving-iron instruments are suitable for reading up to a few kilovolts and down to a few volts: as ammeters the range is from a few milliamperes up to about 500 amperes, above which current transformers can be used for a.c. readings. The d.c. ranges are rather narrower than the a.c. ranges.

A polarized type of moving-iron instrument is also in use. The moving system is simply a soft iron armature carrying a pointer: being polarized by a small permanent magnet the instrument is essentially for d.c. use, with a linear scale. A coil carrying the current to be measured is mounted near or around the armature but has its axis at right angles to that of the normal position of the armature. When current flows, the coil produces a field at right angles to the permanent field: the resultant field is distorted and the armature is deflected. No restoring spring is fitted as the armature is normally controlled by the permanent magnet field. Such instruments are not of a high grade of accuracy but

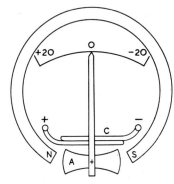

FIG. 12.11. POLARIZED MOVING-IRON INSTRUMENT

have the merit of being very cheap to produce. A diagram showing a simple central zero pattern is given in Fig. 12.11. NS is the permanent magnet, A the armature, and C is a two-turn coil which in the meter illustrated produces a magnetomotive force of ± 40 ampere-turns.

EXAMPLE 12.4 (A). A moving-iron meter has a resistance of 2 000 Ω and the current required to give a full-scale deflexion is 20 mA. How could this instrument be adapted to measure a d.c. voltage of 500 V ? (*C. & G.*)

For a current of 0·02 A at a p.d. of 500 V the total resistance required is 500/0·02 = 25 000 Ω. Since the meter resistance is 2 000 Ω, additional series resistance of (25 000 − 2 000) is required, = 23 000 Ω.

EXAMPLE 12.5 (B). A moving-iron ammeter designed to give a full-scale deflexion with an alternating current of 5 A at a frequency of 50 c/s has an inductance of 0·1 mH and negligible resistance. Calculate the value of a non-inductive shunt which is required to permit the ammeter to measure a maximum current of 15 A at the same frequency. (*C. & G.*)

As the meter resistance is negligible the current will lag 90 degrees behind the voltage. The current in the non-inductive shunt will, however, be in phase with the voltage so that meter and shunt currents will be in quadrature.

At full-scale, the meter current = 5 A and the total current = 15 A.

Shunt current $= \sqrt{15^2 - 5^2} = \sqrt{200} = 14·14$ A

The p.d. across the moving system with 5 A flowing is—

$V = \omega L I = 314 \times 0·1 \times 10^{-3} \times 5 = 0·157$ V

The shunt resistance is $0·157/14·14 = \underline{0·011\ \Omega}$

12.6. Dynamometer Instruments.

In general construction this class of instrument is similar to the moving-coil meter but instead of a permanent magnet the field is provided by an electromagnet. The characteristics of the dynamometer instrument depend upon the excitation of the electromagnet in addition to that of the moving coil : if a direct current of constant value is applied to the field coils the instrument will have the same performance as a moving-coil meter. On the other hand, if the field coils and moving coil are energized (either in series or in parallel) both from the same source, the deflecting torque depends upon the product of the currents in the moving coil and in the field coils : accordingly in this case the instrument will have a square law scale and being no longer polarized it will be equally suitable for A.C. or D.C.

The instrument may be designed as a voltmeter or as an ammeter and used to measure either a.c. or d.c. supplies. The air-gap field is parallel and not radial owing to the absence of any iron core, hence the torque falls off as the deflexion increases : this factor results in some opening out of the scale. The restoring torque is usually provided by a coiled spring : damping is by an air piston and cylinder owing to the undesirability of the presence of a permanent magnet for eddy current damping.

There is no advantage in the use of this instrument for d.c. voltage and current measurements as its power consumption is greater than that of the moving-coil instrument in which most of the power is provided by the permanent magnet. The main field of application for the dynamometer instrument is as a wattmeter. In this case the moving coil is a pressure coil and, connected across the supply leads, it carries a current proportional to the applied p.d. (*V*) : the coil is wound upon a non-magnetic frame and to prevent error due to temperature changes a non-inductive winding of manganin is connected in series with the coil having a resistance some four times as great as the latter. Two field coils are provided, connected in series : they are of heavy gauge wire or strip to carry the load current (*I*) or a known portion of it.

An air core is normally employed throughout but recent developments in low hysteresis nickel-iron alloys make possible the use of a ferromagnetic path and bring about a reduction in power consumption. A schematic diagram showing the connexions of the instrument as a wattmeter is given in Fig. 12.12.

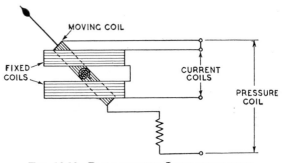

FIG. 12.12. DYNAMOMETER INSTRUMENT USED AS A WATTMETER

Without iron losses the dynamometer measures true power ($VI \cos \phi$ watts) : the scale is linear, the deflexion being proportional to both *V* and *I*. This instrument is liable to be affected by stray magnetic fields but with an air core it is practically independent of frequency and waveform. Errors and power losses due to hysteresis and eddy currents are minimized by reducing all metal parts to a minimum and laminating where necessary.

As a voltmeter or ammeter, the dynamometer instrument is accurate but costly : its range is roughly from 10 V to 100 kV, or from 10 mA to 10 A, using current transformers for higher readings (A.C.). Its use in this case is largely as a *transfer instrument*, that is to say for checking a.c. instruments against a d.c. standard instrument.

Another form of the dynamometer is in the Kelvin-Ampere balance, an instrument used for checking standard and sub-standard instruments. Its operation is dependent upon the electromagnetic forces of attraction or repulsion between adjacent conductors which carry currents in like or unlike directions: these forces are balanced against gravity by means of a travelling weight.

The arrangement of the coils is shown in Fig. 12.13. The conductors are in convolutions forming six "rings" joined in series: four of the rings are fixed and the other two form the ends of a delicately poised balance arm. These two rings are free to

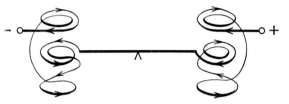

FIG. 12.13. KELVIN-AMPERE BALANCE

move up and down through a small arc, each between one pair of the fixed rings.

The relative current directions are such that the forces from the current urge one movable ring upwards and the other downwards: it is arranged that the current passes in relatively opposite directions in the two movable coils so as to annul disturbances due to possible stray magnetic fields.

When a current passes through the coils the balance arm is deflected from its normal horizontal position: the current strength is determined by the mechanical torque necessary to restore the balance arm to its original position. This torque is applied by means of a jockey weight, provided with a pointer, which may be moved along a finely graduated horizontal scale attached to the balance arm: counterpoise weights are necessary and one of these associated with the particular jockey weight in use is placed in a carrier provided for this purpose and attached to the end of the arm.

Means are provided for ensuring an accurate zero adjustment. The current may be read from the horizontal scale fitted with a vernier.

12.7. Galvanometers.

A galvanometer is an instrument for indicating a small electric current: it is not usually scaled quantitatively.

The Paul unipivot galvanometer is essentially a moving-coil instrument with a high degree of sensitivity obtained by a reduction in bearing friction consequent upon the use of a single pivot for the moving coil. Constructional details are shown in Fig. 12.14. Between the poles of the permanent magnet NS is fixed a soft iron *spherical*

core C: the pole-pieces are hollowed out to form concentric spherical surfaces and so ensure a perfectly uniform air-gap. The coil, of insulated copper wire, is wound upon a light copper frame F and it is provided with a vertical spindle having a single pivot resting upon a jewel cup at the centre of the iron sphere: the centre of gravity of the moving system acts at this point. A single spiral spring provides the controlling torque: the current in the moving coil is led through this spring and through a flexible ligament attached to the lower end of the coil. Eddy current damping is introduced by the copper frame upon which the coil is wound.

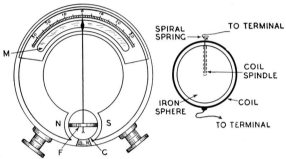

FIG. 12.14. PAUL UNIPIVOT GALVANOMETER: CONSTRUCTIONAL DETAILS

The instrument may, when necessary, be set to zero by means of a small projecting lever to which the controlling spring is attached. A further device is added by which the moving system is raised and clamped for transport whenever the meter is lifted. A mirror M is fitted beneath the pointer adjacent to the scale to avoid reading errors due to parallax.

The coil is so placed to give a central-zero position to the pointer: the scale is uniform with equal divisions representing equal currents. The resistance of the moving coil is 40 to 50 Ω: its sensitivity is such that a full-scale deflexion of 35 divisions either side of zero is produced with a current of 100 μA. On account of this great sensitivity it is desirable to use the meter in conjunction with a variable shunt to avoid damage by excessive currents.

The use of a longer pointer with a galvanometer enables a fine scale to be used and accurately read: the weight of such a pointer adds to the inertia of the moving system and increases the difficulty in providing a delicate and sensitive moving system. By fitting a small mirror to a suspended moving system and directing a beam of light, from a lamp, upon the mirror the reflected beam of light directed upon a scale acts as a long weightless pointer. The

The peak value of a sinusoidal wave of
$$100 \text{ mA r.m.s.} = 100\sqrt{2} \text{ mA}$$
The value indicated by the moving-coil meter
$$= 100\sqrt{2}/\pi = \underline{45} \text{ mA}$$

When the supply has a rectangular waveform, the current through the meters and rectifier will be alternate half-cycles, separated by half-cycle gaps. For a half-wave rectangle, the average, peak, and r.m.s. values of current will be the same. But over a full cycle (i.e. a half-cycle of rectangle followed by zero for half a cycle) the average and the r.m.s. values of current will only equal half the peak value. Since the peak value of the square wave is 2 V, the meters will both read 100/2 = 50 mA.

12.12. Differential Meters. Differential milliammeters are employed to read directly the difference between the currents flowing in two circuits: a common application is in duplex telegraph circuits where a meter is required to indicate any difference

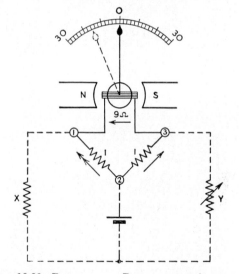

FIG. 12.28. PRINCIPLE OF DIFFERENTIAL AMMETER

between the currents flowing in a real line and in its corresponding artificial balance network.

A moving-coil meter of the central zero type may be made differential by shunting it with an accurately centre-tapped resistor. If such a meter is connected in circuit in the manner shown in Fig. 12.28 then, supposing $X < Y$, more current will flow between terminals 2–1 than between 2–3. The p.d. across terminals 2–1 is then greater than the p.d. across 2–3, so that terminal 3 is at a higher

potential than terminal 1: as a result, current flows through the moving coil in the direction $3 \rightarrow 1$. The arrangement is in effect a form of Wheatstone bridge with equal ratio arms each of one ohm resistance: the direction and magnitude of any current flowing in the moving coil bridged across the network depends upon the values of the circuit resistances X and Y. The instrument terminals are so arranged relative to the scale that the deflexion of the pointer indicates directly which circuit is carrying the greater current.

Another pattern of differential milliammeter (Fig. 12.29) has a double wound moving coil, each winding being separately shunted with a centre-tapped

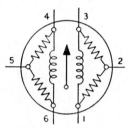

FIG. 12.29. DIFFERENTIAL MILLIAMMETER—
6 TERMINAL PATTERN

resistor fitted internally. The differential meter illustrated in Fig. 12.30 has a $2\frac{1}{4}$ in. scale calibrated 30–0–30 mA with scale divisions showing 2 mA: a full-scale deflexion is produced by a current of 30 mA flowing either between terminals 1 and 2, 2 and 3, 4 and 5, or 5 and 6.

12.13. Ballistic Meters. Ballistic meters are employed to measure the *quantity* of electricity, Q coulombs, which passes when a current of extremely brief duration traverses the moving coil. The moving system is designed so that its period of vibration is large compared with the duration of an applied current impulse, and the damping of the moving system is very slight. The momentary current will then cease before the pointer has appreciably moved from its rest position, and the pointer will move to a maximum position proportional to the quantity of electricity imparted to the coil. Ballistic instruments may be employed for the measurement of short time intervals such as the operating and releasing times of relays.

12.14. The Detector No. 4. This is a small robust portable instrument suitable for making current and voltage measurements over a wide range of values, using both internal and external multiplying resistors and shunts: being of the moving-coil type it is only suitable for d.c. measurements but a rectifier attachment is available to enable the instrument to be used for a.c. voltage measurements.

The moving coil is wound upon an insulated silver frame and connected in series with sufficient swamping resistance to make a total resistance of 10 Ω: the winding consists of 0·005 in. diameter copper wire insulated with single silk and baked in

(i) 0 to 5 V, (ii) 0 to 50 V, (iii) 0 to 50 mA, (iv) 0 t 500 mA. In addition, by connecting the circui under test straight across the moving coil (termina

(a

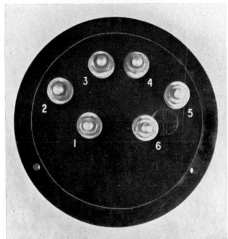

FIG. 12.30. DIFFERENTIAL MILLIAMMETER SHOWING TERMINAL ARRANGEMENT
(Courtesy of Ernest Turner Electrical Instruments, Ltd.)

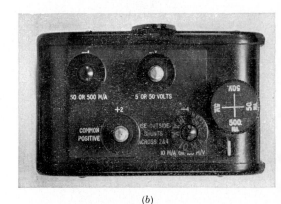

(b)

FIG. 12.31. DETECTOR No. 4
Showing: (a) Internal construction. (b) Terminals and switch.
(Courtesy of P.M.G.)

bakelite. A full-scale reading is given with a p.d. of 0·1 V, i.e. with a current of 10 mA.

Views of the instrument are shown in Fig. 12.31: the internal construction is shown at (a), whilst (b) shows the arrangement of the terminals and switch. The internal connexions of the detector are shown in Fig. 12.32. Using the appropriate terminals and without the use of external resistors or shunts the following ranges may be selected by the switch

+ 2 and − 4), scale readings of 0 to 10 mA or 0 t 100 mV are obtained with the switch in the "50 V position. A fuse of eureka wire, rated to blow a 0·5 A, is included in series with the moving co (Fig. 12.32) when used direct or with extern

METERS AND MEASUREMENTS

For extended current readings, a 5 A and a 25 A shunt are provided: these have connecting lugs accurately spaced to enable them to be connected between terminals + 2 and — 4 (i.e. direct across the moving coil). An illustration of the meter with the 25 A shunt in position is given in Fig. 12.33. With either shunt the switch should be in the 50 V (or 5 V) position.

The voltage range is extended by screwing either one or two 10 000 Ω series resistors on to the extended threads of terminals + 2 or — 3: with the switch in the 50 V position each resistor added increases the scale range by a further 100 V. A view of the instrument with both resistors in position is given in Fig. 12.34: this illustration shows a contact spike—normally housed in the back of the meter—screwed into a socket in the base of the instrument. This spike, which is useful for such purposes as cell testing, becomes the common positive terminal. An instruction plate for the various ranges is mounted upon the side of the instrument.

Fig. 12.34. Detector No. 4 fitted with Voltage Multipliers
(Courtesy of P.M.G.)

Fig. 12.33. Detector No. 4 fitted with 25 A Shunt
(Courtesy of P.M.G.)

shunts: the terminal (— 4) used for these measurements is painted red as a safeguard against inadvertent use which would damage the moving system.

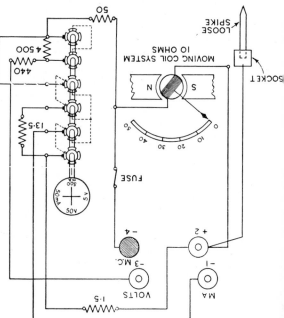

Fig. 12.32. Detector No. 4.—Internal Connexions

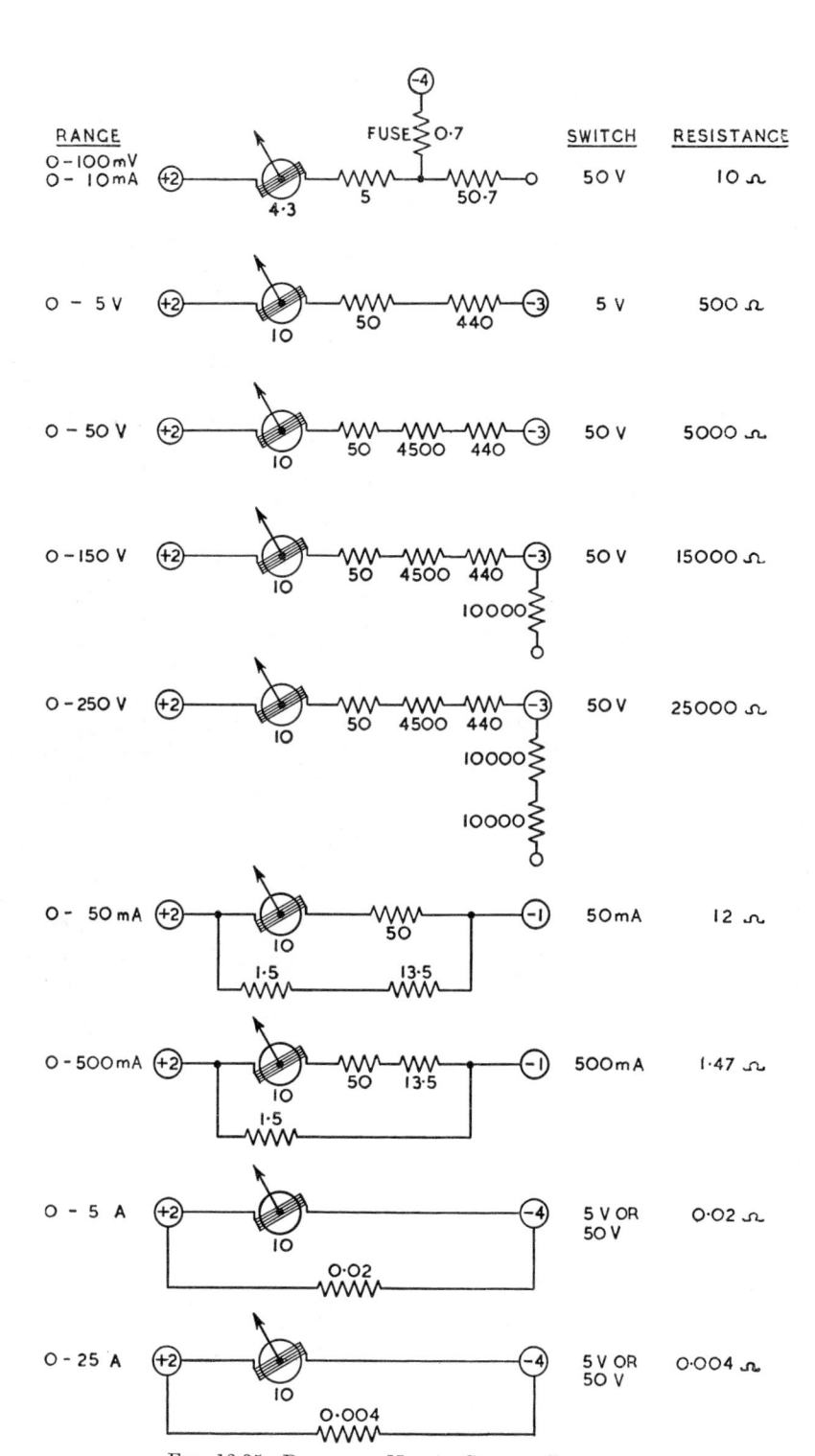

Fig. 12.35. Detector No. 4—Circuit Conditions
for Various Ranges

The meter scale is calibrated in 50 equally spaced divisions. Its current range is then from 0·2 mA to 5 A: its voltage range is from 2 mV to 250 V with a resistance of 100 Ω per volt. The conditions for the various ranges of measurement are given in Table 12.I. The circuit conditions of the Detector No. 4 under these various conditions are shown in Fig. 12.35.

TABLE 12.I

DETECTOR No. 4: RANGES OF MEASUREMENT

Range	Terminals	Switch Position	Value per Division	Total Resistance (ohms)	Shunt or Resistor in Use
10 mA	2 & 4	50 V	0·2 mA	10·0	Moving coil only
50 mA	2 & 1	50 mA	1 mA	12·0	Internal shunt
500 mA	2 & 1	500 mA	10 mA	1·47	Internal shunt
5 A	2 & 4	50 V*	100 mA	0·02	External shunt
25 A	2 & 4	50 V*	500 mA	0·004	External shunt
0·1 V	2 & 4	50 V	2 mV	10	Moving coil only
5 V	2 & 3	5 V	0·1 V	500	Internal resistance
50 V	2 & 3	50 V	1 V	5 000	Internal resistance
150 V	2 & 3	50 V	3 V	15 000	External resistance
250 V	2 & 3	50 V	5 V	25 000	External resistance

(* or 5 V)

12.15. The Avometer. This instrument is a multi-range moving-coil meter suitable for measurements of current and voltage, both A.C. and D.C., and of resistance: a model is also available which gives direct readings of capacitance, power, and power loss. First grade accuracy is given on d.c. measurements and on a.c. readings over the frequency range 25 to 1 000 c/s.

The movement consists of an aluminium former wound with copper wire and supplemented with constantan to reduce temperature error. The coil is pivoted upon hardened and highly polished steel points between conical sapphire jewels and swings in a gap energized by a powerful well-aged "alnico" magnet which ensures constancy in performance of the meter. Two phosphor-bronze hair springs are fitted for the purposes of conveying current to the moving coil and providing the controlling torque. A special type of pointer enables very fine readings to be taken: a mirror is fitted near the scales to prevent parallax errors. The moving system is considerably damped by eddy currents so that the pointer quickly comes to rest.

The model 40 instrument is illustrated in Fig. 12.36. It consists of a moulded panel on the inside of which are mounted the whole of the components such as switches, resistors, transformer and rectifier, as well as the moving system and permanent magnet. This panel fits into a dust-proof aluminium case equipped with a leather carrying strap. All range-switching is accomplished automatically by means of two selecting switches on the panel, each

being plainly marked so that the range in use appears opposite an arrowhead. No external apparatus is necessary and only two terminals are required to connect the instrument for any measurement: the meter leads are fitted with interchangeable spring clips and prods. An automatic cut-out is included to break the circuit in the event of an

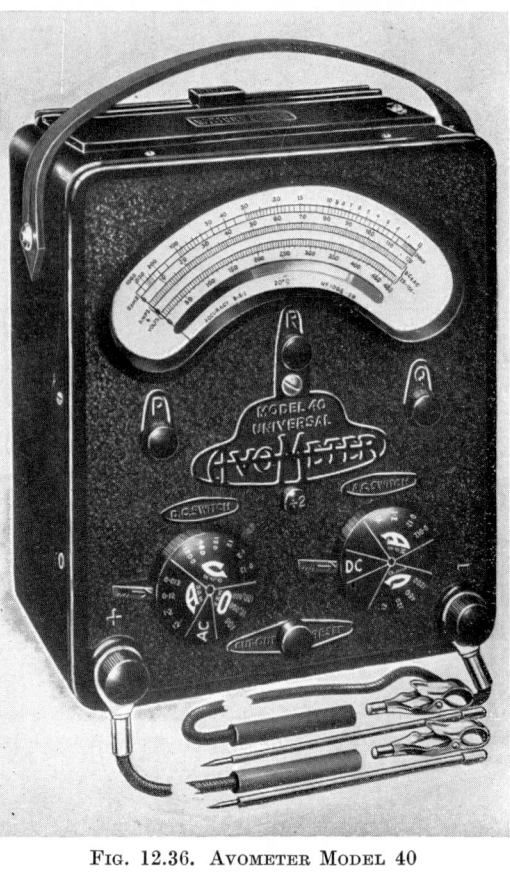

FIG. 12.36. AVOMETER MODEL 40
(Courtesy of Automatic Coil Winder & Electrical Equipment Co., Ltd.)

overload in the moving system: the cut-out is reset by depressing the projecting button after eliminating the cause of the overload. On moderate overloads the cut-out functions by the pointer passing the end of the scale, in either the forward or reverse directions. On severe overloads the cut-out is tripped due to the violent acceleration of the moving coil: the release can occur in this event when the pointer has travelled only about one-quarter of the distance across the scale.

The scales, approximately 5 in. long, are individually calibrated against a sub-standard instrument. The main scale is used for current and voltage

measurements, both a.c. and d.c., and is marked 0–120 with divisions of approximately 1 mm each. Another scale is calibrated 0–480 V in 5-V steps: this scale is used only in conjunction with the "480-V" position of the switch. An additional button marked " ÷ 2 " is provided which doubles the sensitivity of the moving system: if this button is depressed when less than half-scale current and voltage readings are obtained the deflexion is doubled, the normal full-scale values then being halved.

The current and voltage ranges available are tabulated below. External multiplying resistors and shunts are available for further extending these ranges if desired.

TABLE 12.II

Current and Voltage Ranges of Avometer
(Model 40)

Current (A.C. and D.C.)		Voltage (A.C.)		Voltage (D.C.)	
Range	Each divn.	Range	Each divn.	Range	Each divn.
0–6 mA	50 μA	0–6 V	50 mV	0–60 mV	0·5 mV
0–12 mA	100 μA	0–12 V	100 mV	0–120 mV	1 mV
0–60 mA	500 μA	0–60 V	500 mV	0–600 mV	5 mV
0–120 mA	1 mA	0–120 V	1 V	0–1·2 V	10 mV
0–600 mA	5 mA	0–240 V	2 V	0–6 V	50 mV
0–1·2 A	10 mA	0–480 V	5 V	0–12 V	100 mV
0–6 A	50 mA	0–600 V	5 V	0–60 V	500 mV
0–12 A	100 mA	0–1 200 V	10 V	0–120 V	1V
				0–240 V	2V
				0–480 V	5V
				0–600 V	5V
				0–1 200 V	10V

The arrangement of the Avometer when used as a d.c. voltmeter is shown in Fig. 12.37. This circuit, in common with the others, is led through both selecting switches: the meter circuit can then only be completed when one of the switches is in the a.c. or the d.c. position, and the movement is reasonably safeguarded against damage due to switches being left in an incorrect position. A set of series resistors is provided, the appropriate value for any reading being selected by the range switch. The depression of the ÷ 2 button removes the 20-Ω shunt from the moving coil and doubles the current flowing through it: at the same time, the 10-Ω series resistor is short-circuited to maintain the total resistance across the meter terminals at a constant value. On any range, for a full-scale deflexion the meter normally takes a current of 6 mA of which 3 mA only pass through the moving coil: if the ÷ 2 button is depressed, although the meter resistance remains constant, the full-scale current is reduced to 3 mA since the maximum voltage which can be applied is now halved.

The rectifier shunting the moving coil is in the

backward (non-conducting) direction for dire... currents in normal d.c. or a.c. measurement Should an a.c. overload be applied while the met... switches are in the d.c. position, most of the curre...

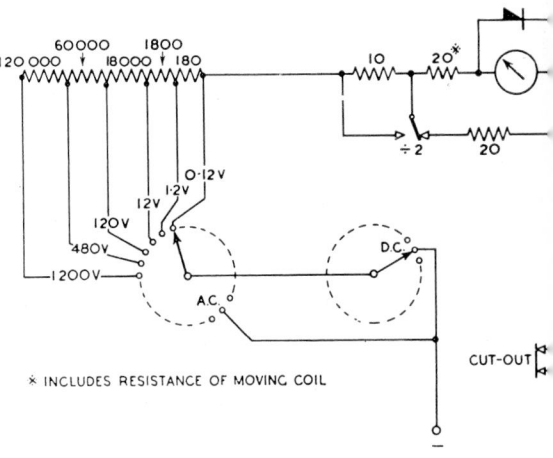

Fig. 12.37. Avometer Model 40—used as D.C. Voltmeter

during reverse half-cycles passes through the rect... fier: during forward half-cycles the full curre... passes through the moving coil and the consequen...

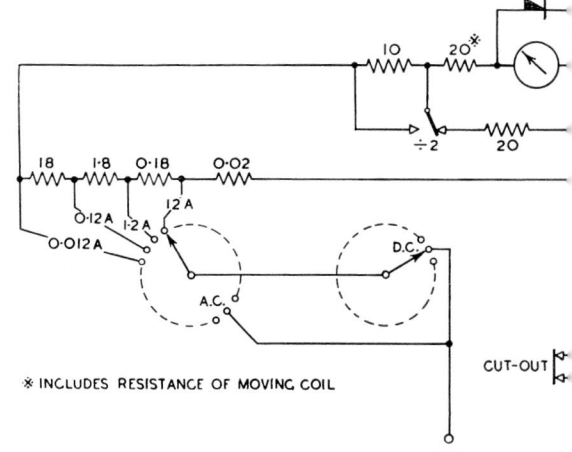

Fig. 12.38. Avometer Model 40—used as D.C. Ammeter

forward movement of the pointer trips the cut-o... as described above.

As a d.c. ammeter (Fig. 12.38) the principle ... the universal shunt is employed: the ÷ 2 facilit... is also available on these ranges.

For a.c. measurements the internal transform... and full-wave bridge rectifier are introduced. As

oltmeter (Fig. 12.39) series resistors, on the pri-
ary side, are selected for the higher voltage ranges:
r the low range (12 V) the voltage step-up trans-
rmer is used. The meter takes a current of
mA (3 mA using the ÷ 2 button) for full-scale
flexion on all a.c. voltage ranges except for the
w voltage (12 V) range: in the latter case the
nsumption is 60 mA (or 30 mA using the ÷ 2
utton). This relatively large current is occasioned
y the large number of ranges achieved with very
w scales, which makes for great simplicity in
ading. A current transformer is used (Fig. 12.40)

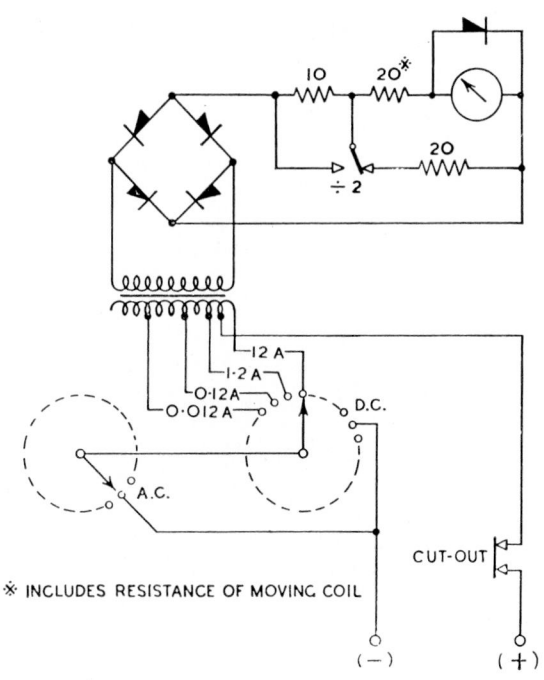

FIG. 12.40. AVOMETER MODEL 40—USED AS
A.C. AMMETER

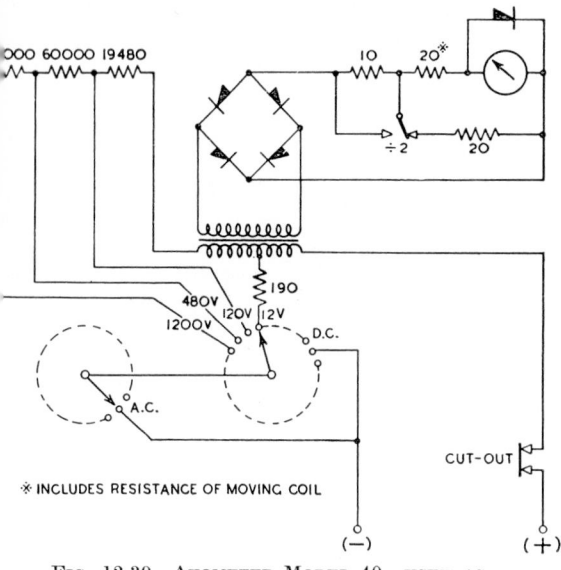

FIG. 12.39. AVOMETER MODEL 40—USED AS
A.C. VOLTMETER

r all current ranges: the ÷ 2 facility is available
r all these scales.

The third scale of the meter is calibrated for
sistance measurements. For this purpose the
eter functions as a milliammeter, using a constant
oltage supply, the scales being calibrated directly
ohms ($I \propto 1/R$). For the two lower ranges,
amely 0–1 000 Ω and 0–10 000 Ω, a 1·5 V cell
side the meter is used: for the higher range,
–100 000 Ω, a 9-V battery, also housed within the
eter, is used. A fourth range, 0–1 MΩ is available
sing an external source of p.d. The general prin-
ple of the ohmmeter circuit is shown in Fig. 12.41.
eparate rheostats are provided for adjusting the
ero when using either the 1·5-V or the 9-V battery
order to allow for any variation in battery volt-
ge. For the 10 000 Ω range shown in the diagram
e rheostat P compensates for variations in voltage
f the 1·5-V cell. The rheostat R compensates for

the resistance of the 1·5-V cell: it is mainly of use
in obtaining greater accuracy on the low range. The
zero on the ohms scales corresponds to full-scale
deflexion, obtained by short-circuiting the testing
leads. For resistance measurements it is only

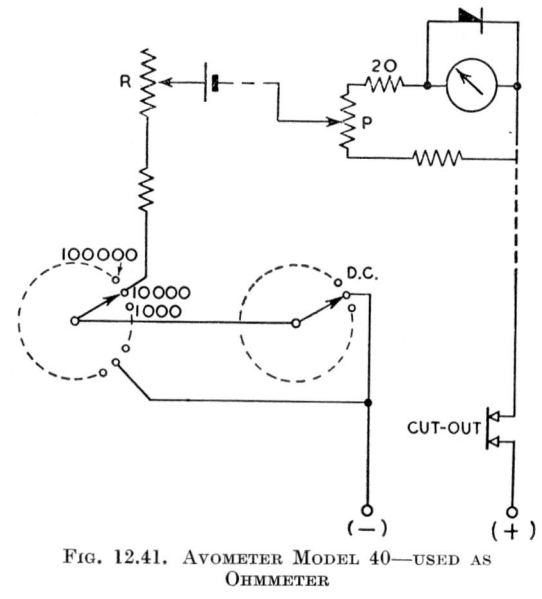

FIG. 12.41. AVOMETER MODEL 40—USED AS
OHMMETER

necessary to connect the leads across the resistor under test to obtain a direct reading in ohms upon the meter scale.

12.16. The Decibelmeter. Measurements of power loss (or gain) over a line or equipment can be made directly in decibel units with reference to some standard of power. In testing telephone plant a power of one milliwatt is used as the reference zero level: this corresponds to a p.d. of 0·775 V across a 600-Ω non-inductive resistor. Routine

FIG. 12.42. DECIBELMETER
(*Courtesy of P.M.G.*)

testing is usually carried out at 800 c/s and other single frequencies, using sinusoidal currents.

A decibelmeter usually takes the form of a high impedance rectifier-voltmeter with a scale calibrated in decibels. One instrument of this type is illustrated in Fig. 12.42: the two switch-arms shown in the accompanying circuit layout (Fig. 12.43) are mechanically coupled together. Three ranges of measurement are given, (i) − 15 to 0 db, (ii) − 5 to + 10 db, and (iii) + 5 to + 20 db. The instrument is accurate to within ± 0·5 db over the frequency range 50–5 000 c/s.

A voltage step-up transformer is employed in conjunction with the rectifier instrument, the turns ratio appropriate to each scale being selected

by a multi-contact switch. The instrument ma be used to measure the power level at some inter mediate point along a line: for this purpose th LEVEL positions of the switch are used and th instrument presents a high impedance shunt acros the line. Alternatively using the TRANS positio of the switch, the line is automatically terminate by a 600-Ω non-inductive impedance and the hig impedance meter is applied across this terminatio

The zero position of these instruments normall

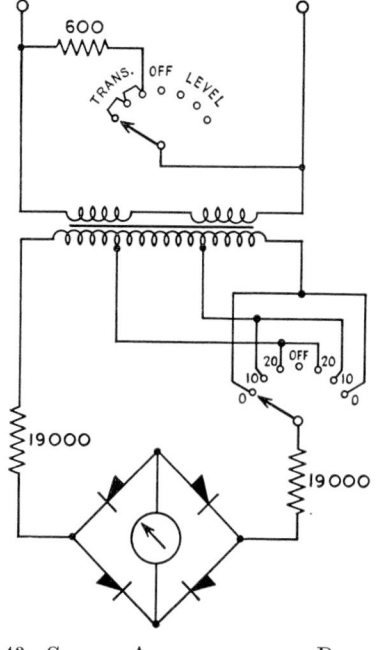

FIG. 12.43. CIRCUIT ARRANGEMENT OF DECIBELMETEI

lies some distance off the scale, a 0-db readin referring of course to the voltage measuremen quoted above: it is important that the zero i accurately adjusted always, this being done wit the terminals of the instrument disconnected.

12.17. The Millisecondmeter. If the restorin spring is removed from a moving-coil meter and th damping force is made very large compared wit the inertia of the moving system, the deflectin force due to a steady current will cause the pointe to move over the scale at a constant speed which i proportional to the value of the current: moreove the pointer will come quickly to rest when th current ceases and remain in position until restore to zero by a reverse current. Such a moving system having a constant velocity, is suitable for measure ment of short time intervals and the principle i used in one form of millisecondmeter.

A current of known magnitude for driving th

eter is conveniently obtained from the discharge
f a capacitor through a resistor with a given time-
onstant. The extent of the discharge is controlled
y the instrument whose time element is being
neasured: for example the operating or releasing
ime-lag of a relay "make" or "break" contact can
e measured by arranging for the commencement of
ne discharge to coincide with the closure or opening
f the relay coil circuit and for the discharge to
ease by operation of the contact being measured.

Such an arrangement produces a logarithmic
cale which may be calibrated directly in milli-
econds. Provided that the supply voltage remains
onstant, readings at 500 milliseconds may be made
vith an accuracy of ± 1.5 per cent, and down to
ne millisecond with but little error. Means are
rovided for adjusting and checking the p.d. across
he capacitor before making a measurement.

12.18. The Wheatstone Bridge. The Wheatstone
ridge is an apparatus employed for the accurate
neasurement of resistance, based upon a *null* or
ero deflexion method: a central-zero galvanometer
s used to indicate when a condition of balance is
btained in a resistance network. Modified forms
f the bridge are used for measurements of capaci-
ance, inductance, and impedance.

The operation of the bridge depends upon (i) the
niform fall of potential in a series circuit, and (ii)
he fact that no current will flow between two
oints when they are at equal potentials.

In the circuit of Fig. 12.44 (*a*), the same potential
xists at A and at A': similarly the potentials at
B and B' are equal. A current I flows from A to B,
nd a current I' flows from A' to B': the magni-
udes of these two currents may differ depending
pon the resistance values AB and $A'B'$. The
otential falls uniformly throughout the resistance
AB from A to B and it also falls uniformly from A'
o B' through the resistance $A'B'$. Whatever the
elationship between AB and $A'B'$, *for every point
n AB there is a corresponding point in $A'B'$ which is
t the same potential.* These two points can be
ocated by joining a galvanometer across them and
onfirming a zero deflexion.

In Fig. 12.44 (*b*), X and X' are assumed to be two
oints at equal potential: no current will flow in a
alvanometer which bridges these two points. If
he upper connexion of the galvanometer is moved
owards A to the point Y, this point will be at a
igher potential than X or X' and a current y flows
rom Y to X' through the galvanometer, producing
deflexion. Alternatively, if the upper connexion
f the galvanometer is moved towards B to point
Z, this point will be at a lower potential than X or
X', and a current flows from X' to Z through the
alvanometer producing a *reversed* deflexion.

Two points of balanced potential may be readily
determined by using a network in which one of the
arms is variable. This arrangement, used in resistance measurement, is depicted in Fig. 12.45. The

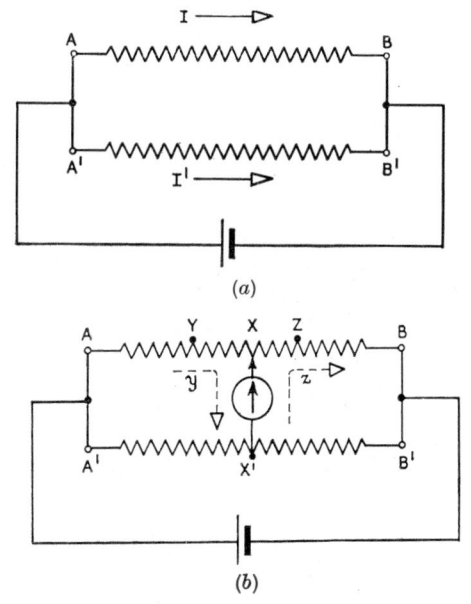

FIG. 12.44. PRINCIPLE OF WHEATSTONE BRIDGE

resistors P and Q, of fixed value, form the "ratio"
arms: X is the unknown resistance being measured
and R is a calibrated variable resistor. Suitable

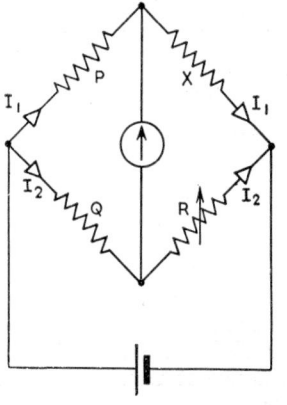

FIG. 12.45. ARRANGEMENT OF BALANCED
WHEATSTONE BRIDGE

adjustment of R produces equal potentials at the
galvanometer terminals, a condition indicated by no
current and zero deflexion. In this balanced condition the same current I_1 flows through P and X:
also the current I_2 is the same through Q and R.
Though I_1 and I_2 may or may not be equal, the p.d.

(I_1P) across P is equal to the p.d. (I_2Q) across Q: similarly the p.d. (I_1X) across X is equal to the p.d. (I_2R) across R. The following equality may now be written—

$$\frac{I_1P}{I_2Q} = \frac{I_1X}{I_2R}$$

Dividing both sides by I_1/I_2—

$$\frac{P}{Q} = \frac{X}{R} \text{ or } X = \frac{P}{Q} \cdot R$$

(If $P = Q$, $P/Q = 1$, and $X = R$.)

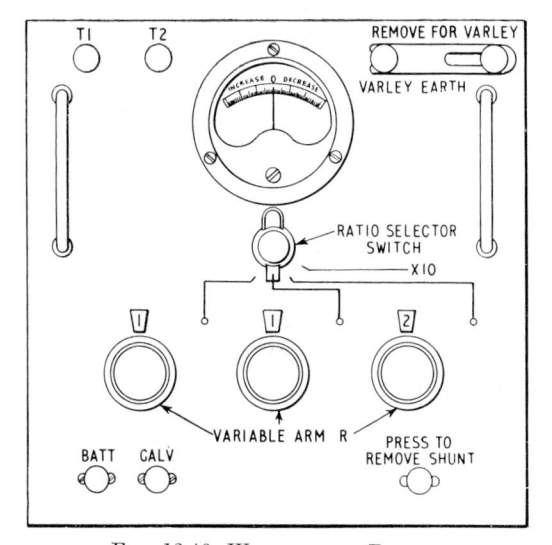

FIG. 12.46. WHEATSTONE BRIDGE

This relationship enables the value of an unknown resistance X to be measured in terms of a known calibrated resistance R ohms, modified by the ratio P/Q. The ratio of the resistors P and Q is made variable by means of a switch, so that the ratio P/Q may have any of the values 100, 10, 1, 1/10, or 1/100. By this means a wide range of unknown resistances can be measured from a limited range of the variable resistor R.

Bridge network problems may be solved with the aid of Kirchhoff's laws, but *provided that the bridge is balanced* the use of Ohm's law is adequate for such problems.

A self-contained portable direct-reading form of Wheatstone bridge is illustrated in Fig. 12.46: a separate compartment, not shown, houses two dry cells and the test leads for connexion to the terminals $T1$ and $T2$. This bridge covers a range of measurement from 1 to 9 990 Ω to three significant figures with an accuracy between ± 0.5 and ± 1.0 per cent. The variable arm of the bridge

contains three direct-reading decade rheostats 9×100, 9×10 and $9 \times 1 \Omega$: the value of resistance selected by rotating any control knob is displayed in a small window.

Three fixed ratio arms give ratios of $1:1$, $10:1$ and $100:1$ to an accuracy of ± 0.1 per cent. Selection of the range is made by a rotary switch whose operation also indicates where the decimal point should be read in relation to the three decade dials.

The galvanometer used is a centre-zero moving coil instrument with a full-scale deflexion of $12.$ μA: a mirror scale avoids errors due to parallax Switches are provided for bringing the galvanometer and the 3 V battery into circuit and also for increasing the effective sensitivity of the galvanometer when required, by disconnecting a $6-\Omega$ shunt and short-circuiting a 600-Ω series resistor from the circuit of the 350-Ω galvanometer.

The Wheatstone bridge is used for conductor resistance measurements and simple fault localization tests on lines: it also forms the basis of more complex line testing equipment. The battery and galvanometer connexions may be interchanged without affecting the bridge principle.

EXAMPLE 12.8 (A). In a particular measurement the ratio arms of the Wheatstone bridge were 1 000 Ω and 100 Ω respectively and the unknown resistance had one terminal common with the 100 Ω ratio arm. At balance the resistance of the balancing arm was 660 Ω. Calculate the value of the unknown resistance.

If on approaching balance, the balancing arm had been set at 649 Ω, indicate on a suitable sketch the direction in which the galvanometer current will flow with the positive battery lead connected to the common terminal of the unknown resistance and the 100 Ω ratio arm.

(C. & G.)

At balance (Fig. 12.47 (a))—

$$100 \times 660 = 1\ 000X, \ X = 66\ \Omega$$

Out of balance (diagram (b))—

If the p.d. across the bridge is V volts, then the p.d. across CD is

$$\frac{66 \times V}{66 + 649} = \frac{66 \times V}{715} = \frac{6 \times V}{65}$$

and the p.d. across AB is

$$\frac{100 \times V}{1\ 100} = \frac{V}{11} = \frac{6 \times V}{66}$$

The potential drop across CD is greater than the p.d. across AB: i.e. B is at a higher potential than D: current in the galvanometer will flow from B to D.

12.19. Ohmmeters. An ohmmeter is an instrument for measuring the electrical resistance of conductors and insulating materials, and provided with a scale graduated in ohms or megohms: in particular the name is applied to instruments of the moving-coil class. Direct reading ohmmeters require some form of electrical energy for their operation: this may

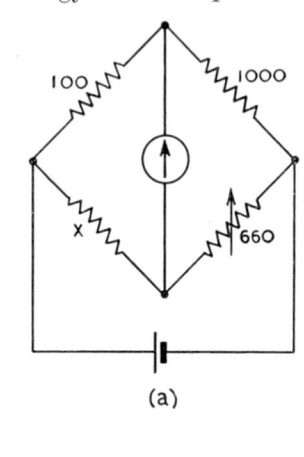

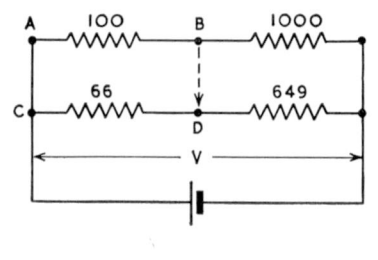

(b)

FIG. 12.47. (Example 12.8)

be provided from a battery, a generator, or a mains supply. Care should be taken to ensure that no current other than the testing current flows in the resistor under test. The meter deflexion is proportional to the current which passes through the resistor under test when a known p.d. is applied across it.

Instruments of this type used for direct reading of conductor resistance comprise a small battery connected to the resistance under test in series with a moving-coil meter which is, in effect, a voltmeter. The scale of such an instrument (Fig. 12.1 (d)) is calibrated from the graph plotted for

$$R = \frac{V - V_1}{V_1} \cdot M$$

where R = the resistance under test
M = the meter resistance

V = the p.d. across the meter for full-scale deflexion

V_1 = the p.d. across the meter with resistance R in series

The measured resistance

$$R = \frac{\text{p.d. across } R}{\text{current in } R \text{ (or meter)}} = \frac{V - V_1}{V_1/M}$$

$$= \frac{V - V_1}{V_1} \cdot M$$

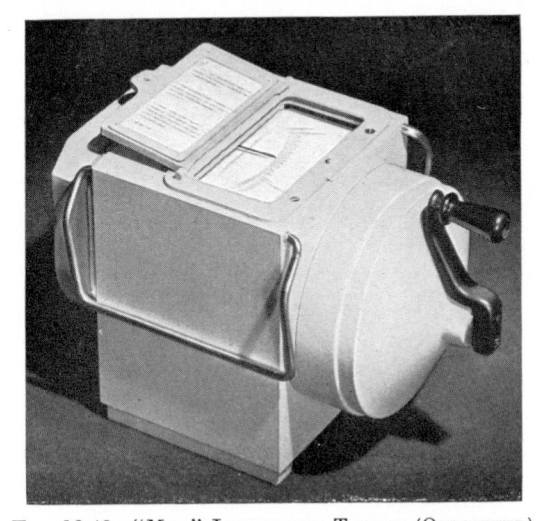

FIG. 12.48. "MEG" INSULATION TESTER (OHMMETER)
(*Courtesy of Evershed & Vignoles, Ltd.*)

The battery voltage is designed to be slightly greater than the full-scale p.d. to allow for zero (i.e. full-scale) adjustment by means of a rheostat: this is necessary to allow for battery variation, for the value V in the expression above must be constant.

In the type of instrument employed for measuring insulation resistance, the moving system comprising both a pressure coil and a current coil, is deflected under the action of mutually opposing electromagnetic forces. The force acting upon the pressure coil is dependent upon the current in that coil, which is practically proportional to the p.d. applied to the instrument terminals. The force acting upon the current coil is proportional to the current which flows in it: this is also the current in the external circuit. These two forces urge the moving system in opposite directions and the position taken up by the pointer is dependent upon the ratio p.d./current, i.e. on the resistance of the external circuit.

The ohmmeter illustrated in Fig. 12.48 consists of two parts, (i) the indicating system described

above, and (ii) a small hand-driven permanent magnet type of d.c. generator. The same permanent magnet system is utilized both for the moving system of the meter and for the generator field. The

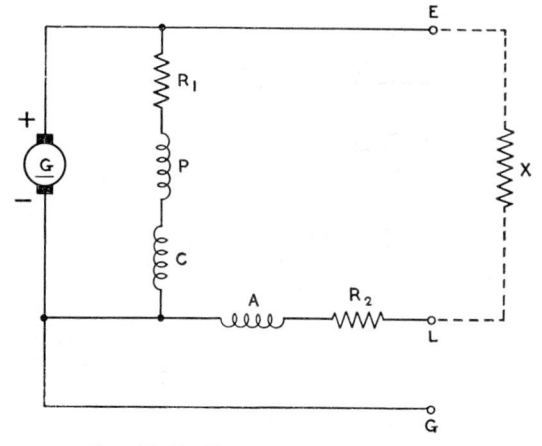

FIG. 12.49. PRINCIPLE OF OHMMETER

general principle of the meter is illustrated in Fig. 12.49. P is the pressure coil and A is the current coil: the generator maintains a constant p.d. across the pressure coil and also across the unknown resistance X connected to the ohmmeter terminals L and E: the same current flows through A and X.

handle through the intermediary of suitable gearing and a clutch. This clutch, of centrifugal type, is designed to slip at a critical speed of rotation— about 100 r.p.m.—in order that the armature speed and e.m.f. of the generator shall remain constant: the generated e.m.f. is 500 V in most instruments of this type. The generator commutator consists of four rings each of two segments, and each segment has a connexion to the armature: four pairs of carbon brushes, insulated from one another, are used. Constancy of terminal voltage is not in itself essential because the ratio V/I is being measured; it is, however, particularly important when testing circuits containing inductance or capacitance (underground lines, for example), for a variable voltage would produce surge currents and give unsteady readings.

The moving system, illustrated in Fig. 12.51, comprises three coils moving about a fixed cylindrical core which is split along its length: the whole system carrying the pointer is supported upon jewelled bearings. There is no mechanical controlling torque: connexions to the coils are made by fine phosphor-bronze strip.

The current coil A carries the current which flows in the external circuit connected to the meter terminals: its function is in every way similar to that of the moving coil of a milliammeter. Its current and torque are inversely proportional to

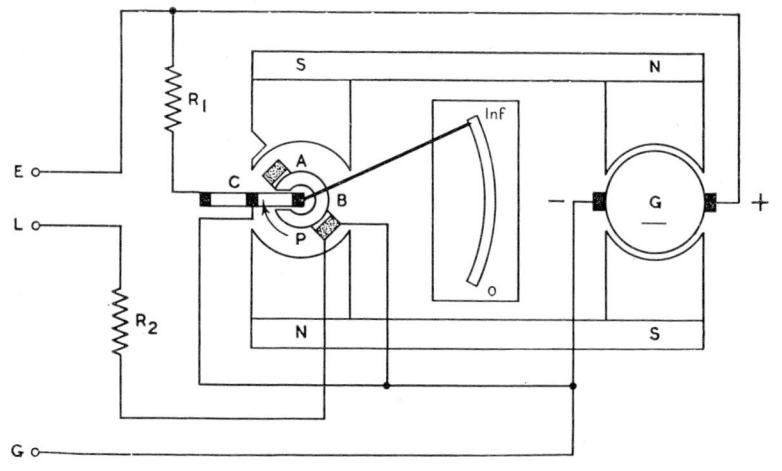

FIG. 12.50. OHMMETER—MAGNETIC AND ELECTRICAL CIRCUITS

The magnetic and electric circuits of the ohmmeter are shown in Fig. 12.50. Two powerful bar magnets fitted with pole-pieces provide the field for the generator at one end and for the moving system at the other. An e.m.f. is generated in the armature when it is rotated from the external

the resistance under test. A protective resistor R_2 is inserted in series to limit the maximum current value.

The pressure coil P with the compensating coil C is arranged approximately at right angles to the current coil. Connected in series they are energized

irect from the generator and provide the control-ing torque. A limiting resistor $R1$ is connected in eries with these coils. The compensating coil is ixed to the outer edge of the pressure coil. It is yound in opposition to the pressure coil, the two oils together forming an *astatic* pair: the combina-tion is largely independent of stray magnetic fields rom sources external to the instrument. A specially haped S pole-piece allows the compensating coil to

When the instrument is idle there is no current and no controlling torque on the moving system: the pointer is entirely free and will remain at any position on the scale. With the generator operating, if no connexion is made between terminals L and E, i.e. if the external resistance is infinitely high, no current will flow in the current coil: the pressure coil is polarized by current from the generator and it will set itself in the position shown in Fig. 12.50,

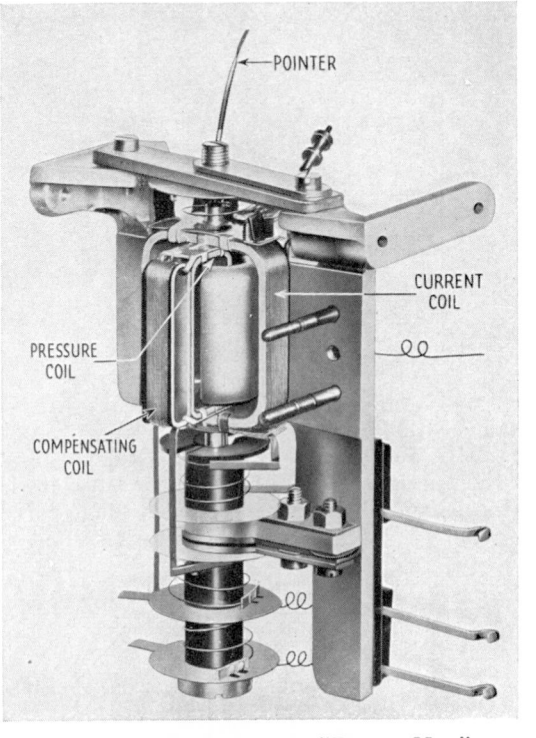

FIG. 12.51. MOVEMENT OF "BRIDGE-MEG" TESTING SET
(*Courtesy of Evershed & Vignoles, Ltd.*)

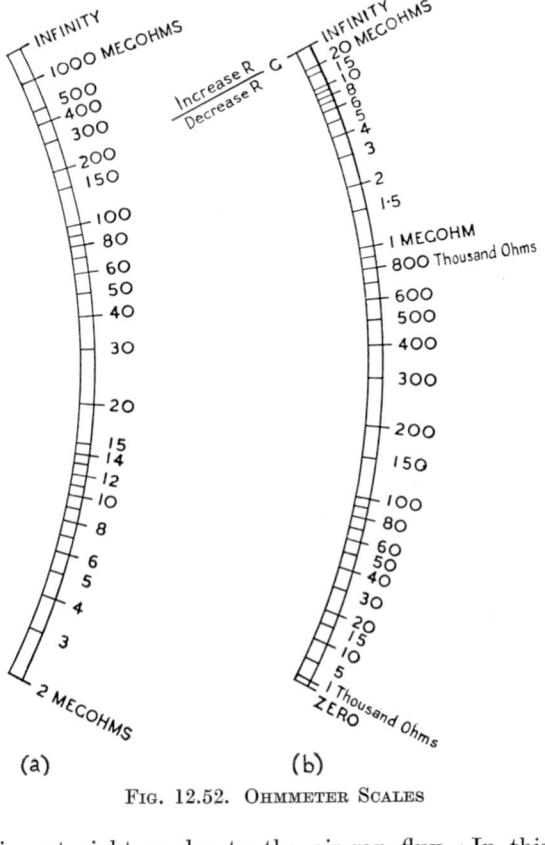

(a)   (b)

FIG. 12.52. OHMMETER SCALES

nove over it and so to oppose the force on the pressure coil.

The two external terminals are marked line (L) and earth (E). A third terminal, the guard terminal, or guard ring (G) is provided to prevent passage hrough the current coil of leakage currents flowing over the surface of the instrument between termi-nals L and E: the guard terminal is connected to the negative terminal of the generator. In measur-ing the insulation resistance of a cable, this guard erminal is connected to the insulating material between conductors and sheath of the cable in order o nullify the effect of any leakage current which passes over the open end of the cable.

i.e. at right angles to the air-gap flux. In this position the pointer is opposite to the INFINITY mark on the scale.

When a resistance is applied across the L and E terminals, a current (inversely proportional to the sum of the external and internal resistances) will flow in the current coil: this coil will tend to set itself at right angles to the flux lines but it is, how-ever, subjected to the opposing torque of the pressure coil. The current coil deflects the astatic system into a gradually increasing magnetic field and the moving system is held in equilibrium due to the balanced torques. The corresponding resistance value is indicated directly by the pointer against the scale.

If a low resistance is connected to the L and E terminals a relatively large current will flow in the current coil and produce a large torque: to counterbalance this the pressure coil is moving towards the position where the magnetic field is strongest. The compensating coil is now in the magnetic field of the projection of the S-pole and the force acting on it opposes the torque on the pressure coil. The moving system takes up a position such that the resultant torque due to the pressure and compensating coils is balanced by the torque of the current coil. The compensating coil in assisting the current coil at the lower resistance readings results in this portion of the scale being opened out. Meters are available to cover various resistance ranges: the scales of two typical ohmmeters are reproduced in Fig. 12.52.

An index adjuster in the form of an external knob is fitted to provide an accurate setting of the pointer over the infinity mark. On turning this knob, a small iron strip is moved across the field between the magnet pole pieces, thus altering slightly the disposition of the field about the pressure coil.

12.20. The Bridge Type Ohmmeter. This instrument combines the functions of an insulation resistance measuring instrument and a Wheatstone bridge. A general view of the instrument is shown in Fig. 12.53.

A change-over switch is provided to select the desired function: when this is set to MEGGER the purpose and conditions of the instrument are exactly as described for the ohmmeter. With the switch operated to BRIDGE the instrument is transformed into a Wheatstone bridge.

The main changes brought about by operating the switch to BRIDGE are as follows—

(i) The introduction of the ratio arms and of the 4-dial calibrated resistance.

(ii) The current coil is connected across the ratio arms and serves as the galvanometer for the bridge.

(iii) The generator system is modified, either by connecting the two armature windings in parallel, or by inserting a limiting resistance to reduce the e.m.f.: in the 500-V instrument the e.m.f. is reduced to 250 V.

(iv) The pressure coil is connected across the generator to provide a controlling torque.

The modified connexions of the ohmmeter when it is set for bridge working are shown in Fig. 12.54.

A separate dial enables the ratio arms to be set for $P/Q = 100, 10, 1, 0\cdot1,$ or $0\cdot01$. The 4-dial decade resistance box gives a maximum resistance of $9\ 999\ \Omega$, variable in steps of one ohm. Resistances may be measured over the range $0\cdot01\ \Omega$ to $999\ 900\ \Omega$.

With the unknown resistance connected to the

L and E terminals the handle is rotated up to the speed at which the clutch slips: the desired ratio having been set, the 4-dial box is manipulated until

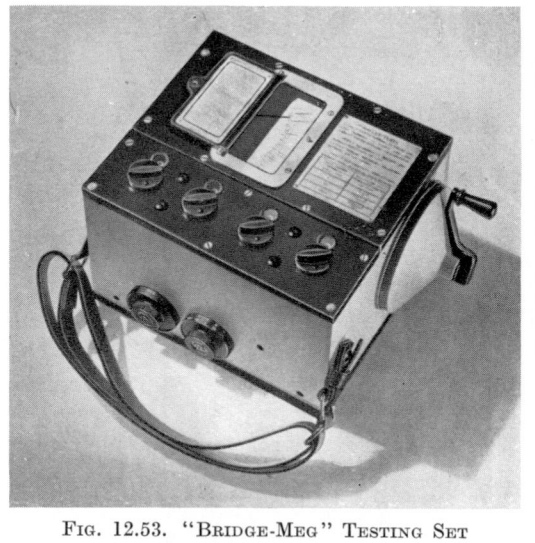

FIG. 12.53. "BRIDGE-MEG" TESTING SET
(Courtesy of Evershed & Vignoles, Ltd.)

a balance is obtained. The whole operation may be completed quickly with this form of bridge.

When no current passes in the current coil—i.e. in the balanced condition—the controlling torque

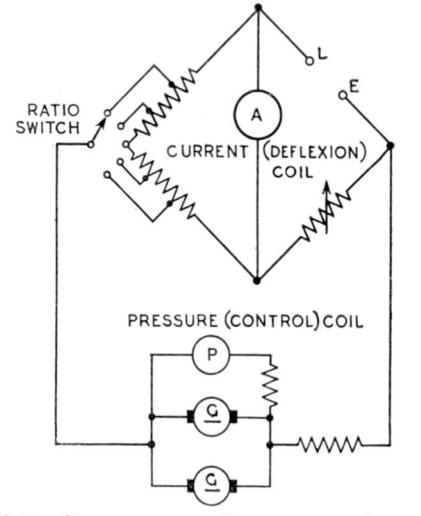

FIG. 12.54. CONNEXIONS OF BRIDGE-TYPE OHMMETER

provided by the pressure coil holds the pointer at the INFINITY mark. When the bridge is unbalanced, current may flow in the current coil in either direction: the pointer may then travel above

or below the infinity mark for which reason the scale (Fig. 12.52 (*b*)) carries the markings "Increase R" and "Decrease R."

via a rectifier unit from a.c. mains: a mains-operated instrument suitable for rack mounting is illustrated in Fig. 12.55B.

FIG. 12.55A. MOTOR-DRIVEN BRIDGE-OHMMETER
(Courtesy of Evershed & Vignoles, Ltd.)

Various patterns of bridge type ohmmeter are available. In Fig. 12.55A is illustrated an instrument which is driven by an externally mounted

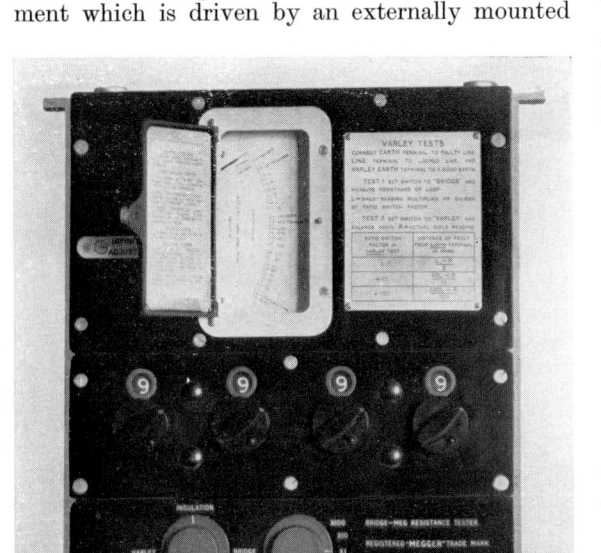

FIG. 12.55B. MAINS-DRIVEN BRIDGE-OHMMETER
(Courtesy of Evershed & Vignoles, Ltd.)

electric motor: a decade resistance box—of the type illustrated in Fig. 2.10—is also mounted externally. Another pattern of bridge-ohmmeter is operated either direct from a d.c. mains supply or

12.21. The Potentiometer. The potentiometer is extensively employed in precision measurements. Using this instrument an e.m.f. or a p.d. can be accurately measured by comparison with a standard cell: using a standard resistance accurate measurements of current and resistance can be made. In all cases, no current flows in any path

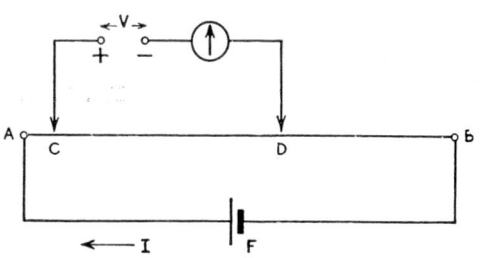

FIG. 12.56. PRINCIPLE OF POTENTIOMETER

where undesirable p.d.s would otherwise introduce errors.

In its simplest form the potentiometer, used as a measuring instrument, consists of a long wire AB (Fig. 12.56) of uniform cross-section stretched over a scale calibrated in equal divisions of length: the uniform wire has a resistance proportional to its length, and if a steady current is maintained in it from a secondary battery F the p.d. between any two points in the wire is proportional to the distance separating those points.

The circuit undergoing measurement is applied to the movable arms CD of the potentiometer (positive to positive) and the position of these is

varied until the p.d. being measured is equal to that tapped off by C and D—a condition indicated by zero deflexion in the galvanometer: if the potentiometer wire AB is calibrated, the value of the p.d. under measurement is known from the length CD.

Two assumptions are made in using this method: (i) that the current flowing in the wire AB is invariable; this is justified if a secondary cell is used and

previous calibration from a standard cell. For this purpose the standard cell is connected to the terminals $\pm A$ and the switch L is set to position AA. Dials C and D are set to read the known e.m.f. of the standard cell, for example 1·018 3 V (arm C on stud 101 and arm D on stud 83, equivalent to $(101 \times 0·01) + (83 \times 0·000\ 1) = 1·018\ 3$). The rheostats H and K are then adjusted until there is

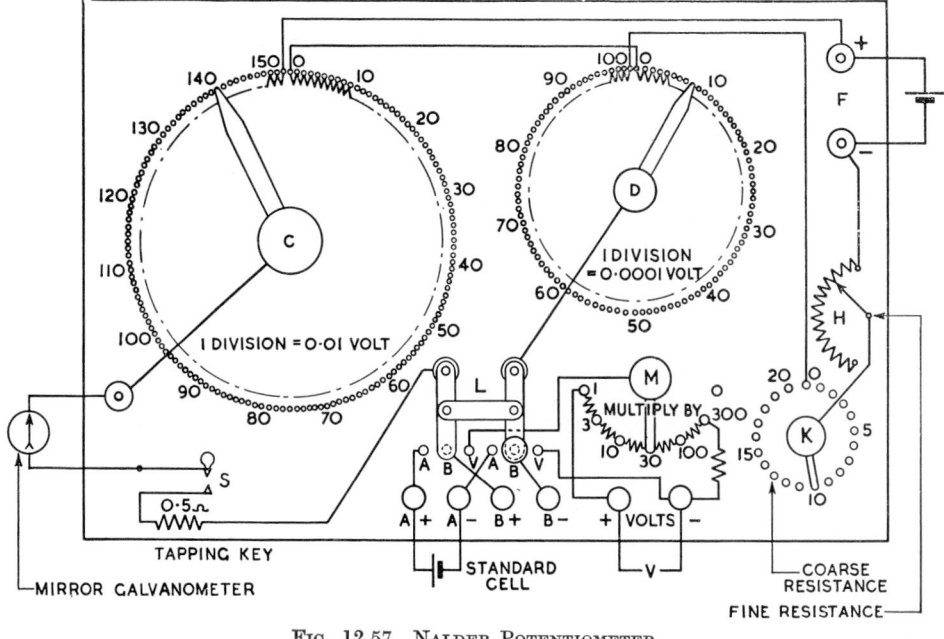

FIG. 12.57. NALDER POTENTIOMETER

the measurements are taken in rapid succession; (ii) that the wire AB is absolutely uniform in resistance; this error may be kept low by good design. It is important that the current flowing in AB should be kept at a low value to prevent rise in temperature.

The layout of the Nalder potentiometer is illustrated in Fig. 12.57. In this instrument the potentiometer resistance is tapped and brought out to contact studs over which switch arms C and D operate. Arm C is associated with 150 equal sections and arm D with 100 equal sections each one-hundredth of those of arm C. A secondary cell joined to the terminals $\pm F$ sends a current through the resistances connected with the dials C and D and then through rheostats K and H. A three-position switch L allows the galvanometer to be connected with one of three sets of terminals marked $\pm A$, $\pm B$, and $VOLTS$.

This instrument may be made direct reading by

no deflexion of the galvanometer when key S is closed. With the switch L in position BB the instrument now reads directly up to 1·51 V (the full range of the C and D switch arms).

An unknown p.d. can be applied to terminals $\pm B$ and arms C and D adjusted until there is no deflexion on the galvanometer when key S is closed. The value of the unknown p.d. can then be read off direct from the instrument: for example, supposing that arm C is on stud 123 and arm D is on stud 35, the p.d. is

$$(123 \times 0·01) + (35 \times 0·000\ 1) = 1·233\ 5\ \text{V}$$

The maximum p.d. which can be read directly is 1·51 V, but if position V of switch L is used in conjunction with the terminals $\pm VOLTS$ the range of the potentiometer is increased by 3, 10, 30, 100, and 300 times depending upon the position of switch M.

The instrument when used as described above is

irect reading for *current* measurements provided
hat a standard 1-Ω resistor is used: the p.d. in
olts measured across the 1-Ω resistor is numerically
qual to the current in amperes flowing through the
esistor.

When the potentiometer is used for resistance
omparisons terminals ± B only should be used and
he p.d. across the resistance should not exceed
·5 V.

Some typical potentiometer measurements are
escribed below: actually they are all measure-
ients of p.d.

(i) MEASUREMENT OF E.M.F. (Fig. 12.58). The
rue e.m.f. E volts of a cell can be measured at its
erminals by any method which takes no current

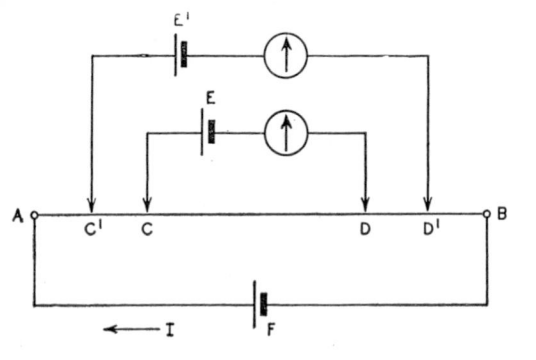

FIG. 12.58. POTENTIOMETER MEASUREMENT OF E.M.F.

rom the cell. The terminal p.d. (V volts) of a cell
; V = E − Ir, where r is the internal resistance.
f the current I = 0, then V = E. Using the
·otentiometer, no current flows in the circuit
rhich includes the cell when balance is obtained,
nd the true e.m.f. is measured.

A steady current is maintained in the potentio-
ieter wire AB to give a steady fall of potential. A
tandard cell E volts is connected in series with a
alvanometer and applied across the variable arms
'D of the potentiometer. One or both of the arms
re then adjusted until no deflexion is shown on the
alvanometer. The e.m.f. of the standard cell is
umerically equal to the p.d. across the points CD
ttained in the balanced state, i.e. the e.m.f. is
·roportional to the resistance CD.

The standard cell is then replaced by the cell E'
olts requiring measurement and the arms adjusted
o some position such as C'D' for which there is
gain no deflexion in the galvanometer—i.e. there
; no current in the cell under test. The e.m.f. of
his cell is proportional to the resistance C'D' and
he following relationship holds: $E/E' = CD/C'D'$.
f the ratio of the resistances ($CD/C'D'$) is accurately

known together with the e.m.f. of the standard cell,
the e.m.f. E' volts of the cell may be calculated.

If the potentiometer has been calibrated (as
described above for the Nalder potentiometer) the
e.m.f. of the cell may be read direct from the
balanced potentiometer.

It is important that the circuit is closed for a
short period only during the unbalanced condition

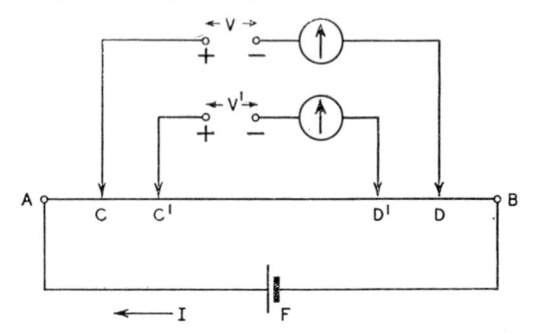

FIG. 12.59. POTENTIOMETER MEASUREMENT OF P.D.

for current will flow in this case and polarization
may occur.

(ii) MEASUREMENT OF P.D. (Fig. 12.59). The
source of p.d. (V' volts) to be measured is applied
in series with a galvanometer, across the variable
arms C'D' of the potentiometer (positive to positive):
one or both of these arms are adjusted until there is
no deflexion on the galvanometer. In this condition

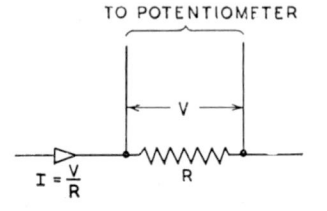

FIG. 12.60. POTENTIOMETER MEASUREMENT OF
CURRENT

the unknown p.d. V' volts is equal to the p.d. across
the points C'D' on account of the current flowing
in the wire AB from the cell F. The p.d. V' volts
is proportional to the resistance C'D'.

If this is repeated with another source of p.d.
V volts and the potentiometer adjusted (to CD)
until a balance is again obtained, the p.d. V volts
is proportional to the resistance CD.

Then $V'/V = C'D'/CD$. If the value of V is
known by previous calibration or by other means,
the exact value of V' may be calculated. If the
potentiometer is calibrated as described above the
value of V' may be read direct.

(iii) MEASUREMENT OF CURRENT (Fig. 12.60).

The current I amperes to be measured is passed through a resistance R ohms whose value is accurately known. The p.d. V volts across this resistance is then measured by a potentiometer as described in (ii) above. The current flowing is calculated from $I = V/R$ amperes. This method is applicable

TO POTENTIOMETER

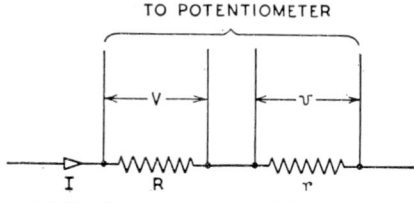

FIG. 12.61. POTENTIOMETER MEASUREMENT OF RESISTANCE

to the measurement of current below 1·5 A using a standard resistance of 1 Ω.

(iv) MEASUREMENT OF RESISTANCE (Fig. 12.61). For this purpose it is necessary to have a resistance whose value is accurately known. The known (R ohms) and unknown (r ohms) resistances are connected in series and a steady current I amperes

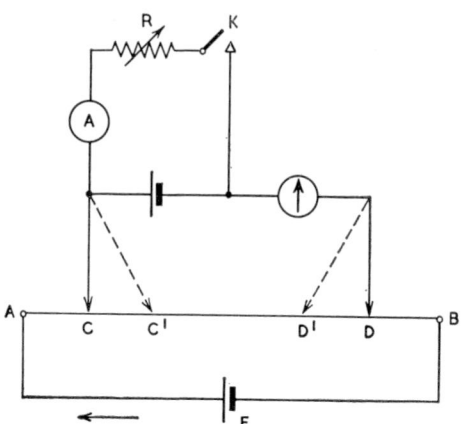

FIG. 12.62. POTENTIOMETER MEASUREMENT OF INTERNAL RESISTANCE

passed through the combination. The p.d. across each resistance is measured by the potentiometer. Then

$$\frac{IR}{Ir} = \frac{V}{v} \text{ and } r = R \cdot \frac{v}{V} \text{ ohms}$$

This method is suitable for p.d.s up to 1·5 V but is especially applicable to the measurement of very low resistances if a standard low resistance is available, since errors due to the resistance of connecting leads are eliminated.

(v) MEASUREMENT OF INTERNAL RESISTANCE OF A CELL (Fig. 12.62). From the relation between the

e.m.f. E volts and terminal p.d. V volts for a cell terms of the external resistance R ohms and t current flowing, viz.

$$I = V/R = E/(R + r)$$

the internal resistance r ohms may be expressed

$$r = R \cdot \frac{(E - V)}{V}$$

The internal resistance may be calculated from th expression after an accurate determination of t values of E and V by the potentiometer.

The e.m.f. of the cell is first measured as describ in (i) above by adjusting the potentiometer to su a position as CD. The key K is now closed to dra a local current from the cell and the potentiomet is readjusted to a position $C'D'$ to measure the p. V volts as described in (ii) above. The resistan R ohms being known for which V is obtained t internal resistance is then calculated from—

$$r = \frac{R(E - V)}{V} = R \cdot \frac{(CD - C'D')}{C'D'}$$

EXAMPLE 12.9 (A). A potentiometer, consisting of 10-Ω resistance wire one metre long, fitted with a slidi tapping point is to be used to measure the direct curre flowing through a 5-Ω resistor in a given circuit. Ad tional connexions can be made to the terminals of t resistor for the purpose of the measurement but the circu must not be broken. A standard cell of e.m.f. 1·018 V, centre-zero galvanometer, a supply battery for the pote tiometer, and the necessary switches are available. Dr carefully the circuit you would use in the measureme of the current.

The potentiometer is adjusted to give a balance at point 30·54 cm from one end when the standard cell connected. With the connexions arranged so as to me sure the external current, the balance is at exactly t mid-point of the potentiometer. Calculate the curre in the 5-Ω resistor.

(C. & C

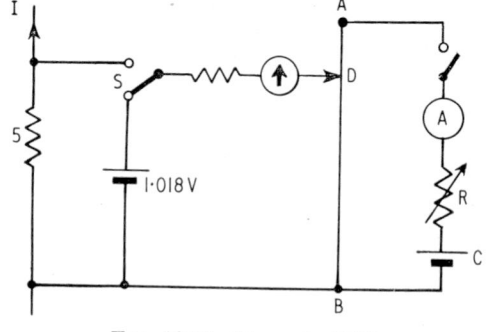

FIG. 12.63. (Example 12.9)

A suitable measuring circuit is shown in Fi 12.63. The 5-Ω resistor carries the current amperes to be measured. AB is the 10-Ω slid wire of the potentiometer, and a steady potenti

drop is maintained along the wire by supplying it with a constant current from a battery C. Resistor R affords pre-adjustment of this current to a convenient value and together with the ammeter A enables this current to be kept constant throughout a measurement.

Since the current in AB is constant and the resistance wire is uniform, by Ohm's Law the voltage drop per unit length along AB is constant. The p.d. between one end B of the wire and the sliding tap D will be proportional to the length DB provided that no current flows through the tapping contact to disturb the constancy of the current in AB.

The point D can be connected via the galvanometer to the 1·018-V standard cell (via a high resistance for safety), the other terminal of the cell being connected to B. Terminals of the standard cell and the supply battery connected to B must be of the same polarity. To calibrate the potentiometer the point D is moved along the slide wire until a position is found where the deflexion of the galvanometer is zero because the p.d. across the length BD of the slide wire equals that of the standard cell. No current flows at this point either in the standard cell or through the tap D. The potential difference from B to D is therefore equal to the e.m.f. of the standard cell, namely 1·018 V.

If now connexions are made by a change-over switch S so that the end of the 5-Ω resistor is connected to the sliding tap D, the sliding point can be readjusted to determine the new balance point. Let x be the new length BD, and d the length when the standard cell was balanced.

Then d represents a potential drop of 1·018 V. The potential gradient along the slide wire

$$= 1·018/d \text{ volts/cm}$$

The p.d. across the 5-Ω resistor

$$= 1·018 \times x/d \text{ volts}$$

In the example, $d = 30·54$ cm, $x = 50$ cm

The p.d. across the 5-Ω resistor

$$= 1·018 \times 50/30·54 = 5/3 \text{ V}$$

Current in the 5-Ω resistor $= \dfrac{5/3}{5} = \underline{\underline{\tfrac{1}{3} \text{ A}}}$

12.22. Measurement of Resistance. Methods of measuring resistance vary, according to the value of the resistance, the accuracy desired and the apparatus available. An approximate determination is sometimes all that is required: for this purpose the voltmeter method, used on exchange test desks, is adequate. For accurate measurements the Wheatstone bridge is used over the

mean resistance range, from an ohm or two to 10^5 or 10^6 ohms. Higher resistance measurements are made on an ohmmeter or if greater precision is required a comparative test is made against a standard resistance using a sensitive reflecting galvanometer. Low resistance tests are accurately made upon a potentiometer. Some methods which have not so far been described are given below.

(i) VOLTMETER-AMMETER METHOD FOR CONDUCTOR RESISTANCE (Fig. 12.64). If the p.d., V volts, across a resistor R ohms and the current I amperes flowing through it can be accurately measured, the value of the resistance can be readily calculated

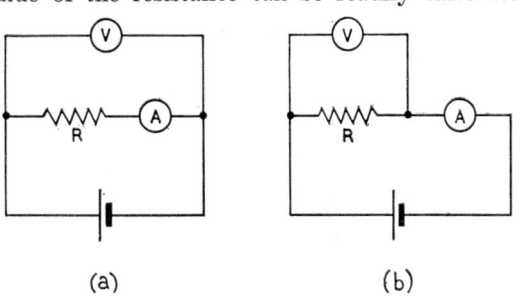

(a) (b)

FIG. 12.64. RESISTANCE MEASUREMENT BY VOLTMETER-AMMETER METHOD

from $R = V/I$ ohms. The difficulty lies in obtaining accurate readings of both V and I.

If an ammeter and a voltmeter are connected in a circuit with an unknown resistance R ohms as shown in Fig. 12.64 (a), the ammeter will read the true current I amperes flowing in the resistance, but the voltmeter reading, V volts, will include the p.d. across the ammeter. If the ammeter resistance is low compared with the value of R, the ratio V/I will give an approximately correct value for R. If the resistance r ohms of the ammeter is known, the voltage drop across the meter is Ir volts and the true p.d. across the unknown resistance is $(V - Ir)$: the true value of the resistor is then $R = \dfrac{(V - Ir)}{I}$.

If I and r are both small, Ir becomes negligible in comparison with V, and $R \simeq V/I$.

Alternatively the circuit may be arranged as shown in Fig. 12.64 (b): here the voltmeter reads the true p.d., V volts, across the resistor R ohms, but the ammeter reading now includes the current taken by the voltmeter. If the voltmeter resistance is high compared with the value of R, the ratio $R = V/I$ is approximately correct. If the voltmeter resistance is known, r ohms, the current in the voltmeter is V/r amperes and the true current flowing in the resistance is $(I - V/r)$ amperes. The correct value of the resistance is then $R = \dfrac{V}{(I - V/r)}$

ohms. If r is high, V/r becomes negligible in comparison with I, and $R \simeq V/I$.

(ii) VOLTMETER METHOD FOR INSULATION OR CONDUCTOR RESISTANCE (Fig. 12.65). This is a simple and speedy method for checking either the conductor loop resistance or the insulation resistance of telephone lines. A sensitive moving-coil meter giving a full-scale deflexion with a current of 0·4 mA is used with a battery of 8 V or 80 V: series resistors of 20 000 Ω and 200 000 Ω respectively are used to limit the current to the figure given above.

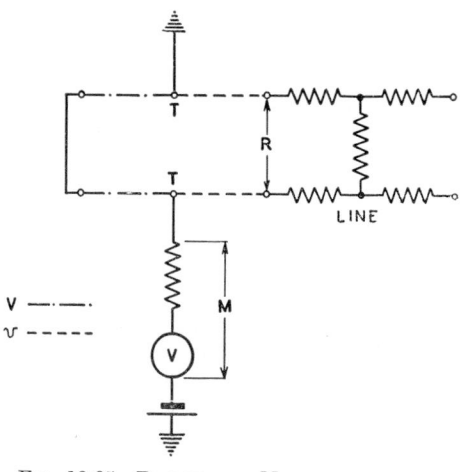

FIG. 12.65. RESISTANCE MEASUREMENT BY
VOLTMETER

For the insulation resistance measurement the testing circuit conditions are shown in Fig. 12.65: the line is open-circuited at the distant end. The battery voltage is first measured by short-circuiting the testing terminals TT: this produces a full deflexion V volts on the meter, which may vary slightly according to the state of the battery. The testing terminals are then connected to the line and a reduced deflexion v volts is obtained. If I amperes is the current in this condition and R ohms is the line resistance, the p.d. across the line is—

$$V - v = IR$$

Also, $v = IM$ where M is the total voltmeter resistance, whence—

$$\frac{V - v}{v} = \frac{R}{M}$$

and $R = M\frac{(V - v)}{v} = M\left(\frac{V}{v} - 1\right)$ ohms

For measuring the conductor resistance, similar conditions apply, the line being short-circuited at the distant end. For greater accuracy, an insulation test is first made from wire to wire and from each wire to earth to ensure that the insulation resistance is of a high order. A test is also made to confirm the absence of any stray potential on the line. This method would only be used as a rough check, the Wheatstone bridge being used for an accurate measurement.

Tables enable the value of R to be read for various deflexions (V and v) for the particular voltmeter (M). In making the conductivity test, a one-tenth shunt is usually applied to the low range of the voltmeter reducing its resistance to

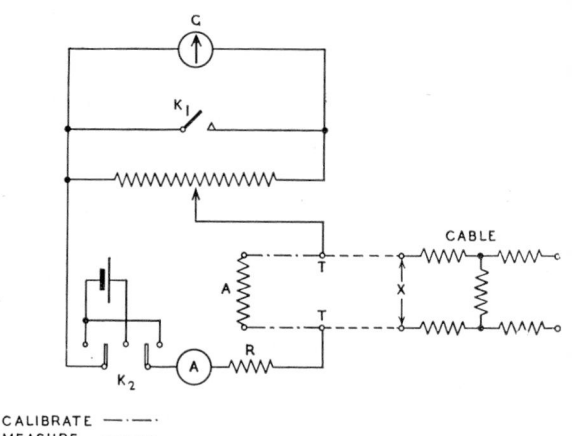

CALIBRATE ─ ─ ─ ─·
MEASURE ─ ─ ─ ─

FIG. 12.66. MEASUREMENT OF INSULATION RESISTANCE
BY DEFLEXION METHOD

2 000 Ω. In all cases, the meter resistance should be comparable to the resistance under test so that $(V/v - 1)$ shall be as large a factor as possible, and any error resulting from incorrect readings shall not be unduly magnified due to M being great.

(iii) DEFLEXION METHOD FOR INSULATION RESISTANCE (Fig. 12.66). This method of measuring insulation resistance is suitable where a more precise measurement is required than that obtainable with an ohmmeter or where the testing voltage must be lower than that used in the ohmmeter (for example, to avoid damaging loading coils): it is used extensively in cable testing.

The method consists in calibrating the deflexion of a galvanometer using a standard resistance—usually a megohm—and then substituting the resistance to be measured. The value of the unknown resistance is calculated from the relation between the two deflexions.

The arrangement of the testing equipment is shown in Fig. 12.66. A reflecting galvanometer G is used in conjunction with a universal shunt and a short-circuiting key $K1$. The testing battery is

pplied through a special form of key $K2$, a detector No. 4, and a protective resistance R of 40 000 Ω. The levers of $K2$ may be moved separately: the battery polarity is reversed by using either the left-hand or the right-hand pair of contacts, and when the outer pair is used the battery is disconnected and the cable is discharged through the 40 000-Ω resistor. All the equipment has high grade insulating properties.

Two tests are made: (i) using the standard megohm, and (ii) with the cable under test. Using a standard megohm resistor across the terminals TT, the testing battery is applied to the circuit, the short-circuiting key $K1$ opened and the universal shunt adjusted to give a useful deflexion on the galvanometer. Let D_1 and M_1 be the deflexion and shunt multiplying power respectively in this test. The short-circuiting key $K1$ is now closed, the shunt set to zero and the battery disconnected.

The above test is repeated using the cable under test in place of the megohm resistor. Let D_2 be the deflexion after one minute's electrification and M_2 the shunt multiplying power used. At the conclusion of this test the line is discharged through the protective resistance after the galvanometer has been short-circuited.

If V is the voltage of the battery—which must be the same for each test—A megohms is the standard resistance, and X megohms is the resistance under test, then if the resistances of the galvanometer and shunt and the internal resistance of the battery are small compared with the other resistances in circuit—

the current flowing through A is I_1

$$= V/(A + R) \text{ microamperes,}$$

the current flowing through X is I_2

$$= V/(X + R) \text{ microamperes.}$$

The current ratio is $I_1/I_2 = (X + R)/(A + R)$, and since the deflexion of the galvanometer is proportional to the current flowing through the galvanometer this ratio is equal to—

$$\frac{D_1 M_1}{D_2 M_2} = \frac{X + R}{A + R}$$

i.e. $$X = \left[\frac{D_1 M_1 (A + R)}{D_2 M_2} - R\right] \text{ megohms}$$

Substituting the known values—

$$X = \frac{(1{\cdot}04 D_1 M_1 - 0{\cdot}04)}{D_2 M_2} \text{ megohms}$$

The value of $D_1 M_1(A + R)$ obtained from a deflexion with a standard resistance is known as the

"galvanometer constant": it is the deflexion that would be given for a total series resistance of one megohm with the shunt in the "× 1" position. This value depends upon the voltage of the testing battery.

(iv) VOLTMETER METHOD FOR INTERNAL RESISTANCE. The approximate value of the internal resistance r ohms of a primary cell may be measured by the use of a high-resistance voltmeter and a 2-Ω resistance. The voltmeter is first applied direct across the cell terminals and an "open-circuit" deflexion V_1 volts is obtained, which approximates to the e.m.f. of the cell. The 2-Ω resistor R is then applied across the cell terminals and the reading V_2 volts taken immediately, before polarization commences.

The voltage drop in the internal resistance is

$$V_1 - V_2 = Ir$$

Also, $$I = \frac{\text{e.m.f.}}{\text{total resistance}} = \frac{V_1}{R + r}$$

$$V_1 - V_2 = \frac{V_1 r}{R + r}$$

$$\frac{R + r}{r} = \frac{V_1}{V_1 - V_2}$$

$$\frac{R}{r} = \left(\frac{V_1}{V_1 - V_2} - 1\right) = \frac{V_2}{V_1 - V_2}$$

and, $$r = R\left(\frac{V_1 - V_2}{V_2}\right) \text{ ohms}$$

(v) EARTH RESISTANCE. The maximum allowable resistance of an earth connexion is usually specified in order to limit the p.d. and interference which may result between circuits.

(a) *Pomeroy's Method* (Fig. 12.67). In this method of determining the resistance of an earth connexion, two measurements are made using two lines connected to independent earth plates. The current passing at the earth plate under test should be approximately equal in each case: for the second measurement the battery connexions are reversed so that the direction of the current is the same for both tests.

The resistance of the earth connexion which terminates LINE 1 is included in the value L: the resistance of the earth connexion under test is represented by X ohms. (The earth resistance in LINE 2 does not enter into the calculation.)

1st Test (Fig. 12.67 (*a*)): $P(R' + X) = QL$

2nd Test (Fig. 12.67 (*b*)): $PR = Q(L + X)$

whence $$X = \frac{P(R - R')}{(P + Q)}$$

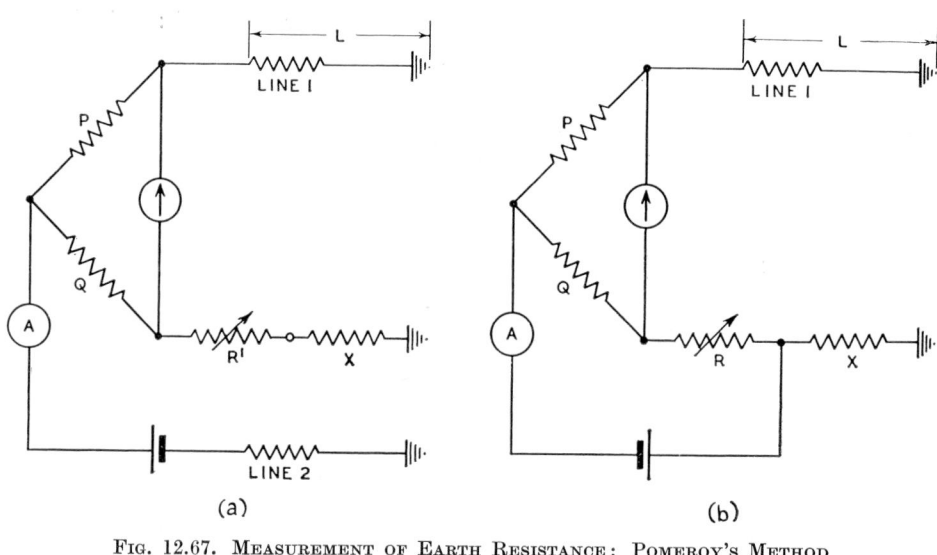

(a)   (b)

FIG. 12.67. MEASUREMENT OF EARTH RESISTANCE: POMEROY'S METHOD

If equal ratio arms are used, $P = Q$ and

$$X = \frac{(R - R')}{2}$$

The accuracy of this method may be impaired by polarization e.m.f.s at the earth plates, or by the presence of stray earth currents.

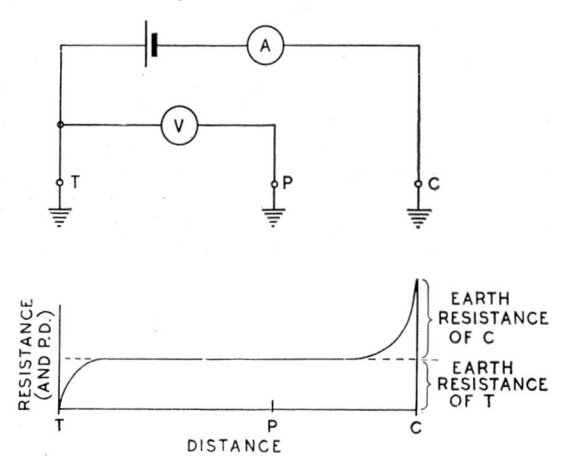

FIG. 12.68. MEASUREMENT OF EARTH RESISTANCE: FALL OF POTENTIAL METHOD

(b) *Fall of Potential Method* (Fig. 12.68). Temporary earth connexions P and C are provided for this measurement. A current I amperes flows from the battery between the earth plate T under test and the "current" earth plate C. Provided that T, P, and C are each separated by several feet, the

potential spike P will be in a region of sensibl constant earth potential: this is because the resi tance between an electrode and the earth itself concentrated very closely in the region of the elec trode. The voltmeter reading (V volts) gives th

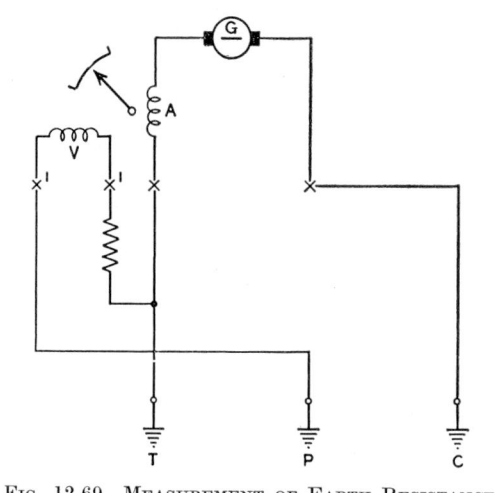

FIG. 12.69. MEASUREMENT OF EARTH RESISTANCE USING "MEGGER" EARTH TESTER

p.d. between the earth plate T and the earth itsel The required earth resistance is equal to

$$R = V/I \text{ ohms}$$

The accuracy of this method also is subject to th absence of polarization e.m.f.s and stray eart currents.

(c) *The "Megger" Earth Tester* (Fig. 12.69). The use of an alternating current for the measurement of earth resistance eliminates errors due to polarization e.m.f.s and stray earth currents: a low frequency is employed to reduce "skin" effects.

In the "Megger" earth tester, a d.c. generator and two commutators are mounted upon a common shaft which is rotated by hand. Except that alternating current is used in the earth circuits the test is based upon the same principle as that described in (b) above, using Potential and Current electrodes P and C in conjunction with the earth plate T under test. The d.c. supply from the generator is converted to A.C. at about 50 c/s by means of the commutator XX. The p.d. picked up between the potential electrode P and the earth plate T is rectified by the synchronous commutator X'X' which produces a d.c. voltage proportional to the a.c. voltage between P and T. A direct reading of resistance is given upon the scale of an ohmmeter. The current coil A and the pressure coil V are mounted upon the same moving system and produce opposing torques so that the deflexion is proportional to the ratio p.d./current.

Stray alternating currents from the earth electrodes cannot introduce errors for they can affect only the voltage coil (V) where their presence may result in a superimposed vibration of the pointer: by turning the handle faster or slower the testing frequency is changed and the stray current frequency is insufficiently close to maintain vibration.

The correct location of electrode P—referred to in (b) above—is important: in testing, a number of measurements should be made for different positions of P—and C also if necessary—until a series of constant resistance readings indicates that a true reading is obtained.

12.23. Inductance Measurement.
Inductance is preferably measured using the a.c. bridge. Simple methods of making approximate measurements are described below.

(i) IMPEDANCE METHOD (Fig. 12.70). The resistance R ohms of the inductor is first measured by using a Wheatstone bridge. An alternating current at 50 c/s, or other known frequency $\omega/(2\pi)$ c/s, is then passed through the coil and the current I amperes and the p.d. V volts read upon the meters.

From the current equation—

$$I = \frac{V}{(R^2 + \omega^2 L^2)^{\frac{1}{2}}}, \quad L = \frac{1}{\omega I}\sqrt{V^2 - I^2 R^2} \text{ henrys}$$

(ii) RESONANCE METHOD (Fig. 12.71). This method uses the property of the series resonant circuit. The inductor is connected in series with a calibrated variable capacitance and an ammeter to

an a.c. supply of known frequency $\omega/(2\pi)$ c/s. The capacitance C farads is adjusted until a maximum reading upon the ammeter indicates resonance. In this condition—

$$\omega L = 1/(\omega C), \text{ and } L = \frac{1}{\omega^2 C} \text{ henrys}$$

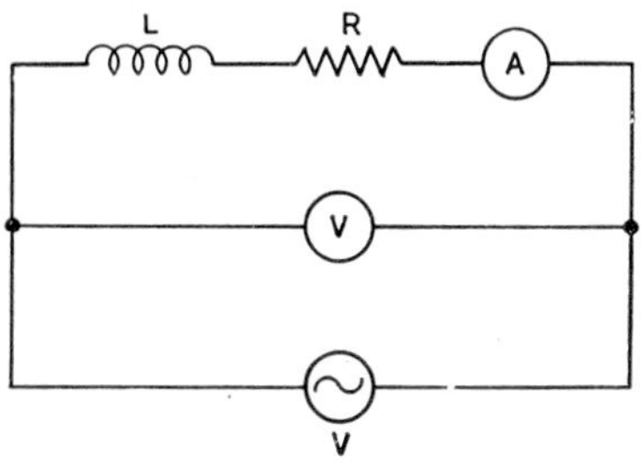

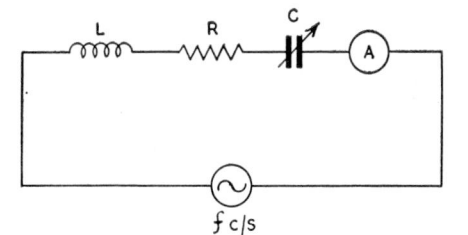

FIG. 12.70. MEASUREMENT OF INDUCTANCE:
IMPEDANCE METHOD

Alternatively a fixed value of capacitance may be used and the frequency of the supply varied until resonance is obtained.

(iii) MUTUAL INDUCTANCE. If the separate inductances L_1 and L_2 of two coils are measured as described in (i) above and their combined inductance L_3 is then measured in the same way, their mutual

FIG. 12.71. MEASUREMENT OF INDUCTANCE:
RESONANCE METHOD

inductance M may be calculated from the expression—

$$L_3 = L_1 + L_2 \pm 2M$$

from which $\quad M = \pm \dfrac{L_3 - (L_1 + L_2)}{2} \text{ henrys}$

12.24. Capacitance Measurement.
Capacitance measurements are preferably made using the a.c. bridge. Three methods of making approximate measurements are described below.

(i) BALLISTIC METHOD (Fig. 12.72). This is a comparative method employing a known capacitance, and a ballistic galvanometer BG the deflexion of which is proportional to the quantity of electricity passing through it. The capacitor under test

(C' microfarads) is charged to a p.d. of V volts by depressing the key K. On releasing the key the capacitor discharges through the galvanometer producing a deflexion D'. The capacitor is replaced by one of known capacitance C microfarads and a

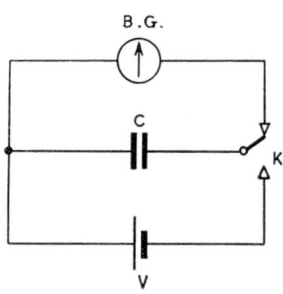

FIG. 12.72. MEASUREMENT OF CAPACITANCE:
BALLISTIC METHOD

deflexion D is obtained. Since the charge Q on a capacitor is equal to the product CV—

$$\frac{D}{D'} = \frac{Q}{Q'} = \frac{CV}{C'V}, \text{ whence } C' = \frac{C \cdot D'}{D} \text{ microfarads}$$

(ii) D.C. BRIDGE METHOD (Fig. 12.73). Using a capacitor of known value C microfarads, the value

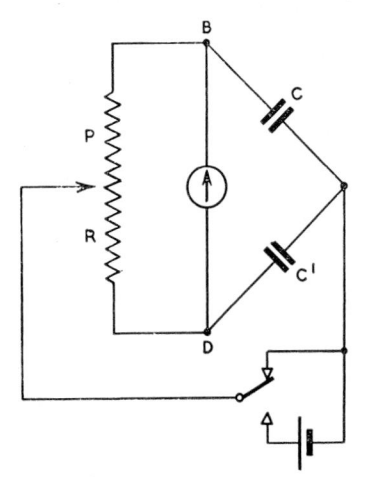

FIG. 12.73. MEASUREMENT OF CAPACITANCE
USING D.C. BRIDGE

C' microfarads of a second capacitor may be measured by the use of a d.c. bridge circuit.

When the battery key is depressed, the capacitors are charged but no deflexion will be obtained in the galvanometer if the points B and D are at the same potential. This balanced state may be obtained by adjustment of the potentiometer, the release of the battery key discharging the capacitors after each trial adjustment of the potentiometer. When the

bridge is balanced, if the charges on the capacitors C and C' are Q and Q' respectively at any instant dt seconds after closing the key, the potential V volts at the point B is equal to that at point D, and

$$V = \frac{Q}{C} = \frac{Q'}{C'}, \text{ whence } \frac{Q}{Q'} = \frac{C}{C'}$$

If the resistance arms are P and R ohms respectively at balance, the current flowing in P is Q/dt amperes

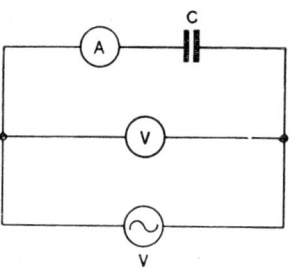

FIG. 12.74. MEASUREMENT OF CAPACITANCE:
IMPEDANCE METHOD

and that through R is Q'/dt amperes. These currents are proportional to the conductances, so that

$$\frac{Q}{Q'} = \frac{R}{P} = \frac{C}{C'}, \text{ and } C' = C \cdot \frac{P}{R} \text{ microfarads}$$

(iii) IMPEDANCE METHOD (Fig. 12.74). Applying an alternating current of known frequency $\omega/(2\pi)$

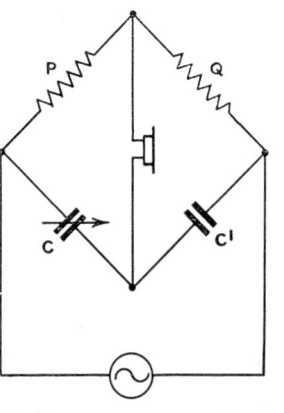

FIG. 12.75. MEASUREMENT OF CAPACITANCE
USING SIMPLE A.C. BRIDGE

c/s at a p.d. of V volts across the capacitor C farads, the current I amperes is measured.

From the current equation $I = V\omega C$—

$$C = \frac{I}{\omega V} \text{ farads}$$

(iv) SIMPLE A.C. BRIDGE (Fig. 12.75). For measurement of pure capacitance, a simplified form

of the a.c. bridge is to be preferred to the methods described above. This a.c. bridge is similar to the d.c. Wheatstone bridge in principle.

An a.c. supply is used, preferably from a variable frequency source so that any testing frequency can be selected. The balanced condition is detected either by minimum tone in a telephone receiver (audio frequencies) or by zero deflexion on a thermo-couple instrument (high frequencies). The unknown capacitance C' microfarads is balanced against a calibrated variable capacitor C microfarads. The resistance ratio P and Q may be variable exactly as for the Wheatstone bridge, permitting a wide range of capacitance to be measured: these ratio arms must be non-inductive, though any inductance should cancel out if equal ratio arms are used.

The bridge actually measures the reactance of the capacitance: this is equal to $1/(2\pi fC)$, i.e. inversely proportional to the capacitance. For capacitances the bridge relationship is accordingly inverted (compared with the resistance bridge), and—

$$\frac{P}{Q} = \frac{C'}{C}, \text{ or } C' = C \cdot \frac{P}{Q} \text{ microfarads}$$

If the capacitance being measured has an appreciable resistance component, i.e. the power-factor is not zero as it would be for a perfect capacitor, this simple bridge is not suitable: in such a case the Max Wien bridge should be used.

12.25. The A.C. Bridge. The alternating current bridge is an extension of the Wheatstone (d.c.) bridge: it is used for measurements of impedance, reactance, inductance, capacitance, and frequency. For each of these purposes some variant of the basic a.c. bridge is employed with the result that many forms of a.c. bridge are available, all differing slightly in detail.

The general arrangement of the a.c. bridge is illustrated in Fig. 12.76. The bridge is energized from an a.c. supply fed through a screened and balanced transformer: a variable frequency oscillator is employed as the a.c. source in order that measurements can readily be made at any desired frequency. A telephone receiver is commonly used as the instrument for detecting the balanced condition: the receiver is preferably of the head-gear pattern so as to leave both hands free for adjustment of the bridge elements. For the bridge to be balanced equal potentials must be obtained at points B and D: the phase angles must also be equal.

If the p.d. applied across the path ABC is V volts, the p.d. across AB is equal to

$$V \times \frac{Z_1/\underline{\phi_1}}{Z_1/\underline{\phi_1} + Z_2/\underline{\phi_2}}$$

With the same p.d. applied across the path ADC, the p.d. across AD is equal to

$$V \times \frac{Z_4/\underline{\phi_4}}{Z_4/\underline{\phi_4} + Z_3/\underline{\phi_3}}$$

From the equality of these potentials across AB and AD at balance it follows that—

$$Z_1/\underline{\phi_1} \times Z_3/\underline{\phi_3} = Z_2/\underline{\phi_2} \times Z_4/\underline{\phi_4}$$

or $$Z_1 Z_3 = Z_2 Z_4$$

and $$(\phi_1 + \phi_3) = (\phi_2 + \phi_4)$$

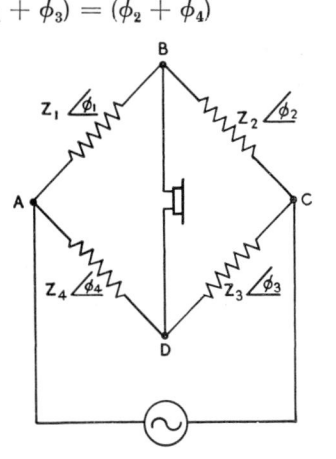

FIG. 12.76. A.C. BRIDGE—GENERAL CASE

From these relationships, the balanced bridge can be solved for any one unknown component.

In the practical design of the bridge, the two ratio arms (P and Q) are usually pure resistances: in this event it is important that they should be entirely non-reactive for all frequencies at which measurements are liable to be made. It is of considerable importance, particularly for high-frequency measurements, that all bridge elements are electrostatically screened so that stray capacitances are either effectively across the bridge diagonals or else are so arranged that they may be balanced out by a preliminary adjustment of the bridge.

A variable capacitor is used to adjust the phase angle of the bridge for balance: this capacitance must have a negligible power-factor. Inductors are rarely used for this purpose since they cannot be readily made adjustable nor with negligible resistance, and their value changes with frequency. Switches are provided to connect the variable capacitance in either the variable (R) arm or in the unknown (Z) arm, and in each case a series or parallel connexion may be adopted as desired by use of the switch: in this way the variable capacitance may be used to measure impedances which

have either a positive or a negative angle. The detecting device is usually a telephone receiver when testing at audio frequencies: an a.c. meter or electronic detector may be used at carrier and radio frequencies. To balance the a.c. bridge requires more skill than the d.c. bridge on account of the two variables R and C whose adjustments are, to some extent, interdependent: this difficulty is increased if the a.c. supply contains harmonic frequencies. The bridge is adjusted for minimum tone in the receiver rather than for no tone.

A number of the more important bridge arrangements are illustrated in Figs. 12.77 to 12.85 and their purpose is briefly described below. In all

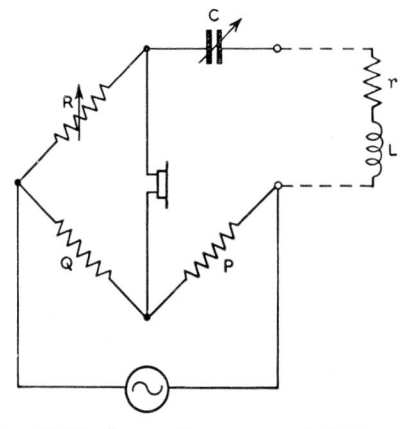

FIG. 12.77. SERIES RESONANCE A.C. BRIDGE

cases the solution depends upon the relationship given above ($Z_1 Z_3 = Z_2 Z_4$): for the more straightforward cases the solution for the bridge is developed below. In all expressions, R, L, and C are in ohms, henrys, and *farads* respectively. In many cases the factor ω^2 enters into the solution: when this occurs the value of ω must be known accurately.

(i) SERIES RESONANCE BRIDGE (Fig. 12.77). This bridge is used for the measurement of inductance when the "Q" value ("Q" $= \omega L/R$) is of a medium or high order, i.e. the inherent resistance of the inductor is low. The variable capacitor in series with the inductor, is tuned to resonance, i.e. to zero phase angle: the bridge can then be balanced by the pure resistance R.

When the bridge is balanced—

$$P \times R = Q \times \{r + j\omega L - j/(\omega C)\}$$

At resonance, $\omega L = 1/(\omega C)$,

$$\text{i.e. } L = 1/\omega^2 C \text{ henrys}$$

Also, $P \times R = Q \times (r + 0)$,

$$\text{i.e. } r = R \cdot P/Q \text{ ohms}$$

From these relationships the following may be obtained—

$$= \frac{1}{\omega C} \sqrt{1 + \frac{P^2 R^2}{Q^2} \cdot \omega^2 C^2}, \text{ and } \phi = \tan^{-1} \frac{Q}{PR\omega C}$$

(ii) MAX WIEN BRIDGE (Fig. 12.78). This bridge is used for the measurement of medium and large capacitances.

At balance—

$$P \times \{R - j/(\omega C)\} = Q \times \{r - j/(\omega c')\}$$

Equating the in-phase components,

$$PR = Qr, \text{ and } r = R \cdot P/Q \text{ ohms}$$

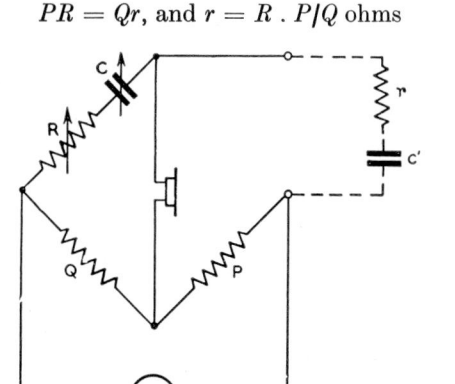

FIG. 12.78. MAX WIEN A.C. BRIDGE

Equating the quadrature components,

$$\frac{P}{\omega C} = \frac{Q}{\omega c'}, \text{ and } c' = C \cdot \frac{Q}{P} \text{ farads}$$

From the above values for r and c' are obtained—

$$Z = \frac{P}{Q} \sqrt{\frac{R^2 \omega^2 C^2 + 1}{\omega^2 C^2}}, \text{ and } \phi = \tan^{-1} \frac{-1}{\omega CR}$$

(iii) MAXWELL INDUCTANCE BRIDGE (Fig. 12.79). This bridge is used for measuring inductances with relatively high inherent resistance, i.e. low Q value ("Q" $= \omega L/R$).

At balance—

$$PQ = (r + j\omega L) \times \frac{1}{(1/R + j\omega C)}$$

$$= \frac{r + j\omega L}{\frac{1}{R} + j\omega C}$$

$$\frac{PQ}{R} + PQj\omega C = r + j\omega L$$

Equating in-phase components,

$$r = PQ/R \text{ ohms}$$

Equating quadrature components,

$$PQj\omega C = j\omega L, \quad L = PQC \text{ henrys}$$

From the above values of r and L, the following are obtained—

$$Z = \frac{PQ}{R}\sqrt{1 + \omega^2 C^2 R^2}, \text{ and } \phi = \tan^{-1} \omega CR$$

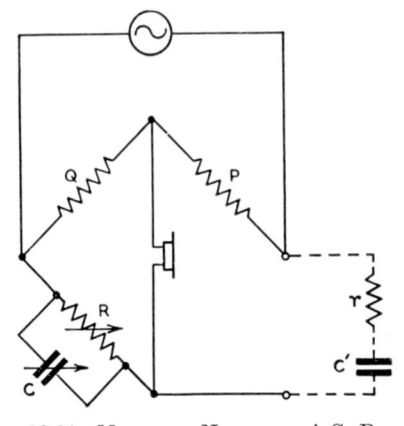

FIG. 12.79. MAXWELL POSITIVE A.C. BRIDGE

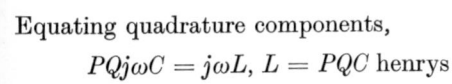

FIG. 12.80. MAXWELL NEGATIVE A.C. BRIDGE

(iv) MAXWELL'S NEGATIVE IMPEDANCE BRIDGE (Fig. 12.80). This bridge is used for measurements of impedances with large negative phase angle.

$$r = \frac{P}{Q} \cdot \frac{R}{1 + \omega^2 C^2 R^2} \text{ ohms}$$

$$c' = \frac{Q}{P} \cdot \left(\frac{1 + \omega^2 C^2 R^2}{\omega^2 C^2 R^2}\right) \text{ farads}$$

$$Z = \frac{PR}{Q\sqrt{1 + \omega^2 C^2 R^2}}$$

$$\phi = \tan^{-1} - \omega CR$$

(v) THE PARALLEL RESONANCE BRIDGE (Fig. 12.81). This bridge is used for impedance measurements when the phase angle is positive.

$$Z = \frac{PR}{\sqrt{Q^2 + P^2 R^2 \omega^2 C^2}} \text{ ohms}$$

$$\phi = \tan^{-1} \frac{P}{Q} \cdot \omega CR$$

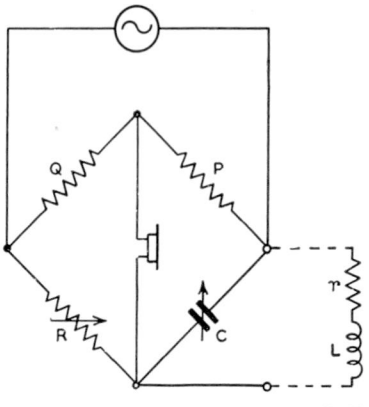

FIG. 12.81. PARALLEL RESONANCE A.C. BRIDGE

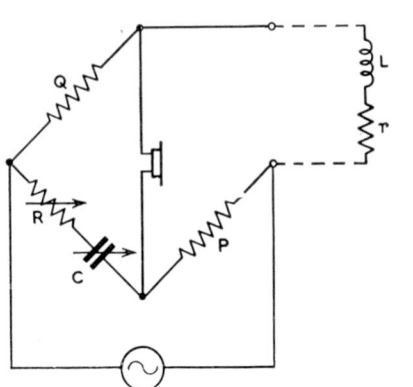

FIG. 12.82. HAY'S A.C. BRIDGE

(vi) HAY'S BRIDGE (Fig. 12.82). This bridge may be used for the measurement of impedances having a large positive phase angle.

$$r = \frac{PQ(\omega^2 C^2 R^2)}{1 + \omega^2 C^2 R^2} \text{ ohms}$$

$$L = \frac{PQC}{1 + \omega^2 C^2 R^2} \text{ henrys}$$

$$Z = \frac{PQ\omega C}{\sqrt{1 + \omega^2 C^2 R^2}}$$

$$\phi = \tan^{-1} \frac{1}{R\omega C}$$

(vii) SCHERING BRIDGE (Fig. 12.83). This bridge is used for impedances with small negative angles, e.g. the measurement of a capacitor and its power-factor.

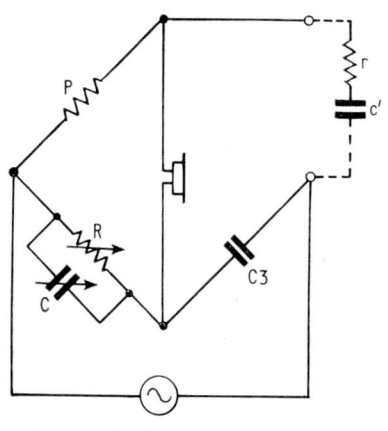

FIG. 12.83. SCHERING A.C. BRIDGE

$$r = PC/C_3 \text{ ohms}$$

$$c' = C_3R/P \text{ farads}$$

$$Z = \frac{P}{\omega C_3 R} \sqrt{1 + \omega^2 C^2 R^2}$$

$$\phi = \tan^{-1} -1/\omega CR$$

(viii) FREQUENCY BRIDGE (Fig. 12.84). This form of bridge is used to measure the frequency of the supply: it may be used as a harmonic analyser—to detect which frequency components are present in a complex waveform.

Admittance of arm $\quad AB = \dfrac{1}{R_1} + j\omega C_1$

$$= \frac{1 + j\omega C_1 R_1}{R_1}$$

Impedance of arm $\quad AB = \dfrac{R_1}{1 + j\omega C_1 R_1}$

$$= \frac{R_1(1 - j\omega C_1 R_1)}{1 + \omega^2 C_1{}^2 R_1{}^2}$$

Impedance of arm $\quad AD = R_2 - j/(\omega C_2)$

$$= \frac{\omega C_2 R_2 - j}{\omega C_2}$$

Phase angle of impedance $AB = \tan^{-1} \omega C_1 R_1$
Phase angle of impedance $AD = \tan^{-1} \omega C_2 R_2$

As these angles are equal at balance

$$\omega C_1 R_1 = \frac{1}{\omega R_2 C_2} \text{ and } \omega = \frac{1}{\sqrt{C_1 C_2 R_1 R_2}} \text{ radn/sec}$$

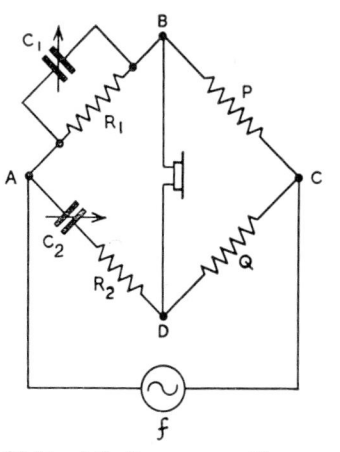

FIG. 12.84. A.C. BRIDGE FOR FREQUENCY MEASUREMENT

(ix) WAGNER EARTH (Fig. 12.85). When using headgear receivers as the detecting instrument on an a.c. bridge, difficulty may be experienced due to the variable capacitance between the detector and earth. The trouble may be overcome by ensuring that, at balance, each of the two points to which the detector is connected is at earth potential.

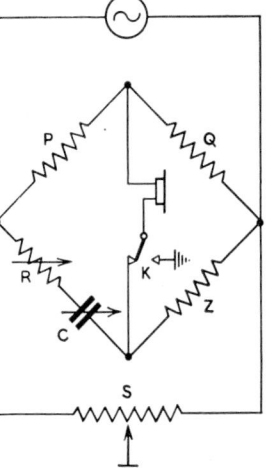

FIG. 12.85. WAGNER EARTH: A.C. BRIDGE

The receiver switch K is first operated to complete the normal bridge circuit and the bridge is balanced as closely as possible. The switch K is then operated to connect the receiver to earth and the rheostat S is adjusted for balance. This ensures that the junction of P and Q is at earth potential: when a rebalance is attempted with the switch K back in its normal position, the receiver is at earth potential and can have no stray capacitance to earth.

CHAPTER XIII

VALVE ELECTRONICS

3.1. Electron Emission. The atoms and molecules of any material are at rest only at the absolute zero of temperature (− 273°C): at other temperatures they are in a continual state of motion. As the temperature is raised the molecular motion becomes increasingly violent until, at a given temperature, which differs for various materials, molecules are thrown off into the surrounding space and evaporation is said to occur.

In a similar manner, the free *electrons* in a material —which are normally in a state of random movement from atom to atom, and in a conductor are formed into a steady drift current by the application of a potential difference—can be dislodged completely and thrown off into the surrounding space if their velocity is raised to a sufficiently high value.

Various methods are available for increasing the electron velocity to the point where the electrons are emitted from the surface of a material. For example, it is well known that conductors will emit electrons from their surface if there exists a potential gradient at their boundary of the order of 10^6 volts per cm, this phenomenon being known as *cold emission*. Electrons may be emitted from certain materials when they are subjected to rays of light energy, this occurrence being known as *photoelectric emission*. Again, when a solid body experiences bombardment from rapidly moving electrons, the impact may be sufficient to cause other electrons to leave the surface of the body. One bombarding electron can liberate several other electrons: the ratio of the number of electrons so liberated to the number of electrons striking the body depends upon the material struck and the velocity of impact. The electrons striking the body are termed "primary electrons" and the electrons liberated are "secondary electrons": the phenomenon is termed *secondary emission*.

More commonly, electron emission is produced by raising the temperature of a material: this liberation of electrons from an electrode by virtue of its temperature is called *thermionic emission*. With many metals, the temperature necessary for electron emission to occur is so high that the material becomes volatile before the desired temperature is attained. Tungsten is a suitable metal for the purpose for, with a melting point in the region of 3 300°C, a useful electron emission is obtained at a temperature of about 2 200°C. If the material is surrounded by air at atmospheric temperature and pressure, however, the motion of the electrons is restricted by collision with the heavy gas molecules.

The emitting surface may be in the form of a tungsten filament enclosed within a glass envelope: when surrounded by gas at minimum pressure— that is to say, as "hard" a vacuum as possible is obtained—electrons will be freely emitted when the filament is brought to a state of incandescence, the number of electrons emitted increasing with the temperature.

The escape of electrons leaves the filament with a more positive charge, producing an attractive force urging the electrons to return to the filament: there is also a force of mutual repulsion between the electrons themselves. Many of the electrons are prevented from returning due to the repulsion of other electrons liberated subsequently: these electrons also repel further electrons which are tending to leave the filament. The net result is that the filament, on attaining the critical temperature, is quickly surrounded by a cloud of electrons setting up a region of negative charge known as the *space charge*. Stability is reached when the number of electrons leaving the filament is balanced by those returning to it.

One of the most important factors on which the electron emission depends is the *work function* of the surface of the material: it is a measure of the work which an electron must do in order to escape from the surface and it can be measured in volts. Typical values are as follows—

	Volts		Volts
Tungsten	4·52	Iron	3·7
Platinum	4·4	Calcium	3·4
Molybdenum	4·3	Thorium	3·4
Carbon	4·1	Magnesium	2·7
Copper	4·0	Lithium	2·3
Tin	3·8	Sodium	1·8

The lower the value of the work function the greater will be the possible electron emission for a given temperature. Electrons are emitted with varying velocities. Thermionic emission follows the equation—

$$I = A T^2 e^{-b/T} \text{ amperes/cm}^2$$

where T is the temperature in degrees Kelvin, (K° = 273 + °C): A is a constant, depending

upon the material: $b = 11\,600 \times$ work function: $e = 2 \cdot 718$.

Important properties of the material for practical use are constancy and efficiency of operation: the tendency is to operate the filament at the relatively low temperature of dull red heat—the "dull emitter" filament as contrasted to the "bright emitter" designed to be used at a relatively high temperature. Pure tungsten is used for the filament in the latter case, now applied only to high power transmitting valves.

For the purpose of electron emission it is immaterial what method of heating the emitting surface—the *cathode*—is adopted: its temperature is most conveniently raised to the desired value by the passage of an electric current which in principle may be either D.C. or A.C. Two main classes of cathode are available according to whether they are heated directly or indirectly. Both classes may be of the dull emitter type in which a treated filament is used to give a greater electron emission per watt of heating power to enable it to be used at lower temperatures: this ensures a longer life to the material by avoiding crystallization and brittleness.

In the directly-heated filament cathode a small percentage of thorium—an impurity commonly present in tungsten—is mixed with the tungsten: during manufacture a heat treatment process brings this thorium to the surface of the tungsten filament as a thin molecular layer. This thorium layer, operating at a temperature of about $1\,700°C$ and with a work function of $2 \cdot 6$, is found to be much more prolific in electrons than is the tungsten filament itself. It is used with anode voltages in excess of $1\,000$ V.

An alternative type of directly-heated filament for anode voltages less than $1\,000$ V consists of a wire of platinum, nickel, or tungsten upon which is deposited a coating of barium or strontium oxides. These materials will readily emit electrons at a temperature of about $1\,100°K$: the work function is $1 \cdot 0$ V. Directly-heated filaments may take the form of a letter I, V, or W to obtain the desired length and surface area. The average power consumption is of the order of 1 A at 2 V, 4 V, or 6 V for low power equipment (e.g. a radio broadcast receiver).

The indirectly-heated cathode consists of a metal tube (Fig. 13.1) usually of nickel, coated upon the outside with barium or strontium oxides. The heater filament is a tungsten wire loop placed inside the tube, the loop being coated with an insulating material such as aluminium oxide which is not affected by heat. This tungsten filament is heated by the passage of a current: typical heater ratings

for small valves are 1 A at 4 V and 0·3 A at 6·3 V. Owing to the relatively large mass of the cathode it takes an appreciable time to warm up and there is a slight delay after switching on the heater wire before electron emission commences.

If residual gases are left in oxide-coated valves during manufacture these gases are liberated when the valve is operated and attack the cathode, oxidizing the excess barium and causing a serious reduction in emission: this effect is termed cathode "poisoning." Another cause of reduced emission

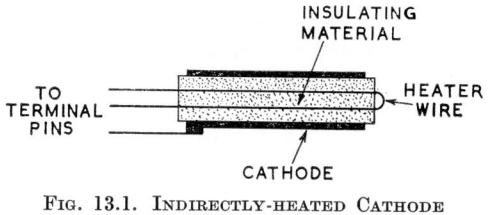

FIG. 13.1. INDIRECTLY-HEATED CATHODE

during the life of a valve is the growth of a high-resistance interface-layer between the granular matrix of the barium-strontium oxides coating the cathode and its supporting metal core: the formation of this layer stems from the presence of such impurities as silicon in nickel cores. This growth can be effectively prevented by the use of platinum, or a low-impurity tungsten-nickel alloy containing 4 per cent tungsten, as the cathode core material.

13.2. The Diode. If a positively charged body (the *anode*) is brought near to a cathode, some of the electrons will be attracted to the anode, reducing the space charge and permitting further electrons to leave the cathode. As the positive anode potential is increased, the space charge is gradually reduced until all electrons which leave the cathode are attracted to the anode: any further increase in anode potential has then no effect on the flow of electrons. A greater flow of electrons can only be obtained by raising the temperature or increasing the size of the cathode surface to produce a greater supply of electrons.

The diode valve comprises two electrodes, the cathode and the anode, enclosed within a glass envelope from which the presence of gas has been excluded. The anode may be in the form of a flat plate—which gives the alternative name "plate" for the anode—or more usually it is of a cylindrical, oval, binocular, or rectangular shape to surround the cathode. With no potential applied to the anode, the potential in the region of the heated cathode is due to the space charge: the potential gradient between cathode and anode may be represented by the graph of Fig. 13.2 (a). When the

node is made positive, if the cathode were cold the potential would fall uniformly from anode to cathode: with the cathode heated, the potential at any point is due to the sum of the positive anode charge and the negative space charge, the potential gradient between anode and cathode taking the form illustrated in Fig. 13.2 (b).

With increasing distance from the cathode the potential becomes increasingly negative until a distance x mm from the cathode is reached: in this region any electron experiences a force drawing it

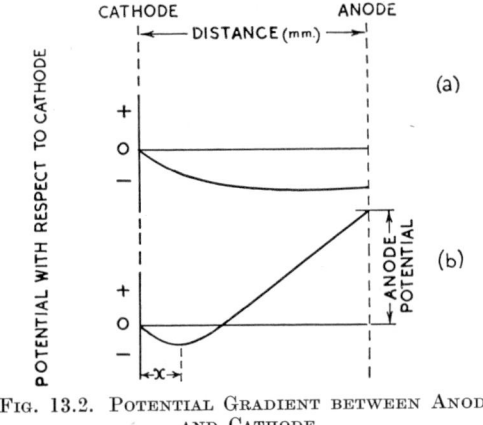

FIG. 13.2. POTENTIAL GRADIENT BETWEEN ANODE AND CATHODE

towards the cathode, whilst at greater distances it is attracted towards the anode on account of the positive potential. Due to the space charge, only those electrons which leave the cathode with sufficient initial velocity to travel beyond the region of negative potential will reach the anode: all other electrons return to the cathode. The region of the space charge has a vital bearing upon the operation of the electronic valve.

The method of applying the operating potentials is shown schematically in Fig. 13.3. A battery or other source of p.d. is applied across the anode and cathode to make the anode positive with respect to the cathode: this potential is designated V_a volts and since its value is normally of the order of 100 V or more the source is referred to as the *high-tension* (H.T.) supply (sometimes as the "B" battery). The filament is heated from a low-tension (L.T.) supply (or "A" battery) providing the required low voltage heater p.d. (V_f volts) across the filament terminals. It is immaterial which end of the filament is positive: with a directly-heated filament, however, (Fig. 13.3 (a)) electrode potentials are referred to the negative end of the filament which results in the connexions shown in Fig. 13.3 (c). The indirectly-heated cathode (Fig. 13.3 (b) and (d)) has the advantage that the cathode is distinct from the

heater filament and its potential can be quite independent of filament potential considerations, In both types it is sometimes convenient to heat the filament directly with alternating current, obtained at the correct voltage from a transformer winding (Fig. 13.3 (e)). In operation, the stream of electrons from cathode to anode is equivalent to the conventional flow of current from anode to cathode: this is termed the *anode current*, designated by the symbol I_a. The essentially unidirectional nature of the current flow provides the

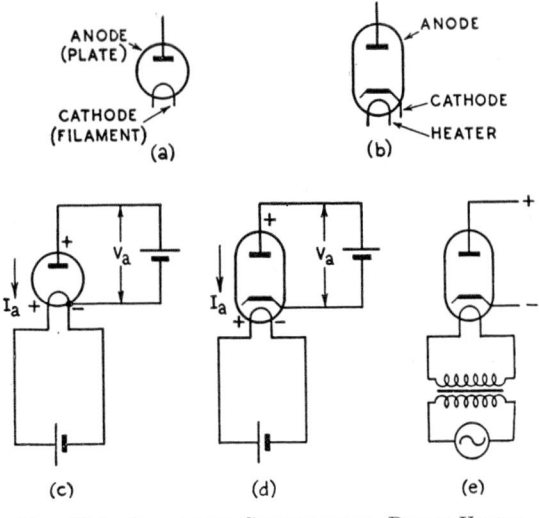

FIG. 13.3. OPERATING CONDITION OF DIODE VALVE

fundamental property of the electronic valve. It will be apparent that the purpose of the low tension or filament supply is solely to raise the temperature of the cathode to promote electron emission: apart from this it takes no part in the electrical operation of the valve unless used for grid biasing purposes. The high-tension supply provides the anode current by driving electrons from anode to cathode in the external circuit of the valve.

If the diode has a straight filament fitted centrally within a cylindrical anode the electron flow can be calculated from the expression—

$$I_a = k \cdot \frac{l}{r} \cdot V_a^{3/2} \text{ amperes}$$

where k is a constant, l cm is the length of the filament and r cm is the radius of the anode: this expression is true up to the point at which saturation commences if the initial velocity of the electrons is neglected.

More generally the expression may be written—

$$I_a = A \cdot V_a^{3/2} \text{ amperes} \qquad . \quad (13.1)$$

where the constant A is dependent upon the electrode shapes and sizes.

The graph for this equation is given in Fig. 13.4. The curve begins to flatten out when the electron flow becomes nearly equal to the total emission of electrons from the cathode, i.e. saturation occurs. With a given filament condition the anode current increases with a rise in anode potential until all available electrons are being drawn to the anode: the anode characteristic then flattens and further increase in anode potential can produce no appreciable increase in anode current. This is the *saturation current* or *total emission* of the filament: it is independent of the anode voltage or dimensions,

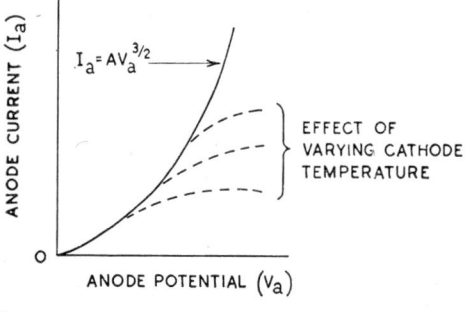

FIG. 13.4. VARIATION OF ANODE CURRENT WITH
ANODE POTENTIAL

but depends upon the length and diameter of the cathode, upon its temperature (which depends upon the heater current and voltage) and also upon the material with which it is made or coated. The magnitude of the anode current increases rapidly with the cathode temperature.

The anode current is made up of discrete charges (electrons) whose emission from the cathode is of random nature: this leads to a varying rate of flow of electrons between cathode and anode producing what is termed "shot effect" or shot noise in any telephone receiver connected in the anode circuit. As might be expected, the shot effect is reduced by the presence of space charge, i.e. when not all the emitted electrons reach the anode or by a decrease in anode current: shot noise is increased with multi-electrode valves due to the random division of the electron stream between the anode and other positive electrodes.

If the valve envelope contains traces of gas, ionization by collision occurs when an electron hits a gas molecule with sufficient velocity to dislodge an electron from the gas molecule. The velocity acquired by the dislodged electron is a function of the anode voltage and the direction which the electron takes: the result of the collision is to increase the anode current. The positive ion

formed is repelled towards the cathode, reducing the space charge and increasing the anode current on this account: these ions may form upon the cathode surface a layer having a different electron affinity from the cathode proper, again affecting the anode current. The charge upon a positive ion travelling from anode to cathode is equivalent to that upon an electron travelling in the reverse direction and a further increase in anode current occurs due to this cause. Furthermore, bombardment of the cathode by the relatively heavy ions is liable to damage it. The presence of gas in a valve —a "soft" valve—produces complex and variable effects. In production every possible trace of gas is exhausted from the valve to make it "hard."

13.3. Diode Rectification. The unidirectional property of the diode makes it suitable for use where *rectification* is required, i.e. the conversion to direct

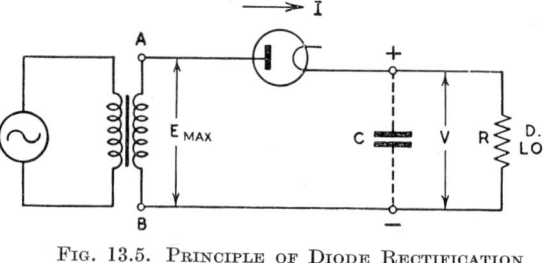

FIG. 13.5. PRINCIPLE OF DIODE RECTIFICATION

current from an alternating current source. The description below relates to the rectification of power supplies: diode rectification or *demodulation* of speech and telegraph signals is dealt with later.

In its simplest form the power rectifying circuit is that shown in Fig. 13.5. A transformer is used to isolate the a.c. and d.c. circuits from one another and to step the a.c. voltage up or down to the desired value: a separate secondary winding (not shown) is employed for the purpose of heating the filament. When the potential at A is sufficiently positive with respect to that at B, a current I amperes flows through the valve into the load resistance R ohms, the current magnitude depending upon the voltage across the diode and upon the valve characteristic (Fig. 13.4). During alternate half-cycles when B is positive to A, the diode is non-conducting because the anode is now at a negative potential with respect to the cathode. The (d.c.) output current and voltage will vary in the manner shown in Fig. 13.6 if the valve is not saturated: the output current consists of a series of unidirectional pulses.

If a "reservoir" capacitance C is connected across the output terminals (Fig. 13.5) it will charge up during the d.c. voltage pulses, and discharge

to the load during the intervals when no supply being transferred from the source, so tending to "smooth" the current output. The p.d. across the pacitor rises during the charging intervals and lls as the charge is withdrawn by the load. Equirium will be established when the charge fed by e rectifier is just equal to that taken by the load: e capacitor will then acquire a mean p.d. which ll be the effective voltage applied to the load.

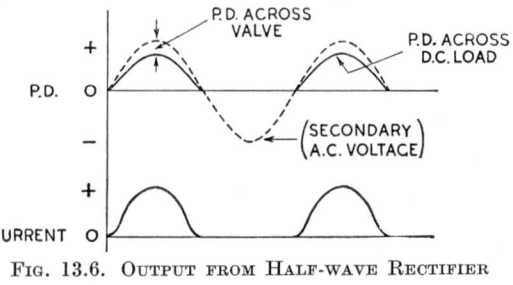

FIG. 13.6. OUTPUT FROM HALF-WAVE RECTIFIER

hese conditions are indicated in Fig. 13.7. The d. across the capacitor presents a back-e.m.f. in e diode circuit, tending to make the anode negave, and no current will flow through the diode til the voltage supplied by the transformer suffiently exceeds the p.d. across the capacitor: this counts for the difference shown in the current lses between Figs. 13.6 and 13.7.

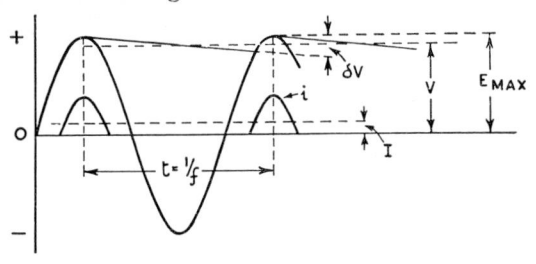

FIG. 13.7. EFFECT OF SMOOTHING CAPACITOR:
HALF-WAVE RECTIFIER

If the load current is small, the average p.d. V lts across the load is nearly equal to E_{max}, the condary voltage of the transformer. It can be ssumed without much error that the capacitor is scharging for the whole time of one cycle, i.e. for $= 1/f$ seconds, where f c/s is the supply frequency. he charge $Q = I \times t = C \times dV$ (the change in ltage) where I and V are the mean current and ltage outputs—see Fig. 13.7.
Substituting $I = V/R$, then $V/(Rf) = C \cdot dV$, or

$$\frac{V}{ } = \frac{1}{RfC}.$$

This relationship gives the extent of output ripple," which is inversely proportional to the

value of the capacitance and load resistance. It the capacitance C or the load resistance R are infinitely high, the capacitor will charge up to the peak value of the applied A.C.

If reliance were placed entirely upon the capacitor to effect smoothing, a large and expensive type of capacitor would be required since it must be capable of withstanding the peak supply voltage and of carrying the load current. Moreover, its low impedance shunting effect upon the load resistance would result in a much heavier charging current from the rectifier, tending to overload the diode emission and reduce the life of the valve.

The pulsating output voltage may be regarded

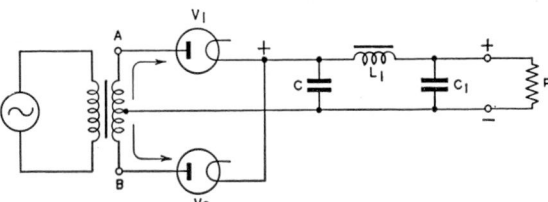

FIG. 13.8. PRINCIPLE OF FULL-WAVE DIODE
RECTIFIER

as being made up from a steady voltage, upon which is superimposed an alternating voltage ripple. This residual ripple may be suppressed by adding a series inductance (L_1) and a further shunt capacitance (C_1)—see Fig. 13.8—which function as a low-pass filter: using a two-stage filter, the ripple can be reduced to negligible proportions.

If heavy currents are involved it is usual to insert an air-gapped ferro-magnetic choke or inductor between the rectifier and the reservoir capacitor: the effect of this is to produce smoothing by limiting the current during the time when the transformer e.m.f. exceeds the p.d. across the capacitor, and prolonging the current thereafter. This reduces the peak current from the diode and enables a smaller rectifier valve to be used, at the same time improving both the ripple and the voltage regulation. On switching off the rectifier the back-e.m.f.s of the inductor and of the reservoir capacitor are additive—another reason for the use of a reservoir capacitor with high dielectric strength.

The single diode circuit of Fig. 13.5 rectifies only alternate half-cycles, the other half-cycle being suppressed: it is termed a *half-wave rectifier*. Full-wave rectification is more commonly employed. In this arrangement (Fig. 13.8) two diodes are connected in anti-phase, one valve rectifying the positive half-cycles and the other the negative. Each anode is connected to one end of the centre-tapped secondary winding of a transformer. During alternate half-cycles of the a.c. supply, the potential at

A will be positive and the potential at *B* will be negative with respect to the centre-point of the transformer. In this condition V_1 will be conducting and V_2 will be non-conducting. While either valve is conducting its impedance is low and the potential at the cathodes will be not much less than that at *A*. During the next half-cycle V_2 conducts and the potential at the cathode follows that at *B*. The output voltage from the valves has the form shown in Fig. 13.9 (*a*). The reservoir capacitor *C* is now charged during each half-cycle,

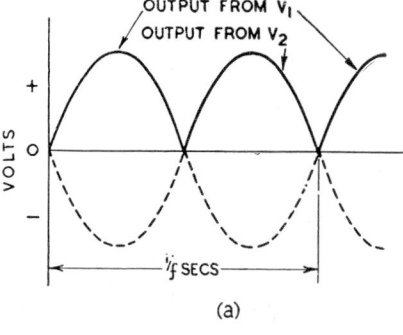

(a)

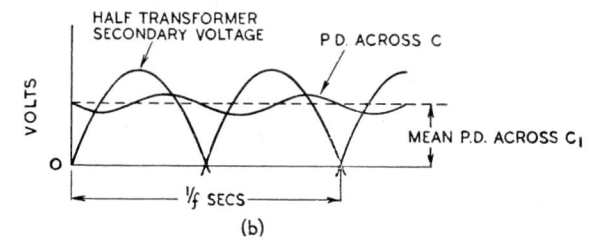

(b)

FIG. 13.9. OUTPUT FROM FULL-WAVE RECTIFIER

the p.d. across the capacitor approaching the peak voltage developed across one-half of the secondary winding of the transformer. During the intervals between peak values the capacitor *C* discharges into the load resistance *R* and the p.d. across *C* falls. The waveform across the capacitor is shown in Fig. 13.9 (*b*). With a full-wave rectifier, the ripple frequency is twice that of the supply frequency, e.g. for a 50 c/s source the ripple frequency will be 100 c/s. If the capacitance is large, the fall in voltage due to the current drawn by the load resistance will be small and this variation will be still further reduced by the low-pass filter L_1C_1. The load p.d. is then sensibly constant and equal to the mean value of the p.d. across *C*, less the voltage drop across the inductor.

For medium and low power use a double-diode

valve is conveniently used in which the two anode are enclosed within the same glass envelope with common cathode. The filament is heated from additional secondary winding upon the transform The arrangement of a typical rectifier unit of t type is shown in Fig. 13.10. The primary windi of the transformer is tapped to suit various mai supply voltages. The maximum possible rectifi voltage available approaches the peak value of t half-secondary voltage, i.e. $300\sqrt{2}$, or appro mately 400 V in the example shown.

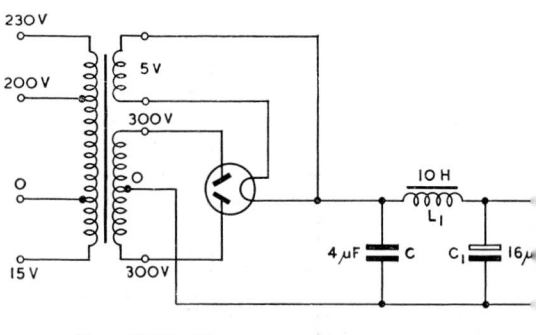

FIG. 13.10. FULL-WAVE RECTIFIER USING
DOUBLE-DIODE VALVE

13.4 The Triode. It has been seen that the regi of the space charge has a critical influence on t movement of electrons which have left the cathod the potential here determines whether electro will travel on to the anode or return to the cathod The function of the valve is considerably enlarg by adding a third electrode in the region of t space charge: this electrode, known as the *gr* or in particular as the *control grid*, is of op mesh or spiral construction so as not to impe the migration of electrons. Any potential impart to the grid by means external to the valve w exert a considerable influence on the electrons in t surrounding area: since the grid is much nearer the cathode than is the anode, it is apparent th its potential will have a much greater relati influence on this space charge than the anode w have for the same potential. In this way it provid a very effective means of regulating the electro flow from cathode to anode: for a given cathod temperature, the electron flow or anode curre (I_a) now depends not only upon the anode potenti (V_a) but also upon the grid potential (V_g). T expression (13.1) for anode current in the diod must be modified for the three-electrode valve, triode, to allow for the increased controlling effe afforded by the grid potential, and becomes—

$$I_a = A(V_a + \mu V_g)^{3/2} \qquad . \quad (13.$$

The grid potential is multiplied by the constant (the *amplification factor*), to take into account the greater influence of the grid relative to the anode: the value of μ *depends only upon the geometry of the valve*, in particular upon the physical dimensions of the grid, cathode, and anode.

With no potential applied, the grid has little influence upon the anode current apart from its slight screening effect upon the cathode. On account of the open construction of the grid the passage of electrons from cathode to anode through the grid is scarcely impeded.

If the grid is given a slight negative potential it will reduce the influence of the positive anode

cathode: the flow of this *grid current* (I_g) is for most purposes undesirable because the resulting p.d. in the grid circuit modifies the potential specifically applied to the grid. On the other hand, the presence of grid current is sometimes put to great practical use in certain types of equipment. The anode current (and grid current) will rise as the positive grid potential is increased until saturation point is reached.

Grid current may also be caused by residual gas inside the valve causing the formation of positive ions which are attracted to a negatively charged grid: this limits the value of resistance which can be connected between grid and cathode since the

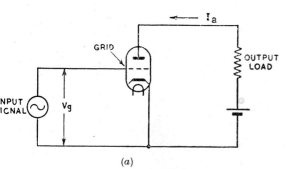
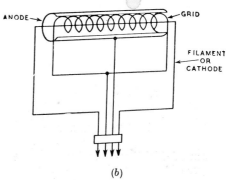

(a)   (b)

FIG. 13.11. GENERAL USE OF TRIODE VALVE

potential in this region: more electrons are repelled back to the cathode and the anode current is reduced. While the negative grid potential is small, the higher positive anode potential will still impart sufficient velocity to the electrons to enable a great number of them to pass to the anode through the meshes of the grid. A gradual increase in negative potential applied to the grid has an increasing neutralizing effect upon the influence of the anode potential, and more and more electrons are repelled to the cathode due to the negative grid potential. The anode current accordingly falls as the grid potential is made more negative, until with a sufficiently negative grid potential the anode current is completely extinguished. It is important to note that, due to the proximity of the grid and cathode, the grid is capable of suppressing the anode current by a negative potential which is numerically considerably lower than the positive anode potential tending to promote anode current.

If the grid is given a positive potential it exerts a considerable accelerating force upon the electrons leaving the cathode: since most of them pass through the meshes of the grid the anode current is increased. Some electrons will terminate upon the grid and flow in the external grid circuit to the

direction of grid current is such as to make the grid more positive.

The general principle of employing a triode is illustrated in Fig. 13.11 (a): the relative positions of the electrodes are indicated in Fig. 13.11 (b). A low power input signal is applied to the grid circuit across the grid and cathode. With the cathode heated and a positive potential applied to the anode, small fluctuations in grid potential will control large changes in anode current. These changes in anode current may be used to produce relatively large voltage changes across the output load impedance in the anode circuit: provided that causes of distortion are avoided the waveform of the output signal will faithfully follow that of the input signal. It may be noted that, assuming that no grid current flows, the grid circuit is voltage-operated and consumes no power: this permits weak input signals, applied to the grid circuit via a voltage step-up transformer to produce appreciable potential changes upon the grid and so control relatively high power in the anode circuit.

The arrangement of the electrodes in a directly-heated triode is illustrated in Fig. 13.12. The grid is mounted concentrically with the V-shaped filament and enclosed within the anode, which is also

concentric with the cathode. Further constructional details are shown in Fig. 13.13 for a directly-
heated triode. The cathode (Fig. 13.13 (a)) is here

operation: an important property is that it does n[ot]
exude excessive quantities of adsorbed gases to caus[e]
ionization. The electrode assembly is mounted upo[n]

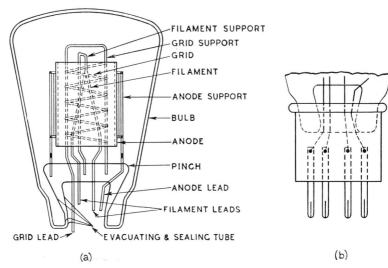

FILAMENT SUPPORT
GRID SUPPORT
GRID
FILAMENT
ANODE SUPPORT
BULB
ANODE
PINCH
ANODE LEAD
FILAMENT LEADS
GRID LEAD
EVACUATING & SEALING TUBE

(a)

(b)

FIG. 13.12. ARRANGEMENT OF ELECTRODES IN TRIODE VALVE

in the form of a W-shaped metal filament coated
with a layer of barium and strontium oxides. The
grid consists of a flattened helix of wire, made from

a glass pinch formed on the top of a re-entra[nt]
tube at the base of a glass envelope. The wir[es]
forming the electrode connexions must mak[e]

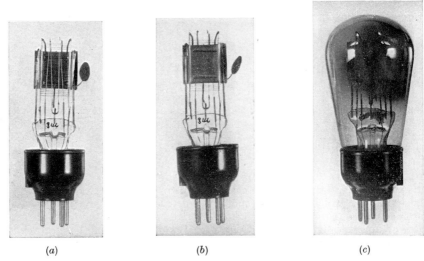

(a)

(b)

(c)

FIG. 13.13. CONSTRUCTIONAL DETAILS OF DIRECTLY-HEATED THREE-ELECTRODE VALVE

either nickel or molybdenum. The anode (shown
cut away at (a) and complete at (b)) is a metal
shield surrounding the grid. Nickel is largely used
for anodes as it can withstand the heat generated
during the manufacturing processes and by normal

vacuum-tight seals where they pass through th[e]
glass pinch. Platinum or copper clad wires [of]
nickel-iron are suitable since they have a therma[l]
coefficient of expansion similar to that of the gla[ss]
to which they adhere satisfactorily. The re-entra[nt]

ibe is provided with a small tube projecting from the interior of the bulb for the purpose of evacuating and sealing the bulb. During the process of evacuation and sealing the electrodes are heated by induced high-frequency eddy currents. After sealing, the residual gases are taken up by the use of a pellet of active substance such as barium, magnesium, or aluminium, known as a "getter": this agent is vaporized by high-frequency heating to combine with the gas, the chemical products condensing on the inner surface of the bulb and producing the characteristic appearance upon the glass. Some uncombined "getter" is condensed upon the surface of the bulb and continues to combine with small quantities of gas which may be liberated within the valve during the course of its life. The pellet of getter material is usually mounted upon a small metal plate or dish (shown projecting to the right in Figs. 13.13 (a) and (b)) in such a position that condensation of the vaporized material upon the electrodes is avoided. The electrode connexions are soldered into contact pins mounted in a base of moulded insulating material to which the base of the glass bulb is cemented (Fig. 13.13 (c)).

13.5. Valve Parameters. The electronic valve has three parameters : (i) the mutual conductance, (ii) the internal or a.c. resistance, and (iii) the amplification factor : these can be evaluated from knowledge of the valve characteristics.

The anode current of a valve can be influenced by three possible variables—the filament temperature, the anode potential, and the grid potential. In practice the valve must be designed to give sufficient emission for the particular purpose for which it is to be used : the cathode is arranged to be operated at a fixed temperature which will provide the required emission and ensure a long life. Accordingly, in examining the characteristic performance of a valve, the cathode is heated under a specified fixed condition, and either the anode potential or the grid potential is varied while observation is made of the resulting anode current. These variations may also affect the flow of grid current.

A testing circuit suitable for examination of the static valve characteristics is shown in Fig. 13.14. The filament battery provides a constant current to raise the cathode to the required temperature. In the anode circuit a potentiometer is connected across the high-tension anode battery to permit the anode potential to be finely adjusted. The anode current is read upon a low-resistance ammeter : a high-resistance voltmeter is connected across the anode and cathode. The battery in the grid circuit is centre-tapped and shunted by a potentiometer : by this arrangement the grid potential can be continuously varied over a wide range of positive and

negative values, read upon the high-resistance voltmeter connected across the grid and cathode. These measurements will give the *static* characteristics of the valve, since they are made with fixed values of electrode potentials, and not with the varying or *dynamic* potentials of normal operation.

Since three variables are concerned, namely the grid potential (V_g), the anode potential (V_a), and the anode current (I_a), the valve operation can be studied by plotting three sets of characteristic curves, each with one of the above factors kept constant, the other two forming the independent and dependent variables. In all cases the cathode

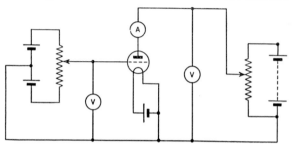

Fig. 13.14. CIRCUIT FOR EXAMINATION OF VALVE CHARACTERISTICS

condition is maintained constant. Grid current (I_g) may be measured separately.

(i) MUTUAL CONDUCTANCE. With the anode potential maintained at a constant value, the grid potential is varied and the corresponding changes in the anode current are observed. Readings of anode current (I_a) are then plotted against those for grid potential (V_g) : a family of such curves is plotted for various values of anode potential (V_a).

The following readings were obtained on a particular triode at the two fixed values of anode potential indicated : the anode current/grid potential graph is plotted in Fig. 13.15.

V_g (V) .	0	-2	-4	-6	-8	-10	-12	-14	-16	-18
I_a (mA) ($V_a = 100$)	10	8	6	4	2	1	0·4	0·1	—	—
I_a (mA) ($V_a = 130$)	15	13	11	9	7	5	3	1·5	0·7	0·2

It will be observed that these graphs have a considerable linear portion which for the two cases are parallel, i.e. the slope of the two graphs is constant over this section. This slope being the ratio current/voltage measures a conductance but since the current and voltage values relate to different circuits—those of the grid and anode—the gradient is known as the *control-grid-to-anode transconductance* or more usually as the MUTUAL

CONDUCTANCE. It is a measure of the control exercised by the grid on the anode current and may be defined as *the ratio of a small change in anode current to the change in grid potential which causes it*, the anode potential being maintained constant. Mutual conductance is denoted by the symbol g_m and

central linear portion with a curved portion a either end: these non-linear regions may hav great significance in the operation of a valve an they are referred to as the "upper anode bend" an "lower anode bend" respectively. The mutua conductance—shown dotted in this diagram—i

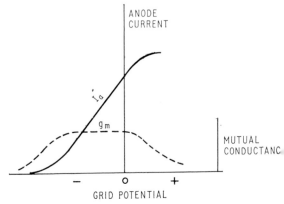

FIG. 13.16. VARIATION OF MUTUAL CONDUCTANCE

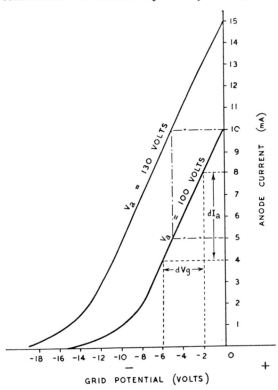

FIG. 13.15. CHARACTERISTIC OF TRIODE VALVE: GRID POTENTIAL/ANODE CURRENT GRAPH

measured, not in mhos, but in "milliamperes per volt." If dI_a milliamperes is the small change in anode current consequent upon a small change dV_g in grid potential then—

$$g_m = dI_a/dV_g \text{ mA/V} \qquad . \qquad . (13.3)$$

In Fig. 13.15, over the linear portion of either graph, $\dfrac{dI_a}{dV_g} = \dfrac{4}{4} = 1$ mA/V (shown by the dotted lines).

The general shape of the mutual characteristic for a valve is shown in Fig. 13.16 for an extended range of grid potential up to the point where saturation occurs. At heavy negative grid potentials the anode current is virtually reduced to zero. At zero or positive values of grid potential saturation commences. The anode current graph comprises a

constant over the linear portion, decreasing as th curved portions are approached.

(ii) VALVE RESISTANCE. With the grid potentia at a constant value, the anode potential i varied and the changes in anode current ar observed: a graph is then plotted of anod current against anode potential. A family of thes curves may then be plotted for various fixed value of grid potential.

The static characteristics over the operatin range of a particular triode are given below fo three different values of constant grid potentia the resulting graphs are plotted in Fig. 13.17.

	I_a (mA)		
V_a (V)	$V_g = 0$	$V_g = -3.0$	$V_g = -6.0$
50	3.2	—	—
100	7.4	—	—
150	11.9	1.5	—
200	17.0	4.8	—
250	—	8.4	1.0
300	—	12.5	3.0
350	—	—	6.0

The linear portions of these graphs are approx mately of the same slope: this slope measures th ratio current/voltage for the internal circuit of th anode current and is called the *internal conductan* of the valve. The reciprocal of this is the voltag current ratio for the same circuit: this is various

nown as the A.C. RESISTANCE or the INTERNAL
IPEDANCE or as the SLOPE RESISTANCE : it may be
efined as *the ratio of a small change in anode poten-
al to the change in anode current which results, the
rid potential remaining constant.* It is measured in
hms and denoted by the symbol r_a. (An external
r load resistance in the anode circuit is denoted by
he capital letter R_a.) Over the linear portion of
he graphs, if dI_a is the small change in anode

within the limits of linearity, say -5 V (the chain-
dotted lines) the increase in current for an increase
of 30 V in anode potential is 5 mA. The valve
slope resistance is

$$dV_a/dI_a = 30/(5 \times 10^{-3}) = 6\,000\ \Omega$$

(iii) AMPLIFICATION FACTOR. Following a change
in grid potential, the anode potential is readjusted
to restore the anode current to its original value. A

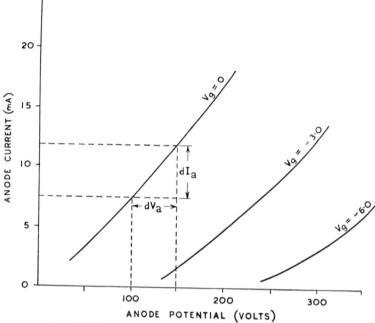

FIG. 13.17. CHARACTERISTIC OF TRIODE VALVE: ANODE
POTENTIAL/ANODE CURRENT GRAPH

irrent resulting from a small change dV_a in anode
otential, then—

$$r_a = dV_a/dI_a \text{ ohms .} \qquad . \quad (13.4)$$

For this evaluation the anode current must be
xpressed in amperes. The value of the impedance
iay vary to some extent with the operating con-
itions of the valve.

In the graph shown (Fig. 13.17) the a.c. resistance

$$r_a = \frac{dV_a}{dI_a} = \frac{150 - 100}{(11 \cdot 9 - 7 \cdot 4) \times 10^{-3}} = \frac{50 \times 10^3}{4 \cdot 5}$$
$$\simeq 11\,000\ \Omega$$

The a.c. resistance may also be determined from
pair of graphs showing the mutual characteristic.
.eferring to Fig. 13.15 for the valve there con-
dered, an increase of $(130 - 100) = 30$ V in anode
otential produces a rise in anode current : con-
dering this for any fixed value of grid potential

series of such measurements is made and the grid
potential changes are plotted against the anode
potential changes required to maintain the anode
current at a constant value.

A set of these curves is plotted in Fig. 13.18. The
slope here is the ratio of the anode voltage change
(dV_a) to the grid voltage change (dV_g) required to
maintain the anode current at a constant value.
This ratio is the AMPLIFICATION FACTOR, which may
be defined as *the ratio of a change in anode potential
to the change in grid potential required to maintain
the anode current constant.* It is denoted by the
symbol μ : being the ratio of two voltages it is a
simple number. Hence—

$$\mu = dV_a/dV_g \qquad . \qquad . \quad (13.5)$$

The amplification factor may be evaluated from
a pair of graphs showing the mutual characteristic,
such as those shown in Fig. 13.15 : it is not usual to

plot the graphs of amplification factor in the form shown in Fig. 13.18. Consider any constant value of anode current within the linear portion of the graph (Fig. 13.15), say $I_a = 8$ mA. This current may be obtained at $V_g = -2$ V when $V_a = 100$ V; and also at $V_g = -7$ V when $V_a = 130$ V. The change in anode volts is $dV_a = (130 - 100) = 30$ V while the corresponding change in grid voltage is $V_g = (7 - 2) = 5$ V: for this valve

$$\mu = dV_a/dV_g = 30/5 = 6$$

A knowledge of the valve parameters enables the most desirable type of valve to be selected for a

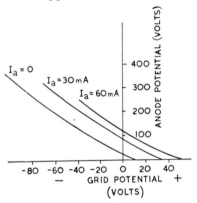

FIG. 13.18. CHARACTERISTIC OF TRIODE VALVE: ANODE POTENTIAL/GRID POTENTIAL GRAPH

particular purpose from the wide range of valves at present available.

A simple relationship exists between the parameters. The amplification factor, $\mu = \dfrac{dV_a}{dV_g}$

Multiply by $\dfrac{dI_a}{dI_a} (= 1)$, $\mu = \dfrac{dV_a}{dV_g} \times \dfrac{dI_a}{dI_a}$

Re-arranging, $\mu = \dfrac{dV_a}{dI_a} \times \dfrac{dI_a}{dV_g}$

whence $\mu = r_a \times g_m$.   .   (13.6)

Grid current (Fig. 13.19) is produced under certain conditions when the grid is positive to the filament, some of the electrons on their way to the anode being attracted and absorbed by the grid. Up to a certain limit this grid current is practically independent of the anode potential. If the anode voltage is high, the velocity of the electrons becomes very great as the positive grid potential increases and electrons strike the grid with such impact as to knock off other electrons (by "secondary emission") which are attracted to the anode. The result is that beyond a certain point the grid current begins to

fall off, becomes zero and then reverses as shown in the graph for $V_a = 200$ or 250 V. At the point where the grid current becomes zero, as many electrons are being liberated from the grid as are absorbed by the grid. When more electrons are being liberated than are being absorbed, the reversed current increases until the positive grid potential becomes of the same order as the anode potential: the secondary electrons are then no longer drawn to the anode and the grid current again falls to zero.

If the valve is "soft," some of the positive ions formed by collision between electrons and gas

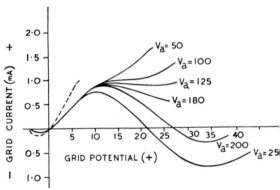

FIG. 13.19. GRID CURRENT CHARACTERISTIC

molecules are attracted to and absorbed by the grid when this is negative to the cathode. This is equivalent to a negative grid current and is sometimes referred to as "backlash" or *reversed grid current*. Absence of reversed grid current is used as a confirmation of the hardness of the valve. When the grid potential is positive these ions are attracted to the cathode and more electrons are absorbed by the grid than is the case with a hard valve. This results in a steepening of the grid current characteristic on the positive side (shown dotted in Fig. 13.19).

EXAMPLE 13.1 (A). If a valve has an amplification factor of 30 and an impedance of 20 000 Ω, what is its mutual conductance?   (C. & G.)

$$\mu = 30$$
$$r_a = 20\,000\ \Omega$$
$$\mu = r_a \times g_m, \text{ or } g_m = \mu/r_a$$
$$g_m = \frac{30 \times 10^{-3}}{20} = 1\cdot5 \times 10^{-3}$$
$$= \underline{1\cdot5 \text{ mA/V}}$$

EXAMPLE 13.2 (A). A triode valve has a characteristic given by: $I_a = 0\cdot002(V_a + 10V_g)^2$, where I_a is in milliamperes, and V_a and V_g are in volts. Plot the characteristic curves for a plate voltage of 160 between values of V_g of $+4$ and -16.

What is the mutual conductance of the valve at zero grid potential with the above plate voltage? (C. & G.)

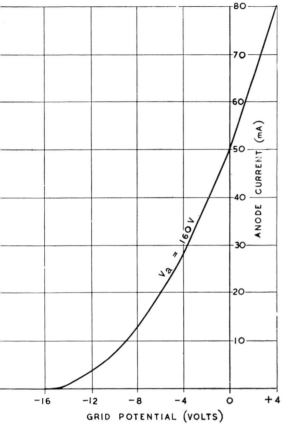

FIG. 13.20 (Example 13.2)

See Fig. 13.20 plotted from the following values—

V_g	$10V_g$	$V_a + 10V_g$	$(V_a + 10V_g)^2$	$I_a = 0.002(V_a + 10V_g)^2$
4	40	200	40.0×10^3	80
2	20	180	32.4×10^3	64.8
0	0	160	25.6×10^3	51.2
−2	−20	140	19.6×10^3	39.2
−4	−40	120	14.4×10^3	28.8
−6	−60	100	10.0×10^3	20.0
−8	−80	80	6.4×10^3	12.8
−10	−100	60	3.6×10^3	7.2
−12	−120	40	1.6×10^3	3.2
−14	−140	20	0.4×10^3	0.8
−16	−160	0	0	0

$$\frac{dI_a}{dV_g} = \frac{64\cdot8 - 39\cdot2}{4} = \frac{25\cdot6}{4} = \underline{6\cdot4 \text{ mA/V}}$$

EXAMPLE 13.3 (A). A three-electrode valve has the following static characteristics—

Grid voltage .	+ 2·5	0	− 2·5	− 5	− 7·5	− 10
Anode current—						
120 V H.T..	7·0	6·35	5·4	4·45	3·5	2·55
80 V H.T..	4·75	3·8	2·85	1·9	1·0	0·5

Plot the characteristic grid voltage/anode current curves and determine the internal impedance at zero grid voltage, the amplification factor and mutual conductance. (C. & G.)

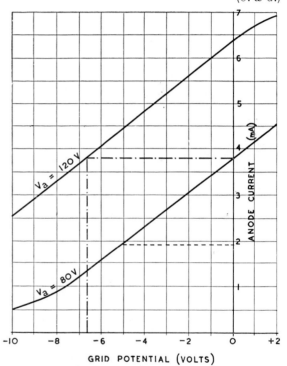

FIG. 13.21 (Example 13.3)

The graphs are plotted in Fig. 13.21. Internal impedance (at $V_g = 0$),

$$\frac{dV_a}{dI_a} = \frac{120 - 80}{(6\cdot35 - 3\cdot8) \times 10^{-3}} = \frac{40 \times 10^3}{2\cdot55} = \underline{15\,700\,\Omega}$$

Amplification factor $= \dfrac{dV_a}{dV_g} = \dfrac{120 - 80}{6\cdot6} = \dfrac{40}{6\cdot6}$

$$\simeq 6$$

Mutual conductance $= \dfrac{dI_a}{dV_g} = \dfrac{3\cdot8 - 1\cdot9}{5}$

$$= \frac{1\cdot9}{5} = \underline{0\cdot38 \text{ mA/V}}$$

13.6. The Valve Amplifier. A varying voltage can be amplified by a suitably designed valve circuit. Since the valve is a voltage-operated device its input circuit consumes no power: weak signals can be applied via a high-ratio step-up voltage transformer to increase the voltage available to operate the valve. These signals are required to operate some instrument such as a relay or a loudspeaker, and for this purpose the valve is designed as a power amplifier. This "output valve" circuit is usually preceded by one or more amplifier valve stages whose function is solely to amplify the signal voltage for application to a further stage either of voltage or power amplification. For both purposes, voltage and power amplification, the principle is the same though the output circuits and the power handling capacities of the valves used will differ.

In employing a valve as an amplifier, an alternating voltage is applied across the grid and cathode (Fig. 13.11) to control changes in anode current: by a suitable choice of output impedance in the anode circuit the ensuing fluctuations in p.d. across this impedance may be made considerably greater than those applied to the grid circuit.

The effect upon the anode current of applying a sine-wave signal to the grid circuit may be examined in conjunction with the mutual characteristic of the valve (Fig. 13.22). The input signal will cause the grid potential to "swing" away from its normal zero potential and to vary between the equal positive and negative peak values of the applied signal. If instantaneous values of grid potential due to the signal are projected on to the graph and thence on to the anode current axis, the instantaneous values of anode current resulting may be plotted.

It is at once apparent that, if the grid is allowed to operate over a range which includes any non-linear portion of the graph, the changes in anode current will not bear a constant relation to the changes in grid potential. In Fig. 13.22 the changes in anode current are greater for negative grid potential changes than for positive grid potential changes owing to the onset of saturation. The anode current waveform is not a faithful reproduction of the grid potential signal: due to *non-linear distortion* a change in waveform has occurred which is equivalent to the introduction of alien harmonics.

The first requirement in using the valve as an amplifier is to limit the excursions of grid potential to the straight portion of the characteristic graph. If the voltage of the input signal is very small—frequently the case with a first stage amplifier—the arrangement depicted by Fig. 13.22, but using a valve with a slightly different characteristic, may

provide distortionless amplification. In most amplifiers, however, it is necessary to "bias" or polarize the grid potential so that in the idle condition it operating point lies midway along the linear portion of the graph. This condition is shown in Fig. 13.23 If the input signal is applied about this biased operating point, then instead of these alteration making the grid potential alternately negative and positive, the signal voltages now make the grid potential *more negative* or *less negative*. For example

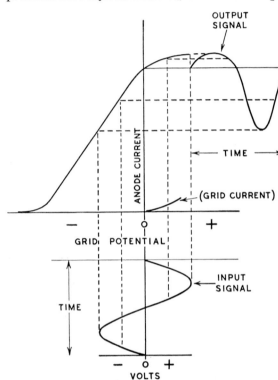

FIG. 13.22. VALVE AMPLIFIER—INPUT AND OUTPUT SIGNALS WITHOUT GRID BIAS VOLTAGE

if the steady bias given to the grid is − 10 V and the applied signal has peaks of ± 5 V, the grid potential will swing between the values of (−10 ± 5 i.e. between − 15 V and − 5 V. Provided that this range falls within the linear portion of the characteristic graph, the changes in anode current bear constant relation to the changes in grid potential and as far as the input circuit is concerned distortionless amplification will result. This condition is however, subject to absence of grid current, and also to suitable design of the anode circuit, described below.

The desired operating point on the grid may be obtained by the inclusion of a battery of suitable oltage in the grid circuit: this *grid bias* (G.B.) attery (or "C" battery) will have its negative rminal connected towards the grid and its positive rminal to the cathode (Fig. 13.24 (*a*)). No power delivered by this battery which can therefore be f small dimensions. More conveniently the reuired bias voltage is derived from the p.d. across resistor connected in series with the cathode: in 'ig. 13.24 (*b*) this resistor R ohms carries the anode urrent I_a. The arrow shows the conventional

d.c. component by providing a shunt circuit which includes a capacitor, or by passing the anode current through the primary winding of a transformer: it is this a.c. component passing through the anode load impedance which provides the a.c. output voltage of the amplifier.

The cathode bias resistor (Fig. 13.24 (*b*)) is shunted with a capacitor to provide a low impedance path for the a.c. component of the anode current since it is undesirable that bias voltages should be

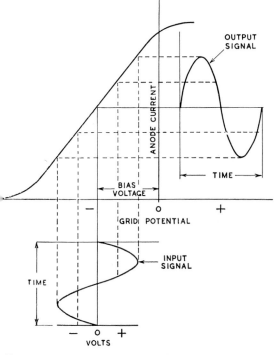

FIG. 13.23. VALVE AMPLIFIER—INPUT AND OUTPUT SIGNALS WITH GRID BIAS VOLTAGE

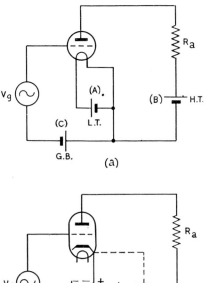

FIG. 13.24. APPLICATION OF GRID BIAS VOLTAGE

Using: (*a*) Grid bias battery. (*b*) Cathode resistor.

urrent direction which makes the grid negative ith respect to the cathode. The bias voltage is mply calculated from $V = I_a R$: if a multiectrode valve is used the cathode current is the m of the current taken by the anode plus one more other electrodes. In some arrangements e filament current may be used to provide bias otentials—see Fig. 2.23.

Though the input signal comprises an alternating oltage the anode current is essentially a fluctuating rect current. It is convenient to regard this anode urrent (Fig. 13.25 (*a*)) as the combination of a eady direct current with an alternating current mponent (Fig. 13.25 (*b*)) having the (undistorted) aveform of the input signal. This a.c. component the anode current may be separated from the

developed by this a.c. component: the value of capacitance should be such that its impedance is small at the lowest frequency transmitted by the amplifier.

Except under *static* conditions (Fig. 13.14)— namely with a constant potential on the grid and no load impedance in the anode circuit—the actual potential on the anode is not equal to that of the H.T. battery nor does it remain constant under working or *dynamic* conditions. A p.d. of $I_a R_a$ volts will exist across a load resistance R_a ohms in the anode circuit which carries a current I_a amperes (Fig. 13.26). The valve anode will actually be at a potential $I_a R_a$ volts less than that of the anode battery. If the anode battery voltage is E volts.

the anode potential V_a is equal to $V_a = (E - I_a R_a)$ volts: furthermore, under working conditions the value of I_a is fluctuating at signal frequency (Fig. 13.25 (a)).

The reduction in potential available to the anode of the valve clearly depends for a given valve upon the magnitude of the load impedance. To examine

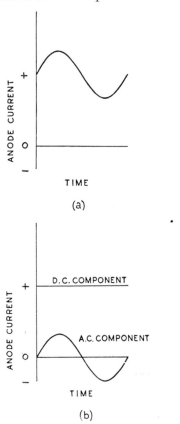

(a)

(b)

FIG. 13.25. A.C. AND D.C. COMPONENTS OF ANODE CURRENT

the working performance of a valve, a study of the static characteristic is insufficient: it is necessary to draw the LOAD LINE which represents the actual operating points of the valve when the grid potential is varying and the anode circuit includes the load impedance. The load line is most usefully constructed across a series of anode potential/anode current graphs (Fig. 13.27). It may also be drawn across the mutual characteristic graphs (Fig. 13.15).

With the anode potential/anode current characteristics (Fig. 13.27) the load line for a pure resistance load may be constructed in the following manner: (i) If the grid is heavily biased negatively so that $I_a = 0$, there is no p.d. ($I_a R_a$) across the

anode load resistance and the full anode battery e.m.f. E volts is available at the anode ($I_a R_a = 0$). The point ($I_a = 0$, $V_a = E$) is plotted at P. (ii) For any value of anode current I_a, the anode potential will be $V_a = E - I_a R_a$ and a second point C can be plotted for any related pair of values of I_a and V_a. Alternatively, a second point Q can be

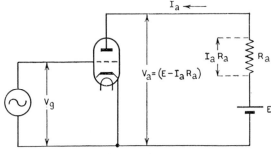

FIG. 13.26. ANODE POTENTIAL UNDER DYNAMIC CONDITIONS

plotted for the value of I_a which makes $V_a = 0$ this assumes that all the H.T. voltage E volts i dropped across the load resistance R_a, i.e. $I_a = E/R_a$

The straight line PQ—the load line—has a slope representing the load resistance. This line is the locus of points representing the anode voltage fo

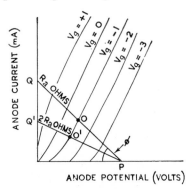

FIG. 13.27. LOAD LINES APPLIED TO ANODE CHARACTERISTIC GRAPHS

various values of anode current: it passes throug the point whose co-ordinates are zero anode curren and the full anode voltage supply. The slope of th load line expressed as the tangent of the angle ϕ i the reciprocal of the anode load resistance R_a, i.e $R_a = 1/\tan \phi$. Thus, if the load resistance i doubled the gradient is halved and for the sam valve, the load line still passes through the point P

The grid would be normally biased to some poin such as O: the application of a sine-wave signal t the grid causes the operating point to swing t

qual distances on either side of O along the load
ie. The range within which the load line is cut
equal sections on both sides of the normal bias
int O by equal changes in grid potential will be
ie range of undistorted output.

For anode loads which have a reactive component
ie load line becomes an ellipse, the dimensions of
hich are a function of the frequency of the signal
well as its peak voltage.

The power developed in the anode load resistance
ay be evaluated from the load line. In Fig. 13.28,
A is the static operating point of the valve (the
ased point of the grid) and BC represents the
tal grid swing, this is twice the peak value of the
id signal voltage. BD is the total change in anode
rrent, and CD is the total change in anode poten-
al: both of these quantities represent twice their

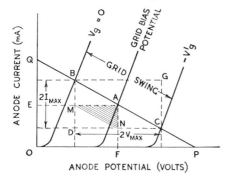

FIG. 13.28. EVALUATION OF OUTPUT POWER

ak values so that I_{max} is $BD/2$ and V_{max} is $CD/2$.
he r.m.s. values are

$$I = BD/(2\sqrt{2}) \text{ and } V = CD/(2\sqrt{2})$$

that the power is

$$\frac{BD}{2\sqrt{2}} \times \frac{CD}{2\sqrt{2}} = \frac{BD \times CD}{8}$$

. one-eighth of the product of the total anode
oltage and anode current swings.

This power output is represented by the area of
ie shaded triangle MAN, i.e. one-eighth of the
ctangle $BDCG = BD \times CD$. The total power
pplied is represented by the rectangle $OEAF$
$= OE \times OF$: under linear operating conditions
ie mean anode current does not vary when a
nusoidal signal is applied to the grid. The differ-
ice between the rectangle $OEAF$ (total power)
d the triangle MAN (useful power) represents
ie power dissipated at the anode—the figure
$EMNF$.

The above assumes that linear characteristics
otain and that grid current is not allowed to flow.

For distortionless output the intercepts AB and
AC should equal one another: if they are not equal
the peak value of one half-cycle of the output
voltage is increased while the peak of the other
half-cycle is reduced. This *non-linear distortion*
introduces a second harmonic component, giving
rise to *second harmonic distortion*.

If the lengths of the intercepts AB and AC differ
by ± 10 per cent, i.e. if the ratio $AB/AC = 1\cdot1/0\cdot9$
$= 1\cdot22$, the magnitude of second harmonic distortion introduced is 5 per cent of the fundamental.
This amount of distortion is not serious and the
ratio $1\cdot22$ is used as a criterion in design.

The load line may also be drawn for the mutual
characteristic: it is shown dotted in Fig. 13.29 for
load resistances of 40 000 Ω and 80 000 Ω. When
the grid bias is sufficiently negative to prevent the

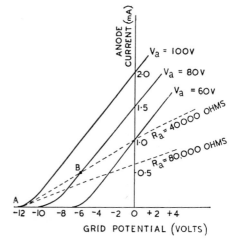

FIG. 13.29. LOAD LINES APPLIED TO MUTUAL
CHARACTERISTIC GRAPHS

flow of anode current, the anode potential is equal
to that of the h.t. supply: in the example shown
this is the point A, ($I_a = 0$, $V_a = 100$). If the
negative grid potential is reduced to permit the
anode current to rise to, say, $0\cdot5$ mA, then considering the 40 000 Ω load, the anode voltage drop
is now $(0\cdot5 \times 10^{-3} \times 40\,000) = 20$ V: from this
the point B, ($I_a = 0\cdot5$, $V_a = 80$ V) is plotted. The
load line is constructed by joining together a series
of such points. The load line is almost straight
except for a small portion near point A. The
straight portion of the load line represents the range
of grid potential and anode current changes which
can occur together without distortion.

If the peak value of the applied signal is so great
that the positive half-cycles make the grid potential
positive, grid current will flow during those intervals. This will cause a potential drop in the grid

circuit which will absorb power from the input circuit and also modify the bias voltage on the grid, so causing distortion. It is important that the grid circuit is not overloaded by a signal voltage whose magnitude causes the flow of grid current.

A change in phase is introduced by the valve. A positive *increase* in grid potential produces an increase in anode current: this increases the p.d. across the anode resistance R_a and *decreases* the potential at the anode, producing a phase change of 180°.

EXAMPLE 13.4 (A). The following values of anode current were obtained with a triode—

Anode voltage	25	50	75	100	Volts
Anode current with $V_g = 0$ . .	0·4	2·8	6·0	8·5	Milli- amps
Anode current with $V_g = -4·2$ . .	0	0·6	3·0	5·7	
Anode current with $V_g = -8·3$ . .	0	0	1·0	2·9	

Plot the anode current/anode voltage characteristic curves.

If a battery of 150 V and a resistance of 15 000 Ω are connected in series with the anode and cathode, what will be the anode current at the above three values of grid voltage?   (*C. & G.*)

See Fig. 13.30. The load line is plotted from the points (i) $I_a = 0$, $V_a = 150$ V; (ii) $V_a = 0$, $I_a = 150/15\,000 = 10$ mA.

From the graph,

when $V_g = 0$, $I_a = 5·3$ mA
               $V_g = -4·2$ V, $I_a = 4·2$ mA
               $V_g = -8·3$ V, $I_a = 3·2$ mA

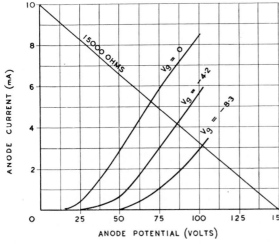

FIG. 13.30 (Example 13.4)

EXAMPLE 13.5 (A). A triode has the following anode characteristics—

$V_g = 0$		$V_g = -40$ V		$V_g = -80$ V	
Anode Volts	Anode Current (mA)	Anode Volts	Anode Current (mA)	Anode Volts	Anode Current (mA)
50	12	175	10	300	7
75	25	200	23	325	17
100	43	225	38	350	28
125	65	250	58		

If the grid bias is − 40 V, the anode voltage supply 350 V, and the external load 6 000 Ω, calculate the power output when the grid swing has an amplitude of 40 V.
(*C. & G.*)

See the diagram, Fig. 13.31.

The slope of the load line is 6 V/mA, i.e. 6 000 Ω resistance requires a p.d. of 6 V to produce 1 mA. The slope ϕ is here shown as the angle between the

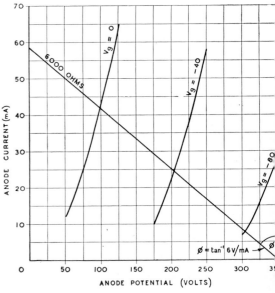

FIG. 13.31 (Example 13.5)

load line and *the anode current axis*. The load line is drawn through the two points

$$(I_a = 0, \ V_a = 350 \text{ V})$$

and $(I_a = 25 \text{ mA}, \ V_a = E - I_a R_a$
               $= 350 - 150 = 200 \text{ V})$

As the grid potential swings from—

− 40 to 0, the anode current varies from
                    24·75 to 41·75 = 17 mA

− 40 to − 80, the anode current varies from
                    24·75 to 7·75 = 17 mA

These are peak current values. The r.m.s. value $= 17/\sqrt{2} = 12$ mA.

Power output $= I_a^2 R_a = (12 \times 10^{-3})^2 \times 6\,000$
$= 0\cdot864$ W

EXAMPLE 13.6 (A). A high-μ triode valve has the following characteristics—

Plate Volt-age	Plate Current in mA at following Grid Potentials						
	$-3\cdot0$	$-2\cdot5$	$-2\cdot0$	$-1\cdot5$	$-1\cdot0$	$-0\cdot5$	0
60	0	0	0	0	0·08	0·4	0·9
80	0	0	0	0·01	0·19	0·59	1·16
100	0	0	0	0·06	0·30	0·79	1·45
120	0	0	0	0·12	0·49	1·02	1·76
140	0	0	0·03	0·24	0·68	1·28	0
160	0	0	0·10	0·40	0·92	1·52	0
180	0	0·03	0·18	0·58	1·16	0	0
200	0	0·08	0·30	0·80	1·41	0	0
220	0·02	0·14	0·48	1·00	0	0	0
240	0·05	0·24	0·68	1·30	0	0	0

Plot the characteristics with the plate voltages as abscissae and the plate currents as ordinates for the given values of grid potentials.

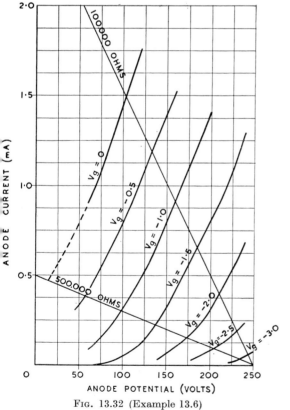

FIG. 13.32 (Example 13.6)

If an external resistance is inserted in the plate circuit, what will be the plate currents with a plate voltage of 250 V and grid voltages of $-2\cdot0$, $-1\cdot5$, $-1\cdot0$, $-0\cdot5$, and 0, when the external resistance is (i) 100 000 Ω, (ii) 500 000 Ω? (C. & G.)

See the diagram, Fig. 13.32. The load lines are drawn both passing through the point

$$(I_a = 0,\; V_a = 250 \text{ V})$$

The slope of the 100 000 Ω load is 100 V/mA, i.e. the anode current is 1 mA at $E - I_a R_a = 250 - 100 = 150$ V, which is here used to plot the second point ($I_a = 1$ mA, $V_a = 150$ V) on the load line.

The slope of the 500 000 Ω load line is 500 V/mA: the second point is plotted at $250 - 250 = 0$ for 0·5 mA ($I_a = 0\cdot5$ mA, $V_a = 0$).

The following values are read from the intersection of the load lines and graphs—

V_a	Plate Current mA	
	100 000 Ω	500 000 Ω
$-2\cdot0$	0·4	0·15
$-1\cdot5$	0·64	0·22
$-1\cdot0$	0·91	0·30
$-0\cdot5$	1·175	0·39
0	1·465	0·47*

* Obtained by extrapolation of the characteristic at zero grid voltage.

VALVE EQUIVALENT GENERATOR

Since a voltage change dV_g on the grid has the same effect upon the anode current I_a as a voltage change $\mu \cdot dV_g$ on the anode, it is convenient to consider the valve as equivalent to a generator having an e.m.f. equal to $\mu \cdot dV_g$ volts and with an internal resistance r_a ohms connected in series with the load impedance Z_a (Fig. 13.33 (a)). The change in circuit current due to a voltage dV_g on the grid is—

$$dI_a = \frac{\mu \cdot dV_g}{r_a + Z_a}$$

and the change in p.d. across the load impedance is

$$dV_a = dI_a \cdot Z_a = \mu \cdot dV_g \frac{Z_a}{r_a + Z_a} \text{ volts}$$

If this expression is multiplied by $r_a/r_a (= 1)$, then—

$$dV_a = \mu \cdot dV_g \frac{Z_a}{r_a + Z_a} \times \frac{r_a}{r_a} = \frac{\mu}{r_a} \cdot dV_g \cdot \left(\frac{r_a Z_a}{r_a + Z_a}\right)$$

The ratio $\mu/r_a = g_m$, the mutual conductance, while the term within brackets is the joint impedance of Z_a and r_a in parallel. The output voltage is that which would result from a current $dI_a = g_m . dV_g$ flowing through Z_a and r_a in parallel. The equivalent circuit is sometimes drawn in the form shown in Fig. 13.33 (b), demonstrating that the valve a.c. resistance is in parallel with the load, and adds to the losses.

The equivalent circuit of Fig. 13.33 (a) is the *constant-voltage* generator form of the equivalent circuit and is useful in the calculations for triode amplifier design. The other equivalent circuit (Fig. 13.33 (b)) is the *constant-current* generator

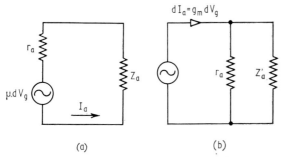

FIG. 13.33. EQUIVALENT CIRCUIT OF VALVE

form of equivalent circuit, used for pentode circuits where $r_a \gg Z_a$.

The change in output p.d., dV_a, expressed as a ratio to the input signal dV_g, gives the actual VOLTAGE AMPLIFICATION produced by the valve circuit as a whole. The voltage amplification factor (v.a.f.) is—

$$\text{v.a.f.} = \frac{dV_a}{dV_g} = \frac{\mu . dV_g}{dV_g} . \frac{Z_a}{r_a + Z_a}$$

$$= \mu . \frac{Z_a}{r_a + Z_a} \quad . \quad . \quad (13.7)$$

Frequently the anode load consists of a pure resistance R_a in which case R_a can be substituted for Z_a in the above expression and

$$\text{v.a.f.} = \mu . \frac{R_a}{r_a + R_a} \quad . \quad . \quad (13.8)$$

For a pure resistance load the voltage amplification will be less than the amplification factor (μ), since $\dfrac{R_a}{r_a + R_a} < 1$. In a voltage amplifier, the load resistance R_a is given a maximum value so that the factor $\dfrac{R_a}{r_a + R_a}$ shall approach as near as possible to unity: this maximum value will have practical limitations on account of the reduction in anode

potential produced and also due to the introduction of distortion. It is found that the value of R cannot be made much greater than three or four times r_a, giving a v.a.f. of 75 to 80 per cent of the value of μ. (If $R_a = 3r_a$, v.a.f. $= \mu . 3r_a/(4r_a) = 75\% \mu$: if $R_a = 4r_a$, v.a.f. $= \mu . 4r_a/(5r_a) = 80\% \mu$.)

The voltage amplification may be expressed in decibels in which case the amplification is usually referred to as the "gain."

If the valve is used as a power amplifier, the optimum value for the load resistance is that required for the maximum transfer of power from a source to a load, for this condition $R_a = r_a$. This assumes that the valve acts as a linear generator, i.e. that the valve is not overloaded so as to introduce distortion. Here again it is found that the load impedance cannot be reduced to this ideal value without the introduction of excessive distortion—the conditions for maximum amplification or power do not coincide with those for minimum distortion.

The voltage amplification may be deduced from the load line. In Fig. 13.28 a change in grid potential (dV_g) equivalent to ($V' - 0$)—the difference between the operating points C and B—produces a change in anode potential (dV_a) equivalent to CL. These values may be read from the graphs and the v.a.f. $= dV_a/dV_g$.

EXAMPLE 13.7 (A). The static characteristics, over the operating range, of a triode valve are given in the accompanying Table. The valve is operated as a low-frequency amplifier with a pure resistance anode load of 20 000 Ω. The static operating point is $V_a = 200$ and $V_g = -3.0$.

Sketch the anode current/anode voltage characteristic and draw the load line. Determine the voltage amplification of the stage. State whether appreciable distortion will occur when a peak voltage of 3.0 V is impressed on the grid circuit.
(C. & G.)

Anode Voltage	Anode Current (mA)		
	$V_g = 0$	$V_g = -3.0$	$V_g = -6.0$
50	3·2	0	0
100	7·4	0	0
150	11·9	1·5	0
200	17·0	4·8	0
250	—	8·4	1·0
300	—	12·5	3·0
350	—	—	6·0

See the diagram, Fig. 13.34.

At the given operating point ($V_a = 200$, $V_g = -3.0$), the anode current is, from the Table, 4.8 mA.

From $E = V_a + I_a R_a$, the H.T. voltage supply is $E = 200 + (4 \cdot 8 \times 10^{-3} \times 20\,000) = 200 + 96 = 296$ V. The load line is drawn between (i) $I_a = 0$, $V_a = 296$, and (ii) $V_a = 0$, $I_a = 296/20\,000 = 14 \cdot 8$ mA.

The load line intersects the characteristics at (i) $V_g = 0$, $V_a = 115$, and (ii) $V_g = -6$, $V_a = 265$, i.e. a change of 6 V in grid potential produces a change of $265 - 115 = 150$ V in anode potential. The voltage amplification is $150/6 = 25$.

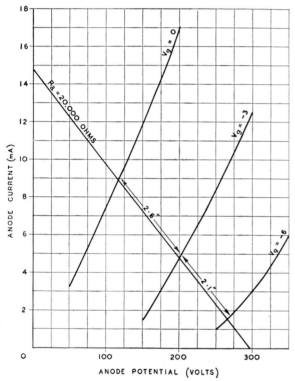

FIG. 13.34 (Example 13.7)

The measured intercept of the load line between the characteristics for $V_g = 0$ and $V_g = -3$ is 2·6 in.: that between the graphs for $V_g = -3$ and $V_g = -6$ is only 2·1 in. The output voltage variations resulting from peak signals of ± 3 V applied to the grid about an operating point of -3 V will be in the ratio of $2 \cdot 6/2 \cdot 1 \; (= 1 \cdot 24)$ for the positive and negative half-cycles. The output wave shape will be unsymmetrical and a little over 5 per cent second harmonic distortion results, a figure which need not be regarded as appreciable.

EXAMPLE 13.8 (A). A certain small output valve having an amplification factor of 10 and an a.c. resistance of 5 000 Ω is used with a load resistance of 10 000 Ω. Estimate the power in the load when a signal of 5 V is applied to the grid. (C. & G.)

$$\mu = 10$$
$$r_a = 5\,000\ \Omega$$
$$R_a = 10\,000\ \Omega$$
$$V_g = 5\ \text{V}$$
$$I_a = \mu \cdot \frac{V_g}{r_a + R_a} = \frac{10 \times 5}{5\,000 + 10\,000}$$
$$= \frac{50}{15\,000} = 1/300\ \text{A}$$

Power in load
$$= I_a^2 R_a = \frac{1 \times 10\,000}{300^2} = \frac{10^4}{9 \times 10^4} = 0 \cdot 11\ \text{W}$$

CLASSIFICATION OF AMPLIFIERS

Amplifiers may be classified according to their use and characteristics. They may be required for d.c. amplification (rarely) or for amplifying signals at audio, radio, or video frequencies: each case requires separate design considerations. They may be designed to give linear amplification over narrow or wide bandwidths. They are also classified, according to the operating conditions, as Class-A, Class-AB, Class-B, or Class-C amplifiers.

The normal low-power audio-frequency amplifiers use Class-A amplification. In this mode the valve is used in such a way that its operation is confined to the substantially linear region of its characteristic. The grid operating point and the amplitude of the input signal are adjusted so that anode current flows at all times during a signal cycle, as indicated in Fig. 13.35 (a).

In Class-AB operation the grid potential and input signal are so arranged that anode current flows for appreciably more than half, but for less than the whole, of the electrical cycle—see Fig. 13.35 (b). For a part of the cycle the grid is driven beyond its cut-off potential and no anode current flows.

With Class-B operation, the grid bias voltage acting alone would reduce the anode current to approximately zero, so that the anode current flows for approximately half of each cycle when an alternating voltage is applied to the grid—see Fig. 13.35 (c).

Classes AB and B may be used for higher power audio-frequency application by using two amplifier valves arranged in "push-pull" operation, i.e. each dealing with alternative half-cycles of the input signal.

Class-C operation is used in certain radio-frequency amplifiers. The valve is operated with the grid bias potential appreciably more negative than that which would reduce the anode current to approximately zero (Fig. 13.35 (d)): the anode current flows for appreciably less than half of

In each case the a.c. component of the output signal in the anode circuit of the first valve is applied to the grid circuit of the succeeding valve: this second valve must have sufficient available

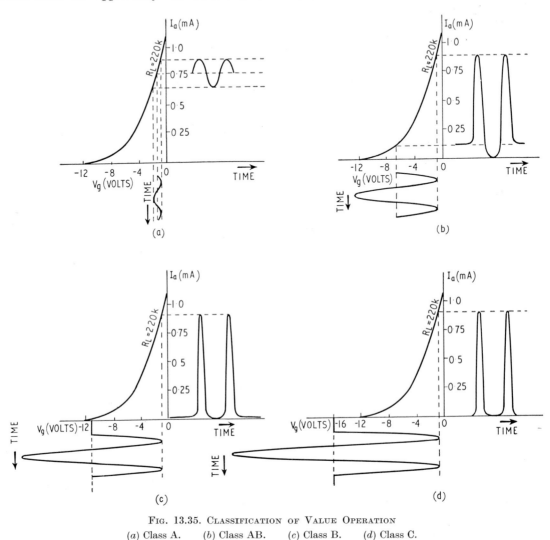

FIG. 13.35. CLASSIFICATION OF VALUE OPERATION

(a) Class A.   (b) Class AB.   (c) Class B.   (d) Class C.

each cycle when an alternating voltage is applied to the grid.

COUPLED AMPLIFIERS

It is frequently necessary to couple two or more amplifiers together in cascade to obtain the requisite voltage or power amplification. There are three different methods by which this is achieved. These are known as (i) resistance-capacitance, (ii) inductance-capacitance, and (iii) transformer coupling.

grid swing and be suitably biased according to the peak value of the signal applied to it.

(i) RESISTANCE-CAPACITANCE COUPLING (Fig. 13.36). In this arrangement the signal p.d. across a pure resistance R_a in the anode circuit is applied to the grid of the second valve by the use of a coupling capacitor C whose function is also to isolate the grid of the second valve from the anode potential of the first valve. The input signal is applied across a high-resistance load R_g in the grid circuit, which is necessary to complete the grid biasing circuit and whose value is comparable to the high input impedance between grid and cathode of the valve. The anode end of the load resistor R_a is connected to the coupling capacitor, the other

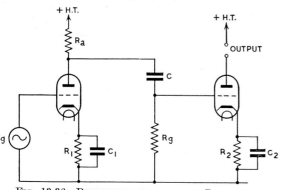

FIG. 13.36. RESISTANCE-CAPACITANCE COUPLING

end of the resistor being, of course, at the unvarying potential of the h.t. supply.

The equivalent coupling circuit is shown in Fig. 13.37. As the a.c. component only is being here considered the batteries, which act simply as a low resistance, can be omitted. The input impedance of the second valve is assumed to be infinitely high and is also omitted.

To obtain the maximum voltage amplification from the first valve the load resistance R_a is made

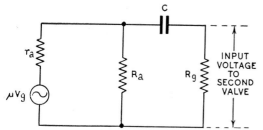

FIG. 13.37. EQUIVALENT CIRCUIT OF RESISTANCE-CAPACITANCE COUPLING

as great as possible, subject to the condition that the anode potential is not reduced excessively nor that an unduly high voltage anode supply is required. The grid input resistor R_g together with the coupling capacitor C are in shunt across the anode load resistor R_a: their combined impedance value must be high compared with that of R_a. The reactance of the coupling capacitor must be low over the frequency range to be transmitted: its value is determined by the lowest frequency of the signals. The value of R_g is normally about five times that of R_a with which it is in shunt.

The cathode bias resistors R_1 and R_2 are shunted by capacitors C_1 and C_2 whose purpose is to provide low-impedance paths to the a.c. component of the anode current.

The voltage amplification of the first valve is equal to

$$\mu \cdot \frac{R_a}{r_a + R_a} \qquad . \qquad . \quad (13.8)$$

Provided that the resistors R_a and R_g are sensibly non-reactive at high frequencies these elements will not introduce signal distortion. The coupling capacitor will have such a value as to introduce negligible frequency distortion except at very low frequencies.

The advantages of resistance-capacitance coupling are that the circuit design is simple, the components are inexpensive and they require little accommodation. In particular the gain/frequency characteristic is approximately linear over a wide

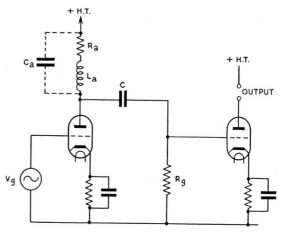

FIG. 13.38. INDUCTANCE-CAPACITANCE COUPLING

range of frequencies: this type of coupling is extensively used for high quality speech and music amplifiers. The voltage amplification may be made to approach the amplification factor of the valve but the voltage of the anode battery must be high to allow for the considerable voltage drop in the anode load resistor.

(ii) INDUCTANCE-CAPACITANCE COUPLING (Fig. 13.38). With this arrangement the anode load impedance takes the form of an inductor or choke, a capacitor being used as the coupling element. The inductance must offer a high reactance at the frequencies of the a.c. component: these currents find a low impedance path through the coupling capacitor.

The value of this load impedance varies with the frequency and is equal to $Z_a = R_a + j\omega L_a$: the resistance component R_a is usually negligibly small. The voltage amplification is determined by substituting $(R_a + j\omega L_a)$ for Z_a in the general equation (13.7), whence—

$$\text{v.a.f.} = \frac{dV_a}{dV_g} = \mu \cdot \frac{(R_a + j\omega L_a)}{r_a + R_a + j\omega L_a}$$

or if the resistance R_a of the inductor can be neglected—

$$\text{v.a.f.} = \frac{dV_a}{dV_g} = \mu \cdot \frac{\omega L_a}{(r_a{}^2 + \omega^2 L_a{}^2)^{\frac{1}{2}}} \quad . \quad (13.9)$$

This assumes that the capacitor C has a low impedance at signal frequencies and that the shunting effect of R_g and of the grid-cathode input

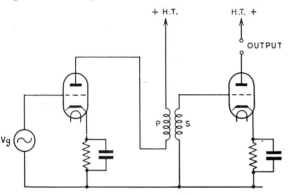

FIG. 13.39. TRANSFORMER COUPLING

impedance is negligible. The voltage amplification increases with the frequency and approaches μ when $\omega L_a \gg r_a$.

For radio-frequency amplification it is usual to shunt the inductor with a capacitor to tune the load circuit broadly to resonance: this particular arrangement is referred to as *tuned anode coupling*. The anode load impedance is then equal to $Z_a = L_a/(C_a R_a)$ at the frequency of resonance and it behaves as a resistance. The properties of the tuned anode circuit affect the degree of selectivity afforded.

The d.c. resistance of the inductor being low, the steady anode potential is almost equal to that of the h.t. supply voltage.

(iii) TRANSFORMER COUPLING (Figs. 13.39 and 13.40). The primary winding of a step-up transformer is connected in series with the anode circuit of the first valve (Fig. 13.39): the a.c. component of the anode current induces a voltage in the secondary winding of the transformer. To obtain a linear gain/frequency response from the amplifier the a.c. voltage across the primary winding of the transformer must be substantially independent of

frequency: for this reason the self-capacitance of the windings must be small and the reactance of the primary winding must be high at all signal frequencies compared with the valve a.c. resistance r_a. The transformer winding carries the whole of the anode current: the magnetic circuit must be designed to prevent saturation and avoid nonlinear distortion due to this cause.

An alternative arrangement (Fig. 13.40)—the *parallel feed circuit*—is sometimes used to separate the a.c. and d.c. components of the anode current. The anode is connected to the h.t. voltage supply via a resistor R_a. In series with a capacitor, to prevent the flow of direct current, the primary winding of the transformer is connected in parallel

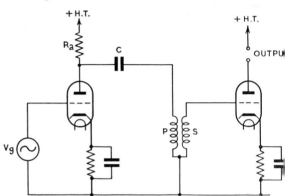

FIG. 13.40. TRANSFORMER COUPLING-PARALLEL FEED

with the anode circuit: this winding carries only the a.c. component of the anode current. For uniform response at all signal frequencies the reactance of the coupling capacitor C must be low compared with the reactance of the transformer primary winding: the reactance of this winding must be high compared with the valve anode impedance r_a.

The overall voltage amplification given by a transformer-coupled amplifier is increased by the voltage transformation, over and above that given by the general expression

$$\mu \cdot \frac{Z_a}{r_a + Z_a}$$

For a transformer coupled amplifier, if the turn ratio is n, then—

$$\text{v.a.f.} = \frac{dV_a}{dV_g} = n\mu \cdot \frac{Z_a}{r_a + Z_a} \quad . \quad (13.10)$$

Z_a is the primary impedance of the transformer including if necessary the impedance of the secondary load. If the resistance of the primary winding is negligibly low and the input impedance of the second valve is infinitely high, the v.a.f. becomes equal to—

$$\text{v.a.f.} = \frac{dV_a}{dV_g} = n\mu \cdot \frac{\omega L_a}{r_a + j\omega L_a}$$

where L_a henrys is the inductance of the primary winding.

With a suitable value of n the transformer coupled amplifier may have a voltage amplification exceeding the value of μ. With a primary winding of low resistance the voltage drop in the anode circuit is small.

If two or more amplifier stages having voltage amplification factors of M_1, M_2 . . . , are connected in cascade, the overall voltage amplification is equal to $M_1 \times M_2 \times \ldots$: and if the gains D_1, D_2 . . . , are expressed in decibels, the total gain is equal to the sum of $D_1 + D_2 + \ldots$ decibels.

At carrier and radio frequencies the self-capacitance of components has an appreciable effect owing to their reduced reactance at these high frequencies. Close attention has to be paid to the spacing, mounting and wiring of all components. Even so, self-capacitance exists between the several electrodes of a valve: undesirable oscillations are produced by the grid-anode capacitance which cannot be satisfactorily circumvented by circuit design external to the valve. For this reason the triode is not suitable for amplification of signals at radio and carrier frequencies, for which purpose the screen grid valve is employed.

EXAMPLE 13.9 (A). In a two-stage radio-frequency voltage amplifier if 90 per cent of the oscillatory voltage developed across the anode circuit of the first valve is applied across the grid circuit of the second valve, calculate the effective voltage amplification of the first stage from the following data: valve amplification factor = 30, a.c. resistance of valve = 10 000 Ω, effective output impedance = 45 000 Ω. (C. & G.)

$$\mu = 30$$
$$r_a = 10\,000 \ \Omega$$
$$Z_a = 45\,000 \ \Omega$$

$$\text{Voltage amplification} = \mu \cdot \frac{Z_a}{r_a + Z_a}$$
$$= \frac{30 \times 45\,000}{10\,000 + 45\,000}$$

$$\text{Effective amplification} = \frac{0 \cdot 9 \times 30 \times 45 \times 10^3}{55 \times 10^3}$$
$$= \underline{\underline{22 \cdot 1}}$$

EXAMPLE 13.10 (B). A single stage thermionic valve amplifier has a tuned anode circuit having a capacitance of 400 pF. an inductance of 300 μH, and a resistance of 12 Ω. If the plate resistance is 40 000 Ω and the amplification factor is 10, what is the radio-frequency voltage across the tuned output circuit when 0·12 V is applied to the grid of the valve? (C. & G.)

$$C_a = 400 \times 10^{-12} \text{ F}$$
$$L_a = 300 \times 10^{-6} \text{ H}$$
$$R_a = 12 \ \Omega$$
$$r_a = 40\,000 \ \Omega$$
$$\mu = 10$$
$$V_g = 0 \cdot 12 \text{ V}$$

The anode load impedance is equivalent to a resistance of

$$Z_a = \frac{L_a}{C_a R_a} = \frac{300 \times 10^{-6}}{400 \times 10^{-12} \times 12} = \frac{3 \times 10^6}{48}$$
$$= 62\,500 \ \Omega$$

$$\text{V.a.f.} = \mu \cdot \frac{Z_a}{r_a + Z_a} = \frac{10 \times 62\,500}{40\,000 + 62\,500}$$
$$= \frac{625}{102 \cdot 5} = 6 \cdot 1$$

Output voltage $= 0 \cdot 12 \times 6 \cdot 1 = \underline{\underline{0 \cdot 73 \text{ V}}}$

EXAMPLE 13.11 (B). In an audio-frequency amplifier the valve has an amplification factor of 40 and an internal impedance of 40 000 Ω. It is coupled to a succeeding stage by a transformer of 1 : 3·5 ratio having a primary inductance of 40 H and a primary resistance of 500 Ω. The secondary load is of infinite impedance. What will be the amplification for frequencies of 40, 100, 1 000, and 10 000 c/s, if the primary of the transformer resonates at 10 000 c/s? (C. & G.)

$$\mu = 40$$
$$r_a = 40\,000 \ \Omega$$
$$n = 3 \cdot 5$$
$$L_a = 40 \text{ H}$$
$$R_a = 500 \ \Omega$$

Since the secondary load is of infinite impedance the anode load may be regarded as an impedance made up of $L_a = 40$ H, $R_a = 500 \ \Omega$, and $C_a =$ value to resonate at 10^4 c/s.

$$\text{The v.a.f.} = n\mu \cdot \frac{\sqrt{R_a^2 + \omega^2 L_a^2}}{\sqrt{(r_a + R_a)^2 + \omega^2 L_a^2}}$$

At 40 c/s :

$$\text{v.a.f.} = \frac{3 \cdot 5 \times 40 \cdot \sqrt{500^2 + (2\pi \times 40 \times 40)^2}}{\sqrt{40\,500^2 + 10\,048^2}}$$

$$= \frac{140 \times 10\,100}{41\,700} = \underline{\underline{34}}$$

At 100 c/s:

$$\text{v.a.f.} = \frac{140 \times \sqrt{500^2 + (2\pi \times 40 \times 100)^2}}{\sqrt{40\,500^2 + 25\,130^2}}$$

$$= \frac{140 \times 25\,130}{47\,670} = \underline{\underline{74}}$$

At 10 000 c/s:

At resonance, $\omega L = 1/(\omega C)$ or $C = 1/(\omega^2 L)$. The effective impedance of the anode load is

$$Z_a = L_a/C_a R_a = \omega^2 L_a^2/R_a$$

$$= \frac{4\pi^2 \times 10^8 \times 1\,600}{500} = 1{\cdot}26 \times 10^{10}\ \Omega$$

As this is very large compared with r_a, v.a.f. $\simeq \underline{\underline{140}}$.

EXAMPLE 13.12 (B). In a two-stage amplifier the first valve has an amplification factor of 20 with a plate impedance of 25 000 Ω and a tuned anode circuit inductance of 4 000 μH and resistance 100 Ω, tuned by a variable capacitor. The second valve has an amplification factor of 6, a plate impedance of 10 000 Ω, and an output impedance consisting of a choke of 10 000 μH inductance. What will be the voltage amplification of the amplifier at a frequency of 100 kc/s? (C. & G.)

It is assumed that the whole of the voltage developed across the anode load of the first valve is applied across the grid circuit of the second valve.

1st Valve		2nd Valve
20	μ	6
25 000	r_a	10 000
4×10^{-3} H	L_a	10^{-2} H
100 Ω	R_a	—
10^5 c/s	f	10^5 c/s

First valve:

Load impedance $= Z_a = \omega^2 L_a^2/R_a$

$$= \frac{(2\pi \times 10^5 \times 4 \times 10^{-3})^2}{100} = 63\,000\ \Omega$$

$$\text{V.a.f.} = \mu \cdot \frac{Z_a}{r_a + Z_a} = \frac{20 \times 63\,000}{25\,000 + 63\,000} = \underline{\underline{14{\cdot}3}}$$

Second valve:

$$X_a = \omega L_a = 2\pi \times 10^5 \times 10^{-2} = 6\,280\ \Omega$$

$$\text{V.a.f.} = \mu \cdot \frac{X_a}{\sqrt{r_a^2 + X_a^2}} = \frac{6 \times 6\,280}{\sqrt{10^8 + (6{\cdot}28^2 \times 10^6)}}$$

$$= \frac{6 \times 6\,280}{1{\cdot}18 \times 10^4} = \underline{\underline{3{\cdot}19}}$$

Overall amplification $= 14{\cdot}3 \times 3{\cdot}19 = \underline{\underline{45{\cdot}6}}$

EXAMPLE 13.13 (B). In an audio-frequency amplifier the valve has an internal impedance of 30 000 Ω and an amplification factor of 40. It is coupled to the succeeding stage by a transformer having a ratio of 1 : 3 and a primary inductance of 30 H. The secondary load is a resistance of 500 000 Ω.

Neglecting the internal capacitances of the valve and the self-capacitance, resistance and leakage of the transformer, what will be the amplification for frequencies of 100 c/s and 10 000 c/s? (C. & G.)

See the diagram of Fig. 13.41 for the equivalent circuit.

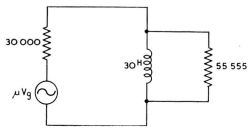

FIG. 13.41 (Example 13.13)

The secondary load impedance (500 000 Ω) referred to the primary circuit of the transformer is 500 000/3² = 55 555 Ω.

At 100 c/s:

The load impedance is $Z/\underline{\phi} = \dfrac{1}{A}\,/\underline{\phi}$ where—

$$A\,\overline{\backslash\phi} = \sqrt{\frac{1}{\omega^2 L^2} + \frac{1}{R^2}}\ \sqrt{\tan^{-1}\frac{R}{\omega L}}$$

$$= \sqrt{\frac{1}{39{\cdot}4 \times 10^4 \times 900} + \frac{1}{30{\cdot}8 \times 10^8}}$$
$$\sqrt{\tan^{-1}\frac{55\,555}{628 \times 30}}$$

$$= \sqrt{\frac{1}{354{\cdot}6 \times 10^6} + \frac{1}{30{\cdot}8 \times 10^8}}$$
$$\overline{\backslash\tan^{-1} 2{\cdot}95}$$

$$= \sqrt{2{\cdot}82 \times 10^{-9} + 3{\cdot}25 \times 10^{-10}}\ \overline{\backslash 71°17'}$$

$$= \sqrt{31{\cdot}45 \times 10^{-10}}\ \overline{\backslash 71°\,17'}$$

$$= 5{\cdot}6 \times 10^{-5}\ \overline{\backslash 71°\,17'}$$

$$Z/\underline{\phi} = 1{\cdot}785 \times 10^4\ /71°\,17'$$

$$X_a = 1{\cdot}785 \times 10^4 \sin 71°\,17'$$

$$= 1{\cdot}785 \times 10^4 \times 0{\cdot}947\,1 = 1{\cdot}694 \times 10^4$$

$$R_a = 1{\cdot}785 \times 10^4 \cos 71°\,17'$$

$$= 1{\cdot}785 \times 10^4 \times 0{\cdot}320\,9 = 0{\cdot}573 \times 10^4$$

$$R_a + r_a = (0{\cdot}573 \times 10^4) + (3 \times 10^4)$$
$$= 3{\cdot}57 \times 10^4$$

$$V.a.f. = n\mu \cdot \frac{Z_a}{\sqrt{(r_a + R_a)^2 + X_a^2}}$$

$$= \frac{40 \times 3 \times 1 \cdot 785 \times 10^4}{\sqrt{(3 \cdot 57 \times 10^4)^2 + (1 \cdot 694 \times 10^4)^2}}$$

$$= \frac{120 \times 1 \cdot 785 \times 10^4}{\sqrt{(12 \cdot 75 \times 10^8) + (2 \cdot 86 \times 10^8)}}$$

$$= \frac{120 \times 1 \cdot 785}{3 \cdot 96} = \underline{\underline{54 \cdot 1}}$$

At 10 000 c/s :

$\omega L_a = 6 \cdot 28 \times 10^4 \times 30 = 18 \cdot 84 \times 10^5 \ \Omega$. The shunting effect of this reactance may be neglected and the anode load regarded as $R_a = 55\ 555\ \Omega$.

$$V.a.f. = \frac{3 \times 40 \times 55\ 555}{30\ 000 + 55\ 555} = \underline{\underline{77 \cdot 8}}$$

13.7. The Valve Oscillator.

An important application of the valve is its use as an oscillator or a.c. generator. Oscillation is normally desired at some frequency which is accurately known and maintained : a major feature of the design of an oscillator is the means adopted to stabilize the frequency within close limits. Oscillators may be required to function at a single fixed frequency or to be capable of variation over an accurately calibrated frequency range.

The various forms of *feedback oscillator* depend in principle on the continuous transfer of energy *from the anode circuit to the grid circuit*, the grid circuit in turn controlling the energy in the anode circuit.

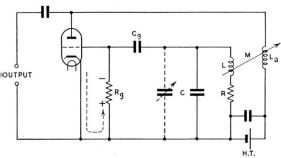

FIG. 13.42. FEEDBACK OSCILLATOR

The feedback type of oscillator is essentially an amplifier with the output connected to the input circuit : the transfer of energy from anode to grid circuit is most conveniently effected by mutual inductance.

The circuit arrangement of such an oscillator is shown in Fig. 13.42. When power is first applied the initial rise in anode current through the inductance L_a induces an e.m.f. in the resonant circuit LRC and produces transient oscillations. The oscillatory voltage developed across the capacitor C is applied between the grid and cathode : this causes the a.c. component of the anode current to oscillate at the same frequency. The oscillations of anode current passing through the inductance L_a induce an oscillatory voltage in the grid circuit, which under suitable conditions is maintained.

Two conditions are required for continuous oscillation. Firstly the voltage induced in the grid circuit must be in the correct phase to maintain the

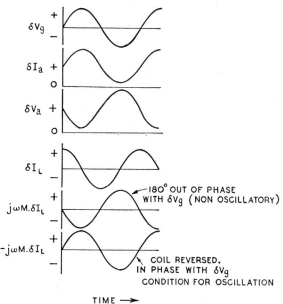

FIG. 13.43. PHASE RELATIONSHIPS IN FEEDBACK OSCILLATOR

initial oscillation. The valve introduces a phase change of 180° from input to output : the voltage induced through the mutual inductance of L_a and L will be in the correct phase provided that the coil connexions are not reversed.

The phase relationship for the current and voltage in the oscillator are indicated in Fig. 13.43. The anode current changes dI_a in a resistive load or in a circuit tuned to resonance are in phase with the alternating grid voltage dV_g : the anode voltage dV_a is 180° out of phase. The current dI_L in the inductance L_a lags approximately 90° on this voltage. The voltage $\pm j\omega M \cdot dI_L$ induced in L will lead or lag by 90° on dI_L according to which end of the coil winding is connected to the grid.

Secondly, the energy fed from anode to grid circuit must exceed the total I^2R losses of the resonant circuit or the oscillation will cease. If these conditions are met, a gradual build up in magnitude of the oscillatory voltage in the grid circuit will result. By equating the power dissipated in the resonant circuit (i.e. in R) to the power fed from the anode circuit through the mutual inductance M henrys, it can be shown that the condition for commencement and maintenance of oscillation is—

$$\mu M = r_a CR + L$$

r_a and μ being the valve a.c. resistance and amplification factor respectively.

The principle causes of frequency instability are variations in the inductance and capacitance of the resonant circuit: these changes may be due to (i) mechanical instability of the components, (ii) temperature changes, which affect the dimensions, the permeability and the permittivity, (iii) changes in stray inductance and capacity due to inadequate screening. Changes in valve characteristics or their electrode voltages, in load impedance, or in other circuit components also affect the frequency stability. Attention to these factors in design permits a stability of 5 parts in 10^5 to be attained.

The amplification provided by the valve will normally be greater than that required to overcome losses and maintain oscillation. As the voltage swing applied to the grid builds up, positive half-cycles will cause the flow of grid current: it will be observed from the diagram that the grid has no steady bias potential applied to it. This flow of grid current in the resistor R_g is in the direction to make the grid negative to the cathode. The grid is automatically given a negative bias potential in this way, the anode current is reduced and the valve oscillation settles down to a steady amplitude determined by the value of R_g in association with the valve characteristics. The grid capacitor C_g is required to prevent the (d.c.) bias voltage across R_g from being shunted by the inductance L. In this respect the valve behaves as a grid rectifier: this device is frequently adopted for limiting a valve output to a predetermined maximum value.

A capacitor is shunted across the h.t. supply to reduce the flow of oscillatory current through that circuit.

The output is fed from the anode via a capacitor which is required to prevent the flow of direct current in the load: with some oscillators, a third winding coupled to L_a and L is used as an output winding. The output signal may be passed through one or more amplifier stages if necessary.

If a variable frequency oscillator is required, a portion of the tuning capacitor C is made variable. The frequency of oscillation, f c/s is given by—

$$f = \frac{1}{2\pi\sqrt{LC}} \qquad . \qquad . \qquad . \quad (10.17)$$

Present-day oscillators are largely crystal controlled giving a frequency stability of 1 part in 10^6.

Oscillation always tends to occur in a high-frequency amplifier, energy being fed back due to the self-capacitance between grid and anode. Various methods are adopted to prevent this undesirable occurrence, a screen grid valve being usually employed.

13.8. The Tetrode. The tetrode, commonly in the form known as the SCREEN GRID valve, has, in addition to cathode, anode, and control grid, an additional grid used as an electrostatic screen between anode and control grid.

The self-capacitance between anode and grid of

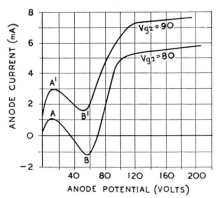

FIG. 13.44. CHARACTERISTIC OF SCREEN GRID VALVE: ANODE POTENTIAL/ANODE CURRENT GRAPH

the three electrode valve provides a path for feeding back energy from anode to grid: this being the principle upon which the feedback oscillator depends, amplifiers using valves of the three-electrode type are unstable at the high frequencies at which the inter-electrode capacitance has appreciable effect. At low frequencies the reactance of this inter-electrode capacitance is sufficiently high to enable the triode amplifier to function without oscillation.

The fourth electrode is in the form of a mesh or spiral of wire, placed between the control grid and anode and given a steady positive potential from the h.t. supply. Its effect is to eliminate the self-capacitance between the control grid and anode.

The anode potential/anode current characteristic of a screen grid valve, shown in Fig. 13.44, is of unusual shape due to the occurrence of *secondary emission*. At low anode potentials a large number of electrons will be drawn from the cathode to the screen grid which is at a fixed positive potential: the anode current will be negligibly small. As the anode potential is raised, electrons will be attracted to it and the anode current commences to rise. With further increase in anode potential, electrons reaching the anode at high velocity will knock out further electrons from the anode: since at this stage the screen grid is at a higher positive potential than the anode, these secondary electrons will be attracted to the screen. The anode current accordingly falls until the anode potential is further raised to equal the screen potential. During this decline the anode current may actually become negative, indicating that more electrons leave the anode than arrive there from the space charge. When the anode potential is raised still further to exceed that of the screen, the secondary electrons will not travel to the screen but they will return to the more positive anode, the anode current again increasing.

A current I_s flows in the screen-cathode circuit and this has variations complementary to those of the anode current I_a; the total cathode current is equal to the sum of I_s and I_a.

Two important points arise from the characteristic graph. (i) The flow of electrons from anode to control grid is prevented by the positive potential of the screen grid, (ii) when the anode current is *falling* despite the *rising* anode potential, the valve behaves as a *negative resistance*: over the region AB or $A'B'$ the graph shows a negative slope corresponding to a negative anode resistance, $r_a = - dV_a/dI_a$.

The detailed shape of the graph will vary to some extent with changes in the fixed values of negative control-grid potential and positive screen-grid potential. The potential of the screen grid is usually fixed at between 50 and 60 per cent of the anode potential: this grid intercepts only a small proportion of the total electron flow. Most of the electrons are accelerated owing to the high potential of the screen grid, and on account of their high velocity they pass through the mesh of the screen to the anode. Variations in anode potential have practically no effect upon the field between the control and screen grids: the valve a.c. resistance is accordingly high. The grid control is, however, comparable to that of the triode since the screen and anode act as the collecting electrodes and thus the mutual conductance is of the same order as for a triode, or rather higher as the turns of the control grid can now be more closely spaced on account of the accelerating field of the screen grid. The product of the a.c. resistance r_a and the mutual conductance g_m is μ, the amplification factor, which in a screen grid valve reaches a much higher value than for a triode.

The mutual characteristic graph for the screen grid valve is similar in shape to that of the triode, the curves for various values of anode voltage being closer together on account of the high a.c. resistance.

If the valve is to function as a stable amplifier, it is essential to operate the valve in such a way that this negative resistance portion of the curve is not embraced. Otherwise instability is likely to occur on account of the oscillator action, described below. It is also necessary to complete the electro-static screening between the external components of the grid and anode circuits.

When used as a power amplifier there will be an a.c. component of the screen current similar to the

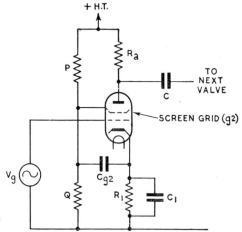

Fig. 13.45. Circuit Principle of Screen Grid Valve Amplifier

a.c. component of the anode current: if any impedance is included in the external circuit of the screen grid this a.c. component will cause the potential of the screen grid to vary about its correct (fixed) operating potential. To prevent this a path to the cathode is provided by a large capacitor C_{g2} (Fig. 13.45) having a negligible impedance at the working frequencies and placing the screen grid at cathode potential for alternating currents. The screen potential is conveniently obtained from a potentiometer (PQ). Resistance-capacitance coupling elements (R_aC) are shown. R_1 is the cathode bias resistor.

The negative resistance characteristic of the screen grid valve is employed in the DYNATRON oscillator (Fig. 13.46). A tuned circuit LC is connected between anode and cathode. The screen grid is held at a *higher* positive potential than the anode. In this condition, owing to the passage of secondary electrons from anode to cathode, the anode current decreases as the anode potential is raised. If the parallel impedance of the tuned circuit is just greater than the value of this negative resistance, oscillations will be maintained. The value of the negative resistance can be adjusted by variations of the negative bias voltage on the control grid.

A good frequency stability up to about 10 Mc/s is produced when the negative resistance is just low enough to maintain a state of oscillation: the oscillation frequency is determined almost completely by the constants of the tuned circuit including the self-capacitance of the internal anode-cathode path.

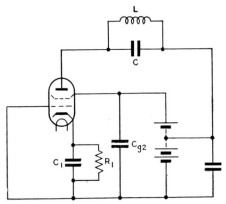

FIG. 13.46. CIRCUIT PRINCIPLE OF DYNATRON OSCILLATOR

A further advantage of the dynatron oscillator lies in the simplicity of the circuit and the fact that no feedback is required.

The BEAM TETRODE is designed to suppress secondary emission from the anode without the use of a suppressor grid. This is achieved by compressing the electron stream into flat beams by the use of deflecting electrodes which are at the same potential as the cathode, and by aligning the grid and screen grid wires. The electron stream is focused at a point between the screen and anode, and the resultant concentration of the electrons lowers the potential between screen and anode: this effectively repels back to the anode the electrons of secondary emission. The anode-current/anode-voltage characteristic curve of the beam tetrode is generally similar to that of the pentode described below, except that the current rises much more steeply at low voltages and flattens out more sharply so that the constant anode current extends over a wider range of anode voltage.

13.9. The Pentode. The pentode is similar in construction to the screen grid tetrode but it is fitted with a fifth electrode: an additional grid, termed the *suppressor grid* is inserted between the screen grid and anode. The suppressor grid is connected directly to the cathode: its function is to repel any

secondary electrons from either the anode or the screen grid. This has the effect of eliminating the dip or kink present in the anode characteristic of the screen grid valve, and it makes the pentode suitable for use as a power amplifier, while retaining the essential properties of the screen grid valve, namely high mutual conductance and amplification factor.

A typical anode characteristic graph for a pentode is given in Fig. 13.47A. The anode current

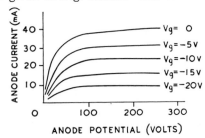

FIG. 13.47A. CHARACTERISTIC OF PENTODE: ANODE CURRENT/ANODE POTENTIAL GRAPH

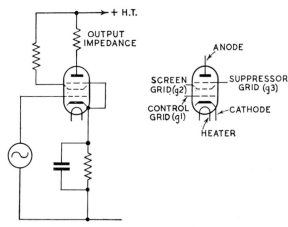

FIG. 13.47B. CIRCUIT PRINCIPLE OF PENTODE POWER AMPLIFIER

rises steeply at low values of anode potential and at an early stage reaches a condition where the anode current is but little affected by the anode potential. The connexions for a pentode used in an amplifier stage are shown in Fig. 13.47B. The pentode is preferably used as a voltage amplifier: when used as a power amplifier into a reactive load, such as a loud speaker for example, the response becomes very dependent upon frequency as the current tends to remain constant.

Constructional details of a pentode valve are shown in Fig. 13.48: the screen grid is connected to the top terminal cap.

It is a characteristic of the pentode that the anode current remains substantially constant over all voltage values beyond a certain minimum. The dynamic resistance of the pentode, $r_a = dV_a/dI_a$, is very high, approaching infinity. The alternating component of the anode current is practically independent of the anode load Z_L: in other words if an alternating voltage v_g is

corresponding variation in mutual conductance also: the adjustment of these parameters is made by variation of the grid bias voltage.

The mutual characteristic graph is shown in Fig. 13.49 (a) for the variable-μ valve, with that for the normal pentode shown in Fig. 13.49 (b) for comparison: in each case the variation in mutual conductance g_m with grid potential is shown by

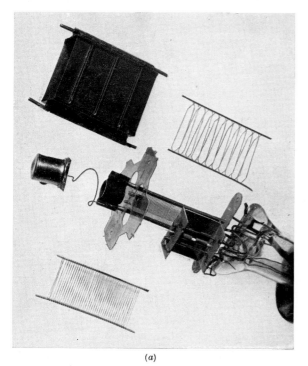

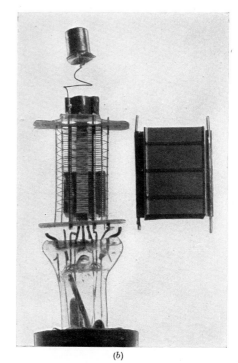

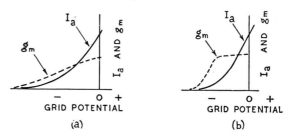

FIG. 13.48. CONSTRUCTIONAL DETAILS OF PENTODE VALVE

applied to the grid-cathode circuit, the anode circuit may be regarded as a constant-current generator. Using the usual symbols,

$$i_a = \frac{\mu v_g}{r_a + Z_L} = \frac{\mu v_g}{r_a(1 + Z_L/r_a)} \simeq \mu v_g/r_a = g_m \cdot v_g$$

if it is assumed that $Z_L/r_a \ll 1$.

A particular form of pentode is the VARIABLE-μ valve. This has the same arrangement of electrodes as the normal pentode but the control grid has a specially designed mesh. The pitch or spacing of the mesh varies progressively from the centre of the grid towards the ends. On account of the construction the control of anode current by the grid is incomplete, and a large negative potential upon the grid is necessary to cut off the anode current completely. The effect of this is to give the valve an adjustable amplification factor and therefore a

the dotted line. The anode current/grid potential graph of the variable-μ valve shows a continuous

FIG. 13.49. MUTUAL CHARACTERISTICS OF VALVES
(a) Variable-μ valve. (b) Pentode.

and gradual change of curvature as the grid potential is varied negatively from zero. The mutual conductance, and amplification factor, vary with grid potential by almost a linear law. With the normal pentode (Fig. 13.49 (b)) the mutual conductance, and therefore the amplification factor, remain almost constant except at the lower bend of the mutual characteristic.

The function of a variable-μ valve is to enable the stage gain to be adjusted automatically according to the strength of incoming signals. A portion of the amplified received signal is rectified—usually by one anode-cathode circuit of a double-diode valve—and the p.d. across a resistor carrying this rectified signal current is fed back to the control grid of the variable-μ amplifier valve. In this way, weak signals can be given an increased gain and the output from the amplifier made sensibly constant for input signals of varying magnitude.

The application of currents at two frequencies to a non-linear device is the principle used in producing modulation. Compared with a normal valve, the variable-μ valve, by its relatively linear characteristic, enables automatic gain control to be effected without the risk of "cross-modulation" occurring between two signal frequencies which may be present simultaneously.

In Table 13.I[1] the parameters of typical low-power (receiving) triode and pentode valves are shown for comparison. Some of the desirable properties of a multi-electrode valve are listed below—

1. High mutual conductance.
2. Low inter-electrode capacitance.
3. Low noise.
4. High input impedance.
5. Low harmonic and intermodulation distortion
6. Low power consumption.
7. Long life.
8. Uniformity between valves of the same type.
9. Small size.
10. Low cost.

Some of these requirements are conflicting others will assume greater prominence for specia purposes. For example in submerged amplifier used in submarine cables at the bottom of a ocean, the need for long life is paramount.

At very high frequencies—V.H.F. (e.g. 10 Mc/s)—electron transit time becomes significant leading to the introduction of valves with ver small electrode spacings. At still higher frequencie completely new techniques become necessary e.g. velocity modulation.

EXAMPLE 13.14 (B). A variable-μ pentode valve has mutual characteristic expressed by the figures given i the Table.

The valve, whose anode slope-resistance is 1 MΩ, used with a 530-μH inductor of Q-factor 300 in a 1-Mc tuned radio-frequency amplifier.

Draw the equivalent circuit, and calculate the stag gain for small signals when the grid bias is (a) −2.5 V and (b) −20 V.

Grid Volts	−25	−20	−15	−10	−7.5	−5	−2.5	0
Anode Current (mA)	0.2	0.5	1.0	1.8	2.6	4.0	6.2	10.4

(C. & G.

TABLE 13.I
PARAMETERS OF TYPICAL RECEIVING VALVES

Type of Valve	Amplification Factor μ	Mutual Conductance g_m (mA/V)	Anode A.C. Resistance r_a (Ω)	Inter-electrode Capacitances			Anode Current at 250 V (mA)	Screen Current at 250 V (mA)
				Anode to Grid (pF)	Anode to Cathode (pF)	Cathode to Grid (pF)		
Medium-impedance triode	20	2.0	10 000	2.5	3	3.5	5	—
Small-power triode	9	3	3 000	3.5	4	7	20	—
Low-slope H.F. pentode	6 000	3	2×10^6	0.003	8	7	5	1.5
High-slope H.F. pentode	7 000	7	10^6	0.003	5	8	10	3
Output pentode	64	8	8 000	0.5	7	14	40	5
Small-power beam tetrode	140	7	20 000	1.0	10	15	80	6

The equivalent circuit is given in Fig. 13.50 (a). The shunt form of equivalent circuit is used owing to the high internal impedance of the valve.

The effective impedance of the tuned circuit at resonance is

$$Z = Q\omega L$$
$$= 300 \times 2\pi \times 10^6 \times 530 \times 10^{-6} = 1 \text{ M}\Omega$$

With the tuned-circuit impedance Z in parallel with the 1-MΩ anode impedance, the valve is

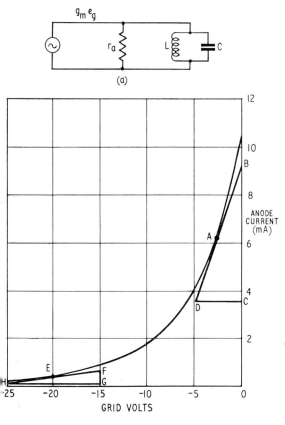

(a)

(b)

FIG. 13.50. (Example 13.14)

supplying current to a load of 0·5 MΩ, i.e. Z_{eff} = 0·5 MΩ.

The valve characteristic curve, plotted from the Table, is shown in Fig. 13.50 (b). If tangents to this graph are drawn at $V_g = -2·5$ V and $V_g = -20$ V, the slopes of these tangents give the two values of mutual conductance required, which will be found to be 1·2 and 0·07 mA/V respectively.

The stage gain is

$$\frac{V_{out}}{V_{in}} = \frac{g_m \cdot e_g \cdot Z_{eff}}{e_g} = g_m \cdot Z_{eff}$$

Gain at $-2·5$ V $= 1·2 \times 0·5 \times 10^6 \times 10^{-3} = \underline{\underline{600}}$

Gain at -20 V $= 0·07 \times 0·5 \times 10^6 \times 10^{-3} = \underline{\underline{35}}$

13.10. Modulation. Electromagnetic radiation does not occur to any marked extent at frequencies within the audible range. For radio communication it is necessary to employ a high-frequency *carrier current* whose characteristics are controlled by the audio- or video-frequency signal to be transmitted in such a way that the signal can be detected at the receiving end. This control is effected by a process of *modulation* in which, for example, the amplitude of the high-frequency carrier wave is varied by the low-frequency impressed signal. The complementary process at the receiving end is referred to variously as *demodulation, detection,* or *rectification*. In addition to their use for radio propagation, modulated carrier currents are also employed in carrier telephone and telegraph systems in which two or more channels of communication are provided by utilizing adjacent frequency bands in the available frequency transmission range of a line.

A carrier current may be fully represented by the expression $I_{max} \sin (\omega t + \phi)$: in order to convey signals any of the three factors I_{max} (amplitude), ω (angular frequency), or ϕ (phase) may be caused to vary by the modulating signal. Two different modulation methods are in general use, (i) amplitude modulation (A.M.) in which the amplitude of the carrier current is varied by the modulating frequency, the carrier frequency remaining constant, (ii) frequency modulation (F.M.) in which the carrier frequency is varied by the modulating frequency, the amplitude of the carrier wave remaining constant. The third method, phase modulation, is not used to any extent.

(i) AMPLITUDE MODULATION. It is found that when a carrier frequency f_c is modulated by an audio frequency f_a the modulated output wave contains the three components (i) the original carrier frequency f_c, (ii) the summation frequency $(f_c + f_a)$, and (iii) the difference frequency $(f_c - f_a)$. The sum and difference frequencies are termed the *side frequencies*. For example, if a 10 kc/s carrier (f_c) is modulated by a 1 000 c/s signal (f_a), the complex modulated signal which results has the three components (i) the carrier frequency, $f_c = 10 000$ c/s, (ii) the upper side frequency, $f_c + f_a = 10 000 + 1 000 = 11 000$ c/s, and (iii) the lower side frequency $f_c - f_a = 10 000 - 1 000 = 9 000$ c/s. This frequency spectrum is represented in Fig. 13.51.

More usually the modulating signal comprises the range or band of frequencies necessary to convey the sound or vision information. If f_1 and f_2 are the limits of this modulating frequency range applied to a carrier frequency f_c then, writing (f_1 to f_2) in place of f_a, the three components are (i) f_c the carrier frequency, (ii) $f_c + (f_1$ to $f_2)$, the *upper side band* and (iii) $f_c - (f_1$ to $f_2)$, the *lower*

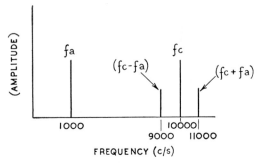

FIG. 13.51. FREQUENCY COMPONENTS OF SIMPLE AMPLITUDE-MODULATED WAVE
(Not to scale)

side band. As an example, using in round figures the speech frequency range from 300 c/s to 3 000 c/s to modulate a 12 kc/s carrier frequency current, the products of modulation are (i) the original carrier frequency, $f_c = 12\ 000$ c/s, (ii) the upper side band, $f_c + (f_1$ to $f_2) = 12\ 000 + (300$ to

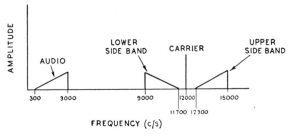

FIG. 13.52. SIDE BAND COMPONENTS OF AMPLITUDE-MODULATED WAVE
(Not to scale)

3 000) = 12 300 to 15 000 c/s, and (iii) the lower side band, $f_c - (f_1$ to $f_2) = 12\ 000 - (300$ to 3 000) = 11 700 to 9 000, or 9 000 to 11 700 c/s. This frequency spectrum is indicated in Fig. 13.52, from which it is apparent that the original frequencies experience inversion in the lower side band.

The products of modulation are represented graphically in Fig. 13.53 for a sine wave modulating frequency of 1 000 c/s applied to a carrier whose frequency is 10 kc/s. At (*a*) is shown the form of the carrier current having a constant frequency and amplitude; (*b*) is a sinusoidal audio-frequency modulating current; (*c*) is the form taken by the

resulting modulated wave; (*d*) is the upper side frequency of 11 000 c/s; (*e*) is the residual carrier frequency; and (*f*) is the lower side frequency of 9 000 c/s.

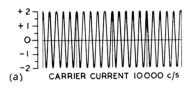

(a)   CARRIER CURRENT 10000 c/s

(b)   AUDIO CURRENT 1 000 c/s

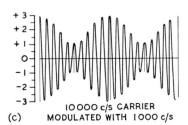

(c)   10 000 c/s CARRIER MODULATED WITH 1 000 c/s

(d)   UPPER SIDE BAND CURRENT 11 000 c/s

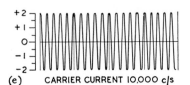

(e)   CARRIER CURRENT 10,000 c/s

(f)   LOWER SIDE BAND CURRENT 9 000 c/s

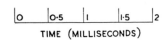

TIME (MILLISECONDS)

FIG. 13.53. INPUT AND OUTPUT COMPONENTS OF AMPLITUDE-MODULATOR

The side bands can be regarded as separate current components propagated with the carrier: any of the three products of modulation can be eliminated by frequency filters or by other means.

The extent to which the carrier amplitude is controlled by the modulating current is termed the 'depth" of modulation or MODULATION FACTOR, usually expressed as a percentage. The modulation factor of an amplitude-modulated wave is defined as *the ratio of half the difference of the maximum and the minimum amplitude to the mean amplitude of the wave.* Using the symbols in Fig. 13.54, the half difference is equal to a and the mean value to b: the modulation percentage is $\left(\dfrac{a}{b} \times 100\right)\%$, which may also be written as

$$\left(\frac{V_{max} - V_0}{V_0}\right) \times 100 \%$$

For example, in Fig. 13.53, the maximum amplitude of the modulated wave is represented by

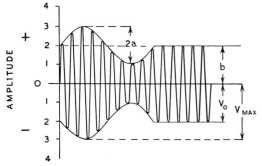

FIG. 13.54. MODULATION FACTOR

units, the minimum falling to 1 unit—a difference of 2 units. The half difference (1 unit) expressed as a ratio to the mean amplitude of the wave (2 units) is 0·5, the modulation factor: the modulation percentage is 50 per cent. This value applies also to the modulated wave shown in Fig. 13.54. In Fig. 13.55 (a), the amplitude of the modulated carrier falls to zero and rises to twice the amplitude of the unmodulated carrier: the carrier is 100 per cent modulated, i.e. completely modulated. For comparison the same components are shown in Fig. 13.55 (b) but with only 25 per cent modulation.

The composition of the modulated carrier wave can be demonstrated mathematically. Suppose that the unmodulated carrier is represented by $i_c = A \cdot \sin \omega_c t$: its peak value is A and its frequency is $f_c = \omega_c/(2\pi)$ c/s. The amplitude of this carrier, i_c, is to be varied in accordance with a lower (audio) frequency modulating sine-wave designated by $i_a = kA \cdot \sin \omega_a t$. The amplitude of this wave is k times that of the carrier wave, k being the modulation factor having a value usually less than 1. The modulating frequency is $f_a = \omega_a/(2\pi)$ c/s. The peak value of the modulated wave is

$$I_m = (A + Ak \cdot \sin \omega_a t) = A(1 + k \cdot \sin \omega_a t)$$

The instantaneous value of the modulated wave is—

$$\begin{aligned}
i_m &= A(1 + k \cdot \sin \omega_a t) \sin \omega_c t \\
&= A(\sin \omega_c t + k \cdot \sin \omega_a t \cdot \sin \omega_c t) \\
&= A[\sin \omega_c t - \frac{k}{2} \cos (\omega_c + \omega_a)t \\
&\qquad + \frac{k}{2} \cos (\omega_c - \omega_a)t] \\
&= A \cdot \sin \omega_c t - \frac{Ak}{2} \cos (\omega_c + \omega_a)t \\
&\qquad + \frac{Ak}{2} \cos (\omega_c - \omega_a)t
\end{aligned}$$

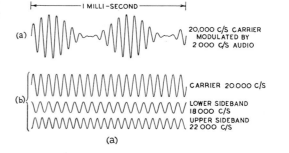

(a)

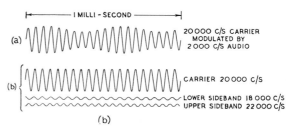

(b)

FIG. 13.55. COMPONENTS OF MODULATED WAVES
(a) 100 per cent modulation. (b) 25 per cent modulation.

Of these three components—
(i) $A \cdot \sin \omega_c t$ is the original (unmodulated) carrier current.

(ii) $\dfrac{Ak}{2} \cdot \cos (\omega_c + \omega_a)t$ is a sine wave with frequency equal to the sum of the carrier and modulating frequencies and is the upper side frequency: its amplitude is one-half that of the modulating current.

(iii) $\dfrac{Ak}{2} \cdot \cos (\omega_c - \omega_a)t$ is a sine wave having a frequency equal to the difference of the carrier and modulating frequencies, and is the lower side frequency: its amplitude is also one-half that of the modulating current.

The percentage modulation in this case is $100\,k$ per cent.

Various methods depending on the employment of a non-linear impedance are available for effecting amplitude modulation. With the grid modulator (Fig. 13.56) the audio-frequency signal is applied to the grid of a valve in series with the carrier voltage of constant frequency, both alternating voltages being applied through transformers. The grid is given a steady bias potential to the lower bend of the mutual characteristic graph. As a result, in the absence of an audio-frequency signal the anode current due to the carrier voltage is small. The comparatively slowly varying audio voltage— Fig. 13.57 (a)—which is added to the carrier voltage (b) may be regarded as producing a variation in the

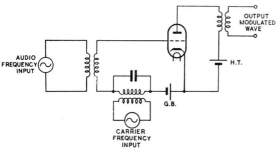

FIG. 13.56. GRID MODULATOR

effective grid bias value and causing the action to take place over different parts of the grid potential/anode current characteristic: the effective grid potential changes are shown at (c).

During negative half-cycles of the audio wave, the grid potential becomes more negative and the carrier anode current is reduced in amplitude by amounts proportional to the negative values of the modulating wave, (d): during positive half-cycles the amplitude of the anode current due to the carrier frequency is increased by amounts proportional to the positive values of the modulating wave. The modulated output wave is shown at (e) with 100 per cent modulation.

In the choke or anode modulator (the Heising system) shown in Fig. 13.58 the anode potential of the carrier frequency amplifier valve is controlled by the audio-frequency modulating current.

The carrier-frequency input is supplied from a constant frequency oscillator. With suitable operating conditions the amplitude of the carrier-frequency output from this amplifier $V1$ is closely proportional to the anode potential: when no audio-frequency signal is applied, the amplified carrier output from $V1$ has a constant amplitude.

The audio-frequency input is fed to the grid of the low-frequency amplifier, or modulating valve $V2$, the anode current for this valve being derived

from the same h.t. source used for the carrier amplifier $V1$ via an audio-frequency choke (AFC) connected in the common feed to both anodes.

When the audio-frequency signal is applied, the anode potential at the point A rises and falls in accordance with the audio-frequency input wave form. The carrier-frequency current in the circuit LC will vary about the mean unmodulated output

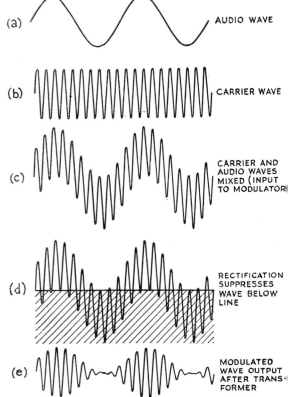

FIG. 13.57. STAGES IN GRID MODULATION

in proportion to the potential at the point A—i.e. the carrier is amplitude-modulated.

The radio-frequency choke (RFC) and the associated capacitor are present to exclude carrier-frequency potentials from the anode of the audio-frequency amplifier. The percentage modulation is determined by the ratio of the peak audio-frequency voltage to the mean d.c. potential on the anode of the carrier-frequency amplifier.

A balanced Carson modulator (Fig. 13.59) is used in certain carrier telephone systems. Two valves are used on the grid modulation principle described in connexion with Fig. 13.56. The input circuits are arranged so that the valves are in phase

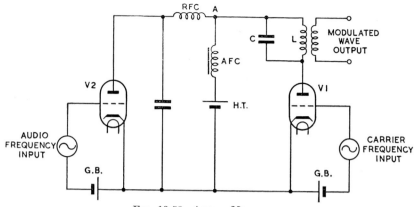

FIG. 13.58. ANODE MODULATOR

opposition to the carrier input but not to the audio signal input.

With the carrier voltage only applied, the grid potentials of the valves vary but they do so in phase with one another, and equal anode currents flow in opposition in the primary winding of the output transformer : the carrier wave is accordingly suppressed from the output.

The audio-frequency voltage applied at the input transformer acts upon the grids of the two valves in opposite senses so that for a positive half-cycle the negative bias of one valve is made more negative, *reducing* the amplitude of carrier-frequency current in its anode circuit : the grid of the second valve is made less negative resulting in an *increase* in carrier current. Since these two modulated carrier currents are unequal an e.m.f. is induced in the secondary

winding due to the difference of these two anode current variations in the primary winding. During negative half-cycles the same effects take place, except that the conditions of the valve grid potentials are interchanged. This is the principle of the "push-pull" amplifier, and it requires that the characteristics of the two valves are closely matched.

When carrier and audio frequencies are applied simultaneously the anode current varies at carrier frequency and its amplitude is modulated at the audio-frequency : modulation products are the upper and lower side bands only, the carrier component being suppressed.

In this, as in most types of modulator, an audio-frequency component and also higher order products of modulation appear in the output. The

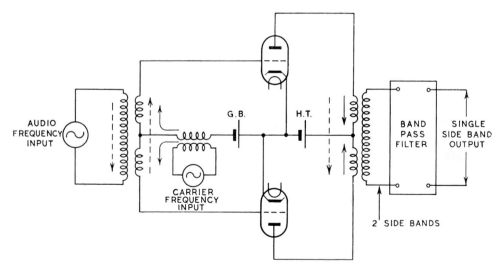

FIG. 13.59. BALANCED GRID MODULATOR

carrier suppression is not complete but is some 30 db below the original power level. These undesired components are eliminated by the frequency filter which is normally inserted in the output of the modulator.

Modulation of one frequency by another always occurs when two frequencies are applied simultaneously to the non-linear characteristic of a valve, a metal rectifier, or an inductor with a ferromagnetic core. If this results in the modulation of the components of a complex wave by one another the effect is known as *intermodulation*. The modulation of the carrier of the desired signal by an undesired signal is termed *cross-modulation*: this

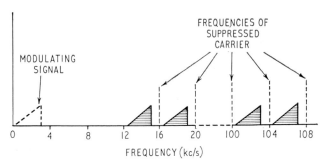

FIG. 13.60. FREQUENCY SPECTRUM FOR 12-CIRCUIT CARRIER TELEPHONE SYSTEM

possibility is present when two or more carrier channel-signals are amplified by the same valve, if the grid swing is not restricted to the linear portion of the characteristic.

Reference to Fig. 13.52 shows that all the component frequencies of the modulating signal are present in each side band, either of which contains in fact the whole of the signal information to be transmitted. For the purpose of transmitting this signal it is clearly sufficient to transmit either side band only, omitting the other and also the carrier wave component. This results in economy of power and in other advantages such as an improved signal/noise ratio. In particular the frequency bandwidth occupied in the transmission medium is reduced to about one-half.

In both radio and line carrier systems, *single side band suppressed carrier* transmission is extensively employed. Using a balanced type of modulator the carrier frequency is suppressed: the wanted side band—which may be either the upper or the lower —is selected by a band-pass filter. This band-pass filter, included in Fig. 13.59, also suppresses the residual carrier current and audio-frequency component. At the receiving point, to effect demodulation it is, however, necessary to re-supply the

carrier wave at the original carrier frequency within very close frequency limits.

If a series of oscillators, each tuned to a different frequency, is used to modulate a number of separate input speech or telegraph signals, the modulated waves may be fed into the same transmission line where they will occupy adjacent positions in the frequency spectrum. Over long distances where the cost of terminal equipment is more than offset by the saving in line plant, considerable economy results from the adoption of carrier systems of telephony and telegraphy which provide two or more separate channels of communication over a single line circuit.

In a 24-circuit carrier telephone system,[2] 24 oscillators are used to generate the carrier frequencies ranging from 16 kc/s to 108 kc/s at 4 kc/s intervals. The lower side band is selected from each balanced modulator by filtering (Fig. 13.59) and the output terminals of the 24 band-pass filters are connected in parallel to the line. The frequency allocation in the line is indicated in Fig. 13.60.

At the receiving terminal the line is connected in parallel with the input terminals of 24 band-pass filters similar to those at the transmitting end. The output of each receiving band-pass filter is fed to a balanced demodulator together with the locally generated carrier at the appropriate frequency. A reproduction of the original modulating signal is selected from each demodulator, using a low-pass filter.

The successful operation of the system is naturally dependent upon many design factors. The most important of these is probably the common amplifier inserted at intervals along the line, which must give a uniform response over the whole frequency band from 12 kc/s to 108 kc/s when carrying the peak input signals of 24 channels simultaneously. This requirement has been met by the development of a negative feedback amplifier in which, by feeding a controlled portion of the amplified output back into the input terminals in opposite phase to the original input, the following advantages are obtained: (i) the variation of gain with frequency is considerably reduced, (ii) non-linearity of the amplifier characteristic is reduced, making cross modulation negligible, (iii) gain stability against variations in battery supply and in components is increased, (iv) the noise content of the amplifier is reduced.

Briefly the operation of the negative feedback amplifier depends upon the following principle. Consider an amplifier which has a gain of A in the absence of feedback, and let B times the output oltage be fed back to *oppose* the input voltage. 'hen if v is the input voltage and V the output oltage, the following relationship applies—

$$(v - BV)A = V$$

o that the *net* gain is

$$\frac{V}{v} = \frac{A}{1 + AB}$$

If AB is large compared with 1, the net gain ecomes closely equal to $1/B$, i.e. dependent largely

amplitude modulation the carrier amplitude is the sum of a constant plus a varying component, so in frequency modulation the instantaneous *frequency* is the sum of a constant and a varying component. The constant component is the carrier frequency, and the instantaneous frequency of the varying component is proportional to the instantaneous value of the modulating current. The maximum amount by which the frequency is changed is proportional to the peak value of the modulating current and for one cycle of the modulating wave the

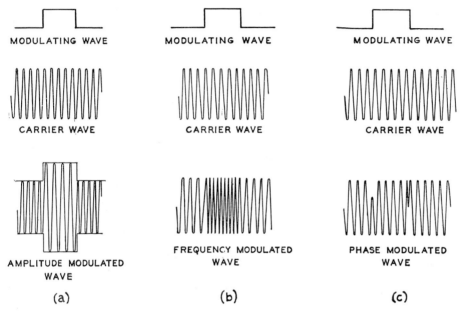

FIG. 13.61. MODULATION OF CARRIER FREQUENCY
(a) By variation of amplitude. (b) By variation of frequency. (c) By variation of phase.

pon the feedback path, and relatively independent f the amplifier gain A.

Using a corresponding though more complex echnique applied to a concentric or *coaxial* type of able having a wide frequency transmission range of p to 12 Mc/s, several hundred telephone channels, ossibly together with a television channel, may be rovided simultaneously over a common line circuit.

(ii) FREQUENCY MODULATION.[3],[4] For the purose of comparison, an amplitude-modulated wave erived from a modulating wave which consists of unidirectional pulse with rectangular wave-shape shown graphically in Fig. 13.61 (a). The modu- ted wave is characterized by constant frequency nd varying amplitude.

The same rectangular waveform and carrier fre- uency are used to produce the frequency-modu- ted wave shown in Fig. 13.61 (b). Just as in

carrier frequency rises from its constant value up to a maximum value, down to a minimum value and back to its unmodulated value: the deviations above and below the carrier frequency are equal for a symmetrical modulating wave. The number of such deviation cycles in one second is equal to the frequency (f) of the modulating wave. The amplitude of the carrier wave is constant, whether modulated or not.

The diagram (Fig. 13.61 (b)) shows only a positive half-cycle, represented by an increase in frequency: on this basis a negative half-cycle would produce a decrease in carrier frequency.

For a frequency-modulated wave the modulation factor is the ratio of half the difference of the maximum and minimum frequencies to the mean frequency of the wave.

The frequency-modulated current is equivalent

to a current at the carrier frequency F together with a series of currents at the frequencies $F \pm f$, $F \pm 2f$, $F \pm 3f$, etc.

The chief advantage of frequency modulation over amplitude modulation is that it gives an improved signal/noise ratio under certain conditions. In order to realize this, however, the use of a sufficient "modulation index"—the ratio of the frequency swing to the frequency of a specified sinusoidal modulation—necessitates a wide frequency band. The equipment at present required for frequency modulation is more elaborate than that needed for amplitude modulation.

(iii) PHASE MODULATION. The effect of phase-modulating the same carrier frequency by the rectangular unidirectional pulse is shown graphically in Fig. 13.61 (c). The amplitude of the phase modulated wave is constant and equal to that of the unmodulated carrier. There is an infinite series of modulation components alternately in phase and in quadrature with the carrier; and also an infinite series of side frequencies spaced from the carrier frequency by amounts corresponding to harmonics of the modulating frequency. Phase and frequency modulation are closely related.

13.11. Demodulation. Before a modulated signal can be used to operate a telephone receiver or similar instrument, it is necessary to extract the audio-frequency component from the modulated wave, because neither the telephone receiver nor the ear will respond to the high carrier frequency. Methods of achieving this include (i) demodulation with the aid of a carrier-frequency current, (ii) diode rectification, (iii) grid circuit rectification using a triode, and (iv) anode current rectification, also using a triode.

The terms demodulation, detection, and rectification tend to be used somewhat indiscriminately; a strict definition of each is given below for reference.

(i) DEMODULATION. Demodulation is defined as *the process of reproduction of an original modulating signal from a modulated wave, i.e. the inverse of modulation.*

In line carrier systems in which single sideband transmission is employed, extraction of the audio-frequency component is carried out by the use of a *demodulator* which may in effect be identical with the modulator used at the transmitting end of the line.

If one of the received side frequencies $(f_c + f_a)$ with the locally generated carrier frequency f_c are together injected into the demodulator, the "modulation" products will be (i) the carrier frequency, f_c, (ii) the summation frequency $(f_c + f_a) + f_c$, and (iii) the difference frequency $(f_c + f_a) - f_c = f_a$. The carrier frequency component is suppressed if a

balanced demodulator (Fig. 13.59) is employed. The summation frequency is a twice-modulated product which is readily eliminated by using a band pass filter to select the desired audio-frequency component f_a.

The products obtained from demodulating the lower sideband taken from Fig. 13.52 are represented in Fig. 13.62. The received sideband

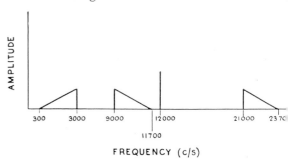

FIG. 13.62. SIDE BAND COMPONENTS OF DEMODULATED WAVE

(9 000 c/s to 11 700 c/s) is applied to a closely stabilized 12 kc/s oscillator forming part of the receiving equipment, using a balanced demodulator to suppress the carrier frequency from the output. The resulting upper side band covers the frequency range $12\,000 + (9\,000 \text{ to } 11\,700) = 21\,000$ c/s to 23 700 c/s: the lower side band, $12\,000 - (9\,000$ to $11\,700)$ c/s $= 300$ to $3\,000$ c/s is the original audio

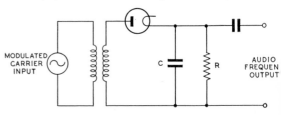

FIG. 13.63. DIODE DEMODULATOR

frequency signal which may be selected by a simple low-pass filter.

(ii) THE DIODE DEMODULATOR OR RECTIFIER. Rectification is defined as *the process of obtaining unidirectional current from an alternating or oscillatory source of supply by means of an asymmetric conducting device.*

The diode is used extensively as a detector of the audio-frequency component in certain classes of radio receiver. The principle of the circuit arrangement for this purpose is shown in Fig. 13.63. Peak values of alternate half-cycles of the modulated input signal (Fig. 13.64 (a)) make the diode anode positive to the cathode. The diode current passed during these intervals charges up the capacitor C until the p.d. across it is very nearly equal to the instantaneous peak value of the modulated carrier voltage. Between positive half-cycles of the modulated carrier the capacitor discharges partially through the shunting resistor R, to an extent dependent upon the time constant of the combination.

device is used. (ii) The use of this term for the action of a frequency-changer is deprecated. (iii) When there was no original modulating signal, use of the term "demodulation" as an alternative for detection is deprecated.)

The grid leak detector, or "cumulative grid rectifier" (Fig. 13.65) operates in such a manner that

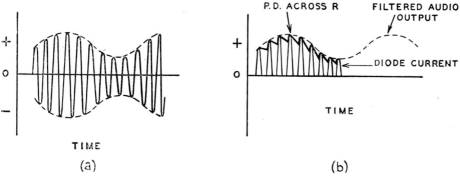

(a)   (b)

FIG. 13.64. INPUT AND OUTPUT CURRENTS OF DIODE DEMODULATOR

This time constant is made long compared with the period of the carrier oscillation, but is still short compared with the period of the highest modulating frequency. The resultant voltage across the load resistance R follows the positive "envelope" of the modulated carrier (Fig. 13.64 (b)) except for the small superimposed carrier frequency ripple: this

its grid-cathode circuit is equivalent to a diode rectifier, the rectified voltage appearing upon the grid then controlling the anode current so that the valve acts as an audio-frequency amplifier. As a result this type of detector has a high sensitivity.

If a modulated high-frequency voltage is applied to the grid of the valve, the grid potential will tend

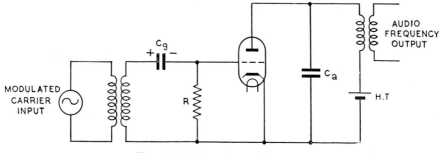

FIG. 13.65. GRID LEAK DETECTOR

ripple may be eliminated by simple resistance-capacitance filtering. The d.c. component may be separated by a capacitor in series with the output terminals, where the resultant voltage is a substantially perfect reproduction of the original modulating signal. The diode rectifier requires a fairly high signal voltage input for satisfactory operation.

(iii) GRID LEAK DETECTOR. Detection is defined as *the process of extracting information from the fluctuations with time of an electromagnetic wave.* (*Notes*. (i) Often an asymmetrical conducting

to oscillate symmetrically about the point of zero grid potential. This, however, will cause grid current to flow during positive half-cycles and the capacitor C_g will become charged with the polarity indicated in the diagram. In the absence of the leak resistor R each successive positive half-cycle would produce a progressively reducing charge owing to the fact that the growing negative potential on the capacitor biases the grid negatively, reducing and ultimately preventing the flow of grid current: the p.d. across the capacitor would finally become equal to the peak value of the signal voltage and the grid would no longer become positive even on peak values of positive half-cycles.

The presence of the resistor R provides a path for the capacitor charge to leak away and the p.d. across the capacitor becomes reduced: grid current then flows at the peaks of positive half-cycles, tending to keep the capacitor charged. Equilibrium is reached when the grid current charges during positive half-cycles are equal to the discharges into the leak resistor over the cycle. This discharge is kept small by making R large—usually it has a value of two or three megohms—and the p.d. across the capacitor C_g becomes very nearly equal to the peak value of the input signal.

As the amplitude of the modulated input signal is continually varying, the p.d. across the capacitor C will follow the modulation envelope: this condition is achieved by a suitable choice of values for R and C_g with regard to their time constant.

This potential upon the grid capacitor C_g controls the anode current which, flowing in the primary winding of the output transformer, produces an amplified reproduction of the original modulation envelope. The modulated input signal is superimposed upon the p.d. across the grid capacitor: the carrier ripple which this produces in the anode current is eliminated from the output by the presence of the anode capacitor C_a which has a low impedance at carrier frequencies.

(iv) ANODE BEND RECTIFICATION. In using a valve as an anode bend rectifier (Fig. 13.66) the

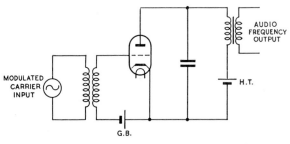

FIG. 13.66. ANODE BEND RECTIFIER

grid is negatively biased to a potential near to the lower bend of the grid potential/anode current characteristic (Fig. 13.67). Symmetrical variations of grid potential due to a modulated signal applied to the grid circuit produce asymmetrical variations in anode current: the mean value of anode current is increased accordingly to the envelope of the modulated carrier input signal. The mean anode current reproduces the original modulating current. This current comprises a steady d.c. component, together with the audio frequency signal and the carrier-frequency ripple. The carrier component is filtered out by the low impedance shunting capacitor in the anode circuit.

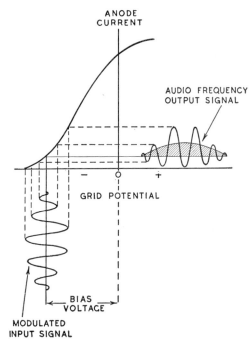

FIG. 13.67. OPERATING CONDITIONS OF ANODE BEND RECTIFIER

The audio-frequency signal may be passed through the primary winding of a transformer to induce an e.m.f. whose waveform is substantially that of the original modulating signal.

13.12. The Valve Voltmeter. A suitably arranged valve circuit, in conjunction with a sensitive moving-coil meter, may be used to measure a.c. voltages. In principle such instruments depend upon the rectifying property of the valve, the meter actually measuring the change in anode current consequent upon an a.c. signal impressed upon the input circuit of the valve. The meter scale may be calibrated in volts to read r.m.s. or peak values according to the operating condition of the valve. The response of the valve is practically independent of frequency and waveform and the instrument may be used for accurate measurement over a very wide frequency range. A big advantage with the use of the valve voltmeter is that it is highly sensitive and it absorbs only a negligible amount of power from the circuit under test.

Whichever method of rectification is used there will usually be some anode current flowing when there is no a.c. voltage applied to the grid of a triode. Unless the design includes some means of balancing out the residual anode current in the meter, the scale zero will not correspond with the instrument zero. It is essential that the rectified current for a given applied voltage should be not only large enough to be read upon the meter but also comparable with the normal anode current.

If anode bend rectification is used this condition for maximum deflexion occurs when there is no separate anode battery, the anode being connected to the positive end of the filament. In an instrument of this type (Fig. 13.68) a single battery is used for heating the cathode, biasing the grid, and providing the positive anode potential: the grid

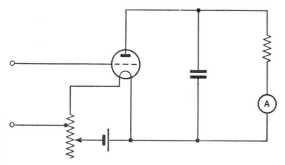

FIG. 13.68. VALVE VOLTMETER USING ANODE BEND RECTIFICATION

bias potential is tapped from a resistor which carries the filament current. Use of a single battery obviates the risk of calibration being upset by variations in a separate grid battery: the filament circuit rheostat is used for zero adjustment. The meter is a sensitive microammeter in series with a high value of swamping resistance: the meter and resistance are shunted by a capacitor to bypass the a.c. component of the rectified current.

In making a measurement the input terminals are first short-circuited to ensure that the grid potential is correct and the rheostat is adjusted to bring the instrument pointer on to the zero of the voltmeter scale (which does not coincide with the normal zero position of the pointer). The voltage under test is then applied across the input terminals to the grid circuit: the rectified current gives a direct reading in volts, the scale having been previously calibrated against a standard instrument. On account of the square law relationship between grid potential and anode current the meter reads r.m.s. values.

A conducting path must exist across the testing terminals to ensure the correct grid bias potential: furthermore this type of voltmeter should not be

used to measure a voltage which includes a d.c. component or the bias potential will be modified and the calibration upset.

A grid-leak type of rectifier (Fig. 13.69) can be used to measure the p.d. of a source containing a d.c. component or one which does not provide a conducting path (e.g. the p.d. across a capacitor).

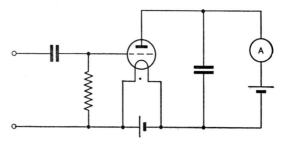

FIG. 13.69. VALVE VOLTMETER USING GRID LEAK RECTIFICATION

The calibration is not appreciably affected by small changes in anode or filament voltage, permissible tolerances being indicated upon the instrument.

For measuring peak values of voltage a diode is used in series with a capacitor (Fig. 13.70). The capacitor charges up to the peak value of the applied voltage and this p.d. (D.C.) may be measured by a

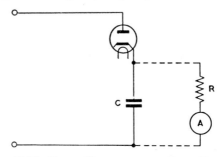

FIG. 13.70. VALVE VOLTMETER FOR PEAK VALUES, USING DIODE

microammeter in series with a suitable resistance, by an electrostatic voltmeter, or by a valve voltmeter applied across the capacitor C. The value of this capacitor should be large in comparison with the diode capacitance but it should not be so great as to produce excessive currents through the diode.

The peak voltmeter may be used for measuring the percentage modulation of a carrier wave (Fig. 13.54): the value of V_0 for the unmodulated carrier is first measured, followed by a reading for V_{max} when the modulating signal is applied.

The usual range of a valve voltmeter is of the order of 0 to 5 volts: instruments are also available for reading up to two or three hundred volts and also for measuring d.c. voltages.

13.13. Metal Rectifiers.[5],[6] The metal rectifier exhibits *asymmetric conduction*, that is to say it has the property of passing current more freely in one direction than in the opposite direction. This type of rectifier is characterized by the use of a thin layer of a semi-conducting material which is formed upon a metal back electrode. A second electrode, the free or counter electrode, is pressed into contact with the semi-conducting layer in order to conduct current into or out of it.

Two examples of this type of rectifier are at present widely used, (i) the copper oxide rectifier

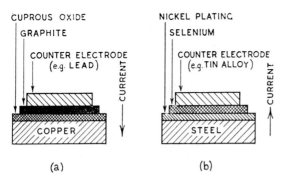

FIG. 13.71. CROSS SECTIONS OF METAL RECTIFIERS
(a) Copper oxide. (b) Selenium.

consisting of a junction between copper and cuprous oxide, and (ii) the selenium rectifier consisting of a junction between selenium and iron. Both of these combinations exhibit also photo-electric properties. Other materials, notably germanium and silicon, have been actively developed during recent years for rectification purposes, and these are gradually coming into widespread use (see Chapter XIV).

Cross sections of typical rectifier elements are shown schematically in Fig. 13.71. In the copper oxide rectifier (Fig. 13.71 (a)) the copper base forms one electrode : to make efficient contact with the copper oxide the surface is covered with a thin layer of graphite against which is firmly pressed the second or counter electrode, for which purpose lead is usually employed. The direction of low resistance —the "forward" direction—is *from the oxide to the copper*.

The selenium rectifier (Fig. 13.71 (b)) has a steel base, usually nickel plated, upon which is formed a thin layer of selenium. Some material such as tin alloy may be used as the counter electrode. The forward direction is *from iron to selenium*.

It is of interest to note that in the copper oxide rectifier the high resistance direction is from metal

to semi-conductor, whereas in the selenium rectifier the high resistance direction is from semi-conductor to metal.

Copper oxide rectifier elements are produced by heating pure copper disks or plates (1 mm thick) in air at a temperature of between 1 000°C and 1 040°C until a film of red cuprous oxide about 0·1 mm thick is formed. One face of the element must remain partially free from oxide : on account of the subsequent method of assembly this is achieved by oxidizing pairs of disks back to back so that oxidation is retarded on the faces to which the air has not free access. The subsequent method of cooling after oxidation has a considerable influence upon the characteristics, and in order to produce a semi-conducting layer of the desired resistance a two-stage annealing process is used in which the disks are finally water-quenched. The cuprous oxide layer is now in the form of a hard bright red crystalline layer adhering very firmly to the copper base, but covered by a thin film of black cupric oxide which has formed during the cooling process. This insulating film of black oxide is removed by the use of mineral acids.

To make effective contact with the cuprous oxide layer, colloidal graphite is painted on to this surface in an aqueous suspension and allowed to dry : contact with the graphite is then made by the use of a soft metal electrode such as lead, under considerable mechanical pressure.

The selenium rectifier element is formed upon a base of iron, which may be nickel plated : the surface is roughened to ensure a good adhesion of the subsequently applied selenium. The selenium is not used in its pure form, additions of other materials (the halogens) being necessary in order to reduce the high resistivity of pure selenium. Selenium exists in three forms, only one of which has a low resistivity suitable for use in a rectifier element. The selenium may be added by melting it upon the iron base at a temperature slightly above the melting point of selenium (217°C) : when this is allowed to cool the selenium layer is in the black vitreous form of extremely high resistivity. Alternatively pulverized selenium in the vitreous (high resistivity) condition is sprinkled evenly upon the cold iron base : these elements are then heated to a temperature of approximately 130°C and at the same time compressed producing a homogeneous layer of selenium in a high resistance crystalline form, with a uniform thickness of approximately 0·1 mm. A further heating process, without pressure and with the selenium surface freely exposed to the atmosphere then raises the temperature to about 200°C to convert the selenium to the desired low resistivity form : it is important at this stage not to reach the

melting point of selenium which would restore it to
the undesirable vitreous form. The immersion of
the element in an alkaline bath at this stage has the
effect of improving the reverse resistance characteristic. The counter electrode is now sprayed on to
the selenium surface: alloys of lead, tin, and bismuth, or of cadmium, tin, and thallium are used,
the particular alloy composition greatly influencing
the results obtained. The reverse or backward
resistance (i.e. in the non-conducting direction) is
very low at this stage and an electrical forming

decreasing slowly with increase of reverse voltage,
but rapidly with increase of forward voltage.

The electrical characteristic is more conveniently
shown by an instantaneous volt-ampere graph.
These graphs are plotted for copper oxide (Fig.
13.73) and selenium (Fig. 13.74) at various temperatures: attention is drawn to the different scales
used for positive and negative values. With increasing voltage in the forward direction the current
is at first very small, but a point—which differs
for the two types—is soon reached where the

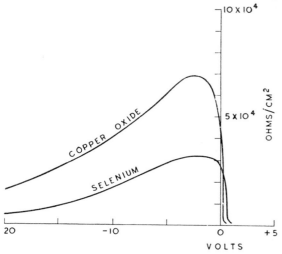

FIG. 13.72. VARIATION OF RECTIFIER RESISTANCE
WITH APPLIED VOLTAGE

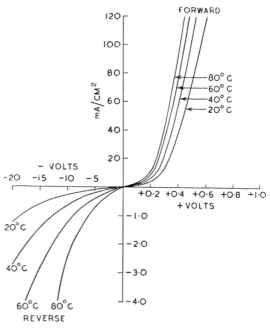

FIG. 13.73. INSTANTANEOUS VOLTAGE/CURRENT
GRAPH FOR COPPER-OXIDE RECTIFIER

process is applied for a few minutes, with the current
in the "non-conducting" direction, to correct this.

Copper oxide elements are produced by treating
blanks of appropriate dimensions: selenium rectifiers are manufactured in large areas, being subdivided into the smaller sizes on completion of all
processes.

The resistance of a metal rectifier in either the
forward or reverse direction is dependent upon the
applied voltage, that is to say, the rectifier does not
obey Ohm's law. In addition to its variation with
applied voltage, the resistance also varies with
temperature and with time: the time effect can be
divided into reversible effects known as "creep" and
the irreversible changes brought about by ageing.

The variation of resistance with applied voltage is
plotted in Fig. 13.72 for new copper oxide and
selenium rectifiers at a temperature of 20°C. These
test voltages were applied just long enough for the
measurements to be taken: under these conditions
the characteristics show the "instantaneous resistance." For both rectifiers the resistance has a
maximum value at approximately zero voltage,

current rises rapidly and the curve gradually
approaches linearity, continuing indefinitely in the
same form. This variable resistance characteristic
of the forward direction of voltage has considerable
practical application quite distinct from the employment of the asymmetric property. The shape of the
reverse voltage/current graph is similar to that of
the forward graph in that the current begins to
increase rapidly after a certain voltage has been
exceeded: however, at reverse voltages higher than
those shown the reverse current increases extremely
rapidly and the rectifiers ultimately break down.
It will be seen from the graphs that the temperature
coefficient of resistance is always negative.

When a voltage is applied to a rectifier in the
forward direction the current which flows is dependent only upon the voltage provided that the

temperature does not change. In the reverse direction, however, the current depends not only upon voltage and temperature, but varies according to the time for which the voltage is imposed. Sometimes the reverse current increases with time, a phenomenon known as "positive" creep: if the current falls with time it is called "negative" creep. In either case the current changes rapidly at first and then tends towards a value which is stable for

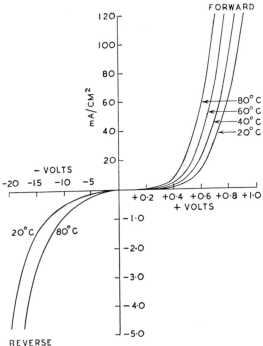

FIG. 13.74. INSTANTANEOUS VOLTAGE/CURRENT GRAPH FOR SELENIUM RECTIFIER

the particular conditions of voltage and temperature. With the copper oxide rectifier this creep is normally positive and is reversible if the rectifier is allowed intervals of rest: with selenium it is generally negative and irreversible, the forming process during manufacture being a manifestation of the creep phenomenon.

At carrier and radio frequencies the self-capacitance of the rectifiers becomes appreciable: this is of the order of 0.02 μF per cm^2 in both types. In general, a cuprous oxide rectifier having a given characteristic would contain more disks in series than an equivalent selenium rectifier and its overall capacitance would therefore be lower.

The theory of operation of the metal rectifier is still incomplete. Investigations into the properties of the cuprous oxide layer itself reveal non-linearity but no asymmetry: variation in the character and

composition of the free electrode does not affect rectification. It is generally considered that a non-conducting "barrier layer" exists at the oxide-copper boundary which behaves in a manner somewhat comparable to the region between the

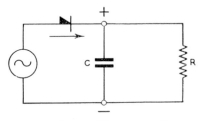

FIG. 13.75. SIMPLE HALF-WAVE RECTIFIER

electrodes of the diode. The conduction is at all events electronic, in contrast to contact rectifiers of the "crystal detector" type.

When an alternating voltage is applied to a single rectifier the current is large during one half-cycle

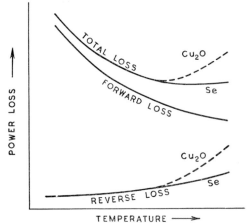

FIG. 13.76. POWER LOSS/TEMPERATURE GRAPHS OF CUPROUS OXIDE (Cu$_2$O) AND SELENIUM (Se) RECTIFIERS

and very small during the other. The simple "half-wave" rectifier applied to a load resistance R is shown in Fig. 13.75: the rectifier symbol is a triangle and plate, the forward direction of current flow being from the triangle to the plate. During each half-cycle the rectifier introduces a power loss —due to a small p.d. and large current in the conducting half-cycle, and to high p.d. with small reverse current during the non-conducting half cycle. The total loss per cycle is the sum of these forward and reverse losses and the rectifier efficiency is dependent upon this loss.

The variation of rectifier losses with temperature is plotted in Fig. 13.76 from which it is seen that

lenium rectifiers afford somewhat greater margin
f safety where high temperatures prevail. Recti-
er power losses appear as heat in the rectifiers:
wing to the deterioration which follows from
xcessive temperatures the rectifier should not be
lowed to operate at a temperature exceeding
5°C in the case of selenium or 55°C for the copper
xide type. Continuous working at high tempera-
ires, in addition to reducing efficiency by increas-
g power loss, also accelerates an irreversible ageing
henomenon which causes the forward resistance
> increase and the reverse resistance to fall.

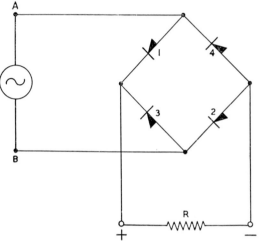

FIG. 13.77. FULL-WAVE BRIDGE RECTIFIER

istability occurs with excessive temperature in
ie copper oxide rectifier due both to the positive
eep and to the fact that as the temperature rises
ie resistance falls and the current rises still
irther.

For the supply of d.c. power, full-wave rectifica-
on is almost always employed. The bridge circuit
nerally used for this purpose is shown in Fig.
3.77, R being the load resistance. When A is
ositive to B, current flows in the conducting
irection from A, through rectifier 1 and the load,
nd then to B through the forward resistance of
ctifier 2: a very small reverse current flows in
ie rectifiers 3 and 4. The p.d. (D.C.) across the load
equal to the applied p.d. (A.C.), less the voltage
rops in rectifiers 1 and 2. The power loss in each
ctifier element is equal to the p.d. across the
ctifier multiplied by the load current: there is
lso the reverse loss in rectifiers 3 and 4, the p.d.
cross rectifier 3 for example being equal to the
pplied voltage less the (forward) p.d. across recti-
er 1. When B is positive to A the conditions are

reversed, rectifiers 3 and 4 being in the conducting
direction with rectifiers 1 and 2 not conducting.
During each cycle, therefore, each rectifier carries
the forward load current for half the time, being
subjected to a reverse voltage during the other half.
A smoothing circuit is usually necessary between
the rectifier bridge and the d.c. load.

A *voltage doubler* circuit (Fig. 13.78) is sometimes
used to produce a d.c. voltage which approximates
to twice that of the secondary e.m.f. of the transformer. During positive half-cycles when A is
positive to B, a charging current flows through the
metal rectifier MRA to charge the capacitor C_A.
For negative half-cycles, B is positive to A and the
capacitor C_B is charged up in series with the
rectifier MRB. Each capacitor charges up, almost
to the voltage present across AB, with the polarity
shown in the diagram: with respect to the d.c. load

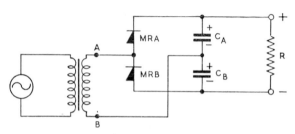

FIG. 13.78. VOLTAGE-DOUBLER RECTIFIER UNIT

resistance R these two charged capacitors are in
series. This arrangement is essentially for high
voltage and small current output, large values of
capacitance being required to present a low
impedance.

Metal rectifiers are extensively used in power
units for providing d.c. supplies over a wide range
of voltage and current outputs. The current-
carrying capacity can be increased by enlarging the
surface area of the rectifier element or if need be by
connecting elements in parallel. For high voltages
a sufficient number of elements is connected in
series. A wide range of elements is available ranging
from 0·005 to 400 cm² (copper oxide) or 0·20 to
200 cm² (selenium): it has not yet been found
practicable to make the selenium elements in such
minute sizes as the copper oxide type.

A selection of rectifier elements used in telecommunication equipment is illustrated in Fig. 13.79.
Elements up to one cm² are best made in the form
of disks which are assembled in insulating tubes:
larger elements up to about 100 cm² are in the
shape of washers for assembly upon a single spindle.
For still larger sizes plates are used with two or
more holes for assembly. Where necessary, cooling

FIG. 13.79. TYPICAL RECTIFIER UNITS USED IN TELECOMMUNICATION EQUIPMENT
(*Courtesy of Westinghouse Brake & Signal Co.*)

fins are incorporated to increase the thermal dissipating surface: to assist heat dissipation the rectifier units should be mounted in such a way that
forced draught cooling is introduced.

For practical use most rectifiers require to be
made up from two or more rectifier elements. In
one form of assembly (Fig. 13.80) the rectifier
"washers" are threaded upon an insulating tube
with alternate lead washers forming the counter
electrodes: spacing washers of conducting material,
and also cooling fins, if necessary, are inserted at
intervals to cool the rectifiers. A bolt passing
through the insulating tube permits the assembly
to be tightly clamped between nuts and spring

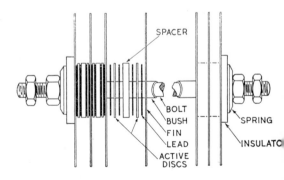

FIG. 13.80. ASSEMBLY OF RECTIFIER ELEMENTS

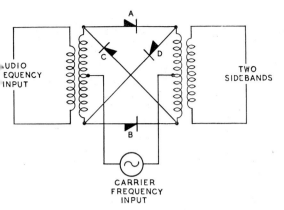

FIG. 13.81. RING MODULATOR

into this circuit are accordingly reversed at every half-cycle of the carrier supply: Fig. 13.82 shows the modulated waveform under ideal conditions. In practice the carrier current has a much higher frequency relative to the audio-frequency than that shown. The output consists only of the upper and lower side band components of the modulated wave. The same device may be used as the complementary demodulator.

A modulator or *static relay* used in multi-channel carrier telegraph systems is shown schematically in Fig. 13.83. A transformer is shunted across the line circuit, the secondary winding being closed with the rectifier networks A and B. Modulation by reversed d.c. signals is effected by varying the value of this secondary impedance reflected to the primary

washers to ensure efficient contact between the active layer and the counter electrode.

Apart from their use in power units, metal rectifiers find wide application in telephone, telegraph, and radio circuit design for a variety of applications where polarization or variable impedance are required. One such application, that in the "ring" modulator, is shown in Fig. 13.81: the device functions as a high-frequency commutator. The carrier voltage produces a current which during positive half-cycles flows through rectifiers A and B, and during negative half-cycles flows through C and D. The magnitude of the carrier voltage must be such that this, and not the audio-frequency signal voltage, effectively determines the instants at which the rectifiers shall become conducting or non-conducting. The audio-frequency currents induced

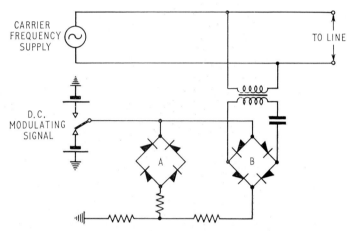

FIG. 13.83. STATIC RELAY

winding. When negative signals are applied at the telegraph transmitter, the metal rectifier bridge A presents a low impedance: the impedance of the rectifier bridge B is high and negligible power from the carrier supply is drawn through the transformer. When positive signals are applied the bridge A offers a high impedance, but the bridge B presents its low forward resistance: this low value of secondary impedance absorbs appreciable power from the carrier power supplied to the line.

13.14. Photo-electricity.[7] The phenomena of photo-electricity include all those processes in which energy in the form of light undergoes a transformation as a result of which some of this energy appears in an electrical form. In all these processes the energy carried by atoms of light—termed *photons*—is absorbed by the electrons of certain materials when subjected to the incidence of light. The particular result of this depends upon the state of the electrons before the energy from the arriving

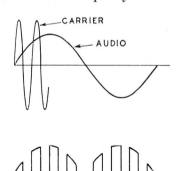

FIG. 13.82. RING-MODULATED WAVE

photons is transferred to them. Any device whose electrical properties undergo a change when it is exposed to light is termed a PHOTO-ELECTRIC CELL.

There are three distinct types of photo-electric cell—

(i) The *conductivity* cell the resistance of which is reduced by incident light.

(ii) The *rectifier* or "barrier layer" cell which generates an e.m.f. when light falls upon it.

(iii) The *emission* cell in which electrons are liberated from a cathode by the action of light.

(i) CONDUCTIVITY CELLS. In a non-conductor there will normally be no free electrons: the effect of light may take the form of liberating some of

that of a rectifier current in the same pair o materials. Consequently the forward resistance c the combination as a rectifier has a shuntin effect upon the cell which renders it desirable t design small cells with high resistance. Coppe oxide cells have forward resistances of the order c hundreds of ohms, while selenium cells of simila size have forward resistances of thousands of ohm

Two types of rectifier cell are in use. In th "back-wall" type (Fig. 13.84 (a)) a very thin laye of semiconductor is deposited on a relatively thic back electrode: contact is made with the out surface of the semiconductor by means of a pe: forated front electrode. The boundary junction

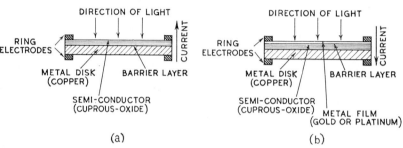

FIG. 13.84. RECTIFIER-TYPE PHOTO-ELECTRIC CELLS
(a) Back-wall pattern. (b) Front-wall pattern.

these electrons and the material will become a conductor when illuminated. This phenomenon is referred to as photo-conductivity. With photo-conducting materials it is found in general that, under a given applied p.d., the quantity of electricity passed is directly proportional to the radiant energy absorbed, and that the quantity of electricity passed under a given illumination increases with the applied p.d. until saturation is reached. Cuprous-oxide and selenium each exhibit photo-conductive effects. Conductivity cells are comparatively slow in response and sometimes erratic in performance. Their sphere of use lies in such applications as control of artificial lighting, burglar alarms, etc.

(ii) RECTIFIER CELLS. An e.m.f. is developed across the boundary between two different substances when in contact and subjected to illumination: cells of this class are known variously as photo-couples, rectifier type or "barrier layer" photo cells. Very large effects are observed when one of the materials is a semiconductor—for example selenium or cuprous oxide—and this phenomenon appears to be closely allied to that found in the metal rectifier. On illumination, a loss of electrons occurs at the boundary which in the copper-cuprous oxide couple leaves the copper oxide with positive polarity, i.e. the photo-electric current tends to flow in the *opposite* direction to

behind the semiconductor which must be in sufficiently thin layer for the light to penetrate t the junction at the back electrode. The "frontwall type (Fig. 13.84 (b)) has a layer of semicon ductor sufficiently thick to be opaque to th incident light: the junction is at the front surfac of the semiconductor. To effect this it is necessar to deposit upon the front surface of the sem conductor a front conducting electrode which form a sufficiently intimate contact with the sem conductor and yet remains transparent to incider light. This may be achieved by sputtering gold c platinum to form a continuous but exceedingly thi metallic film through which a large proportion c the incident light will pass to energize the cell. Th is the more sensitive of the two.

Rectifier type cells are robust and convenient fc use in the *photometer* for comparison of light intens ties in conjunction with a moving coil meter whic may be calibrated to read direct in foot-candle The energy output, however, is small and, owing t the necessity for connecting it to a low-resistanc load, it is not possible to use this type with a valv amplifier. Moreover the capacitance is relativel high—of the order of 0·1 μF per cm^2: it is accord ingly unsuitable for use with light modulated a voice or higher frequencies.

(iii) EMISSION CELLS. With certain material:

ncluding electrical conductors normally containing a large number of free electrons, when the energy of incident light is transferred to them some electrons acquire sufficient energy to leave the conductor: this liberation of electrons from an electrode due to this cause is termed PHOTO-ELECTRIC EMISSION.

In photo-electric emission the number of electrons emitted in a given time (i.e. the flow of current in a suitably arranged circuit) is proportional to the intensity of the illumination. Electrons are only emitted, however, if the energy imparted to them exceeds what they must expend in crossing the boundary of the material. This energy depends upon the frequency of the incident light, i.e. upon its colour. As a result frequencies within the visible spectrum do not cause photo-electric emission from the majority of metals excepting the alkali metals (potassium, caesium, etc.). In photo-cells which are sensitive to visible light energy, the emitting surface contains one of these alkali metals or its compound: the most sensitive cells contain caesium. Even so there is an increase in emission at one particular frequency and a photo-cell exhibits a selective effect for a particular colour. Approximate graphs are shown in Fig. 13.85 for the colour response using various types of cathode: the response of caesium cathodes is very dependent upon the material on which the caesium is deposited and upon the method of manufacture.

An important feature in which photo-electric emission differs from thermionic emission is that in the former the penetration of incident photons is restricted to a thin surface layer only a few hundred atoms in thickness so that only electrons near to the surface come within the region where liberation may occur: as a result, the photo-electric current is relatively small. In thermionic emission the whole mass of the cathode is heated and a much larger number of electrons has the opportunity of becoming energized sufficiently to cross the boundary.

A simple type of photo-emissive cell consists of a photo-electric cathode and a metallic anode insulated from one another and supported inside an evacuated glass envelope. The electrons released from the cathode are collected by the anode maintained at a positive potential. If a suitable battery is connected between anode and cathode, when the cell is in the dark there will be only a very slight current due to *thermionic* emission: a photo-electric current will flow when the cathode is illuminated, this current being proportional to the intensity of illumination but depending also upon the frequency (colour) of the light. Unless a guard ring is used between cathode and anode there will

be a leakage of current over the insulation which greatly exceeds the thermionic dark-current.

An illumination of one *lumen* (the total amount of light falling on a surface of one square foot at a distance of one foot from a source of one candle power) will produce a photo-electric current of the order of 25 μA in a vacuum-type photo-cell. Since the currents obtained from the vacuum type cell are very small some means of amplification *within* the photo-electric cell is highly desirable. The

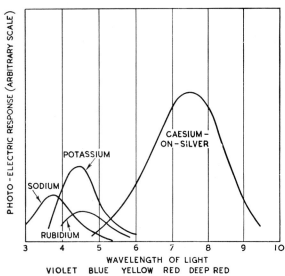

FIG. 13.85. EMISSION TYPE PHOTO-ELECTRIC CELLS: COLOUR CHARACTERISTICS OF VARIOUS CATHODES

emission may be increased by using gas-filled cells, or by the *electron multiplier*.

Gas-filled cells contain an inert gas—usually argon or a mixture of neon and helium—at low pressure. As a result of ionization by collision one electron emitted from the cathode may result in the production of perhaps five pairs of ions: the positive and negative ions contribute to the current to an extent which may produce up to 200 μA per lumen. The linear relationship between illumination and current is not closely followed by the gas-filled cell.

The production of secondary electrons is the basis of the electron multiplier. A vacuum type of photo-cell is fitted with a cathode together with two or more anodes suitably arranged physically and maintained at progressively increasing positive potentials (Fig. 13.86). The material of these electrodes is chosen particularly for its secondary emission properties: up to 8 or 10 secondary electrons may be emitted for each primary electron which bombards an anode. The use of one or more of these intermediate electrodes results in appreciable increase in the electron current in the load resistance R_a.

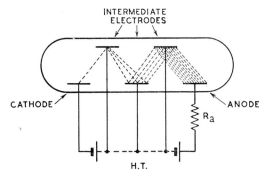

INTERMEDIATE
ELECTRODES

CATHODE

ANODE

R_a

H.T.

FIG. 13.86. THE ELECTRON MULTIPLIER

The photo-emissive cell requires a high voltage battery in order to obtain a sufficient current: it may, however, be connected to a high resistance load to serve as an input to a valve amplifier.

Vacuum and secondary emission type cells respon satisfactorily to the variation in light interrupted a frequencies up to about 1 Mc/s: above this figu the inter-electrode capacitance limits the loa impedance which can be used. In a gas-filled ce however, the comparatively slowly moving io progressively reduce the response to frequencie higher than about 5 000 c/s. Typical photo-electr emission cells of the three classes are illustrated i Fig. 13.87.

13.15. Ionization. A gas at normal temperatu and pressure contains a relatively small number ions and may be regarded practically as a no conductor. If the gas becomes *ionized*, i.e. th number of ions is appreciably increased, it is capab of conducting electricity.

The number of ions may be increased by raisin the temperature of the gas: a gas becomes conduc ing in the neighbourhood of a red-hot body. In th gas-filled valve, ionization by collision betwee moving electrons from the cathode and gas mol cules results in an increased conductivity. A electron leaving a heated cathode at high velocit

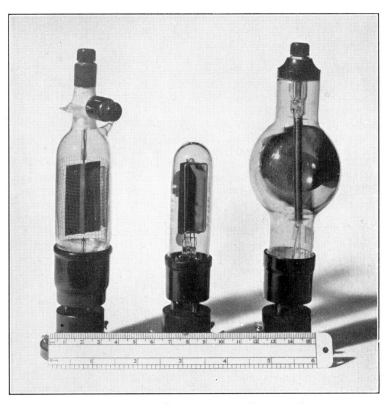

FIG. 13.87. TYPICAL PHOTO-ELECTRIC EMISSION CELLS
(*a*) Vacuum. (*b*) Gas-filled. (*c*) Secondary emission types.
(*Courtesy of "I.P.O.E.E. Journal"*)

may attach itself to a gas molecule, forming a negative ion: ionization due to this cause is usually small. More prolific ionization is due to the disruption of an atom or molecule: as the result of collision one or more electrons may be knocked out of the neutral atom or molecule which becomes a positive ion. In molecules the more usual course of events is for the molecule to split into two fragments, one retaining the extra electron to form a negative ion, the other left with less than its normal complement and forming a positive ion. In the valve the flow of positive ions towards the *cathode* is equivalent to the flow of electrons towards the anode in producing an increase in anode currents. The increase in anode current on ionization is mainly due to neutralization of the space charge by the positive ions. Ionization occurs at the critical anode potential which imparts sufficient energy to the electrons. Ionization may be harmful on account of the bombardment of the cathode by heavy positive ions which reduces the life of the filament.

Some applications based upon the occurrence of ionization are briefly described below.

THE TUNGAR RECTIFIER. The tungar rectifier consists of a gas-filled diode, or double diode, with a tungsten filament and containing argon gas to neutralize the space charge by ionization. The circuit arrangement is generally similar to that of Fig. 13.8, but the use of gas-filled valves has the advantage that the internal resistance is lower.

THE MERCURY ARC RECTIFIER. When heavy direct currents are to be taken from a.c. supplies, mercury arc rectifiers are employed. A typical mercury arc rectifier bulb is shown in Fig. 13.88. It consists of a large evacuated glass bulb containing a small pool of mercury which forms the cathode. Two main anodes of graphite are located in side arms: in addition, two exciter anodes, also of graphite, may be fitted in the positions shown, and a starter electrode is adjacent to the cathode.

The principle on which this rectifier operates is similar to that of a double diode valve but with the presence of ionization: also this rectifier requires the provision of a starting device. The latter is conveniently provided by using a locally operated electro-magnet which causes the starting electrode to dip into the mercury cathode and then withdraw, producing an arc as it leaves the mercury surface. This arc produces a hot "cathode spot" on the mercury surface which commences to evaporate and to emit a particularly dense stream of electrons. Electrons are attracted to one or other of the main anodes during alternate half-cycles: in their passage the electrons strike neutral molecules of mercury vapour and ionization by collision occurs, with consequent increase in anode current. The

energy given up by the positive ions on reaching the cathode is converted to heat and tends to maintain the temperature of the cathode spot. In addition, the heavy positive ions move comparatively slowly and accumulate near the mercury surface producing a positive charge which draws electrons from the mercury surface at a temperature lower than that at which they would normally be emitted. An increase in pressure results from the large quantity of mercury vapour produced. The

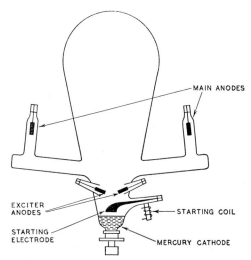

FIG. 13.88. MERCURY ARC RECTIFIER BULB

function of the large bulb is to condense the mercury vapour.

Provided that the necessary anode potential is maintained the process is continuous, once started. A minimum anode current is necessary to maintain a stable cathode spot. The exciter anodes are provided to draw this minimum current irrespective of load variations in the main rectifier load.

A simplified diagram of the mercury arc rectifier circuit is given in Fig. 13.89. In order to prevent the current from falling to zero when the anode potential passes through zero once every half-cycle, an inductance must be included in each of the anode circuits to provide an assisting induced e.m.f. and so maintain the current. The output may be controlled by the regulating reactance: the compensating reactance enables the two anode currents to be balanced.

COLD CATHODE TUBES.[8] The cold cathode tube, a class in which the neon lamp is a well-known example, depends for its operation upon the occurrence of ionization. In the diode form a pair of nickel or iron electrodes are sealed in a well-annealed glass tube, absolutely clean and free from air: the cathode surface may be of metal, or coated with oxides of barium and strontium. After exhaustion a small quantity of a chemically inert gas such as neon, argon or helium, or a mixture of these gases, is introduced into the tube, to a pressure of about 40 mm of mercury, before sealing.

When low values of p.d. are applied to the electrodes there is a small current (about 10^{-14} A) in the tube which consists of electrons and positive ions resulting from ionization of the gas atoms by external ionizing agents, e.g. cosmic radiation and natural radioactivity; this electron current reaches saturation at a relatively low voltage and remains almost constant over a range of applied p.d.

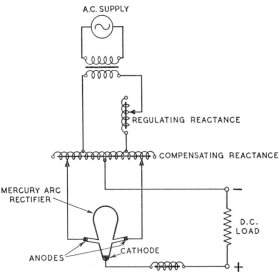

FIG. 13.89. MERCURY ARC FULL-WAVE RECTIFIER

(AB in Fig. 13.90 (a)). As the applied voltage is increased and the electron velocity rises, ionization occurs and the current increases; some electrons and positive ions unite to form molecules in violent oscillation, emitting light waves at a frequency which gives the characteristic colour of the gas used. Positive ions attacking the cathode result in secondary emission and above a certain value of applied voltage (point C) the current rises sharply, until after the "breakdown" voltage (point D) is reached the current continues to increase as the applied voltage is *reduced*, i.e. the tube behaves as a negative resistance (Fig. 13.90 (b)). The discharge is then self-sustaining at a lower voltage than that required to "strike" or "fire" the tube. When the voltage is reduced to a certain value (point E), the current rises at a practically constant voltage, i.e. the resistance falls to zero: at this point it is necessary to operate

the tube with a resistive load to prevent th current from reaching a dangerously high value This is the normal operating point of the tube, an the constancy of voltage over a range of curren values enables the tube to be used as a voltag stabilizer.

The operation of such a tube is influenced b incident radiation such as light: for stability o

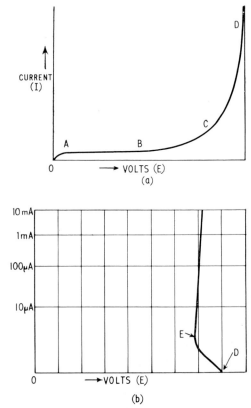

FIG. 13.90. COLD-CATHODE TUBE: CURRENT VOLTAG CHARACTERISTICS

performance it may be necessary to shield the tub from strong sunlight or artificial light and a sma l ocal source of illumination may be provided t cause the emission of the photo-electrons require to assist the initial operation of the tube.

The three-electrode tube has two anodes, one these—the "priming," "trigger," or "striker electrode—being situated more closely to th cathode (Fig. 13.91). Due largely to the shorte path, the priming gap has a substantially lowe breakdown voltage compared with the main ga This enables the tube to be used as a relay in whic the lower voltage applied to the trigger electro will produce a small current in the priming ga and ionize the tube sufficiently to lower the break-down voltage of the main gap. The relation between the priming gap current and the main gap breakdown voltage is termed the *transfer characteristic:* though the primary current may be only of the order of a few microamperes the tube cannot be regarded as a purely voltage-operated device and the impedance of the input circuit must be suitably limited. To extinguish

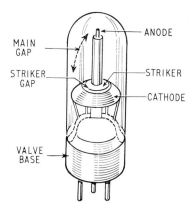

FIG. 13.91. THREE-ELECTRODE COLD-CATHODE TUBE

the glow it is necessary to depress the main anode voltage below the maintaining value.

The principle of transfer electrodes is used in multi-electrode tubes for special purposes: by suitable geometrical arrangement of the electrodes the conducting gap directly influences a following gap by lowering its breakdown voltage.

A finite time is required both to establish the condition of ionization sufficiently for the discharge to be maintained, and also for the ionization products to decay. This limits the rate at which operating pulses can be allowed to follow one another.

For certain purposes cold cathode tubes may conveniently replace thermionic valves with a consequent economy in power consumption: as a secondary feature the operation of such a tube may be confirmed from the presence of the glow.

THE THYRATRON. The thyratron is a triode which contains gas at low pressure: when the grid is negatively biased no anode current will flow until the anode potential reaches a certain critical value. If the anode potential is gradually increased a point is reached when ionization occurs and a very rapid increase of current takes place: it is necessary to include a protective resistance in the anode circuit to limit the maximum current value in this "gas discharge" valve.

A convenient method of gradually raising the

anode potential is to connect it to a capacitor C which is charged through a resistance R (Fig. 13.92), using suitable values for C and R to arrive at the desired time-constant. The capacitor charges at a rate depending upon the product CR: as soon as the critical anode potential is reached the valve becomes conducting and the capacitor is very rapidly discharged. The process is repeated indefinitely, the potential on the anode rising gradually

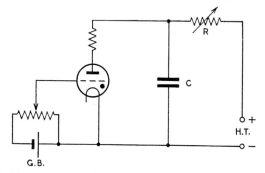

FIG. 13.92. TIME-BASE CIRCUIT FOR CATHODE-RAY TUBE

and collapsing almost instantaneously, producing what is termed a "saw tooth" waveform. The frequency of the operation depends upon the values of resistance and capacitance, and also upon the grid and anode potentials for a given gas.

Charging a capacitor through a resistance does not produce a uniform current and it is usual to charge the capacitor through a pentode valve whose current is practically constant irrespective of the voltage.

A particular application of this device is to produce a "time-base" for operation of the cathode-ray tube: if the resistor is made variable the time duration can be adjusted to any desired value.

13.16. The Cathode-ray Tube. The cathode-ray tube is an instrument for showing pictorially the variations in p.d. or current occurring in a circuit. It relies for its operation upon an electron flow, the electrons being projected in the form of a well-defined and controllable beam on to a fluorescent screen. Used as an oscilloscope the instrument has considerable advantage over oscillograph instruments of the mirror galvanometer pattern whose relatively heavy moving system renders them unsuitable for recording high-frequency variations. The cathode-ray tube may be used for a variety of forms of measurement and waveform analysis: it is also employed as the receiving instrument for television signals.

Constructional details of one form of cathode-ray tube are shown in Fig. 13.93. It consists of a thermionic cathode almost surrounded by an open cylindrical shield—the *modulator electrode*—which is closed at one end by a disk anode with a small

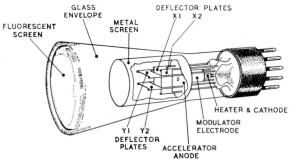

FIG. 13.93. CATHODE-RAY OSCILLOSCOPE: CONSTRUCTIONAL DETAILS

central hole. In some tubes this anode or *accelerator electrode* may be of cylindrical shape. The heater, cathode, accelerator, and modulator electrode are insulated from one another. This assembly of electrodes is sometimes referred to as the "electron gun."

On the further side of the accelerator are two pairs of deflector plates (X1, X2, and Y1, Y2) each pair being mutually at right angles to each other and to the plane of the accelerator. Viewed along the axis of the tube, the area enclosed by the deflector plates is square in cross-section, the length of the sides being sufficient to permit a full-screen deflexion of the electron beam to be obtained on both axes. All the electrodes are rigidly fixed in relation to one another, the insulated connexions from each being brought out through a glass pinch at the heater end of the tube. The entire assembly is enclosed in a glass envelope from which the air is evacuated. The far end of the glass envelope is flattened to form a viewing screen (Fig. 13.94), the inner surface being coated with a fluorescent material.

FIG. 13.94. CATHODE-RAY TUBE, SHOWING FLUORESCENT SCREEN

The corresponding diagrammatic symbol for the cathode-ray tube is shown in Fig. 13.95 with typical electrode connexions: additional electrodes may be added for special purposes. When the cathode is heated and the accelerator maintained at a high positive potential, the electrons emitted are drawn towards the accelerator at high velocity, a considerable proportion of them passing through the small central hole. This action is assisted by the modulating electrode which is maintained at a fairly high negative potential with respect to the cathode: due to this field the electrons are repelled from the modulator electrode to prevent them from dispersing by their mutual repulsion, and are concentrated into a fine beam

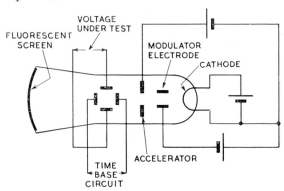

FIG. 13.95. CATHODE-RAY OSCILLOSCOPE: GRAPHICAL SYMBOL SHOWING ELECTRODE CONNEXIONS

along the axis. These electrons travel with sufficient velocity to impinge upon the fluorescent screen, producing a small spot of light whose colour depends upon the material with which the glass has been coated.

The electron beam after passing through the accelerator will be deflected according to the potentials of the deflecting electrodes. These effects are represented in Fig. 13.96 which shows at (a) the screen, the deflecting electrodes at zero potential and the axial position of the light spot. If Y1 is made positive to Y2, the electrodes X1 and X2 remaining at zero potential, the electron beam will be attracted by the positive charge on Y1 and repelled by the negative charge on Y2: the resultant movement of the light spot is indicated by the arrow in diagram (b). Similarly, (diagram (c)) with Y2 positive to Y1, the electron beam moves towards the Y2 electrode. An alternating sine-wave p.d. applied across Y1 and Y2 would cause the light spot to execute a simple harmonic motion between Y1 and Y2: due to the "after-glow" (the time-lag in the extinction of the fluorescent glow) and the persistence of vision by the retina of the eye, the moving light spot would appear to draw a straight line joining the $Y1$ and $Y2$ plates. At (d) and (e) are indicated the force on the electron beam which results from making $X1$ and $X2$ each positive in turn. It is apparent that by the simultaneous application of suitable p.d.s across the two pairs of deflecting electrodes the co-ordinates of the light spot may be varied as desired.

In an oscilloscope, the current or voltage being examined is applied across one pair of plates—those designated $Y1$ and $Y2$ in the diagram: across the other pair of deflecting electrodes $X1–X2$ is applied a p.d. which varies uniformly with time to

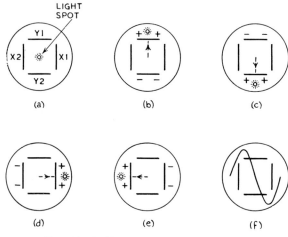

Fig. 13.96. Effects of Potentials on Deflecting Electrodes

form a *time base*. This is conveniently provided by the gas discharge valve circuit given in Fig. 13.92: the p.d. rises at a uniform rate to a maximum value, falling again at zero almost instantaneously. This p.d. applied to the $X1–X2$ electrodes will cause the light spot to traverse the horizontal scale from left to right at a uniform speed and to return to the left instantaneously. By adjusting the time-constant of the time-base circuit to equal the periodic time of the alternating quantity under investigation (or an exact multiple of the periodic time) the waveform will be displayed upon the fluorescent screen as a graph of voltage or current against time. For a pure sine wave the display is shown at (e) in Fig. 13.96.

During the extremely short discharge time of the capacitor in the time-base circuit, the spot is returned to a position on the left-hand side of the oscilloscope screen in readiness for the next steady motion to the right in this continuous cycle of operations. Although the electron stream in the cathode-ray tube is uninterrupted, the speed at

which the light spot is deflected during its return or "fly-back" prevents any perceptible effect upon the screen except where the time-base speed is at its highest setting and the fly-back time may be comparable with the periodic time of the waveform under investigation. The time-base deflection alone is a series of linear movements of the spot from left to right at constant speed, the spot returning with negligible fly-back time. Other types of time-base such as the simple sinusoidal and the elliptical may be provided. When using a time-base for high-frequency measurement a very small change in the time-base adjustment will upset the steady pattern necessary for close examination of the waveform. The time-base can be locked into synchronism by feeding a small fraction of the voltage to be examined into the grid circuit of the gas-filled valve of the time-base generator. For the purpose of making measurements a transparent scale may be fitted to the screen.

The electron beam may be deflected by the presence of a magnetic field at right angles to the beam: the direction of deflexion is at right angles to the direction of the magnetic field. Instead of employing electrostatic deflexion from the $X1–X2$ and $Y1–Y2$ electrodes described above, electromagnetic deflexion may be used by arranging two pairs of coils at right angles to one another outside the tube. This method has the disadvantage that power is consumed by the coils. It follows that the deflexion of the electron beam will always be susceptible to the presence of stray magnetic fields from which the cathode-ray tube must be efficiently screened.

Three alternative methods are available for focusing the electron beam to concentrate it into a small sharply defined area on the fluorescent screen for a sharp image. Such a device functions as an *electron lens*, comparable to the optical lens used for focusing a beam of light.

(i) With electrostatic focusing, the beam is made to converge by the action of electrostatic fields which are due to the potentials of two or more additional electrodes through which the beam passes after leaving the accelerator.

(ii) Alternatively, the beam is caused to converge by means of a magnetic field parallel to the axis of the tube: this is achieved by placing a solenoid over the tube, between the cathode and accelerator.

(iii) The beam may be constricted by the ionization of traces of gas present in the tube. Positive ions are attracted towards the electron beam upon which they exert a concentrating force: this is brought about by the positive ions which on account of their low mobility set up a positive space charge.

In a television receiver, both sets of deflecting electrodes (or coils) are used to scan the area of the screen at the required rate. The intensity of the spot of light is modulated in accordance with the received signals. The modulator electrode in this case functions as a control electrode, comparable to the control grid of a triode valve: in addition to its steady negative bias potential, received signals are applied to this electrode to modulate the intensity of the electron stream.

REFERENCES

1. K. D. BOMFORD: "A Survey of Modern Radio Valves," *I.P.O.E.E. Journal*, **42** (1949), p. 117.
2. G. J. S. LITTLE: "Carrier Telephony," ibid. **29** (1936), p. 34.
3. H. D. BICKLEY: "A Note on Amplitude, Phase and Frequency Modulation," ibid., **34** (1941), p. 42.
4. J. H. H. MERRIMAN, and R. W. WHITE: "Frequency Modulation," *I.P.O.E.E. Paper No.* **183** (1945).
5. A. L. WILLIAMS, and L. E. THOMPSON: "Metal Rectifiers," *I.E.E. Journal*, **88** (1941), p. 353.
6. W. G. RADLEY, C. E. RICHARDS, E. A. SPEIGHT, and E. V. WALKER: "Modern Materials in Telecommunications," *I.P.O.E.E. Journal*, **35** (1942), p. 15.
7. A. C. LYNCH, and J. R. TILLMAN: "Emission Type Photo-electric Cells," ibid. **36** (1943), p. 43.
8. J. A. LAWRENCE: "The Cold Cathode Tube in Telephone Switching Circuits," *I.P.O.E.E. Paper No.* **202** (1952).

CHAPTER XIV

TRANSISTOR ELECTRONICS

14.1 The Transistor. The name *transistor* is derived from "transfer resistor" since it is fundamentally a two-terminal resistor whose value can be controlled by a current injected into a third terminal.

The transistor is an active device made from a semiconductor, capable of controlling an output power some thousands of times greater than the input power. It can with advantage and with economy perform most of the functions previously made possible by the thermionic valve, for example oscillation, amplification, signal detection, and switching. In many applications it has already superseded the thermionic valve. It should however be clearly understood that the transistor does not replace the valve in the simple sense that a valve can be withdrawn from a piece of equipment and its place taken by a transistor: the fundamental physical basis and the conditions of operation of the transistor are so completely different from those of the thermionic valve that circuits and equipment must be specially designed for the incorporation of transistors.

14.2 Transistor versus Valve. Compared with the thermionic valve the primary advantages of the transistor are first the smallness of its dimensions—typically 15 to 20 mm long (excluding leads) and 6 mm diameter—which permits considerable reduction in the size of telecommunication equipment and in requirements for its accommodation; secondly the greater efficiency resulting from a very modest power requirement due to the absence of the need for a heater or for high values of applied voltage; and thirdly the greater life expectancy from a well-designed transistor. Secondary advantages which arise are greater simplicity in the power sources, reduced power consumption, and reduced heat dissipation which means that associated components, e.g. resistors, can themselves be made smaller giving a greater overall compactness to transistor equipments. Unlike the valve the transistor operates instantaneously without any warming-up delay.

Not unnaturally the transistor has certain disadvantages too. These are related to its sensitivity to temperature rise, to its limitations to permissible applied voltages and in power handling; to its limitation in the upper frequency which it will handle, and sometimes to its greater noise factor.

The differences in size between valve and transistor arises from the difference in speed at which the useful charge carriers move between the input and output electrodes. In a receiving valve an electron takes something like 2 mμs* to cross the distance of about 0·5 cm from cathode to anode. In a typical p-n-p transistor the charge carriers traverse the corresponding path (namely the base region between emitter and collector) in about 200 mμs, the distance being about 0·003 cm.

There is some analogy, both from the aspects of physical design and circuit operation, between the transistor and the valve. Of the three transistor electrodes the *emitter* corresponds to the cathode, the *base* corresponds to the control grid, and the *collector* corresponds to the anode. This analogy should however be considered true only in general descriptive terms.

The valve is usually a voltage-operated device: the transistor is current-operated, the emitter-base voltage being always small. The valve shows little or no transmission in the backwards direction (i.e. from anode to grid): all transistors have appreciable backwards transmission even at very low frequencies owing to the finite resistivity of the material forming the base region. Valves depend upon negative charge carriers (electrons) only: the transistor uses both electrons and positive charge carriers known as *holes*.

The thermionic valve can provide a power gain because its input impedance is very great: the transistor on the other hand can provide power gain because its input impedance is low. The high degree of vacuum normally required of the valve is paralleled by the extreme order of purity required in the basic material, usually germanium or silicon, of the transistor.

14.3 The Point-contact Transistor. Following the establishment of the metal rectifier, many attempts were made to use this principle to produce a triode in which a small power input could control a large power output. Success was achieved only when the semiconductor germanium became available. When contact with germanium was made from a thin metal wire, forming a germanium diode, the resistance presented by the combination was either very low or very high, according to the direction of an applied p.d. Furthermore it was found, from using a probe to explore the area of the point-contact, that if a second point-contact was made within 0·01 in. (0·25 mm) of the first

*Milli-microsecond = 10^{-9} seconds.

423

point-contact then there was a relation between the currents flowing in the two point-contacts, provided that appropriate potential conditions were applied to the two point-contacts.

When the first contact, called the *emitter*, is biased by a p.d. applied in the direction to produce *low* resistance and the second contact, called the *collector*, is biased in the *reverse* sense by a p.d. arranged to produce a *high* resistance, the collector current $I_C{}^*$ varies with the emitter current I_E. The ratio of the small changes in these currents is known as the *current gain* α,

hence, $$\alpha = dI_C/dI_E \quad . \quad . \quad (14.1)$$

The value of α can be of the order of 1·0, and since the input resistance at the emitter is low (a few

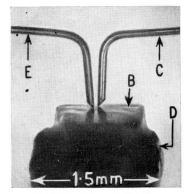

FIG. 14.1. STRUCTURE OF POINT-CONTACT
TRANSISTOR

hundred ohms) while the output resistance at the collector is high (some tens of thousands of ohms) the approximately equal current-changes in both contacts result in a power gain of up to 100.

Fig. 14.1 indicates the structure of a point-contact transistor. The emitter contact-wire may be of beryllium-copper and the collector wire of phosphor-bronze. The diameter of these wires is of the order of 0·002 to 0·005 in. and they are suitably pointed by grinding, shearing, or some similar process. The contact pressure is accurately controlled to about 1 gramme: this may be achieved by deflexion or compression of the wire into an L- or S-shaped spring. The wires may be bonded by an adhesive resin or the entire assembly moulded in a potting resin. The germanium base or wafer has a top surface of about 1 mm² × 0·5 mm thickness: it is soldered to a metal support D which forms the base electrode. With any transistor, encapsulation of the device with hermetic

*A note on letter symbols and subscripts for transistors will be found at the end of this Chapter.

sealing, to exclude moisture and prevent degradation by contamination from gas or vapour at the point contacts, is essential in order to ensure reliability.

Fig. 14.2 indicates the biasing potentials and shows the symbols used for this transistor to designate the emitter (E), the collector (C), and the third electrode—the germanium itself—termed the *base* (B). It will be seen that in this example (the germanium being *n-type*) the emitter has a positive potential applied and the collector has a negative potential applied, while the base is common to both emitter and collector circuits.

It will be appreciated that the production in quantity of point-contact transistors having the degree of mechanical precision indicated and stable

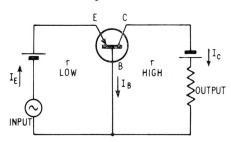

FIG. 14.2. BIAS POTENTIALS FOR POINT-CONTACT
TRANSISTOR: COMMON-BASE MODE

point-contact pressures is a task of no small magnitude. In addition the emitter and collector have to be subjected to a forming process by electrical pulsing to ensure the desired characteristics. Nevertheless these problems have been overcome and point-contact transistors have been the subject of mass-production for a variety of applications. However they are no longer important commercially: their use in telecommunication equipment has not been found favourable on account of their being less linear, more noisy, and less flexible in use as amplifiers when compared with a later form known as the *junction transistor*. Consequently the point-contact transistor will not be further described here.

14.4. Pure (Intrinsic) Germanium: Electrons and Holes. The study of transistors is based particularly on the element germanium and to an increasing extent on silicon.

The electrical characteristics of transistors can be explained only by reference to the theory of the solid state of matter: the number and distribution of the outer or valence electrons forming part of the atom, and also the arrangement of the atoms within the crystal structure of the semiconductor are of particular importance.

It will be seen that the transistor depends upon a monocrystalline structure. By a single crystal is meant an ordered arrangement of the atoms, which persists in all three dimensions right to the surface of the sample: at the surface this uniformity naturally terminates and the crystal properties and effects at the surface are very different. By contrast, a substance in polycrystalline form, consisting of a large number of small single crystals which originally grew along axes with different orientations, has boundary conditions between adjoining crystals or grains which differ from the state within the crystal. The crystal boundaries are imperfections which interfere with the uniform motion of current carriers (e.g. electrons). Molten metals normally produce polycrystalline ingots on cooling: a special metallurgical technique is used to produce monocrystalline germanium.

Germanium appears in the Periodic Table (Appendix D) as element No. 32, below the elements carbon (6) and silicon (14) but above the elements tin (50) and lead (82): all five of these elements have four outer electrons—the loosely-bound valence electrons available for chemical reactions.

Fig. 14.3 shows pictorially the arrangement of germanium atoms in a unit cube of a perfect and absolutely pure single crystal of germanium: the silicon crystal has a similar formation. Both have the crystalline structure of the diamond lattice, namely two inter-penetrating face-centred cubic lattices, one being displaced a quarter of a body-diagonal from the other. Each germanium atom is surrounded by four nearest germanium atoms which occupy the corners of a regular tetrahedron. This pattern persists throughout the single crystal right up to the surface. Every atom is bonded to each of its four neighbouring atoms by one of the four outer or valence electrons acting in conjunction with one valence electron from each neighbouring atom. Each valence bond thus consists of a pair of associated electrons, one from each of two neighbouring atoms, spending most of their time in the region immediately between the centres of the two atoms concerned. When atoms of germanium are arranged in a crystal the valence electrons are no longer exclusively associated with the parent atom but each of the four valence electrons follows an orbit which includes a neighbouring atom. As a result a pair of electrons—the valence bond—performs orbits around each pair of atoms. As the outer electrons form the bonds, very few free electrons are available and pure germanium has a high resistivity, particularly at low temperatures.

Under certain circumstances, for example due to the thermal vibration of the atoms at ordinary room temperatures, a valence bond can be fractured by the removal of one of the pair of electrons, leaving an incomplete one-electron "bond." With germanium the work required to remove the electron is 0·72 electron-volts. The freed electron contributes to the electrical conductivity of the germanium. The electron vacancy in the one-electron bond is termed a *hole* and since its existence can be neutralized only by a single electron the hole is regarded as a positive charge, equal in magnitude but opposite in polarity to the electron.

Each one-electron bond attracts an electron from

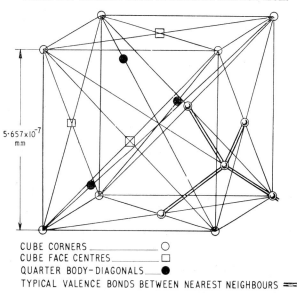

CUBE CORNERS ———————— ○
CUBE FACE CENTRES ———————— □
QUARTER BODY-DIAGONALS ———— ●
TYPICAL VALENCE BONDS BETWEEN NEAREST NEIGHBOURS ⚌

FIG. 14.3. ARRANGEMENT OF ATOMS IN UNIT CUBE OF MONOCRYSTALLINE GERMANIUM

a neighbouring complete bond: this transfer is repeated successively from one bond to a further bond, an electron-vacancy, or hole, occurring in a bond at each successive release of one of the bond-electrons. In this way a condition of displacement of one-electron "bonds," or holes, each with a vacancy for one electron, moves through the crystal in the opposite direction to the freed electrons.

The effect of fracturing the valence bonds is to produce mobile (negative) electrons together with an equal number of (positive) holes: the hole is considered as though it were a charged particle. The crystal as a whole remains electrically neutral.

A crystal of absolutely pure germanium at any normal temperature contains equal numbers of mobile electrons and holes, and is termed *intrinsic* germanium: its conductivity depends only upon the pure germanium itself. This is the pure material which is the starting point for the manufacture of transistors but in its intrinsic form it is not suitable for transistor action to accur: the condition of equilibrium resulting from the equal numbers of mobile electrons and holes must be permanently disturbed, by causing either the electrons or the holes to be in the majority as described below.

If a one-electron "bond" (hole), instead of being filled by another valence electron, is filled by a free conduction electron which has drifted from some other part of the crystal, the process is termed *recombination:* in this event both the hole and the drift electron are neutralized, the electron now becoming a valence electron and completing the bond.

14.5. Doped (Extrinsic) Germanium: Majority and Minority Carriers.

The electrical equilibrium of intrinsic germanium due to the presence of mobile electrons and holes in equal numbers can be permanently disturbed by incorporating minute controlled amounts of impurity elements into the germanium crystal, for example by replacing one atom in about 10^8 germanium atoms by a suitable foreign atom.

To place electrons in the majority, suitable foreign atoms are those which have *five* valence electrons (compared with four in germanium)—for example, arsenic or antimony (Nos. 33 and 51 in the Periodic Table). Antimony is used since it will dissolve substitutionally in the germanium crystal lattice and, after completing the two-electron bonds with one valence electron to each of the four neighbouring germanium atoms, it will have one outer electron remaining free. This spare electron is only loosely bound to the antimony atom (0·01 electron-volt) and may be regarded as free and mobile within the germanium.

On the other hand, to place holes in the majority, elements containing *three* valence electrons (compared with four for germanium) are necessary. Gallium (No. 31) or indium (No. 49) are used as the foreign atoms since they take up only three of the two-electron valence bonds with the germanium atom leaving the fourth germanium valence bond incomplete as a one-electron "bond," or hole: these holes can likewise be regarded as free and mobile within the germanium.

Germanium in which electrons are permanently in the majority is known as *n-type* germanium (negative): similarly if holes are the majority carriers the germanium is known as *p-type* (positive).

The antimony atom has a nucleus with a positive charge equal to $+5q$, neutralized by the negative charge $-5q$ of the five outer electrons. When four of these electrons are bonded to germanium

atoms the fifth electron is left free and mobile, leaving the antimony atom (with one electron deficient) as a positive ion. The n-type material is dotted with immobile positive ions and free electrons. The crystal as a whole is neutral, because the original germanium atoms and also the added antimony atoms are themselves neutral. Similarly p-type germanium is neutral but dotted with immobile negative ions and with holes free to move around.

Foreign atoms (e.g. antimony), which after completing their bonding have a spare electron which they can give up and so make the germanium n-type by putting mobile electrons in the majority as charge carriers, are termed "donors." Foreign atoms (such as indium), which after completing their bonds make free a one-electron "bond" from the crystal and so make the germanium p-type by putting holes in the majority as charge carriers, are termed "acceptors." Germanium containing added donors or acceptors (to make it n-type or p-type) is said to be "doped." The semiconductor is now *extrinsic* germanium because its conductivity depends upon the presence of added impurities. The preparation of extrinsic germanium (or silicon) is essential to the operation of the transistor.

Due to the valence bonds broken by thermal agitation, electrons as well as holes are always present to some extent in both n-type and p-type semiconductors. Electrons present in p-type, and holes present in n-type semiconductors, are known as *minority* carriers—meaning that they comprise less than 50 per cent of the carriers present in the region.

In a doped crystal under equilibrium as at present described, the product of the number of mobile electrons n and holes p is constant for a given material at a given temperature and is equal to the square of the number n_i of electrons (or holes) in the intrinsic material: this may be written as $np = n_i{}^2$. When the majority-carrier concentration is permanently increased by the addition of donor or acceptor impurities, the equilibrium concentration of minority carriers automatically becomes reduced in the same proportion. Over the working temperature range the equilibrium concentration of majority carriers is practically constant but that of minority carriers is very temperature-dependent. The electron and hole concentrations in germanium increase rapidly with the random atomic vibrations of increasing temperature, due to the fracturing of valence bonds. At high temperatures these electron and hole concentrations dominate any added concentrations due to donor or acceptor impurities, and at ufficiently high temperatures extrinsic germanium behaves like intrinsic germanium and the transistor action is lost.

14.6. The Junction Transistor: Excess Minority Carriers.[4]

Development of the junction transistor followed quickly upon the introduction of the early point-contact transistor. Devoid of the unstable point-contacts and needing no electrical forming process the junction triode offers improved stability and performance, particularly greater gain and lower noise value. The principle of its operation is most easily understood from the theoretical model described below.[5] For transistor action to occur it is necessary to inject temporarily into the base extra carriers of the same sign as minority carriers.

The model (Fig. 14.4) represents a p-n-p junction transistor made from a single crystal of germanium, initially pure, and comprising three components, emitter (E), base (B), and collector (C): the pure germanium may be assumed for the

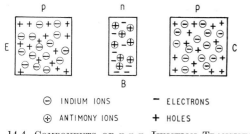

$\ominus$	INDIUM IONS	$-$ ELECTRONS
$\oplus$	ANTIMONY IONS	$+$ HOLES

FIG. 14.4. COMPONENTS OF p-n-p JUNCTION TRANSISTOR

present consideration to contain virtually no free charge carriers, either electrons or holes.

A small quantity of indium is introduced into both the emitter and the collector. These atoms of indium enter the germanium crystal lattice, forming negative indium ions within the lattice and releasing an equivalent number of holes which are free to move within the germanium: similarly a small quantity of antimony introduced

into the base results in positive antimony ions integral with the germanium lattice and releases free electrons. At this stage the indium-doped

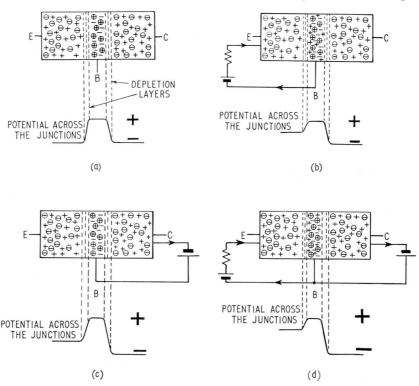

FIG. 14.5. p-n-p JUNCTION TRANSISTOR
(a) As produced.
(b) Emitter biased positively.
(c) Collector biased negatively.
(d) Emitter and collector biased normally.
(*Courtesy of I.E.E.*)

emitter and collector contain mobile holes, the "majority" carriers which make the germanium p-type; while in the antimony-doped base the majority carriers are free electrons making the germanium n-type.

If the emitter, collector, and base are now brought together, holes leave the emitter and collector to migrate to the base while electrons travel in the opposite direction from base to emitter and collector, leaving the base positively charged and the emitter and collector both negatively charged (see Fig. 14.5 (a)). Recombination takes place between holes and electrons in the emitter, the base, and the collector. This migration of carriers across the two junctions followed by recombination continues only until the p.d. between base and emitter, and also between base and collector, is sufficiently high to prevent any further migration of carriers across the junctions. This state may be compared with the space charge from the electron cloud surrounding the heated cathode of a thermionic valve which prevents any further effective electron emission until the positive anode potential is applied. The electric fields established across the two junctions prevent further migration of charge carriers and a state of equilibrium is reached: the regions at the two junctions are known as *depletion layers*, being depleted of free carriers (electrons and holes). This condition of equilibrium represents the state of the transistor as it is manufactured and before it is put into use: it is as depicted in Fig. 14.5 (*a*) which indicates the two junctions, the depletion layers, and the potentials. Emitter and collector are of p-type germanium and the base is n-type, the transistor for this reason being termed a p-n-p transistor.

To put the transistor into use the state of equilibrium must be temporarily disturbed by appropriate bias potentials designed to introduce an excess of minority carriers. In Fig. 14.5 (*b*) the emitter is shown biased with a potential *positive* with respect to the base. This applied potential *reduces* the barrier potential across the emitter-base junction. Free carriers, both holes from the emitter and electrons from the base, can again cross this junction. Since however the transistor is made with a much higher degree of indium concentration in the emitter compared with the antimony concentration in the base, the number of holes greatly exceeds the number of electrons. The current flow can therefore be regarded as virtually that due to migration of holes from emitter to base.

These holes arriving in the base become excess minority carriers. They exist for a finite time before recombining with the electrons present in the base. The average characteristic time, from the instant of injection of the minority carriers (i.e. the holes in the n-type base), required for this recombination to occur is termed the *lifetime* for the particular base material. The lifetime is an important characteristic of the transistor material and may be within the range 1 to 100 μs. As fast as electrons are lost to the base by recombination with the holes they are replaced by further electrons from the negative terminal of the bias potential supply: similarly the supply of holes is maintained by the positive terminal of the bias supply. The net effect of the bias condition is a (conventional) current flow from the positive bias supply to the emitter, migration of holes from emitter to base, and an electron flow from the negative terminal of the bias supply to the base.

Now consider the emitter circuit disconnected but the collector given an opposite bias potential namely a *negative* bias (Fig. 14.5 (*c*)). This additional negative potential *increases* the negative potential at the collector-base junction, preventing the flow of carriers across that junction; consequently there is virtually no current flow in the collector circuit.

Fig. 14.5 (*d*) shows the junction transistor with the appropriate bias potentials applied to both

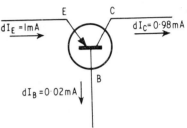

FIG. 14.6. CURRENT CHANGES IN A TRANSISTOR

the emitter and the collector. As described above holes migrate from emitter to base, but due to the "lifetime" factor they do not immediately recombine with electrons in the base: the transistor base is purposely made so narrow (about 0.001 in. that before recombination takes place most of the carriers (holes) come under the influence of the field at the collector-base junction. Due to the negative bias potential this field attracts the holes from the base into the collector, only a few of the holes effecting recombination with electrons in the base. The net effect of the bias potential is thus for a (conventional) current to flow from the emitter through the base to the collector and back by the external bias supply to the emitter in addition a much smaller current flows from emitter to base. The passage of the minority carriers across the base region is slow: it is accompanied by some degree of recombination between minority and majority carriers. This recombination which results in loss of transistor action increase with the emitter-collector spacing which must therefore be kept small.

It is the current flowing in the low-resistance emitter-circuit and with practically the same current value (but minus the small emitter-base current) flowing in the high-resistance collector circuit which gives the power gain of the transistor For explanatory purposes illustrative current value are shown in Fig. 14.6. For a change in emitter current $dI_E = 1$ mA and a small base-current change $dI_B = 0.02$ mA the change in collector current $dI_C = 1 - 0.02 = 0.98$ mA. The current gain is $\alpha = dI_C/dI_E = 0.98/1$. (The term "gain," meaning in fact "ratio," is used even though $II_C < dI_E$.)

The current gain of the junction transistor is determined primarily by the proportion of minority carriers injected by the emitter which diffuse across the base region to the collector junction: this proportion is limited only by the loss of minority carriers by recombination in transit through the base region and by lateral diffusion out of reach of the collector junction.

In this way a power gain is obtained from approximately the same current ($I_C \simeq I_E$) flowing

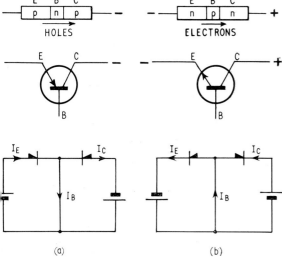

14.7. Symbols, Bias Potentials, and "Representative" Circuits

(a) p-n-p transistor.   (b) n-p-n transistor.

from the low-resistance emitter to the high-resistance collector: for correct impedance match the source impedance and the load impedance would be low and high respectively.

Junction transistors can be made in either p-n-p or n-p-n type. Whether the transistor is p-n-p or n-p-n type the emitter is a rectifying junction biased in the direction of easy current flow (positive bias for a p-n junction): the collector is a second rectifier junction biased in the direction of restricted current flow (negative bias for an n-p junction). The bias is for the purpose of temporarily injecting an excess of minority carriers of the opposite type to the majority carriers which permanently characterize the region. The symbols and bias potentials for these two types of junction transistor are indicated in Fig. 14.7: the reversal of the arrow in the two symbols should be noted.

Summarizing, the action of the junction transistor depends on the current carriers originated at the emitter: these pass through the base in numbers determined by the emitter-base potential, and they are absorbed by the collector which passes a proportional current into the external circuit. In effect, the transistor consists of two diodes connected back-to-back, with potential barriers at each junction: this is suggested in the "representative" circuits at the bottom of Fig. 14.7. Whether p-n-p or n-p-n type, the bias potential applied to the emitter-base circuit neutralizes the potential barrier at the emitter-base junction and it is a *forward* bias: the bias potential applied to the collector-base circuit assists the potential barrier at the collector-base junction and it is a *reverse* bias.

14.7. Energy Levels. The electrons which surround the nucleus of any atom have certain definite energy values which differ for each electron

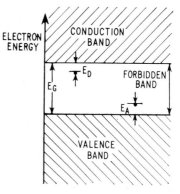

Fig. 14.8. Energy Levels

according to its particular orbit: electrons with lower energy lie in orbits nearer to the nucleus. No two electrons share the identical energy state. Any change in energy level of an electron can be effected only by a change from one fixed energy level to another, involving a corresponding change in orbit and the absorption or emission of the energy difference.

In a crystal comprising a large number of atoms in proximity, interaction takes place between the atoms. For example in the intrinsic germanium atom it has been seen that valence bonds are set up embracing one electron from each of two adjacent atoms. This produces some modification to the fixed energy levels of the electrons. It is found that these energies can have values lying within a particular range or band, the "valence band" of Fig. 14.8, but that energy values within a further range termed the "forbidden band" do not exist. All the bound electrons have energies within the valence band and none can have energies within the forbidden band. Above the forbidden band is a further range of energy levels, the "conduction band." A metal has no forbidden gap and conduction electrons are always present.

The energy range between the conduction and valence bands, the forbidden region or energy gap designated by E_G, is an important parameter which is characteristic of the material. The significance of E_G is that it is the minimum energy necessary to translate a valence electron to become a conduction electron; it is the energy required to liberate one of the electrons of the valence bond to become a free mobile electron. When in the conduction band the electron energy can be further increased by the application of an external electric field or potential gradient to cause it to move carrying its charge $(-q)$ through the crystal. In the limit at a sufficiently high temperature and for a suitable material the electrons acquire sufficient energy to escape from the material entirely, as for example from the cathode of the thermionic valve: in this state the electron can acquire any value of energy.

Considering intrinsic germanium, at very low temperatures all the electron energies are contained within the valence band, none are in the forbidden band nor in the conduction band, and the germanium is an insulating material. As the temperature rises to normal room-temperature values, the increasing thermal excitation of the atoms raises the electron energies to the point where some electrons have sufficient energy to jump from the valence band to the conduction band, involving the fracture of the valence bond and the freeing of an electron for conduction. At this temperature, with numerous free electrons having energies within the conduction band, the germanium conductivity has increased—it is a semiconductor.

It will be seen that materials for which the value of E_G is high have practically no electrons with energies able to "jump the gap" and reach the conduction band: such materials are insulators. Materials which have a smaller value of E_G which can be bridged to permit the existence of electrons within the conduction band are semiconductors. The number of liberated electrons, and hence the conductivity, is strongly dependent upon temperature. In metals there is no energy gap; conduction electrons are always present, and the material is a conductor.

The introduction of impurity atoms into the intrinsic germanium introduces new energy levels which now fall within the forbidden gap. With n-type impurities (donor) these energies E_D lie near to the conduction band, which is to say that the energy required for transfer to the conduction band is relatively small and most of the impurity atoms have given up their electrons to the conduction band at room temperatures: p-type impurities (acceptor) result in energy levels E_A also in the forbidden gap, but just above the valence band (see Fig. 14.8): electrons from p-type impurities are also able to gain the conduction band at room temperatures.

If both n-type and p-type impurities are present together in the germanium, then electrons from both appear in the forbidden energy band as a result compensation takes place in which the acceptor and donor atoms effect a balance until only the numerical excess, whether acceptors or donors, is in fact effective. It will be realized from the diagram that the falling of donor (D) electrons to the acceptor (A) level, with corresponding loss of energy, is more likely to occur than their excitation to the conduction band.

14.8. Refinement and Production of Monocrystalline Germanium.

In Great Britain germanium is extracted from flue dust of which it may form up to 2 per cent, particularly if the source is Northumberland or Durham coal. Another source is in the germanium dioxide which occurs as a by-product in the zinc-refining industry. The extraction of germanium follows a complex process which need not be described here, but the method of refining is of interest.

For transistors the germanium must be of the highest order of purity—the existence of foreign elements even to a few parts in 10^8 would render the germanium unsuitable for transistors. It was found that after extraction of germanium to high standards of commercial purity the remaining impurities, mainly arsenic (a donor impurity) are more soluble in liquid germanium at its melting point (936° C) than in solid germanium. In the process known as *zone refining* a germanium ingot weighing perhaps half a pound, is placed in an inert crucible and slowly drawn through a local induction heating element which melts only a small zone of the germanium at a time. With the changing molten zone adequately stirred, the impurity elements dissolved in the molten germanium are "swept" to one end of the ingot. For a few impurities the reverse effect takes place—these impurities collect in the end which solidifies first as the original ingot leaves the furnace prior to the zone-refining process. In practice, eddy current heating provides the equivalent of stirring and the ingot may pass through more than one heating element so that several spaced molten zones act sequentially to produce the intrinsic germanium. With the ends cut off and discarded following resistivity measurements along the length, the remaining ingot is of considerable purity. At this stage the pure germanium ingot is of polycrystalline form.

The next step in the preparation of germanium suitable for transistors is to convert it to mono-crystalline form. The pure germanium is heated in a graphite crucible to a temperature just above its melting point. A small single-crystal "seed" of germanium, cut in the desired crystal orienta-tion, is lowered into the melt and smoothly and slowly withdrawn (pulled) at the rate of a few inches/hour while being rotated (at about 100 rev/min) at the same time. As growing proceeds, molten germanium is drawn up by surface tension and it solidifies with the same crystal orientation as the seed until the whole of the melt has solidi-fied forming a large single crystal.

Important objectives of the process are to ensure uniformity in resistivity and adequate lifetime of minority carriers, these being two very important parameters in determining the ultimate characteristics of the transistor.

If it is desired to produce an n-type crystal, the molten germanium may be doped for the seed-growing process with a suitable donor impurity (e.g. antimony) to a precisely determined amount. In a similar manner if p-type germanium were required, an acceptor impurity (e.g. gallium), in carefully controlled amount, would be added instead to the molten germanium prior to growing the crystal.

Silicon occurs plentifully in nature in the form of silica (quartz or sand): being highly reactive in the molten state and containing the impurity boron which is not readily removed by zone refining, silicon is not refined by the method described for germanium and other processes are used. Monocrystalline silicon can however be grown from a single-crystal seed, as for germanium, but with important differences in detail due to the high melting point of silicon (1 420°C) and its reactivity with other elements.

14.9. Transistor Production. Wide variations exist in the processes of fabricating transistors of various types, processes still subject to develop-ment in what is even now a young but considerable and expanding industry. Some remarkable metal-lurgical processes are involved, matched by pro-duction methods unique for the mass-production of devices of minute dimensions achieved to a high degree of precision. The methods which survive for commercial production are mainly dictated by economic considerations coupled with the need for the required degree of technical performance, high stability, and reliability.

The following descriptions relate to the broad principles of fabrication of some typical types of transistor, including only the more important stages of the manufacturing processes, and merely hinting at the vital stringent control of conditions which is necessary at all stages. Starting from the availability of the semiconductor material, the basic stages are (i) preparation of the junctions, (ii) attachment of the connecting leads, (iii) encapsulation, (iv) testing and selection.

A junction is a region in the semiconductor where a more or less abrupt transition exists in the rela-tion between the concentrations of donor and acceptor impurities: simple contact between p-type and n-type semiconductors is not sufficient to produce a satisfactory p-n junction. The charac-teristics of a junction may be seriously affected by surface leakage, and the greatest care is required in surface treatment and in subsequent encap-sulation.

The grown and rate-grown methods of producing p-n junctions are briefly described, mainly for the interesting principles involved: they are not now so widely used commercially, since the number of transistors produced in one operation is limited. The early alloy transistor is still one of the most widely employed: although each transistor needs individual fabrication, nevertheless it lends itself to a high degree of mechanization or automation. The diffused transistor, particularly with silicon, has more recently come into production because a very large part of the processing can be carried out on a considerable number of units simul-taneously. The final stages of manufacture—attachment of leads and encapsulation—are neces-sarily carried out on individual transistors.

Germanium transistors tend to be somewhat cheaper than those using silicon. Silicon can be operated at a higher junction-temperature limit (170°C) compared with germanium (85°C) and so can handle greater power.

GROWN JUNCTION TRANSISTORS. The process of growing from a seed a monocrystalline ingot of intrinsic germanium, which can alternatively be grown as an n-type or a p-type crystal, has been described above.

A p-n junction can be grown in a somewhat similar manner from a seed crystal. Starting with the crucible of molten pure germanium, a known amount of n-type impurity is added and the n-type crystal is then grown to a short length: at this stage a known amount of p-type impurity is added, sufficient to overcompensate the n-type impurity, and the crystal then grown will be of p-type.

After a few seconds a return to n-type semi-conductor growing can be achieved by the addition of n-type impurity sufficient to overcome the p-type conductivity. The resulting ingot remains a single crystal throughout with a change from n-type to p-type, and vice versa, at the junctions.

The melt must be effectively stirred to ensure rapid and even distribution from the pellet of added impurity: the timing of successive additions of donor or acceptor pellets and the control of temperature and rate of growth must all be very accurate.

The precise positions of the junctions are located by electrical probing measurements and the slices containing the junctions are cut off. The slice is then diced (Fig. 14.9) to produce perhaps a few

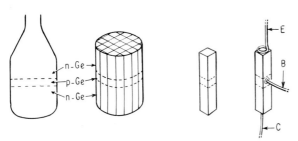

FIG. 14.9. GROWN JUNCTION n-p-n TRANSISTOR—
STAGES IN PRODUCTION

hundred n-p-n junctions, the dimensions of which are about $0.1 \times 0.04 \times 0.04$ in., the base region having a thickness of only 0.001 in. The resistivities are of the order of 10 Ω-cm (collector), 1 Ω-cm (base), and 0.01 Ω-cm (emitter). Connecting leads are applied by soldering wires from the n-regions to the supporting stems: it is important that the soldered connexions are sound and do not form rectifying point-contacts. Soldering a connecting lead to the narrow p-region base is an operation of some delicacy which may be achieved by the use of a gold wire fused to the base region.

RATE-GROWN JUNCTIONS. It has been found that the ratio of impurity content in the solidified ingot to that in the molten germanium varies with the rate at which the crystal is grown. Skilful use is made of this property in growing p-n-p crystals from a single unchanged melt. For this purpose the molten germanium is doped with carefully determined amounts of both antimony and gallium: these two impurities are well mixed with the molten germanium before crystal growing is started. A single-crystal seed is then lowered into the melt and gradually withdrawn as described earlier, except that the rate of withdrawal of the seed is now varied. At low rates of growth a p-type region appears in the crystal, while for faster

rates of growth the region becomes n-type. By controlling the growth-rate carefully, alternately slow and fast, a large number of evenly-spaced n-p and p-n junctions can be produced in the ingot.

ALLOY TRANSISTORS. Fabrication commences with the availability of n-type germanium having a resistivity in the range 1 to 10 Ω-cm: this resistivity may vary throughout the length of the crystal, because during the crystal-growing process the donor-impurity content remains almost constant while the residual volume of molten germanium becomes less and less. The acceptable part of the crystal can be revealed by resistivity measurements.

The n-type crystal is cut into slices about 0.02 in. thick, the cuts being made at right-angles to

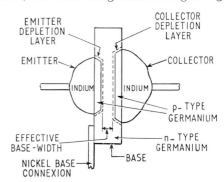

FIG. 14.10. GERMANIUM ALLOY p-n-p TRANSISTOR

the crystal axis using an automatically-controlled high-speed circular saw of copper or steel whose periphery is loaded with diamond dust: ultra-sonic cutting is sometimes used. These slices are then cut into wafers which may be circular, square, or rectangular: even with the use of thin saws the loss of valuable germanium in the sawing process is appreciable. The size of the resulting wafers is about 0.045 in. square or 0.060 in. diameter after the surfaces have been etched with acid and lapped with an abrasive slurry to remove the damaged material resulting from the sawing processes, a uniform thickness of about 0.005 in. is obtained.

Indium pellets or spheres are prepared with diameters of about 0.025 in. for the collector and 0.015 in. for the emitter. The reason for the large collector is to ensure that most of the minority carriers leaving the emitter will reach the collector. A pair of these small indium pellets are fused, on either side of the n-type germanium wafer, to produce a p-n-p type transistor. The three components (Fig. 14.10) are assembled in a graphite jig and held for some minutes at a temperature of 500°C for alloying the indium to the germanium.

he indium melts at 155°C, dissolving the germanium immediately in contact with it. On slowly cooling, these germanium boundaries recrystallize to become p-type, the original undissolved germanium remaining n-type. Precise control at this stage of the process is essential to ensure the correct depth of penetration of the indium in dissolving the germanium and so to determine the base-width which is about 0·002 in.

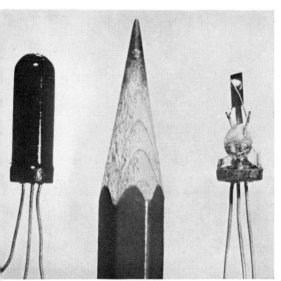

FIG. 14.11. ALLOY TRANSISTOR, AFTER AND BEFORE ENCAPSULATION

(Courtesy of P.M.G.)

A tinned-nickel tab is added to form the base electrode. Contact wires which may be of tinned-tungsten wire or indium-coated nickel wire are then soldered or fused to the indium surfaces: the opposite ends of these wires are welded to supporting stems. After etching, rinsing, and drying, the transistor element is encapsulated (Fig. 14.11) and tested as described later.

Alloy transistors are available in n-p-n and p-n-p types, both germanium and silicon (using aluminium pellets with silicon). They are not suitable for operation at frequencies in excess of 0 Mc/s owing to difficulty in attaining sufficiently precise control of the base-width.

DIFFUSED TRANSISTORS. In this method of producing transistor junctions, the characteristics of the basic doped semiconductor are changed by heating the slices in an atmosphere of acceptor or donor impurity. Usually, donors diffuse through germanium more rapidly than acceptors: with silicon the reverse is true. Consequently p-type germanium is used as the starting material

into which donors are caused to diffuse. The p-n junction occurs at the place where the donor concentration is equal to the acceptor concentration. Diffusion is a slow process which may require up to 72 hours for a diffusion depth of a few thousandths of an inch: it can be controlled by temperature and time to obtain the desired small depth of diffusion. Successive diffusions of different impurities may be applied.

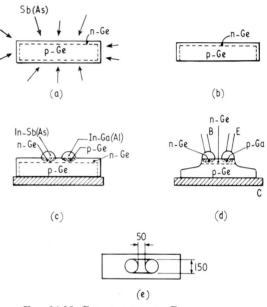

FIG. 14.12. PREPARATION OF DIFFUSED-BASE (MESA) TRANSISTOR

(The dimensions in (e) are in microns: 1 micron = 10^{-6} metre.)

DIFFUSED-BASE TRANSISTORS (MESA).* The stages in the production of a typical p-n-p transistor of this type are illustrated in Fig. 14.12.

(a) The wafer of p-type germanium (which is destined to become the collector) is placed in a furnace at a temperature in the region of 600–700°C and subjected to the vapour of a donor element (antimony or arsenic) which diffuses into the germanium and covers the entire wafer with a surface layer of n-type germanium.

(b) The n-layer is etched away from the underside of the wafer, where the collector contact is to be made.

(c) The emitter region (p-type) and the base contact (n-type) are then produced on the top of the wafer by the alloying method described earlier. Two indium pellets are used, one containing gallium

*The word "mesa" is Spanish for "table": it is also used to mean a tableland. It is indicative of the profile of this class of transistor (e.g. Fig. 14.12 (d)).

(emitter) in solid solution and the other containing antimony (or arsenic). On cooling, the recrystallized germanium contains the impurities gallium and antimony (or arsenic). Gallium, like indium, is an acceptor element, but the solubility of gallium in solid germanium is considerably greater. A strongly-doped p-type emitter region forms under the indium-gallium pellet. Under the other pellet, the indium acceptor atoms are quite overcompensated by the antimony (or arsenic) donor atoms and an n-region results which makes a good electrical contact with the n-layer already produced by diffusion.

(*d*) To reduce the capacitance of the collector,

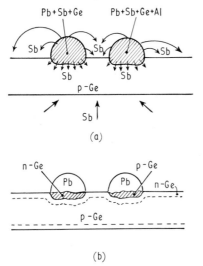

(*a*)

(*b*)

Fig. 14.13. Alloy-diffused Mesa Transistor

the surplus diffused n-layer is etched away as much as possible.

The resulting transistor comprises the original p-type collector, carrying a remnant of the diffused n-type base, topped by an emitter pellet (p-type) and a base pellet (n-type). Connecting leads are soldered to the pellets and a nickel strip is soldered to the underside of the wafer to form the collector contact.

With the pellet dimensions and spacing shown in Fig. 14.12 (*e*), the base may be thinner than 3 microns (3×10^{-4} cm) and the collector and emitter barriers extend over areas smaller than 0·05 mm² and 0·02 mm² respectively. Such a transistor has a good performance at frequencies up to 100 Mc/s.

A refinement of the procedure just described uses vacuum deposition of the alloying materials—using aluminium for the emitter and gold containing antimony for the base contact. Very

small quantities of the materials are transferred and the base-width is more finely controlled. The emitter and base leads are attached to the alloy films by a special technique known as thermocompression bonding. Strictly the term "mesa" is applied only to this method of production.

The Alloy-diffused Mesa Transistor.[5] Practical difficulties in the accurate reproduction of base-width during manufacture are reduced by this somewhat complex process in which diffusing and alloying take place in a single-stage process.

Starting with the p-type germanium wafer two pellets are used as described above, but in this case they are both made of lead containing the donor element antimony, one of them having the acceptor element, aluminium, also present. The alloy-diffusion takes place at 780°C. At this temperature, antimony diffuses fairly rapidly compared to the aluminium which has negligible diffusion, and the donor antimony invades the germanium and makes it n-type (Fig. 14.13 (*a*)) the process being held sufficiently long to produce a base-width of 3 microns. The antimony vapour also attacks the entire surface of the wafer forming an enveloping layer.

On cooling, the acceptor, aluminium, has a solubility in solid germanium greater than that of the donor, antimony. Hence the lead-antimony aluminium pellet gives a p-type germanium (emitter)—Fig. 14.13 (*b*)—while the lead-antimony pellet has produced n-type germanium (base).

The Planar Diffused Transistor.[6],[7] This form of silicon-diffused transistor has recently come into extensive use, largely on account of its economic possibilities of mass-production, coupled with good performance and a very high order of reliability. In manufacture, all but the final stages of the process are performed on a single slice of semiconductor material, about 1 in. in diameter, which is then divided up to form close upon 1 000 transistors. The processing of the slice may comprise up to ten distinct stages, after which the transistor must be separated, mounted upon a header, have the leads connected to base, emitter, and collector, be hermetically sealed, and finally tested. At present restricted to the use of silicon, the planar transistor is available in both n-p-n and p-n-p forms. Furthermore the planar construction is being extended to the production of integrated circuits—for example a complete amplifier, comprising transistors, diodes, resistors, and capacitors, is formed in a single multi-stage process.

The principle of the diffused-silicon planar transistor depends upon the fact that a coating of silicon dioxide on silicon acts as a barrier to the diffusion of most of the Group III and Group V impurity elements which are used for forming p-n junctions. Selected areas are protected against diffusion by photographic masking: this results in a flat or *planar* surface.

The essential stages in the diffusion process are represented in Fig. 14.14.

(*a*) n-type silicon slices, about 50 at a time, are oxidized in a furnace to form a thin glass-like protective layer of silicon dioxide over one surface.

(*b*) The oxide layer is covered with a film of photographic emulsion and exposed to light through a mask consisting of an array of accurately-positioned opaque circles. The film is developed and the unilluminated parts are removed with a solvent. The illuminated areas act as a protective coating against hydrofluoric acid used to etch windows in the oxide layer.

(*c*) In a second furnace treatment, boron is diffused into the silicon wafers. The oxide layer acts as a barrier to diffusion of boron which penetrates the silicon only through the windows in the oxide layer, forming the base region (p-type); before the wafers leave the furnace an oxide layer was reformed over the entire surface.

(*d*) Another window is then opened up in the oxide layer, using photographic masking, very accurately registered, and etching as before.

(*e*) In a third furnace treatment, phosphorus is diffused to form the emitter region (n-type), ending with a newly re-oxidized surface.

(*f*) A third photographic-emulsion operation is used to open up areas for electrical contact with the base and emitter: again highly accurate registration is very important. It will be noted that the p-n junctions are completely protected, both against high-potential gradients and against atmospheric deterioration, by the oxide layer which is effective although one micron or less in thickness.

(*g*) Aluminium is evaporated on to the contact areas: this is the final process applied simultaneously to the batch of transistors.

(*h*) The connexion leads to emitter, base, and collector are added. This and the subsequent processes to encapsulation and testing are individual to each transistor.

MOUNTING AND ENCAPSULATION. The final stage in the manufacture of transistors is to enclose or encapsulate the junction with its connecting wires to protect the delicate device against mechanical damage and to prevent contamination with moisture, vapour, or gases. Leakage currents across the wafer are a principal cause of deterioration in transistor performance. It is usual to fit the transistor to a mounting platform, or header, of glass within a nickel-iron alloy pressing from which the connecting wires lead out: in some

cases the collector is soldered to the metal header to improve the heat dissipation from the collector. This assembly is then plated with nickel or gold and enclosed in a cover or can which is usually

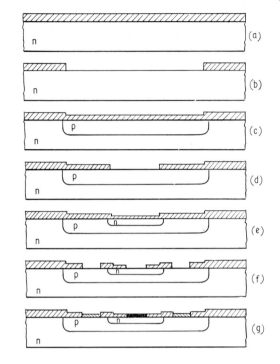

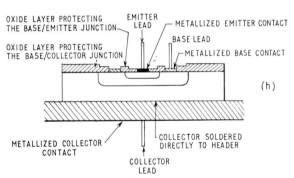

FIG. 14.14. STAGES IN PREPARATION OF THE DIFFUSED PLANAR TRANSISTOR

of nickel or mild steel, but may be glass or plastic, the whole being hermetically sealed. The cover is sometimes filled with a mixture of silicone grease and a powdered desiccant with the object of improving the heat dissipation. The encapsulation is the most vital stage in the whole process, for the life and stability of the transistor depend upon its being able to withstand the effects of temperature, humidity changes, vibration, impact, and the bending and soldering of the connecting wires. The transistor cover must be opaque to the presence of light.

Finally the transistor is subjected to tests to prove the efficacy of the encapsulation and to tests of the electrical parameters, possibly taken at more than one temperature, enabling the transistors to be graded and labelled.

14.10. Modes of Transistor Operation. In Fig. 14.2 the emitter is shown as the input electrode, the collector as the output, with the base common to both the input and the output circuit. It is possible to operate the transistor in other modes:

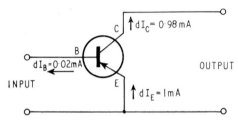

FIG. 14.15. COMMON-EMITTER MODE

indeed this *common-base* configuration is seldom used.

COMMON BASE. In the common-base mode the input impedance is low (50 to 1 000 Ω): the output impedance is very high (up to 1 MΩ). Because the current gain α is less than 1·0 (i.e. the collector output current is less than the emitter input current) the common-base circuit is not suitable for resistance-capacitance coupled amplifiers over a number of similar stages in cascade: resistance-capacitance coupling can be used if combined with one of the other modes, described below. Alternatively it is suitable for use with transformer-coupling: it is also a useful means of matching a low impedance at the input to a high impedance at the output. The input and output signal currents are in phase at low frequencies.

COMMON EMITTER. A more usual method of using the transistor is in the common-emitter arrangement. Here the emitter is common to the input and output circuits, the input signal is applied to the base, and the collector is the output electrode. The current relations of the three electrodes remain the same as in the common-base arrangement (Fig. 14.6). In the example of the common-emitter configuration shown in Fig. 14.15 a small change in base current dI_B of 0·02 mA will now produce a large change in emitter current dI_E of 1·0 mA. The current gain, the ratio of output to input current changes denoted by β

(or sometimes by α^1) for common-emitter configuration, is $\beta = dI_C/dI_B = 0.98/0.02 = 49$

In general terms, since the base current dI_B is the difference between the emitter current dI_E and the collector current dI_C, $dI_B = dI_E - dI_C$ the current gain

$$\beta = dI_C/dI_B = dI_C/(dI_E - dI_C)$$
$$= dI_C/\{dI_E(1 - dI_C/dI_E)\}$$

hence

$$\beta = \alpha/(1 - \alpha) \qquad . \qquad . \quad (14.$$

Because the input is forward biased and the output is reverse biased the input impedance

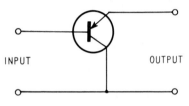

FIG. 14.16. COMMON-COLLECTOR MODE

again low and the output impedance is high however as there is some current feedback through the common internal emitter resistance the input impedance is somewhat higher (say 500 to 3 000 Ω) and the output impedance is somewhat low (say 50 000 to 100 000 Ω) in comparison with the common-base mode of operation. The high current gain (β) in the common-emitter mode taken in conjunction with the output/input impedance ratio gives quite high values of power gain, up to 200. The input and output voltages are 180° out of phase.

COMMON COLLECTOR. The third mode is for the collector electrode to be common to both input and output circuits, as far as the a.c. signals are concerned (Fig. 14.16). The input signal is applied to the base and the output is taken from the load resistance in the emitter circuit. Since the input circuit includes the collector, the input impedance is now high (up to 100 000 Ω) while the output impedance is quite low, of the order of 1 000 Ω.

This common-collector configuration, having characteristics somewhat similar to the cathode follower in valve circuits, is used for special purposes only. With high input and low output impedances this configuration can be used for impedance matching or a buffer stage between, for example, the high-impedance output and low impedance input of two common-emitter stages.

The current gain for the common-collector mode is almost equal to that for the common-emitter arrangement. There is no phase shift between the input and output signal voltages.

Table 14.I below summarizes these characteristics for the three configurations and gives for comparison the comparable analogies of the valve circuit, which should however be regarded as very approximate.

14.11. Transistor Characteristics. As with thermionic valves the most convenient way of describing the electrical characteristics of the transistor is by means of graphs of the voltage-current relationships under static conditions. With the transistor however the input current rather than the input voltage (as for the grid of a valve) is an important independent variable.

The four main quantities which are of interest are the input and output voltages and currents. Of the six possible relationships the following four yield the most valuable information—

(i) The *input characteristic*, showing the variation of input current with input voltage for a fixed value of output voltage: the slope of this graph taken at any suitable point will give the input impedance (or the admittance).

(ii) The *output characteristic*, showing the variation of output current with output voltage for a series of fixed input current values. The slope of this graph at any suitable point will give the output impedance (or admittance).

(iii) The *transfer (mutual) characteristic*, showing the variation of output current with input current for a fixed value of output voltage. This characteristic is a current ratio, and gives the current gain.

(iv) The *feedback characteristic*, showing the input voltage plotted against output voltage for a series of fixed values of input currents. This characteristic is a voltage ratio.

The information in these static characteristic graphs enables the circuit designer to select the appropriate values of d.c. voltage and current at which to operate a given transistor.

These graphs may be plotted for any one of the transistor configurations—common-base, common-emitter or common-collector.

Before studying the characteristic curves it is as well to be clear upon the conventions adopted in relation to the directions of current flow in the transistor. It is usual to designate the *current flowing into a transistor with a positive sign and the current flowing out of the transistor with a negative sign*. The electrode voltages are specified with reference to the potential of the common electrode,

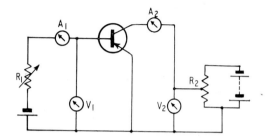

FIG. 14.17. MEASUREMENT OF TRANSISTOR STATIC CHARACTERISTICS

i.e. to the base in common-base and to the emitter in common-emitter. As a result of this the collector current and collector voltage each have a negative sign, and according to mathematical conventions these curves and their axes should appear in the third quadrant (Fig. A.17). This convention is sometimes observed but more usually the first quadrant (x and y both positive) is in fact used. For consistency, the first quadrant will be used throughout in this Chapter.

The basic circuit in which the characteristic currents and voltages of a transistor can be measured is shown in Fig. 14.17 for a p-n-p transistor in the common-emitter mode. For the common-base mode it is only necessary to reverse the emitter and base connexions and also reverse the polarity of the input voltage supply. The rheostat R_1 and the potentiometer R_2 enable preset values of input and output currents and voltages to be applied. As pointed out in Chapter XII it is necessary to make corrections for p.d.s.

TABLE 14.I

COMPARISON OF CIRCUIT CONFIGURATIONS

Mode	Input Electrode	Common Electrode	Output Electrode	Input Impedance	Output Impedance	Current Gain	Valve Analogy
Common Base	Emitter	Base	Collector	Low	Very high	< 1	Earthed grid
Common Emitter	Base	Emitter	Collector	Medium	High	$\gg 1$	Earthed cathode
Common Collector	Base	Collector	Emitter	High	Low	$\gg 1$	Cathode follower

across the ammeters and for the currents taken by the voltmeters.

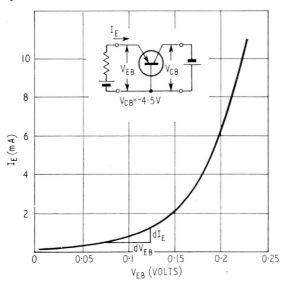

FIG. 14.18. INPUT (I_E/V_{EB}) CHARACTERISTIC—COMMON-BASE MODE

Unlike the thermionic valve, which is a vacuum device with no internal metallic contact between grid and anode, the transistor is a single piece of semiconductor with direct internal contact between input and output. Consequently the input and output circuits are to some extent inter-dependent variations in an output parameter having some effect on the input parameter, and vice versa.

The input impedance of a transistor is not a constant but varies with the applied voltage. To reduce this effect it is usual to supply the input current through a high resistance, with a corresponding increase in the source voltage, so that any change in transistor input resistance becomes negligible in the input circuit as a whole.

The *input* characteristic of a typical p-n-p transistor in the COMMON-BASE MODE is shown in Fig. 14.18. Clearly the input impedance ($= dV_{EB}/dI_E$) is not constant. At the section of the curve chosen,

$$dV_{EB}/dI_E = 0.05/(0.75 \times 10^{-3}) = 66.6 \ \Omega$$

A family of graphs for the *output* characteristic in common-base mode is shown in Fig. 14.19. The collector current I_C is plotted against the collector

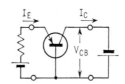

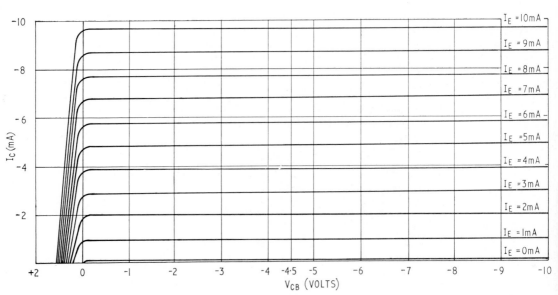

FIG. 14.19. OUTPUT (I_C/V_{CB}) CHARACTERISTIC—COMMON-BASE MODE

voltage V_{CB} for various values (including zero) of emitter current I_E. To indicate that the common-base mode is used, a second subscript B is added and the collector voltage is designated V_{CB}. After the initial sharp rise from zero, the collector current remains almost constant—it is substantially independent of collector voltage. The

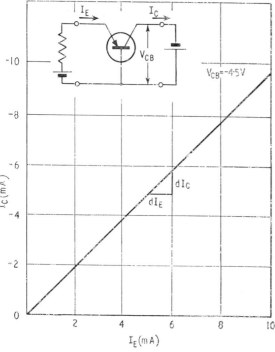

FIG. 14.20. TRANSFER (I_C/I_E) CHARACTERISTIC—COMMON-BASE MODE

values of I_C and I_E are almost equal ($\alpha \simeq 1.0$). From these graphs the following properties emerge—

(i) The collector leakage current I_{CBO} ($= I_{CB}$ at $I_E = 0$) is very small (about 5 μA).

(ii) The collector impedance $Z_C = dV_{CB}/dI_C$ is very large (> 1 MΩ), the graphs being almost parallel to the voltage axis.

(iii) The uniform spacing of the graphs, with equal increments of dI_E, shows α ($= dI_C/dI_E$) to be almost constant—it changes very little with different values of I_E or V_{CB}. For example, at $V_{CB} = 4.5$ V, a change in I_E from 2.0 to 3.0 mA causes the collector current to change from -2.0 mA to -2.95 mA and

$$\alpha = \{-2.0 - (2.95)\}/(3.0 - 2.0) = 0.95$$

The *transfer* characteristic for a transistor in common-base mode is shown in Fig. 14.20. The

characteristic is linear and its slope dI_C/dI_E is the current gain α. As indicated on the graph,

$$\alpha = dI_C/dI_E = \{-4.9 - (-5.8)\}/(6.0 - 5.05) = 0.95$$

When a transistor is used in the COMMON-EMITTER mode the output voltage is the collector-emitter voltage V_{CE} and the input current is the base current I_B (usually in μA).

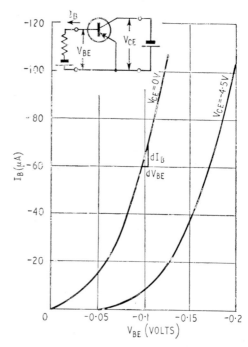

FIG. 14.21. INPUT (I_B/V_{BE}) CHARACTERISTIC—COMMON-EMITTER MODE

The *input* characteristics in common-emitter mode are shown in Fig. 14.21. The slope of the curve (dV_{BE}/dI_B) is the transistor input impedance. This varies widely according to the operating conditions: for example, at the operating point marked in the diagram ($V_{CE} = 0$) the impedance is

$$dV_{BE}/dI_B = 0.0075/(10 \times 10^{-6}) = 750 \ \Omega$$

A family of *output* characteristic curves in common-emitter mode is shown in Fig. 14.22. As the collector voltage is increased the collector current rises steeply (for all finite values of base current) until a sharp "knee" occurs in the curves after which the collector current rises more gradually. The spacing between the curves for equal increments in base current is not uniform and this leads to some non-linearity in operation.

(i) At $I_B = 0$ there is a small collector current which is the leakage current I_{CEO} — the amplified collector-base leakage current.

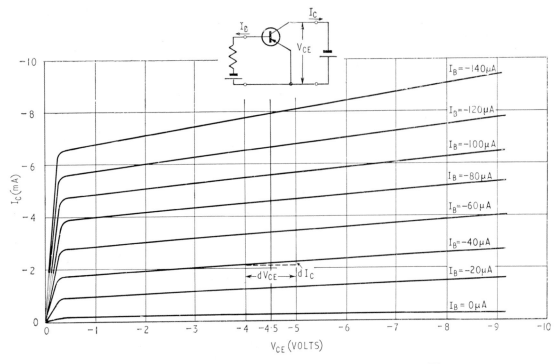

FIG. 14.22. OUTPUT (I_C/V_{CE}) CHARACTERISTIC—COMMON-EMITTER MODE

(ii) The transistor output impedance dV_{CE}/dI_C may be determined from the graph as shown and is

$$\frac{-4-(-5)}{\{-2 \cdot 15-(-2 \cdot 25)\} \times 10^{-3}}$$

$= 1/(0 \cdot 1 \times 10^{-3}) = 10\,000\ \Omega$

(iii) The current gain β can be determined from the curves. For example, at $V_{CE} = -4 \cdot 5$ V,

$$dI_C/dI_E = \frac{\{-1 \cdot 2-(-2 \cdot 2)\} \times 10^{-3}}{\{-20-(-40)\} \times 10^{-6}}$$

$= \dfrac{1 \cdot 0 \times 10^{-3}}{20 \times 10^{-6}} = 50$

Some typical *transfer* characteristics are shown in Fig. 14.23. The current gain ($\beta = dI_C/dI_B$) can also be determined directly from any one of these curves as indicated. The current gain tends to increase a little at the higher collector voltages. These transfer characteristics could be plotted from the information available in the output characteristic curves.

It must be emphasized that the parameters vary according to the configuration, to the d.c. operating point, to the ambient temperature, and where

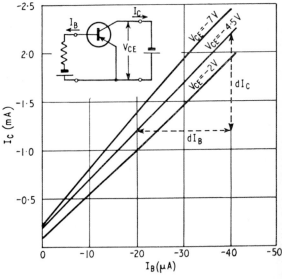

14.23. TRANSFER (I_C/I_B) CHARACTERISTIC— COMMON-EMITTER MODE

appropriate to the measuring frequency. Furthermore, in any batch of transistors nominally of the same type there will be a spread of their characteristics from the nominal values, due to the manufacturing process, for example differences in resistivity.

If small values of a.c. signals are applied to a d.c. working point suitably selected on a straight part of the graph, the superimposed a.c. signals do not drive the transistor far from its working point and linearity between input and output signals is good.

Some of the important properties of the transistor are very dependent upon temperature. The characteristic curves quoted relate to temperatures of about 25°C. At elevated temperatures such as 50°C the leakage current I_{CO} of a junction transistor may be increased tenfold, while the collector resistance r_C falls: the current gain also increases somewhat for grown-junction transistors. As mentioned earlier, at still higher temperatures, of the order of 100°C, the germanium displays intrinsic conduction and performance falls off seriously.

When the collector is dissipating power heat is developed in the collector region. In design a balance will be struck between heat developed and heat dissipated, depending upon the ambient temperature and the manner in which heat is conducted away. Permanent damage can occur to the transistor if the temperature is allowed to rise sufficiently to affect the soldered connexions or melt the indium (M.P. = 155°C) of alloy transistors.

THERMAL RUNAWAY. Collector current increases rapidly with temperature: the collector current produces a rise in temperature which will itself cause a further increase in current with a further increase in temperature, until a condition of *thermal runaway* could occur, with the eventual destruction of the transistor. Such a condition is unlikely to arise in a transistor operated under recommended conditions of voltage and current unless the transistor is virtually faulty with excessive leakage current (I_{CO}). It could occur from the presence of high values of reverse voltage, but this is more a condition possible with rectifiers than with transistors.

PUNCH THROUGH. This is the name given to a condition which can occur when the collector barrier moves through the base to an extent which brings it into contact with the emitter barrier. As the collector voltage is increased, the collector depletion layer increases in width and the effective base-width decreases until eventually "punch through" occurs which effectively joins emitter to collector. A very heavy current may then flow in which event the transistor becomes permanently damaged.

LEAKAGE CURRENT. In the common-base circuit the collector current I_C has its minimum value when the emitter current is zero, $I_E = 0$: in this condition the emitter input is open-circuited and the transistor is then equivalent to a junction diode biased in the reverse direction. The small current flowing in the collector circuit, a few microamperes, is termed the collector leakage current, I_{CBO}.

In the common-emitter mode a greater value of leakage current, I_{CEO} flows when the input circuit (the base) is open-circuited and $I_B = 0$. This higher value is in effect due to the influence of the current gain, β in this case: however the value of β is sometimes much reduced at low values of I_C.

The leakage current varies considerably with temperature of the junction—for germanium, I_{CBO} doubles for every 8°C rise in junction temperature (5°C for silicon): this is reflected in the overall increase of collector current with temperature. The leakage current is much lower with silicon than with germanium.

FREQUENCY RESPONSE. The values of the cut-off frequencies f_α and f_β may be used to compare the frequency responses of transistors. These cut-off frequencies are defined by the current gain (α or β) being reduced to 0·7 of its low-frequency value (i.e. 3 db lower). However, under suitable conditions a transistor circuit may in fact operate beyond these cut-off frequencies.

The current gain α also falls off with increasing frequency at the rate of 6 db per octave—i.e. the value of α is halved when the frequency is doubled. The performance of the current gain α in relation to signal frequency is a function of the width of the base region and (in diffused base devices) of the impurity distribution in the base layer.

NOISE. Noise is believed to be due to fluctuations in diffusion and recombination of carriers and possibly associated with surface leakage at the junctions as well as to normal thermal (Johnson) noise.

14.12. Small-signal Parameters: the Transistor Equivalent Circuit.

The term "small-signal" is based upon the assumption that the transistor operating point does not move far away from its d.c. working point and that the range of characteristics covered by the a.c. signal conditions may be taken as linear.

The small-signal parameters may be considered in relation to the general case of the active four-pole network: in the transistor this reduces in fact to a three-pole network with one common (earth-connected) lead for input and output. The important factors are input and output voltages

(v) and currents (i) with their related impedances or admittances. The quantities v and i are the a.c. signal values, not to be confused with the static d.c. bias values V and I, on which the a.c. signals are superposed.

In what follows the subscripts i and o are used to denote *input* and *output:* while f and r denote *forward* and *reverse*.

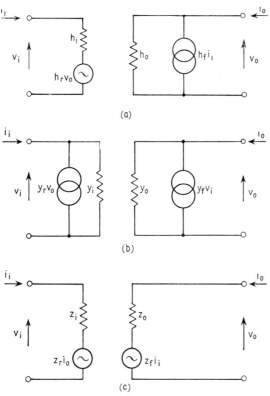

(a)

(b)

(c)

Fig. 14.24. The Transistor as a Four-pole Network

The relationships between the four quantities—the input and output voltages and currents—together with the four characteristics (i) to (iv) in the preceding section may be expressed using standard equations related to the four-pole network. Several different mathematical conventions are in use for this purpose: the more important methods are by the use of hybrid or h-parameters; admittance or y-parameters; and impedance or z-parameters.

The inter-dependence between the input and output of a transistor has already been mentioned: this is allowed for in the circuit analysis by separating components which are, and components which are not, dependent upon the conditions at the remote end of the four-pole network (i.e. the effect of the output on the input and vice versa).

In the circuit analysis, reference is made to the conceptions of constant-voltage and constant-current generators. A constant-voltage generator has zero internal impedance and so it has a terminal p.d. which is independent of the load current flowing: a constant-current generator (represented symbolically by two overlapping circles) has zero admittance (infinite impedance) and the current produced is independent of the load. These generators are used in the simple equivalent circuits of Fig. 14.24 where the transistor is represented by separate input and output circuits.

The h-parameters. The basic voltage and current equations for the network of Fig. 14.24 are—

$$v_i = h_i i_i + h_r v_o \qquad . \qquad . \qquad (14.3)$$

$$i_o = h_f i_i + h_o v_o \qquad . \qquad . \qquad (14.4)$$

If the output terminals of the network are short-circuited to the a.c. signal (e.g. by an adequate value of shunt capacitance), v_o in the equation (14.3) becomes zero, whence $v_i = h_i i_i$ and h_i is clearly the input impedance. Putting $v_o = 0$ in the equation (14.4) $i_o = h_f i_i : h_f$ gives the relation between input and output currents and is the *forward current-transfer ratio*. It is the current gain. Since this is a current ratio, h_f has no dimension (see Appendix B).

Alternatively, if the input is *open*-circuited i_i becomes zero and in equation (14.4) $i_o = h_o v_o$: h_o must be of the form $1/z$ and is the output admittance. In the equation (14.3) if $i_i = 0$ then $v_i = h_r v_o$, giving the relation between input and output voltages. The term h_r is known as the *reverse voltage-feedback ratio*—again it is without dimension, being simply a ratio. These four factors, which here are the four transistor characteristics already enumerated and illustrated by the four graphs in Fig. 14.26, are summarized below—

h_i = input impedance (with output short-circuited to a.c.)

h_r = reverse voltage-feedback ratio (with input open-circuited)

h_f = forward current-transfer ratio (with output short-circuited to a.c.)

h_o = output admittance (with input open-circuited)

It will be appreciated that the first is an impedance, the last an admittance, while the other two are dimensionless: this explains the use of the adjective "hybrid" to these parameters.

THE y-PARAMETERS. Using the quadriple network of Fig. 14.24 (b) the input and output currents may be written as—

$$i_i = y_i v_i + y_r v_o \qquad . \qquad (14.5)$$
$$i_o = y_f v_i + y_o v_o \qquad . \qquad (14.6)$$

As considered for the h-parameters, by short-circuiting the output as far as the a.c. signal is concerned, $v_o = 0$ and

$$i_i = y_i v_i, \; \therefore \; y_i = i_i/v_i$$
$$i_o = y_f v_i, \; \therefore \; y_f = i_o/v_i$$

With the input *short*-circuited, $v_i = 0$ and

$$i_i = y_r v_o, \; \therefore \; y_r = i_i/v_o$$
$$i_o = y_o v_o, \; \therefore \; y_o = i_o/v_o$$

From these derived relationships it is seen that—

y_i = input admittance
y_f = forward transfer (mutual) admittance
y_r = reverse transfer (mutual) admittance
y_o = output admittance

The y-parameters all have the dimensions of an admittance.

THE z-PARAMETERS. In terms of impedances, the equations to the four-pole network (Fig. 14.24 (c)) are—

$$v_i = z_i i_i + z_r i_o \qquad . \qquad (14.7)$$
$$v_o = z_f i_i + z_o i_o \qquad . \qquad (14.8)$$

from which the following values of z_i, z_f, z_r, and z_o may be determined.

$z_i = v_i/i_i$ when $i_o = 0$ (output open-circuited)
$z_f = v_o/i_i$ when $i_o = 0$ (output open-circuited)
$z_r = v_i/i_o$ when $i_i = 0$ (input open-circuited)
$z_o = v_o/i_o$ when $i_i = 0$ (input open-circuited)

The y- and z-parameters are not commonly used because of the practical difficulties in ensuring the required conditions in measurement, of a low-resistance input being short-circuited and a high-resistance output being open-circuited. The h-parameters can be measured directly, a short-circuited output or an open-circuited input being more readily achieved.

THE T-NETWORK PARAMETERS: THE TRANSISTOR EQUIVALENT CIRCUIT. At low frequencies the transistor in common-base configuration can be represented in its simplest form by the equivalent circuit of Fig. 14.25 (a). The emitter and collector slope (a.c.) resistances at the appropriate working conditions are represented by r_e and r_c respectively. The input (emitter) current is i_e and the

output (collector) current is i_c. The constant-current generator (represented by the two overlapping circles) producing a current αi_e from the emitter current i_e, with a current gain a, represents the transistor action. The term a is the internal current gain, but since $r_c \ll r_b$ the currents ai_e and αi_e are very nearly equal and $a = \alpha$.

For correctly-matched source-generator and output-load conditions the power amplification is given by $(\alpha^2/4) \times (r_c/r_e)$. With α of the order of unity, the power gain is largely determined by the ratio r_c/r_e, which in turn may be accounted for by regarding the emitter and collector as diodes biased in the low-impedance and high-impedance directions respectively.

The simple circuit of Fig. 14.25 (a) implies that

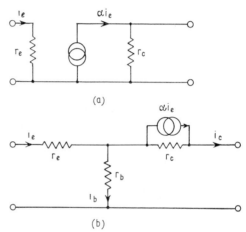

(a)

(b)

FIG. 14.25. TRANSISTOR EQUIVALENT CIRCUITS

the transistor is completely a one-way amplifier, with no backward transmission. Owing to the finite value of the base resistance there is significant backward transmission too. This is taken into account by the resistance r_b of the base region which produces a p.d. in series with the emitter-base circuit: the complete equivalent circuit is then converted to the network shown in Fig. 14.25 (b).

RELATIONSHIP BETWEEN PARAMETERS. Based upon the four-pole network (Fig. 14.24) the fundamental equations apply whatever configuration of network is used, but the values of the parameters depend upon the particular configuration, as well as upon the d.c. operating point, and upon the temperature. Since the h-, y-, and z-parameters refer to the same network and equations there is naturally a relationship between them. Table 14.II gives the relationship for the common-base mode only.

TABLE 14.II

RELATIONSHIP BETWEEN h-, y-, AND z-PARAMETERS:
COMMON-BASE MODE

	h	y	z
r_e	$h_i - \dfrac{h_r(1 + h_f)}{h_o}$	$\dfrac{y_o + y_r}{(y_o y_i - y_r y_f)}$	$z_i - z_r$
r_b	$\dfrac{h_r}{h_o}$	$\dfrac{y_r}{y_r y_f - y_i y_o}$	z_r
r_c	$\dfrac{1 - h_r}{h_o} \simeq \dfrac{1}{h_o}$	$\dfrac{y_c + y_f}{y_i y_o - y_r y_f}$	$z_o - z_r - z_o$
$\propto$	$\dfrac{-h_f + h_r}{1 - h_r} \simeq -h_f$	$\dfrac{y_r - y_f}{y_i + y_r}$	$\dfrac{z_f - z_r}{z_o - z_r} \simeq \dfrac{z_f}{z_o}$

The subscript numbers 11, 12, 21, and 22 were earlier used in place of the subscript letters i, r, f, and o respectively, i.e. $h_{11} \equiv h_i$ etc. For

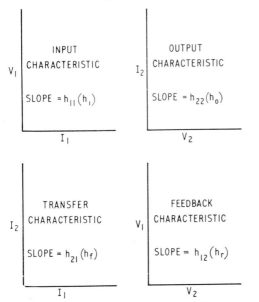

FIG. 14.26. DERIVATION OF h-PARAMETER NUMERICAL SUBSCRIPTS

convenience the derivation of these numerical subscripts is demonstrated by Fig. 14.26 in which, for explanatory reasons, subscripts 1 and 2 are used for input and output. For the common-base mode, 1 relates to the *emitter* input and 2 to the collector output. For the common-emitter mode, 1 relates to the *base* input and 2 to the collector output.

14.13. Semiconductor Diodes.[8] Devices which exhibit an asymmetric resistance-characteristic may be employed as rectifiers. Examples are the thermionic valve and the mercury-arc rectifier.

There are also the so-called "metal" rectifiers of the copper-oxide or selenium type. The copper-oxide rectifier is suitable for low-voltage and low-power applications such as instrumentation and general telecommunication circuits. The selenium rectifier is used for power rectification up to the order of several kilowatts.

The semiconductors germanium and silicon are suitable for use as rectifiers, with the particular advantage that they can handle high voltages, high current-densities and high values of power. N-type germanium is used with indium as an alloy: the forward direction is from indium to

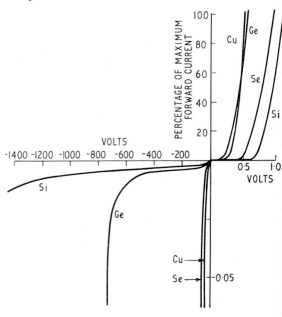

FIG. 14.27. D.C. CHARACTERISTICS OF VARIOUS RECTIFIERS

germanium. N-type silicon with phosphoru impurity is used with aluminium: the forwar direction is from aluminium to silicon.

The relative properties of the four types o rectifier copper-oxide, selenium, germanium, an silicon—are clearly compared in the graphs c Fig. 14.27: attention should be paid to the chang in current and voltage scales for the positive an negative values. At full rated forward curren copper-oxide and germanium have the lowe forward voltage drop and hence lowest losse followed by selenium and silicon in that orde With reverse voltage applied the reverse curren for germanium reaches saturation at low voltage and low current—increasing but little with increa ing reverse voltage until a much higher voltag depending upon base resistivity) is reached. The actual value of reverse current increases with ambient temperature. For silicon the reverse current is much smaller than for germanium and shows less indication of saturation. At the point where the reverse current rises rapidly the high losses cause severe internal heating: if this condition were maintained this would set up a condition of thermal runaway leading to destruction of the rectifier. Relative values at which the runaway condition sets in are about 10–30 V for copper-oxide, 40–60 V for selenium, 500–700 V for germanium, and 1 500–2 000 V for silicon.

The current density at which semiconductor rectifiers may be operated is considerably higher—about 1 000 times higher—than for metal rectifiers. Germanium and silicon can be safely operated at 100 to 300 A/cm², compared to the limit of about 100 mA/cm² (average values) for copper-oxide and selenium rectifiers.

The efficiencies, which vary according to the voltage and power ratings, can be as high as 97 per cent for germanium and 98 per cent for silicon.

The effect of an increase of temperature on all four rectifiers is to reduce the resistance, both forward and reverse: with germanium and silicon the reverse resistance falls little over the working temperature range until a limit is reached beyond which the reverse resistance falls rapidly. For germanium this limit should not exceed about 60°C at the diode base (the junction itself being perhaps 20 centigrade degrees higher) or an ambient temperature of 35°C. For silicon a base temperature of over 100°C may be permitted, the junction temperature being in the range 150 to 200°C.

The rating of a diode rectifier depends upon its forward characteristic, for it is the temperature rise due to the power dissipated by the forward current in association with the voltage drop which limits the current rating. The power-handling capacity of a diode or transistor is determined by the permissible junction temperature: this again depends upon the thermal resistance between the junction and its surroundings for the dissipation of heat away from the junction. Since the heat developed depends upon the time factor (I^2Rt) the rating of a given diode will differ according to its use, e.g. half-wave or full-wave, single-phase or three-phase.

For the low- to medium-power range, e.g. with currents of 5 A to 50 A, conduction cooling is provided by soldering the collector to a copper mounting base which is threaded for bolting to a larger metal surface referred to as a "heat sink" (Figs. 14.28A and 14.28B). This provides a low thermal resistance between the junction and its

surroundings. For greater power loads large cooling fins would also be fitted (Fig. 14.29A). Where considerable heat has to be dissipated additional provision for cooling must be made. This may take the form of convection cooling by air currents, either natural or fan-assisted. Oil

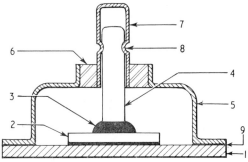

FIG. 14.28A. CONSTRUCTION OF SILICON POWER DIODE (200 A MEAN WHOLE-CYCLE AVERAGE)

1. Base.   6. Insulator.
2. Germanium wafer.   7. Upper terminal.
3. Indium.   8. Crimp.
4. Copper electrode.   9. Hermetic seal.
5. Metal body.

FIG. 14.28B. SILICON POWER DIODE: RECTIFIER CELL

(*Courtesy of Westinghouse Brake & Signal Co. Ltd.*)

or water cooling (Fig. 14.29 (*b*)) may be used for installations where the currents are very high: this is less likely to be needed for silicon rectifiers on account of the higher permissible temperature rise. Due to their small thermal mass, both germanium and silicon rectifiers are sensitive to overloads of forward current and reverse voltage.

The rectifier cells may be used in series or in parallel as required, subject to the normal precautions to avoid excessive voltages or currents due to unequal sharing.

VOLTAGE-REFERENCE DIODES. When a reverse

bias is applied to a p-n junction, the voltage gradually increasing in magnitude from zero, a small reverse current flows which tends to have a constant saturation value until a particular reverse voltage is reached at which the leakage current increases rapidly. This result may be brought about by different physical mechanisms in the semiconductor.

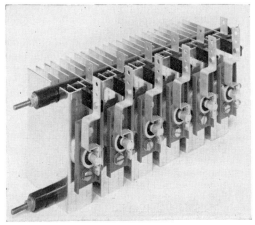

FIG. 14.29A. 200 A SILICON RECTIFIERS WITH COOLING FINS
(Courtesy of Westinghouse Brake & Signal Co. Ltd.)

The reverse current is dependent upon the junction temperature, as with other characteristics. For germanium the reverse current at low voltages doubles approximately for every 10°C rise in

FIG. 14.29B. 120 A GERMANIUM RECTIFIERS ON
WATER-COOLED BUS-BAR
(Courtesy of Westinghouse Brake & Signal Co. Ltd.)

temperature; for silicon, compared with germanium, the reverse current is only 1/100th part at 25°C or 1/1 000th at 100°C.

If leakage current is present to a marked extent in addition to the true junction current, the reverse

current tends to increase with the voltage. The junction temperature rises due to the power dissipated: the reverse current increases with temperature, the effect becomes cumulative, and a condition of thermal runaway occurs.

If however the p-n junction is such that the leakage current is small, the reverse saturation current quickly reaches a constant value which is maintained with increasing reverse voltage until a critical value is reached at which the current increases sharply. This may occur at low voltages below that at which thermal runaway sets in; furthermore the junction temperature does not in this case rise appreciably and the characteristic is stable, i.e. the reverse voltage/current relationship may be reproduced. This phenomenon is termed the *Zener effect*; the "breakdown" current is the Zener current, and a diode exhibiting this effect is known as a Zener diode. This property of the Zener diode is widely used to determine a reference voltage. Typical characteristic graphs for heavily-doped n-type silicon-alloy junctions with breakdown voltages of 5 V and 10 V are shown in Fig. 14.30. The graphs clearly show the marked increase in current at well-defined values of reverse voltage—the Zener voltages.

In p-n junctions with breakdown occurring at

higher voltages, the increase in current occurs less suddenly. This effect is thought to be due to a multiplication of charge carriers at the junction and is referred to as *avalanche breakdown*. Avalanche, Zener, or voltage-reference diodes are silicon-alloy junctions. They have a normal forward conduction characteristic. In a transistor, the avalanche effect is an important factor to be considered in limiting the maximum collector voltage.

ESAKI DIODES. In the Esaki diode, also known as the *tunnel* diode,* heavily doped n- and p-type materials produce an extremely thin junction layer

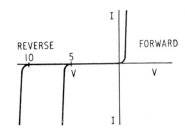

FIG. 14.30. VOLTAGE-REFERENCE DIODE: VOLTAGE/
CURRENT CHARACTERISTIC

through which carriers readily tunnel at low applied voltages. It is taken out of that state by applying a forward bias: as a result the *increase* (beyond zero) of a forward voltage, over a range of a few tenths of a volt, results in a *decrease* of forward current, an effect which may be regarded as a negative resistance characteristic. This is demonstrated in the characteristic graph of Fig. 14.31. The negative resistance region is shown at *nr*, lying between maximum and minimum current values: the dotted line shows the normal characteristic of a normally doped p-n junction. The diode is highly conductive when biased in the direction opposite to that in which the negative resistance characteristic occurs. The values for the forward voltage scale depend upon the materials used—e.g. minimum current occurs at 250 mV (germanium), 400 mV (silicon), or 650 mV (Ga As). The current value depends upon the junction area.

SEMICONDUCTOR DETECTORS. Semiconductor p-n junction diodes are used extensively for signal detection or rectification. The circuit arrangements follow conventional practice. In addition to the accepted advantages of semiconductor diodes, when compared with valves, the important features are small self-capacitance and the ability to work efficiently into low-resistance loads.

*Derived from "quantum mechanical tunnelling".

The germanium diode has an appreciable storage time and is not used at frequencies much in excess of 100 Mc/s: point-contact silicon diodes may be used up to 30 Gc/s or more.

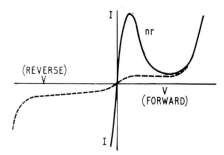

FIG. 14.31. TUNNEL (ESAKI) DIODE: VOLTAGE/
CURRENT CHARACTERISTIC

14.14. Photo-diode and Photo-transistor. When the energy of light is applied to the semi-conductor germanium or silicon the electrical properties are changed. It is for this reason that the normal transistor is protected from the effects of light by enclosing it within an opaque container.

The absorption of light energy (below a certain critical wavelength) generates hole-electron pairs in either n-type or p-type semiconductor: the light imparts its energy to the electrons and is sufficient to raise the electron energy from the valence band to the conduction band. This simple change in conductivity is not of great practical application because the conductivity in the absence of light, at and above ordinary room temperatures, is already fairly high. However the p-n junction, either as a diode or as a transistor, can be usefully employed as a device for converting changes in light intensity into changes in current or voltage.

In a photo-diode or a photo-transistor the function of the transistor emitter is performed instead by the light beam. The sensitivity of a device depends upon the light energy falling close to the p-n junction; consequently close limits are set to the geometry of the device and to the focusing of the incident light beam.

A photo-diode consists essentially of a p-n junction enclosed within a hermetically-sealed case provided with a window. The effect of light falling on the p-n junction when this is biased in the reverse (high-impedance) direction is to increase the reverse current. The current-voltage characteristics of a photo-diode for equal increments of illumination are shown in Fig. 14.32: this diagram also indicates the structure of a photo-diode. It will be seen that a steady leakage current (the *dark* current) flows when incident light is cut off: the dark current is temperature-dependent. The sensitivity may be as much as 50 mA/lumen.* With intense illumination, currents of a few milliamperes may be produced for applied voltages up to 50 V. Response times may be of the order of 10 μs, the limit being set by charge storage.

Another type of photo-diode which operates with little or no external electrical bias is known as a photo-voltaic cell. The best example of this class is the photo-voltaic cell made from silicon, and used also as a solar cell for the purpose of converting sunlight into electrical energy. An n-type silicon wafer has its surface converted to p-type by a diffusion process. The depth of the junction is at a critical value which is related to the absorption of sunlight by the p-layer and also to the desired internal resistance of the photo-cell to limit the internal dissipation of the electrical

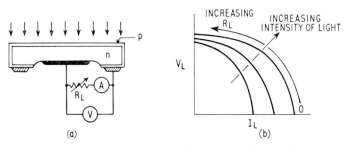

(a)   (b)

FIG. 14.33. CONSTRUCTION OF PHOTO-CELL (SOLAR CELL)

origin. The load resistance varies from zero (at $V = 0$) to infinity (at $I = 0$). The open-circuit voltage generated by a silicon junction is about 0·5 V. In strong sunlight these cells can deliver 10 mW per cm² of area, a conversion efficiency of about 10 per cent. The cell is less sensitive to blue than to red light.

In the photo-transistor, incident light passes through an aperture in the enclosure to reach the sensitive portion of the emitter-base junction. With the collector biased in the normal low-conduction direction and with the base left disconnected, the incident light will generate a collector current additional to the leakage or dark current. A typical sensitivity would be of the order of 300 μA/millilumen, the gain of the transistor being available to produce an enhanced collector current. In both germanium and silicon photo-electric devices the overall efficiency is reduced by some loss of light due to reflexion and scattering of light both in the aperture and at the surface of the semiconductor.

14.15. The Transistor Amplifier.[9] Used as an amplifier, the transistor may be operated in any one of the three modes referred to earlier. The collector is normally associated with the output: either the emitter or the base may be used for the input. As already stated, there are very large spreads in the parameters of transistors even when they are nominally of the same type: furthermore variations occur with a given transistor if operated with different currents or voltages or at different temperatures. In the following descriptions a simplified analysis is made from typical static characteristic curves.

Contrasted against valves, which are voltage-operated with high input impedances, the transistor has a relatively low input impedance. It has been seen that the transistor input current controls the output current. The transistor output is regarded as a function of the input *current* (not voltage). The relationship between these

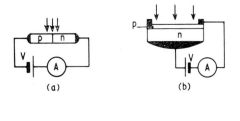

(a)   (b)

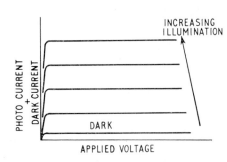

FIG. 14.32. PHOTO-DIODE: CURRENT/VOLTAGE CHARACTERISTICS

energy generated. The structure of this photo-cell is indicated in Fig. 14.33 together with the voltage-current characteristics for increasing illumination and for varying load-resistance values. In the graphs the illumination increases away from the

*Lumen—the luminous flux emitted in unit solid angle by a uniform point source having a uniform luminous intensity of one candle.

currents is substantially linear, and their ratio is the current gain (α or β).

In this section, p-n-p transistors are considered in amplifiers having a purely resistive load.

The input impedance of a transistor—the input voltage/current relationship—is not linear, except when the signal is very small compared with the bias current. Fig. 14.34 shows a typical input-voltage/output-current characteristic (V_{EB}/I_C) for

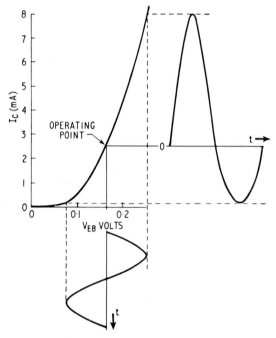

FIG. 14.34. DISTORTION OF LARGE-SIGNAL SINEWAVE DUE TO NON-LINEARITY OF VOLTAGE/CURRENT CHARACTERISTIC

a germanium transistor and illustrates clearly the distortion in the output waveform that would result from applying a large input signal to the non-linear characteristic curve. To overcome this it is usual to add a relatively high resistance in series with the input so that the transistor input impedance forms only a small part of the amplifier input impedance and the linearity is therefore improved.

COMMON-BASE AMPLIFIER. The essential circuit of the common-base p-n-p amplifier is shown in Fig. 14.35. The emitter is given a slight positive (forward) bias from the battery E_E and the resistor R_E. The collector is biased negatively (in reverse) by the battery E_C, through the load resistance R_L. In the static condition the collector current is almost equal to the emitter current.

The input signal is applied via a series resistor R and a capacitor C to the emitter, causing a variation in the number of holes from the emitter through the base to the collector. The variation in collector current produces a varying voltage across the load R_L.

The static output-characteristic curves of a p-n-p transistor in the common-base mode are shown in Fig. 14.36 (a). The load-line can be drawn in the manner previously described for valves. Using

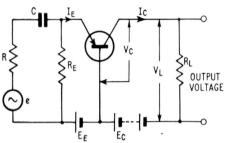

FIG. 14.35. COMMON-BASE AMPLIFIER

the symbols in Fig. 14.35, the collector-base voltage $V_C = E_C - I_C R_L$: since E_C and R_L are constant the relationship between I_C and V_C is linear. From the above,

when $\qquad I_C = E_C/R_L, \ V_C = 0$

and when $\qquad I_C = 0, \ V_C = E_C$

The load-line can be drawn as a straight line between these two points ($I_C = E_C/R_L, \ V_C = 0$) and ($I_C = 0, \ V_C = E_C$). In Fig. 14.36, load-lines for $E_C = -40$ V and $R_L = 5\ 000\ \Omega$ and also $R_L = 10\ 000\ \Omega$ are drawn. In the first case the line passes through ($I_C = -40/5\ 000 = -8$ mA, $V_C = 0$) and ($I_C = 0, \ V_C = -40$ V). In the second case the load-line passes through the points ($I_C = -40/10\ 000 = -4$ mA, $V_C = 0$) and ($I_C = 0, \ V_C = -40$ V).

The emitter current is adjusted (by varying R_E) so that the transistor operates at a suitable point on the load-line, i.e. approximately midway so that I_E, when varied equally above and below its static value, remains within the range covered by the load-line. Suitable operating points (Class-A working) are shown for the two alternative loads, namely $V_C = -21$ V, $I_C = -3\cdot8$ mA for $R_L = 5\ 000\ \Omega$; and $V_C = -21$ V, $I_C = -1\cdot9$ mA for $R_L = 10\ 000\ \Omega$. By adjustment of R_E the static emitter-current would be set at $I_E = -4$ mA (I_C ranging between 0 and -8 mA) and at $I_E = -2$ mA (I_C ranging between 0 and -4 mA) respectively.

The output power, voltage, and current are

determined as follows. If the collector current varies about its static value between $I_{C(max)}$ and $I_{C(min)}$ mA, then the peak value of the alternating component of this current (at the fundamental frequency) is

$$\tfrac{1}{2}(I_{C(max)} - I_{C(min)}) \text{ mA}$$

The r.m.s. value of this is

$$\frac{1}{2\sqrt{2}}(I_{C(max)} - I_{C(min)}) \text{ mA}$$

Similarly if the collector voltage varies about its static value between $V_{C(max)}$ and $V_{C(min)}$ volts, the peak value of the alternating component of the collector voltage (at the fundamental frequency) is

$$\tfrac{1}{2}(V_{C(max)} - V_{C(min)}) \text{ volts}$$

and the r.m.s. value is

$$\frac{1}{2\sqrt{2}}(V_{C(max)} - V_{C(min)}) \text{ volts}$$

The power is the product of the r.m.s. voltage and r.m.s. current—

output power
$$= \tfrac{1}{8}(V_{C(max)} - V_{C(min)})(I_{C(max)} - I_{C(min)}) \text{ mW}$$

As an example, when $R_L = 5\,000\ \Omega$, and I_E varies sinusoidally between 0 and -8 mA, then reading values from Fig. 14.36.

$$\text{Power} = \tfrac{1}{8}\{-39 - (-2)\}\{-7{\cdot}6 - (-0{\cdot}2)\}$$
$$= \tfrac{1}{8}\{-37 \times (-7{\cdot}4)\}$$
$$= 273{\cdot}8/8 = \underline{34 \text{ mW}}$$

The r.m.s. output voltage is $37/2\sqrt{2} = \underline{13 \text{ V}}.$

The r.m.s. output current is $7{\cdot}4/2\sqrt{2} = \underline{2{\cdot}6 \text{ mA}}.$

In the common-base mode $I_C = \alpha I_E$, and $\alpha \simeq 0{\cdot}98$: the collector current is slightly less than the emitter current but the output voltage is much greater than the input voltage, resulting in a power gain. The voltage gain may be ascertained from the output and input characteristic curves Fig. 14.36 (a) and (b). For the 5 000-Ω load-line on the output characteristic the collector voltage V_C varies by $\{-39 - (-2)\} = 37$ V for a change in emitter current from 0 to 8 mA. From the input characteristic, this change of 8 mA requires a change of 0 to 0·21 V only in emitter voltage. The voltage gain is then $37/0{\cdot}21 \simeq 180$ in this case.

Since there is no actual current gain from a

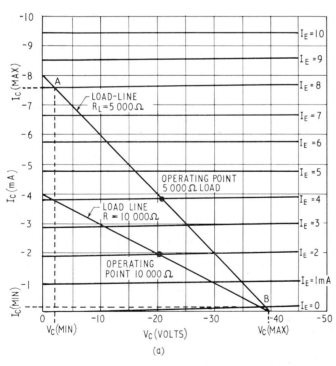
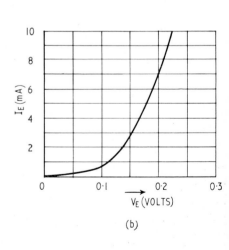

(a)

(b)

FIG. 14.36. CHARACTERISTICS OF p-n-p TRANSISTOR IN COMMON-BASE MODE
(a) Output.   (b) Input.

common-base amplifier (i.e. $\alpha < 1.0$) there is no advantage from coupling two transistor stages together by means of resistance-capacitance coupling.

The circuit arrangement of a two-stage common-base transformer-coupled amplifier is given in Fig. 14.37. Transformers are also used for input and output connexions: these enable the source and load impedances to be varied without affecting the d.c. operating conditions. There are practical advantages from using a single-battery supply for all the amplifier potentials, and a potentiometer is used for this purpose. The emitter will have a small positive bias equal to the p.d. across the 1 000-Ω resistor, less the p.d. across the 390-Ω resistor. The potentiometer should have as low a resistance as possible, yet without wasting excessive power (in this case nearly 50 mW), so that slight variations in I_E will not vary the bias. The 1 000-Ω resistor is decoupled with a capacitor so that the alternating component of I_b will not be fed back to the input. A resistor maintains the emitter bias-current at 5 mA for each transistor.

The transistor input impedance is about 10 Ω. An amplifier input impedance of 600 Ω may be obtained by connecting a resistance of 510 Ω (including the transformer winding resistance) in series with a 3:1 ratio input transformer which presents an equivalent resistance of $3^2 \times 10 = 90$ Ω, and $510 + 90 = 600$ Ω.

At the output to the load, an output impedance of 600 Ω can be obtained by connecting a 600-Ω resistor across the transformer secondary winding giving a joint output load of $600/2 = 300$ Ω. Using a 4:1 ratio output transformer, the collector load is $4^2 \times 300 = 4\ 800$ Ω.

The two stages are coupled by a 31:1 ratio transformer which gives a transformer current gain of 31. The overall gain of the amplifier is 45 db.

The transformers are necessarily large in relation to the transistors and other components which may be a practical disadvantage. In the common-base mode the transistor amplifier has a good gain-stability and can be operated at higher frequencies than in the other two modes: the frequency response is fairly linear provided that the input impedance of the transistor is a small proportion of the total input source impedance.

COMMON-EMITTER AMPLIFIER. The basic arrangement of a common-emitter amplifier is shown in Fig. 14.38. Apart from the connexions to the base

and emitter, which are reversed with respect to the common-base amplifier, this circuit is identical to that of Fig. 14.35. The base, now the input electrode, is given a slight negative potential (forward) bias, with respect to the emitter. The collector-base junction is given a negative (reverse) bias.

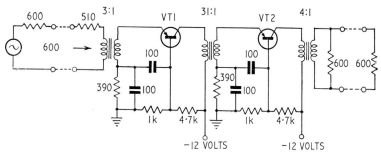

FIG. 14.37. TRANSFORMER-COUPLED TWO-STAGE COMMON-BASE AMPLIFIER

From the curves given in Fig. 14.39 an analysis similar to that undertaken in the common-base amplifier can be made for the common-emitter case. From the characteristic curves, the output power is

$$P = \tfrac{1}{8}\{-7.3 - (-0.5)\}\{-37 - (-3)\}$$
$$= \tfrac{1}{8}\{-6.8 \times (-34)\} = \underline{29\ \text{mW}}$$

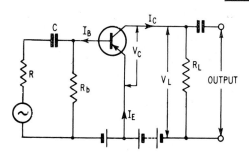

FIG. 14.38. COMMON-EMITTER AMPLIFIER

From the input characteristic of the transistor in the common-emitter mode (Fig. 14.40 (a)), the input impedance, $Z_i = V_B/I_B$, can be plotted (Fig. 14.40(b)). It will be seen that the input impedance is not linear, and also that its values are much higher than for the common-base mode. A large value of series resistance must then be included in the input circuit to correct the non-linearity.

The current gain $\beta = dI_c/dI_b = \alpha/(1 - \alpha)$. The value of α, the current gain in the common-base mode, is approximately 0.98. Hence

$$\beta = 0.98/(1 - 0.98) = 0.98/0.02 \simeq 50$$

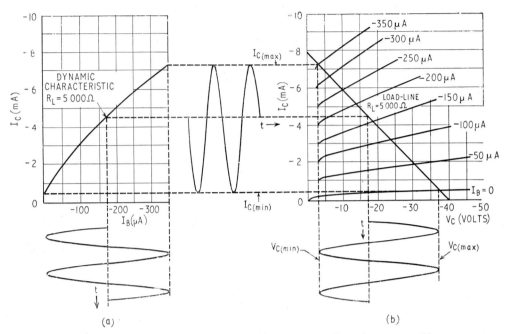

FIG. 14.39. CHARACTERISTICS OF p-n-p TRANSISTOR IN COMMON-EMITTER MODE
(a) Input.   (b) Output.

The common-emitter amplifier also gives a voltage gain. As a result of the high current gain, the common-emitter amplifier has less gain stability than the common-base amplifier. The variations in I_C—with different transistors of the same type, and with changes in ambient temperature—which are relatively small in the common-base mode are greatly magnified in the common-emitter mode on account of its large current gain.

It is of interest to follow the application of an input signal to the dynamic transfer characteristic and the output characteristic curves in Fig. 14.39. The dynamic characteristic curve for $R_L = 5\ 000$ Ω is plotted on the left-hand side from values of

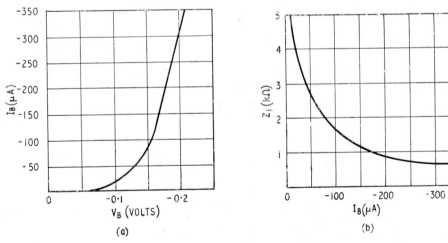

FIG. 14.40. INPUT CHARACTERISTICS: TRANSISTOR IN COMMON-EMITTER MODE
(a) Current/voltage.   (b) Impedance/current.

I_B and I_C taken from the intercepts of the static characteristic curves and the load-line. By projecting the waveform through the characteristic curves it will be seen that the input signal suffers a 180° change of phase on emerging as the output voltage signal. In the left-hand graph (a) the input signal in its first quarter-cycle (voltage and current in phase) is "positive-going" ($-175\ \mu A$

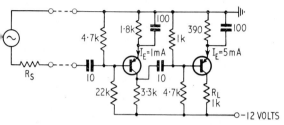

FIG. 14.41. RESISTANCE-CAPACITANCE COUPLED TWO-STAGE AMPLIFIER

to zero): the output signal I_C is also positive-going ($-4\cdot3$ mA to zero). As the output signal V_C, however, it is "negative-going" (-17 to -37 V) — a 180° change of phase. It may be noted that, if the transfer characteristic shown on the left-hand had been drawn for the common-base transistor, the "x-axis" would have been calibrated in positive current units for the emitter current and

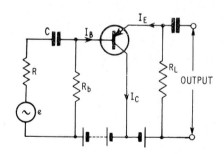

FIG. 14.42. COMMON-COLLECTOR AMPLIFIER

the same input signal shown in Fig. 14.39 (a) would have been negative-going, resulting in no change in phase for the common-base transistor.

Because of the high current-gain available with the common-emitter mode, this amplifier has the big advantage that it can be coupled to a similar amplifier stage using resistance-capacitance coupling. A typical two-stage amplifier using resistance-capacitance coupling is shown in Fig. 14.41. Common-emitter amplifiers are widely used as audio-frequency amplifiers.

THE COMMON-COLLECTOR AMPLIFIER. The basic circuit for an amplifier in this mode is shown in Fig. 14.42. The collector-base junction, given a negative (reverse) bias, forms part of the input circuit which is accordingly of high resistance, of the order of 100 000 Ω. The operation of this circuit can be analysed as for the two preceding amplifiers. The common-collector amplifier does not give a voltage gain, but it gives a current gain and a power gain. Input and output voltages are in phase. Common-collector amplifiers do not find wide application.

BIAS. It has been seen that in a Class-A amplifier a transistor, as indeed for a valve, must be biased at a suitable operating potential so that the input signal is applied over a linear range of the dynamic

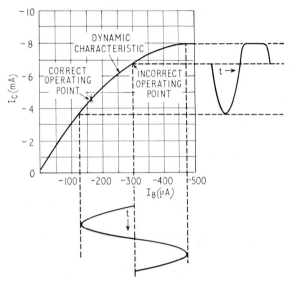

FIG. 14.43. EFFECT OF INCORRECT BIAS

characteristic. If this precept is not observed under all conditions, then the output waveform will be distorted: in an extreme case the output waveform may be "clipped" as demonstrated clearly in Fig. 14.43 for a non-linear dynamic characteristic.

STABILIZATION. In order to guard against the undesired effects which would otherwise occur, due for example to the variation of leakage current with changes in ambient temperature, or with the wide spread of leakage current and current gain from sample to sample, a means of stabilizing the operating potentials is incorporated in the circuit design. Two typical examples are given in Fig. 14.44 (a) and (b) for the common-emitter mode.

In (a) the bias resistor R_B carries the base current, $I_B = V_C/R_B$. The circuit is self-stabilizing in the following manner: an increase in I_C (due, for example, to a temperature rise) produces an increased p.d. across R_L: this reduces V_C and hence reduces I_B also: a fall in I_B causes a fall in I_C (see Fig. 14.39 (a)) so that the original tendency for I_C to rise is compensated.

In (b) more components are required, but better stability is obtained enabling higher temperatures to be tolerated and giving a greater output. The base is held at a negative potential V_B from the $R_1 + R_2$ potential divider connected across the battery. The emitter is negatively biased to a potential V_E by the current I_E flowing in R_E.

EXAMPLE 14.1. Characteristics of a junction transistor are given in the following table—

Collector Volts (V_{CE})	Collector Current (I_C mA)		
	$I_B = 0$	$I_B = 40\ \mu A$	$I_B = 80\ \mu A$
1·0	0·20	1·90	3·7
4·0	0·30	2·05	4·0
7·0	0·40	2·20	4·3

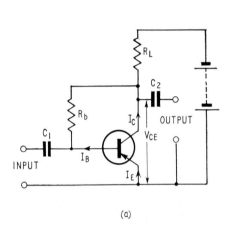

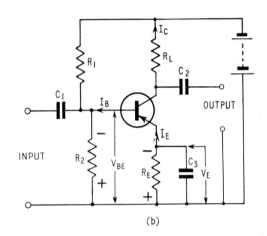

(a)   (b)

FIG. 14.44. STABILIZING CIRCUITS

The emitter-base junction is forward biased a fraction of a volt $(V_B - V_E)$. If I_C increases then I_E increases too by almost the same amount, increasing V_E and reducing the emitter-base bias potential $(V_B - V_E)$. This causes a reduction in I_B causing a fall in I_C which compensates the original rise in I_C.

VOLTAGE REGULATION. Transistor circuits require power supplies at low voltage but with relatively high currents from a low-impedance source. It is important that the supply voltage should remain constant, and for this purpose transistor equipments are usually supplied with some form of automatic voltage-regulator. The basis of operation of the regulator is the comparison of the output voltage with an internal reference voltage: the difference voltage is then used as a control signal, amplified if necessary, to regulate the output voltage. The reference voltage may be conveniently derived from a Zener diode: in the simplest arrangement the Zener diode may be shunted across the supply leads to the load, with due regard to the potentials and currents.

The transistor is connected in a common-emitter stage with a collector load of 1 500 Ω, a supply voltage of 6 V and a d.c. bias of 40 μA.

Plot the characteristics and draw the appropriate load line. Calculate the power dissipated in the transistor.

What will be the total voltage swing at the collector for an a.c. input signal current of 40 μA peak in the base? (C. & G.)

The collector-current/collector-voltage characteristics are plotted in Fig. 14.45.

The load-line is a straight line whose gradient is the inverse of the collector load resistance; it passes through points which represent the extreme working conditions. When the potential of the collector with respect to the emitter is equal to that of the battery voltage, there is no voltage drop in the collector load and the collector current is zero. This gives one point for the load line, point B in the graph at 6·0 V, O mA. At the maximum possible load current all the battery voltage would be dropped across the load resistor and the collector-emitter voltage would be zero. In this case the collector current would be 6/1 500 = 4 mA. This gives a second point ($A = 0$ V, mA) to enable the load-line AB to be drawn to represent the load of 1 500 Ω.

At a bias value of 40 μA the operating point of the transistor is at the point D where the load-line crosses the 40-μA characteristic. Under quiescent

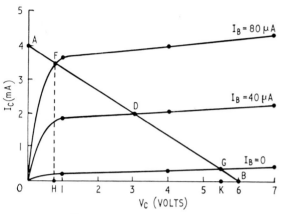

FIG. 14.45. (Example 14.1)

conditions the collector current flowing in the load resistance of 1 500 Ω is (from the graph) 2·0 mA and this is the current drawn from the battery.

Power from battery $= I \times V = 2 \times 6 = 12$ mW

Power dissipated as heat in the 1 500 Ω-load
$$= I^2R = 2^2 \times 1\ 500 = 6 \text{ mW}$$

Power dissipated in the transistor
$$= 12 - 6 = \underline{\underline{6 \text{ mW}}}$$

If an a.c. input signal current of 40 μA peak is applied in the base which is biased at 40 μA, the peak-to-peak input signal will be 80 μA and the current in the base will vary from 0 to 80 μA. The working condition swings up and down the load-line about the point D until it meets the 80- and 0-μA characteristics where they cut the load-line at the points F and G. Dropping perpendiculars from the points F and G to cut the voltage axis at points H and K whose values are 0·6 V and 5·5 V respectively gives

total voltage swing $= 5·5 - 0·6 = \underline{\underline{4·9 \text{ V}}}$

14.16. The Transistor Oscillator.
The principle of the oscillator has already been described for valve circuits. Essentially it is a tuned amplifier in which some of the output energy is fed back in a positive sense to the input to sustain the output. The oscillation is started by the transient condition produced by switching on the power: provided that the signal fed back to the input is exactly in phase with the input the oscillation builds up in

magnitude to a maximum value limited by the circuit design.

The arrangement for a typical LC transistor oscillator is shown in Fig. 14.46. It is essentially a common-emitter amplifier with a parallel-tuned

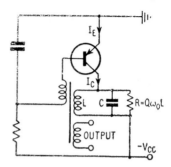

FIG. 14.46. TRANSISTOR OSCILLATOR

output circuit and is equivalent to the tuned-anode valve oscillator. The frequency of oscillation is $f_0 = 1/(2\pi \sqrt{LC})$ c/s. Positive feedback is provided from a secondary winding coupled to L, connected so as to reverse the phase, because of the phase-reversal inherent in the common-emitter amplifier. A third winding is provided for the oscillator output.

14.17. The Transistor Switch.
As with the pentode thermionic valve, which has a similar output characteristic, the junction transistor is used extensively as an on-off switch. The important states to consider are the ON and OFF conditions and, in addition, the transient stage when the transistor is changing between the on and off states.

In one application, symmetrical transistors are used in common-emitter mode: in the symmetrical transistor the collector and emitter are indistinguishable and can be used indiscriminately. The transistor is switched on and off by applying a positive and a negative potential, as required, to control the base current.

With a positive potential to the base—the OFF condition—there is no base current and only a small collector current: the collector circuit then has an impedance of the order of megohms. In the ON position, the negative base potential causes a base current to flow and a heavier collector current flows, with a very low-impedance collector circuit. The switch has a high on-off impedance ratio and little power is dissipated in either ON or OFF state.

If the load-line and output characteristics of Fig. 14.45 are taken by way of example, for switching purposes the transistor is operated in each of the two defined regions—(i) at A, the ON position, the current I_C is high, the voltage V_C is near zero, and the impedance (V/I) is therefore very low: (ii) at B, the OFF position, the base current is positive, I_C is zero and V_C is high $(\simeq V_{CC})$: the impedance (V/I) is therefore very high.

An important factor is the speed of response: this involves four characteristic time intervals— (i) the operating delay time, (ii) the rise time for the current to reach, say, 90 per cent of its final value, (iii) the minority carrier storage time which delays the response, (iv) the decay time for the current to fall to 10 per cent of its maximum value.

A particular form of semiconductor switch is the controlled silicon rectifier, usually termed a silicon controlled rectifier (S.C.R.) but likely to be known in the future as a *thyristor:* commercially it is known by various names such as the *trinistor* (Fig. 14.47). It is a trigger device consisting basically of a four-element three-junction silicon rectifier with a third, controlling electrode or "gate" connected to the central p-region, which can be primed to open the rectifier, which is normally non-conducting in both directions.

The characteristics, together with an indication of the basic p-n-p-n structure and the circuit symbol, are shown in Fig. 14.48. Until a certain level of voltage is established across the rectifier, in the forward direction, the forward characteristic is essentially a mirror-image of the reverse characteristic, i.e. non-conducting in both directions. A further increase in the applied forward voltage V_F to a critical value, the *break-over* voltage V_{BO}, causes the forward characteristic to revert to that associated with a conventional diode. The third electrode, the gate G, enables the value of the

break-over voltage to be varied from the full voltage to a few volts, as required, by the injection of a suitable trigger current. Alternatively if the gate is made positive with respect to the cathode the rectifier will conduct: the gating power is typically 25 mW and it need not be maintained

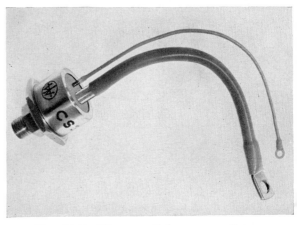

after the rectifier has switched. Once the conducting state has been established the rectifier remains in this condition, the current being determined only by the supply voltage and the load, unless and until the current is reduced below the sustaining value I_S: the rectifier will then revert to its original state of non-conduction in both directions.

The operation of this switching rectifier is

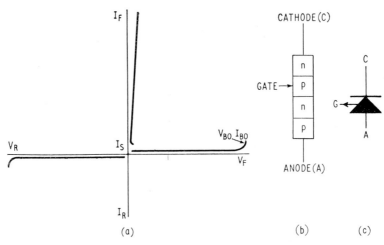

Fig. 14.48. Controlled Silicon Rectifier (Thyristor)

(*a*) Characteristic.   (*b*) Structure.   (*c*) Circuit symbol.

extremely fast, turn-on and turn-off times being measured in microseconds. It is analogous to the thyratron or grid-controlled rectifier but with all the well-known advantages of the semiconductor device. The triggering current can be very small: in the rectifier illustrated the gate current will control a rectifier current up to 26 A with voltage rating up to 400 V peak.

APPENDIX TO CHAPTER XIV

LETTER SYMBOLS FOR SEMICONDUCTOR DEVICES

A FULL list of recommended letter symbols to be used for transistors and semiconductor diodes is contained in *British Standard* 3363 (1961) upon which the following synopsis is based.

1. Quantity Symbols

(i) Instantaneous values: i, v, p.
(ii) Average (d.c.) and r.m.s. values: I, V, P.
(iii) Peak (maximum) values: I_M or I_m, etc.

2. Subscripts to Quantity Symbols

Note 1	Note 3	Note 4
emitter: E, e	input: i (or 11)	reverse-biased: X
base: B, b	output: o (or 22)	open-circuited: O
collector: C, c	forward: f (or 21)	short-circuited: S
	reverse: r (or 12)	

Note 1. Average (d.c.) values and instantaneous total values are indicated by upper-case subscripts, e.g.

$$I_C, i_C; \quad V_{EB}, v_{EB}$$

Values of the varying components are indicated by lower-case subscripts, e.g.

$$I_c, i_c: \quad V_{eb}, v_{eb}$$

Note 2. (i) The first subscript denotes the terminal at which the current (potential, power) is measured, with respect to the reference terminal denoted by the second subscript. The second subscript—which indicates the transistor mode—may be omitted if the meaning is clear without it. For example

V_{EB} = d.c. potential of emitter with reference to the base (i.e. common-base mode).

(ii) Supply voltage is indicated by repeating the first subscript: the reference terminal (if required) then becomes the third subscript, e.g.

$$V_{EE} \text{ or } V_{EEB}$$

Note 3. The letters are preferred to the numerals.

Note 4. X, O, S are used only as third subscripts and relate to the terminal *not* already indicated in the subscript, e.g. I_{CBO} = the collector current, when the collector C is biased (in the high-resistance direction) with reference to the base B, and the other terminal (the emitter E) is open-circuited.

Note 5. The convention to be used is that current flow into a terminal from the external circuit is positive.

[*Additional Note on Primes.* In earlier works it was common practice to use a double prime (e.g. h'') for quantities in common-collector mode; a single-prime (e.g. h') for those in common-emitter mode; and unprimed letters (e.g. h) for common-base configuration.]

REFERENCES

1. J. R. TILLMAN, and F. F. ROBERTS: *An Introduction to the Theory and Practice of Transistors* (Pitman, 1961).
2. J. EVANS: *Fundamental Principles of Transistors* (Heywood, 1962).
3. J. R. TILLMAN *et alii*: "The Transistor," *I.P.O.E.E. Journal*, **47** (1954) p. 92.
4. E. WOLFENDALE: "The Junction Transistor and its Application," *I.E.E. Journal*, **4** (1958), p. 583.
5. P. J. W. JOCHENS: "The Alloy-diffusion Technique for Manufacturing High-frequency Transistors," *Philips Technical Review*, **24** (1963), p. 231.
6. J. T. KENDALL: "The Future of Transistors," *I.E.E. Journal*, **9** (1963), p. 508.
7. J. C. HENDERSON, and SYLVIA J. WILSON: "Design and Technology of Silicon Planar Transistors," *I.P.O.E.E. Journal*, **56** (1964), p. 239.
8. D. ASHBY: "Metal and Semiconductor Rectifiers," *I.E.E. Journal*, **7** (1961), p. 649.
9. J. A. T. FRENCH, D. J. HARDING, and J. R. JARVIS: "Outline of Transistor Characteristics and Applications," *I.P.O.E.E. Journal*, **56** (1963), p. 122.

CHAPTER XV

SOUND

15.1. Sound Waves. Sound is produced by a vibrating body. Any sounding body is in a state of vibration, though it does not follow that all vibrations will produce sound. The ultimate receiver of a sound is the ear: between the vibrating body and the ear is the transmission medium—generally air—which essentially possesses the property known as *elasticity*.

The range of sound transmission is extended enormously by using telephone instruments—the microphone and receiver—which will convert sound energy into electrical energy and vice versa, the transmission path in such cases being electrical over almost the entire distance: nevertheless the acoustic paths at the speaker's and listener's ends are essential portions of the complete transmission system involved in any telephone conversation.

Sound transforming instruments, e.g. microphone and receiver, are termed *transducers*. A transducer is a device which, on receiving waves from one or more transmission systems or media, supplies related waves to one or more other transmission systems or media. (The waves in the input and output may be of the same or different types, e.g. electrical, acoustical, or mechanical.)

Just as ripples spread outward in two dimensions from a disturbance produced on a water surface, so waves of sound spread out from a simple vibrating body in three dimensions through the surrounding medium. In Fig. 15.1 a vibrating body S, which might be one tine of a tuning fork, moves in turn from its normal central position to the two extreme positions shown dotted. As it moves towards the right it causes an increase in pressure or a compression (C) of the adjacent "layer" of air. The air is an elastic medium, that is to say it tends to resist any change in form when acted upon by external forces and to revert to its original shape when those forces are withdrawn. On account of its elasticity the first layer affected, in endeavouring to resume its initial condition reacts upon the adjacent layer of air and compresses it: a condition of compression is successively transmitted in this way from layer to layer or from particle to particle. Ultimately the final layer compresses the stretched membrane or diaphragm R, causing it to move out to the right—the position shown dotted. When the vibrating reed S moves towards the left the pressure on the adjacent air layer is reduced or rarefied: a condition of rarefaction is transmitted from layer to layer

towards the diaphragm which is now drawn towards the left dotted position. In this way the diaphragm sympathetically follows the movements of the vibrating reed. It is important to appreciate that (i) a *condition* of alternate compression and rarefaction is transmitted from the sender S to the receiver R: each layer or particle oscillates through only a very small distance to right and left—there is no bodily movement of the air as a whole, and (ii) the diagram shows only a particular direction

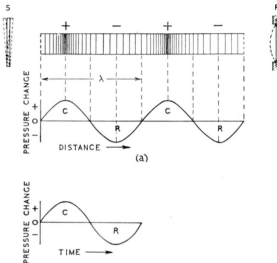

FIG. 15.1. PROPAGATION OF SOUND WAVES

of transmission towards the receiver: the transmission normally occurs in all three dimensions and what have been termed layers of air are in the ideal case concentric spherical shells around the vibrating source.

The analogy may be used of the wave disturbance produced by dropping a stone into a still pool of water. Waves are set up which travel in circles of ever-widening radius to the rim of the pool. The motion of any particular particle of the water is a small oscillation in a vertical plane between the crest and trough of the wave, clearly distinguishable from the motion of the disturbance which travels outwards in a horizontal plane. In this wave the crests and troughs take the place of the compressions and rarefactions of the sound wave. This, however, is actually a case of *transverse* wave

458

motion—the particle motion is in a direction at right angles to the direction of transmission of the condition—but it serves to demonstrate the restricted motion of the particles of the medium in contrast to the continuous propagation of the disturbance. In air the wave motion of sound is *longitudinal*—the particle motion is in the same plane as the transmission of the condition.

If the air were inelastic the first layer adjacent to the vibrating body would suffer compression and remain in that state: no compression or rarefaction would be passed on to the adjacent layer and the pressure changes would not be transmitted. It can be readily demonstrated that sound is not transmitted in a vacuum. Sound is transmitted in varying degrees by different materials according to their elastic properties.

Owing to the elasticity of the medium, pressure changes require a finite time for their transmission. Each particle is subjected alternately to compression and rarefaction as these conditions are radiated outwards from the source. At any given instant successive particles will be undergoing different values of pressure changes in the cycle of variations between maximum positive and negative pressure changes. The distance between any two points which are in the same phase is the wavelength (λ) of the sound wave. If the vibrating body is executing a simple harmonic motion—that of the free vibration of a tuning fork, or the swing of a pendulum—a sinusoidal waveform will be obtained from plotting against time the pressure changes acting upon any given particle.

As the energy of the wave motion is transmitted farther and farther from the source, the wave front approximates to a sphere of steadily expanding radius: the energy becomes gradually spread over a greater area—that of the sphere. Its intensity (energy per unit area) decreases as the spherical area becomes greater and at any distance from the source the intensity is inversely proportional to the square of the distance. In this way even though the total energy remained constant the energy propagated in any given direction is rapidly attenuated: in addition there is, however, some dissipation of energy on account of the frictional resistance between particles and also due to setting into vibration any intermediate obstacles encountered. If any change in the medium occurs there is always some energy lost by reflexion. At a sufficient distance from the source the amplitude of the particle oscillation will be so small that the wave can be considered to have died away.

If the frequency of the vibrating source is f c/s the periodic time is $t = 1/f$ sec: the velocity v with which the sound wave is propagated (i.e. the transmission velocity of the train of compressions and rarefactions) is equal to the wavelength λ divided by the time t, or $v = \lambda/t = \lambda f$. In air the velocity of sound is 1 120 ft/sec at 60°F (approximately 763 miles/hour). This velocity is dependent only upon the nature of the medium—upon its mass per unit volume (density) and elasticity: since the density varies with change in atmospheric pressure and temperature the velocity varies slightly according to these conditions. In water the velocity of sound is 4 680 ft/sec—about four times as great as in air: in iron or steel the velocity is 17 000 ft/sec—some fifteen times as great as in air.

When sound waves strike a denser medium some of the energy is reflected, appearing as an echo if the total transmission time (i.e. from the source to the change of medium and to the listener) is sufficiently great for the reflected and initial sounds to be heard separately. In an interior such as a room or hall any sound heard is always a mixture of the original wave with waves reflected from the walls and other surfaces. A large hall with walls of hard material may have poor acoustic properties on account of repeated reflexions causing every sound to persist too long. In general, soft materials have the property of absorbing the energy of sound waves to a greater extent than comparatively hard materials: if the walls, floor, and ceiling of a room are covered with a sound absorbing material, multiple reflexions are greatly reduced and the reverberation time (the time taken for a sound to die away after its source has ceased) is reduced, so improving the acoustic properties.

Depending upon its mass, size, and shape, a body or an air column has one or more natural frequencies of vibration: at its natural frequency a large amplitude of vibration will be built up from small forces due to resonance. The pendulum is perhaps the most obvious example of mechanical resonance: a large swing is built up from a series of minute impulses provided that these impulses are timed to occur at the natural frequency of the pendulum. Due to mechanical resonance most sound transducers tend to show a greater response at one or more frequencies

15.2. Characteristics of Sound.[1],[2] Sounds may differ from one another according to (i) their loudness or volume, (ii) the pitch, and (iii) the quality.

(i) LOUDNESS. The sensation of loudness depends upon the intensity of the energy reaching the ear: this intensity is proportional to the square of the amplitudes of the vibration of the air particles. The perception of loudness varies not only with individuals but also according to the pitch (frequency) of the sound wave. This fact is demonstrated by the lower graph of Fig. 15.13 which is in effect a curve of equal loudness: the same graph also illustrates the wide range of intensities over which the ear will respond.

The attenuation of energy suffered between the source of sound and the listener is so great that a sound remains audible over a relatively short distance only, despite the fact that the ear is sensitive to extremely minute pressure changes.

The ear responds to sounds of differing loudness according to the *ratio* of their intensities. For example three sounds whose power intensities are equivalent to 0·1 μW, 1·0 μW, and 10 μW (all per cm²) will be detected by the ear as having a loudness ratio of 1 : 2 : 4. The power ratio between each pair taken in order is $1\cdot0/0\cdot1 = 10$, and $10/1 = 10$: this particular power ratio is equivalent to 10 decibels. Increases of sound intensity by equal numbers of decibels are regarded by the ear as equal increments in loudness.

If loudness at any frequency is compared with that at a standard frequency (usually 1 000 c/s) instead of with the same frequency, the unit is termed the *phon*.

(ii) PITCH. If the frequency of vibration is high (or low) the sound produced is said to have a high (or low) *pitch*. The frequency is measured in cycles per second of the vibrating body. If the air particles are performing a complex mode of vibration the pitch is that of the fundamental frequency.

Exceptionally, if the source of sound is itself moving at a high speed—for example the whistle of a rapidly moving locomotive—the pitch depends upon the number of vibrations which reach the ear per second, according to Doppler's Principle.

Differences of pitch are measured not in arithmetic progression but in geometric progression. That is to say that if three notes of frequency 500 c/s, 1 000 c/s, and 2 000 c/s are sounded in succession, the brain and ear record the same difference in pitch between 500 c/s and 1 000 c/s as between 1 000 c/s and 2 000 c/s, the frequency ratio in each case being 2 : 1. Such a frequency ratio is termed an *octave*. In Fig. 15.13 the frequency scale is divided into octaves, i.e. each increasing step has twice the frequency of the previous one. The values shown correspond (approximately) to the range of notes "C" which appear at regular intervals on the pianoforte keyboard.

The human ear has a maximum frequency response range of about 20 c/s to 20 000 c/s (Fig. 15.13) which may be regarded as the audible frequency range: this is a range of 10 or 11 octaves. These limits vary with individuals and also the upper limit tends to fall with increasing years: it is unlikely that many adults are capable of hearing notes whose frequency is greater than 16 000 c/s.

(iii) QUALITY. Sounds of the same pitch and equal intensity but produced by different means are distinguished by their quality or *timbre*. The ear will differentiate between notes of equal loudness and the same pitch when they are produced, for example by the voice, a stringed or a wind instrument.

The note of a tuning fork or the output from a valve oscillator when converted into sound energy may produce a pure sound which has a pure sinusoidal waveform. All other sounds whether produced by a musical instrument or by the voice have a waveform which is more or less complex and may be analysed into a fundamental frequency together with one or more harmonic frequencies. The quality of any sound is determined by the presence of overtones or harmonic frequencies and upon their relative magnitudes and frequencies. The composition of a complex wave from fundamental and harmonic frequencies is discussed in Chapter XI. In sound reproducing systems, such as a telephone transmission system, if fidelity of the original sound is to be preserved it is essential not only to retain harmonic frequencies in their correct relative amplitudes but also to avoid the introduction of spurious harmonic frequencies.

Typical waveforms produced by various musical instruments and the voice are reproduced in Fig. 15.2. It will be observed that for each sustained note the waveform though complex repeats itself at the fundamental frequency. In the same diagram the complex waveform of a note from the clarinet is analysed into its fundamental frequency and the first ten harmonic components. These harmonics are whole-number multiples of the fundamental (pitch) frequency: the relative amplitudes and phase relationships of these component frequencies differ from one another. When the component frequencies are not exact multiples of the fundamental and are scattered indiscriminately over the audible range the impression is described as *noise*.

The ear functions as a wave analyser to complex waveforms: as it responds to the harmonic components according to their frequencies and intensities it is not surprising to find that the relative *displacement* between components while very materially altering the complex waveform, does not produce any marked change in the sound recorded by the ear.

The pitch of a musical note may be judged, if the sound is very complex, as the frequency at which the predominant concentration of energy occurs. If only a small number of component frequencies is present, the ear can usually resolve the sound into its component parts and appreciate the existence of the components at their appropriate pitches. The

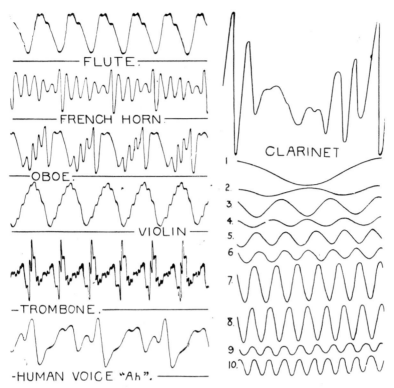

Fig. 15.2. Waveforms of the Voice and Various Musical Instruments

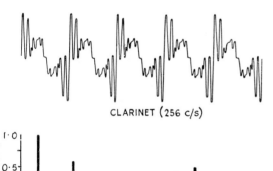

Fig. 15.3. Clarinet at 256 c/s: Waveform
and Components
(*Courtesy of I.P.O.E.E.*)

proportion of the sequence of components, but the pitch is not. For example the series 100 c/s (fundamental), 200, 300, 400, 500, 600, 700, 800, 900, and 1 000 c/s has a pitch of 100 c/s. Elimination of the first seven components (100 to 700 c/s inclusive) leaving only 800, 900, and 1 000 c/s does not affect the pitch, which is always judged as that of a tone having a frequency equal to the difference between successive components. Any three consecutive components in the example quoted give the impression of 100 c/s. This effect explains the illusion of bass response which can be obtained from a sound reproducing system which has a lower cut-off frequency of perhaps 200 c/s or 300 c/s. For example, even after transmission over a telephone circuit which does not reproduce frequencies below 300 c/s the characteristic pitch of a typical male voice with a larynx tone of say 90 c/s remains.

The waveform of a clarinet is shown in Fig. 15.3 together with its harmonic components in spectrum form: this waveform which is for a pitch of 256 c/s (middle C) differs slightly from that given in Fig. 15.2. Most instruments give notes of slightly differing qualities at different parts of their registers: there is also some difference between the quality

special case of a harmonic series is of considerable interest: the pitch is always judged as that of a tone having a frequency equal to the difference between successive components. The quality of the tone is changed by the presence or absence of a

from any two apparently identical instruments. The waveforms for the pianoforte and organ, both at 128 c/s, are of interest (Fig. 15.4): these particular waveforms are somewhat similar but the different timbres are illustrated by their harmonic spectra.

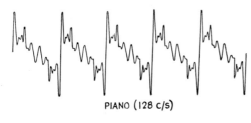

PIANO (128 c/s)

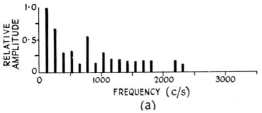

FREQUENCY (c/s)

(a)

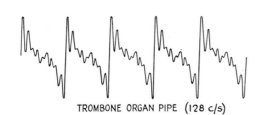

TROMBONE ORGAN PIPE (128 c/s)

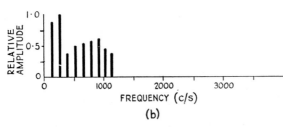

FREQUENCY (c/s)

(b)

FIG. 15.4. PIANO AND ORGAN (TROMBONE STOP) AT 128 c/s: WAVEFORM AND COMPONENTS
(*Courtesy of I.P.O.E.E.*)

The pitch and intensity at which a vowel is uttered affects the waveform so that a vowel may not be readily recognized from its waveform. This is clearly illustrated by Fig. 15.5 which shows the spectra for the long vowel *i* (= *ee* in "feet") sounded at three different frequencies. It will, however, be observed from this diagram that the two main resonance areas remain approximately the

same for the three fundamental frequencies. The waveforms of vowels have the greater part of their total energy round about one or two particular frequencies. These pairs of resonances are shown

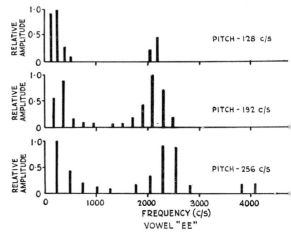

FIG. 15.5. VOWEL EE: HARMONIC SPECTRA
(*Courtesy of I.P.O.E.E.*)

in Fig. 15.6 for the various vowels indicated by their phonetic symbols.[3] The vowel *a* (= *ah* in "father") in the centre is one of the simplest types, being formed by holding the mouth wide open so

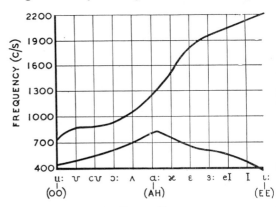

FIG. 15.6. VOWEL RESONANCES
(*Courtesy of I.P.O.E.E.*)

that the two resonances almost merge into one. At the extremes are the characteristic back vowel *u* (= *oo* in "tool") with low-pitched resonances; and the front vowel *i* (= *ee* in "seen") with one high-and one low-pitched resonance. These resonances will of course vary between different speakers and different dialects.

In speech some of the consonants are merely

different ways of starting and ending vowels: they are sufficiently periodic for their waveform to be analysed. Others partake of the nature of vowels usually with multiple resonances. The sibilant sounds *s* and *f* include frequencies of the order of 4 000 c/s or more: the correct transmission of these

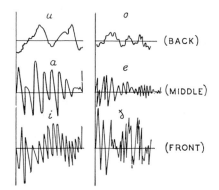

FIG. 15.7. WAVEFORMS OF STANDARD ENGLISH
VOWELS
(*Courtesy of I.P.O.E.E.*)

is not always possible in a telephone system which has an upper frequency cut-off below this value.

Further records of vowels are shown in Fig. 15.7. The upper pair are back vowels with low-pitched resonances: the middle pair are middle vowels with a higher frequency component and less regularity in

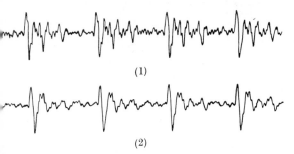

FIG. 15.8. VOWEL "a": (1) BEFORE TRANSMISSION,
(2) AFTER TRANSMISSION
(*Courtesy of I.P.O.E.E.*)

amplitude: the lower pair are front vowels with still higher fundamental frequencies. Finally the waveform of the vowel *a* is shown in Fig. 15.8 without (above) and with (below) distortion. This particular record is of *acoustic* distortion and includes the effect of echo and over-accentuation of components due to resonances.

In speech it is found that the higher harmonic frequencies are of less importance from the point of view of *intelligibility*. It is the function of a telephone system to transmit intelligible speech and this can be done at some sacrifice in the natural quality of the voice (and with considerable economy in cost) by transmitting a restricted audio-frequency range. The frequency range transmitted by some long distance circuits is of the order of 250 c/s to 2 500 c/s at a sensibly constant level, but an upper figure of 3 400 c/s is provided by more recent equipment. Where telephone circuits are provided as links in a broadcast system the greater natural transmission required of the voice necessitates frequency limits of about 100 c/s to 5 000 c/s. For music circuits special transmission equipment is required giving a linear response from 30 c/s up to about 10 000 c/s.

15.3. Voice and Ear. The organs of speech consist of (i) the lungs which provide an air jet, (ii) the vocal cords in the larynx at which the vibration originates, and (iii) the cavities formed by the larynx itself, by the nose and the mouth, which function as resonators. The resonant cavities of the larynx and mouth are capable of adjustment at will, those of the mouth being dependent upon tongue, teeth, and lips.

The vocal cords are two flat membraneous bands stretched across the larynx: their tension is controlled by muscles which can also vary the aperture which forms the air passage. Air passing through this slit is set into vibration: the vocal cords give the pitch to the resulting sound and to a large extent also the characteristic timbre by which any voice is recognized. The vocal cords may be tuned over a range of about two octaves by adjustment of their tension and the aperture. Vowels are produced by adjusting the strength of the harmonic frequencies: this is done by varying resonances in the throat, the mouth, and nasal cavities. In ordinary conversation an average speaker will radiate speech power equivalent to about 10 μW which gives a power intensity of some 1 μW/cm^2 at half an inch from the mouth. Raising the voice or lowering it to a whisper may well cause the power to rise and fall between 1 000 μW and 0·001 μW respectively. An air particle amplitude near to the mouth of about sixty-millionths of an inch represents good speech volume.

The most important speech frequencies are around 600 c/s and 1 800 c/s. The lower frequencies carry the greater part of the energy while the higher frequencies, though small in intensity, are necessary for good articulation.

The hearing system consists essentially of five parts: (i) the outer ear, (ii) the middle ear, (iii) the inner ear, (iv) the nerve connexions to the brain, and (v) the portion of the brain concerned with hearing. The main essentials of the first four parts are illustrated diagrammatically in Fig. 15.9.

The outer ear comprises the pinna and the auditory canal and terminates upon the eardrum: this

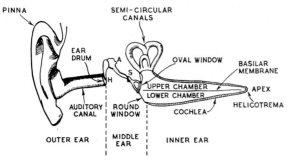

FIG. 15.9. MECHANISM OF THE EAR
(*Courtesy of I.P.O.E.E.*)

is a diaphragm dividing the outer from the middle ear.

The middle ear consists of a linkage of three bones which couple the eardrum to the oval window. On account of their shape these bones are called the

membrane divide the cross-section into an upper and a lower chamber: the stirrup operates into the upper chamber at the oval window. At the tip of the helical chamber the upper and lower chambers communicate by means of a small hole, the *helicotrema* (Fig. 15.9). The outer end of the lower chamber terminates in the round window which is closed by a flexible membrane. The total developed length of the cochlea is about 31 mm. The basilar membrane carries the *organ of Corti* which is equipped with four rows of hair cells (Fig. 15.11) from which nerve connexions to the brain are effected. The hair cells protrude into the fluid which fills the cochlea: they are, in effect, the detectors which are stimulated by the vibrations transmitted from the stirrup to the fluid and the membrane. They are graded in length and tension like the strings of a piano and function as resonators which are heavily loaded and damped.

Transmission through the ear is believed to occur in the following manner. The sound pressure changes developed in the auditory canal cause motion of the eardrum: this motion is transferred via the linkage of bones to the stirrup which

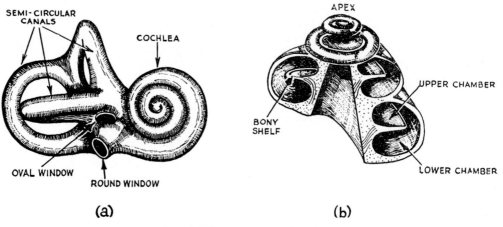

(a)   (b)

FIG. 15.10. DETAILS OF COCHLEA

hammer (H), the *anvil* (A), and the *stirrup* (S). This chain of bones serves as a mechanical transformer coupling the 90 mm² of air at the eardrum to the 3·2 mm² of fluid actuated by the stirrup. A force magnification of 30 to 60 times is produced by this linkage.

The inner ear consists of the cochlea (shown in developed form in Fig. 15.9) and semicircular canals: these canals are believed not to be primarily concerned with hearing. The cochlea, shown in greater detail in Fig. 15.10, is shaped like a shell and has $2\frac{3}{4}$ turns. The bony shelf and the basilar

communicates with the fluid in the cochlea. This fluid is capable of motion via the upper chamber, the helicotrema, and the lower chamber, by virtue of the elasticity of the membrane closing the round window. The fluid, to which motion is directly applied, is contained in the upper chamber which may be regarded as a tube having one yielding wall in the form of a membrane. The form of wave transmission is of such a character as to cause a maximum displacement of the elastic wall at a point along its length, the position of this point depending upon the frequency of the applied alternating force

The organ of Corti, associated with the basilar membrane, is deflected at a particular point causing relative motion between those hair cells which are situated in the vicinity of maximum deflexion and the fluid of the cochlea. In some manner not precisely understood this relative motion causes the elementary nerve fibres associated with the

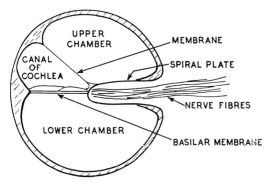

FIG. 15.11. CROSS-SECTION OF COCHLEA

hairs to operate and to send signals in the form of electric charges to the brain. These charges are interpreted by the brain as a sound: the impression of loudness probably depends on the number and magnitude of the charges and the impression of pitch is probably determined from the time pattern of the pulses to the brain. The narrow portion (Fig. 15.12) of the basilar membrane nearest to the oval window is actuated by the highest pitched sounds, whilst the wider portion nearest to the helicotrema is actuated by the lowest pitched sounds. Intermediate values of pitch cause operation at appropriate points graduated between these two extremes. The cochlea performs the dual function of conversion of mechanical energy into electrical energy and of wave analysis of the complex movements of the stirrup. The mechanical system of the middle ear is non-linear, the waveform reaching the inner ear being not necessarily an exact copy of that in the air. Motion of the eardrum (and of the hammer) causes a rocking motion of the stirrup: this rotates about a fixed point at one end of its footplate, a restoring force being provided by the elasticity of the surrounding membrane which seals it into the oval window. Large inward deflexions of the eardrum cause dislocation of the joint between the hammer and anvil: this arrangement

provides a protective device against excessive inward pressures.

The inner ear may be stimulated by means other than mechanical transmission via the middle ear. Sound pressures are transmitted through the air contained in the middle ear cavity and cause motion of the fluid in the cochlea by their action upon the round window. The sensitivity of the ear when operating by this means alone is very low, but it is interesting to note that such operation is in the opposite phase from the normal transmission and therefore tends slightly to reduce normal sensitivity. A more important alternative method of stimulation of the inner ear is by direct mechanical transmission of vibrations through the bony structure of the head to the fluid in the cochlea. This method of operation is utilized in those hearing aids which employ the principle of bone conduction.

The two ears function quite independently: combination of the two separate sets of nerve pulses takes place as a part of the process of interpretation which occurs in the brain.

A definite minimum stimulus is required before any perception by the ear results: also a definite minimum change in the stimulus is necessary before any change in perception results. The minimum stimulus which just causes the impression of sound is known as the "threshold of hearing." The lower graph in Fig. 15.13 shows this threshold for an

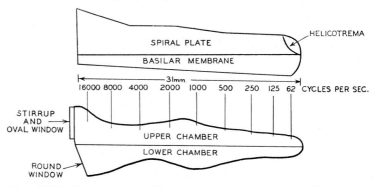

FIG. 15.12. CHARACTERISTIC FREQUENCY AREAS OF BASILAR MEMBRANE

"average" ear over the audible frequency range when the sound pressure is applied to a single ear by means of a telephone receiver, the pressure being defined as that which exists at the entrance to the auditory canal. From this graph it is clear that the limits of audibility are not governed by frequency alone but also depend upon the intensity of the sound energy. For example, at a pressure of 0·0001 N/m² the audible frequency range according to this graph is only from 512 c/s to about 6 000 c/s, while if the power is increased ten thousand fold the frequency range is extended to between 20 c/s and 20 000 c/s. This graph reveals the amazing sensitivity of the ear: the amplitude of motion of the eardrum at the threshold at about 2 000 c/s (where the ear is most sensitive) is about 10^{-10} cm (about 2 per cent of the diameter of a hydrogen molecule). Another striking feature is the comparative insensitivity of the ear to the lower and to very high frequencies.

As the loudness of a sound is increased it passes through the loud and very loud ranges and begins to introduce a sensation of pain. The graph relating the intensities of sounds which just cause a feeling

of convenient size and capable of mass production at low cost while possessing high sensitivity to operate from a simple battery: its performance must be stable and adequate to provide intelligible speech with good articulation, but it need not necessarily include the higher harmonic frequencies for reproducing natural speech. It must also be capable of operation in any position. On the other hand, microphones used for purposes such as radio broadcasting are relatively few in number and their cost is not a primary consideration: high fidelity reproduction up to about 10 000 c/s for natural speech and music transmission is essential.

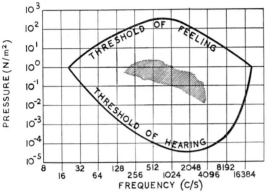

FIG. 15.13. AUDIBILITY LIMITS

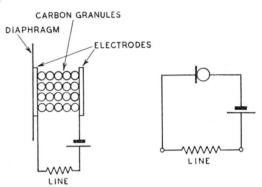

FIG. 15.14. PRINCIPLE OF CARBON GRANULE MICROPHONE

of discomfort, with their frequencies, is the upper curve marked "threshold of feeling" (Fig. 15.13). All audible sounds can be defined by points plotted within the area enclosed by these two curves. The region of most importance in speech is shown shaded. It is interesting to note from the graphs that at the upper and lower limits of audibility the thresholds of hearing and feeling coincide, the two sensations being hardly separable at these frequencies. At the lower limit this is evidenced by the sensations of both hearing and feeling experienced when listening to the sound emitted by the 64 ft stop of the organ, the frequency of this note being 17·5 c/s. The minimum increment of stimulus which is perceptible as an increase in loudness is of the order of 0·25 db for the single ear: this value varies not only with the frequency but also with the sensation level.

15.4. Microphones. The transmitter, or microphone, is an instrument used for converting sound energy into electrical energy for transmission over a circuit.

Types of microphone available are those which depend for their operation upon (i) carbon granules, or (ii) a moving coil in a magnetic field, or (iii) a variable capacitor. For a telephone system important requirements are that the microphone shall be

(i) THE CARBON GRANULE INSET MICROPHONE.[4],[5],[6] An inset pattern of carbon granule microphone is in general use for telephone systems the usual type is a self-contained and sealed microphone which can be readily and completely removed from the telephone instrument. Its operation depends upon the variation in contact resistance of the carbon granules when they are subjected to the pressure changes of sound waves. It follows that this type of microphone does not produce an e.m.f. but functions by modulating the current obtained from an external battery.

The essential components of this microphone are two electrodes between which are loosely packed carbon granules: one electrode is fixed relative to the other which carries a diaphragm to respond to the pressure changes of the sound waves. Movements of this diaphragm vary the resistance of the granules and so control the line current in accordance with the sound waves reaching the diaphragm. An increase in pressure produces a reduction in resistance and an increase in current. The theory of operation of the carbon granule microphone has not yet been established with any certainty. The elementary circuit arrangement is shown in Fig. 15.14 together with the circuit symbol for the microphone which represents symbolically the diaphragm and carbon contact.

Constructional details of the inset microphone are shown in Fig. 15.15. The diaphragm is a single corrugated aluminium cone, rigidly clamped and sealed at its periphery. To prevent the occurrence

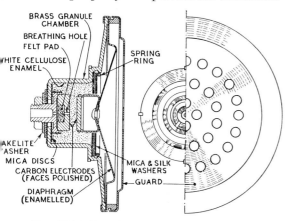

FIG. 15.15. INSET TYPE CARBON GRANULE MICROPHONE (B.P.O. No. 13 PATTERN)
(*Courtesy of P.M.G.*)

of corrosion when used in damp situations or by condensation from the breath, the diaphragm is given a coat of enamel: a perforated metal guard is fitted to protect it from mechanical damage. Attached to the centre of the diaphragm is a small aluminium cylinder whose free end carries a polished carbon electrode projecting into the granule chamber. The fixed carbon electrode is mounted at the base of the brass granule chamber from which it is carefully insulated. A small hole in the fixed electrode permits both back and front of the diaphragm to remain at atmospheric pressure: the felt pad enables the air pressure to be equalized while preventing the escape of granules. The inner surface of the granule chamber is sprayed with a white cellulose (insulating) varnish. Granules are prevented from escaping around the piston—the moving electrode with the aluminium cylinder—by a gland formed from rings of silk held in position by a clamping spring. Sufficient granules are provided so that both electrodes are almost completely immersed for any position in which the microphone may be used. Connexions to the electrodes are made (i) by a pin into the insulated socket to which the back electrode is fitted, and (ii) by springs pressing upon the metal case with which the front electrode and diaphragm are in electrical contact. A photograph showing the component details of an inset microphone is reproduced in Fig. 15.16.

The complete microphone comprising the inset in its case is shown in section in Fig. 15.17: further details will be seen from the photograph of the hand-microtelephone in Fig. 15.24. The moulded mouthpiece also includes a grille whose holes are arranged to be out of alignment with those of the metal guard for greater protection.

Despite the useful properties of the carbon granule microphone it is nevertheless true that much of the distortion of the characteristics of the voice during transmission over a telephone link is due to the inferior performance of this class of microphone with its inherent distortion. With

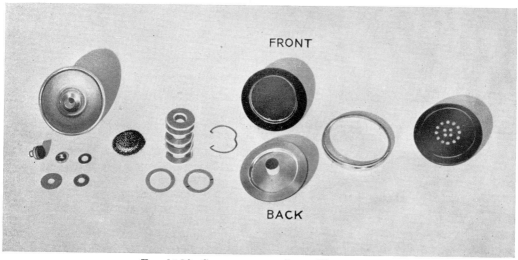

FIG. 15.16. COMPONENTS OF INSET MICROPHONE
(*Courtesy of P.M.G.*)

carbon microphones the electrical output is not directly proportional to the sound input level. The practical effect of this non-linear distortion is to

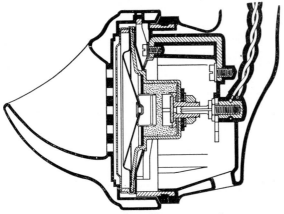

FIG. 15.17. INSET IN MICROPHONE CASE
(Courtesy of P.M.G.)

produce harmonics of the lower speech frequencies and these harmonics tend to mask higher frequencies normally present in the speech, resulting in loss of clarity or articulation. The complete mechanical

defined as the force required for unit deflexion of an elastically controlled body.)

Response curves for three different values of r.m.s. sound pressure are reproduced in Fig. 15.18: these graphs refer to the inset alone. In obtaining these graphs the sound pressure was reduced to one-quarter for each successive test but the sensitivity of the recording instrument was at the same time increased fourfold, so that all three curves would have been coincident if the microphone had exhibited a constant form of frequency characteristic for each value of sound pressure input. It will be seen that this is far from being the case—the microphone introduces amplitude distortion—that is to say, a change in the r.m.s. value of sound pressure input is not followed by a proportionate change in the r.m.s. value of the electrical power output. The three graphs are generally similar in that each shows a maximum sensitivity at about 2 000 c/s. If the sound pressure is further reduced, the sensitivity of the microphone is extremely low for all frequencies below about 450 c/s.

Enclosure of the inset within the case of the telephone instrument produces a marked change in the frequency response (Fig. 15.19): the resonance peak now occurs at about 1 200 c/s with a

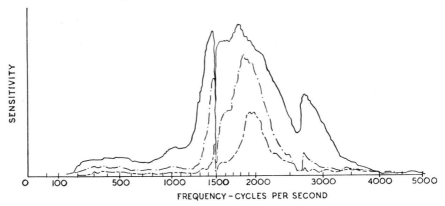

FIG. 15.18. FREQUENCY RESPONSE GRAPH FOR INSET MICROPHONE
(Inset only)
(Courtesy of "I.P.O.E.E. Journal")

system may be conveniently divided into three main parts—

(i) The metal diaphragm and attached electrode: the mass of this system is less than two grammes.

(ii) The air between the back of the diaphragm and the case of the inset.

(iii) The granule column.

The performance of the microphone is dependent upon the mass and stiffness of these parts and upon the electrical characteristic. (Stiffness is

second peak towards 3 000 c/s. It will be seen that the case of the microphone plays a large part in determining the shape of frequency characteristic of the instrument: the main effect of the case is to enclose a volume of air between the moulded grille and the diaphragm of the inset. The resonance of the stiffness due to the volume of air trapped (between the mouthpiece grille and the diaphragm of the inset) with the effective acoustical mass of the holes in the grille appears to account for the

1 200 c/s peak observed with the complete microphone. The mouthpiece horn introduces a resonance peak at about 3 000 c/s which is probably varied both in frequency and magnitude by the position of the speaker's mouth relative to the mouthpiece. The metal guard of the inset itself seems to play comparatively little part in the production of the main resonance peak.

The outstanding distortions occurring with carbon granule microphones may be summarized as (i) frequency characteristic distortion which occurs due to the variation of sensitivity of the microphone as the frequency of the impressed sound pressure is changed, (ii) amplitude distortion which is manifested by a lack of proportionality between the r.m.s. value of the input sound pressure to the microphone and the r.m.s. value of the electrical output from the microphone, (iii) non-linear distortion which is manifested by the generation of unwanted components, e.g. higher harmonics, subharmonics, difference tones, etc., (iv) the generation of unwanted noises not harmonically related to the

$- r$ ohms = the change in resistance
i amps = the change in current
} due to a given increase in sound pressure.

Then
$$I + i = \frac{V}{R - r}$$

$$i = \frac{V}{R - r} - I = \frac{V}{R - r} - \frac{V}{R}$$

$$= V \cdot \left(\frac{1}{R - r} - \frac{1}{R} \right) = V \cdot \frac{r}{R(R - r)}$$

$$= I \cdot \frac{r}{(R - r)}$$

$$= I \cdot \frac{r}{R \left(1 - \dfrac{r}{R} \right)}$$

$$= I \left\{ \frac{r}{R} + \left(\frac{r}{R} \right)^2 + \left(\frac{r}{R} \right)^3 + \ldots \right\}$$

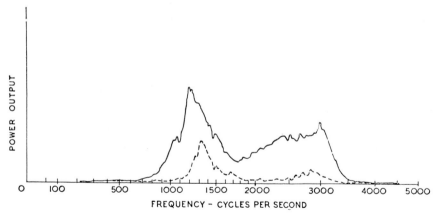

FIG. 15.19. FREQUENCY RESPONSE GRAPH FOR INSET MICROPHONE (FITTED IN TELEPHONE CASE)
(*Courtesy of "I.P.O.E.E. Journal"*)

component frequencies of the sound input to the microphone.

Important properties of carbon for use in a microphone are its high resistance and the fact that it is infusible and does not oxidize. Excessive current in the microphone heats the granules and results in the formation of minute arcs between them producing a frying noise in the associated receiver.

If R ohms = the normal resistance of the microphone,

I amps = the steady current from an applied p.d. of V volts,

If $r = p \sin \omega t$, varying sinusoidally,

$$i = I \cdot \frac{p}{R} \sin \omega t + I \cdot \frac{p^2}{R^2} \sin^2 \omega t$$

$$+ I \cdot \frac{p^3}{R^3} \sin^3 \omega t + \ldots$$

This expression contains components at the fundamental frequency and all its harmonics.

(ii) THE MOVING-COIL MICROPHONE.[7] This type of microphone functions on the generator principle. The diaphragm carries a coil of wire placed in an intense magnetic field of constant value (B). Movements of the diaphragm consequent upon sound pressure changes result in an e.m.f. ($E \propto BLV$) being generated in the conductor. This e.m.f. is proportional to the velocity of motion (V) of the conductor in the air-gap: if the microphone is to have the same sensitivity at all frequencies it is necessary for the velocity of motion of the coil

opposing forces. The constructional details are essentially similar to those of the moving-coil loud speaker. The instrument illustrated in Figs. 15.20 and 15.21 has a cone-shaped diaphragm of soft porous paper 6 cm in diameter carrying a coil of 2 cm diameter: the angle of the cone is 105°.

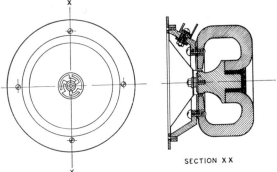

FIG. 15.21. CONSTRUCTIONAL DETAILS OF MOVING-COIL MICROPHONE
(*Courtesy of "I.P.O.E.E. Journal"*)

FIG. 15.20. MOVING-COIL MICROPHONE
(*Courtesy of "I.P.O.E.E. Journal"*)

due to a sound of given intensity to be independent of the pitch of the sound.

In one pattern of moving-coil microphone the mechanical resonance of the suspension system is designed to be well below the useful frequency range. Sound is allowed access to the back as well as the front of the diaphragm, giving an operating force which increases with the frequency owing to the increasing difference in phase and magnitude of the

The combination of coil and cone is suspended so that the coil is free to move in the field of a powerful permanent magnet. This suspension is effected by means of a slack surround of thin leather or of velvet attached to the outer edge of the cone and a centring "spider" of thin paper fixed inside the coil.

The frequency response (shown by the graph of Fig. 15.22) of this microphone is superior to that of the carbon granule type: its electrical power output is, however, small, and the instrument must be used in conjunction with an amplifier.

(iii) THE CAPACITOR MICROPHONE. Capacitor microphones operate by virtue of the change in capacitance of two electrodes, one fixed and the

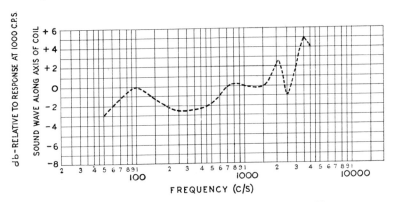

FIG. 15.22. FREQUENCY RESPONSE GRAPH OF MOVING-COIL MICROPHONE
(*Courtesy of "I.P.O.E.E. Journal"*)

other capable of movement with the diaphragm when subject to sound wave pressures. A satisfactory frequency response performance is obtained over a wide frequency range but the output is very low and necessitates an amplifier in close proximity to the microphone.

A microphone has a low impedance—of the order of 50 Ω for the carbon microphone—and the use of a transformer is necessary to match the impedance to the line to which it is connected. The primary winding of such a transformer carries pulsating direct currents and it has an open magnetic circuit: this type of transformer is usually referred to as an *induction coil*.

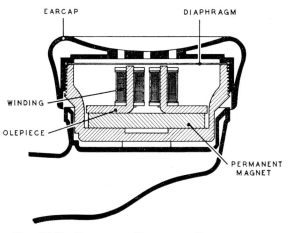

EARCAP   DIAPHRAGM

WINDING

OLEPIECE

PERMANENT MAGNET

FIG. 15.23. TELEPHONE RECEIVER: CROSS-SECTION OF INSET PATTERN

(Courtesy of P.M.G.)

15.5. Receivers and Loud Speakers.
The telephone receiver and the loud speaker are transducers for converting electrical energy into audible sound energy, the latter being designed to handle a relatively greater amount of acoustic power.

(i) RECEIVERS. Telephone receivers in general operate on the principle of the polarized relay. A cross-sectional drawing of this type of receiver is shown in Fig. 15.23: its general appearance will be seen from the photograph of the combined transmitter and receiver in Fig. 15.24. The polarizing magnet is a powerful permanent bar magnet of 33 per cent cobalt steel. It carries two soft iron pole-pieces upon each of which is fitted a coil wound with many turns to a resistance of 80 Ω with the coils connected in series (assisting). The circular diaphragm of stalloy—a silicon-iron alloy —is rigidly clamped at its periphery between the brass case of the receiver and a rim provided in the moulded ear-cap: the diaphragm is 0·01 in. thick

and its normal distance from the pole-pieces is 0·007 in. (the air-gap length). Desirable properties of the diaphragm material are (i) high permeability to produce a low magnetic reluctance, and (ii) a high resistivity to reduce the magnitude of eddy currents, whose effect is to damp down the vibration of the diaphragm and so reduce the efficiency of the receiver.

The bar magnet exerts a steady pull upon the diaphragm. The value of the permanent flux density B depends directly upon the magnetizing force of the bar magnet and inversely upon the reluctance of the magnetic path comprising the magnet itself, the pole pieces, air-gaps, and central

FIG. 15.24. COMPONENTS OF HAND MICROTELEPHONE

(Courtesy of P.M.G.)

portion of the diaphragm. Alternating speech currents flowing in the coils produce in the magnetic circuit an alternating flux which is superimposed upon the steady flux: this causes the diaphragm to vibrate in sympathy with the applied waveform and to originate sound-wave pressure changes in the surrounding air.

If the receiver were not polarized, then instead of the diaphragm being moved inward and outward about its mean position during alternate half-cycles, it would be attracted towards the pole pieces *at every half-cycle*: the frequency of received signals would thus be doubled. In addition the sensitivity of the receiver would be considerably reduced, since the flux is then entirely dependent upon the current strength.

The force F newtons acting upon an unmagnetized piece of ferromagnetic material, when placed in a uniform magnetic field of flux density B Wb/m² with its plane of area A m² at right angles to the field, is $F = B^2A/2\mu_0$ newton. If B_o is the flux due to the permanent magnet alone and $b \sin \omega t$ is that due to the alternating electromagnetic flux,

$$B = B_o + b \sin \omega t$$

and the pull on the diaphragm is

$$F = (B_o + b \sin \omega t)^2 \cdot A/2\mu_0$$
$$= \frac{B_o^2 A}{2\mu_0} + \frac{2A \cdot B_o b \sin \omega t}{2\mu_0} + \frac{A \cdot b^2 \sin^2 \omega t}{2\mu_0}$$

Of these three terms, (i) $B_o^2 \cdot A/(2\mu_0)$ is the steady pull exerted upon the diaphragm by the polarizing magnet, (ii) $2B_o b \sin \omega t \cdot A/(2\mu_0)$, the middle term, is the alternating component at the frequency $[f = \omega/(2\pi)]$ of the received speech signal. The value of b is small compared with B_o: the sound energy output at the desired frequency is proportional to the *product* $B_o b$ and it is the multiplying effect of the permanent flux B_o which is responsible for the high degree of sensitivity of the polarized receiver: (iii) the third term $(b^2 \sin^2 \omega t) \cdot A/(2\mu_0)$ is a small component whose frequency is double that of the signal input frequency, i.e. it introduces second harmonic distortion. The amplitude ratio of this second harmonic to the fundamental frequency is reduced as the polarizing flux is increased.

If the polarizing magnet were absent, the first two terms would disappear and the diaphragm movement would then be dependent only upon the third term $(b^2 \sin^2 \omega t) \cdot A/(2\mu_0)$—a weak pull of double the frequency of the input signal.

In use a capacitor is joined in series with the receiver to prevent the flow of direct current which would be liable to have a demagnetizing effect upon the permanent magnet unless care were taken to connect the terminals with correct polarity. The use of a polarizing electromagnet in place of a permanent magnet is not a satisfactory proposition on account of the reduced current—and hence sensitivity—available when connected over a long line to a remote battery.

In addition to the second harmonic distortion, the mechanical resonance of the diaphragm and the resonances of the air cavities at either side of the diaphragm produce further distortion. The average frequency response characteristic for this type of receiver is plotted in Fig. 15.25: this shows a steep resonance peak at just over 1 000 c/s.

A telephone receiver of more recent design is illustrated in Fig. 15.26: this gives an improved

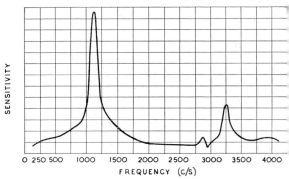

FIG. 15.25. FREQUENCY RESPONSE GRAPH OF TELEPHONE RECEIVER

response characteristic due mainly to the employment of more modern magnetic materials and particular attention to reduction of acoustic resonances. The permanent magnet is of aluminium-nickel-iron alloy and a permendur diaphragm (49 per cent cobalt, 49 per cent iron, and 2 per cent vanadium) is used. The winding resistance is about 50 Ω. The volume of air enclosed behind the diaphragm is reduced by means of an ebonite partition containing a small hole covered by a wire mesh. The size and number of the holes in the ear-cap are considerably reduced and so is the clearance between the diaphragm and the ear-cap: the smaller clearance is achieved by moulding the interior surface of the ear-cap to a conical shape.

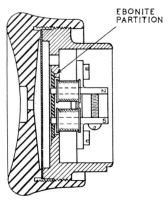

FIG. 15.26. TELEPHONE RECEIVER WITH MODIFIED AIR CAVITIES

The frequency response characteristic for this receiver is shown in Fig. 15.27. Compared with that shown in Fig. 15.25 the frequency response of the improved receiver (Fig. 15.27) shows a less pronounced resonance peak in the region of 1 500 c/s, with a rising sensitivity beyond 2 400 c/s which gives a beneficial improvement in articulation. The resonance at 2 800 c/s is due to the cavity

sensitivity and stability with simplicity of construction: the armature rocks or pivots upon a fulcrum resting upon the supporting permanent magnet (Fig. 15.28). The acoustic function is performed by a light-alloy flared diaphragm having a large effective area (10 cm²): diaphragm and armature are coupled by a thin wire connecting rod which is cemented at one end to the apex of the

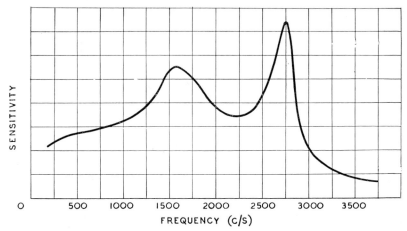

FIG. 15.27. FREQUENCY RESPONSE GRAPH FOR TELEPHONE RECEIVER SHOWN IN FIG. 15.26

in front of the diaphragm and the four small holes in the ear-cap. The receiver will give an audible signal from a power of about 0·5 μW, but about four times this value is regarded as the minimum in practice.

Recently introduced for a new handset telephone is the "rocking-armature" type of receiver (4T), in design a radical departure from the previous types in which a clamped diaphragm fulfilled both magnetic and acoustic functions.

The rocking-armature receiver[8] uses a bipolar form of balanced magnetic system giving a high

diaphragm and, after balancing the two air-gaps, the other end is soldered to a V-recess in the tongue of the armature.

The permanent magnet is of anisotropic Alcomax III. The U-shaped yoke and the armature are of permalloy B. The pole-faces of the yoke and of the armature are ground accurately in the same plane. This permits the use of very small, controlled air-gaps. A ridge is swaged upon the armature at its centre: the circular surface of this ridge rests upon the permanent magnet and acts as the fulcrum. Stability of the armature is ensured by the

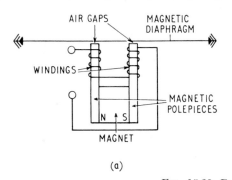

(a)

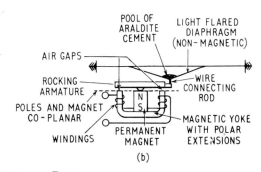

(b)

FIG. 15.28. BASIC ELEMENTS OF RECEIVERS
(a) Earlier receiver.   (b) Rocking-armature receiver.

FIG. 15.29. ROCKING-ARMATURE RECEIVER AND ITS COMPONENT PARTS
(Courtesy of I.P.O.E.E.)

torsional stiffness of its side-limb extensions which support it. The windings upon the two limbs of the yoke are connected in series aiding. The flared diaphragm is clamped between the frame and an inner plate. The delicate movement is protected against damage by enclosing the whole in a sealed capsule which includes inner and outer plates perforated with holes offset. A polythene membrane enclosed between the plates acts as a flap valve, closing the holes in either plate upon a momentary abnormal rise or fall of pressure but readily transmitting the pressure changes of normal amplitude (see Fig. 15.29). A disk of woven silk is cemented to the inner plate.

The improved performance of the new receiver as regards sensitivity and frequency response is contrasted in Fig. 15.30 with the earlier receivers.

When a microphone and a receiver are connected to the same end of a two-wire line, some electrical energy is unavoidably fed from the microphone to the receiver: this reproduction in a telephone receiver of sound picked up by the associated microphone is termed *sidetone*. The presence of sidetone is disadvantageous on account of the masking effect which room noise, picked up by the microphone and

fed to the receiver, has on received signals: if excessive it also causes a speaker unconsciously to

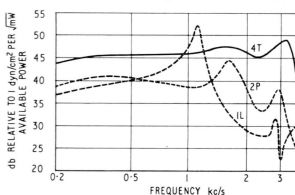

FIG. 15.30. SENSITIVITY/FREQUENCY CHARACTERISTICS OF TELEPHONE RECEIVERS
(Courtesy of I.P.O.E.E.)

lower his voice. When an efficient microphone and receiver are combined in a handset (Fig. 15.24) there is a short acoustic path between them which, on account of their relatively great efficiency and with the existence of sidetone, may set up an oscillating path and cause "howling." For these reasons the induction coil in conjunction with the microphone and receiver is usually arranged in a circuit upon the principle of the a.c. bridge to form an "anti-sidetone" circuit[9] in which the receiver is across two points of approximately zero p.d. with respect to the output from the associated microphone.

The overall frequency response of a typical

A typical design of moving-coil loud-speaker is illustrated in Fig. 15.32. An intense radial magnetic field (Fig. 15.32 (b)) is produced in an annular air-gap between the poles of a magnet which has a cylindrical centre pole surrounded by an outer pole. This magnet may be of the permanent type or energized by a solenoid wound upon the central pole: with the latter method the solenoid may be made to serve also as the smoothing inductance of the power supply for a radio receiver. The coil

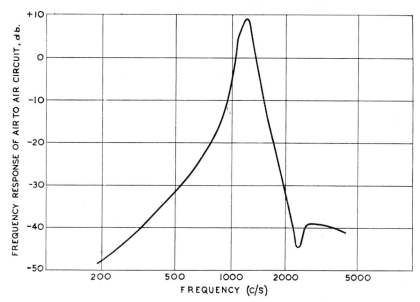

FIG. 15.31. OVERALL FREQUENCY RESPONSE OF TYPICAL
TELEPHONE CIRCUIT
(*Courtesy of "I.P.O.E.E. Journal"*)

elephone system,[10] i.e. the air-to-air path which includes microphone, line, and receiver, is plotted in Fig. 15.31.

(ii) LOUD-SPEAKERS. A loud-speaker, in contrast to a telephone receiver, is required to handle a large acoustic power: sensitivity is not of primary importance but it is generally required that the loud-speaker should have an even response over a wide frequency range up to 9 or 10 kc/s for the natural reproduction of speech and music.

For general purposes the moving-coil pattern of loud-speaker is suitable: in essential construction it is identical with the moving-coil microphone. An important difference, however, is the inclusion of a stout baffle board to ensure that at low frequencies (as for all other frequencies) vibrations of the cone are communicated to the surrounding air and do not merely result in displacement of air from front to back of the diaphragm.

carrying the audio-frequency currents is wound upon a stiff paper cylinder and supported so that it is free to move axially in the air-gap at right angles to the magnetic flux. Audio-frequency currents flowing in this coil produce axial forces in accordance with the left-hand rule which set the cone into vibration with frequency and amplitude corresponding to those of the currents in the coil. The moving-coil former is held in its correct position centrally in the air-gap by a light thin flexible corrugated disk cemented to the frame at its outer periphery (Fig. 15.32 (a)) and formed to a cylindrical lip at its inner edge which is cemented to the coil former. Alternatively, this may be achieved by a centring spider (Fig. 15.20) having its centre fixed in relation to the central pole of the magnet and its edge fixed to the apex of the cone. The paper cone is also formed to a cylindrical shape at the apex and cemented to the moving coil former.

The connexions to the moving coil are brought out by flexible leads. The outer edge of the paper cone is formed into corrugations to give it sufficient axial flexibility: the rim is clamped and cemented between the outer edge of the frame and a stiff paper ring (Fig. 15.32 (c)).

With the higher acoustic output of a loud-speaker used in association with a microphone the the bridge is balanced and no energy can pass from the generator to the impedance Z_R, i.e. from the microphone to the receiver (Fig. 15.33 (b)). In practice, for different telephone calls the value of Z_L varies widely both in magnitude and phase and also changes over the frequency range. It is possible to overcome this difficulty by adding a complex automatic balance control.

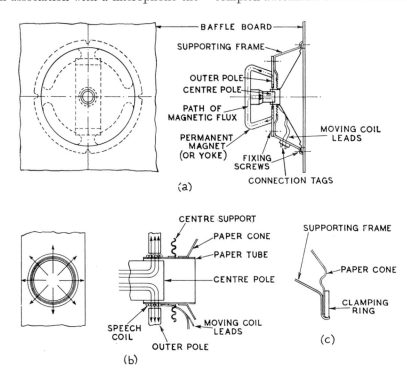

(a)

(b)

(c)

FIG. 15.32. MOVING-COIL LOUD SPEAKER
(Courtesy of "I.P.O.E.E. Journal")

problem of instability due to acoustic coupling between the two transducers, referred to above, becomes aggravated. It is possible to use "voice-switching" in which a voltage developed by the voice signals is used to control variable attenuators and so suppress automatically either the microphone amplifier or the loud-speaker amplifier at all times. Other problems, such as the effects of room noise and reverberation, arise and the cost of an installation is increased. It is not possible here to go into details of this problem, but the arrangement shown in Fig. 15.33 is of interest since it shows how a "hybrid" transformer is used to produce the condition of an a.c. bridge. The line impedance Z_L is simulated in a balancing impedance Z_B. Under ideal conditions (Fig. 15.33 (a)) A modern loud-speaking telephone set[11] without voice-switching is illustrated in Fig. 15.34. The left-hand instrument includes a 3-in. diameter loud-speaker which has a depth of only 0·75 in. achieved by fitting the permanent magnet within the loud-speaker cone: a telephone handset is provided for normal use. The right-hand instrument includes in addition to the telephone dial and on off switch, a three-position volume control switch and a microphone. The electro-magnetic type of microphone is used on account of its superior frequency response and smaller size: the low sensitivity is no disadvantage since separate transistor amplifiers, with power fed from the exchange, are supplied for both microphone and loud-speaker. The microphone and loud-speaker should be placed

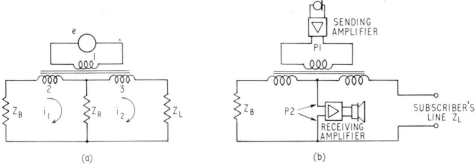

FIG. 15.33. HYBRID CIRCUIT
(*a*) Ideal.   (*b*) Practical.

two to three feet apart in order to reduce acoustic coupling since both amplifiers are in operation during a telephone call.

15.6. Piezo-electricity.[12],[13]

Piezo-electricity relates to the production of electric charges in certain crystals when they are subjected to mechanical pressure; and conversely to the conversion of electrical stress into mechanical strain. ("Piezo" is from a Greek word meaning pressure.)

This inter-relationship of mechanical vibration and electrical oscillation makes the piezo-electric crystal vibrator a suitable vehicle for conversions between electrical and sound energies, particularly where sensitivity to high frequencies is desired. For sound reproduction purposes crystals of Rochelle salt are used because of the relatively greater response of this material. For specialized purposes both transmitters and receivers utilizing piezo-electric crystal elements are available: a more general application is for loud speakers where an improved response over a wide frequency band results from using a moving-coil instrument to reproduce the lower audible frequencies in conjunction with a crystal movement to respond to the upper frequencies. Another use of the piezo-electric crystal as a link in sound reproduction is in the "pick-up" instrument of the electric gramophone.

In the more general field of telecommunication, however, the piezo-electric phenomenon is applied to improved methods of frequency stability and frequency selection, to which the following notes refer.

(i) THE QUARTZ CRYSTAL VIBRATOR. A number of crystalline materials possess the piezo-electric property but, with the possible exception of tourmaline, quartz is the only mineral in which this property can be put to practical use for the purposes stated above.

The external form of the natural quartz crystal is

FIG. 15.34. LOUD-SPEAKING TELEPHONE SETS
(*Courtesy of I.P.O.E.E.*)

a hexagonal prism terminated at each end by hexagonal pyramids (Fig. 15.35). "Left-hand" and "right-hand" crystals occur, the one being a mirror image of the other. A photograph of the crystals,

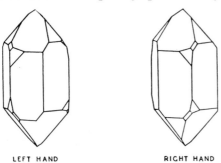

LEFT HAND   RIGHT HAND

FIG. 15.35. QUARTZ CRYSTALS: LEFT-HAND AND RIGHT-HAND FORMS
(*Courtesy of "I.P.O.E.E. Journal"*)

with the base pyramids cut away, appears in Fig. 15.36.

The piezo-electric properties of a crystal vary according to the direction in which it is cut with

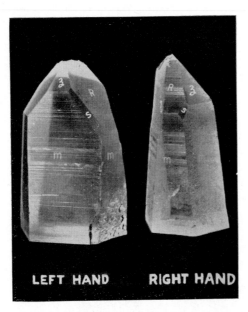

FIG. 15.36. QUARTZ CRYSTALS (BASES CUT SQUARE)
(*Courtesy of "I.P.O.E.E. Journal"*)

respect to the X-axes (parallel to the crystal faces) or the Y-axes (at right angles to the faces). These axes are indicated in Fig. 15.37 which also shows two alternative planes for cutting a flat plate.

The property of liberating electric charges when

the piezo-electric crystal is stressed is due to electrical asymmetry within the atomic groups of which the crystal is built. Inside the crystal the constituent atoms are arranged in a definite pattern

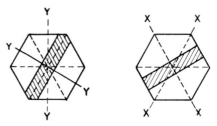

FIG. 15.37. REFERENCE AXES IN QUARTZ CRYSTALS

which is repeated at distances having atomic dimensions. In quartz, silicon and oxygen atoms are arranged with respect to each other to produce silicon dioxide (SiO_2). In Fig. 15.38 the positive charges are shown carried by silicon atoms and the

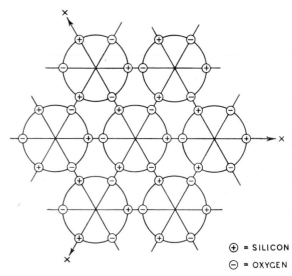

⊕ = SILICON
⊖ = OXYGEN

FIG. 15.38. SYMBOLIC GROUPING OF ATOMS IN QUARTZ
(*Courtesy of "I.P.O.E.E. Journal"*)

negative charges by double oxygen atoms, the diagram relating to the plane containing the directions (marked X) of maximum piezo-electric effect.

An atomic group is shown isolated in Fig. 15.39: in the unstressed crystal at (*a*) the centres of action of the positive and negative charges associated respectively with the silicon and oxygen atoms are coincident and the material is electrically neutral. If the group undergoes a tensile stress—indicated at (*b*)—the atoms are displaced: the centre of action of the three positive charges moves away from the centre in the opposite direction to that of the negative charges and an electric moment results. This separation of charges exists for all the atomic groups within the crystal and the net result is the appearance of charges at the external boundaries along a particular axis. The polarity is reversed on the application of a compressional stress, i.e. an

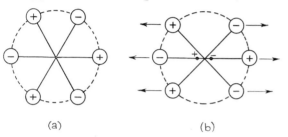

(a)   (b)

FIG. 15.39. QUARTZ CRYSTAL ATOMIC GROUP
(a) Unstressed. (b) Tensile stress.
(Courtesy of "I.P.O.E.E. Journal")

alternating voltage results from alternate pushes and pulls.

The quartz crystal vibrating at its frequency of mechanical resonance may be represented by the equivalent electrical components inductance, capacitance, and resistance (Fig. 15.40). The inductance L, capacitance C, and resistance R have equivalence to the mass, stiffness, and damping factor of the

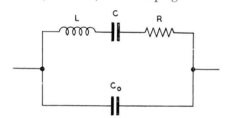

FIG. 15.40. ELECTRICAL EQUIVALENCE OF QUARTZ
CRYSTAL

vibrator: since quartz is a dielectric C_0 represents its electrical capacitance.

In comparison with the normal form of electrical resonant circuit the Q value is extremely high and may lie between 50 000 and 500 000 compared with values of the order of 100 to 500 for the most high-grade inductor and capacitor circuits. The reactance/frequency graph for a quartz crystal is plotted in Fig. 15.41: this shows two points of resonant frequency f_r for the series resonance and f_a for parallel resonance (or anti-resonance). On account of the electrical equivalence of the quartz crystal it is possible to add external capacitance in series or in parallel with C_0 to raise or lower

the series or parallel resonant frequency respectively. (It is not, of course, possible to modify the values of L and C by adding electrical elements.) It follows that metal electrodes used to excite the crystal need not necessarily be in contact with the quartz surface since the intervening air layer would act as the dielectric of a series capacitor. Adjustment of the air-gap may in fact be used for frequency control of the crystal.

The preparation and mounting of quartz crystals demands a specialized and highly skilled technique. Very briefly, the production of a crystal for practical use involves selection of the most suitable axis for cutting a slab from the mother crystal, design of the appropriate dimensions and the subsequent cutting and grinding to obtain these dimensions accurately.

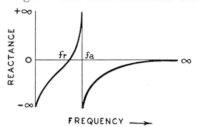

FIG. 15.41. REACTANCE/FREQUENCY RELATION OF
QUARTZ CRYSTAL
(Courtesy of "I.P.O.E.E. Journal")

A standard method of mounting is to use phosphor-bronze wires soldered to silver spots fired by a special process to the quartz surfaces at the nodes—the points of minimum displacement during vibration. Electrodes of gold or silver are then deposited in a thin coating upon the appropriate crystal surfaces. The crystal support wires are soldered to the nickel wires of a mica cage assembly (Fig. 15.42): after a final frequency adjustment the assembly is enclosed in an evacuated glass envelope as for a thermionic valve (Fig. 15.43). This is the more usual form of mounting: it prevents any possibility of frequency instability occurring with changes in atmospheric pressure. Exceptionally, a crystal may be mounted in a thermostatically controlled oven to maintain an accurately constant temperature: this procedure is not necessary except when using the crystal as a standard of frequency.

(ii) THE QUARTZ CRYSTAL OSCILLATOR. Piezo-electric crystals are used for accurate frequency control of valve oscillators. This operation depends upon the application to the quartz crystal of an alternating voltage whose frequency is equal to that of the natural vibration frequency of the crystal. The vibration rate of a material depends upon the dimensions, elasticity, mass, and damping. If a piezo-electric element is placed in an alternating

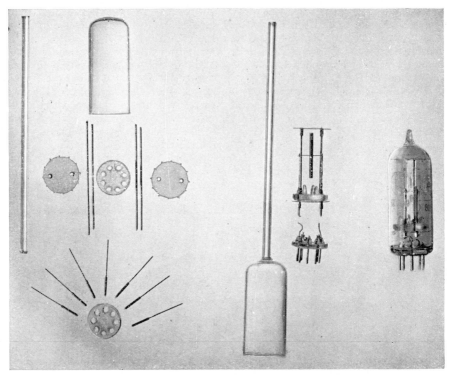

FIG. 15.42. MOUNTING COMPONENTS FOR QUARTZ CRYSTAL
(*Courtesy of P.M.G.*)

electric field it will be forced into mechanical vibration at the frequency of the applied field. Adjustment of this frequency to coincide with the natural vibration frequency of the element causes a large increase in the amplitude of vibration due to the fact that the movement of the element remains in phase with the driving force. If a suitable piece of piezo-electric material is set in vibration by an impulsive force it will continue to vibrate (in the absence of further interference) at its own natural frequency but with gradually diminishing amplitude. During these periodic movements the displacements will give rise to electric charges on the crystal surfaces of sign and magnitude proportional to the movement of the element. If the piezo-electric element, suitably provided with metal electrodes, is connected between the grid and cathode of a thermionic valve, the alternating p.d. produced by the vibrations will be amplified and it will produce larger voltage variations of the same frequency in the anode circuit. In the oscillator these voltages are fed back to the crystal to reinforce the original variations of p.d.: they also reinforce the vibration which will continue so long as the circuit is connected. The medium for feeding

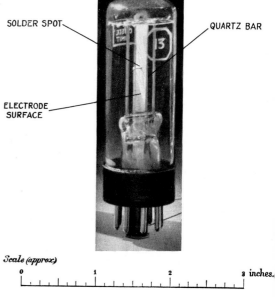

FIG. 15.43. MOUNTED CRYSTAL OSCILLATOR (80 KC/S)
(*Courtesy of "I.P.O.E.E. Journal"*)

back the energy may be an inductor or a capacitor joined between anode and grid provided that anode and grid voltages are in the correct phase relationship. The high Q value of the quartz crystal means that little energy is required to maintain the crystal vibrator in oscillation so that crystals need be only weakly coupled to the associated oscillator valve: in most cases a sufficient feedback path

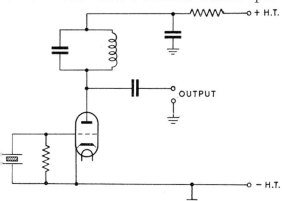

FIG. 15.44. PRINCIPLE OF CRYSTAL CONTROLLED
OSCILLATOR

exists in the form of inter-electrode capacitance. One of the simplest forms of crystal controlled oscillator is illustrated in Fig. 15.44 which also indicates the circuit symbol for a crystal element. On account of the electrical network equivalence of the crystal it is possible to adjust the frequency of a crystal controlled oscillator by adding variable reactance to the crystal element.

In a crystal controlled oscillator the frequency of oscillation is determined primarily by the natural vibration period of the selected quartz crystal, the effect of circuit and supply changes on frequency stability being small. Quartz is an extremely stable substance, the frictional losses in vibration are low and its change of frequency with temperature is

extremely small. In consequence of these factors the frequency stability obtainable with quartz crystals is far superior to the best performance obtainable from inductors and capacitors alone. The frequency variation may well be as little as one part in 10^6 over a period of years.

Quartz-controlled oscillators are available in the range 4 kc/s to 20 Mc/s or more. The resonant frequency of a vibrator depending upon its dimen-

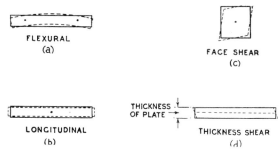

FIG. 15.45. VIBRATION MODES OF QUARTZ CRYSTAL

sions, to cover this wide frequency range solely upon this principle would involve the preparation of impractically large and small crystals. The wide frequency range can be conveniently covered by making use of the various *modes* of vibration which are possible: the diagram of Fig. 15.45 illustrates the deformation produced by four of these modes of vibration.

The frequency range quoted above can be extended upwards or downwards by a method of frequency multiplication and division. Frequency multiplication is effected by the use of a non-linear amplifier to make conditions favourable for harmonic distortion: the desired harmonic frequency component is then selected and suitably amplified.

A quartz crystal-stabilized oscillator is employed as a primary standard of frequency against which the oscillators for carrier systems and radio services are calibrated.

REFERENCES

1. D. MCMILLAN: "Hearing as an Essential Part of the Telephone Circuit," *I.P.O.E.E. Paper*, 1947.
2. N. F. C. B. CAVE: "Sound and Hearing," *I.P.O.E.E. Paper No.* **134.**
3. E. G. RICHARDSON: "Some Acoustical Aspects of Telephony," *I.P.O.E.E. Journal*, **27** (1934), p. 52.
4. D. MCMILLAN: "Some Performance Characteristics of the Subscriber's Telephone Transmitter," ibid., **28** (1935), pp. 167 and 313.
5. C. A. R. PEARCE: "Transmitter Inset No. 13," ibid., **29** (1937), p. 335.
6. D. MCMILLAN: "The Telephone Transmitter: a Suggested Theory of Operation," ibid., **31** (1938), p. 167.
7. D. MCMILLAN: "A Simple Moving Coil Microphone," ibid., **27** (1935), p. 284.
8. J. S. P. ROBERTON: "The Rocking-armature Receiver," ibid., **49** (1956), p. 40.
9. H. J. C. SPENCER: "Some Principles of Anti-sidetone Telephone Circuits," ibid., **48** (1956), p. 208.
10. E. J. BARNES, A. E. WOOD, and D. L. RICHARDS: "Standards of Transmission and Local Line Limits," ibid., **39** (1947), p. 151.
11. W. T. LOWE, and F. A. WILSON: "A Loud-speaking Telephone Without Voice-switching," ibid., **54** (1961), p. 1.
12. C. F. BOOTH, and J. L. CREIGHTON "Piezo-electric Quartz and its use in Telecommunications," *I.P.O.E.E. Paper No.* **191** (1946).
13. J. L. CREIGHTON: "Piezo-electric Quartz Crystals," *I.P.O.E.E. Journal*, **38** (1945), p. 65.

APPENDIX A

MATHEMATICAL NOTES

A.1. Symbols. In addition to the mathematical symbols in common use, the following are used in the text—

$|a - b|$ means difference between a and b.

$\simeq$	,,	approximately equal to.
$\geqslant$	,,	greater than or equal to.
$\leqslant$	,,	less than or equal to.
$\gg$	,,	much greater than.
$\ll$	,,	much less than.
$\propto$	,,	varies as.
∞	,,	infinity.

A.2. Calculus Notation.

(i) RATE OF CHANGE. If x is a function which varies with t, and x_1 represents a certain value

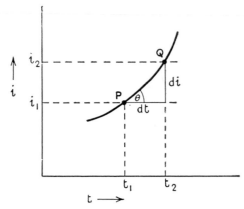

FIG. A.1. SLOPE OF GRAPH

occurring at a time t_1, if this rises or falls to x_2 at the instant t_2, then the change in x is $(x_2 - x_1)$ and this occurs in a time $(t_2 - t_1)$. When these changes are extremely small they are written as dx and dt respectively: thus $(x_2 - x_1) = dx$ and $(t_2 - t_1) = dt$. In this calculus notation the expression dt does *not* mean $d \times t$, but it is a single term (dt) meaning a very small change in the value of t. For example a varying current having a value i at an instant t has a value $(i + di)$ at the instant $(t + dt)$ a small fraction of a second later.

If x changes its value by $dx = (x_2 - x_1)$ in the time interval $dt = (t_2 - t_1)$, the *rate* of change of x, which is $(x_2 - x_1)/(t_2 - t_1) = dx/dt$. For example

$d\phi/dt$ and di/dt represent respectively *rates* of change of flux and of current.

The accompanying diagram (Fig. A.1) shows a part of a graph relating a changing current with time. If the two points P and Q are moved extremely close together, the current change $(i_2 - i_1)$ is di and the time during which this occurs is $(t_2 - t_1) = dt$. If the portion of the curve under consideration is sufficiently small, it approximates to a straight line and the rate of change of current $= di/dt$ is thus equal to $\tan \theta$. The ratio di/dt $= \tan \theta$ represents the *gradient* or *slope* of the curve, i.e. it is the rate at which the vertical ordinate grows with increase of the horizontal abscissa.

(ii) SUMMATION. The symbol Σ is used as a convenient method of indicating the sum of a number of similar terms. For example $\Sigma(R)$ means the sum of a number of similar (not necessarily equal) resistances, $R_1 + R_2 + R_3 + \ldots$: similarly, $\Sigma(r \cos \theta) = r_1 \cos \theta_1 + r_2 \cos \theta_2 + r_3 \cos \theta_3 + \ldots$

A.3. Trigonometry.

(i) RATIOS. In any right-angled triangle (Fig. A.2), for a given angle $\theta°$ the ratio of any pair of sides has a constant value. The three most commonly employed ratios (of the six possible) are known as the sine (sin), cosine (cos), and the tangent (tan). They are determined as follows—

$$\sin \theta = y/r : \cos \theta = x/r : \tan \theta = y/x$$

Alternatively the angle may be expressed in terms of the ratio of the sides: for example $\theta°$ is

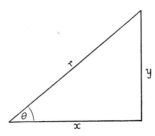

FIG. A.2. TRIGONOMETRICAL RATIOS

the angle whose tangent is y/x. The index $^{-1}$ is used for writing this in the form

$$\theta° = \tan^{-1} y/x$$

which should be read as "$\theta°$ is the angle whose

tangent is y/x ": in a similar manner may be written

$$\theta^° = \cos^{-1} x/r$$
or
$$\theta^° = \sin^{-1} y/r$$

Since $\sin \theta = y/r$, $y = r \sin \theta$: similarly $\cos \theta = x/r$ and $x = r \cos \theta$. In words, the vertical side is always equal to the longest side (opposite the right angle) multiplied by the *sine* of the base angle: the horizontal side is always equal to the longest side multiplied by the *cosine* of the base angle.

From Pythagoras' theorem, the square on the longest side of a right-angled triangle is equal to the sum of the squares on the two shorter sides, or

$$r^2 = (x^2 + y^2) \text{ and } r = (x^2 + y^2)^{\frac{1}{2}}$$

These relationships enable an unknown side or angle to be calculated when two other sides or angles are known: they are invaluable in the solution of vectors.

(ii) Graphs of Sin θ and Cos θ. The accompanying diagram (Fig. A.3) is a graph showing how the sine of an angle varies with the angle. It is constructed by projecting from the rotating radius of a circle on to corresponding points along the axis of the angle $\theta^°$. In the diagram these projections are, for greater clearness, shown only at 30° intervals starting from the axis XX'. For accuracy many more values of $\theta^°$ should be taken.

At any value of $\theta^°$, $\sin \theta = PH/OP = P'H'/OP'$, etc.: OP, the radius of the circle, being constant, $\sin \theta$ is always directly proportional to the projections PH, $P'H'$, etc. These projections of P, P',

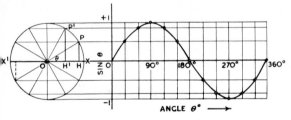

Fig. A.3. Graph of $y = \text{Sin } \theta$

etc., are carried on to the graph as ordinates for the corresponding values of the angle $\theta^°$.

The sine has its maximum value at 90° when PH becomes equal to OP because these lines are then coincident and $\sin 90° = OP/OP = +1$. At angles 0°, 180°, and 360° the ordinate PH vanishes and the value of $\sin \theta$ becomes $0/OP = 0$.

For values between 180° and 360°, the projection PH being below the horizontal axis, is always negative: the radius OP is always regarded as being positive. Sin θ therefore has negative values for all angles between 180° and 360°, reaching a

negative maximum at 270° when PH and OP become coincident and $\sin 270° = -(OP)/OP = -1$.

This curve is characteristic for any expression of the form $y = \sin \theta$: such curves are said to be *sinusoidal* or of sine-wave form.

If OP has the value I_{max}, the projection PH represents the instantaneous value $i = I_{max} \sin \omega t$. In this way the instantaneous value at any angle $\theta = \omega t$ can be determined by graphical means.

A similar construction can be utilized to produce the graph of $y = \cos \theta$ (Fig. A.4). In this case it is more convenient (simply in order to retain the

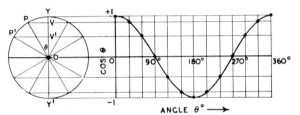

Fig. A.4. Graph of $y = \text{Cos } \theta$

horizontal projection) to take the starting point of the angle on the vertical axis YY'. Since $\cos \theta$ is the ratio $OV/OP = OV'/OP'$, etc., it is always proportional to the projection OV, OV', etc. Projecting these ordinates to their corresponding positions along the axis for the angle $\theta^°$ permits the cosine graph to be completed.

The cosine has zero values at $\theta = 90°$ and $\theta = 270°$. Its maximum positive and negative values are $+1$ and -1 occurring at 0° (or 360°) and at 180° respectively. The shape of the cosine curve is exactly the same as that of the sine curve but it passes through any given value 90° ahead of the corresponding sine curve: the cosine curve may be regarded as a sine curve leading by 90°.

A.4. Vectors. A vector quantity is one whose full description includes *direction* (or angular displacement) as well as magnitude, in contrast to a scalar quantity which is completely defined by stating its magnitude and of course the units in which it is expressed. In addition to the magnitude and direction of a vector quantity, it may be necessary also to know the point of application and the sense. Mass, length, and volume are examples of scalar quantities. Forces, distances, and velocities are vectors since they are not completely described without reference to the direction in which they act. Alternating voltages and currents, reactances and impedances are also vectors on account of their phase displacements: for a full statement of these quantities it is necessary to state the phase angle as well as the magnitude.

17

With vector quantities, operations such as addition and subtraction cannot be performed by the ordinary methods of arithmetic and algebra because the angular differences must be taken into account. Addition and subtraction of vectors may be performed by graphical means from accurately constructed diagrams, or by calculation. In a.c. work

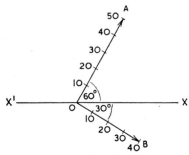

FIG. A.5. VECTOR REPRESENTATION

the use of approximate vector diagrams is frequently an invaluable aid in illustrating the processes: for precise results by graphical methods such diagrams must be drawn as large and accurately as possible.

Vectors may be written in the form $V\underline{/\theta}$ if the angle is positive, and $V\underline{\backslash\theta}$ when the angle is negative. The magnitude V is called the *modulus* and the angle θ the *argument*.

(i) GRAPHICAL REPRESENTATION OF VECTORS. A horizontal line is taken as the standard of reference and the vector is represented by a straight line (drawn from the point of application where this is

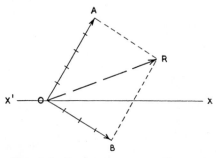

FIG. A.6. PARALLELOGRAM OF VECTORS

necessary). The length of this line represents to some suitable scale the magnitude of the vector, and the angle with the horizontal represents the direction or phase angle: an arrow indicates the *sense* of the direction.

The line OA (Fig. A.5) represents a vector $50\underline{/60°}$ of 50 units magnitude acting at an angle of $\overline{60°}$: the line OB represents another vector $40\backslash\overline{30°}$ of

magnitude 40 units acting at an angle of $-30°$. The arrow heads indicate that the directions are from O to A and O to B, not in the reverse sense.

(ii) THE VECTOR PARALLELOGRAM. Two vectors

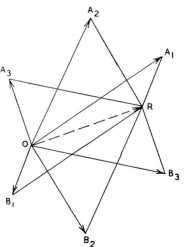

FIG. A.7. ALTERNATIVE PAIRS OF COMPONENTS

can be added together by use of the parallelogram rule. If a parallelogram is constructed on the two lines OA and OB (Fig. A.6) the diagonal OR represents, both in magnitude and direction, the resultant or *vector sum* of OA and OB. For instance two forces OA and OB are exactly equivalent to a single force OR.

Conversely a single vector OR can be split up into its components OA and OB which are together

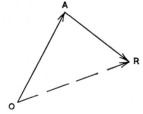

FIG. A.8. TRIANGLE OF VECTORS

equal to OR. There is, however, no limit to the number of alternative pairs of components: three possible cases are illustrated in Fig. A.7. It is usual to select the pair of right-angled components corresponding to the XX' and YY' axes (see (v) below).

(iii) THE VECTOR TRIANGLE. In Fig. A.6, since $OA = BR$ and $OB = AR$, each of the triangles OAR and OBR contains the two components and the resultant. A triangle may be drawn to perform the addition or resolution of vectors (Fig. A.8). It should be noted particularly that the second vector (AR) must be drawn from the point (A) of the first vector (OA), and also that the direction of the resultant (OR) is opposite to the general cyclic sense of the components OA and AR.

Conversely, it is clear from Fig. A.7 that any

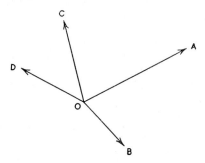

FIG. A.9. VECTORS

number of alternative pairs of components can be drawn to form a triangle on OR.

(iv) THE VECTOR POLYGON. When more than two vectors (Fig. A.9) are to be added together, the resultant OR of the first two OA and OB (see Fig. A.10) can be added to the third vector OC by

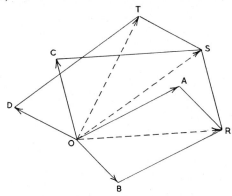

FIG. A.10. SUMMATION OF VECTORS

drawing the parallelogram $OCSR$: its diagonal OS then represents the sum of the three vectors OA, OB, and OC. Adding to this resultant OS the fourth vector OD produces the parallelogram $ODTS$ with a diagonal OT which is the vector sum of OA, OB, OC, and OD.

The same result may be obtained by constructing an open polygon (see Fig. A.11) whose sides, *taken in order*, are equal and parallel to the component vectors: thus OA, OB, OC, and OD in Fig. A.9 are redrawn in Fig. A.11 as OA, AB, BC, and CD respectively. The closing side OD represents their

vector sum both in magnitude and direction. OD in Fig. A.11 is identical with OT in Fig. A.10.

The two points emphasized in connexion with the vector triangle apply with equal force here.

(v) VECTOR COMPONENTS AT RIGHT ANGLES. For the reason demonstrated in Fig. A.7, when splitting

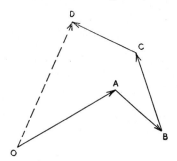

FIG. A.11. POLYGON OF VECTORS

a vector up into two components it is customary to select the pair which lies along the horizontal and vertical axes.

This process is demonstrated in Fig. A.12 for the vector V/θ. Perpendiculars from A are dropped on to the vertical and horizontal axes cutting them at Y and X respectively OX and OY are the components (or *resolutes* since they are mutually at right angles) of the vector V/θ.

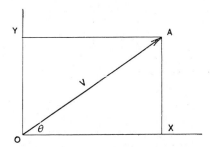

FIG. A.12. RIGHT-ANGLED COMPONENTS

Conversely the line OA at an angle θ is the vector sum of OX and OY: this is a special case of the parallelogram rule.

To add two or more vectors by this method, each vector must first of all be split up into its two resolutes. All components then lie along either the horizontal or the vertical axis. Components on the same axis can be added algebraically: the single pair of components so obtained is then added vectorially by the parallelogram rule. This is illustrated in Fig. A.13 for the four vectors OA, OB, OC, and OD. The vector OA is represented by OA_1

and OA_2: OB by OB_1 and OB_2, and similarly for OC and OD. Like components are then added together in the following manner: $OA_1 + OB_1 = OE$; $OC_1 + OD_1 = OF$; $OB_2 + OC_2 = OG$; and $OA_2 + OD_2 = OH$.

The algebraic sum of OE and OF (i.e. their difference in this case, OE being positive and OF negative) gives OK: the algebraic sum of OG and OH gives OL. Summarizing, OK is the sum of all four horizontal components, and OL the sum of all four vertical components. Completing the right-angled parallelogram $OKML$ gives OM (in magnitude and direction) as the final resultant of OA, OB, OC, and OD.

This graphical method of vector addition lends itself conveniently to mathematical calculation

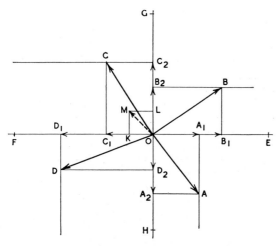

FIG. A.13. ADDITION OF VECTORS BY RESOLUTES

simply by using the trigonometrical ratios (see § **A.3** (i)). The above methods apply equally to the subtraction of vectors if due attention is paid to sign.

(vi) MATHEMATICAL SOLUTION OF VECTORS. The methods described below depend only upon the solution of triangles by the methods of trigonometry.

(a) *Resolution*. The vector V/θ is resolved into its right-angled components (Fig. A.14): vertical components are always in the form $V \sin \theta$ and horizontal components are $V \cos \theta$ (see § **A.3** (i)).

EXAMPLE A.1. What are the horizontal and vertical components of the vectors $600/\underline{45°}$ and $1\,000/\underline{30°}$?

$600/\underline{45°}$—

Horizontal component $= V \cos \theta = 600 \cos 45°$
$$= 600 \,.\, \sqrt{2}/2 = \underline{\underline{424 \cdot 2}}$$

Vertical component $= V \sin \theta = 600 \sin 45°$
$$= 600 \,.\, \sqrt{2}/2 = \underline{\underline{424 \cdot 2}}$$

$1\,000/\underline{30°}$—

Horizontal component $= 1\,000 \cos 30°$
$$= 1\,000 \,.\, \sqrt{3}/2 = \underline{\underline{866}}$$

Vertical component $= 1\,000 \sin 30°$
$$= 1\,000 \times 1/2 = \underline{\underline{500}}$$

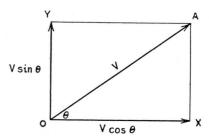

FIG. A.14. MATHEMATICAL RESOLUTION OF VECTOR INTO TWO RIGHT-ANGLED COMPONENTS

(b) *Composition*. Taking the reverse process, i.e. finding the resultant of two components (Fig. A.15) the vector sum of a and b which are in quadrature is $\sqrt{a^2 + b^2}$ in magnitude. The tangent of the phase angle is b/a. Summarizing,
$$V = (a^2 + b^2)^{\frac{1}{2}}, \text{ and } \theta = \tan^{-1} b/a$$

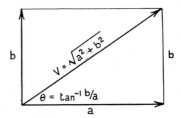

FIG. A.15. MATHEMATICAL COMPOSITION OF VECTORS

EXAMPLE A.2. What is the vector sum of the two right-angled components (i) 500 and 500, (ii) 300 and 400? (The horizontal component is given first in each case.)

(i) $V = (500^2 + 500^2)^{\frac{1}{2}} = \sqrt{50 \times 10^4}$
$$= 100 \times 7 \cdot 07 = \underline{\underline{707}}$$

$\phi = \tan^{-1} 500/500 = \tan^{-1} 1 \cdot 0 : \phi = \underline{\underline{45°}}$

(ii) $V = (300^2 + 400^2)^{\frac{1}{2}} = \sqrt{25 \times 10^4} = \underline{\underline{500}}$

$\phi = \tan^{-1} 400/300 = \tan^{-1} 1 \cdot 33 : \phi = \underline{\underline{53°}}$

(c) *Addition of Two Vectors.* Using as a basis the graphical method of Fig. A.13 the sum of two (or more) vectors can be calculated. Considering the two vectors V/α and R/β (Fig. A.16), the process of addition is as follows—

(i) Resolve each vector into its horizontal and vertical components :*

$$V/\alpha = \overline{V \cos \alpha + V \sin \alpha}$$

$$R/\beta = \overline{R \cos \beta + R \sin \beta}$$

(ii) Take separately the algebraic sums of the horizontal and vertical components. The total horizontal component $= (V \cos \alpha + R \cos \beta)$: the total vertical component $= (V \sin \alpha + R \sin \beta)$.

(iii) To find the sum S, square and add these two total components and take the square root—

$$S = \{(V \cos \alpha + R \cos \beta)^2 + (V \sin \alpha + R \sin \beta)^2\}^{\frac{1}{2}}$$

(iv) The tangent of the resultant angle ϕ is the ratio of these two total components, i.e.

$$\phi = \tan^{-1} \left(\frac{V \sin \alpha + R \sin \beta}{V \cos \alpha + R \cos \beta} \right)$$

EXAMPLE A.3. Find the vector sum of $100/45°$ and $400/60°$.

Sum of horizontal components
$$= 100 \cos 45° + 400 \cos 60°$$
$$= 100 \times 0.707 + 400 \times 0.5$$
$$= 70.7 + 200 = 270.7$$

Sum of vertical components
$$= 100 \sin 45° + 400 \sin 60°$$
$$= 100 \times 0.707 + 400 \times 0.866$$
$$= 70.7 + 346.4 = 417.1$$

Vector magnitude,
$$S = (270.7^2 + 417.1^2)^{\frac{1}{2}} = 497.2$$

$$\phi = \tan^{-1} 417.1/270.7 = \tan^{-1} 1.541 :$$
$$\text{phase angle} = 57.1°$$

If one of the vectors has a negative angle say $R\backslash\overline{\beta}$, then the process is still the same as that given above but $R \sin \beta$ will always be negative ($R \cos \beta$ remaining positive, provided that $\beta < -90$): the sum ($V \sin \alpha + R \sin \beta$) will be positive or negative depending upon whether $R \sin \beta >$ or $< V \sin \alpha$, and the resultant phase angle will be positive or negative accordingly.

EXAMPLE A.4. Find the vector sum of $100/45°$ and $400\backslash\overline{60°}$.

* The horizontal line drawn above these expressions indicates that a vector sum is intended.

Sum of horizontal components
$$= 100 \cos 45° + 400 \cos 60°$$
$$= 100 \times 0.707 + 400 \times 0.5 = 270.7$$

Sum of vertical components
$$= 100 \sin 45° + 400 \sin (-60°)$$
$$= 100 \times 0.707 + 400 (-0.866)$$
$$= 70.7 - 346.4 = -275.7$$

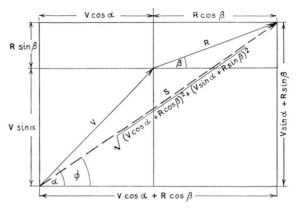

FIG. A.16. MATHEMATICAL ADDITION OF TWO VECTORS

Vector magnitude,
$$S = (270.7^2 + (-275.7)^2)^{\frac{1}{2}} = 386.4$$

$$\phi = \tan^{-1} -275.7/270.7 = \tan^{-1} -1.018\ 6 :$$
$$\text{phase angle} = -45.5°$$

(d) *Difference Between Two Vectors.* This requires the same general process as for addition, but with due attention paid to positive and negative signs.

EXAMPLE A.5. Calculate $400/60° - 100/45°$.

Difference of horizontal components
$$= 400 \times 0.5 - 100 \times 0.707$$
$$= 200 - 70.7 = 129.3$$

Difference of vertical components
$$= 400 \times 0.866 - 100 \times 0.707$$
$$= 346.4 - 70.7 = 275.7$$

Vector magnitude,
$$S = (129.3^2 + 275.7^2)^{\frac{1}{2}} = 304.5$$

$$\phi = \tan^{-1} 275.7/129.3 = \tan^{-1} 2.13 :$$
$$\text{phase angle} = 64.8°$$

EXAMPLE A.6. Calculate $400\underline{/60°} - 100\overline{\backslash 45°}$.

Difference of horizontal components

$$= 400 \times 0.5 - 100 \times 0.707$$
$$= 200 - 70.7 = 129.3$$

Difference of vertical components

$$= 400 \times 0.866 - 100\,(-\,0.707)$$
$$= 346.4 + 70.7 = 417.1$$

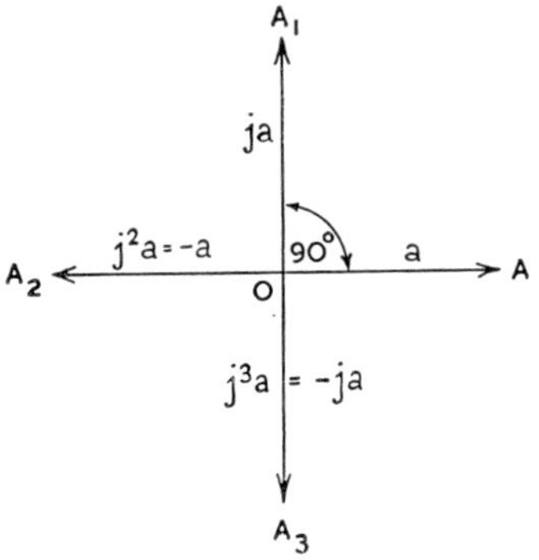

FIG. A.17. SIGNIFICANCE OF THE j-OPERATOR

Vector magnitude,

$$S = (129.3^2 + 417.1^2)^{\frac{1}{2}} = \underline{436.7}$$

$$\phi = \tan^{-1} 417.1/129.3 = \tan^{-1} 3.225\ 5:$$
$$\text{phase angle} = \underline{72.8°}$$

(e) *Addition or Subtraction of Several Vectors (General Case)*. The vector sum of more than two vectors is simply an extension of the above process: it may be expressed as follows—

Magnitude,

$$S = \sqrt{(\Sigma V \cos \theta)^2 + (\Sigma V \sin \theta)^2}$$

Phase angle,

$$\phi = \tan^{-1} \left(\frac{\Sigma V \sin \theta}{\Sigma V \cos \theta} \right)$$

(f) *Multiplication of Vectors*. To multiply together two vectors, multiply the magnitudes and add the angles thus—

$$V\underline{/\alpha} \times R\underline{/\beta} = VR\underline{/\alpha + \beta}$$

or

$$V\underline{/\alpha} + R\overline{\backslash \beta} = VR\underline{/\alpha - \beta}$$

(g) *Division of Vectors*. To find the quotient of two vectors, divide the magnitudes and subtract the angles, thus—

$$\frac{V\underline{/\alpha}}{R\underline{/\beta}} = \frac{V}{R}\underline{/\alpha - \beta}$$

or

$$\frac{V\underline{/\alpha}}{R\overline{\backslash \beta}} = \frac{V}{R}\underline{/\alpha + \beta}$$

(vii) USE OF THE j-OPERATOR. The composition of two right-angled components has been written above as $(a^2 + b^2)^{\frac{1}{2}}$. Expressions such as these may be more conveniently written and also manipulated by the use of the j-*operator*. The j-operator applied to a quantity simply denotes that it is turned through an angle of 90°.

In Fig. A.17 the line OA has, by accepted convention, a positive value to which may be assigned a units. If OA be regarded as a radius vector and turned through an angle of 180°, its magnitude in this new position OA_2 is now by the same convention $(-a)$ units or $-1 \times a$. In other words the effect of multiplying a by -1 is to turn it through two right angles.

If this same process be now performed in two distinct and equal stages, pausing at OA_1 after 90° rotation, it may be considered that the multiplication of a by some factor, say j, turns OA through 90° to the position OA_1: that is to say that if OA is expressed by a, then ja means the same magnitude turned through 90° to the position OA_1. A second similar operation turns OA through a further 90° to the position OA_2. This twice-repeated multiplication of a by j, a total of $(j \times j)$ or j^2 produces the magnitude $(-a)$ in the position OA_2. Since $j^2 a = -1 \times a$ it follows that j^2 may be assigned the magnitude -1 and $j = \sqrt{-1}$. A negative root such as $\sqrt{-1}$ is an imaginary number, but the factor j nevertheless operates as shown to rotate a vector through an angle of 90°.

A third operation by j from 180° produces the position OA_3 at an angle of 270°: hence $OA_3 = j^3 a = (j^2 \times j)a = -ja$ (since $j^2 = -1$). Taking a fourth step through 90° produces $j^4 a = (j^2 \times j^2)a = -1\,.\,-1\,.\,a = +a$: the rotating vector is now at 360°, coincident with its original position. These results are summarized in the following table—

Multiplier	Angle Turned
j	90°
$j^2 \,(= -1)$	180°
$j^3 \,(= -j)$	270°
$j^4 \,(= +1)$	360°

In a.c. circuit calculations the vectors most frequently lie in the first and fourth quadrants, that is to say that their components are referred to the axes of 0°, 90° (j), and 270° ($-j$). The following forms may be written—

Fig. A.18. $V/\underline{\alpha} = a + jb = V \cos \alpha + jV \sin \alpha$

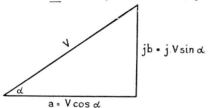

FIG. A.18.   VECTOR WITH POSITIVE ANGLE:
$$V/\underline{\alpha} = a + b$$

Fig. A.19. $R\overline{\backslash\beta} = a - jb = R \cos \beta - j \cdot R \sin \beta$

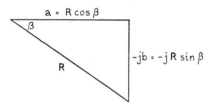

FIG. A.19.   VECTOR WITH NEGATIVE ANGLE:
$$R\overline{\backslash\beta} = a - jb$$

An impedance, for example, would be written—

$$Z/\underline{\phi} = (R + jX)/\tan^{-1} X/R$$

or

$$Z\overline{\backslash\phi} = (R - jX)\overline{\backslash}\tan^{-1} - X/R$$

he presence of the factor j indicating that the quantity X lies at right angles to the quantity R. Although use of the j-operator simplifies both the writing down and the manipulation of vectors, the final value of $(a + jb)$ for example, must still be calculated from Pythagoras' theorem, $V = (a^2 + b^2)^{\frac{1}{2}}$.

(a) *Addition or Subtraction of Vectors.* The rule is to collect separately the "real" terms (i.e. those not involving j) and the "unreal" or so-called "imaginary" terms (i.e. those which involve j), using the ordinary rules of algebra.

$$(a + jb) + (c + jd) = (a + c) + j(b + d)$$
$$= \{(a + c)^2 + (b + d)^2\}^{\frac{1}{2}} \cdot \left/ \tan^{-1} \left(\frac{b + d}{a + c}\right)\right.$$

$$(a + jb) + (c - jd) = (a + c) + j(b - d)$$
$$= \{(a + c)^2 + (b - d)^2\}^{\frac{1}{2}} \cdot \left/ \tan^{-1} \left(\frac{b - d}{a + c}\right)\right.$$

$$(a + jb) - (c + jd) = (a - c) + j(b - d)$$
$$= \{(a - c)^2 + (b - d)^2\}^{\frac{1}{2}} \cdot \left/ \tan^{-1} \left(\frac{b - d}{a - c}\right)\right.$$

$$(a + jb) - (c - jd) = (a - c) + j(b + d)$$
$$= \{(a - c)^2 + (b + d)^2\}^{\frac{1}{2}} \cdot \left/ \tan^{-1} \left(\frac{b + d}{a - c}\right)\right.$$

$$\left(\text{The expression for the tangent is always in the form } \tan^{-1} \frac{imaginary}{real}.\right)$$

(b) *Multiplication of Vectors.* These calculations are made in the algebraic form of $(\overset{\frown}{a + b})\,(\overset{\frown}{c + d})$ $= ac + bc + ad + bd$, substituting $j^2 = -1$ where necessary, thus—

$$(a + jb)(c + jd) = ac + j(bc + ad) + j^2 \cdot bd$$
$$= ac - bd + j(bc + ad) \left/ \tan^{-1} \left(\frac{bc + ad}{ac - bd}\right)\right.$$

$$(a + jb)(c - jd) = ac + j(bc - ad) - j^2 \cdot bd$$
$$= ac + bd + j(bc - ad) \left/ \tan^{-1} \left(\frac{bc - ad}{ac + bd}\right)\right.$$

(c) *Division of Vectors.* This is performed by multiplying *both* numerator and denominator by a factor which will remove from the denominator any term involving j: for example, if the denominator is of the form $(a + b)$ then multiplication of $(a + b)$ by $(a - b)$ eliminates the middle term—

$$\frac{a + jb}{c + jd} = \frac{a + jb}{c + jd} \times \frac{c - jd}{c - jd}$$
$$= \frac{ac + bd + j(bc - ad)}{c^2 + d^2}$$
$$= \frac{ac + bd}{c^2 + d^2} + \frac{j(bc - ad)}{c^2 + d^2} \cdot \left/ \tan^{-1} \left(\frac{bc - ad}{ac + bd}\right)\right.$$

A.5. Proofs Employing the Calculus. Although not essential to the proofs of all formulae given earlier in the book, the following alternative methods will be appreciated by the student who has a working knowledge of the calculus.

(i) ENERGY STORED IN AN ELECTRIC FIELD (§**5.33**). The energy stored in an electric field is equal to the energy expended in charging the conductor, and subsequently restored when the conductor is discharged.

Suppose that the conductor has a charge of q coulombs when the potential is v volts, its capacitance being C farads. The work done in adding a very small charge dq coulombs to the conductor is

$$v \cdot dq = (q/C) \cdot dq \text{ joules}$$

The total work done in charging the conductor

is the sum of these small amounts of energy from zero until the total charge $Q = CV$ is obtained;

$$\text{Energy, } W = \int_0^Q (q/C) \cdot dq = 1/C \cdot \int_0^Q q \cdot dq$$

$$= \frac{1}{C}\left[\frac{Q^2}{2}\right]_0^Q = Q^2/2C$$

$$= CV^2/2 \text{ joules} \quad . \quad . \quad . \quad (5.6)$$

(ii) GROWTH OF CHARGE ON A CAPACITOR (§**5.34**). If a capacitance C farads is charged in series with a resistance R ohms by applying a source of p.d. V volts at an instant $t = 0$, the initial p.d. on the capacitance being zero, the instantaneous current $i = \dfrac{V}{R}$. As the capacitance becomes charged, its instantaneous p.d. v volts acts as a back-e.m.f. and the charging current is reduced to $i = (V - v)/R$,

rewriting, $\qquad\qquad iR = V - v$

substituting, $\qquad\quad v = q/C$ and $i = dq/dt$

$$R \cdot (dq/dt) = V - q/C = (CV - q)/C$$

re-arranging, $CR(dq/dt) = -(q - CV)$

$$\frac{dq}{q - CV} = \frac{-dt}{CR}$$

integrating, $\log_e(q - CV) = -t/CR + k$

$$q - CV = k \cdot e^{-t/CR}$$

substituting $\qquad\quad q = 0$ when $t = 0$

$$0 - CV = k \cdot e^{-0}$$

$$-CV = k$$

$$q = CV - CV \cdot e^{-t/CR}$$

$$= CV(1 - e^{-t/CR}) \quad (5.9)$$

(iii) GROWTH OF CURRENT IN AN INDUCTIVE CIRCUIT (§**7.22**). If a source of p.d. V volts is applied at an instant $t = 0$ to a circuit containing resistance R ohms and inductance L henrys, the instantaneous current i amperes after any elapsed time t seconds gives a p.d. $v = ir$ across the resistance and a back-e.m.f. $E = L \cdot di/dt$ in the inductance: these voltages are together numerically equal to the applied p.d.,

$$V = L \cdot di/dt + iR$$

$$V - iR = L \cdot di/dt$$

re-arranging, $\qquad \dfrac{di}{V - iR} = \dfrac{dt}{L}$

integrating, $-\dfrac{1}{R} \cdot \log_e(V - iR) = \dfrac{t}{L} + k$

$$V - iR = k \cdot e^{-Rt/L}$$

substituting $\quad i = 0$ when $t = 0$

$$V - 0 = k \cdot e^{-0}$$

$$V = k$$

$$V - iR = V \cdot e^{-Rt/L}$$

$$iR = V - V \cdot e^{-Rt/L} = V(1 - e^{-Rt/L})$$

$$i = \frac{V}{R} \cdot (1 - e^{-Rt/L}) \quad . \quad . \quad (7.18)$$

(iv) ENERGY STORED IN AN ELECTROMAGNETIC FIELD (§**7.23**). When a p.d. is applied to an inductance with a resulting current i amperes, the back-e.m.f. at any instant is $E = L \cdot (di/dt)$. The energy expended during a very short time interval, dt seconds is

$$E \times i \times dt = L \cdot (di/dt) \times i \times dt = Li \cdot di \text{ joules}$$

The total energy is found by integrating this expression between the limits $i = 0$ and $i = I$,

$$\text{Energy, } W = L \cdot \int_0^I i \cdot di = L\left[\frac{I^2}{2}\right]_0^I$$

$$= \tfrac{1}{2}LI^2 \text{ joules} \quad . \quad (7.20)$$

(v) AVERAGE VALUE OF A SINE-WAVE ALTERNATING CURRENT (§**10.6**). The instantaneous value is $i = I_{max} \sin \theta$.

A half-wave is completed when $\theta = \omega t$ varies from $0°$ to $180°$, i.e. from 0 to π radians.

$$\text{Average value} = \frac{1}{\pi} \cdot \int_0^\pi I_{max} \sin \theta \cdot d\theta$$

$$= \frac{-I_{max}}{\pi}\left[\cos \theta\right]_0^\pi$$

$$= \frac{-I_{max}}{\pi}\left[-1 - 1\right]$$

$$= \frac{2 I_{max}}{\pi}$$

$$= 0{\cdot}637 I_{max} \quad . \quad . \quad (10.6)$$

(vi) EFFECTIVE VALUE OF A SINE-WAVE ALTERNATING CURRENT (§**10.7**). The instantaneous value is $i = I_{max} \sin \theta$.

Squaring, $i^2 = I^2_{max} \sin^2\theta$ (always positive).

The average value over a half of the original cycle, i.e. when $\theta = \omega t$ varies from 0 to π radians is

$$I^2 = \frac{1}{\pi} \int_0^\pi I^2_{max} \sin^2\theta \cdot d\theta$$

$$= \frac{I^2_{max}}{2\pi} \int_0^\pi (1 - \cos 2\theta) \cdot d\theta$$

$$= \frac{I^2_{max}}{2\pi}\left[\theta - \tfrac{1}{2} \sin 2\theta\right]_0^\pi$$

$$= \frac{I^2_{max}}{2\pi}\left[\pi - \tfrac{1}{2} \sin 2\pi - 0 + \tfrac{1}{2} \sin 0\right]$$

$$= \frac{I^2_{max}}{2}$$

$$I = \frac{I_{max}}{\sqrt{2}} = \frac{I_{max}\sqrt{2}}{2}$$

$$= 0{\cdot}707 I_{max} \quad . \qquad . \qquad . \qquad . \quad (10.7)$$

(vii) INDUCTIVE REACTANCE (§**10.9**). A current $i = I_{max} \sin \omega t$ flowing in an inductance will induce a back-e.m.f.,

$$E = - L(di/dt)$$

$$e = - L \, . \, d(I_{max} \sin \omega t)/dt$$

$$= - \omega L I_{max} \cos \omega t$$

As the applied p.d. v has only to oppose this back-e.m.f. to maintain the current in a pure inductance,

$$v = - e = + \omega L I_{max} \cos \omega t$$

$$= + \omega L I_{max} \sin (\omega t + \pi/2)$$

i.e. the applied voltage leads the current by $\dfrac{\pi}{2}$ radian.

The maximum value,

$$V_{max} = \omega L I_{max}$$

The r.m.s. value,

$$V = \omega L I$$

$$\frac{V}{I} = \omega L = X_L \text{ ohms} \quad . \qquad . \quad (10.9)$$

(viii) CAPACITIVE REACTANCE (§**10.10**). With a voltage $v = V_{max} \sin \omega t$ applied to a capacitor, the charge is

$$q = Cv = C V_{max} \sin \omega t$$

The current $i = dq/dt = d(C V_{max} \sin \omega t)/dt$

$$= \omega C V_{max} \cos \omega t$$

$$= \omega C V_{max} \sin(\omega t + \pi/2)$$

i.e. the current leads the applied voltage by $\dfrac{\pi}{2}$ radian.

The maximum value,

$$I_{max} = \omega C V_{max}$$

The r.m.s. value,

$$I = \omega C V$$

$$\frac{V}{I} = \frac{1}{\omega C} = X_C \text{ ohms} \quad . \qquad . \quad (10.10)$$

APPENDIX B

ELECTRICAL UNITS

(i) FUNDAMENTAL UNITS OF MEASUREMENT. The three fundamental physical units used as the basis from which all electrical units are derived are those of length, mass, and time. The unit of mass is purely arbitrary. It is represented by a prototype mass of one kilogramme, kept at Sèvres, near Paris. The metre was originally designed to be an exact sub-multiple of the earth's circumference. Since 1960, the definition of the metre is—

The metre is equal in length to 1 650 763·73 wavelengths of the radiation in a vacuum corresponding to the transition between the levels $2p_{10}$ and $5d_5$ of the krypton 86 atom. Also since 1956 the definition of the second is—

The second is the fraction 1/31 556 925·974 7 of the tropical year for 0 January 1900 at 12 hours ephemeris time. Ephemeris time (E.T.) is based upon the period of revolution of the earth round the sun.* In the future it is likely that the standard time interval will be based upon the transition between two energy levels of an atom or a molecule.

Three main systems of fundamental units used are, (i) the *C.G.S.* system based upon the *C*entimetre, the *G*ramme, and the *S*econd; (ii) the *M.K.S.* system in which the *M*etre, *K*ilogramme, and *S*econd are the fundamental units; and (iii) the *F.P.S.* system based upon the *F*oot, the *P*ound, and the *S*econd.

The *C.G.S.* system is the foundation upon which the one practical and two theoretical systems of electrical units were built. Prior to Oersted's discovery of the magnetic effect of the current, there was no known relationship between electric charges and magnetic poles: the two systems of units— *electrostatic* and magnetic (later *electromagnetic*)— existed independently. Their inconvenience in application brought into being the *practical* system. The more recently adopted *M.K.S.* system improves upon the convenience of the practical system by translating it into an absolute system.

(ii) DIMENSIONS. From their basis upon the primary units of Length (L), Mass (M), and Time (T) all derived units may be expressed in varying dimensions of these units. For example, a velocity (v) is the length traversed in unit time and has the dimension L/T or LT^{-1}.

An acceleration is the change in velocity in unit time and has the dimension $v/T = LT^{-1}/T = LT^{-2}$.

*L. ESSEN "Atomic Time and Standard Frequency Transmissions," *I.E.E. Journal*, **9** (1963), p. 247.

A force is the product of a mass and an acceleration and so has the dimension MLT^{-2}.

Electrical units may be also written in terms of their dimensions on this basis.

(iii) THE ELECTROSTATIC SYSTEM OF UNITS (E.S. UNITS). This is a system of absolute electrical units based upon the *C.G.S.* system: its primary electrical unit is the *unit of quantity or charge* from which all other electrostatic units were derived.

(iv) THE ELECTROMAGNETIC SYSTEM OF UNITS (E.M. UNITS). This is a system of absolute electrical units based upon the *C.G.S.* system: its primary unit is magnetic—the unit magnetic pole—in terms of which electromagnetic units were later derived, according to the magnetic effect of the current, as follows—

Current. The electromagnetic unit of current is defined as that current which when flowing in an arc of 1 cm length and of 1 cm radius exerts a force of 1 dyne upon a unit magnetic pole at the centre of the arc.

Quantity. The electromagnetic unit of quantity is that quantity of electricity conveyed by 1 electromagnetic unit of current in 1 second.

Potential. One electromagnetic unit of potential difference exists between two points if 1 erg of work is done in moving a quantity of 1 electromagnetic unit from the lower to the higher potential.

Resistance. A conductor has a resistance of 1 electromagnetic unit when a p.d. of 1 electromagnetic unit across its ends produces in it a current of 1 electromagnetic unit.

Capacitance. The electromagnetic unit of capacitance is that which requires 1 electromagnetic unit of quantity to raise its potential by 1 electromagnetic unit.

Inductance. The electromagnetic unit of inductance is that in which an e.m.f. of 1 electromagnetic unit is induced by a current changing at the rate of 1 electromagnetic unit per second.

(v) RELATIONSHIP BETWEEN ELECTROSTATIC AND ELECTROMAGNETIC UNITS. Since there is a connexion between the two phenomena, electricity and magnetism, the two systems of units, electrostatic and electromagnetic, are not independent. They are related by the velocity of light (3×10^{10} cm/sec) i.e. 1 electromagnetic unit of current is equal to 3×10^{10} electrostatic units of current.

The two systems (E.S. and E.M.) being related

by a *velocity* whose dimension is L/T, the dimensions of a given unit will vary for different systems. The multiplying factor which relates the two systems varies accordingly with the dimension of any particular unit: for the more usual units the ratio between the two systems is either c, c^2, $1/c$ or $1/c^2$ (where $c = 3 \times 10^{10}$ cm/sec), together with various powers of 10. These relationships are indicated in Table A.I below.

(vi) THE PRACTICAL SYSTEM OF UNITS. This system of units has long been in practical use owing to the C.G.S. units being in many cases inconveniently large or small The practical system was derived from the electromagnetic system, each practical unit differing from the corresponding electromagnetic unit only by a certain power of 10, the power being selected so as to make the unit of convenient size. These practical units bear the names of eminent physicists and scientists whose work has led to the establishment of the laws of the electrical phenomena.

These practical units are the same as the corresponding units in the M.K.S. system.

Some relationships between the M.K.S. and practical units on the one hand and the electrostatic and electromagnetic units on the other are given in Table A.I below.

TABLE A.I

RELATIONSHIP BETWEEN UNITS

Unit	M.K.S. and Practical System	Measure in E.M.U.	Measure in E.S.U.
Current . .	Ampere	10^{-1}	3×10^9
Quantity . .	Coulomb	10^{-1}	3×10^9
E.M.F. and P.D.	Volt	10^8	$1/(3 \times 10^2)$
Resistance .	Ohm	10^9	$1/(9 \times 10^{11})$
Capacitance .	Farad	10^{-9}	9×10^{11}
Inductance .	Henry	10^9	$1/(9 \times 10^{11})$
Power . .	Watt	10^7	10^7
Energy . .	Joule	10^7 (ergs)	10^7 (ergs)

(vii) THE METRE-KILOGRAMME-SECOND SYSTEM OF UNITS (M.K.S. UNITS). The M.K.S. system of units, originally suggested by Professor Giorgi in 1901, was recommended for adoption by the International Electro-technical Commission in 1938. It is an absolute and completely self-contained system in which the electrical units are the (existing) practical units—the volt, ampere, ohm, coulomb, farad, henry, watt, and joule. The system is based upon the metre, the kilogramme, and the second, together with a fourth fundamental unit μ_0. This fourth defining unit is a constant, which is the connecting link between the electrical and mechanical units: it is referred to as the *permeability of free space* or as the *magnetic space constant* and has the value $\mu_0 = 4\pi \cdot 10^{-7}$ in the "rationalized" system now adopted. The system was at one time referred to as the $M.K.S.\mu_0$ system, in order to indicate these four fundamental units.

Where its presence is necessary, the fundamental constant ε_0—the *permittivity of free space* or *electric space constant*—must also be used. This constant is not independent, but is determined from the relationship $1/\mu_0\varepsilon_0 = c^2$, where c is the velocity of light *in vacuo* ($c \simeq 3 \times 10^8$ metre/second). Substituting this value for c, together with $\mu_0 = 4\pi \cdot 10^{-7}$ (by definition), produces

$$\varepsilon_0 = 1/\mu_0 c^2 = 1/(4\pi \cdot 10^{-7} \cdot c^2) = 8 \cdot 85 \times 10^{-12}.$$

The constant ε_0 is a numeric: μ_0 has the dimensions $L^{-2}T^2$ (since $\mu_0 = 1/\varepsilon_0 c^2$).

The unit of force is called the *newton* (N), which is *that force necessary to give to a mass of one kilogramme an acceleration of one metre per second per second*. The unit of energy or work (= force $\times$ distance) is the newton-metre, equal to the joule. Similarly, the unit of power is the joule per second, or the newton-metre per second, identical with the watt.

The unit of current, the *ampere*, is defined as *that constant current which, when maintained in two parallel rectilinear conductors of infinite length, of negligible cross-section and separated by a distance of one metre (in vacuo), would produce between these conductors a force equal to 2×10^{-7} newton per metre length*.

From these basic definitions for the ampere and the watt (the newton-metre/second), the following electrical units are determined—

Charge or quantity	Q	ampere-second or coulomb
Potential difference	V	watt/ampere or volt
Electric field strength	E	volt/metre
Resistance	R	volt/ampere or ohm
Capacitance	C	coulomb/volt or farad
Magnetic flux	Φ	volt-second or weber
Magnetic flux density	B	weber/metre^2
Inductance	L	weber/ampere or henry

The unit of magnetic flux—the *weber* (Wb)—is determined from the fact that unit rate of change of flux with time produces unit e.m.f. The unit of magnetic flux density is the weber/square metre. The name *tesla* was adopted as the unit of magnetic flux density by the International Electrotechnical Commission in 1956, but the name has not come into general use. There is at present no name given in the M.K.S. system to the unit of magnetizing force (the ampere-turn/metre).

Rationalization relates to the proposal to transfer the factor 4π, which occurs in the basic equations of electrostatics and electromagnetism, from one position to another for specific reasons. Rationalization is not actually essential nor peculiar to the M.K.S. system—it may equally well be applied to the C.G.S. system—but the M.K.S. system adopted is in fact in rationalized form. Rationalization has been defined* as *the alteration of the "unrationalized" systems of electrical and magnetic units, so that unit magnetic pole and unit electric charge respectively should emit unit magnetic and unit electric flux instead of 4π units.*

The rationalized form for an expression is obtained from the traditional form by writing $4\pi\mu_r\mu_0$ in place of μ_r and $4\pi\varepsilon_r\varepsilon_0$ for ε_r where the subscript r indicates "relative." It is clear that if the term 4π is eliminated from some equations, it must make its appearance in certain others from which it would otherwise be absent. On this question it is of interest to quote from Heaviside in favour of rationalization: "If we were to define unit area to be the area of a circle of unit diameter, we could on such a basis construct a system of units. But the area of a rectangle would involve the quantity 4π and various derived formulae would possess the same peculiarity."

The application of rationalization to some typical equations is shown in Table A.II.

(viii) ABBREVIATIONS FOR NAMES OF ELECTRICAL UNITS (to be employed only after numerical values).

A	ampere
Ah	ampere-hour
C	coulomb
c/s	cycles per second
db	decibel
dn	decineper
F	farad
H	henry
J	joule
kc/s	kilocycles per second
Mc/s	megacycles per second
N	newton
Ω	ohm
V	volt
VA	volt-ampere
W	watt
Wb	weber
Wh	watt-hour

TABLE A.II

Equation	Traditional	Rationalized
Inverse Square Law (Electric Charges)	$F = \dfrac{Q_1 Q_2}{\varepsilon_r r^2}$	$F = \dfrac{Q_1 Q_2}{4\pi\varepsilon_r\varepsilon_0 r^2}$
Inverse Square Law (Magnetic Poles)	$F = \dfrac{m_1 m_2}{\mu_r r^2}$	$F = \dfrac{m_1 m_2}{4\pi\mu_r\mu_0 r^2}$
Capacitance of Parallel Plate Capacitor	$C = \dfrac{\varepsilon_r A}{4\pi d}$	$C = \dfrac{\varepsilon_r \varepsilon_0 A}{d}$
Capacitance of Concentric Capacitor	$C = \dfrac{\varepsilon_r}{2\log_e(R/r)}$	$C = \dfrac{2\pi\varepsilon_r\varepsilon_0}{\log_e(R/r)}$

* S. R. ROGET: *A Dictionary of Electrical Terms* (Pitman, 1941).

REFERENCES

1. L. H. A. CARR, G. H. RAWCLIFFE, H. MARRIOTT, and E. BRADSHAW: "Symposium of Papers on the M.K.S. System of Units," *I.E.E. Journal*, **97** (1950).
2. T. McGREEVY: *The M.K.S. System of Units* (Pitman, 1953).

APPENDIX C

LETTER SYMBOLS FOR QUANTITIES

ELECTRICAL ENGINEERING

B	susceptance: flux density (magnetic)
B_R	remanence
C	capacitance
D	flux density (electric)
e	instantaneous e.m.f.
E	electromotive force: electric force: energy
E_{av}	average e.m.f.
E_{max}	maximum e.m.f.
F	magnetomotive force: force
f	frequency
f_0	natural frequency
f_r	resonant frequency
g_m	mutual conductance
G	conductance
H	magnetizing force: field strength
H_C	coercivity
i	instantaneous current
I	current
I_a	anode current
I_{av}	average current
I_g	grid current
I_M	magnetizing current
I_{max}	maximum current
J	current density
k or K	coupling coefficient
L	self inductance
m	strength of pole
M	mutual inductance: magnetic moment: magnetomotive force
p	total number of poles
P	power: number of pairs of poles
Q	quantity
r or R	resistance
R or S	reluctance
T	period: torque
v	instantaneous voltage
V	potential difference
V_a	anode voltage
V_{av}	average voltage
V_f	filament voltage
V_g	grid voltage
V_{max}	maximum voltage
W	work: energy
X	reactance
X_C	capacitive reactance
X_L	inductive reactance
Y	admittance
Z	impedance
α	attenuation coefficient: temperature coefficient
β	phase-change coefficient
γ	propagation coefficient
ε	permittivity
η	efficiency
θ	change in temperature
λ	wavelength
μ	amplification factor: permeability
ρ	resistivity
σ	conductivity
ϕ	phase angle
Φ	magnetic flux
Ψ	induction factor: electric field
ω	angular frequency

PRIMARY, MECHANICAL (ETC.)

A	area
b	breadth
d	diameter
F	force
K	moment of inertia
l	length
m	mass
n	revolutions per second
N	revolutions per minute
r	radius
t	time
T	torque
v or u	velocity
V	volume
W	weight

APPENDIX D

PERIODIC TABLE FOR THE ELEMENTS

Element	Symbol	Atomic Number	K 1s	L 2s	L 2p	M 3s	M 3p	M 3d	N 4s	N 4p	N 4d	N 4f	O 5s	O 5p	O 5d	P 6s	P 6p	Q 7s
Hydrogen	H	1	1	—	—	—	—	—	—	—	—	—	—	—	—	—	—	—
Helium	He	2	2	—	—	—	—	—	—	—	—	—	—	—	—	—	—	—
Lithium	Li	3	2	1	—	—	—	—	—	—	—	—	—	—	—	—	—	—
Beryllium	Be	4	2	2	—	—	—	—	—	—	—	—	—	—	—	—	—	—
Boron	B	5	2	2	1	—	—	—	—	—	—	—	—	—	—	—	—	—
Carbon	C	6	2	2	2	—	—	—	—	—	—	—	—	—	—	—	—	—
Nitrogen	N	7	2	2	3	—	—	—	—	—	—	—	—	—	—	—	—	—
Oxygen	O	8	2	2	4	—	—	—	—	—	—	—	—	—	—	—	—	—
Fluorine	F	9	2	2	5	—	—	—	—	—	—	—	—	—	—	—	—	—
Neon	Ne	10	2	2	6	—	—	—	—	—	—	—	—	—	—	—	—	—
Sodium	Na	11	*Configuration as for Neon*			1	—	—	—	—	—	—	—	—	—	—	—	—
Magnesium	Mg	12				2	—	—	—	—	—	—	—	—	—	—	—	—
Aluminium	Al	13				2	1	—	—	—	—	—	—	—	—	—	—	—
Silicon	Si	14				2	2	—	—	—	—	—	—	—	—	—	—	—
Phosphorus	P	15				2	3	—	—	—	—	—	—	—	—	—	—	—
Sulphur	S	16				2	4	—	—	—	—	—	—	—	—	—	—	—
Chlorine	Cl	17				2	5	—	—	—	—	—	—	—	—	—	—	—
Argon	A	18				2	6	—	—	—	—	—	—	—	—	—	—	—
Potassium	K	19	*Configuration as for Argon*					—	1	—	—	—	—	—	—	—	—	—
Calcium	Ca	20						—	2	—	—	—	—	—	—	—	—	—
Scandium	Sc	21						1	2	—	—	—	—	—	—	—	—	—
Titanium	Ti	22						2	2	—	—	—	—	—	—	—	—	—
Vanadium	V	23						3	2	—	—	—	—	—	—	—	—	—
Chromium	Cr	24						5	1	—	—	—	—	—	—	—	—	—
Manganese	Mn	25						5	2	—	—	—	—	—	—	—	—	—
Iron	Fe	26						6	2	—	—	—	—	—	—	—	—	—
Cobalt	Co	27						7	2	—	—	—	—	—	—	—	—	—
Nickel	Ni	28						8	2	—	—	—	—	—	—	—	—	—
Copper	Cu	29						10	1	—	—	—	—	—	—	—	—	—
Zinc	Zn	30						10	2	—	—	—	—	—	—	—	—	—
Gallium	Ga	31						10	2	1	—	—	—	—	—	—	—	—
Germanium	Ge	32						10	2	2	—	—	—	—	—	—	—	—
Arsenic	As	33						10	2	3	—	—	—	—	—	—	—	—
Selenium	Se	34						10	2	4	—	—	—	—	—	—	—	—
Bromine	Br	35						10	2	5	—	—	—	—	—	—	—	—
Krypton	Kr	36						10	2	6	—	—	—	—	—	—	—	—
Rubidium	Rb	37	*Configuration as for Krypton*								—	—	1	—	—	—	—	—
Strontium	Sr	38									—	—	2	—	—	—	—	—
Yttrium	Yt	39									1	—	2	—	—	—	—	—
Zirconium	Zr	40									2	—	2	—	—	—	—	—
Niobium	Nb	41									4	—	1	—	—	—	—	—
Molybdenum	Mo	42									5	—	1	—	—	—	—	—
Technetium	Tc	43									6	—	1	—	—	—	—	—
Ruthenium	Ru	44									7	—	1	—	—	—	—	—
Rhodium	Rh	45									8	—	1	—	—	—	—	—
Palladium	Pd	46									10	—	—	—	—	—	—	—

PERIODIC TABLE FOR THE ELEMENTS—*(contd.)*

Element	Symbol	Atomic Number	Electron Distribution in Shells							
				N	O	O	O	P	P	P	Q
			4f	5s	5p	5d	6s	6p	6d	7s
Silver . .	Ag	47	—	1	—	—	—	—	—	—
Cadmium . .	Cd	48	—	2	—	—	—	—	—	—
Indium . .	In	49	—	2	1	—	—	—	—	—
Tin . . .	Sn	50	—	2	2	—	—	—	—	—
Antimony . .	Sb	51	—	2	3	—	—	—	—	—
Tellurium . .	Te	52	—	2	4	—	—	—	—	—
Iodine . .	I	53	—	2	5	—	—	—	—	—
Xenon . .	Xe	54	—	2	6	—	—	—	—	—
Caesium . .	Cs	55	—	8		—	1	—	—	—
Barium . .	Ba	56	—	8		—	2	—	—	—
Lanthanum .	La	57	—	8		1	2	—	—	—
*Cerium . .	Ce	58	1	8		1	2	—	—	—
*Praseodymium .	Pr	59	2	8		1	2	—	—	—
*Neodymium .	Nd	60	3	8		1	2	—	—	—
Promethium .	Pm	61	4	8		1	2	—	—	—
*Samarium . .	Sm	62	5	8		1	2	—	—	—
*Europium . .	Eu	63	6	8		1	2	—	—	—
*Gadolinium .	Gd	64	7	8		1	2	—	—	—
*Terbium . .	Tb	65	8	8		1	2	—	—	—
*Dysprosium .	Dy	66	9	8		1	2	—	—	—
*Holmium . .	Ho	67	10	8		1	2	—	—	—
*Erbium . .	Er	68	11	8		1	2	—	—	—
*Thulium . .	Tm	69	12	8		1	2	—	—	—
*Ytterbium .	Yb	70	13	8		1	2	—	—	—
*Lutetium . .	Lu	71	14	8		1	2	—	—	—
*Hafnium . .	Hf	72				2	2	—	—	—
*Tantalum . .	Ta	73				3	2	—	—	—
Tungsten . .	W	74				4	2	—	—	—
Rhenium . .	Re	75				5	2	—	—	—
*Osmium . .	Os	76				6	2	—	—	—
*Iridium . .	Ir	77				9	—	—	—	—
Platinum . .	Pt	78				9	1	—	—	—
Gold . .	Au	79					1	—	—	—
Mercury . .	Hg	80					2	—	—	—
Thallium . .	Tl	81					2	1	—	—
Lead . .	Pb	82					2	2	—	—
Bismuth . .	Bi	83					2	3	—	—
Polonium . .	Po	84					2	4	—	—
*Astatine . .	At	85					2	5	—	—
Radon . .	Rn	86					2	6	—	—
*Francium . .	Fr	87					—	—	—	1
*Radium . .	Ra	88					—	—	—	2
*Actinium . .	Ac	89					—	—	1	2
*Thorium . .	Th	90					—	—	2	2
*Protoactinium .	Pa	91					—	—	3	2
*Uranium . .	U	92					—	—	4	2

Notes within the table body:
- Silver to Xenon: **Configuration for Palladium**
- Caesium to Lutetium: **Shells 1s to 4d contain 46 electrons**
- Hafnium to Platinum: **Shells 1s to 5p contain 68 electrons**
- Gold to Radon: **Shells 1s to 5d contain 78 electrons**
- Francium to Uranium: **Configuration as for Radon**

* Determined by considerations of analogy.

APPENDIX E

GREEK ALPHABET

A	α	alpha	N	ν	nu
B	β	beta	Ξ	ξ	xi
Γ	γ	gamma	O	o	omicron
Δ	δ	delta	Π	π	pi
E	ε	epsilon	P	ρ	rho
Z	ζ	zeta	Σ	σ	sigma
H	η	eta	T	τ	tau
Θ	θ	theta	Υ	υ	upsilon
I	ι	iota	Φ	ϕ	phi
K	κ	kappa	X	χ	chi
Λ	λ	lambda	Ψ	ψ	psi
M	μ	mu	Ω	ω	omega

APPENDIX F

USEFUL NUMBERS AND CONVERSION FACTORS

CONSTANTS:

$\pi = 3{\cdot}141\ 6\ (\simeq 22/7)$

$e = 2{\cdot}718$

CONVERSION FACTORS:

Common logarithms (C) to Naperian logarithms (N),

$$N = C \times 2{\cdot}302\ 6$$

Naperian logarithms (N) to common logarithms (C),

$$C = N \times 0{\cdot}434\ 3$$

2π radians $= 360°$: 1 radian $= 57{\cdot}3°$

1 inch $= 2{\cdot}54$ centimetres.

1 metre $= 39{\cdot}37$ inches.

1 pound $= 453{\cdot}59$ grammes.

1 horse-power (h.p.) $= 33\ 000$ ft-lb/min
$= 746$ watts.

Centigrade (C) to Fahrenheit (F):
$F° = (C° \times 9/5) + 32$.

Fahrenheit (F) to Centigrade (C):
$C° = (F° - 32) \times 5/9$.

CIRCLES AND SPHERES:

$r =$ radius, $d =$ diameter.

Circumference of circle $= 2\pi r = \pi d$.

Area of circle $= \pi r^2 = \pi d^2/4 = 0{\cdot}785\ 4d^2$.

Surface area of sphere $= 4\pi r^2 = \pi d^2$.

Volume of sphere $= 4\pi r^3/3 = \pi d^3/6$.

INDICES. In the numerical expression of very large and very small quantities it is convenient for the purposes of both writing and calculation to express such numbers in units (0 to 9) multiplied by the appropriate power of 10. For example, $100 = 10 \times 10$ and is written as 10^2, so that $576 = 5{\cdot}76 \times 100 = 5{\cdot}76 \times 10^2$; similarly $42\ 000\ 000 = 4{\cdot}2 \times 10^7$.

Multiples less than 1 have a negative index. For example $0{\cdot}01 = 1/100 = 10^{-2}$; a current of 8 mA $= 0{\cdot}008$ A $= 8/1\ 000 = 8 \times 10^{-3}$ A.

The more commonly employed multiples are listed below with their names and symbols.

Prefix	Multiplying Power		Symbol
Tera	$= \times 10^{12}$	$= \times (1\ 000\ 000)^2$	T
Giga	$= \times 10^9$	$= \times 1\ 000\ 000\ 000$	G
Meg(a)	$= \times 10^6$	$= \times 1\ 000\ 000$	M
kilo	$= \times 10^3$	$= \times 1\ 000$	k
centi	$= \times 10^{-2}$	$= \times 1/100$	c
milli	$= \times 10^{-3}$	$= \times 1/1\ 000$	m
micr(o)	$= \times 10^{-6}$	$= \times 1/1\ 000\ 000$	μ
nano	$= \times 10^{-9}$		n
pico	$= \times 10^{-12}$		p
femto	$= \times 10^{-15}$		
atto	$= \times 10^{-18}$		

APPENDIX G

GRAPHICAL SYMBOLS FOR TELECOMMUNICATION

CONDUCTORS CROSSING WITHOUT CONNEXION		VARIABLE CAPACITOR	
CONDUCTORS CONNECTED TOGETHER		ELECTROLYTIC CAPACITOR (THE + AND − SIGNS MAY BE OMITTED IF NO AMBIGUITY AS TO POLARITY WILL RESULT)	
EARTH CONNEXION		NON POLARISED ELECTROLYTIC CAPACITOR	
PRIMARY OR SECONDARY CELL (THE LONG LINE REPRESENTS THE POSITIVE POLE : THE SHORT LINE THE NEGATIVE POLE)		INDUCTOR OR INDUCTANCE	
PRIMARY OR SECONDARY CELL BATTERY (VOLTAGE SHOWN WHERE NECESSARY)	50V	VARIABLE INDUCTANCE	
		INDUCTOR WITH FERROMAGNETIC CORE	
VOLTMETER		TRANSFORMER	
AMMETER		TRANSFORMER WITH FERROMAGNETIC CORE	
GALVANOMETER		"MAKE" CONTACT	
TERMINAL OR CONNEXION	O	LAMP	
RESISTOR (CAN BE USED FOR IMPEDANCE WHERE CONFUSION WILL NOT ARISE)		FUSE	
VARIABLE RESISTOR		METAL RECTIFIER (THE DIRECTION OF HIGHER CONDUCTIVITY IS FROM TRIANGLE TO PLATE. THE + SIGN MAY BE OMITTED)	
SLIDING CONTACT RHEOSTAT		PIEZO-ELECTRIC CRYSTAL	
NON-REACTIVE RESISTOR		GENERATOR	D.C. A.C.
CAPACITOR OR CAPACITANCE		MOTOR	D.C. A.C.

APPENDIX H

EXAMINATION SYLLABUSES OF THE CITY AND GUILDS OF LONDON INSTITUTE

49. Telecommunication Technicians' Course (1965)

ENGINEERING SCIENCE*

1. Mass; force; acceleration due to a constant force. Vector and scalar quantities. Composition and resolution of vectors by graphical methods.

2. Condition for the equilibrium of a body under the action of coplanar forces. Solution of simple problems using graphical methods.

3. Basic principles of moments and couples. Torque. Application to the lever.

4. Simple ideas of tension, compression, and shear. Forces and couples due to springs.

5. Work done by a constant force. Potential and kinetic energy. Heat as a form of energy. Units of energy and power.

6. Electric charge. Elementary concept of current as movement of charge. Potential difference. Capacitance as charge per unit potential difference.

7. The simple electric circuit; electromotive force; resistance. The ampere, the volt, the ohm, the coulomb. Conductors, semiconductors and insulators. Ohm's law. Resistors in series and in parallel. Resistivity and conductivity. Temperature coefficient of resistance. R_0 referred to 0°C only.

8. The heating effect of an electric current. Power and energy in simple d.c. circuits.

9. The chemical effects of an electric current; dependence on the quantity of electricity passed. Corrosion. Comparative treatment of practical cells based on utility without details of construction and action.

10. The magnetic effects of an electric current. Fields due to current-carrying conductors, treated qualitatively. The motor principle and its application to the moving-coil meter.

11. Qualitative treatment of electromagnetic induction. Induced e.m.f. in moving and in stationary circuits. Lenz's law. Mutual and self induction. Electromagnetic damping.

12. Generation of an alternating e.m.f. by the rotation of a coil in a uniform magnetic field. Flow of alternating current in a pure resistor.

13. The use of ammeters and voltmeters. The effect of meter resistance on circuit conditions. Shunts and multipliers.

TELECOMMUNICATION PRINCIPLES A*

1. Kirchhoff's Laws. Solution of simple network problems involving two unknowns. The simple potentiometer and its applications in voltage measurement. The principle of the balanced Wheatstone bridge and its applications in the measurement of resistance.

2. Capacitance. The Farad. Factors governing capacitance. Practical dielectrics. Capacitors in parallel and in series. Energy stored in an electric field.

3. Electromagnetic induction. Self and mutual inductance. The henry. Energy stored in a magnetic field. Total inductance of a series combination ($L_1 + L_2 \pm 2M$).

4. Sinusoidal currents and voltages; peak, half-wave average, and r.m.s. values and their ratios. Phase difference. Reactance. Flow of alternating current through pure resistance, through pure capacitance and through pure inductance. Power in a.c. circuits.

5. Principles of operation of electromagnetic loudspeakers and microphones.

6. Elementary qualitative treatment of the theory of semiconductors. The p–n junction. The germanium transistor: input and output characteristics and current gain in common-base and common-emitter configurations.

7. Thermionic emission. The simple diode; space charge; saturation; rectifying action. The triode; static characteristics and parameters and their determination.

8. The amplifying action of the transistor and of the triode with a pure resistance load. Use of load lines.

9. Types of rectifier, their characteristics and principles of operation: single-phase, half-wave, full-wave and bridge connections only. Smoothing circuits.

10. Descriptive treatment of moving-iron and moving-coil instruments for the measurement of current and voltage. Deflecting and control torques. Damping. Rectifier and thermocouple instruments for the measurement of current and voltage at audio and radio frequencies.

* 1965 Revision.

* 1965 Revision.

Telecommunication Principles B

1. Alternating currents and voltages; r.m.s. and peak values.

2. Capacitance; energy stored in a charged capacitor. Dielectrics employed in telecommunication; permittivity. Capacitors in parallel and in series. Simple treatment of growth and decay of voltage in resistance-capacitance circuits. Time constant. Capacitance with alternating applied voltage. Electrostatic shielding (simple concept).

3. Magnetization curves. Magnetic materials. Permeability, remanence, coercivity. Effect of air gap. Alternating current magnetization. Effect of lamination or granulation; hysteresis magnetic shielding (simple concept).

4. Laws of electromagnetic induction. Concept of self and mutual inductance. Energy stored in inductors carrying current. Spark quenching at contacts.

5. Simple treatment of growth and decay of current in circuit containing inductance and resistance. Time constant. Pure inductance with alternating current.

6. Concept of independence of action of sinusoidal alternating e.m.f.s of different frequencies in the same circuit. Composition of complex waveforms from fundamental and harmonics (by graphical addition of components).

7. Reactance and impedance of circuit elements. Reactance/frequency curves for L and C. Solution of series and parallel circuits containing C, L, and R by vector diagram methods. Resonance in series and parallel circuits.

8. The behaviour over a range of frequencies of series and parallel tuned circuits. Qualitative concept of selectivity. Free oscillation in the ideal loss-free circuit. Qualitative consideration of damping.

9. The simple tuned triode amplifier.

10. Simple transistor amplifiers with resistance load.

11. Concept of transmission by radio and line of signal waveforms upon carrier waves.

12. Instruments for the measurement of current and voltage at audio and radio frequencies, including electrostatic, rectifier, and thermocouple types.

13. Simple a.c. bridges at balance; Maxwell, Hay and Schering bridges.

14. Simple treatment of the characteristics of separately-excited and shunt-connected d.c. generators and motors. The simple a.c. generator.

Telecommunication Principles C

1. Electric strength; energy loss in alternating electric fields; loss angle.

2. The ideal transformer. Voltage ratio; current ratio on load; vector diagram on load. Equivalent input resistance on load. The practical transformer. Effect of magnetizing current and losses.

3. The factors affecting the ranges of frequency utilized for the transmission of speech and music and for television.

4. Amplitude modulation for telegraphy and speech. Expression for sinusoidally amplitude-modulated wave; modulation factor; side frequencies and sidebands.

5. The Q-factor of resonant circuits. Selectivity of resonant circuits.

6. The diode detector for amplitude-modulated waves.

7. Tetrode and pentode valves, their characteristics and their uses in Class A amplifiers. Valve equivalent generators.

8. Simple tuned grid and tuned anode triode oscillators.

9. Simple tuned circuit transistor oscillators.

10. Simple transistor equivalent circuits—definition and use of "h" parameters.

11. Simple treatment of the propagation of alternating currents along an infinite uniform line of low loss. Impedance matching for maximum power transfer. Use of transformers in impedance matching.

12. Simple theoretical treatment of typical electro-acoustic devices in telecommunication.

13. The cathode-ray tube and simple associated circuits.

14. Qualitative consideration of electromagnet radiation. The radiation patterns (polar diagrams) of simple aerials.

Radio and Line Transmission A*

1. The use and advantage of logarithmic units for the expression of ratios of powers, currents and voltages. Definition of the decibel.

2. Sinusoidal variation with time. Frequency. The audio-frequency range. Harmonics. Bandwidth as an essential requirement for the transmission of information.

3. The use of a carrier; amplitude modulation: modulation depth. Waveforms of a carrier amplitude-modulated by a sinusoid. Statement of frequencies comprising the modulated waves of a carrier, amplitude-modulated by (a) a sinusoid, (b) a musical note, and (c) speech.

4. Carrier frequency ranges in common use; frequencies normally transmitted over lines and radio links. Relationship between frequency, wavelength, and velocity of propagation.

5. Block schematic diagrams of a simple line communication system and of a simple radio

* 1965 Revision.

communication system. Introduction to 2-wire and 4-wire terminations. Multi-station broadcasting.

6. Characteristics and performance of common types of resistors, inductors, transformers, and capacitors used in line and radio systems for communication and broadcasting.

7. Characteristics and performance of carbon, crystal, and moving-coil microphones. Moving-iron and moving-coil loudspeakers and telephone receivers.

8. Series and parallel tuned circuits; approximate frequency of resonance (without derivation). Use in selection of narrow bands centred on carriers of different frequencies. Bandwidth, half-power (— 3 db) points.

9. Characteristics and essential features of semiconductor diodes and transistors, thermionic diodes, triodes, tetrodes, beam tetrodes, and pentodes.

10. Descriptive treatment of Class-A, Class-B, and Class-C operation of simple tuned transistor and valve amplifiers. The principle of operation of simple resistance-loaded small-signal transistor and valve amplifiers. Use of load lines. Simple equivalent circuits. Factors affecting stage amplification. Qualitative consideration of the effect upon frequency response of the interstage couplings, and of the input impedance of the subsequent stage.

11. Descriptive treatment of simple triode valve oscillators with tuned circuit in anode or in grid. Simple mutual inductance-coupled transistor oscillators.

12. Descriptive treatment of the detection of amplitude-modulated waves by semiconductor and thermionic devices.

INDEX